ArtScroll Mesorah Series®

Rabbi Nosson Scherman / Rabbi Meir Zlotowitz
General Editors

THE SEIF EDITION

לימות החול

AN ORTHODOX UNION CENTENNIAL PUBLICATION

Published by

Mesorah Publications, ltd

ArtScroll
Transliterated Linear
SIDDUR

WEEKDAY

based on
The Complete ArtScroll Siddur
with translation and commentary by

Rabbi Nosson Scherman

Introductory Essays and Comments by
Rabbi Benjamin Yudin

Designed by
Rabbi Sheah Brander

A PROJECT OF THE

Mesorah Heritage Foundation

AN ORTHODOX UNION CENTENNIAL PUBLICATION

FIRST EDITION
First Impression . . . August 1998
Second Impression . . . December 2002
Third Impression . . . January 2006
Fourth Impression . . . May 2008
Fifth Impression . . . April 2010

THE ARTSCROLL SERIES®
"SIDDUR ZICHRON AVRAHAM"
THE SEIF EDITION OF THE ARTSCROLL TRANSLITERATED LINEAR SIDDUR
WEEKDAY — NUSACH ASHKENAZ

© Copyright 1998 by MESORAH PUBLICATIONS, Ltd.
4401 Second Avenue / Brooklyn, N.Y. 11232 / (718) 921-9000 / www.artscroll.com

ALL RIGHTS RESERVED. *The Hebrew text, punctuation and format, the translation, transliteration, commentary, instructions, prefatory and associated textual contents and introductions of the Gemara and of Rashi's commentary have been enhanced, and the English exposition — including the typographic layout, cover artwork and ornamental graphics — have been designed, edited and revised as to content, form and style.*

> No part of this volume may be reproduced
> IN ANY FORM — PHOTOCOPY, ELECTRONIC MEDIA, OR OTHERWISE
> — EVEN FOR PERSONAL, STUDY GROUP, OR CLASSROOM USE —
> without WRITTEN permission from the copyright holder,
> *except by a reviewer who wishes to quote brief passages*
> *in connection with a review written for inclusion in magazines or newspapers.*

NOTICE IS HEREBY GIVEN THAT THE PUBLICATION OF THIS WORK
INVOLVED EXTENSIVE RESEARCH AND COSTS, AND THE RIGHTS OF
THE COPYRIGHT HOLDER WILL BE STRICTLY ENFORCED.

ISBN 10: 1-57819-151-3
ISBN 13: 978-1-57819-151-2

Typography by CompuScribe at ArtScroll Studios, Ltd.
Printed in the United States of America by Noble Book Press
Custom bound by **Sefercraft, Inc.** / 4401 Second Avenue / Brooklyn, N.Y. 11232

טוֹב שֵׁם מִשֶּׁמֶן טוֹב
A good name is better than good oil
(*Ecclesiastes* 7:1)

This Siddur
is dedicated to the memory of
Abraham Seif ע״ה
אברהם בן יהודה אריה ע״ה
January 13, 1997 / נפטר ה׳ שבט, תשנ״ז

and in honor of his namesake, our grandson
Abraham Seif נ״י
אברהם בן יהודה אריה נ״י
May 25, 2003 / נולד כ״ג אייר, תשס״ג

Little Abraham's great-grandfather built his good name
with uncompromising devotion to *mitzvot,*
unwavering morality, and tenacious integrity,
all blended with a profound love of family and am Yisrael.

No child can have a finer role model
or a more glowing legacy.

This Siddur was originally dedicated
in honor of our father's first *yahrzeit.*
It has already fulfilled our sincere hope
that it would inspire countless Jews to engage
in quiet conversation with God, through prayer.

May it continue to do so,
and may those prayers be a source
of merit for the soul of Abraham Seif ע״ה,
and להבחל״ח for young Abraham and his parents,
and also for Abraham's two siblings, Izzy and Uriel
as they join in bringing new glory to the eternal mission
of our people.

Harriet and Herbert Seif
Orit and Yehuda Seif
Abie, Izzy and Uriel

ꜩ Guide to Reading the Transliteration

Consonants are read as they sound in English, except for "ch" (ח,כ,ך) which is pronounced as in *challah*.

The "silent" Hebrew letters — א and ע, whenever they appear, and ה, when it appears at the end of a word — are not represented. Although the letter ה is not usually pronounced when it appears at the end of a word, there are exceptions to the rule. These exceptions are indicated in Hebrew by a dot inside the letter — הּ. In transliteration the ה appears as a final h and is preceded by a vowel.

A consonant is usually pronounced together with the vowel following it. Thus, הַמֶּלֶךְ, "hamelech," is pronounced "ha-me-lech," and not "ham-el-ech." Hyphens are used to indicate exceptions to this rule.

When two consonants appear in tandem (except for those that are pronounced as a single sound, such as, ch, sh, tz), the first ends a syllable and the second begins a new syllable. Thus, וּבְנֵה, "uvnay," is pronounced "uv-nay"; אֶקְרָא, "ekro," is pronounced "ek-ro" not "e-kro."

Vowels are pronounced as follows:

a	אַ	as in	hurr**a**h
o	אָ	as in	**o**ften
ō	א or אוֹ	as in	p**o**st
ay	אֵ or אֵי	as in	p**ay**
e	אֶ	as in	l**e**g
i	אִ or אִי	as in	mach**i**ne
u	אֻ or אוּ	as in	l**u**nar
oy	אֹי	as in	b**oy**
ai	אַי	as in	**ai**sle

The sounded *sh'va* (בְּ) is represented by an apostrophe (b') and is pronounced similarly to the indistinct **a** in **a**go.

Hyphens are used to separate syllables that might otherwise be slurred into each other (e.g., מֵעֲתָה is transliterated "may-ato" not "ma-yato").

Capital letters are not used in Hebrew. However, for the convenience of the reader, the transliteration uses a capital letter to indicate the beginning of a verse or a sentence. Additionally, capitals are used to indicate Divine Names which may not be pronounced except as part of a Scriptural verse or within a prayer.

Note: Phrases in the transliteration or instructions that are followed by an asterisk (*) are discussed in the commentary below, usually on the same page, but sometimes on the facing or following pages.

THE NAMES OF GOD

The Four-Letter Name of HASHEM [י־ה־ו־ה] indicates that God is timeless and infinite, since the letters of this Name are those of the words הָיָה הֹוֶה וְיִהְיֶה, *He was, He is, and He will be.* This Name appears in some editions with vowel points [יְ־הֹ־וָ־ה] and in others, such as the present edition, without vowels. In either case, this Name is *never* pronounced as it is spelled.

During prayer, or when a blessing is recited, or when Torah verses are read, the Four-Letter Name should be pronounced as if it were spelled אֲדֹנָי, *Adōnoy,* the Name that identifies God as the Master of All. At other times, it should be pronounced הַשֵּׁם, *Hashem,* literally, "the Name."

According to the *Shulchan Aruch,* one should have both meanings — the Master of All and the Timeless, Infinite One — in mind when reciting the Four-Letter Name during prayer (*Orach Chaim* ch. 5). According to the *Vilna Gaon,* however, one need have in mind only the meaning of the Name as it is pronounced — the Master of All (ibid.).

When the Name is spelled אֲדֹנָי in the prayer or verse, all agree that one should have in mind that God is the Master of All.

The Name אֱלֹהִים, *Elōhim, God,* refers to Him as the One Who is all-powerful and Who is in direct overlordship of the universe (ibid.). This is also used as a generic name for the angels, a court, rulers, and even idols. However, when the term אֱלֹהִים is used for the God of Israel, it means the One Omniscient God, Who is uniquely identified with His Chosen People.

In this work, the Four-Letter Name of God is translated "HASHEM," the pronunciation traditionally used for the Name to avoid pronouncing it unnecessarily. This pronunciation should be used when studying the meanings of the prayers. However, if one prays in English, he should say "God" or "Lord" or he should pronounce the Name in the proper Hebrew way — *Adōnoy* — in accord with the ruling of most halachic authorities.

PRONOUNCING THE NAMES OF GOD

The following table gives the pronunciations of the Name when it appears with a prefix. In all these cases, the accent is on the last syllable (*noy*).

בַּי־ה־ו־ה	—	*Ba-dōnoy*
הַי־ה־ו־ה	—	*Ha-adōnoy*
וַי־ה־ו־ה	—	*Va-dōnoy*
כַּי־ה־ו־ה	—	*Ka-dōnoy*
לַי־ה־ו־ה	—	*La-dōnoy*
מֵי־ה־ו־ה	—	*May-adōnoy*
שֶׁי־ה־ו־ה	—	*She-adōnoy*

Sometimes the Name appears with the vowelization יְ־הֹ־וִ־ה. This version of the Name is pronounced as if it were spelled אֱלֹהִים, *Elōhim,* the Name that refers to God as the One Who is all-powerful. When it appears with a prefix לִי־הֹ־וִ־ה, it is pronounced *Lay-lōhim.* We have translated this Name as HASHEM/ELOHIM to indicate that it refers to the aspects inherent in each of those Names.

⊰{ TABLE OF CONTENTS }⊱

	Introductory Essay	2 Background of the Prayers

שַׁחֲרִית / THE MORNING SERVICE

הַשְׁכָּמַת הַבּוֹקֶר/צִיצִית/טַלִּית/תְּפִילִּין	5	Upon Arising/Tzitzis/Tallis/Tefillin
בִּרְכוֹת הַשַּׁחַר	70	Morning Blessings
קַדִּישׁ דְּרַבָּנָן	121	The Rabbis' Kaddish
קַדִּישׁ יָתוֹם	125	The Mourner's Kaddish
פְּסוּקֵי דְזִמְרָה	127	Pesukei D'Zimrah
בִּרְכוֹת קְרִיאַת שְׁמַע	161	The Blessings of the Shema
קְרִיאַת שְׁמַע	169	Shema
שְׁמוֹנֶה עֶשְׂרֵה/עֲמִידָה	179	Shemoneh Esrei/Amidah
הַלֵּל	486	Hallel
תַּחֲנוּן	201	Supplication and Confession
הוֹצָאַת סֵפֶר תּוֹרָה	233	Removal of the Torah from the Ark
הַכְנָסַת סֵפֶר תּוֹרָה	243	Returning the Torah to the Ark
אַשְׁרֵי/וּבָא לְצִיּוֹן	246	Ashrei/Uva L'Tzion
שֵׁשׁ זְכִירוֹת	283	The Six Remembrances
שְׁלֹשׁ עֶשְׂרֵה עִקָּרִים	285	The Thirteen Principles of Faith
עֲשֶׂרֶת הַדִּבְּרוֹת	290	The Ten Commandments

בִּרְכַּת הַמָּזוֹן / GRACE AFTER MEALS

	Introductory Essay	296 **Background of the Prayer**
בִּרְכַּת הַמָּזוֹן	306	Grace After Meals
בְּרָכוֹת אַחֲרוֹנוֹת	326	Blessings After Other Foods
שֶׁבַע בְּרָכוֹת	330	Sheva Berachos
בְּרִית מִילָה	334	Circumcision Ceremony
פִּדְיוֹן הַבֵּן	345	Redemption of the Firstborn Son
תְּפִלַּת הַדֶּרֶךְ	348	Wayfarer's Prayer
בִּרְכוֹת הַנֶּהֱנִין	349	Blessings of Enjoyment
בִּרְכוֹת הוֹדָאָה	351	Blessings of Praise and Gratitude

מִנְחָה / THE AFTERNOON SERVICES

	Introductory Essay	354 **Background of the Prayers**
מִנְחָה	356	Minchah

מַעֲרִיב / THE EVENING SERVICES

	Introductory Essay	400 **Background of the Prayers**
מַעֲרִיב	406	Maariv

	שְׁמַע 408	Shema
שְׁמוֹנֶה עֶשְׂרֵה/עֲמִידָה	420	Shemoneh Esrei/Amidah
סְפִירַת הָעוֹמֶר	448	Counting the Omer
קִדּוּשׁ לְבָנָה	454	Kiddush Levanah

קְרִיאַת שְׁמַע עַל הַמִּטָּה / THE BEDTIME SHEMA

Introductory Essay 465 **Background of the Prayers**
קְרִיאַת שְׁמַע עַל הַמִּטָּה 468 The Bedtime Shema

הַלֵּל / HALLEL

Introductory Essay 483 **Background of the Prayers**
הַלֵּל 486 Hallel

רֹאשׁ חוֹדֶשׁ / ROSH CHODESH

Introductory Essay 500 **Background of the Prayers**
מוּסָף לְרֹאשׁ חוֹדֶשׁ 503 **Mussaf for Rosh Chodesh**

עֶרֶב יוֹם כִּפּוּר / EREV YOM KIPPUR

כַּפָּרוֹת 518 Kaporos/Atonement

חֲנוּכָּה / CHANUKAH

Introductory Essay 528 **Background of the Prayers**
הַדְלָקַת נֵרוֹת חֲנוּכָּה 531 Kindling the Chanukah Lights

פּוּרִים / PURIM

Introductory Essay 537 **Background of the Prayers**
קְרִיאַת הַמְּגִלָּה 542 The Reading of the Megillah

עִנְיְנֵי שְׂמָחוֹת / DEATH AND BEREAVEMENT

Introductory Essay 548 **Coping With Loss**
וִדּוּי 553 Confessional
סֵדֶר לְוָיָה 554 Funeral Services
קַדִּישׁ אַחַר הַקְּבוּרָה 559 Kaddish Following Burial

קְרִיאַת הַתּוֹרָה לְחוֹל 563 THE WEEKDAY TORAH READINGS

←§ Preface

In his quest to express our yearning for the joy of God's ultimate redemption, King David writes: זֶה הַיּוֹם עָשָׂה ה׳ נָגִילָה וְנִשְׂמְחָה בוֹ, *This is the day* HASHEM *has made; let us rejoice and be glad on it.*

This verse includes two distinct expressions of joy: *simchah* and *gilah*. The *Vilna Gaon* explains the difference between the two. *Simchah* is reflected in the thrill of a quick accomplishment; the *simchah* of resolving a difficult problem; the exhilaration of a successful business transaction; the joy of assuming an exalted position of responsibility; or the excitement of finding an item of great worth. *Gilah,* on the other hand, is the joy that comes with the completion of a long process. Where *simchah* is instantaneous, *gilah* is beyond the moment, but well worth the wait and toil. Ultimately, it is a far more fulfilling joy.

While King David yearns for the *simchah* and *gilah* of God's eternal embrace, our quest for purpose in service of God can at times also be reflected in these two expressions. It is with a boundless sense of *simchah* that we introduce to a searching Jewish world this transliterated linear Seif Edition of the ArtScroll Siddur. The joy of creating a project and working towards its fulfillment is truly a moment of *simchah. Gilah,* however, is the status we confidently aspire to enjoy in the months and years ahead. It will be the joy of seeing the benefits that this transliterated linear Siddur will bring to countless people, in the form of enhanced prayer and understanding. It will be the joy of contributing to man's quest for dialogue with our Creator, through the eloquent verses of prayer.

King Solomon also expressed the joys of *simchah* and *gilah*. He wrote: נָגִילָה וְנִשְׂמְחָה בָּךְ, *We will be glad and rejoice in You (Song of Songs* 1:4). The Midrash asks: What does בָּךְ, *in You,* signify? *Yalkut Shimoni* teaches us that the word represents Your [God's] Torah, Your redemption, and, finally, the numerical value of the word, twenty-two, which represents the twenty-two letters of the Hebrew alphabet. Solomon, therefore, prays for the opportunity for Jews to use the twenty-two

PREFACE / xiv

letters of the holy Hebrew language as a vehicle toward unbridled joy. With the introduction of the Seif Siddur, the full creative potential of the Hebrew alphabet is now available to all who yearn for a mystical opportunity to engage God in His holy language.

To praise and beseech God in *Leshon HaKodesh,* the holy language of Hebrew, is an opportunity that is now within the grasp of every Jew. To explore the brilliance of the structure of *tefillah* (prayer) and allow it to penetrate the soul, is now open to every searching Jew. To give the gift of prayer and spiritual meaning to fellow Jews is, in fact, to grant them a gift of eternity — a dialogue with our Creator — at home and in a synagogue.

We are gratified by the overwhelming response of the Jewish community to the Seif Edition of the ArtScroll transliterated linear Sabbath and Festival Siddur. It is with further pride that we introduce the Weekday Siddur and its essays to a community searching to revitalize those singular opportunities to engage God in the dialogue of prayer.

As the Orthodox Union celebrates its Centennial Year, this gift of prayer may be its grandest expression of service to the English-speaking Jewish world. It is fitting, therefore, that one of the highlights of the Centennial Celebration is this overture to all Jews to join in the sublime and uplifting experience of prayer by making it available to all. As the burgeoning spiritually inspired Jewish community seeks greater opportunities to understand the essence of a Jew, the two-volume Seif Edition of the ArtScroll Transliterated Linear Siddur will act as a vehicle of inspiration, motivation and guidance.

We hope and expect that, with God's help, this Siddur will turn *tefillah* (prayer) into an all-embracing experience, from which no Jew will feel excluded by shortcomings of language or background. The line-by-line transliterated and translated Hebrew page is designed to encourage the development of skills to help users eventually read the Siddur in the original Hebrew. At the same time, the treatment allows the reader to progress at his own pace, with translation in place, as he prays.

We are deeply appreciative of the spirit of partnership and purpose that we have shared over the decades with Mesorah Publications and its guiding forces, Rabbi Meir Zlotowitz and Rabbi Nosson Scherman. Their contribution to the revitalization of Torah life is perhaps their greatest legacy. We are grateful to Rabbi Benjamin Yudin, noted Rav, educator and thinker, for his scholarly and inspirational essays and notes on prayer that will distinguish this Siddur as a book of study as well as a book of prayer. We thank Reb Sheah Brander who created the format of the Siddur and whose graphics genius and dedication have

xv / **PREFACE**

made the Seif Edition such a work of beauty. Phyllis Meiner of the Orthodox Union and Avrohom Biderman of Mesorah have coordinated this project from its inception, and this undertaking is a testimony to their diligence and concern. Rabbi Avie Gold did the final editing with his customary skill. Akiva Atwood provided the transliteration. We thank them and all who have toiled in making this Siddur a reality.

The two-volume Seif Edition of the ArtScroll Siddur has been dedicated by Mr. and Mrs. Herbert Seif in memory of Abraham Seif, of blessed memory. May the millions of *tefillos* that will be offered through the creation of the Siddur act as a living legacy to a man of sterling qualities, integrity, and a good name.

Finally, may we, as a united Jewish community, use this newly expanded collective gift of prayer *lehagdil Torah ulehadirah,* to raise the banner of Torah and to extol its values to a searching world.

Rabbi Raphael B. Butler	Mandell I. Ganchrow, M.D.
Executive Vice-President	President
Orthodox Union	Orthodox Union

Introduction

by Rabbi Benjamin Yudin

Prayer: The privileged give and take

What food is to our body, prayer is to our soul. Rav Yehudah HaLevi, in his classic philosophic work *Kuzari,* gives us insight as to the purpose of prayer. Man cannot live without food, and similarly our soul, which is Divine in origin, yearns to be connected with the Divine. Prayer connects us regularly with Hashem.

Our increased understanding of prayer not only impacts upon and makes more meaningful the "prayer encounter and experience" but ideally impacts upon our thinking and actions constantly. To begin with, the one about to pray is to ask himself: What does Hashem owe me? Does He owe me anything? Rabbi Shimon in *Avos* (2:18) teaches, "When you pray, do not make your prayer *keva* (usually translated, a set routine), but rather beg for compassion and supplication before the Omnipresent." The *Mabit* in his *Beis Elohim,* Chapter 1, explains that *keva* in addition refers to the attitude and expectation of the one praying. *Keva* would therefore refer to the one who feels that Hashem has to answer his prayers, it's coming to him, as Hashem owes him something. Rather, our Rabbis are teaching us, one is to pray in the manner of a poor man who approaches and beseeches a rich man for help.

There are different types of *mitzvos,* each with its own identity and purpose. Some *mitzvos* are fulfilled by the performance of a specific action. Shaking a *lulav,* returning a lost object, placing a *mezuzah* on one's door — each is a self-contained *mitzvah,* accomplished upon the completion of the act. While ideally proper thoughts and intentions are to accompany these actions, the mere performance of the act accomplishes the *mitzvah.* In other *mitzvos,* while there is an action performed, noted Rabbi Soloveitchik, the *kiyum,* the ultimate fulfillment of the *mitzvah,* is the personal-psychological-emotional impact that the particular action has on the psyche and character of the individual performing the *mitzvah.* Thus, regarding the laws of mourning, the Rabbis legislated various actions and restrictions for the week of *shivah.* These actions themselves are not the ultimate fulfillment, rather they are the means to impact upon and impress the mourner as to his state of being. Reflection on life, on its purpose and mission, is the ultimate intent of these laws, as King Solomon teaches in *Ecclesiastes* (7:2), "And the living should take it to heart." Similarly, the *mitzvah* of *simchah,* rejoicing on the festivals, the special foods and drink and clothing are meant to create a feeling and state of closeness to Hashem. *Teshuvah —* repentance — is another example of this category. The specific text and recitation of confession is the mechanical, formal, procedural component of this *mitzvah.* The real fulfillment comes only when the individual feels morose and regret for

his past and genuinely yearns for an altered future. This explains why these particular *mitzvos* do not have a blessing preceding them, as the ultimate performance of the *mitzvah* is subjective and not always does the action lead to its ideal effect of molding and shaping character and personality. Prayer, likewise, is in this category of *mitzvos*.

Prayer begins in the synagogue. The process of prayer starts with the recitation of specific prayers composed by the Men of the Great Assembly about 2,500 years ago. The fulfillment of this *mitzvah* is accomplished throughout the day and specifically in the interval between one prayer and the next. Prayer is not only submitting a "shopping list" of needs and requests to Hashem. Rather, by submission of the requests, one comes to realize his total dependence on Hashem. Prior to the recitation of *Shemoneh Esrei,* the Jew introduces his prayer with the verse, "My Lord, open my lips, that my mouth may declare Your praise" (*Psalms* 51:17). Out of the nineteen blessings in the daily *Amidah,* the first three blessings are those of praise and the last three blessings are those of thanksgiving. The middle thirteen blessings are personal and communal requests. Why then is the entire *Shemoneh Esrei* referred to as praise? The *Mabit* (Chapter 2) brilliantly answers that the fact that we have no other address, no other source to make these requests of, is of itself great praise to Hashem. Prayer reminds man that he is in need of Hashem. There is no room for conceit or arrogance when one realizes that all he possesses is a Divine gift. If prayer can remove these negative character and personality traits, then prayer indeed transforms one into a better person.

Jealousy stems from the notion that what the next person has, he might not deserve, or we believe that we are entitled to it as well. However, if we truly understands the ninth blessing of the *Amidah* where we pray for a year of prosperity and acknowledge that all we receive is from Hashem — and that what the next individual has received also comes only from Hashem — then there is no room for jealousy in our lives. Moreover, the tendency to cheat or lie in order to be successful in business is no longer a viable option. We cannot pray to Hashem that He should provide for us and then implement actions that are contrary to His plan for successful living, namely, His Torah. Prayer reminds us thrice daily that despite what is happening about us there is meaning and purpose to life: to serve Hashem.

Perhaps only because prayer impacts, does man have the "license or *chutzpah*" to make the same requests of Hashem that he did but several hours ago. In the morning, one prayed for health for loved ones, livelihood for those out of work, a *shidduch* for those not yet married, and redemption for the Jewish people. At first glance, in the afternoon, at *Minchah* time, when one is about to make the same requests, should he not be stopped by the fact that he already asked Hashem earlier in the day, and He said, "No!" Why ask again? One answer is that ideally he is not the same person he was at *Shacharis;* it is a new day, he is a new person. The morning *Shacharis* prayer has transformed the worshiper into a more sensitive, caring individual, and thus, as a "new person," he can offer what appears to be the same prayer as he did this morning. However, circum-

stances have changed. There is reason to believe that the "new individual" approaching Hashem might receive a different response than the one earlier received.

Communal prayer which the Talmud (*Berachos* 6a, 8a) lauds is one that not only enhances the quality of one's prayer, but binds and connects the worshiper to his people and community. On a practical note, many have been privileged to transform a personal tragedy and loss of loved one to not only a meaningful period of mourning and grieving by the recitation of the *Kaddish,* but to becoming part of a Jewish community. Regular attendance at prayer ideally leads to attendance at classes and growth in one's appreciation of the privilege of being Jewish. Service to the congregation and community in the form of extending one's personal talents and capabilities is often a meaningful extension of praying with a congregation.

Interestingly, often the anticipation of prayer itself plays a significant role in one's day. Ideally, not only the one saying *Kaddish,* but everyone should try to pray all three prayers daily with a *minyan.* Thus one's comings and goings will be centered around where he will be able to find a *minyan* for that time of the day. The Torah ordains, in the second paragraph of the *Shema,* "to serve Him with all your heart and with all your soul" (*Deuteronomy* 11:13); and the *Rambam* teaches that this verse refers to prayer. Ideally, through prayer, the privilege of communication with Hashem, and the very arranging of one's schedule constantly around the recitation of prayers, one comes to the realization that not all of one's time is his own; Hashem already has a lien, a claim on certain key slots of time in one's day, creating an ideal "*eved* - servant" relationship between man and Hashem. While the above-cited verse refers to prayer as Divine service, the purpose of this formal Divine service is to ensure that the entire day and its activities is truly one of "practical Divine service."

We are taught at the beginning of the fifth chapter of Tractate *Berachos* of the ideal frame of mind we are to bring to our prayers. Ideally, we are taught that we are to reflect on the goodness of Hashem prior to the recitation of the *Shemoneh Esrei.* Thus, in the morning we remind ourselves of the Egyptian redemption and His governing and controlling history, enabling us to appreciate that He will likewise speedily transform our exile into redemption. At *Minchah* we precede the recitation of the *Amidah* with the comforting verses of *Ashrei* that speak of Hashem's personal rapport with each individual. If one does not have the ability to contemplate prior to prayer, then the actual prayer service itself must serve to transform the individual. Whatever one was doing comes to an abrupt halt at *Minchah,* impacting upon the individual that however his day is going he has the privilege to stop and have an audience with Hashem. No activity in the day comes before the *Shacharis* prayer and ultimately the night is given greater significance by the recitation of *Maariv.*

Finally, we need to be reminded that prayer is a privilege and not a burden. The famous question regarding the serpent in *Parashas Bereishis* is: What kind of punishment and curse did Hashem place upon it if its food is always available — "And dust shall you eat all the days of your life" (*Genesis* 3:14)?

Rabbi Menachem Mendel of Kotzk explained that as a result of having given the serpent his life supply of food and sustenance, Hashem in effect cut off any rapport and relationship between Himself and the serpent. The serpent has no need to lift up his head and cry to Hashem for help. Prayer affords us the privilege of daily communicating and maintaining a rapport with Hashem. *Ashreinu ma tov chelkainu* translates to: How fortunate are we and how good is our circumstance that we have the privilege of a personal and communal relationship with Hashem.

∽§ Language of Creation

Why transliterate the Siddur — do we not find in the Talmud (*Sotah* 32a) that prayer may be recited in any language? Moreover, are we not taught (*Sanhedrin* 106b) that Hashem is concerned primarily with the sincerity of man, literally that "He desires the heart" of man? The answers to these questions are significant, as the emergence of this Siddur will, it is hoped, enable people who are not yet comfortable and capable of reading Hebrew to pray in Hebrew with the congregation

Rabbi Avraham Yitzchak Kook comments on the daily prayer *Baruch She'emar,* which speaks of God as having uttered the words that brought the universe into being, that words most often are descriptive; they *describe* events or things, but words do not create. God's words were of a different order; the very words themselves were the medium of Creation. God "spoke and the world came into being." What is true regarding Hashem is equally true regarding man's prayer. When he prays he is not only praising God, presenting his needs, and expressing thanksgiving, but he is creating the means, text and opportunity to have a dialogue with Hashem.

∽§ The Holy Tongue

Hebrew is called לְשׁוֹן הַקֹּדֶשׁ, *the holy tongue. Rambam* suggest that the reason for this designation is that there are no words in the Hebrew language for the sexual organs or relations. In other words, the language is sacred because it instills within its people a sense of modesty and purity. *Ramban* proposes that it is called the holy language because it is the language with which Hashem created the world, the language that Adam and Eve spoke. The *Midrash* (*Bereishis Rabbah* 18:6) cites the response of Adam upon seeing Eve — "This shall be called woman for from man she was taken" (*Genesis* 2:23) — as proof that the Torah was given in Hebrew, for the verse teaches that the name *ishah,* woman, comes from the Hebrew word *ish,* man. Moreover, the above-cited *Midrash* teaches: "As the Torah was written by Hashem in Hebrew, so too the world was created with the holy language." As Hashem creates the world anew every day and man is privileged to create dialogue with Hashem, is it not fitting to approach His Divine Presence in His holy language, thereby approaching Him with greater respect, honor and dignity? The primary reason for praying in Hebrew is its richness in spiritual connotations. The holy tongue contains many hidden meanings, nuances, and references that cannot be communicated in a translation. Even if a

translation is correct and accurate, by definition it falls short of the mark, because it can capture only one of the meanings of a phrase. The prophet Jeremiah (23:29) describes the Torah's many meanings in terms of "a hammer that shatters a rock," which splinters into countless fragments; similarly the words of God are so rich in meaning that each word has many varied and legitimate explanations. Thus, praying in Hebrew arms the worshiper with the many forms of praise, petition, and thanksgiving that are inherent in the language.

The *Arizal* taught that no prayer is for naught. Even if a particular prayer is not effective for a person at the specific time he utters it, it is deposited in the Heavenly "bank of prayer," where it is safeguarded and subsequently validated at a time when Hashem sees fit. The richness of Hebrew, therefore, permits us to deposit much more.

⋦ Caliber of the Composers

The Talmud (*Megillah* 17b) teaches that the Men of the Great Assemly, which included many prophets, composed the *Shemoneh Esrei* prayer. Rabbi Joseph B. Soloveitchik, in his *Lonely Man of Faith,* teaches that it was necessary that people of such stature compose the prayers, so that they would be meaningful and expressive of the needs of the Jewish people not only then, but for the next 2,000 years. A case in point: The Talmud (*Berachos* 28b) teaches that when the Sages deemed it necessary to formulate a nineteenth blessing in the *Amidah* against the heretics who were slandering Jews to the Roman government, all agreed that only Shmuel HaKatan was qualified to compose the blessing, because only he could invest it with the perfect balance of love for fellow Jews, and devotion and dedication to the world of Hashem.

We are taught (*Sofrim* 1:7) that when the Torah was translated into Greek, a fast day was declared and darkness descended on the world, and that this tragedy is comparable to the making of the Golden Calf, because "the Torah could not possibly be translated properly." What is true regarding the Torah is equally true regarding prayer; many different meanings are contained in the many psalms and Scriptural verses that abound in our prayer service. By reciting prayers in their original text we invoke the many meanings to help on our behalf, whether we understand or not. An example is the way the *Sfas Emes* understood the verse recited prior to the blowing of the *shofar:* זַמְּרוּ אֱלֹהִים זַמֵּרוּ, usually translated as: *Make music for Hashem, make music,* or *Sing praises to Hashem, sing praises* (*Psalms* 47:7). The brilliant chassidic master taught that the Hebrew root זמר also means *to prune,* as in *Leviticus* 25:4. Thus, he interpreted the above verse homiletically to mean we cut through a strict, harsh measure of judgment, which is alluded to by the Name *Elokim,* which connotes God's strict judgment. Clearly there is much more than meets the eye when we pray in Hebrew.

⋦ Why Hebrew

True, the Talmud teaches that prayer and the *Shema* may be recited in any language, but the commentators offer the following explanation as to why

INTRODUCTION / xxii

Hebrew is preferable. The *Chasam Sofer* (*Teshuvos Choshen Mishpat* 193) writes that it is interesting to note that the debate as to whether to pray in a language one understands or to pray in Hebrew is not a new one. In the days of the Men of the Great Assembly, Hebrew was not the vernacular; the Jewish community, as we are taught in the Book of *Ezra,* spoke Ashdudis, yet the prayers were composed in Hebrew. Moreover, writes Rabbi Ephraim Zalman Margoliyos in his essay *Safah Berurah,* the Mishnah's teaching that prayer may be recited in all languages was only in effect until the composition of the prayers by the Men of the Great Assembly; subsequently we are to pray — preferably — in Hebrew. Similarly, the great *gaon* Rabbi Akiva Eiger, as well, writes that it is forbidden to deviate from the enactment of the Men of the Great Assembly.

Another significant reason for praying in Hebrew is suggested by Rabbi Zvi Hirsh Chayes, who notes the powerful unifying effect that praying in Hebrew has had on the Jewish people. Whenever and wherever a Jew was dispersed he was able to join in prayer with other Jews. Moreover, had we accepted the perhaps more logical approach of praying in the vernacular, thus making the service more accessible to all, then the Torah, being written in Hebrew, might, God forbid, have been forgotten and neglected. *Avodah* — prayer — which, together Torah and kind deeds, is part of the tripod upon which the world stands (*Avos* 1:2), helped preserve and safeguard our holy Torah.

This Siddur enables every worshiper to join the congregation in the fullest sense of the word, as a participant, not as a spectator, stranger, or outsider. In addition, the translation below each line is there to help the worshiper understand his prayers and become more proficient in his knowledge of Hebrew. It is my fervent hope that many newcomers using this Siddur will not only pray from left to right with the transliteration, but will use the transliteration to help them learn the Hebrew language, as well.

~§ Acknowledgments

The Talmud (*Sotah* 13b) teaches that a *mitzvah* is attributed to the one who finishes it. I am most grateful to Hashem for the privilege of finishing the second volume of the Seif Transliterated Siddur. Prayer, as noted in the introduction, is basic to the Jew each and every day. The opportunity afforded to me to introduce the daily prayers to those searching for meaning and undertanding fills me with tremendous personal *hakaras hatov*.

When approached by **Rabbi Raphael B. Butler** of the Orthodox Union and **Rabbi Nosson Scherman** and **Rabbi Meir Zlotowitz** of ArtScroll/Mesorah to pen essays for the beginner, and to make the Siddur more open, understandable and friendly to those not-yet comfortable with the traditional Hebrew Siddur, I soon realized how much there is to learn regarding the background, meaning and philosophy of our prayers, for the relative newcomer to the synagogue as well as for those praying in Hebrew all their lives. I am grateful to the trust that these colleagues placed in me and appreciative of the friendship, direction and support that Rabbi Butler has provided me and this project. His excitement and creativity was a personal source of inspiration. Rabbi Nosson Scherman's meticulous editing has breathed additional life and greater clarity into my essays; for this and for his constant encouragement, I am very grateful. May he, together with **Rabbi Avie Gold** and **Rabbi Avrohom Biderman,** who personally assisted me, be afforded the opportunity to continue to challenge and uplift the Jewish community through their magnificent *harbatzas haTorah*. Rabbis Butler, Zlotowitz and Scherman have given me the opportunity to enrich my spirit with the precious hours carved out of my life — time I spent trying to open the doors of prayer to a wider universe of our fellow Jews.

My task was made easier by the privilege I have had for the past many years of studying on Monday nights with dear friends who have emigrated from the former Soviet Union. Bright men and women denied the opportunity of any Jewish education in their youth, they have taught me that "beginners" can comprehend sophisticated material if presented clearly and logically. Often, in the preparation of these essays, I envisioned myself amidst my loyal students, who subsequently became the barometer as to what materials would be included in this Siddur. To them I affectionately proclaim, as stated in the Talmud (*Taanis* 7a): "I learned much from my teachers, more from the discussion with my colleagues, but most of all, did I learn from my students." Your remarkable religious growth and devotion has inspired me in this entire effort. You and your children have given me great joy in your successful strides in Torah and *mitzvos*. I am especially grateful to my student **Eliyahu Parker** of Jacksonville, Mississippi for his careful review of the *Shemoneh Esrei* essay. His enthusiasm for this project added greatly to my personal gratification.

The completed work has emerged with an identity unexpected at the outset of this project. Originally, the concept of a complete transliterated Siddur was novel unto itself. I applaud the painstaking difficult labor of love of **Rabbi Sheah Brander** and his staff for their excellent transliteration and presentation of the Siddur. It has not only opened the Siddur to countless Jews but I trust the doors of many more synagogues will be open to them as well. They will now have the opportunity of becoming an integral part of the congregation and its prayers. The essays represent my research utilizing some of the major works on *tefillah* including *Otzar HaTefillos, Siddur HaGra, Siddur Iyun Tefillah, Avudraham*, and many more classical works too numerous to mention. In addition, the following works: *World of Prayer* by **Rabbi Elie Munk,** *Meditation on the Siddur* by **Rabbi Jacobson** and the *Encyclopedia of Jewish Prayer* by **Dr. Macy Nulman,** were most helpful in providing background information and scholarship. I thank the very capable librarians of the Gottesman Library at Yeshiva University, where I did most of my writing, for their eagerness to assist and for introducing me to Rabbi Luban's essay on the *Kaddish,* published by Yeshiva University.

A meeting with **Rabbi Benjamin Blech,** former Rabbi of Young Israel of Oceanside and dear colleague at Yeshiva University, yielded the suggestion for headings or captions to summarize the content of each individual prayer. These headings would enable the worshiper to pray in the transliterated Hebrew and have some understanding as to the nature and essence of that particular prayer. These headings were the most challenging part of this project. As stated above, there are often many different themes contained in one prayer, and choosing a particular synopsis was most difficult. Divine providence saw to it that my son, **Rabbi Nisanel Yudin,** would join me in these deliberations. It was truly a fulfillment of *"Es vaheiv besufah"* (*Numbers* 21:14) understood by the Talmud (*Kiddushin* 30b) to refer to the only ideal argument and strife between father and son, namely in the quest for the truth of Torah, yielding and generating greater love between them.

The family's involvement continued with my son **Alexander** reading and editing most of the essays. His constructive suggestions have been incorporated into these essays. I am grateful to my son-in-law **Rabbi Larry Rothwachs** for his assistance in the *Hallel* prayer. I would like to thank my other children, **Joel** and **Susan, Nisanel** and **Ruthie, Steven** and **Devorah, Larry** and **Chaviva, Aryeh,** and **Penina** for their encouragement, support and patience throughout this project and for the many hours spent away from them. Since Adar and the publication of Volume I, my wife Shevi and I are most grateful to Hashem that our son **Aryeh** was married to the former **Atara Williams** and that our son, **Alexander** also became a *chasan* and will soon marry **Rivka Marcus.** We are grateful to Hashem for the special daughters coming into our home and pray for continued Torah *nachas*.

To my mother, **Mrs. Adele Yudin,** to my in-laws, **Irving** and **Sarah Werner,** who served as foundations of strength, love and inspiration, may they be blessed with good health to lead our family for many more years. My father, **Alexander**

xxv / ACKNOWLEDGMENTS

Ziskind, *zt"l,* a man who worked all his life for the betterment and enhancement of Jewish communities and synagogues, inspires me constantly.

I am most grateful to **Rabbi Baruch Simon,** Rosh Yeshiva and colleague at Yeshiva University, for his time, patience and vast encyclopedic array of knowledge that he made available to me. His insights and guidance significantly enhanced this project. I pray that Hashem reward him with the fulfillment of his prayers, enabling him to continue teaching Torah at our Yeshiva for many years.

Unfortunately, since the publication of the first volume, my Rebbe, **Rabbi Aharon Kreiser,** זצ"ל הרב אהרן גדליה בן הרב ישראל יעקב, was taken from our "Wordly Yeshiva." His passing is a great loss not only to the Lakewood Jewish community but indeed to all of *Klal Yisrael,* for rarely does one find a veritable giant both in Torah knowledge and in *chesed*. I had the privilege of visiting him often during the summer months and always when leaving him, I felt both humbled and exhilarated, knowing I had just been exposed to an exceptional individual whose very essence and identity became one with the Torah he studied and the *chesed* he practiced. He was not only constantly and graciously available with his time, guidance and knowledge, but often initiated the concern and sought me out under the pretext that our learning was mutually beneficial. May the learning and inspiration that emerges from this Siddur be a constant elevation to his golden *neshamah* and a merit for his family and *Klal Yisrael*.

I am grateful to **Rabbi Eliyahu Swerdloff,** Rosh Yeshiva of Yeshiva Gedola of Paterson, a dear friend and neighbor, who enhanced the work and guided me; as well as to **Rabbi Hershel Schachter,** Rosh Yeshiva at Yeshiva University, for his friendship, availability and for providing insights of **Rav Soleveitchik**, זצ"ל, on prayer. I feel myself most fortunate that I was able to complete this volume in *Eretz Yisrael* and appreciate the time I learned with **Rabbi Yaacov Wiener** of the Torah and Science Institute.

I would like to thank my congregational family, Shomrei Torah of Fair Lawn, and its distinguished president, **Mr. Rodney Grundman,** for their encouragement and support of my Friday morning radio program on the *Parashah*, enabling me to reach out to a listening audience, and now for their enthusiasm and support of my work on behalf of a reading audience.

In the course of this past year, four of our families and the entire Fair Lawn community sustained especially severe blows. Four young individuals in the prime of their lives and earlier were snatched from our midst. We have learned how important prayer is especially at a time of crisis and are comforted by the teachings of our Rabbis that no prayer is uttered for naught. If our immediate request is not afforded us, our heartfelt prayers are deposited in His special vaults to be energized and ulitized in the appropriate time. May the souls of

ברוך יצחק בן ברוך לייב
אלעזר יהושע בן משה יצחק
יונתן חיים בן משה דוד הכהן
אביעזר דוד בן זלמן

assist in bringing forth our *tefillos* before the *Kisei HaKavod* and may our *tefillos* be a constant *aliyah* for their precious *neshamos*.

ACKNOWLEDGMENTS / xxvi

I wish to thank **Debby Friedman** of Fair Lawn, the go-between myself and the Orthodox Union and **Phyllis Meiner,** for her meticulous transcribing and cheerful encouragement throughout.

On a personal note, how fortuitous that I was privileged to be raised in the Crown Heights community of Brooklyn and knew the late **Abraham Seif,** *z"l*, as a warm, friendly mainstay of the community. His son **Heshe,** a loyal helping friend over the years, and his grandson, **Dr. Jordan Alter,** an officer in my congregation, have refined his legacy through their ongoing devoted service to *Klal Yisrael*.

Finally, in a category all unto herself, there really are no words to describe the debt of gratitude I owe my dear wife **Shevi.** I can best only borrow from the words of Rabbi Akiva who, as we are taught in the Talmud (*Kesubos* 63a), taught and proudly told all that his Torah and that which he was privileged to teach and disseminate to others was only as a result of his wife's righteousness and total self-sacrifice. Shevi has not only encouraged me but has been a *"rebbe"* of *chesed* to me in a very real sense, and therefore all of the lessons of sensitivity, compassion and kindness that I was able to cull from the depths of our *tefillah* stem from her character. May she be blessed with good health and continue to mold our children and grandchildren in her beautiful *middos* of Torah and *maasim tovim*.

Benjamin Yudin

אב תשנ"ח / August 1998

The Background of the Prayers

BACKGROUND OF THE PRAYERS / 2

◆§ The Sources of Our Prayers

◆§ The Patriarchs

The Talmud (*Berachos* 26b) cites two sources as the origin of our daily prayers. The first is our Patriarchs, each of whom instituted a prayer which reflected his life experience. *Shacharis*, the morning prayer, which is recited when the sun is rising, reflects the life of Abraham. Faced with many challenges and difficulties as he embarked on the new mission to proclaim the word of God to an idolatrous world, he emerged triumphant and was treated respectfully by his peers and neighbors.

Minchah, which is recited in the afternoon, when the sun is descending, reflects the circumstance of Isaac, who composed it. In comparison with his father, Abraham, his life was one of subtle decline; he never enjoyed the fame or acceptance that his father did. Nevertheless, Isaac maintained Abraham's teachings and continued his legacy.

Maariv, the evening prayer, was composed by Jacob, whose life was filled with one problem after another, reflected by the dark of night when his prayer is recited. His faith and inspiration during even the darkest times has helped sustain his descendants throughout the "nights" of our history, including the past two millennia of dispersion and frequent oppression.

Maharsha suggests that each of the Patriarchs surely prayed all three times, in keeping with the verse *Evening, morning, and noon, I supplicate and moan, and He has heard my voice* (*Psalms* 55:18), but the life experiences of each was closely identified with a particular prayer.

In all circumstances, each Patriarch turned to God for thanksgiving, guidance, comfort, and inspiration. We, their descendants, proudly maintain this Divine encounter.

◆§ Korbanos / Offerings

The second source for our prayers is the *Korbanos*, the daily offerings that were brought in the Holy Temple in Jerusalem. The Torah ordains that one lamb was to be offered in the morning and a second lamb in the afternoon (*Numbers* 28:4). This was done every day without exception. On the Sabbath and *Yom Tov*, in addition to the morning offering, the Jewish community brought the *mussaf*, or additional offering.

These daily offerings brought atonement to the Jewish nation and renewed the close ties between Hashem and His people. Indeed, the word *korban*, generally — but erroneously — translated as sacrifice, comes from the root *karov* [קרב], which means coming close. Far from a "sacrifice," a word that implies loss, a *korban* is a positive thing — a means of drawing close to God. The Jew begins his day by reiterating his love for Hashem and his willingness to place all of his possessions and resources in His hands, as a means of drawing closer to Him.

◆§ Symbolism of the Offerings

Rabbi Samson Raphael Hirsch explains the symbolism of the offerings as follows. Hashem is our Shepherd, we are taught in Psalm 23. By offering two lambs daily, we proclaim that He leads us morning and evening, through all the different periods of our lives. The flour and wine offerings brought in the Temple signify that all our possessions, from the bare essentials to the luxuries, come from Him and are at His disposal. The institution of *korbanos* represents a reciprocal process: God gives life to man, and man dedicates his life back to Hashem.

The animal that was slaughtered may be seen as man's animalistic elements being placed in the service of God. We control our natural inclinations and attempt to channel them toward Divine service rather than mundane, even unholy, pursuits. Likewise, the fats offered on the Altar symbolize man's excessive indulgence and unused energy, his untapped resources, which could be used more constructively when applied to a higher cause. And the blood sprinkled by the Altar symbolizes man's passions, all of which should be consecrated to Hashem.

The Talmud (*Taanis* 27b) teaches that Abraham asked how the Jewish nation would attain forgiveness without the Temple. God replied that when the people of Israel recite the Scriptural order of the offerings, God will consider it as if they had actually brought the offerings and they will be forgiven. This principle is cited by the prophet who said, "Let our lips substitute for bulls" (*Hosea* 14:3).

◆§ Time Frames

Offerings, as the origin of prayer, impact upon our prayers both legally and philosophically. Prayer must come at fixed times, following the same schedule that governed the sacrificial order, as opposed to randomly chosen moments of individual inspiration. Thus, one should complete the *Shemoneh Esrei* within the first third of the day, just as the morning offering was brought during the first third of the day. (If, however, one was delayed, the *Shacharis Shemoneh Esrei* may be recited until midday, just as the morning *korban* could have been brought until that time, if it had not been brought in its preferred time.)

Similarly, just as our morning prayer corresponds to the daily morning offering, *Minchah*, the afternoon prayer, corresponds to the daily afternoon offering. *Maariv*, the evening prayer, by contrast, is not tied to a specific offering, as no offerings were brought at night. *Maariv* does, however, correspond to the nighttime burning on the Altar of all the fats and organs left over from the preceding day's offerings. It is because *Shacharis* and *Minchah* correspond to specific, required offerings that they are of primary importance, and, therefore, they include the *chazzan's* repetition of *Shemoneh Esrei*. *Maariv*, however, has no such repetition because it does not come in place of a required offering.

The daily recitation of the offering of *Ketores*, the eleven spices that comprised the incense offering, substitutes today for the actual daily offering of *Ketores* every morning and evening on the Golden Altar in the Temple. The Talmud

(*Yoma* 44a) teaches that the *Ketores* atoned for evil speech and served as a daily reminder to the people that there is life and death in the power of the tongue, just as intentional changes in the formula of *Ketores* could incur the Heavenly imposed death penalty.

☙ Not Recitation Alone

Rabbeinu Bachya notes in his commentary on the Torah that it is not the mere recitation of the sacrificial order that is dear to Hashem and that attains its desired end, but rather it is possessing an understanding of the proceedings and their symbolic lessons that achieves this. Thus, our *Shacharis* prayer corresponds to the morning offering that dedicates to God the incoming day's potential; *Minchah* corresponds to the offering that acknowledges Him as Master of all that we have accomplished; and *Maariv* proclaims that even when man is inactive during the night, we declare His absolute and uncontested sovereignty.

The *Levush*, however, contends that our recitation of *Korbanos* is for a different reason. There is a *mitzvah* to study Torah daily, and through the recitation of the *Korbanos*, with its combination of Scripture, Mishnah and Talmud, we accomplish this minimum fulfillment of our daily obligation. That these subject matters were chosen may be more fully understood with the philosophical ideas enumerated above, namely, that the *Korbanos* represent our yearning to become close to God.

☙ Donning the Tallis

Prayer is a great and challenging privilege. To be granted an audience with Hashem, regardless of the outcome, is rewarding. The very encounter is uplifting. Yet, though Hashem grants us this opportunity, too often man fails to capitalize upon the experience. Prayer is called "service of the heart," for Hashem desires our heartfelt commitment when we pray to Him. One way to help accomplish this is by wearing a garment especially for prayer. This is why our rabbis instituted the custom for married men — and, in many communities, single males as well — to wear a *tallis* in conjunction with the morning prayers, to help us focus on our lofty mission, our personal encounter with Hashem.

☙ Tzitzis — the Reminder

The Torah teaches that *tzitzis* (the ritual fringes affixed to a four-cornered garment) help us remember all of God's commandments (see the third paragraph of the *Shema*). Thus we cloak ourselves in a *tallis*, as if to separate ourselves from the mundane pressures and lures of society and envelop ourselves in a special wrap that reminds us of our unique calling and responsibility to

observe the 613 *mitzvos.*

When he stands in prayer, man wishes to be remembered, to be noticed, by God. We therefore don a garment whose essence is remembering, and in remembering Hashem, we hope to be remembered by Him. Perhaps this is why we are taught to give charity before praying (on Shabbos, one may pledge to do so): Though we may not be worthy of having all our requests granted, by giving charity we symbolize our plea that Hashem will reciprocate and be charitable to us.

The Torah ordains that only a four-cornered garment must have *tzitzis,* but since modern wardrobes do not include such garments, we would not have occasion to perform the commandment. Our love for God and desire to carry out His will is so strong, however, that we wear a four-cornered garment in order to affix *tzitzis,* such as the *tallis* during services and the smaller *tallis-katan* worn by males under their shirts. This insistence on creating a means to perform the commandment demonstrates our proactive commitment to find ways to observe even *mitzvos* that do not find their way to us.

The *tallis* is worn by males at every morning service, Shabbos, festivals, and weekdays, except on Tishah B'Av. It is also worn at all the Yom Kippur services and at the afternoon service on Tishah B'Av.

The Talmud teaches that covering one's head with the *tallis* is a sign of respect as well as an aid to concentration. Therefore, many follow this practice during the recitation of the *Amidah,* the most important prayer. Others cover their head earlier in the service, some just before the *Kaddish* prior to *Borchu,* or even before.

৵§ Tefillin

The head and hand *tefillin* each contain four paragraphs from the Torah, which speak of the uniqueness and oneness of Hashem, and recount the miracles He performed for us when He delivered us from Egypt. As Hashem was involved with our nation, and indeed each individual, in the historical past, so is the daily donning of the *tefillin* to remind us of his involvement in every aspect of our national and individual lives, thereby summoning us to daily prayer and thanksgiving. The *tefillin* worn on our arm commemorates His *strong arm* with which he performed the wonders or miracles in Egypt, and because the arm is opposite the heart, we are reminded to channel or subjugate the desires and thoughts of our hearts to His service. The head *tefillin* demonstrates that we commit the soul in our brain, together with our other senses and powers, to serve Hashem.

Originally, *tefillin* were worn all day and removed only at night. Due to their sanctity and the difficulty in being mindful of them constantly, the Rabbis

taught that we should wear the *tefillin* only for the *Shacharis* prayer. Donning the *tefillin* is a privilege. It constitutes one of the few positive Biblical commandments that the Jewish male is able to perform daily. The Torah refers to the *tefillin* as an *os,* a "sign" of the special relationship between Hashem and Israel. The term "sign" is also used to describe the Shabbos and pilgrimage festivals of Pesach, Shavuos and Succos. It is for this reason that we do not don the *tefillin* on Shabbos and Yom Tov, as that would detract from the integral holiness of those days, whose very essence and observance constitute a sign of this special relationship between Hashem and His people.

Because *tefillin* are holy, one should be especially careful in handling them and while wearing them. One should not engage in levity or idle conversation while wearing *tefillin* and, ideally, one should only pray and discuss aspects of Torah law while wearing them. Due to their sanctity, a youngster does not don his *tefillin* until several weeks before his *bar mitzvah*, when he is mature enough to treat them with the proper respect.

Tefillin are a prerequisite for the recitation of the *Shema* and *Amidah*, enabling the worshiper to, in the words of our Rabbis, "wholeheartedly submit to the yoke of the Kingdom of Heaven." If one fails to don *tefillin,* he has not only abstained from the fulfillment of an important Biblical command, but has thereby adversely affected the quality of his prayers. *Tefillin* may be looked upon as "spiritual antenna" enabling one to receive and direct messages on high.

The *mitzvah* of *tallis* is performed prior to the *mitzvah* of *tefillin* for the following two reasons: 1. A *mitzvah* performed more frequently is given priority over one fulfilled less frequently. The *tallis* is worn seven days a week, while *tefillin* are not worn on Shabbos and Yom Tov. 2. When performing *mitzvos,* one follows an ascending order regarding their sanctity, progressing from a lower degree of sanctity to a higher degree. Since the *tallis* is categorized as an "object of *mitzvah,*" while *tefillin* are "objects of holiness," the *tallis* is donned first. The Chafetz Chaim suggests that man internalize this ascension of *mitzvos* and realize that he personally is ascending to a higher degree of holiness when proceeding from *tallis* to *tefillin.*

๛ Kaddish

The *Kaddish* is one of the most important and misunderstood prayers in our liturgy. Although most people think of *Kaddish* as a prayer for the dead, it contains no mention of death whatsoever. Rather, the word *Kaddish* means "sanctification" of Hashem's Name, and that is the function it serves: to declare the holiness of God.

☙ Its Significance

Why is *Kaddish* so significant? Its opening words and the context of where and when they were recited shed light on this question. The prophet Ezekiel warned Israel of the impending destruction of the First Temple and at the same time assured them that eventually the Jewish people would be restored to their former position of spiritual preeminence and enjoy an ideal relationship with Hashem, centered around the Third Temple. Of that time God says, וְהִתְגַּדִּלְתִּי וְהִתְקַדִּשְׁתִּי, *I will be exalted and I will be sanctified* (*Ezekiel* 38:23), the phrase after which the beginning of *Kaddish* is patterned. The prophet says that not only will the people of Israel be redeemed, but, as difficult as it is for us to comprehend, God Himself will be redeemed at that time. When Israel suffers so does He, and when there is evil in this world, not only does man suffer, but God suffers as well. His destiny is inextricably bound to that of the Jewish nation, as we are taught by the symbolism of the burning bush, when He revealed Himself to Moses from the lowly, prickly bush.

The single most important part of *Kaddish* is יְהֵא שְׁמֵהּ רַבָּא מְבָרַךְ לְעָלַם וּלְעָלְמֵי עָלְמַיָּא, May *His great Name be blessed forever and ever*. According to *Machzor Vitri* (cited by *Tosafos, Berachos* 3a), it refers to the Amalekite nation's sneak attack upon Israel shortly after the Exodus from Egypt (*Exodus* 17:8). Amalek thus became the symbol and personification of evil in this world, for it attacked Israel not because it wanted land or possessions; rather, Amalek wanted to destroy Israel. At that time God vowed to blot out the remembrance of Amalek from under the heavens, saying, כִּי יָד עַל כֵּס יָהּ, *For the hand* [of God] *is on the throne of God: HASHEM maintains a war against Amalek from generation to generation* (*Exodus* 17:16). Interestingly, both the word for the throne, כֵּס, instead of כִּסֵּא, and the Name of God are shortened (God's Name in the verse has only two letters instead of all four letters [י-ה-ו-ה]). This suggests that neither His Name, meaning our perception of His essence, nor His throne, will be complete until the evil represented by Amalek is eradicated from this world. Thus, when we declare in *Kaddish* that His Name be blessed forever, we express the wish that His Name and throne be complete.

☙ Faith Amid Crisis

The significance of the *Kaddish* is that it manifests man's ability to express his faith, while acknowledging crisis and difficulties, be they national calamities or personal tragedies. This interpretation can be seen from a fascinating understanding of a Talmudic teaching (*Chullin* 91b). Contrasting the heavenly angels with the nation of Israel, the Talmud concludes that the children of Israel are more beloved and have greater merit before God than even the angels. This is shown by the fact that when the angels praise Hashem, they are permitted to utter His Name only after reciting the three words, "*Kadosh, Kadosh Kadosh,*" *Holy. holy, holy* — קָדוֹשׁ, קָדוֹשׁ, קָדוֹשׁ, ה׳ צְבָאוֹת, while Israel recites His Name after the two words, "*Shema Yisrael*" — שְׁמַע יִשְׂרָאֵל ה׳.

In commenting on this passage, the *Maharsha* suggests that each *Kadosh* of

the angels is inspired by a careful scrutiny and analysis of the Divine Presence in a different sphere, as is seen in the explication of these three levels of holiness that is found in the *Uva L'Tzion* prayer:

> *Holy in the most exalted heaven, the abode of His Presence; Holy on earth, product of His strength; Holy forever and ever is* HASHEM, *Master of Legions.*

The *Maharsha* explains that the angels have a complete understanding of the workings of Hashem. They see how His plan emanates from on high and is executed here on earth and will finally be clear to all in the World to Come. Only when they see the totality of His plan, program and actions do they respond with an enthusiastic sanctification of His Name.

The Jewish people, on the other hand, by virtue of their mortality, are privileged to see and comprehend only the first two stages of holiness. They have faith in His dominion on high and His control of events on earth. Yet mortal man starting from Moses our Teacher cannot understand the totality of His plan, and therefore asks the eternal question: "Why do the righteous suffer and the wicked prosper? (*Berachos* 7a). In his limited vision and understanding, man cannot see how "everything that Hashem does is for the good," as Rabbi Nachum, the illustrious teacher of Rabbi Akiva, was wont to say (*Taanis* 21a).

This lack of comprehension, however, does not deter the Jew from reciting both the *Shema*, which testifies to our faith in Hashem, and the *Kaddish*, which is based on the trust that He knows how and why even death — which is so tragic to the mortal eye — has a far-reaching purpose and meaning beyond our comprehension. We therefore proclaim *"May His Name"* — meaning His essence — *"become great."* May our understanding be expanded from the Two-letter Name of Amalek's time to the full Four-letter Name, and may His throne become unblemished from a perspective of man's noncomprehension to one of recognition and understanding of the Divine way, thereby enhancing God's position and stature in our world today.

⧎ The Bond Between God and Israel

We are accustomed to regard prayer as man either praising God or requesting something from Him. Rabbi Chaim of Volozhin, in his *Nefesh HaChaim* (Ch. 2), presents another intriguing aspect of prayer. Given the special relationship between Hashem and His people, when Israel is in pain, Hashem suffers, too. The *Kaddish* then assumes a most unique role in that man prays not only for the alleviation of his own suffering, but for that of Hashem as well. The Mishnah (*Sanhedrin* 46a) expresses this idea in the following dramatic way. Rabbi Meir taught that when a sinner is executed, Hashem Himself complains that His head and arm hurt, as it were. The Mishnah continues that if He suffers even when the wicked are punished, then how much more so does He feel the suffering of the righteous. What, however, is the meaning of His "head and arm hurt"? Reb Chaim of Volozhin explains that just as a Jew dons *tefillin* to express his appreciation of the fact that Hashem has a relationship with Israel, similarly, the Talmud (*Berachos* 6a) teaches, Hashem, as well, "dons" *tefillin,* as it were, to

9 / BACKGROUND OF THE PRAYERS

symbolize that He and Israel are bound together. When this connection is broken by sin, God's "head and arm," the organs where *tefillin* are worn, are where He feels pain. *Kaddish* is thus man's expression of concern for God's suffering, and a prayer that His Name be sanctified.

◆§ Five Circumstances

Kaddish is recited in five different situations and circumstances:

(1) The *chazzan* (reader) recites it between the different sections of prayer, such as between the *Pesukei D'Zimrah* and the Blessings of the *Shema,* to signify that a section has been completed. This *Kaddish* is referred to as *Chatzi Kaddish*, the Half-*Kaddish,* because it does not include the last two or three verses that are recited at other times. Perhaps the role of this *Kaddish* may be understood in light of the following Talmudic passage (*Berachos* 33b). A *chazzan* leading the prayer service before Rabbi Chanina said in his *Amidah* prayer, "The great, the mighty, the awesome, the glorious, the potent, the feared, the strong, the powerful, the certain and the esteemed God." After the service, Rabbi Chanina said to him, "Did you complete all the praises of your Master?" — meaning that his effusive list of adjectives implied that he was capable of listing *all* of God's praises, something that is clearly impossible. Indeed, the praises that we recite at the beginning of the *Amidah* — *the great, mighty and awesome* — are permitted only because they are found in the Torah (*Deuteronomy* 10:17). Similarly in the case of the Half-*Kaddish,* having concluded a section of His praises, we make it clear that we have not exhausted His praises by reciting *Kaddish,* which states that God's ultimate praise is yet to come, and moreover that *"He is beyond any blessing and song, praise and consolation that are uttered in the world."*

(2) The second *Kaddish* is the *Kaddish Shaleim*, the Full *Kaddish,* which is recited by the reader after the conclusion of the *Shemoneh Esrei*, and which includes *Tiskabeil*, a plea that God accept the just-completed prayer.

(3) The third form is *Kaddish Yasom*, the Mourner's *Kaddish,* which is recited by a son for eleven months after the death of a parent.

(4) The fourth *Kaddish, Kaddish D'Rabbanan*, or the Rabbis' *Kaddish,* is recited after the study of Rabbinic Torah teachings, and especially teachings of an Aggadic nature. It includes a prayer for the welfare of the teachers and students of Torah, for they are essential to Israel's welfare. Indeed, the Talmud teaches that the world survives thanks to this *Kaddish* (*Sotah* 48a).

(5) The fifth *Kaddish* is recited at the cemetery by the son after the completion of the interment. Interestingly, an almost identical *Kaddish* is recited by someone who celebrates a *Siyum*, the completion of a tractate of Talmud or an order of the Mishnah. A possible reason for the applicability of the same *Kaddish* to both situations may be that this *Kaddish* introduces the concept of תְּחִיַּת הַמֵּתִים , the *Resurrection of the Dead*, and it speaks of perfect service of God. This *Kaddish* symbolizes continuity: Just as the dead will live again, so must we strive in our learning to attain a complete state of service to God.

❧ The Key Phrase

The Talmud (*Sotah* 49a) refers to the entire *Kaddish* as *Y'hei Sh'mei Rabba M'varach*, "May His great Name be blessed," the response recited by the congregation upon hearing the recitation of *Kaddish*. This response is so important that Rabbi Yehoshua ben Levi teaches (*Shabbos* 119b): "Whoever responds to the *Kaddish* by saying, '*Amen, may His great Name be blessed for ever and ever*,' with all his might" — meaning with great concentration (*Rashi*) — "any evil decree rendered against that individual is nullified."

Kaddish is so important that the response in it of *Amen, Y'hei Sh'mei Rabba* takes precedence over even that of *Kedushah*, which is recited in the *chazzan's* repetition of the *Amidah*. (In a practical sense, therefore, someone who encounters one *minyan* reciting *Kedushah*, and another reciting *Kaddish*, should respond to the *Kaddish* rather than to *Kedushah* (*Orach Chaim* Ch. 56).

Elijah the Prophet taught Rabbi Yose a lesson that sheds understanding on the *Kaddish* (*Berachos* 3a). Three times every night, God laments the fate of the Jewish nation and exclaims, "Woe to the sons because of whose sins I destroyed My House, burned My Temple, and exiled them among the nations of the world." But when Jews enter their synagogues and houses of study and respond in the *Kaddish*, "*May His great Name be blessed,*" God shakes His head, as it were, and says, "Fortunate is the King Who is praised this way in His house. What is there for the Father Who has exiled His sons, and woe to the sons who have been exiled from their Father's table."

Tosafos (*Berachos* 3a) explains why *Kaddish* is in Aramaic. In Babylonia, the Torah was taught in that language, which was the vernacular of the people. Since the *Kaddish* that follows Torah study is so important, the Rabbis wanted it to be understood by all, so they formulated it in Aramaic. The reason we do not recite *Kaddish* in the vernacular of our respective countries is explained by the *Zohar* (*Terumah*). Since *Y'hei Sh'mei Rabba* is so important, as noted above, and since the portion that is added to the *Kaddish* following Torah study is of great significance, the Rabbis wanted them to be understood by everyone. Aramaic was the common vernacular, so the Sages formulated those parts of *Kaddish* in the language understood by everyone.

The *Zohar* (*Terumah*) teaches that *Y'hei Sh'mei Rabba*, recited with proper concentration and vigor, can destroy evil forces that result from man's misdeeds and prevent God's splendor from being revealed to His children. For this reason it was composed in Aramaic, a language that is utilized by the forces of evil. By exalting God in Aramaic, we bring holiness to the dark corners of earth, where it could not otherwise penetrate. (This would explain why these portions of *Kaddish* were not recited in other languages.)

❧ Connection to Death

While the subject of death is not mentioned in the *Kaddish*, the connection between this prayer and death can be seen both from early sources in our tradition and from the philosophical religious response to this personal tragedy.

In *Kallah Rabbasi* (Ch. 2), one of the minor tractates of the Talmud, we are

taught that Rabbi Akiva chanced to meet what appeared to be a man carrying wood in a cemetery. According to one text, the wood was for his own burning in *Gehinnom* (Purgatory). The load was so heavy he could hardly walk. He was moaning and groaning.

"Is there no one," asked Rabbi Akiva, "who can rescue you from this terrible suffering?"

"No one, unless my son could recite *Kaddish* for my sake." Rabbi Akiva taught the son Torah and the boy recited the *Kaddish,* whereupon the father was released from his punishment.

The idea that a child can earn merit on behalf of a wicked father is found in *Sanhedrin* (104a): "A righteous son can earn merit for a wicked father, but a righteous father cannot earn merit for a wicked son." The Talmud continues, Abraham could not save his wicked son Ishmael from Divine punishment nor could Isaac save his wicked son Esau from Divine punishment. But Abraham could rescue his father Terach. *Rashba* explains this phenomenon. Since parents are the cause of the child's existence in this world, they live on through their progeny. Thus if the child performs righteous deeds, the parents are regarded as partners in the deed, and therefore part of the reward for that deed goes to the parents. The reverse, however, is not true. The existence of the parent is not due to the child. Thus, the righteous deeds of a parent may not be viewed as being performed by the child.

In addition, the benefit of recitation of *Kaddish* by a child may be understood in the following way. In sports there is the concept of an "assist," which means that if one player sets up the play enabling his teammate to score, the one who facilitated the play is also given recognition. Similarly, in the realm of the holy and spiritual, if someone positively motivates and inspires the next one to perform good deeds, then part of the credit is attributed to the one who had the positive influence.

The recitation of *Kaddish* on behalf of a parent is a way of saying, "Though I don't understand why my loved one was snatched from me, his/her faith and courage have motivated me to accept the Divine judgment." This is known as *Tzidduk HaDin*, or justification of the Divine judgment.

Finally, the *Kaddish,* in which we pray for the ultimate sanctification of His Name, is simultaneously a pledge on our part to accept the obligation to help create this sanctification. To live a life of *Kiddush Hashem* is to bring honor and glory to Hashem through our actions. With each recitation of the *Kaddish,* we acknowledge: "All is destined from on high including one's health and wealth, and all accept the fear of Heaven." By not only loving Hashem ourselves, but as taught in *Yoma* (86a), by living in a way that influences others to love Him, we sanctify His Name. The recitation of *Kaddish* is certainly important, but of even greater value is the commitment to live a life of Torah and *mitzvos* that truly sanctifies His Name.

⋙ Worth of an Individual

Moreover, the potential and worth of each individual is highlighted with the

recitation of *Kaddish* specifically for a particular person. The late Rabbi Meir Shapiro, who introduced the concept of *Daf Yomi*, the daily study of a folio of Talmud, noted the significance of each person in the following Talmudic teaching. The Mishnah (*Berachos* 49b) teaches that if three or more men ate a meal together that required the recitation of the Grace After Meals, they preface their blessings with the introductory *"Zimun."* The formula for this introduction changes according to the number of participants. If there are ten men present, the Name of God is added. According to one view in the Talmud, if there are a hundred, a thousand, or ten thousand, respectively, the formula of praise for Hashem is increased. Thus if there are 99 or 999, only one person is missing, but this manifests itself in a noticeable diminution in the praise of His Name and essence. This illustrates the importance of even one Jew. The recitation of *Kaddish* for a departed one proclaims that though the army of Hashem has been diminished by one — thus creating a void, a vacuum of holiness, and a diminution of good deeds in the Jewish community — the life that remains behind must continue to be sanctified.

৵ Verses of Song and Praise: Pesukei D'Zimrah

Pesukei D'Zimrah is a collection of psalms and verses from all three sections of the Written Torah: Torah, Prophets, and Writings. Most of it — indeed its very essence — is composed of chapters and selected verses from King David's Book of *Psalms*.

৵ Praising and Pruning

Rav Simlai taught that prior to beseeching Hashem to allow him to enter *Eretz Yisrael*, Moses first praised Hashem: "You have begun to show Your servant Your greatness and Your strong hand" (*Deuteronomy* 3:24). According to Rashi, Moses referred to God's boundless mercy and willingness to forgive sinners. So too, prior to our petition of prayer, our *Shemoneh Esrei*, we are to praise Hashem (*Berachos* 32a).

Pesukei D'Zimrah helps to prepare us for the *Shemoneh Esrei* by reminding us before Whom we are about to have a personal audience. In addition, the psalms that constitute *Pesukei D'Zimrah* communicate that no one other than Hashem can grant our requests and desires.

Elaborating on this concept, *Menoras HaMaor* suggests that the term *Pesukei*

D'Zimrah might have an additional meaning stemming from the Hebrew verb, זמר, *to prune*. Thus the introduction to the *Shacharis* prayer is designated as "Verses of Pruning." Just as a gardener prunes his vines, removing the unhealthy branches in order to improve the fruit-bearing ability of the superior ones, so too, our recitation of *Pesukei D'Zimrah* removes all spiritual and metaphysical obstructions and hindrances from our prayers, enabling our *tefillos* to enter before the Divine Throne. *Pesukei D'Zimrah* may thus be seen as man's struggle to break through the many layers of impurity in his environment and enable him to connect with the Holy. Our recitation of these verses is our way of sending praises to God and of asking him to decipher our prayers, to cut and paste our yearnings into something worthwhile, as it were. Perhaps this notion is included in the words of the *Yishtabach*, the blessing that concludes *Pesukei D'Zimrah*. There we extol God as הַבּוֹחֵר בְּשִׁירֵי זִמְרָה, *the One Who chooses musical songs of praise*.

Moreover, the Talmud (ibid.) continues, one is not to pray out of sadness, but rather with the happiness that comes from the performance of a *mitzvah*. For this reason, one should recite these verses slowly and with a great deal of feeling and emotion. In fact, the *Shulchan Aruch* writes, one should recite these psalms just as one would count his money: carefully, deliberately, happily. *Quality* of prayer, as opposed to quantity, is the ideal.

Since *Pesukei D'Zimrah* is not a requirement in and of itself, but is a preparation for the *Shema* and *Shemoneh Esrei* — the more essential parts of the service — it is understandable that one who comes to the synagogue late and finds the congregation about to begin the section of *Shema* with its blessings should skip *Pesukei D'Zimrah*, and join the *minyan* for the *Shema* and *Shemoneh Esrei*. As important as *Pesukei D'Zimrah* is in preparing the individual for prayer, not every page of the *siddur* has equal significance. Recitation of the *Amidah* together with the congregation is the primary purpose and fulfillment of congregational prayer.

⋄§ Independent Importance

The second Talmudic source for *Pesukei D'Zimrah* is found in Tractate *Shabbos* (118b). Rav Yosei taught, "Let my portion be with those who complete the *Hallel* every day." (The Talmud explains that the term *Hallel*, as it is used here, means *Pesukei D'Zimrah*, and not what is commonly referred to as *Hallel*, the special collection of psalms recited on Festivals and *Rosh Chodesh*.) The final six chapters of the Book of *Psalms* comprise the essence of *Pesukei D'Zimrah*. They do not contain petitions to God, but uniquely and exclusively praise Him.

⋄§ The Blessings

Pesukei D'Zimrah is preceded and concluded by blessings. The introductory blessing is *Baruch She'amar* and the concluding blessing is *Yishtabach*. According to tradition, the Men of the Great Assembly received the text of *Baruch She'amar* on a note that fell from heaven. Its eighty-seven words correspond to the Hebrew word for refined gold, פָּז, which has the numerical value of eighty-

seven. This alludes to the verse in *Song of Songs* (5:11), *His opening words* — i.e. the introductory words of *Pesukei D'Zimrah* — *are of* פָּז, *the finest gold*.

The concluding blessing, *Yishtabach*, does not include the words אֱלֹקֵינוּ מֶלֶךְ הָעוֹלָם, *our God, King of the universe*, as do most blessings, for *Yishtabach* is, in a sense, the conclusion of *Baruch She'amar*. This shows that all of *Pesukei D'Zimrah* is one unit, and therefore one is not permitted to engage in unnecessary conversation during its *entirety*. Such prayer responses as *amen*, however, are permitted.

◆§ The Central Core

In *Baruch She'amar*, the worshiper says, *through the psalms of David your servant. We shall laud You, Hashem our God, with praises and songs*. *Yehi Chevod* then captures the major themes and motifs of David's psalms. It is a collection of verses taken primarily from *Psalms,* but also from *Chronicles* and *Proverbs*. Incidentally, this helps us understand why this section of the *siddur* is called *Pesukei D'Zimrah*, or *verses* of praise and song. Whereas the *Hallel* recited on Festivals consists of complete psalms, this daily *Hallel* is literally *pesukim* or *verses* of praise, culled from different sources.

◆§ Yehi Chevod

Yehi Chevod contains three separate units. The first discusses God's immanence in the world and how, in this way, man discovers Him as the Creator of the universe. The second section refers to Him as the Master of history, leading mankind towards the realization of His plan, with the chosenness of Israel. Finally, it closes with the assurance that God will forgive our sins when we call to Him, and that He will restore us to our glory when He returns to Zion.

In a sense, *Yehi Chevod* encapsulates the entire Book of *Psalms*. The glory of God, His Kingdom, His relation to His people; petitions for forgiveness; and entreaties for salvation — fundamental ideas that permeate *Psalms* (*Tehillim*) — are contained in the twenty-one verses of *Yehi Chevod*.

◆§ Ashrei and Its Companion Psalms

Yehi Chevod is followed by *Ashrei* (*Psalms* 145) and the final five chapters of *Psalms*.

The Talmud (*Berachos* 4b) states that one reason *Ashrei* was chosen as the primary chapter of *Pesukei D'Zimrah* is because the initials of its verses follow the order of the Hebrew alphabet, from *aleph* to *tav*. This symbolizes that our praise and service of God are complete. But, the Talmud asks, why was *Ashrei* chosen when two other psalms also contain complete alphabetic acrostics? The Talmud responds that *Ashrei* includes the verse, *You open Your hand and satisfy the desire of every living thing,* an inspiring and reassuring testimony to God's mercy. The *Maharsha* understands the significance of *Ashrei* to be that God nourishes us both physically and spiritually.

After *Ashrei,* in Psalm 146, the Psalmist addresses the concept of Divine

Providence directed to each and every person. Each member of *Klal Yisrael* has a purpose, a mission for which God created him, and God cares about him as an individual. This psalm encourages the Jew in exile, promising that God will reign forever, despite the current ascendancy of our enemies.

Psalm 147 extends His Divine Providence to the community of Israel. It is no longer the voice of the individual praising God, but the communal voice recognizing *our* God. If their voice, if their emotion is lacking, then the national symphony of His praise is incomplete. As God heals all wounds so will He heal Israel's wounds. We are reminded that as we endure exile, the Heavenly Jerusalem is being developed by our good deeds and is waiting to descend. Throughout our exile, we must continue to develop the treasures of the Jewish people, our moral and spiritual values.

The psalm makes a striking comparison between nature's obedience to God's command, and our own responsibility to obey His Torah just as unquestioningly, because the Torah way of life should be the natural way for the Jew.

Psalm 148 brings our praises to the next level, rejoicing in the moment when even the non-Jewish nations of the world will recognize and praise the Creator. This will occur only after the Temple in Jerusalem is rebuilt, and the people of Israel will have risen to surpass their former glory.

Psalm 149 reminds us that every generation is confronted with unique challenges and new problems. At the same time, God provides us with the opportunities and wherewithal to solve them. Thus our songs of praise are always infused with new meanings, they never grow stale. The greatest, newest song of all will emanate from Israel's lips when history reaches its climax with the coming of *Mashiach*.

The last psalm contains thirteen variations of the word הַלְלוּ, *give praise,* extolling God for his Thirteen Attributes of Mercy. It concludes with the admission that, while the entire Book of *Psalms* consists of beautifully articulated songs of praise, feelings that words cannot express may best be communicated by the sounds of music or without emitting any sound whatsoever. The human soul can often express God's praises more eloquently than anything else.

◆§ Intercessors and Utterances

Avudraham suggests that the above six psalms serve as "intercessors" for our prayers. They help man attain a purity of soul and an elevation of spirit, enabling him to properly recite the *Shema* and *Shemoneh Esrei*. He suggests further that *Pesukei D'Zimrah* provides a daily reminder of the ten utterances with which Hashem created the world (*Pirkei Avos* 5:1). In his formulation, *Vayevareich David*, which comes after the above six psalms, corresponds to the final statement of Creation, "God blessed them and said to them, 'Be fruitful and multiply; fill the earth and subdue it' " *(Genesis* 1:28). This final charge for man to conquer the world finds its parallel in *Vayevareich David*, where King David says, "Wealth and honor come from You and You rule everything." This is man's response to the trust and faith that God has invested in him, by

recognizing that whatever success he might achieve is due only to the fact that God rules everything and provides man with talent and resources.

David was not allowed to build the First Temple, but nevertheless made the necessary preparations for that purpose. When he entrusted these funds to his son Solomon, he recited this praise, reminding us, writes Rabbi Samson Raphael Hirsch, that it is not God Who needs a dwelling place, but we who need His sanctuary and His Presence in our midst.

Moreover, David reminds the people that whatever they donated was given them by God. For this reason, many either give charity at this point of the prayer or set aside money to be given later in the service.

The daily *Pesukei D'Zimrah* closes with the song that Moses and Israel sang at the occasion of the splitting of the Sea of Reeds. Heretofore, all the praises have been within the context of the natural world, as controlled and supervised by God. This song extols Him for His miraculous involvement in the world. Indeed, suggests Rabbi Elie Munk, the most perfect praise of God is not found in the inspired songs of David, but grows out of the actual events that our ancestors beheld with their own eyes. Only since the day of the miracle at the Sea, when God revealed His mastery of nature and mankind before the eyes of an astonished world, has "His Throne been established for all times."

In his commentary on the Torah, *Ramban* teaches that through God's miraculous control over nature, exhibited by the ten plagues in Egypt and culminating with the splitting of the Sea of Reeds, we come to appreciate and accept Him as the Creator. This song is thus a fitting finale to *Pesukei D'Zimrah*.

As noted above, *Yishtabach* is the closing blessing of *Pesukei D'Zimrah*. It contains fifteen expressions of praise, which alludes to *Psalms* 120-134, the fifteen Songs of Ascent composed by David. We now "ascend" to the next stage of our prayers.

⊷§ The Shema and Its Blessings

The *Shema* is the only text that the Torah obligates a Jew to recite daily. It is our pledge of allegiance to God, acknowledging His sovereignty and Oneness. It is not sufficient merely to recite the *Shema*; one must understand and internalize the content of the declaration, "Hear, O Israel: HASHEM is our God, HASHEM, the One and Only." One who fails to do so, though he has pronounced the words, has not fulfilled the Biblical command.

The Sages ordained blessings in order to enhance our performance of commandments. By reciting a blessing, we focus on the *mitzvah* we are about to perform and on the privilege and responsibility we have in serving Hashem through its performance.

An analogy might help us appreciate the blessings that come before and after the *Shema*. Customarily, a groom gives his fiancée a ring, denoting their serious intention and commitment to a lifetime of devotion to each other. The stone in the center of the ring is its central and most costly aspect. Yet, without the actual ring and setting to house the stone and keep it in place, the precious gem could not be exhibited or fully appreciated. Like this precious gem, the *Shema* has blessings before it and after it, to highlight it and help us appreciate it.

The Sages teach that the morning *Shema* is preceded by two blessings and followed by one blessing. The evening *Shema* is both preceded and followed by two blessings (*Berachos* 11a).

✻§ Themes of the Blessings

The morning and evening blessings begin with inspirational commitments. The opening blessing of the morning describes God's renewal of nature, for we welcome the daylight with excitement, anticipating new opportunities to develop ourselves and our environment. Every night we acknowledge that He brings on evenings, affording us the opportunity to rest our bodies and refresh our souls.

The second blessing of the *Shema*, both morning and evening, which acknowledges the preciousness of Torah, our responsibility to study it, and the gratitude we must feel that God entrusted it to us, is directly related to the *Shema*, the recitation of which is the minimum fulfillment of the commandment to study the Torah, day and night. Thus, the blessing *Ahavah Rabbah*, which precedes the *Shema*, doubles as a form of *Birkas HaTorah*, a blessing for Torah study. (In fact, one who forgot to recite the Torah blessings at the beginning of the *Shacharis* service may discharge that obligation with his recitation of *Ahavah Rabbah*).

In the morning blessing, we pray movingly, "Our Father, the merciful Father, Who acts mercifully, have mercy upon us, instill in our hearts to understand and elucidate, to listen, learn, teach, safeguard, perform, and fulfill all the words of Your Torah's teaching with love." But after such an impassioned request, what if anything do we do about it?

The *Chafetz Chaim,* of blessed memory, in a famous parable, compares our request to that of a poor man who approached a wealthy member of his community and asked for a substantial loan, with which he would establish himself in business. The wealthy man agreed, and asked the borrower to come to his home that evening for the money.

That night the lender stayed home looking forward to the opportunity to help his friend — but the poor man never came. The next day they met in the street and once again the poor man asked his neighbor for the sizable loan, explaining excitedly the potential of his business plan and his genuine need for the money. The rich man responded, "I told you yesterday that the money was yours. All you had to do was come and get it. I will be prepared for you again tonight." That night, as well, the rich man did not leave his home. Again the poor man did not come.

The following day they met again and again the poor man began to ask for the loan. This time the frustrated businessman cut him off. "I was ready every night," he said angrily, "but you never followed through."

Similarly, God surely wishes to enable us to understand, elucidate, listen, learn, teach, safeguard, perform, and fulfill all of His Torah. All He asks is that we come to the house of study. All too often we don't.

৬৯ Commandment to Love

The second blessing of the *Shema* concludes with God's love for Israel. Why is this blessing said exclusively prior to the recitation of the *Shema*, and not in conjunction with the performance of any other *mitzvah*?

The paragraph of *Shema* commands a Jew to love God "with all your heart, with all your soul, and with all your resources." It is understandable that the Torah can demand or prohibit various activities: Return a lost object, do not charge interest when lending money, eat matzah on Pesach. Such *mitzvos* require our physical ability to perform them or strength of character not to violate them — but how can the Torah demand our love, an emotion that swells from within? Love is not something we can control; what tugs at the emotions of one individual might leave the next one unmoved.

The *Sifre* teaches that one comes to love God by studying His Torah and seeing the infinite depths of His wisdom. To know Him is to love Him. No code of morals and ethics composed by mortals, who are bound by their environment and culture, has stood the test of time. Only Hashem, Who created man's nature, is able to legislate eternal ethics and teachings.

It is thus understandable that what follows our declaration of His Oneness is the commandment to love Him and to study His Torah. Commensurate with one's study of Torah is one's love for Hashem.

Rabbi Baruch Epstein (*Baruch She'amar*) offers a different explanation. Love is reciprocal. When someone extends unconditional love to someone else, that person usually responds in turn. Therefore, before we recite the *Shema*, we declare God's unconditional, absolute love for Israel, prompting us to respond with love toward Him.

৬৯ With Every Organ

There are 248 proactive or positive commandments in the Torah, corresponding to the 248 organs in the human body. This phenomenon is given great significance by the Sages, as it signals that man's physical body was created in harmony with the commandments of the Torah, that the commandments do not go against man's nature. This correspondence of *mitzvos* to organs symbolizes that the purpose of our physical existence is to obey the precepts of the Torah.

The total number of words in the three paragraphs of the *Shema* is 245. To help convey the parallelism of 248 organs to the words of the *Shema,* the Sages added three words to the recitation: In the synagogue, the congregation listens to the *chazzan* repeat aloud the final three words, ה׳ אֱלֹהֵיכֶם אֱמֶת, "*Hashem, your God, is true,*" which is considered as if the listeners had uttered the words. One who

prays alone prefaces the *Shema* with three words, אֵל מֶלֶךְ נֶאֱמָן, *"God, trustworthy King."* These words were chosen because their initials spell *amen*, which means faithful or true, thus testifying to our faith in the truths we are about to recite.

◈§ No Contradictions

There is one more critical theme that binds the blessings of the *Shema* with the declaration of the *Shema*: God's absolute Oneness. The text of the opening blessing praises God "Who forms light and creates darkness, makes peace and creates all." The Talmud (*Berachos* 11b) teaches that this blessing is based on the verse in *Isaiah* 45:7 in which God declares that He "forms light and creates darkness, makes peace and creates evil." Our Sages changed the text from "and creates evil" to "and creates all," because, explains the Talmud, it is unseemly to praise God by saying that He creates evil. We speak, rather, in general terms of God creating everything — including that which appears to be evil.

In the evening service, too, the first blessing describes God as the One "Who removes light from before darkness and darkness from before light." The terms day and night are used extensively both by the prophets and in our liturgy to refer to prosperous or troubled times. Light symbolizes life, wisdom, and happiness. Darkness is associated with suffering, failure, and death. Thus we speak of God as the Master of all aspects of life. This refutes the contention of heretical philosophers who reasoned that the "good god" who creates light cannot be the same "bad god" who creates darkness. Therefore, they argued, there must be at least two gods.

Judaism believes that there is One God, that He is good, and that light and darkness, joy and sadness, are all ultimately good, though it is often — or even usually — beyond human capacity to understand how. As the Midrash states: God tells us, "Do not treat Me as the Canaanites and Egyptians treat their deities. When they experience good, they honor their gods, and when misfortune befalls them, they curse their gods. However, when you are showered with blessings, praise Me, and when you experience suffering and travail, praise Me as well."

This charge is beautifully substantiated by the sixth paragraph of the *Hallel* prayer, Psalm 116. Says David the Psalmist, "How can I repay Hashem for all His kindness to me? I will raise the cup of salvations and the Name of Hashem I will invoke." Earlier in the same paragraph, he declares, "The pains of death encircled me; the confines of the grave have found me; trouble and sorrow I would find. Then I would invoke the Name of Hashem." No matter what the circumstances, David invokes God's Name.

◈§ Omnipresent and Indivisible

God's omnipresence allows us to more fully appreciate our declaration: "Hear, O Israel, *Hashem* (the Name of God signifying His Attribute of Love) *Eloheinu* (the Name of God pointing to His Attribute of Justice), Hashem, the One and Only." Both attributes come from the One and only God, writes Rabbi Elie Munk

in *World of Prayer*, "for only if mercy and justice, joy and pain, life and death flow from one source, only if our health and wealth are granted and withheld by the order of the One God, only then are we His, with every fiber of our being, with all our heart, all our soul and all our wealth. Therefore the immediate consequence of His Oneness is וְאָהַבְתָּ, *and you shall love* Hashem, not a theoretical concept echoing in a vacuum, but the direct challenge to lead a moral existence, that we should love and serve God in all the diverse phases of our life and being. Complete, unreserved submission to the One indivisible God makes man into a harmonious and integrated personality."

Rabbi Gedalia Schorr likened this understanding of God to light seen through a prism. Though the viewer sees a myriad of different colors, they all come from a single ray of light. So too, God's many manifestations are truly one.

◆§ The Unique One

Finally the word אֶחָד, *One,* in the context of the *Shema*, has the connotation of "unique." While one often speaks of "one of a kind," by definition there are many others of that kind in different variations. The "one and only ring," for example, that a spouse may receive is invaluable and especially sentimental to her, but it is not truly unique, for there are many other rings like it in the world, or imitations of it can be made. Only, God, however, is unique in the sense that He is incomparable; he is in a category and class unto Himself.

Moreover, we declare that Hashem, Who at present is acknowledged and recognized only by His people Israel — He is now אֱלֹקֵינוּ, **our** *God* — will one day be recognized as the only One, and will be worshiped by all.

◆§ Mode of Recitation

Traditional practice is to recite the first sentence of the *Shema* in a loud voice, with the right hand covering the eyes, thereby blocking all distractions and helping us concentrate on accepting God's absolute sovereignty. This is our testimony to God's Oneness. In the Torah scroll, the letter *ayin* of *Shema* and the letter *daled* of Echad are enlarged — אחד ... שמע. Together these two letters form the word עֵד, *witness*. By pronouncing the *Shema*, every Jew bears witness to God's unity and declares it to all the world.

Immediately after proclaiming God's Kingship with *Shema Yisrael*, we declare, in an undertone, "Blessed is the Name of His glorious Kingdom for all eternity."

The Talmud (*Pesachim* 56a) explains why this verse is said quietly. Prior to his passing, our Patriarch Jacob wanted to reveal to his family future events of Jewish history, including when the Messiah would come. But God, in His infinite wisdom, shut down Jacob's spiritual antenna and withheld this information from him. Jacob feared that perhaps his children were not worthy of hearing this prophecy.

His sons reassured him emphatically, "*Shema Yisrael*, Hear [our father], O Israel, there is no generational or cultural gap; your God is ours, the One and the same."

Hearing this, Jacob immediately responded, "Blessed is the Name of His glorious Kingdom for all eternity."

Nonetheless, the verse *Shema Yisrael* appears in the Torah, but not the verse that Jacob spoke in reply. We wish to include Jacob's words, states the Talmud, but because they are not found in the Torah, we recite them in a whisper.

Aruch HaShulchan suggests that the story of Jacob and his sons may also provide insight into the recitation of the *Shema* itself. Twice daily we address our grandfather Jacob, who was also given the name Israel — "Hear, O Israel" — and reassure him that there is still no generational or cultural gap between us and previous generations of dedicated Jews. We are perpetuating our national belief in the Oneness of Hashem.

⥇ Order of the Passages

The Talmud (*Berachos* 13a) explains the order of the three Biblical paragraphs that make up the *Shema*. In the first paragraph, the Jew accepts upon himself the yoke of the Kingdom of Heaven, for without acknowledgment that the commandments are God given, their performance would have no sanctity. In the second paragraph, he submits to the Divine law, to perform all the *mitzvos* properly, and acknowledges the concept of reward and punishment. And the third paragraph refers to sanctification of the individual, by stressing the responsibility to avoid temptation and to remember God's commandments. The third paragraph also fulfills the commandment to remember the Exodus from Egypt. Simply put, *Krias Shema* comprises the origin of the law, its demands, and its purpose.

Rabbi Joseph B. Soloveitchik noted that both the second and third paragraphs include our acceptance of the commandments. Why twice? He answered that the second paragraph deals with accepting those *mitzvos* that we are capable of doing, while the third paragraph refers to our acceptance of even those *mitzvos* from which we are technically exempt. For example, nowadays, as our garments are not four-cornered cloaks, a man in his regular garb would never be required to wear *tzitzis*. Yet, in our love for God and His *mitzvos,* we commit ourselves to wear special four-cornered garments in order to put *tzitzis* on them. To us, all *mitzvos* are a privilege, and we are eager to find ways to fulfill them.

This attitude, the *Chinuch* maintains, is the purpose of the morning *Shema* — to assist the Jew in sanctifying the challenges of the upcoming day. Realizing that one is an ambassador of the King of kings imposes certain responsibilities and restrictions. Indeed, the word וְאָהַבְתָּ means more than *you shall love* [*Hashem*]; it also implies that you shall want others to love Him, and that you should act in such a way that your speech, actions, demeanor, honesty, and integrity will influence *others* to love God — that your conduct will set an example that will cause others to love the God you serve (*Yoma* 86a). Society ought to see that you are galvanized by the principles of the *Shema* and be motivated to emulate your ways.

❧ How to Love

God commands the Jew to love Him בְּכָל לְבָבְךָ, *with all your heart*. Our Sages point out that the Hebrew word for *your heart* is spelled with two *lameds*, when it should be לִבְּךָ, with one *lamed*. From the structure of this word, the Talmud famously infers that you must serve God with your "two" hearts, i.e., with both of your inclinations, good and evil.

One loves God, *Rabbeinu Yonah* explains, by following one's good inclination to perform *mitzvos* and one loves God just the same by rejecting the evil inclination that presses him to sin.

The *Rambam* takes a different approach to loving God with your "evil" inclination. This, he says, refers to one's baser instincts, his earthly cravings, such as his desire for food and other physical gratifications. By channeling even the most temporal features of one's humanity toward the service of God — by eating kosher food in proper moderation, by having sexual relations only with one's spouse at the permitted time — one elevates the activity and thereby succeeds in serving God with that inclination as well.

God further commands the Jew to love Him בְּכָל נַפְשְׁךָ, *with all your soul*, even if, explains the Mishnah (*Berachos* 61b), your devotion to God costs you your life. This self-sacrifice is demanded of us only in very rare situations: where we are asked to choose between death and one of three cardinal sins — idolatry, adultery or incest, and murder. It is also demanded when the alternative is public desecration of God's Name. In these cases, Jewish law requires one to die rather than sin, and to offer his life in happiness, in martyrdom. The great Rabbi Akiva was joyous while being tortured to death. To his amazed disciples he explained, "All my life I prayed that if faced with this situation, I would be able to maintain my love of God. Now that I succeeded in so doing, should I not be happy?" (ibid.).

The final step is to love God בְּכָל מְאֹדֶךָ, *with all your resources*. A Jew must be prepared to forfeit financial gain rather than violate Torah law. Moreover, those foolish people in every generation who value their money above their lives and will risk their lives to save their money are reminded that they, too, must put their love of God first.

In addition, the Mishnah notes, the phrase means "in whatever measure [מִדָּה] He measures out to you, you should give thanks to Him." This includes any talent with which you are blessed. Channel your pleasant voice, artistic skill, mathematical acumen, to serve Him and the Jewish community, and maintain your faith even if God serves you an apparently bitter portion in life.

❧ Further Commandments

There are three specific commandments in both the first and second paragraphs of the *Shema* — to study and teach Torah, to don the head and arm *tefillin,* and to affix a *mezuzah* to one's doorpost. The obligation to teach Torah to one's children is written in each of the two paragraphs, once referring to one's actual children and once referring to one's students.

The first paragraph of *Shema* closes with the *mitzvos* of *tefillin* and *mezuzah*. These *mitzvos*, writes the *Malbim*, are the actualization of the start of the paragraph: The *tefillin* are worn on the arm across from the heart, directing the Jew to serve Hashem "with all your heart." The head *tefillin* signifies the subjugation of one's intellect to God; this corresponds to "with all your soul." Lastly, the *mezuzah* on the doorpost of one's home shows love of God "with all your resources," as one's home represents his wealth.

The second paragraph of the *Shema* differs from the first in that it is written in the plural form. The first paragraph addresses the individual Jew; the second addresses the Jews as a nation and introduces the concept of reward and punishment. This communicates to us that the good and bad that befall our nation is contingent upon the behavior of all. Reward and punishment, financial gain and drought, security and exile, are not part of some natural process, as *Rambam* explains. Do not be fooled into thinking that some years you are more productive, other years less. Rather, your yield is commensurate with your service and dedication to Hashem.

God's miraculous intervention in human affairs occurs on a national level, based on the merit of the populace as a whole; for the individual, it is not as apparent. It is for this reason that the concept of reward and punishment is not found in the first paragraph, which talks to the individual Jew.

The punishment listed for turning away from God is in the material realm. God promises that "He will restrain the heaven so there will be no rain and the ground will not yield its produce." In the ninth chapter of the Laws of Repentance, *Rambam* notes that lack of financial security causes the individual to devote all of his time and effort toward eking out a living. The dreadful effect is that he will be left with no qualitative time to study Torah or perform acts of kindness, which earn him his share in the World to Come. Thus the ultimate blessing and curse of the second paragraph of the *Shema* is that man's actions determine his ability to attain that lofty reward.

The third paragraph of the *Shema* concludes with the declaration, "I am Hashem your God who has removed you from the land of Egypt." By saying these words we fulfill the daily obligation "that you will remember the day you left Egypt all the days of your life" (*Deuteronomy* 16:3).

◈§ Shemoneh Esrei

Shemoneh Esrei, literally "Eighteen" (the number of blessings it originally comprised), is the most important of our prayers. In a sense, every word that precedes it has been but preparation.

The Talmud (*Megillah* 17b) teaches that Ezra and the Men of the Great

Assembly composed these eighteen blessings from Scriptural sources in the early years of the Second Temple Era. Why do we continue to use a prescribed prayer that was written over two thousand years ago? Why do we not compose our own spontaneous, personal prayers?

Rabbi Joseph B. Soloveitchik provides an answer by pointing to the Talmud's statement: "Rabbi Yochanan taught: One who connects the blessing of redemption [which concludes the Blessings of the *Shema*] to the evening prayer [the *Shemoneh Esrei*] is worthy of the World to Come" (*Berachos* 4b).

What is the connection between prayer and redemption? Rabbi Soloveitchik explains. After recording that Moses killed an Egyptian for beating a Jew, the Torah writes, "And it happened during those many days that the king of Egypt died, and the Children of Israel groaned because of the work, and they cried out" (*Exodus* 2:23). The slaves had been subjected to a miserable existence, yet not even a sigh was heard from them until now. Why had they suffered silently?

Because they were born into slavery and knew no other way of life, they believed that this was their natural lot and they were not impelled to cry out. Not only were their bodies enslaved, notes the *Zohar*, but their power of expression was enslaved as well. The Kabbalists comment that the name of our festival of freedom, Pesach, alludes to the Hebrew words פֶּה שָׂח, *the mouth speaks*, to signify the Jews' newfound freedom to express themselves cogently, an ability that had been robbed from them during their long years of servitude.

Moses' actions changed all that. He demonstrated that a superior lifestyle existed and the people came to recognize their pain and call out to God for redemption. The realization that they were victims of injustice triggered a response from them.

Even so, their response was nothing more than וַיִּזְעָקוּ, a groan, a cry (*Exodus* 2:23). Though they were no longer silent, they did not actually pray, as they did not yet have the capacity to articulate their needs. Speech only follows understanding, and at that point in time, after centuries of enslavement, they did not know how their needs could be addressed and their situation rectified. The redemptive process of the Jewish people thus began with their first recognition of a need – with their emergence from being an enslaved and silent people to being a vocal people.

This historical episode, says Rabbi Soloveitchik, reflects the story of the individual man and sheds light upon why we pray as we do. Man often leads a silent existence, unaware of his genuine needs. He may know what he *wants*, but does not know what he needs. Often, his desires are not in his best spiritual or moral interests, and he loses sight of what his fundamental needs are.

Man's challenge, therefore, is to fashion his personality, to arrange his hierarchy of values so that he can discover and identify those needs and cry out for them, converting his silence into articulate speech. In this manner, he is free to move from a mute, peripheral existence to a speaking part at center stage.

The Torah informs us that Hashem declared, "Let us make man in Our image, after Our likeness" (*Genesis* 1:26). Rabbi Soloveitchik suggests that Hashem says, "Let **us** make." He is addressing man directly, inviting him to join in the

25 / BACKGROUND OF THE PRAYERS

process of creation and development. In this world, man is constantly challenged to develop himself. Unlike the animals who are born with almost their full natural capacity, man has the power to advance his potential by controlling his impulses and fashioning his character.

The primary purpose of prayer is not to change Hashem, but to change us. Prayer thus begins in the heart. It is, in fact, called עֲבוֹדָה שֶׁבְּלֵב, service of the heart. Prayer differs in this regard from most of the Torah's proactive commandments. *Mitzvos* such as eating in a *succah* and affixing a *mezuzah* can be fulfilled simply with a physical act, even without the proper focus upon its Biblical requirement. The *mitzvah* is achieved even without putting one's heart into it.

Prayer is different. Prayer without awareness, without knowing what one is saying or to Whom one is saying it, is drained of its meaning. Prayer has the power to transform each of us into a different person with different values, and it frees us to speak up on our own behalf.

Man alone cannot solve his problems or satisfy his needs. Nor can he ignore them. Judaism rejects the notion of man suffering silently; rather the Torah wants man to cry out to God to rescue him from affliction. But though man's Biblical obligation to pray is satisfied simply by crying out, the Rabbinic structure of prayer calls for identifying, clarifying, and prioritizing one's needs. Enter the *Shemoneh Esrei*, introduced by the Men of the Great Assembly as a litany of specific requests, designed to classify every need.

The development of a fixed prayer, moreover, allows the worshiper not only to be aware of his sundry needs — spiritual, dietary, financial, emotional, and so on — but to understand how to respond to them. They must be channeled properly, toward service of God, as expressed by King Solomon, "In all your activities, know Him" (*Proverbs* 3:6).

This is the great contribution of the Men of the Great Assembly. *Shemoneh Esrei* teaches man thrice daily what his needs really are. Instead of focusing on material acquisitions, we are given the opportunity to clearly find and define our true needs. *Shemoneh Esrei* educates and gives dignity to the worshiper, enabling him to achieve his own private redemption.

⋖ֻ Structure of Shemoneh Esrei

"Rabbi Chanina taught: The first three blessings are compared to a servant who thoughtfully praises his master. The middle blessings [of the weekday *Shemoneh Esrei*] are likened to a servant requesting reward from his master; and the three concluding blessings reflect the servant who received his bounty, who thanks the master and takes leave" (*Megillah* 18a).

⋖ֻ The First Blessing: Patriarchs

The first blessing of the *Shemoneh Esrei* is called *Avos*, or Patriarchs. It invokes Abraham, Isaac, and Jacob, whose personal precedents of prayer serve as one of the sources for our obligation to pray. The Talmud (*Berachos* 28b) teaches that this recital of eighteen blessings corresponds to the eighteen times Hashem's Name is mentioned by King David in Psalm 29.

The first three blessings of the *Shemoneh Esrei* correspond, not only in number but in theme, to the first three phrases of Psalm 29 (*Megillah* 17b)."Render unto Hashem, you sons of the powerful" is understood by the Talmud to refer to the Patriarchs. The second blessing, praising Hashem's might, corresponds to the second phrase "Render unto Hashem honor and might," and the third phrase "Render unto Hashem honor worthy of His Name" inspired the third blessing, which speaks of the holiness of God's Name.

This first blessing differs from most blessings, as the phrase, *Melech ha'olam*, King of the universe, is distinctly missing. The *Tur* suggests that praising Hashem as the "God of Abraham" constitutes an expression of His Kingship, as Abraham promulgated Hashem's rule over the entire world by spreading His word.

We praise Hashem separately as "God of Abraham, God of Isaac, and God of Jacob," because each individual mention denotes a personal discovery of and relationship with Hashem. Each of our Patriarchs labored on his own to perceive God and find the way to serve Him; he did not simply cling to a blind faith as it was passed down to son and grandson (*Panim Me'iros*).

The great Chassidic master, Rabbi Menachem Mendel of Kotzk, explains that this individualized association with Hashem reflects the specialty of each. Thus, "God of Abraham" reflects Abraham's service of Hashem through kindness and good deeds to man; "God of Isaac" focuses on Isaac's service of Hashem through prayer and introspection; and "God of Jacob" refers to Jacob's service of Hashem through Torah study and the pursuit of truth.

The sensitivity of Jews throughout the millennia to respond to the needs of the downtrodden may be attributed to the spiritual genes we inherited from our father Abraham. The phenomenal faith our people have displayed, even with the sword at our necks, to believe and trust in His salvation comes to us from our father Isaac. The designation of Israel as the "People of the Book" and our dedication to the study of Torah emanates from our father Jacob. Consequently, each Jew is charged not to be content with the performance of the Torah's commandments, but also to discover and relate to Hashem in accordance with his unique talents, character, and potential, to forge a personal bond between himself and Hashem.

In addition, this blessing praises Hashem for responding to us in the merit of the Patriarchs, even when we are unworthy. As Hashem protected Abraham, the founder of the Jewish people, when he was cast into the fire by Nimrod (*Genesis* 11:28), so has He safeguarded Abraham's descendants through the ages, despite innumerable attempts to destroy us.

The blessing is also a charge to emulate the kindness and compassion of Abraham and incorporate it into one's everyday activities. For how, asks Rabbi Yonasan Eibeschutz, can one invoke the merit of Abraham if he does not personally aspire to that end?

The importance of this first blessing cannot be underscored enough. Ideally, one should understand what one is saying during the entire *Shemoneh Esrei*, but doing so during the first blessing is crucial. In fact, many authorities hold that

one who prays without this minimum concentration during the first blessing must repeat the entire *Shemoneh Esrei*.

◆§ The Second Blessing: God's Might

The second blessing describes the incomparable power of Hashem, by listing miracles only He can perform. The *sine qua non* of these powers is His ability to revive the dead; man can destroy life, but only Hashem can create life. This phenomenon is completely beyond the realm of anything we personally experience, yet it is one of the cardinal tenets of our faith.

Further, understanding and appreciation of this concept is gleaned from the seemingly natural occurrence of rainfall. The Talmud (*Taanis* 7a) teaches, in the name of Rabbi Abahu, "A day of rain is greater than the day of the resurrection of the dead, for the latter is only for the righteous" (*Isaiah* 66:24), whereas rain benefits both the righteous and the wicked. For this reason, continues the Talmud, the mention of rain was introduced by our Sages in the blessing of the resurrection of the dead. Most natural phenomena occur with regularity, and thus the role of Hashem is not openly evident in them, the *Vilna Gaon* explains. Rain, though, is unpredictable, and is thus a clearer indication of His control over the world. In this way, rain, which sustains human life by causing produce to grow and providing water for human use, is comparable to the resurrection of the dead.

Shibbolei HaLeket points out that the second blessing corresponds to the *Akeidah*, the binding of Isaac on the altar (*Genesis* 22). *Pirkei d'Rabbi Eliezer* (Ch. 31) notes that when Abraham lifted up the knife to slaughter Isaac, Isaac's soul temporarily left him, allowing him to experience firsthand the miracle of resurrection.

Finally, the constant reaffirmation that our physical body will once again come to life challenges us to view our bodies with greater sanctity. The Torah teaches: "Hashem formed [וַיִּיצֶר] man from the dust of the earth" (*Genesis* 2:7). The word וַיִּיצֶר, *formed*, is spelled with an additional letter *yud*, to imply that there were two aspects in the creation of Adam, and indeed of all people — one for his present existence, and the other for the time of his resurrection.

◆§ The Third Blessing: God's Holiness

In his classic philosophic work, *The Kuzari*, the medieval philosopher, Rabbi Yehudah HaLevi, classifies creation into five groups: inanimate objects, vegetation, animals, man, and the Jewish people. The Jew resides at the top of the chain, because at Sinai God designated us as "a kingdom of ministers and a holy nation" (*Exodus* 19:6).

How do we embrace that holiness?

Rashi defines "holy" as separate, apart. The holiness of Hashem lies in the fact that He is completely beyond human comprehension. Man, who is finite and corporeal, cannot comprehend the infinite and the incorporeal, nor can he fully comprehend all the manifestations of Hashem — such as His compassion and graciousness, His judgment and might. The Jewish nation was chosen to lead the

world toward an understanding and acceptance of Hashem's mission.

With each recital of the *Shemoneh Esrei* we renew that commitment toward holiness. This blessing, therefore, exhorts us to emulate Hashem by imparting sanctity to all that we do. The blessing prepares the worshiper for his presentation of requests by putting values in the right perspective. *Mabit* notes that in the *Shemoneh Esrei* we ask Hashem only for what we truly need. By focusing on His holiness and being reminded of our own potential holiness, we elevate the dignity of our requests, because we undertake to use what we receive toward Divine service, subsequently bringing further glory to Hashem's holy Name.

Declaring to Hashem, "You are holy," communicates the readiness of the Jew to sacrifice all, even his life if need be, to sanctify God's Name. In addition, we ought to be mindful of the interpretation of Nachmanides, who understands the command to be holy as a call for moderation in all physical pleasures and materialistic pursuits.

◆§ The Fourth Blessing: Intelligence

Man's essence is his intelligence. When one recognizes that his intelligence comes from Hashem, he reflects upon how Hashem would want him to use this gift. For one to accept a gift and use it to upset the giver is the ultimate ingratitude; therefore, we must not channel our intelligence toward areas of study and endeavors that are devoid of holiness, or worse — immoral and unethical.

Included in this blessing is a request for truthful insight. Often our feelings, impressions, and perspectives lead us to the wrong conclusions. We pray that we correctly understand our situations and ask that we "know Your ways."

Maimonides (*Yesodei HaTorah* 2) writes that the commandment to love and fear Hashem is attained by reflecting upon His vast and detailed world, which reflects His wisdom. The prerequisite for the performance of this *mitzvah* is intelligence, so we beseech Hashem to give us wisdom so that we may use it to appreciate Him.

Moreover, the Torah is expansive and intricate, often difficult to penetrate and to retain. We therefore ask for assistance in mobilizing all the mental powers at our command toward this end.

The worshiper must be ever mindful that his success comes only because his internal computer is "on-line." If for a moment He should withhold the gift of insight, wisdom and discernment, our sophisticated life would be brought to an abrupt halt. It is interesting to note that the *Havdalah* prayer is inserted within this blessing at the conclusion of Shabbos and Yom Tov. The Talmud explains for if there is no *da'as*, intelligence, one cannot discern between Shabbos and the weekday.

◆§ The Fifth Blessing: Repentance

As mentioned above, our request for knowledge was to know Hashem, and once we are privileged to study and reflect on His Being, we are naturally moved to repentance. From day to day as our knowledge and awareness of Him increases,

so does the remorse for the nonchalant attitude with which we treated His presence and commandments in the past. However, we acknowledge that we cannot do it alone. We need His help in our self-improvement.

We request, "Bring us back, our Father, to Your Torah." The *Tur (Orach Chaim* 115) notes that only here and in the next blessing, of forgiveness, do we refer to Hashem as our Father. Since we ask Hashem to teach us Torah, we remind Him that he is our Father, and Jewish law dictates that a father is obligated to teach his son Torah.

The Talmud (*Niddah* 30b) teaches that in the womb the embryo is taught the entire Torah. Then, prior to birth, an angel causes the child to forget the entire Torah. This learning, then, seems futile, but *Etz Yosef* suggests that this initial teaching facilitates learning throughout life, allowing the mature adult to achieve an understanding of Torah that would otherwise be beyond his grasp. "Bring us back, our Father, to Your Torah" is a petition to return to our roots, our earliest encounter with the holiness of Torah.

Next we request, "Bring us near, our King, to Your service." Rabbi Chaim Volozhin (*Nefesh HaChaim* 2:1) points out that the performance of *mitzvos*, while exceedingly important, does not create the same intimacy as Torah study, and thus we refer to Hashem with the more formal appellation of King.

Lastly we request, "Influence us to return in perfect repentance before You." When we are cognizant of Hashem's watching our every action and his awareness of our every thought we are deterred from sin. We therefore petition assistance in repentance "before You," as David expressed in (*Psalms* 16:8), "I have placed the Lord before me always." If one is every mindful and cognizant of His presence, it will deter him from sin. Therefore, we petition assistance in repentance "before *You*" — help us to be mindful of Your presence. This blessing reflects the commitment of the Jew to study Torah, observe the *mitzvos* and to create a personal rapport with Hashem come what may. Success in the business and the professional world often leads one to believe "My power and the might of my hand has procured me this success" (*Deuteronomy* 8:17). The worshiper thrice daily, therefore, reminds himself of his *raison d'etre* and asks for assistance to implement these noble requests. Similarly, trials and tribulations can deflect even the religiously committed from actualizing their mission. Maimonides, himself a successful physician, writes in the laws of *Talmud Torah* (Chapter 1:8): "Every man is obligated to study Torah, whether he is poor or rich, of a healthy and complete body or afflicted by difficulties, whether he is young or old".

Repentance is one of the most difficult commandments in the Torah. *Mitzvos* that relate to an object — *tefillin, mezuzah,* matzah — are relatively easy to do. But to change one's attitude and behavior, to admit that one has been wrong, requires strength and Divine assistance.

✺ The Sixth Blessing: Forgiveness

This blessing follows a logical sequence: Intelligence encourages repentance and repentance brings forgiveness.

The first two requests of this prayer — "Forgive us our Father, for we have

erred, pardon us, our King, for we have willfully sinned" — are a perfect example of one's need to learn and master the Hebrew language and become proficient not only in the translation but in the understanding of the exact and particular use of a specific word. There is sharp contrast between phrase one and phrase two. In phrase one the Rabbis used the word forgive, as opposed to phrase two in which they used the word pardon. This theme is repeated with the use of Father in the first phrase and King in the second. Finally, *chet*, an accidental sin, is contrasted to *pesha,* an intentional sin. This specific choice of language is thus to be understood as follows: Only a father can completely forgive and wipe away the transgression as if it never occurred. But this can only be if the sin was done inadvertently. As King Solomon declares, "For there is not a just man upon earth that does good and sins not" (*Ecclesiastes* 7:20). The first request is: Forgive us, Father, for the affront was unintentional. The second, however, is more serious. *Pesha* denotes a rebellious intentional wrongdoing. Therefore, the relationship is downgraded to that of King, more distant and impersonal as opposed to father, and the best the King can do is pardon, that is, reduce the punishment, but the record is permanently scarred.

The process of repentance begins with the recognition of sin, followed by remorse and a commitment to avoid the sin in the future. Finally, there must be a verbal confession that specifies exactly what was done wrong. One must gather the strength of character to articulate, to Hashem and himself, his transgressions.

It is customary to strike the left side of the chest, over the heart, with one's fist while saying, "We have erred and we have willfully sinned." These symbolic blows represent an acknowledgment of guilt, the heart being the place where sin originates. Regarding sins of man to man, it must be understood that one cannot wrong his fellow and then come to God and ask for forgiveness. True, an affront towards man includes within it a transgression to Hashem, but the first step in the atonement process is to admit one's wrong and ask forgiveness from the one he hurt. Only then can one ask Hashem for His forgiveness as well. The thrice-daily recitation of the *Shemoneh Esrei* is thus one of the primary means of building and maintaining righteousness and moral character, leaving us uplifted and encouraged for the future.

৺ The Seventh Blessing: Redemption

One of the basic tenets of our faith is the belief in Divine supervision of the affairs of each individual. Hashem not only exists, He orchestrates every detail of our lives. This notion testifies to the importance and potential of each individual.

The sequence of this blessing of request in the flow of the *Shemoneh Esrei* is especially noteworthy. Often the various difficulties we experience in this world emanate from our inappropriate actions, our sins. We thus begin by asking Hashem for wisdom that ideally should motivate us to repent and ask for forgiveness. Once we have achieved the repentance that we sought in the previous blessings, we can ask that our difficult circumstances be reversed. It is

now, therefore, fitting or conceivable that our dire circumstances might change as we are ideally no longer the same person to whom the specific decree of tribulation was issued.

All of the blessings of need in the *Shemoneh Esrei* are couched in the plural. Several reasons are given for this, including the idea that the merit of the community is stronger than that of the individual. However, I believe there is a special reason for the plural usage in this *berachah* of redemption, namely, all Israel is considered one whole, one entity. If but one instrument is lacking in the orchestra, the quality of the music is affected. Similarly, if a single Jew and certainly if many are depressed, downtrodden and as a result are unable to fulfill their potential, the entire nation is lacking.

For nearly 2,000 years Jews have wandered in exile and have been persecuted physically, socially and financially for no reason other than the privilege of being born Jewish. When they prayed, it was not only for their personal dignity, but also for the glorification of Hashem.

Today, though we live in relatively prosperous circumstances, we remain ambassadors of Hashem, and we cannot be drawn into the openness of society. Today's Jew stands humbly before his Maker and confesses that he needs His help in this daily struggle to do what he knows is right, but which is not always popular or accepted.

✤§ The Eighth Blessing: Health and Healing

Often, people pay attention to their health only when specific ailments appear, and only then do they realize how fortunate they had been to be blessed with good health, enabling them to function. This blessing sensitizes the worshiper to the precious gift of good health, and asks Hashem to continue that gift.

The Torah mandates that we maintain our bodies. The verse, "Take heed and guard your soul exceedingly" (*Deuteronomy* 4:9), teaches how careful one has to be in creating a safe environment. This today would include the concern for a smoke-free environment.

The Talmud (*Bava Kamma* 85) adds that this verse acts as Hashem's authorization for physicians to heal. Nonetheless, this blessing reminds us that Hashem alone is the healer of mankind, as we are taught, "For I am Hashem, your healer" (*Exodus* 15:26). The doctor is an emissary dispensing Hashem's wishes. A doctor may treat two patients for the same ailment using the same medication, yet one will be cured and the other will succumb to the disease. In the former case, Hashem decreed that he be cured and in the latter, not.

The Talmud (*Megillah* 17b) explains that the blessing of health and healing is the eighth in the *Shemoneh Esrei* because the *mitzvah* of circumcision, which requires healing, is designated for the child's eighth day; therefore it was placed eighth in the sequence of blessings. The commandment of circumcision states "And on the eighth day the flesh of his foreskin shall be circumcised" (*Leviticus* 12:3). Many philosophers, including the *Mabit* and *Maharal,* teach that the number seven corresponds to the natural world, reflecting the unit of days with which Hashem completed creation. The number eight oftentimes denotes a

happening and circumstance that is beyond the realm of the norm. Maimonides, in his *Guide for the Perplexed,* explains the commandment of circumcision as a means of keeping the Jewish male moral, enabling him to comply with the many Biblical and Rabbinic laws that restrict his sexual misconduct. This capacity — to go beyond what is considered the natural behavior of man — is reflected by the performance of this *mitzvah* on the eighth day. Our Rabbis understand the beautiful testimony of *"Ani L'Dodi V'Dodi Li* — I am for my Beloved and my Beloved is for me" (*Song of Songs* 6:3) to mean that the Jewish nation and Hashem compliment one another and respond positively to one another. Circumcision, performed religiously and with great joy, often in the most difficult of conditions, as a reflection of our commitment and loyalty to Hashem, is responded to by Hashem with His gift of healing. *Shibbolei HaLeket* states that when the Angel Raphael healed our father Abraham after his circumcision, the angels in heaven proclaimed, "Blessed are You, Hashem, Who heals the sick of His people Israel." Every one of the 613 commandments is important. How significant is circumcision, that in its merit we are privileged to have His healing in our midst!

It is not only for healing from physical ailments and diseases that we approach Hashem, but, perhaps first and foremost, for healing of the soul. The opening words of this blessing are based on a verse said by Jeremiah (17:14): "Heal me, Hashem, and I will be healed; save me and I will be saved." Yet, the Prophet was not suffering from any physical ailment at that time. Shortly before the Temple was to be destroyed, Jeremiah had the bleak task of prophesying its doom. The Prophet was brokenhearted and asked Hashem to give him the emotional strength to face the impending crisis.

It is customary, when one is aware of specific individuals who are in need of recovery from sickness, that he pray for them by name during this blessing. The *Shemoneh Esrei* is not just an antiquated text composed over 2,500 years ago; this insertion helps the worshipers appreciate their personal encounter with Hashem. Ideally the patient's Hebrew name is mentioned, together with the name of his or her mother.

∽ The Ninth Blessing: Prosperity

Just as we recite blessings prior to eating, so too we recite a blessing prior to acquiring the means to buy the food. Just as the food must be kosher, so too the manner in which we earn our livelihood must be kosher. The Talmud (*Megillah* 17b) teaches in the name of Rabbi Alexandri that the blessing for sustenance is the ninth in the *Shemoneh Esrei,* corresponding to the ninth chapter of *Psalms* wherein David beseeches God to "Break the power of the wicked" (verse 15). The Rabbis teach us that this particular request is directed against those who raise the prices of food unfairly. (Note: When you honor me and check this reference and familiarize yourself with this source — as I trust you will endeavor, with time, to examine all the sources and thus gain each time of the rich background — you will note that this verse is found in Psalm 10 not 9. The commentators *Rashi* and *Tosofot* answer that the first two Psalms were

originally one.)

Different sins have distinct consequences. One who eats non-kosher food, for example, not only violates a Biblical command, but, according to the Talmud, also dulls his heart and limits his capacity for knowledge (*Yoma* 39a). For this reason, suggests Rabbi Yonason Eibeschutz, we pray not simply for the ability to make a living, but to do so with integrity, lest we suffer the negative consequences. Just as bacteria may contaminate or even poison food that is not properly handled, spiritual poisons afflict those who stray from ethical behavior. We therefore pray, "Satisfy us with Your bounty." In doing so, we request that Hashem include His Divine guidance in the manner in which we earn our livelihood. One dare not compromise on his religious principles in order to earn a livelihood.

Torah study and good deeds are the only riches that people take with them when they leave this world (*Avos* 6:9). (Note: See *The Rambam's Laws of Repentance,* Chapter 9, for a clear development of this theme.) Therefore, we pray in this blessing of Prosperity for "*letova* — for good," not only referring to the quality of the produce but the manner in which it will be received and utilized. We pray that we will be ever cognizant that it is Your doing that sustains us as opposed to "My strength and the might of my hand made me all this wealth" (*Deuteronomy* 8:17). Rather, the next verse continues, "You shall remember Hashem, your God: that it was He Who gave you the strength to make wealth." The Aramaic translation and commentary of *Onkelos* understands the above to mean that it is Hashem Who gives one the insights, "brainstorms," or initiative to attain success in one's respective field. The Torah knows only too well the nature of man and therefore cautions: "Jeshurun became fat and kicked" (*Deuteronomy* 32:15). Prosperity, which ideally should earn for the one blessed therewith the title "Jeshurun," meaning upright, straight and just, can lead to kicking and removing the Yoke of Heaven. It is for this reason that we couch our prayer for prosperity "*letova,* for good."

Material blessings are not ends in themselves, but a means toward the ultimate blessing — to serve Hashem without worry. One has to be exceedingly careful not to become consumed by his livelihood, thereby robbing him of the most important aspects of his life. Torah study and *mitzvah* observance are the only riches that one takes with him when he leaves this world. We therefore pray that prosperity come to us "for good," notes the commentary *Iyun Tefillah,* as only Hashem knows what is truly in our best interests and what will sustain us both materially and spiritually.

◈§ The Tenth Blessing: Ingathering of the Exiles

This seventh blessing of petition shifts our focus from our personal needs to those of the community and the Jewish nation.

Many Prophets consoled the Jewish nation by promising the future Ingathering of the Exiles. The text of this blessing is based upon the prophecy of Isaiah (27:13): "And it shall come to pass on that day, a great *shofar* shall be sounded and they who were lost in the land of Ashur [Assyria] and the outcasts in the

land of Mitzrayim [Egypt] shall return and bow down to Hashem on the holy mountain in Jerusalem." Rabbi Avigdor HaLevi Nebenzahl comments that these two nations symbolize the two distinct exiles in which the Jewish people have found themselves over the centuries.

The first exile is characterized by Mitzrayim, a word that comes from the Hebrew root *tzarus,* meaning troubles or difficult circumstances. In this exile, the Jew is trapped, persecuted for observing his religion. The government forbids the study of Torah and the proliferation of Jewish values. Jews, in lands such as the former Soviet Union, were beaten, tortured, imprisoned and killed for observing Torah and *mitzvos.*

The other exile is Ashur, meaning fortunate. In this exile Jews are not molested, but are accepted into society and afforded all the freedom and rights of its citizenship. This produces an exile of spirituality, seen in the assimilation that we suffer from in the United States, with its tragic rate of almost 50 percent intermarriage. The blessing for the Ingathering of Exiles includes both of these circumstances.

To appreciate this blessing one must keep in mind that the natural home of the Jewish people is the Land of Israel. Too many Jews are so comfortable with their lives outside the Land of Israel that they do not realize that theirs is an unnatural condition of Jewish life. We underscore this notion by declaring on each of the major pilgrim Festivals (Pesach, Shavuos, and Succos): "Because of our sins we were exiled from our land." The Jewish people upon accepting the Torah at Sinai were designated as a Holy People, and, ideally, the Holy People are to observe the Holy Torah in the Holy Land.

The Eleventh Blessing: Restoration of Justice

As mentioned above, the natural home for the Jew is the Land of Israel. Throughout the Torah, the Jewish nation is warned that the land is not given to them unconditionally; rather, they must uphold Torah law in order to ensure their claim to the land.

The opening chapter of the Book of *Isaiah* deals with the rebellion of the Jewish people against Hashem: "How has she [Jerusalem] become a harlot? A city that was faithful and full of justice, wherein righteousness would lodge — but now murderers" (verse 21). The Prophet then predicts the future:

"I will restore your judges as at first and your counselors as in the beginning; afterwards you shall be called City of Righteousness, Faithful City" (verse 26).

The Talmud (*Megillah* 17b) teaches that when the ingathering of exiles occurs, it follows that the wicked will be punished and society will be purged of its corrupt leaders, enabling honesty and justice to return to their proper places. This blessing is our pledge to a just society. We pray that we have learned our national lesson: Our disregard for justice uprooted us from our land.

It is not only for judicial authority that we yearn, but for closeness to Hashem's intimate Presence, which will be restored at that time. *Rabbeinu Bachya,* in his commentary to *Genesis* (49:15), teaches that this blessing refers to the peace of mind necessary for rigorous Torah study. Our plea, "Remove

from us sorrow and groan," does not refer to socioeconomic woes but to the impediments that stand in the way of our religious growth and a proper understanding of Hashem.

Moreover, Rabbi Joseph Wanefsky, of Yeshiva University, points to the closing text of this blessing, referring to Hashem as "the King Who loves righteousness and justice." The Talmud (*Sanhedrin* 6b) wonders how these two terms can be combined when they seem to be mutually exclusive. Righteousness usually indicates forgiveness, while justice is the term reserved for application of the law. How could both occur simultaneously?

The Talmud answers that it refers to compromise, whereby both avenues are satisfied. Justice is served but righteousness also perseveres.

Similarly the ingathering of the exiles is going to bring together different groups of Jews — Ashkenazim and Sefardim, Chassidim and Misnagdim, American and Israeli, observant and not-yet observant. All will join in the Messianic melting pot. We will need a body that can unite a diverse nation that has been splintered geographically, culturally and socially for almost 2,000 years. The Sanhedrin will serve to unify and harmonize the ingathering of our exiles.

✎ঃ The Twelfth Blessing: Against Heretics

Originally the *Shemoneh Esrei* was, as its name indicates, eighteen blessings. The Talmud (*Berachos* 28b) teaches that 500 years after the eighteen blessings were composed by the Men of the Great Assembly, Rabban Gamliel II instituted a blessing against heretics, the Sadducees and early Christians who were undermining our national character from both within and without. They informed on fellow Jews to the Roman authorities and rejected the Oral Law.

In our introduction to the *Shemoneh Esrei* we noted that our Rabbis were not able to simply compose prayers unless they had a precedent in the Scriptures upon which to model their prayer. Thus, the Talmud (*Berachos* 28b) suggests that the eighteen blessings in the daily *Amidah* correspond to the eighteen mentions of God's Name that David said in Psalm 29. How then could the Sages add another blessing? The Talmud answers that the nineteenth blessing was established corresponding to verse 3 of this psalm where it is written "the God of Glory thunders"; and while the Name Hashem is not used, the Name *"Keil,"* is used. It is interesting to note that the Name Hashem is identified with His attribute of mercy, and the Name *"Keil"* is associated with His strict judgment, thereby providing a further hint as to the harsh tone of this blessing.

The Talmud (*Berachos* 28b) informs us that it was Shmuel HaKatan who formulated the text of this blessing. At first glance, what is the significance of this historical trivia? There are, however, two important points regarding Shmuel HaKatan that we need to know. Firstly, the Talmud (*Sanhedrin* 11a) notes that he was an especially modest self-effacing person, who went to great lengths not to embarrass anyone. Moreover, when the latter Prophets, Chaggai, Zechariah, and Malachai died, the Divine spirit was withdrawn from the Jewish people. One time, however, a voice came to them from heaven saying that there

is one person who deserves to have God's Divine Presence rest upon him for prophecy, but his generation does not merit this. We are told the Sages turned their eyes to Shmuel HaKatan, knowing that he was that one. The *Yad Ramah* comments that this explains why he was called Shmuel HaKatan, the lesser Shmuel. He was fit for prophecy, as was Samuel the Prophet. This is especially significant as the Talmud (M*egillah* 17b) teaches that it was the Men of the Great Assembly who composed the *Shemoneh Esrei* and among them were several Prophets! The blessings of the *Shemoneh Esrei* were not only composed for that time period, but the authors with their prophetic vision penned blessings that would be appropriate and meaningful throughout the ages. The text of the *Amidah* today is as relevant as it was 2,500 years ago. The blessing against the heretics, as well, is unfortunately still current as every generation has its heretics who wish to undermine our holy tradition. Thus it was necessary to have an individual with the potential and qualifications for prophecy to compose this blessing; indeed, it was Shmuel HaKatan who was chosen.

In addition, in *Pirkei Avos (Ethics of the Fathers)* (4:24) we are taught: "Shmuel HaKatan says: When your enemy falls, be not glad, and when he stumbles let your heart not be joyous." At first glance this is a most difficult Mishnah, as all it seems to do is quote the verse from *Proverbs* (24:17) verbatim. What is Shmuel HaKatan teaching us? Our teachers provide us with the following insightful answer: Whereas throughout the Talmud it is commonplace to have a Mishnah, an exact Rabbinic teaching, without identifying who the author is, in the Mishnah of *Pirkei Avos* this is not the case, and every Mishnah is identified with its author. The reasoning behind this is that ethics are not only taught in the lecture halls as are legal matters, but they are primarily learned by example, by emulating the noble character of others. Thus, throughout *Pirkei Avos* when it says that a particular Rabbi taught a specific lesson, it means that his nature, character and demeanor reflected this teaching. It was a very integral part of his being. If so, what do we know about the man who composed the blessing against the heretics? We know that there was no trace of personal animosity in his heart, no personal vindictiveness or malicious hatred. To quote the words of King David, "For it is a time to act for Hashem, they have voided Your Torah" (*Psalms* 119:126).

The Talmud (*Berachos* 10a) informs us that there were evildoers in Rabbi Meir's neighborhood who caused him considerable distress. Once Rabbi Meir was praying that they should die. The *Tzlach* (commentator on the Talmud) notes that asking that they be killed immediately might insure that whatever portion they had already earned in the World To Come would remain for them. The more they sinned in this world, the more they would be receiving reward in this world and losing their share in the next. Rabbi Meir's wife, Bruriah, said to her husband, "The verse in *Psalms* (104:35) can be read not only 'sinners will cease from the earth' but 'sins and the evil inclination will cease from the earth' "; and indeed this is the proper pronunciation of the text. Accordingly, King David is not praying for the death of sinners, but rather that they should be inspired to repent. Therefore, Bruriah told her husband to pray for mercy for the

evildoers — that they should repent of their wickedness. Rabbi Meir heeded her advice, prayed on their behalf and they indeed repented. Why then are we praying here, "May all Your enemies be cut down speedily"?

There are two answers to this question. First, Maimonides in the *Laws of Prayer* (2:1) writes that the threat during the days of Rabban Gamliel was that the various sects from within the Jewish community were trying to entice others to stray from their Jewish roots. They suggested that the time-honored worship of Hashem was old-fashioned and outmoded, and that all the imposed restrictions of Judaism should be abandoned because its founders had no idea of the spectacular progress of modern times. Moreover, why should the Jew live in fear? Let him assimilate with the dominant religious power and thereby remove a major source of discrimination. The Torah (*Deuteronomy* 13:7-12) deals harshly with the enticer, stressing that he has forfeited every claim to mercy. Although Jews are commanded to love one another, he, the one who attempts to remove a Jew from his religious convictions, is an exception to the rule. Although the court is normally required to seek extenuating circumstances that would permit it to save a transgressor from the death penalty, this is the one and only exception. Thus, the *berachah* reminds us that Judaism is not a democracy. We have a sacred mission to accomplish as delineated by the Torah, and any attempt at undermining that mission is viewed as a threat to our very existence, thereby warranting this harsh, stern language.

In addition, here too, explains the *Vilna Gaon,* we pray for wickedness to perish, so that the wicked will repent and then cause their own sins to be eradicated.

Finally, Rabbi Yonasan Eibeschutz, in his *Ya'aros Devash,* teaches that while reciting this blessing one should keep in mind the Biblical command to remember Amalek's attack upon the fledgling nation of Israel, and our responsibility to erase the memory of Amalek from beneath the heaven and not to forget (*Deuteronomy* 25:17-19). Any nation that attempts to destroy the Jewish people is halachically categorized as Amalek.

⊷ The Thirteenth Blessing: The Righteous

Once we have prayed for the downfall of the wicked, we can now pray for the success of the righteous, as the righteous flourish in an environment free from evil. The sequence of the blessings can now be more clearly understood. First we ask for the ingathering of the exiles to unite our people, then for the establishment of a just society, followed by the removal of sinners. Now, we ask for the righteous to be allowed to create an environment for religious and moral growth and development.

There are five different types of individuals that we identify and pray for in this blessing. The first are the righteous who, according to Rabbi Yaacov Emden in his *siddur Bais Yaacov,* carefully observe Jewish law. The second group, the devout or *chassidim,* are those who go "beyond the letter of the law." The third, the elders, are individuals who hold leadership positions within the community. The fourth, the remnant of their scholars, are the Rabbis who safeguard and

transmit the Oral Torah and tradition, from generation to generation. The fifth category is the righteous converts. Rabbi Eliezer teaches in the Talmud (*Pesachim* 87b) that one of the reasons for Israel's being in exile is to attract and absorb righteous converts.

As the first of the blessings of request was for knowledge, enabling the individual to master Torah study, this blessing is for the creating of a Torah community and a spiritual environment, and this can be accomplished only by personal example and transmission of our sacred law and lore or our people. "The remnant of their scholars" may be understood as familiarizing the younger generation with the great minds and personalities that preceded them. Rabbi Joseph. B. Soloveitchik, described their role in the following exciting fashion:

"The old Rebbe walks into the classroom crowded with students who are young enough to be his grandchildren. He enters as an old man with wrinkled face, his eyes reflecting the fatigue and sadness of old age. The Rebbe is seated and sees before him rows of young beaming faces, clear eyes radiating the joy of being young. For a moment, the Rebbe is gripped with pessimism and with tremors of uncertainty. He asks himself, 'Can there be a dialogue between an old teacher and young students, between a Rebbe in his Indian summer and students enjoying the Spring of their lives?' The Rebbe starts the *shiur,* uncertain as to how it will proceed.

"Suddenly, the door opens and an old man, much older than the Rebbe, enters. He is the grandfather of the Rebbe, Reb Chaim Brisker (1853-1918). The door opens again and another old man comes in. He is older than Reb Chaim, for he lived in the 17th century. His name is Reb Shabbtai Cohen (1622-1663) known as the *Shach,* who must be present when civil law is discussed. Many more visitors arrived, some from the 11th, 12th and 13th centuries, and others harking back to antiquity — *Rabbeinu Tam* (1090-1171), *Rashi* (1040-1105), *Rambam* (1135-1204), *Rabad* (1125-1198), *Rashba* (1245-1310), Rabbi Akiva (40-135), and others. These scholarly giants of the past are bidden to take their seats.

"The Rebbe introduces the guests to his pupils and the dialogue commences. The *Rambam* states a halacha; the *Rabad* disagrees sharply, as is his wont. Some students interrupt to defend the *Rambam,* and they express themselves harshly against the *Rabad,* as young people are apt to do. The Rebbe softly corrects the students and suggests more restrained tones. The *Rashba* smiles gently. The Rebbe tries to analyze what the students meant, and other students intercede. *Rabbeinu Tam* is called upon to stress his opinion, and suddenly, a symposium of generations comes into existence. Young students debate earlier generations with an air of daring familiarity, and a crescendo of discussion ensues.

"All speak one language; all pursue one goal; all are committed to a single vision; and all operate with the same categories (of Talmudic analysis and study). A *mesorah* — tradition, collegiality — is achieved, a friendship, a comradeship of young and old, spanning antiquity, the Middle Ages, and modern times. *V'hu haketz,* this joining of the generations, this merger of identities will ultimately bring about the redemption of the Jewish people. It will fulfill the

words of the last of the Hebrew Prophets, Malachi, "And he [Elijah] shall turn the heart of the fathers to the children and the heart of the children to their fathers" (3:24). The Messianic realization will witness the great dialogue of the generations" (*Reflections of the Rav,* Volume 2, pp. 21-23).

∽§ The Fourteenth Blessing: Rebuilding Jerusalem

This blessing is the natural continuation of the one that precedes it, for only in Jerusalem can the righteous reach their full glory and potential.

The Talmud (*Bava Kamma* 82b) teaches that Jerusalem was not divided among the Tribes. Just as the city of Washington, D.C. does not belong to any individual state in the Union, rather to the entire American people, "We had it first," Jerusalem belonged to all Israel. This was especially important at the time of the three pilgrimage Festivals — Pesach, Shavuos, and Succos — when all Jews came to Jerusalem to spend the holiday. There were no rooms for rent as everyone opened their homes and hearts to the rest of the nation who were coming to "their Jerusalem." The *Chasam Sofer* explains the statement of *Avos,* that no one complained regarding his lodging accommodations, in the following way. In reality it was tight, with many people converging on each dwelling. However, the thrill of being in the confines of His Presence, and of hosting many people and enabling them to bask in the *shechinah* (Divine Presence) outweighed any physical inconvenience. It truly was "a city that is united together" (*Psalms* 122:3).

We have already been privileged in our time to get a glimpse as to how the Third Temple will, please Hashem, unify our people. The Kotel, the "Western Wall," which, miraculously, remains since the Second Temple, attracts Jews and even non-Jews of all backgrounds. "My House is a repository of prayer for all peoples" (*Isaiah* 56:7) will be equally true speedily, in our day.

On Tishah B'Av, the blackest day on the Jewish calendar, the anniversary of the Temple's destruction, we commemorate the event with a special prayer. This prayer, *Nacheim,* is an entreaty for consolation and comfort from Hashem. We insert it in this blessing. "With fire you have destroyed it, and with fire you will rebuild it," we declare. The *Sfas Emes* understands these words metaphorically. In every generation, he writes, there have been righteous individuals who lived, and often died, for upholding Hashem's Torah and *mitzvos.* Their burning commitment has not dissipated. Rather, their loyalty and sacrifice form the walls of fire that will be used by Hashem in the rebuilding of the Third Temple. One should not entertain the notion that the building of the Temple is beyond our reach and scope. The hot tears we shed on Tishah B'Av and throughout the year, and our fervent prayers on behalf of redemption and the rebuilding of the Temple become an integral part of these walls of fire yet to be built.

∽§ The Fifteenth Blessing: Davidic Reign

The opening phrase of this blessing is based upon the verse "In those days, at that time, I will cause a bud of righteousness to sprout forth from David, and he will administer justice and righteousness in the land" (*Jeremiah* 33:15). The

BACKGROUND OF THE PRAYERS / 40

coming of the Messiah is compared to a flower, which we ask Hashem to cause to flourish. While man is limited in his vision, only seeing what is happening immediately to him and his environs, Hashem is putting all the pieces together and creating the environment for the Messiah's arrival. But while the Messiah is already designated and charged with responsibilities, he is in need of man's prayers in order to come forth (*Avodah Shebelev*).

The Talmud (*Shabbos* 31a) teaches that among the first questions to be asked of each individual in the World to Come is, "Did you await and pine for the Messianic salvation?"

Rabbi Avraham Pam says that it is not sufficient to believe that the Messiah will eventually come; rather we have to yearn for his coming each day. Rabbi Pam in his *Atarah L'Melech* cites the *Chofetz Chaim,* who saw in the contemporary events of his day the fulfillment of many conditions cited both in Tractate *Sotah* (49b) and Tractate *Sanhedrin* (98a). In the latter, Rabbi Yochanan taught: "If you see a generation upon which numerous troubles come like a river (that is to say, troubles constantly grow like a river which constantly flows without stopping) expect the Mashiach." Who can deny, says Rabbi Pam, that the tragedies that befell one third of our people during the Holocaust are heralding the imminent arrival of Mashiach. The *Chofetz Chaim* further observes that the incredible scientific and technological breakthroughs of the 20th century are a sure sign of the imminent arrival of the Mashiach. By enabling us to unleash all our locked-up potential before he comes, Hashem gives us a portent of what lies ahead.

Finally, the *Chofetz Chaim* observed that one of the clearest indications that we are in the pre-Messianic era is the hectic pace of world events. He likened this period to the hustle and bustle of last-minute Shabbos preparations, and so too it is Hashem Himself Who has hastened the pace in anticipation of the time that is designated as the complete Shabbos. Even the surge of immorality in the world can be attributed to the pre-Messianic times, as often right before its extinction, something expends a last effort to preserve and maintain itself. Note the intensity of darkness immediately prior to dawn. A candle before extinction flickers brightly, and some individuals rally momentarily before passing on. Since the Prophet Zechariah (13:2) promised, "The impure spirit will be removed from the land," as we approach the time of redemption, immorality tries to prevail, before it is permanently shamed and shunned. Even the U.N., suggests Rabbi Pam, might have been created to chronicle the injustice performed against the Jewish nation.

Rabbi Pam therefore urges that each Jew beseech Hashem to hasten and bring the redemption and Mashiach to our people. The *Chofetz Chaim* cried to Hashem regarding the difficulties and troubles facing the Jewish people and pleaded for the coming of Mashiach saying, "God — *du hust duch tzu gezukt,* you promised us!" Finally, we shall heed the advice of Rabbi Eliezer who taught in *Sanhedrin* (98b): "What can a person do to be spared the travail of the Messiah? One should occupy himself in the study of Torah and in acts of kindness."

Our reciting this blessing should not only awaken within us a yearning for the

Messiah but a commitment to share Torah with others. Just as in Egypt, prior to the redemption, there was a strong campaign for kindness and benevolence among the Jews, and this awakened Divine kindness on our behalf, so too may we be similarly privileged, speedily in our days.

⋄§ The Sixteenth Blessing: Acceptance of Prayer

This last of our thirteen petitions gives us the proper perspective regarding our relationship with Hashem. Standing before Hashem is a privilege. Bringing our requests to Him personally, and acknowledging that He alone has the capacity to grant these requests, is a form of praising Him. Ultimately we are reminded by the language of this blessing that whatever Hashem grants us is a gift and that it does not necessarily come to us because of our merits.

At the conclusion of this blessing, we ask, "Do not turn us away empty-handed from before You, our King." In effect we are saying: Even if our merits are few, please do not reject our prayers completely; at least grant us part of our request (*Avudraham*). The *mitzvah* of prayer, as formulated by our Sages, is to recite the *Shemoneh Esrei*. Today it is nineteen blessings with thirteen requests. If we are not worthy that all of these requests be answered, please, we ask, at least answer as many as possible.

Concerning the phrase "Do not turn us away empty-handed," Rabbi Baruch HaLevi Epstein, in his commentary *Baruch She'Amar,* adds the following insightful idea. We know from the *Taz* in his commentary on *Orach Chaim* (670:1) that in order for a blessing to take effect there must be some substance or material to which the blessing can be applied and extended. It is for this reason, he explained, that the holiday of Chanukah is observed for eight days, though there was enough oil for one day, and therefore at first glance the holiday should only be seven days. He answers that if some of the original oil had not remained from the first day, the miracle could never have taken place. Therefore the first day is also included, and celebrated, as some of the oil of the first day was not consumed, thus allowing for the miracle of the subsequent days to occur. Hashem does not create a miracle from naught as He did at the time of Creation. It is for this reason that the custom is to leave some of the bread on the table at the time of the recitation of the Grace After Meals, so that the blessing of "Our God, Our Father, tend us, nourish us, sustain us, support us" will have something substantive to which to attach itself. Here too we ask, "Do not turn us away empty-handed," thereby allowing some blessing to enrich us.

Finally, the Talmud (*Berachos* 29b) admonishes the one whose prayers are "set," who is not able to add anything new daily. One can include any request in this last of the petitionary blessing. The *Mishnah Berurah* (*Orach Chaim* 119:1) adds that while we may add personal prayers for specific needs within the appropriate blessings of the *Shemoneh Esrei*, these insertions are only made when a need already exists. In this blessing one may include petitions that he maintain good health and prosperity in the future. In reality, all of us have our own personal agenda of activities that are important to us from day to day. A job interview, need for a *shidduch,* a *simchah* taking place that we pray will be

meaningful — all the above and each individual request should be articulated prior to the closing phrase of "For You hear the prayer of your people Israel with compassion," and it should be a sincere heartfelt request, in fulfillment of the directive of King David who taught "From the depths I call You Hashem" (*Psalms* 130:1).

∞§ Expressions of Thanks

The last three blessings of the *Shemoneh Esrei* are the same for every *Amidah*. As a group, they are called *Hoda'ah*, literally Thanksgiving, which is also the theme of the second blessing of the group. While at first glance both the first blessing, *Retzei,* and the final blessing, *Shalom*, Peace, are requests — that God restore the Temple service and endow us with peace — a more careful analysis will show why all three blessings collectively are expressions of thanks.

In essence, in the last section of *Shemoneh Esrei* we are thanking God for granting us the privilege of an audience with Him. In *Retzei*, realizing how fortunate we have been to communicate with Hashem through prayer, we beg that this relationship be expanded, developed, and heightened by the restoration of the Temple Service. In *Modim*, which means not only to thank, but also to acknowledge or confess, we bow in recognition of the fact that we are in the actual presence of the Divine, as it were. Finally, in the last blessing, we say that though in a physical sense we are taking leave of God's Presence, may His spirit accompany us in all our endeavors.

The common denominator is that these three blessings were recited by the *Kohanim* (the Priests), in the Temple, at the conclusion of the morning service. All three elements — the people, the place, and the time — relate to our having entered the realm of the Divine Presence, and for this privilege we are grateful.

∞§ Curse of Independence

In cursing the serpent for tempting Eve to sin, God said, "Upon your belly shall you go and dust shall you eat all the days of your life" (*Genesis* 13:14). Rabbi Menachem Mendel of Kotzk asked wherein lies the curse to the serpent; after all, there is never a shortage of earth and dust to supply the serpent with his needs. Incisively, the Rabbi explained that it was precisely because God provided the serpent with all that he needed, that he was cursed. In essence God said to the serpent, "There will be no need for any communication nor relationship between us; whatever you will need you will have, and you will have no reason to turn to Me, to beseech Me, or to have a relationship with Me." From here we learn what a privilege it is for man to have a relationship with God, and this is why we thank God in these blessings for having granted us the privilege of an audience with Him.

∞§ Restoration of the Temple Service

I believe there are three new concepts in this blessing. The first is one of relationship. We ask God to respond favorably to our prayers not because He *has* to, but because He *wants* to. There is a difference between fulfilling a

commitment because one is bound by contract to do so, and a situation where the donor extends himself because he wants to do so, not motivated by the legal obligation. A husband is obligated by *halachah* to support his wife, but if the relationship is good and loving, he will view his support as a privilege, not a burden. Similarly, we pray that God accept our prayers with favor because He wishes to, and not because of His covenant with our forefathers, or because He must insure our survival since His Name is inextricably associated with ours.

Thus, in the first theme of this blessing, we plead, "May we find favor in Your eyes; may You be pleased with Your people Israel." Enable us to be even closer to You than we are through the direct relationship we are privileged to have by petitioning You through prayer — and that will come about when You restore the Temple service, for the offerings are a means for people to become close to You [קָרְבָּן, *offering*, is from the root קרב, *close*]. As close a rapport as petition and praise of Hashem can bring, the bringing of offerings is an even closer and more intimate relationship.

Secondly, Rabbi Joseph B. Soloveitchik suggested that in this blessing we are asking God not merely to accept our prayers, but rather that we ourselves be elevated in His eyes as if we were offerings. This concept has a basis in *halachah*. *Mishkenos Yaakov* maintains that our recitation of *Retzei*, with its reference to offerings, converts our prayer into an offering. On a personal level, the individual's prayer is ideally looked upon as if it were a personal offering, and when the *chazzan* (reader) repeats this blessing, it converts the public prayer into a public sacrifice. This explains why, when the *Kohanim* ascend to bless the congregation on festivals, we recite the prayer וְהַעֲרֵב, asking God to be pleased with our prayer as if it were a burnt-offering and sacrifice. This prayer is inserted in the middle of *Retzei*, because it is the theme of this blessing. It is thus understandable that if the *Kohen* does not ascend the platform in preparation for the Priestly Blessing while the *chazzan* is reciting *Retzei*, then he may no longer ascend. It is this blessing which enables the *Kohanim* to bless the congregants, as it transforms prayer into sacrifice.

⚜ National Merit

The third new concept in this blessing is expressed by the commentary of the *Maggid Tzedek*, a student of the *Vilna Gaon*. He notes that this prayer asks Hashem to find our prayers acceptable in the merit of "Your people Israel." Even if a person or a particular group of people are not worthy of their prayers being answered, the collective merit of *Am Yisrael*, the metaphysical entity of our people, should warrant this special request. Finally, *Midrash Shocher Tov* (*Psalms* 17:5) observes that many thousands died in the days of King David because the Jewish people had not petitioned Hashem for His Temple to be built and for His presence to reside in their midst. Now if they, who never had a Temple, were held responsible for not praying for one, we, who have had two Temples, should surely bemoan the loss and spiritual vacuum created by its destruction. How much more so must we pray for its rebuilding!

The historical background to this blessing is provided by *Shibbolei HaLeket:*

When the Jewish people sinned with the Golden Calf, Hashem showed his displeasure and announced He was moving out of the camp. It was not until months later, on Yom Kippur, that He forgave the Jewish people and ordered that a Sanctuary be built (*Exodus* 25:8) so that He could dwell again in their midst. They began on the morrow after Yom Kippur and the Sanctuary was dedicated on *Rosh Chodesh* Nissan. When the heavenly fire descended, symbolizing that God's Presence was in their midst (*Leviticus* 9:24), the angels responded with the blessing of "Who returns His Divine Presence to Zion."

∽§ Yaaleh VeYavo

Yaaleh VeYavo is the prayer that is added to the *Amidah* and Grace After Meals on *Rosh Chodesh* and Festivals. The Talmud (*Shabbos* 24a) teaches that on days where there is an obligation to bring a *mussaf* (additional offering beyond the required daily morning offering) one should recite a prayer "that reflects the occasion" in the blessing for the return of the Temple service. It is fitting that this prayer which mentions the occasion of *Rosh Chodesh* or *Chol HaMoed* be incorporated in the blessing of the Temple service, for *Yaaleh VeYavo* petitions God to have compassion on Israel and Jerusalem and to reinstate the Temple service, so that we can fulfill the obligation to bring the offerings mandated by the Torah for the particular occasion. If one did not include this prayer, continues the Talmud, we require him to rectify the omission. [See "Laws."]

The eight expressions beginning *"Rise, come, reach, be noted,* etc." are attributed by the *Vilna Gaon* in his commentary *Avnei Eliyahu* to the fact that the *Shechinah,* Divine Presence, has withdrawn itself above the seven heavens and therefore the eight expressions denote the many levels that our prayers must penetrate.

∽§ The Blessing of Thanksgiving

The Talmud (*Megillah* 18a) emphasizes the close connection between the preceding blessing of restoring the Temple service and thanksgiving; in reality they form one unit, for the rendering of thanks and gratitude is part of the service of Hashem. Rabbi Elie Munk writes emphatically that "Any expression of gratitude not preceded by the acceptance to observe the Divine law is blasphemy." The word *hoda'ah*, thanksgiving, has three connotations: Firstly, to bow down; therefore we bow at the beginning and end of this *berachah*. Secondly, it is an expression of admission and faith, as we express in the words of gratitude and recognition recited upon arising in the morning in which we thank Hashem for restoring our soul. Finally, it refers to thanksgiving (*World of Prayer,* pp. 151-2).

Ideally one should have proper *kavanah*, concentration and understanding of what is being recited throughout the *Amidah*, but the Sages have taught that the first blessing of the faith of the Patriarchs and this blessing of Thanksgiving warrant special attention and concentration.

The *Mabit* (*Beis Elokim*) notes that we bow at the beginning and end of this

blessing because it encompasses all of the praises and the Oneness of Hashem. Thus, to demonstrate that we are humbled by the recitation, we bow in humility. According to *Roke'ach*, we bow to signify our personal acceptance of His Kingship, like a servant prostrating himself before his master. It is thus understandable that a perfunctory mechanical bowing without realizing who, what or why is almost meaningless.

In *Modim* we thank Hashem for binding our identity with His, in the past, present, and future. We offer gratitude to Him for maintaining His oath to Israel never to exchange us for another as His chosen people. We thank Him for our lives and for our souls that He returns to us daily. Notes the *Zohar:* The norm among people is that if one has entrusted a precious object to someone else and he owes that person a great debt, the lender will keep the object as collateral. Similarly, we owe Hashem everything, and each night we entrust our soul to Him. Only due to His abundant kindness does He return our souls daily. *Eitz Yosef* notes that the numerical value of the word מודים, *Modim,* is 100, reminding us of the Rabbinic obligation to recite 100 blessings daily, thus acknowledging throughout the day that He is our Provider, and making our thanksgiving a constant refrain of life.

◆§ Open and Hidden Miracles

Included in this blessing is our thanks to Hashem "for Your miracles that are with us daily, and for Your wonders every evening, morning, and afternoon." *Miracles*, explains the *Eitz Yosef*, are extraordinary events that everyone recognizes to be the result of Hashem's intervention. *Wonders* are the familiar things that we do not regard as miracles, because we have become accustomed to them, such as breathing, raining, and growing. In *Modim,* we are reminded that we are all daily beneficiaries of Hashem's miracles and wonders — but we have become so blasé that we do not even realize their source, and therefore do not adequately thank Hashem. In this blessing, therefore, we offer thanks for the miracles and wonders of which we are aware, and also for the ones that we do not recognize as such.

The basic philosophical principle contained in this blessing is the attribute of *hakaras hatov,* acknowledging the good done for us. All too often man resists this practice as an unwelcome reminder that we are dependent on others. It humbles us to be forced to say thank you or, in other words, I couldn't do it without you. The Talmud (*Bava Kamma* 92a) teaches that one must even thank a waiter. One might argue that, firstly, he is being paid, and secondly, it is not even his food that he is serving. Yet we must accustom ourselves to express appreciation, for unless we recognize the good extended to us by man, we will fail to acknowledge the constant good provided us by God.

The Sages note disapprovingly that Pharaoh was an ingrate. In describing his plan to enslave and persecute the Jews, the Torah says of Pharaoh that he "did not know of Joseph" (*Exodus* 1:8), implying that the new king was unaware of the enormous debt of gratitude he and his people owed their Jewish savior. Our Rabbis tell us that indeed he *did* know of Joseph, but conducted himself as if he

did not. The same Pharaoh later responded to Moses' request that he set free the Jewish nation: "I do not know Hashem, nor will I send out Israel" (5:2). Because Pharaoh did not recognize the good extended to him by man, he was led to deny the good extended to him by God.

◆§ Modim D'Rabbanan

The Talmud (*Sotah* 40b) teaches that when the *chazzan* repeats the blessing of thanksgiving aloud, the congregation is to join with its own declaration of thanks. *Avudraham* suggests that the congregation cannot rely on the *chazzan's Modim*, because only the beneficiaries can express sincere thanks to one who has helped them. Whereas petitions and requests may be submitted on behalf of another, declarations of faith can be uttered only by each individual himself. Similarly, one Jew cannot recite the *Shema*, thereby accepting the tenets of the existence, Oneness, and love of Hashem on behalf of another, just as one cannot don *tefillin* or shake a *lulav* on behalf of another. Such commandments, like the recitation of *Modim*, must be performed personally, and not through an intermediary.

The Talmud cites the personal declarations used by a number of rabbis (Rav, Shmuel, Rav Simlai, and Rabbi Acha bar Yaakov). Rav Pappa held that it is best to include them all, which we do in our text of *Modim D'Rabbanan*, which is appropriately named *Modim* of the Rabbis.

◆§ Conclusion

The blessing ends with praise to God as the One Who deserves thanks. The historical background for this ending, according to *Shibbolei HaLeket*, is found in the Talmud (*Shabbos* 30a). When King Solomon brought the Ark into his newly built Temple, the gates of the Holy of Holies clung to each other miraculously and could not be opened. Solomon recited 24 expressions of prayer, but the gates remained closed. Finally, he pleaded, "Hashem, O God, turn not away the face of Your anointed one. Remember the pieties of David Your servant." As soon as he mentioned the name of David, he was answered and the gates opened. At that moment the angels exclaimed, "Blessed are You, Hashem, Whose Name is good, and to You it is fitting to give thanks."

◆§ Peace: The Final Blessing

The last blessing is that of Peace. As we have pointed out before, our prayers take the place of the sacrificial order that was brought in the Temple. In the Temple, the *Kohanim* would bless the people at the conclusion of the service (*Leviticus* 9:22). Their blessings concluded with a plea for peace, and we, too, conclude our prayers with the blessing of peace and the Priestly Blessing, when appropriate. The Midrash (*Vayikra Rabbah* 9:9) notes that all blessings from God end with peace. Interestingly, the first substantiation of this concept is offered by Rabbi Shimon Ben Yochai from the last verse of Psalm 29, the psalm which, as noted, is the source for the structure of both the weekday and Shabbos *Shemoneh Esrei*. The psalm deals with the revelation at Sinai and ends with

"Hashem will bless His people with peace." The commentaries understand this to mean not only that He will bless His people with peace, but He will bestow all His blessings in an environment of peace, so that the blessings will endure.

The Talmudic sage Chizkiah derived the great importance of peace from Scripture. He noted that many of the 248 positive commandments of the Torah are conditional. For example, if one chances upon his friend's lost object he must return it (*Exodus* 23:4-5), but one is not required to initiate a search for such objects. Similarly, only if one encounters a mother bird roosting on its chicks or eggs must one carry out the prescribed ritual (*Deuteronomy* 22:6-7). However, regarding peace we are taught: "Seek peace and pursue it" (*Psalms* 34:15) — peace is so vital that one is charged to go out of his way to foster it.

The blessing of peace should be understood as an injunction to everyone to pursue peace at all costs. The final blessing after the *Shema* on Friday evenings concludes with "Who spreads the shelter of peace upon us, upon all of His people and upon Jerusalem." The last blessing of the *Amidah* and the Priestly Blessing end with the blessing of peace. And the *Kaddish* concludes with "He Who makes peace in His heights, may He in His compassion make peace upon us and upon all Israel."

Indeed the last Mishnah of the Talmud informs us that the necessary environment to receive blessing is that of peace (*Uktzin* 3:12). Thus, explains Rabbi Yonasan Eibeschutz, we pray for peace and unity and harmony among our people, thereby making us worthy to receive all the diverse blessings of the *Amidah*. One should pray for genuine peace and that strife and argumentation should not characterize the Jewish community. On a personal note, one is to pray that he be rid of anger, for that, too, is an impediment to peace.

Rabbi Zvi Mecklenburg, in his commentary *Eyun Tefillah*, understands the petition of "Bless us with the light of Your countenance" to mean the gift of greater understanding of Your Torah, on all its levels, including those that are beneath the surface and can be understood only with great toil in the study of the Oral Law. In this blessing we ask not only for peace of mind but Divine assistance in mastering the inner hidden secrets of Torah.

✎ Rabbi Meir Makes Peace

This duty of everyone to seek peace is illustrated by a story found in the Jerusalem Talmud (*Sotah* 1:4). The great sage Rabbi Meir used to lecture on Friday evenings at the synagogue in Chamas, and a certain woman attended his lecture religiously. Once the lecture ran longer than usual and, when she returned home late, her husband, who disliked rabbis, vowed that she could not enter his home until she spat in Rabbi Meir's eye. After three weeks of banishment from her home, her friends persuaded her to go to Rabbi Meir, who had been informed by Elijah the Prophet that he was the indirect cause of the marital disharmony. When she arrived, Rabbi Meir feigned distress in his eye. He asked the woman visitor, "Can you assist me by spitting in my eye?" He instructed her to spit seven times, assuring her it would help cure him. She did!

Thereupon he instructed her to tell her husband: "You insisted that I spit

once, and I spat seven times." When his students asked why the great Torah scholar demeaned himself so, he responded, "I, Meir, take my lead from none other than Hashem Himself." As we are taught, for the sake of restoring peace between husband and wife, the Holy Name of God is erased in the waters of the *sotah* (*Numbers* 5:23).

✥ Positive Unity Through Peace

Ashkenazic practice is to recite the *Sim Shalom* text of the blessing for peace only at the times that the Priests offered their blessing in the Temple. This includes every *Shacharis* and *Mussaf,* and *Minchah* on a fast day. In *Avnei Eliyahu*, the *Vilna Gaon* shows how the six forms of goodness we request in *Sim Shalom* correspond to the six blessings contained in the verses of the Priestly Blessings. Thus, the "peace, goodness, blessing, graciousness, kindness, and compassion" mentioned in *Sim Shalom* parallel the six attributes in *Bircas Kohanim*: Bless you, safeguard you, illuminate, be gracious, turn . . . to you, be gracious. The Talmud (*Sotah* 39b) highlights the connection between the Priestly Blessing and the final blessing of the *Amidah* by mandating that the *Kohanim* are not to leave the platform, where they stood as they blessed the congregation, until the *chazzan* has completed the blessing of *Sim Shalom*.

Shibbolei HaLeket ascribes the text of this blessing to the angels who recited it after Joshua's fourteen years of conquest and division of the land, whereupon the Jewish nation attained peace, "each man under his vine and under his fig tree" (*I Kings* 5:5).

Rabbi Baruch HaLevi Epstein in his commentary, *Baruch She'amar*, notes that there is a difference between the verb שִׂים, literally *place*, and תֵּן, *grant*. The former has the connotation of something being carefully placed, in contrast to the latter, which does not denote careful placing (see *Temurah* 34a). Thus when Abraham sent away Hagar and Ishmael, he carefully placed and arranged [שָׂם] the provisions on her shoulder (*Genesis* 21:18). Similarly in our blessing of peace, we pray for "*sim shalom*," meaning that we pray for peace that unifies in a positive way, through common values, purpose and goals, as opposed to the unity that comes from without, through crises and troubles.

✥ Times of Day — and Life

There is a fascinating parallel and symmetry between *Modim*, the blessing of thanksgiving, and *Sim Shalom*, the blessing for peace. In the former we thank God for His wonders and favors in every season, "evening, morning, and afternoon." In the latter we ask for "graciousness, kindness, and compassion." One of my congregants excitedly shared the following thought with me. The times enumerated in *Modim* may refer not only to the literal times of the day, but to the different times in our lives. Unlike the rest of society, in which elderly people try to resist growing old with dignity, by dressing and acting like the young, our tradition associates the "evening" of life with *chein*, charm. Judaism does not spurn its elderly, or regard them as nonproductive members of society;

rather the Torah says, "Ask your father and he will relate it to you, your elders and they will tell you" (*Deuteronomy* 32:7).

The *boker*, morning, is representative of the early, younger years of life, when one sees not only the rising sun, but new opportunities. At this time we recognize God's constant *chesed*, kindness, in guiding our morning, our young selves, toward maturity. Finally, the afternoon represents middle age, which requires a special dose of "His compassion," so that we should be pleased with ourselves, with our accomplishments, and with our contributions to society. The Talmud (*Berachos* 57b) insightfully notes that God implants a positive feeling and desire in each individual artisan and craftsman, so that however one serves society, he should enjoy his work and perform it in a positive way, with a sense of privilege in enhancing society.

Rabbi Moshe Lichtenstein suggests that the main part of the *Amidah* prayer is concluded with the blessing of *Modim* and the recitation of the Priestly Blessing as was the case in the Temple, when the blessing of the *Kohanim* followed the morning sacrifice. That we bow at the beginning and end of *Modim* is a further demonstration that the formal prayer is over and that we are respectfully taking leave of God's Presence. What then is the *Sim Shalom* blessing? It is our request to God that He extend His blessing even after we have left His Divine Presence.

◆§ Krias HaTorah

In addition to the Biblical *mitzvah* incumbent upon each individual to study Torah (*Devarim* 6:7), there is a *mitzvah* from the Prophets to read the Torah in a public forum. We first encounter this phenomenon with Moshe at Sinai when all Israel underwent a conversion process; "He took the Book of the Covenant, (understood by *Rashi* as the Torah from *Bereishis* until the giving of the Torah) and read it to the entire people" (*Shemos* 24:7). We are taught that *Parshat Kedoshim* (*Vayikra*, Chapter 19) Moshe taught to the entire nation as a whole. Similarly, the next to last *mitzvah* of the Torah is that of *hakhel* where on the holiday of Succos, following the *shemittah* — Sabbatical year — the king of Israel read the Torah to the entire nation of Israel (*Devarim* 31:10-13).

The Talmud (*Bava Kamma* 82a) teaches that Ezra the Scribe instituted the practice of publicly reading the Torah on Shabbos afternoon at *Minchah*, and on Monday and Thursday mornings. The Talmud questions the authenticity of this statement by producing an earlier source for public reading of the Torah, namely from the era of Moshe, three days after the splitting of the Red Sea. The Torah teaches, "They went for a three-day period in the Wilderness, but they did not find water" (*Shemos* 15:22). Throughout Scriptures, water is used as a metaphor

for Torah. The Prophet Isaiah (55:1) tells the Jewish nation: "Whoever is thirsty should go to the water." The Talmud (*Taanis* 7a) explains this analogy: Just as water is crucial to life, so is Torah to the life of a Jew. Moreover, just as water seeks its lowest level, so too Torah can only be fully absorbed by one who is humble. Thus not only were the waters found by the Jewish nation bitter until Moshe threw a tree in them, but many explained that the people themselves were bitter. This bitterness is attributed to their going three days without the study of Torah. Thereupon, Moshe enacted that the Torah be read on Shabbos and then on Monday and again on Thursday.

The Talmud resolves this difficulty by informing us that originally the provision was for but one person to read from the Torah, and three verses were sufficient to be read, or three persons read three verses each for a total of nine verses. Ezra then instituted that three individuals be called to the Torah and a minimum of ten verses read.

Rabbi Soloveitchik explained the evolution of this law in the following fascinating way. There is a fundamental difference between the Written Law (Five Books of Moshe and Scriptures) and the Oral Law. With the former, one can fulfill the *mitzvah* of study even if he does not comprehend the material being read. There is value to the recitation of *Psalms* even if one does not know the meaning of the *Psalms*. The Oral Law is different. There one must understand and comprehend to get the *mitzvah*. Thus, the enactment of Moshe was that the Torah be read, not necessarily thoroughly understood by the people. As proof, Maimonides in his *Laws of Prayer* (Chapter 12, Paragraph 1) writes: "Moshe, our teacher, instituted public reading of the Torah on Shabbos, Monday and Thursday mornings, so that there should not be a pause of three days without hearing Torah." The mere hearing of the Torah was not only a fulfillment of the *mitzvah* but it enhanced the listeners. The Midrash compares this to a king who gave vessels with holes to his servants and told them to fill the vessels with water. The foolish ones said, "What is there to be accomplished, as the water will not remain in the vessel?" They therefore did nothing. The intelligent ones followed the directive saying, "At least the vessels will become cleansed." Similarly, the mere listening to the Torah cleansed and added sanctity to those who listened.

Ezra, on the other hand, added the dimension of not less than ten verses. The number ten represents a completeness and wholeness, and denotes a greater degree of clarity and comprehension. As proof, on Rosh Hashanah when we introduce three additional themes and motifs to the *Mussaf* service, the Talmud (*Rosh Hashanah* 32a) teaches, "We are not to have less than ten verses regarding His Kingship, no fewer than ten Remembrances verses, and ten Shofar verses." The reason, explained Rabbi Soloveitchik, is that ten represents a whole unit and is thus more easily understood. Similarly, the world was created with ten statements reflecting this idea of completeness. So too, the Decalogue contains Ten Commandments, and to *Rav Saadia Gaon,* all the *mitzvos* of the Torah may be subsumed under these ten categories. Thus, by Ezra requiring ten verses to be read, he is transforming the reading of the

51 / BACKGROUND OF THE PRAYERS

Written Law to the status of Oral Law. As proof, the *Rambam* (in Chapter 12, Paragraph 10 of the *Laws of Prayer*) writes that in addition to the number of verses, Ezra instituted that the Torah be translated into Aramaic, the vernacular of the Jews of Babylon, so that they would understand what was being read.

We can now appreciate the two different customs regarding the reading of the Torah — whether to stand or to sit during the reading. The Talmud Yerushalmi, (at the beginning of the fourth chapter of *Megillah*) sees the reading of the Torah as a reenactment of the Revelation at Sinai, as the Torah informs us "And they stood at the foot of the mountain" (*Exodus* 19:17). Moreover, Moshe tells the Jewish people "I was standing between Hashem and you at that time" (*Deuteronomy* 5:5). Those who stand for the Torah reading are reliving the manner in which the Torah was given at Sinai. Those who sit during the reading of the Torah are following the teaching of the Talmud (*Megillah* 21a) that after the passing of Rabban Gamliel Torah was studied while sitting. The *Shulchan Aruch* (*Orach Chaim* 146:4) teaches that one does not have to stand during the public reading of the Torah. The *Ramah* says there are those who are strict and stand, as was the practice of the *Maharam*. However, the *Mishnah Berurah* (in paragraph 18 of Chapter 146) adds that regardless of one's practice during the reading of the Torah, one should stand for *Borchu* and the response of "Blessed is Hashem, the blessed One for all eternity," as they constitute a *"davar she'bikdusha"* an acknowledgment of His holiness that requires both a *minyan* and standing.

The Talmud (*Gittin* 59a) teaches that the *Kohen* receives the first *aliyah* to the Torah "in the interest of peace." True, the Torah legislates regarding the *Kohen,* "you shall sanctify him" (*Vayikra* 21:8), which is understood that in all matters of holiness and honor the *Kohen* is to go first, yet in all other matters the *Kohen* may waive and forgo his privilege, and honor another — even a non-*Kohen* — if he so desires. The Rabbis prohibited him from doing so with regard to being called first to the Torah in order to avoid arguments among non-*Kohanim* as to who is worthy to read first in his stead. The *Levi* follows the *Kohen* and the third *aliyah* is for a *Yisroel*.

The honor of being called to the Torah is called an *"aliyah,"* which means, literally, an elevation. There are two reasons for the use of this word. Firstly, often the Torah reading table was elevated in the middle of the synagogue. In addition, the term reflects the spiritual elevation that one is accorded when he is privileged to read from the Torah.

The *Shulchan Aruch* (Chapter 141, paragraph 7) instructs the individual called up for an *aliyah* to take the shortest, most direct route to the Torah reading table, to show his eagerness to study Torah. Conversely, when one leaves and returns to his place, he takes the longer route back, demonstrating his hesitation to leave the Torah. If he is situated in the middle of the synagogue, then he should ascend or approach the *bimah* from the right side and take leave from the left side. In keeping with the Talmud (*Megillah* 31b), the Torah reading on Shabbos *Minchah* and Monday and Thursday commences where the Torah

reading concluded on Shabbos morning.

Finally, it should be understood that the public Torah reading preceded public prayer. Once the rabbis instituted public prayer services, they incorporated the reading of the Torah next to the *Shemoneh Esrei*. On Shabbos *Minchah*, it precedes the *Amidah*, while on Monday and Thursday it follows the *Amidah*. The Torah reading actually complements the *Shemoneh Esrei*. Whereas in prayer man talks to Hashem, in the reading of the Torah, Hashem talks to man. *Rabbeinu Yonah*, in his commentary on *Berachos*, reminds us that while the actual reading of the Torah is a Rabbinic *mitzvah*, if unfortunately one acts disrespectfully and talks during the Torah reading, he is violating a Biblical prohibition by showing irreverence to the Torah.

The Morning Service

﴾ UPON ARISING ﴿

■ The essence of a Jew is gratitude to Hashem:
We awake and thank Hashem for restoring our faculties.

IMMEDIATELY UPON WAKING UP FROM HIS SLEEP, A JEW DECLARES:

MŌ-DE ANI l'fonecho, מוֹדֶה אֲנִי לְפָנֶיךָ,
I gratefully thank You,*

melech chai v'ka-yom, מֶלֶךְ חַי וְקַיָּם,
O living and eternal King,

shehechezarto bi nishmosi שֶׁהֶחֱזַרְתָּ בִּי נִשְׁמָתִי
b'chemlo — בְּחֶמְלָה —
for You have returned my soul within me with compassion —

rabo e-munosecho. רַבָּה אֱמוּנָתֶךָ.
abundant is Your faithfulness!

WASH THE HANDS ACCORDING TO THE RITUAL PROCEDURE:
PICK UP THE VESSEL OF WATER WITH THE RIGHT HAND, PASS IT TO THE LEFT, AND POUR OVER THE RIGHT. THEN WITH THE RIGHT HAND POUR OVER THE LEFT. FOLLOW THIS PROCEDURE UNTIL WATER HAS BEEN POURED OVER EACH HAND THREE TIMES. THEN, RECITE:

RAYSHIS chochmo רֵאשִׁית חָכְמָה
yir-as Adōnoy, יִרְאַת יהוה,
The beginning of wisdom is the fear of HASHEM —

saychel tōv l'chol ōsayhem, שֵׂכֶל טוֹב לְכָל עֹשֵׂיהֶם,
good understanding to all their practitioners;

t'hiloso ōmedes lo-ad. תְּהִלָּתוֹ עֹמֶדֶת לָעַד.
His praise endures forever.

Boruch shaym k'vōd malchusō בָּרוּךְ שֵׁם כְּבוֹד מַלְכוּתוֹ
Blessed is the Name of His glorious kingdom
l'ōlom vo-ed. לְעוֹלָם וָעֶד.
for all eternity.

﴾ DONNING THE TZITZIS ﴿

■ Clothing affords man greater dignity. The Torah commands that we affix *tzitzis*-strands to our four-cornered garments as constant reminders of the privilege the Jewish male has in studying and fulfilling the 613 Biblical commandments. The numeric value of the word *tzitzis* equals 600, and together with 8 strands and 5 knots totals 613.

מוֹדֶה אֲנִי לְפָנֶיךָ — *I gratefully thank You.* A Jew opens his eyes and thanks God for restoring his faculties to him in the morning. Then, he acknowledges that God did so in the expectation that he will serve Him, and that He is abundantly faithful to reward those who do.

◆§ **Donning the Tzitzis**
Since *tzitzis* need not be worn at night, the commandment of *tzitzis* (Numbers 15:38) is classified as a time-related commandment and, as such, is not required of women. It may be fulfilled in two ways: (a) by means of the *tallis katan* (lit., small garment), popularly known simply as "the *tzitzis,*" which is worn all day, usually under the shirt; and (b) by means of the familiar large *tallis,* commonly known simply

55 / SHACHARIS FOR WEEKDAYS — UPON ARISING

HOLD THE *TALLIS KATTAN* IN READINESS TO PUT ON, INSPECT THE *TZITZIS*, AND RECITE THE BLESSING. THEN DON THE *TALLIS KATTAN* AND KISS THE *TZITZIS*. ONE WHO WEARS A *TALLIS* FOR *SHACHARIS* DOES NOT RECITE THIS BLESSING.

BORUCH ato Adōnoy — בָּרוּךְ אַתָּה יהוה
Blessed are You, HASHEM,

Elōhaynu melech ho-ōlom, — אֱלֹהֵינוּ מֶלֶךְ הָעוֹלָם,
our God, King of the universe,

asher kid'shonu b'mitzvōsov, — אֲשֶׁר קִדְּשָׁנוּ בְּמִצְוֹתָיו,
Who has sanctified us with His commandments,

v'tzivonu al mitzvas tzitzis. — וְצִוָּנוּ עַל מִצְוַת צִיצִת.
and has commanded us regarding the commandment of tzitzis.

Y'HI rotzōn mil'fonecho, — יְהִי רָצוֹן מִלְּפָנֶיךָ,
May it be Your will,

Adōnoy Elōhai Vaylōhay avōsai, — יהוה אֱלֹהַי וֵאלֹהֵי אֲבוֹתַי,
HASHEM, my God and the God of my forefathers,

shet'hay chashuvo — שֶׁתְּהֵא חֲשׁוּבָה
   mitzvas tzitzis l'fonecho, — מִצְוַת צִיצִת לְפָנֶיךָ,
that the commandment of tzitzis be as worthy before You

k'ilu kiyamtiho b'chol p'roteho — כְּאִלּוּ קִיַּמְתִּיהָ בְּכָל פְּרָטֶיהָ
as if I had fulfilled it in all its details,

v'dikdukeho v'chav'nōseho, — וְדִקְדּוּקֶיהָ וְכַוָּנוֹתֶיהָ,
implications, and intentions,

v'saryag mitzvōs hat'luyim boh. — וְתַרְיַ"ג מִצְוֹת הַתְּלוּיִם בָּהּ.
as well as the 613 commandments that are dependent upon it.

Omayn selo. — אָמֵן סֶלָה.
Amen, Selah!

⊰{ DONNING THE TALLIS }⊱

■ I recognize that there are teachings, cultures, and morals that are contrary to Torah values. I therefore envelop myself in the *tallis* as I enter the world of prayer.

BEFORE DONNING THE *TALLIS*, INSPECT THE *TZITZIS* WHILE RECITING THESE VERSES:

BOR'CHI NAFSHI es Adōnoy, — בָּרְכִי נַפְשִׁי אֶת יהוה,
Bless HASHEM, O my soul;*

Adōnoy Elōhai godalto m'ōd, — יהוה אֱלֹהַי גָּדַלְתָּ מְּאֹד,
HASHEM, my God, You are very great;

---

as "the *tallis*," which is worn during the morning prayers, in some congregations by all males, and in others only by one who is or has been married.

בָּרְכִי נַפְשִׁי — *Bless ... O my soul.* These two verses describe God figuratively as donning garments of majesty and light. Because the *tallis* symbolizes the splendor of God's com-

hōd v'hodor lovoshto.
הוֹד וְהָדָר לָבָֽשְׁתָּ.
You have donned majesty and splendor;

Ōte ōr kasalmo,
עֹֽטֶה אוֹר כַּשַּׂלְמָה,
cloaked in light as with a garment,

nōte shoma-yim kai-ri-o.
נוֹטֶה שָׁמַֽיִם כַּיְרִיעָה.
stretching out the heavens like a curtain.

■ I pray as I wrap the *tallis* around my body that the Divine soul within me transcend and dominate my physical being.

MANY RECITE THE FOLLOWING DECLARATION OF INTENT BEFORE DONNING THE *TALLIS:*

HARAYNI mis-atayf gufi batzitzis,
הֲרֵינִי מִתְעַטֵּף גּוּפִי בַּצִּיצִת,
I am ready to wrap my body in tzitzis,

kayn tis-atayf nishmosi
כֵּן תִּתְעַטֵּף נִשְׁמָתִי
urmach ayvorai u-shso gidai
וּרְמַ"ח אֵבָרַי וּשְׁסָ"ה גִידַי
so may my soul, my 248 organs and my 365 sinews* be wrapped

b'ōr hatzitzis ho-ōle saryag.
בְּאוֹר הַצִּיצִת הָעוֹלֶה תַּרְיַ"ג.
in the illumination of tzitzis which has the numerical value of 613.

uchshaym she-ani miskase b'talis
וּכְשֵׁם שֶׁאֲנִי מִתְכַּסֶּה בְּטַלִּית
bo-ōlom ha-ze,
בָּעוֹלָם הַזֶּה,
Just as I cover myself with a tallis in this world,

kach ezke lachaluko d'rabonon
כָּךְ אֶזְכֶּה לַחֲלוּקָא דְרַבָּנָן
ultalis no-e
וּלְטַלִּית נָאֶה
so may I merit the rabbinical garb and a beautiful cloak

lo-ōlom habo b'gan ayden.
לָעוֹלָם הַבָּא בְּגַן עֵֽדֶן.
in the World to Come in the Garden of Eden.

V'al y'day mitzvas tzitzis
וְעַל יְדֵי מִצְוַת צִיצִת
Through the commandment of tzitzis

tinotzayl nafshi v'ruchi
תִּנָּצֵל נַפְשִׁי וְרוּחִי
v'nishmosi usfilosi
וְנִשְׁמָתִי וּתְפִלָּתִי
may my life-force, spirit, soul, and prayer be rescued

min hachitzōnim.
מִן הַחִיצוֹנִים.
from the external forces.

V'hatalis yifrōs k'nofov alayhem
וְהַטַּלִּית יִפְרוֹשׂ כְּנָפָיו עֲלֵיהֶם
v'yatzilaym
וְיַצִּילֵם
May the tallis spread its wings over them and rescue them

רְמַ"ח אֵבָרַי וּשְׁסָ"ה גִידַי — *My 248 organs and my 365 sinews.* The Sages' computation of the important organs, two hundred forty-eight, cor-mandments, we liken our wearing of it to wrapping ourselves in God's glory and brilliance.

k'nesher yo-ir kinō,   כְּנֶשֶׁר יָעִיר קִנּוֹ,
   al gōzolov y'rachayf.   עַל גּוֹזָלָיו יְרַחֵף.
like an eagle rousing his nest, fluttering over his eaglets.

Us-hay chashuvo mitzvas tzitzis   וּתְהֵא חֲשׁוּבָה מִצְוַת צִיצִת
May the commandment of tzitzis be worthy

lifnay Hakodōsh boruch hu   לִפְנֵי הַקָּדוֹשׁ בָּרוּךְ הוּא
before the Holy One, Blessed is He,

k'ilu kiyamtiho b'chōl p'roteho   כְּאִלּוּ קִיַּמְתִּיהָ בְּכָל פְּרָטֶיהָ
as if I had fulfilled it in all its details,

v'dikdukeho v'chav'nōseho   וְדִקְדּוּקֶיהָ וְכַוָּנוֹתֶיהָ
implications, and intentions,

v'saryag mitzvōs hat'luyim boh.   וְתַרְיַ"ג מִצְוֹת הַתְּלוּיִם בָּהּ.
as well as the 613 commandments that are dependent upon it.

Omayn selo.   אָמֵן סֶלָה.
Amen, Selah!

UNFOLD THE *TALLIS*, HOLD IT IN READINESS TO WRAP AROUND YOURSELF, AND RECITE THE FOLLOWING BLESSING:

BORUCH ato Adōnoy   **בָּרוּךְ** אַתָּה יהוה
*Blessed are You, H*ASHEM*,*

Elōhaynu melech ho-ōlom,   אֱלֹהֵינוּ מֶלֶךְ הָעוֹלָם,
our God, King of the universe,

asher kid'shonu b'mitzvōsov,   אֲשֶׁר קִדְּשָׁנוּ בְּמִצְוֹתָיו,
Who has sanctified us with His commandments

v'tzivonu l'his-atayf batzitzis.   וְצִוָּנוּ לְהִתְעַטֵּף בַּצִּיצִת.
and has commanded us to wrap ourselves in tzitzis.

WRAP THE *TALLIS* AROUND YOUR HEAD AND BODY, THEN RECITE:

MAH YOKOR chasd'cho Elōhim,   **מַה יָּקָר** חַסְדְּךָ אֱלֹהִים,
How precious is Your kindness, O God!

uvnay odom   וּבְנֵי אָדָם
   b'tzayl k'nofecho yecheso-yun.   בְּצֵל כְּנָפֶיךָ יֶחֱסָיוּן.
The sons of man take refuge in the shadows of Your wings.

Yirv'yun mideshen bay-secho,   יִרְוְיֻן מִדֶּשֶׁן בֵּיתֶךָ,
May they be sated from the abundance of Your house;

v'nachal adonecho sashkaym.   וְנַחַל עֲדָנֶיךָ תַשְׁקֵם.
and may You give them to drink from the stream of Your delights.

---

responds to the number of positive commandments in the Torah, while the three hundred sixty-five sinews corresponds to the number of negative commandments. This symbolizes the principle that man was created to perform God's will.

Ki im'cho m'kōr cha-yim,
b'ōr'cho nir-e ōr.
כִּי עִמְּךָ מְקוֹר חַיִּים,
בְּאוֹרְךָ נִרְאֶה אוֹר.

For with You is the source of life — by Your light we shall see light.

M'shōch chasd'cho l'yōd'e-cho,
מְשֹׁךְ חַסְדְּךָ לְיֹדְעֶיךָ,

Extend Your kindness to those who know You,

v'tzidkos'cho l'yishray layv.
וְצִדְקָתְךָ לְיִשְׁרֵי לֵב.

and Your charity to the upright of heart.

⊰ ORDER OF PUTTING ON TEFILLIN ⊱

■ Every Jewish male is to don the *tefillin* daily — except for Shabbos and Yom Tov — as a sign of God's personal involvement in the historical past of our nation beginning with the Exodus from Egypt, and His constant involvement in my life today.

MANY RECITE THE FOLLOWING DECLARATION OF INTENT BEFORE PUTTING ON *TEFILLIN*:

L'SHAYM YICHUD   לְשֵׁם יִחוּד

For the sake of the unification

Kudsho b'rich hu ush-chintayh
קֻדְשָׁא בְּרִיךְ הוּא וּשְׁכִינְתֵּהּ,

of the Holy One, Blessed is He, and His Presence,

bidchilu urchimu
בִּדְחִילוּ וּרְחִימוּ

in fear and love,

l'yachayd shaym Yud-Kay b'Vov-Kay
b'yi-chudo sh'lim
לְיַחֵד שֵׁם י"ה בְּו"ה
בְּיִחוּדָא שְׁלִים,

to unify the Name — Yud-Kei with Vav-Kei — in perfect unity

b'shaym kol yisro-ayl
בְּשֵׁם כָּל יִשְׂרָאֵל.

in the name of all Israel.

HIN'NI m'chavayn bahanochas t'filin   **הִנְנִי** מְכַוֵּן בַּהֲנָחַת תְּפִלִּין

Behold, in putting on tefillin

l'ka-yaym mitzvas bōr'i,
לְקַיֵּם מִצְוַת בּוֹרְאִי,

I intend to fulfill the commandment of my Creator,

shetzivonu l'honi-ach t'filin,
שֶׁצִּוָּנוּ לְהָנִיחַ תְּפִלִּין,

Who has commanded us to put on tefillin,

kakosuv b'sōrosō:
כַּכָּתוּב בְּתוֹרָתוֹ:

as is written in His Torah:

Ukshartom l'ōs al yodecho,
וּקְשַׁרְתָּם לְאוֹת עַל יָדֶךָ,

"Bind them as a sign upon your arm

⊰ **Putting on Tefillin**

The Scriptural *mitzvah* of *tefillin* does not specify that it should be worn only during prayer. Indeed, throughout the generations, righteous people made it a practice to wear *tefillin* all day, except when they were engaged in activities unbecoming to the sanctity of *tefillin*. However, the halachah requires that one maintain intellectual and bodily purity while wearing *tefillin*, a task that is by no means easy. Consequently, the custom was adopted that *tefillin* be worn only during *Shacharis*.

THE ORDER OF DONNING TEFILLIN

v'ho-yu l'tōtofōs bayn aynecho. וְהָיוּ לְטֹטָפֹת בֵּין עֵינֶיךָ.
and let them be tefillin between your eyes."

v'haym arba parshiyōs aylu — וְהֵם אַרְבַּע פָּרָשִׁיּוֹת אֵלּוּ —
These four portions [contained in the tefillin] —

sh'ma, v'ho-yo im shomō-a, שְׁמַע, וְהָיָה אִם שָׁמֹעַ,
[1] "Shema"; [2] "And it will come to pass, if you will hearken";

kadesh, v'ho-yo ki y'vi-acho — קַדֶּשׁ, וְהָיָה כִּי יְבִאֲךָ —
[3] "Sanctify"; and [4] "And it will come to pass when He shall bring you" —

she-yaysh bo-hem yi-chudō v'achdusō שֶׁיֵּשׁ בָּהֶם יִחוּדוֹ וְאַחְדוּתוֹ
yisborach sh'mō bo-ōlom; יִתְבָּרַךְ שְׁמוֹ בָּעוֹלָם;
contain His Oneness and Unity, may His Name be blessed, in the universe;

v'shenizkōr nisim v'nif-lo-ōs וְשֶׁנִּזְכּוֹר נִסִּים וְנִפְלָאוֹת
so that we will recall the miracles and wonders

she-oso i-monu שֶׁעָשָׂה עִמָּנוּ
b'hōtzi-onu mimitzro-yim; בְּהוֹצִיאָנוּ מִמִּצְרָיִם;
that He did with us when He removed us from Egypt;

va-asher lō hakō-ach v'hamemsholo וַאֲשֶׁר לוֹ הַכֹּחַ וְהַמֶּמְשָׁלָה
bo-elyōnim u-vatachtōnim בָּעֶלְיוֹנִים וּבַתַּחְתּוֹנִים
and that He has the strength and dominion over those above and those below

la-asōs bo-hem kirtzōnō. לַעֲשׂוֹת בָּהֶם כִּרְצוֹנוֹ.
to do with them as He wishes.

V'tzivonu l'honi-ach al ha-yod, וְצִוָּנוּ לְהָנִיחַ עַל הַיָּד,
He has commanded us to put [tefillin] upon the arm

l'zichrōn z'rō-a han'tu-yo, לְזִכְרוֹן זְרוֹעַ הַנְּטוּיָה,
to recall the "outstretched arm" [of the Exodus];

v'shehi neged halayv, וְשֶׁהִיא נֶגֶד הַלֵּב,
and that it be opposite the heart

l'shabayd bo-ze לְשַׁעְבֵּד בָּזֶה
ta-avas u-machsh'vōs libaynu תַּאֲוַת וּמַחְשְׁבוֹת לִבֵּנוּ
thereby to subjugate the desires and thoughts of our heart

la-avōdosō, yisborach sh'mō. לַעֲבוֹדָתוֹ, יִתְבָּרַךְ שְׁמוֹ.
to His service, may His Name be blessed;

V'al horōsh neged hamō-ach, וְעַל הָרֹאשׁ נֶגֶד הַמֹּחַ,
and upon the head opposite the brain,

shehan'shomo sheb'mōchi, שֶׁהַנְּשָׁמָה שֶׁבְּמוֹחִי,
so that the soul that is in my brain,

im sh'or chushai v'chōchōsai,	עִם שְׁאָר חוּשַׁי וְכֹחוֹתַי,
together with my other senses and potentials,	
kulom yih-yu m'shu-bodim	כֻּלָּם יִהְיוּ מְשֻׁעְבָּדִים
la-avōdosō, yisborach sh'mō.	לַעֲבוֹדָתוֹ, יִתְבָּרַךְ שְׁמוֹ.
may all be subjugated to His service, may His Name be blessed.	
U-mi-shefa mitzvas t'filin	וּמִשֶּׁפַע מִצְוַת תְּפִלִּין
May some of the spiritual influence of the commandment of tefillin	
yis-mashaych olai lih-yōs li	יִתְמַשֵּׁךְ עָלַי לִהְיוֹת לִי
be extended upon me so that I have	
cha-yim arukim, v'shefa kōdesh,	חַיִּים אֲרֻכִּים, וְשֶׁפַע קֹדֶשׁ,
a long life, a flow of holiness,	
u-machashovōs k'dōshōs,	וּמַחֲשָׁבוֹת קְדוֹשׁוֹת
b'li harhōr chayt v'ovōn k'lol,	בְּלִי הַרְהוֹר חֵטְא וְעָוֹן כְּלָל;
and holy thoughts, without even an inkling of sin or iniquity;	
v'shelō y'fataynu	וְשֶׁלֹּא יְפַתֵּנוּ
v'lō yisgore vonu yaytzer horo,	וְלֹא יִתְגָּרֶה בָּנוּ יֵצֶר הָרָע,
and that the Evil Inclination will not seduce us nor incite against us,	
v'yanichaynu la-avōd es Adōnoy	וְיַנִּיחֵנוּ לַעֲבֹד אֶת יהוה
ka-asher im l'vovaynu.	כַּאֲשֶׁר עִם לְבָבֵנוּ.
and that it permit us to serve HASHEM as is our hearts' desire.	
Vi-hi rotzōn mil'fonecho,	וִיהִי רָצוֹן מִלְּפָנֶיךָ,
May it be Your will,	
Adōnoy Elōhaynu	יהוה אֱלֹהֵינוּ
Vaylōhay avōsaynu,	וֵאלֹהֵי אֲבוֹתֵינוּ,
HASHEM, our God and the God of our forefathers,	
shet'hay chashuvo mitzvas	שֶׁתְּהֵא חֲשׁוּבָה מִצְוַת
hanochas t'filin	הֲנָחַת תְּפִלִּין
that the commandment of putting on tefillin be considered as worthy	
lifnay Hakodōsh boruch hu,	לִפְנֵי הַקָּדוֹשׁ בָּרוּךְ הוּא
before the Holy One, Blessed is He,	
k'ilu kiyamti-ho b'chol p'rote-ho	כְּאִלּוּ קִיַּמְתִּיהָ בְּכָל פְּרָטֶיהָ
v'dikduke-ho v'chav'nōse-ho,	וְדִקְדּוּקֶיהָ וְכַוָּנוֹתֶיהָ,
as if I had fulfilled it in all its details, implications, and intentions,	
v'saryag mitzvōs hat'lu-yim boh.	וְתַרְיַ"ג מִצְוֹת הַתְּלוּיִם בָּהּ.
as well as the 613 commandments that are dependent upon it.	
Omayn selo.	אָמֵן סֶלָה.
Amen, Selah.	

SHACHARIS FOR WEEKDAYS — THE ORDER OF DONNING TEFILLIN

■ I don *tefillin* on my weaker hand demonstrating my submission to and cognizance of His strong hand that directs and governs all. Moreover, the hand-*tefillin* directs me to sanctify my actions.

STAND WHILE PUTTING ON *TEFILLIN*. PLACE THE ARM-*TEFILLIN* UPON THE LEFT BICEPS (OR THE RIGHT BICEPS OF ONE WHO WRITES LEFT-HANDED), HOLD IT IN PLACE READY FOR TIGHTENING, THEN RECITE THE FOLLOWING BLESSING:

BORUCH ato Adōnoy   בָּרוּךְ אַתָּה יהוה

Elōhaynu melech ho-ōlom,   אֱלֹהֵינוּ מֶלֶךְ הָעוֹלָם,

Blessed are You, Hashem, our God, King of the universe,

asher kid'shonu b'mitzvōsov,   אֲשֶׁר קִדְּשָׁנוּ בְּמִצְוֹתָיו,

Who has sanctified us with His commandments

v'tzivonu l'honi-ach t'filin.   וְצִוָּנוּ לְהָנִיחַ תְּפִלִּין.

and has commanded us to put on tefillin.

■ I don the *tefillin* on my head as a crown of sanctity and holiness. May the lofty ideals and values contained in them elevate my thoughts and aspirations.

TIGHTEN THE ARM-*TEFILLIN* IMMEDIATELY AND WRAP THE STRAP SEVEN TIMES AROUND THE ARM. WITHOUT ANY INTERRUPTION, PUT THE HEAD-*TEFILLIN* IN PLACE, ABOVE THE HAIRLINE AND OPPOSITE THE SPACE BETWEEN THE EYES. BEFORE TIGHTENING THE HEAD-*TEFILLIN*, RECITE THE FOLLOWING BLESSING:

BORUCH ato Adōnoy   בָּרוּךְ אַתָּה יהוה

Elōhaynu melech ho-ōlom,   אֱלֹהֵינוּ מֶלֶךְ הָעוֹלָם,

Blessed are You, Hashem, our God, King of the universe,

asher kid'shonu b'mitzvōsov,   אֲשֶׁר קִדְּשָׁנוּ בְּמִצְוֹתָיו,

Who has sanctified us with His commandments

v'tzivonu al mitzvas t'filin.   וְצִוָּנוּ עַל מִצְוַת תְּפִלִּין.

and has commanded us regarding the commandment of tefillin.

TIGHTEN THE HEAD-*TEFILLIN* IMMEDIATELY AND RECITE:

Boruch shaym k'vōd malchuso   בָּרוּךְ שֵׁם כְּבוֹד מַלְכוּתוֹ

l'ōlom vo-ed.   לְעוֹלָם וָעֶד.

Blessed is the Name of His glorious kingdom for all eternity.

AFTER THE HEAD-*TEFILLIN* IS SECURELY IN PLACE, RECITE:

U-MAYCHOCHMOS'CHO Ayl elyōn,   וּמֵחָכְמָתְךָ אֵל עֶלְיוֹן,

ta-atzil olai,   תַּאֲצִיל עָלַי;

From Your wisdom, O supreme God, may You imbue me;

u-mibinos'cho t'vinayni,   וּמִבִּינָתְךָ תְּבִינֵנִי;

from Your understanding give me understanding;

uvchasd'cho tagdil olai,   וּבְחַסְדְּךָ תַּגְדִּיל עָלַי;

with Your kindness do greatly with me;

u-vigvuros'cho tatzmis ō-y'vai v'komai. וּבִגְבוּרָתְךָ תַּצְמִית אֹיְבַי וְקָמָי.
with Your power cut down my foes and rebels.

v'shemen hatōv torik
   al shivo k'nay ham'nōro,
וְשֶׁמֶן הַטּוֹב תָּרִיק
עַל שִׁבְעָה קְנֵי הַמְּנוֹרָה,
[May] You pour goodly oil upon the seven arms of the Menorah,

l'hashpi-a tuv'cho livri-yōsecho. לְהַשְׁפִּיעַ טוּבְךָ לִבְרִיּוֹתֶיךָ.
to cause Your good to flow to Your creatures.

Pōsay-ach es yodecho, פּוֹתֵחַ אֶת יָדֶךָ,
u-masbi-a l'chol chai rotzōn. וּמַשְׂבִּיעַ לְכָל חַי רָצוֹן.
[May] You open Your hand and satisfy the desire of every living thing.

WRAP THE STRAP THREE TIMES AROUND THE MIDDLE FINGER WHILE RECITING:

V'AYRAS-TICH li l'ōlom. **וְאֵרַשְׂתִּיךְ** לִי לְעוֹלָם,
I will betroth you to Me forever,

V'ayras-tich li b'tzedek uvmishpot
   uvchesed uvrachamim.
וְאֵרַשְׂתִּיךְ לִי בְּצֶדֶק וּבְמִשְׁפָּט
וּבְחֶסֶד וּבְרַחֲמִים.
and I will betroth you to Me with righteousness, justice, kindness, and mercy.

v'ayras-tich li be-emuno, וְאֵרַשְׂתִּיךְ לִי בֶּאֱמוּנָה,
I will betroth you to Me with fidelity,

v'yoda-at es Adōnoy. וְיָדַעַתְּ אֶת יהוה.
and you shall know H<small>ASHEM</small>.

THEN WRAP THE STRAP AROUND THE HAND.

IT IS PROPER TO RECITE THE FOUR SCRIPTURAL PASSAGES THAT ARE CONTAINED IN THE *TEFILLIN* WHILE WEARING THEM. TWO OF THE PASSAGES WILL BE RECITED AS PART OF *SHEMA* (P. 169-174). THE OTHER TWO, CITED BELOW, ARE RECITED EITHER AFTER PUTTING ON THE *TEFILLIN,* OR BEFORE REMOVING THEM.

VAI-DABAYR Adōnoy
   el mōshe laymōr:
וַיְדַבֵּר יהוה
אֶל מֹשֶׁה לֵּאמֹר:
H<small>ASHEM</small> *spoke to Moses, saying:*

kadesh li kol b'chōr, קַדֶּשׁ לִי כָל בְּכוֹר,
Sanctify to Me every firstborn;

peter kol rechem bivnay yisro-ayl פֶּטֶר כָּל רֶחֶם בִּבְנֵי יִשְׂרָאֵל
the first issue of every womb among the Children of Israel,

bo-odom u-vab'haymo, li hu. בָּאָדָם וּבַבְּהֵמָה, לִי הוּא.
both of man and of beast, is Mine.

Va-yōmer mōshe el ho-om: וַיֹּאמֶר מֹשֶׁה אֶל הָעָם:
Moses said to the people:

וְאֵרַשְׂתִּיךְ לִי — *I will betroth you unto Me.* God declares that Israel eternally remains His betrothed. This is symbolized by the wrapping of the *tefillin* strap around the fingers in the manner of a groom placing the betrothal ring on his bride's finger.

zochōr es ha-yōm ha-ze	זָכוֹר אֶת הַיּוֹם הַזֶּה
asher y'tzosem mimitzra-yim,	אֲשֶׁר יְצָאתֶם מִמִּצְרַיִם,

Remember this day on which you departed from Egypt,

mibays avodim,	מִבֵּית עֲבָדִים,

from the house of bondage,

ki b'chōzek yod	כִּי בְּחֹזֶק יָד
hōtzi Adōnoy eschem mi-ze,	הוֹצִיא יהוה אֶתְכֶם מִזֶּה,

for with a strong hand Hashem *removed you from here,*

v'lō yay-ochayl chomaytz.	וְלֹא יֵאָכֵל חָמֵץ.

and therefore no chametz may be eaten.

Ha-yōm atem yōtz'im,	הַיּוֹם אַתֶּם יֹצְאִים,
b'chōdesh ho-oviv.	בְּחֹדֶשׁ הָאָבִיב.

Today you are leaving in the month of springtime.

V'ho-yo ki y'vi-acho Adōnoy	וְהָיָה כִי יְבִיאֲךָ יהוה

And it will come to pass, when Hashem *shall bring you*

el eretz hak'na-ani v'ha-chiti	אֶל אֶרֶץ הַכְּנַעֲנִי וְהַחִתִּי
v'ho-emōri v'ha-chivi v'hai-vusi	וְהָאֱמֹרִי וְהַחִוִּי וְהַיְבוּסִי

to the land of the Canaanites, Hittites, Emorites, Hivvites, and Jebusites,

asher nishba la-avōsecho lo-ses loch,	אֲשֶׁר נִשְׁבַּע לַאֲבֹתֶיךָ לָתֶת לָךְ,

which He swore to your forefathers to give you —

eretz zovas cholov udvosh,	אֶרֶץ זָבַת חָלָב וּדְבָשׁ,

a land flowing with milk and honey —

v'ovad-to es ho-avōdo ha-zōs	וְעָבַדְתָּ אֶת הָעֲבֹדָה הַזֹּאת
ba-chōdesh ha-ze.	בַּחֹדֶשׁ הַזֶּה.

you shall perform this service in this month.

Shivas yomim tōchal matzōs,	שִׁבְעַת יָמִים תֹּאכַל מַצֹּת,

Seven days you shall eat matzos,

u-va-yōm hash'vi-i chag Ladōnoy.	וּבַיּוֹם הַשְּׁבִיעִי חַג לַיהוה.

and on the seventh day there shall be a festival to Hashem.

Matzōs yay-ochayl	מַצּוֹת יֵאָכֵל
ays shivas ha-yomim,	אֵת שִׁבְעַת הַיָּמִים,

Matzos shall be eaten throughout the seven days;

v'lō yayro-e l'cho chomaytz,	וְלֹא יֵרָאֶה לְךָ חָמֵץ,

no chametz may be seen in your possession

v'lō yayro-e l'cho s'ōr	וְלֹא יֵרָאֶה לְךָ שְׂאֹר

nor may leaven be seen in your possession

b'chol g'vulecho.	בְּכָל גְּבֻלֶךָ.

in all your borders.

v'higad-to l'vincho	וְהִגַּדְתָּ לְבִנְךָ
ba-yōm hahu laymōr:	בַּיּוֹם הַהוּא לֵאמֹר:

And you shall tell your son on that day, saying:

ba-avur ze oso Adōnoy li	בַּעֲבוּר זֶה עָשָׂה יהוה לִי
b'tzaysi mimitzro-yim.	בְּצֵאתִי מִמִּצְרָיִם.

"It is because of this that HASHEM acted on my behalf when I left Egypt."

V'ho-yo l'cho l'ōs al yod'cho,	וְהָיָה לְךָ לְאוֹת עַל יָדְךָ,
ulzikorōn bayn aynecho,	וּלְזִכָּרוֹן בֵּין עֵינֶיךָ,

And it shall serve you as a sign on your arm and as a reminder between your eyes —

l'ma-an tih-ye tōras Adōnoy b'ficho,	לְמַעַן תִּהְיֶה תּוֹרַת יהוה בְּפִיךָ,

so that HASHEM's Torah may be in your mouth;

ki b'yod chazoko hōtzi-acho Adōnoy	כִּי בְּיָד חֲזָקָה הוֹצִאֲךָ יהוה
mimitzro-yim.	מִמִּצְרָיִם.

for with a strong hand HASHEM removed you from Egypt.

V'shomarto es hachuko ha-zōs	וְשָׁמַרְתָּ אֶת הַחֻקָּה הַזֹּאת

And you shall observe this ordinance

l'mō-adoh, mi-yomim yomimo.	לְמוֹעֲדָהּ, מִיָּמִים יָמִימָה.

at its designated time from year to year.

V'HO-YO ki y'vi-acho Adōnoy	**וְהָיָה** כִּי יְבִאֲךָ יהוה
el eretz hak'na-ani	אֶל אֶרֶץ הַכְּנַעֲנִי

And it shall come to pass, when HASHEM will bring you to the land of the Canaanites

ka-asher nishba l'cho v'la-avōsecho,	כַּאֲשֶׁר נִשְׁבַּע לְךָ וְלַאֲבֹתֶיךָ,
un-sonoh loch.	וּנְתָנָהּ לָךְ.

as He swore to you and to your forefathers, and will have given it to you.

V'ha-avarto kol peter rechem	וְהַעֲבַרְתָּ כָל פֶּטֶר רֶחֶם
Ladōnoy,	לַיהוה,

Then you shall set apart every first issue of the womb to HASHEM,

v'chol peter sheger b'haymo	וְכָל פֶּטֶר שֶׁגֶר בְּהֵמָה
asher yih-ye l'cho,	אֲשֶׁר יִהְיֶה לְךָ,

and every first issue that is dropped by cattle that belong to you,

haz'chorim Ladōnoy.	הַזְּכָרִים לַיהוה.

the males shall belong to HASHEM.

V'chol peter chamōr tifde v'se,	וְכָל פֶּטֶר חֲמֹר תִּפְדֶּה בְשֶׂה,

Every first issue donkey you shall redeem with a lamb or kid,

v'im lō sifde va-araftō,	וְאִם לֹא תִפְדֶּה וַעֲרַפְתּוֹ,

if you do not redeem it, then you must axe the back of its neck.

v'chōl b'chōr odom b'vonecho tifde.	וְכֹל בְּכוֹר אָדָם בְּבָנֶיךָ תִּפְדֶּה.

And you must redeem every human firstborn among your sons.

V'ho-yo ki yishol'cho vincho mochor	וְהָיָה כִּי יִשְׁאָלְךָ בִנְךָ מָחָר

And it shall be when your son asks you at some future time,

laymōr, ma zōs,	לֵאמֹר, מַה זֹּאת,

saying, "What is this?"

v'omarto aylov,	וְאָמַרְתָּ אֵלָיו,

you shall answer him,

b'chōzek yod	בְּחֹזֶק יָד

"With a strong hand

hōtzi-onu Adōnoy mimitz-ra-yim	הוֹצִיאָנוּ יהוה מִמִּצְרַיִם
mibays avodim.	מִבֵּית עֲבָדִים.

Hashem removed us from Egypt, from the house of bondage.

Vai-hi ki hiksho farō	וַיְהִי כִּי הִקְשָׁה פַרְעֹה
l'shal'chaynu,	לְשַׁלְּחֵנוּ,

And it happened, when Pharaoh stubbornly refused to let us go,

va-ya-harōg Adōnoy	וַיַּהֲרֹג יהוה
kol b'chōr b'eretz mitzra-yim,	כָּל בְּכוֹר בְּאֶרֶץ מִצְרַיִם,

that Hashem killed all the firstborn in the land of Egypt,

mib'chōr odom	מִבְּכֹר אָדָם
v'ad b'chōr b'haymo.	וְעַד בְּכוֹר בְּהֵמָה.

from the firstborn of man to the firstborn of beast.

Al kayn ani zōvay-ach Ladōnoy	עַל כֵּן אֲנִי זֹבֵחַ לַיהוה

Therefore, I sacrifice to Hashem

kol peter rechem haz'chorim,	כָּל פֶּטֶר רֶחֶם הַזְּכָרִים,

all first male issue of the womb,

v'chol b'chōr bonai efde.	וְכָל בְּכוֹר בָּנַי אֶפְדֶּה.

and redeem all the firstborn of my sons."

V'ho-yo l'ōs al yod'cho	וְהָיָה לְאוֹת עַל יָדְכָה

And it shall be a sign upon your arm

ultōtofōs bayn aynecho,	וּלְטוֹטָפֹת בֵּין עֵינֶיךָ,

and totafos between your eyes,

ki b'chōzek yod	כִּי בְּחֹזֶק יָד
hōtzi-onu Adōnoy mimitz-royim.	הוֹצִיאָנוּ יהוה מִמִּצְרָיִם.

for with a strong hand Hashem removed us from Egypt.

> ■ The privilege of entering the synagogue fills me with both reverence and joy.

UPON ENTERING THE SYNAGOGUE THE FOLLOWING VERSES ARE RECITED:

MA TŌVU ōholecho ya-akōv,   מַה טֹּבוּ אֹהָלֶיךָ יַעֲקֹב,
How goodly are your tents,* O Jacob,

mishk'nōsecho yisro-ayl.   מִשְׁכְּנֹתֶיךָ יִשְׂרָאֵל.
your dwelling places, O Israel.

va-ani b'rōv chasd'cho   וַאֲנִי בְּרֹב חַסְדְּךָ
As for me, through Your abundant kindness

ovō vay-secho,   אָבוֹא בֵיתֶךָ,
I will enter Your House;

eshtacha-ve el haychal kodsh'cho   אֶשְׁתַּחֲוֶה אֶל הֵיכַל קָדְשְׁךָ
b'yir-osecho.   בְּיִרְאָתֶךָ.
I will prostrate myself toward Your Holy Sanctuary in awe of You.

Adōnoy   יהוה
O Hashem,

ohavti m'ōn bay-secho,   אָהַבְתִּי מְעוֹן בֵּיתֶךָ,
I love the House where You dwell,

umkōm mishkan k'vōdecho.   וּמְקוֹם מִשְׁכַּן כְּבוֹדֶךָ.
and the place where Your glory resides.

Va-ani eshtacha-ve v'echro-o,   וַאֲנִי אֶשְׁתַּחֲוֶה וְאֶכְרָעָה,
I shall prostrate myself and bow,

evr'cho lifnay Adōnoy ōsi.   אֶבְרְכָה לִפְנֵי יהוה עֹשִׂי.
I shall kneel before Hashem my Maker.

Va-ani,   וַאֲנִי,
As for me,

s'filosi l'cho Adōnoy,   תְפִלָּתִי לְךָ יהוה,
may my prayer to You, Hashem,

ays rotzōn,   עֵת רָצוֹן,
be at an opportune time;

Elōhim b'rov chasdecho,   אֱלֹהִים בְּרָב חַסְדֶּךָ,
O God, in Your abundant kindness,

anayni be-emes yish-e-cho.   עֲנֵנִי בֶּאֱמֶת יִשְׁעֶךָ.
answer me with the truth of Your salvation.

מַה טֹּבוּ אֹהָלֶיךָ — *How goodly are your tents.* The Jewish home achieves its highest level when it incorporates the values of the synagogue and study hall. This collection of verses expresses love and reverence for the synagogue that is the place where God's glory resides among Israel.

MORNING BLESSING

■ I begin the morning prayer, instituted by our Patriarch, Abraham,
by referring to Hashem, as did Abraham,
as the Master of the universe — yet involved in my everyday activities.

ADŌN ŌLOM asher molach, אֲדוֹן עוֹלָם אֲשֶׁר מָלַךְ,
Master of the universe,* Who reigned

b'terem kol y'tzir nivro. בְּטֶרֶם כָּל־יְצִיר נִבְרָא.
before any form was created.

L'ays na-aso v'cheftzō kōl, לְעֵת נַעֲשָׂה בְחֶפְצוֹ כֹּל,
At the time when His will brought all into being —

a-zai melech sh'mō nikro. אֲזַי מֶלֶךְ שְׁמוֹ נִקְרָא.
then as "King" was His Name proclaimed.

V'a-charay kichlōs hakōl, וְאַחֲרֵי כִּכְלוֹת הַכֹּל,
After all has ceased to be,

l'vadō yimlōch nōro. לְבַדּוֹ יִמְלוֹךְ נוֹרָא.
He, the Awesome One, will reign alone.

V'hu ho-yo, v'hu hō-ve, וְהוּא הָיָה וְהוּא הֹוֶה,
It is He Who was, He Who is,

v'hu yih-ye, b'sif-oro. וְהוּא יִהְיֶה בְּתִפְאָרָה.
and He Who shall remain, in splendor.

V'hu e-chod v'ayn shayni, וְהוּא אֶחָד וְאֵין שֵׁנִי,
He is One — there is no second

l'hamshil lō l'hachbiro. לְהַמְשִׁיל לוֹ לְהַחְבִּירָה.
to compare to Him, to declare as His equal.

B'li rayshis b'li sachlis, בְּלִי רֵאשִׁית בְּלִי תַכְלִית,
Without beginning, without conclusion —

v'lō ho-ōz v'hamisro. וְלוֹ הָעֹז וְהַמִּשְׂרָה.
His is the power and dominion.

V'hu Ayli v'chai gō-ali, וְהוּא אֵלִי וְחַי גֹּאֲלִי,
He is my God, my living Redeemer,

v'tzur chevli b'ays tzoro. וְצוּר חֶבְלִי בְּעֵת צָרָה.
Rock of my pain in time of distress.

V'hu nisi u-monōs li, וְהוּא נִסִּי וּמָנוֹס לִי,
He is my banner, a refuge for me,

אֲדוֹן עוֹלָם — *Master of the universe.* This song emphasizes that God is timeless, infinite and omnipotent. Mankind can offer Him only one thing: to proclaim Him as King, by doing His will and praising Him. Despite God's greatness, however, He involves Himself with man's personal needs in time of pain and distress, and therefore man need not fear.

מְנָת כּוֹסִי בְּיוֹם אֶקְרָא.	m'nos kōsi b'yōm ek-ro.
	the portion in my cup on the day I call.
בְּיָדוֹ אַפְקִיד רוּחִי,	B'yodō afkid ruchi,
	Into His hand I shall entrust my spirit
בְּעֵת אִישַׁן וְאָעִירָה.	b'ays i-shan v'o-iro.
	when I go to sleep — and I shall awaken!
וְעִם רוּחִי גְּוִיָּתִי,	V'im ruchi g'vi-yosi,
	With my spirit shall my body remain.
יהוה לִי וְלֹא אִירָא.	Adōnoy li v'lō i-ro.
	Hashem is with me, I shall not fear.

▪ I affirm daily my belief in the Thirteen Principles of Faith accepted by my ancestors at Sinai, as expounded by Maimonides in his famous *Ani Maamin*.

יִגְדַּל אֱלֹהִים חַי וְיִשְׁתַּבַּח,	**YIGDAL** Elōhim chai v'yishtabach,
	Exalted be the Living God* and praised,
נִמְצָא וְאֵין עֵת אֶל מְצִיאוּתוֹ.	nimtzo v'ayn ays el m'tzi-uso.
	He exists — unbounded by time is His existence.*
אֶחָד וְאֵין יָחִיד כְּיִחוּדוֹ,	E-chod v'ayn yo-chid k'yi-chudō,
	He is One — and there is no unity like His Oneness,
נֶעְלָם וְגַם אֵין סוֹף לְאַחְדּוּתוֹ.	nelom v'gam ayn sōf l'achduso.
	inscrutable and infinite is His Oneness.
אֵין לוֹ דְמוּת הַגּוּף וְאֵינוֹ גוּף,	Ayn lō d'mus haguf v'aynō guf,
	He has no semblance of a body nor is He corporeal;*
לֹא נַעֲרוֹךְ אֵלָיו קְדֻשָּׁתוֹ.	lō na-arōch aylov k'du-shoso.
	nor has His holiness any comparison.
קַדְמוֹן לְכָל דָּבָר אֲשֶׁר נִבְרָא,	Kadmōn l'chol dovor asher nivro,
	He preceded every being that was created —
רִאשׁוֹן וְאֵין רֵאשִׁית לְרֵאשִׁיתוֹ.	rishōn v'ayn rayshis l'rayshisō.
	the First, and nothing precedes His precedence.
הִנּוֹ אֲדוֹן עוֹלָם לְכָל נוֹצָר,	Hinō adōn ōlom l'chol nōtzor,
	Behold! He is Master of the universe* to every creature,

יִגְדַּל אֱלֹהִים חַי — *Exalted be the Living God.* This song of uncertain authorship summarizes the Thirteen Principles of Faith expounded by Maimonides and stated succinctly in the famous *Ani Maamin* prayer. They comprise the basic principles that every Jew should believe.

וְאֵין עֵת אֶל מְצִיאוּתוֹ — *Unbounded by time is His existence.* If God's existence were timebound, it would be no different in kind from that of any living, but not eternal, being. The principle of God's timelessness, with neither beginning nor end, implies that He cannot be dependent in any way on any other being, for the timebound is inherently inferior to the timeless. Nothing can exist without God, but He depends on no one and on nothing.

וְאֵינוֹ גוּף — *Nor is He corporeal.* God has no physicality, not even that of invisible, intangible angels.

הִנּוֹ אֲדוֹן עוֹלָם — *Behold! He is Master of the universe.* Because He is absolute Master, there

MORNING BLESSING

Yōre g'dulosō u-malchusō. יוֹרֶה גְּדֻלָּתוֹ וּמַלְכוּתוֹ.
He demonstrates His greatness and His sovereignty.

Shefa n'vu-osō n'sonō, שֶׁפַע נְבוּאָתוֹ נְתָנוֹ,
He granted His flow of prophecy*

el anshay s'gulosō v'sif-artō. אֶל אַנְשֵׁי סְגֻלָּתוֹ וְתִפְאַרְתּוֹ.
to His treasured splendrous people.

Lō kom b'yisro-ayl k'mōshe ōd, לֹא קָם בְּיִשְׂרָאֵל כְּמֹשֶׁה עוֹד,
In Israel none like Moses* arose again —

novi u-mabit es t'munosō. נָבִיא וּמַבִּיט אֶת תְּמוּנָתוֹ.
a prophet who perceived His vision clearly.

Tōras emes nosan l'amō Ayl, תּוֹרַת אֱמֶת נָתַן לְעַמּוֹ אֵל,
God gave His people a Torah of truth,

al yad n'vi-ō ne-eman bay-sō. עַל יַד נְבִיאוֹ נֶאֱמַן בֵּיתוֹ.
by means of His prophet, the most trusted of His household.

Lō yachalif ho-Ayl v'lō yomir dosō, לֹא יַחֲלִיף הָאֵל וְלֹא יָמִיר דָּתוֹ,
God will never amend nor exchange His law

l'ōlomim l'zulosō. לְעוֹלָמִים לְזוּלָתוֹ.
for all eternity, for any other one.

Tzōfe v'yōday-a s'soraynu, צוֹפֶה וְיוֹדֵעַ סְתָרֵינוּ,
He scrutinizes and knows our hiddenmost secrets;

mabit l'sōf dovor b'kadmosō. מַבִּיט לְסוֹף דָּבָר בְּקַדְמָתוֹ.
He perceives a matter's outcome at its inception.

Gōmayl l'ish chesed k'mif-olō, גּוֹמֵל לְאִישׁ חֶסֶד כְּמִפְעָלוֹ,
He recompenses man with kindness according to his deed;

nōsayn l'rosho ro k'rish-osō. נוֹתֵן לְרָשָׁע רָע כְּרִשְׁעָתוֹ.
He places evil on the wicked according to his wickedness.

Yishlach l'kaytz ha-yomin m'shichaynu, יִשְׁלַח לְקֵץ הַיָּמִין מְשִׁיחֵנוּ,
By the End of Days He will send our Messiah,

lifdōs m'chakay kaytz y'shu-osō. לִפְדּוֹת מְחַכֵּי קֵץ יְשׁוּעָתוֹ.
to redeem those longing for His final salvation.

Maysim y'cha-ye Ayl b'rōv chasdō, מֵתִים יְחַיֶּה אֵל בְּרֹב חַסְדּוֹ,
God will revive the dead in His abundant kindness —

boruch aday ad shaym t'hilosō. בָּרוּךְ עֲדֵי עַד שֵׁם תְּהִלָּתוֹ.
Blessed forever is His praised Name.

---

is nothing else to which prayers may be directed.

שֶׁפַע נְבוּאָתוֹ — *His flow of prophecy.* God revealed His will to Israel through His prophets.

כְּמֹשֶׁה — *Like Moses.* Moses' prophecy is peerless; otherwise another "prophet" could conceivably challenge or amend it, thus challenging the authenticity of the Torah.

⊰{ MORNING BLESSINGS }⊱

■ Upon awakening each day, we wash our hands, as did the *Kohanim* of old, to dedicate our daily activities to the service of Hashem.

THIS BLESSING IS RECITED IN THE MORNING, EITHER IMMEDIATELY AFTER THE RITUAL WASHING OF THE HANDS UPON ARISING, OR AT THIS POINT. IT IS REPEATED DURING THE DAY AFTER THE RITUAL WASHING THAT PRECEDES A MEAL AT WHICH BREAD IS EATEN.

BORUCH ato Adōnoy בָּרוּךְ אַתָּה יהוה
Blessed are You, HASHEM,

Elōhaynu melech ho-ōlom, אֱלֹהֵינוּ מֶלֶךְ הָעוֹלָם,
our God, King of the universe,

asher kid'shonu b'mitzvōsov, אֲשֶׁר קִדְּשָׁנוּ בְּמִצְוֹתָיו,
Who has sanctified us with His commandments

v'tzivonu al n'tilas yodo-yim. וְצִוָּנוּ עַל נְטִילַת יָדָיִם.
and has commanded us regarding washing the hands.*

■ We thank Hashem for the daily maintenance of our bodies and the wonders of Divine wisdom performed within ourselves.

THIS BLESSING IS RECITED IN THE MORNING, EITHER IMMEDIATELY AFTER THE RITUAL WASHING OF THE HANDS AFTER RELIEVING ONESELF, OR AT THIS POINT. IT IS REPEATED AFTER THE RITUAL WASHING AFTER RELIEVING ONESELF ANYTIME DURING THE DAY.

BORUCH ato Adōnoy בָּרוּךְ אַתָּה יהוה
Blessed are You, HASHEM,

Elōhaynu melech ho-ōlom, אֱלֹהֵינוּ מֶלֶךְ הָעוֹלָם,
our God, King of the universe,

asher yotzar es ho-odom b'chochmo, אֲשֶׁר יָצַר אֶת הָאָדָם בְּחָכְמָה,
Who fashioned man with wisdom*

u-voro vō n'kovim n'kovim, chalulim chalulim. וּבָרָא בוֹ נְקָבִים נְקָבִים, חֲלוּלִים חֲלוּלִים.
and created within him many openings and many cavities.

Goluy v'yodu-a lifnay chisay ch'vōdecho, גָּלוּי וְיָדוּעַ לִפְנֵי כִסֵּא כְבוֹדֶךָ,
It is obvious and known before Your Throne of Glory

she-im yiposay-ach e-chod mayhem, שֶׁאִם יִפָּתֵחַ אֶחָד מֵהֶם,
that if but one of them were to be ruptured

עַל נְטִילַת יָדָיִם — *Regarding washing the hands.* In the case of blessings, the general rule is that they should be recited in conjunction with the acts to which they apply. Nevertheless, some delay this blessing for washing the hands and the next blessing for relieving oneself so that they will be recited as part of *Shacharis*.

אֲשֶׁר יָצַר אֶת הָאָדָם בְּחָכְמָה — *Who fashioned man with wisdom.* This phrase has two meanings: (a) When God created man, He gave him the gift of wisdom; and (b) God used wisdom when

ō yisosaym e-chod mayhem,   אוֹ יִסָּתֵם אֶחָד מֵהֶם,
or but one of them were to be blocked

i efshar l'hiska-yaym   אִי אֶפְשָׁר לְהִתְקַיֵּם
it would be impossible to survive

v'la-amōd l'fonecho.   וְלַעֲמוֹד לְפָנֶיךָ.
and to stand before You.

Boruch ato Adōnoy,   בָּרוּךְ אַתָּה יהוה,
Blessed are You, HASHEM,

rōfay chol bosor u-mafli la-asōs.   רוֹפֵא כָל בָּשָׂר וּמַפְלִיא לַעֲשׂוֹת.
Who heals all flesh and acts wondrously. *

BLESSINGS OVER THE STUDY OF THE TORAH

ALTHOUGH THE FOLLOWING TWO BLESSINGS ARE RECITED OVER TORAH STUDY, THEY ARE RECITED ONLY ONCE EACH DAY, REGARDLESS OF HOW MANY STUDY SESSIONS ONE HAS DURING THE DAY.

■ First blessing for the Torah: We thank Hashem for the privilege of being commanded to thoroughly study Torah, our most precious possession, and pray for His assistance in our mastering and successfully transmitting the Oral Torah (Talmud).

BORUCH ato Adōnoy   **בָּרוּךְ** אַתָּה יהוה
Blessed are You, HASHEM,

Elōhaynu melech ho-ōlom,   אֱלֹהֵינוּ מֶלֶךְ הָעוֹלָם,
our God, King of the universe,

asher kid'shonu b'mitzvōsov,   אֲשֶׁר קִדְּשָׁנוּ בְּמִצְוֹתָיו,
Who has sanctified us with His commandments

v'tzivonu la-asōk b'divray sōro.   וְצִוָּנוּ לַעֲסוֹק בְּדִבְרֵי תוֹרָה.
and has commanded us to engross ourselves in the words of Torah.

V'ha-arev no Adōnoy Elōhaynu   וְהַעֲרֶב נָא יהוה אֱלֹהֵינוּ
    es divray sōros'cho   אֶת דִּבְרֵי תוֹרָתְךָ
Please, HASHEM, our God, sweeten the words of Your Torah

b'finu uvfi am'cho bays yisro-ayl.   בְּפִינוּ וּבְפִי עַמְּךָ בֵּית יִשְׂרָאֵל.
in our mouth and in the mouth of Your people, the House of Israel.

V'nih-ye anachnu v'tze-etzo-aynu   וְנִהְיֶה אֲנַחְנוּ וְצֶאֱצָאֵינוּ
May we and our offspring

v'tze-etzo-ay am'cho bays yisro-ayl,   וְצֶאֱצָאֵי עַמְּךָ בֵּית יִשְׂרָאֵל,
and the offspring of Your people, the House of Israel —

He created man, as is demonstrated in the precise balance of his organs and functions.

וּמַפְלִיא לַעֲשׂוֹת — *And acts wondrously.* The delicate balance of the organs is a wonder of wonders. Alternatively: It is wondrous that the spiritual soul fuses with the physical body to create a human being.

•≤ **Blessings of the Torah**

The study of Torah is the paramount commandment. Without it, man cannot know God's will; with it, he can penetrate the wisdom of the Creator Himself.

ברכות השחר | שחרית לחול / 72

kulonu yōd'ay sh'mecho	כֻּלָּנוּ יוֹדְעֵי שְׁמֶךָ
all of us — know Your Name	
v'lōm'day sōrosecho lishmoh.	וְלוֹמְדֵי תוֹרָתֶךָ לִשְׁמָהּ.
and study Your Torah for its own sake.*	
Boruch ato Adōnoy,	בָּרוּךְ אַתָּה יהוה,
*Blessed are You, H*ASHEM,	
ham'lamayd tōro l'amō yisro-ayl.	הַמְלַמֵּד תּוֹרָה לְעַמּוֹ יִשְׂרָאֵל.
Who teaches Torah to His people Israel.	

■ Second blessing for the Torah: We thank Hashem for His choosing Israel and giving us the gift of the Written Torah (Scripture).

BORUCH ato Adōnoy	**בָּרוּךְ** אַתָּה יהוה
*Blessed are You, H*ASHEM,	
Elōhaynu melech ho-ōlom,	אֱלֹהֵינוּ מֶלֶךְ הָעוֹלָם,
our God, King of the universe,	
asher bochar bonu mikol ho-amim	אֲשֶׁר בָּחַר בָּנוּ מִכָּל הָעַמִּים
Who selected us from all the peoples	
v'nosan lonu es tōrosō.	וְנָתַן לָנוּ אֶת תּוֹרָתוֹ.
and gave us His Torah.	
Boruch ato Adōnoy,	בָּרוּךְ אַתָּה יהוה,
nōsayn hatōro.	נוֹתֵן הַתּוֹרָה.
*Blessed are You, H*ASHEM, *Giver of the Torah.*	

SCRIPTURAL SELECTION

Y'VORECH'CHO Adōnoy v'yishm'recho.	**יְבָרֶכְךָ** יהוה וְיִשְׁמְרֶךָ.
*May H*ASHEM *bless you and safeguard you.*	
Yo-ayr Adōnoy ponov aylecho	יָאֵר יהוה פָּנָיו אֵלֶיךָ
vichuneko.	וִיחֻנֶּךָּ,
*May H*ASHEM *illuminate His countenance for you and be gracious to you.*	
Yiso Adōnoy ponov aylecho,	יִשָּׂא יהוה פָּנָיו אֵלֶיךָ,
*May H*ASHEM *turn His countenance to you*	
v'yosaym l'cho sholōm.	וְיָשֵׂם לְךָ שָׁלוֹם.
and establish peace for you.	

לִשְׁמָהּ — *For its own sake.* May we study Torah for no other reason than to know it and become imbued with its wisdom.

◆§ **Scriptural and Talmudic Selections**

Whenever a blessing is recited for a *mitzvah*, the *mitzvah* must be performed immediately. Having recited the blessings for the study of Torah, we immediately recite selections from both the Written and Oral Torah. First we recite the Scriptural verses of the Priestly Blessing, then Talmudic selections from the Mishnah (*Pe'ah* 1:1) and Gemara (*Shabbos* 127a). The Talmudic selections discuss the reward for various commandments and conclude with the declaration that Torah study is equivalent to them all, an appropriate addendum to the Blessings of the Torah.

TALMUDIC SELECTIONS

AYLU D'VORIM — אֵלּוּ דְבָרִים

These are the precepts

she-ayn lohem shi-ur: שֶׁאֵין לָהֶם שִׁעוּר:
that have no prescribed measure: *

hapay-o, v'habikurim, הַפֵּאָה, וְהַבִּכּוּרִים,
the corner of a field [which must be left for the poor], the first-fruit offering,

v'hora-yōn, וְהָרֵאָיוֹן,
the pilgrimage,

ugmilus chasodim, וּגְמִילוּת חֲסָדִים,
acts of kindness,

v'salmud tōro. וְתַלְמוּד תּוֹרָה.
and Torah study.

AYLU D'VORIM — אֵלּוּ דְבָרִים

These are the precepts

she-odom ōchayl payrōsayhem שֶׁאָדָם אוֹכֵל פֵּרוֹתֵיהֶם
whose fruits a person enjoys

bo-ōlom ha-ze בָּעוֹלָם הַזֶּה
in this world,

v'hakeren ka-yemes lō וְהַקֶּרֶן קַיֶּמֶת לוֹ
but whose principal remains intact for him *

lo-ōlom habo. לָעוֹלָם הַבָּא.
in the World to Come.

V'aylu hayn: וְאֵלּוּ הֵן:
They are:

kibud ov vo-aym, כִּבּוּד אָב וָאֵם,
the honor due to father and mother,

ugmilus chasodim, וּגְמִילוּת חֲסָדִים,
acts of kindness,

v'hashkomas bays hamidrosh וְהַשְׁכָּמַת בֵּית הַמִּדְרָשׁ
early attendance at the house of study

shacharis v'arvis, שַׁחֲרִית וְעַרְבִית,
morning and evening,

v'hachnosas ōr'chim, וְהַכְנָסַת אוֹרְחִים,
hospitality to guests,

u-vikur chōlim, וּבִקּוּר חוֹלִים,
visiting the sick,

אֵלּוּ דְבָרִים שֶׁאֵין לָהֶם שִׁעוּר — *These are the precepts that have no prescribed measure.* The Torah does not prescribe how much is involved in the performance of the following commandments.

וְהַקֶּרֶן קַיֶּמֶת לוֹ — *But whose principal remains intact for him.* Though one is rewarded for these *mitzvos* in this world, his reward in the World to Come is not diminished.

	שחרית לחול / 74
ברכות השחר	

v'hachnosas kalo,	וְהַכְנָסַת כַּלָּה,
providing for a bride,	
ulvo-yas hamays,	וּלְוָיַת הַמֵּת,
escorting the dead,	
v'iyun t'filo,	וְעִיּוּן תְּפִלָּה,
absorption in prayer,	
vahavo-as sholōm	וַהֲבָאַת שָׁלוֹם
bayn odom lachavayrō.	בֵּין אָדָם לַחֲבֵרוֹ.
bringing peace between man and his fellow.	
V'salmud tōro k'neged kulom.	וְתַלְמוּד תּוֹרָה כְּנֶגֶד כֻּלָּם.
And the study of Torah is equivalent to them all.	

■ *I thank Hashem for the daily restoration of my pure soul.*

ELŌHAI, **אֱלֹהַי,**

My God,

n'shomo shenosato bi t'hōro hi.	נְשָׁמָה שֶׁנָּתַתָּ בִּי טְהוֹרָה הִיא.
the soul You placed within me is pure.	
Ato v'rosoh ato y'tzartoh,	אַתָּה בְרָאתָהּ אַתָּה יְצַרְתָּהּ,
You created it, You fashioned it,	
ato n'fachtoh bi,	אַתָּה נְפַחְתָּהּ בִּי,
You breathed it into me,	
v'ato m'sham'roh b'kirbi,	וְאַתָּה מְשַׁמְּרָהּ בְּקִרְבִּי,
You safeguard it within me,	
v'ato osid lit'loh mimeni,	וְאַתָּה עָתִיד לִטְּלָהּ מִמֶּנִּי,
and eventually You will take it from me,	
ulhachaziroh bi le-osid lovō.	וּלְהַחֲזִירָהּ בִּי לֶעָתִיד לָבֹא.
and restore it to me in Time to Come.	
Kol z'man shehan'shomo v'kirbi,	כָּל זְמַן שֶׁהַנְּשָׁמָה בְקִרְבִּי,
As long as the soul is within me,	
mōde ani l'fonecho,	מוֹדֶה אֲנִי לְפָנֶיךָ,
I gratefully thank You,	
Adōnoy Elōhai Vaylōhay avōsai,	יהוה אֱלֹהַי וֵאלֹהֵי אֲבוֹתַי,
Hashem, my God and the God of my forefathers,	
ribōn kol hama-asim,	רִבּוֹן כָּל הַמַּעֲשִׂים,
Master of all works,	
Adōn kol han'shomōs.	אֲדוֹן כָּל הַנְּשָׁמוֹת.
Lord of all souls.	
Boruch ato Adōnoy,	בָּרוּךְ אַתָּה יהוה,
Blessed are You, Hashem,	

SHACHARIS FOR WEEKDAYS — MORNING BLESSINGS

hamachazir n'shomōs
lifgorim maysim.

הַמַּחֲזִיר נְשָׁמוֹת
לִפְגָרִים מֵתִים.

Who restores souls to dead bodies.

THE *CHAZZAN* RECITES THE FOLLOWING BLESSINGS ALOUD, AND THE CONGREGATION RESPONDS *OMAYN* TO EACH BLESSING. NEVERTHELESS, EACH PERSON MUST RECITE THESE BLESSINGS EITHER BEFORE OR AFTER THE *CHAZZAN* RECITES THEM ALOUD.

■ We greet each new day with the recognition that Hashem gives us the ability to make distinctions and to deal with new situations.

BORUCH ato Adōnoy

בָּרוּךְ אַתָּה יהוה

Blessed* are You, HASHEM,

Elōhaynu melech ho-ōlom,

אֱלֹהֵינוּ מֶלֶךְ הָעוֹלָם,

our God, King of the universe,

asher nosan lasechvi vino

אֲשֶׁר נָתַן לַשֶּׂכְוִי בִינָה

Who gave the heart understanding

l'havchin bayn yom u-vayn loylo.

לְהַבְחִין בֵּין יוֹם וּבֵין לָיְלָה.

to distinguish between day and night.

■ We acknowledge daily the special mission of the 613 commandments which sets us apart from the other nations.

Boruch ato Adōnoy

בָּרוּךְ אַתָּה יהוה

Blessed are You, HASHEM,

Elōhaynu melech ho-ōlom,

אֱלֹהֵינוּ מֶלֶךְ הָעוֹלָם,

our God, King of the universe,

Shelō osani gōy.

שֶׁלֹּא עָשַׂנִי גּוֹי.

for not having made me a gentile.*

■ We acknowledge daily that Judaism frees us from enslavement to passions and desires.

Boruch ato Adōnoy

בָּרוּךְ אַתָּה יהוה

Blessed are You, HASHEM,

Elōhaynu melech ho-ōlom,

אֱלֹהֵינוּ מֶלֶךְ הָעוֹלָם,

our God, King of the universe,

בָּרוּךְ — *Blessed.* This series of fifteen blessings is based on *Berachos* 60b, where the Sages teach that as one experiences the phenomena of the new day, he should bless God for providing them. For example, one thanks God for giving man the crucial ability to make distinctions in life, such as that between day and night; when he rubs his eyes and sees; when he gets dressed, and so on. Some of the phenomena are not readily obvious from the text of the blessing. Among them are: sitting up and stretching ["releases the bound"]; getting out of bed ["straightens the bent"]; standing on the floor ["spreads out the earth ..."]; donning shoes which symbolizes man's ability to go on his way in comfort ["provided me my every need"]; setting out on one's destination ["firms ... footsteps"]; fastening one's clothing ["girds Israel ..."]; putting on a hat, which symbolizes the Jew's reminder of the One Who is above him ["crowns Israel ..."]; feeling the passing of nighttime exhaustion ["gives

שחרית לחול / 76

שֶׁלֹּא עָשַׂנִי עָבֶד.
shelō osani oved.
for not having made me a slave.*

■ We express our gratitude for separate but equal roles:
Men acknowledge daily that they need more *mitzvos* than women do
to heighten their awareness of Hashem and to serve Him.

MEN AND BOYS RECITE:

בָּרוּךְ אַתָּה יהוה
Boruch ato Adōnoy
Blessed are You, HASHEM,

אֱלֹהֵינוּ מֶלֶךְ הָעוֹלָם,
Elōhaynu melech ho-ōlom,
our God, King of the universe,

שֶׁלֹּא עָשַׂנִי אִשָּׁה.
shelō osani i-sho.
for not having made me a woman.*

■ Women acknowledge the daily manifestation of Divine beneficence in
granting them greater strength in moral self-discipline.

WOMEN AND GIRLS RECITE:

בָּרוּךְ אַתָּה יהוה
Boruch ato Adōnoy
Blessed are You, HASHEM,

אֱלֹהֵינוּ מֶלֶךְ הָעוֹלָם,
Elōhaynu melech ho-ōlom,
our God, King of the universe,

שֶׁעָשַׂנִי כִּרְצוֹנוֹ.
she-osani kirtzōnō.
for having made me according to His will.*

■ We acknowledge daily the gift of sight and insight.

בָּרוּךְ אַתָּה יהוה
Boruch ato Adōnoy
Blessed are You, HASHEM,

אֱלֹהֵינוּ מֶלֶךְ הָעוֹלָם,
Elōhaynu melech ho-ōlom,
our God, King of the universe,

פּוֹקֵחַ עִוְרִים.
pōkay-ach ivrim.
Who gives sight to the blind.

---

strength . . . and removes sleep . . ."].

שֶׁלֹּא עָשַׂנִי גוֹי . . . עָבֶד . . . אִשָּׁה — *For not having made me a gentile . . . a slave . . . a woman.* The Torah assigns missions to respective groups of people. Within Israel, for example, the Davidic family, *Kohanim,* and Levites are set apart by virtue of their particular callings, in addition to their shared mission as Jews. All such missions carry extra responsibilities and call for the performance of the *mitzvos* associated with them. We thank God, therefore, for the challenge of improving His universe in accordance with His will. Male, free Jews have responsibilities and duties not shared by others. For this, they express gratitude that, unlike women, they were *not* freed from the obligation to perform the time-related commandments. This follows the Talmudic dictum that an obligatory performance of a commandment is superior to a voluntary one, because it is human nature to resist obligations.

שֶׁעָשַׂנִי כִּרְצוֹנוֹ — *For having made me according to His will.* Women, both historically and because of their nature, are the guardians of tradition, and the molders of character, children, and family. Furthermore, women have often been the protectors of Judaism when the impetuosity and aggressiveness of the male nature led the men astray. The classic precedent was in the wilderness when the men —

■ *We acknowledge daily the gift of our clothing: modesty and dignity.*

Boruch ato Adōnoy   בָּרוּךְ אַתָּה יהוה
*Blessed are You, H*ASHEM,
Elōhaynu melech ho-ōlom,   אֱלֹהֵינוּ מֶלֶךְ הָעוֹלָם,
our God, King of the universe,
malbish arumim.   מַלְבִּישׁ עֲרֻמִּים.
Who clothes the naked.

■ *We acknowledge daily our appreciation to freely move our limbs which were bound in sleep all night.*

Boruch ato Adōnoy   בָּרוּךְ אַתָּה יהוה
*Blessed are You, H*ASHEM,
Elōhaynu melech ho-ōlom,   אֱלֹהֵינוּ מֶלֶךְ הָעוֹלָם,
our God, King of the universe,
matir asurim.   מַתִּיר אֲסוּרִים.
Who releases the bound.

■ *We acknowledge daily our appreciation of the human ability to stand erect.*

Boruch ato Adōnoy   בָּרוּךְ אַתָּה יהוה
*Blessed are You, H*ASHEM,
Elōhaynu melech ho-ōlom,   אֱלֹהֵינוּ מֶלֶךְ הָעוֹלָם,
our God, King of the universe,
zōkayf k'fufim.   זוֹקֵף כְּפוּפִים.
Who straightens the bent.

■ *We acknowledge daily our appreciation of the separation of land and water (enabling us to enjoy life on the earth).*

Boruch ato Adōnoy   בָּרוּךְ אַתָּה יהוה
*Blessed are You, H*ASHEM,
Elōhaynu melech ho-ōlom,   אֱלֹהֵינוּ מֶלֶךְ הָעוֹלָם,
our God, King of the universe,
rōka ho-oretz al hamo-yim. רוֹקַע הָאָרֶץ עַל הַמָּיִם.
Who spreads out the earth upon the waters.

■ *We acknowledge daily that God provides our needs, thus enabling us to adapt to our environment.*

Boruch ato Adōnoy   בָּרוּךְ אַתָּה יהוה
*Blessed are You, H*ASHEM,

not the women — worshiped the Golden Calf. Thus, though women were not given the privilege of the challenge assigned to men, they are created closer to God's ideal of satisfaction. They express their gratitude in the blessing "for having made me according to His will."

Elōhaynu melech ho-ōlom,　　אֱלֹהֵינוּ מֶלֶךְ הָעוֹלָם,
　　our God, King of the universe,
she-oso li kol tzorki.　　שֶׁעָשָׂה לִי כָּל צָרְכִּי.
　　Who has provided me my every need.

■ *We acknowledge daily that God paves the way for man's success.*

Boruch ato Adōnoy　　בָּרוּךְ אַתָּה יהוה
　　Blessed are You, HASHEM,
Elōhaynu melech ho-ōlom,　　אֱלֹהֵינוּ מֶלֶךְ הָעוֹלָם,
　　our God, King of the universe,
hamaychin mitz-aday gover.　　הַמֵּכִין מִצְעֲדֵי גָבֶר.
　　Who firms man's footsteps.

■ *We acknowledge daily our recognition that Hashem has endowed us with the ability to have self-control.*

Boruch ato Adōnoy　　בָּרוּךְ אַתָּה יהוה
　　Blessed are You, HASHEM,
Elōhaynu melech ho-ōlom,　　אֱלֹהֵינוּ מֶלֶךְ הָעוֹלָם,
　　our God, King of the universe,
ōzayr yisro-ayl bigvuro.　　אוֹזֵר יִשְׂרָאֵל בִּגְבוּרָה.
　　Who girds Israel with strength.

■ *We acknowledge daily that covering the head is an honor for the Jewish man and woman.*

Boruch ato Adōnoy　　בָּרוּךְ אַתָּה יהוה
　　Blessed are You, HASHEM,
Elōhaynu melech ho-ōlom,　　אֱלֹהֵינוּ מֶלֶךְ הָעוֹלָם,
　　our God, King of the universe,
ōtayr yisro-ayl b'sif-oro.　　עוֹטֵר יִשְׂרָאֵל בְּתִפְאָרָה.
　　Who crowns Israel with splendor.

■ *We acknowledge daily the Divine gift of both personal and national endurance.*

Boruch ato Adōnoy　　בָּרוּךְ אַתָּה יהוה
　　Blessed are You, HASHEM,
Elōhaynu melech ho-ōlom,　　אֱלֹהֵינוּ מֶלֶךְ הָעוֹלָם,
　　our God, King of the universe,
hanōsayn layo-ayf kō-ach.　　הַנּוֹתֵן לַיָּעֵף כֹּחַ.
　　Who gives strength to the weary.

■ Upon awakening and being energized by Hashem, I pray for Divine assistance in my service of Him.

BORUCH ato Adōnoy   בָּרוּךְ אַתָּה יהוה
Blessed are You, Hashem,

Elōhaynu melech ho-ōlom,   אֱלֹהֵינוּ מֶלֶךְ הָעוֹלָם,
our God, King of the universe,

hama-avir shayno may-aynoy   הַמַּעֲבִיר שֵׁנָה מֵעֵינַי
Who removes sleep from my eyes

usnumo may-af-apoy;   וּתְנוּמָה מֵעַפְעַפָּי;
and slumber from my eyelids;

vi-hi rotzōn mil'fonecho,   וִיהִי רָצוֹן מִלְּפָנֶיךָ,
and may it be Your will,

Adōnoy Elōhaynu   יהוה אֱלֹהֵינוּ
    Vaylōhay avōsaynu,   וֵאלֹהֵי אֲבוֹתֵינוּ,
Hashem, our God, and the God of our forefathers,

shetargilaynu b'sōrosecho   שֶׁתַּרְגִּילֵנוּ בְּתוֹרָתֶךָ
that You accustom us to [study] Your Torah

v'dab'kaynu b'mitzvōsecho,   וְדַבְּקֵנוּ בְּמִצְוֹתֶיךָ,
and attach us to Your commandments;

v'al t'vi-aynu lō liday chayt,   וְאַל תְּבִיאֵנוּ לֹא לִידֵי חֵטְא,
that You do not bring us into the power of error,

v'lō liday avayro v'ovōn,   וְלֹא לִידֵי עֲבֵרָה וְעָוֹן,
nor into the power of transgression and sin;

v'lō liday niso-yōn,   וְלֹא לִידֵי נִסָּיוֹן,
    v'lō liday vizo-yōn,   וְלֹא לִידֵי בִזָּיוֹן,
nor into the power of challenge, nor into the power of scorn;

v'al tashlet bonu yaytzer horo,   וְאַל תַּשְׁלֶט בָּנוּ יֵצֶר הָרָע,
let not the Evil Inclination dominate us;

v'harchikaynu may-odom ro   וְהַרְחִיקֵנוּ מֵאָדָם רָע
    u-maychovayr ro,   וּמֵחָבֵר רָע,
distance us from an evil person and an evil companion;

v'dab'kaynu b'yaytzer hatōv   וְדַבְּקֵנוּ בְּיֵצֶר הַטּוֹב
    uvma-asim tōvim,   וּבְמַעֲשִׂים טוֹבִים,
attach us to the Good Inclination and to good deeds,

v'chōf es yitzraynu l'hishtabed loch,   וְכוֹף אֶת יִצְרֵנוּ לְהִשְׁתַּעְבֶּד לָךְ,
and compel our Evil Inclination to be subservient to You;

80 / שחרית לחול — ברכות השחר

וְתִתְּנֵנוּ הַיּוֹם וּבְכָל יוֹם
usnaynu ha-yōm uvchol yōm
grant us today and every day

לְחֵן וּלְחֶסֶד וּלְרַחֲמִים
l'chayn ulchesed ulrachamim
grace, kindness, and mercy

בְּעֵינֶיךָ וּבְעֵינֵי כָל רוֹאֵינוּ,
b'aynecho uv-aynay chol rō-aynu,
in Your eyes and in the eyes of all who see us;

וְתִגְמְלֵנוּ חֲסָדִים טוֹבִים.
v'sigm'laynu chasodim tōvim.
and bestow beneficent kindnesses upon us.

בָּרוּךְ אַתָּה יהוה,
Boruch ato Adōnoy,
Blessed are You, Hashem,

גּוֹמֵל חֲסָדִים טוֹבִים
לְעַמּוֹ יִשְׂרָאֵל.
gōmayl chasodim tōvim l'amō yisro-ayl.
Who bestows beneficent kindnesses upon His people Israel.

יְהִי רָצוֹן מִלְּפָנֶיךָ,
Y'HI ROTZŌN *mil'fonecho,*
May it be Your will,*

יהוה אֱלֹהַי וֵאלֹהֵי אֲבוֹתַי,
Adōnoy Elōhai Vaylōhay avōsai,
Hashem, my God, and the God of my forefathers,

שֶׁתַּצִּילֵנִי הַיּוֹם וּבְכָל יוֹם
shetatzilayni ha-yōm uvchol yōm
that You rescue me today and every day

מֵעַזֵּי פָנִים וּמֵעַזּוּת פָּנִים,
may-azay fonim u-may-azus ponim,
from brazen men and from brazenness,

מֵאָדָם רָע, וּמֵחָבֵר רָע,
may-odom ro, u-maychovayr ro,
from an evil man, from an evil companion,

וּמִשָּׁכֵן רָע, וּמִפֶּגַע רָע,
u-mishochayn ro, u-mipega ro,
from an evil neighbor, from an evil mishap,

וּמִשָּׂטָן הַמַּשְׁחִית,
u-misoton hamashchis,
from the destructive spiritual impediment,

מִדִּין קָשֶׁה וּמִבַּעַל דִּין קָשֶׁה,
midin koshe u-miba-al din koshe,
from a harsh trial and from a harsh opponent,

בֵּין שֶׁהוּא בֶן בְּרִית,
bayn shehu ven b'ris,
whether he is a member of the covenant*

וּבֵין שֶׁאֵינוֹ בֶן בְּרִית.
u-vayn she-aynō ven b'ris.
or whether he is not a member of the covenant.

יְהִי רָצוֹן — *May it be Your will.* This is a prayer for protection in day-to-day dealings with one's fellowmen. During the recitation, one may add his personal requests for God's help during the day.

בֶּן בְּרִית — *A member of the covenant,* i.e., Abraham's covenant of circumcision, the emblem of Israel's bond with God.

81 / SHACHARIS FOR WEEKDAYS — MORNING BLESSINGS

THE *AKEIDAH*

■ We pray daily that the heroic actions of our Patriarch Abraham in fulfilling God's command to offer Isaac as a sacrifice, though contrary to both Abraham's paternal instincts and religious teachings, ever serve as a source of merit for his descendants. In addition, may we be inspired to serve God with dedication without reservation.

ELŌHAYNU Vaylōhay avōsaynu, אֱלֹהֵינוּ וֵאלֹהֵי אֲבוֹתֵינוּ,
Our God and the God of our forefathers,

zochraynu b'zikorōn tōv l'fonecho, זָכְרֵנוּ בְּזִכָּרוֹן טוֹב לְפָנֶיךָ,
remember us with a favorable memory before You,

u-fokdaynu bifkudas וּפָקְדֵנוּ בִּפְקֻדַּת
y'shu-o v'rachamim יְשׁוּעָה וְרַחֲמִים
and recall us with a recollection of salvation and mercy

mish'may sh'may kedem. מִשְּׁמֵי שְׁמֵי קֶדֶם.
from the primeval loftiest heavens.

Uzchor lonu Adōnoy Elōhaynu וּזְכָר לָנוּ יהוה אֱלֹהֵינוּ
Remember on our behalf — HASHEM, our God —

ahavas hakadmōnim אַהֲבַת הַקַּדְמוֹנִים
the love of the Patriarchs,

avrohom yitzchok v'yisro-ayl אַבְרָהָם יִצְחָק וְיִשְׂרָאֵל
avodecho, עֲבָדֶיךָ,
Abraham, Isaac, and Israel, Your servants;

es hab'ris v'es hachesed אֶת הַבְּרִית וְאֶת הַחֶסֶד
the covenant, the kindness

v'es hash'vu-o וְאֶת הַשְּׁבוּעָה
shenishbato l'avrohom ovinu שֶׁנִּשְׁבַּעְתָּ לְאַבְרָהָם אָבִינוּ
and the oath that You swore to our father Abraham

b'har hamōri-yo, בְּהַר הַמּוֹרִיָּה,
at Mount Moriah,

v'es ho-akaydo וְאֶת הָעֲקֵדָה
and the Akeidah,

she-okad es yitzchok b'nō שֶׁעָקַד אֶת יִצְחָק בְּנוֹ
al gabay hamizbay-ach, עַל גַּבֵּי הַמִּזְבֵּחַ,
when he bound his son Isaac atop the altar,

kakosuv b'sōrosecho: כַּכָּתוּב בְּתוֹרָתֶךָ:
as it is written in Your Torah:

◆§ **The Akeidah**

The *Akeidah* is the story of the most difficult challenge to Abraham's faith in God: He was commanded to sacrifice Isaac, his beloved son and sole heir, to God. Father and son jointly demonstrated their total devotion, whereupon God ordered Abraham to release Isaac. The kabbalistic masters have stressed the great

	שחרית לחול
VAI-HI achar had'vorim ho-ay-le,	וַיְהִי אַחַר הַדְּבָרִים הָאֵלֶּה,

And it happened after these things

v'ho-Elōhim niso es avrohom, וְהָאֱלֹהִים נִסָּה אֶת אַבְרָהָם,

that God tested Abraham

va-yōmer aylov, avrohom, וַיֹּאמֶר אֵלָיו, אַבְרָהָם,

and said to him, "Abraham."

va-yōmer, hinayni. וַיֹּאמֶר, הִנֵּנִי.

And he replied, "Here I am."

Va-yōmer, kach no es bincho, וַיֹּאמֶר, קַח נָא אֶת בִּנְךָ,

And He said, "Please take your son,

es y'chid'cho, asher ohavto, אֶת יְחִידְךָ, אֲשֶׁר אָהַבְתָּ,
es yitzchok, אֶת יִצְחָק,

your only one, whom you love — Isaac —

v'lech l'cho el eretz hamōri-yo, וְלֶךְ לְךָ אֶל אֶרֶץ הַמֹּרִיָּה,

and get yourself to the Land of Moriah;

v'ha-alayhu shom l'ōlo וְהַעֲלֵהוּ שָׁם לְעֹלָה

bring him up there as an offering,

al achad hehorim עַל אַחַד הֶהָרִים

upon one of the mountains

asher ōmar aylecho. אֲשֶׁר אֹמַר אֵלֶיךָ.

which I shall indicate to you."

Va-yashkaym avrohom babōker, וַיַּשְׁכֵּם אַבְרָהָם בַּבֹּקֶר,

So Abraham awoke early in the morning

va-yachavōsh es chamōrō, וַיַּחֲבֹשׁ אֶת חֲמֹרוֹ,

and he saddled his donkey;

va-yikach es sh'nay n'orov itō, וַיִּקַּח אֶת שְׁנֵי נְעָרָיו אִתּוֹ,

he took his two young men with him,

v'ays yitzchok b'nō, וְאֵת יִצְחָק בְּנוֹ,

and Isaac, his son.

vai-vaka atzay ōlo, וַיְבַקַּע עֲצֵי עֹלָה,

He split the wood for the offering,

---

importance of the daily recitation of the *Akeidah*. In response to their writings, the *Akeidah* has been incorporated into the great majority of *siddurim*, although it is not recited in all congregations. In some congregations, it is recited individually rather than as part of the public morning service. According to the kabbalistic teachings, this recitation of Abraham and Isaac's readiness to put love of God ahead of life itself is a source of Heavenly mercy whenever Jewish lives are threatened; the *Akeidah* should inspire us toward greater love of God, by following the example of Abraham and Isaac; and the recitation brings atonement to someone who repents sincerely, for he identifies himself with these two Patriarchs who placed loyalty to God above all other considerations.

va-yokom va-yaylech el hamokōm	וַיָּקָם וַיֵּלֶךְ אֶל הַמָּקוֹם
and rose and went toward the place	
asher omar lō ho-Elōhim.	אֲשֶׁר אָמַר לוֹ הָאֱלֹהִים.
which God had indicated to him.	
Ba-yōm hash'lishi,	בַּיּוֹם הַשְּׁלִישִׁי,
On the third day,	
va-yiso avrohom es aynov,	וַיִּשָּׂא אַבְרָהָם אֶת עֵינָיו,
Abraham looked up,	
va-yar es hamokōm mayrochōk.	וַיַּרְא אֶת הַמָּקוֹם מֵרָחֹק.
and perceived the place from afar.	
Va-yōmer avrohom el n'orov,	וַיֹּאמֶר אַבְרָהָם אֶל נְעָרָיו,
And Abraham said to his young men,	
sh'vu lochem pō im hachamōr,	שְׁבוּ לָכֶם פֹּה עִם הַחֲמוֹר,
"Stay here by yourselves with the donkey,	
va-ani v'hana-ar nayl'cho ad kō	וַאֲנִי וְהַנַּעַר נֵלְכָה עַד כֹּה,
while I and the lad will go yonder;	
v'nishtacha-ve	וְנִשְׁתַּחֲוֶה
we will prostrate ourselves	
v'no-shuvo alaychem.	וְנָשׁוּבָה אֲלֵיכֶם.
and we will return* to you."	
Va-yikach avrohom es atzay ho-ōlo,	וַיִּקַּח אַבְרָהָם אֶת עֲצֵי הָעֹלָה,
And Abraham took the wood for the offering,	
va-yosem al yitzchok b'nō,	וַיָּשֶׂם עַל יִצְחָק בְּנוֹ,
and placed it on Isaac, his son.	
va-yikach b'yodō es ho-aysh v'es hama-acheles,	וַיִּקַּח בְּיָדוֹ אֶת הָאֵשׁ וְאֶת הַמַּאֲכֶלֶת,
He took in his hand the fire and the knife,	
va-yayl'chu sh'nayhem yachdov.	וַיֵּלְכוּ שְׁנֵיהֶם יַחְדָּו.
and the two of them went together.	
Va-yōmer yitzchok el avrohom oviv,	וַיֹּאמֶר יִצְחָק אֶל אַבְרָהָם אָבִיו,
Then Isaac spoke to Abraham his father	
va-yōmer, ovi,	וַיֹּאמֶר, אָבִי,
and said, "My father —,"	
va-yōmer, hineni v'ni.	וַיֹּאמֶר, הִנֶּנִּי בְנִי.
and he said, "Here I am, my son."	

וְנִשְׁתַּחֲוֶה וְנָשׁוּבָה — *We will prostrate ourselves and we will return.* An unintended prophecy issued from Abraham's lips. Instead of saying "I will return" — without Isaac — he said "we," for such, indeed was God's intention.

Va-yōmer, hinay ho-aysh v'ho-aytzim,	וַיֹּאמֶר, הִנֵּה הָאֵשׁ וְהָעֵצִים,
v'a-yay ha-se l'ōlo.	וְאַיֵּה הַשֶּׂה לְעֹלָה.

And he said, "Here are the fire and the wood, but where is the lamb for the offering?"

Va-yōmer avrohom,	וַיֹּאמֶר אַבְרָהָם,
Elōhim yir-e lō ha-se l'ōlo, b'ni.	אֱלֹהִים יִרְאֶה לּוֹ הַשֶּׂה לְעֹלָה, בְּנִי.

And Abraham said, "God will seek out for Himself the lamb* for the offering, my son."

Va-yayl'chu sh'nayhem yachdov.	וַיֵּלְכוּ שְׁנֵיהֶם יַחְדָּו.

And the two of them went together.

Va-yovō-u el hamokōm	וַיָּבֹאוּ אֶל הַמָּקוֹם
asher omar lō ho-Elōhim,	אֲשֶׁר אָמַר לוֹ הָאֱלֹהִים,

They arrived at the place which God indicated to him.

va-yiven shom avrohom es hamizbay-ach,	וַיִּבֶן שָׁם אַבְרָהָם אֶת הַמִּזְבֵּחַ,

Abraham built the altar there,

va-ya-arōch es ho-aytzim,	וַיַּעֲרֹךְ אֶת הָעֵצִים,

and arranged the wood;

va-ya-akōd es yitzchok b'nō,	וַיַּעֲקֹד אֶת יִצְחָק בְּנוֹ,

he bound Isaac, his son,

va-yosem ōsō al hamizbay-ach	וַיָּשֶׂם אֹתוֹ עַל הַמִּזְבֵּחַ
mima-al lo-aytzim.	מִמַּעַל לָעֵצִים.

and he placed him on the altar atop the wood.

Va-yishlach avrohom es yodō,	וַיִּשְׁלַח אַבְרָהָם אֶת יָדוֹ,

Abraham stretched out his hand,

va-yikach es hama-acheles lishchōt es b'nō.	וַיִּקַּח אֶת הַמַּאֲכֶלֶת לִשְׁחֹט אֶת בְּנוֹ.

and took the knife to slaughter his son.

Va-yikro aylov mal-ach Adōnoy min ha-shoma-yim,	וַיִּקְרָא אֵלָיו מַלְאַךְ יהוה מִן הַשָּׁמַיִם,

*And an angel of H*ASHEM *called to him from heaven,*

אֱלֹהִים יִרְאֶה לּוֹ הַשֶּׂה — *God will seek out for Himself the lamb.* Isaac understood from this reply that he would be the sacrificial lamb. Nevertheless, though Isaac was in the prime of life at the age of thirty-seven and Abraham was a century his senior, "the two of them went together," united in their dedication.

Va-yōmer, avrohom, avrohom,	וַיֹּאמֶר, אַבְרָהָם, אַבְרָהָם,
and he said, "Abraham! Abraham!"	
va-yōmer, hinayni.	וַיֹּאמֶר, הִנֵּנִי.
And he said, "Here I am."	
Va-yōmer,	וַיֹּאמֶר,
And he [the angel quoting Hashem] said,	
al tishlach yod'cho el hana-ar,	אַל תִּשְׁלַח יָדְךָ אֶל הַנַּעַר,
"Do not stretch out your hand against the lad	
v'al ta-as lō m'umo,	וְאַל תַּעַשׂ לוֹ מְאוּמָה,
and do not do anything to him,	
ki ato yodati	כִּי עַתָּה יָדַעְתִּי
for now I know	
ki y'ray Elōhim ato,	כִּי יְרֵא אֱלֹהִים אַתָּה,
that you are a God-fearing man,	
v'lō chosachto es bincho	וְלֹא חָשַׂכְתָּ אֶת בִּנְךָ
es y'chid'cho mimeni.	אֶת יְחִידְךָ מִמֶּנִּי.
since you have not withheld your son, your only one, from Me."	
Va-yiso avrohom es aynov	וַיִּשָּׂא אַבְרָהָם אֶת עֵינָיו
And Abraham raised his eyes	
va-yar, v'hinay a-yil, achar,	וַיַּרְא, וְהִנֵּה אַיִל, אַחַר,
and saw — behold a ram! — afterwards,	
ne-echaz bas'vach b'karnov.	נֶאֱחַז בַּסְּבַךְ בְּקַרְנָיו.
caught in the thicket by its horns.	
va-yaylech avrohom	וַיֵּלֶךְ אַבְרָהָם
va-yikach es ho-a-yil,	וַיִּקַּח אֶת הָאַיִל,
So Abraham went and took the ram	
Va-ya-alayhu l'ōlo tachas b'nō.	וַיַּעֲלֵהוּ לְעֹלָה תַּחַת בְּנוֹ.
and brought it as an offering instead of his son.	
Va-yikro avrohom	וַיִּקְרָא אַבְרָהָם
shaym hamokōm hahu	שֵׁם הַמָּקוֹם הַהוּא
And Abraham named that site	
Adōnoy yir-e,	יהוה יִרְאֶה,
"Hashem Yireh,"	
asher yay-o-mayr ha-yōm,	אֲשֶׁר יֵאָמֵר הַיּוֹם,
as it is said this day:	
b'har Adōnoy yayro-e.	בְּהַר יהוה יֵרָאֶה.
On the mountain Hashem will be seen.	

Va-yikro mal-ach Adōnoy el avrohom,	וַיִּקְרָא מַלְאַךְ יהוה אֶל אַבְרָהָם,

The angel of H<small>ASHEM</small> called to Abraham,

shaynis min ha-shomo-yim.	שֵׁנִית מִן הַשָּׁמָיִם.

a second time from heaven,

Va-yōmer,	וַיֹּאמֶר,

and he said,

bi nishbati n'um Adōnoy,	בִּי נִשְׁבַּעְתִּי נְאֻם יהוה,

" 'By Myself I swear,' declared H<small>ASHEM</small>,

ki ya-an asher osiso es hadovor ha-ze,	כִּי יַעַן אֲשֶׁר עָשִׂיתָ אֶת הַדָּבָר הַזֶּה,

'that since you have done this thing,

v'lō chosachto es bincho es y'chide-cho.	וְלֹא חָשַׂכְתָּ אֶת בִּנְךָ אֶת יְחִידֶךָ.

and have not withheld your son, your only one,

Ki voraych avorech'cho,	כִּי בָרֵךְ אֲבָרֶכְךָ,

I shall surely bless you

v'harbo arbe es zar-acho	וְהַרְבָּה אַרְבֶּה אֶת זַרְעֲךָ

and greatly increase your offspring

k'chōch'vay ha-shoma-yim,	כְּכוֹכְבֵי הַשָּׁמַיִם,

like the stars of the heavens

v'chachōl asher al s'fas ha-yom,	וְכַחוֹל אֲשֶׁר עַל שְׂפַת הַיָּם,

and like the sand on the seashore;

v'yirash zar-acho ays sha-ar ōy'vov.	וְיִרַשׁ זַרְעֲךָ אֵת שַׁעַר אֹיְבָיו.

and your offspring shall inherit the gate of its enemy;

V'hisbor'chu v'zar-acho kōl gō-yay ho-oretz,	וְהִתְבָּרְכוּ בְזַרְעֲךָ כֹּל גּוֹיֵי הָאָרֶץ,

and all the nations of the earth shall bless themselves by your offspring,

aykev asher shomato b'kōli.	עֵקֶב אֲשֶׁר שָׁמַעְתָּ בְּקֹלִי.

because you have listened to My voice.' "

Va-yoshov avrohom el n'orov,	וַיָּשָׁב אַבְרָהָם אֶל נְעָרָיו,

Abraham returned to his young men,

va-yokumu va-yayl'chu yachdov el b'ayr shova,	וַיָּקֻמוּ וַיֵּלְכוּ יַחְדָּו אֶל בְּאֵר שָׁבַע,

and they rose and went together to Beer Sheba,

va-yayshev avrohom biv-ayr shova.	וַיֵּשֶׁב אַבְרָהָם בִּבְאֵר שָׁבַע.

and Abraham stayed at Beer Sheba.

RIBŌNŌ SHEL ŌLOM,   רִבּוֹנוֹ שֶׁל עוֹלָם,
Master of the universe!

y'hi rotzōn mil'fonecho,   יְהִי רָצוֹן מִלְּפָנֶיךָ,
May it be Your will,

Adōnoy Elōhaynu   יהוה אֱלֹהֵינוּ
    Vaylōhay avōsaynu,   וֵאלֹהֵי אֲבוֹתֵינוּ,
Hashem, our God, and the God of our forefathers,

shetizkor lonu b'ris avōsaynu.   שֶׁתִּזְכָּר לָנוּ בְּרִית אֲבוֹתֵינוּ.
that You remember for our sake the covenant of our forefathers.

k'mō shekovash avrohom ovinu   כְּמוֹ שֶׁכָּבַשׁ אַבְרָהָם אָבִינוּ
Just as Abraham our forefather suppressed

es rachamov miben y'chidō,   אֶת רַחֲמָיו מִבֶּן יְחִידוֹ,
his mercy for his only son

v'rotzo lishchōt ōsō   וְרָצָה לִשְׁחוֹט אוֹתוֹ
and was willing to slaughter him

k'day la-asōs r'tzōnecho,   כְּדֵי לַעֲשׂוֹת רְצוֹנֶךָ,
in order to do Your will,

kayn yichb'shu rachamecho   כֵּן יִכְבְּשׁוּ רַחֲמֶיךָ
    es ka-as-cho may-olaynu,   אֶת כַּעַסְךָ מֵעָלֵינוּ,
so may Your mercy suppress Your anger from upon us

v'yogōlu rachamecho al midōsecho,   וְיָגֹלּוּ רַחֲמֶיךָ עַל מִדּוֹתֶיךָ,
and may Your mercy overwhelm Your attributes.

v'sikonays itonu   וְתִכָּנֵס אִתָּנוּ
    lifnim mi-shuras dinecho,   לִפְנִים מִשּׁוּרַת דִּינֶךָ,
May You overstep with us the line of Your law

v'sisnahayg imonu,   וְתִתְנַהֵג עִמָּנוּ,
    Adōnoy Elōhaynu,   יהוה אֱלֹהֵינוּ,
and deal with us — O Hashem, our God —

b'midas hachesed   בְּמִדַּת הַחֶסֶד
    uvmidas horachamim.   וּבְמִדַּת הָרַחֲמִים.
with the attribute of kindness and the attribute of mercy.

Uvtuv'cho hagodōl,   וּבְטוּבְךָ הַגָּדוֹל,
    yoshuv charōn ap'cho   יָשׁוּב חֲרוֹן אַפֶּךָ
In Your great goodness may You turn aside Your burning wrath

may-am'cho u-may-ir'cho   מֵעַמְּךָ וּמֵעִירְךָ
    u-may-artz'cho u-minachalose-cho.   וּמֵאַרְצְךָ וּמִנַּחֲלָתֶךָ.
from Your people, Your city, Your land, and Your heritage.

וְקַיֶּם לָנוּ, יהוה אֱלֹהֵינוּ,
V'ka-yem lonu, Adōnoy Elōhaynu,
Fulfill for us, Hashem, our God,

אֶת הַדָּבָר שֶׁהִבְטַחְתָּנוּ
es hadovor she-hivtachtonu
the word You pledged

עַל יְדֵי מֹשֶׁה עַבְדֶּךָ,
al y'day mōshe avdecho,
through Moses, Your servant,

כָּאָמוּר:
ko-omur:
as it is said:

וְזָכַרְתִּי אֶת בְּרִיתִי יַעֲקוֹב,
V'zocharti es b'risi ya-akōv,
"I shall remember My covenant with Jacob;

וְאַף אֶת בְּרִיתִי יִצְחָק,
v'af es b'risi yitzchok,
also My covenant with Isaac,

וְאַף אֶת בְּרִיתִי אַבְרָהָם אֶזְכֹּר,
v'af es b'risi avrohom ezkōr,
and also My covenant with Abraham shall I remember;

וְהָאָרֶץ אֶזְכֹּר.
v'ho-oretz ezkōr.
and the land shall I remember."

לְעוֹלָם יְהֵא אָדָם
L'ŌLOM y'hay odom
יְרֵא שָׁמַיִם
y'ray shoma-yim
Always* let a person be God-fearing

בְּסֵתֶר וּבַגָּלוּי,
b'sayser u-vagoluy,
privately and publicly,

וּמוֹדֶה עַל הָאֱמֶת,
u-mōde al ho-emes,
acknowledge the truth,*

וְדוֹבֵר אֱמֶת בִּלְבָבוֹ,
v'dōvayr emes bilvovō,
speak the truth within his heart,

וְיַשְׁכֵּם וְיֹאמַר:
v'yashkaym v'yōmar:
and arise early and proclaim:

רִבּוֹן כָּל הָעוֹלָמִים,
Ribōn kol ho-ōlomim,
Master of all worlds!

לֹא עַל צִדְקוֹתֵינוּ
lō al tzidkōsaynu
Not in the merit of our righteousness

לְעוֹלָם — *Always*. The section beginning here and extending until *Offerings* is in its totality a profound and succinct summation of basic Jewish faith and loyalty to God. What is more, it is a ringing declaration of joyous pride in our Jewishness, a pride that overcomes all persecutions and that moves us to pray for the time when all will recognize the truth of the Torah's message, and we will proudly proclaim that message which the anti-Semites of the world attempt to silence.

Furthermore, the declarations contained in this section represent the manner in which a Jew should conduct himself always, not merely on ceremonial occasions.

וּמוֹדֶה עַל הָאֱמֶת — [*Let him*] *acknowledge the truth*. One who seeks the truth is not ashamed to concede his errors. But if he cares more about his reputation than the truth, he will stubbornly persist in falsehood and sin.

anachnu mapilim	אֲנַחְנוּ מַפִּילִים
tachanunaynu l'fonecho,	תַּחֲנוּנֵינוּ לְפָנֶיךָ,

do we cast our supplications before You,

ki al rachamecho horabim.	כִּי עַל רַחֲמֶיךָ הָרַבִּים.

but in the merit of Your abundant mercy.

Mo anachnu, me cha-yaynu,	מָה אֲנַחְנוּ, מֶה חַיֵּינוּ,

What are we? What is our life?

me chasdaynu, ma tzidkōsaynu	מֶה חַסְדֵּנוּ, מַה צִּדְקוֹתֵינוּ,
ma y'shu-osaynu,	מַה יְשׁוּעָתֵנוּ,

What is our kindness? What is our righteousness? What is our salvation?

ma kōchaynu, ma g'vurosaynu.	מַה כֹּחֵנוּ, מַה גְּבוּרָתֵנוּ.

What is our strength? What is our might?

Ma nōmar l'fonecho,	מַה נֹּאמַר לְפָנֶיךָ,

What can we say before You,

Adōnoy Elōhaynu	יהוה אֱלֹהֵינוּ
Vaylōhay avōsaynu,	וֵאלֹהֵי אֲבוֹתֵינוּ,

HASHEM, our God, and the God of our forefathers —

halō kol hagibōrim k'a-yin l'fonecho,	הֲלֹא כָּל הַגִּבּוֹרִים כְּאַיִן לְפָנֶיךָ,

are not all the mighty like nothing before You,

v'anshay ha-shaym k'lō ho-yu,	וְאַנְשֵׁי הַשֵּׁם כְּלֹא הָיוּ,

the renowned as if they had never existed,

vachachomim kivli mado,	וַחֲכָמִים כִּבְלִי מַדָּע,

the wise as if devoid of wisdom

unvōnim kivli haskayl.	וּנְבוֹנִים כִּבְלִי הַשְׂכֵּל.

and the perceptive as if devoid of intelligence?

Ki rōv ma-asayhem tōhu,	כִּי רוֹב מַעֲשֵׂיהֶם תֹּהוּ,

For most of their deeds are desolate

vimay cha-yayhem hevel l'fonecho,	וִימֵי חַיֵּיהֶם הֶבֶל לְפָנֶיךָ,

and the days of their lives are empty before You.

U-mōsar ho-odom	וּמוֹתַר הָאָדָם
min hab'haymo o-yin,	מִן הַבְּהֵמָה אָיִן,

The pre-eminence of man over beast is non-existent

ki hakōl hovel.	כִּי הַכֹּל הָבֶל.

for all is vain.

Avol anachnu am'cho,	אֲבָל אֲנַחְנוּ עַמָּךְ,
b'nay v'risecho,	בְּנֵי בְרִיתֶךָ,

But we are Your people, members of Your covenant,

בְּנֵי אַבְרָהָם אֹהַבְךָ	b'nay avrohom ōhavcho

children of Abraham, Your beloved,

שֶׁנִּשְׁבַּעְתָּ לּוֹ בְּהַר הַמּוֹרִיָּה, shenishbato lō b'har hamōri-yo,

to whom You took an oath at Mount Moriah;

זֶרַע יִצְחָק יְחִידוֹ zera yitzchok y'chidō

the offspring of Isaac, his only son,

שֶׁנֶּעֱקַד עַל גַּבֵּי הַמִּזְבֵּחַ, shene-ekad al gabay hamizbay-ach,

who was bound atop the altar;

עֲדַת יַעֲקֹב בִּנְךָ בְּכוֹרֶךָ, adas ya-akōv bincho b'chōrecho,

the community of Jacob, Your firstborn son,

שֶׁמֵּאַהֲבָתְךָ שֶׁאָהַבְתָּ אוֹתוֹ shemay-ahavos'cho she-ohavto ōsō

whom — because of the love with which You adored him

וּמִשִּׂמְחָתְךָ שֶׁשָּׂמַחְתָּ בּוֹ, u-misimchos'cho shesomachto bō,

and the joy with which You delighted in him —

קָרָאתָ אֶת שְׁמוֹ יִשְׂרָאֵל וִישֻׁרוּן. koroso es shmō yisro-ayl vi-shurun.

You named him Israel and Jeshurun.

לְפִיכָךְ אֲנַחְנוּ חַיָּבִים **L'FI-CHOCH** anachnu cha-yovim

Therefore, we are obliged

לְהוֹדוֹת לְךָ, וּלְשַׁבֵּחֲךָ, l'hōdōs l'cho, ulshabaychacho,
וּלְפָאֶרְךָ, ulfo-ercho,

to thank You, praise You, glorify You,

וּלְבָרֵךְ וּלְקַדֵּשׁ ulvoraych ulkadaysh

bless, sanctify,

וְלָתֵת שֶׁבַח וְהוֹדָיָה לִשְׁמֶךָ. v'losays shevach v'hōdo-yo lishmecho.

and offer praise and thanks to Your Name.

אַשְׁרֵינוּ, מַה טּוֹב חֶלְקֵנוּ, Ashraynu, ma tōv chelkaynu,

We are fortunate — how good is our portion,

וּמַה נָּעִים גּוֹרָלֵנוּ, u-ma no-im gōrolaynu,
וּמַה יָּפָה יְרֻשָּׁתֵנוּ. u-ma yofo y'rushosaynu.

how pleasant our lot, and how beautiful our heritage!

❖ אַשְׁרֵינוּ, Ashraynu,

We are fortunate

שֶׁאֲנַחְנוּ מַשְׁכִּימִים she-anachnu mashkimim
וּמַעֲרִיבִים, עֶרֶב וָבֹקֶר, u-ma-arivim, erev vovōker,

for we come early and stay late, evening and morning,

וְאוֹמְרִים פַּעֲמַיִם בְּכָל יוֹם. v'ōm'rim pa-ama-yim b'chol yōm.

and proclaim twice each day.

SHACHARIS FOR WEEKDAYS

SH'MA yisro-ayl,   שְׁמַע יִשְׂרָאֵל,
Hear, O Israel.*

Adōnoy Elohaynu, Adōnoy e-chod.   יהוה אֱלֹהֵינוּ, יהוה אֶחָד.
Hᴀꜱʜᴇᴍ *is our God,* Hᴀꜱʜᴇᴍ, *the One and Only.*

IN AN UNDERTONE:
Boruch shaym k'vōd malchuso   בָּרוּךְ שֵׁם כְּבוֹד מַלְכוּתוֹ
l'ōlom vo-ed.   לְעוֹלָם וָעֶד.
Blessed is the Name of His glorious kingdom for all eternity.

ATO hu   אַתָּה הוּא
ad shelō nivro ho-ōlom,   עַד שֶׁלֹּא נִבְרָא הָעוֹלָם,
It was You* before the world was created,

ato hu mi-shenivro ho-ōlom,   אַתָּה הוּא מִשֶּׁנִּבְרָא הָעוֹלָם,
it is You since the world was created,

ato hu bo-ōlom ha-ze,   אַתָּה הוּא בָּעוֹלָם הַזֶּה,
it is You in This World,

v'ato hu lo-ōlom habo.   וְאַתָּה הוּא לָעוֹלָם הַבָּא.
and it is You in the World to Come.

Kadaysh es shimcho   ❖ קַדֵּשׁ אֶת שִׁמְךָ
Sanctify Your Name

al makdi-shay sh'mecho,   עַל מַקְדִּישֵׁי שְׁמֶךָ,
through those who sanctify Your Name,

v'kadaysh es shimcho b'ōlomecho.   וְקַדֵּשׁ אֶת שִׁמְךָ בְּעוֹלָמֶךָ.
and sanctify Your Name in Your universe.

u-vi-shu-os'cho   וּבִישׁוּעָתְךָ
Through Your salvation

torim v'sagbi-ah karnaynu.   תָּרִים וְתַגְבִּיהַּ קַרְנֵנוּ.
may You exalt and raise our pride.

Boruch ato Adōnoy,   בָּרוּךְ אַתָּה יהוה,
Blessed are You, Hᴀꜱʜᴇᴍ,

m'kadaysh es shimcho borabim.   מְקַדֵּשׁ אֶת שִׁמְךָ בָּרַבִּים.
Who sanctifies Your Name among the multitudes.

CONGREGATION RESPONDS: Omayn — אָמֵן

שְׁמַע יִשְׂרָאֵל — *Hear, O Israel.* During the fifth century, a Persian king forbade the Jews in his empire to recite the *Shema*. He stationed guards in every synagogue during the time that the *Shema* would ordinarily be recited. To counteract his design, the people recited *Shema* at home, before going to the synagogue. When the ban was lifted, the first verse of the *Shema* was made a part of the introductory prayers of the morning synagogue service.

אַתָּה הוּא — *It was You...* God is eternal and unchanging, unaffected by time or place.

ATO hu Adōnoy Elōhaynu,	אַתָּה הוּא יהוה אֱלֹהֵינוּ,
It is You Who are HASHEM, our God,	
ba-shoma-yim u-vo-oretz	בַּשָּׁמַיִם וּבָאָרֶץ
in heaven and on earth	
u-vishmay ha-shoma-yim ho-elyōnim.	וּבִשְׁמֵי הַשָּׁמַיִם הָעֶלְיוֹנִים.
and in the loftiest heavens.	
Emes, ato hu rishōn,	אֱמֶת, אַתָּה הוּא רִאשׁוֹן,
True — You are the First	
v'ato hu acharōn,	וְאַתָּה הוּא אַחֲרוֹן,
and You are the Last,*	
u-mibal-odecho ayn Elōhim.	וּמִבַּלְעָדֶיךָ אֵין אֱלֹהִים.
and other than You there is no God.	
Kabaytz kōvecho	קַבֵּץ קֹוֶיךָ
may-arba kanfōs ho-oretz.	מֵאַרְבַּע כַּנְפוֹת הָאָרֶץ.
Gather in those who [place] their hope in You, from the four corners of the earth.	
Yakiru v'yayd'u kol bo-ay ōlom	יַכִּירוּ וְיֵדְעוּ כָּל בָּאֵי עוֹלָם
Let all who walk the earth recognize and know	
ki ato hu ho-Elōhim l'vad'cho	כִּי אַתָּה הוּא הָאֱלֹהִים לְבַדֶּךָ
that You alone are the God	
l'chōl maml'chōs ho-oretz.	לְכֹל מַמְלְכוֹת הָאָרֶץ.
over all the kingdoms of the earth.	
Ato osiso	אַתָּה עָשִׂיתָ
es ha-shoma-yim v'es ho-oretz,	אֶת הַשָּׁמַיִם וְאֶת הָאָרֶץ,
You have made the heavens, the earth,	
es ha-yom, v'es kol asher bom.	אֶת הַיָּם, וְאֶת כָּל אֲשֶׁר בָּם.
the sea, and all that is in them.	
U-mi b'chol ma-asay yodecho	וּמִי בְּכָל מַעֲשֵׂה יָדֶיךָ
Who among all Your handiwork,	
bo-elyōnim ō vatachtōnim	בָּעֶלְיוֹנִים אוֹ בַתַּחְתּוֹנִים
those above and those below,	
she-yōmar l'cho, ma ta-ase.	שֶׁיֹּאמַר לְךָ, מַה תַּעֲשֶׂה.
can say to You, "What are You doing?"	
Ovinu sheba-shoma-yim,	אָבִינוּ שֶׁבַּשָּׁמַיִם,
Our Father in Heaven,	

אַתָּה הוּא רִאשׁוֹן וְאַתָּה הוּא אַחֲרוֹן — *You are the First and You are the Last.* This means that God pre-existed everything and will outlast everything, not that He had a beginning or will have an end, for God is infinite and timeless.

asay imonu chesed	עֲשֵׂה עִמָּנוּ חֶסֶד
do kindness with us	
ba-avur shimcho hagodōl	בַּעֲבוּר שִׁמְךָ הַגָּדוֹל
shenikro olaynu,	שֶׁנִּקְרָא עָלֵינוּ,
for the sake of Your great Name that has been proclaimed upon us.	
v'ka-yem lonu Adōnoy Elōhaynu	וְקַיֶּם לָנוּ יהוה אֱלֹהֵינוּ
Fulfill for us, HASHEM, our God,	
ma shekosuv:	מַה שֶּׁכָּתוּב:
what is written:	
Bo-ays ha-hi ovi eschem,	בָּעֵת הַהִיא אָבִיא אֶתְכֶם,
"'At that time I will bring you	
u-vo-ays kab'tzi eschem,	וּבָעֵת קַבְּצִי אֶתְכֶם,
and at that time I will gather you in,	
ki etayn eschem l'shaym v'lis-hilo	כִּי אֶתֵּן אֶתְכֶם לְשֵׁם וְלִתְהִלָּה
for I will set you up for renown and praise	
b'chōl amay ho-oretz,	בְּכֹל עַמֵּי הָאָרֶץ,
among all the peoples of the earth,	
b'shuvi es sh'vusaychem	בְּשׁוּבִי אֶת שְׁבוּתֵיכֶם
l'aynaychem, omar Adōnoy.	לְעֵינֵיכֶם, אָמַר יהוה.
when I bring back your captivity, before your own eyes,' said HASHEM."	

OFFERINGS

■ Our Patriarch Abraham was taught that as long as Israel was privileged to bring offerings to Hashem, it would maintain a close relationship with Him. In the absence thereof, our Sages taught that Hashem cherishes the recitation of the Biblical verses of the prescribed offerings, and regards our recitation as if we actually offered them.

VAI-DABAYR Adōnoy	**וַיְדַבֵּר** יהוה
el mōshe laymōr.	אֶל מֹשֶׁה לֵּאמֹר.
HASHEM spoke to Moses, saying:	
V'osiso kiyōr n'chōshes,	וְעָשִׂיתָ כִּיּוֹר נְחֹשֶׁת,
*Make a laver of copper,**	

◆§ Offerings

From the beginning of its existence as a nation, Israel *saw* — whether or not it understood why or how — that the sacrificial service effected a closeness to God and the manifestation of His Presence. The offerings represented the Jew's submission to God of his self and his resources.

In the inspiring words of Rabbi S. R. Hirsch (*Horeb* §624): "The Temple has fallen, the Altar has disappeared, the harps of the singers are heard no more, but their spirit has become the heritage of Israel; it still infuses the word which alone survives as an expression of the inward Divine service."

The offerings whose laws are about to be recited are all communal ones; the Sages chose them because they illustrate our wish that Israel become united as a single nation in God's service.

וְעָשִׂיתָ כִּיּוֹר נְחֹשֶׁת — *Make a laver of copper.* Before the *Kohanim* could begin the Temple

v'chanō n'chōshes, l'rochtzo,	וְכַנּוֹ נְחֹשֶׁת, לְרָחְצָה,
and its base of copper, for washing;	
v'nosato ōsō bayn ōhel mō-ayd u-vayn hamizbay-ach,	וְנָתַתָּ אֹתוֹ בֵּין אֹהֶל מוֹעֵד וּבֵין הַמִּזְבֵּחַ,
and place it between the Tent of Appointment and the Altar	
v'nosato shomo mo-yim.	וְנָתַתָּ שָׁמָּה מָיִם.
and put water there.	
V'rochatzu aharōn u-vonov mimenu,	וְרָחֲצוּ אַהֲרֹן וּבָנָיו מִמֶּנּוּ,
Aaron and his sons are to wash from it	
es y'dayhem v'es raglayhem.	אֶת יְדֵיהֶם וְאֶת רַגְלֵיהֶם.
their hands and feet.	
B'vō-om el ōhel mō-ayd	בְּבֹאָם אֶל אֹהֶל מוֹעֵד
When they arrive at the Tent of Appointment	
yirchatzu ma-yim	יִרְחֲצוּ מַיִם
they are to wash with water	
v'lō yomusu,	וְלֹא יָמֻתוּ,
so that they not die;*	
ō v'gishtom el hamizbay-ach l'shorays	אוֹ בְגִשְׁתָּם אֶל הַמִּזְבֵּחַ לְשָׁרֵת
or when they approach the Altar to serve,	
l'haktir i-she Ladōnoy.	לְהַקְטִיר אִשֶּׁה לַיהוה.
to burn a fire-offering to HASHEM.	
V'rochatzu y'dayhem v'raglayhem	וְרָחֲצוּ יְדֵיהֶם וְרַגְלֵיהֶם
They are to wash their hands and feet	
v'lō yomusu,	וְלֹא יָמֻתוּ,
so that they not die;	
v'hoy'so lohem chok ōlom,	וְהָיְתָה לָהֶם חָק עוֹלָם,
and this shall be an eternal decree for them —	
lō ulzar-ō l'dōrōsom.	לוֹ וּלְזַרְעוֹ לְדֹרֹתָם.
for him and for his offspring — throughout their generations.	
VAI-DABAYR Adōnoy el mōshe laymōr.	**וַיְדַבֵּר** יהוה אֶל מֹשֶׁה לֵּאמֹר.
HASHEM *spoke to Moses, saying:*	

---

service, they had to take sanctified water and pour it over their hands and feet. This water was drawn from a large copper laver in the Temple Courtyard. In preparation for our verbal sacrificial service therefore, we wash ourselves with water from the laver, as it were.

וְלֹא יָמֻתוּ — *So that they not die.* The offense of performing the service without washing did *not* incur a court-imposed death penalty, but the violator made himself liable to a Heavenly punishment for his display of contempt.

SHACHARIS FOR WEEKDAYS — OFFERINGS

Tzav es aharōn v'es bonov laymōr, צַו אֶת אַהֲרֹן וְאֶת בָּנָיו לֵאמֹר,
Instruct Aaron and his sons, saying:

zōs tōras ho-ōlo, זֹאת תּוֹרַת הָעֹלָה,
This is the teaching of the elevation-offering;

hi ho-ōlo al mōk'do הִוא הָעֹלָה עַל מוֹקְדָה
al hamizbay-ach עַל הַמִּזְבֵּחַ
it is the elevation-offering that stays on the pyre on the Altar

kol ha-lailo ad habōker, כָּל הַלַּיְלָה עַד הַבֹּקֶר,
all night until morning,

v'aysh hamizbay-ach tukad bō. וְאֵשׁ הַמִּזְבֵּחַ תּוּקַד בּוֹ.
and the fire of the Altar should be kept burning on it.

V'lovash hakōhayn midō vad, וְלָבַשׁ הַכֹּהֵן מִדּוֹ בַד,
The Kohen should don his linen garment,

u-michn'say vad yilbash al b'sorō, וּמִכְנְסֵי בַד יִלְבַּשׁ עַל בְּשָׂרוֹ,
and he is to don linen breeches upon his flesh;

v'hayrim es hadeshen וְהֵרִים אֶת הַדֶּשֶׁן
he is to pick up the ashes

asher tōchal ho-aysh אֲשֶׁר תֹּאכַל הָאֵשׁ
of what the fire consumed

es ho-ōlo al hamizbay-ach, אֶת הָעֹלָה עַל הַמִּזְבֵּחַ,
of the elevation-offering upon the Altar

v'somō aytzel hamizbay-ach. וְשָׂמוֹ אֵצֶל הַמִּזְבֵּחַ.
and place it next to the Altar.

U-foshat es b'godov, וּפָשַׁט אֶת בְּגָדָיו,
Then he should remove his garments*

v'lovash b'godim achayrim, וְלָבַשׁ בְּגָדִים אֲחֵרִים,
and don other garments;

v'hōtzi es hadeshen וְהוֹצִיא אֶת הַדֶּשֶׁן
then he should remove the ashes

el michutz lamachane, אֶל מִחוּץ לַמַּחֲנֶה,
to the outside of the camp

◆§ The Taking of Ashes

These verses are recited here because they concern the first service of the day: to remove a small portion of the ashes from the previous day's offerings.

וּפָשַׁט אֶת בְּגָדָיו — *Then he should remove his garments.* Unlike the previous verse that discusses a daily *mitzvah*, this verse discusses the cleaning of the Altar, which was done whenever the accumulation of ashes atop the Altar interfered with the service. The ashes were removed and taken to a designated place outside of Jerusalem. The verse advises that the *Kohen* should wear less expensive or well-worn priestly garments when performing this service because the ashes would tend to soil his clothing. In the words of the Talmud, "The outfit one wears while cooking his master's meal, one should not wear while filling his master's goblet" (*Yoma* 23a).

el mokōm tohōr.	אֶל מָקוֹם טָהוֹר.
to a pure place.	
V'ho-aysh al hamizbay-ach	וְהָאֵשׁ עַל הַמִּזְבֵּחַ
The fire on the Altar	
tukad bō, lō sichbe,	תּוּקַד בּוֹ, לֹא תִכְבֶּה,
shall be kept burning on it, it may not be extinguished,	
u-vi-ayr oleho hakōhayn aytzim	וּבִעֵר עָלֶיהָ הַכֹּהֵן עֵצִים
and the Kohen shall burn wood upon it	
babōker babōker,	בַּבֹּקֶר בַּבֹּקֶר,
every morning.	
v'orach oleho ho-ōlo,	וְעָרַךְ עָלֶיהָ הָעֹלָה,
He is to prepare the elevation-offering upon it	
v'hiktir oleho	וְהִקְטִיר עָלֶיהָ
and burn upon it	
chelvay hash'lomim.	חֶלְבֵי הַשְּׁלָמִים.
the fats of the peace-offering.	
Aysh tomid tukad al hamizbay-ach,	אֵשׁ תָּמִיד תּוּקַד עַל הַמִּזְבֵּחַ,
A permanent fire should remain burning on the Altar;	
lō sichbe.	לֹא תִכְבֶּה.
it may not be extinguished.	
Y'HI ROTZŌN mil'fonecho,	**יְהִי רָצוֹן** מִלְּפָנֶיךָ,
May it be Your will,	
Adōnoy Elōhaynu Vaylōhay avōsaynu,	יהוה אֱלֹהֵינוּ וֵאלֹהֵי אֲבוֹתֵינוּ,
HASHEM, our God, and the God of our forefathers,	
shet'rachaym olaynu	שֶׁתְּרַחֵם עָלֵינוּ
that You have mercy on us	
v'simchol lonu al kol chatōsaynu,	וְתִמְחָל לָנוּ עַל כָּל חַטֹּאתֵינוּ,
and pardon us for all our errors,	
us-chaper lonu es kol avonōsaynu,	וּתְכַפֶּר לָנוּ אֶת כָּל עֲוֹנוֹתֵינוּ,
atone for us all our iniquities,	
v'sislach l'chol p'sho-aynu,	וְתִסְלַח לְכָל פְּשָׁעֵינוּ,
and forgive all our willful sins;	
v'sivne bays hamikdosh bimhayro v'yomaynu,	וְתִבְנֶה בֵּית הַמִּקְדָּשׁ בִּמְהֵרָה בְיָמֵינוּ,
and that You rebuild the Holy Temple speedily, in our days,	
v'nakriv l'fonecho korban hatomid	וְנַקְרִיב לְפָנֶיךָ קָרְבַּן הַתָּמִיד
so that we may offer to You the continual-offering	

97 / SHACHARIS FOR WEEKDAYS — OFFERINGS

she-y'chapayr ba-adaynu,   שֶׁיְּכַפֵּר בַּעֲדֵנוּ,
that it may atone for us,
k'mō shekosavto olaynu   כְּמוֹ שֶׁכָּתַבְתָּ עָלֵינוּ
b'sōrosecho   בְּתוֹרָתֶךָ
as You have prescribed for us in Your Torah
al y'day mōshe avdecho,   עַל יְדֵי מֹשֶׁה עַבְדֶּךָ,
through Moses, Your servant,
mipi ch'vōdecho, ko-omur: מִפִּי כְבוֹדֶךָ, כָּאָמוּר:
from Your glorious mouth, as it is said:

SOME STAND WHILE RECITING THE FOLLOWING PARAGRAPH

VAI-DABAYR Adōnoy   **וַיְדַבֵּר** יהוה
el mōshe laymōr.   אֶל מֹשֶׁה לֵּאמֹר.
HASHEM spoke to Moses, saying:
Tzav es b'nay yisro-ayl   צַו אֶת בְּנֵי יִשְׂרָאֵל
v'omarto alayhem,   וְאָמַרְתָּ אֲלֵהֶם,
Command the Children of Israel and tell them:
es korboni lachmi l'i-shai,   אֶת קָרְבָּנִי לַחְמִי לְאִשַּׁי,
My offering, My food* for My fires,
ray-ach nichōchi,   רֵיחַ נִיחֹחִי,
My satisfying aroma,
tishm'ru l'hakriv li b'mō-adō.   תִּשְׁמְרוּ לְהַקְרִיב לִי בְּמוֹעֲדוֹ.
you are to be scrupulous to offer Me in its appointed time.
V'omarto lohem,   וְאָמַרְתָּ לָהֶם,
And you are to tell them:
ze ho-i-she asher takrivu Ladōnoy,   זֶה הָאִשֶּׁה אֲשֶׁר תַּקְרִיבוּ לַיהוה,
This is the fire-offering that you are to bring to HASHEM:
k'vosim b'nay shono s'mimim,   כְּבָשִׂים בְּנֵי שָׁנָה תְמִימִם,
[male] first-year lambs, unblemished,
sh'na-yim la-yōm, ōlo somid.   שְׁנַיִם לַיּוֹם, עֹלָה תָמִיד.
two a day, as a continual elevation-offering.
Es hakeves e-chod ta-ase vabōker,   אֶת הַכֶּבֶשׂ אֶחָד תַּעֲשֶׂה בַבֹּקֶר,
One lamb-service you are to perform in the morning

קָרְבָּנִי לַחְמִי — *My offering, My food.* The offering referred to here is the *tamid* or continual-offering that is brought continually, day in and day out; it is a communal offering purchased with the annual half-*shekel* contributions, collected especially for this purpose. The offering is called "food" in the figurative sense, referring to the parts that are burned on the Altar. The "satisfying aroma" does not refer to the aroma *per se*, for just as God does not require our "food," He does not benefit from the aroma of burning flesh. Rather, the aroma of the burning offering is pleasing to God because it represents the culmination of our performance of His will. God is pleased, for He has spoken, and His will has been done.

v'ays hakeves ha-shayni	וְאֵת הַכֶּבֶשׂ הַשֵּׁנִי
ta-ase bayn ho-arbo-yim.	תַּעֲשֶׂה בֵּין הָעַרְבָּיִם.

and the second lamb-service you are to perform in the afternoon;

Va-asiris ho-ayfo sōles l'mincho,	וַעֲשִׂירִית הָאֵיפָה סֹלֶת לְמִנְחָה,

with a tenth-ephah of fine flour for a meal-offering,

b'lulo b'shemen kosis	בְּלוּלָה בְּשֶׁמֶן כָּתִית
r'vi-is hahin.	רְבִיעִת הַהִין.

mixed with a quarter-hin of crushed olive oil.

Ōlas tomid, ho-asuyo b'har sinai,	עֹלַת תָּמִיד, הָעֲשֻׂיָה בְּהַר סִינַי,

It is the continual elevation-offering that was done at Mount Sinai,

l'ray-ach nichō-ach, i-she Ladōnoy.	לְרֵיחַ נִיחֹחַ, אִשֶּׁה לַיהוה.

for a satisfying aroma, a fire-offering to H<small>ASHEM</small>.

v'niskō r'vi-is hahin	וְנִסְכּוֹ רְבִיעִת הַהִין
lakeves ho-e-chod,	לַכֶּבֶשׂ הָאֶחָד,

And its libation is a quarter-hin for each lamb,

bakōdesh hasaych	בַּקֹּדֶשׁ הַסֵּךְ
nesech shaychor Ladōnoy.	נֶסֶךְ שֵׁכָר לַיהוה.

to be poured on the Holy [Altar], a fermented libation to H<small>ASHEM</small>.

V'ays hakeves ha-shayni	וְאֵת הַכֶּבֶשׂ הַשֵּׁנִי

And the second lamb-service

ta-ase bayn ho-arbo-yim,	תַּעֲשֶׂה בֵּין הָעַרְבָּיִם,

you are to perform in the afternoon,

k'minchas habōker	כְּמִנְחַת הַבֹּקֶר
uchniskō ta-ase,	וּכְנִסְכּוֹ תַּעֲשֶׂה,

like the meal-offering of the morning and its libation are you to make,

i-shay ray-ach nichō-ach Ladōnoy.	אִשֵּׁה רֵיחַ נִיחֹחַ לַיהוה.

a fire-offering for a satisfying aroma to H<small>ASHEM</small>.

V'shochat ōsō	וְשָׁחַט אֹתוֹ
al yerech hamizbay-ach tzofōno	עַל יֶרֶךְ הַמִּזְבֵּחַ צָפֹנָה

He is to slaughter it on the north side of the Altar

lifnay Adōnoy,	לִפְנֵי יהוה,

before H<small>ASHEM</small>,

v'zor'ku b'nay aharōn hakōhanim	וְזָרְקוּ בְּנֵי אַהֲרֹן הַכֹּהֲנִים
es domō	אֶת דָּמוֹ

and Aaron's sons the Kohanim are to dash its blood

al hamizbay-ach soviv.	עַל הַמִּזְבֵּחַ סָבִיב.

upon the Altar, all around.

SHACHARIS FOR WEEKDAYS — OFFERINGS

Y'HI ROTZŌN milfonecho,
יְהִי רָצוֹן מִלְּפָנֶיךָ,
May it be Your will,

Adōnoy Elōhaynu Vaylōhay avōsaynu,
יהוה אֱלֹהֵינוּ וֵאלֹהֵי אֲבוֹתֵינוּ,
Hashem, our God and the God of our forefathers,

shet'hay amiro zu
שֶׁתְּהֵא אֲמִירָה זוֹ
that this recital be

chashuvo umkubeles
חֲשׁוּבָה וּמְקֻבֶּלֶת
umrutzo l'fonecho
וּמְרֻצָּה לְפָנֶיךָ
worthy and acceptable, and favorable before You

k'ilu hikravnu korban hatomid
כְּאִלּוּ הִקְרַבְנוּ קָרְבַּן הַתָּמִיד
as if we had offered the continual-offering

b'mō-adō u-vimkōmō uch-hilchosō.
בְּמוֹעֲדוֹ וּבִמְקוֹמוֹ וּכְהִלְכָתוֹ.
in its set time, in its place, and according to its requirement.

INCENSE

▪ Eleven blended spices were offered daily in the Temple, symbolizing the complete and total integration of the Jewish nation including those not-yet observant. This unity is able to protect and safeguard our people from plague — from within and without.

ATO hu Adōnoy Elōhaynu
אַתָּה הוּא יהוה אֱלֹהֵינוּ
It is You, Hashem, our God,

she-hiktiru avōsaynu l'fonecho
שֶׁהִקְטִירוּ אֲבוֹתֵינוּ לְפָנֶיךָ
before Whom our forefathers burned

es k'tōres hasamim
אֶת קְטֹרֶת הַסַּמִּים
the incense-spices

bizman shebays hamikdosh ka-yom,
בִּזְמַן שֶׁבֵּית הַמִּקְדָּשׁ קַיָּם,
in the time when the Holy Temple stood,

ka-asher tziviso ōsom
כַּאֲשֶׁר צִוִּיתָ אוֹתָם
al y'day mōshe n'vi-e-cho,
עַל יְדֵי מֹשֶׁה נְבִיאֶךָ,
as You commanded them through Moses Your prophet,

kakosuv b'sōrosecho:
כַּכָּתוּב בְּתוֹרָתֶךָ:
as is written in Your Torah:

VA-YŌMER Adōnoy el mōshe,
וַיֹּאמֶר יהוה אֶל מֹשֶׁה,
Hashem said to Moses:

kach l'cho samim,
קַח לְךָ סַמִּים,
Take yourself spices *

◆§ **Incense**
Incense, blended according to a strictly pre-scribed formula, was burned morning and evening on the Golden Altar, located inside the Temple building.

וַיֹּאמֶר ה׳ ... קַח לְךָ סַמִּים — *Hashem said to Moses: Take yourself spices.* As enumerated below in the Talmudic passage beginning "The Rabbis taught," eleven different spices were used in the incense mixture, but only four of

no-tof ushchayles v'chelb'no,	נָטָף וּשְׁחֵלֶת וְחֶלְבְּנָה,

— stacte, onycha, and galbanum —

samim ulvōno zako,	סַמִּים וּלְבֹנָה זַכָּה,

spices and pure frankincense;

bad b'vad yih-ye.	בַּד בְּבַד יִהְיֶה.

they shall all be of equal weight.*

V'osiso ōsoh k'tōres,	וְעָשִׂיתָ אֹתָהּ קְטֹרֶת,

You shall make it into incense,

rōkach, ma-asay rōkayach,	רֹקַח, מַעֲשֵׂה רוֹקֵחַ,

a spice-compound, the handiwork of an expert spice-compounder,

m'muloch, tohōr, kōdesh.	מְמֻלָּח, טָהוֹר, קֹדֶשׁ.

thoroughly mixed, pure and holy.

V'shochakto mimeno hodayk,	וְשָׁחַקְתָּ מִמֶּנָּה הָדֵק,

You shall grind some of it finely

v'nosato mimeno lifnay ho-aydus	וְנָתַתָּה מִמֶּנָּה לִפְנֵי הָעֵדֻת

and place some of it before the Testimony

b'ōhel mō-ayd	בְּאֹהֶל מוֹעֵד

in the Tent of Appointment,

asher ivo-ayd l'cho shomo,	אֲשֶׁר אִוָּעֵד לְךָ שָׁמָּה,

where I shall designate a time to meet you;

kōdesh kodoshim tih-ye lochem.	קֹדֶשׁ קָדָשִׁים תִּהְיֶה לָכֶם.

it shall be a Holy of Holies for you.

V'ne-emar:	וְנֶאֱמַר:

It is also written:

v'hiktir olov aharōn k'tōres samim,	וְהִקְטִיר עָלָיו אַהֲרֹן קְטֹרֶת סַמִּים,

Aaron shall burn upon it the incense-spices

babōker babōker,	בַּבֹּקֶר בַּבֹּקֶר,

every morning;

b'haytivō es hanayrōs yaktireno.	בְּהֵיטִיבוֹ אֶת הַנֵּרֹת יַקְטִירֶנָּה.

when he cleans the lamps he is to burn it.

Uvha-alōs aharōn es hanayrōs bayn ho-arba-yim,	וּבְהַעֲלֹת אַהֲרֹן אֶת הַנֵּרֹת בֵּין הָעַרְבַּיִם,

And when Aaron ignites the lamps in the afternoon,

בַּד בְּבַד יִהְיֶה — *They shall all be of equal weight.* The four spices given by name are of equal weight. The other seven, however, were different from these four, as will be seen from the Talmudic passage that follows.

them — stacte, onycha, galbanum, and frankincense — are named in the Scriptural verse. It should be noted that the exact translations of the spices are not known with absolute certainty.

yaktireno,	יַקְטִירֶנָּה,
he is to burn it,	
k'tōres tomid lifnay Adōnoy	קְטֹרֶת תָּמִיד לִפְנֵי יהוה
as continual incense before H<small>ASHEM</small>	
l'dōrōsaychem.	לְדֹרֹתֵיכֶם.
throughout your generations.	

TONU RABONON,	**תָּנוּ רַבָּנָן,**
The Rabbis taught:	
Pitum hak'tōres kaytzad.	פִּטּוּם הַקְּטֹרֶת כֵּיצַד.
How is the incense mixture formulated? *	
Sh'lōsh may-ōs v'shishim	שְׁלֹשׁ מֵאוֹת וְשִׁשִּׁים
ush'mōno monim ho-yu voh.	וּשְׁמוֹנָה מָנִים הָיוּ בָהּ.
Three hundred sixty-eight maneh were in it:	
Sh'lōsh mayōs	שְׁלֹשׁ מֵאוֹת
v'shishim vachami-sho	וְשִׁשִּׁים וַחֲמִשָּׁה
three hundred sixty-five	
k'minyan y'mōs hachamo —	כְּמִנְיַן יְמוֹת הַחַמָּה —
corresponding to the days of the solar year —	
mone l'chol yōm,	מָנֶה לְכָל יוֹם,
a maneh for each day,	
p'ras b'shacharis	פְּרָס בְּשַׁחֲרִית
half in the morning	
ufras bayn ho-arbo-yim;	וּפְרָס בֵּין הָעַרְבָּיִם;
and half in the afternoon;	
ushlōsho monim y'sayrim,	וּשְׁלֹשָׁה מָנִים יְתֵרִים,
and three extra maneh,	
shemayhem machnis kōhayn godōl	שֶׁמֵּהֶם מַכְנִיס כֹּהֵן גָּדוֹל
from which the Kohen Godol would bring [into the Holy of Holies]	
m'lō chof'nov	מְלֹא חָפְנָיו
both his handfuls	
b'yōm hakipurim.	בְּיוֹם הַכִּפֻּרִים.
on Yom Kippur.	
U-machazirom l'machteshes	וּמַחֲזִירָם לַמַּכְתֶּשֶׁת
He would return them to the mortar	
b'erev yōm hakipurim,	בְּעֶרֶב יוֹם הַכִּפֻּרִים,
on the day before Yom Kippur,	

---

* תָּנוּ רַבָּנָן פִּטּוּם הַקְּטֹרֶת כֵּיצַד — *The Rabbis taught: How is the incense mixture formulated?* This passage explains how the incense mixture was prepared and it gives the names and amounts that are not specified in Scripture.

v'shōchakon yofe yofe	וְשׁוֹחֲקָן יָפֶה יָפֶה
k'day shet'hay dako min hadako.	כְּדֵי שֶׁתְּהֵא דַקָּה מִן הַדַּקָּה.

and grind them very thoroughly so that it would be exceptionally fine.

v'achad osor samonim ho-yu voh, v'aylu hayn:	וְאַחַד עָשָׂר סַמָּנִים הָיוּ בָהּ, וְאֵלּוּ הֵן:

Eleven kinds of spices were in it, as follows:

hatzori, v'hatzipōren, hachelb'no, v'hal'vōno,	הַצֳּרִי, וְהַצִּפֹּרֶן, הַחֶלְבְּנָה, וְהַלְּבוֹנָה,

(1) stacte, (2) onycha, (3) galbanum, (4) frankincense —

mishkal shiv-im shiv-im mone;	מִשְׁקַל שִׁבְעִים שִׁבְעִים מָנֶה;

each weighing seventy maneh;

mōr, uktzi-o, shibōles nayrd, v'charkōm,	מוֹר, וּקְצִיעָה, שִׁבֹּלֶת נֵרְדְּ, וְכַרְכֹּם,

(5) myrrh, (6) cassia, (7) spikenard, (8) saffron —

mishkal shisho osor shisho osor mone;	מִשְׁקַל שִׁשָּׁה עָשָׂר שִׁשָּׁה עָשָׂר מָנֶה;

each weighing sixteen maneh;

hakōsht sh'naym osor,	הַקֹּשְׁטְ שְׁנֵים עָשָׂר,

(9) costus — twelve [maneh];

v'kilufo sh'lōsho,	וּקְלוּפָה שְׁלֹשָׁה,

(10) aromatic bark — three;

v'kinomōn tish-o.	וְקִנָּמוֹן תִּשְׁעָה.

and (11) cinnamon — nine.

Bōris karshino tish-o kabin,	בֹּרִית כַּרְשִׁינָה תִּשְׁעָה קַבִּין,

[Additionally] Carshinah lye, nine kav;

yayn kafrisin s'in t'loso v'kabin t'loso,	יֵין קַפְרִיסִין סְאִין תְּלָתָא וְקַבִּין תְּלָתָא,

Cyprus wine, three se'ah and three kav —

v'im ayn lō yayn kafrisin,	וְאִם אֵין לוֹ יֵין קַפְרִיסִין,

if he has no Cyprus wine,

mayvi chamar chivaryon atik,	מֵבִיא חֲמַר חִוַּרְיָן עַתִּיק,

he brings old white wine;

melach s'dōmis rōva hakov;	מֶלַח סְדוֹמִית רֹבַע הַקַּב;

Sodom salt, a quarter-kav;

ma-a-le oshon kol she-hu.	מַעֲלֶה עָשָׁן כָּל שֶׁהוּא.

and a minute amount of maaleh ashan.*

Rabi noson habavli ōmayr: רַבִּי נָתָן הַבַּבְלִי אוֹמֵר:
Rabbi Nassan the Babylonian says:

af kipas ha-yardayn kol shehu. אַף כִּפַּת הַיַּרְדֵּן כָּל שֶׁהוּא.
Also a minute amount of Jordan amber.

V'im nosan boh d'vash, p'soloh. וְאִם נָתַן בָּהּ דְּבַשׁ, פְּסָלָהּ.
If he placed fruit-honey into it, he invalidated it.

V'im chisar achas mikol samoneho, וְאִם חִסַּר אַחַת מִכָּל סַמָּנֶיהָ,
But if he left out any of its spices,

cha-yov miso. חַיָּב מִיתָה.
he is liable to the death penalty.

RABON shim-ōn ben gamli-ayl ōmayr: **רַבָּן** שִׁמְעוֹן בֶּן גַּמְלִיאֵל אוֹמֵר:
Rabban Shimon ben Gamliel says:

Hatzori aynō elo s'rof הַצֳּרִי אֵינוֹ אֶלָּא שְׂרָף
The stacte is simply the sap

hanōtayf may-atzay hak'tof. הַנּוֹטֵף מֵעֲצֵי הַקְּטָף.
that drips from balsam trees.

Bōris karshino lomo hi vo-o, בֹּרִית כַּרְשִׁינָה לָמָה הִיא בָאָה,
Why is Carshinah lye used?

k'day l'yapōs boh es hatzipōren, כְּדֵי לְיַפּוֹת בָּהּ אֶת הַצִּפֹּרֶן,
To bleach the onycha,

k'day shet'hay no-o. כְּדֵי שֶׁתְּהֵא נָאָה.
to make it pleasing.

Yayn kafrisin lomo hu vo, יֵין קַפְרִיסִין לָמָה הוּא בָא,
Why is Cyprus wine used?

k'day lishrōs bō es hatzipōren, כְּדֵי לִשְׁרוֹת בּוֹ אֶת הַצִּפֹּרֶן,
So that the onycha could be soaked in it,

k'day shet'hay azo. כְּדֵי שֶׁתְּהֵא עַזָּה.
to make it pungent.

Vahalō may ragla-yim yofin loh, וַהֲלֹא מֵי רַגְלַיִם יָפִין לָהּ,
Even though mei raglayim is more suitable for that,

elo she-ayn machnisin אֶלָּא שֶׁאֵין מַכְנִיסִין
may ragla-yim bamikdosh מֵי רַגְלַיִם בַּמִּקְדָּשׁ
nevertheless they do not bring mei raglayim into the Temple

mip'nay hakovōd. מִפְּנֵי הַכָּבוֹד.
out of respect.

מַעֲלֶה עָשָׁן — *Maaleh ashan* [lit. *a smoke-raising herb*]. As implied by its name, the addition of this herb caused the smoke of the incense to ascend straight as a pillar.

TANYO, rabi noson ōmayr: תַּנְיָא, רַבִּי נָתָן אוֹמֵר:
It is taught: Rabbi Nassan says:

K'shehu shōchayk, ōmayr: כְּשֶׁהוּא שׁוֹחֵק, אוֹמֵר:
As one would grind [the incense] another would say,

hodayk haytayv, haytayv hodayk,   הָדֵק הֵיטֵב, הֵיטֵב הָדֵק,
"Grind thoroughly, thoroughly grind,"

mip'nay shehakōl yofe lab'somim.   מִפְּנֵי שֶׁהַקּוֹל יָפֶה לַבְּשָׂמִים.
because the sound is beneficial for the spices.

Pit'moh lachatzo-in, k'shayro;   פִּטְּמָהּ לַחֲצָאִין, כְּשֵׁרָה;
If one mixed it in half-quantities, it was fit for use,

lishlish v'lirvi-a, lō shomonu.   לִשְׁלִישׁ וְלִרְבִיעַ, לֹא שָׁמָעְנוּ.
but as to a third or a quarter — we have not heard the law.

Omar rabi y'hudo: Ze hak'lol —   אָמַר רַבִּי יְהוּדָה: זֶה הַכְּלָל —
Rabbi Yehudah said: This is the general rule —

im k'midosoh, k'shayro lachatzo-in;   אִם כְּמִדָּתָהּ, כְּשֵׁרָה לַחֲצָאִין;
In its proper proportion, it is fit for use in half the full amount;

v'im chisar achas mikol samoneho,   וְאִם חִסַּר אַחַת מִכָּל סַמָּנֶיהָ,
but if he left out any one of its spices,

cha-yov miso.   חַיָּב מִיתָה.
he is liable to the death penalty.

TANYO, bar kaporo ōmayr: תַּנְיָא, בַּר קַפָּרָא אוֹמֵר:
It is taught: [The Sage] Bar Kappara says:

Achas l'shishim ō l'shiv-im shono   אַחַת לְשִׁשִּׁים אוֹ לְשִׁבְעִים שָׁנָה
Once every sixty or seventy years,

hoy'so vo-o   הָיְתָה בָאָה
    shel shira-yim lachatzo-in.   שֶׁל שִׁירַיִם לַחֲצָאִין.
the accumulated leftovers reached half the yearly quantity.

V'ōd tonay bar kaporo: וְעוֹד תָּנֵי בַּר קַפָּרָא:
Bar Kappara taught further:

Ilu ho-yo nōsayn boh   אִלּוּ הָיָה נוֹתֵן בָּהּ
    kōr'tōv shel d'vash,   קוֹרְטוֹב שֶׁל דְּבַשׁ,
Had one put a kortov of fruit-honey into it,*

ayn odom yochōl la-amōd   אֵין אָדָם יָכוֹל לַעֲמוֹד
    mip'nay raychoh.   מִפְּנֵי רֵיחָהּ.
no person could have resisted its scent.

קוֹרְטוֹב שֶׁל דְּבַשׁ — *A kortov of fruit-honey.* Honey or any other fruit juice or produce would have made the scent irresistible, but the Torah forbids the use of fruit products in the incense.

V'lomo ayn m'or'vin boh d'vash,   וְלָמָה אֵין מְעָרְבִין בָּהּ דְּבַשׁ,
Why did they not mix fruit-honey into it?

mip'nay shehatōro om'rō: מִפְּנֵי שֶׁהַתּוֹרָה אָמְרָה:
Because the Torah says:

Ki chol s'ōr v'chol d'vash   כִּי כָל שְׂאֹר וְכָל דְּבַשׁ
"For any leaven or any fruit-honey,

lō saktiru mimenu   לֹא תַקְטִירוּ מִמֶּנּוּ
   i-she Ladōnoy.   אִשֶּׁה לַיהוה.
you are not to burn from them a fire-offering to HASHEM.*"*

———————— RECITE THREE TIMES. ————————

ADŌNOY tz'vo-ōs imonu,   **יהוה** צְבָאוֹת עִמָּנוּ,
HASHEM, *Master of Legions, is with us,*

misgōv lonu Elōhay ya-akōv, selo.   מִשְׂגָּב לָנוּ אֱלֹהֵי יַעֲקֹב, סֶלָה.
a stronghold for us is the God of Jacob, Selah!

———————— RECITE THREE TIMES. ————————

ADŌNOY tz'vo-ōs,   **יהוה** צְבָאוֹת,
HASHEM, *Master of Legions,*

ashray odom bōtay-ach boch.   אַשְׁרֵי אָדָם בֹּטֵחַ בָּךְ.
praiseworthy is the person who trusts in You.

———————— RECITE THREE TIMES. ————————

ADŌNOY hōshi-o,   **יהוה** הוֹשִׁיעָה,
HASHEM, *save!*

hamelech ya-anaynu v'yōm kor-aynu.   הַמֶּלֶךְ יַעֲנֵנוּ בְיוֹם קָרְאֵנוּ.
May the King answer us on the day we call!

———————————————————————

ATO sayser li,   **אַתָּה** סֵתֶר לִי,
You are a shelter for me;

mitzar titz'rayni,   מִצַּר תִּצְּרֵנִי,
from distress You preserve me;

ronay falayt, t'sōv'vayni, selo.   רָנֵּי פַלֵּט, תְּסוֹבְבֵנִי, סֶלָה.
with glad song of rescue, You envelop me, Selah!

V'or'vo Ladōnoy   וְעָרְבָה לַיהוה
   minchas y'hudo virusholo-yim,   מִנְחַת יְהוּדָה וִירוּשָׁלָיִם,
May the offering of Judah and Jerusalem be pleasing to HASHEM,

kimay ōlom   כִּימֵי עוֹלָם
   uchshonim kadmōni-yōs.   וּכְשָׁנִים קַדְמֹנִיּוֹת.
as in days of old and in former years.

שחרית לחול / 106   קרבנות

ABA-YAY havo m'sadayr sayder hama-arocho *Abaye listed* the order of the Altar service*	**אַבַּיֵּי** הֲוָה מְסַדֵּר סֵדֶר הַמַּעֲרָכָה
mish'mo digmoro v'alibo d'abo sho-ul: *based on the tradition and according to Abba Shaul:*	מִשְּׁמָא דִגְמָרָא וְאַלִּבָּא דְאַבָּא שָׁאוּל:
Ma-arocho g'dōlo *The arrangement of the large pyre*	מַעֲרָכָה גְדוֹלָה
kōdemes l'ma-arocho sh'niyo shel k'tōres; *precedes that of the secondary pyre for the incense-offering;*	קוֹדֶמֶת לְמַעֲרָכָה שְׁנִיָּה שֶׁל קְטֹרֶת;
u-ma-arocho sh'niyo shel k'tōres *the secondary pyre for the incense-offering*	וּמַעֲרָכָה שְׁנִיָּה שֶׁל קְטֹרֶת
kōdemes l'sidur sh'nay gizray aytzim; *precedes the placement of two logs;*	קוֹדֶמֶת לְסִדּוּר שְׁנֵי גִזְרֵי עֵצִים;
v'sidur sh'nay gizray aytzim *the placement of two logs*	וְסִדּוּר שְׁנֵי גִזְרֵי עֵצִים
kōdaym l'dishun mizbay-ach hap'nimi; *precedes the removal of ashes from the Inner Altar;*	קוֹדֵם לְדִשּׁוּן מִזְבֵּחַ הַפְּנִימִי;
v'dishun mizbay-ach hap'nimi *the removal of ashes from the Inner Altar*	וְדִשּׁוּן מִזְבֵּחַ הַפְּנִימִי
kōdaym lahatovas chomaysh nayrōs; *precedes the cleaning of five lamps [of the Menorah];*	קוֹדֵם לַהֲטָבַת חָמֵשׁ נֵרוֹת;
vahatovas chomaysh nayrōs *the cleaning of the five lamps*	וַהֲטָבַת חָמֵשׁ נֵרוֹת
kōdemes l'dam hatomid; *precedes the [dashing of the] blood of the continual-offering;*	קוֹדֶמֶת לְדַם הַתָּמִיד;
v'dam hatomid kōdaym *the blood of the continual-offering precedes*	וְדַם הַתָּמִיד קוֹדֵם
lahatovas sh'tay nayrōs; *the cleaning of the [other] two lamps;*	לַהֲטָבַת שְׁתֵּי נֵרוֹת;
vahatovas sh'tay nayrōs *the cleaning of the two lamps*	וַהֲטָבַת שְׁתֵּי נֵרוֹת

אַבַּיֵּי הֲוָה מְסַדֵּר — *Abaye listed.* To conclude the description of the daily Temple service, we recite its full order as transmitted by the Talmudic sage Abaye. Although he lived several generations after the Destruction, he taught the order, as it had been transmitted orally, in the name of Abba Shaul, a sage who lived in the time of the Second Temple.

kōdemes liktōres;	קוֹדֶמֶת לִקְטֹרֶת;

precedes the incense;

uktōres kōdemes l'ayvorim;	וּקְטֹרֶת קוֹדֶמֶת לְאֵבָרִים;

the incense precedes the [burning of the] limbs;

v'ayvorim l'mincho;	וְאֵבָרִים לְמִנְחָה;

the [burning of the] limbs [precedes] the meal-offering;

u-mincho lachavitin;	וּמִנְחָה לַחֲבִתִּין;

the meal-offering [precedes] the pancakes;

vachavitin lin-sochin;	וַחֲבִתִּין לִנְסָכִין;

the pancakes [precede] the wine-libations;

un-sochin l'musofin;	וּנְסָכִין לְמוּסָפִין;

the wine-libations [precede] the mussaf-offering;

u-musofin l'vozichin;	וּמוּסָפִין לְבָזִיכִין;

the mussaf-offering [precedes] the bowls [of frankincense];

u-vozichin kōd'min	וּבָזִיכִין קוֹדְמִין

the bowls precede

l'somid shel bayn ho-arbo-yim,	לְתָמִיד שֶׁל בֵּין הָעַרְבָּיִם,

the afternoon continual-offering,

shene-emar: v'orach oleho ho-ōlo,	שֶׁנֶּאֱמַר: וְעָרַךְ עָלֶיהָ הָעֹלָה,

for it is said: "And he is to arrange the elevation-offering upon it

v'hiktir oleho chelvay hash'lomim.	וְהִקְטִיר עָלֶיהָ חֶלְבֵי הַשְּׁלָמִים.

and burn the fats of the peace-offering upon it";

oleho hashlaym	עָלֶיהָ הַשְׁלֵם
kol hakorbonōs kulom.	כָּל הַקָּרְבָּנוֹת כֻּלָּם.

"upon it" [the elevation-offering] you are to complete all the [day's] offerings.

ONO B'CHŌACH g'dulas y'min'cho	**אָנָּא בְּכֹחַ** גְּדֻלַּת יְמִינְךָ

We beg You! With the strength* of Your right hand's greatness,

tatir tz'ruro.	תַּתִּיר צְרוּרָה.

untie the bundled sins.

Kabayl rinas am'cho	קַבֵּל רִנַּת עַמְּךָ

Accept the prayer of Your people;

sag'vaynu taharaynu nōro.	שַׂגְּבֵנוּ טַהֲרֵנוּ נוֹרָא.

strengthen us, purify us, O Awesome One.

No, gibōr,	נָא גִבּוֹר

Please, O Strong One —

אָנָּא בְּכֹחַ — *We beg You! With the strength* . . . This prayer — ascribed to the *Tanna* Rabbi Nechunia ben Hakanah — has profound mystical significance. It is inserted at this point because it is an eloquent prayer that God save Israel from Exile. After having recited the order of the Temple service, it is a most fitting time for us to pray for the Redemption.

dōr'shay yichud'cho	דּוֹרְשֵׁי יִחוּדְךָ
k'vovas shom'raym.	כְּבָבַת שָׁמְרֵם.

those who foster Your Oneness, guard them like the pupil of an eye.

Bor'chaym taharaym rachamaym   בָּרְכֵם טַהֲרֵם רַחֲמֵם

Bless them, purify them, show them pity,

tzidkos'cho tomid gom-laym.   צִדְקָתְךָ תָּמִיד גָּמְלֵם.

may Your righteousness always recompense them.

Chasin kodōsh   חֲסִין קָדוֹשׁ
   b'rōv tuv'cho nahayl adosecho.   בְּרוֹב טוּבְךָ נַהֵל עֲדָתֶךָ.

Powerful Holy One, with Your abundant goodness guide Your congregation.

Yochid gay-e l'am'cho p'nay   יָחִיד גֵּאֶה לְעַמְּךָ פְּנֵה

One and only Exalted One, turn to Your people,

zōch'ray k'dushosecho.   זוֹכְרֵי קְדֻשָּׁתֶךָ.

who proclaim Your holiness.

Shav-osaynu kabayl   שַׁוְעָתֵנוּ קַבֵּל
   ush-ma tza-akosaynu   וּשְׁמַע צַעֲקָתֵנוּ

Accept our entreaty and hear our cry,

yōday-a ta-alumōs.   יוֹדֵעַ תַּעֲלֻמוֹת.

O Knower of mysteries.

Boruch shaym k'vōd malchusō   בָּרוּךְ שֵׁם כְּבוֹד מַלְכוּתוֹ
   l'ōlom vo-ed.   לְעוֹלָם וָעֶד.

Blessed is the Name of His glorious Kingdom forever and ever.

RIBŌN HO-ŌLOMIM,   **רִבּוֹן הָעוֹלָמִים,**

Master of the worlds,

ato tzivisonu l'hakriv   אַתָּה צִוִּיתָנוּ לְהַקְרִיב
   korban hatomid b'mō-adō,   קָרְבַּן הַתָּמִיד בְּמוֹעֲדוֹ,

You commanded us to bring the continual-offering at its set time,

v'lih-yōs kōhanim ba-avōdosom,   וְלִהְיוֹת כֹּהֲנִים בַּעֲבוֹדָתָם,

and that the Kohanim be at their assigned service,

ulviyim b'duchonom,   וּלְוִיִּם בְּדוּכָנָם,
   v'yisro-ayl b'ma-amodom.   וְיִשְׂרָאֵל בְּמַעֲמָדָם.

the Levites on their platform, and the Israelites at their station.

V'ato ba-avōnōsaynu   וְעַתָּה בַּעֲוֹנוֹתֵינוּ

But now, through our sins,

chorav bays hamikdosh   חָרַב בֵּית הַמִּקְדָּשׁ
   uvotayl hatomid,   וּבֻטַּל הַתָּמִיד,

the Holy Temple is destroyed, the continual-offering is discontinued,

v'ayn lonu lō chōhayn ba-avōdosō,	וְאֵין לָנוּ לֹא כֹהֵן בַּעֲבוֹדָתוֹ,
and we have neither Kohen at his service,	
v'lō layvi b'duchonō,	וְלֹא לֵוִי בְּדוּכָנוֹ,
v'lō yisro-ayl b'ma-amodō.	וְלֹא יִשְׂרָאֵל בְּמַעֲמָדוֹ.
*nor Levite on his platform, nor Israelite at his station.**	
V'ato omarto:	וְאַתָּה אָמַרְתָּ:
Unshal'mo forim s'fosaynu.	וּנְשַׁלְּמָה פָרִים שְׂפָתֵינוּ.
But You said: "Let our lips compensate for the bulls" —	
Lochayn y'hi rotzōn mil'fonecho,	לָכֵן יְהִי רָצוֹן מִלְּפָנֶיךָ,
therefore may it be Your will,	
Adōnoy Elōhaynu	יהוה אֱלֹהֵינוּ
Vaylōhay avōsaynu,	וֵאלֹהֵי אֲבוֹתֵינוּ,
HASHEM*, our God, and the God of our forefathers,*	
she-y'hay si-ach sifsōsaynu	שֶׁיְּהֵא שִׂיחַ שִׂפְתוֹתֵינוּ
that the prayer of our lips	
choshuv umkubol umrutze l'fonecho,	חָשׁוּב וּמְקֻבָּל וּמְרֻצֶּה לְפָנֶיךָ,
be worthy, acceptable, and favorable before You,	
k'ilu hikravnu	כְּאִלּוּ הִקְרַבְנוּ
korban hatomid b'mō-adō,	קָרְבַּן הַתָּמִיד בְּמוֹעֲדוֹ,
as if we had brought the continual-offering at its set time	
v'omadnu al ma-amodō.	וְעָמַדְנוּ עַל מַעֲמָדוֹ.
and we had stood at its station.	

THE FOLLOWING PARAGRAPH IS RECITED ONLY ON *ROSH CHODESH*:

UVROSHAY chodshaychem	**וּבְרָאשֵׁי** חָדְשֵׁיכֶם
On the first days of your months	
takrivu ōlo Ladōnoy,	תַּקְרִיבוּ עֹלָה לַיהוה,
you are to bring an elevation-offering to HASHEM,	
porim b'nay vokor sh'na-yim,	פָּרִים בְּנֵי בָקָר שְׁנַיִם,
v'a-yil e-chod,	וְאַיִל אֶחָד,
two young bulls, one ram,	
k'vosim b'nay shono shiv-o,	כְּבָשִׂים בְּנֵי שָׁנָה שִׁבְעָה,
t'mimim.	תְּמִימִם.
seven [male] first-year lambs, unblemished.	

לֹא כֹהֵן בַּעֲבוֹדָתוֹ, וְלֹא לֵוִי בְּדוּכָנוֹ, וְלֹא יִשְׂרָאֵל בְּמַעֲמָדוֹ — *Neither Kohen at his service, nor Levite on his platform, nor Israelite at his station.* All three categories of Jews were represented in the daily communal service. The *Kohanim* performed the service, the Levites stood on a platform to sing the psalm of the day, and the rest of the nation were represented by delegates who recited special prayers and Scriptural passages.

	קרבנות

| Ush-lōsho esrōnim sō-les mincho | וּשְׁלֹשָׁה עֶשְׂרֹנִים סֹלֶת מִנְחָה |
| b'lulo va-shemen | בְּלוּלָה בַשֶּׁמֶן |

And three tenth-ephah of fine flour for a meal-offering mixed with olive oil

| lapor ho-e-chod, | לַפָּר הָאֶחָד, |

for each bull,

| ush-nay esrōnim sō-les mincho | וּשְׁנֵי עֶשְׂרֹנִים סֹלֶת מִנְחָה |
| b'lulo va-shemen | בְּלוּלָה בַשֶּׁמֶן |

and two tenth-ephah of fine flour for a meal-offering mixed with olive oil

| lo-a-yil ho-e-chod. | לָאַיִל הָאֶחָד. |

for each ram.

| v'isorōn isorōn, sō-les mincho | וְעִשָּׂרֹן עִשָּׂרוֹן, סֹלֶת מִנְחָה |
| b'lulo vashemen, | בְּלוּלָה בַשֶּׁמֶן, |

And a tenth-ephah of fine flour for a meal-offering mixed with olive oil

| lakeves ho-e-chod, | לַכֶּבֶשׂ הָאֶחָד, |

for each lamb —

| ōlo ray-ach nichō-ach, | עֹלָה רֵיחַ נִיחֹחַ, |
| i-she Ladōnoy. | אִשֶּׁה לַיהוה. |

an elevation-offering, a satisfying aroma, a fire-offering to HASHEM.

| V'nis-kayhem, | וְנִסְכֵּיהֶם |

And their libations —

| chatzi hahin yih-ye lapor | חֲצִי הַהִין יִהְיֶה לַפָּר, |

there is to be a half-hin for a bull,

| ush-lishis hahin lo-a-yil, | וּשְׁלִישִׁת הַהִין לָאַיִל, |

a third-hin for a ram,

| urvi-is hahin lakeves — yo-yin; | וּרְבִיעִת הַהִין לַכֶּבֶשׂ — יָיִן; |

a quarter-hin for a lamb — of wine.

| zōs ōlas chōdesh b'chodshō | זֹאת עֹלַת חֹדֶשׁ בְּחָדְשׁוֹ |

This is the elevation-offering of the month upon its renewal,

| l'chodshay ha-shono. | לְחָדְשֵׁי הַשָּׁנָה. |

for the months of the year.

| Us-ir izim e-chod | וּשְׂעִיר עִזִּים אֶחָד |
| l'chatos Ladōnoy, | לְחַטָּאת לַיהוה, |

And one he-goat for a sin-offering to HASHEM.

| al ōlas hatomid yay-o-se, | עַל עֹלַת הַתָּמִיד יֵעָשֶׂה, |

In addition to the continual elevation-offering, should it be made —

| v'niskō. | וְנִסְכּוֹ. |

and its libation.

MISHNAH SELECTION

MISHNAH ONE

AY-ZEHU M'KŌMON shel z'vochim shel z'vochim. אֵיזֶהוּ מְקוֹמָן שֶׁל זְבָחִים.
What is the location* of the offerings?

Kodshay kodoshim קָדְשֵׁי קָדָשִׁים
  sh'chitoson batzofōn, שְׁחִיטָתָן בַּצָּפוֹן.
The most-holy offerings, their slaughter is in the north.*

Por v'so-ir shel yōm hakipurim פַּר וְשָׂעִיר שֶׁל יוֹם הַכִּפּוּרִים
The bull and the he-goat of Yom Kippur

sh'chitoson batzofōn, שְׁחִיטָתָן בַּצָּפוֹן,
  their slaughter is in the north,

v'kibul domon bichli shorays וְקִבּוּל דָּמָן בִּכְלִי שָׁרֵת
  batzofōn. בַּצָּפוֹן.
and the reception of their blood in a service-vessel is in the north.

V'domon to-un hazo-yo וְדָמָן טָעוּן הַזָּיָה
Their blood requires sprinkling

al bayn habadim, עַל בֵּין הַבַּדִּים,
  between the poles [of the Holy Ark],*

v'al haporōches, וְעַל הַפָּרֹכֶת,
  and toward the Curtain* [of the Holy of Holies]

v'al mizbach hazohov. וְעַל מִזְבַּח הַזָּהָב.
  and upon the Golden Altar;

matono achas mayhen m'akoves. מַתָּנָה אַחַת מֵהֶן מְעַכָּבֶת.
[the absence of] any one of these applications [of blood] prevents [atonement].

Sh'yoray hadom ho-yo shōfaych שְׁיָרֵי הַדָּם הָיָה שׁוֹפֵךְ
The leftover blood he would pour

≈§ What Is the Location

The Talmud (*Kiddushin* 30a) teaches that one should study Scripture, Mishnah [i.e., the compilation of laws that are the basis of the Talmud discussions], and Gemara [i.e., the discussions of the laws] every day. In fulfillment of that injunction, the Sages instituted that appropriate passages from each of these three categories be included in this section of *Shacharis*. Since Scriptural passages regarding the Temple offerings are part of the service in any case, the Sages chose a chapter of the Mishnah on the same subject. Chapter 5 of *Zevachim*, which begins אֵיזֶהוּ מְקוֹמָן, *What is the location,* was chosen for three reasons: (a) It discusses all the sacrifices; (b) it is the only chapter in the Mishnah in which there is no halachic dispute; and (c) its text is of very ancient origin, possibly even from the days of Moses.

אֵיזֶהוּ מְקוֹמָן — *What is the location* in the Courtyard where they were slaughtered and the part of the Altar upon which their blood was placed?

בַּצָּפוֹן — *In the north,* i.e., in the Courtyard to the north of the Altar.

עַל בֵּין הַבַּדִּים — *Between the poles [of the Holy Ark].* On Yom Kippur, the *Kohen Gadol* brought the blood of this offering into the Holy of Holies and sprinkled part of it toward the Holy Ark, between the two poles of the Ark that extended from either side of it toward the Sanctuary.

וְעַל הַפָּרֹכֶת — *And toward the Curtain* that separated the Holy of Holies from the Sanctuary. Toward this Curtain, too, the *Kohen Gadol*

al y'sōd ma-arovi	עַל יְסוֹד מַעֲרָבִי
shel mizbay-ach hachitzōn;	שֶׁל מִזְבֵּחַ הַחִיצוֹן;

onto the western base of the Outer Altar;

im lō nosan, lō ikayv.	אִם לֹא נָתַן, לֹא עִכֵּב.

but if he did not apply it [the leftover blood on the base], he has not prevented [atonement].

MISHNAH TWO

PORIM hanis-rofim	**פָּרִים** הַנִּשְׂרָפִים

The bulls that are completely burned*

us-irim hanis-rofim	וּשְׂעִירִים הַנִּשְׂרָפִים

and he-goats that are completely burned,*

sh'chitoson batzofōn,	שְׁחִיטָתָן בַּצָּפוֹן,

their slaughter is in the north,

v'kibul domon bichli shorays batzofōn.	וְקִבּוּל דָּמָן בִּכְלִי שָׁרֵת בַּצָּפוֹן.

and the reception of their blood in a service-vessel is in the north.

V'domon to-un hazo-yo	וְדָמָן טָעוּן הַזָּיָה

Their blood requires sprinkling

al haporōches	עַל הַפָּרֹכֶת

toward the Curtain

v'al mizbach hazohov.	וְעַל מִזְבַּח הַזָּהָב.

and upon the Golden Altar;

matono achas mayhen m'akoves.	מַתָּנָה אַחַת מֵהֶן מְעַכֶּבֶת.

[the absence of] any one of these applications prevents [atonement].

Sh'yoray hadom ho-yo shōfaych	שְׁיָרֵי הַדָּם הָיָה שׁוֹפֵךְ

The leftover blood he would pour

al y'sōd ma-arovi	עַל יְסוֹד מַעֲרָבִי
shel mizbay-ach hachitzōn;	שֶׁל מִזְבֵּחַ הַחִיצוֹן;

onto the western base of the Outer Altar;

im lō nosan, lō ikayv.	אִם לֹא נָתַן, לֹא עִכֵּב.

but if he did not apply it, he has not prevented [atonement].

---

sprinkled blood.

פָּרִים הַנִּשְׂרָפִים — *The bulls that are completely burned.* With the exception of the Yom Kippur offerings mentioned above, only two kinds of bull offerings are completely burned, no part of them being eaten by the *Kohanim*. They are (a) the bull brought if the Sanhedrin erred in a halachic ruling, and, as a result of following that ruling, a majority of the people violated a commandment; (b) the bull brought by the *Kohen Gadol* if he made an erroneous halachic decision and himself acted on this ruling.

שְׂעִירִים הַנִּשְׂרָפִים — *He-goats that are completely burned.* If the Sanhedrin (highest court) erroneously permitted an act that was a violation of the laws against idol worship, and a majority of the community followed their ruling, their atonement consists of a he-goat that is completely burned.

Aylu vo-aylu	אֵלּוּ וָאֵלּוּ

Both these and those [the Yom Kippur offerings]

nis-rofin b'vays hadoshen.	נִשְׂרָפִין בְּבֵית הַדֶּשֶׁן.

are burned in the place where the [Altar] ashes are deposited.

MISHNAH THREE

CHATŌS hatzibur v'ha-yochid,	**חַטֹּאת** הַצִּבּוּר וְהַיָּחִיד,

Sin-offerings of the community and of the individual —

aylu hayn chatōs hatzibur:	אֵלּוּ הֵן חַטֹּאת הַצִּבּוּר:

the communal sin-offerings are the following:

s'iray roshay chodoshim	שְׂעִירֵי רָאשֵׁי חֳדָשִׁים
v'shel mō-adōs,	וְשֶׁל מוֹעֲדוֹת

The he-goats of Rosh Chodesh and Festivals:

sh'chitoson batzofōn,	שְׁחִיטָתָן בַּצָּפוֹן,

Their slaughter is in the north,

v'kibul domon bichli shorays batzofōn.	וְקִבּוּל דָּמָן בִּכְלִי שָׁרֵת בַּצָּפוֹן.

and the reception of their blood in a service-vessel is in the north.

V'domon to-un arba matonōs	וְדָמָן טָעוּן אַרְבַּע מַתָּנוֹת

Their blood requires four applications,

al arba k'ronōs.	עַל אַרְבַּע קְרָנוֹת.

[one] on [each of] the four corners [of the Altar].

Kaytzad,	כֵּיצַד,

How is it done?

olo vakevesh, u-fono lasōvayv	עָלָה בַכֶּבֶשׁ, וּפָנָה לַסּוֹבֵב

He [the Kohen] ascended the [Altar] ramp, and turned to the surrounding ledge

u-vo lō l'keren d'rōmis mizrochis,	וּבָא לוֹ לְקֶרֶן דְּרוֹמִית מִזְרָחִית,

and came (first) to the southeast [corner],

mizrochis tz'fōnis,	מִזְרָחִית צְפוֹנִית,

[then to] the northeast [corner],

tz'fōnis ma-arovis,	צְפוֹנִית מַעֲרָבִית,

[then to] the northwest,

ma-arovis d'rōmis.	מַעֲרָבִית דְּרוֹמִית.

and [finally] the southwest.

Sh'yoray hadom ho-yo shōfaych	שְׁיָרֵי הַדָּם הָיָה שׁוֹפֵךְ

The leftover blood he would pour out

al y'sōd d'rōmi.	עַל יְסוֹד דְּרוֹמִי.

on the southern base.

V'ne-e-cholin lifnim min hak'lo-im,	וְנֶאֱכָלִין לִפְנִים מִן הַקְּלָעִים,

They are eaten within the [Courtyard] curtains,*

l'zich-ray ch'huno, b'chol ma-achol,	לְזִכְרֵי כְהֻנָּה, בְּכָל מַאֲכָל,

by males of the priesthood, prepared in any manner,

l'yōm volailo, ad chatzōs.	לְיוֹם וָלַיְלָה, עַד חֲצוֹת.

on the day [of offering] and on the following night until midnight.

MISHNAH FOUR

HO-ŌLO kōdesh kodoshim.	**הָעוֹלָה** קֹדֶשׁ קָדָשִׁים.

The elevation-offering is among the most-holy offerings:

sh'chitosoh batzofōn,	שְׁחִיטָתָהּ בַּצָּפוֹן,

Its slaughter is in the north,

v'kibul domoh bichli shorays batzofōn.	וְקִבּוּל דָּמָהּ בִּכְלִי שָׁרֵת בַּצָּפוֹן.

and the reception of its blood in a service-vessel is in the north.

V'domoh to-un sh'tay matonōs shehayn arba;	וְדָמָהּ טָעוּן שְׁתֵּי מַתָּנוֹת שֶׁהֵן אַרְבַּע;

Its blood requires two applications that are [equivalent to] four.*

ut-uno hafshayt v'nitu-ach,	וּטְעוּנָה הַפְשֵׁט וְנִתּוּחַ,

It requires flaying and dismemberment,*

v'cholil lo-i-shim.	וְכָלִיל לָאִשִּׁים.

and it is entirely consumed by the fire.

MISHNAH FIVE

ZIVCHAY shalmay tzibur va-ashomōs,	**זִבְחֵי** שַׁלְמֵי צִבּוּר וַאֲשָׁמוֹת,

Communal peace-offerings and [personal] guilt-offerings* —

aylu hayn ashomōs:	אֵלוּ הֵן אֲשָׁמוֹת:

the guilt-offerings are the following:

asham g'zaylōs,	אֲשַׁם גְּזֵלוֹת,

the guilt-offering for thefts,*

וְנֶאֱכָלִין לִפְנִים מִן הַקְּלָעִים — *They are eaten within the [Courtyard] curtains.* After the specified fats are removed to be burned on the Altar, the flesh of the sin-offerings is distributed to be eaten by male *Kohanim*. It could be prepared and eaten only within the Temple Courtyard. The term "curtains" is borrowed from the period in the wilderness, when the Tabernacle Courtyard was enclosed not by walls, but by curtains.

שְׁתֵּי מַתָּנוֹת שֶׁהֵן אַרְבַּע — *Two applications that are [equivalent to] four.* Their blood was thrown from the service-vessel at two corners of the Altar walls: the northeast and the southwest. The blood would spread out to the two adjacent walls. Thus, the two applications of blood would put blood on all four walls of the Altar.

וְנִתּוּחַ — *And dismemberment.* The elevation-offering was cut up in a prescribed way; only then was it completely burned.

אֲשָׁמוֹת — *Guilt-offerings.* There are six kinds of guilt-offerings, all of which are listed in this mishnah. They are:

(a) אֲשַׁם גְּזֵלוֹת — *. . . for thefts.* If someone owed money — whether a loan, a theft, an

OFFERINGS

asham m'ilōs, אֲשַׁם מְעִילוֹת,
the guilt-offering for misuse of sacred objects,*

asham shifcho charufo, אֲשַׁם שִׁפְחָה חֲרוּפָה,
the guilt-offering [for violating] a betrothed maidservant,*

asham nozir, asham m'tzoro, אֲשַׁם נָזִיר, אֲשַׁם מְצֹרָע,
the guilt-offering of a Nazirite,* the guilt-offering of a metzora,*

oshom toluy. אָשָׁם תָּלוּי.
and a guilt-offering in case of doubt.*

Sh'chitoson batzofōn, שְׁחִיטָתָן בַּצָּפוֹן,
Their slaughter is in the north,

v'kibul domon bichli shorays וְקִבּוּל דָּמָן בִּכְלִי שָׁרֵת
batzofōn, בַּצָּפוֹן,
and the reception of their blood in a service-vessel is in the north.

V'domon to-un sh'tay matonōs וְדָמָן טָעוּן שְׁתֵּי מַתָּנוֹת
shehayn arba. שֶׁהֵן אַרְבַּע.
Their blood requires two applications that are [equivalent to] four.

V'ne-e-cholin lifnim min hak'lo-im, וְנֶאֱכָלִין לִפְנִים מִן הַקְּלָעִים,
They are eaten within the [Courtyard] curtains,

l'zich-ray ch'huno, b'chol ma-achol לְזִכְרֵי כְהֻנָּה, בְּכָל מַאֲכָל,
by males of the priesthood, prepared in any manner,

l'yōm volailo, ad chatzōs. לְיוֹם וָלַיְלָה, עַד חֲצוֹת.
on the day [of offering] and on the following night until midnight.

---

article held in safekeeping, or whatever — and intentionally swore falsely that he did not owe it, in addition to returning the money or article he is required to bring a guilt-offering as an atonement. See *Leviticus* 5:20-26.

(b) אֲשַׁם מְעִילוֹת — ... *for misuse of sacred objects.* If someone unintentionally used objects belonging to the Sanctuary for his personal benefit he must atone by bringing a guilt-offering. See *Leviticus* 5:14-16.

(c) אֲשַׁם שִׁפְחָה חֲרוּפָה — ... *[for violating] a betrothed maidservant.* The woman involved was a non-Jewish slave who had been owned by two Jewish partners. One of the partners freed her, thus making her half free and half slave. But since a freed non-Jewish slave has the same status as a proselyte, this half-free maidservant is half Jewish and half non-Jewish and is forbidden to marry either a non-Jew or a Jew. She is, however, permitted to a Jewish indentured servant, who is permitted to both a Jewish woman and a non-Jewish maidservant. If she became betrothed to a Jewish indentured servant and subsequently had relations with another man, the adulterer must bring a guilt-offering in atonement.

(d) אֲשַׁם נָזִיר — ... *of a Nazirite,* who became טָמֵא, *ritually contaminated,* through contact with a corpse. See *Numbers* 6:9-12.

(e) אֲשַׁם מְצֹרָע — ... *of a metzora.* One afflicted by the leprous-like disease of *tzaraas* described in *Leviticus* (ch. 13) regains his complete ritual purity upon bringing a series of offerings after he is cured. See *Leviticus* 14:10-12.

(f) אָשָׁם תָּלוּי — ... *in case of doubt.* This is the only guilt-offering not prescribed for a specific offense or phenomenon. It is required whenever there is a question of whether one has become liable to bring a sin-offering. As long as such a doubt exists, the possible transgressor can protect himself from punishment through a guilt-offering. However, if and when it becomes established that the offense was indeed committed, the person must bring his sin-offering. See *Leviticus* 5:17-19.

MISHNAH SIX

HATÔDO v'ayl nozir | **הַתּוֹדָה** וְאֵיל נָזִיר
The thanksgiving-offering* and the ram of a Nazirite*

kodoshim kalim. | קָדְשִׁים קַלִּים.
are offerings of lesser holiness:*

Sh'chitoson b'chol mokôm bo-azoro, | שְׁחִיטָתָן בְּכָל מָקוֹם בָּעֲזָרָה,
Their slaughter is anywhere in the Courtyard,

v'domon to-un sh'tay matonôs shehayn arba. | וְדָמָן טָעוּן שְׁתֵּי מַתָּנוֹת שֶׁהֵן אַרְבַּע.
and their blood requires two applications that are [equivalent to] four.

V'ne-echolin b'chol ho-ir, | וְנֶאֱכָלִין בְּכָל הָעִיר,
They are eaten throughout the City [of Jerusalem],

l'chol odom, b'chol ma-achol, | לְכָל אָדָם, בְּכָל מַאֲכָל,
by anyone, prepared in any manner,

l'yôm volailo, ad chatzôs. | לְיוֹם וָלַיְלָה, עַד חֲצוֹת.
on the day [of offering] and on the following night until midnight.

Hamurom may-hem ka-yôtzay vohem, | הַמּוּרָם מֵהֶם כַּיּוֹצֵא בָהֶם,
The [priestly] portion separated from them is treated like them,

elo she-hamurom ne-e-chol | אֶלָּא שֶׁהַמּוּרָם נֶאֱכָל
except that that separated portion may be eaten

lakôhanim, linshayhem v'livnayhem ul-avdayhem. | לַכֹּהֲנִים, לִנְשֵׁיהֶם וְלִבְנֵיהֶם וּלְעַבְדֵיהֶם.
only by the Kohanim, by their wives, by their children, and by their slaves.

MISHNAH SEVEN

SH'LOMIM kodoshim kalim. | **שְׁלָמִים** קָדְשִׁים קַלִּים.
The peace-offerings* are offerings of lesser holiness:

sh'chitoson b'chol mokôm bo-azoro, | שְׁחִיטָתָן בְּכָל מָקוֹם בָּעֲזָרָה,
Their slaughter is anywhere in the Courtyard,

v'domon to-un sh'tay matonôs shehayn arba. | וְדָמָן טָעוּן שְׁתֵּי מַתָּנוֹת שֶׁהֵן אַרְבַּע.
and their blood requires two applications that are [equivalent to] four.

הַתּוֹדָה — *The thanksgiving-offering.* This offering is brought by someone who survives serious danger or illness. See *Leviticus* 7:12.

אֵיל נָזִיר — *Ram of a Nazirite,* which is brought when a Nazirite completes the period of abstinence he has accepted upon himself. See *Number* 6:13-21.

קָדְשִׁים קַלִּים — *Offerings of lesser holiness.* Their greater leniency is obvious from a comparison of the laws in this mishnah with those above.

שְׁלָמִים — *Peace-offerings.* The peace-offerings may be eaten for two days and the intervening night, while thanksgiving-offerings (mishnah 6) are eaten for only one day and a night.

V'ne-e-cholin b'chol ho-ir,	וְנֶאֱכָלִין בְּכָל הָעִיר,

They are eaten throughout the City [of Jerusalem]

l'chol odom, b'chol ma-achol,	לְכָל אָדָם, בְּכָל מַאֲכָל,

by anyone, prepared in any manner,

lishnay yomim v'lailo e-chod.	לִשְׁנֵי יָמִים וְלַיְלָה אֶחָד.

for two days and one night [the day of offering, the following night, and the next day].

Hamurom mayhem kayōtzay vohem,	הַמּוּרָם מֵהֶם כַּיּוֹצֵא בָהֶם,

The [priestly] portion separated from them is treated like them,

elo shehamurom ne-e-chol	אֶלָּא שֶׁהַמּוּרָם נֶאֱכָל

except that that separated portion may be eaten

lakōhanim, linshayhem v'livnayhem ulavdayhem.	לַכֹּהֲנִים, לִנְשֵׁיהֶם וְלִבְנֵיהֶם וּלְעַבְדֵיהֶם.

only by the Kohanim, by their wives, by their children and by their slaves.

MISHNAH EIGHT

HAB'CHŌR v'hama-asayr v'hapesach	**הַבְּכוֹר** וְהַמַּעֲשֵׂר וְהַפֶּסַח

The firstborn, the animal tithe and the pesach-offering

kodoshim kalim,	קָדָשִׁים קַלִּים,

are offerings of lesser holiness:

sh'chitoson b'chol mokōm bo-azoro,	שְׁחִיטָתָן בְּכָל מָקוֹם בָּעֲזָרָה,

Their slaughter is anywhere in the Courtyard,

v'domon to-un matono e-chos,	וְדָמָן טָעוּן מַתָּנָה אֶחָת,

and their blood requires a single application,

u-vilvod she-yitayn k'neged ha-y'sōd.	וּבִלְבַד שֶׁיִּתֵּן כְּנֶגֶד הַיְסוֹד.

provided he applies it above the base.

Shino va-achiloson:	שָׁנָה בַאֲכִילָתָן:

They differ in their consumption:

hab'chōr ne-echol lakōhanim,	הַבְּכוֹר נֶאֱכָל לַכֹּהֲנִים,

The firstborn is eaten by Kohanim,

v'hama-asayr l'chol odom.	וְהַמַּעֲשֵׂר לְכָל אָדָם.

and the tithe by anyone;

v'ne-e-cholin b'chol ho-ir,	וְנֶאֱכָלִין בְּכָל הָעִיר,

they are eaten throughout the City [of Jerusalem],

b'chol ma-achol,	בְּכָל מַאֲכָל,

prepared in any manner,

lishnay yomim v'lailo e-chod.	לִשְׁנֵי יָמִים וְלַיְלָה אֶחָד.

for two days and one night.

	ברייתא דר' ישמעאל

Hapesach aynō ne-e-chol elo valailo,   הַפֶּסַח אֵינוּ נֶאֱכָל אֶלָּא בַּלַּיְלָה,
The pesach-offering is not eaten except at night;

v'aynō ne-e-chol elo ad chatzōs,   וְאֵינוּ נֶאֱכָל אֶלָּא עַד חֲצוֹת,
and it is not eaten except until midnight;

v'aynō ne-e-chol elo lim-nuyov,   וְאֵינוּ נֶאֱכָל אֶלָּא לִמְנוּיָיו,
and it is not eaten except by those registered for it;*

v'aynō ne-e-chol elo tzoli.   וְאֵינוּ נֶאֱכָל אֶלָּא צָלִי.
and it is not eaten [in any manner] except roasted.

TALMUD SELECTION

RABI YISHMO-AYL ōmayr: רַבִּי יִשְׁמָעֵאל אוֹמֵר:
Rabbi Yishmael* says:

Bishlōsh esray midōs   בִּשְׁלֹשׁ עֶשְׂרֵה מִדּוֹת
Through thirteen rules

hatōro nid-reshes bo-hayn.   הַתּוֹרָה נִדְרֶשֶׁת בָּהֶן.
is the Torah elucidated:

Mikal vochōmer;   מִקַּל וָחֹמֶר;
(1) Through a conclusion inferred from a lenient law to a strict one, and vice versa;

u-mig'zayro shovo;   וּמִגְּזֵרָה שָׁוָה;
(2) through tradition that similar words in different contexts are meant to clarify one another;

mibinyan ov mikosuv e-chod,   מִבִּנְיַן אָב מִכָּתוּב אֶחָד,
(3) through a general principle derived from one verse,

u-mibinyan ov mish'nay ch'suvim;   וּמִבִּנְיַן אָב מִשְּׁנֵי כְתוּבִים;
and a general principle derived from two verses;

mik'lol u-frot;   מִכְּלָל וּפְרָט;
(4) through a general statement limited by a specification;

הַפֶּסַח ... לִמְנוּיָיו — *The pesach-offering ... by those registered for it.* Those who eat from a particular *pesach*-offering must reserve their share in it before the slaughter (see *Exodus* 12:4).

רַבִּי יִשְׁמָעֵאל / Rabbi Yishmael
As noted above, the Sages prefaced *Shacharis* with selections from Scripture, Mishnah, and Gemara. As used in the Talmud, Mishnah means a listing of laws and Gemara means the logic behind and the application of the laws. As a selection from Gemara, the Sages chose one that lists the thirteen methods used in Scriptural interpretation. It shows us how the very brief statements of the Torah can be mined to reveal a host of principles and teachings. This is why such use of these thirteen rules is called *derash*, which implies investigation; we seek to elicit principles and laws from the sometimes cryptic words of the Torah.

The Torah was composed by God according to the rules of logic and textual analysis contained in this passage. (These rules are also known as hermeneutic principles.) The oral tradition governs the way in which these rules are applied and we have no authority to use them in a manner that contradicts or is not sanctioned by the Oral Law. Thus, when we speak of Rabbinic exegesis, or the way in which the Torah is expounded, we do not speak of the invention of new laws, but of the means by

u-mip'rot uch-lol;	וּמִפְּרָט וּכְלָל;

(5) through a specification broadened by a general statement;

k'lol u-frot uch-lol,	כְּלָל וּפְרָט וּכְלָל,

(6) through a general statement followed by a specification followed, in turn, by another general statement —

i ato don elo k'ayn hap'rot;	אִי אַתָּה דָן אֶלָּא כְּעֵין הַפְּרָט;

you may only infer whatever is similar to the specification;

mik'lol shehu tzorich lif-rot,	מִכְּלָל שֶׁהוּא צָרִיךְ לִפְרָט,

(7) when a general statement requires a specification

u-mip'rot shehu tzorich lich-lol;	וּמִפְּרָט שֶׁהוּא צָרִיךְ לִכְלָל;

or a specification requires a general statement to clarify its meaning;

kol dovor sheho-yo bich-lol	כָּל דָּבָר שֶׁהָיָה בִּכְלָל

(8) anything that was included in a general statement,

v'yotzo min hak'lol l'lamayd,	וְיָצָא מִן הַכְּלָל לְלַמֵּד,

but was then singled out from the general statement in order to teach something,

lō l'lamayd al atzmō yotzo,	לֹא לְלַמֵּד עַל עַצְמוֹ יָצָא,

was not singled out to teach only about itself,

elo l'lamayd al hak'lol kulō yotzo;	אֶלָּא לְלַמֵּד עַל הַכְּלָל כֻּלּוֹ יָצָא;

but to apply its teaching to the entire generality;

kol dovor sheho-yo bich-lol	כָּל דָּבָר שֶׁהָיָה בִּכְלָל

(9) anything that was included in a general statement,

v'yotzo lit-ōn tō-an e-chod	וְיָצָא לִטְעוֹן טוֹעַן אֶחָד
shehu ch'in-yonō,	שֶׁהוּא כְעִנְיָנוֹ,

but was then singled out to discuss a provision similar to the general category,

yotzo l'hokayl v'lō l'hachamir;	יָצָא לְהָקֵל וְלֹא לְהַחֲמִיר;

has been singled out to be more lenient rather than more severe;

kol dovor sheho-yo bich-lol	כָּל דָּבָר שֶׁהָיָה בִּכְלָל

(10) anything that was included in a general statement,

v'yotzo lit-ōn tō-an achayr	וְיָצָא לִטְעוֹן טַעַן אַחֵר

but was then singled out to discuss a provision

shelō ch'inyonō,	שֶׁלֹּא כְעִנְיָנוֹ,

not similar to the general category,

---

which the Oral Law was implied in the Torah itself. It should also be noted that the great majority of the laws had been handed down through the centuries from teacher to student, and they were well known without a need to search for their Scriptural sources. Consequently, in the Talmud era, when the Sages attempted to set forth the Scriptural derivation of such well-known laws, there were disputes concerning the exact Scriptural interpretations.

Unfortunately, even a brief explanation of the Thirteen Rules is not within the purview of this *siddur*.

yotzo l'hokayl ul-hachamir;	יָצָא לְהָקֵל וּלְהַחֲמִיר;

has been singled out both to be more lenient and more severe;

kol dovor sheho-yo bich-lol	כָּל דָּבָר שֶׁהָיָה בִּכְלָל

(11) anything that was included in a general statement,

v'yotzo lidōn badovor hechodosh,	וְיָצָא לִדּוֹן בַּדָּבָר הֶחָדָשׁ,

but was then singled out to be treated as a new case,

i ato yochōl l'hachazirō lich-lolō,	אִי אַתָּה יָכוֹל לְהַחֲזִירוֹ לִכְלָלוֹ,

cannot be returned to its general statement

ad she-yachazirenu hakosuv	עַד שֶׁיַּחֲזִירֶנּוּ הַכָּתוּב
lich-lolō b'fayrush;	לִכְלָלוֹ בְּפֵרוּשׁ;

unless Scripture returns it explicitly to its general statement;

dōvōr halomayd may-inyonō,	דָּבָר הַלָּמֵד מֵעִנְיָנוֹ,

(12) a matter elucidated from its context,

v'dovor halomayd misōfō;	וְדָבָר הַלָּמֵד מִסּוֹפוֹ;

or from the following passage;

v'chayn sh'nay ch'suvim	וְכֵן שְׁנֵי כְתוּבִים
hamach-chishim ze es ze,	הַמַּכְחִישִׁים זֶה אֶת זֶה,

(13) similarly, two passages that contradict one another —

ad she-yovō hakosuv ha-sh'lishi	עַד שֶׁיָּבוֹא הַכָּתוּב הַשְּׁלִישִׁי

until a third passage comes

v'yachri-a baynayhem.	וְיַכְרִיעַ בֵּינֵיהֶם.

and reconciles them.

Y'HI ROTZŌN mil'fonecho,	**יְהִי רָצוֹן** מִלְּפָנֶיךָ,

May it be Your will,

Adōnoy Elōhaynu	יהוה אֱלֹהֵינוּ
Vaylōhay avōsaynu	וֵאלֹהֵי אֲבוֹתֵינוּ,

HASHEM, our God and the God of our forefathers,

sheyibone bays hamikdosh	שֶׁיִּבָּנֶה בֵּית הַמִּקְדָּשׁ
bimhayro v'yomaynu,	בִּמְהֵרָה בְיָמֵינוּ,

that the Holy Temple be rebuilt, speedily in our days,

v'sayn chelkaynu b'sōrosecho.	וְתֵן חֶלְקֵנוּ בְּתוֹרָתֶךָ.

and grant us our share in Your Torah,

V'shom na-avodcho b'yir-o	וְשָׁם נַעֲבָדְךָ בְּיִרְאָה

and may we serve You there with reverence

kimay ōlom uchshonim kadmōniyōs.	כִּימֵי עוֹלָם וּכְשָׁנִים קַדְמוֹנִיּוֹת.

as in days of old and in former years.

THE RABBIS' KADDISH

IN THE PRESENCE OF A *MINYAN*, MOURNERS RECITE THE RABBIS' *KADDISH*.

MOURNER:

YISGADAL v'yiskadash sh'mayh rabo. יִתְגַּדַּל וְיִתְקַדַּשׁ שְׁמֵהּ רַבָּא.
May His great Name grow exalted and sanctified

CONGREGATION RESPONDS: Omayn — אָמֵן

B'ol'mo di v'ro chir-usayh. בְּעָלְמָא דִּי בְרָא כִרְעוּתֵהּ.
in the world that He created as He willed.

V'yamlich malchusayh, וְיַמְלִיךְ מַלְכוּתֵהּ,
May He give reign to His kingship

b'cha-yaychōn uvyōmaychōn בְּחַיֵּיכוֹן וּבְיוֹמֵיכוֹן
in your lifetimes and in your days

uvcha-yay d'chol bays yisro-ayl, וּבְחַיֵּי דְכָל בֵּית יִשְׂרָאֵל,
and in the lifetimes of the entire Family of Israel,

ba-agolo u-vizman koriv. בַּעֲגָלָא וּבִזְמַן קָרִיב.
swiftly and soon.

V'imru: Omayn. וְאִמְרוּ: אָמֵן.
Now respond: Amen.

CONGREGATION RESPONDS:

Omayn. Y'hay sh'mayh rabo m'vorach l'olam ul-ol'may ol'ma-yo. אָמֵן. יְהֵא שְׁמֵהּ רַבָּא מְבָרַךְ לְעָלַם וּלְעָלְמֵי עָלְמַיָּא.
Amen. May His great Name be blessed forever and ever.

MOURNER CONTINUES:

Y'hay sh'mayh rabo m'vorach l'olam ul-ol'may ol'ma-yo, יְהֵא שְׁמֵהּ רַבָּא מְבָרַךְ לְעָלַם וּלְעָלְמֵי עָלְמַיָּא,
May His great Name be blessed forever and ever;

yisborach v'yishtabach v'yispo-ar יִתְבָּרַךְ וְיִשְׁתַּבַּח וְיִתְפָּאַר
blessed, praised, glorified,

v'yisrōmam v'yisnasay וְיִתְרוֹמַם וְיִתְנַשֵּׂא
exalted, extolled,

v'yis-hador v'yis-ale v'yis-halol וְיִתְהַדָּר וְיִתְעַלֶּה וְיִתְהַלָּל
mighty, upraised, and lauded

sh'mayh d'kudsho b'rich hu שְׁמֵהּ דְּקֻדְשָׁא בְּרִיךְ הוּא
be the Name of the Holy One, Blessed is He,

CONGREGATION RESPONDS:

B'rich hu.   *Blessed is He.*   בְּרִיךְ הוּא.

קדיש דרבנן

MOURNER CONTINUES:

°לְעֵלָּא מִן כָּל
°l'aylo min kol
beyond any

FROM ROSH HASHANAH TO YOM KIPPUR SUBSTITUTE:

°לְעֵלָּא לְעֵלָּא מִכָּל
°l'aylo l'aylo mikol
exceedingly beyond any

בִּרְכָתָא וְשִׁירָתָא
birchoso v'shiroso
תֻּשְׁבְּחָתָא וְנֶחֱמָתָא,
tushb'choso v'nechemoso,
blessing and song, praise and consolation

דַּאֲמִירָן בְּעָלְמָא.
da-amiron b'ol'mo.
that are uttered in the world.

וְאִמְרוּ: אָמֵן.
V'imru: Omayn.
Now respond: Amen.

CONGREGATION RESPONDS: Omayn — אָמֵן

עַל יִשְׂרָאֵל וְעַל רַבָּנָן,
Al yisro-el v'al rabo-non
Upon Israel, and upon the teachers,

וְעַל תַּלְמִידֵיהוֹן,
v'al talmiday-hōn,
וְעַל כָּל תַּלְמִידֵי תַלְמִידֵיהוֹן,
v'al kol talmiday salmiday-hōn,
upon their disciples and upon all of their disciples

וְעַל כָּל מָאן דְּעָסְקִין בְּאוֹרַיְתָא,
v'al kol man d'os'kin b'ōrai-so,
and upon all those who engage in the study of Torah,

דִּי בְאַתְרָא הָדֵין,
dee v'as-ro hodayn,
וְדִי בְכָל אֲתַר וַאֲתַר.
v'dee b'chol asar va-asar.
who are here or anywhere else.

יְהֵא לְהוֹן וּלְכוֹן שְׁלָמָא רַבָּא,
Y'hay l'hōn ulchōn sh'lomo rabo,
May they and you have abundant peace,

חִנָּא וְחִסְדָּא וְרַחֲמִין,
chi-no v'chis-do v'racha-min,
grace, kindness, and mercy,

וְחַיִּין אֲרִיכִין, וּמְזוֹנֵי רְוִיחֵי,
v'cha-yin arichin, um-zōnay r'vichay,
long life, ample nourishment,

וּפֻרְקָנָא מִן קֳדָם אֲבוּהוֹן
u-furkono min kodom a-vu-hōn
and salvation from before their Father

דִּי בִשְׁמַיָּא (וְאַרְעָא).
dee vishma-yo (v'ar-o).
Who is in Heaven (and on earth).

וְאִמְרוּ: אָמֵן.
V'imru: Omayn.
Now respond: Amen.

CONGREGATION RESPONDS: Omayn — אָמֵן

יְהֵא שְׁלָמָא רַבָּא מִן שְׁמַיָּא,
Y'hay sh'lomo rabo min sh'mayo
May there be abundant peace from Heaven,

SHACHARIS FOR WEEKDAYS — INTRODUCTORY PSALM

v'cha-yim olaynu v'al kol yisro-ayl. וְחַיִּים עָלֵינוּ וְעַל כָּל יִשְׂרָאֵל.
V'imru: Omayn: וְאִמְרוּ: אָמֵן.
Now respond: Amen.

CONGREGATION RESPONDS: Omayn — אָמֵן

MOURNER BOWS, THEN TAKES THREE STEPS BACK, BOWS LEFT AND SAYS:

Ō-se sholōm bimrōmov עֹשֶׂה שָׁלוֹם בִּמְרוֹמָיו,
He Who makes peace in His heights,

MOURNER BOWS RIGHT AND SAYS:

hu b'racha-mov ya-a-se sholōm olaynu הוּא בְּרַחֲמָיו יַעֲשֶׂה שָׁלוֹם עָלֵינוּ,
may He, in His compassion, make peace upon us,

MOURNER BOWS FORWARD AND SAYS:

v'al kol yisro-ayl. V'imru: Omayn: וְעַל כָּל יִשְׂרָאֵל. וְאִמְרוּ: אָמֵן.
and upon all Israel. Now respond: Amen.

CONGREGATION RESPONDS: Omayn — אָמֵן

MOURNER REMAINS IN PLACE FOR A FEW MOMENTS, THEN TAKES THREE STEPS FORWARD.

■ **Psalm 30:** This psalm of inauguration provides a perspective on the frequent afflictions and frustrations that commonly precede success. Just as the darkest part of night precedes sunrise, so human agony should be accepted as the preparation for success and jubilation.

MIZMŌR SHIR — מִזְמוֹר שִׁיר

chanukas haba-yis l'dovid. חֲנֻכַּת הַבַּיִת לְדָוִד.
A psalm — a song* for the inauguration of the Temple* — by David.

Arōmimcho Adōnoy ki dilisoni, אֲרוֹמִמְךָ יהוה כִּי דִלִּיתָנִי,
I will exalt You, HASHEM, for You have drawn me up

v'lō simachto ōy'vai li. וְלֹא שִׂמַּחְתָּ אֹיְבַי לִי.
and not let my foes rejoice over me.

Adōnoy Elōhoy, יהוה אֱלֹהָי,
shivati aylecho vatirpo-ayni. שִׁוַּעְתִּי אֵלֶיךָ וַתִּרְפָּאֵנִי.
HASHEM, my God, I cried out to You and You healed me.

Adōnoy he-eliso min sh'ōl nafshi, יהוה הֶעֱלִיתָ מִן שְׁאוֹל נַפְשִׁי,
HASHEM, You have raised my soul from the lower world,

chi-yisani mi-yordi vōr. חִיִּיתַנִי מִיָּרְדִי בוֹר.
You have preserved me from my descent to the Pit.

מִזְמוֹר שִׁיר — *A psalm, a song.* Psalm 30 was sung to inaugurate the morning Temple service, and thus is an appropriate prelude to the prayers that take the place of that service. It is also a fitting conclusion to the Scriptural and Talmudical passages regarding the offerings.

חֲנֻכַּת הַבַּיִת — *The inauguration of the Temple.* How is this psalm, which deals only with David's illness, related to the dedication of the Temple? The Temple's purpose is best achieved when each individual Jew recognizes God's presence and help in his personal life. Accordingly, by never

	מזמור שיר

| Zam'ru Ladōnoy chasidov, | זַמְּרוּ לַיהוה חֲסִידָיו, |
| v'hōdu l'zaycher kodshō. | וְהוֹדוּ לְזֵכֶר קָדְשׁוֹ. |

Make music to HASHEM, *His devout ones, and give thanks to His Holy Name.*

| Ki rega b'apō, cha-yim bir-tzōnō, | כִּי רֶגַע בְּאַפּוֹ, חַיִּים בִּרְצוֹנוֹ, |

For His anger endures but a moment; life results from His favor.

| bo-erev yolin bechi, v'labōker rino. | בָּעֶרֶב יָלִין בֶּכִי וְלַבֹּקֶר רִנָּה. |

In the evening one lies down weeping, but with dawn — a cry of joy!

| Va-ani omarti v'shalvi, | וַאֲנִי אָמַרְתִּי בְשַׁלְוִי, |
| bal emōt l'ōlom. | בַּל אֶמּוֹט לְעוֹלָם. |

I had said in my serenity, "I will never falter."

| Adōnoy birtzōn'cho | יהוה בִּרְצוֹנְךָ |
| he-emadto l'har'ri ōz, | הֶעֱמַדְתָּה לְהַרְרִי עֹז, |

But, HASHEM, *through Your favor You supported my greatness with might;*

| histarto fonecho ho-yisi nivhol. | הִסְתַּרְתָּ פָנֶיךָ הָיִיתִי נִבְהָל. |

should You but conceal Your face, I would be confounded.

| Aylecho Adōnoy ekro, | אֵלֶיךָ יהוה אֶקְרָא, |
| v'el Adōnoy eschanon. | וְאֶל אֲדֹנָי אֶתְחַנָּן. |

To You, HASHEM, *I would call and to my Lord I would appeal.*

| Mah betza b'domi, | מַה בֶּצַע בְּדָמִי, |
| b'rid-ti el shochas, | בְּרִדְתִּי אֶל שָׁחַת, |

What gain is there in my death, when I descend to the Pit?

| ha-yōd'cho ofor, ha-yagid amitecho. | הֲיוֹדְךָ עָפָר, הֲיַגִּיד אֲמִתֶּךָ. |

Will the dust acknowledge You? Will it declare Your truth?

| Sh'ma Adōnoy v'chonayni, | שְׁמַע יהוה וְחָנֵּנִי, |
| Adōnoy he-yay ōzayr li. | יהוה הֱיֵה עֹזֵר לִי. |

Hear, HASHEM, *and favor me;* HASHEM, *be my Helper!*

| ❖ Hofachto misp'di l'mochōl li, | הָפַכְתָּ מִסְפְּדִי לְמָחוֹל לִי, |

You have changed for me my lament into dancing;

| pitachto saki, vat'az'rayni simcho. | פִּתַּחְתָּ שַׂקִּי, וַתְּאַזְּרֵנִי שִׂמְחָה. |

You undid my sackcloth and girded me with gladness.

| L'ma-an y'zamercho chovōd | לְמַעַן יְזַמֶּרְךָ כָבוֹד |
| v'lō yidōm, | וְלֹא יִדֹּם, |

So that my soul might make music to You and not be stilled,

| Adōnoy Elōhai l'ōlom ōdeko. | יהוה אֱלֹהַי לְעוֹלָם אוֹדֶךָּ. |

HASHEM, *my God, forever will I thank You.*

---

losing his faith in God, and by ultimately being vindicated through God's deliverance, David is the perfect embodiment of the Temple's role in the life of the nation.

⊰{ MOURNER'S KADDISH }⊱

■ Man was created to serve God and sanctify His Name. This service and sanctification is actualized by living one's life in accordance with the laws and customs of Judaism. This includes both those commandments directed toward God and those that govern our relationship to man.

When an individual passes on, there is a void in this world which is caused by the loss of the sanctification that the deceased had contributed. Therefore, the surviving son (or other relative) addresses this void by announcing through the *Kaddish*, "May the great Name of God continue to be holy." There is no specific reference to death in the *Kaddish*, for it is a message of life. And life that continues is to be sanctified.

The recitation of the *Kaddish* is a great merit for the soul of the deceased. *Kaddish* is recited for eleven months following the death, and is also recited on the *Yahrzeit* (anniversary of the passing).

IN THE PRESENCE OF A *MINYAN*, MOURNERS RECITE THE MOURNER'S *KADDISH*.

MOURNER:

YISGADAL v'yiskadash sh'mayh rabo.   יִתְגַּדַּל וְיִתְקַדַּשׁ שְׁמֵהּ רַבָּא.

May His great Name grow exalted and sanctified

CONGREGATION RESPONDS: Omayn — אָמֵן

B'ol'mo di v'ro chir-usayh.   בְּעָלְמָא דִּי בְרָא כִרְעוּתֵהּ.

in the world that He created as He willed.

V'yamlich malchusayh,   וְיַמְלִיךְ מַלְכוּתֵהּ,

May He give reign to His kingship

b'cha-yaychōn uvyōmaychōn   בְּחַיֵּיכוֹן וּבְיוֹמֵיכוֹן

in your lifetimes and in your days

uvcha-yay d'chol bays yisro-ayl,   וּבְחַיֵּי דְכָל בֵּית יִשְׂרָאֵל,

and in the lifetimes of the entire Family of Israel,

ba-agolo u-vizman koriv.   בַּעֲגָלָא וּבִזְמַן קָרִיב.

swiftly and soon.

V'imru: Omayn.   וְאִמְרוּ: אָמֵן.

Now respond: Amen.

CONGREGATION RESPONDS:

Omayn. Y'hay sh'mayh rabo m'vorach l'olam ul-ol'may ol'ma-yo.   אָמֵן. יְהֵא שְׁמֵהּ רַבָּא מְבָרַךְ לְעָלַם וּלְעָלְמֵי עָלְמַיָּא.

Amen. May His great Name be blessed forever and ever.

MOURNER CONTINUES:

Y'hay sh'mayh rabo m'vorach l'olam ul-ol'may ol'ma-yo,   יְהֵא שְׁמֵהּ רַבָּא מְבָרַךְ לְעָלַם וּלְעָלְמֵי עָלְמַיָּא,

May His great Name be blessed forever and ever;

yisborach v'yishtabach v'yispo-ar v'yisrōmam v'yisnasay   יִתְבָּרַךְ וְיִשְׁתַּבַּח וְיִתְפָּאַר וְיִתְרוֹמַם וְיִתְנַשֵּׂא

blessed, praised, glorified, exalted, extolled,

v'yis-hador v'yis-ale v'yis-halol	וְיִתְהַדָּר וְיִתְעַלֶּה וְיִתְהַלָּל
mighty, upraised, and lauded	
sh'mayh d'kudsho b'rich hu	שְׁמֵהּ דְּקֻדְשָׁא בְּרִיךְ הוּא
be the Name of the Holy One, Blessed is He,	

CONGREGATION RESPONDS:

B'rich hu. — *Blessed is He.* — בְּרִיךְ הוּא.

MOURNER CONTINUES:

°l'aylo min kol — °לְעֵלָּא מִן כָּל
beyond any

FROM ROSH HASHANAH TO YOM KIPPUR SUBSTITUTE:

°l'aylo l'aylo mikol — °לְעֵלָּא לְעֵלָּא מִכָּל
exceedingly beyond any

birchoso v'shiroso	בִּרְכָתָא וְשִׁירָתָא
blessing and song,	
tushb'choso v'nechemoso,	תֻּשְׁבְּחָתָא וְנֶחֱמָתָא,
praise and consolation	
da-amiron b'ol'mo.	דַּאֲמִירָן בְּעָלְמָא.
that are uttered in the world.	
V'imru: Omayn.	וְאִמְרוּ: אָמֵן.
Now respond: Amen.	

CONGREGATION RESPONDS: Omayn — אָמֵן

Y'hay sh'lomo rabo min sh'mayo	יְהֵא שְׁלָמָא רַבָּא מִן שְׁמַיָּא,
May there be abundant peace from Heaven,	
v'cha-yim olaynu v'al kol yisro-ayl.	וְחַיִּים עָלֵינוּ וְעַל כָּל יִשְׂרָאֵל.
and life, upon us and upon all Israel.	
V'imru: Omayn:	וְאִמְרוּ: אָמֵן.
Now respond: Amen.	

CONGREGATION RESPONDS: Omayn — אָמֵן

MOURNER BOW, THEN TAKES THREE STEPS BACK, BOWS LEFT AND SAYS:

Ō-se sholōm bimrōmov — עֹשֶׂה שָׁלוֹם בִּמְרוֹמָיו,
He Who makes peace in His heights,

MOURNER BOWS RIGHT AND SAYS:

hu ya-a-se sholōm olaynu — הוּא יַעֲשֶׂה שָׁלוֹם עָלֵינוּ,
may He make peace upon us,

MOURNER BOWS FORWARD AND SAYS:

v'al kol yisro-ayl. V'imru: Omayn. — וְעַל כָּל יִשְׂרָאֵל. וְאִמְרוּ: אָמֵן.
and upon all Israel. Now respond: Amen.

CONGREGATION RESPONDS: Omayn — אָמֵן

MOURNER REMAINS IN PLACE FOR A FEW MOMENTS, THEN TAKES THREE STEPS FORWARD.

⊰ PESUKEI D'ZIMRAH — פסוקי דזמרה ⊱

SOME RECITE THIS STATEMENT OF INTENT BEFORE *PESUKEI D'ZIMRAH*:

Harayni m'zamayn es pi / הֲרֵינִי מְזַמֵּן אֶת פִּי
I now prepare my mouth

l'hōdōs ulhalayl ulshabay-ach es bor'i. / לְהוֹדוֹת וּלְהַלֵּל וּלְשַׁבֵּחַ אֶת בּוֹרְאִי
to thank, to laud and to praise my Creator.

SOME INCLUDE THIS KABBALISTIC STATMENT:

L'shaym yichud kudsho brich hu ush-chintayh / לְשֵׁם יִחוּד קֻדְשָׁא בְּרִיךְ הוּא וּשְׁכִינְתֵּיהּ
For the sake of the Unification of the Holy One, Blessed is He, and His Presence,

al y'day hahu tomir v'ne-elam, / עַל יְדֵי הַהוּא טָמִיר וְנֶעְלָם,
through Him Who is hidden and inscrutable —

b'shaym kol yisro-ayl. / בְּשֵׁם כָּל יִשְׂרָאֵל.
[I pray] in the name of all Israel.

CONVERSATION IS FORBIDDEN FROM THIS POINT UNTIL AFTER *SHEMONEH ESREI*
(EXCEPT FOR CERTAIN PRAYER RESPONSES).

■ This blessing consists of two separate sections. The first is an introductory series of thanksgiving sentences focusing on Hashem as the Creator Who manifests Himself through His beneficence to His creations. The second section begins with *Boruch ato*, and is the blessing whereby we extol Hashem for accepting human praise in general, and specifically the praises that follow this blessing.

BORUCH SHE-OMAR / בָּרוּךְ שֶׁאָמַר

v'ho-yo ho-ōlom, / וְהָיָה הָעוֹלָם,
Blessed is He Who spoke,* and the world came into being;*

boruch hu, / בָּרוּךְ הוּא.
blessed is He.

Boruch ō-se v'rayshis, / בָּרוּךְ עֹשֶׂה בְרֵאשִׁית,
Blessed is He Who maintains Creation;

boruch ōmayr v'ō-se, / בָּרוּךְ אוֹמֵר וְעֹשֶׂה,
blessed is He Who speaks and does;*

⊰• **Pesukei D'zimrah/Verses of Praise**

The Sages taught that one should set forth the praises of God before making requests of Him (*Berachos* 32a). In this section of *Shacharis*, we concentrate on God's revelation in nature and history — on how His glory can be seen in Creation and in the unfolding of events.

Because it is a separate section of *Shacharis* with a purpose all its own, *Pesukei D'zimrah* is introduced with a blessing — *Baruch She-amar* — and concluded with a blessing —

Yishtabach (p. 159).

בָּרוּךְ שֶׁאָמַר — *Blessed is He Who spoke.* There is an ancient tradition that this prayer was transcribed approximately 2,400 years ago from a script that fell from heaven.

שֶׁאָמַר וְהָיָה הָעוֹלָם — *Who spoke, and the world came into being.* God is the Creator Who brought all of Creation into being and maintains it with no more than His word.

אוֹמֵר וְעֹשֶׂה — *Who speaks and does.* God brings His promise into being even when people no

שחרית לחול / 128 פסוקי דזמרה

בָּרוּךְ גּוֹזֵר וּמְקַיֵּם,
boruch gōzayr umka-yaym,
blessed is He Who decrees and fulfills;

בָּרוּךְ מְרַחֵם עַל הָאָרֶץ,
boruch m'rachaym al ho-oretz,
blessed is He Who has mercy on the earth;*

בָּרוּךְ מְרַחֵם עַל הַבְּרִיּוֹת,
boruch m'rachaym al hab'riyōs,
blessed is He Who has mercy on the creatures;

בָּרוּךְ מְשַׁלֵּם שָׂכָר טוֹב לִירֵאָיו,
boruch m'shalaym sochor tōv liray-ov,
blessed is He Who gives goodly reward to those who fear Him;*

בָּרוּךְ חַי לָעַד וְקַיָּם לָנֶצַח,
boruch chai lo-ad v'ka-yom lonetzach,
blessed is He Who lives forever and endures to eternity;*

בָּרוּךְ פּוֹדֶה וּמַצִּיל,
boruch pōde u-matzil,
blessed is He Who redeems and rescues;*

בָּרוּךְ שְׁמוֹ.
boruch sh'mō.
blessed is His Name!*

בָּרוּךְ אַתָּה יהוה אֱלֹהֵינוּ מֶלֶךְ הָעוֹלָם,
Boruch ato Adōnoy Elōhaynu melech ho-ōlom,
Blessed are You, Hashem, *our God, King of the universe,*

הָאֵל הָאָב הָרַחֲמָן
ho-Ayl ho-ov horachamon
the God, the merciful Father,*

הַמְהֻלָּל בְּפֶה עַמּוֹ,
ham'hulol b'fe amō,
Who is lauded by the mouth of His people,

מְשֻׁבָּח וּמְפֹאָר בִּלְשׁוֹן חֲסִידָיו וַעֲבָדָיו,
m'shuboch umfō-or bilshōn chasidov va-avodov,
praised and glorified by the tongue of His devout ones and His servants

וּבְשִׁירֵי דָוִד עַבְדֶּךָ.
uvshiray dovid avdecho.
and through the psalms of David Your servant.

---

longer seem to deserve His generosity. Conversely, "He decrees and fulfills"; when He warns of punishment, the sinner cannot escape unless he repents sincerely.

מְרַחֵם עַל הָאָרֶץ — *Who has mercy on the earth.* God has compassion on the earth and all its creatures, human or otherwise.

מְשַׁלֵּם שָׂכָר טוֹב לִירֵאָיו — *Who gives goodly reward to those who fear Him.* His reward may not be dispensed in This World, but it will surely be dispensed in the World to Come. Whatever the case, no good deed goes unrewarded.

חַי לָעַד וְקַיָּם לָנֶצַח — *Who lives forever and endures to eternity.* Not only is God's existence infinite and eternal, but He continues to involve Himself in the affairs of the universe.

פּוֹדֶה וּמַצִּיל — *Who redeems* people from moral decline *and rescues* them from physical danger.

בָּרוּךְ שְׁמוֹ — *Blessed is His Name!* The Name by which we call God can in no way express His true essence. Nevertheless, in His kindness to man, He allows us to glimpse some of His properties and express them in a Name.

הָאֵל הָאָב הָרַחֲמָן — *The God, the merciful Father.* We acknowledge that He is the all-powerful God, yet is filled with mercy, like a father whose behavior is a constant expression of mercy, even when he must be harsh.

129 / SHACHARIS FOR WEEKDAYS — PESUKEI D'ZIMRAH

N'halelcho Adōnoy Elōhaynu — נְהַלֶּלְךָ יהוה אֱלֹהֵינוּ,
We shall laud You, HASHEM, our God,

bish-vochōs u-viz-mirōs. — בִּשְׁבָחוֹת וּבִזְמִרוֹת.
with praises and songs;

n'gadelcho un-shabaychacho — נְגַדֶּלְךָ וּנְשַׁבֵּחֲךָ
we shall exalt You, we shall praise You,

unfo-ercho v'nazkir shimcho — וּנְפָאֶרְךָ וְנַזְכִּיר שִׁמְךָ
we shall glorify You, we shall mention Your Name

v'namlich'cho, malkaynu Elōhaynu. — וְנַמְלִיכְךָ, מַלְכֵּנוּ אֱלֹהֵינוּ.
and we shall proclaim Your reign, our King, our God.

❖ Yochid, chay ho-ōlomim, — ❖ יָחִיד, חֵי הָעוֹלָמִים,
O Unique One, Life-giver of the worlds,

melech m'shuboch umfō-or — מֶלֶךְ מְשֻׁבָּח וּמְפֹאָר
a-day ad sh'mō hagodōl. — עֲדֵי עַד שְׁמוֹ הַגָּדוֹל.
King Whose great Name is eternally praised and glorified.

Boruch ato Adōnoy, — בָּרוּךְ אַתָּה יהוה,
Blessed are You, HASHEM,

melech m'hulol batishbochōs. — מֶלֶךְ מְהֻלָּל בַּתִּשְׁבָּחוֹת.
the King Who is lauded with praises.

CONGREGATION RESPONDS: Omayn — אָמֵן

■ The following prayer comprises three parts: In the first, we praise Hashem for His guiding the course of history, whereby we realize that seemingly unrelated events all lead to His ultimate plan for mankind: man living by His Torah. In the second part, beginning *Shiru Ladōnoy*, we excitedly anticipate the time when all nations will acknowledge Hashem. And in the third part, beginning *V'hu rachum*, we plead for Hashem's mercy to actualize our aspirations.

HŌDU Ladōnoy kir-u vishmō, — הוֹדוּ לַיהוה קִרְאוּ בִשְׁמוֹ,
Give thanks to HASHEM,* declare His Name,

hōdi-u vo-amim alilōsov. — הוֹדִיעוּ בָעַמִּים עֲלִילוֹתָיו.
make His acts known among the peoples.

Shiru lō, zam'ru lō, — שִׁירוּ לוֹ, זַמְּרוּ לוֹ,
Sing to Him, make music to Him,

sichu b'chol nifl'ōsov. — שִׂיחוּ בְּכָל נִפְלְאוֹתָיו.
speak of all His wonders.

הוֹדוּ לַה׳ — *Give thanks to* HASHEM. The first twenty-nine verses of this lengthy prayer form a jubilant song that David intended to be sung when the Holy Ark was brought to Jerusalem. In its entirety this song calls upon Israel to maintain its faith in God and its confidence that He will bring it salvation from exile and persecution.

His-hal'lu b'shaym kodshō,	הִתְהַלְלוּ בְּשֵׁם קָדְשׁוֹ,

Glory in His holy Name,

yismach layv m'vakshay Adōnoy.	יִשְׂמַח לֵב מְבַקְשֵׁי יהוה.

*be glad of heart, you who seek H*ASHEM.

Dirshu Adōnoy v'uzō,	דִּרְשׁוּ יהוה וְעֻזּוֹ,

*Search out H*ASHEM *and His might,*

bak'shu fonov tomid.	בַּקְּשׁוּ פָנָיו תָּמִיד.

seek His Presence always.

Zich-ru nifl'ōsov asher oso,	זִכְרוּ נִפְלְאֹתָיו אֲשֶׁר עָשָׂה,

Remember His wonders that He wrought,

mōfsov u-mishp'tay fihu.	מֹפְתָיו וּמִשְׁפְּטֵי פִיהוּ.

His marvels and the judgments of His mouth.

Zera yisro-ayl avdō,	זֶרַע יִשְׂרָאֵל עַבְדּוֹ,

O seed of Israel, His servant,

b'nay ya-akōv b'chirov.	בְּנֵי יַעֲקֹב בְּחִירָיו.

O children of Jacob, His chosen ones —

Hu Adōnoy Elōhaynu,	הוּא יהוה אֱלֹהֵינוּ,

*He is H*ASHEM, *our God,*

b'chol ho-oretz mishpotov.	בְּכָל הָאָרֶץ מִשְׁפָּטָיו.

over all the earth are His judgments.

Zichru l'ōlom b'risō,	זִכְרוּ לְעוֹלָם בְּרִיתוֹ,

Remember His covenant forever —

dovor tzivo l'elef dōr.	דָּבָר צִוָּה לְאֶלֶף דּוֹר.

the word He commanded for a thousand generations —

Asher koras es avrohom,	אֲשֶׁר כָּרַת אֶת אַבְרָהָם,

that He made with Abraham

ushvu-osō l'yitzchok.	וּשְׁבוּעָתוֹ לְיִצְחָק.

and His vow to Isaac.

Va-ya-amidehō l'ya-akōv l'chōk,	וַיַּעֲמִידֶהָ לְיַעֲקֹב לְחֹק,

Then He established it for Jacob as a statute,

l'yisro-ayl b'ris ōlom.	לְיִשְׂרָאֵל בְּרִית עוֹלָם.

for Israel as an everlasting covenant,

Laymōr, l'cho etayn eretz k'no-an,	לֵאמֹר, לְךָ אֶתֵּן אֶרֶץ כְּנָעַן,

saying, "To you I shall give the Land of Canaan,

chevel nachalaschem.	חֶבֶל נַחֲלַתְכֶם.

the lot of your heritage."

Bih-yōs'chem m'say mispor,	בִּהְיוֹתְכֶם מְתֵי מִסְפָּר,

When you were but few in number,

kim-at v'gorim boh.	כִּמְעַט וְגָרִים בָּהּ.
hardly dwelling there,	
Va-yis-hal'chu migōy el gōy,	וַיִּתְהַלְּכוּ מִגּוֹי אֶל גּוֹי,
and they wandered from nation to nation,	
u-mimamlocho el am achayr.	וּמִמַּמְלָכָה אֶל עַם אַחֵר.
from one kingdom to another people.	
Lō hini-ach l'ish l'oshkom,	לֹא הִנִּיחַ לְאִישׁ לְעָשְׁקָם,
He let no man rob them,	
va-yōchach alayhem m'lochim.	וַיּוֹכַח עֲלֵיהֶם מְלָכִים.
and He rebuked kings for their sake.	
Al tig'u bim-shichoy,	אַל תִּגְּעוּ בִמְשִׁיחָי,
"Dare not touch My anointed ones,	
u-vinvi-ai al toray-u.	וּבִנְבִיאַי אַל תָּרֵעוּ.
and to My prophets do no harm."	
Shiru Ladōnoy kol ho-oretz,	שִׁירוּ לַיהוה כָּל הָאָרֶץ,
Sing to H*ashem*, *everyone on earth,*	
bas'ru mi-yōm el yōm y'shu-osō.	בַּשְּׂרוּ מִיּוֹם אֶל יוֹם יְשׁוּעָתוֹ.
announce His salvation daily.	
Sap'ru vagōyim es k'vōdō,	סַפְּרוּ בַגּוֹיִם אֶת כְּבוֹדוֹ,
Relate His glory among the nations,	
b'chol ho-amim nifl'ōsov.	בְּכָל הָעַמִּים נִפְלְאוֹתָיו.
among all the peoples His wonders.	
Ki godōl Adōnoy umhulol m'ōd,	כִּי גָדוֹל יהוה וּמְהֻלָּל מְאֹד,
That H*ashem* *is great and exceedingly lauded,*	
v'nōro hu al kol elōhim.	וְנוֹרָא הוּא עַל כָּל אֱלֹהִים.
and awesome is He above all heavenly powers.	
Ki kol elōhay ho-amim elilim.	❖ כִּי כָּל אֱלֹהֵי הָעַמִּים אֱלִילִים,
For all the gods of the peoples are nothings —	
(PAUSE BRIEFLY)	
Vadōnoy shoma-yim oso.	וַיהוה שָׁמַיִם עָשָׂה.
but H*ashem* *made heaven!*	
Hōd v'hodor l'fonov,	הוֹד וְהָדָר לְפָנָיו,
Glory and majesty are before Him,	
ōz v'chedvo bimkōmō.	עֹז וְחֶדְוָה בִּמְקֹמוֹ.
might and delight are in His place.	
Hovu Ladōnoy mishp'chōs amim,	הָבוּ לַיהוה מִשְׁפְּחוֹת עַמִּים,
Render to H*ashem*, *O families of the peoples,*	

hovu Ladōnoy kovōd vo-ōz.	הָבוּ לַיהוה כָּבוֹד וָעֹז.

render to HASHEM honor and might.

Hovu Ladōnoy k'vōd sh'mō,	הָבוּ לַיהוה כְּבוֹד שְׁמוֹ,

Render to HASHEM honor worthy of His Name,

s'u mincho u-vō-u l'fonov,	שְׂאוּ מִנְחָה וּבֹאוּ לְפָנָיו,

take an offering and come before Him,

hishtachavu Ladōnoy b'hadras kōdesh.	הִשְׁתַּחֲווּ לַיהוה בְּהַדְרַת קֹדֶשׁ.

prostrate yourselves before HASHEM in His intensely holy place.

Chilu mil'fonov kol ho-oretz,	חִילוּ מִלְּפָנָיו כָּל הָאָרֶץ,

Tremble before Him, everyone on earth,

af tikōn tayvayl bal timōt.	אַף תִּכּוֹן תֵּבֵל בַּל תִּמּוֹט.

indeed, the world is fixed so that it cannot falter.

Yism'chu ha-shoma-yim v'sogayl ho-oretz,	יִשְׂמְחוּ הַשָּׁמַיִם וְתָגֵל הָאָרֶץ,

The heavens will be glad and the earth will rejoice

v'yōm'ru vagōyim Adōnoy moloch.	וְיֹאמְרוּ בַגּוֹיִם, יהוה מָלָךְ.

and say among the nations, "HASHEM has reigned!"

Yir-am ha-yom umlō-ō,	יִרְעַם הַיָּם וּמְלוֹאוֹ,

The sea and its fullness will roar,

ya-alōtz hasode v'chol asher bō.	יַעֲלֹץ הַשָּׂדֶה וְכָל אֲשֶׁר בּוֹ.

the field and everything in it will exult.

Oz y'ran'nu atzay ha-yo-ar,	אָז יְרַנְּנוּ עֲצֵי הַיָּעַר,

Then the trees of the forest will sing with joy

milifnay Adōnoy,	מִלִּפְנֵי יהוה,

before HASHEM,

ki vo lishpōt es ho-oretz.	כִּי בָא לִשְׁפֹּט אֶת הָאָרֶץ.

for He will have arrived to judge the earth.

Hōdu Ladōnoy ki tōv,	הוֹדוּ לַיהוה כִּי טוֹב,

Give thanks to HASHEM, for He is good,

ki l'ōlom chasdō.	כִּי לְעוֹלָם חַסְדּוֹ.

for His kindness endures forever.

V'imru hōshi-aynu Elōhay yish-aynu,	וְאִמְרוּ הוֹשִׁיעֵנוּ אֱלֹהֵי יִשְׁעֵנוּ,

And say, "Save us, O God of our salvation,

v'kab'tzaynu v'hatzilaynu min hagōyim,	וְקַבְּצֵנוּ וְהַצִּילֵנוּ מִן הַגּוֹיִם,

gather us and rescue us from the nations,

PESUKEI D'ZIMRAH

l'hōdōs l'shaym kodshecho,   לְהֹדוֹת לְשֵׁם קָדְשֶׁךָ,
to thank Your Holy Name

l'hishtabay-ach bis-hilosecho.   לְהִשְׁתַּבֵּחַ בִּתְהִלָּתֶךָ.
and to glory in Your praise!"

Boruch Adōnoy Elōhay yisro-ayl   בָּרוּךְ יהוה אֱלֹהֵי יִשְׂרָאֵל
Blessed is HASHEM, the God of Israel,

min ho-ōlom v'ad ho-ōlom,   מִן הָעוֹלָם וְעַד הָעֹלָם,
from this world to the World to Come —

va-yōm'ru chol ho-om,   וַיֹּאמְרוּ כָל הָעָם,
and let the entire people say,

omayn, v'halayl Ladōnoy.   אָמֵן, וְהַלֵּל לַיהוה.
"Amen and praise to God!"

❖ Rōm'mu Adōnoy Elōhaynu   ❖ רוֹמְמוּ יהוה אֱלֹהֵינוּ
Exalt HASHEM, our God,

v'hishta-chavu lahadōm raglov,   וְהִשְׁתַּחֲווּ לַהֲדֹם רַגְלָיו,
and bow at His footstool;

kodōsh hu.   קָדוֹשׁ הוּא.
He is holy!

Rōm'mu Adōnoy Elōhaynu   רוֹמְמוּ יהוה אֱלֹהֵינוּ
Exalt HASHEM, our God,

v'hishta-chavu l'har kodshō,   וְהִשְׁתַּחֲווּ לְהַר קָדְשׁוֹ,
and bow at His holy mountain;

ki kodōsh Adōnoy Elōhaynu.   כִּי קָדוֹשׁ יהוה אֱלֹהֵינוּ.
for holy is HASHEM, our God.

V'hu rachum y'chapayr ovōn   וְהוּא רַחוּם יְכַפֵּר עָוֹן
He, the Merciful One, is forgiving of iniquity

v'lō yashchis,   וְלֹא יַשְׁחִית,
and does not destroy;

v'hirbo l'hoshiv apō,   וְהִרְבָּה לְהָשִׁיב אַפּוֹ,
frequently, He withdraws His anger,

v'lō yo-ir kol chamosō.   וְלֹא יָעִיר כָּל חֲמָתוֹ.
not arousing His entire rage.

Ato Adōnoy,   אַתָּה יהוה,

lō sichlo rachamecho mimeni,   לֹא תִכְלָא רַחֲמֶיךָ מִמֶּנִּי,
You, HASHEM — withhold not Your mercy from me;

chasd'cho va-amit'cho tomid yitz'runi.   חַסְדְּךָ וַאֲמִתְּךָ תָּמִיד יִצְּרוּנִי.
may Your kindness and Your truth always protect me.

שחרית לחול / 134   פסוקי דזמרה

Z'chōr rachamecho Adōnoy vachasodecho,	זְכֹר רַחֲמֶיךָ יהוה וַחֲסָדֶיךָ,

Remember Your mercies, H<small>ASHEM</small>, and Your kindnesses,

ki may-ōlom haymo.	כִּי מֵעוֹלָם הֵמָּה.

for they are from the beginning of the world.

T'nu ōz Laylōhim,	תְּנוּ עֹז לֵאלֹהִים,

Render might to God,

al yisro-ayl ga-avosō,	עַל יִשְׂרָאֵל גַּאֲוָתוֹ,

Whose majesty hovers over Israel

v'uzō bash'chokim.	וְעֻזּוֹ בַּשְּׁחָקִים.

and Whose might is in the clouds.

Nōro Elōhim mimikdoshecho,	נוֹרָא אֱלֹהִים מִמִּקְדָּשֶׁיךָ,

You are awesome, O God, from Your Sanctuaries,

Ayl yisro-ayl	אֵל יִשְׂרָאֵל

O God of Israel —

hu nōsayn ōz v'sa-atzumōs lo-om,	הוּא נֹתֵן עֹז וְתַעֲצֻמוֹת לָעָם,

it is He Who grants might and power to the people,

boruch Elōhim.	בָּרוּךְ אֱלֹהִים.

blessed is God.

Ayl n'komōs Adōnoy,	אֵל נְקָמוֹת יהוה,

O God of vengeance, H<small>ASHEM</small>,

Ayl n'komōs hōfi-a.	אֵל נְקָמוֹת הוֹפִיעַ.

O God of vengeance, appear!

Hinosay shōfayt ho-oretz,	הִנָּשֵׂא שֹׁפֵט הָאָרֶץ,

Arise, O Judge of the earth,

hoshayv g'mul al gay-im.	הָשֵׁב גְּמוּל עַל גֵּאִים.

render recompense to the haughty.

Ladōnoy hai-shu-o,	לַיהוה הַיְשׁוּעָה,

Salvation is H<small>ASHEM</small>'s,

al am'cho virchosecho selo.	עַל עַמְּךָ בִרְכָתֶךָ סֶּלָה.

upon Your people is Your blessing, Selah.

❖ Adōnoy tz'vo-ōs imonu,	❖ יהוה צְבָאוֹת עִמָּנוּ,

H<small>ASHEM</small>, Master of Legions, is with us,

misgov lonu, Elōhay ya-akōv selo.	מִשְׂגָּב לָנוּ אֱלֹהֵי יַעֲקֹב סֶלָה.

a stronghold for us is the God of Jacob, Selah.

Adōnoy tz'vo-ōs,	יהוה צְבָאוֹת,

H<small>ASHEM</small>, Master of Legions,

ashray odom bōtay-ach boch.	אַשְׁרֵי אָדָם בֹּטֵחַ בָּךְ.

praiseworthy is the person who trusts in You.

Adōnoy hōshi-o,	יהוה הוֹשִׁיעָה,

HASHEM, save!

hamelech ya-anaynu v'yōm kor-aynu.	הַמֶּלֶךְ יַעֲנֵנוּ בְיוֹם קָרְאֵנוּ.

May the King answer us on the day we call.

Hōshi-o es amecho,	הוֹשִׁיעָה אֶת עַמֶּךָ,
u-voraych es nachalosecho,	וּבָרֵךְ אֶת נַחֲלָתֶךָ,

Save Your people and bless Your heritage,

ur-aym v'nas'aym ad ho-ōlom.	וּרְעֵם וְנַשְּׂאֵם עַד הָעוֹלָם.

tend them and elevate them forever.

Nafshaynu chik'so Ladōnoy,	נַפְשֵׁנוּ חִכְּתָה לַיהוה,

Our soul longed for HASHEM —

ezraynu u-moginaynu hu.	עֶזְרֵנוּ וּמָגִנֵּנוּ הוּא.

our help and our shield is He.

Ki vō yismach libaynu,	כִּי בוֹ יִשְׂמַח לִבֵּנוּ,

For in Him will our hearts be glad,

ki v'shaym kodshō votochnu.	כִּי בְשֵׁם קָדְשׁוֹ בָטָחְנוּ.

for in His Holy Name we trusted.

Y'hi chasd'cho Adōnoy olaynu,	יְהִי חַסְדְּךָ יהוה עָלֵינוּ,

May Your kindness, HASHEM, be upon us,

ka-asher yi-chalnu loch.	כַּאֲשֶׁר יִחַלְנוּ לָךְ.

just as we awaited You.

Har-aynu Adōnoy chasdecho,	הַרְאֵנוּ יהוה חַסְדֶּךָ,

Show us Your kindness, HASHEM,

v'yesh-acho titayn lonu.	וְיֶשְׁעֲךָ תִּתֶּן לָנוּ.

and grant us Your salvation.

Kumo ez-roso lonu,	קוּמָה עֶזְרָתָה לָּנוּ,

Arise — assist us,

ufdaynu l'ma-an chasdecho.	וּפְדֵנוּ לְמַעַן חַסְדֶּךָ.

and redeem us by virtue of Your kindness.

Onōchi Adōnoy Elōhecho,	אָנֹכִי יהוה אֱלֹהֶיךָ

I am HASHEM, your God,

hama-alcho may-eretz mitzroyim,	הַמַּעַלְךָ מֵאֶרֶץ מִצְרָיִם,

Who raised you from the land of Egypt;

harchev picho va-amal-ayhu.	הַרְחֶב פִּיךָ וַאֲמַלְאֵהוּ.

open wide your mouth and I will fill it.

Ashray ho-om shekocho lō,	אַשְׁרֵי הָעָם שֶׁכָּכָה לּוֹ,
Praiseworthy is the people for whom this is so,	
ashray ho-om She-adōnoy Elōhov.	אַשְׁרֵי הָעָם שֶׁיהוה אֱלֹהָיו.
praiseworthy is the people whose God is Hashem.	
❖ Va-ani b'chasd'cho votachti,	❖ וַאֲנִי בְּחַסְדְּךָ בָטַחְתִּי,
As for me, I trust in Your kindness;	
yogayl libi bishu-osecho,	יָגֵל לִבִּי בִּישׁוּעָתֶךָ,
my heart will rejoice in Your salvation.	
oshiro Ladōnoy, ki gomal oloy.	אָשִׁירָה לַיהוה, כִּי גָמַל עָלָי.
I will sing to Hashem, *for He dealt kindly with me.*	

THE FOLLOWING PSALM, WHICH IS RECITED WHILE STANDING,
IS OMITTED ON EREV YOM KIPPUR AND EREV PESACH.

■ **Psalm 100:** In recognition of God's daily extricating us from dangers, even from those unbeknownst to us, we view it as a privilege to serve Him with joy.

MIZMŌR L'SŌDO,	**מִזְמוֹר לְתוֹדָה,**
A psalm of thanksgiving,	
hori-u Ladōnoy kol ho-oretz.	הָרִיעוּ לַיהוה כָּל הָאָרֶץ.
call out to Hashem *everyone on earth.*	
Ivdu es Adōnoy b'simcho,	עִבְדוּ אֶת יהוה בְּשִׂמְחָה,
Serve Hashem *with gladness,*	
bō-u l'fonov birnono.	בֹּאוּ לְפָנָיו בִּרְנָנָה.
come before Him with joyous song.	
D'u ki Adōnoy hu Elōhim	דְּעוּ כִּי יהוה הוּא אֱלֹהִים,
Know that Hashem, *He is God,*	
hu osonu, v'lō anachnu,	הוּא עָשָׂנוּ, וְלוֹ אֲנַחְנוּ,
it is He Who made us and we are His,	
amō v'tzōn mar-isō.	עַמּוֹ וְצֹאן מַרְעִיתוֹ.
His people and the sheep of His pasture.	
Bō-u sh'orov b'sōdo,	בֹּאוּ שְׁעָרָיו בְּתוֹדָה,
chatzayrōsov bis-hilo,	חֲצֵרֹתָיו בִּתְהִלָּה,
Enter His gates with thanksgiving, His Courtyards with praise,	
hōdu lō bor'chu sh'mō.	הוֹדוּ לוֹ, בָּרְכוּ שְׁמוֹ.
give thanks to Him, bless His Name.	
❖ Ki tōv Adōnoy, l'ōlom chasdō,	❖ כִּי טוֹב יהוה, לְעוֹלָם חַסְדּוֹ,
For Hashem *is good, His kindness endures forever,*	
v'ad dōr vodōr emunosō	וְעַד דֹּר וָדֹר אֱמוּנָתוֹ.
and from generation to generation is His faithfulness.	

■ *I sing in anticipation of the time when the kingship, honor and glory of Hashem will be manifested by man's noble ways.*

Y'HI CH'VŌD Adōnoy l'ōlom, יְהִי כְבוֹד יהוה לְעוֹלָם,
*May the glory of H*ASHEM* endure forever,*

yismach Adōnoy b'ma-asov. יִשְׂמַח יהוה בְּמַעֲשָׂיו.
*let H*ASHEM *rejoice in His works.*

Y'hi shaym Adōnoy m'vōroch, יְהִי שֵׁם יהוה מְבֹרָךְ,
*Blessed be the Name of H*ASHEM,

may-ato v'ad ōlom. מֵעַתָּה וְעַד עוֹלָם.
from this time and forever.

Mimizrach shemesh ad m'vō-ō, מִמִּזְרַח שֶׁמֶשׁ עַד מְבוֹאוֹ,
From the rising of the sun to its setting,

m'hulol shaym Adōnoy. מְהֻלָּל שֵׁם יהוה.
*H*ASHEM*'s Name is praised.*

Rom al kol gō-yim Adōnoy, רָם עַל כָּל גּוֹיִם יהוה,
*High above all nations is H*ASHEM,

al ha-shoma-yim k'vōdō. עַל הַשָּׁמַיִם כְּבוֹדוֹ.
above the heavens is His glory.

Adōnoy shimcho l'ōlom, יהוה שִׁמְךָ לְעוֹלָם,
*"H*ASHEM*" is Your Name forever,*

Adōnoy zichr'cho l'dōr vodōr. יהוה זִכְרְךָ לְדֹר וָדֹר.
*"H*ASHEM*" is Your memorial throughout the generations.*

Adōnoy ba-shoma-yim haychin kis-ō, יהוה בַּשָּׁמַיִם הֵכִין כִּסְאוֹ,
*H*ASHEM *has established His throne in the heavens,*

u-malchusō bakōl mosholo. וּמַלְכוּתוֹ בַּכֹּל מָשָׁלָה.
and His kingdom reigns over all.

Yism'chu ha-shoma-yim יִשְׂמְחוּ הַשָּׁמַיִם
v'sogayl ho-oretz, וְתָגֵל הָאָרֶץ,
The heavens will be glad and the earth will rejoice,

v'yōm'ru vagō-yim Adōnoy moloch. וְיֹאמְרוּ בַגּוֹיִם יהוה מָלָךְ.
*they will proclaim among the nations, "H*ASHEM *has reigned!"*

יְהִי כְבוֹד ה׳ — *May the glory of H*ASHEM. This is a collection of verses, primarily from *Psalms*, that revolves around two themes: the sovereignty of God and the role of Israel. Central to prayer and to the purpose of Creation is the Kingship of Heaven, which means that every being exists as part of God's plan and is dedicated to His service. This idea is found in nature itself, for, as the Psalmist says lyrically, man attains awareness of God when he contemplates the beauty and perfection of the universe. The last five verses speak of God's choosing the Jewish people and pleads for His mercy and attentiveness to their prayers.

Adōnoy melech, Adōnoy moloch,	יְהוָה מֶלֶךְ, יְהוָה מָלָךְ,
Adōnoy yimlōch l'ōlom vo-ed.	יְהוָה יִמְלֹךְ לְעֹלָם וָעֶד.

HASHEM reigns, HASHEM has reigned, HASHEM shall reign for all eternity.*

Adōnoy melech ōlom vo-ed,	יְהוָה מֶלֶךְ עוֹלָם וָעֶד,

HASHEM reigns forever and ever,

ov'du gō-yim may-artzō.	אָבְדוּ גוֹיִם מֵאַרְצוֹ.

when the nations will have perished from His earth.*

Adōnoy hayfir atzas gō-yim,	יְהוָה הֵפִיר עֲצַת גּוֹיִם,

HASHEM annuls the counsel of nations,

hayni machsh'vōs amim.	הֵנִיא מַחְשְׁבוֹת עַמִּים.

He balks the designs of peoples.

Rabōs machashovōs b'lev ish,	רַבּוֹת מַחֲשָׁבוֹת בְּלֶב אִישׁ,

Many designs are in man's heart,

va-atzas Adōnoy hi sokum.	וַעֲצַת יְהוָה הִיא תָקוּם.

but the counsel of HASHEM — only it will prevail.

Atzas Adōnoy l'ōlom ta-amōd,	עֲצַת יְהוָה לְעוֹלָם תַּעֲמֹד,

The counsel of HASHEM will endure forever,

machsh'vōs libō l'dōr vodōr.	מַחְשְׁבוֹת לִבּוֹ לְדֹר וָדֹר.

the designs of His heart throughout the generations.

Ki hu omar va-yehi,	כִּי הוּא אָמַר וַיֶּהִי,
hu tzivo va-ya-amōd.	הוּא צִוָּה וַיַּעֲמֹד.

For He spoke and it came to be; He commanded and it stood firm.

Ki vochar Adōnoy b'tziyōn,	כִּי בָחַר יְהוָה בְּצִיּוֹן,
ivoh l'mōshov lō.	אִוָּהּ לְמוֹשָׁב לוֹ.

For God selected Zion, He desired it for His dwelling place.

Ki ya-akōv bochar lō Yoh,	כִּי יַעֲקֹב בָּחַר לוֹ יָהּ,
yisro-ayl lisgulosō.	יִשְׂרָאֵל לִסְגֻלָּתוֹ.

For God selected Jacob as His own, Israel as His treasure.

Ki lō yitōsh Adōnoy amō,	כִּי לֹא יִטֹּשׁ יְהוָה עַמּוֹ,

For HASHEM will not cast off His people,

v'nachalosō lō ya-azōv.	וְנַחֲלָתוֹ לֹא יַעֲזֹב.

nor will He forsake His heritage.

... ה׳ מֶלֶךְ — HASHEM *reigns,* HASHEM *has reigned,* HASHEM *shall reign for all eternity.* This is one of the most familiar verses in the entire liturgy, but, surprisingly enough, it is not found in Scripture. Rather, each phrase comes from a different part of Scripture. In combination, the three phrases express the eternity of God's reign.

אָבְדוּ גוֹיִם מֵאַרְצוֹ — *When the nations will have perished from His earth.* The verse refers only to the *evil* people among the nations, for their deeds prevent others from acknowledging God.

V'hu rachum y'chapayr ovōn v'lō yashchis,	׃ וְהוּא רַחוּם יְכַפֵּר עָוֹן וְלֹא יַשְׁחִית,

He, the Merciful One, is forgiving of iniquity and does not destroy;

v'hirbo l'hoshiv apō,   וְהִרְבָּה לְהָשִׁיב אַפּוֹ,

frequently He withdraws His anger,

v'lō yo-ir kol chamosō.   וְלֹא יָעִיר כָּל חֲמָתוֹ.

not arousing His entire rage.

Adōnoy hōshi-o,   יהוה הוֹשִׁיעָה,

HASHEM, save!

hamelech ya-anaynu v'yōm kor-aynu.   הַמֶּלֶךְ יַעֲנֵנוּ בְיוֹם קָרְאֵנוּ.

May the King answer us on the day we call.

■ The alphabetic acrostic of *Ashrei* motivates the supplicant to praise God, His Kingship, and His providing the needs of every living creature. The Sages highlight the importance of *Ashrei* by declaring that whoever recites this psalm three times daily is directing himself towards meriting a place in the World to Come (*Berachos* 4b).

ASHRAY yōsh'vay vay-secho,   **אַשְׁרֵי** יוֹשְׁבֵי בֵיתֶךָ,

Praiseworthy are those who dwell in Your house;

ōd y'hal'lucho selo.   עוֹד יְהַלְלוּךָ סֶּלָה.

may they always praise You, Selah!

Ashray ho-om shekocho lō,   אַשְׁרֵי הָעָם שֶׁכָּכָה לוֹ,

Praiseworthy is the people for whom this is so,

ashray ho-om she-Adōnoy Elōhov.   אַשְׁרֵי הָעָם שֶׁיהוה אֱלֹהָיו.

praiseworthy is the people whose God is HASHEM.

T'hilo l'dovid,   תְּהִלָּה לְדָוִד,

A psalm of praise by David:

arōmimcho Elōhai hamelech,   אֲרוֹמִמְךָ אֱלוֹהַי הַמֶּלֶךְ,

I will exalt You, my God the King,

va-avor'cho shimcho l'ōlom vo-ed.   וַאֲבָרְכָה שִׁמְךָ לְעוֹלָם וָעֶד.

and I will bless Your Name forever and ever.

B'chol yōm avor'cheko,   בְּכָל יוֹם אֲבָרְכֶךָּ,

Every day I will bless You,*

◆§ Ashrei

Ashrei comprises Psalm 145, with the addition of two introductory verses and a closing verse from elsewhere in *Psalms*. This psalm possesses two virtues: (a) The initials of the psalm's respective verses follow the order of the *alef-beis;* and (b) it contains the inspiring and the reassuring testimony to God's mercy, "You open Your hand and satisfy the desire of every living thing."

The Midrash records that the Psalmist and Sages used the *alef-beis* formula in chapters that they wanted people to follow more easily or to memorize. Moreover, the *alef-beis* structure symbolizes that we praise God with every sound available to our organs of speech.

בְּכָל יוֹם אֲבָרְכֶךָּ — *Every day I will bless You.* True, no mortal can pretend to know God's

וַאֲהַלְלָה שִׁמְךָ לְעוֹלָם וָעֶד.	va-ahal'lo shimcho l'ōlom vo-ed.

and I will laud Your Name forever and ever.

גָּדוֹל יהוה וּמְהֻלָּל מְאֹד,	Godōl Adōnoy umhulol m'ōd,

Hashem is great and exceedingly lauded,

וְלִגְדֻלָּתוֹ אֵין חֵקֶר.	v'ligduloso̊ ayn chayker.

and His greatness is beyond investigation.

דּוֹר לְדוֹר יְשַׁבַּח מַעֲשֶׂיךָ,	Dōr l'dōr y'shabach ma-asecho,

Each generation will praise Your deeds to the next,*

וּגְבוּרֹתֶיךָ יַגִּידוּ.	ugvurōsecho yagidu.

and of Your mighty deeds they will tell.

הֲדַר כְּבוֹד הוֹדֶךָ,	Hadar k'vōd hōdecho,

The splendrous glory of Your power

וְדִבְרֵי נִפְלְאֹתֶיךָ אָשִׂיחָה.	v'divray nifl'ōsecho osicho.

and Your wondrous deeds I shall discuss.

וֶעֱזוּז נוֹרְאוֹתֶיךָ יֹאמֵרוּ,	Ve-ezuz nōr'ōsecho yōmayru,

And of Your awesome power they will speak,

וּגְדוּלָּתְךָ אֲסַפְּרֶנָּה.	ugdulos'cho asap'reno.

and Your greatness I shall relate.

זֵכֶר רַב טוּבְךָ יַבִּיעוּ,	Zecher rav tuv'cho yabi-u,

A recollection of Your abundant goodness they will utter

וְצִדְקָתְךָ יְרַנֵּנוּ.	v'tzidkos'cho y'ranaynu.

and of Your righteousness they will sing exultantly.

חַנּוּן וְרַחוּם יהוה,	Chanun v'rachum Adōnoy,

Gracious and merciful is Hashem,

אֶרֶךְ אַפַּיִם וּגְדָל חָסֶד.	erech apa-yim ugdol chosed.

slow to anger, and great in [bestowing] kindness.

טוֹב יהוה לַכֹּל,	Tōv Adōnoy lakōl,

Hashem is good to all,

וְרַחֲמָיו עַל כָּל מַעֲשָׂיו.	v'rachamov al kol ma-asov.

and His mercies are on all His works.

יוֹדוּךָ יהוה כָּל מַעֲשֶׂיךָ,	Yōducho Adōnoy kol ma-asecho,

All Your works shall thank You, Hashem,

וַחֲסִידֶיךָ יְבָרְכוּכָה.	vachasidecho y'vor'chucho.

and Your devout ones will bless You.

דּוֹר לְדוֹר יְשַׁבַּח מַעֲשֶׂיךָ — *Each generation will praise Your deeds to the next.* We cannot understand God's essence or His ways, for He is infinite. We must rely on the traditions from essence, but each of us *is* equipped to appreciate life, health, sustenance, sunshine, rainfall, and so on. For these and their daily renewal, we give daily blessings.

SHACHARIS FOR WEEKDAYS / PESUKEI D'ZIMRAH

K'vōd malchus'cho yōmayru,   בְּבוֹד מַלְכוּתְךָ יֹאמֵרוּ,
Of the glory of Your kingdom they will speak,

ugvuros'cho y'dabayru.   וּגְבוּרָתְךָ יְדַבֵּרוּ.
and of Your power they will tell,

L'hōdi-a livnay ho-odom g'vurōsov,   לְהוֹדִיעַ לִבְנֵי הָאָדָם גְּבוּרֹתָיו,
to inform human beings of His mighty deeds,

uchvōd hadar malchusō.   וּכְבוֹד הֲדַר מַלְכוּתוֹ.
and the glorious splendor of His kingdom.

Malchus'cho malchus kol ōlomim,   מַלְכוּתְךָ מַלְכוּת כָּל עֹלָמִים,
Your kingdom is a kingdom spanning all eternities,

u-memshalt'cho b'chol dōr vodōr.   וּמֶמְשַׁלְתְּךָ בְּכָל דּוֹר וָדֹר.
and Your dominion is throughout every generation.

Sōmaych Adōnoy l'chol hanōf'lim,   סוֹמֵךְ יהוה לְכָל הַנֹּפְלִים,
HASHEM supports all the fallen ones*

v'zōkayf l'chol hak'fufim.   וְזוֹקֵף לְכָל הַכְּפוּפִים.
and straightens all the bent.

Aynay chōl aylecho y'sabayru,   עֵינֵי כֹל אֵלֶיךָ יְשַׂבֵּרוּ,
The eyes of all look to You with hope

v'ato nōsayn lohem   וְאַתָּה נוֹתֵן לָהֶם
es ochlom b'ito.   אֶת אָכְלָם בְּעִתּוֹ.
and You give them their food in its proper time.

CONCENTRATE INTENTLY WHILE RECITING THE NEXT VERSE. IT IS CUSTOMARY TO TOUCH THE ARM-TEFILLIN WHEN SAYING Pōsay-ach ... AND THE HEAD-TEFILLIN WHILE SAYING u-masbi-a ...

Pōsay-ach es yodecho,   פּוֹתֵחַ אֶת יָדֶךָ,
u-masbi-a l'chol chai rotzōn.   וּמַשְׂבִּיעַ לְכָל חַי רָצוֹן.
You open Your hand* and satisfy the desire of every living thing.

Tzadik Adōnoy b'chol d'rochov,   צַדִּיק יהוה בְּכָל דְּרָכָיו,
Righteous is HASHEM in all His ways

---

earlier generations.

סוֹמֵךְ ה' לְכָל הַנֹּפְלִים — *HASHEM supports all the fallen ones.* Although *Ashrei* follows an alphabetical format, the fourteenth letter of the *alef-beis*, the נ, is omitted. That letter begins the Hebrew word נְפִילָה, "downfall," and in context with the verse of the next letter ס — "HASHEM supports all the fallen ones" — could be taken as an allusion to Israel's future downfall, Heaven forbid; but the Psalmist refused to use a letter that could suggest such tragedy. That omission implies that even when Israel does suffer reverses, those reverses will never be final. Rather, as the next verse declares, God supports the fallen.

פּוֹתֵחַ אֶת יָדֶךָ — *You open Your hand.* This verse should be recited with great joy at the knowledge that God cares for every creature.

יָדֶךָ — *Your hand.* It is axiomatic to Jewish belief that God has no physicality, not even that of the invisible, intangible angels. Because we are physical beings, we cannot grasp God's essence. We cannot conceive of a Being totally unaffected by material conditions or the laws of nature and physics. When Scripture speaks of "the hand of God" or "the eyes of God" and so forth, it does not imply that God has corporeality. Rather, it speaks this way to enable us to understand the concepts being conveyed.

וְחָסִיד בְּכָל מַעֲשָׂיו.
v'chosid b'chol ma-asov.
and magnanimous* in all His deeds.

קָרוֹב יהוה לְכָל קֹרְאָיו,
Korōv Adōnoy l'chol kōr'ov,
Hashem is close to all who call upon Him —

לְכֹל אֲשֶׁר יִקְרָאֻהוּ בֶאֱמֶת.
l'chōl asher yikro-uhu ve-emes.
to all who call upon Him sincerely.

רְצוֹן יְרֵאָיו יַעֲשֶׂה,
R'tzōn y'ray-ov ya-a-se,
The will of those who fear Him He will do,

וְאֶת שַׁוְעָתָם יִשְׁמַע וְיוֹשִׁיעֵם.
v'es shav-osom yishma v'yōshi-aym.
and their cry He will hear, and save them.

שׁוֹמֵר יהוה אֶת כָּל אֹהֲבָיו,
Shōmayr Adōnoy es kol ōhavov,
Hashem protects all who love Him,

וְאֵת כָּל הָרְשָׁעִים יַשְׁמִיד.
v'ays kol hor'sho-im yashmid.
but all the wicked He will destroy.

❖ תְּהִלַּת יהוה יְדַבֶּר פִּי,
T'hilas Adōnoy y'daber pi,
May my mouth declare the praise of Hashem

וִיבָרֵךְ כָּל בָּשָׂר שֵׁם קָדְשׁוֹ לְעוֹלָם וָעֶד.
vivoraych kol bosor shaym kodshō, l'ōlom vo-ed.
and may all flesh bless His Holy Name forever and ever.

וַאֲנַחְנוּ נְבָרֵךְ יָהּ,
Va-anachnu n'voraych Yoh,
We will bless God

מֵעַתָּה וְעַד עוֹלָם, הַלְלוּיָהּ.
may-ato v'ad ōlom, hal'luyoh.
from this time and forever: Praise God!

■ Psalm 146: I recognize that You alone can address my material and emotional needs.

הַלְלוּיָהּ, / HAL'LUYOH,
Praise God!

הַלְלִי נַפְשִׁי אֶת יהוה.
hal'li nafshi es Adōnoy.
Praise Hashem, O my soul!*

אֲהַלְלָה יהוה בְּחַיָּי,
Ahal'lo Adōnoy b'cha-yoy,
I will praise Hashem while I live,

אֲזַמְּרָה לֵאלֹהַי בְּעוֹדִי.
azam'ro Laylōhai b'ōdi.
I will make music to my God while I exist.

צַדִּיק ... וְחָסִיד — *Righteous ... and magnanimous.* God judges people righteously, according to their deeds. Nevertheless, even when justice calls for grievous punishment, He is magnanimous in softening the blow, for He is merciful.

הַלְלוּיָהּ הַלְלִי נַפְשִׁי אֶת ה' — *Praise God! Praise Hashem, O my soul!* Psalm 146 is a a hymn of encouragement for Jews in exile. It begins with the Psalmist insisting that he will praise God as long as he lives and warning his fellow Jews not to rely on human beings. After describing

Al tivt'chu vindivim,	אַל תִּבְטְחוּ בִנְדִיבִים,

Do not rely on nobles,

B'ven odom she-ayn lō s'shu-o.	בְּבֶן אָדָם שֶׁאֵין לוֹ תְשׁוּעָה.

nor on a human being, for he holds no salvation.

Taytzay ruchō, yoshuv l'admosō,	תֵּצֵא רוּחוֹ, יָשֻׁב לְאַדְמָתוֹ,

When his spirit departs he returns to his earth,

ba-yōm hahu ov'du eshtōnōsov.	בַּיּוֹם הַהוּא אָבְדוּ עֶשְׁתֹּנֹתָיו.

on that day his plans all perish.

Ashray she-Ayl ya-akōv b'ezrō,	אַשְׁרֵי שֶׁאֵל יַעֲקֹב בְּעֶזְרוֹ,

Praiseworthy is one whose help is Jacob's God,

sivrō al Adōnoy Elōhov.	שִׂבְרוֹ עַל יהוה אֱלֹהָיו.

whose hope is in HASHEM, *his God.*

Ō-se shoma-yim vo-oretz,	עֹשֶׂה שָׁמַיִם וָאָרֶץ,

He is the Maker of heaven and earth,

es ha-yom v'es kol asher bom,	אֶת הַיָּם וְאֶת כָּל אֲשֶׁר בָּם,

the sea and all that is in them,

ha-shōmayr emes l'ōlom.	הַשֹּׁמֵר אֱמֶת לְעוֹלָם.

Who safeguards truth forever.

Ō-se mishpot la-ashukim,	עֹשֶׂה מִשְׁפָּט לָעֲשׁוּקִים,

He does justice for the exploited;

nōsayn lechem lor'ayvim,	נֹתֵן לֶחֶם לָרְעֵבִים,

He gives bread to the hungry;

Adōnoy matir asurim.	יהוה מַתִּיר אֲסוּרִים.

HASHEM *releases the bound.*

Adōnoy pōkay-ach ivrim,	יהוה פֹּקֵחַ עִוְרִים,

HASHEM *gives sight to the blind;*

Adōnoy zōkayf k'fufim,	יהוה זֹקֵף כְּפוּפִים,

HASHEM *straightens the bent;*

Adōnoy ōhayv tzadikim.	יהוה אֹהֵב צַדִּיקִים.

HASHEM *loves the righteous.*

Adōnoy shōmayr es gayrim,	יהוה שֹׁמֵר אֶת גֵּרִים,

HASHEM *protects strangers;*

yosōm v'almono y'ōdayd,	יָתוֹם וְאַלְמָנָה יְעוֹדֵד,

orphan and widow He encourages;

v'derech r'sho-im y'avays.	וְדֶרֶךְ רְשָׁעִים יְעַוֵּת.

but the way of the wicked He contorts.

God as the One Who cares for the underprivileged and oppressed, the Psalmist concludes that God will reign forever — despite the current ascendancy of our enemies.

Yimlōch Adōnoy l'ōlom,　　יִמְלֹךְ יהוה לְעוֹלָם,
Hashem shall reign forever,

Elōha-yich tziyōn, l'dōr vodōr,　　אֱלֹהַיִךְ צִיּוֹן, לְדֹר וָדֹר,
your God, O Zion, from generation to generation.

hal'luyoh　　הַלְלוּיָהּ.
Praise God!

■ Psalm 147: I, as part of the Jewish people, praise Hashem for His ongoing redemption of Israel and for the Torah that emanates from Jerusalem.

HAL'LUYOH,　　הַלְלוּיָהּ,
Praise God!

ki tōv zam'ro Elōhaynu,　　כִּי טוֹב זַמְּרָה אֱלֹהֵינוּ,
For it is good* to make music to our God,

ki no-im novo s'hilo.　　כִּי נָעִים נָאוָה תְהִלָּה.
for praise is pleasant and befitting.

Bōnay y'rushola-yim Adōnoy,　　בּוֹנֵה יְרוּשָׁלַיִם יהוה,
The Builder of Jerusalem is Hashem,

nidchay yisro-ayl y'chanays.　　נִדְחֵי יִשְׂרָאֵל יְכַנֵּס.
the outcast of Israel He will gather in.

Horōfay lishvuray layv,　　הָרוֹפֵא לִשְׁבוּרֵי לֵב,
He is the Healer of the brokenhearted,

umchabaysh l'atz'vōsom.　　וּמְחַבֵּשׁ לְעַצְּבוֹתָם.
and the One Who binds up their sorrows.

Mōne mispor lakōchovim,　　מוֹנֶה מִסְפָּר לַכּוֹכָבִים,
He counts the number of the stars,*

l'chulom shaymōs yikro.　　לְכֻלָּם שֵׁמוֹת יִקְרָא.
to all of them He assigns names.

Godōl Adōnaynu v'rav kō-ach,　　גָּדוֹל אֲדוֹנֵינוּ וְרַב כֹּחַ,
Great is our Lord and abundant in strength,

lisvunosō ayn mispor.　　לִתְבוּנָתוֹ אֵין מִסְפָּר.
His understanding is beyond calculation.

הַלְלוּיָהּ כִּי טוֹב — *Praise God! For it is good.* Psalm 147 continues the theme of redemption, placing its primary focus on Jerusalem, the center from which holiness, redemption, and Torah will emanate. In this sense, Jerusalem cannot be considered rebuilt until the Redemption, because the city's spiritual grandeur cannot be recaptured by mere architecture and growing numbers of people.

מוֹנֶה מִסְפָּר לַכּוֹכָבִים — *He counts the number of the stars.* Having given the assurance that God will rebuild Jerusalem and gather in Israel with joy, the Psalmist then proceeds to illustrate God's ability to do so. The next series of verses catalogue His might, compassion, and attention to individual needs.

The stars number in the billions, but God is aware of each one and gives it a "name" that denotes its purpose in the universe. Thus, nothing goes unnoticed or unprovided for.

M'ōdayd anovim Adōnoy,	מְעוֹדֵד עֲנָוִים יהוה,

Hashem encourages the humble,

mashpil r'sho-im aday oretz.	מַשְׁפִּיל רְשָׁעִים עֲדֵי אָרֶץ.

He lowers the wicked down to the ground.

enu Ladōnoy b'sōdo,	עֱנוּ לַיהוה בְּתוֹדָה,

Call out to Hashem with thanks,

zam'ru Laylōhaynu b'chinōr.	זַמְּרוּ לֵאלֹהֵינוּ בְכִנּוֹר.

with the harp sing to our God —

Ham'chase shoma-yim b'ovim,	הַמְכַסֶּה שָׁמַיִם בְּעָבִים,

Who covers the heavens with clouds,

hamaychin lo-oretz motor,	הַמֵּכִין לָאָרֶץ מָטָר,

Who prepares rain for the earth,

hamatzmi-ach horim chotzir.	הַמַּצְמִיחַ הָרִים חָצִיר.

Who makes mountains sprout with grass.

Nōsayn livhaymo lachmoh,	נוֹתֵן לִבְהֵמָה לַחְמָהּ,

He gives to an animal its food,

livnay ōrayv asher yikro-u.	לִבְנֵי עֹרֵב אֲשֶׁר יִקְרָאוּ.

to young ravens that cry out.

Lō vigvuras hasus yechpotz,	לֹא בִגְבוּרַת הַסּוּס יֶחְפָּץ,

Not in the strength of the horse does He desire,

lō v'shōkay ha-ish yirtze.	לֹא בְשׁוֹקֵי הָאִישׁ יִרְצֶה.

and not in the legs of man does He favor.

Rōtze Adōnoy es y'ray-ov,	רוֹצֶה יהוה אֶת יְרֵאָיו,

Hashem favors those who fear Him,

es ham'yachalim l'chasdō.	אֶת הַמְיַחֲלִים לְחַסְדּוֹ.

those who hope for His kindness.

Shab'chi y'rushola-yim es Adōnoy,	שַׁבְּחִי יְרוּשָׁלַיִם אֶת יהוה,

Praise Hashem, O Jerusalem,

hal'li Elōha-yich tziyōn.	הַלְלִי אֱלֹהַיִךְ צִיּוֹן.

laud your God, O Zion.

Ki chizak b'richay sh'oro-yich,	כִּי חִזַּק בְּרִיחֵי שְׁעָרָיִךְ,

For He has strengthened the bars of your gates,

bayrach bona-yich b'kirbaych.	בֵּרַךְ בָּנַיִךְ בְּקִרְבֵּךְ.

and blessed your children in your midst.

Hasom g'vulaych sholōm,	הַשָּׂם גְּבוּלֵךְ שָׁלוֹם,

He Who makes your borders peaceful,

chaylev chitim yasbi-aych.	חֵלֶב חִטִּים יַשְׂבִּיעֵךְ.
and with the cream of the wheat He sates you;	
Hashōlay-ach imrosō oretz,	הַשֹּׁלֵחַ אִמְרָתוֹ אָרֶץ,
He Who dispatches His utterance earthward;	
ad m'hayrō yorutz d'vorō.	עַד מְהֵרָה יָרוּץ דְּבָרוֹ.
how swiftly His commandment runs!	
Hanōsayn sheleg katzomer,	הַנֹּתֵן שֶׁלֶג כַּצָּמֶר,
k'fōr ko-ayfer y'fazayr.	כְּפוֹר כָּאֵפֶר יְפַזֵּר.
He Who gives snow like fleece, He scatters frost like ashes.	
Mashlich karchō ch'fitim,	מַשְׁלִיךְ קַרְחוֹ כְפִתִּים,
He hurls His ice like crumbs —	
lifnay korosō mi ya-amōd.	לִפְנֵי קָרָתוֹ מִי יַעֲמֹד.
before His cold, who can stand?	
Yishlach d'vorō v'yamsaym,	יִשְׁלַח דְּבָרוֹ וְיַמְסֵם,
He issues His command and it melts them,	
yashayv ruchō yiz'lu mo-yim.	יַשֵּׁב רוּחוֹ יִזְּלוּ מָיִם.
He blows His wind — the waters flow.	
❖ Magid d'vorov l'ya-akōv,	❖ מַגִּיד דְּבָרָיו לְיַעֲקֹב,
He relates His Word to Jacob,*	
chukov u-mishpotov l'yisro-ayl.	חֻקָּיו וּמִשְׁפָּטָיו לְיִשְׂרָאֵל.
His statutes and judgments to Israel.	
Lō oso chayn l'chol gōy,	לֹא עָשָׂה כֵן לְכָל גּוֹי,
He did not do so for any other nation,	
u-mishpotim bal y'do-um,	וּמִשְׁפָּטִים בַּל יְדָעוּם,
such judgments — they know them not.	
hal'luyoh.	הַלְלוּיָהּ.
Praise God!	

■ **Psalm 148:** I sing in anticipation and excitement of the time when all the world will be imbued with the knowledge of Hashem.

HAL'LUYOH,	**הַלְלוּיָהּ,**
Praise God!	
hal'lu es Adōnoy min ha-shoma-yim,	הַלְלוּ אֶת יהוה מִן הַשָּׁמַיִם,
Praise HASHEM from the heavens;*	

מַגִּיד דְּבָרָיו לְיַעֲקֹב — *He relates His Word to Jacob.* Lest you wonder at the many centuries that have gone by without Israel's redemption, do not forget that the Torah itself — the very purpose of Creation — was not given to man until 2,448 years after Creation. That God sees fit to delay is no cause for despair.

הַלְלוּיָהּ הַלְלוּ אֶת ה׳ מִן הַשָּׁמַיִם — *Praise God! Praise HASHEM from the heavens.* The Psalmist begins by calling upon the heavenly beings to praise God, and then he calls to earthly beings. God's praises echo from the heavens and de-

SHACHARIS FOR WEEKDAYS — PESUKEI D'ZIMRAH

hal'luhu bam'rōmim.
הַלְלוּהוּ בַּמְּרוֹמִים.
praise Him in the heights;

Hal'luhu chol mal-ochov,
הַלְלוּהוּ כָל מַלְאָכָיו,
praise Him, all His angels;

hal'luhu kol tz'vo-ov.
הַלְלוּהוּ כָּל צְבָאָיו.
praise Him, all His legions;*

Hal'luhu shemesh v'yoray-ach,
הַלְלוּהוּ שֶׁמֶשׁ וְיָרֵחַ,
praise Him, sun and moon;

hal'luhu kol kōch'vay ōr.
הַלְלוּהוּ כָּל כּוֹכְבֵי אוֹר.
praise Him, all bright stars;

Hal'luhu sh'may ha-shomo-yim,
הַלְלוּהוּ שְׁמֵי הַשָּׁמָיִם,
praise Him, the most exalted of the heavens

v'hama-yim asher may-al ha-shomo-yim.
וְהַמַּיִם אֲשֶׁר מֵעַל הַשָּׁמָיִם.
and the waters that are above the heavens.

Y'hal'lu es shaym Adōnoy,
יְהַלְלוּ אֶת שֵׁם יהוה,
Let them praise the Name of HASHEM,

ki hu tzivo v'nivro-u.
כִּי הוּא צִוָּה וְנִבְרָאוּ.
for He commanded and they were created.

Va-ya-amidaym lo-ad l'ōlom,
וַיַּעֲמִידֵם לָעַד לְעוֹלָם,
And He established them forever and ever,

chok nosan v'lō ya-avōr.
חָק נָתַן וְלֹא יַעֲבוֹר.
He issued a decree* that will not change.

Hal'lu es Adōnoy min ho-oretz,
הַלְלוּ אֶת יהוה מִן הָאָרֶץ,
Praise HASHEM *from the earth,*

taninim v'chol t'hōmōs.
תַּנִּינִים וְכָל תְּהֹמוֹת.
sea giants and all watery depths;

Aysh u-vorod, sheleg v'kitōr,
אֵשׁ וּבָרָד, שֶׁלֶג וְקִיטוֹר,
fire and hail; snow and vapor;

ru-ach s'oro ō-so d'vorō.
רוּחַ סְעָרָה עֹשָׂה דְבָרוֹ.
stormy wind fulfilling His word;

Hehorim v'chol g'vo-ōs,
הֶהָרִים וְכָל גְּבָעוֹת,
mountains and all hills;

aytz p'ri v'chol arozim.
עֵץ פְּרִי וְכָל אֲרָזִים.
fruitful trees and all cedars;

---

scend to earth, where the devout echo the heavenly songs with their own praises.

מַלְאָכָיו ... צְבָאָיו — *His angels ... His legions.* The *angels* are spiritual beings without physical form while the *legions* are the heavenly bodies, which are so numerous that they are likened to legions.

חָק נָתַן — *He issued a decree* that the sun shine by day and the moon by night, and this *decree* can never be disobeyed.

Hacha-yo v'chol b'haymo,	הַחַיָּה וְכָל בְּהֵמָה,
remes v'tzipōr konof.	רֶמֶשׂ וְצִפּוֹר כָּנָף.

beasts and all cattle; crawling things and winged fowl;

Malchay eretz v'chol l'umim,   מַלְכֵי אֶרֶץ וְכָל לְאֻמִּים,
kings of the earth and all governments;

sorim v'chol shōf'tay oretz.   שָׂרִים וְכָל שֹׁפְטֵי אָרֶץ.
princes and all judges on earth;

Bachurim v'gam b'sulōs,   בַּחוּרִים וְגַם בְּתוּלוֹת,
young men and also maidens;*

z'kaynim im n'orim.   זְקֵנִים עִם נְעָרִים.
old men together with youths.

Y'hal'lu es shaym Adōnoy,   ❖ יְהַלְלוּ אֶת שֵׁם יהוה,
*Let them praise the Name of H*ASHEM,

ki nisgov sh'mō l'vadō,   כִּי נִשְׂגָּב שְׁמוֹ לְבַדּוֹ,
for His Name alone will have been exalted;

hōdō al eretz v'shomo-yim.   הוֹדוֹ עַל אֶרֶץ וְשָׁמָיִם.
His glory is above earth and heaven.

Va-yorem keren l'amō,   וַיָּרֶם קֶרֶן לְעַמּוֹ,
And He will have exalted the pride of His people,

t'hilo l'chol chasidov,   תְּהִלָּה לְכָל חֲסִידָיו,
causing praise for all His devout ones,

livnay yisro-ayl am k'rōvō,   לִבְנֵי יִשְׂרָאֵל עַם קְרֹבוֹ,
for the Children of Israel, His intimate people.

hal'luyoh.   הַלְלוּיָהּ.
Praise God!

■ Psalm 149: I sing in anticipation of the ultimate redemption and Israel's triumph over the enemies of Hashem.

HAL'LUYOH,   הַלְלוּיָהּ,
Praise God!

shiru Ladōnoy shir chodosh,   שִׁירוּ לַיהוה שִׁיר חָדָשׁ,
*Sing to H*ASHEM*, a new song**

t'hilosō bikhal chasidim.   תְּהִלָּתוֹ בִּקְהַל חֲסִידִים.
let His praise be in the congregation of the devout.

בַּחוּרִים וְגַם בְּתוּלוֹת — *Young men and also maidens.* The use here of the word וְגַם, "and also," is noteworthy. The Psalmist does not say that young men *and* women will be together, because such mingling would be immodest. Only later, when he speaks of old men and youths does the Psalmist say עִם, "with" — that they will be together.

הַלְלוּיָהּ שִׁירוּ לַה׳ שִׁיר חָדָשׁ — *Praise God! Sing to H*ASHEM *a new song.* In every generation, God confronts us with new challenges and problems, yet He provides us with the ability to solve them.

Yismach yisro-ayl b'ō-sov,	יִשְׂמַח יִשְׂרָאֵל בְּעֹשָׂיו,

Let Israel exult in its Maker,

b'nay tziyōn yogilu v'malkom.   בְּנֵי צִיּוֹן יָגִילוּ בְמַלְכָּם.

let the Children of Zion rejoice in their King.

Y'hal'lu sh'mō v'mochōl,   יְהַלְלוּ שְׁמוֹ בְמָחוֹל,

Let them praise His Name with dancing,

b'sōf v'chinōr y'zam'ru lō.   בְּתֹף וְכִנּוֹר יְזַמְּרוּ לוֹ.

with drums and harp let them make music to Him.

Ki rōtze Adōnoy b'amō,   כִּי רוֹצֶה יהוה בְּעַמּוֹ,

For HASHEM *favors His people,*

y'fo-ayr anovim bishu-o.   יְפָאֵר עֲנָוִים בִּישׁוּעָה.

He adorns the humble with salvation.

Ya-l'zu chasidim b'chovōd,   יַעְלְזוּ חֲסִידִים בְּכָבוֹד,

Let the devout exult in glory,

y'ran'nu al mishk'vōsom.   יְרַנְּנוּ עַל מִשְׁכְּבוֹתָם.

let them sing joyously upon their beds.

Rōm'mōs Ayl bigrōnom,   רוֹמְמוֹת אֵל בִּגְרוֹנָם,

The lofty praises of God are in their throats,

v'cherev pifiyōs b'yodom.   וְחֶרֶב פִּיפִיּוֹת בְּיָדָם.

and a double-edged sword is in their hand —

La-asōs n'komo bagōyim,   לַעֲשׂוֹת נְקָמָה בַּגּוֹיִם,

to execute vengeance among the nations,

tōchaychōs bal-umim.   תּוֹכֵחוֹת בַּלְאֻמִּים.

rebukes among the governments.

❖ Lesōr malchayhem b'zikim,   לֶאְסֹר מַלְכֵיהֶם בְּזִקִּים,

To bind their kings with chains,

v'nichb'dayhem b'chavlay varzel.   וְנִכְבְּדֵיהֶם בְּכַבְלֵי בַרְזֶל.

and their nobles with fetters of iron,

La-asōs bohem mishpot kosuv,   לַעֲשׂוֹת בָּהֶם מִשְׁפָּט כָּתוּב,

to execute upon them written judgment — *

hodor hu l'chol chasidov,   הָדָר הוּא לְכָל חֲסִידָיו,

that will be the splendor of all His devout ones.

hal'luyoh.   הַלְלוּיָהּ.

Praise God!

For this, our songs of praise never grow stale, because they are always infused with new meaning. But the greatest, newest song of all will spring from Israel's lips when history reaches its climax with the coming of Messiah.

לַעֲשׂוֹת בָּהֶם מִשְׁפָּט כָּתוּב — *To execute upon them written judgment.* The future judgment upon the nations has been written in the Prophets. The execution of that judgment will bring the reign of justice to earth, and that will be the

■ Psalm 150: I conclude that the ultimate praise of Hashem can neither be articulated nor played on any instrument, but emanates from the soul.

HAL'LUYOH, הַלְלוּיָהּ,
Praise God!

hal'lu Ayl b'kodshō, הַלְלוּ אֵל בְּקָדְשׁוֹ,
Praise God in His Sanctuary; *

hal'luhu birki-a uzō. הַלְלוּהוּ בִּרְקִיעַ עֻזּוֹ.
praise Him in the firmament of His power.

Hal'luhu bigvurōsov, הַלְלוּהוּ בִגְבוּרֹתָיו,
Praise Him for His mighty acts;

hal'luhu k'rōv gudlō. הַלְלוּהוּ כְּרֹב גֻּדְלוֹ.
praise Him as befits His abundant greatness.

Hal'luhu b'sayka shōfor, הַלְלוּהוּ בְּתֵקַע שׁוֹפָר,
Praise Him with the blast of the shofar;

hal'luhu b'nayvel v'chinōr. הַלְלוּהוּ בְּנֵבֶל וְכִנּוֹר.
praise Him with lyre and harp.

Hal'luhu b'sōf u-mochōl, הַלְלוּהוּ בְּתֹף וּמָחוֹל,
Praise Him with drum and dance;

hal'luhu b'minim v'ugov. הַלְלוּהוּ בְּמִנִּים וְעֻגָב.
praise Him with organ and flute.

Hal'luhu b'tziltz'lay shoma, הַלְלוּהוּ בְצִלְצְלֵי שָׁמַע,
Praise Him with clanging cymbals;

hal'luhu b'tziltz'lay s'ru-o. הַלְלוּהוּ בְצִלְצְלֵי תְרוּעָה.
praise Him with resonant trumpets.

Kōl han'shomo t'halayl Yoh ❖ כֹּל הַנְּשָׁמָה תְּהַלֵּל יָהּ,
Let all souls praise * *God,*

hal'luyoh. הַלְלוּיָהּ.
Praise God!

Kōl han'shomo t'halayl Yoh כֹּל הַנְּשָׁמָה תְּהַלֵּל יָהּ,
Let all souls praise God,

hal'luyoh. הַלְלוּיָהּ.
Praise God!

---

splendor — the pride and vindication — of the righteous who have always lived that way.

הַלְלוּיָהּ הַלְלוּ אֵל בְּקָדְשׁוֹ — *Praise God! Praise God in His Sanctuary.* In this, the final psalm in the Book of *Psalms,* the Psalmist sums up his task by saying that man must enrich his spiritual self by recognizing God's greatness and kindness and by praising Him. The Psalmist's long list of musical instruments reflects the full spectrum of human emotions and spiritual potential, all of which can be aroused by music.

כֹּל הַנְּשָׁמָה תְּהַלֵּל — *Let all souls praise.* Far greater than the most sublime instrumental songs of praise is the song of the human soul. God's greatest praise is the soul that utilizes its full potential in His service.

SHACHARIS FOR WEEKDAYS — PESUKEI D'ZIMRAH

BORUCH Adōnoy l'ōlom, בָּרוּךְ יהוה לְעוֹלָם,
Blessed is HASHEM forever,
omayn v'omayn. אָמֵן וְאָמֵן.
Amen and Amen.

Boruch Adōnoy mitziyōn, בָּרוּךְ יהוה מִצִּיּוֹן,
shōchayn y'rusholoyim, שֹׁכֵן יְרוּשָׁלָיִם,
Blessed is HASHEM from Zion, Who dwells in Jerusalem.
hal'luyoh. הַלְלוּיָהּ.
Praise God!

Boruch Adōnoy בָּרוּךְ יהוה
Elōhim Elōhay yisro-ayl, אֱלֹהִים אֱלֹהֵי יִשְׂרָאֵל,
Blessed is HASHEM, God, the God of Israel,
ō-say niflo-ōs l'vadō. עֹשֵׂה נִפְלָאוֹת לְבַדּוֹ.
Who alone does wonders.

U-voruch shaym k'vōdō l'ōlom, ❖ וּבָרוּךְ שֵׁם כְּבוֹדוֹ לְעוֹלָם,
Blessed is His glorious Name forever,
v'yimolay ch'vōdō es kol ho-oretz, וְיִמָּלֵא כְבוֹדוֹ אֶת כָּל הָאָרֶץ,
and may all the earth be filled with His glory,
omayn v'omayn. אָמֵן וְאָמֵן.
Amen and Amen.

■ I affirm, as did King David, that beyond the psalms of praise that I have offered, the personal circumstances of my life inspire me to further thank Hashem.

THE FOLLOWING IS RECITED WHILE STANDING:

VAIVORECH dovid es Adōnoy וַיְבָרֶךְ דָּוִיד אֶת יהוה
And David blessed HASHEM*
l'aynay kol hakohol, לְעֵינֵי כָּל הַקָּהָל,
in the presence of the entire congregation —
va-yōmer dovid: וַיֹּאמֶר דָּוִיד:
David said,
Boruch ato Adōnoy, בָּרוּךְ אַתָּה יהוה,
"Blessed are You, HASHEM,
Elōhay yisro-ayl ovinu, אֱלֹהֵי יִשְׂרָאֵל אָבִינוּ,
the God of Israel our forefather,
may-ōlom v'ad ōlom. מֵעוֹלָם וְעַד עוֹלָם.
from this world to the World to Come.

וַיְבָרֶךְ דָּוִיד — *And David blessed* HASHEM. The first four verses of this prayer (*I Chronicles* 29:10-13) were uttered by David at one of the supreme moments of his life: Although he had been denied Divine permission to build the Holy Temple, he had assembled the necessary contributions and materials so that his heir, Solomon, could be ready to build it upon assuming the throne. In the presence of the assembled congregation, he thanked and blessed

	152 / שחרית לחול

L'cho Adōnoy hag'dulo
לְךָ יהוה הַגְּדֻלָּה
Yours, Hashem, is the greatness,*

v'hag'vuro v'hatif-eres
וְהַגְּבוּרָה וְהַתִּפְאֶרֶת
the strength, the splendor,

v'hanaytzach v'hahōd,
וְהַנֵּצַח וְהַהוֹד,
the triumph, and the glory,

ki chōl ba-shoma-yim u-vo-oretz;
כִּי כֹל בַּשָּׁמַיִם וּבָאָרֶץ;
even everything in heaven and earth;

l'cho Adōnoy hamamlocho
לְךָ יהוה הַמַּמְלָכָה
Yours, Hashem, is the kingdom,

v'hamisnasay l'chōl l'rōsh.
וְהַמִּתְנַשֵּׂא לְכֹל לְרֹאשׁ.
and the sovereignty over every leader.

IT IS CUSTOMARY TO SET ASIDE SOMETHING FOR CHARITY AT THIS POINT.

V'ho-ōsher v'hakovōd mil'fonecho,
וְהָעֹשֶׁר וְהַכָּבוֹד מִלְּפָנֶיךָ,
Wealth and honor come from You

v'ato mōshayl bakōl,
וְאַתָּה מוֹשֵׁל בַּכֹּל,
and You rule everything —

uvyod'cho kō-ach ugvuro,
וּבְיָדְךָ כֹּחַ וּגְבוּרָה,
in Your hand is power and strength,

uvyod'cho l'gadayl ulchazayk lakōl.
וּבְיָדְךָ לְגַדֵּל וּלְחַזֵּק לַכֹּל.
and it is in Your hand to make anyone great or strong.

V'ato Elōhaynu
וְעַתָּה אֱלֹהֵינוּ
So now, our God,

mōdim anachnu loch,
מוֹדִים אֲנַחְנוּ לָךְ,
we thank You

umhal'lim l'shaym tif-artecho.
וּמְהַלְלִים לְשֵׁם תִּפְאַרְתֶּךָ.
and praise Your splendrous Name."

Ato hu Adōnoy l'vadecho,
אַתָּה הוּא יהוה לְבַדֶּךָ,
It is You alone, Hashem,*

ato osiso es ha-shoma-yim,
אַתָּה עָשִׂיתָ אֶת הַשָּׁמַיִם,
You have made the heaven,

God for having allowed him to set aside resources for the Divine service.

לְךָ ה' הַגְּדֻלָּה — *Yours, Hashem, is the greatness.* In his moment of public glory, David scrupulously made clear that his every achievement was made possible by God and that it was meant to be utilized in His service. Lest anyone think that his attainments are to his own credit, David proclaims that God is Master of everything in heaven and earth and, because He has "sovereignty over every leader," He decrees who shall gain exalted positions and who shall be toppled.

אַתָּה הוּא ה' לְבַדֶּךָ — *It is You alone, Hashem.* The next six verses (*Nechemiah* 9:6-1) were recited by the people, led by the Levites, the day after the newly returned Jews had completed their first Succos festival in Jerusalem after returning from their Babylonian exile. They gathered in devotion and repentance and echoed the resolve voiced by David nearly five hundred years earlier.

SHACHARIS FOR WEEKDAYS — PESUKEI D'ZIMRAH

sh'may ha-shoma-yim v'chol tz'vo-om, שְׁמֵי הַשָּׁמַיִם וְכָל צְבָאָם,
the most exalted heaven and all their legions,

ho-oretz v'chol asher oleho, הָאָרֶץ וְכָל אֲשֶׁר עָלֶיהָ,
the earth and everything upon it,

ha-yamim v'chol asher bohem, הַיַּמִּים וְכָל אֲשֶׁר בָּהֶם,
the seas and everything in them,

v'ato m'cha-ye es kulom, וְאַתָּה מְחַיֶּה אֶת כֻּלָּם,
and You give them all life;*

utzvo ha-shoma-yim וּצְבָא הַשָּׁמַיִם
   l'cho mishta-chavim. לְךָ מִשְׁתַּחֲוִים.
and the heavenly legions bow to You.

Ato hu Adōnoy ho-Elōhim ❖ אַתָּה הוּא יהוה הָאֱלֹהִים
*It is You, H*ASHEM*, the God*

asher bocharto b'avrom, אֲשֶׁר בָּחַרְתָּ בְּאַבְרָם,
Who selected Abram,*

v'hōtzaysō may-ur kasdim, וְהוֹצֵאתוֹ מֵאוּר כַּשְׂדִּים,
and You brought him out of Ur Kasdim

v'samto sh'mō avrohom. וְשַׂמְתָּ שְׁמוֹ אַבְרָהָם.
and You made his name Abraham.*

U-motzoso es l'vovō וּמָצָאתָ אֶת לְבָבוֹ
   ne-emon l'fonecho — נֶאֱמָן לְפָנֶיךָ —
You found his heart faithful before You —

— **V'CHORŌS** imō hab'ris — **וְכָרוֹת** עִמּוֹ הַבְּרִית
and You established the covenant with him

losays es eretz hak'na-ani לָתֵת אֶת אֶרֶץ הַכְּנַעֲנִי
to give the land of the Canaanite,

ha-chiti ho-emōri v'hap'rizi, הַחִתִּי הָאֱמֹרִי וְהַפְּרִזִּי,
   v'haivusi v'hagirgoshi, וְהַיְבוּסִי וְהַגִּרְגָּשִׁי,
Hittite, Emorite, Perizzite, Jebusite, and Girgashite,

וְאַתָּה מְחַיֶּה אֶת כֻּלָּם — *And You give them all life.* Even inanimate objects have "life" in the sense that they have whatever conditions are necessary for their continued existence.

אֲשֶׁר בָּחַרְתָּ בְּאַבְרָם — *Who selected Abram.* After cataloguing the endless array of Creation and its components, we acknowledge that from them all, God chose Abraham and his offspring as His chosen ones — an astonishing testimony to the Patriarch and the nation he founded.

וְשַׂמְתָּ שְׁמוֹ אַבְרָהָם — *And you made his name Abraham.* The change of name signified that Abram's mission had been changed and elevated. His original name — Abram — means "father of Aram," because he had been a spiritual father of his native Aram. The new name — Abraham — means "father of a multitude [of nations]," marking him as the spiritual mentor of all mankind.

פסוקי דזמרה

losays l'zar-ō,	לָתֵת לְזַרְעוֹ,

to give it to his offspring;

vatokem es d'vorecho,	וַתָּקֶם אֶת דְּבָרֶיךָ,
ki tzadik oto.	כִּי צַדִּיק אָתָּה.

and You affirmed Your word, for You are righteous.

Vatayre es oni avōsaynu	וַתֵּרֶא אֶת עֳנִי אֲבֹתֵינוּ
b'mitzroyim,	בְּמִצְרָיִם,

You observed the suffering of our forefathers in Egypt,

v'es za-akosom shomato	וְאֶת זַעֲקָתָם שָׁמַעְתָּ
al yam suf.	עַל יַם סוּף.

and their outcry You heard at the Sea of Reeds.

Vatitayn ō-sōs u-mōf'sim b'far-ō	וַתִּתֵּן אֹתֹת וּמֹפְתִים בְּפַרְעֹה

You imposed signs and wonders upon Pharaoh

uvchol avodov uvchol am artzō,	וּבְכָל עֲבָדָיו וּבְכָל עַם אַרְצוֹ,

and upon all his servants, and upon all the people of his land.

ki yodato ki hayzidu alayhem,	כִּי יָדַעְתָּ כִּי הֵזִידוּ עֲלֵיהֶם,

For You knew that they sinned willfully* against them,

vata-as l'cho shaym k'ha-yōm ha-ze.	וַתַּעַשׂ לְךָ שֵׁם כְּהַיּוֹם הַזֶּה.

and You brought Yourself renown as [clear as] this very day.

❖ V'ha-yom bokato lifnayhem,	❖ וְהַיָּם בָּקַעְתָּ לִפְנֵיהֶם,

You split the Sea before them

va-ya-avru v'sōch ha-yom ba-yabosho,	וַיַּעַבְרוּ בְתוֹךְ הַיָּם בַּיַּבָּשָׁה,

and they crossed in the midst of the Sea on dry land;

v'es rōd'fayhem	וְאֶת רֹדְפֵיהֶם
hishlachto vimtzōlōs,	הִשְׁלַכְתָּ בִמְצוֹלֹת,

but their pursuers You hurled into the depths,

k'mō even b'ma-yim azim.	כְּמוֹ אֶבֶן בְּמַיִם עַזִּים.

like a stone into turbulent waters.

■ Each day I repeat the Song recited by Moses and Israel at the Splitting of the Sea of Reeds. In addition to my appreciation of Hashem in the natural world order, my recognition of His performing miraculous events constitutes the full praise of Hashem.

VA-YŌSHA Adōnoy ba-yōm hahu   **וַיּוֹשַׁע** יהוה בַּיּוֹם הַהוּא

HASHEM saved* — on that day —

כִּי הֵזִידוּ — *That they sinned willfully.* The Egyptians sinned against the Jews by mistreating and enslaving them. Had the servitude not been so harsh and hatefully cruel, the Egyptians would not have suffered such devastation.

וַיּוֹשַׁע ה׳ — *HASHEM saved.* In these two verses the Torah sums up the miracle at the Sea as a prelude to Moses' song. The miracles of the Exodus, beginning with the Ten Plagues, illustrate that God controls every facet of nature at

es yisro-ayl mi-yad mitzro-yim,	אֶת יִשְׂרָאֵל מִיַּד מִצְרָיִם,
Israel from the hand of Egypt,	
va-yar yisro-ayl es mitzra-yim	וַיַּרְא יִשְׂרָאֵל אֶת מִצְרַיִם
and Israel saw the Egyptians	
mays al s'fas ha-yom.	מֵת עַל שְׂפַת הַיָּם.
dead on the seashore.	
❖ Va-yar yisro-ayl es ha-yod hag'dōlo	❖ וַיַּרְא יִשְׂרָאֵל אֶת הַיָּד הַגְּדֹלָה
Israel saw the great hand	
asher oso Adōnoy b'mitzra-yim,	אֲשֶׁר עָשָׂה יהוה בְּמִצְרַיִם,
that HASHEM inflicted upon Egypt	
va-yir'u ho-om es Adōnoy,	וַיִּירְאוּ הָעָם אֶת יהוה,
and the people feared HASHEM,	
va-ya-aminu Badōnoy uvmōshe avdō.	וַיַּאֲמִינוּ בַּיהוה וּבְמֹשֶׁה עַבְדּוֹ.
and they had faith in HASHEM and in Moses, His servant.	
OZ YOSHIR mōshe uvnay yisro-ayl	**אָז יָשִׁיר** מֹשֶׁה וּבְנֵי יִשְׂרָאֵל
Then Moses and the Children of Israel chose to sing	
es ha-shiro ha-zōs Ladōnoy,	אֶת הַשִּׁירָה הַזֹּאת לַיהוה,
this song to HASHEM,	
va-yōm'ru laymōr,	וַיֹּאמְרוּ לֵאמֹר,
and they said the following:	
oshiro Ladōnoy ki go-ō go-o,	אָשִׁירָה לַיהוה כִּי גָאֹה גָּאָה,
I shall sing to HASHEM for He is exalted above the arrogant,	
sus v'rōch'vō romo va-yom.	סוּס וְרֹכְבוֹ רָמָה בַיָּם.
having hurled horse with its rider into the sea.	
Ozi v'zimros Yoh vai-hi li lishu-o,	עָזִּי וְזִמְרָת יָהּ וַיְהִי לִי לִישׁוּעָה,
God is my might and my praise, and He was a salvation for me.	
ze Ayli v'anvayhu,	זֶה אֵלִי וְאַנְוֵהוּ,
This is my God,* and I will build Him a Sanctuary;	
Elōhay ovi va-arōm'menhu.	אֱלֹהֵי אָבִי וַאֲרֹמְמֶנְהוּ.
the God of my father, and I will exalt Him.	
Adōnoy ish milchomo Adōnoy sh'mō.	יהוה אִישׁ מִלְחָמָה, יהוה שְׁמוֹ.
HASHEM is Master of war, through His Name HASHEM.*	

---

will. Thus, they remain the testimony to God as the all-powerful Creator: No human being saw the Creation of the universe, but millions of Jews witnessed the Exodus. The climax of those miraculous events was the Splitting of the Sea, an event celebrated by Moses and the entire nation in the glorious Song of the Sea (*Exodus* 14:30-15:19).

זֶה אֵלִי — *This is my God.* So obvious was God's presence that the Jews could point to it, as it were, and say, "This is my God."

ה' שְׁמוֹ — *Through His Name HASHEM.* Mortal kings require legions and armaments, but God overcomes His enemies with nothing more than His Name.

Mark'vōs par-ō v'chaylō yoro va-yom,	מַרְכְּבֹת פַּרְעֹה וְחֵילוֹ יָרָה בַיָּם,
Pharaoh's chariots and army He threw into the sea;	
u-mivchar sholishov tub'u v'yam suf.	וּמִבְחַר שָׁלִשָׁיו טֻבְּעוּ בְיַם־סוּף.
and the pick of his officers were mired in the Sea of Reeds.	
T'hōmōs y'chasyumu,	תְּהֹמֹת יְכַסְיֻמוּ,
Deep waters covered them;	
yor'du vimtzōlōs k'mō oven.	יָרְדוּ בִמְצוֹלֹת כְּמוֹ אָבֶן.
they descended in the depths like stone.	
Y'min'cho Adōnoy nedori bakō-ach,	יְמִינְךָ יהוה נֶאְדָּרִי בַּכֹּחַ,
Your right hand,* HASHEM, is adorned with strength;	
Y'min'cho Adōnoy tir-atz ōyayv.	יְמִינְךָ יהוה תִּרְעַץ אוֹיֵב.
Your right hand, HASHEM, smashes the enemy.	
Uvrōv g'ōn'cho tahorōs komecho,	וּבְרֹב גְּאוֹנְךָ תַּהֲרֹס קָמֶיךָ,
In Your abundant grandeur You shatter Your opponents;	
t'shalach charōn'cho	תְּשַׁלַּח חֲרֹנְךָ
yōch'laymō kakash.	יֹאכְלֵמוֹ כַּקַּשׁ.
You dispatch Your wrath, it consumes them like straw.	
Uvru-ach apecho ne-ermu ma-yim,	וּבְרוּחַ אַפֶּיךָ נֶעֶרְמוּ מַיִם,
At a blast from Your nostrils the waters were heaped up;	
nitz'vu ch'mō nayd nōz'lim,	נִצְּבוּ כְמוֹ נֵד נֹזְלִים,
straight as a wall stood the running water,	
kof'u s'hōmōs b'lev yom.	קָפְאוּ תְהֹמֹת בְּלֶב יָם.
the deep waters congealed in the heart of the sea.	
Omar ōyayv,	אָמַר אוֹיֵב,
The enemy declared:	
erdōf asig achalayk sholol,	אֶרְדֹּף אַשִּׂיג אֲחַלֵּק שָׁלָל,
"I will pursue, I will overtake, I will divide plunder;	
timlo-aymō nafshi,	תִּמְלָאֵמוֹ נַפְשִׁי,
I will satisfy my lust with them;	
orik charbi, tōrishaymō yodi.	אָרִיק חַרְבִּי, תּוֹרִישֵׁמוֹ יָדִי.
I will unsheathe my sword, my hand will impoverish them."	
Noshafto v'ruchacho kisomō yom,	נָשַׁפְתָּ בְרוּחֲךָ כִּסָּמוֹ יָם,
You blew with Your wind — the sea enshrouded them;	
tzol'lu ka-ōferes b'ma-yim, adirim.	צָלְלוּ כַּעוֹפֶרֶת בְּמַיִם, אַדִּירִים.
the mighty ones sank like lead in the waters.	

יְמִינְךָ — *Your right hand*. Of course God has no physical characteristic. All the Scriptural references to physicality are allegorical. The right hand symbolizes power. Similarly, below, God's wrath is described as a blast from His nostrils, because angry people tend to snort.

Mi chomōcho bo-aylim Adōnoy,	מִי כָמֹֽכָה בָּאֵלִם יהוה,

Who is like You among the heavenly powers, HASHEM!

mi komōcho nedor bakōdesh,	מִי כָּמֹֽכָה נֶאְדָּר בַּקֹּֽדֶשׁ,

Who is like You, mighty in holiness,

nōro s'hilōs ō-say fele.	נוֹרָא תְהִלֹּת עֹֽשֵׂה פֶֽלֶא.

too awesome for praise, doing wonders!

Notiso y'min'cho, tivlo-aymō oretz.	נָטִֽיתָ יְמִינְךָ, תִּבְלָעֵֽמוֹ אָֽרֶץ.

You stretched out Your right hand — the earth swallowed them.

Nochiso v'chasd'cho am zu go-olto,	נָחִֽיתָ בְחַסְדְּךָ עַם זוּ גָּאָֽלְתָּ,

You guided with Your kindness this people that You redeemed;

nayhalto v'oz'cho el n'vay kodshecho.	נֵהַֽלְתָּ בְעָזְּךָ אֶל נְוֵה קָדְשֶֽׁךָ.

You led with Your might to Your holy abode.*

Shom'u amim yirgozun,	שָׁמְעוּ עַמִּים יִרְגָּזוּן,

Peoples heard — they were agitated;

chil ochaz yōsh'vay p'loshes.	חִיל אָחַז יֹשְׁבֵי פְּלָֽשֶׁת.

convulsive terror gripped the dwellers of Philistia.

Oz nivhalu alufay edōm,	אָז נִבְהֲלוּ אַלּוּפֵי אֱדוֹם,

Then the chieftains of Edom were confounded,

aylay mō-ov yōchazaymō ro-ad,	אֵילֵי מוֹאָב יֹאחֲזֵֽמוֹ רָֽעַד,

trembling gripped the powers of Moab,

nomōgu kōl yōsh'vay ch'no-an.	נָמֹֽגוּ כֹּל יֹשְׁבֵי כְנָֽעַן.

all the dwellers of Canaan dissolved.

Tipōl alayhem aymoso vofachad,	תִּפֹּל עֲלֵיהֶם אֵימָֽתָה וָפַֽחַד,

May fear and terror befall them,

bigdōl z'rō-acho yid'mu ko-oven,	בִּגְדֹל זְרוֹעֲךָ יִדְּמוּ כָּאָֽבֶן,

at the greatness of Your arm may they be still as stone;

ad ya-avōr am'cho Adōnoy,	עַד יַעֲבֹר עַמְּךָ יהוה,

until Your people passes through, HASHEM,

ad ya-avōr am zu koniso.	עַד יַעֲבֹר עַם זוּ קָנִֽיתָ.

until this people You have acquired passes through.

T'vi-aymō v'sito-aymō	תְּבִאֵֽמוֹ וְתִטָּעֵֽמוֹ

You shall bring them and implant them

b'har nachalos'cho,	בְּהַר נַחֲלָתְךָ,

on the mount of Your heritage,

אֶל נְוֵה קָדְשֶֽׁךָ — *To Your holy abode*, i.e., the Holy Temple. Although the Temple would not be built for over four hundred years, it is typical for prophetic song to combine the past with the future, because in the Divine perception they are interrelated.

מָכוֹן לְשִׁבְתְּךָ פָּעַלְתָּ יהוה, — mochōn l'shivt'cho po-alto Adōnoy,
the foundation of Your dwelling-place, which You, HASHEM, have made:

מִקְּדָשׁ אֲדֹנָי כּוֹנְנוּ יָדֶיךָ. — mik'dosh Adōnoy kōn'nu yodecho.
the Sanctuary, my Lord, that Your hands established.

יהוה יִמְלֹךְ לְעֹלָם וָעֶד. — Adōnoy yimlōch l'ōlom vo-ed.
HASHEM shall reign for all eternity.*

יהוה יִמְלֹךְ לְעֹלָם וָעֶד. — Adōnoy yimlōch l'ōlom vo-ed.
HASHEM shall reign for all eternity.

(יהוה מַלְכוּתֵהּ קָאֵם, — (Adōnoy malchusayh ko-aym,
לְעָלַם וּלְעָלְמֵי עָלְמַיָּא.) — l'olam ul-ol'may ol'ma-yo.)
(HASHEM — His kingdom is established forever and ever.)

כִּי בָא סוּס פַּרְעֹה — Ki vo sus par-ō
When Pharaoh's cavalry came —

בְּרִכְבּוֹ וּבְפָרָשָׁיו בַּיָּם, — b'richbō uvforoshov ba-yom,
with his chariots and horsemen — into the sea

וַיָּשֶׁב יהוה עֲלֵהֶם — va-yoshev Adōnoy alayhem
אֶת מֵי הַיָּם, — es may ha-yom,
and HASHEM turned back the waters of the sea upon them,

וּבְנֵי יִשְׂרָאֵל — uvnay yisro-ayl
הָלְכוּ בַיַּבָּשָׁה בְּתוֹךְ הַיָּם. — hol'chu va-yabosho b'sōch ha-yom.
the Children of Israel walked on the dry bed amid the sea.

❖ כִּי לַיהוה הַמְּלוּכָה, — Ki Ladōnoy ham'lucho,
וּמֹשֵׁל בַּגּוֹיִם. — u-mōshayl bagōyim.
For the sovereignty is HASHEM's* and He rules over nations.

וְעָלוּ מוֹשִׁעִים בְּהַר צִיּוֹן, — V'olu mōshi-im b'har tziyōn,
The saviors will ascend Mount Zion

לִשְׁפֹּט אֶת הַר עֵשָׂו, — lishpōt es har ay-sov,
to judge Esau's mountain,

וְהָיְתָה לַיהוה הַמְּלוּכָה. — v'hoy'so Ladōnoy ham'lucho.
and the kingdom will be HASHEM's.

וְהָיָה יהוה לְמֶלֶךְ — V'ho-yo Adōnoy l'melech
עַל כָּל הָאָרֶץ, — al kol ho-oretz,
Then HASHEM will be King over all the world,

ה' יִמְלֹךְ לְעֹלָם וָעֶד — *HASHEM shall reign for all eternity.* This verse is repeated to signify that it is the climax of the Song — that God's sovereignty shall be recognized forever. Because of the importance of this idea the Aramaic Targum of this verse is also recited.

כִּי לַה' הַמְּלוּכָה — *For the sovereignty is HASHEM's.* The collected verses attached to the Song are appropriate to the climactic verse that God will reign forever.

SHACHARIS FOR WEEKDAYS — PESUKEI D'ZIMRAH

ba-yōm hahu yih-ye Adōnoy e-chod ushmō e-chod.
בַּיּוֹם הַהוּא יִהְיֶה יהוה אֶחָד וּשְׁמוֹ אֶחָד.

on that day HASHEM will be One and His Name will be One.

SOME CONGREGATIONS CONCLUDE:

(Uvsōros'cho kosuv lamōr:
(וּבְתוֹרָתְךָ כָּתוּב לֵאמֹר:

(And in Your Torah it is written:

Sh'ma yisro-ayl Adōnoy Elōhaynu Adōnoy e-chod.)
שְׁמַע יִשְׂרָאֵל יהוה אֱלֹהֵינוּ יהוה אֶחָד.)

Hear O Israel: Hashem is our God, Hashem, the One and Only.)

■ *The praises of Hashem are never ending. In the closing blessing of Pesukei D'Zimrah I pray that the Name of Hashem will be praised forever.*

STAND WHILE RECITING THE FOLLOWING BLESSING:

YISHTABACH shimcho lo-ad malkaynu,
יִשְׁתַּבַּח שִׁמְךָ לָעַד מַלְכֵּנוּ,

May Your Name be praised forever — our King,

ho-Ayl hamelech hagodōl v'hakodōsh, ba-shoma-yim u-vo-oretz.
הָאֵל הַמֶּלֶךְ הַגָּדוֹל וְהַקָּדוֹשׁ, בַּשָּׁמַיִם וּבָאָרֶץ.

the God, the great and holy King — in heaven and on earth.

Ki l'cho no-e Adōnoy Elōhaynu Vaylōhay avōsaynu,
כִּי לְךָ נָאֶה יהוה אֱלֹהֵינוּ וֵאלֹהֵי אֲבוֹתֵינוּ,

Because for You is fitting — O HASHEM, our God and the God of our forefathers —

shir ushvocho, halayl v'zimro,
שִׁיר וּשְׁבָחָה, הַלֵּל וְזִמְרָה,

song and praise, lauding and hymns,

ōz u-memsholo, netzach, g'dulo ug-vuro,
עֹז וּמֶמְשָׁלָה, נֶצַח גְּדֻלָּה וּגְבוּרָה,

power and dominion, triumph, greatness and strength,

t'hilo v'sif-eres, k'dusho u-malchus,
תְּהִלָּה וְתִפְאֶרֶת, קְדֻשָּׁה וּמַלְכוּת,

praise and splendor, holiness and sovereignty,

b'rochōs v'hōdo-ōs may-ato v'ad ōlom.
בְּרָכוֹת וְהוֹדָאוֹת מֵעַתָּה וְעַד עוֹלָם.

blessings and thanksgivings from this time and forever.

Boruch ato Adōnoy,
❖ בָּרוּךְ אַתָּה יהוה,

Blessed are You, HASHEM,

Ayl melech godōl batishbochōs,
אֵל מֶלֶךְ גָּדוֹל בַּתִּשְׁבָּחוֹת,

God, King exalted through praises,*

גָּדוֹל בַּתִּשְׁבָּחוֹת — *Exalted through praises.* The implication is not that God requires our praises in order to become exalted, for His infinite greatness is beyond our capacity to compre-

160 / שחרית לחול — פסוקי דזמרה

אֵל הַהוֹדָאוֹת, אֲדוֹן הַנִּפְלָאוֹת,
Ayl hahōdo-ōs, adōn haniflo-ōs,
God of thanksgivings, Master of wonders,

הַבּוֹחֵר בְּשִׁירֵי זִמְרָה,
habōchayr b'shiray zimro,
Who chooses musical songs of praise —

מֶלֶךְ אֵל חֵי הָעוֹלָמִים.
melech Ayl chay ho-ōlomim.
King, God, Life-giver of the world.*

CONGREGATION RESPONDS: Omayn – אָמֵן

FROM ROSH HASHANAH UNTIL YOM KIPPUR SOME CONGREGATIONS RECITE THE FOLLOWING (PSALM 130). THE ARK IS OPENED. EACH VERSE IS RECITED ALOUD BY THE CHAZZAN, THEN REPEATED BY THE CONGREGATION.

SHIR HAMA-ALŌS, שִׁיר הַמַּעֲלוֹת,
A song of ascents:

מִמַּעֲמַקִּים קְרָאתִיךָ יהוה.
mima-amakim k'rosicho Adōnoy.
From the depths I called You, HASHEM.

אֲדֹנָי שִׁמְעָה בְקוֹלִי,
Adōnoy shim-o v'kōli,
My Lord, hear my voice,

תִּהְיֶינָה אָזְנֶיךָ קַשֻּׁבוֹת לְקוֹל תַּחֲנוּנָי.
tih-yeno oz-necho kashuvōs l'kōl tachanunoy.
may Your ears be attentive to the sound of my pleas.

אִם עֲוֹנוֹת תִּשְׁמָר יָהּ,
Im avonōs tishmor Yoh,
If You preserve iniquities, O God,

אֲדֹנָי מִי יַעֲמֹד.
Adōnoy mi ya-amōd.
my Lord, who could survive?

כִּי עִמְּךָ הַסְּלִיחָה,
Ki im'cho has'licho,
For with You is forgiveness,

לְמַעַן תִּוָּרֵא.
l'ma-an tivoray.
that You may be feared.

קִוִּיתִי יהוה קִוְּתָה נַפְשִׁי,
Kivisi Adōnoy kiv'so nafshi,
I put my confidence in HASHEM, *my soul put confidence,*

וְלִדְבָרוֹ הוֹחָלְתִּי.
v'lidvorō hōcholti.
and I hoped for His word.

נַפְשִׁי לַאדֹנָי,
Nafshi LaAdōnoy,
מִשֹּׁמְרִים לַבֹּקֶר,
mishōm'rim labōker,
I yearn for my Lord, among those longing for the dawn,

שֹׁמְרִים לַבֹּקֶר.
shōm'rim labōker.
those longing for the dawn.

---

hend, much less express. Rather, it is His will that we have the privilege of exalting Him, despite our inability to do so adequately.

חֵי הָעוֹלָמִים — *Life-giver of the world.* This essential principle of Jewish belief reiterates that Creation is an ongoing process — God

SHEMA AND ITS BLESSINGS

Yachayl yisro-ayl el Adōnoy,   יַחֵל יִשְׂרָאֵל אֶל יהוה,
Let Israel hope for HASHEM,

ki im Adōnoy ha-chesed,   כִּי עִם יהוה הַחֶסֶד,
for with HASHEM *is kindness,*

v'harbay imō f'dus.   וְהַרְבֵּה עִמּוֹ פְדוּת.
and with Him is abundant redemption.

V'hu yifde es yisro-ayl,   וְהוּא יִפְדֶּה אֶת יִשְׂרָאֵל,
mikōl avonōsov.   מִכֹּל עֲוֹנוֹתָיו.
And He shall redeem Israel from all its iniquities.

THE *CHAZZAN* RECITES *HALF-KADDISH*.
(Congregational responses are indicated by parentheses.)

יִתְגַּדַּל וְיִתְקַדַּשׁ שְׁמֵהּ רַבָּא. (Omayn – אָמֵן). בְּעָלְמָא דִּי בְרָא כִרְעוּתֵהּ. וְיַמְלִיךְ מַלְכוּתֵהּ, בְּחַיֵּיכוֹן וּבְיוֹמֵיכוֹן וּבְחַיֵּי דְכָל בֵּית יִשְׂרָאֵל, בַּעֲגָלָא וּבִזְמַן קָרִיב. וְאִמְרוּ: אָמֵן.

(אָמֵן. יְהֵא שְׁמֵהּ רַבָּא מְבָרַךְ לְעָלַם וּלְעָלְמֵי עָלְמַיָּא.)
(Omayn. Y'hay sh'mayh rabo m'vorach l'olam ul-ol'may ol'ma-yo.)

יְהֵא שְׁמֵהּ רַבָּא מְבָרַךְ לְעָלַם וּלְעָלְמֵי עָלְמַיָּא. יִתְבָּרַךְ וְיִשְׁתַּבַּח וְיִתְפָּאַר וְיִתְרוֹמַם וְיִתְנַשֵּׂא וְיִתְהַדָּר וְיִתְעַלֶּה וְיִתְהַלָּל שְׁמֵהּ דְקֻדְשָׁא בְּרִיךְ הוּא (בְּרִיךְ הוּא – B'rich hu). °לְעֵלָּא מִן כָּל
[substitute *from Rosh Hashanah to Yom Kippur* — °לְעֵלָּא לְעֵלָּא מִכָּל]
בִּרְכָתָא וְשִׁירָתָא תֻּשְׁבְּחָתָא וְנֶחֱמָתָא, דַּאֲמִירָן בְּעָלְמָא. וְאִמְרוּ: אָמֵן.
(אָמֵן – Omayn).

CHAZZAN SUMMONS THE CONGREGATION TO JOIN IN THE FORTHCOMING PRAYERS,
BOWING AT Bor'chu AND STRAIGHTENING UP AT Adōnoy:

BOR'CHU es Adōnoy ham'vōroch.   **בָּרְכוּ** אֶת יהוה הַמְבֹרָךְ.
Bless HASHEM, *the blessed One.*

CONGREGATION, FOLLOWED BY *CHAZZAN*, RESPONDS:
BOWING AT Bor'chu AND STRAIGHTENING UP AT Adōnoy.

Boruch Adōnoy   בָּרוּךְ יהוה
ham'vōroch l'ōlom vo-ed.   הַמְבֹרָךְ לְעוֹלָם וָעֶד.
Blessed is HASHEM, *the blessed One, for all eternity.*

BLESSINGS OF THE SHEMA

■ First blessing preceding the *Shema:* I praise Hashem for His governing the universe and acknowledge that everything emanates from Hashem — both that which is visibly and understandably good and that which is not.

---

created and continues to create. Because He gives life constantly, our thanks and praise are likewise constant.

◆§ **Blessings of the Shema**

The blessing of the *Shema* comprise the third section of *Shacharis,* whose central fea-

שחרית לחול / 162   קריאת שמע וברכותיה

IT IS CUSTOMARY TO TOUCH THE ARM-TEFILLIN WHEN SAYING yōtzayr ōr
AND THE HEAD-TEFILLIN WHILE SAYING u-vōray chōshech.

BORUCH ato Adōnoy   בָּרוּךְ אַתָּה יהוה
Blessed are You, HASHEM,

Elōhaynu melech ho-ōlom,   אֱלֹהֵינוּ מֶלֶךְ הָעוֹלָם,
our God, King of the universe,

yōtzayr ōr u-vōray chōshech,   יוֹצֵר אוֹר וּבוֹרֵא חֹשֶׁךְ,
Who forms light and creates darkness,*

ō-se sholōm u-vōray es hakōl.   עֹשֶׂה שָׁלוֹם וּבוֹרֵא אֶת הַכֹּל.
makes peace and creates all.

HAMAY-IR lo-oretz v'ladorim oleho   הַמֵּאִיר לָאָרֶץ וְלַדָּרִים עָלֶיהָ
b'rachamim,   בְּרַחֲמִים,
He Who illuminates the earth and those who dwell upon it,* *with compassion;*

uvtuvō m'chadaysh   וּבְטוּבוֹ מְחַדֵּשׁ
b'chol yōm tomid   בְּכָל יוֹם תָּמִיד
and in His goodness renews daily, perpetually,

ma-asay v'rayshis.   מַעֲשֵׂה בְרֵאשִׁית.
the work of Creation.

Mo rabu ma-asecho Adōnoy,   מָה רַבּוּ מַעֲשֶׂיךָ יהוה,
How great are Your works, HASHEM,

kulom b'chochmo osiso,   כֻּלָּם בְּחָכְמָה עָשִׂיתָ,
You make them all with wisdom,

mol'o ho-oretz kinyonecho.   מָלְאָה הָאָרֶץ קִנְיָנֶךָ.
the world is full of Your possessions.

Hamelech ham'rōmom   הַמֶּלֶךְ הַמְרוֹמָם
l'vadō may-oz,   לְבַדּוֹ מֵאָז,
The King Who was exalted in solitude before Creation,

---

ture is the *Shema*. The recitation of *Shema* is mandated by the Torah and is the basic acknowledgment of God's sovereignty and Oneness. The morning *Shema* is accompanied by three blessings (two before it and one after it), which (a) express God's mastery over nature, (b) pray for intellectual and moral attainment through the study of Torah, and (c) describe God's role in the flow of history.

יוֹצֵר אוֹר וּבוֹרֵא חֹשֶׁךְ — *Who forms light and creates darkness.* Since the beginning of time, the term light has symbolized new life, wisdom, happiness — all the things associated with goodness. Darkness, however, is associated with suffering, failure and death. The philosophers of idolatry claimed that the good god who creates light cannot also be the bad one who creates darkness. Therefore, they reasoned, there must be at least two gods. In modern times, the same argument is presented in different terms: How can there be a God if He allows bad things to happen? This blessing refutes the argument that anything people find unpleasant either is not an act of God or proves that He lacks power. To the contrary, we believe unequivocally that God is One; what appears to our limited human intelligence to be contradictory or evil is really part of the plan of the One Merciful God, despite our failure to understand it.

הַמֵּאִיר לָאָרֶץ וְלַדָּרִים עָלֶיהָ — *He Who illuminates the earth and those who dwell upon it.* The

ham'shuboch v'ham'fō-or	הַמְשֻׁבָּח וְהַמְפֹאָר
v'hamisnasay mimōs ōlom.	וְהַמִּתְנַשֵּׂא מִימוֹת עוֹלָם.

Who is praised, glorified, and upraised since days of old.

Elōhay ōlom,	אֱלֹהֵי עוֹלָם,

Eternal God,

b'rachamecho horabim	בְּרַחֲמֶיךָ הָרַבִּים
rachaym olaynu,	רַחֵם עָלֵינוּ,

with Your abundant compassion be compassionate to us —

adōn u-zaynu, tzur misgabaynu,	אֲדוֹן עֻזֵּנוּ, צוּר מִשְׂגַּבֵּנוּ,

O Master of our power, our rocklike stronghold,

mogayn yish-aynu, misgov ba-adaynu.	מָגֵן יִשְׁעֵנוּ, מִשְׂגָּב בַּעֲדֵנוּ.

O Shield of our salvation, be a stronghold for us.

Ayl boruch g'dōl day-o,	אֵל בָּרוּךְ גְּדוֹל דֵּעָה,

The blessed God,* Who is great in knowledge,

haychin u-fo-al zohoray chamo,	הֵכִין וּפָעַל זָהֳרֵי חַמָּה,

prepared and worked on the rays of the sun;

tōv yotzar kovōd lishmō,	טוֹב יָצַר כָּבוֹד לִשְׁמוֹ,

the Beneficent One fashioned honor for His Name,

m'ōrōs nosan s'vivōs u-zō,	מְאוֹרוֹת נָתַן סְבִיבוֹת עֻזּוֹ,

emplaced luminaries all around His power;

pinōs tz'vo-ov k'dōshim	פִּנּוֹת צְבָאָיו קְדוֹשִׁים
rōm'may Shadai,	רוֹמְמֵי שַׁדַּי,

the leaders of His legions, holy ones, Who exalt the Almighty,

tomid m'sap'rim	תָּמִיד מְסַפְּרִים
k'vōd Ayl ukdushosō.	כְּבוֹד אֵל וּקְדֻשָּׁתוֹ.

constantly relate the honor of God and His sanctity.

Tisborach Adōnoy Elōhaynu	תִּתְבָּרַךְ יהוה אֱלֹהֵינוּ

May You be blessed, HASHEM, our God,

al shevach ma-asay yodecho,	עַל שֶׁבַח מַעֲשֵׂה יָדֶיךָ,

beyond the praises of Your handiwork

v'al m'ōray ōr she-osiso,	וְעַל מְאוֹרֵי אוֹר שֶׁעָשִׂיתָ,

and beyond the bright luminaries that You have made —

y'fo-aru-cho, selo.	יְפָאֲרוּךָ, סֶּלָה.

may they glorify You — Selah!

---

earth's dwellers enjoy the light, but so does the earth itself, because sunlight makes vegetation possible.

אֵל בָּרוּךְ — *The blessed God.* From here, the next twenty-two words follow the order of the *alef-beis.*

■ *We recount the daily praise of Hashem respectfully offered by the angels and celestial beings.*

TISBORACH tzuraynu malkaynu v'gō-alaynu,   תִּתְבָּרֵךְ צוּרֵנוּ מַלְכֵּנוּ וְגוֹאֲלֵנוּ,

May You be blessed, our Rock,* our King and our Redeemer,

bōray k'dōshim.   בּוֹרֵא קְדוֹשִׁים.

Creator of holy ones;

Yishtabach shimcho lo-ad malkaynu,   יִשְׁתַּבַּח שִׁמְךָ לָעַד מַלְכֵּנוּ,

may Your Name be praised forever, our King,

yōtzayr m'shor'sim,   יוֹצֵר מְשָׁרְתִים,

O Fashioner of ministering angels;

va-asher m'shor'sov kulom ōm'dim b'rum ōlom,   וַאֲשֶׁר מְשָׁרְתָיו כֻּלָּם עוֹמְדִים בְּרוּם עוֹלָם,

all of Whose ministering angels stand at the summit of the universe

u-mashmi-im b'yiro yachad b'kōl   וּמַשְׁמִיעִים בְּיִרְאָה יַחַד בְּקוֹל

and proclaim — with awe, together, loudly —

divray Elōhim cha-yim u-melech ōlom.   דִּבְרֵי אֱלֹהִים חַיִּים וּמֶלֶךְ עוֹלָם.

the words of the living God and King of the universe.

Kulom ahuvim, kulom b'rurim, kulom gibōrim,   כֻּלָּם אֲהוּבִים, כֻּלָּם בְּרוּרִים, כֻּלָּם גִּבּוֹרִים,

They are all beloved; they are all flawless; they are all mighty;

v'chulom ōsim b'aymo uvyir-o r'tzōn kōnom.   וְכֻלָּם עוֹשִׂים בְּאֵימָה וּבְיִרְאָה רְצוֹן קוֹנָם.

they all do the will of their Maker with dread and reverence.

❖ V'chulom pōs'chim es pihem   וְכֻלָּם פּוֹתְחִים אֶת פִּיהֶם

And they all open their mouth

bikdusho uvtohoro, b'shiro uvzimro,   בִּקְדֻשָּׁה וּבְטָהֳרָה, בְּשִׁירָה וּבְזִמְרָה,

in holiness and purity, in song and hymn —

umvor'chim umshab'chim umfo-arim uma-aritzim umakdishim umamlichim —   וּמְבָרְכִים וּמְשַׁבְּחִים וּמְפָאֲרִים וּמַעֲרִיצִים וּמַקְדִּישִׁים וּמַמְלִיכִים —

and bless, praise, glorify, revere, sanctify and declare the kingship of —

תִּתְבָּרֵךְ צוּרֵנוּ — *May You be blessed, our Rock.* The previous paragraph expressed man's praise of God. Now we turn to the angels' praise of Him. Since there have been people who worshiped the heavenly bodies as independent gods, we now cite the prayers of the heav-

ES SHAYM ho-Ayl, אֶת שֵׁם הָאֵל
the Name of God,

hamelech hagodōl hagibōr v'hanōro, הַמֶּלֶךְ הַגָּדוֹל הַגִּבּוֹר וְהַנּוֹרָא
kodōsh hu. קָדוֹשׁ הוּא.
the great, mighty, and awesome King; holy is He.

❖ V'chulom m'kab'lim alayhem ❖ וְכֻלָּם מְקַבְּלִים עֲלֵיהֶם
Then they all accept upon themselves

ōl malchus shoma-yim ze mi-ze, עֹל מַלְכוּת שָׁמַיִם זֶה מִזֶּה,
the yoke of heavenly sovereignty from one another,*

v'nōs'nim r'shus ze lo-ze, וְנוֹתְנִים רְשׁוּת זֶה לָזֶה,
and grant permission to one another

l'hakdish l'yōtz'rom, לְהַקְדִּישׁ לְיוֹצְרָם,
to sanctify the One Who formed them,

b'nachas ru-ach בְּנַחַת רוּחַ
b'sofo v'ruro u-vin-imo. בְּשָׂפָה בְרוּרָה וּבִנְעִימָה.
with tranquility, with clear articulation, and with sweetness.

K'dusho kulom k'e-chod קְדֻשָּׁה כֻּלָּם כְּאֶחָד
ōnim v'ōm'rim b'yir-o: עוֹנִים וְאוֹמְרִים בְּיִרְאָה:
All of them as one proclaim His holiness and say with awe:

CONGREGATION RECITES ALOUD:

kodōsh kodōsh kodōsh קָדוֹשׁ קָדוֹשׁ קָדוֹשׁ
Adōnoy tz'vo-ōs, יהוה צְבָאוֹת,
"Holy, holy, holy* is HASHEM, *Master of Legions,*

m'lō chol ho-oretz k'vōdo. מְלֹא כָל הָאָרֶץ כְּבוֹדוֹ.
the whole world is filled with His glory."

❖ V'ho-ōfanim v'cha-yōs hakōdesh ❖ וְהָאוֹפַנִּים וְחַיּוֹת הַקֹּדֶשׁ
Then the Ofanim* and the holy Chayos,

b'ra-ash godōl בְּרַעַשׁ גָּדוֹל
misnas'im l'umas s'rofim. מִתְנַשְּׂאִים לְעֻמַּת שְׂרָפִים.
with great noise, raise themselves towards the Seraphim.

---

enly legions, for they know that the sun and the moon are but God's creations and servants.

וְכֻלָּם מְקַבְּלִים... זֶה מִזֶּה — *Then they all accept... from one another.* Unlike people whose competitive jealousies cause them to thwart and outdo one another, angels urge one another to take the initiative in serving and praising God. Conflict is the foe of perfection, harmony is its ally.

קָדוֹשׁ קָדוֹשׁ קָדוֹשׁ — *Holy, holy, holy.* God is *holy* with relation to the physical world, *holy* with relation to the spiritual world and *holy* with relation to the World to Come.

וְהָאוֹפַנִּים — *Then the Ofanim.* The categories of angels are not translated since we lack the vocabulary to define them. Maimonides notes that there are ten levels of angels: *Chayos, Ofanim, Eraylim, Chashmalim, Serafim, Melachim, Elohim, B'nei Elohim, Cheruvim* and *Ishim.*

שחרית לחול / 166

קריאת שמע וברכותיה

L'u-mosom m'shab'chim v'ōm'rim: לְעֻמָּתָם מְשַׁבְּחִים וְאוֹמְרִים:

Facing them they give praise saying:

CONGREGATION RECITES ALOUD:

Boruch k'vōd adōnoy mim'kōmō.   בָּרוּךְ כְּבוֹד יהוה מִמְּקוֹמוֹ.

*"Blessed is the glory of H*ASHEM *from His place."*

■ We complete the first blessing citing Hashem's continuing renewal of Creation and His addressing the specific needs of mankind.

L'AYL boruch n'imōs yitaynu.   **לְאֵל** בָּרוּךְ נְעִימוֹת יִתֵּנוּ.

To the blessed God they shall offer sweet melodies;

L'melech Ayl chai v'ka-yom,   לְמֶלֶךְ אֵל חַי וְקַיָּם,

to the King, the living and enduring God,

z'mirōs yōmayru,   זְמִרוֹת יֹאמֵרוּ,

v'sishbochōs yashmi-u.   וְתִשְׁבָּחוֹת יַשְׁמִיעוּ.

they shall sing hymns and proclaim praises.

Ki hu l'vadō pō-ayl g'vurōs,   כִּי הוּא לְבַדּוֹ פּוֹעֵל גְּבוּרוֹת,

For He alone effects mighty deeds,

ōse chadoshōs, ba-al milchomōs,   עֹשֶׂה חֲדָשׁוֹת, בַּעַל מִלְחָמוֹת,

makes new things, is Master of wars,

zōray-a tz'dokōs, matzmi-ach y'shu-ōs,   זוֹרֵעַ צְדָקוֹת, מַצְמִיחַ יְשׁוּעוֹת,

sows kindnesses,* makes salvations flourish,

bōray r'fu-ōs, nōro s'hilōs,   בּוֹרֵא רְפוּאוֹת, נוֹרָא תְהִלּוֹת,

creates cures, is too awesome for praise,

adōn hanifl̄o-ōs.   אֲדוֹן הַנִּפְלָאוֹת.

is Lord of wonders.

Ham'chadaysh b'tuvō   הַמְחַדֵּשׁ בְּטוּבוֹ

b'chol yōm tomid   בְּכָל יוֹם תָּמִיד

In His goodness He renews daily, perpetually,

ma-asay v'rayshis.   מַעֲשֵׂה בְרֵאשִׁית.

the work of Creation.

Ko-omur: L'ōsay ōrim g'dōlim,   כָּאָמוּר: לְעֹשֵׂה אוֹרִים גְּדֹלִים,

As it is said: "[Give thanks] to Him Who makes the great luminaries,

ki l'ōlom chasdō.   כִּי לְעוֹלָם חַסְדּוֹ.

for His kindness endures forever."

Ōr chodosh al tziyōn to-ir,   ❖ אוֹר חָדָשׁ עַל צִיּוֹן תָּאִיר,

May You shine a new light* on Zion,

זוֹרֵעַ צְדָקוֹת — *Sows kindnesses.* God does not erely reward man for his good deeds; He rewards him even for the chain reaction that results from human kindness. Thus, an act of kindness is like a seed that can produce luxuriant vegetation.

אוֹר חָדָשׁ — *A new light.* The *new* light is actually a

SHEMA AND ITS BLESSINGS

v'nizke chulonu m'hayro l'ōrō. וְנִזְכֶּה כֻלָּנוּ מְהֵרָה לְאוֹרוֹ.

and may we all speedily merit its light.

Boruch ato Adōnoy, בָּרוּךְ אַתָּה יהוה,
yōtzayr ham'ōrōs. יוֹצֵר הַמְּאוֹרוֹת.

Blessed are You, HASHEM, Who fashions the luminaries.

CONGREGATION RESPONDS: Omayn — אָמֵן

▪ *Second blessing preceding the* Shema: *We appreciate the love of Israel that God demonstrated by choosing Israel and giving them the gift of Torah; and we request Divine assistance in living according to His Torah.*

AHAVO RABO ahavtonu **אַהֲבָה רַבָּה** אֲהַבְתָּנוּ
Adōnoy Elōhaynu, יהוה אֱלֹהֵינוּ,

With an abundant love* have You loved us, HASHEM, our God;

chemlo g'dōlo visayro חֶמְלָה גְדוֹלָה וִיתֵרָה
chomalto olaynu. חָמַלְתָּ עָלֵינוּ.

with exceedingly great pity have You pitied us.

Ovinu malkaynu, אָבִינוּ מַלְכֵּנוּ,

Our Father, our King,

ba-avur avōsaynu shebot'chu v'cho, בַּעֲבוּר אֲבוֹתֵינוּ שֶׁבָּטְחוּ בְךָ,

for the sake of our forefathers who trusted in You

vat'lam'daym chukay cha-yim, וַתְּלַמְּדֵם חֻקֵּי חַיִּים,

and whom You taught the decrees of life,

kayn t'chonaynu uslam'daynu. כֵּן תְּחָנֵּנוּ וּתְלַמְּדֵנוּ.

may You be equally gracious to us and teach us.

Ovinu ho-ov horachamon, אָבִינוּ הָאָב הָרַחֲמָן
Our Father, the merciful Father,

ham'rachaym, rachaym olaynu, הַמְרַחֵם, רַחֵם עָלֵינוּ,

Who acts mercifully, have mercy upon us,

v'sayn b'libaynu l'hovin ulhaskil, וְתֵן בְּלִבֵּנוּ לְהָבִין וּלְהַשְׂכִּיל,

instill in our hearts to understand and elucidate,

lishmō-a lilmōd ul'lamayd, לִשְׁמֹעַ לִלְמֹד וּלְלַמֵּד,
lishmōr v'la-asōs ul-ka-yaym לִשְׁמֹר וְלַעֲשׂוֹת וּלְקַיֵּם

to listen, learn, teach, safeguard, perform, and fulfill

---

return of the original brilliance of Creation. That light was concealed for the enjoyment of the righteous in the Messianic era. May it soon shine upon Zion.

אַהֲבָה רַבָּה — *With an abundant love*. Up to now, we have blessed God for having created the luminaries, but there is a light even greater than that of the brightest stars and the sun — the light of the Torah. Now, in this second blessing before *Shema*, we thank God for the Torah and pray that He grant us the wisdom to understand it properly.

es kol divray	אֶת כָּל דִּבְרֵי
salmud tōrosecho b'ahavo.	תַלְמוּד תּוֹרָתֶךָ בְּאַהֲבָה.

all the words of Your Torah's teaching with love.

V'ho-ayr aynaynu b'sōrosecho,   וְהָאֵר עֵינֵינוּ בְּתוֹרָתֶךָ,

Enlighten our eyes* in Your Torah,

v'dabayk libaynu b'mitzvōsecho,   וְדַבֵּק לִבֵּנוּ בְּמִצְוֹתֶיךָ,

attach our hearts to Your commandments,

v'yachayd l'vovaynu   וְיַחֵד לְבָבֵנוּ

and unify our hearts

l'a-havo ul-yiro es sh'mecho,   לְאַהֲבָה וּלְיִרְאָה אֶת שְׁמֶךָ,

to love and fear Your Name,

v'lō nayvōsh l'ōlom vo-ed: וְלֹא נֵבוֹשׁ לְעוֹלָם וָעֶד.

and may we not feel inner shame for all eternity.*

Ki v'shaym kod-sh'cho	כִּי בְשֵׁם קָדְשְׁךָ
hagodōl v'hanōro botoch'nu,	הַגָּדוֹל וְהַנּוֹרָא בָטָחְנוּ,

Because we have trusted in Your great and awesome holy Name,

nogilo v'nism'cho bi-shu-osecho.   נָגִילָה וְנִשְׂמְחָה בִּישׁוּעָתֶךָ.

may we exult and rejoice in Your salvation.

ONE WHO IS WEARING A *TALLIS* SHOULD GATHER THE FOUR *TZITZIS* (FRINGES) INTO HIS LEFT HAND AND HOLD THEM UNTIL AFTER THE *SHEMA*, AS INDICATED BELOW (P. 173).

Vahavi-aynu l'sholōm	וַהֲבִיאֵנוּ לְשָׁלוֹם
may-arba kanfōs ho-oretz,	מֵאַרְבַּע כַּנְפוֹת הָאָרֶץ,

Bring us in peacefulness from the four corners of the earth

v'sōlichaynu kōm'miyus l'artzaynu,   וְתוֹלִיכֵנוּ קוֹמְמִיּוּת לְאַרְצֵנוּ.

and lead us with upright pride to our land.

Ki Ayl pō-ayl y'shu-ōs oto,   כִּי אֵל פּוֹעֵל יְשׁוּעוֹת אָתָּה,

For You effect salvations, O God;

u-vonu vocharto mikol am v'loshōn.   וּבָנוּ בָחַרְתָּ מִכָּל עַם וְלָשׁוֹן.

and You have chosen us from among every people and tongue.

V'kayravtonu l'shimcho hagodōl	❖ וְקֵרַבְתָּנוּ לְשִׁמְךָ הַגָּדוֹל
selo be-emes	סֶלָה בֶּאֱמֶת,

And You have brought us close to Your great Name forever, in truth,

---

וְהָאֵר עֵינֵינוּ — *Enlighten our eyes.* This begins a series of brief supplications with one general purpose: A Jew's involvement with Torah study and observance must saturate all his activities, even his business, leisure, and social life.

וְלֹא נֵבוֹשׁ לְעוֹלָם וָעֶד — *And may we not feel inner shame for all eternity.* "Inner shame" refers to the humiliation one feels deep within himself when he knows he has done wrong — even though the people around him may sing his praises. The cost of such shame is borne primarily in the World to Come, where it can diminish one's eternal bliss or even destroy it entirely. Therefore we pray that our eternity not be marred by inner shame.

SHACHARIS FOR WEEKDAYS — SHEMA AND ITS BLESSINGS

l'hōdōs l'cho ul-yachedcho b'ahava. לְהוֹדוֹת לְךָ וּלְיַחֶדְךָ בְּאַהֲבָה.
to offer praiseful thanks to You, and proclaim Your Oneness with love.

Boruch ato Adōnoy, בָּרוּךְ אַתָּה יהוה,
Blessed are You, HASHEM,

habōchayr b'amō yisro-ayl b'ahavo. הַבּוֹחֵר בְּעַמּוֹ יִשְׂרָאֵל בְּאַהֲבָה.
Who chooses His people Israel with love.

CONGREGATION RESPONDS: Omayn — אָמֵן

THE SHEMA

■ The *Shema* is our acceptance of and submission to the absolute Sovereignty of God.

IMMEDIATELY BEFORE THE RECITATION OF THE *SHEMA*, CONCENTRATE ON FULFILLING THE POSITIVE COMMANDMENT OF RECITING THE *SHEMA* DAILY, ONCE IN THE EVENING AND ONCE IN THE MORNING. ENUNCIATE EACH WORD CLEARLY AND DO NOT RUN THE WORDS TOGETHER. ONE PRAYING WITHOUT A *MINYAN* BEGINS WITH THE FOLLOWING THREE-WORD FORMULA:

Ayl melech ne-emon. אֵל מֶלֶךְ נֶאֱמָן.
God, trustworthy King.

RECITE THE fIRST VERSE ALOUD, WITH YOUR RIGHT HAND COVERING YOUR EYES, AND CONCENTRATE INTENTLY UPON ACCEPTING GOD'S ABSOLUTE SOVEREIGNTY.

SH'MA yisro-ayl, שְׁמַע יִשְׂרָאֵל,
Adōnoy Elōhaynu, Adōnoy e-chod. יהוה אֱלֹהֵינוּ, יהוה אֶחָד.
Hear, O Israel: HASHEM is our God,* HASHEM, the One [and Only].*

IN AN UNDERTONE:

Boruch shaym k'vōd malchusō l'ōlom vo-ed. בָּרוּךְ שֵׁם כְּבוֹד מַלְכוּתוֹ לְעוֹלָם וָעֶד.
Blessed is the Name* of His glorious kingdom for all eternity.

■ We return God's love by studying His Torah and committing ourselves to observe the Torah with all our resources and being.

WHILE RECITING THE FOLLOWING PARAGRAPH, CONCENTRATE ON ACCEPTING THE COMMANDMENT TO LOVE GOD.

V'OHAVTO ays Adōnoy Elōhecho, וְאָהַבְתָּ אֵת יהוה ׀ אֱלֹהֶיךָ,
You shall love* HASHEM, your God,

שְׁמַע יִשְׂרָאֵל — *Hear, O Israel: HASHEM is our God.* At this point in history, He is only "our God," for He is not acknowledged universally. Ultimately, however, all will recognize Him as "the One and Only" God.

אֶחָד — *The One [and only].* The Hebrew word has two connotations: (a) There is no God other than HASHEM and, (b) though we perceive God in many roles — kind, angry, merciful, wise, judging, and so on — these different attitudes are not contradictory, even though human intelligence does not comprehend their harmony. This can be compared to a ray of light seen through a prism. Though one may see a myriad of different colors, they are all a single ray of light. So, too, God's many manifestations are truly one.

בָּרוּךְ שֵׁם — *Blessed is the Name.* Having proclaimed God as our King, we show gratitude for the privilege of serving the One Whose kingdom is eternal and unbounded.

וְאָהַבְתָּ — *You shall love.* We should serve God with all our emotions and desires ("with all your heart"), even to the point of giving up our life ("with all your soul"), and our wealth ("with all your resources") for God.

בְּכָל לְבָבְךָ, וּבְכָל נַפְשְׁךָ, וּבְכָל מְאֹדֶךָ.
b'chol l'vov'cho, uvchol nafsh'cho, uvchol m'ōdecho.

with all your heart, with all your soul and with all your resources.

וְהָיוּ הַדְּבָרִים הָאֵלֶּה, אֲשֶׁר אָנֹכִי מְצַוְּךָ הַיּוֹם,
V'ho-yu had'vorim ho-ayle, asher onōchi m'tzav'cho ha-yōm,

Let these matters that I command you today*

עַל לְבָבֶךָ.
al l'vovecho.

be upon your heart.

וְשִׁנַּנְתָּם לְבָנֶיךָ,
V'shinantom l'vonecho,

Teach them thoroughly to your children

וְדִבַּרְתָּ בָּם,
v'dibarto bom

and speak of them

בְּשִׁבְתְּךָ בְּבֵיתֶךָ, וּבְלֶכְתְּךָ בַדֶּרֶךְ,
b'shivt'cho b'vaysecho, uvlecht'cho vaderech

while you sit in your home, while you walk on the way,

וּבְשָׁכְבְּךָ וּבְקוּמֶךָ.
uv'shochb'cho, uvkumecho.

when you retire and when you arise.

IT IS CUSTOMARY TO TOUCH THE ARM-TEFILLIN WHEN SAYING Ukshartom . . .
AND THE HEAD-TEFILLIN WHILE SAYING v'ho-yu l'tōtofōs . . .

וּקְשַׁרְתָּם לְאוֹת עַל יָדֶךָ,
Ukshartom l'ōs al yodecho,

And you shall bind them* as a sign upon your arm

וְהָיוּ לְטֹטָפֹת בֵּין עֵינֶיךָ.
v'ho-yu l'tōtofōs bayn aynecho.

and they shall be tefillin between your eyes.

וּכְתַבְתָּם עַל מְזֻזוֹת בֵּיתֶךָ, וּבִשְׁעָרֶיךָ.
Uchsavtom al m'zuzōs baysecho u-visho-recho.

And write them on the doorposts of your house and upon your gates.

▪ We declare Israel's collective commitment to observe God's *mitzvos,* and the recognition that our national success or failure is dependent on this observance.

וְהָיָה, אִם־שָׁמֹעַ תִּשְׁמְעוּ אֶל מִצְוֹתַי,
V'HO-YO im shomō-a tishm'u el mitzvōsai,

And it will come to pass that if you continually hearken to My comandments

אֲשֶׁר אָנֹכִי מְצַוֶּה אֶתְכֶם הַיּוֹם,
asher onōchi m'tza-ve eschem ha-yōm,

that I command you today,

אֲשֶׁר אָנֹכִי מְצַוְּךָ הַיּוֹם — *That I command you today.* But have they all been commanded today? — This teaches that although the Torah and *mitzvos* were given to us thousands of years ago, we are not to regard the commandments as an ancient rite that we follow out of loyalty and habit. Rather, we are to regard them with as much freshness and enthusiasm as if God had given them to us this very day.

וּקְשַׁרְתָּם — *And you shall bind them.* By binding *tefillin* on our arm, next to our heart, and on our head, we consecrate our physical, emo-

171 / SHACHARIS FOR WEEKDAYS — SHEMA AND ITS BLESSINGS

l'ahavo es Adōnoy Elōhaychem, לְאַהֲבָה אֶת יהוה אֱלֹהֵיכֶם
ul-ovdō וּלְעָבְדוֹ,
to love H<small>ASHEM</small>, *your God, and to serve Him,*

b'chol-lvavchem uvchol nafsh'chem. בְּכָל לְבַבְכֶם וּבְכָל נַפְשְׁכֶם.
with all your heart and with all your soul —

V'nosati m'tar artz'chem b'itō, וְנָתַתִּי מְטַר אַרְצְכֶם בְּעִתּוֹ,
then I will provide rain for your land in its proper time,

yōre u-malkōsh, יוֹרֶה וּמַלְקוֹשׁ,
the early rains and the late rains,

v'osafto d'gonecho v'sirōsh'cho וְאָסַפְתָּ דְגָנֶךָ וְתִירֹשְׁךָ
v'yitzhorecho. וְיִצְהָרֶךָ.
that you may gather in your grain, your wine, and your oil.

V'nosati aysev וְנָתַתִּי עֵשֶׂב
b'sod'cho livhemtecho, בְּשָׂדְךָ לִבְהֶמְתֶּךָ,
I will provide grass in your field for your cattle

v'ochalto v'sovo-to. וְאָכַלְתָּ וְשָׂבָעְתָּ.
and you will eat and you will be satisfied.

Hi-shom'ru lochem, הִשָּׁמְרוּ לָכֶם,
Beware* for yourselves,

pen yifte l'vavchem, פֶּן יִפְתֶּה לְבַבְכֶם,
lest your heart be seduced

v'sartem va-avadtem וְסַרְתֶּם וַעֲבַדְתֶּם
elōhim a-chayrim אֱלֹהִים אֲחֵרִים,
and you turn astray and serve gods of others

v'hishtachavisem lohem. וְהִשְׁתַּחֲוִיתֶם לָהֶם.
and bow to them.*

V'choro af Adōnoy bochem, וְחָרָה אַף יהוה בָּכֶם,
Then the wrath of H<small>ASHEM</small> *will blaze against you;*

v'otzar es ha-shoma-yim וְעָצַר אֶת הַשָּׁמַיִם,
v'lō yih-ye motor, וְלֹא יִהְיֶה מָטָר,
He will restrain the heaven so there will be no rain

v'ho-adomo lō sitayn es y'vuloh וְהָאֲדָמָה לֹא תִתֵּן אֶת יְבוּלָהּ,
and the ground will not yield its produce;

---

tional, and intellectual capacities to God's service. The *mezuzah* on our doorpost consecrates our home to Him.

וְאָכַלְתָּ וְשָׂבָעְתָּ הִשָּׁמְרוּ — *And you will eat and you will be satisfied. Beware* . . . Prosperity is often the greatest challenge to religious devotion.

People who are rich in wealth but poor in sophistication often succumb to temptation.

יִפְתֶּה . . . וְהִשְׁתַּחֲוִיתֶם לָהֶם — *Be seduced . . . and bow to them*, i.e., to strange gods. An imperceptible, seemingly innocent surrender to temptation can be the beginning of a course that will

va-avadtem m'hayro	וַאֲבַדְתֶּם מְהֵרָה
and you will swiftly be banished	
may-al ho-oretz hatōvo	מֵעַל הָאָרֶץ הַטֹּבָה
from the goodly land	
asher Adōnoy nōsayn lochem.	אֲשֶׁר יהוה נֹתֵן לָכֶם.
which H‍ASHEM *gives you.*	
V'samtem es d'vorai ayle	וְשַׂמְתֶּם אֶת דְּבָרַי אֵלֶּה,
You shall place these words of Mine	
al l'vavchem v'al nafsh'chem	עַל לְבַבְכֶם וְעַל נַפְשְׁכֶם,
upon your heart and upon your soul;	

IT IS CUSTOMARY TO TOUCH THE ARM-TEFILLIN WHEN SAYING ukshartem ōsom . . .
AND THE HEAD-TEFILLIN WHILE SAYING v'ho-yu l'tōtofōs . . .

ukshartem ōsom l'ōs al yedchem,	וּקְשַׁרְתֶּם אֹתָם לְאוֹת עַל יֶדְכֶם,
and you shall bind them for a sign upon your arm	
v'ho-yu l'tōtofōs bayn aynaychem.	וְהָיוּ לְטוֹטָפֹת בֵּין עֵינֵיכֶם.
and they shall be tefillin between your eyes.	
V'limadtem ōsom es b'naychem,	וְלִמַּדְתֶּם אֹתָם אֶת בְּנֵיכֶם,
You shall teach them to your children,	
l'dabayr bom,	לְדַבֵּר בָּם,
to discuss them,	
b'shivt'cho b'vay-secho,	בְּשִׁבְתְּךָ בְּבֵיתֶךָ,
uvlecht'cho vaderech,	וּבְלֶכְתְּךָ בַדֶּרֶךְ,
while you sit in your home, while you walk on the way,	
uv'shochb'cho uvkumecho.	וּבְשָׁכְבְּךָ וּבְקוּמֶךָ.
when you retire and when you arise.	
Uchsavtom al m'zuzōs baysecho	וּכְתַבְתָּם עַל מְזוּזוֹת בֵּיתֶךָ,
u-vish-orecho.	וּבִשְׁעָרֶיךָ.
And write them on the doorposts of your house and upon your gates.	
L'ma-an yirbu y'maychem	לְמַעַן יִרְבּוּ יְמֵיכֶם
vimay v'naychem	וִימֵי בְנֵיכֶם,
In order to prolong your days and the days of your children	
al ho-adomo asher nishba	עַל הָאֲדָמָה אֲשֶׁר נִשְׁבַּע
Adōnoy la-avōsaychem	יהוה לַאֲבֹתֵיכֶם
upon the ground that H‍ASHEM *has sworn to your ancestors*	
losays lohem,	לָתֵת לָהֶם,
to give them,	

---

end in the basest of sins.

SHACHARIS FOR WEEKDAYS — SHEMA AND ITS BLESSINGS

kimay hashoma-yim al ho-oretz.   כִּימֵי הַשָּׁמַיִם עַל הָאָרֶץ.
like the days of the heavens on the earth.

■ We acknowledge of the Divine providence over Israel as demonstrated by the Exodus from Egypt, thus obligating us to observe His *mitzvos*.

BEFORE RECITING THIS PARAGRAPH, THE *TZITZIS*, WHICH HAVE BEEN HELD IN THE LEFT HAND, ARE TAKEN IN THE RIGHT HAND ALSO. THE *TZITZIS* ARE KISSED AT EACH MENTION OF *TZITZIS*, AND AT THE END OF THE PARAGRAPH, AND ARE PASSED BEFORE THE EYES AT ur'isem ōsō.

VA-YŌMER Adōnoy   וַיֹּאמֶר יהוה
    el mōshe laymōr.   אֶל מֹשֶׁה לֵּאמֹר.
        And HASHEM *said to Moses saying:*

Dabayr el b'nay yisro-ayl,   דַּבֵּר אֶל בְּנֵי יִשְׂרָאֵל,
    v'omarto alayhem,   וְאָמַרְתָּ אֲלֵהֶם,
        Speak to the Children of Israel and say to them

v'osu lohem tzitzis   וְעָשׂוּ לָהֶם צִיצִת,
        that they are to make themselves tzitzis

al kanfay vigdayhem   עַל כַּנְפֵי בִגְדֵיהֶם
        on the corners of their garments,

l'dōrōsom,   לְדֹרֹתָם,
        throughout their generations.

v'nos'nu al tzitzis hakonof   וְנָתְנוּ עַל צִיצִת הַכָּנָף,
    p'sil t'chayles.   פְּתִיל תְּכֵלֶת.
And they are to place upon the tzitzis of each corner a thread of turquoise wool.

V'hoyo lochem l'tzitzis,   וְהָיָה לָכֶם לְצִיצִת,
        And it shall constitute tzitzis for you,

ur-isem ōsō   וּרְאִיתֶם אֹתוֹ,
        that you may see it

uz-chartem   וּזְכַרְתֶּם
    es kol mitzvōs Adōnoy,   אֶת כָּל מִצְוֹת יהוה,
        and remember all the commandments of HASHEM

va-asisem ōsom,   וַעֲשִׂיתֶם אֹתָם,
        and perform them;

v'lō sosuru acharay l'vavchem   וְלֹא תָתוּרוּ אַחֲרֵי לְבַבְכֶם
    v'acharay aynaychem,   וְאַחֲרֵי עֵינֵיכֶם,
        and you shall not explore after your heart and after your eyes

asher atem zōnim acharayhem.   אֲשֶׁר אַתֶּם זֹנִים אַחֲרֵיהֶם.
        after which you stray.

L'ma-an tizk'ru   לְמַעַן תִּזְכְּרוּ
    va-asisem es kol mitzvōsoy,   וַעֲשִׂיתֶם אֶת כָּל מִצְוֹתָי,
        So that you may remember and perform all My commandments;

vih-yisem k'dōshim Laylōhaychem.	וִהְיִיתֶם קְדֹשִׁים לֵאלֹהֵיכֶם.
and be holy to your God.	

CONCENTRATE ON FULFILLING THE COMMANDMENT TO REMEMBER THE EXODUS FROM EGYPT.

Ani Adōnoy Elohaychem,	אֲנִי יהוה אֱלֹהֵיכֶם,
I am Hashem, your God,	
asher hōtzaysi eschem	אֲשֶׁר הוֹצֵאתִי אֶתְכֶם
may-eretz mitzra-yim,	מֵאֶרֶץ מִצְרַיִם,
Who has removed you from the land of Egypt*	
lih-yōs lochem Laylōhim,	לִהְיוֹת לָכֶם לֵאלֹהִים,
to be a God to you;	
ani Adōnoy Elōhaychem. Emes . . .	. . . אֱמֶת. אֲנִי יהוה אֱלֹהֵיכֶם
I am Hashem your God. It is true . . .	

— Chazzan repeats יהוה אֱלֹהֵיכֶם אֱמֶת.

■ The blessing following the *Shema*: This blessing marks our transition from the *Shema* to the *Shemoneh Esrei* with profuse expressions of praise for His manifold acts of redemption.

V'YATZIV v'nochōn v'ka-yom	**וְיַצִּיב** וְנָכוֹן וְקַיָּם
And certain,* established and enduring,	
v'yoshor v'ne-emon v'ohuv v'choviv	וְיָשָׁר וְנֶאֱמָן וְאָהוּב וְחָבִיב
fair and faithful, beloved and cherished,	
v'nechmod v'no-im v'nōro v'adir	וְנֶחְמָד וְנָעִים וְנוֹרָא וְאַדִּיר
delightful and pleasant, awesome and powerful,	
umsukon umkubol v'tōv v'yofe	וּמְתֻקָּן וּמְקֻבָּל וְטוֹב וְיָפֶה
correct and accepted, good and beautiful	
hadovor ha-ze olaynu l'ōlom vo-ed.	הַדָּבָר הַזֶּה עָלֵינוּ לְעוֹלָם וָעֶד.
is this affirmation to us forever and ever.	
Emes Elōhay ōlom malkaynu,	אֱמֶת אֱלֹהֵי עוֹלָם מַלְכֵּנוּ,
True — the God of the universe is our King;	
tzur ya-akōv mogayn yish-aynu,	צוּר יַעֲקֹב מָגֵן יִשְׁעֵנוּ,
the Rock of Jacob is the Shield of our salvation.	
l'dōr vodōr hu ka-yom,	לְדֹר וָדֹר הוּא קַיָּם,
From generation to generation He endures	

אֲשֶׁר הוֹצֵאתִי אֶתְכֶם מֵאֶרֶץ מִצְרַיִם — *Who has removed you from the land of Egypt.* By freeing Israel from Egypt, God laid claim to the nation's eternal allegiance. No Jew is free to absolve himself of that obligation.

אֱמֶת . . . וְיַצִּיב — *True . . . and certain.* This paragraph begins the third and final blessing of the *Shema*, which ends with "Who redeemed Israel." Like its counterpart in the Evening Service, this blessing continues our fulfillment of the requirement to recall the Exodus, morning and evening.

ushmō ka-yom, v'chis-ō nochōn, וּשְׁמוֹ קַיָּם, וְכִסְאוֹ נָכוֹן,
and His Name endures and His throne is well established;

umalchusō ve-emunosō וּמַלְכוּתוֹ וֶאֱמוּנָתוֹ
lo-ad ka-yomes. לָעַד קַיֶּמֶת.
His sovereignty and faithfulness endure forever.

Udvorov cho-yim v'ka-yomim, וּדְבָרָיו חָיִים וְקַיָּמִים,
His words are living and enduring,

ne-emonim v'nechemodim lo-ad נֶאֱמָנִים וְנֶחֱמָדִים לָעַד
faithful and delightful forever

(ONE WHO IS WEARING A TALLIS KISSES THE TZITZIS AND RELEASES THEM)

ul-ōl'may ōlomim. וּלְעוֹלְמֵי עוֹלָמִים.
and to all eternity;

Al avōsaynu v'olaynu, עַל אֲבוֹתֵינוּ וְעָלֵינוּ,
for our forefathers and for us,

al bonaynu v'al dōrōsaynu, עַל בָּנֵינוּ וְעַל דּוֹרוֹתֵינוּ,
for our children and for our generations,

v'al kol dōrōs וְעַל כָּל דּוֹרוֹת
zera yisro-ayl avodecho. זֶרַע יִשְׂרָאֵל עֲבָדֶיךָ.
and for all the generations of Your servant Israel's offspring.

■ *Our expressions of confidence that Hashem, in His goodness, will continue to redeem Israel*

AL HORISHŌNIM עַל הָרִאשׁוֹנִים

v'al ho-acharōnim, וְעַל הָאַחֲרוֹנִים,
Upon the earlier and upon the later generations,

dovor tōv v'ka-yom l'ōlom vo-ed, דָּבָר טוֹב וְקַיָּם לְעוֹלָם וָעֶד,
this affirmation is good and enduring forever.

emes ve-emuno chōk v'lō ya-avōr. אֱמֶת וֶאֱמוּנָה חֹק וְלֹא יַעֲבֹר.
True and faithful, it is an unbreachable decree.

Emes sho-ato hu Adōnoy אֱמֶת שָׁאַתָּה הוּא יהוה
It is true that You are HASHEM,

Elōhaynu Vaylōhay avōsaynu, אֱלֹהֵינוּ וֵאלֹהֵי אֲבוֹתֵינוּ,
our God and the God of our forefathers,

malkaynu melech avōsaynu, ❖ מַלְכֵּנוּ מֶלֶךְ אֲבוֹתֵינוּ,
our King and the King of our forefathers,

gō-alaynu gō-ayl avōsaynu, גֹּאֲלֵנוּ גֹּאֵל אֲבוֹתֵינוּ,
our Redeemer, the Redeemer of our forefathers;

שחרית לחול / 176

yōtz'raynu tzur y'shu-osaynu,	יוֹצְרֵנוּ צוּר יְשׁוּעָתֵנוּ,
our Molder, the Rock of our salvation;	
pōdaynu u-matzilaynu	פּוֹדֵנוּ וּמַצִּילֵנוּ
our Liberator and our Rescuer —	
may-ōlom sh'mecho,	מֵעוֹלָם שְׁמֶךָ,
this has ever been Your Name.	
ayn Elōhim zulosecho.	אֵין אֱלֹהִים זוּלָתֶךָ.
There is no God but You.	

▪ A detailed description of our past redemption and the joy we expressed then provides the basis for our confidence and surety of future redemption.

EZRAS avōsaynu	**עֶזְרַת** אֲבוֹתֵינוּ
*The Helper of our forefathers***	
ato hu may-ōlom,	אַתָּה הוּא מֵעוֹלָם,
have You ever been, forever,	
mogayn u-mōshi-a	מָגֵן וּמוֹשִׁיעַ
Shield and Savior	
livnayhem acharayhem	לִבְנֵיהֶם אַחֲרֵיהֶם
b'chol dōr vodōr.	בְּכָל דּוֹר וָדוֹר.
for their children after them in every generation.	
B'rum ōlom mōshovecho,	בְּרוּם עוֹלָם מוֹשָׁבֶךָ,
At the zenith of the universe is Your dwelling,	
u-mishpotecho v'tzidkos'cho	וּמִשְׁפָּטֶיךָ וְצִדְקָתְךָ
ad afsay oretz.	עַד אַפְסֵי אָרֶץ.
and Your justice and Your righteousness extend to the ends of the earth.	
Ashray ish she-yishma l'mitzvōsecho,	אַשְׁרֵי אִישׁ שֶׁיִּשְׁמַע לְמִצְוֹתֶיךָ,
Praiseworthy is the person who obeys Your commandments	
v'sōros'cho udvor'cho yosim al libō.	וְתוֹרָתְךָ וּדְבָרְךָ יָשִׂים עַל לִבּוֹ.
and takes to his heart Your teaching and Your word.	
Emes ato hu odōn l'amecho	אֱמֶת אַתָּה הוּא אָדוֹן לְעַמֶּךָ
True — You are the Master for Your people	
u-melech gibōr loriv rivom.	וּמֶלֶךְ גִּבּוֹר לָרִיב רִיבָם.
and a mighty King to take up their grievance.	
Emes ato hu rishōn	אֱמֶת אַתָּה הוּא רִאשׁוֹן
True — You are the First	
v'ato hu acharōn,	וְאַתָּה הוּא אַחֲרוֹן,
and You are the Last,	

עֶזְרַת אֲבוֹתֵינוּ — *The Helper of our forefathers.* This passage elaborates upon the Exodus within the context of God's eternal supervision of Israel and mastery over its destiny.

u-mibal-odecho ayn lonu melech	וּמִבַּלְעָדֶיךָ אֵין לָנוּ מֶלֶךְ
gō-ayl u-mōshi-a.	גּוֹאֵל וּמוֹשִׁיעַ.

and other than You we have no king, redeemer, or savior.

Mimitzra-yim g'altonu	מִמִּצְרַיִם גְּאַלְתָּנוּ
Adōnoy Elōhaynu,	יהוה אֱלֹהֵינוּ,

From Egypt You redeemed us, HASHEM, our God,

u-mibays avodim p'disonu.	וּמִבֵּית עֲבָדִים פְּדִיתָנוּ.

and from the house of slavery You liberated us.

Kol b'chōrayhem horogto,	כָּל בְּכוֹרֵיהֶם הָרָגְתָּ,

All their firstborn You slew,

uvchōr'cho go-olto,	וּבְכוֹרְךָ גָּאָלְתָּ,

but Your firstborn You redeemed;

v'yam suf bokato,	וְיַם סוּף בָּקַעְתָּ,

the Sea of Reeds You split;

v'zaydim tibato,	וְזֵדִים טִבַּעְתָּ,

the wanton sinners You drowned;

vididim he-evarto,	וִידִידִים הֶעֱבַרְתָּ,

the dear ones You brought across;

vaichasu ma-yim tzorayhem,	וַיְכַסּוּ מַיִם צָרֵיהֶם,

and the water covered their foes

e-chod mayhem lō nōsor.	אֶחָד מֵהֶם לֹא נוֹתָר.

— not one of them was left.

Al zōs shib'chu ahuvim	עַל זֹאת שִׁבְּחוּ אֲהוּבִים
v'rōm'mu Ayl,	וְרוֹמְמוּ אֵל,

For this, the beloved praised and exalted God;

v'nos'nu y'didim	וְנָתְנוּ יְדִידִים

the dear ones offered

z'mirōs shirōs v'sishbochōs,	זְמִרוֹת שִׁירוֹת וְתִשְׁבָּחוֹת,
b'rochōs v'hōdo-ōs,	בְּרָכוֹת וְהוֹדָאוֹת,

hymns, songs, praises, blessings, and thanksgivings

l'melech Ayl chai v'ka-yom,	לְמֶלֶךְ אֵל חַי וְקַיָּם,

to the King, the living and enduring God —

rom v'niso, godōl v'nōro,	רָם וְנִשָּׂא, גָּדוֹל וְנוֹרָא,

exalted and uplifted, great and awesome,

mashpil gay-im, u-magbi-ah sh'folim,	מַשְׁפִּיל גֵּאִים, וּמַגְבִּיהַּ שְׁפָלִים,

Who humbles the haughty and lifts the lowly;

mōtzi asirim, u-fōde anovim,	מוֹצִיא אֲסִירִים, וּפוֹדֶה עֲנָוִים,

withdraws the captive, liberates the humble,

וְעוֹזֵר דַּלִּים,
v'ōzayr dalim,
and helps the poor;

וְעוֹנֶה לְעַמּוֹ בְּעֵת שַׁוְּעָם אֵלָיו.
v'ōne l'amō b'ays shav-om aylov.
Who responds to His people upon their outcry to Him.

RISE FOR *SHEMONEH ESREI*. SOME TAKE THREE STEPS BACKWARD
AT THIS POINT; OTHERS DO SO BEFORE tzur yisro-ayl, "ROCK OF ISRAEL."

❖ תְּהִלּוֹת לְאֵל עֶלְיוֹן,
T'hilōs l'Ayl elyōn,
Praises to the Supreme God,

בָּרוּךְ הוּא וּמְבֹרָךְ.
boruch hu umvōroch.
the blessed One Who is blessed.

מֹשֶׁה וּבְנֵי יִשְׂרָאֵל
לְךָ עָנוּ שִׁירָה
Mōshe uvnay yisro-ayl l'cho onu shiro
Moses and the Children of Israel exclaimed a song to You

בְּשִׂמְחָה רַבָּה וְאָמְרוּ כֻלָּם:
b'simcho rabo v'om'ru chulom:
with great joy and they all said:

מִי כָמֹכָה בָּאֵלִם יהוה,
mi chomōcho bo-aylim Adōnoy,
"Who is like You among the heavenly powers, HASHEM!

מִי כָּמֹכָה נֶאְדָּר בַּקֹּדֶשׁ,
mi komōcho nedor bakōdesh,
Who is like You, mighty in holiness,

נוֹרָא תְהִלֹּת עֹשֵׂה פֶלֶא.
nōro s'hilōs ōsay fele.
too awesome for praise, doing wonders."

❖ שִׁירָה חֲדָשָׁה
Shiro chadosho
With a new song

שִׁבְּחוּ גְאוּלִים לְשִׁמְךָ
עַל שְׂפַת הַיָּם,
shib'chu g'ulim l'shimcho al s'fas ha-yom,
the redeemed ones praised Your Name at the seashore,

יַחַד כֻּלָּם הוֹדוּ וְהִמְלִיכוּ
וְאָמְרוּ:
yachad kulom hōdu v'himlichu v'om'ru:
all of them in unison gave thanks, acknowledged [Your] sovereignty, and said:

יהוה יִמְלֹךְ לְעֹלָם וָעֶד.
Adōnoy yimlōch l'ōlom vo-ed.
"HASHEM shall reign for all eternity."

❖ **צוּר** יִשְׂרָאֵל,
TZUR yisro-ayl,
Rock of Israel,*

קוּמָה בְּעֶזְרַת יִשְׂרָאֵל,
kumo b'ezras yisro-ayl,
arise to the aid of Israel

צוּר יִשְׂרָאֵל — *Rock of Israel.* Since the end of *Shema*, we have concentrated on an elaboration of the miracles of the Exodus. We do not lose sight, however, of our faith that there is another, greater redemption yet to come. Thus we conclude with a plea that God rise up again to redeem Israel from this exile as He did in ancient Egypt.

179 / SHACHARIS FOR WEEKDAYS — SHEMONEH ESREI

ufday chin-umecho y'hudo v'yisro-ayl. וּפְדֵה כִנְאֻמֶךָ יְהוּדָה וְיִשְׂרָאֵל.
and liberate, as You pledged, Judah and Israel.

Gō-alaynu Adōnoy tz'vo-ōs sh'mō, גֹּאֲלֵנוּ יהוה צְבָאוֹת שְׁמוֹ,
Our Redeemer — Hashem, Master of Legions, is His Name —

k'dōsh yisro-ayl. קְדוֹשׁ יִשְׂרָאֵל.
the Holy One of Israel.

Boruch ato Adōnoy go-al yisro-ayl. בָּרוּךְ אַתָּה יהוה, גָּאַל יִשְׂרָאֵל.
Blessed are You, Hashem, Who redeemed Israel.

◆⟨ SHEMONEH ESREI — AMIDAH ⟩◆

■ *Shemoneh Esrei* (or the *Amidah*) is known as "Service of the Heart." By definition, it must be understood and comprehended. Failure to do so is compared by the Sages to a "body without a soul." Two independent kinds of awareness are necessary for the *Amidah*:

1. To understand the meaning of that which we are saying. The format of this *siddur* is most helpful in this regard. Please take your time to recite the prayer with the conviction that accompanies comprehension.

2. To visualize that we are privileged literally to be standing before God. You are talking to Him directly. In each blessing, when we recite the word *ato*, "You," we should understand to Whom the "You" is referring.

IN THE SYNAGOGUE THE *SHEMONEH ESREI** IS RECITED WHILE FACING THE ARK; ELSEWHERE IT IS RECITED WHILE FACING THE DIRECTION OF THE LAND OF ISRAEL. TAKE THREE STEPS BACKWARD, LEFT, RIGHT, LEFT, THEN THREE STEPS FORWARD, RIGHT, LEFT, RIGHT. REMAIN STANDING WITH FEET TOGETHER DURING *SHEMONEH ESREI*. RECITE IT WITH QUIET DEVOTION AND WITHOUT ANY INTERRUPTION. ALTHOUGH IT SHOULD NOT BE AUDIBLE TO OTHERS, ONE MUST PRAY LOUDLY ENOUGH TO HEAR ONESELF.

Adōnoy s'fosai tiftoch, אֲדֹנָי שְׂפָתַי תִּפְתָּח,
My Lord, open my lips,

u-fi yagid t'hilosecho. וּפִי יַגִּיד תְּהִלָּתֶךָ.
that my mouth may declare Your praise.*

■ **First Blessing:** In the merit of our Patriarchs whose actions reflected Godliness, Hashem pledged to always be with Israel and protect them.

◆⟨ Shemoneh Esrei

Moses advanced through three levels of holiness as he approached God when he ascended Mount Sinai. Therefore, as we approach God with our requests, we take three steps backward to symbolize our separation from the mundane, then three steps forward to symbolize our advance toward God.

Shemoneh Esrei has three sections: (a) In the first three blessings, we pay homage to God, like a slave praising his master before daring to make a request; (b) in the middle section of thirteen (originally twelve) blessings, we make our requests; (c) in the last three blessings, we take leave, expressing our gratitude and confidence in our Master's graciousness.

But even the middle section is not merely a catalogue of selfish requests. Rather, in each blessing, we first acknowledge God's mastery, and only then make our request. Thus, each blessing is an affirmation of God's power.

וּפִי יַגִּיד תְּהִלָּתֶךָ — *That my mouth may declare Your praise.* This introductory verse acknowledges that one needs God's help to articulate and comprehend the prayers properly. But why do we ask God for assistance "to declare Your praise"? We should ask, "Assist me to formulate my requests." The answer is that our thrice-daily approach with our requests is in itself a constant praise of God, for it demonstrates that He alone can fulfill our needs.

שחרית לחול

BEND THE KNEES AT Boruch; BOW AT ato; STRAIGHTEN UP AT Adōnoy.

BORUCH ato Adōnoy   בָּרוּךְ אַתָּה יהוה
Blessed are You, HASHEM,*

Elōhaynu Vaylōhay avōsaynu,   אֱלֹהֵינוּ וֵאלֹהֵי אֲבוֹתֵינוּ,
our God and the God of our forefathers,

Elōhay avrohom, Elōhay yitzchok,   אֱלֹהֵי אַבְרָהָם, אֱלֹהֵי יִצְחָק,
Vaylōhay ya-akōv,   וֵאלֹהֵי יַעֲקֹב,
God of Abraham, God of Isaac, and God of Jacob;

ho-Ayl hagodōl hagibōr v'hanōro,   הָאֵל הַגָּדוֹל הַגִּבּוֹר וְהַנּוֹרָא,
Ayl elyōn,   אֵל עֶלְיוֹן,
the great, mighty, and awesome God, the supreme God,

gōmayl chasodim tōvim   גּוֹמֵל חֲסָדִים טוֹבִים
v'kōnay hakōl,   וְקוֹנֵה הַכֹּל,
Who bestows beneficial kindnesses and creates everything,

v'zōchayr chasday ovōs,   וְזוֹכֵר חַסְדֵי אָבוֹת,
Who recalls the kindnesses of the Patriarchs

u-mayvi gō-ayl livnay v'nayhem,   וּמֵבִיא גוֹאֵל לִבְנֵי בְנֵיהֶם,
and brings a Redeemer to their children's children,

l'ma-an sh'mō b'ahavo.   לְמַעַן שְׁמוֹ בְּאַהֲבָה.
for His Name's sake, with love.

FROM ROSH HASHANAH TO YOM KIPPUR ADD:

Zochraynu l'cha-yim,   זָכְרֵנוּ לְחַיִּים,
melech chofaytz bacha-yim,   מֶלֶךְ חָפֵץ בַּחַיִּים,
Remember us for life, O King Who desires life,

v'chosvaynu b'sayfer hacha-yim,   וְכָתְבֵנוּ בְּסֵפֶר הַחַיִּים,
l'ma-ancho Elōhim cha-yim.   לְמַעַנְךָ אֱלֹהִים חַיִּים.
and inscribe us in the Book of Life — for Your sake, O Living God.

Melech ōzayr u-mōshi-a u-mogayn.   מֶלֶךְ עוֹזֵר וּמוֹשִׁיעַ וּמָגֵן.
O King, Helper, Savior, and Shield.

BEND THE KNEES AT Boruch; BOW AT ato; STRAIGHTEN UP AT Adōnoy.

Boruch ato Adōnoy,   בָּרוּךְ אַתָּה יהוה,
mogayn avrohom.   מָגֵן אַבְרָהָם.
Blessed are You, HASHEM, Shield of Abraham.

בָּרוּךְ אַתָּה ה׳ — *Blessed are You, HASHEM.* This formula, used to begin and/or end every blessing, is a declaration of fact: God *is* blessed in the sense that He is perfect and complete. Additionally, the phrase means, "You, HASHEM, are the Source of blessing."

SHACHARIS FOR WEEKDAYS — SHEMONEH ESREI

■ *Second Blessing: God's might as it is manifest in nature and man*

ATO gibōr l'ōlom Adōnoy,
אַתָּה גִּבּוֹר לְעוֹלָם אֲדֹנָי,
You are eternally mighty, my Lord,

m'cha-yay maysim ato,
מְחַיֵּה מֵתִים אַתָּה,
the Resuscitator of the dead are You;*

rav l'hōshi-a.
רַב לְהוֹשִׁיעַ.
abundantly able to save,

BETWEEN SHEMINI ATZERES AND PESACH, ADD:

Mashiv horu-ach u-mōrid hageshem.
מַשִּׁיב הָרוּחַ וּמוֹרִיד הַגֶּשֶׁם.
Who makes the wind blow and makes the rain descend;

M'chalkayl cha-yim b'chesed,
מְכַלְכֵּל חַיִּים בְּחֶסֶד,
Who sustains the living with kindness;

m'cha-yay maysim b'rachamim rabim,
מְחַיֵּה מֵתִים בְּרַחֲמִים רַבִּים,
resuscitates the dead with abundant mercy,

sōmaych nōf'lim, v'rōfay chōlim,
סוֹמֵךְ נוֹפְלִים, וְרוֹפֵא חוֹלִים,
supports the fallen, heals the sick,

u-matir asurim,
וּמַתִּיר אֲסוּרִים,
releases the confined,

umka-yaym emunosō li-shaynay ofor.
וּמְקַיֵּם אֱמוּנָתוֹ לִישֵׁנֵי עָפָר.
and maintains His faith to those asleep in the dust.

Mi cho-mōcho ba-al g'vurōs,
מִי כָמוֹךָ בַּעַל גְּבוּרוֹת,
Who is like You, O Master of mighty deeds,

u-mi dōme loch,
וּמִי דוֹמֶה לָּךְ,
and who is comparable to You,

melech maymis umcha-ye
u-matzmi-ach y'shu-o.
מֶלֶךְ מֵמִית וּמְחַיֶּה
וּמַצְמִיחַ יְשׁוּעָה.
O King Who causes death and restores life and makes salvation sprout!

FROM ROSH HASHANAH TO YOM KIPPUR ADD:

Mi cho-mōcho av horachamim,
מִי כָמוֹךָ אַב הָרַחֲמִים,
Who is like You, O Merciful Father,

zōchayr y'tzurov l'cha-yim
b'rachamim.
זוֹכֵר יְצוּרָיו לְחַיִּים
בְּרַחֲמִים.
Who recalls His creatures mercifully for life!

מְחַיֵּה מֵתִים — *The Resuscitator of the dead.* This concept is found three times in this section, alluding to the three kinds of resuscitation: He causes man to awaken every morning after deathlike slumber; He sends the rain that has the life-sustaining quality of making vegetation grow; and He will bring about the literal resuscitation of the dead in the Messianic era.

V'ne-emon ato l'hacha-yōs maysim. וְנֶאֱמָן אַתָּה לְהַחֲיוֹת מֵתִים.
And You are faithful to resuscitate the dead.

Boruch ato Adōnoy, בָּרוּךְ אַתָּה יהוה,
   m'cha-yay hamaysim. מְחַיֵּה הַמֵּתִים.
   *Blessed are You, H*ASHEM*, Who resuscitates the dead.*

■ Third Blessing: Regarding the holiness of God's Name

DURING THE *CHAZZAN'S* REPETITION, *KEDUSHAH** IS RECITED; INDIVIDUALS CONTINUE ON P. 183.
STAND WITH FEET TOGETHER AND AVOID ANY INTERRUPTIONS. RISE ON TOES
WHEN SAYING *Kodōsh, kodōsh, kodōsh; Boruch; AND Yimlōch.*

CONGREGATION, THEN *CHAZZAN*:

N'KADAYSH es shimcho bo-ōlom, נְקַדֵּשׁ אֶת שִׁמְךָ בָּעוֹלָם,
We shall sanctify Your Name in this world,
k'shaym shemakdishim ōsō כְּשֵׁם שֶׁמַּקְדִּישִׁים אוֹתוֹ
bishmay morōm, בִּשְׁמֵי מָרוֹם,
just as they sanctify it in heaven above,
Kakosuv al yad n'vi-echo, כַּכָּתוּב עַל יַד נְבִיאֶךָ,
as it is written by the hand of Your prophet,
v'koro ze el ze v'omar: וְקָרָא זֶה אֶל זֶה וְאָמַר:
"And one [angel] will call another and say:

ALL IN UNISON:

Kodōsh, kodōsh, kodōsh קָדוֹשׁ קָדוֹשׁ קָדוֹשׁ
Adōnoy Tz'vo-ōs, יהוה צְבָאוֹת,
'Holy, holy, holy is H*ASHEM*, Master of Legions,*
m'lō chol ho-oretz k'vōdō. מְלֹא כָל הָאָרֶץ כְּבוֹדוֹ.
the whole world is filled with His glory.'"

CHAZZAN:

L'u-mosom boruch yōmayru: לְעֻמָּתָם בָּרוּךְ יֹאמֵרוּ:
Those facing them say, "Blessed":

ALL IN UNISON:

Boruch k'vōd Adōnoy, mim'kōmō. בָּרוּךְ כְּבוֹד יהוה, מִמְּקוֹמוֹ.
*"Blessed is the glory of H*ASHEM *from His place."*

CHAZZAN:

Uvdivray kodsh'cho kosuv laymōr: וּבְדִבְרֵי קָדְשְׁךָ כָּתוּב לֵאמֹר:
And in Your holy Writings the following is written:

◈§ **Kedushah.** *Kedushah,* "Sanctification," expresses the concept that God is exalted above and separated from the limitations of material existence. A *minyan* (quorum of ten men over the age of *bar mitzvah*) becomes the representative of the nation and echoes the angels who sing God's praises in Heaven by proclaiming His holiness and glory.

קָדוֹשׁ קָדוֹשׁ קָדוֹשׁ — *Holy, holy, holy.* God is holy with relation to the physical world, holy with relation to the spiritual world and holy with relation to the World to Come.

SHACHARIS FOR WEEKDAYS — SHEMONEH ESREI

ALL IN UNISON:

Yimlōch Adōnoy l'ōlom,   יִמְלֹךְ יהוה לְעוֹלָם,
"Hashem shall reign forever —
Elōha-yich tziyōn l'dōr vodōr,   אֱלֹהַיִךְ צִיּוֹן לְדֹר וָדֹר,
hal'luyoh.   הַלְלוּיָהּ.
your God, O Zion — from generation to generation: Praise God!"

CHAZZAN CONCLUDES:

לְדוֹר וָדוֹר נַגִּיד גָּדְלֶךָ וּלְנֵצַח נְצָחִים קְדֻשָּׁתְךָ נַקְדִּישׁ, וְשִׁבְחֲךָ אֱלֹהֵינוּ מִפִּינוּ לֹא יָמוּשׁ לְעוֹלָם וָעֶד, כִּי אֵל מֶלֶךְ גָּדוֹל וְקָדוֹשׁ אָתָּה. בָּרוּךְ אַתָּה יהוה, °הָאֵל הַקָּדוֹשׁ.

°הַמֶּלֶךְ הַקָּדוֹשׁ. — from Rosh Hashanah to Yom Kippur substitute
THE *CHAZZAN* CONTINUES ato chōnayn BELOW.

ATO kodōsh v'shimcho kodōsh,   **אַתָּה** קָדוֹשׁ וְשִׁמְךָ קָדוֹשׁ,
You are holy and Your Name is holy,
ukdōshim b'chol yōm   וּקְדוֹשִׁים בְּכָל יוֹם
y'hal'lucho, selo.   יְהַלְלוּךָ סֶּלָה.
and holy ones praise You, every day, forever.
Boruch ato Adōnoy,   בָּרוּךְ אַתָּה יהוה,
°ho-Ayl hakodōsh.   °הָאֵל הַקָּדוֹשׁ.
Blessed are You, Hashem, the holy God.

FROM ROSH HASHANAH TO YOM KIPPUR SUBSTITUTE:

°hamelech hakodōsh.   °הַמֶּלֶךְ הַקָּדוֹשׁ.
the holy King.

■ **Fourth Blessing: Supplication for the gift of intellect**

ATO chōnayn l'odom da-as,   **אַתָּה** חוֹנֵן לְאָדָם דַּעַת,
You graciously endow man with wisdom*
umlamayd le-enōsh bino.   וּמְלַמֵּד לֶאֱנוֹשׁ בִּינָה.
and teach insight to a frail mortal.
Chonaynu may-it'cho   חָנֵּנוּ מֵאִתְּךָ
day-o bino v'haskayl.   דֵּעָה בִּינָה וְהַשְׂכֵּל.
Endow us graciously from Yourself with wisdom, insight, and discernment.
Boruch ato Adōnoy,   בָּרוּךְ אַתָּה יהוה,
chōnayn hado-as.   חוֹנֵן הַדָּעַת.
Blessed are You, Hashem, gracious Giver of wisdom.

דַּעַת — *Wisdom.* This blessing begins the middle section of the *Shemoneh Esrei,* in which man makes his requests of God. The first plea is for wisdom and understanding, because man's intelligence is the characteristic that sets him apart from animals.

■ Fifth Blessing: Supplication for Divine assistance in repentance

HASHIVAYNU ovinu l'sōrosecho,   הֲשִׁיבֵנוּ אָבִינוּ לְתוֹרָתֶךָ,
Bring us back,* our Father, to Your Torah,

v'kor'vaynu malkaynu la-avōdosecho,   וְקָרְבֵנוּ מַלְכֵּנוּ לַעֲבוֹדָתֶךָ,
and bring us near, our King, to Your service,

v'hachaziraynu bis-shuvo sh'laymo l'fonecho.   וְהַחֲזִירֵנוּ בִּתְשׁוּבָה שְׁלֵמָה לְפָנֶיךָ.
and return us in perfect repentance before You.

Boruch ato Adōnoy,   בָּרוּךְ אַתָּה יהוה,
horōtze bis-shuvo.   הָרוֹצֶה בִּתְשׁוּבָה.
Blessed are You, HASHEM, Who desires repentance.

■ Sixth Blessing: Supplication for forgiveness

STRIKE THE LEFT SIDE OF THE CHEST WITH THE RIGHT FIST
WHILE RECITING THE WORDS ki chotonu AND ki fo-shonu.

S'LACH lonu ovinu ki chotonu,   סְלַח לָנוּ אָבִינוּ כִּי חָטָאנוּ,
Forgive us, our Father, for we have erred;

m'chal lonu malkaynu ki fo-shonu,   מְחַל לָנוּ מַלְכֵּנוּ כִּי פָשָׁעְנוּ,
pardon us, our King, for we have willfully sinned;

ki mōchayl v'sōlay-ach oto.   כִּי מוֹחֵל וְסוֹלֵחַ אָתָּה.
for You pardon and forgive.

Boruch ato Adōnoy,   בָּרוּךְ אַתָּה יהוה,
chanun hamarbe lislō-ach.   חַנּוּן הַמַּרְבֶּה לִסְלוֹחַ.
*Blessed are You, HASHEM,
the gracious One Who pardons abundantly.*

■ Seventh Blessing: Supplication for personal redemption
from the perils and problems of daily life

R'AY v'on-yaynu, v'rivo rivaynu,   רְאֵה בְעָנְיֵנוּ, וְרִיבָה רִיבֵנוּ,
Behold our affliction, take up our grievance,

ug-olaynu m'hayro l'ma-an sh'mecho,   וּגְאָלֵנוּ מְהֵרָה לְמַעַן שְׁמֶךָ,
and redeem us speedily for Your Name's sake,

ki gō-ayl chozok oto.   כִּי גּוֹאֵל חָזָק אָתָּה.
for You are a powerful Redeemer.

Boruch ato Adōnoy, gō-ayl yisro-ayl.   בָּרוּךְ אַתָּה יהוה, גּוֹאֵל יִשְׂרָאֵל.
Blessed are You, HASHEM, Redeemer of Israel.

הֲשִׁיבֵנוּ – *Bring us back.* God never compels anyone to repent, but if we make a sincere beginning, God will make our way easier.

SHACHARIS FOR WEEKDAYS — SHEMONEH ESREI

ON A FAST DAY, THE *CHAZZAN* RECITES THE FOLLOWING BLESSING AT THIS POINT:

עֲנֵנוּ יהוה עֲנֵנוּ, בְּיוֹם צוֹם תַּעֲנִיתֵנוּ, כִּי בְצָרָה גְדוֹלָה אֲנָחְנוּ. אַל תֵּפֶן אֶל רִשְׁעֵנוּ, וְאַל תַּסְתֵּר פָּנֶיךָ מִמֶּנּוּ, וְאַל תִּתְעַלַּם מִתְּחִנָּתֵנוּ. הֱיֵה נָא קָרוֹב לְשַׁוְעָתֵנוּ, יְהִי נָא חַסְדְּךָ לְנַחֲמֵנוּ, טֶרֶם נִקְרָא אֵלֶיךָ עֲנֵנוּ, כַּדָּבָר שֶׁנֶּאֱמַר: וְהָיָה טֶרֶם יִקְרָאוּ וַאֲנִי אֶעֱנֶה, עוֹד הֵם מְדַבְּרִים וַאֲנִי אֶשְׁמָע. כִּי אַתָּה יהוה הָעוֹנֶה בְּעֵת צָרָה, פּוֹדֶה וּמַצִּיל בְּכָל עֵת צָרָה וְצוּקָה. בָּרוּךְ אַתָּה יהוה, הָעוֹנֶה בְּעֵת צָרָה.

■ **Eighth Blessing: Supplication for health and healing of body and soul**

R'FO-AYNU Adōnoy, v'nayrofay,   **רְפָאֵנוּ** יהוה וְנֵרָפֵא,
*Heal us, H*ASHEM *— then we will be healed;**

hōshi-aynu v'nivoshay-o,   הוֹשִׁיעֵנוּ וְנִוָּשֵׁעָה,
ki s'hilosaynu oto,   כִּי תְהִלָּתֵנוּ אָתָּה,
save us — then we will be saved, for You are our praise;

v'ha-alay r'fu-o sh'laymo   וְהַעֲלֵה רְפוּאָה שְׁלֵמָה
l'chol makōsaynu,   לְכָל מַכּוֹתֵינוּ,
and bring complete recovery for all our ailments,

ki Ayl melech   כִּי אֵל מֶלֶךְ
rōfay ne-emon v'rachamon oto.   רוֹפֵא נֶאֱמָן וְרַחֲמָן אָתָּה.
for You are God, King, the faithful and compassionate Healer.

Boruch ato Adōnoy,   בָּרוּךְ אַתָּה יהוה,
rōfay chōlay amō yisro-ayl.   רוֹפֵא חוֹלֵי עַמּוֹ יִשְׂרָאֵל.
*Blessed are You, H*ASHEM, *Who heals the sick of His people Israel.*

■ **Ninth Blessing: Supplication for a year of prosperity**

FOR THE FOLLOWING BLESSING, SUMMER IS DEFINED AS THE PERIOD FROM PESACH THROUGH *SHACHARIS* OF DECEMBER 4TH (OR 5TH, IN THE YEAR BEFORE A CIVIL LEAP YEAR); WINTER IS DEFINED AS THE REST OF THE YEAR.

BORAYCH olaynu, Adōnoy Elōhaynu,   **בָּרֵךְ** עָלֵינוּ יהוה אֱלֹהֵינוּ
es ha-shono ha-zōs   אֶת הַשָּׁנָה הַזֹּאת
*Bless on our behalf, O H*ASHEM, *our God, this year*

v'es kol minay s'vu-oso l'tōvo,   וְאֶת כָּל מִינֵי תְבוּאָתָהּ לְטוֹבָה,
and all its kinds of crops for the best,

רְפָאֵנוּ ה' וְנֵרָפֵא — *Heal us, H*ASHEM *— then we will be healed.* The *Zohar* teaches that at times human beings or angels are sent as God's agents to heal illness. In such cases, however, the cure may be only partial or temporary. Or the pain or other symptoms may be relieved, while the illness itself remains uncured. But if God Himself undertakes to cure the patient, the result will not be a temporary or a partial measure, "then we will be healed."

IN SUMMER SAY	
v'sayn b'rocho	וְתֵן בְּרָכָה
and give a blessing	
IN WINTER SAY	
v'sayn tal u-motor livrocho	וְתֵן טַל וּמָטָר לִבְרָכָה
and give dew and rain for a blessing	

al p'nay ho-adomo, עַל פְּנֵי הָאֲדָמָה,
on the face of the earth,
v'sab'aynu mituvecho, וְשַׂבְּעֵנוּ מִטּוּבֶךָ,
and satisfy us from Your bounty,*
u-voraych sh'nosaynu וּבָרֵךְ שְׁנָתֵנוּ
   ka-shonim hatōvōs. כַּשָּׁנִים הַטּוֹבוֹת.
and bless our year like the best years.
Boruch ato Adōnoy, בָּרוּךְ אַתָּה יהוה,
   m'voraych ha-shonim. מְבָרֵךְ הַשָּׁנִים.
Blessed are You, Hashem, Who blesses the years.

■ **Tenth Blessing: Supplication for the ingathering of the exiles**

T'KA b'shōfor godōl l'chayrusaynu, תְּקַע בְּשׁוֹפָר גָּדוֹל לְחֵרוּתֵנוּ,
Sound the great shofar for our freedom,
v'so nays l'kabaytz golu-yōsaynu, וְשָׂא נֵס לְקַבֵּץ גָּלֻיּוֹתֵינוּ,
raise a banner to gather our exiles
v'kab'tzaynu yachad וְקַבְּצֵנוּ יַחַד
   may-arba kanfōs ho-oretz. מֵאַרְבַּע כַּנְפוֹת הָאָרֶץ.
and gather us together from the four corners of the earth.
Boruch ato Adōnoy, בָּרוּךְ אַתָּה יהוה,
   m'kabaytz nidchay amō yisro-ayl. מְקַבֵּץ נִדְחֵי עַמּוֹ יִשְׂרָאֵל.
Blessed are You, Hashem, Who gathers in the dispersed of His people Israel.

■ **Eleventh Blessing: Supplication for the restoration of justice to the Jewish judiciary**

HOSHIVO shōf'taynu k'vorishōno, הָשִׁיבָה שׁוֹפְטֵינוּ כְּבָרִאשׁוֹנָה,
   v'yō-atzaynu k'vat'chilo, וְיוֹעֲצֵינוּ כְּבַתְּחִלָּה,
Restore our judges as in earliest times and our counselors as at first;
v'hosayr mimenu yogōn va-anocho, וְהָסֵר מִמֶּנּוּ יָגוֹן וַאֲנָחָה,
remove from us sorrow and groan;

מִטּוּבֶךָ — *From Your bounty.* Food acquired through tainted means lacks the holiness to nourish the soul. Therefore, we ask that God satisfy us from His bounty, not from earnings to which we are not entitled.

SHACHARIS FOR WEEKDAYS — SHEMONEH ESREI

umlōch olaynu ato, Adōnoy, l'vad'cho   וּמְלוֹךְ עָלֵינוּ אַתָּה יהוה לְבַדֶּךָ
b'chesed uvrachamim,   בְּחֶסֶד וּבְרַחֲמִים,
and reign over us, You, HASHEM, alone, with kindness and with compassion,
v'tzad'kaynu bamishpot.   וְצַדְּקֵנוּ בַּמִּשְׁפָּט.
and justify us through judgment.

Boruch ato Adōnoy,   בָּרוּךְ אַתָּה יהוה,
°melech ōhayv tz'doko u-mishpot.   °מֶלֶךְ אוֹהֵב צְדָקָה וּמִשְׁפָּט.
Blessed are You, HASHEM, the King Who loves righteousness and judgment.

FROM ROSH HASHANAH TO YOM KIPPUR SUBSTITUTE:

°hamelech hamishpot.   °הַמֶּלֶךְ הַמִּשְׁפָּט.
the King of Judgment.

■ **Twelfth Blessing:** Supplication for the eradication
of heretic influences that threaten Jewish life

V'LAMALSHINIM al t'hi sikvo,   **וְלַמַּלְשִׁינִים** אַל תְּהִי תִקְוָה,
And for the slanderers* let there be no hope;
v'chol horish-o k'rega tōvayd,   וְכָל הָרִשְׁעָה כְּרֶגַע תֹּאבֵד,
and may all wickedness perish in an instant;
v'chol ō-y'vecho m'hayro yikoraysu.   וְכָל אֹיְבֶיךָ מְהֵרָה יִכָּרֵתוּ.
and may all Your enemies be cut down speedily.
V'hazaydim m'hayro s'akayr   וְהַזֵּדִים מְהֵרָה תְעַקֵּר
us-shabayr usmagayr v'sachni-a   וּתְשַׁבֵּר וּתְמַגֵּר וְתַכְנִיעַ
The wanton sinners — may You speedily uproot, smash, cast down, and humble —
bimhayro v'yomaynu.   בִּמְהֵרָה בְיָמֵינוּ.
speedily in our days.

Boruch ato Adōnoy,   בָּרוּךְ אַתָּה יהוה,
shōvayr ō-y'vim u-machni-a zaydim.   שׁוֹבֵר אֹיְבִים וּמַכְנִיעַ זֵדִים.
Blessed are You, HASHEM, Who breaks enemies and humbles wanton sinners.

■ **Thirteenth Blessing:** Supplication on behalf of the righteous
and recognition of their significance

AL hatzadikim v'al hachasidim   **עַל** הַצַּדִּיקִים וְעַל הַחֲסִידִים,
On the righteous, on the devout,

וְלַמַּלְשִׁינִים — *And for the slanderers.* This blessing is not one of the original eighteen blessings of the *Shemoneh Esrei.* It was composed, and approved, by the Sanhedrin, a short time after the destruction of the Second Temple, in response to the threats of such heretical Jewish sects as the Sadducees, Boethusians, Essenes, and early Christians. These sects tried to lead Jews astray through example and persuasion, and they used their political power to oppress observant Jews and to slander them to the anti-Semitic Roman government.

It was incorporated into the *Shemoneh Esrei* so that the populace would be aware of the danger posed by these sects.

Despite the disappearance from within Is-

v'al ziknay am'cho bays yisro-ayl,	וְעַל זִקְנֵי עַמְּךָ בֵּית יִשְׂרָאֵל,

on the elders of Your people the Family of Israel,

v'al p'laytas sōf'rayhem, וְעַל פְּלֵיטַת סוֹפְרֵיהֶם,

on the remnant of their scholars,

v'al gayray hatzedek v'olaynu, וְעַל גֵּרֵי הַצֶּדֶק וְעָלֵינוּ,

on the righteous converts and on ourselves —

yehemu rachamecho, Adōnoy Elōhaynu, יֶהֱמוּ רַחֲמֶיךָ יהוה אֱלֹהֵינוּ,

may Your compassion be aroused, HASHEM, our God;

v'sayn sochor tōv וְתֵן שָׂכָר טוֹב

and give goodly reward

l'chol habōt'chim b'shimcho be-emes, לְכָל הַבּוֹטְחִים בְּשִׁמְךָ בֶּאֱמֶת,

to all who sincerely believe in Your Name;

v'sim chelkaynu imohem l'ōlom, וְשִׂים חֶלְקֵנוּ עִמָּהֶם לְעוֹלָם,

and place our lot with them forever,

v'lō nayvōsh ki v'cho botoch-nu. וְלֹא נֵבוֹשׁ כִּי בְךָ בָּטָחְנוּ.

and we will not feel ashamed, for we trust in You.

Boruch ato Adōnoy, בָּרוּךְ אַתָּה יהוה,
   mish-on u-mivtoch latzadikim. מִשְׁעָן וּמִבְטָח לַצַּדִּיקִים.

Blessed are You, HASHEM, Mainstay and Assurance of the righteous.

■ **Fourteenth Blessing:** Supplication for the physical
and spiritual rebuilding of Jerusalem

V'LIRUSHOLA-YIM ir'cho וְלִירוּשָׁלַיִם עִירְךָ
   b'rachamim toshuv, בְּרַחֲמִים תָּשׁוּב,

And to Jerusalem,* Your city, may You return in compassion,

v'sishkōn b'sōchoh וְתִשְׁכּוֹן בְּתוֹכָהּ
   ka-asher dibarto, כַּאֲשֶׁר דִּבַּרְתָּ,

and may You rest within it, as You have spoken;

uvnay ōsoh b'korōv b'yomaynu וּבְנֵה אוֹתָהּ בְּקָרוֹב בְּיָמֵינוּ
   binyan ōlom, בִּנְיַן עוֹלָם,

may You rebuild it soon in our days as an eternal structure,

v'chisay dovid וְכִסֵּא דָוִד
   m'hayro l'sōchoh tochin. מְהֵרָה לְתוֹכָהּ תָּכִין.

and the throne of David may You speedily establish within it.

---

rael of the particular sects against whom it was directed, it is always relevant, because there are still those who seek to destroy the spiritual continuity of Israel.

וְלִירוּשָׁלַיִם — *And to Jerusalem.* After seeking God's blessing on our leaders and righteous people, we seek His blessing for the Holy City. No blessing is complete until the seat of holi-

SHEMONEH ESREI

Boruch ato Adōnoy,
bōnay y'rusholo-yim.

בָּרוּךְ אַתָּה יהוה,
בּוֹנֵה יְרוּשָׁלָיִם.

Blessed are You, Hashem, the Builder of Jerusalem.

■ **Fifteenth Blessing:** Supplication that the Messiah restore the Davidic reign

ES TZEMACH dovid avd'cho
m'hayro satzmi-ach,

אֶת צֶמַח דָּוִד עַבְדְּךָ
מְהֵרָה תַצְמִיחַ,

The offspring of Your servant David may You speedily cause to flourish,

v'karnō torum bi-shu-osecho,

וְקַרְנוֹ תָּרוּם בִּישׁוּעָתֶךָ,

and enhance his pride through Your salvation,

ki li-shu-os'cho kivinu kol hayom.

כִּי לִישׁוּעָתְךָ קִוִּינוּ כָּל הַיּוֹם.

for we hope for Your salvation all day long.

Boruch ato Adōnoy,
matzmi-ach keren y'shu-o.

בָּרוּךְ אַתָּה יהוה,
מַצְמִיחַ קֶרֶן יְשׁוּעָה.

Blessed are You, Hashem, Who causes the pride of salvation to flourish.

■ **Sixteenth Blessing:** Supplication for God's acceptance of our prayer

SH'MA KOLAYNU Adōnoy Elōhaynu,

שְׁמַע קוֹלֵנוּ יהוה אֱלֹהֵינוּ,

Hear our voice, * Hashem our God,*

chus v'rachaym olaynu,

חוּס וְרַחֵם עָלֵינוּ,

pity and be compassionate to us,

v'kabayl b'rachamim uvrotzōn
es t'filosaynu,

וְקַבֵּל בְּרַחֲמִים וּבְרָצוֹן
אֶת תְּפִלָּתֵנוּ,

and accept — with compassion and favor — our prayer,

ki Ayl shōmay-a
t'filōs v'sachanunim oto,

כִּי אֵל שׁוֹמֵעַ
תְּפִלּוֹת וְתַחֲנוּנִים אָתָּה.

for God Who hears prayers and supplications are You;

umil'fonecho, malkaynu,
raykom al t'shivaynu,

וּמִלְּפָנֶיךָ מַלְכֵּנוּ
רֵיקָם אַל תְּשִׁיבֵנוּ,

from before Yourself, our King, turn us not away empty-handed,

Ki ato shōmay-a t'filas
am'cho yisro-ayl b'rachamim.

כִּי אַתָּה שׁוֹמֵעַ תְּפִלַּת
עַמְּךָ יִשְׂרָאֵל בְּרַחֲמִים.

for You hear the prayer of Your people Israel with compassion.

Boruch ato Adōnoy, shōmay-a t'filo.

בָּרוּךְ אַתָּה יהוה, שׁוֹמֵעַ תְּפִלָּה.

Blessed are You, Hashem, Who hears prayer.

---

ness, Jerusalem, is rebuilt in all its grandeur. שְׁמַע קוֹלֵנוּ — *Hear our voice.* In the middle section of *Shemoneh Esrei* we have asked God to grant our specific needs. We now close the section with a general plea that He take note of our call and grant our requests.

שמונה עשרה / שחרית לחול

■ Seventeenth Blessing: Prayer for restoration of the Temple service

R'TZAY, Adōnoy Elōhaynu   **רְצֵה** יהוה אֱלֹהֵינוּ
Be favorable,* Hashem, our God,

b'am'cho yisro-ayl u-visfilosom,   בְּעַמְּךָ יִשְׂרָאֵל וּבִתְפִלָּתָם,
toward Your people Israel and their prayer

v'hoshayv es ho-avōdo   וְהָשֵׁב אֶת הָעֲבוֹדָה
    lidvir bay-secho.   לִדְבִיר בֵּיתֶךָ.
and restore the service to the Holy of Holies of Your Temple.

V'i-shay yisro-ayl, usfilosom   וְאִשֵּׁי יִשְׂרָאֵל וּתְפִלָּתָם
    b'ahavo s'kabayl b'rotzōn,   בְּאַהֲבָה תְקַבֵּל בְּרָצוֹן,
The fire-offerings of Israel and their prayer accept with love and favor,

us-hi l'rotzōn tomid   וּתְהִי לְרָצוֹן תָּמִיד
    avōdas yisro-ayl amecho.   עֲבוֹדַת יִשְׂרָאֵל עַמֶּךָ.
and may the service of Your people Israel always be favorable to You.

■ Yaaleh Veyavo: We petition God to have compassion on Israel and Jerusalem, and to reinstate the Temple service, to enable us to bring the appropriate offerings for the particular occasion.

ON *ROSH CHODESH* AND *CHOL HAMOED* RECITE THE FOLLOWING:

ELŌHAYNU Vaylōhay avōsaynu,   **אֱלֹהֵינוּ** וֵאלֹהֵי אֲבוֹתֵינוּ,
Our God and the God of our forefathers,

ya-a-le v'yovō v'yagi-a v'yayro-e   יַעֲלֶה, וְיָבֹא, וְיַגִּיעַ, וְיֵרָאֶה,
may there rise, come, reach, be noted,

v'yayro-tze v'yi-shoma v'yipokayd   וְיֵרָצֶה, וְיִשָּׁמַע, וְיִפָּקֵד,
be favored, be heard, be considered,

v'yizochayr zichrōnaynu u-fikdōnaynu,   וְיִזָּכֵר זִכְרוֹנֵנוּ וּפִקְדוֹנֵנוּ,
and be remembered — the remembrance and consideration of ourselves;

v'zichrōn avōsaynu,   וְזִכְרוֹן אֲבוֹתֵינוּ,
the remembrance of our forefathers;

v'zichrōn moshi-ach   וְזִכְרוֹן מָשִׁיחַ
    ben dovid avdecho,   בֶּן דָּוִד עַבְדֶּךָ,
the remembrance of Messiah, son of David, Your servant;

v'zichrōn y'rushola-yim   וְזִכְרוֹן יְרוּשָׁלַיִם
    ir kod-shecho,   עִיר קָדְשֶׁךָ,
the remembrance of Jerusalem, Your Holy City;

רְצֵה — *Be favorable.* This begins the final section of *Shemoneh Esrei*. Like a servant who is grateful for having had the opportunity to express himself before his master, we thank God for hearing us out.

SHEMONEH ESREI

v'zichrōn kol am'cho bays yisro-ayl l'fonecho,   וְזִכְרוֹן כָּל עַמְּךָ בֵּית יִשְׂרָאֵל לְפָנֶיךָ,

and the remembrance of Your entire people the Family of Israel — before You

lif-layto l'tōvo   לִפְלֵיטָה לְטוֹבָה

for deliverance, for goodness,

l'chayn ul-chesed ul-rachamim,   לְחֵן וּלְחֶסֶד וּלְרַחֲמִים,

for grace, for kindness, and for compassion,

l'cha-yim ul-sholōm   לְחַיִּים וּלְשָׁלוֹם

for life, and for peace

——— ON ROSH CHODESH ———

b'yōm rōsh hachōdesh ha-ze.   בְּיוֹם רֹאשׁ הַחֹדֶשׁ הַזֶּה.

on this day of Rosh Chodesh.

——— ON PESACH ———

b'yōm chag hamatzōs ha-ze.   בְּיוֹם חַג הַמַּצּוֹת הַזֶּה.

on this day of the Festival of Matzos.

——— ON SUCCOS ———

b'yōm chag hasukōs ha-ze.   בְּיוֹם חַג הַסֻּכּוֹת הַזֶּה.

on this day of the Succos Festival.

DURING THE *CHAZZAN'S* REPETITION, THE CONGREGATION RESPONDS AMEN AS INDICATED.

Zoch-raynu Adōnoy Elōhaynu bō l'tōvo (Omayn),   זָכְרֵנוּ יהוה אֱלֹהֵינוּ בּוֹ לְטוֹבָה (אָמֵן),

Remember us on it, HASHEM, our God, for goodness (Amen),

u-fokdaynu vō livrocho (Omayn),   וּפָקְדֵנוּ בוֹ לִבְרָכָה (אָמֵן),

consider us on it for blessing (Amen),

v'hōshi-aynu vō l'cha-yim (Omayn).   וְהוֹשִׁיעֵנוּ בוֹ לְחַיִּים (אָמֵן).

and help us on it for life (Amen).

U-vidvar y'shu-o v'rachamim,   וּבִדְבַר יְשׁוּעָה וְרַחֲמִים,

In the matter of salvation and compassion,

chus v'chonaynu v'rachaym olaynu v'hōshi-aynu,   חוּס וְחָנֵּנוּ וְרַחֵם עָלֵינוּ וְהוֹשִׁיעֵנוּ,

pity, be gracious and compassionate with us and help us,

ki aylecho aynaynu,   כִּי אֵלֶיךָ עֵינֵינוּ,

for our eyes are turned to You,

ki Ayl melech chanun v'rachum oto.   כִּי אֵל מֶלֶךְ חַנּוּן וְרַחוּם אָתָּה.

because You are God, the gracious and compassionate King.

שמונה עשרה / שחרית לחול

V'SECHEZENO aynaynu
וְתֶחֱזֶינָה עֵינֵינוּ
May our eyes behold

b'shuv'cho l'tziyōn b'rachamim.
בְּשׁוּבְךָ לְצִיּוֹן בְּרַחֲמִים.
Your return to Zion in compassion.

Boruch ato Adōnoy,
בָּרוּךְ אַתָּה יהוה,
hamachazir sh'chinosō l'tziyōn.
הַמַּחֲזִיר שְׁכִינָתוֹ לְצִיּוֹן.
Blessed are You, HASHEM, Who restores His Presence unto Zion.

■ Eighteenth Blessing: Acknowledgment of our debt of gratitude

---

BOW AT Mōdim anachnu loch; STRAIGHTEN UP AT Adōnoy.
IN HIS REPETITION THE CHAZZAN SHOULD RECITE THE ENTIRE MODIM ALOUD,
WHILE THE CONGREGATION RECITES MODIM OF THE RABBIS (P. 193) SOFTLY.

MŌDIM anachnu loch,
מוֹדִים אֲנַחְנוּ לָךְ,
We gratefully thank You,

sho-ato hu Adōnoy Elōhaynu
שָׁאַתָּה הוּא יהוה אֱלֹהֵינוּ
for it is You Who are HASHEM, our God,

Vaylōhay avōsaynu
וֵאלֹהֵי אֲבוֹתֵינוּ
and the God of our forefathers

l'ōlom vo-ed,
לְעוֹלָם וָעֶד,
forever and ever;

tzur cha-yaynu, mogayn yish-aynu
צוּר חַיֵּינוּ, מָגֵן יִשְׁעֵנוּ
Rock of our lives,* Shield of our salvation

ato hu l'dōr vodōr.
אַתָּה הוּא לְדוֹר וָדוֹר.
are You from generation to generation.

Nōde l'cho unsapayr t'hilosecho
נוֹדֶה לְךָ וּנְסַפֵּר תְּהִלָּתֶךָ
We shall thank You and relate Your praise —

al cha-yaynu ham'surim b'yodecho,
עַל חַיֵּינוּ הַמְּסוּרִים בְּיָדֶךָ,
for our lives, which are committed to Your power,

v'al nishmōsaynu hap'kudōs loch,
וְעַל נִשְׁמוֹתֵינוּ הַפְּקוּדוֹת לָךְ,
and for our souls that are entrusted to You,

v'al nisecho sheb'chol yōm i-monu,
וְעַל נִסֶּיךָ שֶׁבְּכָל יוֹם עִמָּנוּ,
and for Your miracles that are with us every day,

v'al nifl'ōsecho v'tōvōsecho
sheb'chol ays,
וְעַל נִפְלְאוֹתֶיךָ וְטוֹבוֹתֶיךָ
שֶׁבְּכָל עֵת,
and for Your wonders and favors in every season —

erev vovōker v'tzohoro-yim.
עֶרֶב וָבֹקֶר וְצָהֳרָיִם.
evening, morning, and afternoon.

צוּר חַיֵּינוּ — *Rock of our lives.* Our parents are the "rocks" from which our bodies are hewn, but it is from You that we receive life itself.

Hatōv ki lō cholu rachamecho,	הַטּוֹב כִּי לֹא כָלוּ רַחֲמֶיךָ,

The Beneficent One, for Your compassions were never exhausted,

v'ham'rachaym ki lō samu chasodecho,	וְהַמְרַחֵם כִּי לֹא תַמּוּ חֲסָדֶיךָ,

and the Compassionate One, for Your kindnesses never ended —

may-ōlom kivinu loch.	מֵעוֹלָם קִוִּינוּ לָךְ.

always have we put our hope in You.

MODIM OF THE RABBIS*

RECITED SOFTLY BY CONGREGATION WHILE CHAZZAN RECITES THE REGULAR *MODIM* ALOUD

MŌDIM anachnu loch,	**מוֹדִים** אֲנַחְנוּ לָךְ,

We gratefully thank You,

sho-ato hu Adōnoy Elōhaynu	שָׁאַתָּה הוּא יהוה אֱלֹהֵינוּ
Vaylōhay avōsaynu,	וֵאלֹהֵי אֲבוֹתֵינוּ,

for it is You Who are HASHEM, our God and the God of our forefathers,

Elōhay chol bosor,	אֱלֹהֵי כָל בָּשָׂר,

the God of all flesh,

yōtz'raynu, yōtzayr b'rayshis.	יוֹצְרֵנוּ, יוֹצֵר בְּרֵאשִׁית.

our Molder, the Molder of the universe.

B'rochōs v'hōdo-ōs l'shimcho	בְּרָכוֹת וְהוֹדָאוֹת לְשִׁמְךָ
hagodōl v'hakodōsh,	הַגָּדוֹל וְהַקָּדוֹשׁ,

Blessings and thanks are due Your great and holy Name

al sheheche-yisonu v'ki-yamtonu.	עַל שֶׁהֶחֱיִיתָנוּ וְקִיַּמְתָּנוּ.

for You have given us life and sustained us.

Kayn t'cha-yaynu uska-y'maynu,	כֵּן תְּחַיֵּנוּ וּתְקַיְּמֵנוּ,

So may You continue to give us life and sustain us

v'se-esōf golu-yōsaynu	וְתֶאֱסוֹף גָּלֻיּוֹתֵינוּ
l'chatzrōs kod-shecho,	לְחַצְרוֹת קָדְשֶׁךָ,

and gather our exiles to the Courtyards of Your Sanctuary,

lishmōr chukecho v'la-asōs r'tzōnecho,	לִשְׁמוֹר חֻקֶּיךָ וְלַעֲשׂוֹת רְצוֹנֶךָ,

to observe Your decrees, to do Your will

ul-ovd'cho b'layvov sholaym,	וּלְעָבְדְּךָ בְּלֵבָב שָׁלֵם,

and to serve You wholeheartedly.

al she-anachnu mōdim loch.	עַל שֶׁאֲנַחְנוּ מוֹדִים לָךְ.

[We thank You] for inspiring us to thank You.

Boruch Ayl hahōdo-ōs.	בָּרוּךְ אֵל הַהוֹדָאוֹת.

Blessed is the God of thanksgivings.

ᴈ Modim of the Rabbis

When the *chazzan* bows and recites *Modim* in the manner of a slave accepting the total authority of his master, the congregation must join him in accepting God's sovereignty. Therefore, each member of the congregation must make his own declaration of submission.

ON CHANUKAH AND PURIM CONTINUE BELOW. ON ALL OTHER DAYS TURN TO P. 197.

ON CHANUKAH AND PURIM ADD THE FOLLOWING:

AL HANISIM, v'al hapurkon, עַל הַנִּסִּים, וְעַל הַפֻּרְקָן,
For the miracles, and for the salvation,

v'al hag'vurōs, v'al hat'shu-ōs, וְעַל הַגְּבוּרוֹת, וְעַל הַתְּשׁוּעוֹת,
and for the mighty deeds, and for the victories,

v'al hamilchomōs, וְעַל הַמִּלְחָמוֹת,
and for the battles

she-osiso la-avōsaynu שֶׁעָשִׂיתָ לַאֲבוֹתֵינוּ
which You performed for our forefathers

ba-yomim hohaym baz'man ha-ze. בַּיָּמִים הָהֵם בַּזְּמַן הַזֶּה.
in those days, at this time.

ON CHANUKAH CONTINUE HERE; ON PURIM TURN TO P. 196.

BIMAY matisyohu ben yōchonon בִּימֵי מַתִּתְיָהוּ בֶּן יוֹחָנָן
In the days of Mattisyahu, the son of Yochanan,

kōhayn godōl chashmōno-i u-vonov, כֹּהֵן גָּדוֹל חַשְׁמוֹנַאי וּבָנָיו,
the High Priest, the Hasmonean, and his sons —

k'she-om'do malchus yovon כְּשֶׁעָמְדָה מַלְכוּת יָוָן
hor'sho-o al am'cho yisro-ayl, הָרְשָׁעָה עַל עַמְּךָ יִשְׂרָאֵל,
when the wicked Greek kingdom rose up against Your people Israel

l'hashkichom tōrosecho, לְהַשְׁכִּיחָם תּוֹרָתֶךָ,
to make them forget Your Torah

ulha-avirom maychukay r'tzōnecho. וּלְהַעֲבִירָם מֵחֻקֵּי רְצוֹנֶךָ.
and compel them to stray from the statutes of Your will.

V'ato b'rachamecho horabim, וְאַתָּה בְּרַחֲמֶיךָ הָרַבִּים,
But You, in Your abundant mercy,

omadto lohem b'ays tzorosom, עָמַדְתָּ לָהֶם בְּעֵת צָרָתָם,
stood up for them in the time of their distress;

ravto es rivom, danto es dinom, רַבְתָּ אֶת רִיבָם, דַּנְתָּ אֶת דִּינָם,
You took up their grievance, You judged their claim,

nokamto es nikmosom. נָקַמְתָּ אֶת נִקְמָתָם.
and You avenged their wrong.

Mosarto gibōrim b'yad chaloshim, מָסַרְתָּ גִבּוֹרִים בְּיַד חַלָּשִׁים,
You delivered the strong into the hand of the weak,

◆§ **Chanukah**

לְהַשְׁכִּיחָם תּוֹרָתֶךְ וּלְהַעֲבִירָם מֵחֻקֵּי רְצוֹנֶךְ — *To make them forget Your Torah and compel them to stray from the statutes of Your Will.* The Syrian-Greeks knew that the key to the Jewish religion is the study of Torah; if Torah study were neglected, then the decline of ritual observance would be inevitable and swift. Therefore,

SHACHARIS FOR WEEKDAYS — SHEMONEH ESREI

ON CHANUKAH CONTINUE HERE:

v'rabim b'yad m'atim,   וְרַבִּים בְּיַד מְעַטִּים,
the many into the hand of the few,

utmay-im b'yad t'horim,   וּטְמֵאִים בְּיַד טְהוֹרִים,
the impure into the hand of the pure,

ursho-im b'yad tzadikim   וּרְשָׁעִים בְּיַד צַדִּיקִים,
the wicked into the hand of the righteous,

v'zaydim b'yad ōs'kay sōrosecho.   וְזֵדִים בְּיַד עוֹסְקֵי תוֹרָתֶךָ.
and the wanton into the hand of the diligent students of Your Torah.

Ulcho osiso   וּלְךָ עָשִׂיתָ
For Yourself You made

shaym godōl v'kodōsh b'ōlomecho,   שֵׁם גָּדוֹל וְקָדוֹשׁ בְּעוֹלָמֶךָ,
a great and holy Name in Your world,

ul-am'cho yisro-ayl   וּלְעַמְּךָ יִשְׂרָאֵל
and for Your people Israel

osiso t'shu-o g'dōlo u-furkon   עָשִׂיתָ תְּשׁוּעָה גְדוֹלָה וּפֻרְקָן
You performed a great victory and salvation

k'ha-yōm ha-ze.   כְּהַיּוֹם הַזֶּה.
as this very day.

V'achar kayn bo-u vonecho   וְאַחַר כֵּן בָּאוּ בָנֶיךָ
   lidvir bay-secho,   לִדְבִיר בֵּיתֶךָ,
Thereafter, Your children came to the Holy of Holies of Your House,

u-finu es haycholecho,   וּפִנּוּ אֶת הֵיכָלֶךָ,
they cleansed Your Temple,

v'tiharu es mikdoshecho,   וְטִהֲרוּ אֶת מִקְדָּשֶׁךָ,
they purified the site of Your Holiness;

v'hidliku nayrōs   וְהִדְלִיקוּ נֵרוֹת
   b'chatzrōs kod-shecho,   בְּחַצְרוֹת קָדְשֶׁךָ,
and they kindled lights in the Courtyards of Your Sanctuary;

v'kov'u   וְקָבְעוּ
   sh'mōnas y'may chanuko aylu,   שְׁמוֹנַת יְמֵי חֲנֻכָּה אֵלּוּ,
and they established these eight days of Chanukah

l'hōdōs ulhalayl   לְהוֹדוֹת וּלְהַלֵּל
   l'shimcho hagodōl.   לְשִׁמְךָ הַגָּדוֹל.
to express thanks and praise to Your great Name.

CONTINUE ON P. 197.

---

they concentrated first on causing Torah to be forgotten, knowing that the deterioration of observance would soon follow.

ON PURIM CONTINUE HERE:

בִּימֵי מָרְדְּכַי וְאֶסְתֵּר
BIMAY mord'chai v'estayr
In the days of Mordechai and Esther,

בְּשׁוּשַׁן הַבִּירָה,
b'shushan habiro,
in Shushan, the capital,

כְּשֶׁעָמַד עֲלֵיהֶם הָמָן הָרָשָׁע,
k'she-omad alayhem homon horosho,
when Haman, the wicked, rose up against them*

בִּקֵּשׁ לְהַשְׁמִיד לַהֲרֹג וּלְאַבֵּד
bikaysh l'hashmid laharōg ul-abayd
and sought to destroy, to slay, and to exterminate

אֶת כָּל הַיְּהוּדִים,
es kol ha-y'hudim,

מִנַּעַר וְעַד זָקֵן, טַף וְנָשִׁים
mina-ar v'ad zokayn, taf v'noshim
all the Jews, young and old, infants and women,

בְּיוֹם אֶחָד,
b'yōm echod,
on the same day,

בִּשְׁלוֹשָׁה עָשָׂר לְחֹדֶשׁ שְׁנֵים עָשָׂר, הוּא חֹדֶשׁ אֲדָר,
bishlōsho osor l'chōdesh sh'naym osor, hu chōdesh ador,
on the thirteenth of the twelfth month which is the month of Adar,

וּשְׁלָלָם לָבוֹז.
ushlolom lovōz.
and to plunder their possessions.

וְאַתָּה בְּרַחֲמֶיךָ הָרַבִּים
V'ato b'rachamecho horabim
But You, in Your abundant mercy,

הֵפַרְתָּ אֶת עֲצָתוֹ,
hayfarto es atzosō,
nullified his counsel

וְקִלְקַלְתָּ אֶת מַחֲשַׁבְתּוֹ,
v'kilkalto es machashavtō,
and frustrated his intention

וַהֲשֵׁבְוֹתָ לּוֹ גְּמוּלוֹ בְּרֹאשׁוֹ,
vahashayvōso lō g'mulō b'rōshō,
and caused his design to return upon his own head.

וְתָלוּ אוֹתוֹ וְאֶת בָּנָיו עַל הָעֵץ.
V'solu ōsō v'es bonov al ho-aytz.
And they hanged him and his sons on the gallows.

⤶ **Purim**

כְּשֶׁעָמַד עֲלֵיהֶם — *When ... rose up against them.* The paragraph describing the miracle of Purim is far briefer than that describing Chanukah. The danger of Purim was straightforward — the extermination of the nation — and requires no elaboration. The peril of Chanukah was more subtle. It involved assimilation and impurity. The unaware do not perceive danger unless it is starkly physical in nature. Therefore, it requires a more elaborate explanation.

SHACHARIS FOR WEEKDAYS — SHEMONEH ESREI

V'AL kulom yisborach v'yisrōmam shimcho, malkaynu

וְעַל כֻּלָּם יִתְבָּרַךְ וְיִתְרוֹמַם שִׁמְךָ מַלְכֵּנוּ

For all these, may Your Name be blessed and exalted, our King,

tomid l'ōlom vo-ed.

תָּמִיד לְעוֹלָם וָעֶד.

continually forever and ever.

FROM ROSH HASHANAH TO YOM KIPPUR ADD:

Uchsōv l'cha-yim tōvim kol b'nay v'risecho.

וּכְתוֹב לְחַיִּים טוֹבִים כָּל בְּנֵי בְרִיתֶךָ.

And inscribe all the children of Your covenant for a good life.

V'chōl hacha-yim yōducho selo,

וְכֹל הַחַיִּים יוֹדוּךָ סֶּלָה,

Everything alive will gratefully acknowledge You, Selah!

vihal'lu es shimcho be-emes,

וִיהַלְלוּ אֶת שִׁמְךָ בֶּאֱמֶת,

and praise Your Name sincerely,

ho-Ayl y'shu-osaynu
v'ezrosaynu selo.

הָאֵל יְשׁוּעָתֵנוּ וְעֶזְרָתֵנוּ סֶלָה.

O God of our salvation and help, Selah!

BEND THE KNEES AT Boruch; BOW AT ato; STRAIGHTEN UP AT Adōnoy.

Boruch ato Adōnoy,
hatōv shimcho
ulcho no-e l'hōdōs.

בָּרוּךְ אַתָּה יהוה,
הַטּוֹב שִׁמְךָ
וּלְךָ נָאֶה לְהוֹדוֹת.

Blessed are You, HASHEM, Your Name is "The Beneficent One" and to You it is fitting to give thanks.

■ **Nineteenth Blessing:** Prayer for peace and harmony amongst the Jewish people

---

THE CHAZZAN RECITES THE PRIESTLY BLESSING DURING HIS REPETITION, EXCEPT IN A HOUSE OF MOURNING.

אֱלֹהֵינוּ, וֵאלֹהֵי אֲבוֹתֵינוּ, בָּרְכֵנוּ בַבְּרָכָה הַמְשֻׁלֶּשֶׁת בַּתּוֹרָה
הַכְּתוּבָה עַל יְדֵי מֹשֶׁה עַבְדֶּךָ, הָאֲמוּרָה מִפִּי אַהֲרֹן וּבָנָיו,
כֹּהֲנִים עַם קְדוֹשֶׁךָ, כָּאָמוּר:

יְבָרֶכְךָ יהוה, וְיִשְׁמְרֶךָ. — Cong.) — כֵּן יְהִי רָצוֹן — kayn y'hi rotzōn)
יָאֵר יהוה פָּנָיו אֵלֶיךָ וִיחֻנֶּךָּ. — Cong.) — כֵּן יְהִי רָצוֹן — kayn y'hi rotzōn)
יִשָּׂא יהוה פָּנָיו אֵלֶיךָ וְיָשֵׂם לְךָ שָׁלוֹם.
— Cong.) — כֵּן יְהִי רָצוֹן — kayn y'hi rotzōn)

וְכֹל הַחַיִּים — *Everything alive.* As long as there is life, people can express their thanks to God.

This passage refers specifically to the universal praise that will come in the time of the Messiah.

SIM SHOLŌM tōvo uvrocho,	שִׂים שָׁלוֹם, טוֹבָה, וּבְרָכָה,

Establish peace, goodness, blessing,

chayn vochesed v'rachamim   חֵן וָחֶסֶד וְרַחֲמִים

graciousness, kindness, and compassion

olaynu v'al kol yisro-ayl amecho.   עָלֵינוּ וְעַל כָּל יִשְׂרָאֵל עַמֶּךָ.

upon us and upon all of Your people Israel.

Bor'chaynu, ovinu, kulonu k'e-chod b'ōr ponecho,   בָּרְכֵנוּ, אָבִינוּ, כֻּלָּנוּ כְּאֶחָד בְּאוֹר פָּנֶיךָ,

Bless us, our Father, all of us as one, with the light of Your countenance,

ki v'ōr ponecho nosato lonu, Adōnoy Elōhaynu,   כִּי בְאוֹר פָּנֶיךָ נָתַתָּ לָּנוּ, יהוה אֱלֹהֵינוּ,

for with the light of Your countenance, You, HASHEM, our God, gave us

tōras cha-yim v'ahavas chesed,   תּוֹרַת חַיִּים וְאַהֲבַת חֶסֶד,

the Torah of life and a love of kindness,

utz-doko uvrocho v'rachamim v'cha-yim v'sholōm.   וּצְדָקָה וּבְרָכָה וְרַחֲמִים וְחַיִּים וְשָׁלוֹם.

righteousness, blessing, compassion, life, and peace.

V'tōv b'aynecho l'voraych es am'cho yisro-ayl,   וְטוֹב בְּעֵינֶיךָ לְבָרֵךְ אֶת עַמְּךָ יִשְׂרָאֵל,

And may it be good in Your eyes to bless Your people Israel

b'chol ays uvchol sho-o bish-lōmecho.   בְּכָל עֵת וּבְכָל שָׁעָה בִּשְׁלוֹמֶךָ.

at every time and at every hour, with Your peace.

°Boruch ato Adōnoy, ham'voraych es amō yisro-ayl ba-sholōm.   °בָּרוּךְ אַתָּה יהוה, הַמְבָרֵךְ אֶת עַמּוֹ יִשְׂרָאֵל בַּשָּׁלוֹם.

°Blessed are You, HASHEM, Who blesses His people Israel with peace.

° FROM ROSH HASHANAH TO YOM KIPPUR SUBSTITUTE THE FOLLOWING:

B'sayfer cha-yim b'rocho v'sholōm, ufarnoso tōvo,   בְּסֵפֶר חַיִּים בְּרָכָה וְשָׁלוֹם, וּפַרְנָסָה טוֹבָה,

In the book of life, blessing, and peace, and good livelihood,

nizochayr v'nikosayv l'fonecho,   נִזָּכֵר וְנִכָּתֵב לְפָנֶיךָ,

may we be remembered and inscribed before You —

anachnu v'chol am'cho bays yisro-ayl,   אֲנַחְנוּ וְכָל עַמְּךָ בֵּית יִשְׂרָאֵל,

we and Your entire people the Family of Israel —

SHACHARIS FOR WEEKDAYS — SHEMONEH ESREI

l'cha-yim tōvim ulsholōm.
לְחַיִּים טוֹבִים וּלְשָׁלוֹם.
for a good life and for peace.

Boruch ato Adōnoy,
ō-se ha-sholōm.
בָּרוּךְ אַתָּה יהוה,
עוֹשֶׂה הַשָּׁלוֹם.
Blessed are You, HASHEM, Who makes the peace.

THE *CHAZZAN'S* REPETITION ENDS HERE (TURN TO PAGE 150). INDIVIDUALS CONTINUE:

Yih-yu l'rotzōn imray fi
v'hegyōn libi l'fonecho,
יִהְיוּ לְרָצוֹן אִמְרֵי פִי
וְהֶגְיוֹן לִבִּי לְפָנֶיךָ,
May the expressions of my mouth and the thoughts of my heart find favor* before You,

Adōnoy tzuri v'gō-ali.
יהוה צוּרִי וְגֹאֲלִי.
HASHEM, my Rock and my Redeemer.

■ I pray that, having completed my *Amidah*, I have been changed in a positive way, especially with regard to my interpersonal relationships.

ELŌHAI, n'tzōr l'shōni mayro,
אֱלֹהַי, נְצוֹר לְשׁוֹנִי מֵרָע,
My God, guard my tongue from evil*

usfosai midabayr mirmo,
וּשְׂפָתַי מִדַּבֵּר מִרְמָה,
and my lips from speaking deceitfully.

V'limkal'lai nafshi sidōm,
וְלִמְקַלְלַי נַפְשִׁי תִדּוֹם,
To those who curse me, let my soul be silent;

v'nafshi ke-ofor lakōl tih-ye.
וְנַפְשִׁי כֶּעָפָר לַכֹּל תִּהְיֶה.
and let my soul be like dust* to everyone.

P'sach libi b'sōrosecho,
פְּתַח לִבִּי בְּתוֹרָתֶךָ,
Open my heart to Your Torah,*

uvmitzvōsecho tirdōf nafshi.
וּבְמִצְוֹתֶיךָ תִּרְדּוֹף נַפְשִׁי.
then my soul will pursue Your commandments.

יִהְיוּ לְרָצוֹן — *May . . . find favor.* We conclude *Shemoneh Esrei* with this brief prayer that our prayers find favor before God. Kabbalistic literature attaches great sanctity to this verse and stresses that it be recited slowly and fervently.

אֱלֹהַי, נְצוֹר לְשׁוֹנִי מֵרָע — *My God, guard my tongue from evil.* We pray that God protect us from situations that would tempt us to speak ill of others.

The Midrash relates that Rabban Shimon ben Gamliel once sent his servant, Tavi, to buy "good food." Tavi, who was famous for his wisdom, brought back a tongue. Thereupon Rabban Shimon sent him to buy some "bad food." Again, he returned with a tongue. Rabban Shimon asked him to explain how the same food could be both good and bad. Tavi said, "From a tongue can come good or bad. When a tongue speaks *good*, there is nothing better, but when a tongue speaks *ill*, there is nothing worse."

נַפְשִׁי תִדּוֹם . . . כֶּעָפָר — *Let my soul be silent . . . like dust.* We should ignore barbs and insults, because the less we care about our prestige, the less we will allow selfishness to interfere with our service of God, our relations with others and our efforts at self-improvement.

פְּתַח לִבִּי בְּתוֹרָתֶךָ — *Open my heart to Your Torah.* Our goal is to serve God in a positive manner by studying Torah and fulfilling its commandments: both those between man and God and those between man and man.

V'chol hachōsh'vim olai ro-o,	וְכָל הַחוֹשְׁבִים עָלַי רָעָה,

As for all those who design evil against me,

m'hayro hofayr atzosom	מְהֵרָה הָפֵר עֲצָתָם
v'kalkayl machashavtom.	וְקַלְקֵל מַחֲשַׁבְתָּם.

speedily nullify their counsel and disrupt their design.

Asay l'ma-an sh'mecho,	עֲשֵׂה לְמַעַן שְׁמֶךָ,

Act for Your Name's sake;

asay l'ma-an y'minecho,	עֲשֵׂה לְמַעַן יְמִינֶךָ,

act for Your right hand's sake;

asay l'ma-an k'dushosecho,	עֲשֵׂה לְמַעַן קְדֻשָּׁתֶךָ,

act for Your sanctity's sake;

asay l'ma-an tōrosecho.	עֲשֵׂה לְמַעַן תּוֹרָתֶךָ.

act for Your Torah's sake.

L'ma-an yaychol'tzun y'didecho,	לְמַעַן יֵחָלְצוּן יְדִידֶיךָ,

That Your beloved ones may be given rest;

hōshi-o y'min'cho va-anayni.	הוֹשִׁיעָה יְמִינְךָ וַעֲנֵנִי.

let Your right hand save, and respond to me.

Yih-yu l'rotzōn imray fi	יִהְיוּ לְרָצוֹן אִמְרֵי פִי
v'hegyōn libi l'fonecho,	וְהֶגְיוֹן לִבִּי לְפָנֶיךָ,

May the expressions of my mouth and the thoughts of my heart find favor before You,

Adōnoy tzuri v'gō-ali.	יהוה צוּרִי וְגֹאֲלִי.

HASHEM, my Rock and my Redeemer.

BOW. TAKE THREE STEPS BACK. BOW LEFT AND SAY:

Ō-se sholōm bimrōmov,	עֹשֶׂה שָׁלוֹם בִּמְרוֹמָיו,

He Who makes peace in His heights,

BOW RIGHT AND SAY:

hu ya-a-se sholōm olaynu,	הוּא יַעֲשֶׂה שָׁלוֹם עָלֵינוּ,

may He make peace upon us,

BOW FORWARD AND SAY:

v'al kol yisro-ayl. V'imru: Omayn.	וְעַל כָּל יִשְׂרָאֵל. וְאִמְרוּ: אָמֵן.

and upon all Israel. Now respond: Amen.

Y'HI ROTZŌN mil'fonecho,	**יְהִי רָצוֹן** מִלְּפָנֶיךָ

May it be Your will,

Adōnoy Elōhaynu	יהוה אֱלֹהֵינוּ
Vaylōhay avōsaynu,	וֵאלֹהֵי אֲבוֹתֵינוּ,

HASHEM, our God and the God of our forefathers,

SHACHARIS FOR WEEKDAYS — SHEMONEH ESREI

she-yibo-ne bays hamikdosh
bimhayro v'yomaynu, שֶׁיִּבָּנֶה בֵּית הַמִּקְדָּשׁ
בִּמְהֵרָה בְיָמֵינוּ,
that the Holy Temple be rebuilt, speedily in our days;

v'sayn chelkaynu b'sōrosecho, וְתֵן חֶלְקֵנוּ בְּתוֹרָתֶךָ,
and grant us our share in Your Torah;

v'shom na-avod-cho b'yiro, וְשָׁם נַעֲבָדְךָ בְּיִרְאָה,
and may we serve You there with reverence,

kimay ōlom uchshonim kadmōniyōs. כִּימֵי עוֹלָם וּכְשָׁנִים קַדְמוֹנִיּוֹת.
as in days of old and in former years.

V'or'vo Ladōnoy
minchas y'hudo virusholo-yim וְעָרְבָה לַיהוה
מִנְחַת יְהוּדָה וִירוּשָׁלָיִם,
Then the offering of Judah and Jerusalem will be pleasing to HASHEM,

kimay ōlom uchshonim kadmōniyōs. כִּימֵי עוֹלָם וּכְשָׁנִים קַדְמוֹנִיּוֹת.
as in days of old and in former years.

THE INDIVIDUAL'S RECITATION OF *SHEMONEH ESREI* ENDS HERE.
REMAIN STANDING IN PLACE UNTIL THE *CHAZZAN* REACHES *KEDUSHAH* —
OR AT LEAST FOR A FEW MOMENTS — THEN TAKE THREE STEPS FORWARD.

ON ROSH CHODESH AND CHANUKAH, THE SERVICE CONTINUES WITH HALLEL (P. 486).

SUPPLICATION AND CONFESSION

EXCEPT FOR CERTAIN FESTIVE DAYS (SEE BOX BELOW), ONE OR MORE SECTIONS
OF SUPPLICATION AND CONFESSION ARE RECITED AT THIS POINT, AS FOLLOWS:
[SOME CONGREGATIONS BEGIN THIS SECTION BY RECITING THE *VIDUI*-CONFESSION (P. 202).]

❏ ON MONDAYS AND THURSDAYS, *TACHANUN* BEGINS ON P. 212
❏ ON OTHER DAYS, *TACHANUN* BEGINS ON P. 225
❏ BETWEEN ROSH HASHANAH AND YOM KIPPUR, *AVINU MALKEINU* (P. 206) IS RECITED BEFORE *TACHANUN*.
❏ ON FAST DAYS (WITH THE EXCEPTION OF TISHAH B'AV), *AVINU MALKEINU* (P. 206) IS RECITED BEFORE *TACHANUN*. MANY CONGREGATIONS RECITE *SELICHOS* BEFORE *AVINU MALKEINU*.

> ### ✦§ Occasions and Days on Which the Supplication and Confession Section Is Omitted
>
> (a) In a house of mourning during the *shivah* period;
> (b) In the presence of a bridegroom, from the day of his wedding until after the *Sheva Berachos* week (if both bride and groom have been previously married, their period of celebration extends for only three days);
> (c) In the synagogue where a circumcision will take place later that day, or in the presence of a primary participant (i.e., the father, the *mohel* or the *sandak*) in a circumcision that will take place later that day;
> (d) *Rosh Chodesh*; the entire month of Nissan; *Lag B'Omer*; from *Rosh Chodesh* Sivan until the day after Shavuos (some congregations do not resume until 14 Sivan); Tishah B'Av; 15 Av; between Yom Kippur and the day after Succos (some congregations do not resume until 2 Cheshvan); Chanukah; Tu B'Shevat; Purim and Shushan Purim (in a leap year this applies also to 14-15 Adar I); or at *Minchah* of the day preceding any of the days listed above;
> (e) On Erev Rosh Hashanah and Erev Yom Kippur;
> (f) In some congregations, it is omitted on Pesach Sheni (14 Iyar).

VIDUI/CONFESSION

SOME CONGREGATIONS RECITE *VIDUI* BEFORE *TACHANUN*. IT IS RECITED WHILE STANDING.

ELOHAYNU Vaylōhay avōsaynu, אֱלֹהֵינוּ וֵאלֹהֵי אֲבוֹתֵינוּ,
Our God and the God of our forefathers,

tovō l'fonecho t'filosaynu, תָּבֹא לְפָנֶיךָ תְּפִלָּתֵנוּ,
may our prayer come before You,

v'al tisalam mit'chinosaynu, וְאַל תִּתְעַלַּם מִתְּחִנָּתֵנוּ,
Do not ignore our supplication,

she-ayn onu azay fonim שֶׁאֵין אָנוּ עַזֵּי פָנִים
ukshay ōref, וּקְשֵׁי עֹרֶף,
for we are not so brazen and obstinate

lōmar l'fonecho לוֹמַר לְפָנֶיךָ
as to say before You,

Adōnoy Elōhaynu יהוה אֱלֹהֵינוּ
Vaylōhay avōsaynu, וֵאלֹהֵי אֲבוֹתֵינוּ,
Hashem, our God and the God of our forefathers,

tzadikim anachnu v'lō chotonu, צַדִּיקִים אֲנַחְנוּ וְלֹא חָטָאנוּ,
that we are righteous and have not sinned,

avol anachnu va-avōsaynu אֲבָל אֲנַחְנוּ וַאֲבוֹתֵינוּ
chotonu. חָטָאנוּ.
for in truth, we and our forefathers have sinned.

STRIKE THE LEFT SIDE OF THE CHEST WITH THE RIGHT FIST WHILE RECITING
EACH OF THE SINS IN THE FOLLOWING CONFESSION LITANY.

OSHAMNU, bogadnu, אָשַׁמְנוּ, בָּגַדְנוּ,
We have become guilty; we have betrayed;

gozalnu, dibarnu dōfi. גָּזַלְנוּ, דִּבַּרְנוּ דֹפִי.
we have robbed; we have spoken slander;

He-evinu, v'hirshanu, הֶעֱוִינוּ, וְהִרְשַׁעְנוּ,
we have caused perversion; we have caused wickedness;

zadnu, chomasnu, tofalnu sheker. זַדְנוּ, חָמַסְנוּ, טָפַלְנוּ שֶׁקֶר.
we have sinned willfully; we have extorted; we have accused falsely;

Yo-atznu ro, kizavnu, יָעַצְנוּ רָע, כִּזַּבְנוּ,
we have given evil counsel; we have been deceitful;

◈§ Confession

The custom of confessing as a prelude to *Tachanun* is based on the *Zohar*. The confession, beginning with the last phrase of the opening paragraph (*avol anachnu va-avōsaynu chotonu*), should be said while one stands with head and body slightly bowed to symbolize contrition and submission. It is customary to strike oneself lightly opposite the heart with the right fist while saying each individual expression of sin. This act symbolizes that sin is caused by the desires of the heart and that the

latznu, moradnu,	לַצְנוּ, מָרַדְנוּ,

we have scorned; we have rebelled;

ni-atznu, sorarnu,	נִאַצְנוּ, סָרַרְנוּ,

we have provoked; we have turned away;

ovinu, poshanu,	עָוִינוּ, פָּשַׁעְנוּ,

we have been perverse; we have acted wantonly;

tzorarnu, kishinu ōref.	צָרַרְנוּ, קִשִּׁינוּ עֹרֶף.

we have persecuted; we have been obstinate;

Roshanu, shichasnu,	רָשַׁעְנוּ, שִׁחַתְנוּ,

we have been wicked; we have corrupted;

ti-avnu, to-inu, tito'nu.	תִּעַבְנוּ, תָּעִינוּ, תִּעְתָּעְנוּ.

we have been abominable; we have strayed; You have let us go astray.

SARNU mimitzvōsecho	**סַרְנוּ** מִמִּצְוֹתֶיךָ
u-mimishpotecho hatōvim,	וּמִמִּשְׁפָּטֶיךָ הַטּוֹבִים

We have turned away from Your commandments and from Your good laws

v'lō shovo lonu.	וְלֹא שָׁוָה לָנוּ.

but to no avail.

V'atoh tzadik	וְאַתָּה צַדִּיק
al kol habo olaynu,	עַל כָּל הַבָּא עָלֵינוּ,

Yet You are righteous in all that has come upon us,

ki emes osiso	כִּי אֱמֶת עָשִׂיתָ

for You have acted truthfully

va-anachnu hirsho'nu.	וַאֲנַחְנוּ הִרְשָׁעְנוּ.

while we have caused wickedness.

ONE PRAYING WITHOUT A *MINYAN* OMITS THE REMAINDER OF THE *VIDUI*/CONFESSION.

AYL ERECH APA-YIM ato,	**אֵל אֶרֶךְ אַפַּיִם** אַתָּה,

O God — You are slow to anger,

u-va-al horachamim nikrayso,	וּבַעַל הָרַחֲמִים נִקְרֵאתָ,

You are called the Master of Mercy,

v'derech t'shuvo hōrayso.	וְדֶרֶךְ תְּשׁוּבָה הוֹרֵיתָ.

and You have taught the way of repentance.

---

beginning of repentance is the resolve to curb one's passions (*Matanos Kehunah* to *Koheles Rabbah*, ch. 7).

The confession is formulated in the plural because the Jewish people are like a single body and each of us is like one of its organs. We are responsible for one another, for the good or evil of every Jew affects us all.

The confession follows the order of the *aleph-beis* because God created the universe with the sacred letters (see Overview to ArtScroll *Wisdom of the Hebrew Alphabet*), and our sins have damaged that Creation. By expressing our repentance through the very letters whose accomplishments we have tainted, we help repair the damage our sins have caused.

G'dulas rachamecho vachasodecho,	גְּדֻלַּת רַחֲמֶיךָ וַחֲסָדֶיךָ,

The greatness of Your mercy and Your kindness

tizkōr hayōm uvchol yōm	תִּזְכּוֹר הַיּוֹם וּבְכָל יוֹם

may You remember this day and every day

l'zera y'didecho.	לְזֶרַע יְדִידֶיךָ.

to the offspring of Your beloved Ones.

Tayfen aylaynu b'rachamim,	תֵּפֶן אֵלֵינוּ בְּרַחֲמִים,

Turn to us in mercy

ki ato hu ba-al horachamim.	כִּי אַתָּה הוּא בַּעַל הָרַחֲמִים.

for You are the Master of Mercy.

B'sachanun uvisfilo pōnecho n'kadaym,	בְּתַחֲנוּן וּבִתְפִלָּה פָּנֶיךָ נְקַדֵּם,

With supplication and prayer we approach Your Presence

k'hōdato le-onov mikedem.	כְּהוֹדַעְתָּ לֶעָנָיו מִקֶּדֶם.

in the manner that You made known to the humble [Moses] in ancient times.

Maycharōn ap'cho shuv,	מֵחֲרוֹן אַפְּךָ שׁוּב,

Turn back from Your fierce anger;

k'mō v'sōros'cho kosuv.	כְּמוֹ בְתוֹרָתְךָ כָּתוּב.

as is written in Your Torah.

Uvtzayl k'nofecho nechese v'nislōnon,	וּבְצֵל כְּנָפֶיךָ נֶחֱסֶה וְנִתְלוֹנָן,

In the shadow of Your wings may we find shelter and lodging

k'yōm va-yayred Adōnoy be-onon.	כְּיוֹם וַיֵּרֶד יהוה בֶּעָנָן.

as on the day "Hashem descended in a cloud" [to appear to Moses on Sinai].

❖ Ta-avōr al pesha v'simche oshom,	❖ תַּעֲבוֹר עַל פֶּשַׁע וְתִמְחֶה אָשָׁם,

Overlook sin and erase guilt

k'yōm va-yisyatzayv imō shom.	כְּיוֹם וַיִּתְיַצֵּב עִמּוֹ שָׁם.

as on the day "He [God] stood there with him [Moses]."

Ta-azin shavosaynu v'sakshiv me-nu ma-amar,	תַּאֲזִין שַׁוְעָתֵנוּ וְתַקְשִׁיב מֶנּוּ מַאֲמָר,

Give heed to our cry and be attentive to our declaration

k'yōm va-yikro v'shaym Adōnoy,	כְּיוֹם וַיִּקְרָא בְשֵׁם יהוה,

as on the day "He called out with the Name Hashem,"

v'shom ne-emar:	וְשָׁם נֶאֱמַר:

and there it was said:

SHACHARIS FOR WEEKDAYS — SUPPLICATION AND CONFESSION

CONGREGATION, THEN CHAZZAN:

Va-ya-avōr Adōnoy al ponov va-yikro: וַיַּעֲבֹר יהוה עַל פָּנָיו וַיִּקְרָא:

And HASHEM passed before him [Moses] and proclaimed:

ALL RECITE (THE WORDS IN BOLD TYPE ARE RECITED ALOUD AND IN UNISON):

ADŌNOY, Adōnoy, Ayl, rachum,   **יהוה, יהוה, אֵל, רַחוּם,**

HASHEM, HASHEM, God, Compassionate

v'chanun, erech apa-yim,   **וְחַנּוּן, אֶרֶךְ אַפַּיִם,**

and Gracious, Slow to anger,

v'rav chesed, ve-emes,   **וְרַב חֶסֶד, וֶאֱמֶת,**

and Abundant in Kindness and Truth,

nōtzayr chesed lo-alofim,   **נֹצֵר חֶסֶד לָאֲלָפִים,**

Preserver of kindness for thousands [of generations],

nōsay ovōn, vofesha,   **נֹשֵׂא עָוֹן, וָפֶשַׁע,**

Forgiver of iniquity, willful sin,

v'chato-o, v'nakay.   **וְחַטָּאָה, וְנַקֵּה.**

and error, and Who cleanses.

v'solachto la-avōnaynu   וְסָלַחְתָּ לַעֲוֺנֵנוּ

May You forgive our iniquities

ulchatosaynu unchaltonu.   וּלְחַטָּאתֵנוּ וּנְחַלְתָּנוּ.

and our errors and make us Your heritage.

S'lach lonu ovinu ki chotonu,   סְלַח לָנוּ אָבִינוּ כִּי חָטָאנוּ,

Forgive us, our Father, for we have erred;

m'chal lonu malkaynu ki foshonu.   מְחַל לָנוּ מַלְכֵּנוּ כִּי פָשָׁעְנוּ.

pardon us, our King, for we have willfully sinned;

Ki ato Adōnoy tōv v'saloch,   כִּי אַתָּה אֲדֹנָי טוֹב וְסַלָּח,

for You, my Lord, are good and forgiving

v'rav chesed l'chol kōr'echo.   וְרַב חֶסֶד לְכָל קֹרְאֶיךָ.

and abundantly kind to all who call upon You.

THE *VIDUI*/CONFESSION ENDS HERE.

ᴥ§ The Thirteen Attributes of Mercy

The *Zohar* teaches that the Thirteen Attributes of Mercy should always be recited with *Tachanun*.

The verse of the Thirteen Attributes may be said only in the presence of a *minyan*. If there is no *minyan*, it may be recited not in the form of a prayer, but in the manner of reading from the Torah, that is, with the musical cantillation (*trop*) of the Torah reading (*Orach Chaim* 565:5).

⊰ AVINU MALKEINU ⊱

■ Cognizant of our relationship to Hashem as both a loving Father and omnipotent King, we beseech Him in times of crisis.

FROM ROSH HASHANAH TO YOM KIPPUR AND ON FAST DAYS, *AVINU MALKEINU* IS RECITED. EVERYONE STANDS UP AND THE ARK IS OPENED.

OVINU MALKAYNU, אָבִינוּ מַלְכֵּנוּ,
chotonu l'fonecho. חָטָאנוּ לְפָנֶיךָ.
Our Father, our King, we have sinned before You.

Ovinu malkaynu, אָבִינוּ מַלְכֵּנוּ,
ayn lonu melech elo oto. אֵין לָנוּ מֶלֶךְ אֶלָּא אָתָּה.
Our Father, our King, we have no King but You.

Ovinu malkaynu, אָבִינוּ מַלְכֵּנוּ,
asay i-monu l'ma-an sh'mecho. עֲשֵׂה עִמָּנוּ לְמַעַן שְׁמֶךָ.
Our Father, our King, deal [kindly] with us for Your Name's sake.

──────── ON FAST DAYS ────────

Ovinu malkaynu, אָבִינוּ מַלְכֵּנוּ,
boraych olaynu shono tōvo. בָּרֵךְ עָלֵינוּ שָׁנָה טוֹבָה.
Our Father, our King, bless us with a good year.

──────── BETWEEN ROSH HASHANAH AND YOM KIPPUR ────────

Ovinu malkaynu, אָבִינוּ מַלְכֵּנוּ,
chadaysh olaynu shono tōvo. חַדֵּשׁ עָלֵינוּ שָׁנָה טוֹבָה.
Our Father, our King, inaugurate upon us a good year.

Ovinu malkaynu, batayl אָבִינוּ מַלְכֵּנוּ, בַּטֵּל
may-olaynu kol g'zayrōs koshōs. מֵעָלֵינוּ כָּל גְּזֵרוֹת קָשׁוֹת.
Our Father, our King, nullify all harsh decrees upon us.

Ovinu malkaynu, אָבִינוּ מַלְכֵּנוּ,
batayl machsh'vōs sōn'aynu. בַּטֵּל מַחְשְׁבוֹת שׂוֹנְאֵינוּ.
Our Father, our King, nullify the thoughts of those who hate us.

Ovinu malkaynu, אָבִינוּ מַלְכֵּנוּ,
hofayr atzas ōy'vaynu. הָפֵר עֲצַת אוֹיְבֵינוּ.
Our Father, our King, thwart the counsel of our enemies.

⊰ **Avinu Malkeinu**

Avinu Malkeinu, which is recited on fast days and during the Ten Days of Repentance between Rosh Hashanah and Yom Kippur, combines pleas for our personal and national needs with expressions of repentance. The prayer is based on an incident in the life of Rabbi Akiva as related in the Talmud (*Taanis* 25b). During a drought, the Sages proclaimed a day of public fast and prayer, but no rain fell. Thereupon Rabbi Akiva said five brief supplications, each beginning *Our Father, our King*, and it began to rain.

Over the course of the generations, various communities added brief prayers with this beginning. This explains why Rabbi Akiva's five

AVINU MALKEINU

Ovinu malkaynu,
 kalay kol tzar u-mastin
 may-olaynu.

אָבִינוּ מַלְכֵּנוּ,
כַּלֵּה כָּל צַר וּמַשְׂטִין
מֵעָלֵינוּ.

Our Father, our King, exterminate every foe and adversary from upon us.

Ovinu malkaynu, s'sōm piyōs
 mastinaynu umkatrigaynu.

אָבִינוּ מַלְכֵּנוּ, סְתוֹם פִּיּוֹת
מַשְׂטִינֵנוּ וּמְקַטְרִיגֵנוּ.

*Our Father, our King,
seal the mouths of our adversaries and accusers.*

Ovinu malkaynu,
 kalay dever v'cherev v'ro-ov
 ushvi u-mashchis v'vōn ushmad
 mib'nay v'risecho.

אָבִינוּ מַלְכֵּנוּ,
כַּלֵּה דֶּבֶר וְחֶרֶב וְרָעָב
וּשְׁבִי וּמַשְׁחִית וְעָוֹן וּשְׁמַד
מִבְּנֵי בְרִיתֶךָ.

*Our Father, our King, exterminate pestilence, sword, famine, captivity,
destruction, iniquity, and eradication from the members of Your covenant.*

Ovinu malkaynu,
 m'na magayfo minachalosecho.

אָבִינוּ מַלְכֵּנוּ,
מְנַע מַגֵּפָה מִנַּחֲלָתֶךָ.

Our Father, our King, withhold the plague from Your heritage.

Ovinu malkaynu,
 s'lach umchal l'chol a-vōnōsaynu.

אָבִינוּ מַלְכֵּנוּ,
סְלַח וּמְחַל לְכָל עֲווֹנוֹתֵינוּ.

Our Father, our King, forgive and pardon all our iniquities.

Ovinu malkaynu,
 m'chay v'ha-avayr
 p'sho-aynu v'chatōsaynu
 mineged aynecho.

אָבִינוּ מַלְכֵּנוּ,
מְחֵה וְהַעֲבֵר
פְּשָׁעֵינוּ וְחַטֹּאתֵינוּ
מִנֶּגֶד עֵינֶיךָ.

*Our Father, our King, wipe away and remove
our willful sins and errors from Your sight.*

Ovinu malkaynu,
 m'chōk b'rachamecho harabim
 kol shitray chōvōsaynu.

אָבִינוּ מַלְכֵּנוּ,
מְחוֹק בְּרַחֲמֶיךָ הָרַבִּים
כָּל שִׁטְרֵי חוֹבוֹתֵינוּ.

*Our Father, our King, erase through Your abundant compassion
all records of our guilt.*

---

supplications have grown to over forty, and, in the Sephardic rite, over fifty. The introductory formula expresses our dual relationship to God: because He created and loves us, He is our merciful *Father;* because it is our duty to serve Him, He is our *King.*

The Sabbath and festivals are days of joy and contentment when it is not proper to pray for specific needs or to recall sad thoughts. *Avinu Malkeinu* is inappropriate on these days because: (a) many of its verses parallel specific requests of the weekday *Shemoneh Esrei*, such as those for health, prosperity, forgiveness, etc., which are omitted on festive days; and (b) it was composed originally for times of distress.

אבינו מלכנו

EACH OF THE NEXT NINE VERSES IS RECITED RESPONSIVELY: *CHAZZAN*, THEN CONGREGATION. THE FIRST FOUR VERSES ARE IDENTICAL FOR FAST DAYS AND BETWEEN ROSH HASHANAH AND YOM KIPPUR; THE LAST FIVE VERSES ARE DIFFERENT. SEE BELOW.

Ovinu malkaynu, אָבִינוּ מַלְכֵּנוּ,
    hachaziraynu הַחֲזִירֵנוּ
    bis-shuvo sh'laymo l'fonecho. בִּתְשׁוּבָה שְׁלֵמָה לְפָנֶיךָ.
Our Father, our King, return us to You in perfect repentance.

Ovinu malkaynu, אָבִינוּ מַלְכֵּנוּ,
    sh'lach r'fu-o sh'laymo שְׁלַח רְפוּאָה שְׁלֵמָה
    l'chōlay amecho. לְחוֹלֵי עַמֶּךָ.
Our Father, our King, send complete recovery to the sick of Your people.

Ovinu malkaynu, אָבִינוּ מַלְכֵּנוּ,
    k'ra rō-a g'zar dinaynu. קְרַע רוֹעַ גְּזַר דִּינֵנוּ.
Our Father, our King, tear up the evil decree of our verdict.

Ovinu malkaynu, אָבִינוּ מַלְכֵּנוּ,
    zochraynu b'zikorōn tōv זָכְרֵנוּ בְּזִכָּרוֹן טוֹב
    l'fonecho. לְפָנֶיךָ.
Our Father, our King, recall us with a favorable memory before you.

——————— ON FAST DAYS CONTINUE HERE ———————

Ovinu malkaynu, אָבִינוּ מַלְכֵּנוּ,
    zochraynu l'cha-yim tōvim. זָכְרֵנוּ לְחַיִּים טוֹבִים.
Our Father, our King, remember us for good life.

Ovinu malkaynu, אָבִינוּ מַלְכֵּנוּ,
    zochraynu lig-ulo vishu-o. זָכְרֵנוּ לִגְאֻלָּה וִישׁוּעָה.
Our Father, our King, remember us for redemption and salvation.

Ovinu malkaynu, אָבִינוּ מַלְכֵּנוּ,
    zochraynu l'farnoso v'chalkolo. זָכְרֵנוּ לְפַרְנָסָה וְכַלְכָּלָה.
Our Father, our King, remember us for sustenance and support.

Ovinu malkaynu, אָבִינוּ מַלְכֵּנוּ,
    zochraynu lizchuyōs. זָכְרֵנוּ לִזְכֻיּוֹת.
Our Father, our King, remember us for merits.

Ovinu malkaynu, אָבִינוּ מַלְכֵּנוּ,
    zochraynu lislicho umchilo. זָכְרֵנוּ לִסְלִיחָה וּמְחִילָה.
Our Father, our King, remember us for forgiveness and pardon.

AVINU MALKEINU

———— BETWEEN ROSH HASHANAH AND YOM KIPPUR CONTINUE HERE ————

Ovinu malkaynu,   אָבִינוּ מַלְכֵּנוּ,
kosvaynu   כָּתְבֵנוּ
b'sayfer cha-yim tōvim.   בְּסֵפֶר חַיִּים טוֹבִים.
Our Father, our King, inscribe us in the book of good life.

Ovinu malkaynu,   אָבִינוּ מַלְכֵּנוּ,
kosvaynu   כָּתְבֵנוּ
b'sayfer g'ulo vi-shu-o.   בְּסֵפֶר גְּאֻלָּה וִישׁוּעָה.
Our Father, our King, inscribe us in the book of redemption and salvation.

Ovinu malkaynu,   אָבִינוּ מַלְכֵּנוּ,
kosvaynu   כָּתְבֵנוּ
b'sayfer parnoso v'chalkolo.   בְּסֵפֶר פַּרְנָסָה וְכַלְכָּלָה.
Our Father, our King, inscribe us in the book of sustenance and support.

Ovinu malkaynu,   אָבִינוּ מַלְכֵּנוּ,
kosvaynu b'sayfer z'chuyōs.   כָּתְבֵנוּ בְּסֵפֶר זְכִיּוֹת.
Our Father, our King, inscribe us in the book of merits.

Ovinu malkaynu,   אָבִינוּ מַלְכֵּנוּ,
kosvaynu   כָּתְבֵנוּ
b'sayfer s'licho umchilo.   בְּסֵפֶר סְלִיחָה וּמְחִילָה.
Our Father, our King, inscribe us in the book of forgiveness and pardon.

———— END OF RESPONSIVE READING; ON ALL DAYS CONTINUE HERE ————

Ovinu malkaynu,   אָבִינוּ מַלְכֵּנוּ,
hatzmach lonu y'shu-o b'korōv.   הַצְמַח לָנוּ יְשׁוּעָה בְּקָרוֹב.
Our Father, our King, make salvation sprout for us soon.

Ovinu malkaynu,   אָבִינוּ מַלְכֵּנוּ,
horaym keren yisro-ayl amecho.   הָרֵם קֶרֶן יִשְׂרָאֵל עַמֶּךָ.
Our Father, our King, raise high the pride of Israel, Your people.

Ovinu malkaynu,   אָבִינוּ מַלְכֵּנוּ,
horaym keren m'shichecho.   הָרֵם קֶרֶן מְשִׁיחֶךָ.
Our Father, our King, raise high the pride of Your anointed.

Ovinu malkaynu,   אָבִינוּ מַלְכֵּנוּ,
malay yodaynu mibirchōsecho.   מַלֵּא יָדֵינוּ מִבִּרְכוֹתֶיךָ.
Our Father, our King, fill our hands from Your blessings.

Ovinu malkaynu,   אָבִינוּ מַלְכֵּנוּ,
malay asomaynu sovo.   מַלֵּא אֲסָמֵינוּ שָׂבָע.
Our Father, our King, fill our storehouses with abundance.

Ovinu malkaynu, sh'ma kōlaynu, chus v'rachaym olaynu.	אָבִינוּ מַלְכֵּנוּ, שְׁמַע קוֹלֵנוּ, חוּס וְרַחֵם עָלֵינוּ.

Our Father, our King, hear our voice, pity and be compassionate to us.

Ovinu malkaynu, kabayl b'rachamim uvrotzōn es t'filosaynu.	אָבִינוּ מַלְכֵּנוּ, קַבֵּל בְּרַחֲמִים וּבְרָצוֹן אֶת תְּפִלָּתֵנוּ.

Our Father, our King, accept — with compassion and favor — our prayer.

Ovinu malkaynu, p'sach sha-aray shoma-yim lisfilosaynu.	אָבִינוּ מַלְכֵּנוּ, פְּתַח שַׁעֲרֵי שָׁמַיִם לִתְפִלָּתֵנוּ.

Our Father, our King, open the gates of heaven to our prayer.

Ovinu malkaynu, zochōr ki ofor anochnu.	אָבִינוּ מַלְכֵּנוּ, זְכוֹר כִּי עָפָר אֲנָחְנוּ.

Our Father, our King, remember that we are but dust.

Ovinu malkaynu, no al t'shivaynu raykom mil'fonecho.	אָבִינוּ מַלְכֵּנוּ, נָא אַל תְּשִׁיבֵנוּ רֵיקָם מִלְּפָנֶיךָ.

Our Father, our King, please do not turn us from You empty-handed.

Ovinu malkaynu, t'hay hasho-o ha-zōs sh'as rachamim v'ays rotzōn mil'fonecho.	אָבִינוּ מַלְכֵּנוּ, תְּהֵא הַשָּׁעָה הַזֹּאת שְׁעַת רַחֲמִים וְעֵת רָצוֹן מִלְּפָנֶיךָ.

Our Father, our King, may this moment be a moment of compassion and a time of favor before You.

Ovinu malkaynu, chamōl olaynu v'al ōlolaynu v'tapaynu.	אָבִינוּ מַלְכֵּנוּ, חֲמוֹל עָלֵינוּ וְעַל עוֹלָלֵינוּ וְטַפֵּנוּ.

Our Father, our King, take pity upon us, and upon our children and our infants.

Ovinu malkaynu, asay l'ma-an harugim al shaym kodshecho.	אָבִינוּ מַלְכֵּנוּ, עֲשֵׂה לְמַעַן הֲרוּגִים עַל שֵׁם קָדְשֶׁךָ.

Our Father, our King, act for the sake of those who were murdered for Your Holy Name.

Ovinu malkaynu, asay l'ma-an t'vuchim al yichudecho.	אָבִינוּ מַלְכֵּנוּ, עֲשֵׂה לְמַעַן טְבוּחִים עַל יִחוּדֶךָ.

Our Father, our King, act for the sake of those who were slaughtered for Your Oneness.

SHACHARIS FOR WEEKDAYS — AVINU MALKEINU

Ovinu malkaynu,
   asay l'ma-an
   bo-ay vo-aysh u-vama-yim
   al kidush sh'mecho.

אָבִינוּ מַלְכֵּנוּ,
עֲשֵׂה לְמַעַן
בָּאֵי בָאֵשׁ וּבַמַּיִם
עַל קִדּוּשׁ שְׁמֶךָ.

Our Father, our King, act for the sake of those who went into fire and water for the sanctification of Your Name.

Ovinu malkaynu,
   n'kōm l'aynaynu
   nikmas dam avodecho hashofuch.

אָבִינוּ מַלְכֵּנוּ,
נְקוֹם לְעֵינֵינוּ
נִקְמַת דַּם עֲבָדֶיךָ הַשָּׁפוּךְ.

Our Father, our King, avenge before our eyes the spilled blood of Your servants.

Ovinu malkaynu,
   asay l'ma-ancho
   im lō l'ma-anaynu.

אָבִינוּ מַלְכֵּנוּ,
עֲשֵׂה לְמַעַנְךָ
אִם לֹא לְמַעֲנֵנוּ.

Our Father, our King, act for Your sake if not for our sake.

Ovinu malkaynu,
   asay l'ma-ancho v'hōshi-aynu.

אָבִינוּ מַלְכֵּנוּ,
עֲשֵׂה לְמַעַנְךָ וְהוֹשִׁיעֵנוּ.

Our Father, our King, act for Your sake and save us.

Ovinu malkaynu,
   asay l'ma-an
   rachamecho horabim.

אָבִינוּ מַלְכֵּנוּ,
עֲשֵׂה לְמַעַן
רַחֲמֶיךָ הָרַבִּים.

Our Father, our King, act for the sake of Your abundant compassion.

Ovinu malkaynu,
   asay l'ma-an shimcho hagodōl
   hagibōr v'hanōro,
   shenikro olaynu.

אָבִינוּ מַלְכֵּנוּ,
עֲשֵׂה לְמַעַן שִׁמְךָ הַגָּדוֹל
הַגִּבּוֹר וְהַנּוֹרָא,
שֶׁנִּקְרָא עָלֵינוּ.

Our Father, our King, act for the sake of Your great, mighty, and awesome Name that is proclaimed upon us.

Ovinu malkaynu,
   chonaynu va-anaynu,
   ki ayn bonu ma-asim,
   asay i-monu tz'doko vochesed
   v'hoshi-aynu.

אָבִינוּ מַלְכֵּנוּ,
חָנֵּנוּ וַעֲנֵנוּ,
כִּי אֵין בָּנוּ מַעֲשִׂים,
עֲשֵׂה עִמָּנוּ צְדָקָה וָחֶסֶד
וְהוֹשִׁיעֵנוּ.

Our Father, our King, be gracious with us and answer us, though we have no worthy deeds; treat us with charity and kindness, and save us.

THE AVINU MALKEINU PRAYER ENDS HERE. THE SERVICE CONTINUES WITH TACHANUN: ON MONDAYS AND THURSDAYS ON P. 212; ON OTHER DAYS ON P. 225.

⊰ TACHANUN / SUPPLICATION ⊱

ON MONDAY AND THURSDAY, *TACHANUN* BEGINS HERE. ON OTHER DAYS, *TACHANUN* BEGINS ON P. 225 SEE P. 201 FOR DAYS AND OCCASIONS WHEN *TACHANUN* IS OMITTED.

V'HU RACHUM y'chapayr ovōn v'lō yashchis,   וְהוּא רַחוּם יְכַפֵּר עָוֹן וְלֹא יַשְׁחִית,

He, the Merciful One,* is forgiving of iniquity and does not destroy,

v'hirbo l'hoshiv apō,   וְהִרְבָּה לְהָשִׁיב אַפּוֹ

frequently withdrawing His anger,

v'lō yo-ir kol chamosō.   וְלֹא יָעִיר כָּל חֲמָתוֹ.

not arousing His entire rage.

Ato, Adōnoy,   אַתָּה יהוה,

You, Hashem —

lō sichlo rachamecho mimenu,   לֹא תִכְלָא רַחֲמֶיךָ מִמֶּנּוּ,

withhold not Your mercy from us;

chasd'cho va-amit'cho tomid yitz'runu.   חַסְדְּךָ וַאֲמִתְּךָ תָּמִיד יִצְּרוּנוּ.

may Your kindness and Your truth always protect us.

Hōshi-aynu, Adōnoy Elōhaynu,   הוֹשִׁיעֵנוּ יהוה אֱלֹהֵינוּ

Save us, Hashem, our God,

v'kab'tzaynu min hagōyim,   וְקַבְּצֵנוּ מִן הַגּוֹיִם,

and gather us from among the peoples,

l'hōdōs l'shaym kod'shecho,   לְהוֹדוֹת לְשֵׁם קָדְשֶׁךָ,

to give thanks to Your Holy Name,

l'hishtabayach bis-hilosecho.   לְהִשְׁתַּבֵּחַ בִּתְהִלָּתֶךָ.

and to glory in Your praise.

Im avonōs tishmor yoh,   אִם עֲוֹנוֹת תִּשְׁמָר יָהּ,

If You preserve iniquities, O God,

Adōnoy mi ya-amōd?   אֲדֹנָי מִי יַעֲמֹד.

my Lord, who could survive?

⊰• **Tachanun**

The Talmud (*Bava Metzia* 59a) teaches that if one submissively places his head upon his arm in fervent, intense prayer immediately after *Shemoneh Esrei*, his prayer is warmly accepted by God and can achieve great results. Therefore, there must be no significant interruption between *Shemoneh Esrei* and this prayer, תַּחֲנוּן, *Tachanun*, lit. *supplication*, a term that implies an especially heartfelt plea for God's gracious compassion. The essential part of *Tachanun* is *putting down the head* (p. 225).

On Mondays and Thursdays, the *Tachanun* service is augmented with additional supplications prior to and following the "putting down the head." The choice of these two days for special prayers is based on one of the earliest events in Israel's national history. According to the Midrashic tradition, Moses ascended Mount Sinai to receive the Second Tablets on Thursday, the first day of Elul, and descended forty days later on Monday, Yom Kippur. Since those were days when God accepted Israel's repentance for the sin of the Golden Calf, and demonstrated His love for Israel with the greatest of all gifts — the Torah, in the form of

SUPPLICATION

Ki im'cho has'licho,   כִּי עִמְּךָ הַסְּלִיחָה,
l'ma-an tivoray.   לְמַעַן תִּוָּרֵא.
For with You is forgiveness, that You may be feared.

Lō chachato-aynu ta-ase lonu,   לֹא כַחֲטָאֵינוּ תַּעֲשֶׂה לָּנוּ,
Do not treat us according to our sins,

v'lō cha-avonōsaynu tigmōl olaynu.   וְלֹא כַעֲוֹנוֹתֵינוּ תִּגְמֹל עָלֵינוּ.
do not repay us according to our iniquities.

Im avōnaynu onu vonu,   אִם עֲוֹנֵינוּ עָנוּ בָנוּ,
Though our iniquities testify against us,

Adōnoy, asay l'ma-an sh'mecho.   יהוה עֲשֵׂה לְמַעַן שְׁמֶךָ.
O HASHEM, act for Your Name's sake.

Z'chōr rachamecho, Adōnoy,   זְכֹר רַחֲמֶיךָ יהוה
Remember Your mercies, HASHEM,

vachasodecho, ki mayōlom haymo.   וַחֲסָדֶיךָ, כִּי מֵעוֹלָם הֵמָּה.
and Your kindnesses, for they are from the beginning of the world.

Ya-anaynu Adōnoy b'yōm tzoro,   יַעֲנֵנוּ יהוה בְּיוֹם צָרָה,
May HASHEM answer us on the day of distress,

y'sag'vaynu shaym Elōhay ya-akōv.   יְשַׂגְּבֵנוּ שֵׁם אֱלֹהֵי יַעֲקֹב.
may the Name of Jacob's God make us impregnable.

Adōnoy, hōshi-o!   יהוה הוֹשִׁיעָה,
HASHEM, save —

hamelech, ya-anaynu v'yōm kor'aynu.   הַמֶּלֶךְ יַעֲנֵנוּ בְיוֹם קָרְאֵנוּ.
the King will answer us on the day we call.

Ovinu malkaynu! chonaynu va-anaynu,   אָבִינוּ מַלְכֵּנוּ חָנֵּנוּ וַעֲנֵנוּ,
Our Father, our King, be gracious with us and answer us

ki ayn bonu ma-asim   כִּי אֵין בָּנוּ מַעֲשִׂים,
though we have no worthy deeds;

tz'doko asay imonu   צְדָקָה עֲשֵׂה עִמָּנוּ
treat us with charity

l'ma-an sh'mecho.   לְמַעַן שְׁמֶךָ.
for Your Name's sake.

---

the Second Tablets — Monday and Thursday remain days of Divine mercy (see *Bava Kamma* 82a; *Tos. s.v.* כדי). Ezra instituted that rabbinical courts should convene on Monday and Thursday, and Kabbalistic literature teaches that on these days the Heavenly Court judges man. Consequently, extra supplications were introduced into the *Tachanun* recited each Monday and Thursday. These supplications must be said while standing and, because of their nature, with great feeling.

וְהוּא רַחוּם — *He, the Merciful One.* In a mystical comment on this verse, *Zohar* teaches that God, in His mercy, does not allow the forces of impurity to prevent our prayers from reaching Him. Were they to succeed, we could never hope to achieve forgiveness.

Adōnaynu Elōhaynu!	אֲדוֹנֵֽינוּ אֱלֹהֵֽינוּ,

Our Master, our God,

sh'ma kōl tachanunaynu,	שְׁמַע קוֹל תַּחֲנוּנֵֽינוּ,

hear the sound of our supplications;

uz'chor lonu es b'ris avōsaynu,	וּזְכָר לָֽנוּ אֶת בְּרִית אֲבוֹתֵֽינוּ

recall for us the covenant of our forefathers

v'hōshi-aynu l'ma-an sh'mecho.	וְהוֹשִׁיעֵֽנוּ לְמַֽעַן שְׁמֶֽךָ.

and save us for Your Name's sake.

V'ato, Adōnoy Elōhaynu,	וְעַתָּה אֲדֹנָי אֱלֹהֵֽינוּ,

And now, My Lord our God,

asher hōtzayso es am'cho	אֲשֶׁר הוֹצֵֽאתָ אֶת עַמְּךָ

Who has taken Your people

may-eretz mitzra-yim b'yod chazoko,	מֵאֶֽרֶץ מִצְרַֽיִם בְּיָד חֲזָקָה,

out of the land of Egypt with a strong hand

vata-as l'cho shaym kayōm ha-ze,	וַתַּֽעַשׂ לְךָ שֵׁם כַּיּוֹם הַזֶּה,

and gained Yourself renown as of this day —

chotonu rosho'nu.	חָטָֽאנוּ רָשָֽׁעְנוּ.

we have sinned and acted wickedly.

Adōnoy! k'chol tzidkōsecho,	אֲדֹנָי, כְּכָל צִדְקֹתֶֽיךָ

My Lord, in keeping with all Your righteousness,

yoshov no ap'cho vachamos'cho	יָֽשָׁב נָא אַפְּךָ וַחֲמָתְךָ

please let Your anger and Your fury turn away

may-ir'cho y'rushola-yim	מֵעִירְךָ יְרוּשָׁלַֽיִם,
har kod'shecho.	הַר קָדְשֶֽׁךָ.

from Your city Jerusalem, Your holy mountain;

Ki vachato-aynu	כִּי בַחֲטָאֵֽינוּ
u-va-avonōs avōsaynu,	וּבַעֲוֺנוֹת אֲבוֹתֵֽינוּ,

for because of our sins and the iniquities of our ancestors,

y'rushola-yim v'am'cho l'cherpo	יְרוּשָׁלַֽיִם וְעַמְּךָ לְחֶרְפָּה

Jerusalem and Your people have become the scorn

l'chol s'vivōsaynu.	לְכָל סְבִיבֹתֵֽינוּ.

of all those around us.

V'ato, sh'ma, Elōhaynu,	וְעַתָּה שְׁמַע אֱלֹהֵֽינוּ

And now, pay heed, our God,

el t'filas avd'cho v'el tachanunov,	אֶל תְּפִלַּת עַבְדְּךָ וְאֶל תַּחֲנוּנָיו,

to the prayer of Your servant and to his supplications,

SUPPLICATION

v'ho-ayr ponecho	וְהָאֵר פָּנֶיךָ
al mikdosh'cho ha-shomaym,	עַל מִקְדָּשְׁךָ הַשָּׁמֵם,

and let Your countenance shine upon Your desolate Sanctuary

l'maan Adōnoy!   לְמַעַן אֲדֹנָי.

for my Lord's sake.

HATAY, Elōhai, ozn'cho ush'mo,   **הַטֵּה** אֱלֹהַי אָזְנְךָ וּשֲׁמָע,

Incline Your ear, my God,* and listen,

p'kach aynecho ur-ay shōm'mōsaynu,   פְּקַח עֵינֶיךָ וּרְאֵה שֹׁמְמֹתֵינוּ,

open Your eyes and see our desolation

v'ho-ir asher nikro shimcho oleho.   וְהָעִיר אֲשֶׁר נִקְרָא שִׁמְךָ עָלֶיהָ,

and that of the city upon which Your Name is proclaimed;

Ki lō al tzidkōsaynu,   כִּי לֹא עַל צִדְקֹתֵינוּ

for not because of our righteousness

anachnu mapilim	אֲנַחְנוּ מַפִּילִים
tachanunaynu l'fonecho,	תַּחֲנוּנֵינוּ לְפָנֶיךָ,

do we cast down our supplications before You,

ki al rachamecho horabim.   כִּי עַל רַחֲמֶיךָ הָרַבִּים.

rather because of Your abundant compassion.

Adōnoy sh'mo-o, Adōnoy s'locho,   אֲדֹנָי שְׁמָעָה, אֲדֹנָי סְלָחָה,

O my Lord, heed; O my Lord, forgive;

Adōnoy hakshivo va-asay,	אֲדֹנָי הַקְשִׁיבָה וַעֲשֵׂה,
al t'achar,	אַל תְּאַחַר,

O my Lord, be attentive and act, do not delay;

l'ma-ancho, Elōhai,   לְמַעַנְךָ אֱלֹהַי,

for Your sake, my God,

ki shimcho nikro	כִּי שִׁמְךָ נִקְרָא
al ir'cho v'al amecho.	עַל עִירְךָ וְעַל עַמֶּךָ.

for Your Name is proclaimed upon Your city and upon Your people.

Ovinu ho-ov horachamon!   אָבִינוּ הָאָב הָרַחֲמָן,

Our Father, the merciful Father —

haraynu ōs l'tōvo,   הַרְאֵנוּ אוֹת לְטוֹבָה

show us an omen for good

v'kabaytz n'futzōsaynu	וְקַבֵּץ נְפוּצוֹתֵינוּ
may-arba kanfōs ho-oretz.	מֵאַרְבַּע כַּנְפוֹת הָאָרֶץ,

and gather in our dispersed from the four corners of the world;

הַטֵּה אֱלֹהַי אָזְנְךָ — *Incline Your ear, my God.* Despite the sins we have just confessed, we plead with God to heed our call. Even if we are not deserving, at least let Him help us for the sake of His Name that is desecrated by the destruction of His city and the persecution of His people.

תחנון

Yakiru v'yayd'u kol hagōyim,	יַכִּירוּ וְיֵדְעוּ כָּל הַגּוֹיִם,

let all the nations recognize and realize

ki ato Adōnoy Elōhaynu.	כִּי אַתָּה יהוה אֱלֹהֵינוּ.

that You are HASHEM, *our God.*

V'ato, Adōnoy, ovinu oto,	וְעַתָּה יהוה אָבִינוּ אָתָּה,

And now, HASHEM, *You are our Father;*

anachnu hachōmer v'ato yōtz'raynu,	אֲנַחְנוּ הַחֹמֶר וְאַתָּה יֹצְרֵנוּ,

we are the clay and You are our Molder

u-ma-asay yod'cho kulonu.	וּמַעֲשֵׂה יָדְךָ כֻּלָּנוּ.

and Your handiwork are we all.

Hōshi-aynu l'ma-an sh'mecho,	הוֹשִׁיעֵנוּ לְמַעַן שְׁמֶךָ,

Save us for Your Name's sake,

tzuraynu malkaynu v'gō-alaynu!	צוּרֵנוּ מַלְכֵּנוּ וְגוֹאֲלֵנוּ.

our Rock, our King, and our Redeemer.

Chuso Adōnoy, al amecho,	חוּסָה יהוה עַל עַמֶּךָ

Pity Your people, HASHEM;

v'al titayn nachalos'cho l'cherpo	וְאַל תִּתֵּן נַחֲלָתְךָ לְחֶרְפָּה

let not Your heritage be an object of scorn,

limshol bom gōyim.	לִמְשָׁל בָּם גּוֹיִם.

for nations to dominate.

Lomo yōmru vo-amim:	לָמָּה יֹאמְרוּ בָעַמִּים,
a-yay Elōhayhem.	אַיֵּה אֱלֹהֵיהֶם.

Why should they say among the peoples, "Where is their God?"

Yodanu ki chotonu,	יָדַעְנוּ כִּי חָטָאנוּ

We know that we have sinned

v'ayn mi ya-amōd ba-adaynu,	וְאֵין מִי יַעֲמֹד בַּעֲדֵנוּ,

and there is no one to stand up for us —

shimcho hagodōl ya-amod lonu	שִׁמְךָ הַגָּדוֹל יַעֲמָד לָנוּ
b'ays tzoro.	בְּעֵת צָרָה.

let Your great Name stand up for us in time of distress.

Yodanu ki ayn bonu ma-asim,	יָדַעְנוּ כִּי אֵין בָּנוּ מַעֲשִׂים,

We know that there are no worthy deeds in us —

tz'doko, asay i-monu	צְדָקָה עֲשֵׂה עִמָּנוּ
l'ma-an sh'mecho.	לְמַעַן שְׁמֶךָ.

treat us with charity for Your Name's sake.

K'rachaym ov al bonim,	כְּרַחֵם אָב עַל בָּנִים,

As a father has mercy on his children,

SUPPLICATION

kayn t'rachaym Adōnoy olaynu,	כֵּן תְּרַחֵם יהוה עָלֵינוּ,
so may You have mercy on us,	
v'hōshi-aynu l'ma-an sh'mecho.	וְהוֹשִׁיעֵנוּ לְמַעַן שְׁמֶךָ.
O Hashem, and save us for Your Name's sake.	
Chamōl al amecho,	חֲמֹל עַל עַמֶּךָ,
rachaym al nachalosecho,	רַחֵם עַל נַחֲלָתֶךָ,
Have compassion on Your people, have mercy on Your heritage;	
chuso no k'rōv rachamecho,	חוּסָה נָּא כְּרֹב רַחֲמֶיךָ.
have pity, we beg You, according to Your abundant mercy.	
Chonaynu va-anaynu,	חָנֵּנוּ וַעֲנֵנוּ,
Be gracious with us and answer us,	
ki l'cho, Adōnoy, hatz'doko,	כִּי לְךָ יהוה הַצְּדָקָה,
for Yours, Hashem, is the righteousness,	
ōsay niflo-ōs b'chol ays.	עֹשֵׂה נִפְלָאוֹת בְּכָל עֵת.
He Who does wonders always.	
HABET NO, rachem no al am'cho	**הַבֶּט נָא** רַחֵם נָא עַל עַמְּךָ
Look, we beg You,* and have mercy on Your people	
m'hayro l'ma-an sh'mecho.	מְהֵרָה לְמַעַן שְׁמֶךָ.
speedily for Your Name's sake.	
B'rachamecho horabim,	בְּרַחֲמֶיךָ הָרַבִּים,
Adōnoy Elōhaynu,	יהוה אֱלֹהֵינוּ,
In Your abundant mercy, Hashem, our God,	
chus v'rachaym	חוּס וְרַחֵם
v'hōshi-o tzōn mar-isecho,	וְהוֹשִׁיעָה צֹאן מַרְעִיתֶךָ,
pity, have mercy upon, and save the sheep of Your pasture;	
v'al yimshol bonu ketzef,	וְאַל יִמְשָׁל בָּנוּ קָצֶף,
ki l'cho aynaynu s'luyōs.	כִּי לְךָ עֵינֵינוּ תְלוּיוֹת.
let not anger dominate us, for on You do our eyes depend.	
Hōshi-aynu l'ma-an sh'mecho,	הוֹשִׁיעֵנוּ לְמַעַן שְׁמֶךָ,
Save us for Your Name's sake;	
rachaym olaynu l'ma-an b'risecho,	רַחֵם עָלֵינוּ לְמַעַן בְּרִיתֶךָ.
have mercy on us for the sake of Your covenant.	
Habito va-anaynu b'ays tzoro,	הַבִּיטָה וַעֲנֵנוּ בְּעֵת צָרָה,
Look and answer us in time of distress,	

הַבֶּט נָא — *Look, we beg You.* This prayer for compassion stresses our helplessness and total dependence on Him. It introduces the concept that we are the "sheep of God's pasture." Like sheep we depend totally on the guidance and protection of our Shepherd.

שחרית לחול / 218   תחנון

כִּי לְךָ יהוה הַיְשׁוּעָה.   ki l'cho Adōnoy hai-shu-o.
for salvation is Yours, Hashem.

בְּךָ תוֹחַלְתֵּנוּ, אֱלוֹהַּ סְלִיחוֹת,   B'cho sōchaltaynu, Elōha s'lichōs!
Upon You is our hope, O God of forgiveness;

אָנָּא סְלַח נָא אֵל טוֹב וְסַלָּח,   ono s'lach no, Ayl tōv v'saloch,
please forgive now, O good and forgiving God,

כִּי אֵל מֶלֶךְ חַנּוּן וְרַחוּם אָתָּה.   ki Ayl melech chanun v'rachum oto.
for You are God, the gracious and compassionate King.

אָנָּא מֶלֶךְ חַנּוּן וְרַחוּם,   **ONO** melech chanun v'rachum,
Please, O gracious and compassionate King,*

זְכוֹר וְהַבֵּט   z'chōr v'habayt
לִבְרִית בֵּין הַבְּתָרִים,   livris bayn hab'sorim,
remember and look to the Covenant between the Parts;

וְתֵרָאֶה לְפָנֶיךָ עֲקֵדַת יָחִיד   v'sayro-e l'fonecho akaydas yochid,
לְמַעַן יִשְׂרָאֵל.   l'ma-an yisro-ayl.
may there appear before You the binding of the only son — for Israel's sake.

אָבִינוּ מַלְכֵּנוּ חָנֵּנוּ וַעֲנֵנוּ,   Ovinu malkaynu, chonaynu v'anaynu,
Our Father, our King — be gracious with us and answer us,

כִּי שִׁמְךָ הַגָּדוֹל נִקְרָא עָלֵינוּ.   ki shimcho hagodōl nikro olaynu,
for Your great Name has been proclaimed upon us.

עֹשֵׂה נִפְלָאוֹת בְּכָל עֵת,   Ōsay niflo-ōs b'chol ays,
O Maker of miracles at all times,

עֲשֵׂה עִמָּנוּ כְּחַסְדֶּךָ.   asay i-monu k'chasdecho,
treat us according to Your kindness.

חַנּוּן וְרַחוּם   Chanun v'rachum,
Gracious and Compassionate One,

הַבִּיטָה וַעֲנֵנוּ בְּעֵת צָרָה,   habito va-anaynu b'ays tzoro,
look and answer us in time of distress,

כִּי לְךָ יהוה הַיְשׁוּעָה.   ki l'cho Adōnoy hai-shu-o.
for Yours, Hashem, is the salvation.

אָבִינוּ מַלְכֵּנוּ, מַחֲסֵנוּ,   Ovinu malkaynu machasaynu,
Our Father, our King, our Protector,

אָנָּא — *Please.* This supplication emphasizes the experiences of the Patriarchs, Abraham and Isaac. It singles out the בְּרִית בֵּין הַבְּתָרִים, *Covenant Between the Parts* (Genesis ch. 15), and the *Akeidah* of Isaac (Genesis ch. 22). In the Covenant, God sealed a treaty with Abraham that his descendants would inherit *Eretz Yisrael* and always be God's nation. The covenant was made in response to Abraham's wish to know how he could be sure that sinfulness or changing conditions would not prevent his offspring from inheriting the Land. Thus, it remains an eternal assurance to Israel, despite exile and oppression.

al ta-as i-monu k'rō-a ma-alolaynu. אַל תַּעַשׂ עִמָּנוּ כְּרֹעַ מַעֲלָלֵינוּ.
do not treat us according to the evil of our deeds.

Z'chōr rachamecho Adōnoy v'chasodecho, זְכֹר רַחֲמֶיךָ יהוה וַחֲסָדֶיךָ,
*Recall Your mercies, H*ASHEM*, and Your kindnesses;*

uchrōv tuv'cho hōshi-aynu, וּכְרֹב טוּבְךָ הוֹשִׁיעֵנוּ,
according to Your abundant goodness save us

vachamol no olaynu, וַחֲמָל נָא עָלֵינוּ,
and have pity on us, we beg You,

ki ayn lonu elōha achayr כִּי אֵין לָנוּ אֱלוֹהַּ אַחֵר
mibalodecho tzuraynu: מִבַּלְעָדֶיךָ צוּרֵנוּ.
for we have no god other than You, our Rock.

Al ta-azvaynu Adōnoy Elōhaynu, אַל תַּעַזְבֵנוּ יהוה אֱלֹהֵינוּ,
*Do not forsake us, H*ASHEM*, our God,*

al tirchak mimenu, אַל תִּרְחַק מִמֶּנּוּ,
be not distant from us,

ki nafshaynu k'tzoro, כִּי נַפְשֵׁנוּ קָצְרָה,
for our soul is diminished

maycherev u-mish'vi, מֵחֶרֶב וּמִשְּׁבִי
u-midever u-mimagayfo. וּמִדֶּבֶר וּמִמַּגֵּפָה.
by sword and captivity, pestilence and plague.

u-mikol tzoro v'yogōn hatzilaynu, וּמִכָּל צָרָה וְיָגוֹן הַצִּילֵנוּ
ki l'cho kivinu, כִּי לְךָ קִוִּינוּ,
And from every distress and woe rescue us, for we hope to You;

v'al tachlimaynu Adōnoy Elōhaynu, וְאַל תַּכְלִימֵנוּ יהוה אֱלֹהֵינוּ,
*do not humiliate us, H*ASHEM*, our God.*

v'ho-ayr ponecho bonu, וְהָאֵר פָּנֶיךָ בָּנוּ,
Illuminate Your countenance within us,

uz'chor lonu es b'ris avōsaynu, וּזְכָר לָנוּ אֶת בְּרִית אֲבוֹתֵינוּ,
recall for us the covenant of our forefathers,

v'hōshi-aynu l'ma-an sh'mecho. וְהוֹשִׁיעֵנוּ לְמַעַן שְׁמֶךָ.
and save us for Your Name's sake.

R'ay v'tzorōsaynu, רְאֵה בְצָרוֹתֵינוּ
u-shma kōl t'filosaynu, וּשְׁמַע קוֹל תְּפִלָּתֵנוּ,
Observe our troubles and hear the voice of our prayer,

ki ato shōmay-a t'filas kol pe. כִּי אַתָּה שׁוֹמֵעַ תְּפִלַּת כָּל פֶּה.
for You hear the prayer of every mouth.

תחנון

AYL RACHUM v'chanun,	אֵל רַחוּם וְחַנּוּן,

O compassionate and gracious God,

rachaym olaynu v'al kol ma-asecho,   רַחֵם עָלֵינוּ וְעַל כָּל מַעֲשֶׂיךָ
have mercy on us and on all Your works,

ki ayn komōcho.   כִּי אֵין כָּמוֹךָ.
for there is none like You.

Adōnoy Elōhaynu,   יהוה אֱלֹהֵינוּ,
Please, HASHEM, our God —

ono so no f'sho-aynu,   אָנָּא שָׂא נָא פְשָׁעֵינוּ.
forgive our willful sins.

Ovinu malkaynu tzuraynu v'gō-alaynu,   אָבִינוּ מַלְכֵּנוּ צוּרֵנוּ וְגוֹאֲלֵנוּ,
Our Father, our King, our Rock and Redeemer,

Ayl chai v'ka-yom, ha-chasin bakō-ach,   אֵל חַי וְקַיָּם הֶחָסִין בַּכֹּחַ,
living and enduring God, Who is mighty in strength,

chosid votōv al kol ma-asecho,   חָסִיד וָטוֹב עַל כָּל מַעֲשֶׂיךָ,
generous and good to all Your works;

ki ato hu Adōnoy Elōhaynu.   כִּי אַתָּה הוּא יהוה אֱלֹהֵינוּ.
for You are HASHEM, our God.

Ayl erech apa-yim, u-molay rachamim,   אֵל אֶרֶךְ אַפַּיִם וּמָלֵא רַחֲמִים,
O God Who is slow to anger and full of mercy,

asay i-monu k'rōv rachamecho,   עֲשֵׂה עִמָּנוּ כְּרֹב רַחֲמֶיךָ,
treat us according to Your abundant mercy

v'hōshi-aynu l'ma-an sh'mecho.   וְהוֹשִׁיעֵנוּ לְמַעַן שְׁמֶךָ.
and save us for Your Name's sake.

Sh'ma malkaynu t'filosaynu,   שְׁמַע מַלְכֵּנוּ תְּפִלָּתֵנוּ,
Hear our King, our prayer

u-miyad ōy'vaynu hatzilaynu.   וּמִיַּד אוֹיְבֵינוּ הַצִּילֵנוּ.
and from our foes rescue us;

Sh'ma malkaynu t'filosaynu   שְׁמַע מַלְכֵּנוּ תְּפִלָּתֵנוּ
hear, our King, our prayer

u-mikol tzoro v'yogōn hatzilaynu.   וּמִכָּל צָרָה וְיָגוֹן הַצִּילֵנוּ.
and from every distress and woe rescue us.

Ovinu malkaynu oto,   אָבִינוּ מַלְכֵּנוּ אָתָּה,
You are our Father, our King,

אֵל רַחוּם וְחַנּוּן — *O compassionate and gracious God.* In this supplication, we refer to God not only as the Master of Israel, but as the God of all creatures and as the All-Powerful. He is the Master of history and, as such, has given us our role in it. Only if He shows us mercy and forgives our shortcomings can we serve Him. Therefore we beg Him not to cast us aside and abandon us.

v'shimcho olaynu nikro,	וְשִׁמְךָ עָלֵינוּ נִקְרָא,
and Your Name is proclaimed upon us —	
al tanichaynu.	אַל תַּנִּיחֵנוּ.
do not set us aside.	
Al ta-azvaynu ovinu,	אַל תַּעַזְבֵנוּ אָבִינוּ,
Do not abandon us, our Father,	
v'al tit'shaynu bōr'aynu,	וְאַל תִּטְּשֵׁנוּ בּוֹרְאֵנוּ,
do not cast us away, our Creator;	
v'al tishkochaynu yōtz'raynu,	וְאַל תִּשְׁכָּחֵנוּ יוֹצְרֵנוּ,
do not forget us, our Molder;	
ki Ayl melech	כִּי אֵל מֶלֶךְ
chanun v'rachum oto.	חַנּוּן וְרַחוּם אָתָּה.
for You are God, the gracious and compassionate King.	
AYN KOMŌCHO chanun v'rachum	**אֵין כָּמוֹךָ** חַנּוּן וְרַחוּם
Adōnoy Elōhaynu,	יהוה אֱלֹהֵינוּ,
There is none like You,* gracious and compassionate, Hashem, our God.	
ayn komōcho ayl erech apa-yim,	אֵין כָּמוֹךָ אֵל אֶרֶךְ אַפַּיִם
There is none like You, God Who is slow to anger	
v'rav chesed ve-emes,	וְרַב חֶסֶד וֶאֱמֶת.
and is abundant in kindness and truth.	
Hōshi-aynu b'rachamecho horabim,	הוֹשִׁיעֵנוּ בְּרַחֲמֶיךָ הָרַבִּים,
Save us with Your abundant mercy;	
mayra-ash u-mayrōgez hatzilaynu.	מֵרַעַשׁ וּמֵרֹגֶז הַצִּילֵנוּ.
from storm and anger save us.	
Z'chōr la-avodecho	זְכֹר לַעֲבָדֶיךָ
l'avrohom l'yitzchok ulya-akōv,	לְאַבְרָהָם לְיִצְחָק וּלְיַעֲקֹב,
Remember Your servants Abraham, Isaac, and Jacob;	
al tayfen el kosh'yaynu,	אַל תֵּפֶן אֶל קָשְׁיֵנוּ,
regard not our stubbornness,	
v'el rishaynu, v'el chatosaynu.	וְאֶל רִשְׁעֵנוּ וְאֶל חַטֹּאתֵנוּ.
our wickedness, and our sinfulness.	
Shuv maycharōn apecho,	שׁוּב מֵחֲרוֹן אַפֶּךָ
Turn back from Your flaring anger	

אֵין כָּמוֹךָ — *There is none like You.* This supplication consists mainly of verses from various parts of Scripture. Their unifying theme is an acknowledgment that we cannot justify our deeds. Nevertheless we have confidence that — against all odds and against our enemies' confident predictions of our doom — God's mercy is constant and He will help us find the way to repentance and forgiveness.

v'hinochaym al horo-o l'amecho.	וְהִנָּחֵם עַל הָרָעָה לְעַמֶּךָ.

and relent from the evil meant for Your people.

V'hosayr mimenu makas ha-moves,	וְהָסֵר מִמֶּנּוּ מַכַּת הַמָּוֶת

Remove from us the scourge of death

ki rachum oto, ki chayn darkecho,	כִּי רַחוּם אָתָּה, כִּי כֵן דַּרְכֶּךָ,

for You are compassionate, for such is Your manner:

ōse chesed chinom,	עוֹשֶׂה חֶסֶד חִנָּם
b'chol dōr vodōr.	בְּכָל דּוֹר וָדוֹר.

doing undeserved kindness in every generation.

Chuso Adōnoy al amecho,	חוּסָה יהוה עַל עַמֶּךָ

Have pity upon Your people, HASHEM,

v'hatzilaynu mizamecho,	וְהַצִּילֵנוּ מִזַּעְמֶךָ,

rescue us from Your wrath;

v'hosayr mimenu makas hamagayfo,	וְהָסֵר מִמֶּנּוּ מַכַּת הַמַּגֵּפָה
ugzayro kosho,	וּגְזֵרָה קָשָׁה,

remove from us the scourge of plague and harsh decree,

ki ato shōmayr yisro-ayl.	כִּי אַתָּה שׁוֹמֵר יִשְׂרָאֵל.

for You are the Guardian of Israel.

L'cho Adōnoy hatz'doko,	לְךָ אֲדֹנָי הַצְּדָקָה

Yours, my Lord, is the righteousness

v'lonu bōshes haponim.	וְלָנוּ בֹּשֶׁת הַפָּנִים.

and ours is the shamefacedness.

Ma nis-ōnayn, mah nōmar,	מַה נִּתְאוֹנֵן, מַה נֹּאמַר,

What complaint can we make? What can we say?

ma n'dabayr, uma nitztadok.	מַה נְּדַבֵּר, וּמַה נִּצְטַדָּק.

What can we declare? What justification can we offer?

Nachp'so d'rochaynu v'nachkōro,	נַחְפְּשָׂה דְרָכֵינוּ וְנַחְקֹרָה,

Let us examine our ways and analyze —

v'noshuvo aylecho,	וְנָשׁוּבָה אֵלֶיךָ,

and return to You,

ki y'min'cho f'shuto	כִּי יְמִינְךָ פְּשׁוּטָה
l'kabayl shovim.	לְקַבֵּל שָׁבִים.

for Your right hand is extended to accept penitents.

Ono Adōnoy hōshi-o no,	אָנָּא יהוה הוֹשִׁיעָה נָּא,

Please, HASHEM, save now;

ono Adōnoy hatzlicho no.	אָנָּא יהוה הַצְלִיחָה נָּא.

please, HASHEM, bring success now!

SUPPLICATION

Ono Adōnoy anaynu, v'yōm kor'aynu. אָנָּא יהוה עֲנֵנוּ בְיוֹם קָרְאֵנוּ.
Please, HASHEM, answer us on the day we call.

L'cho Adōnoy chikinu, לְךָ יהוה חִכִּינוּ,
For You, HASHEM, we have waited;

l'cho Adōnoy kivinu, לְךָ יהוה קִוְּינוּ,
for You, HASHEM, we have hoped;

l'cho Adōnoy n'yachayl. לְךָ יהוה נְיַחֵל.
for You, HASHEM, we long.

Al techeshe us-anaynu, אַל תֶּחֱשֶׁה וּתְעַנֵּנוּ,
Do not be silent while letting us suffer,

ki no-amu gōyim, כִּי נָאֲמוּ גוֹיִם,
ov'do sikvosom. אָבְדָה תִקְוָתָם.
for the nations have declared, "Their hope is lost."

kol berech v'chol kōmo, כָּל בֶּרֶךְ וְכָל קוֹמָה
l'cho l'vad tishtachave. לְךָ לְבַד תִּשְׁתַּחֲוֶה.
Let every knee and every erect being bow to You alone

HAPŌSAYACH YOD bis-shuvo **הַפּוֹתֵחַ יָד** בִּתְשׁוּבָה
You Who opens a hand* for repentance,

l'kabayl pōsh'im v'chato-im, לְקַבֵּל פּוֹשְׁעִים וְחַטָּאִים,
to welcome rebels and sinners:

nivhalo nafshaynu נִבְהֲלָה נַפְשֵׁנוּ
mayrōv itz'vōnaynu, מֵרֹב עִצְּבוֹנֵנוּ,
our soul is confounded by the abundance of our depression —

al tishkochaynu netzach. אַל תִּשְׁכָּחֵנוּ נֶצַח.
forget us not eternally.

Kumo v'hōshi-aynu, ki chosinu voch. קוּמָה וְהוֹשִׁיעֵנוּ, כִּי חָסִינוּ בָךְ.
Arise and save us for we take refuge in You.

Ovinu malkaynu, אָבִינוּ מַלְכֵּנוּ,
Our Father, our King,

im ayn bonu tz'doko אִם אֵין בָּנוּ צְדָקָה
u-ma-asim tōvim, וּמַעֲשִׂים טוֹבִים,
if we lack righteousness and good deeds,

z'chor lonu es b'ris avōsaynu, זְכָר לָנוּ אֶת בְּרִית אֲבוֹתֵינוּ
recall for us the covenant of our forefathers

הַפּוֹתֵחַ יָד — *You Who opens a hand.* Sometimes a person has become so sinful that there is no reason to think that he can still repent. Even then, however, there is hope. As the Sages put it, God opens a place for the penitent beneath His Own Heavenly Throne, as it were. The point is that God's mercy exceeds all imaginable boundaries (*Etz Yosef*).

וְעֵדוֹתֵינוּ בְּכָל יוֹם,	v'aydōsaynu b'chol yōm
יהוה אֶחָד.	Adōnoy e-chod.

and our daily testimonies that "Hashem is the One and Only."

הַבִּיטָה בְעָנְיֵנוּ,	Habito v'on'yaynu,

Look upon our affliction,

כִּי רַבּוּ מַכְאוֹבֵינוּ,	ki rabu mach-ōvaynu,
וְצָרוֹת לְבָבֵנוּ.	v'tzorōs l'vovaynu.

for many are our sufferings and the distresses of our hearts.

חוּסָה יהוה עָלֵינוּ,	Chuso Adōnoy olaynu,
בְּאֶרֶץ שִׁבְיֵנוּ,	v'eretz shivyaynu,

Have pity upon us, Hashem, in the land of our captivity

וְאַל תִּשְׁפֹּךְ חֲרוֹנְךָ עָלֵינוּ,	v'al tishpōch charōn'cho olaynu,

and do not pour Your wrath upon us –

כִּי אֲנַחְנוּ עַמְּךָ בְּנֵי בְרִיתֶךָ.	ki anachnu am'cho b'nay v'risecho.

for we are Your people, the members of Your covenant.

אֵל, הַבִּיטָה דַּל כְּבוֹדֵנוּ בַּגּוֹיִם,	Ayl habito dal k'vōdaynu bagōyim,

O God, look upon the impoverishment of our honor among the nations

וְשִׁקְּצוּנוּ כְּטֻמְאַת הַנִּדָּה.	v'shik'tzunu k'tumas hanido.

and how they abhor us like menstrual impurity.

עַד מָתַי עֻזְּךָ בַּשֶּׁבִי,	Ad mosai uz'cho bashvi,

How long will Your strength be in bondage

וְתִפְאַרְתְּךָ בְּיַד צָר.	v'sifart'cho b'yad tzor.

and Your splendor in the enemy's power?

עוֹרְרָה גְבוּרָתְךָ	Ōr'ro g'vuros'cho
וְקִנְאָתְךָ עַל אוֹיְבֶיךָ.	v'kinos'cho al ōy'vecho.

Arouse Your strength and Your zeal against Your enemies.

הֵם יֵבוֹשׁוּ	Haym yayvōshu
וְיֵחַתּוּ מִגְּבוּרָתָם,	v'yaychatu mig'vurosom,

Let them be shamed and broken of their strength;

וְאַל יִמְעֲטוּ לְפָנֶיךָ תְּלָאוֹתֵינוּ.	v'al yimatu l'fonecho t'lo-ōsaynu.

and may our travails not seem petty to You.

מַהֵר יְקַדְּמוּנוּ רַחֲמֶיךָ	Mahayr y'kad'munu rachamecho
בְּיוֹם צָרָתֵנוּ,	b'yōm tzorosaynu,

May Your mercies meet us swiftly in our time of distress;

וְאִם לֹא לְמַעֲנֵנוּ,	v'im lō l'ma-anaynu,

and if not for our sake,

l'ma-ancho f'al, לְמַעַנְךָ פְּעַל,
act for Your own sake

v'al tashchis zaycher sh'ayrisaynu. וְאַל תַּשְׁחִית זֵכֶר שְׁאֵרִיתֵנוּ.
and do not destroy our remnant's remembrance.

V'chōn ōm ham'ya-chadim shimcho וְחֹן אם הַמְיַחֲדִים שִׁמְךָ
Be gracious to the nation that ascribes Oneness to Your Name

pa-ama-yim b'chol yōm tomid פַּעֲמַיִם בְּכָל יוֹם תָּמִיד
b'ahavo v'ōm'rim: בְּאַהֲבָה וְאוֹמְרִים:
twice daily, constantly with love, saying:

Sh'ma yisro-ayl, שְׁמַע יִשְׂרָאֵל
Adōnoy Elōhaynu, Adōnoy e-chod. יהוה אֱלֹהֵינוּ יהוה אֶחָד.
*"Hear, O Israel, H*ASHEM*, is our God, H*ASHEM*, the One and Only."*

⌘ TACHANUN / PUTTING DOWN THE HEAD ⌘

■ *Shemoneh Esrei* presupposes the worth of man, that he is crowned with intelligence, that he is created in the image of God, and that he is justified to petition God with his many needs. We therefore recite it in a standing, erect position.

But perhaps man has failed to be worthy of being answered. If so, we now approach God assuming the stance of a lowly animal, sitting and putting down our head, and beseeching that He heed our pleas as He fills the needs of all creatures. Then we pray while sitting, and finally conclude *Tachanun* while standing.

Avudraham notes that just as Moses in his encounter with God at Sinai underwent these three different bodily positions, so do we.

IN THE PRESENCE OF A TORAH SCROLL, THE FOLLOWING IS RECITED WITH THE HEAD RESTING ON THE ARM, PREFERABLY WHILE SEATED. ELSEWHERE, IT IS RECITED WITH THE HEAD ERECT.

VA-YŌMER dovid el gad, וַיֹּאמֶר דָּוִד אֶל גָּד,
tzar li m'ōd, צַר לִי מְאֹד,
And David said to Gad, "I am exceedingly distressed.

nip'lo no v'yad Adōnoy, נִפְּלָה נָּא בְיַד יהוה,
*Let us fall into H*ASHEM*'s hand*

⌘ PUTTING DOWN THE HEAD ⌘

Tachanun consists mainly of *Psalms* 6:2-11. However, two verses, both of which reflect the theme of *Tachanun,* are inserted to introduce the primary psalm.

The act of נְפִילַת אַפַּיִם, *putting down the head,* i.e., 'burying' one's face in submissive supplication, is based on the behavior of Moses, Aaron and Joshua. These three cast themselves down before God in times of stress and tragedy (*Numbers* 16:22; *Joshua* 7:6).

This portion of *Tachanun* is recited with the head down and resting on the left arm, and preferably in a sitting position. One wearing *tefillin* on the left arm rests his head on his right arm out of respect for the *tefillin.* The head should not rest on the bare arm; rather the arm should be covered with a sleeve, *tallis,* or even a cloth. This posture is an indication of the feelings of despair and guilt that combine with the undying hope that God's mercy will rescue the supplicant no matter how hopeless his plight. Since Joshua cast himself down in the presence of the Holy Ark, the act of falling on the face is done only in the presence of a Torah scroll, i.e., an Ark containing a Torah scroll. If a Torah is not present, *Tachanun* is recited with the head held erect.

וַיֹּאמֶר דָּוִד — *And David said.* King David had sinned by taking a census of the Jews in a manner contrary to that prescribed in the Torah (see *Exodus* 30:12). God, through the

ki rabim rachamov,	כִּי רַבִּים רַחֲמָיו,

for His mercies are abundant,

uvyad odom al epōlo.	וּבְיַד אָדָם אַל אֶפֹּלָה.

but let me not fall into human hands."

RACHUM V'CHANUN / רַחוּם וְחַנּוּן

chotosi l'fonecho. — חָטָאתִי לְפָנֶיךָ.

O compassionate and gracious One, I have sinned before You,*

Adōnoy molay rachamim, — יהוה מָלֵא רַחֲמִים,

Hashem, Who is full of mercy,

rachaym olai v'kabayl tachanunoy. — רַחֵם עָלַי וְקַבֵּל תַּחֲנוּנָי.

have mercy on me and accept my supplications.

Adōnoy al b'ap'cho sōchichayni, — יהוה אַל בְּאַפְּךָ תוֹכִיחֵנִי,

Hashem, do not rebuke me in Your anger,

v'al bachamos'cho s'yas'rayni. — וְאַל בַּחֲמָתְךָ תְיַסְּרֵנִי.

nor chastise me in Your rage.

Chonayni Adōnoy, ki umlal oni, — חָנֵּנִי יהוה, כִּי אֻמְלַל אָנִי,

Favor me, Hashem, for I am feeble;

r'fo-ayni Adōnoy, ki nivhalu atzomoy. — רְפָאֵנִי יהוה, כִּי נִבְהֲלוּ עֲצָמָי.

heal me, Hashem, for my bones shudder.

V'nafshi nivhalo m'ōd, — וְנַפְשִׁי נִבְהֲלָה מְאֹד,

My soul is utterly confounded,

v'ato Adōnoy ad mosoy. — וְאַתָּה יהוה, עַד מָתָי.

and You, Hashem, how long?

Shuvo Adōnoy chal'tzo nafshi, — שׁוּבָה יהוה, חַלְּצָה נַפְשִׁי,

Desist, Hashem, release my soul;

hōshi-ayni l'ma-an chasdecho. — הוֹשִׁיעֵנִי לְמַעַן חַסְדֶּךָ.

save me as befits Your kindness.

---

agency of the prophet Gad, gave King David a choice of three calamities, one of which he and his people would have to suffer in atonement for his sin: seven years of hunger; three months of defeat in battle; or a three-day death plague. David chose the last because that one would be inflicted directly by God, Whose mercy is everpresent, even when His wrath is aroused. His choice proved the correct one when God mercifully halted the plague after a duration of only half a day. Similarly, in *Tachanun*, we cast ourselves upon God's compassion.

רַחוּם וְחַנּוּן — *O compassionate and gracious*

One. This verse is not of Scriptural origin. It is based on the dictum that God tempers the judgment of someone who confesses that he has sinned (*Etz Yosef*).

אַל בְּאַפְּךָ 'ה — *Hashem, do not . . . in Your anger.* David composed this psalm when he was sick and in pain. he intended his prayer for every person in distress, and particularly for Israel when it suffered oppression and deprivation.

Even if he must be punished for his deeds, David pleaded, let God do so gradually, but not in *anger,* for then it would be beyond human endurance (*Radak*).

Ki ayn bamo-ves zichrecho,	כִּי אֵין בַּמָּוֶת זִכְרֶךָ,

For there is no mention of You in death;

bish-ōl mi yōde loch.	בִּשְׁאוֹל מִי יוֹדֶה לָּךְ.

in the Lower World who will thank You?

Yogati b'anchosi,	יָגַעְתִּי בְּאַנְחָתִי,

I am wearied with my sigh,

a-sche v'chol lailo mitosi,	אַשְׂחֶה בְכָל לַיְלָה מִטָּתִי,

every night I drench my bed,

b'dim-osi arsi amse.	בְּדִמְעָתִי עַרְשִׂי אַמְסֶה.

with my tears I soak my couch.

O-sh'sho mika-as ayni,	עָשְׁשָׁה מִכַּעַס עֵינִי,

My eye is dimmed because of anger,

os'ko b'chol tzōr'roy.	עָתְקָה בְּכָל צוֹרְרָי.

aged by my tormentors.

Suru mimeni kol pō-alay oven,	סוּרוּ מִמֶּנִּי כָּל פֹּעֲלֵי אָוֶן,

Depart from me, all evildoers,

ki shoma Adōnoy kōl bich-yi.	כִּי שָׁמַע יהוה קוֹל בִּכְיִי.

for HASHEM has heard the sound of my weeping.

Shoma Adōnoy t'chinosi,	שָׁמַע יהוה תְּחִנָּתִי,

HASHEM has heard my plea,

Adōnoy t'filosi yikoch.	יהוה תְּפִלָּתִי יִקָּח.

HASHEM will accept my prayer.

Yayvōshu v'yibohalu m'ōd kol ōy'voy,	יֵבֹשׁוּ וְיִבָּהֲלוּ מְאֹד כָּל אֹיְבָי,

Let all my foes be shamed and utterly confounded,

yoshuvu yayvōshu roga.	יָשֻׁבוּ יֵבֹשׁוּ רָגַע.

they will regret and be instantly shamed

THE HEAD IS RAISED AT THIS POINT.

ON MONDAYS AND THURSDAYS *TACHANUN* CONTINUES HERE.
ON OTHER DAYS TURN TO P. 231.

ADŌNOY Elōhay yisro-ayl	**יהוה** אֱלֹהֵי יִשְׂרָאֵל,

HASHEM, God of Israel,

shuv maycharōn apecho,	שׁוּב מֵחֲרוֹן אַפֶּךָ,

turn back from Your flaring anger

v'hinochaym al horo-o l'amecho.	וְהִנָּחֵם עַל הָרָעָה לְעַמֶּךָ.

and relent from the evil meant for Your people.

HABAYT mi-shoma-yim ur'ay,   הַבֵּט מִשָּׁמַיִם וּרְאֵה
Look from heaven and perceive

ki hoyinu la-ag vokeles ba-gōyim,   כִּי הָיִינוּ לַעַג וָקֶלֶס בַּגּוֹיִם,
that we have become an object of scorn and derision among the nations;

nechshavnu k'tzōn latevach yuvol,   נֶחְשַׁבְנוּ כְּצֹאן לַטֶּבַח יוּבָל,
we are regarded as the sheep led to slaughter,

laharōg ul-abayd   לַהֲרֹג וּלְאַבֵּד
    ulmako ulcherpo.   וּלְמַכָּה וּלְחֶרְפָּה.
to be killed, destroyed, beaten, and humiliated.

Uvchol zōs   וּבְכָל זֹאת
    shimcho lō shochoch-nu,   שִׁמְךָ לֹא שָׁכָחְנוּ,
But despite all this we have not forgotten Your Name –

no al tishkochaynu.   נָא אַל תִּשְׁכָּחֵנוּ.
we beg You not to forget us.

Adōnoy Elōhay yisro-ayl   יהוה אֱלֹהֵי יִשְׂרָאֵל,
H<small>ASHEM</small>, *God of Israel,*

shuv maycharōn apecho,   שׁוּב מֵחֲרוֹן אַפֶּךָ,
turn back from Your flaring anger

v'hinochaym al horo-o l'amecho.   וְהִנָּחֵם עַל הָרָעָה לְעַמֶּךָ.
and relent from the evil meant for Your people.

ZORIM ōm'rim   זָרִים אוֹמְרִים
Foreigners say,

ayn tōcheles v'sikvo.   אֵין תּוֹחֶלֶת וְתִקְוָה.
'There is no expectation nor hope!'

Chōn ōm l'shimcho m'kavo.   חֹן אֹם לְשִׁמְךָ מְקַוֶּה.
Be gracious to the nation whose hope is in Your Name.

Tohōr, y'shu-osaynu kor'vo.   טָהוֹר, יְשׁוּעָתֵנוּ קָרְבָה.
O Pure One, bring near Your salvation!

Yoganu v'lō hunach lonu,   יָגַעְנוּ וְלֹא הוּנַח לָנוּ,
We are exhausted but are allowed no rest.

rachamecho yichb'shu   רַחֲמֶיךָ יִכְבְּשׁוּ
    es ka-ascho may-olaynu.   אֶת כַּעַסְךָ מֵעָלֵינוּ.
May Your mercies conquer Your anger against us.

Ono shuv maycharōn'cho,   אָנָּא שׁוּב מֵחֲרוֹנְךָ,
We beg You, turn back from Your anger

v'rachaym s'gulo asher bochor'to.	וְרַחֵם סְגֻלָּה אֲשֶׁר בָּחָרְתָּ.

and have mercy on the treasured nation that You have chosen.

Adōnoy Elōhay yisro-ayl	יהוה אֱלֹהֵי יִשְׂרָאֵל,

HASHEM, God of Israel,

shuv maycharōn apecho,	שׁוּב מֵחֲרוֹן אַפֶּךָ,

turn back from Your flaring anger

v'hinochaym al horo-o l'amecho.	וְהִנָּחֵם עַל הָרָעָה לְעַמֶּךָ.

and relent from the evil meant for Your people.

CHUSO Adōnoy olaynu b'rachamecho,	**חוּסָה** יהוה עָלֵינוּ בְּרַחֲמֶיךָ,

HASHEM, pity us in Your mercy

v'al tit'naynu biday achzorim.	וְאַל תִּתְּנֵנוּ בִּידֵי אַכְזָרִים.

and do not turn us over to sadists.

Lomo yōmru hagōyim,	לָמָּה יֹאמְרוּ הַגּוֹיִם,

Why should the nations say,

a-yay no Elōhayhem.	אַיֵּה נָא אֱלֹהֵיהֶם,

"Where is their God now?"

L'ma-ancho asay i-monu chesed,	לְמַעַנְךָ עֲשֵׂה עִמָּנוּ חֶסֶד

For Your sake, treat us with kindness

v'al t'achar.	וְאַל תְּאַחַר.

and do not delay.

Ono shuv maycharōn'cho,	אָנָּא שׁוּב מֵחֲרוֹנְךָ,

We beg You, turn back from Your anger

v'rachaym s'gulo asher bochor'to.	וְרַחֵם סְגֻלָּה אֲשֶׁר בָּחָרְתָּ.

and have mercy on the treasured nation that You have chosen.

Adōnoy Elōhay yisro-ayl	יהוה אֱלֹהֵי יִשְׂרָאֵל,

HASHEM, God of Israel,

shuv maycharōn apecho,	שׁוּב מֵחֲרוֹן אַפֶּךָ,

turn back from Your flaring anger

v'hinochaym al horo-o l'amecho.	וְהִנָּחֵם עַל הָרָעָה לְעַמֶּךָ.

and relent from the evil meant for Your people.

KŌLAYNU sishma v'sochōn,	**קוֹלֵנוּ** תִשְׁמַע וְתָחֹן,

Listen to our voice and be gracious –

v'al tit'shaynu b'yad ōy'vaynu,	וְאַל תִּטְּשֵׁנוּ בְּיַד אוֹיְבֵינוּ,

do not cast us off into the hand of our enemies

limchōs es sh'maynu.	לִמְחוֹת אֶת שְׁמֵנוּ.

to blot out our name.

Z'chōr asher nishbato la-avōsaynu,   זְכֹר אֲשֶׁר נִשְׁבַּעְתָּ לַאֲבוֹתֵינוּ,

Remember what You swore to our forefathers:

k'chōch'vay ha-shoma-yim arbe es zar-achem,   כְּכוֹכְבֵי הַשָּׁמַיִם אַרְבֶּה אֶת זַרְעֲכֶם,

"Like the stars of the heaven will I multiply your offspring" —

v'ato nish-arnu m'at mayharbay.   וְעַתָּה נִשְׁאַרְנוּ מְעַט מֵהַרְבֵּה.

but now we are few left from many.

Uvchol zōs shimcho lō shochoch-nu,   וּבְכָל זֹאת שִׁמְךָ לֹא שָׁכָחְנוּ,

But despite all this, we have not forgotten Your Name —

no al tishkochaynu.   נָא אַל תִּשְׁכָּחֵנוּ.

we beg You not to forget us.

Adōnoy Elōhay yisro-ayl   יהוה אֱלֹהֵי יִשְׂרָאֵל,

Hashem, God of Israel,

shuv maycharōn apecho,   שׁוּב מֵחֲרוֹן אַפֶּךָ,

turn back from Your flaring anger

v'hinochaym al horo-o l'amecho.   וְהִנָּחֵם עַל הָרָעָה לְעַמֶּךָ.

and relent from the evil meant for Your people.

OZ'RAYNU Elōhay yishaynu   **עָזְרֵנוּ** אֱלֹהֵי יִשְׁעֵנוּ

Assist us, O God of our salvation,

al d'var k'vōd sh'mecho,   עַל דְּבַר כְּבוֹד שְׁמֶךָ,

for the sake of Your Name's glory;

v'hatzilaynu v'chapayr al chatōsaynu   וְהַצִּילֵנוּ וְכַפֵּר עַל חַטֹּאתֵינוּ

rescue us, and atone for our sins

l'ma-an sh'mecho.   לְמַעַן שְׁמֶךָ.

for Your Name's sake.

Adōnoy Elōhay yisro-ayl,   יהוה אֱלֹהֵי יִשְׂרָאֵל,

Hashem, God of Israel,

shuv maycharōn apecho,   שׁוּב מֵחֲרוֹן אַפֶּךָ,

turn back from Your flaring anger

v'hinochaym al horo-o l'amecho.   וְהִנָּחֵם עַל הָרָעָה לְעַמֶּךָ.

and relent from the evil meant for Your people.

SHACHARIS FOR WEEKDAYS — SUPPLICATION

ON ALL DAYS TACHANUN CONTINUES HERE. REMAIN SEATED WITH HEAD RAISED.

SHŌMAYR yisro-ayl, שׁוֹמֵר יִשְׂרָאֵל,
   sh'mōr sh'ayris yisro-ayl, שְׁמוֹר שְׁאֵרִית יִשְׂרָאֵל,
      O Guardian of Israel, protect the remnant of Israel;
v'al yōvad yisro-ayl, וְאַל יֹאבַד יִשְׂרָאֵל,
      let not Israel be destroyed —
ho-ōm'rim, sh'ma yisro-ayl. הָאוֹמְרִים, שְׁמַע יִשְׂרָאֵל.
      those who proclaim, "Hear O Israel."

Shōmayr gōy e-chod, שׁוֹמֵר גּוֹי אֶחָד,
   sh'mōr sh'ayris am e-chod, שְׁמוֹר שְׁאֵרִית עַם אֶחָד,
      O Guardian of the unique nation, protect the remnant of the unique people;
v'al yōvad gōy e-chod, וְאַל יֹאבַד גּוֹי אֶחָד,
      let not the unique nation be destroyed —
ham'yachadim shimcho, הַמְיַחֲדִים שִׁמְךָ,
      those who proclaim the Oneness of Your Name,
Adōnoy Elōhaynu, Adōnoy e-chod. יהוה אֱלֹהֵינוּ יהוה אֶחָד.
      "HASHEM is our God, HASHEM — the One and Only!"

Shōmayr gōy kodōsh, שׁוֹמֵר גּוֹי קָדוֹשׁ,
   sh'mōr sh'ayris am kodōsh, שְׁמוֹר שְׁאֵרִית עַם קָדוֹשׁ,
      O Guardian of the holy nation, protect the remnant of the holy people;
v'al yōvad gōy kodōsh, וְאַל יֹאבַד גּוֹי קָדוֹשׁ,
      let not the holy nation be destroyed —
hamshal'shim b'sholōsh k'dushōs l'kodōsh. הַמְשַׁלְּשִׁים בְּשָׁלֹשׁ קְדֻשּׁוֹת לְקָדוֹשׁ.
      those who proclaim three-fold sanctifications to the Holy One.

Misratze v'rachamim מִתְרַצֶּה בְּרַחֲמִים
      Become favorable through compassion
u-mispa-yays b'sachanunim, וּמִתְפַּיֵּס בְּתַחֲנוּנִים,
      and become appeased through supplications;
hisratze v'hispa-yays l'dōr oni, הִתְרַצֵּה וְהִתְפַּיֵּס לְדוֹר עָנִי,
      become favorable and appeased to the poor generation
ki ayn ōzayr. כִּי אֵין עוֹזֵר.
      for there is no helper.

Ovinu malkaynu, chonaynu va-anaynu, אָבִינוּ מַלְכֵּנוּ, חָנֵּנוּ וַעֲנֵנוּ,
      Our Father, our King, be gracious with us and answer us,
ki ayn bonu ma-asim, כִּי אֵין בָּנוּ מַעֲשִׂים,
      though we have no worthy deeds;

asay imonu tz'doko vochesed v'hōshi-aynu.	עֲשֵׂה עִמָּֽנוּ צְדָקָה וָחֶֽסֶד וְהוֹשִׁיעֵֽנוּ.

treat us with charity and kindness, and save us.

RISE AFTER SAYING Va-anachnu lo nayda. REMAIN STANDING UNTIL THE END OF TACHANUN.

VA-ANACHNU lō nayda ma na-ase, ki olecho aynaynu.	**וַאֲנַֽחְנוּ** לֹא נֵדַע מַה נַּעֲשֶׂה, כִּי עָלֶֽיךָ עֵינֵֽינוּ.

We know not what to do — but our eyes are upon You.

Z'chōr rachamecho Adōnoy	זְכֹר רַחֲמֶֽיךָ יהוה

Remember Your mercies, HASHEM,

vachasodecho, ki may-ōlom haymo.	וַחֲסָדֶֽיךָ, כִּי מֵעוֹלָם הֵֽמָּה.

and Your kindnesses, for they are from the beginning of the world.

Y'hi chasd'cho Adōnoy olaynu, ka-asher yichalnu loch.	יְהִי חַסְדְּךָ יהוה עָלֵֽינוּ, כַּאֲשֶׁר יִחַֽלְנוּ לָךְ.

May Your kindness be upon us, HASHEM, just as we awaited You.

Al tizkor lonu avonōs rishōnim,	אַל תִּזְכָּר לָֽנוּ עֲוֹנוֹת רִאשׁוֹנִים,

Recall not against us the sins of the ancients;

mahayr y'kad'munu rachamecho, ki dalōnu m'ōd.	מַהֵר יְקַדְּמֽוּנוּ רַחֲמֶֽיךָ, כִּי דַלּֽוֹנוּ מְאֹד.

may Your mercies meet us swiftly, for we have become exceedingly impoverished.

Chonaynu Adōnoy chonaynu, ki rav sovanu vuz.	חָנֵּֽנוּ יהוה חָנֵּֽנוּ, כִּי רַב שָׂבַֽעְנוּ בוּז.

Be gracious to us, HASHEM, be gracious to us, for we are abundantly sated with scorn.

B'rōgez rachaym tizkōr.	בְּרֹֽגֶז רַחֵם תִּזְכּוֹר.

Amid rage — remember to be merciful!

Ki hu yoda yitzraynu, zochur ki ofor anochnu.	כִּי הוּא יָדַע יִצְרֵֽנוּ, זָכוּר כִּי עָפָר אֲנָֽחְנוּ.

For He knew our nature, He remembers that we are dust.

❖ Oz'raynu Elōhay yish-aynu	❖ עָזְרֵֽנוּ אֱלֹהֵי יִשְׁעֵֽנוּ

Assist us, O God of our salvation,

al d'var k'vōd sh'mecho,	עַל דְּבַר כְּבוֹד שְׁמֶֽךָ,

for the sake of Your Name's glory;

v'hatzilaynu v'chapayr al chatōsaynu	וְהַצִּילֵֽנוּ וְכַפֵּר עַל חַטֹּאתֵֽינוּ

rescue us and atone for our sins

l'ma-an sh'mecho.	לְמַֽעַן שְׁמֶֽךָ.

for Your Name's sake.

TACHANUN ENDS HERE.

SHACHARIS FOR WEEKDAYS — TORAH READING

THE *CHAZZAN* RECITES *HALF-KADDISH*.
(Congregational responses are indicated by parentheses.)

יִתְגַּדַּל וְיִתְקַדַּשׁ שְׁמֵהּ רַבָּא. (אָמֵן—Omayn). בְּעָלְמָא דִּי בְרָא כִרְעוּתֵהּ. וְיַמְלִיךְ מַלְכוּתֵהּ, בְּחַיֵּיכוֹן וּבְיוֹמֵיכוֹן וּבְחַיֵּי דְכָל בֵּית יִשְׂרָאֵל, בַּעֲגָלָא וּבִזְמַן קָרִיב. וְאִמְרוּ: אָמֵן.

(אָמֵן. יְהֵא שְׁמֵהּ רַבָּא מְבָרַךְ לְעָלַם וּלְעָלְמֵי עָלְמַיָּא.)
(Omayn. Y'hay sh'mayh rabo m'vorach l'olam ul-ol'may ol'ma-yo.)

יְהֵא שְׁמֵהּ רַבָּא מְבָרַךְ לְעָלַם וּלְעָלְמֵי עָלְמַיָּא. יִתְבָּרַךְ וְיִשְׁתַּבַּח וְיִתְפָּאַר וְיִתְרוֹמַם וְיִתְנַשֵּׂא וְיִתְהַדָּר וְיִתְעַלֶּה וְיִתְהַלָּל שְׁמֵהּ דְּקֻדְשָׁא בְּרִיךְ הוּא (בְּרִיךְ הוּא — B'rich hu). °לְעֵלָּא מִן כָּל [substitute Yom Kippur to Hashanah Rosh from — °לְעֵלָּא לְעֵלָּא מִכָּל] בִּרְכָתָא וְשִׁירָתָא תֻּשְׁבְּחָתָא וְנֶחֱמָתָא, דַּאֲמִירָן בְּעָלְמָא. וְאִמְרוּ: אָמֵן.
(אָמֵן—Omayn).

ON DAYS THAT THE TORAH IS NOT READ, THE SERVICE CONTINUES WITH *ASHREI* (P. 246).

⸻ REMOVAL OF THE TORAH FROM THE ARK ⸻

ALL RISE AND REMAIN STANDING UNTIL THE TORAH IS PLACED ON THE *BIMAH*.

■ The Torah is read every Monday and Thursday, assuring that the Jew studies Torah regularly, not allowing three days to pass without its study. In sharp contrast to prayer — which reflects man's speaking to Hashem — the Torah reading represents Hashem's communicating with us.

THE FOLLOWING PARAGRAPH IS OMITTED ON MOST DAYS THAT *TACHANUN* IS NOT RECITED.

■ I confess my shortcomings and pray for His mercy, recognizing my unworthiness to enter the personal encounter with Hashem which the Torah represents.

AYL erech apa-yim   **אֵל** אֶרֶךְ אַפַּיִם
   v'rav chesed v'emes   וְרַב חֶסֶד וֶאֱמֶת,
      O God, slow to anger and abundant in kindness and truth,
al tastayr ponecho mimenu.   אַל תַּסְתֵּר פָּנֶיךָ מִמֶּנּוּ.
      do not chastise us in Your anger.
Chuso Adonoy al yisro-ayl amecha   חוּסָה יהוה עַל יִשְׂרָאֵל עַמֶּךָ,
      Pity, HASHEM, Your people
v'hatzilaynu mikol ro.   וְהַצִּילֵנוּ מִכָּל רָע.
      and save us from any evil.
Chotonu l'cho odōn,   חָטָאנוּ לְךָ אָדוֹן,
      We have sinned against You, Master;
s'lach no k'rōv rachamecho Ayl.   סְלַח נָא כְּרֹב רַחֲמֶיךָ אֵל.
      forgive us, we beg You, in accordance with Your abundant mercies, O God.

■ Citing verses from our historical past and glorious future, we proclaim that Torah study is to accompany the Jew wherever he is.

THE ARK IS OPENED. BEFORE THE TORAH IS REMOVED THE CONGREGATION RECITES:

VAIHI BINSÔ-A ho-orōn
va-yōmer mōshe,

וַיְהִי בִּנְסֹעַ הָאָרֹן
וַיֹּאמֶר מֹשֶׁה,

When the Ark would travel,* Moses would say,

kumo Adōnoy v'yofutzu ōy'vecho

קוּמָה יהוה וְיָפֻצוּ אֹיְבֶיךָ

"Arise, HASHEM, and let Your foes be scattered,

v'yonusu m'san-echo miponecho.

וְיָנֻסוּ מְשַׂנְאֶיךָ מִפָּנֶיךָ.

let those who hate You flee from You."

Ki mitziyōn taytzay sōro,

כִּי מִצִּיּוֹן תֵּצֵא תוֹרָה,

For from Zion the Torah will come forth

udvar Adōnoy mirusholo-yim.

וּדְבַר יהוה מִירוּשָׁלָיִם.

and the word of HASHEM from Jerusalem.

Boruch shenosan tōro
l'amō yisro-ayl bikdushosō.

בָּרוּךְ שֶׁנָּתַן תּוֹרָה
לְעַמּוֹ יִשְׂרָאֵל בִּקְדֻשָּׁתוֹ.

Blessed is He Who gave the Torah to His people Israel in His holiness.

■ According to kabbalistic tradition, the opening of the Ark in the synagogue portrays the opening of Hashem's heavenly Gates of Mercy. We therefore utilize this lofty moment to affirm our close relationship to Him and pray for personal and national success.

B'RICH SH'MAYH d'moray ol'mo,

בְּרִיךְ שְׁמֵהּ דְּמָרֵא עָלְמָא,

Blessed is the Name* of the Master of the universe,

b'rich kisroch v'asroch.

בְּרִיךְ כִּתְרָךְ וְאַתְרָךְ.

blessed is Your crown and Your place.

Y'hay r'usoch im amoch yisro-ayl l'olam,

יְהֵא רְעוּתָךְ עִם עַמָּךְ יִשְׂרָאֵל לְעָלַם,

May Your favor remain with Your people Israel forever;

u-furkan y'minoch achazay l'amoch

וּפֻרְקַן יְמִינָךְ אַחֲזֵי לְעַמָּךְ

may You display the salvation of Your right hand* to Your people

---

וַיְהִי בִּנְסֹעַ הָאָרֹן — *When the Ark would travel.* When the Ark is opened we declare, as Moses did when the Ark traveled for forty years in the wilderness, that God's word is invincible. Having acknowledged this, we can read from the Torah with the proper awareness. We continue that it is God's will that the Torah's message go forth to the entire world, and by blessing Him for having given us the Torah, we accept our responsibility to carry out its commands and spread its message.

בְּרִיךְ שְׁמֵהּ — *Blessed is the Name.* The *Zohar* declares that when the congregation prepares to read from the Torah, the heavenly gates of mercy are opened and God's love for Israel is aroused. Therefore, it is an auspicious occasion for the recital of this prayer which asks for God's compassion; pleads that He display His salvation in the finally rebuilt Holy Temple; declares our faith in Him and His Torah; and asks that He make us receptive to its wisdom.

יְמִינָךְ — *Your right hand.* It is axiomatic to Jew-

b'vays makd'shoch	בְּבֵית מַקְדְּשָׁךְ,
in Your Holy Temple,	
ul-amtuyay lono mituv n'horoch,	וּלְאַמְטוּיֵי לָנָא מִטּוּב נְהוֹרָךְ,
and to benefit us with the goodness of Your luminescence	
ulkabayl tz'lōsono b'rachamin.	וּלְקַבֵּל צְלוֹתָנָא בְּרַחֲמִין.
and to accept our prayers with mercy.	
Y'hay ra-avo kodomoch	יְהֵא רַעֲוָא קֳדָמָךְ,
May it be Your will	
d'sōrich lon cha-yin b'tivuso,	דְּתוֹרִיךְ לָן חַיִּין בְּטִיבוּתָא,
that You extend our lives with goodness	
v'lehevay ano f'kido b'gō tzadika-yo,	וְלֶהֱוֵי אֲנָא פְּקִידָא בְּגוֹ צַדִּיקַיָּא,
and that I be numbered among the righteous;	
l'mircham olai	לְמִרְחַם עָלַי
that You have mercy on me	
ulmintar yosi v'yas kol di li,	וּלְמִנְטַר יָתִי וְיָת כָּל דִּי לִי,
and protect me, all that is mine	
v'di l'amoch yisro-ayl.	וְדִי לְעַמָּךְ יִשְׂרָאֵל.
and that is Your people Israel's.	
Ant hu zon l'chōlo, umfarnays l'chōlo,	אַנְתְּ הוּא זָן לְכֹלָּא, וּמְפַרְנֵס לְכֹלָּא,
It is You Who nourishes all and sustains all;	
ant hu shalit al kōlo,	אַנְתְּ הוּא שַׁלִּיט עַל כֹּלָּא,
it is You Who controls everything;	
ant hu d'shalit al malcha-yo, u-malchuso diloch hi.	אַנְתְּ הוּא דְּשַׁלִּיט עַל מַלְכַיָּא, וּמַלְכוּתָא דִילָךְ הִיא.
it is You Who controls kings, and kingship is Yours.	
Ano avdo d'kudsho b'rich hu,	אֲנָא עַבְדָּא דְּקֻדְשָׁא בְּרִיךְ הוּא,
I am a servant of the Holy One, Blessed is He,	
d'sogidno kamayh u-mikamo dikar ōraisayh	דְּסָגִידְנָא קַמֵּהּ וּמִקָּמָא דִּיקַר אוֹרַיְתֵהּ
and I prostrate myself before Him and before the glory of His Torah	
b'chol idon v'idon.	בְּכָל עִדָּן וְעִדָּן.
at all times.	

---

ish belief that God had no physicality, not even that of the invisible, intangible angels. Because we are physical beings, we cannot grasp God's essence. We cannot conceive of a Being totally unaffected by material conditions or the laws of nature and physics. When Scripture speaks of "the hand of God" or "the eyes of God," it does not imply that God has corporeality. Rather, it speaks this way to enable us to understand the concepts being conveyed.

קריאת התורה	**236** / שחרית לחול

Lo al enosh rochitzno,	לָא עַל אֱנָשׁ רָחִיצְנָא,

Not in any man do I put trust,

v'lo al bar elohin somichno,	וְלָא עַל בַּר אֱלָהִין סָמִיכְנָא,

nor on any angel do I rely —

elo be-Eloho dishma-yo,	אֶלָּא בֶּאֱלָהָא דִשְׁמַיָּא,

only on the God of heaven,

d'hu Eloho k'shōt,	דְּהוּא אֱלָהָא קְשׁוֹט,

Who is the God of truth,

v'ōraisayh k'shōt,	וְאוֹרַיְתֵהּ קְשׁוֹט,
unvi-ōhi k'shōt,	וּנְבִיאוֹהִי קְשׁוֹט,

Whose Torah is true, and whose prophets are true,

u-masgay l'mebad tav-von ukshōt.	וּמַסְגֵּא לְמֶעְבַּד טַבְוָן וּקְשׁוֹט.

and Who acts liberally with kindness and truth.

Bayh ano rochitz,	בֵּהּ אֲנָא רָחִיץ,

In Him do I trust,

v'lishmayh kadisho yakiro	וְלִשְׁמֵהּ קַדִּישָׁא יַקִּירָא
ano aymar tushb'chon.	אֲנָא אֵמַר תֻּשְׁבְּחָן.

and to His glorious and holy Name do I declare praises.

Y'hay ra-avo kodomoch,	יְהֵא רַעֲוָא קֳדָמָךְ,

May it be Your will

d'siftach libo-i b'ōraiso,	דְּתִפְתַּח לִבָּאִי בְּאוֹרַיְתָא,

that You open my heart to the Torah,

v'sashlim mish-alin d'libo-i,	וְתַשְׁלִים מִשְׁאֲלִין דְּלִבָּאִי,

and that You fulfill the wishes of my heart

v'libo d'chol amoch yisro-ayl,	וְלִבָּא דְכָל עַמָּךְ יִשְׂרָאֵל,

and the heart of Your entire people Israel,

l'tav ulcha-yin v'lishlom. Omayn.	לְטַב וּלְחַיִּין וְלִשְׁלָם. אָמֵן.

for good, for life, and for peace. Amen.

THE TORAH SCROLL IS REMOVED FROM THE ARK AND PRESENTED TO THE *CHAZZAN*, WHO ACCEPTS IT IN HIS RIGHT ARM. THE *CHAZZAN* TURNS TO THE ARK, BOWS WHILE RAISING THE TORAH, AND RECITES:

Gad'lu Ladōnoy iti	גַּדְּלוּ לַיהוה אִתִּי

Declare the greatness of HASHEM *with me,*

unrōm'mo sh'mō yachdov.	וּנְרוֹמְמָה שְׁמוֹ יַחְדָּו.

and let us exalt His Name together.

THE *CHAZZAN* TURNS TO HIS RIGHT AND CARRIES THE TORAH TO THE *BIMAH*. THE TORAH IS KISSED AS IT IS CARRIED TO THE *BIMAH*. THE CONGREGATION RESPONDS:

L'CHO Adōnoy hag'dulo	**לְךָ** יהוה הַגְּדֻלָּה

Yours, HASHEM, *is the greatness,*

v'hag'vuro v'hatif-eres	וְהַגְּבוּרָה וְהַתִּפְאֶרֶת
v'hanaytzach v'hahōd,	וְהַנֵּצַח וְהַהוֹד,

the strength, the splendor, the triumph, and the glory;

ki chōl ba-shoma-yim u-vo-oretz,   כִּי כֹל בַּשָּׁמַיִם וּבָאָרֶץ,

even everything in heaven and earth;

l'cho Adōnoy hamamlocho   לְךָ יהוה הַמַּמְלָכָה

Yours, HASHEM, is the kingdom,

v'hamisnasay l'chōl l'rōsh.   וְהַמִּתְנַשֵּׂא לְכֹל לְרֹאשׁ.

and the sovereignty over every leader.

Rōm'mu Adōnoy Elōhaynu,   רוֹמְמוּ יהוה אֱלֹהֵינוּ,

Exalt HASHEM, our God,

v'hishta-chavu lahadōm raglov,	וְהִשְׁתַּחֲווּ לַהֲדֹם רַגְלָיו,
kodōsh hu.	קָדוֹשׁ הוּא.

and bow at His footstool; He is Holy!

Rōm'mu Adōnoy Elōhaynu,   רוֹמְמוּ יהוה אֱלֹהֵינוּ,

Exalt HASHEM, our God,

v'hishta-chavu l'har kodshō,   וְהִשְׁתַּחֲווּ לְהַר קָדְשׁוֹ,

and bow to His holy mountain;

ki kodōsh Adōnoy Elōhaynu.   כִּי קָדוֹשׁ יהוה אֱלֹהֵינוּ.

for holy is HASHEM, our God.

AV HORACHAMIM,   אַב הָרַחֲמִים,

hu y'rachaym am amusim,   הוּא יְרַחֵם עַם עֲמוּסִים,

May the Father of compassion have mercy on the people that is borne by Him,

v'yizkōr b'ris aysonim,   וְיִזְכֹּר בְּרִית אֵיתָנִים,

and may He remember the covenant of the spiritually mighty.

v'yatzil nafshōsaynu	וְיַצִּיל נַפְשׁוֹתֵינוּ
min hasho-ōs horo-ōs,	מִן הַשָּׁעוֹת הָרָעוֹת,

May He rescue our souls from the bad times,

v'yig-ar b'yaytzer hora	וְיִגְעַר בְּיֵצֶר הָרָע
min han'su-im,	מִן הַנְּשׂוּאִים,

and upbraid the Evil Inclination to leave those borne by Him,

v'yochōn ōsonu liflaytas ōlomim,   וְיָחֹן אוֹתָנוּ לִפְלֵיטַת עוֹלָמִים,

graciously make us an eternal remnant,

vimalay mish-alōsaynu   וִימַלֵּא מִשְׁאֲלוֹתֵינוּ

and fulfill our requests

b'mido tōvo y'shu-o v'rachamim.   בְּמִדָּה טוֹבָה יְשׁוּעָה וְרַחֲמִים.

in good measure, for salvation and mercy.

THE TORAH IS PLACED ON THE *BIMAH* AND PREPARED FOR READING.
THE *GABBAI* USES THE FOLLOWING FORMULA TO CALL A *KOHEN* TO THE TORAH:

וְתִגָּלֶה וְתֵרָאֶה מַלְכוּתוֹ עָלֵינוּ בִּזְמַן קָרוֹב, וְיָחֹן פְּלֵיטָתֵנוּ וּפְלֵיטַת עַמּוֹ בֵּית יִשְׂרָאֵל לְחֵן וּלְחֶסֶד וּלְרַחֲמִים וּלְרָצוֹן. וְנֹאמַר אָמֵן. הַכֹּל הָבוּ גֹדֶל לֵאלֹהֵינוּ וּתְנוּ כָבוֹד לַתּוֹרָה. כֹּהֵן° קְרַב, יַעֲמֹד (NAME) בֶּן (FATHER'S NAME) הַכֹּהֵן.

——— °IF NO *KOHEN* IS PRESENT, THE *GABBAI* SAYS: ———

אֵין כַּאן כֹּהֵן, יַעֲמֹד (insert name) בֶּן (father's name) יִשְׂרָאֵל (לֵוִי) בִּמְקוֹם כֹּהֵן.

בָּרוּךְ שֶׁנָּתַן תּוֹרָה לְעַמּוֹ יִשְׂרָאֵל בִּקְדֻשָּׁתוֹ.

CONGREGATION, THEN *GABBAI*:

V'atem had'vaykim   וְאַתֶּם הַדְּבֵקִים
Badōnoy Elōhaychem,   בַּיהוה אֱלֹהֵיכֶם,
You who cling to HASHEM, your God,
cha-yim kul'chem ha-yōm.   חַיִּים כֻּלְּכֶם הַיּוֹם
you are all alive today.

❧ READING OF THE TORAH ❧

THE APPROPRIATE PORTIONS FOR THE READING MAY BE FOUND BEGINNING ON P. 565.

THE READER SHOWS THE *OLEH* (PERSON CALLED TO THE TORAH) THE PLACE IN THE TORAH. THE *OLEH* TOUCHES THE TORAH WITH A CORNER OF HIS *TALLIS*, OR THE BELT OR MANTLE OF THE TORAH, AND KISSES IT. HE THEN BEGINS THE BLESSING, BOWING AT Bor'chu AND STRAIGHTENING UP AT Adōnoy.

BOR'CHU es Adōnoy ham'vōroch.   בָּרְכוּ אֶת יהוה הַמְבֹרָךְ.
Bless HASHEM, the blessed One.

CONGREGATION, FOLLOWED BY *OLEH*, RESPONDS,
BOWING AT Boruch AND STRAIGHTENING UP AT Adōnoy.

Boruch Adōnoy ham'vōroch   בָּרוּךְ יהוה הַמְבֹרָךְ
l'ōlom vo-ed.   לְעוֹלָם וָעֶד.
Blessed is HASHEM, the blessed One, for all eternity.

OLEH CONTINUES:

BORUCH ato Adōnoy   בָּרוּךְ אַתָּה יהוה
Elōhaynu melech ho-ōlom,   אֱלֹהֵינוּ מֶלֶךְ הָעוֹלָם,
Blessed are You, HASHEM, our God, King of the universe,
asher bochar bonu mikol ho-amim   אֲשֶׁר בָּחַר בָּנוּ מִכָּל הָעַמִּים,
Who selected us from all the peoples
v'nosan lonu es tōrosō.   וְנָתַן לָנוּ אֶת תּוֹרָתוֹ.
and gave us His Torah.
Boruch ato Adōnoy, nōsayn hatōro.   בָּרוּךְ אַתָּה יהוה, נוֹתֵן הַתּוֹרָה.
Blessed are You, HASHEM, Giver of the Torah.
CONGREGATION RESPONDS: Omayn — אָמֵן.

239 / SHACHARIS FOR WEEKDAYS — TORAH READING

AFTER HIS TORAH PORTION HAS BEEN READ, THE OLEH RECITES:

BORUCH ato Adōnoy בָּרוּךְ אַתָּה יהוה
   Elōhaynu melech ho-ōlom, אֱלֹהֵינוּ מֶלֶךְ הָעוֹלָם,
*Blessed are You, H*ASHEM*, our God, King of the universe,*
asher nosan lonu tōras emes, אֲשֶׁר נָתַן לָנוּ תּוֹרַת אֱמֶת,
Who gave us the Torah of truth
v'cha-yay ōlom nota b'sōchaynu. וְחַיֵּי עוֹלָם נָטַע בְּתוֹכֵנוּ.
and implanted eternal life within us.
Boruch ato Adōnoy, nōsayn hatōro. בָּרוּךְ אַתָּה יהוה, נוֹתֵן הַתּוֹרָה.
*Blessed are You, H*ASHEM*, Giver of the Torah.*
CONGREGATION RESPONDS: Omayn — אָמֵן.

THANKSGIVING BLESSING*

THE FOLLOWING IS RECITED BY ONE WHO SURVIVED A DANGEROUS SITUATION:

BORUCH ato Adōnoy בָּרוּךְ אַתָּה יהוה
   Elōhaynu melech ho-ōlom, אֱלֹהֵינוּ מֶלֶךְ הָעוֹלָם,
*Blessed are You, H*ASHEM*, our God, King of the universe,*
hagōmayl l'cha-yovim tōvōs, הַגּוֹמֵל לְחַיָּבִים טוֹבוֹת,
Who bestows good things upon the guilty,
sheg'molani kol tōv. שֶׁגְּמָלַנִי כָּל טוֹב.
Who has bestowed every goodness upon me.

CONGREGATION RESPONDS:

Omayn. Mi sheg'mol'cho kol tōv, אָמֵן. מִי שֶׁגְּמָלְךָ כָּל טוֹב,
Amen. May He Who has bestowed goodness upon you
hu yigmol'cho kol tōv selo. הוּא יִגְמָלְךָ כָּל טוֹב, סֶלָה.
continue to bestow every goodness upon you, selah.

BAR MITZVAH BLESSING*

AFTER A BAR MITZVAH BOY COMPLETES HIS FIRST ALIYAH, HIS FATHER RECITES:

Boruch shep'torani בָּרוּךְ שֶׁפְּטָרַנִי
may-ōnshō shelo-ze. מֵעָנְשׁוֹ שֶׁלָּזֶה.
Blessed is the One Who has freed me from the punishment* due this boy.

•§ **Thanksgiving Blessing**

In Temple times, one who had been spared from a life-threatening situation would bring a thanksgiving-offering. Now, the obligation to thank God is discharged by reciting the thanksgiving blessing during the Torah reading, within three days of the event. The types of events that require the blessing are: (a) completion of a sea journey; (b) completion of a hazardous land journey; (c) recovery from a major illness; (d) release from captivity. By extension, however, the blessing should be recited whenever someone has been spared from a life-threatening situation.

•§ **Bar Mitzvah Blessing**

Since the calling to the Torah is symbolic of religious adulthood, the father recites the blessing after his son has completed his first *aliyah*.

שֶׁפְּטָרַנִי מֵעָנְשׁוֹ — *Who has freed me from the punishment.* There are two interpretations of the

PRAYER FOR A SICK PERSON

FOR A MAN

מִי שֶׁבֵּרַךְ אֲבוֹתֵינוּ אַבְרָהָם יִצְחָק וְיַעֲקֹב, מֹשֶׁה אַהֲרֹן דָּוִד וּשְׁלֹמֹה, הוּא יְבָרֵךְ וִירַפֵּא אֶת הַחוֹלֶה (PATIENT'S NAME) בֶּן (PATIENT'S MOTHER'S NAME) בַּעֲבוּר שֶׁ (SUPPLICANT'S NAME) יִתֵּן לִצְדָקָה בַּעֲבוּרוֹ.° בִּשְׂכַר זֶה, הַקָּדוֹשׁ בָּרוּךְ הוּא יִמָּלֵא רַחֲמִים עָלָיו, לְהַחֲלִימוֹ וּלְרַפֹּאתוֹ וּלְהַחֲזִיקוֹ וּלְהַחֲיוֹתוֹ, וְיִשְׁלַח לוֹ מְהֵרָה רְפוּאָה שְׁלֵמָה מִן הַשָּׁמַיִם, לִרְמַ״ח אֵבָרָיו, וּשְׁסָ״ה גִּידָיו, בְּתוֹךְ שְׁאָר חוֹלֵי יִשְׂרָאֵל, רְפוּאַת הַנֶּפֶשׁ וּרְפוּאַת הַגּוּף הַשְׁתָּא, בַּעֲגָלָא וּבִזְמַן קָרִיב. וְנֹאמַר. אָמֵן.   CONGREGATION RESPONDS: Omayn — אָמֵן.

FOR A WOMAN

מִי שֶׁבֵּרַךְ אֲבוֹתֵינוּ אַבְרָהָם יִצְחָק וְיַעֲקֹב, מֹשֶׁה אַהֲרֹן דָּוִד וּשְׁלֹמֹה, הוּא יְבָרֵךְ וִירַפֵּא אֶת הַחוֹלָה (PATIENT'S NAME) בַּת (PATIENT'S MOTHER'S NAME) בַּעֲבוּר שֶׁ (SUPPLICANT'S NAME) יִתֵּן לִצְדָקָה בַּעֲבוּרָהּ.° בִּשְׂכַר זֶה, הַקָּדוֹשׁ בָּרוּךְ הוּא יִמָּלֵא רַחֲמִים עָלֶיהָ, לְהַחֲלִימָהּ וּלְרַפֹּאתָהּ וּלְהַחֲזִיקָהּ וּלְהַחֲיוֹתָהּ, וְיִשְׁלַח לָהּ מְהֵרָה רְפוּאָה שְׁלֵמָה מִן הַשָּׁמַיִם, לְכָל אֵבָרֶיהָ, וּלְכָל גִּידֶיהָ, בְּתוֹךְ שְׁאָר חוֹלֵי יִשְׂרָאֵל, רְפוּאַת הַנֶּפֶשׁ וּרְפוּאַת הַגּוּף, הַשְׁתָּא, בַּעֲגָלָא וּבִזְמַן קָרִיב. וְנֹאמַר. אָמֵן.   CONGREGATION RESPONDS: Omayn — אָמֵן.

° SOME SUBSTITUTE — בַּעֲבוּר שֶׁכָּל הַקָּהָל מִתְפַּלְּלִים בַּעֲבוּרוֹ (בַּעֲבוּרָהּ)

IN MANY CONGREGATIONS THE *GABBAI* RECITES THE FOLLOWING IN MEMORY OF THE DECEASED, EITHER ON OR PRIOR TO THE DAY OF A *YAHRZEIT*.

FOR A MAN

אֵל מָלֵא רַחֲמִים, שׁוֹכֵן בַּמְּרוֹמִים, הַמְצֵא מְנוּחָה נְכוֹנָה עַל כַּנְפֵי הַשְּׁכִינָה, בְּמַעֲלוֹת קְדוֹשִׁים וּטְהוֹרִים כְּזֹהַר הָרָקִיעַ מַזְהִירִים, אֶת נִשְׁמַת (NAME OF THE DECEASED) שֶׁהָלַךְ לְעוֹלָמוֹ, בַּעֲבוּר שֶׁבְּלִי נֶדֶר אֶתֵּן צְדָקָה בְּעַד הַזְכָּרַת נִשְׁמָתוֹ, בְּגַן עֵדֶן תְּהֵא מְנוּחָתוֹ, לָכֵן בַּעַל הָרַחֲמִים יַסְתִּירֵהוּ בְּסֵתֶר כְּנָפָיו לְעוֹלָמִים, וְיִצְרוֹר בִּצְרוֹר הַחַיִּים אֶת נִשְׁמָתוֹ, יהוה הוּא נַחֲלָתוֹ, וְיָנוּחַ בְּשָׁלוֹם עַל מִשְׁכָּבוֹ. וְנֹאמַר: אָמֵן.   CONGREGATION: Omayn — אָמֵן.

FOR A WOMAN

אֵל מָלֵא רַחֲמִים, שׁוֹכֵן בַּמְּרוֹמִים, הַמְצֵא מְנוּחָה נְכוֹנָה עַל כַּנְפֵי הַשְּׁכִינָה, בְּמַעֲלוֹת קְדוֹשִׁים וּטְהוֹרִים כְּזֹהַר הָרָקִיעַ מַזְהִירִים, אֶת נִשְׁמַת (NAME OF THE DECEASED) שֶׁהָלְכָה לְעוֹלָמָהּ, בַּעֲבוּר שֶׁבְּלִי נֶדֶר אֶתֵּן צְדָקָה בְּעַד הַזְכָּרַת נִשְׁמָתָהּ, בְּגַן עֵדֶן תְּהֵא מְנוּחָתָהּ, לָכֵן בַּעַל הָרַחֲמִים יַסְתִּירֶהָ בְּסֵתֶר כְּנָפָיו לְעוֹלָמִים, וְיִצְרוֹר בִּצְרוֹר הַחַיִּים אֶת נִשְׁמָתָהּ, יהוה הוּא נַחֲלָתָהּ, וְתָנוּחַ בְּשָׁלוֹם עַל מִשְׁכָּבָהּ. וְנֹאמַר: אָמֵן.   CONGREGATION: Omayn — אָמֵן.

word "punishment": (a) Until the *bar mitzvah*, the father was responsible for his child's behavior and could be punished if it was deficient; or, (b) until the *bar mitzvah*, the child could have suffered for the failures of his parents. According to the second interpretation, the father is grateful that his own sins will no longer harm his child.

WHEN THE TORAH READING HAS BEEN COMPLETED THE READER RECITES HALF-*KADDISH*.
(Congregational responses are indicated by parentheses.)

יִתְגַּדַּל וְיִתְקַדַּשׁ שְׁמֵהּ רַבָּא. (אָמֵן –Omayn). בְּעָלְמָא דִּי בְרָא כִרְעוּתֵהּ. וְיַמְלִיךְ מַלְכוּתֵהּ, בְּחַיֵּיכוֹן וּבְיוֹמֵיכוֹן וּבְחַיֵּי דְכָל בֵּית יִשְׂרָאֵל, בַּעֲגָלָא וּבִזְמַן קָרִיב. וְאִמְרוּ: אָמֵן.

(אָמֵן. יְהֵא שְׁמֵהּ רַבָּא מְבָרַךְ לְעָלַם וּלְעָלְמֵי עָלְמַיָּא.)

(Omayn. Y'hay sh'mayh rabo m'vorach l'olam ul-ol'may ol'ma-yo.)

יְהֵא שְׁמֵהּ רַבָּא מְבָרַךְ לְעָלַם וּלְעָלְמֵי עָלְמַיָּא. יִתְבָּרַךְ וְיִשְׁתַּבַּח וְיִתְפָּאַר וְיִתְרוֹמַם וְיִתְנַשֵּׂא וְיִתְהַדָּר וְיִתְעַלֶּה וְיִתְהַלָּל שְׁמֵהּ דְּקֻדְשָׁא בְּרִיךְ הוּא (בְּרִיךְ הוּא – B'rich hu). °לְעֵלָּא מִן כָּל [לְעֵלָּא לְעֵלָּא מִכָּל° – from Rosh Hashanah to Yom Kippur substitute] בִּרְכָתָא וְשִׁירָתָא תֻּשְׁבְּחָתָא וְנֶחֱמָתָא, דַּאֲמִירָן בְּעָלְמָא. וְאִמְרוּ: אָמֵן. (אָמֵן –Omayn).

HAGBAHAH AND GELILAH / RAISING THE TORAH

THE TORAH IS RAISED FOR ALL TO SEE. EACH PERSON LOOKS AT THE TORAH AND RECITES ALOUD:

V'ZŌS hatōro asher som mōshe   וְזֹאת הַתּוֹרָה אֲשֶׁר שָׂם מֹשֶׁה
lifnay b'nay yisro-ayl   לִפְנֵי בְּנֵי יִשְׂרָאֵל,

This is the Torah* that Moses placed before the Children of Israel,

al pi Adōnoy b'yad mōshe.   עַל פִּי יהוה בְּיַד מֹשֶׁה.

upon the command of HASHEM, through Moses' hand.

ON MONDAY AND THURSDAY, THE *CHAZZAN* RECITES THE FOLLOWING PRAYER.
IT IS OMITTED ON DAYS WHEN *TACHANUN* IS NOT RECITED.

Y'HI ROTZŌN milifnay   יְהִי רָצוֹן מִלְּפְנֵי
ovinu sheba-shoma-yim   אָבִינוּ שֶׁבַּשָּׁמַיִם,

May it be the will* of our Father Who is in heaven

l'chōnayn es bays cha-yaynu,   לְכוֹנֵן אֶת בֵּית חַיֵּינוּ,

to establish the House of our lives

ulhoshiv es sh'chinosō b'sōchaynu,   וּלְהָשִׁיב אֶת שְׁכִינָתוֹ בְּתוֹכֵנוּ,
bimhayro v'yomaynu,   בִּמְהֵרָה בְיָמֵינוּ,

and to settle His Presence within us, speedily in our days —

v'nōmar: Omayn.   וְנֹאמַר: אָמֵן.

and let us say: Amen.

וְזֹאת הַתּוֹרָה — *This is the Torah*. As the congregation looks at the words and columns of the unrolled, upheld Torah Scroll, it declares the cardinal tenet of faith that the Torah we now have is the same one that God transmitted to Moses.

יְהִי רָצוֹן — *May it be the will*. This very ancient series of prayers dates from the days of Rav Amram Gaon (9th century), whose *siddur* prescribed that it be recited after the Torah reading on Monday and Thursday. Apparently, the merit of communal Torah makes the time most fitting to beseech God for the fulfillment of His people's yearnings.

Y'HI ROTZŌN milifnay ovinu sheba-shoma-yim	יְהִי רָצוֹן מִלְּפָנֶי אָבִינוּ שֶׁבַּשָּׁמַיִם,

May it be the will of our Father Who is in heaven

l'rachaym olaynu v'al p'laytosaynu,   לְרַחֵם עָלֵינוּ וְעַל פְּלֵיטָתֵנוּ,

to have mercy upon us and upon our remnant

v'limnō-a mashchis   וְלִמְנֹעַ מַשְׁחִית
umagayfo mayolaynu,   וּמַגֵּפָה מֵעָלֵינוּ,

and to keep destruction and plague away from us

umayal kol amō bays yisro-ayl,   וּמֵעַל כָּל עַמּוֹ בֵּית יִשְׂרָאֵל.

and from all His people the Family of Israel —

v'nōmar: Omayn.   וְנֹאמַר: אָמֵן.

and let us say: Amen.

Y'HI ROTZŌN milifnay   יְהִי רָצוֹן מִלְּפָנֶי
ovinu sheba-shoma-yim   אָבִינוּ שֶׁבַּשָּׁמַיִם,

May it be the will of our Father Who is in heaven

l'ka-yem bonu chachmay yisro-ayl,   לְקַיֵּם בָּנוּ חַכְמֵי יִשְׂרָאֵל,

to preserve among us the sages of Israel,

haym un'shayhem   הֵם וּנְשֵׁיהֶם
uvnayhem uvnōsayhem,   וּבְנֵיהֶם וּבְנוֹתֵיהֶם

them, their wives, their sons, their daughters,

v'salmidayhem   וְתַלְמִידֵיהֶם
v'salmiday salmidayhem,   וְתַלְמִידֵי תַלְמִידֵיהֶם,

their disciples and the students of their disciples

b'chol m'kōmōs mōsh'vōsayhem,   בְּכָל מְקוֹמוֹת מוֹשְׁבוֹתֵיהֶם.

in all their dwelling places —

v'nōmar omayn.   וְנֹאמַר: אָמֵן.

and let us say: Amen.

Y'HI ROTZŌN milifnay   יְהִי רָצוֹן מִלְּפָנֶי
ovinu shebashoma-yim   אָבִינוּ שֶׁבַּשָּׁמַיִם,

May it be the will of our Father Who is in heaven

shenishma v'nisbasayr   שֶׁנִּשְׁמַע וְנִתְבַּשֵּׂר

that we may hear and be informed of

b'sōrōs tōvōs   בְּשׂוֹרוֹת טוֹבוֹת,
y'shu-ōs v'nechomōs,   יְשׁוּעוֹת וְנֶחָמוֹת,

good tidings, salvations, and consolations,

vikabaytz nidochaynu   וִיקַבֵּץ נִדָּחֵינוּ

and that our dispersed be gathered

may-arba kanfōs ho-oretz,   מֵאַרְבַּע כַּנְפוֹת הָאָרֶץ.
from the four corners of the earth —

v'nōmar: Omayn.   וְנֹאמַר: אָמֵן.
and let us say: Amen.

THE ENTIRE CONGREGATION, FOLLOWED BY THE CHAZZAN, RECITES ALOUD:

ACHAYNU kol bays yisro-ayl,   **אַחֵינוּ** כָּל בֵּית יִשְׂרָאֵל,
Our brothers, the entire family of Israel,

han'sunim b'tzoro uv-shivyo,   הַנְּתוּנִים בְּצָרָה וּבְשִׁבְיָה,
who are delivered into distress and captivity,

ho-ōm'dim bayn ba-yom
    u-vayn ba-yabosho,   הָעוֹמְדִים בֵּין בַּיָּם וּבֵין בַּיַּבָּשָׁה,
whether they are on sea or dry land —

hamokōm y'rachaym alayhem,   הַמָּקוֹם יְרַחֵם עֲלֵיהֶם,
may the Omnipresent One have mercy on them

v'yōtzi-aym mitzoro lirvocho,   וְיוֹצִיאֵם מִצָּרָה לִרְוָחָה,
and remove them from distress to relief,

u-may-afaylo l'ōro,
    u-mishibud ligulo,   וּמֵאֲפֵלָה לְאוֹרָה, וּמִשִּׁעְבּוּד לִגְאֻלָּה,
from darkness to light, from subjugation to redemption,

hashto ba-agolo u-vizman koriv,   הַשְׁתָּא בַּעֲגָלָא וּבִזְמַן קָרִיב.
now, speedily, and soon —

v'nōmar: Omayn.   וְנֹאמַר: אָמֵן.
and let us say: Amen.

RETURNING THE TORAH

THE CHAZZAN TAKES THE TORAH IN HIS RIGHT ARM AND RECITES:

Y'HAL'LU es shaym Adōnoy,   **יְהַלְלוּ** אֶת שֵׁם יהוה,
Let them praise the Name of HASHEM,

ki nisgov sh'mō l'vadō —   כִּי נִשְׂגָּב שְׁמוֹ לְבַדּוֹ —
for His Name alone will have been exalted —

CONGREGATION RESPONDS:

— hōdō al eretz v'shomoyim   — הוֹדוֹ עַל אֶרֶץ וְשָׁמָיִם.
— His glory is above earth and heaven.

Va-yorem keren l'amō,   וַיָּרֶם קֶרֶן לְעַמּוֹ,
And He will have exalted the pride of His people,

t'hilo l'chol chasidov,   תְּהִלָּה לְכָל חֲסִידָיו,
causing praise for all His devout ones,

livnay yisro-ayl am k'rōvō, hal'luyoh.   לִבְנֵי יִשְׂרָאֵל עַם קְרֹבוֹ, הַלְלוּיָהּ.
for the Children of Israel, His intimate people. Praise God!

As the Torah is carried to the Ark the following psalm is recited.

L'DOVID MIZMÔR, לְדָוִד מִזְמוֹר,
Of David a psalm:

Ladōnoy ho-oretz umlō-oh, לַיהוה הָאָרֶץ וּמְלוֹאָהּ,
    tayvayl v'yōsh'vay voh. תֵּבֵל וְיֹשְׁבֵי בָהּ.
Hashem's is the earth and its fullness, the inhabited land and those who dwell in it.

Ki hu al yamim y'sodoh, כִּי הוּא עַל יַמִּים יְסָדָהּ,
    v'al n'horōs y'chōn'neho. וְעַל נְהָרוֹת יְכוֹנְנֶהָ.
For He founded it upon seas, and established it upon rivers.

Mi ya-ale v'har Adōnoy, מִי יַעֲלֶה בְהַר יהוה,
Who may ascend the mountain of Hashem,

u-mi yokum bimkōm kodshō. וּמִי יָקוּם בִּמְקוֹם קָדְשׁוֹ.
and who may stand in the place of His sanctity?

N'ki chapa-yim u-var layvov, נְקִי כַפַּיִם וּבַר לֵבָב,
One with clean hands and pure heart,

asher lō noso lashov nafshi אֲשֶׁר לֹא נָשָׂא לַשָּׁוְא נַפְשִׁי
    v'lō nishba l'mirmo. וְלֹא נִשְׁבַּע לְמִרְמָה.
who has not sworn in vain by My soul and has not sworn deceitfully.

Yiso v'rocho may-ays Adōnoy, יִשָּׂא בְרָכָה מֵאֵת יהוה,
He will receive a blessing from Hashem

utzdoko may-Elōhay yish-ō. וּצְדָקָה מֵאֱלֹהֵי יִשְׁעוֹ.
and just kindness from the God of his salvation.

Ze dōr dōr'shov, זֶה דּוֹר דֹּרְשָׁיו,
This is the generation of those who seek Him,

m'vakshay fonecho, ya-akōv, selo. מְבַקְשֵׁי פָנֶיךָ, יַעֲקֹב, סֶלָה.
those who strive for Your Presence — Jacob, Selah.

S'u sh'orim ro-shaychem, שְׂאוּ שְׁעָרִים רָאשֵׁיכֶם,
    v'hinos'u pischay ōlom, וְהִנָּשְׂאוּ פִּתְחֵי עוֹלָם,
Raise up your heads, O gates, and be uplifted, you everlasting entrances,

v'yovō melech hakovōd. וְיָבוֹא מֶלֶךְ הַכָּבוֹד.
so that the King of Glory may enter.

Mi ze melech hakovōd, מִי זֶה מֶלֶךְ הַכָּבוֹד,
Who is this King of Glory? —

Adōnoy izuz v'gibōr, יהוה עִזּוּז וְגִבּוֹר,
    Adōnoy gibōr milchomo. יהוה גִּבּוֹר מִלְחָמָה.
Hashem, the mighty and strong, Hashem, the strong in battle.

S'u sh'orim ro-shaychem,	שְׂאוּ שְׁעָרִים רָאשֵׁיכֶם,
us-u pischay ōlom,	וּשְׂאוּ פִּתְחֵי עוֹלָם,

Raise up your heads, O gates, and raise up, you everlasting entrances,

v'yovō melech hakovōd.	וְיָבֹא מֶלֶךְ הַכָּבוֹד.

so that the King of Glory may enter.

Mi hu ze melech hakovōd,	מִי הוּא זֶה מֶלֶךְ הַכָּבוֹד,

Who then is the King of Glory?

Adōnoy Tz'vo-ōs	יהוה צְבָאוֹת
hu melech hakovōd, selo.	הוּא מֶלֶךְ הַכָּבוֹד, סֶלָה.

HASHEM, Master of Legions, He is the King of Glory. Selah!

AS THE TORAH IS PLACED INTO THE ARK, THE FOLLOWING VERSES ARE RECITED:

UVNUCHŌ yōmar,	**וּבְנֻחֹה** יֹאמַר,

And when it rested he would say,

shuvo Adōnoy	שׁוּבָה יהוה
riv'vōs alfay yisro-ayl.	רִבְבוֹת אַלְפֵי יִשְׂרָאֵל.

"Reside tranquilly, O HASHEM, among the myriad thousands of Israel."

Kumo Adōnoy limnuchosecho,	קוּמָה יהוה לִמְנוּחָתֶךָ,
ato va-arōn u-zecho.	אַתָּה וַאֲרוֹן עֻזֶּךָ.

Arise, HASHEM, to Your resting place, You and the Ark of Your strength.

Kōhanecho yilb'shu tzedek,	כֹּהֲנֶיךָ יִלְבְּשׁוּ צֶדֶק,
vachasidecho y'ranaynu.	וַחֲסִידֶיךָ יְרַנֵּנוּ.

Let Your priests be clothed in righteousness, and Your devout ones will sing joyously.

Ba-avur dovid avdecho,	בַּעֲבוּר דָּוִד עַבְדֶּךָ,
al toshayv p'nay m'shichecho.	אַל תָּשֵׁב פְּנֵי מְשִׁיחֶךָ.

For the sake of David, Your servant, turn not away the face of Your anointed.

Ki lekach tōv nosati lochem,	כִּי לֶקַח טוֹב נָתַתִּי לָכֶם,
tōrosi al ta-azōvu.	תּוֹרָתִי אַל תַּעֲזֹבוּ.

For I have given you a good teaching, do not forsake My Torah.

❖ Aytz cha-yim hi lamachazikim boh,	❖ עֵץ חַיִּים הִיא לַמַּחֲזִיקִים בָּהּ,
v'sōm'cheho m'u-shor.	וְתֹמְכֶיהָ מְאֻשָּׁר.

It is a tree of life for those who grasp it, and its supporters are praiseworthy.

D'rocheho darchay nō-am,	דְּרָכֶיהָ דַרְכֵי נֹעַם,
v'chol n'sivōseho sholōm.	וְכָל נְתִיבוֹתֶיהָ שָׁלוֹם.

Its ways are ways of pleasantness and all its paths are peace.

Hashivaynu Adōnoy aylecho v'noshuvo,	הֲשִׁיבֵנוּ יהוה אֵלֶיךָ וְנָשׁוּבָה,
chadaysh yomaynu k'kedem.	חַדֵּשׁ יָמֵינוּ כְּקֶדֶם.

Bring us back to You, HASHEM, and we shall return, renew our days as of old.

ASHREI — UVA LETZION
THE CONCLUDING SECTION OF SHACHARIS IS RECITED EVERY DAY.

■ The alphabetic acrostic of *Ashrei* motivates the supplicant to praise God, His Kingship, and His providing the needs of every living creature. The Sages highlight the importance of *Ashrei* by declaring that whoever recites this psalm three times daily is directing himself towards meriting a place in the World to Come (*Berachos* 4b).

ASHRAY yōsh'vay vay-secho, אַשְׁרֵי יוֹשְׁבֵי בֵיתֶךָ,
Praiseworthy are those who dwell in Your house;

ōd y'hal'lucho selo. עוֹד יְהַלְלוּךָ סֶּלָה.
may they always praise You, Selah!

Ashray ho-om shekocho lō, אַשְׁרֵי הָעָם שֶׁכָּכָה לּוֹ,
Praiseworthy is the people for whom this is so,

ashray ho-om she-Adōnoy Elōhov. אַשְׁרֵי הָעָם שֱׁיהוה אֱלֹהָיו.
praiseworthy is the people whose God is HASHEM.

T'hilo l'dovid, תְּהִלָּה לְדָוִד,
A psalm of praise by David:

arōmimcho Elōhai hamelech, אֲרוֹמִמְךָ אֱלוֹהַי הַמֶּלֶךְ,
I will exalt You, my God the King,

va-avor'cho shimcho l'ōlom vo-ed. וַאֲבָרְכָה שִׁמְךָ לְעוֹלָם וָעֶד.
and I will bless Your Name forever and ever.

B'chol yōm avor'cheko, בְּכָל יוֹם אֲבָרְכֶךָּ,
Every day I will bless You,

va-ahal'lo shimcho l'ōlom vo-ed. וַאֲהַלְלָה שִׁמְךָ לְעוֹלָם וָעֶד.
and I will laud Your Name forever and ever.

Godōl Adōnoy umhulol m'ōd, גָּדוֹל יהוה וּמְהֻלָּל מְאֹד,
HASHEM *is great and exceedingly lauded,*

v'ligdulosō ayn chayker. וְלִגְדֻלָּתוֹ אֵין חֵקֶר.
and His greatness is beyond investigation.

Dōr l'dōr y'shabach ma-asecho, דּוֹר לְדוֹר יְשַׁבַּח מַעֲשֶׂיךָ,
Each generation will praise Your deeds to the next,

ugvurōsecho yagidu. וּגְבוּרֹתֶיךָ יַגִּידוּ.
and of Your mighty deeds they will tell.

Hadar k'vōd hōdecho, הֲדַר כְּבוֹד הוֹדֶךָ,
The splendrous glory of Your power

v'divray nifl'ōsecho osicho. וְדִבְרֵי נִפְלְאֹתֶיךָ אָשִׂיחָה.
and Your wondrous deeds I shall discuss.

Ve-ezuz nōr'ōsecho yōmayru, וֶעֱזוּז נוֹרְאוֹתֶיךָ יֹאמֵרוּ,
And of Your awesome power they will speak,

ugdulos'cho asap'reno.	וּגְדוּלָתְךָ אֲסַפְּרֶנָּה.

and Your greatness I shall relate.

Zecher rav tuv'cho yabi-u,	זֵכֶר רַב טוּבְךָ יַבִּיעוּ,

A recollection of Your abundant goodness they will utter

v'tzidkos'cho y'ranaynu.	וְצִדְקָתְךָ יְרַנֵּנוּ.

and of Your righteousness they will sing exultantly.

Chanun v'rachum Adōnoy,	חַנּוּן וְרַחוּם יהוה,

Gracious and merciful is HASHEM,

erech apa-yim ugdol chosed.	אֶרֶךְ אַפַּיִם וּגְדָל חָסֶד.

slow to anger, and great in [bestowing] kindness.

Tōv Adōnoy lakōl,	טוֹב יהוה לַכֹּל,

HASHEM is good to all,

v'rachamov al kol ma-asov.	וְרַחֲמָיו עַל כָּל מַעֲשָׂיו.

and His mercies are on all His works.

Yōducho Adōnoy kol ma-asecho,	יוֹדוּךָ יהוה כָּל מַעֲשֶׂיךָ,

All Your works shall thank You, HASHEM,

vachasidecho y'vor'chucho.	וַחֲסִידֶיךָ יְבָרְכוּכָה.

and Your devout ones will bless You.

K'vōd malchus'cho yōmayru,	כְּבוֹד מַלְכוּתְךָ יֹאמֵרוּ,
ugvuros'cho y'dabayru.	וּגְבוּרָתְךָ יְדַבֵּרוּ.

Of the glory of Your kingdom they will speak, and of Your power they will tell,

L'hōdi-a livnay ho-odom g'vurōsov,	לְהוֹדִיעַ לִבְנֵי הָאָדָם גְּבוּרֹתָיו,

to inform human beings of His mighty deeds,

uchvōd hadar malchusō.	וּכְבוֹד הֲדַר מַלְכוּתוֹ.

and the glorious splendor of His kingdom.

Malchus'cho malchus kol ōlomim,	מַלְכוּתְךָ מַלְכוּת כָּל עֹלָמִים,

Your kingdom is a kingdom spanning all eternities,

u-memshalt'cho b'chol dōr vodōr.	וּמֶמְשַׁלְתְּךָ בְּכָל דּוֹר וָדֹר.

and Your dominion is throughout every generation.

Sōmaych Adōnoy l'chol hanōf'lim,	סוֹמֵךְ יהוה לְכָל הַנֹּפְלִים,
v'zōkayf l'chol hak'fufim.	וְזוֹקֵף לְכָל הַכְּפוּפִים.

HASHEM supports all the fallen ones and straightens all the bent.

Aynay chōl aylecho y'sabayru,	עֵינֵי כֹל אֵלֶיךָ יְשַׂבֵּרוּ,

The eyes of all look to You with hope

v'ato nōsayn lohem	וְאַתָּה נוֹתֵן לָהֶם
es ochlom b'ito.	אֶת אָכְלָם בְּעִתּוֹ.

and You give them their food in its proper time.

CONCENTRATE INTENLY WHILE RECITING THE NEXT VERSE.

פּוֹתֵחַ אֶת יָדֶךָ, וּמַשְׂבִּיעַ לְכָל חַי רָצוֹן.
Pōsay-ach es yodecho, u-masbi-a l'chol chai rotzōn.
You open Your hand, and satisfy the desire of every living thing.

צַדִּיק יהוה בְּכָל דְּרָכָיו,
Tzadik Adōnoy b'chol d'rochov,
Righteous is HASHEM *in all His ways*

וְחָסִיד בְּכָל מַעֲשָׂיו.
v'chosid b'chol ma-asov.
and magnanimous in all His deeds.

קָרוֹב יהוה לְכָל קֹרְאָיו,
Korōv Adōnoy l'chol kōr'ov,
HASHEM *is close to all who call upon Him —*

לְכֹל אֲשֶׁר יִקְרָאֻהוּ בֶאֱמֶת.
l'chōl asher yikro-uhu ve-emes.
to all who call upon Him sincerely.

רְצוֹן יְרֵאָיו יַעֲשֶׂה,
R'tzōn y'ray-ov ya-ase,
The will of those who fear Him He will do,

וְאֶת שַׁוְעָתָם יִשְׁמַע וְיוֹשִׁיעֵם.
v'es shav-osom yishma v'yōshi-aym.
and their cry He will hear, and save them.

שׁוֹמֵר יהוה אֶת כָּל אֹהֲבָיו,
Shōmayr Adōnoy es kol ōhavov,
HASHEM *protects all who love Him,*

וְאֵת כָּל הָרְשָׁעִים יַשְׁמִיד.
v'ays kol hor'sho-im yashmid.
but all the wicked He will destroy.

❖ תְּהִלַּת יהוה יְדַבֶּר פִּי,
T'hilas Adōnoy y'daber pi,
May my mouth declare the praise of HASHEM

וִיבָרֵךְ כָּל בָּשָׂר שֵׁם קָדְשׁוֹ לְעוֹלָם וָעֶד.
vi-voraych kol bosor shaym kodshō l'ōlom vo-ed.
and may all flesh bless His Holy Name forever and ever.

וַאֲנַחְנוּ נְבָרֵךְ יָהּ, מֵעַתָּה וְעַד עוֹלָם, הַלְלוּיָהּ.
Va-anachnu n'voraych Yoh, may-ato v'ad ōlom, hal'luyoh.
We will bless God from this time and forever. Praise God!

THE FOLLOWING PSALM IS RECITED EACH WEEKDAY MORNING EXCEPT: ROSH CHODESH, EREV PESACH, CHOL HAMOED, TISHAH B'AV, EREV YOM KIPPUR, CHANUKAH, PURIM AND SHUSHAN PURIM, THE 14TH AND 15TH OF ADAR I (PURIM KATTAN), AND IN A HOUSE OF MOURNING.

■ We beseech Hashem in time of distress and express our faith in His being the true source of our salvation.

LAMNATZAYACH mizmōr l'dovid: לַמְנַצֵּחַ מִזְמוֹר לְדָוִד.
For the conductor; a psalm of David.

Ya-ancho Adōnoy b'yōm tzoro, יַעַנְךָ יהוה בְּיוֹם צָרָה,
May HASHEM *answer you on the day of distress,*

y'sagevcho shaym Elōhay ya-akōv.	יְשַׂגֶּבְךָ שֵׁם אֱלֹהֵי יַעֲקֹב.

may the Name of Jacob's God make you impregnable.

Yishlach ezr'cho mikōdesh,	יִשְׁלַח עֶזְרְךָ מִקֹּדֶשׁ,
u-mitziyōn yisodeko.	וּמִצִּיּוֹן יִסְעָדֶךָּ.

May He dispatch your help from the Sanctuary, and support you from Zion.

Yizkōr kol minchōsecho,	יִזְכֹּר כָּל מִנְחֹתֶיךָ,

May He remember all your offerings,

v'ōlos'cho y'dash'ne selo.	וְעוֹלָתְךָ יְדַשְּׁנֶה סֶלָה.

and consider your burnt sacrifices generous, Selah.

Yiten l'cho chilvovecho,	יִתֶּן לְךָ כִלְבָבֶךָ
v'chol atzos'cho y'malay.	וְכָל עֲצָתְךָ יְמַלֵּא.

May He grant you your heart's desire, and fulfill your every plan.

N'ran'no bi-shu-osecho,	נְרַנְּנָה בִּישׁוּעָתֶךָ,

May we sing for joy at your salvation,

uvshaym Elōhaynu nidgōl,	וּבְשֵׁם אֱלֹהֵינוּ נִדְגֹּל,

and raise our banner in the Name of our God;

y'malay Adōnoy kol mish-alōsecho.	יְמַלֵּא יהוה כָּל מִשְׁאֲלוֹתֶיךָ.

may HASHEM fulfill all your requests.

Ato yodati,	עַתָּה יָדַעְתִּי
ki hōshi-a Adōnoy m'shichō,	כִּי הוֹשִׁיעַ יהוה מְשִׁיחוֹ,

Now I know that HASHEM has saved His anointed one;

ya-anayhu mishmay kod'shō,	יַעֲנֵהוּ מִשְּׁמֵי קָדְשׁוֹ,

He will answer him from His sacred heaven,

bigvurōs yaysha y'minō.	בִּגְבוּרוֹת יֵשַׁע יְמִינוֹ.

with the omnipotent salvations of His right arm.

Ayle vorechev, v'ayle vasusim,	אֵלֶּה בָרֶכֶב, וְאֵלֶּה בַסּוּסִים,

Some with chariots, and some with horses,

va-anachnu	וַאֲנַחְנוּ
b'shaym Adōnoy Elōhaynu nazkir.	בְּשֵׁם יהוה אֱלֹהֵינוּ נַזְכִּיר.

but we — in the Name of HASHEM, our God — call out.

Haymo kor'u v'nofolu,	הֵמָּה כָּרְעוּ וְנָפָלוּ,
va-anachnu kamnu vanisōdod.	וַאֲנַחְנוּ קַמְנוּ וַנִּתְעוֹדָד.

They slumped and fell, but we arose and were invigorated.

Adōnoy hōshi-o	❖ יהוה הוֹשִׁיעָה,

HASHEM save!

hamelech ya-anaynu v'yōm kor-aynu.	הַמֶּלֶךְ יַעֲנֵנוּ בְיוֹם קָרְאֵנוּ.

May the King answer us on the day we call.

■ The recitation of "The Order of *Kedushah*," which follows, is one of the merits upon which the world continues to endure (*Sotah* 49a).

UVO L'TZIYŌN gō-ayl,   וּבָא לְצִיּוֹן גּוֹאֵל,
 "A redeemer shall come to Zion*
ulshovay fesha b'ya-akōv,   וּלְשָׁבֵי פֶשַׁע בְּיַעֲקֹב,
 and to those of Jacob who repent from willful sin,"
n'um Adōnoy.   נְאֻם יהוה.
 the words of HASHEM.
Va-ani, zōs b'risi ōsom,   וַאֲנִי, זֹאת בְּרִיתִי אוֹתָם,
 omar Adōnoy,   אָמַר יהוה,
 "And as for Me, this is My covenant* with them," said HASHEM,
ruchi asher olecho,   רוּחִי אֲשֶׁר עָלֶיךָ,
 "My spirit that is upon you
udvorai asher samti b'ficho,   וּדְבָרַי אֲשֶׁר שַׂמְתִּי בְּפִיךָ,
 and My words that I have placed in your mouth
lō yomushu mipicho   לֹא יָמוּשׁוּ מִפִּיךָ
 u-mipi zar-acho   וּמִפִּי זַרְעֲךָ
shall not be withdrawn from your mouth, nor from the mouth of your offspring,
u-mipi zera zar-acho,   וּמִפִּי זֶרַע זַרְעֲךָ,
 nor from the mouth of your offspring's offspring,"*
omar Adōnoy,   אָמַר יהוה,
 said HASHEM,
may-ato v'ad ōlom.   מֵעַתָּה וְעַד עוֹלָם.
 "from this moment and forever."

❖ V'ato kodōsh,   ❖ וְאַתָּה קָדוֹשׁ
 yōshayv t'hilōs yisro-ayl.   יוֹשֵׁב תְּהִלּוֹת יִשְׂרָאֵל.
 You are the Holy One, enthroned upon the praises of Israel.*

וּבָא לְצִיּוֹן גּוֹאֵל — *A redeemer shall come to Zion.* God pledges that Messiah will come to redeem the city Zion and the people of Israel. Not only those who remained righteous throughout the ordeal of exile will be saved, but even those who have strayed will rejoin the righteous in the glorious future, provided they return to the ways of God.

זֹאת בְּרִיתִי — *This is My covenant.* God affirms that His covenant with Israel will always remain in force: that His spirit [of prophecy] and His words [as written in His Torah] will remain with Israel forever.

מִפִּיךָ וּמִפִּי זַרְעֲךָ וּמִפִּי זֶרַע זַרְעֲךָ — *From your mouth, nor from the mouth of your offspring,* nor from the mouth of your offspring's offspring. Three generations are mentioned here. This is a Divine assurance that if a family produces three consecutive generations of profound Torah scholars, the blessing of Torah knowledge will not be withdrawn from its posterity (*Bava Metzia* 85a). In a broader sense, we see the fulfillment of this blessing in the miracle that Torah greatness has remained with Israel throughout centuries of exile and flight from country to country and from continent to continent.

יוֹשֵׁב תְּהִלּוֹת יִשְׂרָאֵל — *Enthroned upon the praises of Israel.* Although God is praised by myriad angels, He values the praises of Israel

V'koro ze el ze v'omar: וְקָרָא זֶה אֶל זֶה וְאָמַר:
And one [angel] will call another and say:

――――― THE ENTIRE CONGREGATION RECITES ALOUD AND IN UNISON ―――――

Kodōsh, kodōsh, kodōsh, קָדוֹשׁ, קָדוֹשׁ, קָדוֹשׁ,
   Adōnoy Tz'vo-ōs, יהוה צְבָאוֹת,
"Holy, holy, holy* is HASHEM, *Master of Legions,*
m'lō chol ho-oretz k'vōdō. מְלֹא כָל הָאָרֶץ כְּבוֹדוֹ.
the whole world is filled with His glory."

―――――

Umkab'lin dayn min dayn v'om'rin: וּמְקַבְּלִין דֵּין מִן דֵּין וְאָמְרִין:
And they receive permission from one another and say:
Kadish bish-may m'rōmo ilo-o קַדִּישׁ בִּשְׁמֵי מְרוֹמָא עִלָּאָה
   bays sh'chin'tayh; בֵּית שְׁכִינְתֵּהּ,
"Holy in the most exalted heaven, the abode of His Presence;
kadish al ar-o ōvad g'vurtayh; קַדִּישׁ עַל אַרְעָא עוֹבַד גְּבוּרְתֵּהּ,
holy on earth, product of His strength;
kadish l'olam ul-ol'may ol'ma-yo, קַדִּישׁ לְעָלַם וּלְעָלְמֵי עָלְמַיָּא,
   Adonoy Tz'vo-ōs, יהוה צְבָאוֹת,
holy forever and ever is HASHEM, *Master of Legions —*
malyo chol ar-o ziv y'korayh. מַלְיָא כָל אַרְעָא זִיו יְקָרֵהּ.
the entire world is filled with the radiance of His glory."
Vatiso-ayni ru-ach, וַתִּשָּׂאֵנִי רוּחַ,
And a wind lifted me;*
vo-eshma acharai kōl ra-ash godōl: וָאֶשְׁמַע אַחֲרַי קוֹל רַעַשׁ גָּדוֹל:
and I heard behind me the sound of a great noise:

――――― THE ENTIRE CONGREGATION RECITES ALOUD AND IN UNISON ―――――

Boruch k'vōd Adōnoy mim'kōmō. בָּרוּךְ כְּבוֹד יהוה מִמְּקוֹמוֹ.
"Blessed is the glory of HASHEM *from His place."*

―――――

Untolasni rucho, וּנְטָלַתְנִי רוּחָא,
And a wind lifted me;
v'shim-ays basrai kol zi-a sagi וְשִׁמְעֵת בַּתְרַי קָל זִיעַ סַגִּיא
and I heard behind me the sound of the powerful movement

---

above all; as the Talmud teaches (*Chullin* 90b), the angels are not permitted to sing their praises on High until the Jews sing theirs on earth.

קָדוֹשׁ — *Holy.* The song of the angels is discussed on page 165 above.

וַתִּשָּׂאֵנִי רוּחַ — *And a wind lifted me.* These words were uttered by the prophet Ezekiel, after he had been commanded to undertake a difficult mission on behalf of the exiled Jew. God sent a wind to lift him and transport him to Babylon, and as he was lifted, Ezekiel heard the song of the angels. This suggests that the person who ignores his own convenience in order to serve God can expect to climb spiritual heights beyond his normal capacity.

שחרית לחול / 252 — אשרי־ובא לציון

dimshab'chin v'om'rin:
of those who praised saying:
דִּמְשַׁבְּחִין וְאָמְרִין:

B'rich y'koro Dadōnoy
"*Blessed is the honor of* HASHEM
בְּרִיךְ יְקָרָא דַיהוה

may-asar bays sh'chintayh.
from the place of the abode of His Presence."
מֵאֲתַר בֵּית שְׁכִינְתֵּהּ.

――――― THE ENTIRE CONGREGATION RECITES ALOUD AND IN UNISON ―――――

Adōnoy yimlōch l'ōlom vo-ed.
HASHEM *shall reign for all eternity.*
יהוה יִמְלֹךְ לְעֹלָם וָעֶד.

―――

Adōnoy malchusayh ko-aym
l'olam ul-ol'may ol'ma-yo.
HASHEM — *His kingdom is established forever and ever.*
יהוה מַלְכוּתֵהּ קָאֵם
לְעָלַם וּלְעָלְמֵי עָלְמַיָּא.

Adōnoy Elōhay avrohom
yitzchok v'yisro-ayl avōsaynu,
HASHEM, *God of Abraham, Isaac, and Israel, our forefathers,*
יהוה אֱלֹהֵי אַבְרָהָם
יִצְחָק וְיִשְׂרָאֵל אֲבֹתֵינוּ,

shomro zōs l'ōlom,
may You preserve this forever
שָׁמְרָה זֹּאת לְעוֹלָם,

l'yaytzer machsh'vōs l'vav amecho,
as the realization of the thoughts in Your people's heart,
לְיֵצֶר מַחְשְׁבוֹת לְבַב עַמֶּךָ,

v'hochayn l'vovom aylecho.
and may You direct their heart to You.
וְהָכֵן לְבָבָם אֵלֶיךָ.

V'hu rachum,
y'chapayr ovōn v'lō yashchis,
He, the Merciful One, is forgiving of iniquity and does not destroy;
וְהוּא רַחוּם,
יְכַפֵּר עָוֹן וְלֹא יַשְׁחִית,

v'hirbo l'hoshiv apō,
v'lō yo-ir kol chamosō.
frequently He withdraws His anger, not arousing His entire rage.
וְהִרְבָּה לְהָשִׁיב אַפּוֹ,
וְלֹא יָעִיר כָּל חֲמָתוֹ.

Ki ato Adōnoy tōv v'saloch,
For You, my Lord, are good and forgiving,
כִּי אַתָּה אֲדֹנָי טוֹב וְסַלָּח,

v'rav chesed l'chol kōr'echo.
and abundantly kind to all who call upon You.
וְרַב חֶסֶד לְכָל קֹרְאֶיךָ.

Tzidkos'cho tzedek l'ōlom,
v'sōros'cho emes.
Your righteousness is righteous forever,* and Your Torah is truth.
צִדְקָתְךָ צֶדֶק לְעוֹלָם,
וְתוֹרָתְךָ אֱמֶת.

―――

צִדְקָתְךָ צֶדֶק לְעוֹלָם — *Your righteousness is righteous forever.* People question the ways of God because they do not see the righteous rewarded nor the wicked punished. But this question is a product of shortsightedness. God's justice is not measured in months or years. His reward

Titayn emes l'ya-akōv,	תִּתֵּן אֱמֶת לְיַעֲקֹב,
chesed l'avrohom,	חֶסֶד לְאַבְרָהָם,

Grant truth to Jacob, kindness to Abraham,

asher nishbato la-avōsaynu	אֲשֶׁר נִשְׁבַּעְתָּ לַאֲבֹתֵינוּ
mimay kedem.	מִימֵי קֶדֶם.

as You swore to our forefathers from ancient times.

Boruch Adōnoy	בָּרוּךְ אֲדֹנָי
yōm yōm ya-amos lonu,	יוֹם יוֹם יַעֲמָס לָנוּ,

Blessed is my Lord, for every single day He burdens us [with blessings],*

ho-Ayl y'shu-osaynu selo.	הָאֵל יְשׁוּעָתֵנוּ סֶלָה.

the God of our salvation, Selah.

Adōnoy Tz'vo-ōs i-monu,	יהוה צְבָאוֹת עִמָּנוּ,

Hashem, Master of Legions, is with us,

misgov lonu Elōhay ya-akōv selo.	מִשְׂגָּב לָנוּ אֱלֹהֵי יַעֲקֹב סֶלָה.

a stronghold for us is the God of Jacob, Selah.

Adōnoy Tz'vo-ōs,	יהוה צְבָאוֹת,
ashray odom bōtay-ach boch.	אַשְׁרֵי אָדָם בֹּטֵחַ בָּךְ.

Hashem, Master of Legions, praiseworthy is the man who trusts in You.

Adōnoy hōshi-o,	יהוה הוֹשִׁיעָה,

Hashem, save!

hamelech ya-anaynu v'yōm kor-aynu.	הַמֶּלֶךְ יַעֲנֵנוּ בְיוֹם קָרְאֵנוּ.

May the King answer us on the day we call.

Boruch hu Elōhaynu	בָּרוּךְ הוּא אֱלֹהֵינוּ
sheb'ro-onu lichvōdō,	שֶׁבְּרָאָנוּ לִכְבוֹדוֹ,

Blessed is He, our God, Who created us for His glory,

v'hivdilonu min hatō-im,	וְהִבְדִּילָנוּ מִן הַתּוֹעִים,

separated us from those who stray,

v'nosan lonu tōras emes,	וְנָתַן לָנוּ תּוֹרַת אֱמֶת,

gave us the Torah of truth

v'cha-yay ōlom nota b'sōchaynu.	וְחַיֵּי עוֹלָם נָטַע בְּתוֹכֵנוּ.

and implanted eternal life within us.

Hu yiftach libaynu b'sōroso	הוּא יִפְתַּח לִבֵּנוּ בְּתוֹרָתוֹ

May He open our heart* through His Torah

---

lasts forever, so it does not matter if it is delayed during the temporary stay of our souls in our earthly bodies.

יַעֲמָס לָנוּ — *He burdens us [with blessings].* God gives us the daily responsibility to perform countless commandments because He desires to load us with blessings.

הוּא יִפְתַּח לִבֵּנוּ — *May He open our heart.* This verse contains a major principle of the nature of Torah study. Though it is a rigorous and

v'yosaym b'libaynu ahavosō v'yir-osō,	וְיָשֵׂם בְּלִבֵּנוּ אַהֲבָתוֹ וְיִרְאָתוֹ
and imbue our heart with love and awe of Him	
v'la-asōs r'tzōnō ul-ovdō b'layvov sholaym,	וְלַעֲשׂוֹת רְצוֹנוֹ וּלְעָבְדוֹ בְּלֵבָב שָׁלֵם,
and that we may do His will and serve Him wholeheartedly,	
l'ma-an lō niga lorik,	לְמַעַן לֹא נִיגַע לָרִיק,
so that we do not struggle in vain	
v'lō naylayd labeholo.	וְלֹא נֵלֵד לַבֶּהָלָה.
nor produce for futility.	
Y'hi rotzōn mil'fonecho	יְהִי רָצוֹן מִלְּפָנֶיךָ
May it be Your will,	
Adōnoy Elōhaynu Vaylōhay avōsaynu,	יהוה אֱלֹהֵינוּ וֵאלֹהֵי אֲבוֹתֵינוּ,
Hᴀsʜᴇᴍ, *our God and the God of our forefathers,*	
shenishmōr chukecho bo-ōlom ha-ze,	שֶׁנִּשְׁמֹר חֻקֶּיךָ בָּעוֹלָם הַזֶּה,
that we observe Your decrees in this world,	
v'nizke v'nichye v'nir-e	וְנִזְכֶּה וְנִחְיֶה וְנִרְאֶה
and merit that we live and see	
v'nirash tōvo uvrocho	וְנִירַשׁ טוֹבָה וּבְרָכָה
and inherit goodness and blessing	
lishnay y'mōs hamoshi-ach,	לִשְׁנֵי יְמוֹת הַמָּשִׁיחַ
in the years of Messianic times	
ulcha-yay ho-ōlom habo.	וּלְחַיֵּי הָעוֹלָם הַבָּא.
and for the life of the World to Come.	
L'ma-an y'zamercho chovōd v'lō yidōm,	לְמַעַן יְזַמֶּרְךָ כָבוֹד וְלֹא יִדֹּם,
So that my soul might sing to You and not be stilled,	
Adōnoy Elōhai l'ōlom ōdeko.	יהוה אֱלֹהַי לְעוֹלָם אוֹדֶךָּ.
Hᴀsʜᴇᴍ, *my God, forever will I thank You.*	
Boruch hagever asher yivtach Badōnoy,	בָּרוּךְ הַגֶּבֶר אֲשֶׁר יִבְטַח בַּיהוה,
Blessed is the man who trusts in Hᴀsʜᴇᴍ,	

demanding intellectual pursuit, it cannot be mastered without pure motives, faith and love of God, and Divine help. If someone studies Torah only for the sake of the prestige it will give him to outwit less accomplished scholars, he will not succeed: His struggle for knowledge will be in vain. Or if someone has attained Torah knowledge in a commendable way, but later discards his faith, he will have lost the merit of his study — and his efforts will have proved to be futile.

v'ho-yo Adōnoy mivtachō. וְהָיָה יהוה מִבְטַחוֹ.
then H͟ASHEM *will be his security.*

Bitchu Vadōnoy aday ad, בִּטְחוּ בַיהוה עֲדֵי עַד,
Trust in H͟ASHEM *forever,*

ki b'Yoh Adōnoy tzur ōlomim. כִּי בְּיָהּ יהוה צוּר עוֹלָמִים.
for in God, H͟ASHEM, *is the strength of the worlds.*

❖ v'yivt'chu v'cho yōd'ay sh'mecho, ❖ וְיִבְטְחוּ בְךָ יוֹדְעֵי שְׁמֶךָ,
Those knowing Your Name will trust in You,

ki lō ozavto dōr'shecho Adōnoy. כִּי לֹא עָזַבְתָּ דֹּרְשֶׁיךָ, יהוה.
and You forsake not those Who seek You, H͟ASHEM.

Adōnoy chofaytz l'ma-an tzidkō, יהוה חָפֵץ לְמַעַן צִדְקוֹ,
H͟ASHEM *desired, for the sake of its [Israel's] righteousness,*

yagdil tōro v'yadir. יַגְדִּיל תּוֹרָה וְיַאְדִּיר.
that the Torah be made great and glorious.

THE *CHAZZAN* RECITES FULL *KADDISH*
(congregational responses are indicated by parentheses):

יִתְגַּדַּל וְיִתְקַדַּשׁ שְׁמֵהּ רַבָּא. (Omayn—אָמֵן). בְּעָלְמָא דִּי בְרָא כִרְעוּתֵהּ. וְיַמְלִיךְ מַלְכוּתֵהּ, בְּחַיֵּיכוֹן וּבְיוֹמֵיכוֹן וּבְחַיֵּי דְכָל בֵּית יִשְׂרָאֵל, בַּעֲגָלָא וּבִזְמַן קָרִיב. וְאִמְרוּ: אָמֵן.
(אָמֵן. יְהֵא שְׁמֵהּ רַבָּא מְבָרַךְ לְעָלַם וּלְעָלְמֵי עָלְמַיָּא.)
(Omayn. Y'hay sh'mayh rabo m'vorach l'olam ul-ol'may ol'ma-yo.)

יְהֵא שְׁמֵהּ רַבָּא מְבָרַךְ לְעָלַם וּלְעָלְמֵי עָלְמַיָּא. יִתְבָּרַךְ וְיִשְׁתַּבַּח וְיִתְפָּאַר וְיִתְרוֹמַם וְיִתְנַשֵּׂא וְיִתְהַדָּר וְיִתְעַלֶּה וְיִתְהַלָּל שְׁמֵהּ דְּקֻדְשָׁא בְּרִיךְ הוּא (B'rich hu—בְּרִיךְ הוּא). °לְעֵלָּא מִן כָּל [°לְעֵלָּא לְעֵלָּא מִכָּל] — from Rosh Hashanah to Yom Kippur substitute] בִּרְכָתָא וְשִׁירָתָא תֻּשְׁבְּחָתָא וְנֶחֱמָתָא, דַּאֲמִירָן בְּעָלְמָא. וְאִמְרוּ: אָמֵן.
(אָמֵן—Omayn).

תִּתְקַבֵּל צְלוֹתְהוֹן וּבָעוּתְהוֹן דְּכָל (בֵּית) יִשְׂרָאֵל קֳדָם אֲבוּהוֹן דִּי בִשְׁמַיָּא. וְאִמְרוּ: אָמֵן. (אָמֵן—Omayn).

יְהֵא שְׁלָמָא רַבָּא מִן שְׁמַיָּא, וְחַיִּים עָלֵינוּ וְעַל כָּל יִשְׂרָאֵל. וְאִמְרוּ: אָמֵן. (אָמֵן—Omayn).

Bow. Take three steps back. Bow left and say, . . . עֹשֶׂה; bow right and say, . . . הוּא יַעֲשֶׂה; bow forward and say, . . . וְעַל כָּל. Remain in place for a few moments, then take three steps forward.

עֹשֶׂה שָׁלוֹם בִּמְרוֹמָיו, הוּא יַעֲשֶׂה שָׁלוֹם עָלֵינוּ, וְעַל כָּל יִשְׂרָאֵל. וְאִמְרוּ: אָמֵן. (אָמֵן—Omayn).

■ As we take leave of the synagogue and God's presence, we fortify ourselves with the resolve and commitment that the lofty ideals of prayer can be implemented and actualized in our mundane pursuits.

STAND WHILE RECITING *ALEINU*.

OLAYNU l'shabay-ach la-adōn hakōl, עָלֵינוּ לְשַׁבֵּחַ לַאֲדוֹן הַכֹּל,
It is our duty to praise* the Master of all,

losays g'dulo l'yōtzayr b'rayshis, לָתֵת גְּדֻלָּה לְיוֹצֵר בְּרֵאשִׁית,
to ascribe greatness to the Molder of primeval Creation,

shelō osonu k'gōyay ho-arotzōs, שֶׁלֹּא עָשָׂנוּ כְּגוֹיֵי הָאֲרָצוֹת,
for He has not made us like the nations of the lands

v'lō somonu
  k'mishp'chōs ho-adomo, וְלֹא שָׂמָנוּ כְּמִשְׁפְּחוֹת הָאֲדָמָה.
and has not emplaced us like the families of the earth;

shelō som chelkaynu kohem, שֶׁלֹּא שָׂם חֶלְקֵנוּ כָּהֶם,
for He has not assigned our portion like theirs

v'gōrolaynu k'chol hamōnom וְגוֹרָלֵנוּ כְּכָל הֲמוֹנָם.
nor our lot like all their multitudes.

SOME CONGREGATIONS OMIT THE PARENTHESIZED VERSE:

(Shehaym mishta-chavim l'hevel vorik, (שֶׁהֵם מִשְׁתַּחֲוִים לְהֶבֶל וָרִיק,
u-mispal'lim el ayl lō yōshi-a.) וּמִתְפַּלְּלִים אֶל אֵל לֹא יוֹשִׁיעַ.)
(For they bow to vanity and emptiness and pray to a god which helps not.)

BOW WHILE RECITING THE NEXT PHRASE.

Va-anachnu kōr'im u-mishta-chavim וַאֲנַחְנוּ כּוֹרְעִים וּמִשְׁתַּחֲוִים
u-mōdim, וּמוֹדִים,
But we bend our knees, bow, and acknowledge our thanks

lifnay melech malchay ham'lochim, לִפְנֵי מֶלֶךְ מַלְכֵי הַמְּלָכִים
before the King Who reigns over kings,

Hakodōsh boruch hu. הַקָּדוֹשׁ בָּרוּךְ הוּא.
the Holy One, Blessed is He.

Shehu nō-te shoma-yim שֶׁהוּא נוֹטֶה שָׁמַיִם
v'yōsayd oretz, וְיֹסֵד אָרֶץ,
He stretches out heaven and establishes earth's foundation,

u-mōshav y'korō וּמוֹשַׁב יְקָרוֹ
ba-shoma-yim mima-al, בַּשָּׁמַיִם מִמַּעַל,
the seat of His homage is in the heavens above

עָלֵינוּ לְשַׁבֵּחַ — *It is our duty to praise.* According to many early sources, this declaration of faith and dedication was composed by Joshua after he led Israel across the Jordan. It was added to the daily prayers to implant faith in the Oneness of God's kingship, and the conviction that

ush-chinas u-zō b'gov-hay m'rōmim. וּשְׁכִינַת עֻזּוֹ בְּגָבְהֵי מְרוֹמִים.
and His powerful Presence is in the loftiest heights.

Hu Elōhaynu ayn ōd. הוּא אֱלֹהֵינוּ, אֵין עוֹד.
He is our God and there is none other.

Emes malkaynu, efes zulosō, אֱמֶת מַלְכֵּנוּ, אֶפֶס זוּלָתוֹ,
True is our King, there is nothing beside Him,

kakosuv b'sōrosō: כַּכָּתוּב בְּתוֹרָתוֹ:
as it is written in His Torah:

V'yodato ha-yōm vaha-shayvōso el l'vovecho, וְיָדַעְתָּ הַיּוֹם וַהֲשֵׁבֹתָ אֶל לְבָבֶךָ,
"You are to know this day and take to your heart

ki Adōnoy hu ho-Elōhim כִּי יהוה הוּא הָאֱלֹהִים
that HASHEM *is the only God —*

ba-shoma-yim mima-al v'al ho-oretz mitochas, ayn ōd. בַּשָּׁמַיִם מִמַּעַל וְעַל הָאָרֶץ מִתָּחַת, אֵין עוֹד.
in heaven above and on the earth below — there is none other."

AL KAYN n'kave l'cho Adōnoy Elōhaynu **עַל כֵּן** נְקַוֶּה לְּךָ יהוה אֱלֹהֵינוּ
Therefore we put our hope in You, HASHEM, *our God,*

lir-ōs m'hayro b'sif-eres u-zecho, לִרְאוֹת מְהֵרָה בְּתִפְאֶרֶת עֻזֶּךָ,
that we may soon see Your mighty splendor,

l'ha-avir gilulim min ho-oretz, לְהַעֲבִיר גִּלּוּלִים מִן הָאָרֶץ,
to remove detestable idolatry from the earth,

v'ho-elilim korōs yikoraysun, וְהָאֱלִילִים כָּרוֹת יִכָּרֵתוּן,
and false gods will be utterly cut off,

l'sakayn ōlom b'malchus Shadai. לְתַקֵּן עוֹלָם בְּמַלְכוּת שַׁדַּי.
to perfect the universe through the Almighty's sovereignty.

V'chol b'nay vosor yikr'u vishmecho, וְכָל בְּנֵי בָשָׂר יִקְרְאוּ בִשְׁמֶךָ,
Then all humanity will call upon Your Name,

l'hafnōs aylecho kol rish-ay oretz. לְהַפְנוֹת אֵלֶיךָ כָּל רִשְׁעֵי אָרֶץ.
to turn all the earth's wicked toward You.

Yakiru v'yayd'u kol yōsh'vay sayvayl, יַכִּירוּ וְיֵדְעוּ כָּל יוֹשְׁבֵי תֵבֵל,
All the world's inhabitants will recognize and know

ki l'cho tichra kol berech, כִּי לְךָ תִּכְרַע כָּל בֶּרֶךְ,
that to You every knee should bend,

He will one day "remove detestable idolatry from the earth...," thus preventing Jews from being tempted to follow the beliefs and life styles of the nations among whom they dwell.

tishova kol loshōn.	תִּשָּׁבַע כָּל לָשׁוֹן.

every tongue should swear.

L'fonecho Adōnoy Elōhaynu yichr'u v'yipōlu,   לְפָנֶיךָ יהוה אֱלֹהֵינוּ יִכְרְעוּ וְיִפֹּלוּ,

*Before You, H*ashem*, our God, they will bend every knee and cast themselves down,*

v'lichvōd shimcho y'kor yitaynu,   וְלִכְבוֹד שִׁמְךָ יְקָר יִתֵּנוּ,

and to the glory of Your Name they will render homage,

vikab'lu chulom es ōl malchusecho,   וִיקַבְּלוּ כֻלָּם אֶת עוֹל מַלְכוּתֶךָ,

and they will all accept upon themselves the yoke of Your kingship

v'simlōch alayhem m'hayro l'ōlom vo-ed.   וְתִמְלֹךְ עֲלֵיהֶם מְהֵרָה לְעוֹלָם וָעֶד.

that You may reign over them soon and for all eternity.

Ki hamalchus shel'cho hi ul-ōl'may ad timlōch b'chovōd,   כִּי הַמַּלְכוּת שֶׁלְּךָ הִיא וּלְעוֹלְמֵי עַד תִּמְלוֹךְ בְּכָבוֹד,

For the kingdom is Yours and You will reign for all eternity in glory,

kakosuv b'sōrosecho: כַּכָּתוּב בְּתוֹרָתֶךָ:

as it is written in Your Torah:

Adōnoy yimlōch l'ōlom vo-ed.   יהוה יִמְלֹךְ לְעֹלָם וָעֶד.

*"*Hashem *shall reign for all eternity."*

V'ne-emar: ❖ וְנֶאֱמַר:

And it is said:

V'ho-yo Adōnoy l'melech al kol ho-oretz,   וְהָיָה יהוה לְמֶלֶךְ עַל כָּל הָאָרֶץ,

*"*Hashem *will be King over all the world —*

ba-yōm hahu yih-ye Adōnoy e-chod, ushmō e-chod.   בַּיּוֹם הַהוּא יִהְיֶה יהוה אֶחָד וּשְׁמוֹ אֶחָד.

on that day Hashem *will be One and His Name will be One."*

SOME CONGREGATIONS RECITE THE FOLLOWING AT THIS POINT.

AL TIRO mipachad pis-ōm,   **אַל תִּירָא** מִפַּחַד פִּתְאֹם,

Do not fear sudden terror,

u-mishō-as r'sho-im ki sovō.   וּמִשֹּׁאַת רְשָׁעִים כִּי תָבֹא.

or the holocaust of the wicked when it comes.

Utzu aytzo v'sufor, dab'ru dovor v'lō yokum,   עֻצוּ עֵצָה וְתֻפָר, דַּבְּרוּ דָבָר וְלֹא יָקוּם,

Plan a conspiracy and it will be annulled; speak your piece and it shall not stand,

ki i-monu Ayl.   כִּי עִמָּנוּ אֵל.

for God is with us.

V'ad zikno ani hu,   וְעַד זִקְנָה אֲנִי הוּא,
Even till your seniority, I remain unchanged;

v'ad sayvo ani esbōl,   וְעַד שֵׂיבָה אֲנִי אֶסְבֹּל,
and even till your ripe old age, I shall endure;

ani osisi va-ani eso,   אֲנִי עָשִׂיתִי וַאֲנִי אֶשָּׂא,
va-ani esbōl va-amalayt.   וַאֲנִי אֶסְבֹּל וַאֲמַלֵּט.
I created [you] and I shall bear [you]; I shall endure and rescue.

⊰ MOURNER'S KADDISH ⊱

■ Man was created to serve God and sanctify His Name. This service and sanctification is actualized by living one's life in accordance with the laws and customs of Judaism. This includes both those commandments directed toward God and those that govern our relationship to man.

When an individual passes on, there is a void in this world which is caused by the loss of the sanctification that the deceased had contributed. Therefore, the surviving son (or other relative) addresses this void by announcing through the *Kaddish*, "May the great Name of God continue to be holy." There is no specific reference to death in the *Kaddish*, for it is a message of life. And life that continues is to be sanctified.

The recitation of the *Kaddish* is a great merit for the soul of the deceased. *Kaddish* is recited for eleven months following the death, and is also recited on the *Yahrzeit* (anniversary of the passing).

KADDISH IS RECITED ONLY IN THE PRESENCE OF A MINYAN.

MOURNER:

YISGADAL v'yiskadash sh'mayh rabo.   **יִתְגַּדַּל** וְיִתְקַדַּשׁ שְׁמֵהּ רַבָּא.
May His great Name grow exalted and sanctified

CONGREGATION RESPONDS: Omayn — אָמֵן

B'ol'mo di v'ro chir-usayh.   בְּעָלְמָא דִּי בְרָא כִרְעוּתֵהּ.
in the world that He created as He willed.

V'yamlich malchusayh,   וְיַמְלִיךְ מַלְכוּתֵהּ,
May He give reign to His kingship

b'cha-yaychōn uvyōmaychōn   בְּחַיֵּיכוֹן וּבְיוֹמֵיכוֹן
in your lifetimes and in your days

uvcha-yay d'chol bays yisro-ayl,   וּבְחַיֵּי דְכָל בֵּית יִשְׂרָאֵל,
and in the lifetimes of the entire Family of Israel,

ba-agolo u-vizman koriv.   בַּעֲגָלָא וּבִזְמַן קָרִיב.
swiftly and soon.

V'imru: Omayn.   וְאִמְרוּ: אָמֵן.
Now respond: Amen.

CONGREGATION RESPONDS:

Omayn. Y'hay sh'mayh rabo m'vorach   אָמֵן. יְהֵא שְׁמֵהּ רַבָּא מְבָרַךְ
l'olam ul-ol'may ol'ma-yo.   לְעָלַם וּלְעָלְמֵי עָלְמַיָּא.
Amen. May His great Name be blessed forever and ever;

קדיש יתום

MOURNER CONTINUES:

Y'hay sh'mayh rabo m'vorach
l'olam ul-ol'may ol'ma-yo,

יְהֵא שְׁמֵהּ רַבָּא מְבָרַךְ
לְעָלַם וּלְעָלְמֵי עָלְמַיָּא,

May His great Name be blessed forever and ever;

yisborach v'yishtabach v'yispo-ar

יִתְבָּרַךְ וְיִשְׁתַּבַּח וְיִתְפָּאַר

blessed, praised, glorified,

v'yisrōmam v'yisnasay

וְיִתְרוֹמַם וְיִתְנַשֵּׂא

exalted, extolled,

v'yis-hador v'yis-ale v'yis-halol

וְיִתְהַדָּר וְיִתְעַלֶּה וְיִתְהַלָּל

mighty, upraised, and lauded

sh'mayh d'kudsho b'rich hu

שְׁמֵהּ דְּקֻדְשָׁא בְּרִיךְ הוּא

be the Name of the Holy One, Blessed is He,

CONGREGATION RESPONDS:

B'rich hu.   *Blessed is He.*   בְּרִיךְ הוּא.

MOURNER CONTINUES:

°l'aylo min kol   °לְעֵלָּא מִן כָּל

beyond any

FROM ROSH HASHANAH TO YOM KIPPUR SUBSTITUTE:

°l'aylo l'aylo mikol   °לְעֵלָּא לְעֵלָּא מִכָּל

exceedingly beyond any

birchoso v'shiroso

בִּרְכָתָא וְשִׁירָתָא

blessing and song,

tushb'choso v'nechemoso,

תֻּשְׁבְּחָתָא וְנֶחֱמָתָא,

praise and consolation

da-amiron b'ol'mo.

דַּאֲמִירָן בְּעָלְמָא.

that are uttered in the world.

V'imru: Omayn.   וְאִמְרוּ: אָמֵן.

Now respond: Amen.

CONGREGATION RESPONDS: Omayn — אָמֵן

Y'hay sh'lomo rabo min sh'mayo

יְהֵא שְׁלָמָא רַבָּא מִן שְׁמַיָּא,

May there be abundant peace from Heaven,

v'cha-yim olaynu v'al kol yisro-ayl.

וְחַיִּים עָלֵינוּ וְעַל כָּל יִשְׂרָאֵל.

and life, upon us and upon all Israel.

V'imru: Omayn.   וְאִמְרוּ: אָמֵן.

Now respond: Amen.

CONGREGATION RESPONDS: Omayn — אָמֵן

MOURNER BOWS, THEN TAKES THREE STEPS BACK, BOWS LEFT AND SAYS:

Ō-se sholōm bimrōmov   עֹשֶׂה שָׁלוֹם בִּמְרוֹמָיו,

He Who makes peace in His heights,

SHACHARIS FOR WEEKDAYS — SONG OF THE DAY

MOURNER BOWS RIGHT AND SAYS:

hu ya-a-se sholōm olaynu   הוּא יַעֲשֶׂה שָׁלוֹם עָלֵינוּ,

may He make peace upon us,

MOURNER BOWS FORWARD AND SAYS:

v'al kol yisro-ayl. V'imru: Omayn.   וְעַל כָּל יִשְׂרָאֵל. וְאִמְרוּ: אָמֵן.

and upon all Israel. Now respond: Amen.

CONGREGATION RESPONDS: Omayn — אָמֵן

MOURNER REMAINS IN PLACE FOR A FEW MOMENTS, THEN TAKES THREE STEPS FORWARD.

❈ SONG OF THE DAY ❈

A DIFFERENT PSALM IS ASSIGNED AS THE SONG OF THE DAY FOR EACH DAY OF THE WEEK.

FOR SUNDAY

■ I remember the Shabbos daily: On the first day of Creation, Hashem created the world to benefit man, and challenged him to aspire to perfection.

Ha-yōm yōm rishōn ba-shabos,   הַיּוֹם יוֹם רִאשׁוֹן בַּשַּׁבָּת,

Today is the first day* of the Sabbath,

shebō ho-yu hal'viyim   שֶׁבּוֹ הָיוּ הַלְוִיִּם

ōm'rim b'vays hamikdosh: אוֹמְרִים בְּבֵית הַמִּקְדָּשׁ:

on which the Levites would recite in the Holy Temple:

L'DOVID mizmōr,   **לְדָוִד** מִזְמוֹר,

Of David a psalm.

Ladōnoy ho-oretz umlō-oh,   לַיהוה הָאָרֶץ וּמְלוֹאָהּ,

Hashem's is the earth* and its fullness,

tayvayl v'yōsh'vay voh.   תֵּבֵל וְיֹשְׁבֵי בָהּ.

the inhabited land and those who dwell in it.

Ki hu al yamim y'sodoh,   כִּי הוּא עַל יַמִּים יְסָדָהּ,

For He founded it upon seas,*

⋅≼ Song of the Day

As part of the morning Temple service, the Levites chanted a psalm that was suited to the significance of that particular day of the week. As a memorial to the Temple, these psalms have been incorporated into *Shacharis*. The introductory sentence, "Today is the first day of the Sabbath . . ." helps fulfill the Torah's command to remember the Sabbath always. By counting the days of the week with reference to the forthcoming Sabbath we tie our existence to the Sabbath. The Talmud (*Rosh Hashanah* 31a) explains why each of these psalms were assigned to its particular day.

הַיּוֹם יוֹם רִאשׁוֹן — *Today is the first day.* Psalm 24 teaches that everything belongs to God. The Talmud assigns this psalm to the first day of the week because on the first day of Creation, God was the sole Power — even the angels had not yet been created. He took possession of His newly created world with the intention of ceding it to man.

לַה' הָאָרֶץ — *Hashem's is the earth.* Since the world belongs to God, anyone who derives pleasure from His world without reciting the proper blessing expressing thanks to the Owner is regarded as a thief (*Berachos* 35a).

כִּי הוּא עַל יַמִּים יְסָדָהּ — *For He founded it upon seas.* The entire planet was covered with water until God commanded it to gather in seas and rivers and to expose the dry land.

שחרית לחול

וְעַל נְהָרוֹת יְכוֹנְנֶהָ.
v'al n'horōs y'chōn'neho.
and established it upon rivers.

מִי יַעֲלֶה בְהַר יהוה,
Mi ya-ale v'har Adōnoy,
Who may ascend* the mountain of HASHEM,

וּמִי יָקוּם בִּמְקוֹם קָדְשׁוֹ.
u-mi yokum bimkōm kodshō.
and who may stand in the place of His sanctity?

נְקִי כַפַּיִם וּבַר לֵבָב,
N'ki chapa-yim u-var layvov,
One with clean hands* and pure heart,

אֲשֶׁר לֹא נָשָׂא לַשָּׁוְא נַפְשִׁי,
asher lō noso la-shov nafshi,
who has not sworn in vain by My soul*

וְלֹא נִשְׁבַּע לְמִרְמָה.
v'lō nishba l'mirmo.
and has not sworn deceitfully.

יִשָּׂא בְרָכָה מֵאֵת יהוה,
Yiso v'rocho may-ays Adōnoy,
He will receive a blessing* from HASHEM

וּצְדָקָה מֵאֱלֹהֵי יִשְׁעוֹ.
utzdoko may-Elōhay yish-ō.
and just kindness from the God of his salvation.

זֶה דּוֹר דֹּרְשָׁיו,
Ze dōr dōr'shov,
This is the generation of those who seek Him,

מְבַקְשֵׁי פָנֶיךָ יַעֲקֹב סֶלָה.
m'vakshay fonecho ya-akōv selo.
those who strive for Your Presence — Jacob, Selah.

שְׂאוּ שְׁעָרִים רָאשֵׁיכֶם,
S'u sh'orim ro-shaychem,
Raise up your heads, O gates,

וְהִנָּשְׂאוּ פִּתְחֵי עוֹלָם,
v'hinos'u pischay ōlom,
and be uplifted, you everlasting entrances,

וְיָבוֹא מֶלֶךְ הַכָּבוֹד.
v'yovō melech hakovōd.
so that the King of Glory may enter.

מִי זֶה מֶלֶךְ הַכָּבוֹד,
Mi ze melech hakovōd,
Who is this King of Glory? —

יהוה עִזּוּז וְגִבּוֹר,
Adōnoy izuz v'gibōr

יהוה גִּבּוֹר מִלְחָמָה.
Adōnoy gibōr milchomo.
HASHEM, the mighty and strong, HASHEM, the strong in battle.

מִי יַעֲלֶה — *Who may ascend ...?* God's most intense Presence is in the Temple, so those who wish to draw near and to perceive His splendor must be especially worthy. By extension, one who wishes to enjoy spiritual elevation must refine his behavior.

נְקִי כַפַּיִם — *One with clean hands.* This verse answers the previous question. To ascend, one must have hands clean from dishonest gain; must be honest in dealing with man; and must be reverent toward God.

נַפְשִׁי — *My soul.* God is the "speaker." He refers to one who swears falsely as having treated God's soul, as it were, with disrespect.

יִשָּׂא בְרָכָה — *He will receive a blessing..* By honoring God's Name in heart and behavior, he earns God's blessing, kindness and salvation.

SHACHARIS FOR WEEKDAYS — SONG OF THE DAY

S'u sh'orim ro-shaychem,   שְׂאוּ שְׁעָרִים רָאשֵׁיכֶם,
Raise up your heads, O gates,

us-u pischay ōlom,   וּשְׂאוּ פִּתְחֵי עוֹלָם,
and raise up, you everlasting entrances,

v'yovō melech hakovōd.   וְיָבֹא מֶלֶךְ הַכָּבוֹד.
so that the King of Glory may enter.

Mi hu ze melech hakovōd,   מִי הוּא זֶה מֶלֶךְ הַכָּבוֹד,
Who then is the King of Glory?

Adōnoy Tz'vo-ōs,   יהוה צְבָאוֹת,
   hu melech hakovōd selo.   הוּא מֶלֶךְ הַכָּבוֹד סֶלָה.
HASHEM, Master of Legions, He is the King of Glory. Selah!

IF A MOURNER IS PRESENT, HE RECITES THE MOURNER'S *KADDISH* (PAGE 259).

FOR MONDAY

■ I remember the Shabbos daily: On the second day of Creation, Hashem separated Heaven and Earth. As he rules the Heavens above, so does He reign on earth in Jerusalem.

Ha-yōm yōm shayni ba-shabos,   הַיּוֹם יוֹם שֵׁנִי בַּשַּׁבָּת,
Today is the second day* of the Sabbath,

shebō ho-yu hal'viyim   שֶׁבּוֹ הָיוּ הַלְוִיִּם
   ōm'rim b'vays hamikdosh: אוֹמְרִים בְּבֵית הַמִּקְדָּשׁ:
on which the Levites would recite in the Holy Temple:

SHIR mizmōr livnay kōrach.   **שִׁיר** מִזְמוֹר לִבְנֵי קֹרַח.
A song, a psalm, by the sons of Korach.

Godōl Adōnoy umhulol m'ōd,   גָּדוֹל יהוה וּמְהֻלָּל מְאֹד,
Great is HASHEM and much praised,

b'ir Elōhaynu har kodshō.   בְּעִיר אֱלֹהֵינוּ, הַר קָדְשׁוֹ.
in the city of our God, Mount of His Holiness.

Y'fay nōf m'sōs kol ho-oretz   יְפֵה נוֹף, מְשׂוֹשׂ כָּל הָאָרֶץ,
Fairest of sites, joy of all the earth

har tziyōn yark'say tzofōn,   הַר צִיּוֹן יַרְכְּתֵי צָפוֹן,
   kiryas melech rov.   קִרְיַת מֶלֶךְ רָב.
is Mount Zion, by the northern sides of the great king's city.

Elōhim b'arm'nōseho.   אֱלֹהִים בְּאַרְמְנוֹתֶיהָ
   nōda l'misgov.   נוֹדַע לְמִשְׂגָּב.
In her palaces God is known as the Stronghold.

הַיּוֹם יוֹם שֵׁנִי — *Today is the second day*. Psalm 48 speaks of Jerusalem, the seat of God's holiness and kingship over the entire world. On the second day of Creation, God separated between the heavenly and earthly components of the universe and ruled over both.

Ki hinay ham'lochim nō-adu,	כִּי הִנֵּה הַמְּלָכִים נוֹעֲדוּ,
ov'ru yachdov.	עָבְרוּ יַחְדָּו.

For behold — the kings assembled, they came together.

Haymo ro-u kayn tomohu,	הֵמָּה רָאוּ כֵּן תָּמָהוּ,

They saw and they were astounded,

nivhalu nechpozu.	נִבְהֲלוּ נֶחְפָּזוּ.

they were confounded and hastily fled.

R'odo achozosam shom,	רְעָדָה אֲחָזָתַם שָׁם,
chil kayōlaydo.	חִיל כַּיּוֹלֵדָה.

Trembling gripped them there, convulsions like a woman in birth travail.

B'ru-ach kodim	בְּרוּחַ קָדִים
t'shabayr oniyōs tarshish.	תְּשַׁבֵּר אֳנִיּוֹת תַּרְשִׁישׁ.

With an east wind You smashed the ships of Tarshish.

Ka-asher shomanu kayn ro-inu	כַּאֲשֶׁר שָׁמַעְנוּ כֵּן רָאִינוּ

As we heard,* so we saw

b'ir Adōnoy Tz'vo-ōs,	בְּעִיר יהוה צְבָאוֹת,
b'ir Elōhaynu,	בְּעִיר אֱלֹהֵינוּ,

in the city of HASHEM, Master of Legions, in the city of our God —

Elōhim y'chōn'neho ad ōlom	אֱלֹהִים יְכוֹנְנֶהָ עַד עוֹלָם
selo.	סֶלָה.

may God establish it to eternity, Selah!

Diminu Elōhim chasdecho,	דִּמִּינוּ אֱלֹהִים חַסְדֶּךָ,
b'kerev haycholecho.	בְּקֶרֶב הֵיכָלֶךָ.

We hoped, O God, for Your kindness, in the midst of Your Sanctuary.

K'shimcho Elōhim kayn t'hilos'cho,	כְּשִׁמְךָ אֱלֹהִים כֵּן תְּהִלָּתְךָ,
al katzvay eretz,	עַל קַצְוֵי אֶרֶץ,

Like Your Name, O God, so is Your praise — to the ends of the earth;

tzedek mol'o y'mine-cho.	צֶדֶק מָלְאָה יְמִינֶךָ.

righteousness fills Your right hand.

Yismach har tziyōn,	יִשְׂמַח הַר צִיּוֹן,
togaylno b'nōs y'hudo,	תָּגֵלְנָה בְּנוֹת יְהוּדָה,

May Mount Zion be glad, may the daughters of Judah rejoice,

l'ma-an mishpotecho.	לְמַעַן מִשְׁפָּטֶיךָ.

because of Your judgments.

כַּאֲשֶׁר שָׁמַעְנוּ — *As we heard.* From our ancestors we heard of God's miraculous salvations — but we will see similar wonders as well.

כְּשִׁמְךָ אֱלֹהִים — *Like Your Name, O God.* The prophets gave You exalted Names, and we can testify that Your praise, given You for actual deeds, justifies those glorious titles.

SHACHARIS FOR WEEKDAYS — SONG OF THE DAY

Sōbu tziyōn v'hakifuho,   סֹבּוּ צִיּוֹן וְהַקִּיפוּהָ,
    sifru migdoleho.   סִפְרוּ מִגְדָּלֶיהָ.
Walk about Zion and encircle her, count her towers.

Shisu lib'chem l'chaylo,   ❖ שִׁיתוּ לִבְּכֶם לְחֵילָה,
    pas'gu arm'nōseho,   פַּסְּגוּ אַרְמְנוֹתֶיהָ,
Mark well in your hearts her ramparts, raise up her palaces,

l'ma-an t'sap'ru l'dōr acharōn.   לְמַעַן תְּסַפְּרוּ לְדוֹר אַחֲרוֹן.
that you may recount it to the succeeding generation —

Ki ze Elōhim Elōhaynu ōlom vo-ed,   כִּי זֶה אֱלֹהִים אֱלֹהֵינוּ עוֹלָם וָעֶד,
that this is God, our God, forever and ever,

hu y'nahagaynu al mus.   הוּא יְנַהֲגֵנוּ עַל־מוּת.
He will guide us like children.*

IF A MOURNER IS PRESENT, HE RECITES THE MOURNER'S *KADDISH* (PAGE 259).

FOR TUESDAY

■ I remember the Shabbos daily: On the third day of Creation, Hashem made the Earth visible. This psalm teaches that law and order are essential for its continued existence.

Ha-yōm, yōm sh'lishi ba-shabos,   הַיּוֹם יוֹם שְׁלִישִׁי בַּשַּׁבָּת,
Today is the third day* of the Sabbath,

shebō ho-yu hal'viyim   שֶׁבּוֹ הָיוּ הַלְוִיִּם
    ōm'rim b'vays hamikdosh: אוֹמְרִים בְּבֵית הַמִּקְדָּשׁ:
on which the Levites would recite in the Holy Temple:

MIZMŌR l'osof,   **מִזְמוֹר** לְאָסָף,
A psalm of Assaf.

Elōhim nitzov ba-adas Ayl,   אֱלֹהִים נִצָּב בַּעֲדַת אֵל,
God stands in the Divine assembly,

b'kerev elōhim yishpōt.   בְּקֶרֶב אֱלֹהִים יִשְׁפֹּט.
in the midst of judges shall He judge.

Ad mosai tishp'tu ovel,   עַד מָתַי תִּשְׁפְּטוּ עָוֶל,
Until when* will you judge lawlessly

עַל־מוּת — *Like children.* This can be read as one word — עֲלָמוֹת, "youth," or as two words — עַל מוּת, "beyond death." That is, God will guide us like a father caring for his young, and will continue to guide us in the World to Come.

הַיּוֹם יוֹם שְׁלִישִׁי — *Today is the third day.* On the third day, God caused the dry land to become visible and fit for habitation. He did so in order that man follow the Torah's laws and deal justly with other people. Therefore Psalm 82, which has as its theme the maintenance of equity and justice, a prerequisite for the continued existence of the world that was revealed on the third day, was chosen as that day's song. But this message is not limited only to courts. In his own personal life, every person is a judge, for his opinions and decisions about people can affect their lives in a thousand different ways.

עַד מָתַי — *Until when . . . ?* The next three verses are addressed directly to judges who fail to carry out their responsibilities.

שיר של יום

שחרית לחול

uf'nay r'sho-im tisu, selo.	וּפְנֵי רְשָׁעִים תִּשְׂאוּ סֶלָה.

and favor the presence of the wicked, Selah?

Shiftu dol v'yosōm,
   oni vorosh hatz-diku.

שִׁפְטוּ דַל וְיָתוֹם,
עָנִי וָרָשׁ הַצְדִּיקוּ.

Judge the needy and the orphan, vindicate the poor and impoverished.

Pal'tu dal v'evyōn,
   mi-yad r'sho-im hatzilu.

פַּלְּטוּ דַל וְאֶבְיוֹן,
מִיַּד רְשָׁעִים הַצִּילוּ.

Rescue the needy and destitute, from the hand of the wicked deliver them.

Lō yod'u v'lō yovinu,
   bacha-shaycho yis-halochu,

לֹא יָדְעוּ וְלֹא יָבִינוּ,
בַּחֲשֵׁכָה יִתְהַלָּכוּ,

They do not know* nor do they understand, in darkness they walk;

yimōtu kol mōs'day oretz.

יִמּוֹטוּ כָּל מוֹסְדֵי אָרֶץ.

all foundations of the earth collapse.

Ani omarti elōhim atem,
   uvnay elyōn kulchem.

אֲנִי אָמַרְתִּי אֱלֹהִים אַתֶּם,
וּבְנֵי עֶלְיוֹן כֻּלְּכֶם.

I said, "You are angelic, sons of the Most High are you all."

Ochayn k'odom t'musun,
   uchachad hasorim tipōlu.

אָכֵן כְּאָדָם תְּמוּתוּן,
וּכְאַחַד הַשָּׂרִים תִּפֹּלוּ.

But like men you shall die, and like one of the princes you shall fall.

❖ Kumo Elōhim shofto ho-oretz,

קוּמָה אֱלֹהִים שָׁפְטָה הָאָרֶץ,

Arise, O God, judge the earth,

ki ato sinchal b'chol hagōyim.

כִּי אַתָּה תִנְחַל בְּכָל הַגּוֹיִם.

for You allot the heritage* among all the nations.

IF A MOURNER IS PRESENT, HE RECITES THE MOURNER'S *KADDISH* (PAGE 259).

FOR WEDNESDAY

■ I remember the Shabbos daily: On the fourth day of Creation, Hashem created the sun, moon and stars. We are reminded that they, as well as the rest of Creation, are to be used in the service of Hashem.

Ha-yōm yōm r'vi-i ba-shabos,

הַיּוֹם יוֹם רְבִיעִי בַּשַּׁבָּת,

Today is the fourth day* of the Sabbath,

shebō ho-yu hal'viyim
   ōm'rim b'vays hamikdosh:

שֶׁבּוֹ הָיוּ הַלְוִיִּם
אוֹמְרִים בְּבֵית הַמִּקְדָּשׁ:

on which the Levites would recite in the Holy Temple:

לֹא יָדְעוּ — *They do not know.* The Psalmist exclaims that many judges are unaware of their awesome responsibility; they walk in darkness, blinded by prejudice and selfishness.

כִּי אַתָּה תִנְחַל — *For You allot the heritage.* The Psalmist addresses God: You sought to avoid strife by allotting a fair share to all nations. Now step in to judge the earth and undo man's destructiveness.

הַיּוֹם יוֹם רְבִיעִי — *Today is the fourth day.* On the fourth day, God created the sun, moon, and the stars. But instead of recognizing them as God's

SONG OF THE DAY

AYL N'KOMŌS Adōnoy, אֵל נְקָמוֹת יהוה,
Ayl n'komōs hōfi-a. אֵל נְקָמוֹת הוֹפִיעַ.
O God of vengeance, HASHEM; O God of vengeance, appear!

Hinosay shōfayt ho-oretz, הִנָּשֵׂא שֹׁפֵט הָאָרֶץ,
hoshayv g'mul al gay-im. הָשֵׁב גְּמוּל עַל גֵּאִים.
Arise, O Judge of the earth, render recompense to the haughty.

Ad mosai r'sho-im, Adōnoy, עַד מָתַי רְשָׁעִים, יהוה,
ad mosai r'sho-im ya-alōzu. עַד מָתַי רְשָׁעִים יַעֲלֹזוּ.
How long shall the wicked — O HASHEM — how long shall the wicked exult?

Yabi-u y'dab'ru osok, יַבִּיעוּ יְדַבְּרוּ עָתָק,
They speak freely, they utter malicious falsehood,
yis-am'ru kol pō-alay o-ven. יִתְאַמְּרוּ כָּל פֹּעֲלֵי אָוֶן.
they glorify themselves, all workers of iniquity.

Am'cho Adōnoy y'dak'u, עַמְּךָ יהוה יְדַכְּאוּ,
v'nachlos'cho y'anu. וְנַחֲלָתְךָ יְעַנּוּ.
Your nation, HASHEM, they crush, and they afflict Your heritage.

Almono v'gayr yaharōgu, אַלְמָנָה וְגֵר יַהֲרֹגוּ,
visōmim y'ratzaychu. וִיתוֹמִים יְרַצֵּחוּ.
The widow and the stranger they slay, and the orphans they murder.

Va-yōm'ru lō yir-e Yoh, וַיֹּאמְרוּ לֹא יִרְאֶה יָּהּ,
v'lō yovin Elōhay ya-akōv. וְלֹא יָבִין אֱלֹהֵי יַעֲקֹב.
And they say, "God will not see, nor will the God of Jacob understand."

Binu bō-arim bo-om בִּינוּ בֹּעֲרִים בָּעָם,
Understand, you boors among the people;
uchsilim mosai taskilu. וּכְסִילִים מָתַי תַּשְׂכִּילוּ.
and you fools, when will you gain wisdom?

Hanōta ōzen ha-lō yishmo, הֲנֹטַע אֹזֶן הֲלֹא יִשְׁמָע,
He Who implants the ear, shall He not hear?
im yōtzayr a-yin ha-lō yabit. אִם יֹצֵר עַיִן הֲלֹא יַבִּיט.
He Who fashions the eye, shall He not see?

Ha-yōsayr gōyim ha-lō yōchi-ach, הֲיֹסֵר גּוֹיִם הֲלֹא יוֹכִיחַ,
He Who chastises nations, shall He not rebuke? —
ham'lamayd odom do-as. הַמְלַמֵּד אָדָם דָּעַת.
He Who teaches man knowledge.

---

servants, man eventually came to regard the luminaries as independent gods that should be worshiped. Because of this idolatry, God showed Himself to be, as Psalm 94 describes Him, the God of vengeance, for despite his almost endless patience and mercy, He does not

Adōnoy yōday-a machsh'vōs odom,	יהוה יֹדֵעַ מַחְשְׁבוֹת אָדָם,
ki haymo hovel.	כִּי הֵמָּה הָבֶל.

Hashem knows the thoughts of man, that they are futile.

Ashray hagever,	אַשְׁרֵי הַגֶּבֶר
asher t'yas'renu Yoh,	אֲשֶׁר תְּיַסְּרֶנּוּ יָהּ,

Praiseworthy is the man* whom God disciplines,

u-mitōros'cho s'lam'denu.	וּמִתּוֹרָתְךָ תְלַמְּדֶנּוּ.

and whom You teach from Your Torah.

L'hashkit lō mimay ro,	לְהַשְׁקִיט לוֹ מִימֵי רָע,
ad yikore lorosho shochas.	עַד יִכָּרֶה לָרָשָׁע שָׁחַת.

To give him rest from the days of evil, until a pit is dug for the wicked.

Ki lō yitōsh Adōnoy amō,	כִּי לֹא יִטֹּשׁ יהוה עַמּוֹ,
v'nachalosō lō ya-azōv.	וְנַחֲלָתוֹ לֹא יַעֲזֹב.

For Hashem will not cast off His people, nor will He forsake His heritage.

Ki ad tzedek yoshuv mishpot,	כִּי עַד צֶדֶק יָשׁוּב מִשְׁפָּט,

For justice shall revert to righteousness,

v'acharov kol yishray layv.	וְאַחֲרָיו כָּל יִשְׁרֵי לֵב.

and following it will be all of upright heart.

Mi yokum li im m'rayim,	מִי יָקוּם לִי עִם מְרֵעִים,

Who will rise up for me against evildoers?

mi yis-yatzayv li im pō-alay o-ven.	מִי יִתְיַצֵּב לִי עִם פֹּעֲלֵי אָוֶן.

Who will stand up for me against the workers of iniquity?

Lulay Adōnoy ezrosō li,	לוּלֵי יהוה עֶזְרָתָה לִּי,

Had Hashem not been a help to me,

kim-at shoch'no dumo nafshi.	כִּמְעַט שָׁכְנָה דוּמָה נַפְשִׁי.

my soul would soon have dwelt in silence.

Im omarti moto ragli,	אִם אָמַרְתִּי מָטָה רַגְלִי,
chasd'cho Adōnoy yis-odayni.	חַסְדְּךָ יהוה יִסְעָדֵנִי.

If I said, "My foot falters," Your kindness, Hashem, supported me.

B'rōv sar-apai b'kirbi,	בְּרֹב שַׂרְעַפַּי בְּקִרְבִּי,

When my forebodings were abundant within me,

tanchumecho y'sha-ashu nafshi.	תַּנְחוּמֶיךָ יְשַׁעַשְׁעוּ נַפְשִׁי.

Your comforts cheered my soul.

---

tolerate evil forever.

אַשְׁרֵי הַגֶּבֶר — *Praiseworthy is the man.* The wicked ask why the righteous suffer, if God truly controls everything. The Psalmist answers that God afflicts the righteous only when it is to their benefit: to chastise them, to make them realize the futility of physical pleasures, or to atone for their sins.

hay'chovr'cho kisay havōs, הַיְחָבְרְךָ כִּסֵּא הַוּוֹת,
Can the throne of destruction be associated with You? —

yōtzayr omol alay chōk. יֹצֵר עָמָל עֲלֵי חֹק.
those who fashion evil into a way of life.

Yogōdu al nefesh tzadik, יָגֽוֹדּוּ עַל נֶפֶשׁ צַדִּיק,
They join together against the soul of the righteous,

v'dom noki yarshi-u. וְדָם נָקִי יַרְשִֽׁיעוּ.
and the blood of the innocent they condemn.

Vai-hi Adōnoy li l'misgov, וַיְהִי יהוה לִי לְמִשְׂגָּב,
    Vaylōhai l'tzur machsi. וֵאלֹהַי לְצוּר מַחְסִי.
Then HASHEM became a stronghold for me, and my God, the Rock of my refuge.

Va-yoshev alayhem es ōnom, וַיָּֽשֶׁב עֲלֵיהֶם אֶת אוֹנָם,
He turned upon them their own violence,

uvro-osom yatzmisaym, וּבְרָעָתָם יַצְמִיתֵם,
    yatzmisaym Adōnoy Elōhaynu. יַצְמִיתֵם יהוה אֱלֹהֵֽינוּ.
and with their own evil He will cut them off, HASHEM, our God, will cut them off.

L'chu n'ran'no Ladōnoy, ❖ לְכוּ נְרַנְּנָה לַיהוה,
    nori-o l'tzur yishaynu. נָרִֽיעָה לְצוּר יִשְׁעֵֽנוּ.
Come — let us sing to HASHEM, let us call out to the Rock of our salvation.

N'kad'mo fonov b'sōdo, נְקַדְּמָה פָנָיו בְּתוֹדָה,
    bizmirōs nori-a lō. בִּזְמִרוֹת נָרִֽיעַ לוֹ.
Let us greet Him with thanksgiving, with praiseful songs let us call out to Him.

Ki Ayl godōl Adōnoy, כִּי אֵל גָּדוֹל יהוה,
    u-melech godōl al kol elōhim: וּמֶֽלֶךְ גָּדוֹל עַל כָּל אֱלֹהִים.
For a great God is HASHEM, and a great King above all heavenly powers.

IF A MOURNER IS PRESENT, HE RECITES THE MOURNER'S *KADDISH* (PAGE 259).

FOR THURSDAY

■ I remember the Shabbos daily: On the fifth day of Creation, Hashem created an exciting variety of birds and fish, adding color to our world. If only man would appreciate the Divine origin of nature . . .

Ha-yōm yōm chami-shi ba-shabos, הַיּוֹם יוֹם חֲמִישִׁי בַּשַּׁבָּת,
Today is the fifth day* of the Sabbath,

shebō ho-yu hal'viyim שֶׁבּוֹ הָיוּ הַלְוִיִּם
    ōm'rim b'vays hamikdosh: אוֹמְרִים בְּבֵית הַמִּקְדָּשׁ:
on which the Levites would recite in the Holy Temple:

היום יום חמישי — *Today is the fifth day.* On the fifth day of Creation, God made the birds and the fish, which bring joy to the world. When people observe the vast variety of colorful birds and

שחרית לחול / שיר של יום

LAM'NATZAYACH al hagitis l'osof. לַמְנַצֵּחַ עַל הַגִּתִּית לְאָסָף.
For the Conductor, upon the gittis, by Assaf.

Harninu Laylōhim u-zaynu, הַרְנִינוּ לֵאלֹהִים עוּזֵּנוּ,
Sing joyously to the God of our might,

hori-u Laylōhay ya-akōv. הָרִיעוּ לֵאלֹהֵי יַעֲקֹב.
call out to the God of Jacob.

S'u zimro us-nu sōf, שְׂאוּ זִמְרָה וּתְנוּ תֹף,
   kinōr no-im im novel. כִּנּוֹר נָעִים עִם נָבֶל.
Raise a song and sound the drum, the sweet harp with the lyre.

Tik-u vachōdesh shōfor, תִּקְעוּ בַחֹדֶשׁ שׁוֹפָר,
   bakese l'yōm chagaynu. בַּכֶּסֶה לְיוֹם חַגֵּנוּ.
Blow the shofar at the moon's renewal,* at the time appointed for our festive day.

Ki chōk l'yisro-ayl hu, כִּי חֹק לְיִשְׂרָאֵל הוּא,
   mishpot Laylōhay ya-akōv. מִשְׁפָּט לֵאלֹהֵי יַעֲקֹב.
Because it is a decree for Israel, a judgment day for the God of Jacob.

Aydus bihōsayf somō, עֵדוּת בִּיהוֹסֵף שָׂמוֹ,
He imposed it as a testimony for Joseph,*

b'tzaysō al eretz mitzro-yim, בְּצֵאתוֹ עַל אֶרֶץ מִצְרָיִם,
when he went forth over the land of Egypt —

s'fas lō yoda-ti eshmo. שְׂפַת לֹא יָדַעְתִּי אֶשְׁמָע.
"I understood a language I never knew!"

Hasirōsi misayvel shichmō, הֲסִירוֹתִי מִסֵּבֶל שִׁכְמוֹ,
   kapov midud ta-avōr'no. כַּפָּיו מִדּוּד תַּעֲבֹרְנָה.
I removed his shoulder from the burden, his hands let go of the kettle.

Batzoro koroso, vo-achal'tzeko, בַּצָּרָה קָרָאתָ, וָאֲחַלְּצֶךָּ,
In distress you called out, and I released you,

e-encho b'sayser ra-am, אֶעֶנְךָ בְּסֵתֶר רַעַם,
I answered you with thunder when you hid,

evchon'cho al may m'rivo selo. אֶבְחָנְךָ עַל מֵי מְרִיבָה, סֶלָה.
I tested you at the Waters of Strife, Selah.

---

fish, they are awed by the tremendous scope of God's creative ability, and they are stirred to praise Him with songs such as Psalm 81.

תִּקְעוּ בַחֹדֶשׁ שׁוֹפָר — *Blow the shofar at the moon's renewal.* The moon's renewal is a poetic term for the first day of the lunar month, when the moon becomes visible again. This verse refers to Rosh Hashanah, which occurs on the first day of Tishrei and is the day when the *shofar* is blown.

עֵדוּת בִּיהוֹסֵף שָׂמוֹ — *He imposed it as a testimony for Joseph.* This verse is based on Joseph's life. The Talmud teaches that on Rosh Hashanah Joseph was released from prison and appointed viceroy of Egypt. In honor of that event, God ordained the *mitzvah* of shofar on Rosh Hashanah as a *testimony* of Joseph's freedom.

הַרְחֶב פִּיךָ — *Open wide your mouth,* with requests, and I will fulfill them. God urges

SONG OF THE DAY

Sh'ma ami v'o-ido boch,	שְׁמַע עַמִּי וְאָעִידָה בָּךְ,

Listen, My nation, and I will attest to you;

yisro-ayl im tishma li.	יִשְׂרָאֵל אִם תִּשְׁמַע לִי.

O Israel, if you would but listen to Me.

Lō yih-ye v'cho ayl zor,	לֹא יִהְיֶה בְךָ אֵל זָר,

There shall be no strange god within you,

v'lō sishta-chave l'ayl naychor.	וְלֹא תִשְׁתַּחֲוֶה לְאֵל נֵכָר.

nor shall you bow before an alien god.

Onōchi Adōnoy Elōhecho,	אָנֹכִי יהוה אֱלֹהֶיךָ,
hama-alcho may-eretz mitzro-yim,	הַמַּעַלְךָ מֵאֶרֶץ מִצְרָיִם,

I am HASHEM, your God, Who elevated you from the land of Egypt,

harchev picho vo-amalayhu.	הַרְחֶב פִּיךָ וַאֲמַלְאֵהוּ.

open wide your mouth* and I will fill it.

V'lō shoma ami l'kōli,	וְלֹא שָׁמַע עַמִּי לְקוֹלִי,
v'yisro-ayl lō ovo li.	וְיִשְׂרָאֵל לֹא אָבָה לִי.

But My people did not heed My voice and Israel did not desire Me.

Vo-ashal'chayhu b'shrirus libom,	וָאֲשַׁלְּחֵהוּ בִּשְׁרִירוּת לִבָּם,
yayl'chu b'mō-atzōsayhem.	יֵלְכוּ בְּמוֹעֲצוֹתֵיהֶם.

So I let them follow their heart's fantasies, they follow their own counsels.

Lu ami shōmay-a li,	לוּ עַמִּי שֹׁמֵעַ לִי,
yisro-ayl bidrochai y'halaychu.	יִשְׂרָאֵל בִּדְרָכַי יְהַלֵּכוּ.

If only My people would heed Me, if Israel would walk in My ways.

Kimat ō-y'vayhem achni-a,	כִּמְעַט אוֹיְבֵיהֶם אַכְנִיעַ,

In an instant I would subdue their foes,

v'al tzorayhem oshiv yodi:	וְעַל צָרֵיהֶם אָשִׁיב יָדִי.

and against their tormentors turn My hand.

M'sanay Adōnoy y'chachashu lō,	מְשַׂנְאֵי יהוה יְכַחֲשׁוּ לוֹ,

Those who hate HASHEM lie to Him —

vihi itom l'ōlom.	וִיהִי עִתָּם לְעוֹלָם.

so their destiny is eternal.

❖ Va-ya-achilayhu maychaylev chito,	❖ וַיַּאֲכִילֵהוּ מֵחֵלֶב חִטָּה,

But He would feed him with the cream of the wheat,

u-mitzur d'vash asbi-eko.	וּמִצּוּר דְּבַשׁ אַשְׂבִּיעֶךָ.

and with honey from a rock sate you.

IF A MOURNER IS PRESENT, HE RECITES THE MOURNER'S *KADDISH* (PAGE 259).

Israel to ask all that its heart desires. By asking God for *everything* that he needs, a person demonstrates his faith that God's power and generosity know no bounds.

שחרית לחול / 272 — שיר של יום

FOR FRIDAY

■ I remember the Shabbos daily: On the sixth day, at the completion of Creation, Hashem is described as being in His full grandeur, and "dressing" Himself like a person adorned in special Sabbath clothing.

Ha-yōm yōm shishi ba-shabos,   הַיּוֹם יוֹם שִׁשִּׁי בַּשַּׁבָּת,
Today is the sixth day* of the Sabbath,
shebō ho-yu hal'viyim
ōm'rim b'vays hamikdosh: שֶׁבּוֹ הָיוּ הַלְוִיִּם
אוֹמְרִים בְּבֵית הַמִּקְדָּשׁ:
on which the Levites would recite in the Holy Temple:

ADŌNOY MOLOCH gay-us lovaysh,   יהוה מָלָךְ, גֵּאוּת לָבֵשׁ,
HASHEM *will have reigned, He will have donned grandeur;*
lovaysh Adōnoy ōz his-azor,   לָבֵשׁ יהוה עֹז הִתְאַזָּר,
HASHEM *will have donned might and girded Himself;*
af tikōn tayvayl bal timōt.   אַף תִּכּוֹן תֵּבֵל בַּל תִּמּוֹט.
He even made the world firm so that it should not falter.
Nochōn kis-acho may-oz,
may-ōlom oto.   נָכוֹן כִּסְאֲךָ מֵאָז,
מֵעוֹלָם אָתָּה.
Your throne was established from of old, eternal are You.
Nos'u n'horōs, Adōnoy,
nos'u n'horōs kōlom,   נָשְׂאוּ נְהָרוֹת יהוה,
נָשְׂאוּ נְהָרוֹת קוֹלָם,
Like rivers they raised, O HASHEM, *like rivers they raised their voice;*
yis-u n'horōs doch'yom.   יִשְׂאוּ נְהָרוֹת דָּכְיָם.
like rivers they shall raise their destructiveness.
Mikōlōs ma-yim rabim,
adirim mishb'ray yom,   מִקֹּלוֹת מַיִם רַבִּים,
אַדִּירִים מִשְׁבְּרֵי יָם,
More than the roars of many waters, mightier than the waves of the sea —
adir bamorōm Adōnoy.   אַדִּיר בַּמָּרוֹם יהוה.
HASHEM *is mighty on high.*
Aydōsecho ne-emnu m'ōd   ❖ עֵדֹתֶיךָ נֶאֶמְנוּ מְאֹד
Your testimonies are exceedingly trustworthy about
l'vays'cho no-avo kōdesh,
Adōnoy l'ōrech yomim.   לְבֵיתְךָ נַאֲוָה קֹדֶשׁ,
יהוה לְאֹרֶךְ יָמִים.
Your House, the Sacred Dwelling — O HASHEM, *may it be for lengthy days.*

IF A MOURNER IS PRESENT, HE RECITES THE MOURNER'S *KADDISH* (PAGE 259).

הַיּוֹם יוֹם שִׁשִּׁי — *Today is the sixth day.* Psalm 93 was designated as the song of Friday, when the footsteps of the Sabbath begin to be heard, because it describes God in His full grandeur and power as He was when He completed the six days of Creation. Moreover, it describes Him as "donning" grandeur and "girding" Himself like one dressing in his Sabbath finery.

SONG OF THE DAY

> ■ *Rosh Chodesh* Elul, forty days after the incident of the Golden Calf, was the third time Moses ascended Mt. Sinai, and forty days later, on Yom Kippur, he brought with him the message of God's forgiveness. Every year we relive this momentous chapter in our history, highlighting the special opportunity for repentance and forgiveness by reciting this psalm, which contains allusions to the holidays of Rosh Hashanah, Yom Kippur, and Succos.

FROM *ROSH CHODESH* ELUL THROUGH SHEMINI ATZERES, THE FOLLOWING PSALM IS RECITED.

L'DOVID, Adōnoy ōri v'yish-i mimi iro, לְדָוִד, יהוה אוֹרִי וְיִשְׁעִי, מִמִּי אִירָא,

Of David; HASHEM is my light and my salvation, whom shall I fear?

Adōnoy mo-ōz cha-yai, mimi efchod. יהוה מָעוֹז חַיַּי, מִמִּי אֶפְחָד.

HASHEM is my life's strength, whom shall I dread?

Bikrōv olai m'ray-im בִּקְרֹב עָלַי מְרֵעִים

When evildoers approach me

le-echōl es b'sori, לֶאֱכֹל אֶת בְּשָׂרִי,

to devour my flesh,

tzorai v'ō-y'vai li, צָרַי וְאֹיְבַי לִי,

my tormentors and my foes against me —

haymo kosh'lu v'nofolu. הֵמָּה כָּשְׁלוּ וְנָפָלוּ.

it is they who stumble and fall.

Im ta-chane olai ma-chane, lō yiro libi, אִם תַּחֲנֶה עָלַי מַחֲנֶה, לֹא יִירָא לִבִּי,

Though an army would besiege me, my heart would not fear;

im tokum olai milchomo, b'zōs ani vōtay-ach. אִם תָּקוּם עָלַי מִלְחָמָה, בְּזֹאת אֲנִי בוֹטֵחַ.

though war would arise against me, in this I trust.

Achas sho-alti may-ays Adōnoy, ōsoh avakaysh, אַחַת שָׁאַלְתִּי מֵאֵת יהוה, אוֹתָהּ אֲבַקֵּשׁ,

One thing I asked of HASHEM, that shall I seek:

shivti b'vays Adōnoy kol y'may cha-yai, שִׁבְתִּי בְּבֵית יהוה כָּל יְמֵי חַיַּי,

that I dwell in the House of HASHEM all the days of my life;

la-chazōs b'nō-am Adōnoy, ulvakayr b'haycholō. לַחֲזוֹת בְּנֹעַם יהוה, וּלְבַקֵּר בְּהֵיכָלוֹ.

to behold the sweetness of HASHEM and to contemplate in His Sanctuary.

Ki yitzp'nayni b'sukō b'yōm ro-o, כִּי יִצְפְּנֵנִי בְּסֻכֹּה בְּיוֹם רָעָה,

Indeed, He will hide me in His shelter on the day of evil;

yastirayni b'sayser oholō, יַסְתִּירֵנִי בְּסֵתֶר אָהֳלוֹ,

He will conceal me in the concealment of His Tent,

b'tzur y'rōm'mayni.	בְּצוּר יְרוֹמְמֵנִי.

He will lift me upon a rock.

V'ato yorum rōshi	וְעַתָּה יָרוּם רֹאשִׁי
al ō-y'vai s'vivōsai,	עַל אֹיְבַי סְבִיבוֹתַי,

Now my head is raised above my enemies around me,

v'ezb'cho v'oholō zivchay s'ru-o,	וְאֶזְבְּחָה בְאָהֳלוֹ זִבְחֵי תְרוּעָה,

and in His Tent I will slaughter offerings accompanied by joyous song;

oshiro va-azam'ro Ladōnoy.	אָשִׁירָה וַאֲזַמְּרָה לַיהוה.

I will sing and make music to HASHEM.

Sh'ma Adōnoy kōli ekro,	שְׁמַע יהוה קוֹלִי אֶקְרָא,
v'chonayni va-anayni.	וְחָנֵּנִי וַעֲנֵנִי.

HASHEM, hear my voice when I call, and be gracious toward me and answer me.

L'cho omar libi bak'shu fonoy,	לְךָ אָמַר לִבִּי בַּקְּשׁוּ פָנָי,

In Your behalf, my heart has said, "Seek My Presence";

es ponecho Adōnoy avakaysh.	אֶת פָּנֶיךָ יהוה אֲבַקֵּשׁ.

Your Presence, HASHEM, do I seek.

Al tastayr ponecho mimeni,	אַל תַּסְתֵּר פָּנֶיךָ מִמֶּנִּי,
al tat b'af avdecho,	אַל תַּט בְּאַף עַבְדֶּךָ,

Conceal not Your Presence from me, repel not Your servant in anger.

ezrosi ho-yiso,	עֶזְרָתִי הָיִיתָ,

You have been my Helper,

al tit'shayni v'al ta-azvayni,	אַל תִּטְּשֵׁנִי וְאַל תַּעַזְבֵנִי,
Elōhay yish-i.	אֱלֹהֵי יִשְׁעִי.

abandon me not, forsake me not, O God of my salvation.

Ki ovi v'imi azovuni,	כִּי אָבִי וְאִמִּי עֲזָבוּנִי,
Vadōnoy ya-asfayni.	וַיהוה יַאַסְפֵנִי.

Though my father and mother have forsaken me, HASHEM will gather me in.

Hōrayni Adōnoy dar-kecho,	הוֹרֵנִי יהוה דַּרְכֶּךָ,
un-chayni b'ōrach mi-shōr,	וּנְחֵנִי בְּאֹרַח מִישׁוֹר,

Teach me Your way, HASHEM, and lead me on the path of integrity,

l'ma-an shōr'roy.	לְמַעַן שׁוֹרְרָי.

because of my watchful foes.

Al tit'nayni b'nefesh tzoroy,	אַל תִּתְּנֵנִי בְּנֶפֶשׁ צָרָי,

Deliver me not to the wishes of my tormentors,

ki komu vi	כִּי קָמוּ בִי
ayday sheker vifay-ach chomos.	עֵדֵי שֶׁקֶר, וִיפֵחַ חָמָס.

for there have arisen against me false witnesses who breathe violence.

Lulay he-emanti	׃ לוּלֵא הֶאֱמַנְתִּי
Had I not trusted	
lir-ōs b'tuv Adōnoy b'eretz cha-yim.	לִרְאוֹת בְּטוּב יהוה בְּאֶרֶץ חַיִּים.
that I would see the goodness of HASHEM *in the land of life!*	
Kavay el Adōnoy,	קַוֵּה אֶל יהוה,
Hope to HASHEM,	
chazak v'ya-amaytz libecho,	חֲזַק וְיַאֲמֵץ לִבֶּךָ,
strengthen yourself and He will give your heart courage;	
v'kavay el Adōnoy.	וְקַוֵּה אֶל יהוה.
and hope to HASHEM.	

IF A MOURNER IS PRESENT, HE RECITES THE MOURNER'S *KADDISH* (PAGE 259).

■ Psalm 104: My soul bursts forth blessing Hashem; His greatness and His glory, His goodness and His wisdom are manifested in the brilliance of the world He created.

MANY CONGREGATIONS RECITE PSALM 104 ON *ROSH CHODESH:*

BOR'CHI NAFSHI es Adōnoy,	**בָּרְכִי נַפְשִׁי** אֶת יהוה,
Bless HASHEM, *O my soul.**	
Adōnoy Elōhai godalto m'ōd,	יהוה אֱלֹהַי גָּדַלְתָּ מְּאֹד,
HASHEM, *my God, You are very great;*	
hōd v'hodor lovoshto.	הוֹד וְהָדָר לָבָשְׁתָּ.
You have donned majesty and splendor;	
Ōte ōr kasalmo,	עֹטֶה אוֹר כַּשַּׂלְמָה,
covering with light as with a garment,	
nōte shoma-yim kai-ri-o.	נוֹטֶה שָׁמַיִם כַּיְרִיעָה.
stretching out the heavens like a curtain.	
Ham'kore vama-yim aliyōsov,	הַמְקָרֶה בַמַּיִם עֲלִיּוֹתָיו,
He Who roofs His upper chambers with water;	
hasom ovim r'chuvō,	הַשָּׂם עָבִים רְכוּבוֹ,
He Who makes clouds His chariot;	
ham'halaych al kanfay ru-ach.	הַמְהַלֵּךְ עַל כַּנְפֵי רוּחַ.
He Who walks on winged wind.	
Ōse mal-ochov ruchōs,	עֹשֶׂה מַלְאָכָיו רוּחוֹת,
He makes the winds His messengers,	

בָּרְכִי נַפְשִׁי אֶת ה׳ — *Bless Hashem, O my soul.* Psalm 104 is recited on *Rosh Chodesh* because the Psalmist alludes to the new moon in the verse: "He made the moon for Festivals."

These words are not merely a casual allusion to the new month. Rather, they set the tone of this entire composition, whose main theme is God's complete mastery over every aspect of Creation. Throughout the monthly lunar cycle, the size of the moon visibly waxes and wanes, to demonstrate dramatically that God has total mastery over His creations. No other natural phenomenon conveys this message as vividly and forcefully as the moon's cycle. Thus, the

מְשָׁרְתָיו אֵשׁ לֹהֵט.
m'shor'sov aysh lōhayt.
the flaming fire His attendants.

יָסַד אֶרֶץ עַל מְכוֹנֶיהָ,
בַּל תִּמּוֹט עוֹלָם וָעֶד.
Yosad eretz al m'chōneho,
bal timōt ōlom vo-ed.
He established the earth upon its foundations, that it falter not forever and ever.

תְּהוֹם כַּלְּבוּשׁ כִּסִּיתוֹ,
T'hōm kal'vush kisisō,
The watery deep, as with a garment You covered it;

עַל הָרִים יַעַמְדוּ מָיִם.
al horim ya-amdu mo-yim.
upon the mountains, water would stand.

מִן גַּעֲרָתְךָ יְנוּסוּן,
מִן קוֹל רַעַמְךָ יֵחָפֵזוּן.
Min ga-aros'cho y'nusun,
min kōl ra-amcho yaychofayzun.
From Your rebuke they flee, from the sound of Your thunder they rush away.

יַעֲלוּ הָרִים, יֵרְדוּ בְקָעוֹת,
Ya-alu horim, yayr'du v'ko-ōs,
They ascend mountains, they descend to valleys,

אֶל מְקוֹם זֶה יָסַדְתָּ לָהֶם.
el m'kōm ze yosadto lohem.
to the special place You founded for them.

גְּבוּל שַׂמְתָּ בַּל יַעֲבֹרוּן,
G'vul samto bal ya-avōrun,
You set a boundary they cannot overstep,

בַּל יְשׁוּבוּן לְכַסּוֹת הָאָרֶץ.
bal y'shuvun l'chasōs ho-oretz.
they cannot return to cover the earth.

הַמְשַׁלֵּחַ מַעְיָנִים בַּנְּחָלִים,
Ham'shalay-ach ma-yonim ban'cholim,
He sends the springs into the streams,

בֵּין הָרִים יְהַלֵּכוּן.
bayn horim y'halaychun.
they flow between the mountains.

יַשְׁקוּ כָּל חַיְתוֹ שָׂדָי,
יִשְׁבְּרוּ פְרָאִים צְמָאָם.
Yashku kol chaisō sodoy,
yishb'ru f'ro-im tz'mo-om.
They water every beast of the field, they quench the wild creatures' thirst.

עֲלֵיהֶם עוֹף הַשָּׁמַיִם יִשְׁכּוֹן,
Alayhem ōf ha-shoma-yim yishkōn,
Near them dwell the heaven's birds,

---

theme of the New Moon complements the theme of this entire hymn of praise to the Master of Creation.

By calling upon his soul to bless God, the Psalmist suggests that the human soul is God's great gift to man and, in effect, thanks God for the ability to reason, articulate, and rise to spiritual heights.

הַמְשַׁלֵּחַ מַעְיָנִים בַּנְּחָלִים — *He sends the springs into the streams*. The Psalmist describes poeti-cally how God instituted a natural system whereby the earth would be watered to provide for people and vegetation.

מַצְמִיחַ חָצִיר לַבְּהֵמָה וְעֵשֶׂב לַעֲבֹדַת הָאָדָם — *He causes vegetation to sprout for the cattle, and plants through man's labor*. For animals, which cannot engage in agriculture, God causes vegetation to sprout. Man, however, must labor to earn his daily bread. Before he can partake of food, he must first sow, reap, thresh, knead,

mibayn ofo-yim yit'nu kōl.	מִבֵּין עֳפָאיִם יִתְּנוּ קוֹל.

from among the branches they give forth song.

Mashke horim may-aliyōsov,	מַשְׁקֶה הָרִים מֵעֲלִיּוֹתָיו,

He waters the mountains from His upper chambers,

mip'ri ma-asecho tisba ho-oretz.	מִפְּרִי מַעֲשֶׂיךָ תִּשְׂבַּע הָאָרֶץ.

from the fruit of Your works the earth is sated.

Matzmi-ach chotzir lab'haymo,	מַצְמִיחַ חָצִיר לַבְּהֵמָה,

He causes vegetation to sprout for the cattle,

v'aysev la-avōdas ho-odom,	וְעֵשֶׂב לַעֲבֹדַת הָאָדָם,

and plants through man's labor,*

l'hōtzi lechem min ho-oretz.	לְהוֹצִיא לֶחֶם מִן הָאָרֶץ.

to bring forth bread from the earth,

V'ya-yin y'samach l'vav enōsh,	וְיַיִן יְשַׂמַּח לְבַב אֱנוֹשׁ,

and wine that gladdens man's heart,*

l'hatzhil ponim mi-shomen,	לְהַצְהִיל פָּנִים מִשָּׁמֶן,

to make the face glow from oil,

v'lechem l'vav enōsh yis-od.	וְלֶחֶם לְבַב אֱנוֹשׁ יִסְעָד.

and bread that sustains the heart of man.

Yisb'u atzay Adōnoy,	יִשְׂבְּעוּ עֲצֵי יהוה,
arzay l'vonōn asher noto.	אַרְזֵי לְבָנוֹן אֲשֶׁר נָטָע.

The trees of HASHEM are sated, the cedars of Lebanon that He has planted;

Asher shom tziporim y'kanaynu,	אֲשֶׁר שָׁם צִפֳּרִים יְקַנֵּנוּ,

there where the birds nest,

chasido b'rōshim baysoh.	חֲסִידָה בְּרוֹשִׁים בֵּיתָהּ.

the chassidah with its home among cypresses;

Horim hag'vōhim la-y'aylim,	הָרִים הַגְּבֹהִים לַיְּעֵלִים,
s'lo-im machse lash'fanim.	סְלָעִים מַחְסֶה לַשְׁפַנִּים.

high mountains for the wild goats,* rocks as refuge for the gophers.

Oso yoray-ach l'mō-adim,	עָשָׂה יָרֵחַ לְמוֹעֲדִים,

He made the moon for Festivals,*

---

and bake his bread.

וְיַיִן יְשַׂמַּח לְבַב אֱנוֹשׁ — **And wine that gladdens man's heart.** God creates the grapes from which wine is pressed. When drunk in sensible amounts, wine gladdens the heart and drives away melancholy. It heightens the intellect and even prepares the mind for prophecy.

הָרִים הַגְּבֹהִים לַיְּעֵלִים — **High mountains for the wild goats.** At first glance, the remote and barren mountains appear to serve no purpose; but in fact they were created to provide a habitat for the wild mountain goats.

Contrary to the theory that species survived only by adapting themselves to hostile environments, the Psalmist says that God created the setting to suit the needs of the species.

עָשָׂה יָרֵחַ לְמוֹעֲדִים — **He made the moon for Festivals**, i.e., the moon and its cycles were made to facilitate the lunar calendar, upon which the Torah bases the dating of the Festivals.

shemesh yoda m'vō-ō.	שֶׁמֶשׁ יָדַע מְבוֹאוֹ.

the sun knows its destination.

To-shes chōshech vi-hi loylo,	תָּשֶׁת חֹשֶׁךְ וִיהִי לָיְלָה,

You make darkness and it is night,

bō sirmōs kol chaisō yo-ar.	בּוֹ תִרְמֹשׂ כָּל חַיְתוֹ יָעַר.

in which every forest beast stirs.

Hak'firim shō-agim latoref,	הַכְּפִירִים שֹׁאֲגִים לַטָּרֶף,
ulvakaysh may-Ayl ochlom.	וּלְבַקֵּשׁ מֵאֵל אָכְלָם.

The young lions roar after their prey, and to seek their food from God.

Tizrach ha-shemesh yay-osayfun,	תִּזְרַח הַשֶּׁמֶשׁ יֵאָסֵפוּן,

The sun rises and they are gathered in,

v'el m'ōnōsom yirbotzun.	וְאֶל מְעוֹנֹתָם יִרְבָּצוּן.

and in their dens they crouch.

Yaytzay odom l'fo-olō,	יֵצֵא אָדָם לְפָעֳלוֹ,
v'la-avōdosō aday orev.	וְלַעֲבֹדָתוֹ עֲדֵי עָרֶב.

Man goes forth to his work, and to his labor until evening.

Mo rabu ma-asecho Adōnoy,	מָה רַבּוּ מַעֲשֶׂיךָ יהוה,

How abundant are Your works, HASHEM;

kulom b'chochmo osiso,	כֻּלָּם בְּחָכְמָה עָשִׂיתָ,

with wisdom You made them all,*

mol'o ho-oretz kinyonecho.	מָלְאָה הָאָרֶץ קִנְיָנֶךָ.

the earth is full of Your possessions.*

Ze ha-yom godōl urchav yodo-yim,	זֶה הַיָּם, גָּדוֹל וּרְחַב יָדָיִם,

Behold this sea — great and of broad measure;

shom remes v'ayn mispor,	שָׁם רֶמֶשׂ וְאֵין מִסְפָּר,

there are creeping things without number,

cha-yōs k'tanōs im g'dōlōs.	חַיּוֹת קְטַנּוֹת עִם גְּדֹלוֹת.

small creatures and great ones.

Shom oniyōs y'halaychun,	שָׁם אֳנִיּוֹת יְהַלֵּכוּן,

There ships travel,

livyoson ze yotzarto l'sachek bō.	לִוְיָתָן זֶה יָצַרְתָּ לְשַׂחֶק בּוֹ.

this Leviathan You fashioned to sport with.

Kulom aylecho y'sabayrun,	כֻּלָּם אֵלֶיךָ יְשַׂבֵּרוּן,

All of them look to You with hope,

כֻּלָּם בְּחָכְמָה עָשִׂיתָ — *With wisdom You made them all.* No creature evolved by chance; each one was designed by God in His *wisdom* and demonstrates His omnipotence.

מָלְאָה הָאָרֶץ קִנְיָנֶךָ — *The earth is full of Your possessions.* God allows nothing to go to waste. Every spot is full of wondrous creations which testify to God's absolute mastery.

לָתֵת אָכְלָם בְּעִתּוֹ.	losays ochlom b'itō.

to provide their food in its [proper] time.

תִּתֵּן לָהֶם, יִלְקֹטוּן,	Titayn lohem, yilkōtun,

You give to them, they gather it in;

תִּפְתַּח יָדְךָ, יִשְׂבְּעוּן טוֹב.	tiftach yod'cho, yisb'un tōv.

You open Your hand, they are sated with good.

תַּסְתִּיר פָּנֶיךָ יִבָּהֵלוּן,	Tastir ponecho yibohaylun,

When You hide Your face, they are dismayed;

תֹּסֵף רוּחָם יִגְוָעוּן,	tōsayf ruchom yigvo-un
וְאֶל עֲפָרָם יְשׁוּבוּן.	v'el aforom y'shuvun.

when You retrieve their spirit, they perish and to their dust they return.

תְּשַׁלַּח רוּחֲךָ יִבָּרֵאוּן,	T'shalach ruchacho yiboray-un

When You send forth Your breath, they are created,

וּתְחַדֵּשׁ פְּנֵי אֲדָמָה.	us-chadaysh p'nay adomo.

and You renew the surface of the earth.

יְהִי כְבוֹד יהוה לְעוֹלָם,	Y'hi ch'vōd Adōnoy l'ōlom,

May the glory of HASHEM endure forever,

יִשְׂמַח יהוה בְּמַעֲשָׂיו.	yismach Adōnoy b'ma-asov.

let HASHEM rejoice in His works.

הַמַּבִּיט לָאָרֶץ וַתִּרְעָד,	Hamabit lo-oretz vatir-od,

He looks toward the earth and it trembles,

יִגַּע בֶּהָרִים וְיֶעֱשָׁנוּ.	yiga behorim v'ye-eshonu.

He touches the mountains and they smoke.

אָשִׁירָה לַיהוה בְּחַיָּי,	O-shiro Ladōnoy b'cha-yoy,
אֲזַמְּרָה לֵאלֹהַי בְּעוֹדִי.	azam'ro Laylōhai b'ōdi.

I will sing to HASHEM while I live, I will sing praises to my God while I endure.

יֶעֱרַב עָלָיו שִׂיחִי,	Ye-erav olov sichi
אָנֹכִי אֶשְׂמַח בַּיהוה.	onōchi esmach Badōnoy.

May my words be sweet to Him — I will rejoice in HASHEM.

יִתַּמּוּ חַטָּאִים מִן הָאָרֶץ,	Yitamu chato-im min ho-oretz
וּרְשָׁעִים עוֹד אֵינָם,	ursho-im ōd aynom,

Sinners will cease from the earth, and the wicked will be no more —

בָּרְכִי נַפְשִׁי אֶת יהוה,	bor'chi nafshi es Adōnoy,
הַלְלוּיָהּ.	hal'luyoh.

Bless HASHEM, O my soul. Praise God!

IF A MOURNER IS PRESENT, HE RECITES THE MOURNER'S *KADDISH* (PAGE 259).

■ *Psalm* 49 teaches that man should use his sojourn on earth to enhance his spiritual development so that he will be better prepared for the World to Come. This concept is a source of comfort for those who have lost a close relative; therefore it is customary to recite this psalm after *Shacharis* and *Maariv* in the home of someone observing *shivah*, the seven-day period of mourning.

IN A HOUSE OF MOURNING, PSALM 49 IS RECITED:

LAM'NATZAY-ACH livnay kōrach mizmōr. לַמְנַצֵּחַ לִבְנֵי קֹרַח מִזְמוֹר.
For the Conductor, by the sons of Korach, a psalm.

Shim-u zōs kol ho-amim, שִׁמְעוּ זֹאת כָּל הָעַמִּים,
Hear this all you peoples,

ha-azinu kol yōsh'vay choled. הַאֲזִינוּ כָּל יֹשְׁבֵי חָלֶד.
give ear all you dwellers of decaying earth.

Gam b'nay odom, gam b'nay ish, גַּם בְּנֵי אָדָם, גַּם בְּנֵי אִישׁ,
Sons of Adam and sons of man alike;

yachad o-shir v'evyōn. יַחַד עָשִׁיר וְאֶבְיוֹן.
together — rich man, poor man.

Pi y'dabayr chochmōs, פִּי יְדַבֵּר חָכְמוֹת,
My mouth shall speak wisdom,

v'hogus libi s'vunōs. וְהָגוּת לִבִּי תְבוּנוֹת.
and the meditations of my heart are insightful.

A-te l'moshol ozni, אַטֶּה לְמָשָׁל אָזְנִי,
I will incline my ear to the parable,

eftach b'chinōr chidosi. אֶפְתַּח בְּכִנּוֹר חִידָתִי.
with a harp I will solve my riddle.

Lomo iro bimay ro, לָמָּה אִירָא בִּימֵי רָע,
Why should I have to fear in days of evil,

avon akayvai y'subayni. עֲוֹן עֲקֵבַי יְסֻבֵּנִי.
when the injunctions that I trod upon will surround me?

Habōt'chim al chaylom, הַבֹּטְחִים עַל חֵילָם,
Those who rely on their possessions,

uvrōv oshrom yis-halolu. וּבְרֹב עָשְׁרָם יִתְהַלָּלוּ.
and of their great wealth they are boastful —

Och lō fodō yifde ish, אָח לֹא פָדֹה יִפְדֶּה אִישׁ,
yet a man cannot redeem a brother,

lō yitayn Laylōhim kofrō. לֹא יִתֵּן לֵאלֹהִים כָּפְרוֹ.
nor give to God his ransom.

V'yaykar pidyōn nafshom,	וְיֵקַר פִּדְיוֹן נַפְשָׁם,
Too costly is their soul's redemption	
v'chodal l'ōlom.	וְחָדַל לְעוֹלָם.
and unattainable forever.	
Vichi ōd lənetzach,	וִיחִי עוֹד לָנֶצַח,
Can one live eternally,	
lō yir-e ha-shochas.	לֹא יִרְאֶה הַשָּׁחַת.
never to see the pit?	
Ki yir-e chachomim yomusu,*	כִּי יִרְאֶה חֲכָמִים יָמוּתוּ,
Though he sees that wise men die,*	
yachad k'sil vova-ar yōvaydu,	יַחַד כְּסִיל וָבַעַר יֹאבֵדוּ,
that the foolish and boorish perish together	
v'oz'vu la-achayrim chaylom.	וְעָזְבוּ לַאֲחֵרִים חֵילָם.
and leave their possessions to others — [nevertheless,]	
Kirbom botaymō l'ōlom,	קִרְבָּם בָּתֵּימוֹ לְעוֹלָם,
in their imagination their houses are forever,	
mish-k'nōsom l'dōr vodōr,	מִשְׁכְּנֹתָם לְדוֹר וָדֹר,
their dwellings for generation after generation;	
kor'u vish-mōsom alay adomōs.	קָרְאוּ בִשְׁמוֹתָם עֲלֵי אֲדָמוֹת.
they have proclaimed their names throughout the lands.	
V'odom bikor bal yolin,	וְאָדָם בִּיקָר בַּל יָלִין,
But as for man — in glory he shall not repose,	
nimshal kab'haymōs nidmu.	נִמְשַׁל כַּבְּהֵמוֹת נִדְמוּ.
he is likened to the silenced animals.	
Ze darkom, kesel lomō,	זֶה דַרְכָּם, כֵּסֶל לָמוֹ,
This is their way — folly is theirs,	
v'a-charayhem b'fihem yirtzu, selo.	וְאַחֲרֵיהֶם בְּפִיהֶם יִרְצוּ, סֶלָה.
yet of their destiny their mouths speak soothingly, Selah!	
Katzōn lish-ōl shatu,	כַּצֹאן לִשְׁאוֹל שַׁתּוּ,
Like sheep, they are destined for the Lower World,	

כִּי יִרְאֶה חֲכָמִים יָמוּתוּ — *Though he sees that wise men die.* Sinners are deluded because they see that even good people die. If death grasps everyone equally, then why should the wealthy not indulge his pleasures?

אַךְ אֱלֹהִים יִפְדֶּה נַפְשִׁי — *But God will redeem my soul.* Having completed his observations regarding the doom facing the wicked, the Psalmist now expresses his confidence that *he* can look forward to the splendor of the World to Come.

mo-ves yir-aym,	מָוֶת יִרְעֵם,

death shall consume them;

va-yirdu vom y'shorim labōker,	וַיִּרְדּוּ בָם יְשָׁרִים לַבֹּקֶר,

and the upright shall dominate them at daybreak,

v'tzurom l'valōs sh'ōl	וְצוּרָם לְבַלּוֹת שְׁאוֹל

their essence is doomed to rot in the grave,

miz'vul lō.	מִזְּבֻל לוֹ.

each from his dwelling.

Ach Elōhim yifde nafshi	אַךְ אֱלֹהִים יִפְדֶּה נַפְשִׁי

But God will redeem my soul*

miyad sh'ōl,	מִיַּד שְׁאוֹל,

from the grip of the Lower World,

ki yikochayni selo.	כִּי יִקָּחֵנִי סֶלָה.

for He will take me, Selah!

Al tiro ki ya-ashir ish,	אַל תִּירָא כִּי יַעֲשִׁר אִישׁ,

Fear not when a man grows rich,

ki yirbe k'vōd bay-sō.	כִּי יִרְבֶּה כְּבוֹד בֵּיתוֹ.

when he increases the splendor of his house.

Ki lō v'mōsō yikach hakōl,	כִּי לֹא בְמוֹתוֹ יִקַּח הַכֹּל,

For upon his death he will not take anything,

lō yayrayd acharov k'vōdō.	לֹא יֵרֵד אַחֲרָיו כְּבוֹדוֹ.

his splendor will not descend after him.

Ki nafshō b'cha-yov y'voraych,	כִּי נַפְשׁוֹ בְּחַיָּיו יְבָרֵךְ,

Though he may bless himself in his lifetime,

v'yōducho ki saytiv loch.	וְיוֹדֻךָ כִּי תֵיטִיב לָךְ.

others will praise you if you improve yourself.

Tovō ad dōr avōsov,	תָּבוֹא עַד דּוֹר אֲבוֹתָיו,

It shall come to the generation of its fathers —

ad naytzach lō yir-u ōr.	עַד נֵצַח לֹא יִרְאוּ אוֹר.

unto eternity they shall see no light.

❖ Odom bikor v'lō yovin,	❖ אָדָם בִּיקָר וְלֹא יָבִין,

Man is glorious but understands not,

nimshal kab'haymōs nidmu.	נִמְשַׁל כַּבְּהֵמוֹת נִדְמוּ.

he is likened to the silenced animals.

IF A MOURNER IS PRESENT, HE RECITES THE MOURNER'S *KADDISH* (PAGE 259).

READINGS FOLLOWING SHACHARIS
THE SIX REMEMBRANCES

- The Torah commands that these six historical themes be remembered always, to impact our daily existence.

1. THE EXODUS FROM EGYPT (Deuteronomy 16:3)

- As Hashem redeemed the Jewish people from Egypt, so He directs my daily life.

L'MA-AN tizkor es yōm tzays'cho may-eretz mitzra-yim

לְמַעַן תִּזְכֹּר אֶת יוֹם צֵאתְךָ מֵאֶרֶץ מִצְרַיִם

That you may remember the day of your departure from the land of Egypt

kōl y'may cha-yecho.

כֹּל יְמֵי חַיֶּיךָ.

all the days of your life.

2. RECEIVING THE TORAH AT MOUNT SINAI (Deuteronomy 4:9-10)

- No other people can claim that their entire nation experienced Revelation, and I recall daily the awe and reverence that accompanied the giving of the Torah.

RAK hi-shomer l'cho ushmōr naf-sh'cho m'ōd,

רַק הִשָּׁמֶר לְךָ וּשְׁמֹר נַפְשְׁךָ מְאֹד,

Only beware and guard yourself carefully,

pen tish-kach es had'vorim asher ro-u ay-necho,

פֶּן תִּשְׁכַּח אֶת הַדְּבָרִים אֲשֶׁר רָאוּ עֵינֶיךָ,

lest you forget the things your eyes have seen

u-fen yosuru mil'vov'cho kol y'may cha-yecho,

וּפֶן יָסוּרוּ מִלְּבָבְךָ כֹּל יְמֵי חַיֶּיךָ,

and lest they stray from your heart all the days of your life.

v'hoda-tom l'vonecho,

וְהוֹדַעְתָּם לְבָנֶיךָ,

And you are to make them known to your children

v'livnay vonecho,

וְלִבְנֵי בָנֶיךָ,

and to your children's children —

yom asher omad-to lifnay Adōnoy Elōhecho b'chōrayv.

יוֹם אֲשֶׁר עָמַדְתָּ לִפְנֵי יהוה אֱלֹהֶיךָ בְּחֹרֵב.

the day you stood before HASHEM, *your God, at Sinai.*

◆§ The Six Remembrances

Kabbalistic literature teaches that it is desirable to recite the six Scriptural passages that command us always to bear in mind specific events. Thus, these major themes in our history are kept alive in our consciousness.

1. The Exodus. The Exodus is essential to Israel's mission. The idea that God redeemed Israel from degrading slavery should inspire us with confidence in the future redemption.

2. Receiving the Torah at Mount Sinai. Israel's redemption — its very existence — is based on the mission entrusted to us when God presented us with the Torah, represented by the Ten Commandments, at Sinai. If we are not the nation of Torah, we are nothing.

3. AMALEK'S ATTACK (Deuteronomy 25:17-19)

■ *I remember with the Jewish poeple our obligation to remember and eradicate evil from society.*

ZOCHŌR ays asher   זָכוֹר אֵת אֲשֶׁר
oso l'cho amolayk,   עָשָׂה לְךָ עֲמָלֵק,
Remember what Amalek did to you
baderech b'tzayschem mimitzro-yim.   בַּדֶּרֶךְ בְּצֵאתְכֶם מִמִּצְרָיִם.
on the way, as you departed from Egypt.
Asher kor'cho baderech   אֲשֶׁר קָרְךָ בַּדֶּרֶךְ,
How he encountered you on the way
vaizanayv b'cho   וַיְזַנֵּב בְּךָ
kol hanechesholim acharecho,   כָּל הַנֶּחֱשָׁלִים אַחֲרֶיךָ,
and cut down the weaklings trailing behind you,
v'ato o-yayf v'yogay-a   וְאַתָּה עָיֵף וְיָגֵעַ,
v'lo yoray Elōhim.   וְלֹא יָרֵא אֱלֹהִים.
while you were faint and exhausted, and he did not fear God.
V'ho-yo b'honiach   וְהָיָה בְּהָנִיחַ
Adōnoy Elōhecho l'cho   יהוה אֱלֹהֶיךָ לְךָ
It shall be that when HASHEM, your God, lets you rest,
mikol o-y'vecho misoviv,   מִכָּל אֹיְבֶיךָ מִסָּבִיב,
from all your surrounding enemies,
bo-oretz asher Adōnoy Elōhecho   בָּאָרֶץ אֲשֶׁר יהוה אֱלֹהֶיךָ
nōsayn l'cho nachlo l'rishto,   נֹתֵן לְךָ נַחֲלָה לְרִשְׁתָּהּ,
in the land that HASHEM, your God, gives you as a heritage to bequeath;
tim-che es zaycher amolayk   תִּמְחֶה אֶת זֵכֶר עֲמָלֵק
mitachas ha-shoma-yim   מִתַּחַת הַשָּׁמָיִם,
you are to erase the memory of Amalek from beneath the heaven.
lo tishkoch.   לֹא תִּשְׁכָּח.
Do not forget.

4. THE GOLDEN CALF (Deuteronomy 9:7)

■ *I recall how we angered Hashem by worshiping the Golden Calf, and am reminded that man is vulnerable to quickly fall from a spiritual high to an abysmal low.*

Z'CHŌR al tishkach   זְכֹר, אַל תִּשְׁכַּח,
Remember, do not forget,

---

3. Amalek's attack. Amalek's ability to attack Israel resulted from Israel's failure to study thr Torah zealously (*Tanchuma, Beshalach*). Thus the episode of Amalek cautions us to hold the Torah precious. Also, the fate of Amalek — total extinction — reminds us that evil has no future.

4. The Golden Calf. One of the most dismal episodes in Jewish history, this sin caused Israel to

es asher hiktzafto אֶת אֲשֶׁר הִקְצַפְתָּ
es Adōnoy Elōhecho bamidbor. אֶת יהוה אֱלֹהֶיךָ, בַּמִּדְבָּר.
how you angered HASHEM, *your God, in the Wilderness.*

5. MIRIAM (Deuteronomy 24:9)

■ Miriam failed to realize the uniqueness of her brother Moshe (*Bamidbar* 12:1-2). I am charged to refrain from speaking evil or slandering our leaders and all people.

ZOCHŌR es asher oso זָכוֹר אֵת אֲשֶׁר עָשָׂה
Adōnoy Elōhecho l'mir-yom, יהוה אֱלֹהֶיךָ לְמִרְיָם,
Remember, what HASHEM, *your God, did to Miriam,*
baderech b'tzayschem mimitzrō-yim. בַּדֶּרֶךְ בְּצֵאתְכֶם מִמִּצְרָיִם.
on the way when you departed from Egypt.

6. THE SABBATH (Exodus 20:8)

■ By remembering Shabbos daily, I draw inspiration and sanctity from the previous Shabbos and anticipate the forthcoming Shabbos.

ZOCHŌR es yōm ha-shabos זָכוֹר אֶת יוֹם הַשַּׁבָּת
l'kad'shō. לְקַדְּשׁוֹ.
Remember the Sabbath day to hallow it.

THE THIRTEEN PRINCIPLES OF FAITH

■ Maimonides codified Thirteen Articles of Faith that embrace the totality of the Jewish belief system.

---- 1 ----

ANI MA-AMIN be-emuno sh'laymo, אֲנִי מַאֲמִין בֶּאֱמוּנָה שְׁלֵמָה,
I believe with complete faith

fall from the spiritual pedestal it had ascended upon receiving the Ten Commandments. This teaches us to have faith in God's promise and never deviate from His Torah, even if we think that we have found a better way to serve Him.

5. Miriam. Miriam criticized her brother Moses, on the grounds that he did not live with his wife. She failed to consider that a man of Moses' humility and unselfishness would not have done so unless he had been commanded always to hold himself in readiness for prophecy, a condition that mandated abstinence. Miriam was punished with *tzara'as*, a disease similar to leprosy, and was healed because of Moses' prayers. This teaches us never to slander another person.

6. The Sabbath. By refraining from work on the seventh day, the day that God rested upon completing Creation, the Jew offers enduring testimony that God created the world. Throughout the week, we remember the Sabbath by directing our preparations toward its honor.

ᴥ§ **The Thirteen Principles of Faith**

Historically, Judaism never separated belief from performance. As the centuries rolled by, however, philosophical speculation and dogmas of faith became prevalent among other religions and, in time, began to influence a number of Jews. To counteract this trend, medieval Rabbinical authorities felt the need to respond by defining the principles of Judaism. The 'Thirteen Principles of Faith' are based upon the formulation of *Rambam* [Maimonides] in his *Commentary to Mishnah* (*Sanhedrin*, ch. 10) and have achieved virtually universal acceptance.

The Thirteen Principles fall into three general categories: (a) the nature of belief in God; (b) the authenticity of the Torah, its validity and immutability; and (c) man's responsibility and ultimate reward.

A) The Nature of Belief in God

1. *God's Existence.* There is no partnership in Creation. God is the sole Creator and the uni-

	שֶׁהַבּוֹרֵא יִתְבָּרַךְ שְׁמוֹ
shehaboray yisborach sh'mo	

that the Creator, Blessed is His Name,

hu boray u-manhig הוּא בּוֹרֵא וּמַנְהִיג
   l'chol hab'ru-im, לְכָל הַבְּרוּאִים,

creates and guides all creatures,

v'hu l'vado oso v'ose v'ya-ase וְהוּא לְבַדּוֹ עָשָׂה וְעוֹשֶׂה וְיַעֲשֶׂה
   l'chol hama-asim. לְכָל הַמַּעֲשִׂים.

and that He alone made, makes, and will make everything.

--- 2 ---

ANI MA-AMIN be-emuno sh'laymo, **אֲנִי מַאֲמִין** בֶּאֱמוּנָה שְׁלֵמָה,

I believe with complete faith

shehaboray yisborach sh'mo שֶׁהַבּוֹרֵא יִתְבָּרַךְ שְׁמוֹ

that the Creator, Blessed is His Name,

hu yochid הוּא יָחִיד

is unique

v'ayn y'chidus komohu וְאֵין יְחִידוּת כָּמוֹהוּ
   b'shum ponim, בְּשׁוּם פָּנִים,

and there is no uniqueness like His in any way,

v'hu l'vado Elohaynu, וְהוּא לְבַדּוֹ אֱלֹהֵינוּ,

and that He alone is our God, Who was,

ho-yo hō-ve v'yih-ye. הָיָה הֹוֶה וְיִהְיֶה.

Who is, and Who always will be.

--- 3 ---

ANI MA-AMIN be-emuno sh'laymo, **אֲנִי מַאֲמִין** בֶּאֱמוּנָה שְׁלֵמָה,

I believe with complete faith

shehaboray yisborach sh'mō שֶׁהַבּוֹרֵא יִתְבָּרַךְ שְׁמוֹ

that the Creator, Blessed is His Name,

aynō guf, אֵינוֹ גוּף,

is not physical

v'lō yasiguhu masigay haguf, וְלֹא יַשִּׂיגוּהוּ מַשִּׂיגֵי הַגּוּף,

and is not affected by physical phenomena,

v'ayn lō shum dimyōn k'lol. וְאֵין לוֹ שׁוּם דִּמְיוֹן כְּלָל.

and that there is no comparison whatsoever to Him.

---

verse continues to exist only because He wills it so. He could exist if everything else were to come to an end, but it is inconceivable that there could be any form of existence independent of Him.

2. *God is a complete and total Unity.* He is not a collection of limbs and organs. He cannot be split as can a rock or divided into component elements as can everything in Creation.

3. *God is not physical* nor can His essence be grasped by the human imagination; because we are physical, we cannot conceive of a Being

4

ANI MA-AMIN be-emuno sh'laymo, אֲנִי מַאֲמִין בֶּאֱמוּנָה שְׁלֵמָה,
I believe with complete faith

shehaboray yisborach sh'mo שֶׁהַבּוֹרֵא יִתְבָּרַךְ שְׁמוֹ
that the Creator, Blessed is His Name,

hu rishōn v'hu acharōn. הוּא רִאשׁוֹן וְהוּא אַחֲרוֹן.
is the very first and the very last.

5

ANI ma-amin be-emuno sh'laymo, אֲנִי מַאֲמִין בֶּאֱמוּנָה שְׁלֵמָה,
I believe with complete faith

shehaboray yisborach sh'mō שֶׁהַבּוֹרֵא יִתְבָּרַךְ שְׁמוֹ
that the Creator, Blessed is His Name —

lō l'vadō ro-uy l'his-palayl, לוֹ לְבַדּוֹ רָאוּי לְהִתְפַּלֵּל,
to Him alone is it proper to pray

v'ayn ro-uy l'his-palayl l'zulosō. וְאֵין לְזוּלָתוֹ רָאוּי לְהִתְפַּלֵּל.
and it is not proper to pray to any other.

6

ANI MA-AMIN be-emuno sh'laymo, אֲנִי מַאֲמִין בֶּאֱמוּנָה שְׁלֵמָה,
I believe with complete faith

shekol divray n'vi-im emes. שֶׁכָּל דִּבְרֵי נְבִיאִים אֱמֶת.
that all the words of the prophets are true.

7

ANI MA-AMIN be-emuno sh'laymo, אֲנִי מַאֲמִין בֶּאֱמוּנָה שְׁלֵמָה,
I believe with complete faith

shen'vu-as mōshe rabaynu שֶׁנְּבוּאַת מֹשֶׁה רַבֵּנוּ
olov ha-sholōm עָלָיו הַשָּׁלוֹם
that the prophecy of Moses our teacher, peace be upon him,

---

totally unaffected by material conditions or the laws of nature and physics. The Torah speaks of God's 'eyes,' 'hands,' and so forth only to help man grasp the concepts being conveyed.

4. *God is eternal and the First Source.* Everything in the created universe has a moment when it came into existence; by definition no creature can be infinite. God transcends time, however, because time itself is His creation.

5. *Prayers should be directed to God.* It is tempting to beseech the angels or natural forces, because God has entrusted them with carrying out His will. However, this is illusory. None of them have any power independent of what God assigns them. Therefore, prayers should be directed only toward God Himself.

B) Authenticity of the Torah

6. *God communicates with man.* In order for man to carry out his Divinely ordained mission, he must know what it is. Prophecy is the means by which God communicates His wishes to man. It is a gift that man can attain upon reaching heights of self-perfection.

7. *Moses' prophecy is unique.* Moses' prophecy is not only true, but of a quality unapproached by that of any other prophet before or since. It is essential that his prophecy be unrivaled so that no later 'prophet' could ever claim that he

	שחרית לחול / 288
hoy'so amitis,	הָיְתָה אֲמִתִּית,

was true,

v'shehu ho-yo ov lan'vi-im,   וְשֶׁהוּא הָיָה אָב לַנְּבִיאִים,

and that he was the father of the prophets —

lakōd'mim l'fonov   לַקּוֹדְמִים לְפָנָיו

   v'labo-im acharov.   וְלַבָּאִים אַחֲרָיו.

both those who preceded him and those who followed him.

――――――― 8 ―――――――

ANI MA-AMIN be-emuno sh'laymo,   **אֲנִי מַאֲמִין** בֶּאֱמוּנָה שְׁלֵמָה,

I believe with complete faith

shekol hatōro ham'tzuyo   שֶׁכָּל הַתּוֹרָה הַמְּצוּיָה

that the entire Torah now in our hands

ato b'yodaynu hi han'suno   עַתָּה בְּיָדֵינוּ הִיא הַנְּתוּנָה

is the same one that was given

l'mōshe rabaynu olov ha-sholōm.   לְמֹשֶׁה רַבֵּנוּ עָלָיו הַשָּׁלוֹם.

to Moses our teacher, peace be upon him.

――――――― 9 ―――――――

ANI MA-AMIN be-emuno sh'laymo,   **אֲנִי מַאֲמִין** בֶּאֱמוּנָה שְׁלֵמָה,

I believe with complete faith

shezōs hatōro lō s'hay muchlefes   שֶׁזֹּאת הַתּוֹרָה לֹא תְהֵא מֻחְלֶפֶת

that this Torah will not be exchanged

v'lō s'hay tōro acheres   וְלֹא תְהֵא תוֹרָה אַחֶרֶת

nor will there be another Torah

may-ays habōray yisborach sh'mō.   מֵאֵת הַבּוֹרֵא יִתְבָּרַךְ שְׁמוֹ.

from the Creator, Blessed is His Name.

――――――― 10 ―――――――

ANI MA-AMIN be-emuno sh'laymo,   **אֲנִי מַאֲמִין** בֶּאֱמוּנָה שְׁלֵמָה,

I believe with complete faith

shehabōray yisborach sh'mo   שֶׁהַבּוֹרֵא יִתְבָּרַךְ שְׁמוֹ

that the Creator, Blessed is His Name,

---

had received a 'Torah' that was superior to that of Moses.

8. *The entire Torah is God-given.* Every word in the Torah was dictated to Moses by God, and all the verses of the Torah have equal sanctity.

9. *The Torah is unchangeable.* Since both the Written and Oral Law were God-given, they cannot be improved upon in any manner.

C) Man's Responsibility and Ultimate Reward

10. *God knows man's thoughts and deeds.* Man's individual deeds are important to God and so are the hopes and thoughts that drive him. God is aware of everything man thinks and does.

yōday kol ma-asay v'nay odom יוֹדֵעַ כָּל מַעֲשֵׂה בְּנֵי אָדָם

knows all the deeds of human beings

v'chol machsh'vōsom, shene-emar: וְכָל מַחְשְׁבוֹתָם, שֶׁנֶּאֱמַר:

and their thoughts, as it is said,

Ha-yōtzayr yachad libom, הַיֹּצֵר יַחַד לִבָּם,

ha-mayvin el kol ma-asayhem. הַמֵּבִין אֶל כָּל מַעֲשֵׂיהֶם.

"He fashions their hearts all together, He comprehends all their deeds."

———————————— 11 ————————————

ANI MA-AMIN be-emuno sh'laymo, **אֲנִי מַאֲמִין** בֶּאֱמוּנָה שְׁלֵמָה,

I believe with complete faith

shehabōray yisborach sh'mō שֶׁהַבּוֹרֵא יִתְבָּרַךְ שְׁמוֹ

that the Creator, Blessed is His Name,

gōmayl tōv l'shōm'ray mitzvōsov גּוֹמֵל טוֹב לְשׁוֹמְרֵי מִצְוֹתָיו

rewards with good those who observe His commandments,

u-ma-anish l'ōv'ray mitzvōsov. וּמַעֲנִישׁ לְעוֹבְרֵי מִצְוֹתָיו.

and punishes those who violate His commandments.

———————————— 12 ————————————

ANI MA-AMIN be-emuno sh'laymo, **אֲנִי מַאֲמִין** בֶּאֱמוּנָה שְׁלֵמָה,

I believe with complete faith

b'vi-as ha-moshi-ach, בְּבִיאַת הַמָּשִׁיחַ,

in the coming of the Messiah,

v'af al pi she-yismamay-ah, וְאַף עַל פִּי שֶׁיִּתְמַהְמֵהַּ,

and even though he may delay,

im kol zeh achake lo עִם כָּל זֶה אֲחַכֶּה לּוֹ

b'chol yōm she-yovō. בְּכָל יוֹם שֶׁיָּבוֹא.

nevertheless I anticipate every day that he will come.

———————————— 13 ————————————

ANI MA-AMIN be-emuno sh'laymo, **אֲנִי מַאֲמִין** בֶּאֱמוּנָה שְׁלֵמָה,

I believe with complete faith

shetih-yeh t'chiyas ha-maysim שֶׁתִּהְיֶה תְּחִיַּת הַמֵּתִים

that there will be a resuscitation of the dead

---

11. *Reward and punishment.* No deed goes unrewarded or unpunished. This includes the dictum that one cannot cancel out a bad deed with a good one; each is treated independently.

12. *The Messiah will come.* We are to conduct our lives according to the Torah and remain faithful that the Messiah will come at the time deemed by God to be proper. This faith includes the principle that the Messianic king will descend only from the Davidic dynasty.

13. *The dead will live again* in the Messianic era, when the world will attain a new spiritual

b'ays sheya-ale rotzōn	בְּעֵת שֶׁיַּעֲלֶה רָצוֹן
whenever the wish emanates	
may-ays habōray yisborach sh'mo	מֵאֵת הַבּוֹרֵא יִתְבָּרַךְ שְׁמוֹ
from the Creator, Blessed is His Name	
v'yisale zichrō lo-ad	וְיִתְעַלֶּה זִכְרוֹ לָעַד
and exalted is His mention,	
ulnaytzach n'tzochim.	וּלְנֵצַח נְצָחִים.
forever and for all eternity.	

THE TEN COMMANDMENTS

■ Belief in the Revelation at Sinai is a basic tenet of Judaism, and we are commanded to always remember this seminal event. Even as we recite the Ten Commandments, we bear in mind that all of the Written and Oral Torah are Hashem's word.

VAIDABER Elōhim	וַיְדַבֵּר אֱלֹהִים
God spoke	
es kol had'vorim ho-ayle	אֵת כָּל הַדְּבָרִים הָאֵלֶּה
lay-mōr.	לֵאמֹר.
all these statements, saying:	

——————— 1 ———————

ONOCHI Adōnoy Elōhecho,	אָנֹכִי יהוה אֱלֹהֶיךָ,
I am HASHEM, *your God,*	
asher hotzaysicho	אֲשֶׁר הוֹצֵאתִיךָ
Who has taken you out	
may-eretz mitzra-yim	מֵאֶרֶץ מִצְרַיִם
of the land of Egypt,	
mibays avodim.	מִבֵּית עֲבָדִים.
from the house of slavery.	

——————— 2 ———————

LŌ yih-ye l'cho	לֹא יִהְיֶה לְךָ
elōhim achayrim	אֱלֹהִים אֲחֵרִים
You shall not recognize the gods of others	
al ponoy.	עַל פָּנָי.
in My presence.	

and physical level of perfection. Those who have not been found too unworthy to enter this exalted state will live again to enjoy it.

⏴ **The Ten Commandments**

During the Temple era, the Ten Commandments were recited as a part of the *Shema* service each morning. Later, certain heretics denied the validity of the rest of the Torah, but accepted only the Ten Commandments as the word of God. To prove their point, they recited the Ten Commandments each day, while the rest of the Torah was not. To

Lō sa-a-se l'cho fesel	לֹא תַעֲשֶׂה לְךָ פֶסֶל

You shall not make yourself a carved image

v'chol t'muna	וְכָל תְּמוּנָה

nor any likeness

asher ba-shoma-yim mima-al	אֲשֶׁר בַּשָּׁמַיִם מִמַּעַל,

of that which is in the heavens above

va-asher bo-oretz mitochas	וַאֲשֶׁר בָּאָרֶץ מִתָּחַת,

or on the earth below

va-asher bama-yim mitachas lo-oretz.	וַאֲשֶׁר בַּמַּיִם מִתַּחַת לָאָרֶץ.

or in the water beneath the earth.

Lo sishtacha-ve lo-hem	לֹא תִשְׁתַּחֲוֶה לָהֶם

You shall not prostrate yourself to them

v'lo so-ovdaym	וְלֹא תָעָבְדֵם

nor worship them,

ki onōchi Adōnoy Elohecho,	כִּי אָנֹכִי יהוה אֱלֹהֶיךָ,

*for I am H*ASHEM*, your God —*

Ayl kano,	אֵל קַנָּא,

a jealous God,

pōkayd avon avos al bonim,	פֹּקֵד עֲוֹן אָבֹת עַל בָּנִים,

Who visits the sin of fathers upon children

al shilayshim v'al ribay-im l'sōnoy,	עַל שִׁלֵּשִׁים, וְעַל רִבֵּעִים לְשֹׂנְאָי,

to the third and fourth generations, for My enemies;

v'ō-se chesed la-alofim	וְעֹשֶׂה חֶסֶד לַאֲלָפִים,

but Who shows kindness for thousands [of generations]

l'ō-havai ulshōm'ray mitzvōsoy.	לְאֹהֲבַי, וּלְשֹׁמְרֵי מִצְוֹתָי.

to those who love Me and observe My commandments.

——— 3 ———

LŌ siso	**לֹא** תִשָּׂא

You shall not take

es shaym Adōnoy Elōhecho la-shov,	אֶת שֵׁם יהוה אֱלֹהֶיךָ לַשָּׁוְא,

*the Name of H*ASHEM*, your God, in vain,*

---

counteract their claims, the Talmudic Sages (*Berachos* 12a) removed the Ten Commandments from the formal public prayer service and forbade their reinsertion into the service of their recitation in any public forum (except when they appear in the course of the regular Torah readings). Moreover, even an individual may not recite them as a part of the formal service. Nevertheless, an individual may (and, according to some authorities, should) recite them either before or after his regular prayers.

ki lō y'nake Adōnoy	כִּי לֹא יְנַקֶּה יהוה
for HASHEM will not absolve	
ays asher yiso es sh'mo la-shov.	אֵת אֲשֶׁר יִשָּׂא אֶת שְׁמוֹ לַשָּׁוְא.
anyone who takes His Name in vain.	

--- 4 ---

ZOCHŌR es	זָכוֹר אֶת
yom ha-shabos l'kad'sho.	יוֹם הַשַּׁבָּת לְקַדְּשׁוֹ.
Remember the Sabbath day to sanctify it.	
Shay-shes yomim ta-avod	שֵׁשֶׁת יָמִים תַּעֲבֹד
Six days shall you work	
v'osiso kol m'lachtecho,	וְעָשִׂיתָ כָּל מְלַאכְתֶּךָ,
and accomplish all your work;	
v'yom hash'vi-i	וְיוֹם הַשְּׁבִיעִי
but the seventh day	
shabos Ladōnoy Elōhecho.	שַׁבָּת לַיהוה אֱלֹהֶיךָ.
is Sabbath to HASHEM, your God;	
Lo sa-a-se kol m'locho	לֹא תַעֲשֶׂה כָל מְלָאכָה,
you shall not do any work —	
ato u-vin'cho uvitecho,	אַתָּה וּבִנְךָ וּבִתֶּךָ,
you, your son, your daughter,	
avd'cho va-amos'cho uv-hemtecho,	עַבְדְּךָ וַאֲמָתְךָ וּבְהֶמְתֶּךָ,
your slave, your maidservant, your animal,	
v'gayr'cho asher bish-orecho.	וְגֵרְךָ אֲשֶׁר בִּשְׁעָרֶיךָ.
and your convert within your gates —	
Ki shayshes yomim oso Adōnoy	כִּי שֵׁשֶׁת יָמִים עָשָׂה יהוה
for in six days HASHEM made	
es ha-shoma-yim v'es ho-oretz,	אֶת הַשָּׁמַיִם וְאֶת הָאָרֶץ,
the heavens and the earth,	
es ha-yom v'es kol asher bom,	אֶת הַיָּם וְאֶת כָּל אֲשֶׁר בָּם,
the sea and all that is in them,	
va-yonach ba-yōm hash'vi-i.	וַיָּנַח בַּיּוֹם הַשְּׁבִיעִי.
and He rested on the seventh day.	
Al kayn bayrach Adōnoi	עַל כֵּן בֵּרַךְ יהוה
es yom ha-shabos vai-kad'shay-hu.	אֶת יוֹם הַשַּׁבָּת וַיְקַדְּשֵׁהוּ.
Therefore, HASHEM blessed the Sabbath day and sanctified it.	

5

KABAYD es ovicho v'es i-mecho
כַּבֵּד אֶת אָבִיךָ וְאֶת אִמֶּךָ,
Honor your father and your mother,

l'ma-an ya-arichun yo-mecho
לְמַעַן יַאֲרִכוּן יָמֶיךָ
so that your days will be lengthened

al ho-adomo
עַל הָאֲדָמָה
upon the land

asher Adōnoy Elōhecho nōsayn loch.
אֲשֶׁר יהוה אֱלֹהֶיךָ נֹתֵן לָךְ.
that H<small>ASHEM</small>, *your God, gives you.*

6

LŌ sir-tzach.
לֹא תִרְצָח
You shall not kill;

7

LŌ sin-of.
לֹא תִנְאָף
you shall not commit adultery;

8

LŌ sig-nōv.
לֹא תִגְנֹב
you shall not steal;

9

LŌ sa-a-ne b'ray-acho ayd shoker.
לֹא תַעֲנֶה בְרֵעֲךָ עֵד שָׁקֶר.
you shall not bear false witness against your fellow.

10

LŌ sach-mod bays ray-echo,
לֹא תַחְמֹד בֵּית רֵעֶךָ,
You shall not covet your fellow's house.

lo sach-mod ay-shes ray-echo,
לֹא תַחְמֹד אֵשֶׁת רֵעֶךָ,
You shall not covet your fellow's wife,

v'avdō va-amosō
וְעַבְדּוֹ וַאֲמָתוֹ
his slave, his maidservant,

v'shōrō vachamōrō,
וְשׁוֹרוֹ וַחֲמֹרוֹ,
his ox, his donkey,

v'chol asher l'ray-echo.
וְכֹל אֲשֶׁר לְרֵעֶךָ.
nor anything that belongs to your fellow.

Grace After Meals

Sheva Berachos
Bris / Circumcision
Pidyon Haben /
   Redeeming the Firstborn

～§ Bircas HaMazon / Grace After Meals

Bircas HaMazon, Grace After Meals, has the distinction of being the only Biblically mandated blessing, based on the verse, "And you shall eat and be satisfied and you shall bless Hashem, your God, for the good land that He gave you" (*Deuteronomy* 8:10). But what exactly constitutes this blessing and the fulfillment of this command?

The *Ramban* understands the Torah obligation to be a simple message of acknowledgment and thanks for our sustenance. This follows one opinion in the Talmud *(Berachos* 40b), which teaches, "Binyamin the shepherd ate bread and said, 'Blessed is the Merciful One, Master of this bread,' and Rav said, 'He has fulfilled the obligation of reciting Grace After Meals.' " According to this view, all the other prayers and blessings contained in *Bircas HaMazon* are Rabbinical additions.

The *Rashba,* on the other hand, considers the first three blessings of *Bircas HaMazon* — for the food; for the land of Israel; and for Jerusalem and the Temple — to be required by the Torah. Only the fourth blessing and the prayers that follow are Rabbinic additions. Most authorities agree with the opinion of the *Rashba.*

The *Meshech Chochmah* notes that the function of Grace After Meals is to maintain the dependence of the Jew to His maker. The Torah warns — in the context of the commandment of *Bircas HaMazon* — "Take heed, lest you forget Hashem ... Lest you eat and are satisfied ... and your heart become haughty and you forget Hashem. And you say in your innermost heart, 'My power and the might of my hand has secured me this wealth.' Therefore, remember Hashem, for it is He Who has given you the opportunity to prosper" (*Deuteronomy* 8:11-18).

Prior to eating, a person recognizes how much he needs Hashem to provide him with food. A person is more likely to forget his Provider and neglect thanking Him after he eats and is satisfied. *Bircas HaMazon* , therefore, reiterates this dependence and expresses this thanks *after* the meal is eaten.

～§ The First Blessing

Moses composed the first blessing of Grace After Meals, thanking Hashem "Who nourishes all," when the manna fell from heaven and sustained the nation of Israel for forty years in the desert *(Berachos* 48b). The Lubavitcher Rebbe, Rabbi Menachem Schneerson, notes that to thank Hashem for our nourishment we recite the very same blessing that our ancestors did in the wilderness. The manna was clearly a miracle from Hashem; the food which we eat is no less less miraculous and is also of Divine origin, although this may be less obvious.   As Rabbi Samson Raphael Hirsch writes, "It makes every little piece of bread looked on as being as much the direct gift from Hashem as was the manna

dropped from heaven to the wanderers in the wilderness" (*Deuteronomy* 8:10).

In this blessing, we thank Hashem for granting us nourishment with "grace, kindness, and mercy." Rabbi Yechezkel Sarna, *Rosh Yeshivah* of the Chevron Yeshivah in Jerusalem, understood this to be thanking Hashem for the wide variety of foods with which he provides us. While Hashem could have given us but a few sources of nourishment, in His kindness He chose to to offer us a broad array from which to select. Moreover, adds Rabbi Avigdor Nebenzahl of Jerusalem, we thank Hashem for the lively and appealing colors of the foods with which He provides us. We could have been fed in black-and-white. The many different colors of foods enhance our enjoyment and bear testimony to His pleasure in providing for His creatures.

The first blessing stresses that Hashem personally sustains all — "from the horned buffalo to the brood of vermin" (*Avodah Zarah* 3b) — and does not delegate that responsibility to an angel or emissary. That Hashem provides for everyone, without basing their sustenance on individual merit, reflects His attribute of compassion.

This blessing also directs us to the purpose of eating. The values and aspirations of a Jew ought to follow the words of *Proverbs* (3:6), "In all your ways, know Him." This credo mandates that we take temporal physical activities and elevate them to the level of Divine service by articulating that their purpose is not only physical pleasure but to maintain a healthy body in order to better serve Hashem.

৺ঌ The Second Blessing

The next blessing of Grace After Meals offers thanks for Hashem's gift of Eretz Yisrael. We are reminded of the uniqueness of Eretz Yisrael, a holy land which demands both circumcision and the observance of Torah to assure our continued possesion thereof. The Torah mandates, "And you shall eat and be satisfied and you shall bless Hashem, your God, *for the good land* that He gave you" (*Deuteronomy* 8:10).

Every time a Jew eats a slice of bread — the barest necessity of life — he is reminded that Hashem gave the Jewish people the land of Israel, reflecting His personal rapport with His nation. The land of Israel responds to the Jew as to no one else. In his absence the land does not yield its potential — in keeping with the Torah's promise, "I will make the land desolate, and your foes who dwell upon it will be desolate" (*Leviticus* 26:32).

We stand today, amazed at how the land of Israel responds to her sons and daughters, who have returned to her after nearly 2,000 years (reflecting the prophecy of *Ezekiel* 36:8). Although we may live in other lands, we nonetheless must realize that Israel is the source of all blessings that affect our produce and sustenance (see *Rashi*, *Deuteronomy* 11:12).

৺ঌ The Third Blessing

The third blessing asks for the restoration of Jerusalem. Our land is not

considered complete until the Holy City and the Temple are rebuilt and the monarchy of David is restored.

The Temple represented not only the dwelling place of the Divine, but also the personal rapport between Hashem and His people. On the pilgrim festivals, the *Kohanim* would draw the curtain from in front of the Ark revealing the golden cherubs embracing one another (*Yoma* 54a). The lesson to the people was: See how beloved you are before Hashem.

The *Kohanim* also showed the people the showbread, which sat on a special table in the Temple and never went stale (*Chagigah* 26b). This miracle underscored Hashem's personal involvement in the livelihood of each Jewish family. We therefore beseech Hashem to provide for us now as He provided for us then, and we pray that our sustenance come directly from him so that we never need to rely on another human being for our nourishment and needs.

The Talmudic commentary, *Mordechai,* considers the institution of a Jewish monarchy an extension of Hashem's Kingship. The king represents the unity of our people and is responsible to teach, through his own behavior, Torah values and morality. Thus, while a teacher may release his students from their obligation to show him honor, and even parents may free their children from their formal responsibilities to honor and respect, a king — who represents Hashem — may never step down from his venerated position. As our High Holy Day prayers put it, "Hashem crowns kings, but ultimately all kingship is His."

ৰ্ঙ The Shabbos and Festivals

On Shabbos and Festivals one is obligated to eat bread and to include specific mentions of those days in *Bircas HaMazon* (*Orach Chaim* 188).

The prayer added on Shabbos, *Retzei*, and the one added on the Festivals, *Yaaleh VeYavo*, ask for a resumption of the additional sacrificial offerings brought on those days in the Temple. Moreover, *Retzei*, notes *Avudraham*, is a petition for the redemption of our people in merit of our observing the Shabbos. These prayers are therefore appropriately placed within the third blessing.

ৰ্ঙ Ending the Third Blessing

Though one does not commonly answer Amen to his own blessing, Amen is said following this blessing to separate the first three blessings, which are mandated by the Torah, from the fourth blessing, which is Rabbinic in nature.

ৰ্ঙ The Fourth Blessing

When the Jewish resistance of Bar-Kochba was defeated by the Romans at Beitar in the second century, hundreds of thousands of Jews were killed. For years the Romans refused to turn over their remains for burial and did so only due to the strenuous efforts of Rabban Gamliel the Elder. Miraculously, it was discovered, the bodies had not decomposed. The day of their burial, the Sages in Yavneh composed the fourth blessing of *Bircas HaMazon*, *HaTov VeHaMeitiv* —

Who is good and confers good: *tov*, that the bodies did not decay, and *meitiv*, that they were given a proper Jewish burial. The *Tzlach* suggests that as the dead bodies miraculously retained their completeness, so too does Israel maintain its spirituality even without its Holy Temple.

Why does this blessing conclude Grace After Meals? The *Meshech Chochmah* (*Deuteronomy* 8:10) suggests that Grace After Meals reflects the development of the Jewish people. The miraculous manna is the theme of the first blessing, followed by the Jewish nation being brought to the land of Israel and, finally, the gifts of Jerusalem and the Temple where God's miracles and providence were experienced openly and constantly.

The fourth blessing, invoking the miracle at Beitar, represents the survival of our people in exile, in the face of wanderings, persecution, and genocide. More than once did many of our people abandon hope and think that our peoplehood had come to an end, God forbid, as has indeed happened to many other nations and cultures. But through it all, the prophecy of Isaiah has held true: "No weapon formed against you shall prosper" (54:17). The fourth blessing teaches that though Israel is like a sheep surrounded by 70 wolves, the miracle of Beitar — which occurred following the destruction of the Second Temple — reminds us that Hashem's care and providence guard us even in difficult times.

Nonetheless, this blessing is still considered a Rabbinic addition to *Bircas HaMazon* and that designation has ramifications. The Talmud *(Berachos* 45b) teaches that Abaye would recite Amen following this blessing so that workers would hear and know to return to work. This was because a worker was entitled to eat and also recite Grace After Meals on company time. But his responsibility to his employer would necessitate his skipping this fourth blessing.

This practice of Abaye shows the extent of integrity that an employee must have toward his work, and how scrupulous one must be in his business dealings.

⋴ᡸ Giving Thanks to Hashem

The Heavenly angels brought a challenge to Hashem. On the one hand, they said, it is written that You do not show favor and do not accept bribes (*Devarim* 10:17). But do You not show favor to the Jewish people? For indeed it is written, "May God show you favor" (*Numbers* 6:26).

Hashem answers: Shall I not show favor to Israel? For, after all, I have written in the Torah, "And you shall eat, be satisfied and bless Hashem, your God" (*Deuteronomy* 8:10), which requires them to recite *Bircas HaMazon* only if they have eaten enough to be satisfied. Yet, My people are demanding of themselves and are careful to recite Grace After Meals for virtually any meal — even the size of an olive or an egg! Just as they favor Me, so must I favor them (*Berachos* 20b).

There is no question but that one who has eaten but an olive's worth or even an egg's worth of bread is still hungry. Yet, the Jew's capacity to offer thanksgiving to God, even when he is still hungry, not only warrants God's Divine favor but strengthens His relationship with His people.

∽§ Bris Milah / Circumcision

Hashem, while perfect, did not create a perfect world. He left room for man to leave his imprint by enhancing his environment. As we say in the *Kiddush* on Friday night, "God blessed the seventh day and hallowed it, because on it he abstained from all His work which God created to make." These final two words need not refer to Hashem but to man; Hashem charges man with the responsibility of making something out of this world and perfecting His creation.

The foreskin denotes imperfection and is repugnant (*Nedarim* 31b). The *Sefer HaChinuch* suggests that boys are born with foreskins to impress upon man that perfection does not come automatically. Just as he is to bring his body to a state of completion, so too he must perfect his character and soul with good deeds.

Maimonides, in his *Guide for the Perplexed*, suggests that the *mitzvah* of circumcision assists the Jew in complying with the many laws related to moral behavior. Circumcision, he suggests, allows the Jewish male to procreate, but, at the same time, weakens his sex drive, enabling him to comply with the many moral restrictions of the Torah.

Rabbi Samson Raphael Hirsch understands Hashem's directive to Abraham, "Walk before Me and be perfect" (*Genesis* 17:1), to mean there is to be a perfect harmony between the body and soul. Do not believe that your soul is holy and belongs to heaven, while your body can follow its animalistic instincts. Rather, one must serve Hashem with one's body. *Milah* helps us appreciate that even the most animal-like action can be performed in holiness for the perpetuation of the world. *Milah* reminds the Jew that his body does not belong to him but to Hashem; it is for him to use not abuse (*Horeb*, Book 2, Chapter 36).

Abraham, the father of the Jewish nation, was tested with circumcision, which separated him from the rest of society. As such, Abraham was concerned that he would no longer be able to reach out and spread the word of Hashem to as many people as before (*Midrash Rabbah, Bereishis* 46:2). Essentially, Hashem responded that "quality is more important than quantity." Just as the Jew is spiritually different from the gentile, so too Hashem wants him to be physically different. Hashem chose the organ of procreation to mark this difference, signifying the Jew's uniqueness.

Onkelos of Rome was the nephew of Caesar and wanted to convert. He traveled to Israel and asked that the Rabbis teach him Torah. They told him that circumcision is a prerequisite for acquiring Torah, so he underwent *milah* and studied much Torah, eventually translating the entire Torah into the Aramaic text that is still found in today's volumes.

When he returned to his uncle, Caesar asked why he looked different. "I have been circumcised and have studied Torah," he told him.

"You should never have done that!" Caesar exclaimed and slapped him.

Onkelos responded, "One cannot successfully study Torah without circumci-

sion, as it is written 'He relates his word to Yaakov' (*Psalms* 147:19) — to those who are circumcised as Yaakov."

This connection is reiterated each time we recite the second blessing of the Grace After Meals in which we thank Hashem "for Your Covenant which You sealed in our flesh, and for Your Torah which You taught us."

The *milah* takes place on the eighth day after birth. The *mitzvah* of *milah* is so important that it is even performed when the eighth day is Shabbos. The *Maharal* and others note that in Jewish tradition the number seven denotes nature and the natural order of things. The world was created in seven days. Eight signifies that which is beyond the natural. *Milah,* which is performed on the eighth day, reflects the miraculous survival of the Jewish people despite the hostilities and terror we have experienced over the millennia. At the *bris milah*, we recite the verse, "And I said to you: In your blood, live!" (*Ezekiel* 16:6). *Milah* represents our willingness to give our lives for Hashem, demonstrated by the blood of circumcision — and it is this willingness and this *mitzvah* that have guaranteed our survival.

There are also similarities between *milah* and *korbanos*, the offerings brought in the Temple. An animal is not fit to be offered on the Altar until it has reached the age of eight days. Moreover, the one who holds the baby while he is being circumcised is considered to have brought an offering in the Temple.

The *bris milah* ceremony begins with a married couple (usually of child-bearing age), known as the *kvater* and *kvateren,* holding the baby. The woman passes the baby to her husband and he carries the boy to a designated chair known as "the Chair of Elijah." The *mohel* then welcomes Elijah the Prophet, who, tradition tells us, attends every *bris milah.* The baby is then given to the father who places his son on the lap of the *sandek.* The *mohel* recites the blessing and circumcises the child. Then the father recites a blessing. After the baby is bandaged, more blessings are recited over a cup of wine and the baby is named. A festive meal follows.

The Talmud states, "Any commandment that the Jewish people accepted upon themselves with joy — such as circumcision, as it is written, 'I rejoice over your word like one who finds abundant spoils' (*Psalms* 119:162) — they still perform with joy" (*Shabbos* 130a). Our Sages understood King David's psalm of joy to refer to his circumcision. David had visited the bathhouse and became distressed that in his nakedness he was bereft of *mitzvos*. Then he became filled with joy as he realized that his circumcision provided him with constant testimony of being sanctified by God's commandments.

May we be privileged to merit the blessing of circumcision which has been engraved upon us as a seal of the holy covenant that exists between God and His People.

Pidyon Haben / Redemption of the Firstborn Son

The *Sforno* (*Numbers* 3:13) provides an insightful background to the *mitzvah* of *pidyon haben* — redeeming the firstborn son. Originally, the firstborn — the *bechor* — had the privilege of serving Hashem, but had no intrinsic sanctity. He functioned normally within society.

In one of the first episodes recounted in the Torah, Cain, a *bechor*, is afforded the privilege of bring an offering to Hashem. Only after his offering is rejected does his younger brother, Abel, bring his offering. Jacob, too, struggled with his brother, Esau, for the birthright. "Shall this wicked man stand and bring the offerings?" Jacob asked (*Bereishis Rabbah* 63:18).

With the last of the ten plagues in Egypt — the killing of the firstborn — Hashem imbued the *bechor* with greater sanctity. Because of his leadership role, the firstborn bears responsibility for his family and, ultimately, for his nation. The firstborn Egyptians were killed for the sins of Egypt, but with the Angel of Death present, the Jewish firstborn were also vulnerable and needed greater protection. Hashem, therefore, sanctified them to save them at their moment of peril.

The sin of the Golden Calf changed that. Having participated in its construction, the firstborn lost their favored status and the opportunity to officiate in the Tabernacle and Temple. Hashem chose the Levites, who did not participate during the tragedy of the Golden Calf, to replace the firstborn and minister in His Sanctuary. Nonetheless, the innate holiness of the firstborn never left them and they need to be redeemed from their sanctity in order to engage in secular, ordinary labor.

The firstborn male child, as well as the first offspring of kosher animals and the first fruits, are among the 24 gifts that the Torah provides for the *Kohen*. Since the *Kohen* did not possess land in Israel, the Torah ordained that the Jew pay frequent visits to the *Kohen*, providing him and his family with their daily needs. In turn, the *Kohen* taught the Jew and his children Torah.

The *Sefer HaChinuch* (*mitzvah* 18) writes that this *mitzvah* teaches the Jew that everything he possesses belongs to Hashem. Every beginning is special. First fruits, firstborn animals, and especially firstborn children are most precious. By giving these over to Hashem, through the *mitzvah*, one demonstrates his recognition that all these and everything that follows come from Hashem.

During the *pidyon haben* banquet, the father holds the boy before the *Kohen* and declares, "This, my firstborn son, he is the first issue of the womb of his mother, and the Holy One, Blessed is He, commanded to redeem him."

The *Kohen* responds, "Which do you prefer: to give me your firstborn son, who

is the first issue of the womb of his mother, or to redeem him for five *sela'im*, as required by the Torah."

"I wish to redeem my son," the father answers, "and here is the money for his redemption as required by the Torah." He then recites the appropriate blessings and hands the five coins to the *Kohen*. (In the United States, five silver dollars are used.)

The *Kohen* accepts the money, blesses the child and recites the blessing over a cup of wine. The festive meal then continues.

If one is a firstborn male and neither of his parents is a *Kohen* or a *Levi*, he must be redeemed. If this *mitzvah* was not performed when he was an infant, *he must redeem himself as an adult*. One should consult his rabbi for guidance in this matter.

⋖§ Sheva Berachos

Moses instituted a week of rejoicing for a couple following their wedding. Some attribute this celebration to the instruction of Laban to Jacob, who wished to marry Rachel after having been tricked into marrying Leah. "Complete the week of this one," Laban said, "and we will give you the other one too" (*Genesis* 29:27). Others attribute it to Samson, who posed a riddle "during the seven days of feasting" (*Judges* 14:12).

The seven marriage blessings are recited throughout the week of celebration at every meal prepared on behalf of the bride and groom, provided there is a "new face" in attendance (*Even HaEzer* 62:5). This "new face" — *panim chadashos* — represents a further proliferation of the happiness and joy of the wedding. The joy of the bride and groom is not only theirs personally but a celebration for the nation of Israel. *Tosafos* comments that on Shabbos *panim chadashos* are not needed because on Shabbos we are all considered new individuals, possessing an additional soul.

Rashi (*Kesubos* 8a) explains the nature of these blessings. The first blessing, "Who has created everything for His glory," is a blessing in honor of the guests Who have come to rejoice with the bride and groom and are, in essence, emulating Hashem Who Himself gladdened and rejoiced with Adam and Eve.

The second blessing, "Who fashioned the man," brings to mind the teaching of the Talmud, "Originally it was the will of Hashem to create two separate beings, but in the end He created one" (*Berachos* 61a). The *Raavad* understands this teaching as explaining the term "*eizer kenegdo* — a helpmate to complement him" (*Genesis* 2:18). The ability of husband and wife to fuse into one being comes from Hashem's creation of them as one, having both partners in mind in this creation process.

The third blessing speaks of the physical and spiritual perpetuation of man. A primary purpose of marriage is to procreate and populate the world. Indeed, the first *mitzvah* in the Torah is "to be fruitful and multiply" (*Geneiss* 1:28). This blessing acknowledges our responsibility and gives thanks to Hashem Who enables us to participate in the building of His world.

The fourth blessing highlights the concept that Zion and the Jewish nation, described by the Prophet Isaiah (54:1) as the barren one, rejoice because the building of an individual family in Israel contributes to the collective good of our people. "The whole is equal to the sum of all its parts" is not only an important axiom in geometry, but basic to the Jewish nation. The Talmud teaches, "The Messiah will not come until all the souls in *Guf* [the region inhabited by the souls of the unborn] have been assigned" (*Yevamos* 62a). The anticipation of a new Jewish family gladdens Zion.

The fifth blessing wishes the bride and groom success in attaining joy and happiness. The *Sefer HaChinuch* explains the 582nd *mitzvah* of, "He shall be free to his home for one year, and he shall gladden his wife whom he has married" (*Deuteronomy* 24:5) with great psychological depth. The bride and groom each bring different personalities and natures into the marriage. Hashem therefore urges that the couple spend time, especially during their first year together, blending their distinct natures and developing an attachment and affection for one another — to the exclusion of all others. Just as Adam and Eve in the Garden of Eden were infatuated with one another and were completely alone, so too we wish the newlyweds that they achieve this solitude with each other, in their eyes and thoughts.

Ten different expressions of happiness and joy are expressed in the last blessing. The verses from *Jeremiah* (33:10-11) are cited: "Let there soon be heard in the cities of Judah and the streets of Jerusalem the sound of joy and the sound of gladness, the voice of the groom and the voice of the bride." The author of the *Tanya* asks a most fundamental question. We know that at a Jewish wedding, under the *chuppah,* the bride is silent. Only the groom speaks the words, "You are betrothed to me." What then does the Prophet mean by "the voice of the bride"?

He answers that every wedding reminds us of the wedding between Hashem and the Jewish people. Hashem is figuratively characterized as the groom and the Jewish people as His bride. Hashem proposed to us by offering us His Torah, by the recitation of the Ten Commandments, and we responded, *"Naaseh venishma* — We will do and we will hear" (*Exodus* 24:7). The Prophet thus calls to mind the time when once again the Jewish nation — the bride — will pledge her loyalty to Hashem.

A Jewish wedding has the capacity to connect all its participants to a national wedding with Hashem. The *chuppah*, which reminds us of Mount Sinai, gives us the opportunity of raising an individual celebration to the national level (*Rabbeinu Bachya*).

In addition, the blessing begins by extolling Hashem who created *"sason vesimchah* — joy and gladness." What is the difference between these two

words? The *Vilna Gaon* (*Job* 3-21) explains. On Shabbos morning, in the hymn *"Keil Adon,"* we sing about the moon and the sun, *"semeichim betzeisam vesasim bevo'am* — glad as they go forth, and exultant as they return." *Semeichim* describes their feelings as they set out, reflecting the anticipation of their missions. *Sason* describes the feelings they have after fulfilling the will of Hashem, the joy of accomplishment. Thus, the bride and groom, who have found each other and are now whole, give thanks to Hashem "Who created *sason* for the accomplishment of finding each other, and the *simchah* of anticipating a life together built on Torah and *mitzvos.*"

The reward for the *mitzvah* of rejoicing with the groom and bride is greater than the acquisition and understanding of Torah (*Berachos* 6b). This insightful remark sums up the purpose of marriage. We are rewarded "measure for measure" for our efforts in undertaking *mitzvos*. One would therefore assume that dancing and singing before the bride and groom and sharing with them words of Torah would be rewarded with a similar celebration at one's own wedding. But in telling us that the reward is Torah, the Talmud teaches that ultimately a marriage is an opportunity for a Torah life in its fullest, purest sense.

⊰{ GRACE AFTER MEALS }⊱

IT IS CUSTOMARY TO RECITE PSALM 137 IN MEMORY OF THE TEMPLE'S DESTRUCTION, BEFORE *BIRCAS HAMAZON* ON WEEKDAYS. ON THE SABBATH AND FESTIVALS, AND ON SUCH OCCASIONS AS THE MEALS CELEBRATING A MARRIAGE, *BRIS*, OR *PIDYON HABEN*, IT IS IMPROPER TO INTRUDE UPON THE JOY WITH MEMORIES OF TRAGEDY, AND PSALM 126 (P. 307) IS RECITED INSTEAD.

■ Psalm 137: Despite his wanderings, the Jew's mission remains rooted in the heart of Jerusalem, to promote Torah, *mitzvos* and knowledge of God in the world. Otherwise, all his prodigious skills might as well be forgotten.

AL naharōs bovel,   עַל נַהֲרוֹת בָּבֶל,
By the rivers of Babylon* —

shom yo-shavnu gam bo-chinu   שָׁם יָשַׁבְנוּ גַּם בָּכִינוּ,
b'zoch'raynu es tziyōn.   בְּזָכְרֵנוּ אֶת צִיּוֹן.
there we sat and also wept when we remembered Zion.

Al arovim b'sōchoh   עַל עֲרָבִים בְּתוֹכָהּ
tolinu kinōrōsaynu.   תָּלִינוּ כִּנֹּרוֹתֵינוּ.
On the willows within it we hung our lyres.

Ki shom sh'aylunu shōvaynu   כִּי שָׁם שְׁאֵלוּנוּ שׁוֹבֵינוּ
divray shir   דִּבְרֵי שִׁיר
For there our captors requested words of song from us,

v'sōlolaynu simcho,   וְתוֹלָלֵינוּ שִׂמְחָה,
with our lyres [playing] joyous [music],

shiru lonu mishir tziyōn.   שִׁירוּ לָנוּ מִשִּׁיר צִיּוֹן.
"Sing for us from Zion's song!"

Aych no-shir es shir Adōnoy   אֵיךְ נָשִׁיר אֶת שִׁיר יהוה,
al admas naychor.   עַל אַדְמַת נֵכָר.
"How can we sing the song of HASHEM upon the alien's soil?"

Im eshko-chaych y'rusholo-yim   אִם אֶשְׁכָּחֵךְ יְרוּשָׁלָיִם,
tishkach y'mini.   תִּשְׁכַּח יְמִינִי.
If I forget you, O Jerusalem, let my right hand forget its skill.

⊰§ Grace After Meals

The commandment to thank God after a meal is of Scriptural origin: "And you shall eat and you shall be satisfied and you shall bless HASHEM, your God, for the good Land which He gave you" (*Deuteronomy* 8:10). As the verse indicates, the Scriptural requirement applies only when one has eaten his fill — *you shall eat and you shall be satisfied.* From earliest times, however, the Jewish people has undertaken to express its gratitude to God even after a modest meal, provided one had eaten at least as much bread as a *kezayis*, the volume of an olive.

The first to compose a text for Grace After Meals was Moses, whose text is still recited as the first blessing of the Grace. Although Moses' blessing was composed in gratitude for the manna in the wilderness, it makes no mention of the manna. The message appears rather clear: When we thank God for giving us food, we are recognizing that there is no intrinsic difference between the manna and the livelihood one wrests from the earth through sweat and hard toil; both are gifts from Heaven.

עַל נַהֲרוֹת בָּבֶל — *By the rivers of Babylon.* God endowed King David with a prophetic vision in

GRACE AFTER MEALS

Tidbak l'shōni l'chiki	תִּדְבַּק לְשׁוֹנִי לְחִכִּי,

Let my tongue adhere to my palate

im lō ezk'raychi	אִם לֹא אֶזְכְּרֵכִי,

if I fail to recall you,

im lō a-ale es y'rushola-yim	אִם לֹא אַעֲלֶה אֶת יְרוּשָׁלַיִם
al rōsh simchosi.	עַל רֹאשׁ שִׂמְחָתִי.

if I fail to elevate Jerusalem above my foremost joy. *

Z'chōr Adōnoy livnay edōm	זְכֹר יהוה לִבְנֵי אֱדוֹם
ays yōm y'rusholo-yim,	אֵת יוֹם יְרוּשָׁלָיִם,

Remember, Hashem, for the offspring of Edom, the day of Jerusalem —

ho-ōm'rim oru oru ad ha-y'sōd boh.	הָאֹמְרִים עָרוּ עָרוּ, עַד הַיְסוֹד בָּהּ.

for those who say "Destroy! Destroy! to its very foundation."

Bas bovel hash'dudo	בַּת בָּבֶל הַשְּׁדוּדָה

O violated daughter of Babylon —

ashray shey'shalem loch	אַשְׁרֵי שֶׁיְּשַׁלֶּם לָךְ

praiseworthy is he who repays you

es g'mulaych shegomalt lonu.	אֶת גְּמוּלֵךְ שֶׁגָּמַלְתְּ לָנוּ.

in accordance with the manner that you treated us.

Ashray she-yōchayz v'nipaytz	אַשְׁרֵי שֶׁיֹּאחֵז וְנִפֵּץ
es ōlola-yich el hasola.	אֶת עֹלָלַיִךְ אֶל הַסָּלַע.

Praiseworthy is he who will clutch and dash your infants against the rock.

CONTINUE ON P. 308

■ Psalm 126: When the Exile ends, we will return to Jerusalem triumphantly and joyously.

SHIR hama-alōs,	**שִׁיר** הַמַּעֲלוֹת,

A song of ascents.

b'shuv Adōnoy es shivas tziyōn,	בְּשׁוּב יהוה אֶת שִׁיבַת צִיּוֹן,

When Hashem will return the captivity of Zion, *

ho-yinu k'chōl'mim.	הָיִינוּ כְּחֹלְמִים.

we will be like dreamers. *

---

which he foresaw the destruction of the First Temple at the hands of Babylon and the Second Temple at the hands of Edom/Rome (*Gittin* 57b).

אִם לֹא אַעֲלֶה ... עַל רֹאשׁ שִׂמְחָתִי — *If I fail to elevate ... above my foremost joy.* At every occasion of personal joy, the memory of Jerusalem must be foremost (*Ibn Ezra*). From this verse stems the custom that a bridegroom places ashes on his head before the marriage ceremony; and the custom that a glass is broken after the ceremony in memory of Jerusalem (*Rama*).

בְּשׁוּב ה' אֶת שִׁיבַת צִיּוֹן — *When Hashem will return the captivity of Zion.* The Psalmist wrote prophetically about the return from the exile.

הָיִינוּ כְּחֹלְמִים — *We will be like dreamers*. When the long-awaited return to Zion finally comes to pass, the recollection of the past oppression of the exile will swiftly fade away and seem like a bad dream.

Oz yimolay s'chōk pinu ulshōnaynu rino,	אָז יִמָּלֵא שְׂחוֹק פִּינוּ וּלְשׁוֹנֵנוּ רִנָּה,

Then our mouth will be filled with laughter and our tongue with glad song.

oz yōm'ru vagōyim,　　　　　אָז יֹאמְרוּ בַגּוֹיִם,

Then they will declare among the nations,

higdil Adōnoy la-asōs im ayle.　　הִגְדִּיל יהוה לַעֲשׂוֹת עִם אֵלֶּה.

"Hashem has done greatly with these."

Higdil Adōnoy la-asōs i-monu,　　הִגְדִּיל יהוה לַעֲשׂוֹת עִמָּנוּ,

Hashem has done greatly with us,

ho-yinu s'maychim.　　　　הָיִינוּ שְׂמֵחִים.

we were gladdened.

Shuvo Adōnoy es sh'visaynu　　שׁוּבָה יהוה אֶת שְׁבִיתֵנוּ,
ka-afikim banegev.　　　　כַּאֲפִיקִים בַּנֶּגֶב.

O Hashem — return our captivity like springs in the desert.

Hazōr'im b'dim-o b'rino yik-tzōru.　　הַזֹּרְעִים בְּדִמְעָה בְּרִנָּה יִקְצֹרוּ.

Those who tearfully sow* will reap in glad song.

Holōch yaylaych u-vochō　　　הָלוֹךְ יֵלֵךְ וּבָכֹה
nōsay meshech ha-zora,　　　נֹשֵׂא מֶשֶׁךְ הַזָּרַע,

He walks along weeping, he who bears the measure of seeds,*

bō yovō v'rino, nōsay alumōsov.　　בֹּא יָבֹא בְרִנָּה, נֹשֵׂא אֲלֻמֹּתָיו.

but will return in exultation, a bearer of his sheaves.

ON ALL OCCASIONS, CONTINUE HERE:

T'HILAS Adonoy y'daber pi,　　תְּהִלַּת יהוה יְדַבֶּר פִּי,

May my mouth declare the praise of Hashem

vivoraych kol bosor　　　　וִיבָרֵךְ כָּל בָּשָׂר
shem kodshō l'ōlom vo-ed.　　שֵׁם קָדְשׁוֹ לְעוֹלָם וָעֶד.

and may all flesh bless His Holy Name forever.

Va-anachnu n'voraych Yoh,　　וַאֲנַחְנוּ נְבָרֵךְ יָהּ,

We will bless Hashem

may-ato v'ad ōlom, hal'luyoh.　　מֵעַתָּה וְעַד עוֹלָם, הַלְלוּיָהּ.

from this time and forever, Praise God!

הַזֹּרְעִים בְּדִמְעָה — *Those who tearfully sow.* The Psalmist compares those whose primary concern is with the study of Torah and with the performance of the commandments to farmers. The seeds of Israel's spiritual mission may become drenched in tears of unbearable suffering, but the crop, the eventual harvest of homage to righteousness and truth, will be reaped in joy.

הָלוֹךְ יֵלֵךְ וּבָכֹה נֹשֵׂא מֶשֶׁךְ הַזָּרַע — *He walks along weeping, he who bears the measure of seeds.* The poor man weeps in fear that his precious seeds may go to waste. God sees his plight and has mercy on him, enabling him to reap a bountiful crop. So too, exiled Israel carries the burden of spiritual seeds in a hostile world, fearful lest its efforts be wasted. Yet, God will reward its

GRACE AFTER MEALS

Hōdu Ladonoy ki tov, / הוֹדוּ לַיהוה כִּי טוֹב,
ki l'ōlom chasdo. / כִּי לְעוֹלָם חַסְדּוֹ.
Give thanks to God for He is good, His kindness endures forever.

Mi y'malayl g'vurōs Adonoy, / מִי יְמַלֵּל גְּבוּרוֹת יהוה,
Who can express the mighty acts of HASHEM?

yashmi-a kol t'hilosō. / יַשְׁמִיעַ כָּל תְּהִלָּתוֹ.
Who can declare all His praise?

Hin'ni muchon umzumon / הִנְנִי מוּכָן וּמְזֻמָּן
Behold I am prepared and ready

l'ka-yaym mitzvas asay / לְקַיֵּם מִצְוַת עֲשֵׂה
shel birkas hamozōn, / שֶׁל בִּרְכַּת הַמָּזוֹן,
to perform the positive commandment of Grace After Meals,

shene-emar: v'ochalto v'sovoto, / שֶׁנֶּאֱמַר: וְאָכַלְתָּ וְשָׂבָעְתָּ,
for it is said: "And you shall eat and you shall be satisfied

u-vayrachto es Adōnoy Elōhecho, / וּבֵרַכְתָּ אֶת יהוה אֱלֹהֶיךָ,
and you shall bless HASHEM, *your God,*

al ho-oretz hatōvo / עַל הָאָרֶץ הַטֹּבָה
asher nosan loch. / אֲשֶׁר נָתַן לָךְ.
for the good land which He gave you."

ZIMUN/INVITATION

IF THREE OR MORE MALES, AGED THIRTEEN OR OLDER, PARTICIPATE IN A MEAL, A LEADER IS APPOINTED TO FORMALLY INVITE THE OTHERS TO JOIN HIM IN RECITING GRACE AFTER MEALS.

LEADER:

Rabōsai n'voraych. / רַבּוֹתַי נְבָרֵךְ.
Gentlemen, let us bless.

OTHERS:

Y'hi shaym Adōnoy m'vōroch / יְהִי שֵׁם יהוה מְבֹרָךְ
Blessed be the Name of HASHEM*

may-ato v'ad ōlom. / מֵעַתָּה וְעַד עוֹלָם.
from this time and forever!

LEADER:

Y'hi shaym Adōnoy m'vōroch / יְהִי שֵׁם יהוה מְבֹרָךְ
Blessed be the Name of HASHEM*

may-ato v'ad ōlom. / מֵעַתָּה וְעַד עוֹלָם.
from this time and forever!

---

sacrifice with the bounty of the World to Come. יְהִי שֵׁם ה' מְבֹרָךְ — *Blessed be the Name of Hashem.* The leader, too, repeats the blessings because it would be sacrilegious for him to ask others to bless God while he, being part of the group, refrains from joining them.

IF TEN MEN JOIN IN THE ZIMUN, THE WORD IN PARENTHESES IS ADDED.

Bir-shus moronon v'rabonon
v'rabōsai,
בִּרְשׁוּת מָרָנָן וְרַבָּנָן
וְרַבּוֹתַי,

With the permission* of my masters, rabbis and teachers,

n'voraych (Elōhaynu)
she-ochalnu mi-shelō.
נְבָרֵךְ (אֱלֹהֵינוּ)
שֶׁאָכַלְנוּ מִשֶּׁלּוֹ.

let us bless [our God,] He of Whose we have eaten.*

THOSE WHO HAVE EATEN RESPOND:

Boruch (Elōhaynu)
she-ochalnu mi-shelō
בָּרוּךְ (אֱלֹהֵינוּ)
שֶׁאָכַלְנוּ מִשֶּׁלּוֹ

Blessed is [our God,] He of Whose we have eaten

uvtuvō cho-yinu.
וּבְטוּבוֹ חָיִינוּ.

and through Whose goodness we live.

THOSE WHO HAVE NOT EATEN RESPOND:

Boruch (Elōhaynu) umvōroch sh'mo
בָּרוּךְ (אֱלֹהֵינוּ) וּמְבֹרָךְ שְׁמוֹ

Blessed is [our God] and blessed is His Name

tomid l'ōlom vo-ed.
תָּמִיד לְעוֹלָם וָעֶד.

continuously forever and ever.

LEADER:

Boruch (Elōhaynu)
she-ochalnu mi-shelō
בָּרוּךְ (אֱלֹהֵינוּ)
שֶׁאָכַלְנוּ מִשֶּׁלּוֹ

Blessed is [our God,] He of Whose we have eaten

uvtuvō cho-yinu.
וּבְטוּבוֹ חָיִינוּ.

and through Whose goodness we live.

ALL:

Boruch hu u-voruch sh'mō.
בָּרוּךְ הוּא וּבָרוּךְ שְׁמוֹ.

Blessed is He and Blessed is His Name.

THE ZIMUN LEADER SHOULD RECITE GRACE AFTER MEALS (OR, AT LEAST, THE FIRST BLESSING) ALOUD. OTHER THAN TO RESPOND AMEN AT THE CONCLUSION OF EACH BLESSING, IT IS FORBIDDEN TO INTERRUPT GRACE AFTER MEALS FOR ANY RESPONSE OTHER THAN THOSE PERMITTED DURING THE SHEMA.

■ First blessing: for nourishment. I thank Hashem for miraculously providing and sustaining me and all living beings with nourishment, as He sustained the Jewish people daily for forty years in the wilderness.

BORUCH ato Adōnoy
בָּרוּךְ אַתָּה יהוה

Blessed are You, HASHEM,

בִּרְשׁוּת — *With the permission.* Since one of the group assumes the privilege of leading them all in the recitation, he requests their permission.

שֶׁאָכַלְנוּ מִשֶּׁלּוֹ — *Of Whose we have eaten.* This text is ancient. The Talmud relates that Abraham would invite wayfarers to his home and

Elōhaynu melech ho-ōlom,	אֱלֹהֵינוּ מֶלֶךְ הָעוֹלָם,

our God, King of the universe,

ha-zon es ho-ōlom kulō, b'tuvō,	הַזָּן אֶת הָעוֹלָם כֻּלּוֹ, בְּטוּבוֹ,

Who nourishes the entire world, in His goodness —

b'chayn b'chesed uvrachamim	בְּחֵן בְּחֶסֶד וּבְרַחֲמִים,

with grace, with kindness, and with mercy.

hu nōsayn lechem l'chol bosor,	הוּא נוֹתֵן לֶחֶם לְכָל בָּשָׂר,

He gives nourishment to all flesh,

ki l'ōlom chasdō.	כִּי לְעוֹלָם חַסְדּוֹ.

for His kindness is eternal.

Uvtuvō hagodōl,	וּבְטוּבוֹ הַגָּדוֹל,

And through His great goodness,

tomid lō chosar lonu,	תָּמִיד לֹא חָסַר לָנוּ,

we have never lacked,

v'al yechsar lonu	וְאַל יֶחְסַר לָנוּ
mozōn l'ōlom vo-ed.	מָזוֹן לְעוֹלָם וָעֶד.

and may we never lack, nourishment, for all eternity.

ba-avur sh'mō hagodōl,	בַּעֲבוּר שְׁמוֹ הַגָּדוֹל,

For the sake of His Great Name,

ki hu Ayl zon umfarnays lakōl,	כִּי הוּא אֵל זָן וּמְפַרְנֵס לַכֹּל,

because He is God* Who nourishes and sustains all,

u-maytiv lakōl,	וּמֵטִיב לַכֹּל,

and benefits all,

u-maychin mozōn l'chōl b'riyōsov	וּמֵכִין מָזוֹן לְכָל בְּרִיּוֹתָיו
asher boro.	אֲשֶׁר בָּרָא.

and He prepares food for all of His creatures which He has created.

❖ Boruch ato Adōnoy,	❖ בָּרוּךְ אַתָּה יהוה,
ha-zon es hakōl.	הַזָּן אֶת הַכֹּל.

Blessed are You, HASHEM, Who nourishes all.

ALL PRESENT RESPOND: Omayn — אָמֵן

---

serve them lavishly. When they were sated and refreshed and ready to continue on their way, they would thank him. He would insist that their thanks belonged not to him, but to God, the One from Whose bounty they had eaten (*Sotah* 10b).

⥽ **First Blessing: for the Nourishment**

Bircas HaMazon comprises four blessings, of which the first three are Scripturally ordained and the fourth was instituted by the Sages. The first blessing was, as noted above, composed by Moses in gratitude for the manna with which God sustained Israel daily in the wilderness (*Berachos* 48b).

בַּעֲבוּר שְׁמוֹ הַגָּדוֹל כִּי הוּא אֵל — *For the sake of His Great Name, because He is God.* We declare that the motive of our request for eternally abundant food is not selfish, but for the sake of His Great Name so that we may be better able to serve Him.

ברכת המזון / 312

■ Second Blessing: for the Land of Israel. I thank Hashem for giving us the Holy Land and the opportunity it affords me to permeate it with *mitzvos*.

NŌ-DE l'cho, Adōnoy Elōhaynu,   נוֹדֶה לְךָ, יהוה אֱלֹהֵינוּ,
We thank You, Hashem, our God,

al shehinchalto la-avōsaynu   עַל שֶׁהִנְחַלְתָּ לַאֲבוֹתֵינוּ
because You have given to our forefathers as a heritage*

eretz chemdo tōvo urchovo,   אֶרֶץ חֶמְדָּה טוֹבָה וּרְחָבָה,
a desirable, good and spacious Land;

V'al shehōtzaysonu Adōnoy Elōhaynu   וְעַל שֶׁהוֹצֵאתָנוּ יהוה אֱלֹהֵינוּ
may-eretz mitzra-yim,   מֵאֶרֶץ מִצְרַיִם,
because You removed us, Hashem, our God, from the land of Egypt

ufdisonu mibays avodim,   וּפְדִיתָנוּ מִבֵּית עֲבָדִים,
and You redeemed us from the house of bondage;

v'al b'ris'cho shechosamto bivsoraynu,   וְעַל בְּרִיתְךָ שֶׁחָתַמְתָּ בִּבְשָׂרֵנוּ,
and for Your covenant which You sealed in our flesh;*

v'al tōros'cho shelimad-tonu,   וְעַל תּוֹרָתְךָ שֶׁלִּמַּדְתָּנוּ,
for Your Torah which You taught us

v'al chu-kecho shehōdatonu,   וְעַל חֻקֶּיךָ שֶׁהוֹדַעְתָּנוּ,
and for Your statutes which You made known to us;

v'al cha-yim chayn vo-chesed shechōnantonu,   וְעַל חַיִּים חֵן וָחֶסֶד שֶׁחוֹנַנְתָּנוּ,
for life, grace, and lovingkindness which You granted us;

v'al achilas mozōn   וְעַל אֲכִילַת מָזוֹן
and for the provision of food

sho-ato zon umfarnays ōsonu tomid,   שָׁאַתָּה זָן וּמְפַרְנֵס אוֹתָנוּ תָּמִיד,
with which You nourish and sustain us constantly,

b'chol yōm uvchol ays uvchol sho-o.   בְּכָל יוֹם וּבְכָל עֵת וּבְכָל שָׁעָה.
in every day, in every season, and in every hour.

⛊ Second Blessing: for the Land

This blessing was formulated by Joshua (*Berachos* 48a). He witnessed Moses' overwhelming desire to enter the Land of Israel and knew how anxious the Patriarchs were to be buried there. Therefore when Joshua was privileged to enter the Land, he composed this blessing in its honor.

עַל שֶׁהִנְחַלְתָּ לַאֲבוֹתֵינוּ — *Because You have given to our forefathers as a heritage.* The Land of Israel is referred to as "a heritage," implying that it remains eternally the inheritance of Israel. Thus, the long exile means only that God denied us access to it in punishment for our sins, not that it ceased to be ours.

וְעַל בְּרִיתְךָ שֶׁחָתַמְתָּ בִּבְשָׂרֵנוּ — *And for Your covenant which You sealed in our flesh.* The reference is to circumcision, mention of which is required in the blessing of the Land because the Land was promised to Abraham in the merit of circumcision (see *Genesis* 17:7-8).

Women are not subject to the commandment of circumcision. Nevertheless, women do say, "For Your covenant which You sealed in our flesh." Although women do not require circumcision, they are considered as equivalent to circumcised men in this regard.

GRACE AFTER MEALS

ON CHANUKAH AND PURIM CONTINUE BELOW. ON ALL OTHER DAYS TURN TO P. 315.

AL hanisim, v'al hapurkon, עַל הַנִּסִּים, וְעַל הַפֻּרְקָן,
For the miracles, and for the salvation,
v'al hag'vurōs, v'al hat'shu-ōs, וְעַל הַגְּבוּרוֹת, וְעַל הַתְּשׁוּעוֹת,
v'al hamilchomōs, וְעַל הַמִּלְחָמוֹת,
and for the mighty deeds, and for the victories, and for the battles
she-osiso la-avōsaynu שֶׁעָשִׂיתָ לַאֲבוֹתֵינוּ
ba-yomim hohaym baz'man ha-ze. בַּיָּמִים הָהֵם בַּזְּמַן הַזֶּה.
which You performed for our forefathers in those days, at this time.

ON CHANUKAH CONTINUE HERE; ON PURIM TURN TO P. 314.

BIMAY matisyohu ben yōchonon בִּימֵי מַתִּתְיֶהוּ בֶּן יוֹחָנָן
In the days of Mattisyahu, the son of Yochanan,
kōhayn godōl chashmōno-i u-vonov, כֹּהֵן גָּדוֹל חַשְׁמוֹנַאי וּבָנָיו,
the High Priest, the Hasmonean, and his sons —
k'she-om'do malchus yovon כְּשֶׁעָמְדָה מַלְכוּת יָוָן
hor'sho-o al am'cho yisro-ayl, הָרְשָׁעָה עַל עַמְּךָ יִשְׂרָאֵל,
when the wicked Greek kingdom rose up against Your people Israel
l'hashkichom tōrosecho, לְהַשְׁכִּיחָם תּוֹרָתֶךָ,
to make them forget Your Torah
ulha-avirom may-chukay r'tzōnecho. וּלְהַעֲבִירָם מֵחֻקֵּי רְצוֹנֶךָ.
and compel them to stray from the statutes of Your will.
V'ato b'rachamecho horabim, וְאַתָּה בְּרַחֲמֶיךָ הָרַבִּים,
But You, in Your abundant mercy,
omadto lohem b'ays tzorosom, עָמַדְתָּ לָהֶם בְּעֵת צָרָתָם,
stood up for them in the time of their distress;
ravto es rivom, danto es dinom, רַבְתָּ אֶת רִיבָם, דַּנְתָּ אֶת דִּינָם,
You took up their grievance, You judged their claim,
nokamto es nikmosom. נָקַמְתָּ אֶת נִקְמָתָם.
and You avenged their wrong.
Mosarto gibōrim b'yad chaloshim, מָסַרְתָּ גִבּוֹרִים בְּיַד חַלָּשִׁים,
You delivered the strong into the hand of the weak,
v'rabim b'yad m'atim, וְרַבִּים בְּיַד מְעַטִּים,
the many into the hand of the few,
utmay-im b'yad t'hōrim, וּטְמֵאִים בְּיַד טְהוֹרִים,
the impure into the hand of the pure,
ursho-im b'yad tzadikim וּרְשָׁעִים בְּיַד צַדִּיקִים,
the wicked into the hand of the righteous,

ON CHANUKAH CONTINUE:

וְזֵדִים בְּיַד עוֹסְקֵי תוֹרָתֶךָ.
v'zaydim b'yad ōs'kay sōrosecho.
and the wanton into the hand of the diligent students of Your Torah.

וּלְךָ עָשִׂיתָ שֵׁם גָּדוֹל וְקָדוֹשׁ בְּעוֹלָמֶךָ,
Ulcho osiso shaym godōl v'kodōsh b'ōlomecho,
For Yourself You made a great and holy Name in Your world,

וּלְעַמְּךָ יִשְׂרָאֵל עָשִׂיתָ תְּשׁוּעָה גְדוֹלָה וּפֻרְקָן
ul-am'cho yisro-ayl osiso t'shu-o g'dōlo u-furkon
and for Your people Israel You performed a great victory and salvation

כְּהַיּוֹם הַזֶּה.
k'ha-yōm ha-ze.
as this very day.

וְאַחַר כֵּן בָּאוּ בָנֶיךָ לִדְבִיר בֵּיתֶךָ,
V'achar kayn bo-u vonecho lidvir bay-secho,
Thereafter, Your children came to the Holy of Holies of Your House,

וּפִנּוּ אֶת הֵיכָלֶךָ,
u-finu es haycholecho,

וְטִהֲרוּ אֶת מִקְדָּשֶׁךָ,
v'tiharu es mikdoshecho,
they cleansed Your Temple, they purified the site of Your Holiness

וְהִדְלִיקוּ נֵרוֹת בְּחַצְרוֹת קָדְשֶׁךָ,
v'hidliku nayrōs b'chatzrōs kod-shecho,
and they kindled lights in the Courtyards of Your Sanctuary;

וְקָבְעוּ שְׁמוֹנַת יְמֵי חֲנֻכָּה אֵלּוּ,
v'kov'u sh'mōnas y'may chanuko aylu,
and they established these eight days of Chanukah

לְהוֹדוֹת וּלְהַלֵּל לְשִׁמְךָ הַגָּדוֹל.
l'hōdōs ulhalayl l'shimcho hagodōl.
to express thanks and praise to Your great Name.

CONTINUE V'al hakōl, P. 315

ON PURIM CONTINUE HERE:

בִּימֵי מָרְדְּכַי וְאֶסְתֵּר בְּשׁוּשַׁן הַבִּירָה,
BIMAY mord'chai v'estayr b'shushan habiro,
In the days of Mordechai and Esther, in Shushan, the capital,

כְּשֶׁעָמַד עֲלֵיהֶם הָמָן הָרָשָׁע,
k'she-omad alayhem homon horosho,
when Haman, the wicked, rose up against them

בִּקֵּשׁ לְהַשְׁמִיד לַהֲרֹג וּלְאַבֵּד
bikaysh l'hashmid laharōg ul-abayd
and sought to destroy, to slay, and to exterminate

אֶת כָּל הַיְּהוּדִים,
es kol ha-y'hudim,

מִנַּעַר וְעַד זָקֵן, טַף וְנָשִׁים
mina-ar v'ad zokayn, taf v'noshim
all the Jews, young and old, infants and women,

בְּיוֹם אֶחָד,
b'yōm e-chod,
on the same day,

ON PURIM CONTINUE:

bish-lōsho osor l'chōdesh   בִּשְׁלוֹשָׁה עָשָׂר לַחֹדֶשׁ
sh'naym osor, hu chōdesh ador,   שְׁנֵים עָשָׂר, הוּא חֹדֶשׁ אֲדָר,
on the thirteenth of the twelfth month which is the month of Adar,
ushlolom lovōz.   וּשְׁלָלָם לָבוֹז.
and to plunder their possessions.
V'ato b'rachamecho horabim   וְאַתָּה בְּרַחֲמֶיךָ הָרַבִּים
But You, in Your abundant mercy,
hayfarto es atzosō,   הֵפַרְתָּ אֶת עֲצָתוֹ,
nullified his counsel
v'kilkalto es machashavtō,   וְקִלְקַלְתָּ אֶת מַחֲשַׁבְתּוֹ,
and frustrated his intention
vaha-shayvōso lō g'mulō b'rōshō,   וַהֲשֵׁבוֹתָ לּוֹ גְּמוּלוֹ בְּרֹאשׁוֹ,
and caused his design to return upon his own head.
V'solu ōsō v'es bonov al ho-aytz.   וְתָלוּ אוֹתוֹ וְאֶת בָּנָיו עַל הָעֵץ.
And they hanged him and his sons on the gallows.

ON ALL DAYS CONTINUE HERE:

V'AL HAKŌL, Adōnoy Elōhaynu,   **וְעַל הַכֹּל** יהוה אֱלֹהֵינוּ
For all, Hashem, our God,
anachnu mōdim loch,   אֲנַחְנוּ מוֹדִים לָךְ,
umvor'chim ōsoch,   וּמְבָרְכִים אוֹתָךְ,
we thank You and bless You.
yisborach shimcho b'fi kol chai   יִתְבָּרַךְ שִׁמְךָ בְּפִי כָּל חַי
May Your Name be blessed by the mouth of all the living,
tomid l'ōlom vo-ed.   תָּמִיד לְעוֹלָם וָעֶד.
continuously for all eternity.
Kakosuv: V'ochalto v'sovoto,   כַּכָּתוּב: וְאָכַלְתָּ וְשָׂבָעְתָּ,
As it is written: "And you shall eat and you shall be satisfied
u-vayrachto es Adōnoy Elōhecho,   וּבֵרַכְתָּ אֶת יהוה אֱלֹהֶיךָ,
and you shall bless Hashem, your God,
al ho-oretz hatōvo   עַל הָאָרֶץ הַטֹּבָה
asher nosan loch.   אֲשֶׁר נָתַן לָךְ.
for the good land which He gave you."
Boruch ato Adōnoy,   ❖ בָּרוּךְ אַתָּה יהוה,
al ho-oretz v'al hamozōn.   עַל הָאָרֶץ וְעַל הַמָּזוֹן.
Blessed are You, Hashem, for the land and for the nourishment.

ALL PRESENT RESPOND: **Omayn** — אָמֵן

■ Third Blessing: for Jerusalem. I ask Hashem to rebuild Jerusalem and the Third Temple which will again enable us to be cognizant of the fact that He provides us with all our needs.

RACHAYM Adōnoy Elōhaynu   רַחֶם יהוה אֱלֹהֵינוּ
Have mercy, HASHEM, our God,

al yisro-ayl amecho,   עַל יִשְׂרָאֵל עַמֶּךָ,
v'al y'rushola-yim i-recho,   וְעַל יְרוּשָׁלַיִם עִירֶךָ,
on Israel Your people; on Jerusalem, Your city;

v'al tziyōn mishkan k'vōdecho,   וְעַל צִיּוֹן מִשְׁכַּן כְּבוֹדֶךָ,
on Zion, the resting place of Your Glory;

v'al malchus bays dovid   וְעַל מַלְכוּת בֵּית דָּוִד
m'shichecho,   מְשִׁיחֶךָ,
on the monarchy of the house of David, Your anointed;*

v'al haba-yis hagodōl v'hakodōsh   וְעַל הַבַּיִת הַגָּדוֹל וְהַקָּדוֹשׁ
shenikro shimcho olov.   שֶׁנִּקְרָא שִׁמְךָ עָלָיו.
and on the great and holy House upon which Your Name is called.

Elōhaynu ovinu,   אֱלֹהֵינוּ אָבִינוּ
Our God, our Father —

r'aynu, zunaynu, parn'saynu   רְעֵנוּ זוּנֵנוּ פַּרְנְסֵנוּ
v'chalk'laynu v'harvichaynu,   וְכַלְכְּלֵנוּ וְהַרְוִיחֵנוּ,
tend us, nourish us, sustain us, support us, relieve us;

v'harvach lonu Adōnoy Elōhaynu   וְהַרְוַח לָנוּ יהוה אֱלֹהֵינוּ
m'hayro mikol tzorōsaynu.   מְהֵרָה מִכָּל צָרוֹתֵינוּ.
HASHEM, our God, grant us speedy relief from all our troubles.

V'no al tatzrichaynu,   וְנָא אַל תַּצְרִיכֵנוּ,
Adōnoy Elōhaynu,   יהוה אֱלֹהֵינוּ,
Please, make us not needful — HASHEM, our God —

lō liday mat'nas bosor vodom,   לֹא לִידֵי מַתְּנַת בָּשָׂר וָדָם,
v'lō liday halvo-osom,   וְלֹא לִידֵי הַלְוָאָתָם,
of the gifts of human hands nor of their loans,

◈§ **Third Blessing: for Jerusalem**

The third blessing is the final one required by the Torah. It was composed in stages by David and Solomon. David, who occupied Jerusalem, made reference to "Israel, Your people, and Jerusalem, Your city." Solomon, following his construction of the Temple, added, "the great and holy House" (*Berachos* 48b).

Their blessing was a prayer that God preserve the tranquility of the Land. Following the destruction and exile, the blessing was changed to embody a prayer for the return of the Land, the Temple, and the Davidic dynasty.

מַלְכוּת בֵּית דָּוִד מְשִׁיחֶךָ — *The monarchy of the house of David, Your anointed.* It is mandatory that the monarchy of David's dynasty be mentioned in this blessing (*Berachos* 49a), because it was David who sanctified Jerusalem, and because the consolation for the exile will not be complete until David's kingdom is restored.

GRACE AFTER MEALS

ki im l'yod'cho ham'lay-o hap'su-cho hak'dōsho v'hor'chovo,
כִּי אִם לְיָדְךָ הַמְּלֵאָה הַפְּתוּחָה הַקְּדוֹשָׁה וְהָרְחָבָה,
but only of Your Hand that is full, open, holy, and generous,

shelō nayvōsh v'lō nikolaym l'ōlom vo-ed.
שֶׁלֹּא נֵבוֹשׁ וְלֹא נִכָּלֵם לְעוֹלָם וָעֶד.
that we not feel inner shame nor be humiliated forever and ever.

ON THE SABBATH ADD THE FOLLOWING.

R'TZAY v'hachalitzaynu Adōnoy Elōhaynu
רְצֵה וְהַחֲלִיצֵנוּ יהוה אֱלֹהֵינוּ
May it please You, HASHEM, our God — give us rest

b'mitzvōsecho,
בְּמִצְוֹתֶיךָ,
through Your commandments

uvmitzvas yōm hash'vi-i
וּבְמִצְוַת יוֹם הַשְּׁבִיעִי
and through the commandment of the seventh day,

ha-shabos hagodōl v'hakodōsh ha-ze,
הַשַּׁבָּת הַגָּדוֹל וְהַקָּדוֹשׁ הַזֶּה,
this great and holy Sabbath.

Ki yōm ze godōl v'kodōsh hu l'fonecho,
כִּי יוֹם זֶה גָּדוֹל וְקָדוֹשׁ הוּא לְפָנֶיךָ,
For this day is great and holy before You

lishbos bō v'lonu-ach bō b'ahavo k'mitzvas r'tzōnecho.
לִשְׁבָּת בּוֹ וְלָנוּחַ בּוֹ בְּאַהֲבָה כְּמִצְוַת רְצוֹנֶךָ.
to rest on it and be content on it in love, as ordained by Your will.

U-virtzōn'cho honi-ach lonu, Adōnoy Elōhaynu,
וּבִרְצוֹנְךָ הָנִיחַ לָנוּ, יהוה אֱלֹהֵינוּ,
May this be Your will — calm us, HASHEM, our God,

shelō s'hay tzoro v'yogōn va-anocho b'yōm m'nuchosaynu.
שֶׁלֹּא תְהֵא צָרָה וְיָגוֹן וַאֲנָחָה בְּיוֹם מְנוּחָתֵנוּ.
so that there be no distress, grief, or lament on this day of our contentment.

V'har-aynu Adōnoy Elōhaynu
וְהַרְאֵנוּ יהוה אֱלֹהֵינוּ
And show us, HASHEM, our God,

b'nechomas tziyōn i-recho,
בְּנֶחָמַת צִיּוֹן עִירֶךָ,
the consolation of Zion, Your city,

uv'vinyan y'rushola-yim ir kodshecho,
וּבְבִנְיַן יְרוּשָׁלַיִם עִיר קָדְשֶׁךָ,
and the rebuilding of Jerusalem, City of Your holiness,

ki ato hu ba-al hai-shu-ōs u-va-al hanechomōs.
כִּי אַתָּה הוּא בַּעַל הַיְשׁוּעוֹת וּבַעַל הַנֶּחָמוֹת.
for You are the Master of salvations and Master of consolations.

ON *ROSH CHODESH* AND FESTIVALS (INCLUDING *CHOL HAMOED*) RECITE:

ELÔHAYNU Vaylōhay avōsaynu, אֱלֹהֵינוּ וֵאלֹהֵי אֲבוֹתֵינוּ,
Our God and the God of our forefathers,

ya-a-le v'yovō v'yagi-a v'yayro-e יַעֲלֶה, וְיָבֹא, וְיַגִּיעַ, וְיֵרָאֶה,
may there rise, come, reach, be noted,

v'yayro-tze v'yi-shoma v'yipokayd וְיֵרָצֶה, וְיִשָּׁמַע, וְיִפָּקֵד,
be favored, be heard, be considered,

v'yizochayr zichrōnaynu u-fikdōnaynu, וְיִזָּכֵר זִכְרוֹנֵנוּ וּפִקְדּוֹנֵנוּ,
and be remembered — the remembrance and consideration of ourselves;

v'zichrōn avōsaynu, וְזִכְרוֹן אֲבוֹתֵינוּ,
the remembrance of our forefathers;

v'zichrōn moshi-ach ben dovid avdecho, וְזִכְרוֹן מָשִׁיחַ בֶּן דָּוִד עַבְדֶּךָ,
the remembrance of Messiah, son of David, Your servant;

v'zichrōn y'rushola-yim ir kod'shecho, וְזִכְרוֹן יְרוּשָׁלַיִם עִיר קָדְשֶׁךָ,
the remembrance of Jerusalem, Your Holy City;

v'zichrōn kol am'cho bays yisro-ayl וְזִכְרוֹן כָּל עַמְּךָ בֵּית יִשְׂרָאֵל
l'fonecho, לְפָנֶיךָ,
and the remembrance of Your entire people the Family of Israel — before You

lif-layto l'tōvo לִפְלֵיטָה לְטוֹבָה
for deliverance, for goodness,

l'chayn ulchesed ulrachamim, לְחֵן וּלְחֶסֶד וּלְרַחֲמִים,
for grace, for kindness, and for compassion,

l'cha-yim ulsholōm לְחַיִּים וּלְשָׁלוֹם
for life, and for peace

——————— ON ROSH CHODESH ———————

b'yōm rōsh ha-chōdesh ha-ze. בְּיוֹם רֹאשׁ הַחֹדֶשׁ הַזֶּה.
on this day of Rosh Chodesh.

——————— ON PESACH ———————

b'yōm chag hamatzōs ha-ze. בְּיוֹם חַג הַמַּצּוֹת הַזֶּה.
on this day of the Festival of Matzos.

——————— ON SHAVUOS ———————

b'yōm chag ha-shovu-ōs ha-ze. בְּיוֹם חַג הַשָּׁבֻעוֹת הַזֶּה.
on this day of the Festival of Shavuos.

——————— ON SUCCOS ———————

b'yōm chag ha-sukōs ha-ze. בְּיוֹם חַג הַסֻּכּוֹת הַזֶּה.
on this day of the Succos Festival.

——————— ON SHEMINI ATZERES AND SIMCHAS TORAH ———————

b'yōm ha-shmini בְּיוֹם הַשְּׁמִינִי
chag ho-atzeress ha-ze. חַג הָעֲצֶרֶת הַזֶּה.
on the eighth day, this Festival of the Assembly.

zoch'raynu Adōnoy Elōhaynu bō l'tōvo,	זָכְרֵנוּ יהוה אֱלֹהֵינוּ בּוֹ לְטוֹבָה,

Remember us on it, HASHEM, our God, for goodness,

u-fokdaynu vō livrocho,   וּפָקְדֵנוּ בּוֹ לִבְרָכָה,

consider us on it for blessing

v'hōshi-aynu vō l'cha-yim.   וְהוֹשִׁיעֵנוּ בּוֹ לְחַיִּים.

and help us on it for life.

U-vidvar y'shu-o v'rachamim,   וּבִדְבַר יְשׁוּעָה וְרַחֲמִים,

In the matter of salvation and compassion,

chus v'chonaynu   חוּס וְחָנֵּנוּ

v'rachaym olaynu v'hōshi-aynu,   וְרַחֵם עָלֵינוּ וְהוֹשִׁיעֵנוּ,

pity, be gracious and compassionate with us and help us,

ki aylecho aynaynu,   כִּי אֵלֶיךָ עֵינֵינוּ,

for our eyes are turned to You,

ki Ayl (melech) chanun v'rachum oto.   כִּי אֵל (מֶלֶךְ) חַנּוּן וְרַחוּם אָתָּה.

because You are God, the gracious and compassionate (King).

❖ **UVNAY** y'rushola-yim ir hakōdesh   ❖ **וּבְנֵה** יְרוּשָׁלַיִם עִיר הַקֹּדֶשׁ

Rebuild Jerusalem,* the Holy City,

bimhayro v'yomaynu.   בִּמְהֵרָה בְיָמֵינוּ.

soon in our days.

Boruch ato Adōnoy,   בָּרוּךְ אַתָּה יהוה,

bōnay (v'rachamov) y'rusholo-yim.   בּוֹנֵה (בְרַחֲמָיו) יְרוּשָׁלָיִם.

Blessed are You, HASHEM, Who rebuilds Jerusalem (in His mercy).

Omayn.   אָמֵן.

Amen.*

ALL PRESENT RESPOND: Omayn — אָמֵן

■ Fourth Blessing: for God's goodness. I thank Hashem for the constant goodness that He provides for me and for the entire Jewish nation, especially in our difficult times.

BORUCH ato Adōnoy   **בָּרוּךְ** אַתָּה יהוה

Blessed are You, HASHEM,

Elōhaynu melech ho-ōlom,   אֱלֹהֵינוּ מֶלֶךְ הָעוֹלָם,

our God, King of the universe,

וּבְנֵה יְרוּשָׁלַיִם — *Rebuild Jerusalem.* This is the conclusion of the third blessing, and thus returns to the theme with which the blessings began — a plea for God's mercy on Jerusalem (*Pesachim* 104a).

אָמֵן — *Amen.* This blessing is unique in that one responds *Amen* after his own blessing. The purpose of this unusual formula is to serve as a demarcation between the first three blessings, which are ordained by the Torah, and the next blessing, which is Rabbinic in origin.

◈§ **Fourth Blessing: for God's Goodness**

The essence of this blessing is the phrase "Who is good and Who does good." The blessing was composed by the court of Rabban Gamliel the Elder in Yavneh in gratitude to God for

ho-Ayl ovinu malkaynu	הָאֵל אָבִינוּ מַלְכֵּנוּ
the Almighty, our Father, our King,	
adiraynu bōr'aynu	אַדִּירֵנוּ בּוֹרְאֵנוּ
our Sovereign, our Creator,	
gō-alaynu yōtz'raynu,	גּוֹאֲלֵנוּ יוֹצְרֵנוּ,
our Redeemer, our Maker,	
k'dōshaynu k'dōsh ya-akōv,	קְדוֹשֵׁנוּ קְדוֹשׁ יַעֲקֹב,
our Holy One, Holy One of Jacob,	
rō-aynu rō-ay yisro-ayl.	רוֹעֵנוּ רוֹעֵה יִשְׂרָאֵל.
our Shepherd, the Shepherd of Israel,	
Hamelech hatōv	הַמֶּלֶךְ הַטּוֹב
the King Who is good	
v'hamaytiv lakōl,	וְהַמֵּטִיב לַכֹּל,
and Who does good for all.	
sheb'chol yōm vo-yōm	שֶׁבְּכָל יוֹם וָיוֹם
For every single day*	
hu haytiv, hu maytiv,	הוּא הֵטִיב, הוּא מֵטִיב,
He did good, He does good,	
hu yaytiv lonu.	הוּא יֵיטִיב לָנוּ.
and He will do good to us.	
Hu g'molonu, hu gōm'laynu,	הוּא גְמָלָנוּ, הוּא גוֹמְלֵנוּ,
He was bountiful with us, He is bountiful with us,	
hu yigm'laynu lo-ad,	הוּא יִגְמְלֵנוּ לָעַד,
and He will forever be bountiful with us –	
l'chayn ulchesed	לְחֵן וּלְחֶסֶד
with grace and with kindness,	
ulrachamim ulrevach,	וּלְרַחֲמִים וּלְרֶוַח,
with mercy and with relief,	
hatzolo v'hatzlocho,	הַצָּלָה וְהַצְלָחָה,
salvation, success,	
b'rocho vi-shu-o,	בְּרָכָה וִישׁוּעָה
blessing, help,	
nechomo, parnoso v'chalkolo,	נֶחָמָה פַּרְנָסָה וְכַלְכָּלָה
consolation, sustenance, support,	
v'rachamim v'cha-yim	❖ וְרַחֲמִים וְחַיִּים
mercy, life,	

שֶׁבְּכָל יוֹם וָיוֹם — *For every single day.* It is not nearly sufficient to thank God for His graciousness to past generations of Jews. We must be conscious of the fact that His goodness and preserving the bodies of the victims of the Roman massacre at Betar, and for eventually allowing them to be brought to burial (*Berachos* 48b).

GRACE AFTER MEALS

v'sholōm v'chol tōv,	וְשָׁלוֹם וְכָל טוֹב,
peace, and all good;	
u-mikol tuv l'ōlom al y'chas'raynu.	וּמִכָּל טוּב לְעוֹלָם אַל יְחַסְּרֵנוּ.
and of all good things may He never deprive us.	

ALL PRESENT RESPOND: Omayn — אָמֵן

HORACHAMON,   הָרַחֲמָן,
The compassionate One!*

hu yimlōch olaynu l'ōlom vo-ed.	הוּא יִמְלוֹךְ עָלֵינוּ לְעוֹלָם וָעֶד.
May He reign over us forever.	
Horachamon, hu yisborach	הָרַחֲמָן, הוּא יִתְבָּרַךְ
The compassionate One! May He be blessed	
ba-shoma-yim u-vo-oretz.	בַּשָּׁמַיִם וּבָאָרֶץ.
in heaven and on earth.	
Horachamon,	הָרַחֲמָן,
The compassionate One!	
hu yishtabach l'dōr dōrim,	הוּא יִשְׁתַּבַּח לְדוֹר דּוֹרִים,
May He be praised throughout all generations,	
v'yispo-ar bonu lo-ad	וְיִתְפָּאַר בָּנוּ לָעַד
and may He be glorified through us forever	
ulnaytzach n'tzochim,	וּלְנֵצַח נְצָחִים,
to the ultimate ends,	
v'yis-hadar bonu lo-ad	וְיִתְהַדַּר בָּנוּ לָעַד
and be honored through us forever	
ul-ōl'may ōlomim.	וּלְעוֹלְמֵי עוֹלָמִים.
and for all eternity.	
Horachamon,	הָרַחֲמָן
The compassionate One!	
hu y'farn'saynu b'chovōd.	הוּא יְפַרְנְסֵנוּ בְּכָבוֹד.
May He sustain us in honor.	
Horachamon,	הָרַחֲמָן,
The compassionate One!	
hu yishbōr ulaynu	הוּא יִשְׁבּוֹר עֻלֵּנוּ
may-al tzavoraynu,	מֵעַל צַוָּארֵנוּ,
May He break the yoke of oppression from our necks	
v'hu yōli-chaynu	וְהוּא יוֹלִיכֵנוּ
kōm'miyus l'artzaynu.	קוֹמְמִיּוּת לְאַרְצֵנוּ.
and guide us erect to our Land.	

---

bounty are daily, constant occurrences.
הָרַחֲמָן — *The compassionate One!* The four blessings of *Bircas HaMazon* end with לְעוֹלָם אַל יְחַסְּרֵנוּ, "may He never deprive us." The remainder of *Bircas HaMazon* is a collection of brief prayers for God's compassion.

Horachamon,	הָרַחֲמָן,
hu yishlach lonu b'rocho	הוּא יִשְׁלַח לָנוּ בְּרָכָה
m'rubo baba-yis ha-ze,	מְרֻבָּה בַּבַּיִת הַזֶּה,

The compassionate One! May He send us abundant blessing to this house

v'al shulchon ze she-ochalnu olov.	וְעַל שֻׁלְחָן זֶה שֶׁאָכַלְנוּ עָלָיו.

and upon this table at which we have eaten.

Horachamon,	הָרַחֲמָן,
hu yishlach lonu es	הוּא יִשְׁלַח לָנוּ אֶת
ayliyohu hanovi zochur latōv,	אֵלִיָּהוּ הַנָּבִיא זָכוּר לַטּוֹב,

The compassionate One! May He send us Elijah, the Prophet — he is remembered for good

vivaser lonu b'sōrōs tōvōs	וִיבַשֶּׂר לָנוּ בְּשׂוֹרוֹת טוֹבוֹת
y'shu-ōs v'nechomōs.	יְשׁוּעוֹת וְנֶחָמוֹת.

to proclaim to us good tidings, salvations, and consolations.

AT ONE'S OWN TABLE (INCLUDE THE APPLICABLE WORDS IN PARENTHESES):

Horachamon,	הָרַחֲמָן,
hu y'voraych ōsi	הוּא יְבָרֵךְ אוֹתִי
(v'es ishti/v'es bali. v'es zari)	(וְאֶת אִשְׁתִּי/וְאֶת בַּעֲלִי. וְאֶת זַרְעִי)

The compassionate One! May He bless me (my wife/my husband and my children)

v'es kol asher li.	וְאֶת כָּל אֲשֶׁר לִי.

and all that is mine.

GUESTS RECITE THE FOLLOWING (CHILDREN AT THEIR PARENTS' TABLE INCLUDE THE APPLICABLE WORDS IN PARENTHESES):

Horachamon,	הָרַחֲמָן,
hu y'voraych es (ovi mōri)	הוּא יְבָרֵךְ אֶת (אָבִי מוֹרִי)
ba-al haba-yis ha-ze,	בַּעַל הַבַּיִת הַזֶּה,

The compassionate One! May He bless (my father, my teacher) the master of this house,

v'es (imi mōrosi)	וְאֶת (אִמִּי מוֹרָתִי)
ba-alas haba-yis ha-ze,	בַּעֲלַת הַבַּיִת הַזֶּה,

and (my mother, my teacher) the lady of this house,

ALL CONTINUE:

ōsom v'es bay-som v'es zar-om	אוֹתָם וְאֶת בֵּיתָם וְאֶת זַרְעָם

them, their house, their family,

v'es kol asher lohem,	וְאֶת כָּל אֲשֶׁר לָהֶם,

and all that is theirs.

ōsonu v'es kol asher lonu,	אוֹתָנוּ וְאֶת כָּל אֲשֶׁר לָנוּ,

Ours and all that is ours —

k'mō shenisbor'chu avōsaynu avrohom yitzchok v'ya-akōv	כְּמוֹ שֶׁנִּתְבָּרְכוּ אֲבוֹתֵינוּ אַבְרָהָם יִצְחָק וְיַעֲקֹב

just as our forefathers Abraham, Isaac, and Jacob were blessed

bakōl mikōl kōl.	בַּכֹּל מִכֹּל כֹּל,

in everything, from everything, with everything.

kayn y'voraych ōsonu kulonu yachad	כֵּן יְבָרֵךְ אוֹתָנוּ כֻּלָּנוּ יַחַד

So may He bless us all together

bivrocho sh'laymo.	בִּבְרָכָה שְׁלֵמָה.

with a perfect blessing.

V'nōmar: Omayn.	וְנֹאמַר: אָמֵן.

And let us say: Amen!

BAMORŌM — בַּמָּרוֹם

On high,

y'lam'du alayhem v'olaynu z'chus,	יְלַמְּדוּ עֲלֵיהֶם וְעָלֵינוּ זְכוּת,

may merit be pleaded upon them and upon us,

shet'hay l'mishmeres sholōm,	שֶׁתְּהֵא לְמִשְׁמֶרֶת שָׁלוֹם.

for a safeguard of peace.*

V'niso v'rocho may-ays Adōnoy,	וְנִשָּׂא בְרָכָה מֵאֵת יהוה,

May we receive a blessing from HASHEM

utzdoko may-Elōhay yish-aynu,	וּצְדָקָה מֵאֱלֹהֵי יִשְׁעֵנוּ,

and just kindness from the God of our salvation,

v'nimtzo chayn v'saychel tōv	וְנִמְצָא חֵן וְשֵׂכֶל טוֹב

and find favor and good understanding

b'aynay Elōhim v'odom.	בְּעֵינֵי אֱלֹהִים וְאָדָם.

in the eyes of God and man.

ON THE SABBATH ADD:

Horachamon, hu yanchilaynu	הָרַחֲמָן, הוּא יַנְחִילֵנוּ

The compassionate One! May He cause us to inherit

yōm shekulō shabos umnucho	יוֹם שֶׁכֻּלּוֹ שַׁבָּת וּמְנוּחָה

the day which will be completely a Sabbath and rest day

l'cha-yay ho-ōlomim.	לְחַיֵּי הָעוֹלָמִים.

for eternal life.

לְמִשְׁמֶרֶת שָׁלוֹם — *For a safeguard of peace,* i.e., to assure that the home will be contented and peaceful.

יוֹם שֶׁכֻּלּוֹ שַׁבָּת — *The day which will be completely a Sabbath,* an allusion to the World to Come after the Final Redemption.

ברכת המזון / 324

ON *ROSH CHODESH* ADD:

Horachamon,   הָרַחֲמָן
The compassionate One!

hu y'chadaysh olaynu   הוּא יְחַדֵּשׁ עָלֵינוּ
es ha-chōdesh ha-ze   אֶת הַחֹדֶשׁ הַזֶּה
May He inaugurate this month upon us

l'tōvo v'livrocho.   לְטוֹבָה וְלִבְרָכָה.
for goodness and for blessing.

ON FESTIVALS ADD:

Horachamon, hu yanchilaynu   הָרַחֲמָן הוּא יַנְחִילֵנוּ
The compassionate One! May He cause us to inherit

yōm shekulō tōv.   יוֹם שֶׁכֻּלּוֹ טוֹב.
the day which is completely good.

ON *SUCCOS* ADD:

Horachamon, hu yokim lonu   הָרַחֲמָן הוּא יָקִים לָנוּ
The compassionate One! May He erect for us

es sukas dovid hanōfoles.   אֶת סֻכַּת דָּוִיד הַנֹּפֶלֶת.
David's fallen booth.*

HORACHAMON, hu y'zakaynu   **הָרַחֲמָן** הוּא יְזַכֵּנוּ
The compassionate One! May He make us worthy

limōs hamoshi-ach   לִימוֹת הַמָּשִׁיחַ
of the days of Messiah

ulcha-yay ho-ōlom habo.   וּלְחַיֵּי הָעוֹלָם הַבָּא.
and the life of the World to Come.

──────── ON WEEKDAYS: ────────

Magdil y'shu-ōs malkō,   מַגְדִּל יְשׁוּעוֹת מַלְכּוֹ
He Who makes great the salvations of His king

──────── ON THE SABBATH, FESTIVALS, *CHOL HAMOED*, AND *ROSH CHODESH*: ────────

Migdōl y'shu-ōs malkō,   מִגְדּוֹל יְשׁוּעוֹת מַלְכּוֹ
He Who is a tower of salvations to His king

v'ōse chesed limshichō   וְעֹשֶׂה חֶסֶד לִמְשִׁיחוֹ
and does kindness for His anointed,

l'dovid ulzar-ō ad ōlom.   לְדָוִד וּלְזַרְעוֹ עַד עוֹלָם.
to David and to his descendants forever.

סֻכַּת דָּוִיד הַנֹּפֶלֶת — *David's fallen booth.* This phrase was used by God when He promised to restore the kingship of the Davidic dynasty which is figuratively called *succah*. The word *succah* means "protection," and refers to the king's protection of his people.

325 / GRACE AFTER MEALS

Ōse sholōm bimrōmov, עֹשֶׂה שָׁלוֹם בִּמְרוֹמָיו,
He Who makes peace in His heights,*

hu ya-ase sholōm olaynu הוּא יַעֲשֶׂה שָׁלוֹם עָלֵינוּ
may He make peace upon us

v'al kol yisro-ayl. V'imru: Omayn. וְעַל כָּל יִשְׂרָאֵל. וְאִמְרוּ, אָמֵן.
and upon all Israel. Now respond: Amen!

Y'RU es Adōnoy k'dōshov, **יְראוּ** אֶת יהוה קְדֹשָׁיו,
Fear HASHEM*, you — His holy ones —*

ki ayn machsōr liray-ov. כִּי אֵין מַחְסוֹר לִירֵאָיו.
for there is no deprivation for His reverent ones.*

K'firim roshu v'ro-ayvu, כְּפִירִים רָשׁוּ וְרָעֵבוּ,
Young lions may be in need and hunger,

v'dōr'shay Adōnoy וְדֹרְשֵׁי יהוה
lō yachs'ru chol tōv. לֹא יַחְסְרוּ כָל טוֹב.
but those who seek HASHEM *will not lack any good.*

Hōdu Ladōnoy ki tōv, הוֹדוּ לַיהוה כִּי טוֹב,
Give thanks to God for He is good;

ki l'ōlom chasdō. כִּי לְעוֹלָם חַסְדּוֹ.
His kindness endures forever.

Pōsay-ach es yodecho, פּוֹתֵחַ אֶת יָדֶךָ,
You open Your hand

u-masbi-a l'chol chai rotzōn. וּמַשְׂבִּיעַ לְכָל חַי רָצוֹן.
and satisfy the desire of every living thing.

Boruch hagever בָּרוּךְ הַגֶּבֶר
asher yivtach Badōnoy, אֲשֶׁר יִבְטַח בַּיהוה,
Blessed is the man who trusts in HASHEM*,*

v'ho-yo Adōnoy mivtachō. וְהָיָה יהוה מִבְטַחוֹ.
then HASHEM *will be his security.**

Na-ar ho-yisi gam zokanti, נַעַר הָיִיתִי גַּם זָקַנְתִּי,
I was a youth and also have aged,

By extension, this also refers to the Temple, which is called David's because he longed to build it and prepared for its construction. As the abode of God's Presence, it, too, protects Israel.

עֹשֶׂה שָׁלוֹם בִּמְרוֹמָיו — *He Who makes peace in His heights.* Even the heavenly beings require God to make peace among them — how much more so fractious man!

יְראוּ . . . כִּי אֵין מַחְסוֹר לִירֵאָיו — *Fear . . . for there is no deprivation for His reverent ones.* Those who fear God are content, even if they are lacking in material possessions. But the wicked are never satisfied; whatever they have only whets their appetite for more.

אֲשֶׁר יִבְטַח בַּה׳ וְהָיָה ה׳ מִבְטחוֹ — *Who trusts in* HASHEM*, then* HASHEM *will be his security.* God will be a fortress of trust to a person in direct proportion to the amount of trust one places in God.

v'lō ro-isi tzadik ne-ezov,	וְלֹא רָאִיתִי צַדִּיק נֶעֱזָב,

and I have not seen a righteous man forsaken,

v'zar-ō m'vakaysh lochem.	וְזַרְעוֹ מְבַקֶּשׁ לָחֶם.

with his children begging for bread.*

Adōnoy ōz l'amō yitayn,	יהוה עֹז לְעַמּוֹ יִתֵּן,

HASHEM *will give might to His people;*

Adōnoy y'voraych es amō va-sholōm.	יהוה יְבָרֵךְ אֶת עַמּוֹ בַשָּׁלוֹם.

HASHEM *will bless His people with peace.*

⊰ BLESSINGS AFTER OTHER FOODS ⊱
THE THREE-FACETED BLESSING*

THE FOLLOWING BLESSING IS RECITED AFTER PARTAKING OF:
(A) GRAIN PRODUCTS (OTHER THAN BREAD OR MATZAH) MADE FROM WHEAT, BARLEY, RYE, OATS, OR SPELT; (B) GRAPE WINE OR GRAPE JUICE; (C) GRAPES, FIGS, POMEGRANATES, OLIVES, OR DATES. (IF FOODS FROM TWO OR THREE OF THESE GROUPS WERE EATEN, THEN THE INSERTIONS FOR EACH GROUP ARE CONNECTED WITH THE CONJUNCTIVE ו, THUS וְעַל.
THE ORDER IN SUCH A CASE IS GRAIN, WINE, FRUIT.)

Boruch ato Adōnoy,	**בָּרוּךְ** אַתָּה יהוה

Blessed are You, HASHEM*,*

Elōhaynu melech ho-ōlom,	אֱלֹהֵינוּ מֶלֶךְ הָעוֹלָם,

our God, King of the universe,

———— AFTER GRAIN PRODUCTS: ————

al hamichyo v'al hakalkolo,	עַל הַמִּחְיָה וְעַל הַכַּלְכָּלָה,

for the nourishment* and the sustenance*

———— AFTER WINE: ————

al hagefen v'al p'ri hagefen,	עַל הַגֶּפֶן וְעַל פְּרִי הַגֶּפֶן,

for the vine and the fruit of the vine*

———— AFTER FRUITS: ————

al ho-aytz v'al p'ri ho-aytz,	עַל הָעֵץ וְעַל פְּרִי הָעֵץ,

for the tree and the fruit of the tree

וְלֹא רָאִיתִי צַדִּיק נֶעֱזָב . . . — *And I have not seen a righteous man forsaken, with his children begging for bread.* I have never seen a righteous man consider himself forsaken even if his children must beg for bread. Whatever his lot in life, he trusts that God brings it upon him for a constructive and merciful purpose.

⊰ **The Three-Faceted Blessing**

A special blessing of thanks is recited after partaking of any of the seven species for which the Torah praises the Land of Israel (see *Deuteronomy* 8:8). This blessing is a single blessing that is an abridgment of the three Scripturally ordained blessings of *Bircas HaMazon*.

הַמִּחְיָה — *Nourishment.* This is a generic term referring to all foods made from five species of grain: wheat, barley, rye, oats, and spelt.

כַּלְכָּלָה — *Sustenance.* This concludes the first section of the Three-Part Blessing. It is parallel to the first blessing of *Bircas HaMazon* which thanks God for the blessing of food.

עַל הַגֶּפֶן וְעַל פְּרִי הַגֶּפֶן — *For the vine and the fruit of the vine.* Wine has its own particular blessings, both before partaking of it and after. The uniqueness of wine is due to its special qualities: In sensible amounts it glad-

v'al t'nuvas haso-de,	וְעַל תְּנוּבַת הַשָּׂדֶה,

and for the produce of the field;

v'al eretz chemdo tova urchovo,	וְעַל אֶרֶץ חֶמְדָּה טוֹבָה וּרְחָבָה,

for the desirable, good, and spacious Land*

sherotziso v'hinchalto la-avōsaynu,	שֶׁרָצִיתָ וְהִנְחַלְתָּ לַאֲבוֹתֵינוּ,

that You were pleased to give our forefathers as a heritage,

le-echōl mipiryoh	לֶאֱכוֹל מִפִּרְיָהּ

to eat of its fruit

v'lisbō-a mituvoh.	וְלִשְׂבֹּעַ מִטּוּבָהּ.

and to be satisfied with its goodness.

Rachaym no Adōnoy Elōhaynu	רַחֶם נָא יהוה אֱלֹהֵינוּ

Have mercy,* we beg You, HASHEM, our God,

al yisro-ayl amecho,	עַל יִשְׂרָאֵל עַמֶּךָ,

on Israel, Your people;

v'al y'rushola-yim i-recho,	וְעַל יְרוּשָׁלַיִם עִירֶךָ,

on Jerusalem, Your city;

v'al tzi-yōn mishkan k'vodecho,	וְעַל צִיּוֹן מִשְׁכַּן כְּבוֹדֶךָ,

on Zion, the resting place of Your glory;

v'al mizb'checho v'al haycholecho.	וְעַל מִזְבְּחֶךָ וְעַל הֵיכָלֶךָ.

on Your Altar, and on Your Temple.

Uvnay y'rushola-yim ir hakōdesh	וּבְנֵה יְרוּשָׁלַיִם עִיר הַקֹּדֶשׁ

Rebuild Jerusalem, the Holy City,

bimhayro v'yomaynu,	בִּמְהֵרָה בְיָמֵינוּ,

speedily in our days.

v'ha-alaynu l'sōchoh,	וְהַעֲלֵנוּ לְתוֹכָהּ,

Bring us up into it

v'samchaynu b'vinyonoh,	וְשַׂמְּחֵנוּ בְּבִנְיָנָהּ,

and gladden us in its rebuilding

v'nochal mipiryoh,	וְנֹאכַל מִפִּרְיָהּ,

and let us eat from its fruit

v'nisba mituvoh,	וְנִשְׂבַּע מִטּוּבָהּ,

and be satisfied with its goodness

---

dens and satiates and is used in the performance of such commandments as *Kiddush* and *Havdalah* (*Berachos* 35b).

וְעַל אֶרֶץ חֶמְדָּה — *And for the desirable . . . Land.* This begins the second section of the blessing.

It parallels the second blessing of *Bircas HaMazon* in thanking God for *Eretz Yisrael.*

רַחֵם — *Have mercy.* This begins the third section of the blessing, paralleling the third blessing of *Bircas HaMazon.*

unvorech'cho oleho	וּנְבָרֶכְךָ עָלֶיהָ
and bless You upon it	
bikdusho uvtohoro.	בִּקְדֻשָּׁה וּבְטָהֳרָה.
in holiness and purity.	

--- ON THE SABBATH: ---

Urtzay v'ha-chalitzaynu	וּרְצֵה וְהַחֲלִיצֵנוּ
b'yōm ha-shabos ha-ze.	בְּיוֹם הַשַּׁבָּת הַזֶּה.
And be pleased to let us rest on this Sabbath day.	

--- ON ROSH CHODESH: ---

V'zochraynu l'tōvo	וְזָכְרֵנוּ לְטוֹבָה
b'yōm rōsh hachōdesh ha-ze.	בְּיוֹם רֹאשׁ הַחֹדֶשׁ הַזֶּה.
And remember us (for goodness) on this day of Rosh Chodesh.	

--- ON PESACH: ---

V'sam'chaynu b'yōm	וְשַׂמְּחֵנוּ בְּיוֹם
chag hamatzōs ha-ze.	חַג הַמַּצּוֹת הַזֶּה.
And gladden us on this day of the Festival of Matzos.	

--- ON SHAVUOS: ---

V'sam'chaynu b'yōm	וְשַׂמְּחֵנוּ בְּיוֹם
chag ha-shovu-ōs ha-ze.	חַג הַשָּׁבֻעוֹת הַזֶּה.
And gladden us on this day of the Festival of Shavuos.	

--- ON SUCCOS: ---

V'sam'chaynu b'yōm	וְשַׂמְּחֵנוּ בְּיוֹם
chag ha-sukōs ha-ze.	חַג הַסֻּכּוֹת הַזֶּה.
And gladden us on this day of the Festival of Succos.	

--- ON SHEMINI ATZERES AND SIMCHAS TORAH: ---

V'sam'chaynu b'yōm ha-shmini	וְשַׂמְּחֵנוּ בְּיוֹם הַשְּׁמִינִי
chag ho-atzeres ha-ze.	חַג הָעֲצֶרֶת הַזֶּה.
And gladden us on the eighth day, this Festival of the Assembly.	

Ki ato Adōnoy	כִּי אַתָּה יהוה
For You, HASHEM,	
tōv u-maytiv lakōl,	טוֹב וּמֵטִיב לַכֹּל,
are good and do good to all*	
v'nōde lecho al ho-oretz	וְנוֹדֶה לְךָ עַל הָאָרֶץ
and we thank You for the Land	

אַתָּה... טוֹב וּמֵטִיב לַכֹּל — *You ... are good and do good to all.* This section of the blessing parallels the fourth, Rabbinically instituted, blessing of *Bircas HaMazon.*.

BLESSINGS

--- AFTER GRAIN PRODUCTS: ---

v'al hamichyo,   וְעַל הַמִּחְיָה.
and for the nourishment.

Boruch ato Adōnoy,   בָּרוּךְ אַתָּה יהוה,
   al ho-oretz v'al hamichyo.   עַל הָאָרֶץ וְעַל הַמִּחְיָה.
Blessed are You, HASHEM, for the Land and for the nourishment.

--- AFTER WINE: ---

IF THE WINE IS FROM *ERETZ YISRAEL,* SUBSTITUTE THE WORD IN BRACKETS.

v'al p'ri hagefen [gafnoh],   וְעַל פְּרִי הַגֶּפֶן [גַּפְנָהּ].
and for the fruit of the [its] vine

Boruch ato Adōnoy, al ho-oretz   בָּרוּךְ אַתָּה יהוה, עַל הָאָרֶץ
   v'al p'ri hagefen [gafnoh],   וְעַל פְּרִי הַגֶּפֶן [גַּפְנָהּ].
Blessed are You, HASHEM, for the Land and for the fruit of the [its] vine.

--- AFTER FRUITS: ---

IF THE FRUIT IS FROM *ERETZ YISRAEL,* SUBSTITUTE THE WORD IN BRACKETS.

v'al hapayrōs [payrō-seho].   וְעַל הַפֵּרוֹת [פֵּרוֹתֶיהָ].
and for the [its] fruit.

Boruch ato Adōnoy, al ho-oretz   בָּרוּךְ אַתָּה יהוה, עַל הָאָרֶץ
   v'al hapayrōs [payrō-seho].   וְעַל הַפֵּרוֹת [פֵּרוֹתֶיהָ].
Blessed are You, HASHEM, for the Land and for the [its] fruit.

BOREI NEFASHOS

AFTER EATING OR DRINKING ANY FOOD TO WHICH NEITHER THE GRACE AFTER MEALS NOR THE THREE-FACETED BLESSING APPLIES, SUCH AS FRUITS OTHER THAN THE ABOVE, VEGETABLES, OR BEVERAGES OTHER THAN WINE, RECITE:

Boruch ato Adōnoy,   **בָּרוּךְ** אַתָּה יהוה
Blessed are You, HASHEM,

Elōhaynu melech ho-ōlom,   אֱלֹהֵינוּ מֶלֶךְ הָעוֹלָם,
our God, King of the universe,

bōray n'foshōs rabōs v'chesrōnon,   בּוֹרֵא נְפָשׁוֹת רַבּוֹת וְחֶסְרוֹנָן,
Who creates numerous living things with their deficiencies;

al kol ma sheboro(so)   עַל כָּל מַה שֶּׁבָּרָא(תָ)
for all that You have created

l'hacha-yōs bohem nefesh kol chai.   לְהַחֲיוֹת בָּהֶם נֶפֶשׁ כָּל חָי.
with which to maintain the life of every being.

Boruch chay ho-ōlomim.   בָּרוּךְ חֵי הָעוֹלָמִים.
Blessed is He, the life of the worlds.

⊰{ SHEVA BERACHOS }⊱

■ The Rabbis enacted that the festivities and celebration of the wedding should continue for seven days. During this time, if a *minyan* (quorum of ten or more men), with at least one person who was not present at the *chupah*, eat together with the bride and groom, the seven marriage blessings, *sheva berachos*, are added to the *Bircas HaMazon*/Grace After Meals.

WHEN THE *SHEVA BERACHOS* ARE RECITED, THE FOLLOWING *ZIMUN*, RECITED BY THE LEADER WITH A CUP OF WINE IN HAND, IS USED:

LEADER:

Rabōsai, n'voraych.   רַבּוֹתַי נְבָרֵךְ.

Gentlemen, let us bless.

OTHERS:

Y'hi shaym Adōnoy m'vōroch   יְהִי שֵׁם יהוה מְבֹרָךְ
may-ato v'ad ōlom.   מֵעַתָּה וְעַד עוֹלָם.

Blessed is the Name of Hashem *from this time and forever!*

LEADER:

Y'hi shaym Adōnoy m'vōroch   יְהִי שֵׁם יהוה מְבֹרָךְ
may-ato v'ad ōlom.   מֵעַתָּה וְעַד עוֹלָם.

Blessed is the Name of Hashem *from this time and forever!*

D'vai hosayr v'gam chorōn,   דְּוַי הָסֵר וְגַם חָרוֹן,

Banish pain and also wrath,

v'oz ilaym b'shir yorōn,   וְאָז אִלֵּם בְּשִׁיר יָרוֹן,

and then the mute will exult in song.

n'chaynu b'mag'lay tzedek,   נְחֵנוּ בְּמַעְגְּלֵי צֶדֶק,

Guide us in paths of righteousness;

sh'ay birkas b'nay aharōn.   שְׁעֵה בִּרְכַּת בְּנֵי אַהֲרֹן.

heed the blessing of the children of Aaron.

Bir-shus moronon v'rabonon v'rabōsai,   בִּרְשׁוּת מָרָנָן וְרַבָּנָן וְרַבּוֹתַי,

With the permission of the distinguished people present

n'voraych Elōhaynu   נְבָרֵךְ אֱלֹהֵינוּ
shehasimcho bimōnō,   שֶׁהַשִּׂמְחָה בִמְעוֹנוֹ,

let us bless our God in Whose abode is this celebration,

(v')she-ochalnu mi-shelō.   (וְ)שֶׁאָכַלְנוּ מִשֶּׁלּוֹ.

of Whose we have eaten.

OTHERS:

Boruch Elōhaynu   בָּרוּךְ אֱלֹהֵינוּ
shehasimchoh bimōnō,   שֶׁהַשִּׂמְחָה בִמְעוֹנוֹ,

Blessed is our God in Whose abode is this celebration,

331 / BLESSINGS SHEVA BERACHOS

(v')she-ochalnu mi-shelo (וְ)שֶׁאָכַלְנוּ מִשֶּׁלוֹ,
uvtuvō cho-yinu. וּבְטוּבוֹ חָיִינוּ.
of Whose we have eaten, and through Whose goodness we live.

LEADER:

Boruch Elōhaynu בָּרוּךְ אֱלֹהֵינוּ
shehasimcho bimōnō, שֶׁהַשִּׂמְחָה בִמְעוֹנוֹ,
Blessed is our God whose abode is this celebration,
(v')she-ochalnu mi-shelō (וְ)שֶׁאָכַלְנוּ מִשֶּׁלוֹ,
uvtuvō cho-yinu. וּבְטוּבוֹ חָיִינוּ.
of Whose we have eaten, and through Whose goodness we live.

ALL:

Boruch hu u'voruch sh'mō. בָּרוּךְ הוּא וּבָרוּךְ שְׁמוֹ.
Blessed is He and Blessed is His Name.

BIRCAS HAMAZON IS RECITED (P. 310).
AFTER BIRCAS HAMAZON A SECOND CUP IS POURED AND THE FOLLOWING SEVEN BLESSINGS
ARE RECITED. WHOEVER RECITES A BLESSING SHOULD HOLD THE CUP AS HE DOES SO.

■ First Blessing: *Rashi* explains that this blessing honors the guests who have assembled to perform the mitzvah of rejoicing with the bride and groom.

BORUCH ato Adōnoy בָּרוּךְ אַתָּה יהוה
Elōhaynu melech ho-ōlom, אֱלֹהֵינוּ מֶלֶךְ הָעוֹלָם,
Blessed are You, HASHEM, our God, King of the universe,
shehakōl boro lichvōdō. שֶׁהַכֹּל בָּרָא לִכְבוֹדוֹ.
Who has created everything for His glory.

ALL PRESENT RESPOND: Omayn — אָמֵן

■ Second Blessing: This blessing begins the recounting of Creation, noting a time that man was created incomplete.

BORUCH ato Adōnoy בָּרוּךְ אַתָּה יהוה
Elōhaynu melech ho-ōlom, אֱלֹהֵינוּ מֶלֶךְ הָעוֹלָם,
Blessed are You, HASHEM, our God, King of the universe,
yōtzayr ho-odom. יוֹצֵר הָאָדָם.
Who fashioned the Man.

ALL PRESENT RESPOND: Omayn — אָמֵן

■ Third Blessing: We thank Hashem for creating man and woman, endowing them with the ability to emulate Hashem and to perpetuate these traits to future generations.

BORUCH ato Adōnoy בָּרוּךְ אַתָּה יהוה
Elōhaynu melech ho-ōlom, אֱלֹהֵינוּ מֶלֶךְ הָעוֹלָם,
Blessed are You, HASHEM, our God, King of the universe,

asher yotzar es ho-odom b'tzalmō,	אֲשֶׁר יָצַר אֶת הָאָדָם בְּצַלְמוֹ,
b'tzelem d'mus tavniso	בְּצֶלֶם דְּמוּת תַּבְנִיתוֹ

Who fashioned the Man in His image, in the image of his likeness

v'hiskin lō mimenu binyan aday ad.	וְהִתְקִין לוֹ מִמֶּנּוּ בִּנְיַן עֲדֵי עַד.

and prepared for him — from himself — a building for eternity.

Boruch ato Adōnoy,	בָּרוּךְ אַתָּה יהוה,
yōtzayr ho-odom.	יוֹצֵר הָאָדָם.

Blessed are You, HASHEM, Who fashioned the Man.

ALL PRESENT RESPOND: Omayn — אָמֵן

■ **Fourth Blessing:** Marriage and children represent the potential of the return to Zion and the joy that will encompass Jerusalem.

SŌS tosis v'sogayl ho-akoro,	**שׂוֹשׂ** תָּשִׂישׂ וְתָגֵל הָעֲקָרָה,

Bring intense joy and exultation to the barren one

b'kibutz boneho l'sōchoh b'simcho.	בְּקִבּוּץ בָּנֶיהָ לְתוֹכָהּ בְּשִׂמְחָה.

through the ingathering of her children amidst her in gladness.

Boruch ato Adōnoy,	בָּרוּךְ אַתָּה יהוה,
m'samay-ach tziyōn b'voneho.	מְשַׂמֵּחַ צִיּוֹן בְּבָנֶיהָ.

Blessed are You, HASHEM, Who gladdens Zion through her children.

ALL PRESENT RESPOND: Omayn — אָמֵן

■ **Fifth Blessing:** May Hashem help the newlyweds to always find love and happiness exclusively with each other, as did Adam and Eve.

SAMAY-ACH t'samach	**שַׂמֵּחַ** תְּשַׂמַּח
ra-yim ho-ahuvim,	רֵעִים הָאֲהוּבִים,

Gladden the beloved companions

k'samaychacho y'tzir'cho	כְּשַׂמֵּחֲךָ יְצִירְךָ
b'gan ayden mikedem.	בְּגַן עֵדֶן מִקֶּדֶם.

as You gladdened Your creature in the Garden of Eden from aforetime.

Boruch ato Adōnoy,	בָּרוּךְ אַתָּה יהוה,
m'samay-ach choson v'chalo.	מְשַׂמֵּחַ חָתָן וְכַלָּה.

Blessed are You, HASHEM, Who gladdens groom and bride.

ALL PRESENT RESPOND: Omayn — אָמֵן

■ **Sixth Blessing:** The wedding experience arouses the most deeply felt emotions between man and woman. We pray that these feelings will ultimately be shared between Hashem and the Jewish People, whose relationship is compared to that of a bride and groom.

BORUCH ato Adōnoy	**בָּרוּךְ** אַתָּה יהוה

Blessed are You, HASHEM,

BLESSINGS — SHEVA BERACHOS

Elōhaynu melech ho-ōlom, אֱלֹהֵינוּ מֶלֶךְ הָעוֹלָם,
our God, King of the universe,

asher boro sosōn v'simcho, אֲשֶׁר בָּרָא שָׂשׂוֹן וְשִׂמְחָה,
choson v'chalo, חָתָן וְכַלָּה,
Who created joy and gladness, groom and bride,

gilo, rino, ditzo v'chedvo, גִּילָה רִנָּה, דִּיצָה וְחֶדְוָה,
mirth, glad song, pleasure, delight,

ahavo v'achavo v'sholōm v'ray-us. אַהֲבָה וְאַחֲוָה, וְשָׁלוֹם וְרֵעוּת.
love, brotherhood, peace, and companionship.

M'hayro Adōnoy Elōhaynu מְהֵרָה יהוה אֱלֹהֵינוּ
Hashem, *our God, let there soon*

yi-shoma b'oray y'hudo יִשָּׁמַע בְּעָרֵי יְהוּדָה
uvchutzōs y'rusholō-yim, וּבְחֻצוֹת יְרוּשָׁלָיִם,
be heard in the cities of Judah and the streets of Jerusalem

kōl sosōn v'kōl simcho, קוֹל שָׂשׂוֹן וְקוֹל שִׂמְחָה,
the sound of joy and the sound of gladness,

kōl choson v'kōl kalo, קוֹל חָתָן וְקוֹל כַּלָּה,
the voice of the groom and the voice of the bride,

kōl mitzhalōs chasonim maychuposom, קוֹל מִצְהֲלוֹת חֲתָנִים מֵחֻפָּתָם,
the sound of the grooms' jubilance from their canopies

un-orim mimishtay n'ginosom. וּנְעָרִים מִמִּשְׁתֵּה נְגִינָתָם.
and of youths from their song-filled feasts.

BORUCH atoh Adōnoy, בָּרוּךְ אַתָּה יהוה,
Blessed are You, Hashem

m'samay-ach choson im hakalo. מְשַׂמֵּחַ חָתָן עִם הַכַּלָּה.
Who gladdens the groom with the bride.

ALL PRESENT RESPOND: Omayn — אָמֵן

■ Seventh Blessing: *The above blessings were enhanced by their recitation over a cup of wine.*

THE LEADER OF BIRCAS HAMAZON RECITES THE SEVENTH BLESSING:

BORUCH ato Adōnoy בָּרוּךְ אַתָּה יהוה
Elōhaynu melech ho-ōlom, אֱלֹהֵינוּ מֶלֶךְ הָעוֹלָם,
Blessed are You, Hashem, *our God, King of the universe,*

bōray p'ri hagofen. בּוֹרֵא פְּרִי הַגָּפֶן.
Who creates the fruit of the vine.

ALL PRESENT RESPOND: Omayn — אָמֵן

◈{ CIRCUMCISION }◈

■ The commandment of circumcision performed on the eighth day is one of the most important positive commandments of our Torah. It marks both a physical identification with one's people and, according to Maimonides, assists the Jew to live a more moral lifestyle. A baby born naturally (not caesarean) on Shabbos, is circumcised on the eighth day, which falls on the following Shabbos.

WHEN THE INFANT IS BROUGHT IN, THE ENTIRE ASSEMBLAGE GREETS HIM:

■ Baruch Haba: We rise in honor of the *kvater* and *kvateren* (godparents) who, by bringing in the baby, enable the circumcision to take place.

BORUCH HABO!
בָּרוּךְ הַבָּא!

Blessed is he who arrives!

THE *MOHEL* THEN RECITES:

וַיְדַבֵּר יהוה אֶל מֹשֶׁה לֵּאמֹר. פִּינְחָס בֶּן אֶלְעָזָר בֶּן אַהֲרֹן הַכֹּהֵן הֵשִׁיב אֶת חֲמָתִי מֵעַל בְּנֵי יִשְׂרָאֵל, בְּקַנְאוֹ אֶת קִנְאָתִי בְּתוֹכָם, וְלֹא כִלִּיתִי אֶת בְּנֵי יִשְׂרָאֵל בְּקִנְאָתִי. לָכֵן אֱמֹר, הִנְנִי נֹתֵן לוֹ אֶת בְּרִיתִי שָׁלוֹם.

TWO SEATS ARE PREPARED, ONE UPON WHICH THE *SANDAK* WILL SIT HOLDING THE BABY DURING THE CIRCUMCISION, AND ONE FOR ELIYAHU (ELIJAH) THE PROPHET. THE BABY IS FIRST PLACED UPON THE "THRONE OF ELIYAHU" BY THE FATHER OR ONE OF THE PROMINENT GUESTS, WHEREUPON THE *MOHEL* SAYS:

■ We acknowledge the presence of Elijah the prophet — who, according to tradition, attends every *Bris Milah* — by according him a seat of honor.

זֶה הַכִּסֵּא שֶׁל אֵלִיָּהוּ הַנָּבִיא, זָכוּר לַטּוֹב. לִישׁוּעָתְךָ קִוִּיתִי יהוה. שִׂבַּרְתִּי לִישׁוּעָתְךָ יהוה, וּמִצְוֺתֶיךָ עָשִׂיתִי. אֵלִיָּהוּ מַלְאַךְ הַבְּרִית, הִנֵּה שֶׁלְּךָ לְפָנֶיךָ, עֲמוֹד עַל יְמִינִי וְסָמְכֵנִי. שִׂבַּרְתִּי לִישׁוּעָתְךָ יהוה. שָׂשׂ אָנֹכִי עַל אִמְרָתֶךָ, כְּמוֹצֵא שָׁלָל רָב. שָׁלוֹם רָב לְאֹהֲבֵי תוֹרָתֶךָ, וְאֵין לָמוֹ מִכְשׁוֹל. אַשְׁרֵי, תִּבְחַר וּתְקָרֵב, יִשְׁכֹּן חֲצֵרֶיךָ —

ALL PRESENT RESPOND:

Nis-b'o b'tuv baysecho   נִשְׂבְּעָה, בְּטוּב בֵּיתֶךָ,
k'dōsh haycholecho.   קְדֹשׁ הֵיכָלֶךָ.

May we be satisfied by the goodness of Your House, Your Holy Temple.

WHEN THE *MOHEL* IS READY TO PERFORM THE CIRCUMCISION, THE BABY'S FATHER SAYS:

Hin'ni muchon umzumon   הִנְנִי מוּכָן וּמְזֻמָּן
l'ka-yaym mitzvas a-say   לְקַיֵּם מִצְוַת עֲשֵׂה

Behold, I am prepared and ready to perform the positive commandment

BLESSINGS — CIRCUMCISION

shetzivani habōray yisborach,   שֶׁצִוָּנִי הַבּוֹרֵא יִתְבָּרַךְ,
that the Creator, Blessed is He, has commanded me,
lomōl es b'ni.   לָמוֹל אֶת בְּנִי.
to circumcise my son.

IN SOME CONGREGATIONS, AT THIS POINT THE FATHER VERBALLY APPOINTS THE *MOHEL* TO PERFORM CIRCUMCISION ON HIS SON. THE *MOHEL* THEN TAKES THE INFANT AND PROCLAIMS JOYOUSLY:

אָמַר הַקָּדוֹשׁ בָּרוּךְ הוּא לְאַבְרָהָם אָבִינוּ, הִתְהַלֵּךְ לְפָנַי וֶהְיֵה תָמִים. הִנְנִי מוּכָן וּמְזֻמָּן לְקַיֵּם מִצְוַת עֲשֵׂה שֶׁצִוָּנוּ הַבּוֹרֵא יִתְבָּרַךְ לָמוֹל.

IMMEDIATELY BEFORE PERFORMING THE CIRCUMCISION, THE MOHEL RECITES:

BORUCH ato Adōnoy   **בָּרוּךְ** אַתָּה יהוה
Elōhaynu melech ho-ōlom,   אֱלֹהֵינוּ מֶלֶךְ הָעוֹלָם,
Blessed are You, HASHEM, our God, King of the universe,
asher kid'shonu b'mitzvōsov   אֲשֶׁר קִדְּשָׁנוּ בְּמִצְוֹתָיו,
Who has sanctified us with His commandments,
v'tzivonu al ha-milo.   וְצִוָּנוּ עַל הַמִּילָה.
and has commanded us regarding circumcision.

ALL PRESENT RESPOND: Omayn — אָמֵן

AS THE *MOHEL* PERFORMS THE CIRCUMCISION, THE FATHER
(OR, IF THE FATHER IS NOT PRESENT, THE *SANDAK*) RECITES:

BORUCH ato Adōnoy   **בָּרוּךְ** אַתָּה יהוה
Elōhaynu melech ho-ōlom,   אֱלֹהֵינוּ מֶלֶךְ הָעוֹלָם,
Blessed are You, HASHEM, our God, King of the universe,
asher kid'shonu b'mitzvōsov   אֲשֶׁר קִדְּשָׁנוּ בְּמִצְוֹתָיו,
Who has sanctified us with His commandments,
v'tzivonu l'hachnisō bivriso   וְצִוָּנוּ לְהַכְנִיסוֹ בִּבְרִיתוֹ
and has commanded us to bring him into the covenant
shel avrohom ovinu.   שֶׁל אַבְרָהָם אָבִינוּ.
of Abraham, our forefather.

ALL RESPOND, LOUDLY AND JOYFULLY:

Omayn. K'shaym shenichnas lab'ris,   אָמֵן. כְּשֵׁם שֶׁנִּכְנַס לַבְּרִית,
Amen. Just as he entered into the covenant,
kayn yikonays l'sōro   כֵּן יִכָּנֵס לְתוֹרָה
ulchupo ulma-asim tōvim.   וּלְחֻפָּה וּלְמַעֲשִׂים טוֹבִים.
so may he enter into the Torah, the marriage canopy, and good deeds.

WHEN THE CIRCUMCISION IS COMPLETE, THE BABY IS GIVEN TO ONE OF THE PROMINENT

ברית מילה

GUESTS TO HOLD, WHILE THE FOLLOWING PRAYERS (INCLUDING THE GIVING OF THE NAME) ARE RECITED. THE HONOR OF RECITING THEM MAY BE GIVEN TO ONE PERSON, OR THEY MAY BE DIVIDED BETWEEN TWO PEOPLE. IF SO, THE FIRST PERSON RECITES THE TWO BLESSINGS AND THE SECOND PERSON RECITES THE PRAYER DURING WHICH THE BABY IS GIVEN HIS NAME.

BORUCH ato Adōnoy
Elōhaynu melech ho-ōlom,
בָּרוּךְ אַתָּה יהוה
אֱלֹהֵינוּ מֶלֶךְ הָעוֹלָם,
Blessed are You, HASHEM, our God, King of the universe,

bōray p'ri hagofen.
בּוֹרֵא פְּרִי הַגָּפֶן.
Who creates the fruit of the vine.

ALL PRESENT RESPOND: Omayn — אָמֵן

■ Circumcision not only assists the Jew in living a moral life, but protects him in the Afterworld as well.

BORUCH ato Adōnoy
Elōhaynu melech ho-ōlom,
בָּרוּךְ אַתָּה יהוה
אֱלֹהֵינוּ מֶלֶךְ הָעוֹלָם,
Blessed are You, HASHEM, our God, King of the universe,

asher kidash y'did mibeten,
אֲשֶׁר קִדַּשׁ יְדִיד מִבֶּטֶן,
Who sanctified the beloved one from the womb

v'chōk bish-ayrō som,
וְחֹק בִּשְׁאֵרוֹ שָׂם,
and placed the mark of the decree in his flesh,

v'tze-etzo-ov chosam
b'ōs b'ris kōdesh.
וְצֶאֱצָאָיו חָתַם
בְּאוֹת בְּרִית קֹדֶשׁ.
and sealed his offspring with the sign of the holy covenant.

Al kayn bischar zōs,
עַל כֵּן בִּשְׂכַר זֹאת,
Therefore, as reward for this,

Ayl chai chelkaynu tzuraynu,
אֵל חַי, חֶלְקֵנוּ צוּרֵנוּ,
O Living God, our Portion, our Rock,

tzavay l'hatzil y'didus
צַוֵּה לְהַצִּיל יְדִידוּת
may You issue the command to rescue the beloved soul

sh'ayraynu mi-shachas,
שְׁאֵרֵנוּ מִשַּׁחַת,
within our flesh from destruction,

l'ma-an b'risō
asher som bivsoraynu.
לְמַעַן בְּרִיתוֹ
אֲשֶׁר שָׂם בִּבְשָׂרֵנוּ.
for the sake of His covenant that He has placed in our flesh.

Boruch ato Adōnoy,
kōrays hab'ris
בָּרוּךְ אַתָּה יהוה,
כּוֹרֵת הַבְּרִית.
Blessed are You, HASHEM, Who establishes the covenant.

ALL PRESENT RESPOND: Omayn — אָמֵן

GIVING THE NAME

■ The name given to the baby often reflects the hope that the baby perpetuate the character and personality of the one for whom he is being named, or the meaning of the name itself.

ELŌHAYNU Vaylōhay avōsaynu, אֱלֹהֵינוּ וֵאלֹהֵי אֲבוֹתֵינוּ,
Our God and the God of our forefathers,

ka-yaym es ha-yeled ha-ze קַיֵּם אֶת הַיֶּלֶד הַזֶּה
l'oviv ul-i-mo, לְאָבִיו וּלְאִמּוֹ,
preserve this child for his father and mother,

v'yikoray sh'mō b'yisro-ayl וְיִקָּרֵא שְׁמוֹ, בְּיִשְׂרָאֵל
and may his name be called in Israel

… ben … בֶּן …
(BABY'S HEBREW NAME) *son of* (FATHER'S HEBREW NAME).

Yismach ho-ov b'yōtzay chalotzov, יִשְׂמַח הָאָב בְּיוֹצֵא חֲלָצָיו,
May his father rejoice in the issue of his loins

v'sogayl i-mō bifri vitnoh, וְתָגֵל אִמּוֹ בִּפְרִי בִטְנָהּ.
and may his mother exult in the fruit of her womb,

Kakosuv: Yismach ovicho v'i-mecho, כַּכָּתוּב: יִשְׂמַח אָבִיךָ וְאִמֶּךָ,
as it is written: "May your father and mother rejoice

v'sogayl yōladtecho. V'ne-emar: וְתָגֵל יוֹלַדְתֶּךָ. וְנֶאֱמַר:
and may she who gave birth to you exult." And it is said:

Vo-e-evōr ola-yich וָאֶעֱבֹר עָלַיִךְ
"Then I passed by you

vo-er-aych misbōseses b'domoyich, וָאֶרְאֵךְ מִתְבּוֹסֶסֶת בְּדָמָיִךְ,
and saw you downtrodden in your blood,

vo-ōmar loch b'doma-yich cha-yi, וָאֹמַר לָךְ בְּדָמַיִךְ חֲיִי,
and I said to you: 'In your blood, live!'

vo-ōmar loch b'doma-yich cha-yi. וָאֹמַר לָךְ בְּדָמַיִךְ חֲיִי.
and I said to you: 'In your blood, live!'"

V'ne-emar: Zochar l'ōlom b'risō, וְנֶאֱמַר: זָכַר לְעוֹלָם בְּרִיתוֹ,
And it is said: "He remembered His covenant forever;

dovor tzivo l'elef dōr, דָּבָר צִוָּה לְאֶלֶף דּוֹר,
the word of His command for a thousand generations —

asher koras es avrohom אֲשֶׁר כָּרַת אֶת אַבְרָהָם,
that He made with Abraham

ush'vu-osō l'yischok. וּשְׁבוּעָתוֹ לְיִשְׂחָק.
and His vow to Isaac.

ברית מילה

Vaya-amideho l'ya-akōv l'chōk,	וַיַּעֲמִידֶהָ לְיַעֲקֹב לְחֹק,
l'yisro-ayl b'ris ōlom.	לְיִשְׂרָאֵל בְּרִית עוֹלָם.

Then He established it for Jacob as a statute, for Israel as an everlasting statute.'

v'ne-emar: Va-yomol avrohom	וְנֶאֱמַר. וַיָּמָל אַבְרָהָם
es yitzchok b'nō,	אֶת יִצְחָק בְּנוֹ,

And it is said: "Abraham circumcised his son Isaac

ben sh'mōnas yomim,	בֶּן שְׁמֹנַת יָמִים,

at the age of eight days

ka-asher tzivo ōsō Elōhim.	כַּאֲשֶׁר צִוָּה אֹתוֹ אֱלֹהִים.

as God had commanded him."

THE READER PAUSES WHILE ALL PRESENT RECITE THE FOLLOWING, WHICH HE THEN REPEATS:

Hōdu Ladōnoy ki tōv,	הוֹדוּ לַיהוה כִּי טוֹב,
ki l'ōlom chasdō.	כִּי לְעוֹלָם חַסְדּוֹ.

Give thanks to HASHEM for He is good; His kindness endures forever!

Hōdu Ladōnoy ki tōv,	הוֹדוּ לַיהוה כִּי טוֹב,
ki l'ōlom chasdō.	כִּי לְעוֹלָם חַסְדּוֹ.

Give thanks to HASHEM for He is good; His kindness endures forever!

THE READER CONTINUES:

. . . ben . . .	. . . בֶּן . . .

(BABY'S HEBREW NAME) son of (FATHER'S HEBREW NAME).

zeh hakotōn godōl yih-ye.	זֶה הַקָּטָן גָּדוֹל יִהְיֶה.

May this little one become great.

THE READER PAUSES WHILE ALL PRESENT RECITE THE FOLLOWING, WHICH HE THEN REPEATS:

K'shaym shenichnas lab'ris,	כְּשֵׁם שֶׁנִּכְנַס לַבְּרִית,

Just as he has entered the covenant

kayn yikonays l'sōro	כֵּן יִכָּנֵס לְתוֹרָה,

so may he enter into the Torah,

ulchupo ulma-asim tōvim.	וּלְחֻפָּה, וּלְמַעֲשִׂים טוֹבִים.

the marriage canopy, and good deeds.

THE ONE WHO RECITED THE BLESSINGS DRINKS SOME WINE. THE MOHEL BLESSES THE CHILD.
BOTH THE MOHEL AND FATHER THEN RECITE THE FOLLOWING PRAYER:

Ribōnō shel ōlam	**רִבּוֹנוֹ** שֶׁל עוֹלָם,
y'hi rotzōn mil'fonecho	יְהִי רָצוֹן מִלְּפָנֶיךָ,

Master of the universe, may it be Your will

she-y'hay choshuv umru-tze	שֶׁיְּהֵא חָשׁוּב וּמְרֻצֶּה
umkubol l'fonecho,	וּמְקֻבָּל לְפָנֶיךָ,

that he be worthy, favored, and acceptable before You

k'ilu hikravti-hu	כְּאִלוּ הִקְרַבְתִּיהוּ
lifnay chi-say ch'vōdecho.	לִפְנֵי כִסֵּא כְבוֹדֶךָ.

as if I had offered him before the throne of Your glory,

V'ato b'rachamecho horabim	וְאַתָּה, בְּרַחֲמֶיךָ הָרַבִּים,

and may You, in Your abundant mercy,

sh'lach al y'day	שְׁלַח עַל יְדֵי
malochecho hak'dōshim	מַלְאָכֶיךָ הַקְּדוֹשִׁים

send through Your holy angels

n'shomo k'dōsho ut-hōro	נְשָׁמָה קְדוֹשָׁה וּטְהוֹרָה

a holy and pure soul

——— THE FATHER SAYS: ———

livni (BABY'S HEBREW NAME)	לִבְנִי

to my son, (...)

——— THE *MOHEL* SAYS: ———

l'(BABY'S HEBREW NAME) ben (FATHER'S HEBREW NAME)	לְ (BABY'S HEBREW NAME) בֶּן (BABY'S HEBREW NAME)

to (...) son of (...)

---

ha-nimōl ato l'shimcho hagodōl,	הַנִּמּוֹל עַתָּה לְשִׁמְךָ הַגָּדוֹל,

who has now been circumcised for the sake of Your Great Name,

v'she-yih-ye libō posu-ach	וְשֶׁיִּהְיֶה לִבּוֹ פָּתוּחַ
k'pischō shel ulom,	כְּפִתְחוֹ שֶׁל אוּלָם,

and may his heart be as open as the entrance of the Temple,

b'sōros'cho hak'dōsho,	בְּתוֹרָתְךָ הַקְּדוֹשָׁה,

to Your holy Torah

lilmōd ul'lamayd	לִלְמוֹד וּלְלַמֵּד,
lishmōr v'la-asos.	לִשְׁמוֹר וְלַעֲשׂוֹת.

to learn and to teach, to observe and to perform.

V'sen lō arichus yomim v'shonim	וְתֶן לוֹ אֲרִיכוּת יָמִים וְשָׁנִים,

Give him long days and years,

cha-yim shel yiras chayt,	חַיִּים שֶׁל יִרְאַת חֵטְא,
cha-yim shel ōsher v'chovod,	חַיִּים שֶׁל עֹשֶׁר וְכָבוֹד,

a life of fear of sin, a life of wealth and honor,

cha-yim shet'malay	חַיִּים שֶׁתְּמַלֵּא
mishalos libō l'tova.	מִשְׁאֲלוֹת לִבּוֹ לְטוֹבָה.

a life in which You fulfill all the wishes of his heart for good.

Omayn, v'chayn y'hi rotzōn.	אָמֵן, וְכֵן יְהִי רָצוֹן.

Amen — may such be Your will.

ZIMUN FOR THE CIRCUMCISION FEAST

IF A *MINYAN* IS PRESENT, THIS *ZIMUN* IS RECITED WITH A CUP OF WINE IN HAND:

LEADER:

Rabōsai, n'voraych. — רַבּוֹתַי נְבָרֵךְ.

Gentlemen, let us bless.

OTHERS:

Y'hi shaym Adōnoy m'vōroch — יְהִי שֵׁם יהוה מְבֹרָךְ

Blessed be the Name of HASHEM

may-ato v'ad ōlom. — מֵעַתָּה וְעַד עוֹלָם.

from this time and forever!

LEADER:

Y'hi shaym Adōnoy m'vōroch — יְהִי שֵׁם יהוה מְבֹרָךְ

Blessed be the Name of HASHEM

may-ato v'ad ōlom. — מֵעַתָּה וְעַד עוֹלָם.

from this time and forever!

Nōde l'shimcho b'sōch emunai, — נוֹדֶה לְשִׁמְךָ בְּתוֹךְ אֱמוּנַי,

We give thanks to Your Name among my faithful;

b'ruchim atem Ladōnoy. — בְּרוּכִים אַתֶּם לַיהוה.

blessed are you to HASHEM.

OTHERS:

Nōde l'shimcho b'sōch emunai, — נוֹדֶה לְשִׁמְךָ בְּתוֹךְ אֱמוּנַי,

We give thanks to Your Name among my faithful;

b'ruchim atem Ladōnoy. — בְּרוּכִים אַתֶּם לַיהוה.

blessed are you to HASHEM.

LEADER:

Bir-shus Ayl oyōm v'nōro, — בִּרְשׁוּת אֵל אָיוֹם וְנוֹרָא,

With permission of the Almighty — fearful and awesome,

misgov l'itōs batzoro, — מִשְׂגָּב לְעִתּוֹת בַּצָּרָה,

the Refuge in times of trouble,

Ayl nezor bigvuro, — אֵל נֶאְזָר בִּגְבוּרָה,

the Almighty girded with strength,

adir bamorōm Adōnoy. — אַדִּיר בַּמָּרוֹם יהוה.

the Mighty on high — HASHEM.

OTHERS:

Nōde l'shimcho b'sōch emunai, — נוֹדֶה לְשִׁמְךָ בְּתוֹךְ אֱמוּנַי,

We give thanks to Your Name among my faithful;

b'ruchim atem Ladōnoy. — בְּרוּכִים אַתֶּם לַיהוה.

blessed are you to HASHEM.

LEADER:

Bir-shus hatōro hak'dōsho,   בִּרְשׁוּת הַתּוֹרָה הַקְּדוֹשָׁה,
With the permission of the holy Torah,

t'hōro hi v'gam p'rusho,   טְהוֹרָה הִיא וְגַם פְּרוּשָׁה,
it is pure and explicit,

tzivo lonu mōrosho,   צִוָּה לָנוּ מוֹרָשָׁה,
commanded to us as a heritage,

mōshe eved Adōnoy.   מֹשֶׁה עֶבֶד יהוה.
by Moses, servant of HASHEM.

OTHERS:

Nōde l'shimcho b'sōch emunai,   נוֹדֶה לְשִׁמְךָ בְּתוֹךְ אֱמוּנַי,
We give thanks to Your Name among my faithful;

b'ruchim atem Ladōnoy.   בְּרוּכִים אַתֶּם לַיהוה.
blessed are you to HASHEM.

LEADER:

Bir-shus hakōhanim v'hal-viyim,   בִּרְשׁוּת הַכֹּהֲנִים הַלְוִיִּם
With the permission of the Kohanim (from the tribe of) Levi,

ekro Laylōhay ho-ivriyim,   אֶקְרָא לֵאלֹהֵי הָעִבְרִיִּים,
I call upon the God of the Hebrews,

ahōdenu b'chol iyim,   אֲהוֹדֶנּוּ בְּכָל אִיִּים,
I will thank Him unto all islands,

avor'cho es Adōnoy.   אֲבָרְכָה אֶת יהוה.
I will give blessing to HASHEM.

OTHERS:

Nōde l'shimcho b'sōch emunai,   נוֹדֶה לְשִׁמְךָ בְּתוֹךְ אֱמוּנַי,
We give thanks to Your Name among my faithful;

b'ruchim atem Ladōnoy.   בְּרוּכִים אַתֶּם לַיהוה.
blessed are you to HASHEM.

LEADER:

Bir-shus moronon v'rabanan v'rabōsai,   בִּרְשׁוּת מָרָנָן וְרַבָּנָן וְרַבּוֹתַי,
With permission of the distinguished people present,

eft'cho b'shir pi usfosai,   אֶפְתְּחָה בְּשִׁיר פִּי וּשְׂפָתַי,
I open in song my mouth and lips,

v'sōmarno atzmōsai,   וְתֹאמַרְנָה עַצְמוֹתַי,
and my bones shall proclaim,

boruch habo b'shaym Adōnoy.   בָּרוּךְ הַבָּא בְּשֵׁם יהוה.
"Blessed is he who comes in the Name of HASHEM.*"*

ברית מילה

OTHERS:

Nōde l'shimcho b'sōch emunai, נוֹדֶה לְשִׁמְךָ בְּתוֹךְ אֱמוּנָי,
We give thanks to Your Name among my faithful;
b'ruchim atem Ladōnoy. בְּרוּכִים אַתֶּם לַיהוה.
blessed are you to HASHEM.

LEADER:

Bir-shus moronon v'rabonon v'rabōsai, בִּרְשׁוּת מָרָנָן וְרַבָּנָן וְרַבּוֹתַי,
With the permission of my masters, rabbis and teachers,
n'voraych (Elōhaynu) she-ochalnu mi-shelō. נְבָרֵךְ (אֱלֹהֵינוּ) שֶׁאָכַלְנוּ מִשֶּׁלּוֹ.
let us bless [our God,] He of Whose we have eaten.

OTHERS:

Boruch (Elōhaynu) she-ochalnu mi-shelō בָּרוּךְ (אֱלֹהֵינוּ) שֶׁאָכַלְנוּ מִשֶּׁלּוֹ
Blessed is [our God,] He of Whose we have eaten
uvtuvō cho-yinu. וּבְטוּבוֹ חָיִינוּ.
and through Whose goodness we live.

LEADER:

Boruch (Elōhaynu) she-ochalnu mi-shelō בָּרוּךְ (אֱלֹהֵינוּ) שֶׁאָכַלְנוּ מִשֶּׁלּוֹ
Blessed is [our God,] He of Whose we have eaten
uvtuvō cho-yinu. וּבְטוּבוֹ חָיִינוּ.
and through Whose goodness we live.

ALL:

Boruch hu u-voruch sh'mō. בָּרוּךְ הוּא וּבָרוּךְ שְׁמוֹ.
Blessed is He and Blessed is His Name.

CONTINUE WITH *BIRCAS HAMAZON* (P. 310) UNTIL '…IN THE EYES OF GOD AND OF MAN' (P. 323).

THEN A DESIGNATED PERSON (OR PERSONS) RECITES THE FOLLOWING PRAYERS ALOUD.

SOMEONE OTHER THAN THE FATHER SHOULD RECITE THE FOLLOWING STANZA.

HORACHAMON hu y'voraych **הָרַחֲמָן** הוּא יְבָרֵךְ
The compassionate One! May He bless
avi ha-yeled v'imō, אֲבִי הַיֶּלֶד וְאִמּוֹ,
the father and mother of the child;
v'yizku l'gad'lō וְיִזְכּוּ לְגַדְּלוֹ
and may they merit to raise him,
ulchan'chō ulchak'mō, וּלְחַנְּכוֹ וּלְחַכְּמוֹ,
to educate him, and to make him wise,

CIRCUMCISION

miyōm hash'mini vohol-o	מִיּוֹם הַשְּׁמִינִי וָהָלְאָה

from the eighth day onward

yayrotze domō,	יֵרָצֶה דָמוֹ,

may his blood be pleasing,

vi-hi Adōnoy Elōhov i-mō.	וִיהִי יהוה אֱלֹהָיו עִמּוֹ.

and may HASHEM, his God, be with him.

SOMEONE OTHER THAN THE SANDAK SHOULD RECITE THE FOLLOWING STANZA.

HORACHAMON hu y'voraych	הָרַחֲמָן הוּא יְבָרֵךְ

The compassionate One! May He bless

ba-al b'ris hamilo,	בַּעַל בְּרִית הַמִּילָה,

the master of the circumcision covenant,

asher sos la-asōs tzedek b'gilo,	אֲשֶׁר שָׂשׂ לַעֲשׂוֹת צֶדֶק בְּגִילָה,

who rejoiced to do justice with glee,

vi-shalaym po-olō	וִישַׁלֵּם פָּעֳלוֹ

and may his deed be rewarded,

u-maskurtō k'fulo,	וּמַשְׂכֻּרְתּוֹ כְּפוּלָה,

his recompense be doubled,

v'yit'nayhu l'malo l'mo'lo.	וְיִתְּנֵהוּ לְמַעְלָה לְמָעְלָה.

and may He place him ever higher.

HORACHAMON hu y'vorayc	הָרַחֲמָן הוּא יְבָרֵךְ

The compassionate One! May He bless

rach hanimōl lishmōno,	רַךְ הַנִּמּוֹל לִשְׁמוֹנָה,

the tender circumcised eight-day-old

v'yih-yu yodov v'libō lo-ayl emuno,	וְיִהְיוּ יָדָיו וְלִבּוֹ לָאֵל אֱמוּנָה,

and may his strength and heart be a trust to God,

v'yiz-ke lir-ōs p'nay hash'chino,	וְיִזְכֶּה לִרְאוֹת פְּנֵי הַשְּׁכִינָה,

and may he merit to perceive the Divine Presence,

sholōsh p'omim bashono.	שָׁלֹשׁ פְּעָמִים בַּשָּׁנָה.

three times a year.

HORACHAMON hu y'voraych	הָרַחֲמָן הוּא יְבָרֵךְ

The compassionate One! May He bless

hamol b'sar ho-or'lo,	הַמָּל בְּשַׂר הָעָרְלָה,

him who circumcised the uncut flesh,

u-fora u-motzatz d'may hamilo,	וּפָרַע וּמָצַץ דְּמֵי הַמִּילָה,

and revealed and drew the bloods of the circumcision,

ish hayoray v'rach halayvov	אִישׁ הַיָּרֵא וְרַךְ הַלֵּבָב
avōdosō p'sulo,	עֲבוֹדָתוֹ פְּסוּלָה,

the service of the coward and the faint-hearted is unfit

im sh'lōsh ayleh	(וְ)אִם שָׁלֹשׁ אֵלֶּה
lō ya-ase lo.	לֹא יַעֲשֶׂה לָהּ.

— *(and) if he does not perform upon it these three acts.*

SOMEONE OTHER THAN THE *MOHEL* SHOULD RECITE THE FOLLOWING STANZA.

HORACHAMON hu yishlach lonu   **הָרַחֲמָן** הוּא יִשְׁלַח לָנוּ

The compassionate One! May He send us

m'shichō hōlaych tomim,	מְשִׁיחוֹ הוֹלֵךְ תָּמִים,

His anointed who goes with wholesomeness,

bizchus chasan lamulōs domim,	בִּזְכוּת חֲתַן לַמּוּלוֹת דָּמִים,

in the merit of the groom bloodied for the sake of circumcision,

l'vasayr b'sōrōs tōvōs	לְבַשֵּׂר בְּשׂוֹרוֹת טוֹבוֹת

to proclaim good tidings

v'nichumim,	וְנִחוּמִים,

and consolations,

l'am e-chod m'fuzor umfōrod	לְעַם אֶחָד מְפֻזָּר וּמְפֹרָד

to the one nation dispersed and splintered

bayn ho-amim.	בֵּין הָעַמִּים.

among the nations.

HORACHAMON hu yishlach lonu   **הָרַחֲמָן** הוּא יִשְׁלַח לָנוּ

The compassionate One! May He send us

kōhayn tzedek asher lukach l'aylōm,	כֹּהֵן צֶדֶק אֲשֶׁר לֻקַּח לְעֵילוֹם,

the righteous Kohen who was taken into hiding,

ad huchan kisō	עַד הוּכַן כִּסְאוֹ

until His throne is established

ka-shemesh v'yoholōm,	כַּשֶּׁמֶשׁ וְיָהֲלוֹם,

bright as sun and diamond,

va-yolet ponov b'adartō va-yiglōm,	וַיָּלֶט פָּנָיו בְּאַדַּרְתּוֹ וַיִּגְלֹם,

he who covered his face with his cloak and enwrapped himself,

b'ris ho-y'so itō	בְּרִיתִי הָיְתָה אִתּוֹ

My covenant was with him

hacha-yim v'hasholōm.	הַחַיִּים וְהַשָּׁלוֹם.

for life and peace.

CONTINUE WITH THE CONCLUSION OF *BIRCAS HAMAZON* (P. 324).

⊰{ REDEMPTION OF THE FIRSTBORN SON }⊱

■ **Pidyon Haben:** Redemption of the firstborn reflects the teaching of the Torah that all "firsts" belong to Hashem. When the Jewish firstborn were spared the deathblow of the tenth plague in Egypt, Hashem imbued them with greater sanctity, inviting them to serve as His emissaries. After these firstborn participated in the sin of the Golden Calf, their privileges were transferred to the Kohanim. This ceremony represents the formal redemption of the firstborn male.

THE FATHER AND THE *KOHEN* STAND.
HOLDING HIS CHILD, THE FATHER DECLARES TO THE *KOHEN*:

ZE b'ni v'chōri,   זֶה, בְּנִי בְכוֹרִי,
This is my firstborn son;

hu pe-ter rechem l'i-mo,   הוּא פֶּטֶר רֶחֶם לְאִמּוֹ,
he is the first issue of his mother's womb

v'hakodōsh boruch hu   וְהַקָּדוֹשׁ בָּרוּךְ הוּא
and the Holy One, Blessed is He,

tzivo lifdōsō she-ne-emar: צִוָּה לִפְדּוֹתוֹ. שֶׁנֶּאֱמַר:
has commanded to redeem him, as it is said:

U'f-duyov miben chōdesh tif-de   וּפְדוּיָו מִבֶּן חֹדֶשׁ תִּפְדֶּה,
"And those who must be redeemed, from the age of a month are you to redeem,

b'erk'cho kesef chamayshes sh'kolim,   בְּעֶרְכְּךָ, כֶּסֶף חֲמֵשֶׁת שְׁקָלִים,
according to your estimate, five silver shekels

b'shekel hakōdesh esrim gayro hu   בְּשֶׁקֶל הַקֹּדֶשׁ עֶשְׂרִים גֵּרָה הוּא.
in the shekel of the Sanctuary, which is twenty gerah."

V'ne-e-mar: Kadesh li kol b'chōr   וְנֶאֱמַר: קַדֶּשׁ לִי כָל בְּכוֹר,
And it is said: "Sanctify for Me every firstborn,

pe-ter kol rechem bivnay yisroayl,   פֶּטֶר כָּל רֶחֶם בִּבְנֵי יִשְׂרָאֵל,
the first issue of every womb among the Children of Israel,

bo-odom u'vab'haymo li hu.   בָּאָדָם וּבַבְּהֵמָה לִי הוּא.
both of man and of beast, is Mine."

THE *KOHEN* ASKS:

MAI bo-is t'fay,   מַאי בָּעִית טְפֵי,
Which do you prefer:

litayn li bincho b'chōr'cho   לִיתֵּן לִי בִּנְךָ בְּכוֹרְךָ
to give away your firstborn son,

shehu pe-ter rechem l'i-mō,   שֶׁהוּא פֶּטֶר רֶחֶם לְאִמּוֹ,
who is the first issue of his mother's womb,

ō bo-is lifdōsō   אוֹ בָּעִית לִפְדּוֹתוֹ
or do you prefer to redeem him

פדיון הבן

b'ad chomaysh s'lo-im   בְּעַד חָמֵשׁ סְלָעִים
for five shekels

k'dimcha-yavt mid'ōraiso.   כִּדְמְחַיַּבְתְּ מִדְּאוֹרַיְתָא?
as you are required to do by the Torah?

THE FATHER REPLIES:

CHOFAYTZ ani lifdōs es b'ni,   חָפֵץ אֲנִי לִפְדּוֹת אֶת בְּנִי,
I wish to redeem my son.

v'hay-loch d'may fid-yōnō   וְהֵילָךְ דְּמֵי פִדְיוֹנוֹ
I present you with the cost of his redemption

k'dimcha-yavt mid'ōraiso.   כִּדְמְחַיַּבְתְּ מִדְּאוֹרַיְתָא.
as I am required to do by the Torah.

WITH THE REDEMPTION MONEY IN HAND, THE FATHER RECITES THE FOLLOWING BLESSINGS:

BORUCH ato Adōnoy   בָּרוּךְ אַתָּה יהוה
Elōhaynu melech ho-ōlom,   אֱלֹהֵינוּ מֶלֶךְ הָעוֹלָם,
Blessed are You, Hashem, our God, King of the universe,

asher kid'shonu b'mitzvōsov,   אֲשֶׁר קִדְּשָׁנוּ בְּמִצְוֹתָיו,
Who has sanctified us with His commandments

v'tzivonu al pidyōn habayn.   וְצִוָּנוּ עַל פִּדְיוֹן הַבֵּן.
and has commanded us regarding the redemption of a son.

ALL PRESENT RESPOND: Omayn — אָמֵן

BORUCH ato Adōnoy   בָּרוּךְ אַתָּה יהוה
Elōhaynu melech ho-ōlom,   אֱלֹהֵינוּ מֶלֶךְ הָעוֹלָם,
Blessed are You, Hashem, our God, King of the universe,

shehecheyonu v'kiy'monu   שֶׁהֶחֱיָנוּ וְקִיְּמָנוּ
v'higi-onu laz'man ha-ze.   וְהִגִּיעָנוּ לַזְּמַן הַזֶּה.
Who has kept us alive, sustained us, and brought us to this season.

ALL PRESENT RESPOND: Omayn — אָמֵן

THE KOHEN ACCEPTS THE MONEY AND, WHILE SWINGING IT
IN A CIRCULAR MOTION OVER THE INFANT'S HEAD, SAYS:

ZE tachas ze. Ze chiluf ze.   זֶה תַּחַת זֶה. זֶה חִלּוּף זֶה.
This is instead of that; this is in exchange for that;

Ze mochul al ze.   זֶה מָחוּל עַל זֶה.
this is pardoned because of that.

V'yikonays ze habayn l'cha-yim,   וְיִכָּנֵס זֶה הַבֵּן לְחַיִּים,
May this son enter into life,

l'sōro ul-yiras shoma-yim.   לְתוֹרָה וּלְיִרְאַת שָׁמָיִם.
into Torah and into fear of Heaven.

REDEMPTION OF THE FIRSTBORN

Y'hi rotzōn shek'shaym   יְהִי רָצוֹן שֶׁכְּשֵׁם
shenichnas l'fidyōn   שֶׁנִּכְנַס לַפִּדְיוֹן

May it be Your will that just as he has entered into this redemption,

kayn yikonays l'soro ulchupa   כֵּן יִכָּנֵס לְתוֹרָה וּלְחֻפָּה
ulma-asim tovim. Omayn.   וּלְמַעֲשִׂים טוֹבִים. אָמֵן.

so may he enter into the Torah, the marriage canopy, and good deeds, Amen.

THE *KOHEN* PLACES HIS RIGHT HAND ON THE INFANT'S HEAD AND BLESSES HIM:

Y'SIMCHO Elōhim   **יְשִׂמְךָ** אֱלֹהִים
May God make you

k'efra-yim v'chim-nashe.   כְּאֶפְרַיִם וְכִמְנַשֶּׁה.
like Ephraim and like Menashe.

Y'vorechcho Adōnoy v'yishm'recho.   יְבָרֶכְךָ יהוה וְיִשְׁמְרֶךָ.
May HASHEM bless you and safeguard you.

Yo-ayr Adōnoy   יָאֵר יהוה
May HASHEM illuminate

ponov aylecho vi-chuneko.   פָּנָיו אֵלֶיךָ וִיחֻנֶּךָּ.
His countenance for you and be gracious to you.

Yiso Adōnoy ponov aylecho   יִשָּׂא יהוה פָּנָיו אֵלֶיךָ,
May HASHEM turn His countenance to you

v'yosaym l'cho sholōm.   וְיָשֵׂם לְךָ שָׁלוֹם.
and establish peace for you.

Ki ōrech yomim ush-nōs cha-yim   כִּי אֹרֶךְ יָמִים וּשְׁנוֹת חַיִּים
For lengthy days, and years of life,

v'sholōm yōsifu loch.   וְשָׁלוֹם יוֹסִיפוּ לָךְ.
and peace shall He increase for you.

Adōnoy yishmor'cho mikol ro,   יהוה יִשְׁמָרְךָ מִכָּל רָע,
HASHEM will protect you from every evil;

yishmōr es nafshecho.   יִשְׁמֹר אֶת נַפְשֶׁךָ.
He will guard your soul.

BORUCH ato Adōnoy   **בָּרוּךְ** אַתָּה יהוה
Blessed are You, HASHEM,

Elōhaynu melech ho-ōlom,   אֱלֹהֵינוּ מֶלֶךְ הָעוֹלָם,
our God, King of the universe,

bōray p'ri hagofen.   בּוֹרֵא פְּרִי הַגָּפֶן.
Who creates the fruit of the vine.

ALL PRESENT RESPOND: Omayn — אָמֵן

≼{ WAYFARER'S PRAYER }≽

ONE WHO SETS OUT ON A JOURNEY RECITES THE FOLLOWING PRAYER ONCE HE LEAVES THE CITY LIMITS.

Y'HI rotzōn mil'fonecho   יְהִי רָצוֹן מִלְּפָנֶיךָ
May it be Your will,

Adōnoy Elōhaynu Vaylōhay avōsaynu,   יהוה אֱלֹהֵינוּ וֵאלֹהֵי אֲבוֹתֵינוּ,
Hashem, our God and the God of our forefathers,

shetōlichaynu l'sholōm,   שֶׁתּוֹלִיכֵנוּ לְשָׁלוֹם,
    v'satzidaynu l'sholōm,   וְתַצְעִידֵנוּ לְשָׁלוֹם,
that You lead us toward peace, emplace our footsteps toward peace,

v'sadrichaynu l'sholōm,   וְתַדְרִיכֵנוּ לְשָׁלוֹם,
guide us toward peace,

v'sagi-aynu limchōz cheftzaynu   וְתַגִּיעֵנוּ לִמְחוֹז חֶפְצֵנוּ
    l'cha-yim ulsimcho ulsholōm,   לְחַיִּים וּלְשִׂמְחָה וּלְשָׁלוֹם,
and make us reach our desired destination for life, gladness, and peace

——————— ONE WHO IS PLANNING TO RETURN ON THE SAME DAY ADDS ———————

v'sachaziraynu l'vaysaynu l'sholōm   וְתַחֲזִירֵנוּ לְבֵיתֵנוּ לְשָׁלוֹם,
and return us to our homes in peace.

———————

v'satzilaynu mikaf kol ō-yayv v'ōrayv   וְתַצִּילֵנוּ מִכַּף כָּל אוֹיֵב וְאוֹרֵב
May You rescue us from the hand of every foe, ambush,

(v'listim v'chayōs ro-ōs) baderech   (וְלִסְטִים וְחַיּוֹת רָעוֹת) בַּדֶּרֶךְ,
(bandits, and evil animals) along the way,

u-mikol minay furoniyōs   וּמִכָּל מִינֵי פֻרְעָנִיּוֹת
    hamisrag'shōs lovō lo-ōlom.   הַמִּתְרַגְּשׁוֹת לָבוֹא לָעוֹלָם.
and from all manner of punishments that assemble to come to earth.

V'sishlach b'rocho   וְתִשְׁלַח בְּרָכָה
    b'chol ma-asay yodaynu,   בְּכָל מַעֲשֵׂה יָדֵינוּ,
May You send blessing in our (every) handiwork,

v'sit'naynu l'chayn ulchesed ulrachamim   וְתִתְּנֵנוּ לְחֵן וּלְחֶסֶד וּלְרַחֲמִים
and grant us grace, kindness, and mercy

b'aynecho uv-aynay chol rō-aynu,   בְּעֵינֶיךָ וּבְעֵינֵי כָל רוֹאֵינוּ,
in Your eyes and in the eyes of all who see us.

V'sishma kōl tachanunaynu,   וְתִשְׁמַע קוֹל תַּחֲנוּנֵינוּ,
May You hear the sound of our supplication,

ki Ayl shōmaya t'filo v'sachanun oto.   כִּי אֵל שׁוֹמֵעַ תְּפִלָּה וְתַחֲנוּן אָתָּה.
because You are God Who hears prayer and supplication.

Boruch ato Adōnoy, shōmay-a t'filo.   בָּרוּךְ אַתָּה יהוה, שׁוֹמֵעַ תְּפִלָּה.
Blessed are You, Hashem, Who hears prayer.

⊰ BLESSINGS FOR ENJOYMENT ⊱
BLESSINGS BEFORE FOOD OR DRINK

UPON WASHING THE HANDS BEFORE EATING BREAD:

Boruch ato Adōnoy,   בָּרוּךְ אַתָּה יהוה
     Elōhaynu melech ho-ōlom,   אֱלֹהֵינוּ מֶלֶךְ הָעוֹלָם,
       Blessed are You, HASHEM our God, King of the universe,
asher kid'shonu b'mitzvōsov,   אֲשֶׁר קִדְּשָׁנוּ בְּמִצְוֹתָיו,
       Who has sanctified us with His commandments,
v'tzivonu al n'tilas yodo-yim.   וְצִוָּנוּ עַל נְטִילַת יָדָיִם.
       and commanded us regarding washing the hands.

BEFORE EATING BREAD:

Boruch ato Adōnoy,   בָּרוּךְ אַתָּה יהוה
     Elōhaynu melech ho-ōlom,   אֱלֹהֵינוּ מֶלֶךְ הָעוֹלָם,
       Blessed are You, HASHEM, our God, King of the universe,
ha-mōtzi lechem min ho-oretz.   הַמּוֹצִיא לֶחֶם מִן הָאָרֶץ.
       Who brings forth bread from the earth.

BEFORE EATING PRODUCTS OF WHEAT, BARLEY, RYE, OATS OR SPELT
(AND RICE, ACCORDING TO MANY OPINIONS):

Boruch ato Adōnoy,   בָּרוּךְ אַתָּה יהוה
     Elōhaynu melech ho-ōlom,   אֱלֹהֵינוּ מֶלֶךְ הָעוֹלָם,
       Blessed are You, HASHEM, our God, King of the universe,
bōray minay m'zōnōs.   בּוֹרֵא מִינֵי מְזוֹנוֹת.
       Who creates species of nourishment.

BEFORE DRINKING GRAPE WINE OR GRAPE JUICE:

Boruch ato Adōnoy,   בָּרוּךְ אַתָּה יהוה
     Elōhaynu melech ho-ōlom,   אֱלֹהֵינוּ מֶלֶךְ הָעוֹלָם,
       Blessed are You, HASHEM, our God, King of the universe,
bōray p'ri hagofen.   בּוֹרֵא פְּרִי הַגָּפֶן.
       Who creates the fruit of the vine.

BEFORE EATING TREE-GROWN FRUIT:

Boruch ato Adōnoy,   בָּרוּךְ אַתָּה יהוה
     Elōhaynu melech ho-ōlom,   אֱלֹהֵינוּ מֶלֶךְ הָעוֹלָם,
       Blessed are You, HASHEM, our God, King of the universe,
bōray p'ri ho-aytz.   בּוֹרֵא פְּרִי הָעֵץ.
       Who creates the fruit of the tree.

BEFORE EATING PRODUCE THAT GREW DIRECTLY FROM THE EARTH:

Boruch ato Adōnoy,   בָּרוּךְ אַתָּה יהוה
Elōhaynu melech ho-ōlom,   אֱלֹהֵינוּ מֶלֶךְ הָעוֹלָם,
*Blessed are You, H*ASHEM*, our God, King of the universe,*
bōray p'ri ho-adomo.   בּוֹרֵא פְּרִי הָאֲדָמָה.
Who creates the fruit of the ground.

BEFORE EATING OR DRINKING ANY OTHER FOODS:

Boruch ato Adōnoy,   בָּרוּךְ אַתָּה יהוה
Elōhaynu melech ho-ōlom,   אֱלֹהֵינוּ מֶלֶךְ הָעוֹלָם,
*Blessed are You, H*ASHEM*, our God, King of the universe,*
shehakōl nih-ye bidvorō.   שֶׁהַכֹּל נִהְיֶה בִּדְבָרוֹ.
through Whose word everything came to be.

UPON ENTERING A PERFUMERY OR UPON SMELLING FRAGRANCES OF (A) NON-VEGETABLE ORIGIN (E.G., MUSK); (B) UNDETERMINED ORIGIN; OR (C) A BLEND OF SPICES OF DIFFERENT ORIGINS:

Boruch ato Adōnoy   בָּרוּךְ אַתָּה יהוה
Elōhaynu melech ho-ōlom,   אֱלֹהֵינוּ מֶלֶךְ הָעוֹלָם,
*Blessed are You, H*ASHEM*, our God, King of the universe,*
bōray minay v'somim.   בּוֹרֵא מִינֵי בְשָׂמִים.
Who creates species of fragrance.

UPON AFFIXING A *MEZUZAH* TO A DOORPOST:

Boruch ato Adōnoy,   בָּרוּךְ אַתָּה יהוה
Elōhaynu melech ho-ōlom,   אֱלֹהֵינוּ מֶלֶךְ הָעוֹלָם,
*Blessed are You, H*ASHEM*, our God, King of the universe,*
asher kid'shonu b'mitzvōsov,   אֲשֶׁר קִדְּשָׁנוּ בְּמִצְוֹתָיו,
Who has sanctified us with His commandments,
v'tzivonu likbō-a m'zuzo.   וְצִוָּנוּ לִקְבֹּעַ מְזוּזָה.
and has commanded us to affix a mezuzah.

UPON IMMERSING IN A *MIKVEH* METAL OR GLASS UTENSILS (USED FOR THE PREPARATION OR SERVING OF FOOD OR DRINK) THAT HAVE BEEN MADE BY OR PURCHASED FROM A GENTILE:

Boruch ato Adōnoy,   בָּרוּךְ אַתָּה יהוה
Elōhaynu melech ho-ōlom,   אֱלֹהֵינוּ מֶלֶךְ הָעוֹלָם,
*Blessed are You, H*ASHEM*, our God, King of the universe,*
asher kid'shonu b'mitzvōsov,   אֲשֶׁר קִדְּשָׁנוּ בְּמִצְוֹתָיו,
Who has sanctified us with His commandments,

IF ONLY ONE UTENSIL IS IMMERSED, CONCLUDE WITH THE WORD IN PARENTHESES

v'tzivonu al t'vilas kaylim (keli).   וְצִוָּנוּ עַל טְבִילַת כֵּלִים (כְּלִי).
and has commanded us regarding the immersion of vessels (a vessel).

❧ BLESSINGS OF PRAISE AND GRATITUDE ❧

BLESSINGS OVER PHENOMENA AND EVENTS

THE FIRST THREE BLESSINGS OF THIS SECTION MAY BE RECITED ONLY ONCE EACH DAY, UNLESS THE SKIES HAVE CLEARED COMPLETELY AND THEN THE CLOUDS RETURNED. EXCEPT AS OTHERWISE INDICATED, THE REMAINING BLESSINGS ARE RECITED ONLY IF THIRTY DAYS HAVE ELAPSED SINCE THE PHENOMENON WAS LAST SEEN. IF UNSURE WHETHER TO RECITE ONE OF THE BLESSINGS IN THIS SECTION ON A PARTICULAR OCCASION, RECITE THE BLESSING BUT OMIT THE OPENING CLAUSE, "BLESSED . . . UNIVERSE," AND SUBSTITUTE, "BLESSED IS HE."

UPON EXPERIENCING AN EARTHQUAKE, OR SEEING LIGHTNING, A COMET, EXCEPTIONALLY LOFTY MOUNTAINS, OR EXCEPTIONALLY LARGE RIVERS (IN THEIR NATURAL COURSE):

Boruch ato Adōnoy   בָּרוּךְ אַתָּה יהוה
    Elōhaynu melech ho-ōlom,   אֱלֹהֵינוּ מֶלֶךְ הָעוֹלָם,
       Blessed are You, Hashem, our God, King of the universe,
ōse ma-asay v'rayshis.   עֹשֶׂה מַעֲשֵׂה בְרֵאשִׁית.
       Who makes the work of Creation.

UPON HEARING THUNDER:

Boruch ato Adōnoy   בָּרוּךְ אַתָּה יהוה
    Elōhaynu melech ho-ōlom,   אֱלֹהֵינוּ מֶלֶךְ הָעוֹלָם,
       Blessed are You, Hashem, our God, King of the universe,
shekōchō ugvurosō molay ōlom.   שֶׁכֹּחוֹ וּגְבוּרָתוֹ מָלֵא עוֹלָם.
       for His strength and His power fill the universe.

UPON SEEING A RAINBOW IN THE SKY:

Boruch ato Adōnoy   בָּרוּךְ אַתָּה יהוה
    Elōhaynu melech ho-ōlom,   אֱלֹהֵינוּ מֶלֶךְ הָעוֹלָם,
       Blessed are You, Hashem, our God, King of the universe,
zōchayr hab'ris,   זוֹכֵר הַבְּרִית,
    v'ne-emon biv-risō,   וְנֶאֱמָן בִּבְרִיתוֹ,
       Who remembers the covenant, is trustworthy in His covenant,
v'ka-yom b'ma-amorō.   וְקַיָּם בְּמַאֲמָרוֹ.
       and fulfills His word.

UPON SEEING FRUIT TREES IN BLOOM DURING THE SPRING (ONLY ONCE A YEAR):

Boruch ato Adōnoy   בָּרוּךְ אַתָּה יהוה
    Elōhaynu melech ho-ōlom,   אֱלֹהֵינוּ מֶלֶךְ הָעוֹלָם,
       Blessed are You, Hashem, our God, King of the universe,
shelō chisayr b'ōlomō dovor,   שֶׁלֹּא חִסַּר בְּעוֹלָמוֹ דָּבָר,
       for nothing is lacking in His universe,

u-voro vō b'ri-yōs tōvōs
v'i-lonōs tōvim

וּבָרָא בוֹ בְּרִיּוֹת טוֹבוֹת
וְאִילָנוֹת טוֹבִים,

and He created in it good creatures and good trees,

l'hanōs bo-hem b'nay odom.

לְהַנּוֹת בָּהֶם בְּנֵי אָדָם.

to cause mankind pleasure with them.

VARIOUS BLESSINGS

UPON HEARING UNUSUALLY GOOD NEWS WHICH BENEFITS BOTH ONESELF AND OTHERS:

Boruch ato Adōnoy
Elōhaynu melech ho-ōlom,

בָּרוּךְ אַתָּה יהוה
אֱלֹהֵינוּ מֶלֶךְ הָעוֹלָם,

Blessed are You, HASHEM, our God, King of the universe,

hatōv v'hamaytiv.

הַטּוֹב וְהַמֵּטִיב.

Who is good and does good.

UPON HEARING UNUSUALLY BAD NEWS:

Boruch ato Adōnoy
Elōhaynu melech ho-ōlom,

בָּרוּךְ אַתָּה יהוה
אֱלֹהֵינוּ מֶלֶךְ הָעוֹלָם,

Blessed are You, HASHEM, our God, King of the universe,

dayan ho-emes.

דַּיַּן הָאֱמֶת.

the true Judge.

UPON (A) EATING SEASONAL FRUITS OF A NEW SEASON FOR THE FIRST TIME; (B) PURCHASING A NEW GARMENT OF SIGNIFICANT VALUE TO THE WEARER [E.G., A NEW SUIT OR DRESS]; (C) PERFORMANCE OF A SEASONAL MITZVAH; OR (D) DERIVING SIGNIFICANT BENEFIT FROM AN EVENT [IF OTHERS ALSO BENEFIT, THE BLESSING IS THE SAME AS FOR HEARING UNUSUALLY GOOD NEWS (ABOVE):

Boruch ato Adōnoy
Elōhaynu melech ho-ōlom,

בָּרוּךְ אַתָּה יהוה
אֱלֹהֵינוּ מֶלֶךְ הָעוֹלָם,

Blessed are You, HASHEM, our God, King of the universe,

shehecheyonu v'kiy'manu v'higi-onu
laz'man ha-ze.

שֶׁהֶחֱיָנוּ וְקִיְּמָנוּ וְהִגִּיעָנוּ
לַזְּמַן הַזֶּה.

Who has kept us alive, sustained us, and brought us to this season.

UPON DONNING A NEW GARMENT OF SIGNIFICANT VALUE TO THE WEARER [E.G., A NEW SUIT OR DRESS]:

Boruch ato Adōnoy
Elōhaynu melech ho-ōlom,

בָּרוּךְ אַתָּה יהוה
אֱלֹהֵינוּ מֶלֶךְ הָעוֹלָם,

Blessed are You, HASHEM, our God, King of the universe,

malbish arumim.

מַלְבִּישׁ עֲרֻמִּים.

Who clothes the naked.

The Afternoon Service

৺ Minchah

৺ Elijah's Proof

One should be especially careful regarding the prayer of *Mincha*. Rabbi Chelbo said in the name of Rav Huna, "A person should be diligent with regard to the *Minchah* prayer for Elijah the Prophet was answered only through the *Minchah* prayer" (see *I Kings* 18:19-39). Elijah challenged almost a thousand false prophets, "Let them give us two bulls; let them choose one bull for themselves, cut it, and put it on the wood, but not apply fire, and I will prepare one bull and place it on the wood, and I will not apply fire. You shall call out in the name of your god and I shall call out in the Name of Hashem, and whichever God responds with fire, He is the [true] God" (vs. 23-24). The false prophets shouted their incantations and mortified their bodies, but to no avail. No "god" heeded them. When they were done, Elijah drenched his offering with water, uttered a simple prayer — and a Heavenly fire consumed the offering. Masses of Jews had gathered to see who would prevail. Thunderstruck, they called out, "Hashem is the God! Hashem is the God!"

Rashba comments that the false prophets believed that the sun had independent power and that God does not control the world. Therefore Elijah waited until the end of the day when the sun was setting, demonstrating that precisely when their god was waning, the fire would descend and Hashem would manifest His absolute dominion and control. Our daily recitation of *Minchah* echoes Elijah's demonstration that Hashem controls nature always.

৺ Minchah's Uniqueness

The *Tur* (*Orach Chaim* Ch. 232) explains the special significance of *Minchah* by contrasting it with the other prayers of the day. Whereas *Shacharis* is recited before a person becomes preoccupied with all the pressures and details of earning a livelihood, and *Maariv* is recited in the evening, after one has distanced himself from the concerns of the workday, *Minchah* is often recited while one is still at work. To extricate oneself not only physically but mentally, and to focus on the Jew's special relationship with God and the responsibilities that accompany that relationship, is often a great challenge and sacrifice. In the words of Ben Hei Hei (*Pirkei Avos* 5:26): "The reward is in proportion to the exertion."

Avudraham comments that the afternoon prayer is called *Minchah* to allude to the translation of *Onkelos* on the verse "They [i.e., Adam and Eve] heard the sound of Hashem God manifesting Itself in the garden toward evening" (*Genesis* 3:8). *Onkelos* translates the latter phrase *limnach yuma*, "as the day was setting." Adam and Eve transgressed the word of God late in the afternoon, the

time of *Minchah*, and God responded by granting them an audience with Himself, as it were, an opportunity to reflect upon their actions and repent. Similarly, we are given the same opportunity as the day wanes; it is an *opportune time* (*Psalms* 69:14) to reflect upon the day's activities. Perhaps the Aramaic *limnach yuma* can also mean "when the day is coming to a rest"; just as on Shabbos, a day of rest, *yom menuchah*, we should reflect on the activities of the week, and on Yom Kippur we review the activities of the year, each day at *Minchah* we review and scrutinize the proceedings of the day.

Avudraham further suggests that as the setting sun "bows" respectfully to God, we, too, should emulate nature and utilize the moment to draw closer to Him.

At *Minchah*, with the day drawing to a close, we should be filled with pride at having had the privilege to serve Hashem that day. We draw this lesson from the *Vilna Gaon's* comment on a passage from the liturgical poem *Keil Adon*, which is added to the first blessing of the *Shema* on Shabbos morning: [The sun and the heavenly bodies are] "Glad as they go forth and exultant as they return." They embark on their daily mission with happy anticipation that they will serve God, and upon completion of their mission at sunset, they are filled with exultation stemming from the satisfaction of fulfilling His mission.

⊰{ WEEKDAY MINCHAH }⊱

■ We begin *Minchah* with the *Ashrei* prayer — "Praiseworthy are those who dwell in Your house" — extolling those who sit, pause, and reflect on God's greatness. The focus on Scriptural verses of praise and consolation enables us to rise and stand before God in a more cheerful disposition.

The alphabetic acrostic of *Ashrei* motivates the supplicant to praise God, His Kingship, and His providing the needs of every living creature. The Sages highlight the importance of *Ashrei* by declaring that whoever recites this psalm three times daily is directing himself towards meriting a place in the World to Come (*Berachos* 4b).

ASHRAY yōsh'vay vay-secho,   **אַשְׁרֵי** יוֹשְׁבֵי בֵיתֶךָ,
Praiseworthy are those who dwell in Your house;

ōd y'hal'lucho selo.   עוֹד יְהַלְלוּךָ סֶּלָה.
may they always praise You, Selah!

Ashray ho-om shekocho lō,   אַשְׁרֵי הָעָם שֶׁכָּכָה לּוֹ,
Praiseworthy is the people for whom this is so,

ashray ho-om she-Adōnoy Elōhov.   אַשְׁרֵי הָעָם שֶׁיהוה אֱלֹהָיו.
*praiseworthy is the people whose God is H*ASHEM.

T'hilo l'dovid,   תְּהִלָּה לְדָוִד,
A psalm of praise by David:

arōmimcho Elōhai hamelech,   אֲרוֹמִמְךָ אֱלוֹהַי הַמֶּלֶךְ,
I will exalt You, my God the King,

va-avor'cho shimcho l'ōlom vo-ed.   וַאֲבָרְכָה שִׁמְךָ לְעוֹלָם וָעֶד.
and I will bless Your Name forever and ever.

B'chol yōm avor'cheko,   בְּכָל יוֹם אֲבָרְכֶךָּ,
Every day I will bless You,

va-ahal'lo shimcho l'ōlom vo-ed.   וַאֲהַלְלָה שִׁמְךָ לְעוֹלָם וָעֶד.
and I will laud Your Name forever and ever.

Godōl Adōnoy umhulol m'ōd,   גָּדוֹל יהוה וּמְהֻלָּל מְאֹד,
*H*ASHEM *is great and exceedingly lauded,*

v'ligduloso ayn chayker.   וְלִגְדֻלָּתוֹ אֵין חֵקֶר.
and His greatness is beyond investigation.

Dōr l'dōr y'shabach ma-asecho,   דּוֹר לְדוֹר יְשַׁבַּח מַעֲשֶׂיךָ,
Each generation will praise Your deeds to the next,

ugvurōsecho yagidu.   וּגְבוּרֹתֶיךָ יַגִּידוּ.
and of Your mighty deeds they will tell.

⊰§ **Minchah**
Minchah corresponds to the *tamid*, the daily afternoon offering in the Temple (*Berachos* 26b), so it is recited only when it was permissible to offer the *tamid*: from half an hour after midday until evening.

Hadar k'vōd hōdecho,	הֲדַר כְּבוֹד הוֹדֶךָ,

The splendrous glory of Your power

v'divray nifl'ōsecho osicho.	וְדִבְרֵי נִפְלְאֹתֶיךָ אָשִׂיחָה.

and Your wondrous deeds I shall discuss.

Ve-ezuz nōr'ōsecho yōmayru,	וֶעֱזוּז נוֹרְאוֹתֶיךָ יֹאמֵרוּ,

And of Your awesome power they will speak,

ugdulos'cho asap'reno.	וּגְדוּלָּתְךָ אֲסַפְּרֶנָּה.

and Your greatness I shall relate.

Zecher rav tuv'cho yabi-u,	זֵכֶר רַב טוּבְךָ יַבִּיעוּ,

A recollection of Your abundant goodness they will utter

v'tzidkos'cho y'ranaynu.	וְצִדְקָתְךָ יְרַנֵּנוּ.

and of Your righteousness they will sing exultantly.

Chanun v'rachum Adōnoy,	חַנּוּן וְרַחוּם יהוה,

*Gracious and merciful is H*ASHEM*,*

erech apa-yim ugdol chosed.	אֶרֶךְ אַפַּיִם וּגְדָל חָסֶד.

slow to anger, and great in [bestowing] kindness.

Tōv Adōnoy lakōl,	טוֹב יהוה לַכֹּל,

*H*ASHEM *is good to all,*

v'rachamov al kol ma-asov.	וְרַחֲמָיו עַל כָּל מַעֲשָׂיו.

and His mercies are on all His works.

Yōducho Adōnoy kol ma-asecho,	יוֹדוּךָ יהוה כָּל מַעֲשֶׂיךָ,

*All Your works shall thank You, H*ASHEM*,*

vachasidecho y'vor'chucho.	וַחֲסִידֶיךָ יְבָרְכוּכָה.

and Your devout ones will bless You.

K'vōd malchus'cho yōmayru,	כְּבוֹד מַלְכוּתְךָ יֹאמֵרוּ,
ugvuros'cho y'dabayru.	וּגְבוּרָתְךָ יְדַבֵּרוּ.

Of the glory of Your kingdom they will speak, and of Your power they will tell,

L'hōdi-a livnay ho-odom g'vurōsov,	לְהוֹדִיעַ לִבְנֵי הָאָדָם גְּבוּרֹתָיו,

to inform human beings of His mighty deeds,

uchvōd hadar malchusō.	וּכְבוֹד הֲדַר מַלְכוּתוֹ.

and the glorious splendor of His kingdom.

Malchus'cho malchus kol ōlomim,	מַלְכוּתְךָ מַלְכוּת כָּל עֹלָמִים,

Your kingdom is a kingdom spanning all eternities,

u-memshalt'cho b'chol dōr vodōr.	וּמֶמְשַׁלְתְּךָ בְּכָל דּוֹר וָדֹר.

and Your dominion is throughout every generation.

Sōmaych Adōnoy l'chol hanōf'lim,	סוֹמֵךְ יהוה לְכָל הַנֹּפְלִים,

*H*ASHEM *supports all the fallen ones*

v'zōkayf l'chol hak'fufim.	וְזוֹקֵף לְכָל הַכְּפוּפִים.

and straightens all the bent.

Aynay chōl aylecho y'sabayru,	עֵינֵי כֹל אֵלֶיךָ יְשַׂבֵּרוּ,

The eyes of all look to You with hope

v'ato nōsayn lohem es ochlom b'ito.	וְאַתָּה נוֹתֵן לָהֶם אֶת אָכְלָם בְּעִתּוֹ.

and You give them their food in its proper time.

CONCENTRATE INTENTLY WHILE RECITING THE NEXT VERSE.

Pōsay-ach es yodecho,	**פּוֹתֵחַ** אֶת יָדֶךָ,

You open Your hand

u-masbi-a l'chol chai rotzōn.	וּמַשְׂבִּיעַ לְכָל חַי רָצוֹן.

and satisfy the desire of every living thing.

Tzadik Adōnoy b'chol d'rochov,	**צַדִּיק** יהוה בְּכָל דְּרָכָיו,

Righteous is HASHEM in all His ways

v'chosid b'chol ma-asov.	וְחָסִיד בְּכָל מַעֲשָׂיו.

and magnanimous in all His deeds.

Korōv Adōnoy l'chol kōr'ov,	**קָרוֹב** יהוה לְכָל קֹרְאָיו,

HASHEM is close to all who call upon Him —

l'chōl asher yikro-uhu ve-emes.	לְכֹל אֲשֶׁר יִקְרָאֻהוּ בֶאֱמֶת.

to all who call upon Him sincerely.

R'tzōn y'ray-ov ya-ase,	**רְצוֹן** יְרֵאָיו יַעֲשֶׂה,

The will of those who fear Him He will do,

v'es shav-osom yishma v'yōshi-aym.	וְאֶת שַׁוְעָתָם יִשְׁמַע וְיוֹשִׁיעֵם.

and their cry He will hear, and save them.

Shōmayr Adōnoy es kol ōhavov,	**שׁוֹמֵר** יהוה אֶת כָּל אֹהֲבָיו,

HASHEM protects all who love Him,

v'ays kol hor'sho-im yashmid.	וְאֵת כָּל הָרְשָׁעִים יַשְׁמִיד.

but all the wicked He will destroy.

T'hilas Adōnoy y'daber pi,	❖ **תְּהִלַּת** יהוה יְדַבֶּר פִּי,

May my mouth declare the praise of HASHEM

vivoraych kol bosor shaym kodshō, l'ōlom vo-ed.	וִיבָרֵךְ כָּל בָּשָׂר שֵׁם קָדְשׁוֹ לְעוֹלָם וָעֶד.

and may all flesh bless His Holy Name forever and ever.

Va-anachnu n'voraych Yoh,	וַאֲנַחְנוּ נְבָרֵךְ יָהּ,

We will bless God

may-ato v'ad ōlom, hal'luyoh.	מֵעַתָּה וְעַד עוֹלָם, הַלְלוּיָהּ.

from this time and forever: Praise God!

MINCHAH FOR WEEKDAYS — SHEMONEH ESREI

THE *CHAZZAN* RECITES *HALF-KADDISH*.
(Congregational responses are indicated by parentheses.)

יִתְגַּדַּל וְיִתְקַדַּשׁ שְׁמֵהּ רַבָּא. (אָמֵן – Omayn). בְּעָלְמָא דִּי בְרָא כִרְעוּתֵהּ. וְיַמְלִיךְ מַלְכוּתֵהּ, בְּחַיֵּיכוֹן וּבְיוֹמֵיכוֹן וּבְחַיֵּי דְכָל בֵּית יִשְׂרָאֵל, בַּעֲגָלָא וּבִזְמַן קָרִיב. וְאִמְרוּ: אָמֵן.

(אָמֵן. יְהֵא שְׁמֵהּ רַבָּא מְבָרַךְ לְעָלַם וּלְעָלְמֵי עָלְמַיָּא.)
(Omayn. Y'hay sh'mayh rabo m'vorach l'olam ul-ol'may ol'ma-yo.)

יְהֵא שְׁמֵהּ רַבָּא מְבָרַךְ לְעָלַם וּלְעָלְמֵי עָלְמַיָּא. יִתְבָּרַךְ וְיִשְׁתַּבַּח וְיִתְפָּאַר וְיִתְרוֹמַם וְיִתְנַשֵּׂא וְיִתְהַדָּר וְיִתְעַלֶּה וְיִתְהַלָּל שְׁמֵהּ דְּקֻדְשָׁא בְּרִיךְ הוּא (בְּרִיךְ הוּא – B'rich hu). °לְעֵלָּא מִן כָּל [°לְעֵלָּא לְעֵלָּא מִכָּל — from Rosh Hashanah to Yom Kippur substitute] בִּרְכָתָא וְשִׁירָתָא תֻּשְׁבְּחָתָא וְנֶחָמָתָא, דַּאֲמִירָן בְּעָלְמָא. וְאִמְרוּ: אָמֵן. (אָמֵן – Omayn).

> **ON PUBLIC FAST DAYS:** If at least seven members of the *minyan* are fasting, the Torah and *Haftarah* are read. The services of removing the Torah from the Ark and returning it to the Ark appear on pages 233-245. After the Torah has been returned to the Ark, the *chazzan* repeats Half-*Kaddish* and *Shemoneh Esrei* is recited.

☙ SHEMONEH ESREI — AMIDAH ❧

■ *Shemoneh Esrei* (or the *Amidah*) is known as "Service of the Heart." By definition, it must be understood and comprehended. Failure to do so is compared by the Sages to a "body without a soul." Two independent kinds of awareness are necessary for the *Amidah*:

1. To understand the meaning of that which we are saying. The format of this *siddur* is most helpful in this regard. Please take your time to recite the prayer with the conviction that accompanies comprehension.

2. To visualize that we are privileged literally to be standing before God. You are talking to Him directly. In each blessing, when we recite the word *ato*, "You," we should understand to Whom the "You" is referring.

IN THE SYNAGOGUE THE *SHEMONEH ESREI* IS RECITED WHILE FACING THE ARK; ELSEWHERE IT IS RECITED WHILE FACING THE DIRECTION OF THE LAND OF ISRAEL. TAKE THREE STEPS BACKWARD, LEFT, RIGHT, LEFT, THEN THREE STEPS FORWARD, RIGHT, LEFT, RIGHT. REMAIN STANDING WITH FEET TOGETHER DURING *SHEMONEH ESREI*. RECITE IT WITH QUIET DEVOTION AND WITHOUT ANY INTERRUPTION. ALTHOUGH IT SHOULD NOT BE AUDIBLE TO OTHERS, ONE MUST PRAY LOUDLY ENOUGH TO HEAR ONESELF.

Ki shaym Adōnoy ekro,   כִּי שֵׁם יהוה אֶקְרָא,
hovu gōdel Laylōhaynu.   הָבוּ גֹדֶל לֵאלֹהֵינוּ.

When I call out the Name of H<small>ASHEM</small>, *ascribe greatness to our God.*

Adōnoy s'fosai tiftoch,   אֲדֹנָי שְׂפָתַי תִּפְתָּח,
u-fi yagid t'hilosecho.   וּפִי יַגִּיד תְּהִלָּתֶךָ.

My Lord, open my lips, that my mouth may declare Your praise.

- **First Blessing:** In the merit of our Patriarchs whose actions reflected Godliness, Hashem pledged to always be with Israel and protect them.

BEND THE KNEES AT Boruch; BOW AT ato; STRAIGHTEN UP AT Adōnoy.

BORUCH ato Adōnoy   בָּרוּךְ אַתָּה יהוה
Blessed are You, HASHEM,

Elōhaynu Vaylōhay avōsaynu,   אֱלֹהֵינוּ וֵאלֹהֵי אֲבוֹתֵינוּ,
our God and the God of our forefathers,

Elōhay avrohom, Elōhay yitzchok,   אֱלֹהֵי אַבְרָהָם, אֱלֹהֵי יִצְחָק,
Vaylōhay ya-akōv,   וֵאלֹהֵי יַעֲקֹב,
God of Abraham, God of Isaac, and God of Jacob;

ho-Ayl hagodōl hagibōr v'hanōro,   הָאֵל הַגָּדוֹל הַגִּבּוֹר וְהַנּוֹרָא,
Ayl elyōn,   אֵל עֶלְיוֹן,
the great, mighty, and awesome God, the supreme God,

gōmayl chasodim tōvim   גּוֹמֵל חֲסָדִים טוֹבִים
v'kōnay hakōl,   וְקוֹנֵה הַכֹּל,
Who bestows beneficial kindnesses and creates everything,

v'zōchayr chasday ovōs,   וְזוֹכֵר חַסְדֵי אָבוֹת,
Who recalls the kindnesses of the Patriarchs

u-mayvi gō-ayl livnay v'nayhem,   וּמֵבִיא גוֹאֵל לִבְנֵי בְנֵיהֶם,
and brings a Redeemer to their children's children,

l'ma-an sh'mō b'ahavo.   לְמַעַן שְׁמוֹ בְּאַהֲבָה.
for His Name's sake, with love.

FROM ROSH HASHANAH TO YOM KIPPUR ADD:

Zochraynu l'cha-yim,   זָכְרֵנוּ לְחַיִּים,
melech chofaytz bacha-yim,   מֶלֶךְ חָפֵץ בַּחַיִּים,
Remember us for life, O King Who desires life,

v'chosvaynu b'sayfer hacha-yim,   וְכָתְבֵנוּ בְּסֵפֶר הַחַיִּים,
l'ma-ancho Elōhim cha-yim.   לְמַעַנְךָ אֱלֹהִים חַיִּים.
and inscribe us in the Book of Life — for Your sake, O Living God.

Melech ōzayr u-mōshi-a u-mogayn.   מֶלֶךְ עוֹזֵר וּמוֹשִׁיעַ וּמָגֵן.
O King, Helper, Savior, and Shield.

BEND THE KNEES AT Boruch; BOW AT ato; STRAIGHTEN UP AT Adōnoy.

Boruch ato Adōnoy,   בָּרוּךְ אַתָּה יהוה,
mogayn avrohom.   מָגֵן אַבְרָהָם.
Blessed are You, HASHEM, Shield of Abraham.

MINCHAH FOR WEEKDAYS — SHEMONEH ESREI

■ *Second Blessing: God's might as it is manifest in nature and man*

ATO gibōr l'ōlom Adōnoy, אַתָּה גִּבּוֹר לְעוֹלָם אֲדֹנָי,
You are eternally mighty, my Lord,

m'cha-yay maysim ato, rav l'hōshi-a. מְחַיֵּה מֵתִים אַתָּה, רַב לְהוֹשִׁיעַ.
the Resuscitator of the dead are You, abundantly able to save,

---
BETWEEN SHEMINI ATZERES AND PESACH, ADD:

Mashiv horu-ach u-mōrid hageshem. מַשִּׁיב הָרוּחַ וּמוֹרִיד הַגֶּשֶׁם.
Who makes the wind blow and makes the rain descend;

M'chalkayl cha-yim b'chesed, מְכַלְכֵּל חַיִּים בְּחֶסֶד,
Who sustains the living with kindness;

m'cha-yay maysim b'rachamim rabim, מְחַיֵּה מֵתִים בְּרַחֲמִים רַבִּים,
resuscitates the dead with abundant mercy,

sōmaych nōf'lim, v'rōfay chōlim, סוֹמֵךְ נוֹפְלִים, וְרוֹפֵא חוֹלִים,
u-matir asurim, וּמַתִּיר אֲסוּרִים,
supports the fallen, heals the sick, releases the confined,

umka-yaym emunosō li-shaynay ofor. וּמְקַיֵּם אֱמוּנָתוֹ לִישֵׁנֵי עָפָר.
and maintains His faith to those asleep in the dust.

Mi cho-mōcho ba-al g'vurōs, מִי כָמוֹךָ בַּעַל גְּבוּרוֹת,
u-mi dōme loch, וּמִי דּוֹמֶה לָּךְ,
Who is like You, O Master of mighty deeds, and who is comparable to You,

melech maymis umcha-ye מֶלֶךְ מֵמִית וּמְחַיֶּה
u-matzmi-ach y'shu-o. וּמַצְמִיחַ יְשׁוּעָה.
O King Who causes death and restores life and makes salvation sprout!

FROM ROSH HASHANAH TO YOM KIPPUR ADD:

Mi cho-mōcho av horachamim, מִי כָמוֹךָ אַב הָרַחֲמִים,
Who is like You, O Merciful Father,

zōchayr y'tzurov l'cha-yim זוֹכֵר יְצוּרָיו לְחַיִּים
b'rachamim. בְּרַחֲמִים.
Who recalls His creatures mercifully for life!

V'ne-emon ato l'hacha-yōs maysim. וְנֶאֱמָן אַתָּה לְהַחֲיוֹת מֵתִים.
And You are faithful to resuscitate the dead.

Boruch ato Adōnoy, בָּרוּךְ אַתָּה יהוה,
m'cha-yay hamaysim. מְחַיֵּה הַמֵּתִים.
*Blessed are You, H*ASHEM*, Who resuscitates the dead.*

DURING THE CHAZZAN'S REPETITION, KEDUSHAH (P. 362) IS RECITED;
INDIVIDUALS CONTINUE ON P. 363.

■ Third Blessing: Regarding the holiness of God's Name

DURING *KEDUSHAH* STAND WITH FEET TOGETHER AND AVOID ANY INTERRUPTIONS. RISE ON TOES WHEN SAYING Kodōsh, kodōsh, kodōsh; Boruch; AND Yimlōch.

CONGREGATION, THEN *CHAZZAN*:

N'KADAYSH es shimcho bo-ōlom,   נְקַדֵּשׁ אֶת שִׁמְךָ בָּעוֹלָם,
We shall sanctify Your Name in this world,

k'shaym shemakdishim ōsō   כְּשֵׁם שֶׁמַּקְדִּישִׁים אוֹתוֹ
bishmay morōm,   בִּשְׁמֵי מָרוֹם,
just as they sanctify it in heaven above,

Kakosuv al yad n'vi-echo,   כַּכָּתוּב עַל יַד נְבִיאֶךָ,
as it is written by the hand of Your prophet,

v'koro ze el ze v'omar: וְקָרָא זֶה אֶל זֶה וְאָמַר:
"And one [angel] will call another and say:

ALL IN UNISON:

Kodōsh, kodōsh, kodōsh   קָדוֹשׁ קָדוֹשׁ קָדוֹשׁ
Adōnoy Tz'vo-ōs,   יהוה צְבָאוֹת,
'Holy, holy, holy is HASHEM, *Master of Legions,*

m'lō chol ho-oretz k'vōdō.   מְלֹא כָל הָאָרֶץ כְּבוֹדוֹ.
the whole world is filled with His glory.'"

CHAZZAN:

L'u-mosom boruch yōmayru: לְעֻמָּתָם בָּרוּךְ יֹאמֵרוּ:
Those facing them say, "Blessed":

ALL IN UNISON:

Boruch k'vōd Adōnoy, mim'kōmō.   בָּרוּךְ כְּבוֹד יהוה, מִמְּקוֹמוֹ.
"Blessed is the glory of HASHEM *from His place."*

CHAZZAN:

Uvdivray kodsh'cho kosuv laymōr: וּבְדִבְרֵי קָדְשְׁךָ כָּתוּב לֵאמֹר:
And in Your holy Writings the following is written:

ALL IN UNISON:

Yimlōch Adōnoy l'ōlom,   יִמְלֹךְ יהוה לְעוֹלָם,
*"*HASHEM *shall reign forever —*

Elōha-yich tziyōn l'dōr vodōr,   אֱלֹהַיִךְ צִיּוֹן לְדֹר וָדֹר,
hal'luyoh.   הַלְלוּיָהּ.
your God, O Zion — from generation to generation: Praise God!"

CHAZZAN CONCLUDES:

לְדוֹר וָדוֹר נַגִּיד גָּדְלֶךָ וּלְנֵצַח נְצָחִים קְדֻשָּׁתְךָ נַקְדִּישׁ, וְשִׁבְחֲךָ אֱלֹהֵינוּ מִפִּינוּ לֹא יָמוּשׁ לְעוֹלָם וָעֶד, כִּי אֵל מֶלֶךְ גָּדוֹל וְקָדוֹשׁ אָתָּה. בָּרוּךְ אַתָּה יהוה, °הָאֵל הַקָּדוֹשׁ.

° הַמֶּלֶךְ הַקָּדוֹשׁ. — from Rosh Hashanah to Yom Kippur substitute

THE *CHAZZAN* CONTINUES ato chōnayn (P. 363).

MINCHAH FOR WEEKDAYS — SHEMONEH ESREI

ATO kodōsh v'shimcho kodōsh,   אַתָּה קָדוֹשׁ וְשִׁמְךָ קָדוֹשׁ,
You are holy and Your Name is holy,

ukdōshim b'chol yōm   וּקְדוֹשִׁים בְּכָל יוֹם
y'hal'lucho, selo.   יְהַלְלוּךָ סֶּלָה.
and holy ones praise You, every day, forever.

Boruch ato Adōnoy,   בָּרוּךְ אַתָּה יהוה,
°ho-Ayl hakodōsh.   °הָאֵל הַקָּדוֹשׁ.
*Blessed are You, H*ASHEM*, the holy God.*

> **FROM ROSH HASHANAH TO YOM KIPPUR SUBSTITUTE:**
> °hamelech hakodōsh.   °הַמֶּלֶךְ הַקָּדוֹשׁ.
> *the holy King.*

■ **Fourth Blessing: Supplication for the gift of intellect**

ATO chōnayn l'odom da-as,   אַתָּה חוֹנֵן לְאָדָם דַּעַת,
You graciously endow man with wisdom

umlamayd le-enōsh bino.   וּמְלַמֵּד לֶאֱנוֹשׁ בִּינָה.
and teach insight to a frail mortal.

Chonaynu may-it'cho   חָנֵּנוּ מֵאִתְּךָ
day-o bino v'haskayl.   דֵּעָה בִּינָה וְהַשְׂכֵּל.
Endow us graciously from Yourself with wisdom, insight, and discernment.

Boruch ato Adōnoy,   בָּרוּךְ אַתָּה יהוה,
chōnayn hado-as.   חוֹנֵן הַדָּעַת.
*Blessed are You, H*ASHEM*, gracious Giver of wisdom.*

■ **Fifth Blessing: Supplication for Divine assistance in repentance**

HASHIVAYNU ovinu l'sōrosecho,   הֲשִׁיבֵנוּ אָבִינוּ לְתוֹרָתֶךָ,
Bring us back, our Father, to Your Torah,

v'kor'vaynu malkaynu   וְקָרְבֵנוּ מַלְכֵּנוּ
la-avōdosecho,   לַעֲבוֹדָתֶךָ,
and bring us near, our King, to Your service,

v'hachaziraynu bis-shuvo sh'laymo   וְהַחֲזִירֵנוּ בִּתְשׁוּבָה שְׁלֵמָה
l'fonecho.   לְפָנֶיךָ.
and return us in perfect repentance before You.

Boruch ato Adōnoy,   בָּרוּךְ אַתָּה יהוה,
horōtze bis-shuvo.   הָרוֹצֶה בִּתְשׁוּבָה.
*Blessed are You, H*ASHEM*, Who desires repentance.*

■ Sixth Blessing: Supplication for forgiveness

STRIKE THE LEFT SIDE OF THE CHEST WITH THE RIGHT FIST
WHILE RECITING THE WORDS ki chotonu AND ki fo-shonu.

S'LACH lonu ovinu ki chotonu,   סְלַח לָנוּ אָבִינוּ כִּי חָטָאנוּ,
Forgive us, our Father, for we have erred;

m'chal lonu malkaynu ki fo-shonu,   מְחַל לָנוּ מַלְכֵּנוּ כִּי פָשָׁעְנוּ,
pardon us, our King, for we have willfully sinned;

ki mōchayl v'sōlay-ach oto.   כִּי מוֹחֵל וְסוֹלֵחַ אָתָּה.
for You pardon and forgive.

Boruch ato Adōnoy,   בָּרוּךְ אַתָּה יהוה,
  chanun hamarbe lislō-ach.   חַנּוּן הַמַּרְבֶּה לִסְלֹחַ.
Blessed are You, HASHEM, the gracious One Who pardons abundantly.

■ Seventh Blessing: Supplication for personal redemption from the perils and problems of daily life

R'AY v'on-yaynu, v'rivo rivaynu,   רְאֵה בְעָנְיֵנוּ, וְרִיבָה רִיבֵנוּ,
Behold our affliction, take up our grievance,

ug-olaynu m'hayro l'ma-an sh'mecho,   וּגְאָלֵנוּ מְהֵרָה לְמַעַן שְׁמֶךָ,
and redeem us speedily for Your Name's sake,

ki gō-ayl chozok oto.   כִּי גּוֹאֵל חָזָק אָתָּה.
for You are a powerful Redeemer.

Boruch ato Adōnoy, gō-ayl yisro-ayl.   בָּרוּךְ אַתָּה יהוה, גּוֹאֵל יִשְׂרָאֵל.
Blessed are You, HASHEM, Redeemer of Israel.

ON A FAST DAY, THE CHAZZAN RECITES THE FOLLOWING BLESSING AT THIS POINT:

עֲנֵנוּ יהוה עֲנֵנוּ, בְּיוֹם צוֹם תַּעֲנִיתֵנוּ, כִּי בְצָרָה גְדוֹלָה אֲנָחְנוּ. אַל תֵּפֶן אֶל רִשְׁעֵנוּ, וְאַל תַּסְתֵּר פָּנֶיךָ מִמֶּנּוּ, וְאַל תִּתְעַלַּם מִתְּחִנָּתֵנוּ. הֱיֵה נָא קָרוֹב לְשַׁוְעָתֵנוּ, יְהִי נָא חַסְדְּךָ לְנַחֲמֵנוּ, טֶרֶם נִקְרָא אֵלֶיךָ עֲנֵנוּ, כַּדָּבָר שֶׁנֶּאֱמַר: וְהָיָה טֶרֶם יִקְרָאוּ וַאֲנִי אֶעֱנֶה, עוֹד הֵם מְדַבְּרִים וַאֲנִי אֶשְׁמָע. כִּי אַתָּה יהוה הָעוֹנֶה בְּעֵת צָרָה, פּוֹדֶה וּמַצִּיל בְּכָל עֵת צָרָה וְצוּקָה. בָּרוּךְ אַתָּה יהוה, הָעוֹנֶה בְּעֵת צָרָה.

■ Eighth Blessing: Supplication for health and healing of body and soul

R'FO-AYNU Adōnoy, v'nayrofay,   רְפָאֵנוּ יהוה וְנֵרָפֵא,
Heal us, HASHEM — then we will be healed;

hōshi-aynu v'nivoshay-o,   הוֹשִׁיעֵנוּ וְנִוָּשֵׁעָה,
  ki s'hilosaynu oto,   כִּי תְהִלָּתֵנוּ אָתָּה.
save us — then we will be saved, for You are our praise;

v'ha-alay r'fu-o sh'laymo l'chol makōsaynu,	וְהַעֲלֵה רְפוּאָה שְׁלֵמָה לְכָל מַכּוֹתֵינוּ,

and bring complete recovery for all our ailments,

ki Ayl melech rōfay ne-emon v'rachamon oto.	כִּי אֵל מֶלֶךְ רוֹפֵא נֶאֱמָן וְרַחֲמָן אָתָּה.

for You are God, King, the faithful and compassionate Healer.

Boruch ato Adōnoy, rōfay chōlay amō yisro-ayl.	בָּרוּךְ אַתָּה יהוה, רוֹפֵא חוֹלֵי עַמּוֹ יִשְׂרָאֵל.

Blessed are You, HASHEM, Who heals the sick of His people Israel.

■ **Ninth Blessing: Supplication for a year of prosperity**

FOR THE FOLLOWING BLESSING, SUMMER IS DEFINED AS THE PERIOD FROM PESACH THROUGH *MINCHAH* OF DECEMBER 4TH (OR 5TH, IN THE YEAR BEFORE A CIVIL LEAP YEAR); WINTER IS DEFINED AS THE REST OF THE YEAR.

BORAYCH olaynu, Adōnoy Elōhaynu, es ha-shono ha-zōs	**בָּרֵךְ** עָלֵינוּ יהוה אֱלֹהֵינוּ אֶת הַשָּׁנָה הַזֹּאת

Bless on our behalf, O HASHEM, our God, this year

v'es kol minay s'vu-oso l'tōvo,	וְאֶת כָּל מִינֵי תְבוּאָתָהּ לְטוֹבָה,

and all its kinds of crops for the best,

IN SUMMER SAY

v'sayn b'rocho	וְתֵן בְּרָכָה

and give a blessing

IN WINTER SAY

v'sayn tal u-motor livrocho	וְתֵן טַל וּמָטָר לִבְרָכָה

and give dew and rain for a blessing

---

al p'nay ho-adomo,	עַל פְּנֵי הָאֲדָמָה,

on the face of the earth,

v'sab'aynu mituvecho,	וְשַׂבְּעֵנוּ מִטּוּבֶךָ,

and satisfy us from Your bounty,

u-voraych sh'nosaynu kashonim hatōvōs.	וּבָרֵךְ שְׁנָתֵנוּ כַּשָּׁנִים הַטּוֹבוֹת.

and bless our year like the best years.

Boruch ato Adōnoy, m'voraych ha-shonim.	בָּרוּךְ אַתָּה יהוה, מְבָרֵךְ הַשָּׁנִים.

Blessed are You, HASHEM, Who blesses the years.

■ **Tenth Blessing: Supplication for the ingathering of the exiles**

T'KA b'shōfor godōl l'chayrusaynu,	**תְּקַע** בְּשׁוֹפָר גָּדוֹל לְחֵרוּתֵנוּ,

Sound the great shofar for our freedom,

v'so nays l'kabaytz golu-yōsaynu,	וְשָׂא נֵס לְקַבֵּץ גָּלֻיּוֹתֵינוּ,

raise a banner to gather our exiles

v'kab'tzaynu yachad	וְקַבְּצֵנוּ יַחַד
may-arba kanfōs ho-oretz.	מֵאַרְבַּע כַּנְפוֹת הָאָרֶץ.

and gather us together from the four corners of the earth.

Boruch ato Adōnoy,	בָּרוּךְ אַתָּה יהוה,
m'kabaytz nidchay amō yisro-ayl.	מְקַבֵּץ נִדְחֵי עַמּוֹ יִשְׂרָאֵל.

Blessed are You, HASHEM, Who gathers in the dispersed of His people Israel.

■ **Eleventh Blessing**: Supplication for the restoration of justice to the Jewish judiciary

---

HOSHIVO shōf'taynu k'vorishōno,	**הָשִׁיבָה** שׁוֹפְטֵינוּ כְּבָרִאשׁוֹנָה,
v'yō-atzaynu k'vat'chilo,	וְיוֹעֲצֵינוּ כְּבַתְּחִלָּה,

Restore our judges as in earliest times and our counselors as at first;

v'hosayr mimenu yogōn va-anocho,	וְהָסֵר מִמֶּנּוּ יָגוֹן וַאֲנָחָה,

remove from us sorrow and groan;

umlōch olaynu ato, Adōnoy, l'vad'cho	וּמְלוֹךְ עָלֵינוּ אַתָּה יהוה לְבַדְּךָ

and reign over us, You, HASHEM, alone,

b'chesed uvrachamim,	בְּחֶסֶד וּבְרַחֲמִים,

with kindness and with compassion,

v'tzad'kaynu bamishpot.	וְצַדְּקֵנוּ בַּמִּשְׁפָּט.

and justify us through judgment.

Boruch ato Adōnoy,	בָּרוּךְ אַתָּה יהוה,
°melech ōhayv tz'doko u-mishpot.	°מֶלֶךְ אוֹהֵב צְדָקָה וּמִשְׁפָּט.

Blessed are You, HASHEM, the King Who loves righteousness and judgment.

FROM ROSH HASHANAH TO YOM KIPPUR SUBSTITUTE:

°hamelech hamishpot.	°הַמֶּלֶךְ הַמִּשְׁפָּט.

the King of Judgment.

■ **Twelfth Blessing**: Supplication for the eradication of heretic influences that threaten Jewish life

---

V'LAMALSHINIM al t'hi sikvo,	**וְלַמַּלְשִׁינִים** אַל תְּהִי תִקְוָה,

And for the slanderers let there be no hope;

v'chol horish-o k'rega tōvayd,	וְכָל הָרִשְׁעָה כְּרֶגַע תֹּאבֵד,

and may all wickedness perish in an instant;

v'chol ō-y'vecho m'hayro yikoraysu.	וְכָל אוֹיְבֶיךָ מְהֵרָה יִכָּרֵתוּ.

and may all Your enemies be cut down speedily.

V'hazaydim m'hayro s'akayr	וְהַזֵּדִים מְהֵרָה תְעַקֵּר

The wanton sinners — may You speedily uproot,

us-shabayr usmagayr v'sachni-a	וּתְשַׁבֵּר וּתְמַגֵּר וְתַכְנִיעַ

smash, cast down, and humble –

bimhayro v'yomaynu.	בִּמְהֵרָה בְיָמֵינוּ.

speedily in our days.

Boruch ato Adōnoy,	בָּרוּךְ אַתָּה יהוה,
shōvayr ō-y'vim u-machni-a zaydim.	שׁוֹבֵר אֹיְבִים וּמַכְנִיעַ זֵדִים.

Blessed are You, HASHEM, Who breaks enemies and humbles wanton sinners.

■ **Thirteenth Blessing: Supplication on behalf of the righteous and recognition of their significance**

AL hatzadikim v'al hachasidim	**עַל** הַצַּדִּיקִים וְעַל הַחֲסִידִים,

On the righteous, on the devout,

v'al ziknay am'cho bays yisro-ayl,	וְעַל זִקְנֵי עַמְּךָ בֵּית יִשְׂרָאֵל,

on the elders of Your people the Family of Israel,

v'al p'laytas sōf'rayhem,	וְעַל פְּלֵיטַת סוֹפְרֵיהֶם,

on the remnant of their scholars,

v'al gayray hatzedek v'olaynu,	וְעַל גֵּרֵי הַצֶּדֶק וְעָלֵינוּ,

on the righteous converts and on ourselves –

yehemu rachamecho,	יֶהֱמוּ רַחֲמֶיךָ
Adōnoy Elōhaynu,	יהוה אֱלֹהֵינוּ,

may Your compassion be aroused, HASHEM, our God;

v'sayn sochor tōv	וְתֵן שָׂכָר טוֹב

and give goodly reward

l'chol habōt'chim b'shimcho be-emes,	לְכָל הַבּוֹטְחִים בְּשִׁמְךָ בֶּאֱמֶת,

to all who sincerely believe in Your Name;

v'sim chelkaynu i-mohem l'ōlom,	וְשִׂים חֶלְקֵנוּ עִמָּהֶם לְעוֹלָם,

and place our lot with them forever,

v'lō nayvōsh ki v'cho botoch-nu.	וְלֹא נֵבוֹשׁ כִּי בְךָ בָּטָחְנוּ.

and we will not feel ashamed, for we trust in You.

Boruch ato Adōnoy,	בָּרוּךְ אַתָּה יהוה,
mish-on u-mivtoch latzadikim.	מִשְׁעָן וּמִבְטָח לַצַּדִּיקִים.

Blessed are You, HASHEM, Mainstay and Assurance of the righteous.

■ **Fourteenth Blessing: Supplication for the physical and spiritual rebuilding of Jerusalem**

V'LIRUSHOLA-YIM ir'cho	**וְלִירוּשָׁלַיִם** עִירְךָ
b'rachamim toshuv,	בְּרַחֲמִים תָּשׁוּב,

And to Jerusalem, Your city, may You return in compassion,

	שמונה עשרה

v'sishkōn b'sōchoh
  ka-asher dibarto,
וְתִשְׁכּוֹן בְּתוֹכָהּ
  כַּאֲשֶׁר דִּבַּרְתָּ,

and may You rest within it, as You have spoken;

uvnay ōsoh b'korōv b'yomaynu
  binyan ōlom,
וּבְנֵה אוֹתָהּ בְּקָרוֹב בְּיָמֵינוּ
  בִּנְיַן עוֹלָם,

may You rebuild it soon in our days as an eternal structure,

v'chisay dovid
  m'hayro l'sōchoh tochin
וְכִסֵּא דָוִד
  מְהֵרָה לְתוֹכָהּ תָּכִין.

and the throne of David may You speedily establish within it.

°°Boruch ato Adōnoy,
bōnay y'rusholo-yim.
°°בָּרוּךְ אַתָּה יהוה,
בּוֹנֵה יְרוּשָׁלָיִם.

°°*Blessed are You,* HASHEM, *the Builder of Jerusalem.*

°° DURING *MINCHAH* OF TISHAH B'AV SUBSTITUTE THE FOLLOWING CONCLUSION:

NACHAYM Adōnoy Elōhaynu   **נַחֵם** יהוה אֱלֹהֵינוּ

O HASHEM, *our God, console*

es avaylay tziyōn,
  v'es avaylay y'rusholo-yim,
אֶת אֲבֵלֵי צִיּוֹן,
  וְאֶת אֲבֵלֵי יְרוּשָׁלָיִם,

the mourners of Zion and the mourners of Jerusalem,

v'es ho-ir ho-avaylo
  v'hacharayvo v'hab'zuyo
  v'hashōmaymo.
וְאֶת הָעִיר הָאֲבֵלָה
  וְהַחֲרֵבָה וְהַבְּזוּיָה
  וְהַשּׁוֹמֵמָה.

and the city that is mournful, ruined, scorned, and desolate:

Ho-avaylo mib'li vonēho,   הָאֲבֵלָה מִבְּלִי בָנֶיהָ,

mournful without her children,

v'hacharayvo mim'ōnōseho,   וְהַחֲרֵבָה מִמְּעוֹנוֹתֶיהָ,

ruined without her abodes,

v'hab'zuyo mik'vōdoh,   וְהַבְּזוּיָה מִכְּבוֹדָהּ,

scorned without her glory,

v'hashōmaymo may-ayn yōshayv.   וְהַשּׁוֹמֵמָה מֵאֵין יוֹשֵׁב.

and desolate without inhabitant.

V'hi yōsheves v'rōshoh chofuy   וְהִיא יוֹשֶׁבֶת וְרֹאשָׁהּ חָפוּי

She sits with her head covered

k'i-sho akoro shelō yolodo.   כְּאִשָּׁה עֲקָרָה שֶׁלֹּא יָלָדָה.

like a barren woman who never gave birth.

Vai-val'uho ligyōnōs,
  va-yiroshuho ōv'day zorim,
וַיְבַלְּעוּהָ לִגְיוֹנוֹת,
  וַיִּירָשׁוּהָ עוֹבְדֵי זָרִים,

Legions have devoured her, and idolaters have conquered her;

va-yotilu es am'cho yisro-ayl lechorev,	וַיַּטִּילוּ אֶת עַמְּךָ יִשְׂרָאֵל לֶחָרֶב,
they have cast Your people Israel to the sword	
va-yahargu v'zodōn chasiday elyōn.	וַיַּהַרְגוּ בְזָדוֹן חֲסִידֵי עֶלְיוֹן.
and wantonly murdered the devout servants of the Supreme One.	
Al kayn tziyōn b'mar tivke,	עַל כֵּן צִיּוֹן בְּמַר תִּבְכֶּה,
Therefore, Zion weeps bitterly	
virushola-yim titayn kōloh.	וִירוּשָׁלַיִם תִּתֵּן קוֹלָהּ.
and Jerusalem raises her voice.	
Libi libi al chal'layhem.	לִבִּי לִבִּי עַל חַלְלֵיהֶם,
My heart, my heart — [it aches] for their slain!	
May-ai may-ai al chal'layhem,	מֵעַי מֵעַי עַל חַלְלֵיהֶם.
My innards, my innards — [they ache] for their slain!	
Ki ato Adōnoy bo-aysh hitzatoh.	כִּי אַתָּה יהוה בָּאֵשׁ הִצַּתָּהּ.
For You, HASHEM, with fire You consumed her	
u-vo-aysh ato osid livnōsoh,	וּבָאֵשׁ אַתָּה עָתִיד לִבְנוֹתָהּ,
and with fire You will rebuild her,	
ko-omur: va-ani ehye loh, n'um Adōnoy,	כָּאָמוּר: וַאֲנִי אֶהְיֶה לָּהּ, נְאֻם יהוה,
as it is said: "I will be for her, the words of HASHEM,	
chōmas ays soviv	חוֹמַת אֵשׁ סָבִיב
a wall of fire around	
ulchovōd e-yeh v'sōchoh.	וּלְכָבוֹד אֶהְיֶה בְתוֹכָהּ.
and I will be glorious in her midst."	
Boruch ato Adōnoy, m'nachaym tziyōn u-vōnay y'rusholo-yim.	בָּרוּךְ אַתָּה יהוה, מְנַחֵם צִיּוֹן וּבוֹנֵה יְרוּשָׁלָיִם.
Blessed are You, HASHEM, Who consoles Zion and rebuilds Jerusalem.	

■ Fifteenth Blessing: Supplication that the Messiah restore the Davidic reign

ES TZEMACH dovid avd'cho m'hayro satzmi-ach,	**אֶת צֶמַח** דָּוִד עַבְדְּךָ מְהֵרָה תַצְמִיחַ,
The offspring of Your servant David may You speedily cause to flourish,	
v'karnō torum bi-shu-osecho,	וְקַרְנוֹ תָּרוּם בִּישׁוּעָתֶךָ,
and enhance his pride through Your salvation,	
ki lishu-os'cho kivinu kol ha-yom.	כִּי לִישׁוּעָתְךָ קִוִּינוּ כָּל הַיּוֹם.
for we hope for Your salvation all day long.	

Boruch ato Adōnoy,
matzmi-ach keren y'shu-o.

בָּרוּךְ אַתָּה יהוה,
מַצְמִיחַ קֶרֶן יְשׁוּעָה.

*Blessed are You, H*ASHEM*, Who causes the pride of salvation to flourish.*

■ Sixteenth Blessing: Supplication for God's acceptance of our prayer

SH'MA KOLAYNU Adōnoy Elōhaynu,   שְׁמַע קוֹלֵנוּ יהוה אֱלֹהֵינוּ,

*Hear our voice, H*ASHEM*, our God,*

chus v'rachaym olaynu,

חוּס וְרַחֵם עָלֵינוּ,

pity and be compassionate to us,

v'kabayl b'rachamim uvrotzōn
es t'filosaynu,

וְקַבֵּל בְּרַחֲמִים וּבְרָצוֹן
אֶת תְּפִלָּתֵנוּ,

and accept — with compassion and favor — our prayer,

ki Ayl shōmay-a
t'filōs v'sachanunim oto,

כִּי אֵל שׁוֹמֵעַ
תְּפִלּוֹת וְתַחֲנוּנִים אָתָּה.

for God Who hears prayers and supplications are You;

u-mil'fonecho, malkaynu,

וּמִלְּפָנֶיךָ מַלְכֵּנוּ

from before Yourself, our King,

raykom al t'shivaynu,

רֵיקָם אַל תְּשִׁיבֵנוּ,

turn us not away empty-handed,

ON A FAST DAY, AN INDIVIDUAL WHO IS FASTING RECITES THE FOLLOWING.

ANAYNU, Adōnoy, anaynu,   **עֲנֵנוּ** יהוה עֲנֵנוּ,

*Answer us, H*ASHEM*, answer us,*

b'yōm tzōm ta-anisaynu,

בְּיוֹם צוֹם תַּעֲנִיתֵנוּ,

on this day of our fast,

ki v'tzoro g'dōlo anoch'nu,

כִּי בְצָרָה גְדוֹלָה אֲנָחְנוּ.

for we are in great distress;

al tayfen el rish-aynu,

אַל תֵּפֶן אֶל רִשְׁעֵנוּ,

do not pay attention to our wickedness,

v'al tastayr ponecho mimenu,

וְאַל תַּסְתֵּר פָּנֶיךָ מִמֶּנּוּ,

do not hide Your Face from us,

v'al tisalam mit'chinosaynu,

וְאַל תִּתְעַלַּם מִתְּחִנָּתֵנוּ.

and do not ignore our supplication;

he-yay no korōv l'shav-osaynu,

הֱיֵה נָא קָרוֹב לְשַׁוְעָתֵנוּ,

please be near to our outcry;

y'hi no chasd'cho l'nachamaynu,

יְהִי נָא חַסְדְּךָ לְנַחֲמֵנוּ,

please let Your kindness comfort us —

terem nikro aylecho anaynu,	טֶרֶם נִקְרָא אֵלֶיךָ עֲנֵנוּ,
before we call to You answer us,	
kadovor shene-emar:	כַּדָּבָר שֶׁנֶּאֱמַר:
as it is said:	
V'ho-yo terem yikro-u va-ani e-ene,	וְהָיָה טֶרֶם יִקְרָאוּ וַאֲנִי אֶעֱנֶה,
"And it will be that before they call, I will answer;	
ōd haym m'dab'rim va-ani eshmo.	עוֹד הֵם מְדַבְּרִים וַאֲנִי אֶשְׁמָע.
while they yet speak, I will hear."	
Ki ato, Adōnoy, ho-ōne b'ays tzoro,	כִּי אַתָּה יהוה הָעוֹנֶה בְּעֵת צָרָה,
For You, HASHEM, are the One Who responds in time of distress,	
pōde u-matzil	פּוֹדֶה וּמַצִּיל
b'chol ays tzoro v'tzuko.	בְּכָל עֵת צָרָה וְצוּקָה.
Who redeems and rescues in every time of distress and woe.	
ki ato shōmay-a t'filas	כִּי אַתָּה שׁוֹמֵעַ תְּפִלַּת
am'cho yisro-ayl b'rachamim.	עַמְּךָ יִשְׂרָאֵל בְּרַחֲמִים.
For You hear the prayer of Your people Israel with compassion.	
Boruch ato Adōnoy,	בָּרוּךְ אַתָּה יהוה,
shōmay-a t'filo.	שׁוֹמֵעַ תְּפִלָּה.
Blessed are You, HASHEM, Who hears prayer.	

■ **Seventeenth Blessing: Prayer for restoration of the Temple service**

R'TZAY, Adōnoy Elōhaynu	**רְצֵה** יהוה אֱלֹהֵינוּ
Be favorable, HASHEM, our God,	
b'am'cho yisro-ayl u-visfilosom,	בְּעַמְּךָ יִשְׂרָאֵל וּבִתְפִלָּתָם,
toward Your people Israel and their prayer	
v'hoshayv es ho-avōdo	וְהָשֵׁב אֶת הָעֲבוֹדָה
and restore the service	
lidvir bay-secho.	לִדְבִיר בֵּיתֶךָ.
to the Holy of Holies of Your Temple.	
V'i-shay yisro-ayl, usfilosom	וְאִשֵּׁי יִשְׂרָאֵל וּתְפִלָּתָם
The fire-offerings of Israel and their prayer	
b'ahavo s'kabayl b'rotzōn,	בְּאַהֲבָה תְקַבֵּל בְּרָצוֹן,
accept with love and favor,	
us-hi l'rotzōn tomid	וּתְהִי לְרָצוֹן תָּמִיד
avōdas yisro-ayl amecho.	עֲבוֹדַת יִשְׂרָאֵל עַמֶּךָ.
and may the service of Your people Israel always be favorable to You.	

- Yaaleh Veyavo: We petition God to have compassion on Israel and Jerusalem, and to reinstate the Temple service, to enable us to bring the appropriate offerings for the particular occasion.

ON *ROSH CHODESH* AND *CHOL HAMOED* RECITE THE FOLLOWING:

ELOHAYNU Vaylōhay avōsaynu, אֱלֹהֵינוּ וֵאלֹהֵי אֲבוֹתֵינוּ,
Our God and the God of our forefathers,

ya-a-le v'yovō v'yagi-a v'yayro-e יַעֲלֶה, וְיָבֹא, וְיַגִּיעַ, וְיֵרָאֶה,
may there rise, come, reach, be noted,

v'yayro-tze v'yi-shoma v'yipokayd וְיֵרָצֶה, וְיִשָּׁמַע, וְיִפָּקֵד,
be favored, be heard, be considered,

v'yizochayr zichrōnaynu u-fikdōnaynu, וְיִזָּכֵר זִכְרוֹנֵנוּ וּפִקְדוֹנֵנוּ,
and be remembered — the remembrance and consideration of ourselves;

v'zichrōn avōsaynu, וְזִכְרוֹן אֲבוֹתֵינוּ,
the remembrance of our forefathers;

v'zichrōn moshi-ach וְזִכְרוֹן מָשִׁיחַ
ben dovid avdecho, בֶּן דָּוִד עַבְדֶּךָ,
the remembrance of Messiah, son of David, Your servant;

v'zichrōn y'rushola-yim וְזִכְרוֹן יְרוּשָׁלַיִם
ir kod-shecho, עִיר קָדְשֶׁךָ,
the remembrance of Jerusalem, Your Holy City;

v'zichrōn kol am'cho bays yisro-ayl וְזִכְרוֹן כָּל עַמְּךָ בֵּית יִשְׂרָאֵל
l'fonecho, לְפָנֶיךָ,
and the remembrance of Your entire people the Family of Israel — before You

lif-layto l'tōvo לִפְלֵיטָה לְטוֹבָה
for deliverance, for goodness,

l'chayn ul-chesed ul-rachamim, לְחֵן וּלְחֶסֶד וּלְרַחֲמִים,
for grace, for kindness, and for compassion,

l'cha-yim ul-sholōm לְחַיִּים וּלְשָׁלוֹם
for life, and for peace

——— ON ROSH CHODESH ———
b'yōm rōsh ha-chōdesh ha-ze. בְּיוֹם רֹאשׁ הַחֹדֶשׁ הַזֶּה.
on this day of Rosh Chodesh

——— ON PESACH ———
b'yōm chag ha-matzōs ha-ze. בְּיוֹם חַג הַמַּצּוֹת הַזֶּה.
on this day of the Festival of Matzos.

——— ON SUCCOS ———
b'yōm chag ha-sukōs ha-ze. בְּיוֹם חַג הַסֻּכּוֹת הַזֶּה.
on this day of the Succos Festival.

MINCHAH FOR WEEKDAYS — SHEMONEH ESREI

DURING THE *CHAZZAN'S* REPETITION, THE CONGREGATION RESPONDS AMEN AS INDICATED.

Zoch-raynu Adōnoy Elōhaynu   זָכְרֵנוּ יהוה אֱלֹהֵינוּ
bō l'tōvo (Omayn),   בּוֹ לְטוֹבָה (אָמֵן),
Remember us on it, HASHEM, our God, for goodness (Amen),

u-fokdaynu vō livrocho (Omayn),   וּפָקְדֵנוּ בוֹ לִבְרָכָה (אָמֵן),
consider us on it for blessing (Amen),

v'hōshi-aynu vō l'cha-yim (Omayn).   וְהוֹשִׁיעֵנוּ בוֹ לְחַיִּים (אָמֵן).
and help us on it for life (Amen).

U-vidvar y'shu-o v'rachamim,   וּבִדְבַר יְשׁוּעָה וְרַחֲמִים,
In the matter of salvation and compassion,

chus v'chonaynu   חוּס וְחָנֵּנוּ
v'rachaym olaynu v'hōshi-aynu,   וְרַחֵם עָלֵינוּ וְהוֹשִׁיעֵנוּ,
pity, be gracious and compassionate with us and help us,

ki aylecho aynaynu,   כִּי אֵלֶיךָ עֵינֵינוּ,
for our eyes are turned to You,

ki Ayl melech   כִּי אֵל מֶלֶךְ
chanun v'rachum oto.   חַנּוּן וְרַחוּם אָתָּה.
because You are God, the gracious and compassionate King.

V'SECHEZENO aynaynu   **וְתֶחֱזֶינָה** עֵינֵינוּ
b'shuv'cho l'tziyōn b'rachamim.   בְּשׁוּבְךָ לְצִיּוֹן בְּרַחֲמִים.
May our eyes behold Your return to Zion in compassion.

Boruch ato Adōnoy,   בָּרוּךְ אַתָּה יהוה,
hamachazir sh'chinosō l'tziyōn.   הַמַּחֲזִיר שְׁכִינָתוֹ לְצִיּוֹן.
Blessed are You, HASHEM, Who restores His Presence unto Zion.

■ Eighteenth Blessing: Acknowledgment of our debt of gratitude

---

BOW AT Mōdim anachnu loch; STRAIGHTEN UP AT Adōnoy.
IN HIS REPETITION THE *CHAZZAN* SHOULD RECITE THE ENTIRE *MODIM* ALOUD,
WHILE THE CONGREGATION RECITES *MODIM OF THE RABBIS* (P. 374) SOFTLY.

MŌDIM anachnu loch,   **מוֹדִים** אֲנַחְנוּ לָךְ,
We gratefully thank You,

sho-ato hu Adōnoy Elōhaynu   שָׁאַתָּה הוּא יהוה אֱלֹהֵינוּ
for it is You Who are HASHEM, our God,

Vaylōhay avōsaynu   וֵאלֹהֵי אֲבוֹתֵינוּ
and the God of our forefathers

l'ōlom vo-ed,   לְעוֹלָם וָעֶד,
forever and ever;

tzur cha-yaynu, mogayn yish-aynu ato hu l'dōr vodōr. *Rock of our lives, Shield of our salvation are You from generation to generation.*	צוּר חַיֵּינוּ, מָגֵן יִשְׁעֵנוּ אַתָּה הוּא לְדוֹר וָדוֹר.
Nōde l'cho unsapayr t'hilosecho *We shall thank You and relate Your praise —*	נוֹדֶה לְּךָ וּנְסַפֵּר תְּהִלָּתֶךָ
al cha-yaynu ham'surim b'yodecho, *for our lives, which are committed to Your power,*	עַל חַיֵּינוּ הַמְּסוּרִים בְּיָדֶךָ,
v'al nishmōsaynu hap'kudōs loch, *and for our souls that are entrusted to You,*	וְעַל נִשְׁמוֹתֵינוּ הַפְּקוּדוֹת לָךְ,
v'al nisecho sheb'chol yōm i-monu, *and for Your miracles that are with us every day,*	וְעַל נִסֶּיךָ שֶׁבְּכָל יוֹם עִמָּנוּ,
v'al nifl'ōsecho v'tōvōsecho sheb'chol ays, *and for Your wonders and favors in every season —*	וְעַל נִפְלְאוֹתֶיךָ וְטוֹבוֹתֶיךָ שֶׁבְּכָל עֵת,
erev vovōker v'tzohoro-yim. *evening, morning, and afternoon.*	עֶרֶב וָבֹקֶר וְצָהֳרָיִם.
Hatōv ki lō cholu rachamecho, *The Beneficent One, for Your compassions were never exhausted,*	הַטּוֹב כִּי לֹא כָלוּ רַחֲמֶיךָ,
v'ham'rachaym ki lō samu chasodecho, *and the Compassionate One, for Your kindnesses never ended —*	וְהַמְרַחֵם כִּי לֹא תַמּוּ חֲסָדֶיךָ,
may-ōlom kivinu loch. *always have we put our hope in You.*	מֵעוֹלָם קִוִּינוּ לָךְ.

MODIM OF THE RABBIS

RECITED SOFTLY BY CONGREGATION WHILE *CHAZZAN* RECITES THE REGULAR MODIM ALOUD

MŌDIM anachnu loch, *We gratefully thank You,*	**מוֹדִים** אֲנַחְנוּ לָךְ,
sho-ato hu Adōnoy Elōhaynu Vaylōhay avōsaynu, *for it is You Who are H*ASHEM*, our God and the God of our forefathers,*	שָׁאַתָּה הוּא יהוה אֱלֹהֵינוּ וֵאלֹהֵי אֲבוֹתֵינוּ,
Elōhay chol bosor, *the God of all flesh,*	אֱלֹהֵי כָל בָּשָׂר,
yōtz'raynu, yōtzayr b'rayshis. *our Molder, the Molder of the universe.*	יוֹצְרֵנוּ, יוֹצֵר בְּרֵאשִׁית.
B'rochōs v'hōdo-ōs l'shimcho hagodōl v'hakodōsh, *Blessings and thanks are due Your great and holy Name*	בְּרָכוֹת וְהוֹדָאוֹת לְשִׁמְךָ הַגָּדוֹל וְהַקָּדוֹשׁ,
al sheheche-yisonu v'ki-yamtonu. *for You have given us life and sustained us.*	עַל שֶׁהֶחֱיִיתָנוּ וְקִיַּמְתָּנוּ.

SHEMONEH ESREI

Kayn t'cha-yaynu uska-y'maynu,   כֵּן תְּחַיֵּנוּ וּתְקַיְּמֵנוּ,
So may You continue to give us life and sustain us

v'se-esōf golu-yōsaynu   וְתֶאֱסוֹף גָּלֻיּוֹתֵינוּ
l'chatzrōs kod-shecho,   לְחַצְרוֹת קָדְשֶׁךָ,
and gather our exiles to the Courtyards of Your Sanctuary,

lishmōr chukecho v'la-asōs r'tzōnecho,   לִשְׁמוֹר חֻקֶּיךָ וְלַעֲשׂוֹת רְצוֹנֶךָ,
ul-ovd'cho b'layvov sholaym,   וּלְעָבְדְּךָ בְּלֵבָב שָׁלֵם,
to observe Your decrees, to do Your will and to serve You wholeheartedly.

al she-anachnu mōdim loch.   עַל שֶׁאֲנַחְנוּ מוֹדִים לָךְ.
[We thank You] for inspiring us to thank You.

Boruch Ayl hahōdo-ōs.   בָּרוּךְ אֵל הַהוֹדָאוֹת.
Blessed is the God of thanksgivings.

ON CHANUKAH AND PURIM CONTINUE BELOW. ON ALL OTHER DAYS TURN TO P. 377.

ON CHANUKAH AND PURIM ADD THE FOLLOWING:

AL hanisim, v'al hapurkon,   **עַל** הַנִּסִּים, וְעַל הַפֻּרְקָן,
For the miracles, and for the salvation,

v'al hag'vurōs, v'al hat'shu-ōs,   וְעַל הַגְּבוּרוֹת, וְעַל הַתְּשׁוּעוֹת,
v'al hamilchomōs,   וְעַל הַמִּלְחָמוֹת,
and for the mighty deeds, and for the victories, and for the battles

she-osiso la-avōsaynu   שֶׁעָשִׂיתָ לַאֲבוֹתֵינוּ
which You performed for our forefathers

ba-yomim hohaym baz'man ha-ze.   בַּיָּמִים הָהֵם בַּזְּמַן הַזֶּה.
in those days, at this time.

ON CHANUKAH CONTINUE HERE; ON PURIM TURN TO P. 377.

BIMAY matisyohu ben yōchonon   **בִּימֵי** מַתִּתְיָהוּ בֶּן יוֹחָנָן
In the days of Mattisyahu, the son of Yochanan,

kōhayn godōl chashmōno-i u-vonov,   כֹּהֵן גָּדוֹל חַשְׁמוֹנָאִי וּבָנָיו,
the High Priest, the Hasmonean, and his sons —

k'she-om'do malchus yovon   כְּשֶׁעָמְדָה מַלְכוּת יָוָן
hor'sho-o al am'cho yisro-ayl,   הָרְשָׁעָה עַל עַמְּךָ יִשְׂרָאֵל,
when the wicked Greek kingdom rose up against Your people Israel

l'hashkichom tōrosecho,   לְהַשְׁכִּיחָם תּוֹרָתֶךָ,
to make them forget Your Torah

ulha-avirom maychukay r'tzōnecho.   וּלְהַעֲבִירָם מֵחֻקֵּי רְצוֹנֶךָ.
and compel them to stray from the statutes of Your will.

V'ato b'rachamecho horabim,   וְאַתָּה בְּרַחֲמֶיךָ הָרַבִּים,
But You, in Your abundant mercy,

omadto lohem b'ays tzorosom,	עָמַדְתָּ לָהֶם בְּעֵת צָרָתָם,

stood up for them in the time of their distress;

ravto es rivom, danto es dinom,	רַבְתָּ אֶת רִיבָם, דַּנְתָּ אֶת דִּינָם,

You took up their grievance, You judged their claim,

nokamto es nikmosom.	נָקַמְתָּ אֶת נִקְמָתָם.

and You avenged their wrong.

Mosarto gibōrim b'yad chaloshim,	מָסַרְתָּ גִבּוֹרִים בְּיַד חַלָּשִׁים,

You delivered the strong into the hand of the weak,

v'rabim b'yad m'atim,	וְרַבִּים בְּיַד מְעַטִּים,

the many into the hand of the few,

utmay-im b'yad t'hōrim,	וּטְמֵאִים בְּיַד טְהוֹרִים,
ursho-im b'yad tzadikim	וּרְשָׁעִים בְּיַד צַדִּיקִים,

the impure into the hand of the pure, the wicked into the hand of the righteous,

v'zaydim b'yad ōs'kay sōrosecho.	וְזֵדִים בְּיַד עוֹסְקֵי תוֹרָתֶךָ.

and the wanton into the hand of the diligent students of Your Torah.

Ulcho osiso	וּלְךָ עָשִׂיתָ
shaym godōl v'kodōsh b'ōlomecho,	שֵׁם גָּדוֹל וְקָדוֹשׁ בְּעוֹלָמֶךָ,

And for Yourself You made a great and holy Name in Your world,

ul-am'cho yisro-ayl	וּלְעַמְּךָ יִשְׂרָאֵל

and for Your people Israel

osiso t'shu-o g'dōlo u-furkon	עָשִׂיתָ תְּשׁוּעָה גְדוֹלָה וּפֻרְקָן
k'ha-yōm ha-ze.	כְּהַיּוֹם הַזֶּה.

You performed a great victory and salvation as this very day.

V'achar kayn bo-u vonecho	וְאַחַר כֵּן בָּאוּ בָנֶיךָ
lidvir bay-secho,	לִדְבִיר בֵּיתֶךָ,

Thereafter, Your children came to the Holy of Holies of Your House,

u-finu es haycholecho,	וּפִנּוּ אֶת הֵיכָלֶךָ,
v'tiharu es mikdoshecho,	וְטִהֲרוּ אֶת מִקְדָּשֶׁךָ,

they cleansed Your Temple, they purified the site of Your Holiness;

v'hidliku nayrōs	וְהִדְלִיקוּ נֵרוֹת
b'chatzrōs kod-shecho,	בְּחַצְרוֹת קָדְשֶׁךָ,

and they kindled lights in the Courtyards of Your Sanctuary;

v'kov'u sh'mōnas y'may chanuko aylu,	וְקָבְעוּ שְׁמוֹנַת יְמֵי חֲנֻכָּה אֵלּוּ,

and they established these eight days of Chanukah

l'hōdōs ulhalayl	לְהוֹדוֹת וּלְהַלֵּל
l'shimcho hagodōl.	לְשִׁמְךָ הַגָּדוֹל.

to express thanks and praise to Your great Name.

CONTINUE ON P. 377

ON PURIM CONTINUE HERE:

BIMAY mord'chai v'estayr
b'shushan habiro,   בִּימֵי מָרְדְּכַי וְאֶסְתֵּר בְּשׁוּשַׁן הַבִּירָה,
In the days of Mordechai and Esther, in Shushan, the capital,

k'she-omad alayhem homon horosho,   כְּשֶׁעָמַד עֲלֵיהֶם הָמָן הָרָשָׁע,
when Haman, the wicked, rose up against them

bikaysh l'hashmid laharōg ul-abayd
es kol ha-y'hudim,   בִּקֵּשׁ לְהַשְׁמִיד לַהֲרֹג וּלְאַבֵּד אֶת כָּל הַיְּהוּדִים,
and sought to destroy, to slay, and to exterminate all the Jews,

mina-ar v'ad zokayn, taf v'noshim
b'yōm e-chod,   מִנַּעַר וְעַד זָקֵן, טַף וְנָשִׁים בְּיוֹם אֶחָד,
young and old, infants and women, on the same day,

bishlōsho osor
l'chōdesh sh'naym osor,
hu chōdesh ador,   בִּשְׁלוֹשָׁה עָשָׂר לְחֹדֶשׁ שְׁנֵים עָשָׂר, הוּא חֹדֶשׁ אֲדָר,
on the thirteenth of the twelfth month which is the month of Adar,

ushlolom lovōz.   וּשְׁלָלָם לָבוֹז.
and to plunder their possessions.

V'ato b'rachamecho horabim   וְאַתָּה בְּרַחֲמֶיךָ הָרַבִּים
But You, in Your abundant mercy,

hayfarto es atzosō,
v'kilkalto es machashavtō,   הֵפַרְתָּ אֶת עֲצָתוֹ, וְקִלְקַלְתָּ אֶת מַחֲשַׁבְתּוֹ,
nullified his counsel and frustrated his intention

vaha-shayvōso lō g'mulō b'rōshō,   וַהֲשֵׁבְוֹתָ לּוֹ גְּמוּלוֹ בְּרֹאשׁוֹ,
and caused his design to return upon his own head.

V'solu ōsō v'es bonov al ho-aytz.   וְתָלוּ אוֹתוֹ וְאֶת בָּנָיו עַל הָעֵץ.
And they hanged him and his sons on the gallows.

ON ALL DAYS CONTINUE HERE:

V'AL kulom yisborach v'yisrōmam
shimcho, malkaynu   וְעַל כֻּלָּם יִתְבָּרַךְ וְיִתְרוֹמַם שִׁמְךָ מַלְכֵּנוּ
For all these, may Your Name be blessed and exalted, our King,

tomid l'ōlom vo-ed.   תָּמִיד לְעוֹלָם וָעֶד.
continually forever and ever.

FROM ROSH HASHANAH TO YOM KIPPUR ADD:

Uchsōv l'cha-yim tōvim
kol b'nay v'risecho.   וּכְתוֹב לְחַיִּים טוֹבִים כָּל בְּנֵי בְרִיתֶךָ.
And inscribe all the children of Your covenant for a good life.

וְכֹל הַחַיִּים יוֹדוּךָ סֶּלָה,   V'chōl hacha-yim yōducho selo,
Everything alive will gratefully acknowledge You, Selah!

וִיהַלְלוּ אֶת שִׁמְךָ בֶּאֱמֶת,   vihal'lu es shimcho be-emes,
and praise Your Name sincerely,

הָאֵל יְשׁוּעָתֵנוּ וְעֶזְרָתֵנוּ סֶלָה.   ho-Ayl y'shu-osaynu v'ezrosaynu selo.
O God of our salvation and help, Selah!

BEND THE KNEES AT Boruch; BOW AT ato; STRAIGHTEN UP AT Adōnoy.

בָּרוּךְ אַתָּה יהוה,   Boruch ato Adōnoy,
Blessed are You, HASHEM,

הַטּוֹב שִׁמְךָ וּלְךָ נָאֶה לְהוֹדוֹת.   hatōv shimcho ulcho no-e l'hōdōs.
Your Name is "The Beneficent One" and to You it is fitting to give thanks.

■ Nineteenth Blessing: Prayer for peace and harmony amongst the Jewish people

---

ON PUBLIC FAST DAYS THE *CHAZZAN* RECITES THE PRIESTLY BLESSING DURING HIS REPETITION, EXCEPT IN A HOUSE OF MOURNING.

אֱלֹהֵינוּ, וֵאלֹהֵי אֲבוֹתֵינוּ, בָּרְכֵנוּ בַּבְּרָכָה הַמְשֻׁלֶּשֶׁת בַּתּוֹרָה הַכְּתוּבָה עַל יְדֵי מֹשֶׁה עַבְדֶּךָ, הָאֲמוּרָה מִפִּי אַהֲרֹן וּבָנָיו, כֹּהֲנִים עַם קְדוֹשֶׁךָ, כָּאָמוּר:

יְבָרֶכְךָ יהוה, וְיִשְׁמְרֶךָ.   — Cong.) כֵּן יְהִי רָצוֹן — kayn y'hi rotzōn)

יָאֵר יהוה פָּנָיו אֵלֶיךָ וִיחֻנֶּךָּ.   — Cong.) כֵּן יְהִי רָצוֹן — kayn y'hi rotzōn)

יִשָּׂא יהוה פָּנָיו אֵלֶיךָ וְיָשֵׂם לְךָ שָׁלוֹם.
     — Cong.) כֵּן יְהִי רָצוֹן — kayn y'hi rotzōn)

ON PUBLIC FAST DAYS Sim sholōm (P. 379) IS RECITED INSTEAD OF Sholōm rov.

שָׁלוֹם רָב עַל יִשְׂרָאֵל   **SHOLŌM ROV** al yisro-ayl
עַמְּךָ תָּשִׂים לְעוֹלָם,   am'cho tosim l'ōlom,
Establish abundant peace upon Your people Israel forever,

כִּי אַתָּה הוּא מֶלֶךְ   ki ato hu melech,
אָדוֹן לְכָל הַשָּׁלוֹם.   odōn l'chol ha-sholōm.
for You are King, Master of all peace.

וְטוֹב בְּעֵינֶיךָ לְבָרֵךְ   V'tōv b'aynecho l'voraych
אֶת עַמְּךָ יִשְׂרָאֵל,   es am'cho yisro-ayl,
And may it be good in Your eyes to bless Your people Israel

בְּכָל עֵת וּבְכָל שָׁעָה   b'chol ays uvchol sho-o
בִּשְׁלוֹמֶךָ.   bish-lōmecho.
at every time and at every hour, with Your peace.

MINCHAH FOR WEEKDAYS — SHEMONEH ESREI

ON PUBLIC FAST DAYS SUBSTITUTE:

SIM SHOLŌM tōvo uvrocho, chayn vochesed v'rachamim — שִׂים שָׁלוֹם, טוֹבָה, וּבְרָכָה, חֵן וָחֶסֶד וְרַחֲמִים

Establish peace, goodness, blessing, graciousness, kindness, and compassion

olaynu v'al kol yisro-ayl amecho. — עָלֵינוּ וְעַל כָּל יִשְׂרָאֵל עַמֶּךָ.

upon us and upon all of Your people Israel.

Bor'chaynu, ovinu, kulonu k'e-chod b'ōr ponecho, — בָּרְכֵנוּ, אָבִינוּ, כֻּלָּנוּ כְּאֶחָד בְּאוֹר פָּנֶיךָ,

Bless us, our Father, all of us as one, with the light of Your countenance,

ki v'ōr ponecho nosato lonu, Adōnoy Elōhaynu, — כִּי בְאוֹר פָּנֶיךָ נָתַתָּ לָּנוּ, יהוה אֱלֹהֵינוּ,

for with the light of Your countenance, You, HASHEM, our God, gave us

tōras cha-yim v'ahavas chesed, — תּוֹרַת חַיִּים וְאַהֲבַת חֶסֶד,

the Torah of life and a love of kindness,

utz-doko uvrocho v'rachamim v'cha-yim v'sholōm. — וּצְדָקָה וּבְרָכָה וְרַחֲמִים וְחַיִּים וְשָׁלוֹם.

righteousness, blessing, compassion, life, and peace.

V'tōv b'aynecho l'voraych es am'cho yisro-ayl, — וְטוֹב בְּעֵינֶיךָ לְבָרֵךְ אֶת עַמְּךָ יִשְׂרָאֵל,

And may it be good in Your eyes to bless Your people Israel

b'chol ays uvchol sho-o bishlōmecho. — בְּכָל עֵת וּבְכָל שָׁעָה בִּשְׁלוֹמֶךָ.

at every time and at every hour, with Your peace.

°Boruch ato Adōnoy, ham'voraych es amō yisro-ayl ba-sholōm. — בָּרוּךְ אַתָּה יהוה, הַמְבָרֵךְ אֶת עַמּוֹ יִשְׂרָאֵל בַּשָּׁלוֹם.

°*Blessed are You, HASHEM, Who blesses His people Israel with peace.*

° FROM ROSH HASHANAH TO YOM KIPPUR SUBSTITUTE THE FOLLOWING:

B'sayfer cha-yim b'rocho v'sholōm, u-farnoso tōvo, — בְּסֵפֶר חַיִּים בְּרָכָה וְשָׁלוֹם, וּפַרְנָסָה טוֹבָה,

In the book of life, blessing, and peace, and good livelihood,

nizochayr v'nikosayv l'fonecho, — נִזָּכֵר וְנִכָּתֵב לְפָנֶיךָ,

may we be remembered and inscribed before You —

anachnu v'chol am'cho bays yisro-ayl, — אֲנַחְנוּ וְכָל עַמְּךָ בֵּית יִשְׂרָאֵל,

we and Your entire people the Family of Israel —

l'cha-yim tōvim ulsholōm. — לְחַיִּים טוֹבִים וּלְשָׁלוֹם.

for a good life and for peace.

Boruch ato Adōnoy, ō-se ha-sholōm. — בָּרוּךְ אַתָּה יהוה, עוֹשֶׂה הַשָּׁלוֹם.

Blessed are You, HASHEM, Who makes the peace.

THE *CHAZZAN'S* REPETITION ENDS HERE. INDIVIDUALS CONTINUE.

Yih-yu l'rotzōn imray fi / יִהְיוּ לְרָצוֹן אִמְרֵי פִי
v'hegyōn libi l'fonecho, / וְהֶגְיוֹן לִבִּי לְפָנֶיךָ,
May the expressions of my mouth and the thoughts of my heart find favor before You,
Adōnoy tzuri v'gō-ali. / יהוה צוּרִי וְגוֹאֲלִי.
Hashem, my Rock and my Redeemer.

▪ I pray that, having completed my *Amidah*, I have been changed in a positive way, especially with regard to my interpersonal relationships.

ELŌHAI, n'tzōr l'shōni mayro, / **אֱלֹהַי,** נְצוֹר לְשׁוֹנִי מֵרָע,
My God, guard my tongue from evil
usfosai midabayr mirmo, / וּשְׂפָתַי מִדַּבֵּר מִרְמָה,
and my lips from speaking deceitfully.
V'limkal'lai nafshi sidōm, / וְלִמְקַלְלַי נַפְשִׁי תִדּוֹם,
To those who curse me, let my soul be silent;
v'nafshi ke-ofor lakōl tih-ye. / וְנַפְשִׁי כֶּעָפָר לַכֹּל תִּהְיֶה.
and let my soul be like dust to everyone.
P'sach libi b'sōrosecho, / פְּתַח לִבִּי בְּתוֹרָתֶךָ,
uvmitzvōsecho tirdōf nafshi. / וּבְמִצְוֹתֶיךָ תִּרְדּוֹף נַפְשִׁי.
Open my heart to Your Torah, then my soul will pursue Your commandments.
V'chol hachōsh'vim olai ro-o, / וְכָל הַחוֹשְׁבִים עָלַי רָעָה,
As for all those who design evil against me,
m'hayro hofayr atzosom / מְהֵרָה הָפֵר עֲצָתָם
v'kalkayl machashavtom. / וְקַלְקֵל מַחֲשַׁבְתָּם.
speedily nullify their counsel and disrupt their design.
Asay l'ma-an sh'mecho, / עֲשֵׂה לְמַעַן שְׁמֶךָ,
asay l'ma-an y'minecho, / עֲשֵׂה לְמַעַן יְמִינֶךָ,
Act for Your Name's sake; act for Your right hand's sake;
asay l'ma-an k'dushosecho, / עֲשֵׂה לְמַעַן קְדֻשָּׁתֶךָ,
asay l'ma-an tōrosecho. / עֲשֵׂה לְמַעַן תּוֹרָתֶךָ.
act for Your sanctity's sake; act for Your Torah's sake.
L'ma-an yaychol'tzun y'didecho, / לְמַעַן יֵחָלְצוּן יְדִידֶיךָ,
That Your beloved ones may be given rest;
hōshi-o y'min'cho va-anayni. / הוֹשִׁיעָה יְמִינְךָ וַעֲנֵנִי.
let Your right hand save, and respond to me.
Yih-yu l'rotzōn imray fi / יִהְיוּ לְרָצוֹן אִמְרֵי פִי
v'hegyōn libi l'fonecho, / וְהֶגְיוֹן לִבִּי לְפָנֶיךָ,
May the expressions of my mouth and the thoughts of my heart find favor before You,

MINCHAH FOR WEEKDAYS — SHEMONEH ESREI

Adōnoy tzuri v'gō-ali.   יהוה צוּרִי וְגֹאֲלִי.
HASHEM, my Rock and my Redeemer.

BOW. TAKE THREE STEPS BACK. BOW LEFT AND SAY:

Ō-se sholōm bimrōmov,   עֹשֶׂה שָׁלוֹם בִּמְרוֹמָיו,
He Who makes peace in His heights,

BOW RIGHT AND SAY:

hu ya-a-se sholōm olaynu,   הוּא יַעֲשֶׂה שָׁלוֹם עָלֵינוּ,
may He make peace upon us,

BOW FORWARD AND SAY:

v'al kol yisro-ayl. V'imru: Omayn.   וְעַל כָּל יִשְׂרָאֵל. וְאִמְרוּ: אָמֵן.
and upon all Israel. Now respond: Amen.

Y'HI ROTZŌN mil'fonecho,   **יְהִי רָצוֹן** מִלְּפָנֶיךָ
May it be Your will,

Adōnoy Elōhaynu   יהוה אֱלֹהֵינוּ
    Vaylōhay avōsaynu,   וֵאלֹהֵי אֲבוֹתֵינוּ,
HASHEM, our God and the God of our forefathers,

she-yibo-ne bays hamikdosh   שֶׁיִּבָּנֶה בֵּית הַמִּקְדָּשׁ
    bimhayro v'yomaynu,   בִּמְהֵרָה בְיָמֵינוּ,
that the Holy Temple be rebuilt, speedily in our days;

v'sayn chelkaynu b'sōrosecho,   וְתֵן חֶלְקֵנוּ בְּתוֹרָתֶךָ,
and grant us our share in Your Torah;

v'shom na-avod-cho b'yiro,   וְשָׁם נַעֲבָדְךָ בְּיִרְאָה,
and may we serve You there with reverence,

kimay ōlom   כִּימֵי עוֹלָם
    uchshonim kadmōniyōs.   וּכְשָׁנִים קַדְמוֹנִיּוֹת.
as in days of old and in former years.

V'or'vo Ladōnoy   וְעָרְבָה לַיהוה
    minchas y'hudo virusholo-yim   מִנְחַת יְהוּדָה וִירוּשָׁלָיִם,
Then the offering of Judah and Jerusalem will be pleasing to HASHEM,

kimay ōlom   כִּימֵי עוֹלָם
    uchshonim kadmōniyōs.   וּכְשָׁנִים קַדְמוֹנִיּוֹת.
as in days of old and in former years.

THE INDIVIDUAL'S RECITATION OF *SHEMONEH ESREI* ENDS HERE.
REMAIN STANDING IN PLACE UNTIL THE *CHAZZAN* REACHES *KEDUSHAH* —
OR AT LEAST FOR A FEW MOMENTS — THEN TAKE THREE STEPS FORWARD.
WHEN *TACHANUN* IS NOT RECITED, THE *CHAZZAN* RECITES THE FULL *KADDISH* (P. 392);
INDIVIDUALS CONTINUE WITH *ALEINU* (P. 392).
FOR OCCASIONS AND DAYS THAT *TACHANUN* IS OMITTED, SEE P. 201.

⸺ AVINU MALKEINU ⸺

■ Cognizant of our relationship to Hashem as both a loving Father and omnipotent King, we beseech Him in times of crisis.

FROM ROSH HASHANAH TO YOM KIPPUR AND ON FAST DAYS, *AVINU MALKEINU* IS RECITED. EVERYONE STANDS UP AND THE ARK IS OPENED.

OVINU MALKAYNU, אָבִינוּ מַלְכֵּנוּ,
chotonu l'fonecho. חָטָאנוּ לְפָנֶיךָ.
Our Father, our King, we have sinned before You.

Ovinu malkaynu, אָבִינוּ מַלְכֵּנוּ,
ayn lonu melech elo oto. אֵין לָנוּ מֶלֶךְ אֶלָּא אָתָּה.
Our Father, our King, we have no King but You.

Ovinu malkaynu, אָבִינוּ מַלְכֵּנוּ,
asay imonu l'ma-an sh'mecho. עֲשֵׂה עִמָּנוּ לְמַעַן שְׁמֶךָ.
Our Father, our King, deal [kindly] with us for Your Name's sake.

⸺ ON FAST DAYS ⸺

Ovinu malkaynu, אָבִינוּ מַלְכֵּנוּ,
boraych olaynu shono tōvo. בָּרֵךְ עָלֵינוּ שָׁנָה טוֹבָה.
Our Father, our King, bless us with a good year.

⸺ BETWEEN ROSH HASHANAH AND YOM KIPPUR ⸺

Ovinu malkaynu, אָבִינוּ מַלְכֵּנוּ,
chadaysh olaynu shono tōvo. חַדֵּשׁ עָלֵינוּ שָׁנָה טוֹבָה.
Our Father, our King, inaugurate upon us a good year.

Ovinu malkaynu, batayl אָבִינוּ מַלְכֵּנוּ, בַּטֵּל
may-olaynu kol g'zayrōs koshōs. מֵעָלֵינוּ כָּל גְּזֵרוֹת קָשׁוֹת.
Our Father, our King, nullify all harsh decrees upon us.

Ovinu malkaynu, אָבִינוּ מַלְכֵּנוּ,
batayl machsh'vōs sōn'aynu. בַּטֵּל מַחְשְׁבוֹת שׂוֹנְאֵינוּ.
Our Father, our King, nullify the thoughts of those who hate us.

Ovinu malkaynu, אָבִינוּ מַלְכֵּנוּ,
hofayr atzas ōy'vaynu. הָפֵר עֲצַת אוֹיְבֵינוּ.
Our Father, our King, thwart the counsel of our enemies.

⸺⸺

❧ **Avinu Malkeinu**

Avinu Malkeinu, which is recited on fast days and during the Ten Days of Repentance between Rosh Hashanah and Yom Kippur, combines pleas for our personal and national needs with expressions of repentance. The prayer is based on an incident in the life of Rabbi Akiva as related in the Talmud (*Taanis* 25b). During a drought, the Sages proclaimed a day of public fast and prayer, but no rain fell. Thereupon Rabbi Akiva said five brief supplications, each beginning *Our Father, our King*, and it began to rain.

Over the course of the generations, various communities added brief prayers with this beginning. This explains why Rabbi Akiva's five

AVINU MALKEINU

Ovinu malkaynu,
   kalay kol tzar u-mastin
   may-olaynu.

אָבִינוּ מַלְכֵּנוּ,
כַּלֵּה כָּל צַר וּמַשְׂטִין
מֵעָלֵינוּ.

Our Father, our King, exterminate every foe and adversary from upon us.

Ovinu malkaynu, s'ōm piyōs
mastinaynu umkatrigaynu.

אָבִינוּ מַלְכֵּנוּ, סְתוֹם פִּיּוֹת
מַשְׂטִינֵנוּ וּמְקַטְרִיגֵנוּ.

Our Father, our King,
seal the mouths of our adversaries and accusers.

Ovinu malkaynu,
   kalay dever v'cherev v'ro-ov
   ushvi u-mashchis v'ovōn ush-mad
   mib'nay v'risecho.

אָבִינוּ מַלְכֵּנוּ,
כַּלֵּה דֶּבֶר וְחֶרֶב וְרָעָב
וּשְׁבִי וּמַשְׁחִית וְעָוֹן וּשְׁמַד
מִבְּנֵי בְרִיתֶךָ.

Our Father, our King, exterminate pestilence, sword, famine, captivity,
destruction, iniquity, and eradication from the members of Your covenant.

Ovinu malkaynu,
   m'na magayfo minachalosecho.

אָבִינוּ מַלְכֵּנוּ,
מְנַע מַגֵּפָה מִנַּחֲלָתֶךָ.

Our Father, our King, withhold the plague from Your heritage.

Ovinu malkaynu,
s'lach umchal l'chol avōnōsaynu.

אָבִינוּ מַלְכֵּנוּ,
סְלַח וּמְחַל לְכָל עֲוֹנוֹתֵינוּ.

Our Father, our King, forgive and pardon all our iniquities.

Ovinu malkaynu,
   m'chay v'ha-avayr
   p'sho-aynu v'chatōsaynu
   mineged aynecho.

אָבִינוּ מַלְכֵּנוּ,
מְחֵה וְהַעֲבֵר
פְּשָׁעֵינוּ וְחַטֹּאתֵינוּ
מִנֶּגֶד עֵינֶיךָ.

Our Father, our King, wipe away and remove
our willful sins and errors from Your sight.

Ovinu malkaynu,
   m'chōk b'rachamecho harabim
   kol shitray chōvōsaynu.

אָבִינוּ מַלְכֵּנוּ,
מְחוֹק בְּרַחֲמֶיךָ הָרַבִּים
כָּל שִׁטְרֵי חוֹבוֹתֵינוּ.

Our Father, our King, erase through Your abundant compassion
all records of our guilt.

---

supplications have grown to over forty, and, in the Sephardic rite, over fifty. The introductory formula expresses our dual relationship to God: because He created and loves us, He is our merciful *Father;* because it is our duty to serve Him, He is our *King.*

The Sabbath and festivals are days of joy and contentment when it is not proper to pray for specific needs or to recall sad thoughts. *Avinu Malkeinu* is inappropriate on these days because: (a) Many of its verses parallel specific requests of the weekday *Shemoneh Esrei*, such as those for health, prosperity, forgiveness, etc., which are omitted on festive days; and (b) it was composed originally for times of distress.

EACH OF THE NEXT NINE VERSES IS RECITED RESPONSIVELY: *CHAZZAN*, THEN CONGREGATION. THE FIRST FOUR VERSES ARE IDENTICAL FOR FAST DAYS AND BETWEEN ROSH HASHANAH AND YOM KIPPUR; THE LAST FIVE VERSES ARE DIFFERENT. SEE BELOW.

Ovinu malkaynu,
   hachaziraynu
   bis-shuvo sh'laymo l'fonecho.
    Our Father, our King, return us to You in perfect repentance.

אָבִֽינוּ מַלְכֵּֽנוּ,
הַחֲזִירֵֽנוּ
בִּתְשׁוּבָה שְׁלֵמָה לְפָנֶֽיךָ.

Ovinu malkaynu,
   sh'lach r'fu-o sh'laymo
   l'chōlay amecho.
    Our Father, our King, send complete recovery to the sick of Your people.

אָבִֽינוּ מַלְכֵּֽנוּ,
שְׁלַח רְפוּאָה שְׁלֵמָה
לְחוֹלֵי עַמֶּֽךָ.

Ovinu malkaynu,
   k'ra rō-a g'zar dinaynu.
    Our Father, our King, tear up the evil decree of our verdict.

אָבִֽינוּ מַלְכֵּֽנוּ,
קְרַע רֽוֹעַ גְּזַר דִּינֵֽנוּ.

Ovinu malkaynu,
   zochraynu b'zikorōn tōv
   l'fonecho.
    Our Father, our King, recall us with a favorable memory before you.

אָבִֽינוּ מַלְכֵּֽנוּ,
זָכְרֵֽנוּ בְּזִכָּרוֹן טוֹב
לְפָנֶֽיךָ.

——————— ON FAST DAYS CONTINUE HERE ———————

Ovinu malkaynu,
   zochraynu l'cha-yim tōvim.
    Our Father, our King, remember us for good life.

אָבִֽינוּ מַלְכֵּֽנוּ,
זָכְרֵֽנוּ לְחַיִּים טוֹבִים.

Ovinu malkaynu,
   zochraynu lig-ulo vi-shu-o.
    Our Father, our King, remember us for redemption and salvation.

אָבִֽינוּ מַלְכֵּֽנוּ,
זָכְרֵֽנוּ לִגְאֻלָּה וִישׁוּעָה.

Ovinu malkaynu,
   zochraynu l'farnoso v'chalkolo.
    Our Father, our King, remember us for sustenance and support.

אָבִֽינוּ מַלְכֵּֽנוּ,
זָכְרֵֽנוּ לְפַרְנָסָה וְכַלְכָּלָה.

Ovinu malkaynu,
   zochraynu lizchuyōs.
    Our Father, our King, remember us for merits.

אָבִֽינוּ מַלְכֵּֽנוּ,
זָכְרֵֽנוּ לִזְכֻיּוֹת.

Ovinu malkaynu,
   zochraynu lislicho umchilo.
    Our Father, our King, remember us for forgiveness and pardon.

אָבִֽינוּ מַלְכֵּֽנוּ,
זָכְרֵֽנוּ לִסְלִיחָה וּמְחִילָה.

AVINU MALKEINU

---— BETWEEN ROSH HASHANAH AND YOM KIPPUR CONTINUE HERE ———

Ovinu malkaynu,
  kosvaynu
  b'sayfer cha-yim tōvim

אָבִינוּ מַלְכֵּנוּ,
כָּתְבֵנוּ
בְּסֵפֶר חַיִּים טוֹבִים.

Our Father, our King, inscribe us in the book of good life.

Ovinu malkaynu,
  kosvaynu
  b'sayfer g'ulo vishu-o.

אָבִינוּ מַלְכֵּנוּ,
כָּתְבֵנוּ
בְּסֵפֶר גְּאֻלָּה וִישׁוּעָה.

Our Father, our King, inscribe us in the book of redemption and salvation.

Ovinu malkaynu,
  kosvaynu
  b'sayfer parnoso v'chalkolo.

אָבִינוּ מַלְכֵּנוּ,
כָּתְבֵנוּ
בְּסֵפֶר פַּרְנָסָה וְכַלְכָּלָה.

Our Father, our King, inscribe us in the book of sustenance and support.

Ovinu malkaynu,
  kosvaynu b'sayfer z'chuyōs.

אָבִינוּ מַלְכֵּנוּ,
כָּתְבֵנוּ בְּסֵפֶר זְכֻיּוֹת.

Our Father, our King, inscribe us in the book of merits.

Ovinu malkaynu,
  kosvaynu
  b'sayfer s'licho umchilo.

אָבִינוּ מַלְכֵּנוּ,
כָּתְבֵנוּ
בְּסֵפֶר סְלִיחָה וּמְחִילָה.

Our Father, our King, inscribe us in the book of forgiveness and pardon.

——— END OF RESPONSIVE READING; ON ALL DAYS CONTINUE HERE ———

Ovinu malkaynu,
  hatzmach lonu y'shu-o b'korōv.

אָבִינוּ מַלְכֵּנוּ,
הַצְמַח לָנוּ יְשׁוּעָה בְּקָרוֹב.

Our Father, our King, make salvation sprout for us soon.

Ovinu malkaynu,
  horaym keren yisro-ayl amecho.

אָבִינוּ מַלְכֵּנוּ,
הָרֵם קֶרֶן יִשְׂרָאֵל עַמֶּךָ.

Our Father, our King, raise high the pride of Israel, Your people.

Ovinu malkaynu,
  horaym keren m'shichecho.

אָבִינוּ מַלְכֵּנוּ,
הָרֵם קֶרֶן מְשִׁיחֶךָ.

Our Father, our King, raise high the pride of Your anointed.

Ovinu malkaynu,
  malay yodaynu mibirchōsecho.

אָבִינוּ מַלְכֵּנוּ,
מַלֵּא יָדֵינוּ מִבִּרְכוֹתֶיךָ.

Our Father, our King, fill our hands from Your blessings.

Ovinu malkaynu,
  malay asomaynu sovo.

אָבִינוּ מַלְכֵּנוּ,
מַלֵּא אֲסָמֵינוּ שָׂבָע.

Our Father, our King, fill our storehouses with abundance.

Ovinu malkaynu, sh'ma kōlaynu, אָבִינוּ מַלְכֵּנוּ, שְׁמַע קוֹלֵנוּ,
chus v'rachaym olaynu. חוּס וְרַחֵם עָלֵינוּ.
Our Father, our King, hear our voice, pity and be compassionate to us.

Ovinu malkaynu, אָבִינוּ מַלְכֵּנוּ,
kabayl b'rachamim uvrotzōn קַבֵּל בְּרַחֲמִים וּבְרָצוֹן
es t'filosaynu. אֶת תְּפִלָּתֵנוּ.
Our Father, our King, accept — with compassion and favor — our prayer.

Ovinu malkaynu, אָבִינוּ מַלְכֵּנוּ,
p'sach sha-aray shoma-yim פְּתַח שַׁעֲרֵי שָׁמַיִם
lisfilosaynu. לִתְפִלָּתֵנוּ.
Our Father, our King, open the gates of heaven to our prayer.

Ovinu malkaynu, אָבִינוּ מַלְכֵּנוּ,
zochōr ki ofor anochnu. זָכוֹר כִּי עָפָר אֲנָחְנוּ.
Our Father, our King, remember that we are but dust.

Ovinu malkaynu, אָבִינוּ מַלְכֵּנוּ,
no al t'shivaynu raykom נָא אַל תְּשִׁיבֵנוּ רֵיקָם
mil'fonecho. מִלְּפָנֶיךָ.
Our Father, our King, please do not turn us from You empty-handed.

Ovinu malkaynu, אָבִינוּ מַלְכֵּנוּ,
t'hay hasho-o ha-zōs תְּהֵא הַשָּׁעָה הַזֹּאת
sh'as rachamim v'ays rotzōn שְׁעַת רַחֲמִים וְעֵת רָצוֹן
mil'fonecho. מִלְּפָנֶיךָ.
Our Father, our King, may this moment be a moment of compassion and a time of favor before You.

Ovinu malkaynu, chamōl olaynu אָבִינוּ מַלְכֵּנוּ, חֲמוֹל עָלֵינוּ
v'al ōlolaynu v'tapaynu. וְעַל עוֹלָלֵינוּ וְטַפֵּנוּ.
Our Father, our King, take pity upon us, and upon our children and our infants.

Ovinu malkaynu, אָבִינוּ מַלְכֵּנוּ,
asay l'ma-an harugim עֲשֵׂה לְמַעַן הֲרוּגִים
al shaym kodshecho. עַל שֵׁם קָדְשֶׁךָ.
Our Father, our King, act for the sake of those who were murdered for Your Holy Name.

Ovinu malkaynu, אָבִינוּ מַלְכֵּנוּ,
asay l'ma-an t'vuchim עֲשֵׂה לְמַעַן טְבוּחִים
al yichudecho. עַל יִחוּדֶךָ.
Our Father, our King, act for the sake of those who were slaughtered for Your Oneness.

AVINU MALKEINU

Ovinu malkaynu,   אָבִינוּ מַלְכֵּנוּ,
  asay l'ma-an   עֲשֵׂה לְמַעַן
  bo-ay vo-aysh u-vama-yim   בָּאֵי בָאֵשׁ וּבַמַּיִם
  al kidush sh'mecho.   עַל קִדּוּשׁ שְׁמֶךָ.

Our Father, our King, act for the sake of those who went into fire and water for the sanctification of Your Name.

Ovinu malkaynu,   אָבִינוּ מַלְכֵּנוּ,
  n'kōm l'aynaynu   נְקוֹם לְעֵינֵינוּ
  nikmas dam avodecho hashofuch.   נִקְמַת דַּם עֲבָדֶיךָ הַשָּׁפוּךְ.

Our Father, our King, avenge before our eyes the spilled blood of Your servants.

Ovinu malkaynu,   אָבִינוּ מַלְכֵּנוּ,
  asay l'ma-ancho   עֲשֵׂה לְמַעַנְךָ
  im lō l'ma-anaynu.   אִם לֹא לְמַעֲנֵנוּ.

Our Father, our King, act for Your sake if not for our sake.

Ovinu malkaynu,   אָבִינוּ מַלְכֵּנוּ,
  asay l'ma-ancho v'hōshi-aynu.   עֲשֵׂה לְמַעַנְךָ וְהוֹשִׁיעֵנוּ.

Our Father, our King, act for Your sake and save us.

Ovinu malkaynu,   אָבִינוּ מַלְכֵּנוּ,
  asay l'ma-an   עֲשֵׂה לְמַעַן
  rachamecho horabim.   רַחֲמֶיךָ הָרַבִּים.

Our Father, our King, act for the sake of Your abundant compassion.

Ovinu malkaynu,   אָבִינוּ מַלְכֵּנוּ,
  asay l'ma-an shimcho hagodōl   עֲשֵׂה לְמַעַן שִׁמְךָ הַגָּדוֹל
  hagibōr v'hanōro,   הַגִּבּוֹר וְהַנּוֹרָא,
  shenikro olaynu.   שֶׁנִּקְרָא עָלֵינוּ.

Our Father, our King, act for the sake of Your great, mighty, and awesome Name that is proclaimed upon us.

Ovinu malkaynu,   אָבִינוּ מַלְכֵּנוּ,
  chonaynu va-anaynu,   חָנֵּנוּ וַעֲנֵנוּ,
  ki ayn bonu ma-asim,   כִּי אֵין בָּנוּ מַעֲשִׂים,
  asay i-monu tz'doko vochesed   עֲשֵׂה עִמָּנוּ צְדָקָה וָחֶסֶד
  v'hoshi-aynu.   וְהוֹשִׁיעֵנוּ.

Our Father, our King, be gracious with us and answer us, though we have no worthy deeds; treat us with charity and kindness, and save us.

THE AVINU MALKEINU PRAYER ENDS HERE.
THE SERVICE CONTINUES WITH TACHANUN (P. 388).

❖{ TACHANUN / PUTTING DOWN THE HEAD }❖

■ *Shemoneh Esrei* presupposes the worth of man, that he is crowned with intelligence, that he is created in the image of God, and that he is justified to petition God with his many needs. We therefore recite it in a standing, erect position.

But perhaps man has failed to be worthy of being answered. If so, we now approach God assuming the stance of a lowly animal, sitting and putting down our head, and beseeching that He heed our pleas as He fills the needs of all creatures. Then we pray while sitting, and finally conclude *Tachanun* while standing.

Avudraham notes that just as Moses in his encounter with God at Sinai underwent these three different bodily positions, so do we.

IN THE PRESENCE OF A TORAH SCROLL, THE FOLLOWING IS RECITED WITH THE HEAD RESTING ON THE ARM, PREFERABLY WHILE SEATED. ELSEWHERE, IT IS RECITED WITH THE HEAD ERECT.

VA-YŌMER dovid el gad, וַיֹּאמֶר דָּוִד אֶל גָּד,
tzar li m'ōd, צַר לִי מְאֹד,
And David said to Gad, 'I am exceedingly distressed.
nip'lo no v'yad Adōnoy, נִפְּלָה נָּא בְיַד יהוה,
Let us fall into HASHEM*'s hand*
ki rabim rachamov, כִּי רַבִּים רַחֲמָיו,
for His mercies are abundant,
uvyad odom al epōlo. וּבְיַד אָדָם אַל אֶפֹּלָה.
but let me not fall into human hands."

RACHUM V'CHANUN רַחוּם וְחַנּוּן
chotosi l'fonecho. חָטָאתִי לְפָנֶיךָ.
O compassionate and gracious One, I have sinned before You,
Adōnoy molay rachamim, יהוה מָלֵא רַחֲמִים,
HASHEM, Who is full of mercy,
rachaym olai v'kabayl tachanunoy. רַחֵם עָלַי וְקַבֵּל תַּחֲנוּנָי.
have mercy on me and accept my supplications.
Adōnoy al b'ap'cho sōchichayni, יהוה אַל בְּאַפְּךָ תוֹכִיחֵנִי,
HASHEM, do not rebuke me in Your anger,
v'al bachamos'cho s'yas'rayni. וְאַל בַּחֲמָתְךָ תְיַסְּרֵנִי.
nor chastise me in Your rage.
Chonayni Adōnoy, ki umlal oni, חָנֵּנִי יהוה, כִּי אֻמְלַל אָנִי,
Favor me, HASHEM, *for I am feeble;*
r'fo-ayni Adōnoy, רְפָאֵנִי יהוה,
heal me, HASHEM,
ki nivhalu atzomoy. כִּי נִבְהֲלוּ עֲצָמָי.
for my bones shudder.

TACHANUN

V'nafshi nivhalo m'ōd,	וְנַפְשִׁי נִבְהֲלָה מְאֹד,

My soul is utterly confounded,

v'ato Adōnoy ad mosoy.	וְאַתָּה יהוה, עַד מָתָי.

and You, HASHEM, how long?

Shuvo Adōnoy chal'tzo nafshi,	שׁוּבָה יהוה, חַלְּצָה נַפְשִׁי,

Desist, HASHEM, release my soul;

hōshi-ayni l'ma-an chasdecho.	הוֹשִׁיעֵנִי לְמַעַן חַסְדֶּךָ.

save me as befits Your kindness.

Ki ayn bamoves zichrecho,	כִּי אֵין בַּמָּוֶת זִכְרֶךָ,

For there is no mention of You in death;

bish-ōl mi yōde loch.	בִּשְׁאוֹל מִי יוֹדֶה לָּךְ.

in the Lower World who will thank You?

Yogati b'anchosi,	יָגַעְתִּי בְּאַנְחָתִי,

I am wearied with my sigh,

as-cheh v'chol lailo mitosi,	אַשְׂחֶה בְכָל לַיְלָה מִטָּתִי,

every night I drench my bed,

b'dim-osi arsi amse.	בְּדִמְעָתִי עַרְשִׂי אַמְסֶה.

with my tears I soak my couch.

O-sh'sho mika-as ayni,	עָשְׁשָׁה מִכַּעַס עֵינִי,

My eye is dimmed because of anger,

os'ko b'chol tzōr'roy.	עָתְקָה בְּכָל צוֹרְרָי.

aged by my tormentors.

Suru mimeni kol pō-alay oven,	סוּרוּ מִמֶּנִּי כָּל פֹּעֲלֵי אָוֶן,

Depart from me, all evildoers,

ki shoma Adōnoy kōl bich-yi.	כִּי שָׁמַע יהוה קוֹל בִּכְיִי.

for HASHEM has heard the sound of my weeping.

Shoma Adōnoy t'chinosi,	שָׁמַע יהוה תְּחִנָּתִי,

HASHEM has heard my plea,

Adōnoy t'filosi yikoch.	יהוה תְּפִלָּתִי יִקָּח.

HASHEM will accept my prayer.

Yayvōshu v'yibohalu m'ōd kol ōy'voy,	יֵבֹשׁוּ וְיִבָּהֲלוּ מְאֹד כָּל אֹיְבָי,

Let all my foes be shamed and utterly confounded,

yoshuvu yayvōshu roga.	יָשֻׁבוּ יֵבֹשׁוּ רָגַע.

they will regret and be instantly shamed

THE HEAD IS RAISED AT THIS POINT.

SHŌMAYR yisro-ayl,	שׁוֹמֵר יִשְׂרָאֵל,
sh'mōr sh'ayris yisro-ayl,	שְׁמוֹר שְׁאֵרִית יִשְׂרָאֵל,

O Guardian of Israel, protect the remnant of Israel;

v'al yōvad yisro-ayl,	וְאַל יֹאבַד יִשְׂרָאֵל,
ho-ōm'rim, sh'ma yisro-ayl.	הָאוֹמְרִים, שְׁמַע יִשְׂרָאֵל.

let not Israel be destroyed — those who proclaim, "Hear O Israel."

Shōmayr gōy e-chod.	שׁוֹמֵר גּוֹי אֶחָד,
sh'mōr sh'ayris am e-chod,	שְׁמוֹר שְׁאֵרִית עַם אֶחָד,

O Guardian of the unique nation, protect the remnant of the unique people;

v'al yōvad gōy e-chod, וְאַל יֹאבַד גּוֹי אֶחָד,

let not the unique nation be destroyed —

ham'yachadim shimcho, הַמְיַחֲדִים שִׁמְךָ,

those who proclaim the Oneness of Your Name,

Adōnoy Elōhaynu, Adōnoy e-chod. יהוה אֱלֹהֵינוּ יהוה אֶחָד.

"HASHEM is our God, HASHEM — the One and Only!"

Shōmayr gōy kodōsh,	שׁוֹמֵר גּוֹי קָדוֹשׁ,
sh'mōr sh'ayris am kodōsh,	שְׁמוֹר שְׁאֵרִית עַם קָדוֹשׁ,

O Guardian of the holy nation, protect the remnant of the holy people;

v'al yōvad gōy kodōsh, וְאַל יֹאבַד גּוֹי קָדוֹשׁ,

let not the holy nation be destroyed —

hamshal'shim b'sholōsh k'dushōs	הַמְשַׁלְּשִׁים בְּשָׁלֹשׁ קְדֻשּׁוֹת
l'kodōsh.	לְקָדוֹשׁ.

those who proclaim three-fold sanctifications to the Holy One.

Misratze v'rachamim מִתְרַצֶּה בְּרַחֲמִים

Become favorable through compassion

u-mispa-yays b'sa-chanunim, וּמִתְפַּיֵּס בְּתַחֲנוּנִים,

and become appeased through supplications;

hisratze v'hispa-yays l'dōr oni,	הִתְרַצֶּה וְהִתְפַּיֵּס לְדוֹר עָנִי,
ki ayn ōzayr.	כִּי אֵין עוֹזֵר.

become favorable and appeased to the poor generation for there is no helper.

Ovinu malkaynu, chonaynu va-anaynu, אָבִינוּ מַלְכֵּנוּ, חָנֵּנוּ וַעֲנֵנוּ,

Our Father, our King, be gracious with us and answer us,

ki ayn bonu ma-asim, כִּי אֵין בָּנוּ מַעֲשִׂים,

though we have no worthy deeds;

asay i-monu tz'doko vochesed	עֲשֵׂה עִמָּנוּ צְדָקָה וָחֶסֶד
v'hōshi-aynu.	וְהוֹשִׁיעֵנוּ.

treat us with charity and kindness, and save us.

TACHANUN

RISE AFTER SAYING Va-anachnu lo nayda.
REMAIN STANDING UNTIL THE END OF TACHANUN.

VA-ANACHNU lō nayda
ma na-ase,   וַאֲנַחְנוּ לֹא נֵדַע מַה נַּעֲשֶׂה,
We know not what to do —
ki olecho aynaynu.   כִּי עָלֶיךָ עֵינֵינוּ.
but our eyes are upon You.

Z'chōr rachamecho Adōnoy   זְכֹר רַחֲמֶיךָ יהוה
Remember Your mercies, HASHEM,
vachasodecho, ki may-ōlom haymoh.   וַחֲסָדֶיךָ, כִּי מֵעוֹלָם הֵמָּה.
and Your kindnesses, for they are from the beginning of the world.

Y'hi chasd'cho Adōnoy olaynu,   יְהִי חַסְדְּךָ יהוה עָלֵינוּ,
ka-asher yichalnu loch.   כַּאֲשֶׁר יִחַלְנוּ לָךְ.
May Your kindness be upon us, HASHEM, just as we awaited You.

Al tizkor lonu avonōs rishōnim,   אַל תִּזְכָּר לָנוּ עֲוֹנוֹת רִאשׁוֹנִים,
Recall not against us the sins of the ancients;
mahayr y'kad'munu rachamecho,   מַהֵר יְקַדְּמוּנוּ רַחֲמֶיךָ,
ki dalōnu m'ōd.   כִּי דַלּוֹנוּ מְאֹד.
may Your mercies meet us swiftly, for we have become exceedingly impoverished.

Chonaynu Adōnoy chonaynu,   חָנֵּנוּ יהוה חָנֵּנוּ,
ki rav sovanu vuz.   כִּי רַב שָׂבַעְנוּ בוּז.
Be gracious to us, HASHEM, be gracious to us, for we are abundantly sated with scorn.

B'rōgez rachaym tizkōr.   בְּרֹגֶז רַחֵם תִּזְכּוֹר.
Amid rage — remember to be merciful!

Ki hu yoda yitzraynu,   כִּי הוּא יָדַע יִצְרֵנוּ,
zochur ki ofor anochnu.   זָכוּר כִּי עָפָר אֲנָחְנוּ.
For He knew our nature, He remembers that we are dust.

❖ Oz'raynu Elōhay yish-aynu   עָזְרֵנוּ אֱלֹהֵי יִשְׁעֵנוּ
Assist us, O God of our salvation,
al d'var k'vōd sh'mecho,   עַל דְּבַר כְּבוֹד שְׁמֶךָ,
for the sake of Your Name's glory;
v'hatzilaynu
v'chapayr al chatōsaynu   וְהַצִּילֵנוּ וְכַפֵּר עַל חַטֹּאתֵינוּ
rescue us and atone for our sins
l'ma-an sh'mecho.   לְמַעַן שְׁמֶךָ.
for Your Name's sake.

TACHANUN ENDS HERE.

THE *CHAZZAN* RECITES FULL *KADDISH*
(congregational responses are indicated by parentheses):

יִתְגַּדַּל וְיִתְקַדַּשׁ שְׁמֵהּ רַבָּא. (אָמֵן – Omayn). בְּעָלְמָא דִּי בְרָא כִרְעוּתֵהּ. וְיַמְלִיךְ מַלְכוּתֵהּ, בְּחַיֵּיכוֹן וּבְיוֹמֵיכוֹן וּבְחַיֵּי דְכָל בֵּית יִשְׂרָאֵל, בַּעֲגָלָא וּבִזְמַן קָרִיב. וְאִמְרוּ: אָמֵן.

(אָמֵן. יְהֵא שְׁמֵהּ רַבָּא מְבָרַךְ לְעָלַם וּלְעָלְמֵי עָלְמַיָּא.)
(Omayn. Y'hay sh'mayh rabo m'vorach l'olam ul-ol'may ol'ma-yo.)

יְהֵא שְׁמֵהּ רַבָּא מְבָרַךְ לְעָלַם וּלְעָלְמֵי עָלְמַיָּא. יִתְבָּרַךְ וְיִשְׁתַּבַּח וְיִתְפָּאַר וְיִתְרוֹמַם וְיִתְנַשֵּׂא וְיִתְהַדָּר וְיִתְעַלֶּה וְיִתְהַלָּל שְׁמֵהּ דְּקֻדְשָׁא בְּרִיךְ הוּא (בְּרִיךְ הוּא – B'rich hu). °לְעֵלָּא מִן כָּל [°לְעֵלָּא לְעֵלָּא מִכָּל – from Rosh Hashanah to Yom Kippur substitute] בִּרְכָתָא וְשִׁירָתָא תֻּשְׁבְּחָתָא וְנֶחָמָתָא, דַּאֲמִירָן בְּעָלְמָא. וְאִמְרוּ: אָמֵן. (אָמֵן – Omayn).

תִּתְקַבֵּל צְלוֹתְהוֹן וּבָעוּתְהוֹן דְּכָל (בֵּית) יִשְׂרָאֵל קֳדָם אֲבוּהוֹן דִּי בִשְׁמַיָּא. וְאִמְרוּ: אָמֵן. (אָמֵן – Omayn).

יְהֵא שְׁלָמָא רַבָּא מִן שְׁמַיָּא, וְחַיִּים עָלֵינוּ וְעַל כָּל יִשְׂרָאֵל. וְאִמְרוּ: אָמֵן. (אָמֵן – Omayn).

Bow. Take three steps back. Bow left and say, . . . עֹשֶׂה; bow right and say, . . . הוּא יַעֲשֶׂה; bow forward and say, . . . וְעַל כָּל. Remain in place for a few moments, then take three steps forward.

עֹשֶׂה שָׁלוֹם בִּמְרוֹמָיו, הוּא יַעֲשֶׂה שָׁלוֹם עָלֵינוּ, וְעַל כָּל יִשְׂרָאֵל. וְאִמְרוּ: אָמֵן. (אָמֵן – Omayn).

■ As we take leave of the synagogue and God's presence, we fortify ourselves with the resolve and commitment that the lofty ideals of prayer can be implemented and actualized in our mundane pursuits.

STAND WHILE RECITING *ALEINU*.

OLAYNU l'shabay-ach la-adōn hakōl, **עָלֵינוּ** לְשַׁבֵּחַ לַאֲדוֹן הַכֹּל,
It is our duty to praise the Master of all,

losays g'dulo l'yōtzayr b'rayshis, לָתֵת גְּדֻלָּה לְיוֹצֵר בְּרֵאשִׁית,
to ascribe greatness to the Molder of primeval Creation,

shelō osonu k'gōyay ho-arotzōs, שֶׁלֹּא עָשָׂנוּ כְּגוֹיֵי הָאֲרָצוֹת,
for He has not made us like the nations of the lands

v'lō somonu וְלֹא שָׂמָנוּ
k'mishp'chōs ho-adomo, כְּמִשְׁפְּחוֹת הָאֲדָמָה.
and has not emplaced us like the families of the earth;

shelō som chelkaynu kohem, שֶׁלֹּא שָׂם חֶלְקֵנוּ כָּהֶם,
for He has not assigned our portion like theirs

ALEINU

v'gōrolaynu k'chol hamōnom — וְגוֹרָלֵנוּ כְּכָל הֲמוֹנָם.
nor our lot like all their multitudes.

SOME CONGREGATIONS OMIT THE PARENTHESIZED VERSE:

(Shehaym mishta-chavim l'hevel vorik (שֶׁהֵם מִשְׁתַּחֲוִים לְהֶבֶל וָרִיק,
u-mispal'lim el ayl lō yōshi-a.) וּמִתְפַּלְלִים אֶל אֵל לֹא יוֹשִׁיעַ.)
(For they bow to vanity and emptiness and pray to a god which helps not.)

BOW WHILE RECITING THE NEXT PHRASE.

Va-anachnu kōr'im u-mishta-chavim וַאֲנַחְנוּ כּוֹרְעִים וּמִשְׁתַּחֲוִים
u-mōdim, וּמוֹדִים,
But we bend our knees, bow, and acknowledge our thanks

lifnay melech malchay ham'lochim, לִפְנֵי מֶלֶךְ מַלְכֵי הַמְּלָכִים,
before the King Who reigns over kings,

Hakodōsh boruch hu. הַקָּדוֹשׁ בָּרוּךְ הוּא.
the Holy One, Blessed is He.

Shehu nō-te shoma-yim שֶׁהוּא נוֹטֶה שָׁמַיִם
v'yōsayd oretz, וְיֹסֵד אָרֶץ,
He stretches out heaven and establishes earth's foundation,

u-mōshav y'korō וּמוֹשַׁב יְקָרוֹ
ba-shoma-yim mima-al, בַּשָּׁמַיִם מִמַּעַל,
the seat of His homage is in the heavens above

ush-chinas u-zō b'gov-hay m'rōmim. וּשְׁכִינַת עֻזּוֹ בְּגָבְהֵי מְרוֹמִים.
and His powerful Presence is in the loftiest heights.

Hu Elōhaynu ayn ōd. הוּא אֱלֹהֵינוּ, אֵין עוֹד.
He is our God and there is none other.

Emes malkaynu, efes zulosō, אֱמֶת מַלְכֵּנוּ, אֶפֶס זוּלָתוֹ,
True is our King, there is nothing beside Him,

kakosuv b'sōrosō: כַּכָּתוּב בְּתוֹרָתוֹ:
as it is written in His Torah:

V'yodato ha-yōm vaha-shayvōso וְיָדַעְתָּ הַיּוֹם וַהֲשֵׁבֹתָ
el l'vovecho, אֶל לְבָבֶךָ,
"You are to know this day and take to your heart

ki Adōnoy hu ho-Elōhim כִּי יהוה הוּא הָאֱלֹהִים
that HASHEM *is the only God —*

ba-shoma-yim mima-al בַּשָּׁמַיִם מִמַּעַל
v'al ho-oretz mitochas, ayn ōd. וְעַל הָאָרֶץ מִתָּחַת, אֵין עוֹד.
in heaven above and on the earth below — there is none other."

עלינו

AL KAYN n'kave l'cho
Therefore we put our hope in You,
עַל כֵּן נְקַוֶּה לְּךָ

Adōnoy Elōhaynu
H<small>ASHEM</small>, our God,
יהוה אֱלֹהֵינוּ

lir-ōs m'hayro
   b'sif-eres u-zecho,
that we may soon see Your mighty splendor,
לִרְאוֹת מְהֵרָה בְּתִפְאֶרֶת עֻזֶּךָ,

l'ha-avir gilulim min ho-oretz,
to remove detestable idolatry from the earth,
לְהַעֲבִיר גִּלּוּלִים מִן הָאָרֶץ,

v'ho-elilim korōs yikoraysun,
and false gods will be utterly cut off,
וְהָאֱלִילִים כָּרוֹת יִכָּרֵתוּן,

l'sakayn ōlom b'malchus Shadai.
to perfect the universe through the Almighty's sovereignty.
לְתַקֵּן עוֹלָם בְּמַלְכוּת שַׁדַּי.

V'chol b'nay vosor
   yikr'u vishmecho,
Then all humanity will call upon Your Name,
וְכָל בְּנֵי בָשָׂר יִקְרְאוּ בִשְׁמֶךָ,

l'hafnōs aylecho kol rish-ay oretz.
to turn all the earth's wicked toward You.
לְהַפְנוֹת אֵלֶיךָ כָּל רִשְׁעֵי אָרֶץ.

Yakiru v'yayd'u
   kol yōsh'vay sayvayl,
All the world's inhabitants will recognize and know
יַכִּירוּ וְיֵדְעוּ כָּל יוֹשְׁבֵי תֵבֵל,

ki l'cho tichra kol berech,
that to You every knee should bend,
כִּי לְךָ תִּכְרַע כָּל בֶּרֶךְ,

tishova kol loshōn.
every tongue should swear.
תִּשָּׁבַע כָּל לָשׁוֹן.

L'fonecho Adōnoy Elōhaynu
Before You, H<small>ASHEM</small>, our God,
לְפָנֶיךָ יהוה אֱלֹהֵינוּ

yichr'u v'yipōlu,
they will bend every knee and cast themselves down,
יִכְרְעוּ וְיִפֹּלוּ,

v'lichvōd shimcho y'kor yitaynu,
and to the glory of Your Name they will render homage,
וְלִכְבוֹד שִׁמְךָ יְקָר יִתֵּנוּ,

vikab'lu chulom
   es ōl malchusecho,
and they will all accept upon themselves the yoke of Your kingship
וִיקַבְּלוּ כֻלָּם אֶת עוֹל מַלְכוּתֶךָ,

v'simlōch alayhem m'hayro
that You may reign over them soon
וְתִמְלֹךְ עֲלֵיהֶם מְהֵרָה

395 / MINCHAH FOR WEEKDAYS — ALEINU

l'ōlom vo-ed. לְעוֹלָם וָעֶד.
and for all eternity.

Ki hamalchus shel'cho hi כִּי הַמַּלְכוּת שֶׁלְּךָ הִיא
For the kingdom is Yours

ul-ōl'may ad timlōch b'chovōd, וּלְעוֹלְמֵי עַד תִּמְלוֹךְ בְּכָבוֹד,
and You will reign for all eternity in glory,

kakosuv b'sōrosecho: כַּכָּתוּב בְּתוֹרָתֶךָ:
as it is written in Your Torah:

Adōnoy yimlōch l'ōlom vo-ed. יהוה יִמְלֹךְ לְעֹלָם וָעֶד.
"Hashem shall reign for all eternity."

❖ V'ne-emar: ❖ וְנֶאֱמַר:
And it is said:

V'ho-yo Adōnoy l'melech וְהָיָה יהוה לְמֶלֶךְ
  al kol ho-oretz, עַל כָּל הָאָרֶץ,
"Hashem will be King over all the world —

ba-yōm hahu yih-ye בַּיּוֹם הַהוּא יִהְיֶה
  Adōnoy e-chod, ushmō e-chod. יהוה אֶחָד וּשְׁמוֹ אֶחָד.
on that day Hashem will be One and His Name will be One."

SOME CONGREGATIONS RECITE THE FOLLOWING AT THIS POINT.

AL TIRO mipachad pis-ōm, **אַל תִּירָא** מִפַּחַד פִּתְאֹם,
Do not fear sudden terror,

u-mishō-as r'sho-im ki sovō. וּמִשֹּׁאַת רְשָׁעִים כִּי תָבֹא.
or the holocaust of the wicked when it comes.

Utzu aytzo v'sufor, עֻצוּ עֵצָה וְתֻפָר,
Plan a conspiracy and it will be annulled;

dab'ru dovor v'lō yokum, דַּבְּרוּ דָבָר וְלֹא יָקוּם,
speak your piece and it shall not stand,

ki i-monu Ayl. כִּי עִמָּנוּ אֵל.
for God is with us.

V'ad zikno ani hu, וְעַד זִקְנָה אֲנִי הוּא,
Even till your seniority, I remain unchanged;

v'ad sayvo ani esbōl, וְעַד שֵׂיבָה אֲנִי אֶסְבֹּל,
and even till your ripe old age, I shall endure;

ani osisi va-ani eso, אֲנִי עָשִׂיתִי וַאֲנִי אֶשָּׂא,
I created [you] and I shall bear [you];

va-ani esbōl va-amalayt. וַאֲנִי אֶסְבֹּל וַאֲמַלֵּט.
I shall endure and rescue.

קדיש יתום — מנחה לחול

⊰{ MOURNER'S KADDISH }⊱

■ Man was created to serve God and sanctify His Name. This service and sanctification is actualized by living one's life in accordance with the laws and customs of Judaism. This includes both commandments directed toward God and those that govern our relationship to man.

When an individual passes on, there is a void in this world which is caused by the loss of the sanctification that the deceased had contributed. Therefore, the surviving son (or other relative) addresses this void by announcing through the *Kaddish*, "May the great Name of God continue to be holy." There is no specific reference to death in the *Kaddish*, for it is a message of life. And life that continues is to be sanctified.

The recitation of the *Kaddish* is a great merit for the soul of the deceased. *Kaddish* is recited for eleven months following the death, and is also recited on the *Yahrzeit* (anniversary of the passing).

KADDISH IS RECITED ONLY IN THE PRESENCE OF A *MINYAN*.

MOURNER:

YISGADAL v'yiskadash sh'mayh rabo. יִתְגַּדַּל וְיִתְקַדַּשׁ שְׁמֵהּ רַבָּא.
May His great Name grow exalted and sanctified

CONGREGATION RESPONDS: Omayn — אָמֵן

B'ol'mo di v'ro chir-usayh. בְּעָלְמָא דִּי בְרָא כִרְעוּתֵהּ.
in the world that He created as He willed.

V'yamlich malchusayh, וְיַמְלִיךְ מַלְכוּתֵהּ,
May He give reign to His kingship

b'cha-yaychōn uvyōmaychōn בְּחַיֵּיכוֹן וּבְיוֹמֵיכוֹן
in your lifetimes and in your days

uvcha-yay d'chol bays yisro-ayl, וּבְחַיֵּי דְכָל בֵּית יִשְׂרָאֵל,
and in the lifetimes of the entire Family of Israel,

ba-agolo u-vizman koriv. בַּעֲגָלָא וּבִזְמַן קָרִיב.
swiftly and soon.

V'imru: Omayn. וְאִמְרוּ: אָמֵן.
Now respond: Amen.

CONGREGATION RESPONDS:

Omayn. Y'hay sh'mayh rabo m'vorach אָמֵן. יְהֵא שְׁמֵהּ רַבָּא מְבָרַךְ
l'olam ul-ol'may ol'ma-yo. לְעָלַם וּלְעָלְמֵי עָלְמַיָּא.
Amen. May His great Name be blessed forever and ever;

MOURNER CONTINUES:

Y'hay sh'mayh rabo m'vorach יְהֵא שְׁמֵהּ רַבָּא מְבָרַךְ
l'olam ul-ol'may ol'ma-yo, לְעָלַם וּלְעָלְמֵי עָלְמַיָּא,
May His great Name be blessed forever and ever;

yisborach v'yishtabach v'yispo-ar יִתְבָּרַךְ וְיִשְׁתַּבַּח וְיִתְפָּאַר
blessed, praised, glorified,

v'yisrōmam v'yisnasay וְיִתְרוֹמַם וְיִתְנַשֵּׂא
exalted, extolled,

MOURNER'S KADDISH

v'yis-hador v'yis-ale v'yis-halol	וְיִתְהַדָּר וְיִתְעַלֶּה וְיִתְהַלָּל

mighty, upraised, and lauded

sh'mayh d'kudsho b'rich hu	שְׁמֵהּ דְּקֻדְשָׁא בְּרִיךְ הוּא

be the Name of the Holy One, Blessed is He,

CONGREGATION RESPONDS:

| B'rich hu. | Blessed is He. | בְּרִיךְ הוּא. |

MOURNER CONTINUES:

°l'aylo min kol	°לְעֵלָּא מִן כָּל

beyond any

FROM ROSH HASHANAH TO YOM KIPPUR SUBSTITUTE:

°l'aylo l'aylo mikol	°לְעֵלָּא לְעֵלָּא מִכָּל

exceedingly beyond any

birchoso v'shiroso	בִּרְכָתָא וְשִׁירָתָא

blessing and song,

tushb'choso v'nechemoso,	תֻּשְׁבְּחָתָא וְנֶחֱמָתָא,

praise and consolation

da-amiron b'ol'mo.	דַּאֲמִירָן בְּעָלְמָא.

that are uttered in the world.

V'imru: Omayn.	וְאִמְרוּ: אָמֵן.

Now respond: Amen.

CONGREGATION RESPONDS: Omayn — אָמֵן

Y'hay sh'lomo rabo min sh'mayo	יְהֵא שְׁלָמָא רַבָּא מִן שְׁמַיָּא,

May there be abundant peace from Heaven,

v'cha-yim olaynu v'al kol yisro-ayl.	וְחַיִּים עָלֵינוּ וְעַל כָּל יִשְׂרָאֵל.

and life, upon us and upon all Israel.

V'imru: Omayn.	וְאִמְרוּ: אָמֵן.

Now respond: Amen.

CONGREGATION RESPONDS: Omayn — אָמֵן

MOURNER BOWS, THEN TAKES THREE STEPS BACK, BOWS LEFT AND SAYS:

Ō-se sholōm bimrōmov	עֹשֶׂה שָׁלוֹם בִּמְרוֹמָיו,

He Who makes peace in His heights,

MOURNER BOWS RIGHT AND SAYS:

hu ya-a-se sholōm olaynu	הוּא יַעֲשֶׂה שָׁלוֹם עָלֵינוּ,

may He make peace upon us,

MOURNER BOWS FORWARD AND SAYS:

v'al kol yisro-ayl. V'imru: Omayn.	וְעַל כָּל יִשְׂרָאֵל. וְאִמְרוּ: אָמֵן.

and upon all Israel. Now respond: Amen.

CONGREGATION RESPONDS: Omayn — אָמֵן

MOURNER REMAINS IN PLACE FOR A FEW MOMENTS, THEN TAKES THREE STEPS FORWARD.

The Evening Service

◆§ Maariv

Jacob instituted *Maariv* (*Berachos* 26b). A cursory look at his life indicates why he became the composer of the prayer of the night. The Torah tells us, "And a man wrestled with him [Jacob] until the break of dawn" (*Genesis* 32:25). The Sages explain that the "man" was the guardian angel of Esau, who tried to overcome Jacob. *Ramban* comments that the "night" of this prophetic text refers to the long exile that Jacob's offspring would experience at the hands of Esau's descendants — Israel's current, seemingly endless exile. Away from the land of Israel, facing foes that attempt either to exterminate or absorb us, Jacob's struggle with the guardian angel of Esau portended the future travail of the Jewish people. Furthermore, as Jacob was about to leave *Eretz Yisrael* for Egypt, God appeared to him in "night visions" (*Genesis* 46:2). *Meshech Chochmah* notes that the term "night visions" is used only with regard to Jacob. As he was about to leave *Eretz Yisrael* and venture into the darkness of exile, God taught him that even in the dark of night, the Divine Presence would still be found in Israel. As our Rabbis have comforted us, when the Jewish people go into exile, the Divine Presence joins them in exile (*Megillah* 29a).

Jacob's trials and difficulties seem endless. He was forced to flee from family, home, and country because his brother wished to kill him. He worked honestly and diligently for his father-in-law for twenty years, was deceived countless times, and because of the great resentment that others had for his success, he had to flee again. Only Divine intervention saved his life. He had problems with his children. His daughter was kidnaped and defiled, his firstborn failed to show him proper respect, and his favored treatment of Joseph led his other sons to sell Joseph, lie to their father, and plunge him into sadness for twenty-two years.

◆§ Prayer of Faith

For close to 2,000 years, the Jewish nation has been exiled from its land and has suffered communal and personal persecution, humiliation, and difficulty. Nevertheless, they derived strength from the great faith of Jacob, as expressed in his *Maariv*, the prayer of the distressed. "To relate Your kindness in the dawn and Your faith in the nights," exclaims the psalmist (*Psalms* 92:3). The Sages (*Berachos* 12a) understood this verse as a reflection of the *Shacharis* and *Maariv* prayers. *Dawn* symbolizes the hope-filled time when we can see the redemption, success, and prosperity of our nation; *nights* symbolize times when we are beset by failure, problems, and foreboding. The prayer of the night, which is characterized by *faith*, calls upon Israel to believe that God will redeem His chosen ones in the future, as He had saved them from exile and persecution from the time they were in Egypt and onward. On a personal note, faith and trust are understood by the *Chazon Ish* not to mean that the outcome of every problem will be as we

desire or that we will understand why it should be so, but rather the comforting knowledge that God is in control, that the outcome is not haphazard, and "whatever the Omnipotent does is for the best," though we may not understand how (*Emunah U'Vitachon*).

I recently heard of two Jewish mothers sitting in the intensive care waiting room, while their children were undergoing serious surgery. One mother, a Torah-observant, believing Jewess, was reciting *Tehillim / Psalms*. The other was not-yet observant and had no way to cope with the situation, other than bite her nails and curse the day. The *Maariv* prayer, in effect, declares: To the faithful, committed Jew there are no questions; to the Jew bereft of faith there are no answers.

ೞ Structure of Maariv

The structure of *Maariv* consists of the Biblical recitation of the *Shema* — the declaration of our faith — as the Torah legislates, "Speak of them [the words of the *Shema*] . . . when you retire and when you arise" (*Deuteronomy* 6:7) and the recitation of the *Shemoneh Esrei*. As in the *Shacharis* prayer, the *Shema* is surrounded by blessings. While in the morning there are three blessings, in the evening there are two blessings before and two after the recitation of the *Shema*. The total number of seven blessings that encompass the two recitations of the *Shema* reflect the sentiment: "Seven times a day I have praised You for Your righteous ordinances" (*Psalms* 119:164; *Berachos* 11a, *Rashi*).

ೞ The Blessings

The themes of the evening and morning blessings are identical. The first blessing extols God as the Creator Who still controls the cosmos. The second blessing is an expression of our deeply felt gratitude to God for the gift of His Torah and His unconditional love for the Jewish people. It is most appropriate that we focus on the Torah at night, for we recognize that it is only due to our loyalty to Torah study and observance that we have endured the many, long, difficult exiles. Moreover, the Sages teach that while there is a commandment to study Torah both day and night, one acquires the majority of one's Torah insight and understanding in the quietude of the night (*Eruvin* 65a). *Rambam* extols the virtues of Torah study at night (*Hil. Talmud Torah* 3:13).

The third blessing, immediately after the *Shema*, recounts the wondrous events that gave way to the Exodus from Egypt. It begins "True and faithful is all this" and *Chidushei HaRim* explains that *truth* refers to something we know to be true because our senses tell us so, or because we have conclusive evidence. *Faith*, on the other hand, refers to that which we believe, though we have never seen it, nor do we have proof that it happened. We know the Exodus to be true, because it was witnessed by millions of people. The future redemption is not yet an accomplished fact, but we have perfect faith that God will bring it about, as He promised through the Prophets.

The fourth blessing, *Hashkiveinu*, is understood by the Sages (*Berachos* 4a) as an extension of the previous blessing of redemption. We affirm that He is our Protector from the challenges and afflictions associated with the terrors of night, literally and figuratively.

✥ Additional Blessings

Ashkenazic Jews outside of Israel add *Baruch Hashem L'Olam*, a collection of Scriptural verses. *Tur* (*Orach Chaim* 236) explains its origin. In the Geonic Era (750-1,000 C.E.) the synagogues were located in the fields and people were afraid to remain there until after the conclusion of the complete *Shemoneh Esrei*, so the rabbis of the time composed a shorter prayer, containing the Name Hashem eighteen times, corresponding to the eighteen blessings of *Shemoneh Esrei*. *Tosafos* (*Berachos* 4b) suggests that *Baruch Hashem L'Olam* was added to enable latecomers to catch up to the congregation, thus enabling all to leave in safety together. Though the full *Maariv* has been recited in synagogues for many centuries, the former custom was not abandoned, and *Baruch Hashem* is still recited before *Shemoneh Esrei* by nearly all Ashkenazi congregations.

✥ Sefiras HaOmer

✥ Origin of the Mitzvah

Sefiras HaOmer refers to the daily counting of the seven weeks that connect Pesach and Shavuos. Pesach is the holiday of our freedom from slavery. We are taught in *Avos* (6:2), "The Tablets are God's handiwork and the script was God's script engraved (*charus*) on the Tablets" (*Exodus* 32:16). The Mishnah continues, "Do not read חָרוּת [*charus*], *engraved*, but חֵרוּת [*cheirus*], *freedom*, for you can have no freer man than one who engages in the study of Torah." It is understandable, therefore, that Nachmanides (*Ramban*), in his commentary on the Torah, suggests that the forty-nine days between Pesach and Shavuos are comparable to "Chol HaMoed," the Intermediate Days of Pesach and Succos. Just as the Intermediate Days connect the first and last days of Pesach and Succos, so too the days between our festivals of freedom and of receiving the Torah are bridged by the days of *Sefiras HaOmer*. Moreover, as a bride and groom count the days in anticipation of their wedding, so do the Jewish people not only relive the Exodus from Egypt on the night of the Pesach Seder, but anticipate and yearn for the receiving of the Torah each and every year.

When Hashem appeared to Moses at the burning bush, He said to him, "... this is your sign that I have sent you: When you take the people out of Egypt, you will

serve Hashem on this mountain" (*Exodus* 3:12). The word serve is written in Hebrew as תַעַבְדוּן, with a final *nun*, which at first glance is unnecessary. Based on the *nun*'s numerical equivalent of fifty, the Sages interpret it as an allusion to the fifty days from Pesach to Shavuos. The *Ran's* commentary at the end of Tractate *Pesachim* adds that, based on the above, the Jewish nation took the initiative of counting from the Exodus until they arrived at Sinai and received the Torah. Hashem was so pleased with this demonstration of eagerness on the part of His nation, that He made the count from Pesach to Shavuos an annual *mitzvah* (*Exodus* 23:15).

✦§ Terms of the Mitzvah

The counting of the *Omer* is done at night following the *Maariv* service. Since the Torah ordains seven full — complete [תְּמִימוֹת] — weeks, we count at night, as the day in Jewish law begins with evening. Each night we recite a blessing prior to the counting of the *Omer*. Someone who forgot to count at night may count during the following day (until sunset) without a blessing, and can continue to count the rest of the days with a blessing. But if someone missed a complete day, he continues counting the rest of the days without a blessing.

✦§ From Animal to Man

The *omer* is a measure of grain. We first encounter this word in conjunction with the manna that descended in the desert, when Moses instructed the people to gather an *omer* of manna per person (*Exodus* 16:15-16). An *omer* was enough to feed a person for a day. Another use of the *omer* was in conjunction with Pesach. The Torah commands that on the second night of Pesach, barley should be harvested and brought to the Temple. An *omer* of it was parched over fire, ground and then sifted until it was especially fine flour. A *Kohen* would wave it in all directions on behalf of the nation. The *Omer* offering permitted the new crop of grain (wheat, barley, rye, oats, spelt) to be eaten.

It is interesting to note that the offering on Pesach was of barley and on Shevuos there was an offering of *Shtei HaLechem*, two loaves made of wheat. Rabbi Samson Refael Hirsch, in his commentary on the Torah, notes that barley was generally used for animal food, and wheat was used for humans. On Pesach, before we receive the Torah, we are symbolically on the level of unsophisticated animals and therefore the offering is barley. Fifty days later when we accept the Torah, we graduate from barley to wheat, from the low level of an animal to the dignity and worthiness of man.

✦§ Counting Sabbaths

Rabbi Samson Refael Hirsch notes that first time the Torah mentions the *mitzvah* of *Sefiras HaOmer*, it speaks of שֶׁבַע שַׁבָּתוֹת, *seven Sabbaths* (*Leviticus* 23:15), rather than seven *weeks*, as it does in *Deuteronomy* 16:9. The *sefirah* count is to transform a free nation into a religious nation. At first glance this usage seems strange. However, it is difficult only if people believes they are the

masters of their destiny, that they are the ones who create their culture, that they are the ones building society, that they are in control of their destiny. Shabbos reminds the Jew that that is not the case. "For in six days Hashem made the heavens and the earth . . ." (*Exodus* 31:17). We are neither the creators nor the builders, and thus the Shabbos element helps prepare us to receive the Torah on Shavuos.

◆§ Mourning

Historically, *Sefirah* was a period of joy, spiritually because the nation was preparing for Shavuos, and materially because the crops were approaching the harvest. Then, during the time of the Mishnah, it became a time of mourning. The Talmud (*Yevamos* 62b) states that Rabbi Akiva had 12,000 pairs of students and they perished during a thirty-three day period between Pesach and Shavuos, because they were lax in showing respect to one another. Approximately 1,000 years later, the Crusaders in 1096 destroyed most of the Torah communities of Germany, especially during this time period. As a result of both of these tragic events the custom in Israel is to abstain from haircuts and weddings for a period of thirty-three days during the counting of the *Omer*. Some have the practice to observe the first thirty-three days of the *Omer*, until Lag B'Omer, when according to their tradition the students of Rabbi Akiva stopped dying. Others begin the period of mourning from the second day of *Rosh Chodesh* Iyar and observe the subsequent thirty-three days, with the exception of Lag B'Omer itself.

◆§ Kiddush Levanah

◆§ Welcoming the Divine Presence

Rav Yochanan (*Sanhedrin* 42a) teaches that, "Whoever recites the blessing over the new moon in its proper time, it is as if he has welcomed the presence of the *Shechinah*, the Divine Presence." This is explained by the students of *Rabbeinu Yonah* at the end of the fourth chapter of Tractate *Berachos*: In reality, man with his intelligence should perceive God in all of nature constantly. The recurring photosynthesis in plant life should be enough to convince everyone of the Divine orchestration of nature. King David realized this when he sang, "The heavens declare the glory of Hashem, and the firmament tells of His handiwork" (*Psalms* 19:2). However, the constancy and consistency of nature dulls man's awareness of Hashem. The waxing and maning of the moon is an exception to this; the daily change is a reminder of God's guiding hand.

While one cannot see Hashem, He is seen through His might and wonders, as the Prophet Isaiah (45:15) taught, "Indeed, You are a God who conceals Himself, the God of Israel is the Savior." Hashem has established Himself as the God of Israel by executing wonders on their behalf; by His salvation of them, extricating them from their enemies, He is revealed to mankind and slowly recognized by all. Thus a fascinating philosophical principle emerges: Often man is put in a difficult situation only to come to the realization that it was Hashem Who assisted him, teaches Rabbi Yerucham Levovitz, the renowned *Mashgiach* of the Mirrer Yeshivah. Most think that a community or person faces a crisis, and then they beseech Hashem for His assistance, when in reality they were put in the crisis only to force them to call on Hashem. "Let Me hear your supplicating voice, for your voice is sweet" (*Song of Songs* 2:14).

This is how the *Aruch HaShulchan* explains the text of the *Borei Nefashos* blessing: "Blessed are You Hashem . . . Who creates numerous living things with their deficiencies." Incredible! We thank Hashem for creating us deficient and lacking; for when we realize we are lacking, we turn to Hashem and therefore acquire "the life of the worlds," our needs and sustenance for this world and our share in the World to Come. Similarly, the renewal of the moon each month portrays Hashem's presence, and as a result of this renewal we are cognizant of His *Shechinah,* Divine Presence, everywhere.

⋅⋄ Longing for the Future

A second theme of this blessing is the optimism and encouragement for the Jewish nation, "who are destined to renew themselves like [the moon]." During Israel's long exile, the monthly renewal of the moon serves as assurance that Israel will be again renewed and rejuvenated. The Midrash (*Shemos Rabbah* 15:25) shows that as the moon reaches its full potential on the fifteenth day of the month, similarly there were fifteen generations from Abraham to King Solomon, when the Jewish people reached their full potential and built the First Temple. Then came fifteen generations of decline until Nebuchadnezzar blinded the Jewish King Zedekiah (*II Kings* 25:7); these are reflected in the moon's hiddenness at the end of the month. For this reason, says the *Rama* (*Orach Chaim* 426), we recite three times, "David King of Israel, is alive and enduring," as his kingship will be renewed, like the moon. Due to the significant allusion to Hashem as the Creator and to the rebirth of the Jewish nation, it is preferable to recite *Kiddush Levanah* after the *Maariv* service following Shabbos, when people are dressed in their Shabbos finery. Moreover, says the *Rama,* the recitation of *Kiddush Levanah* should be followed by festive dancing as at a wedding, demonstrating our trust and optimism.

⊰{ WEEKDAY MAARIV }⊱

CONGREGATION, THEN CHAZZAN:

V'HU rachum y'chapayr ovon   וְהוּא רַחוּם יְכַפֵּר עָוֹן
He, the Merciful One, is forgiving of iniquity

v'lō yashchis,   וְלֹא יַשְׁחִית,
and does not destroy;

v'hirbo l'hoshiv apō   וְהִרְבָּה לְהָשִׁיב אַפּוֹ,
frequently He withdraws His anger,

v'lō yo-ir kol chamosō.   וְלֹא יָעִיר כָּל חֲמָתוֹ.
not arousing His entire rage.

Adōnoy hōshi-o   יהוה הוֹשִׁיעָה,
HASHEM, save!

hamelech ya-anaynu v'yōm kor'aynu.   הַמֶּלֶךְ יַעֲנֵנוּ בְיוֹם קָרְאֵנוּ.
May the King answer us on the day we call.

CHAZZAN SUMMONS THE CONGREGATION TO JOIN IN THE FORTHCOMING PRAYERS,
BEGIN AT Bor'chu AND STRAIGHTENING UP AT Adōnoy..

BOR'CHU es Adōnoy ham'vōroch.   בָּרְכוּ אֶת יהוה הַמְבֹרָךְ.
Bless HASHEM, the blessed One.

CONGREGATION, FOLLOWED BY CHAZZAN, RESPONDS,
BOWING AT Boruch AND STRAIGHTENING UP AT Adōnoy:

Boruch Adōnoy   בָּרוּךְ יהוה
ham'vōroch l'ōlom vo-ed.   הַמְבֹרָךְ לְעוֹלָם וָעֶד.
Blessed is HASHEM, the blessed One, for all eternity.

■ First blessing preceding the *Shema:* We recognize God's ongoing management of the world, as He allows us to benefit from the recurring cycles of night and day.

BORUCH ato Adōnoy,   בָּרוּךְ אַתָּה יהוה
Elōhaynu melech ho-ōlom,   אֱלֹהֵינוּ מֶלֶךְ הָעוֹלָם,
Blessed are You, HASHEM, our God, King of the universe,

asher bidvorō ma-ariv arovim,   אֲשֶׁר בִּדְבָרוֹ מַעֲרִיב עֲרָבִים,
Who by His word brings on evenings,

b'chochmo pōsay-ach sh'orim,   בְּחָכְמָה פּוֹתֵחַ שְׁעָרִים,
with wisdom opens gates,

u-visvuno m'shane itim,   וּבִתְבוּנָה מְשַׁנֶּה עִתִּים,
with understanding alters periods,

u-machalif es haz'manim,   וּמַחֲלִיף אֶת הַזְּמַנִּים,
changes the seasons,

umsadayr es hakōchovim,   וּמְסַדֵּר אֶת הַכּוֹכָבִים
and orders the stars

b'mishm'rōsayhem boroki-a kirtzōnō.	בְּמִשְׁמְרוֹתֵיהֶם בָּרָקִיעַ כִּרְצוֹנוֹ.

in their heavenly constellations as He wills.

Bōray yōm voloylo,	בּוֹרֵא יוֹם וָלָיְלָה,

He creates day and night,

gōlayl ōr mip'nay chōshech,	גּוֹלֵל אוֹר מִפְּנֵי חֹשֶׁךְ

removing light before darkness

v'chōshech mip'nay ōr,	וְחֹשֶׁךְ מִפְּנֵי אוֹר,

and darkness before light;

u-ma-avir yōm u-mayvi loylo,	וּמַעֲבִיר יוֹם וּמֵבִיא לָיְלָה,

He causes day to pass and brings night,

u-mavdil bayn yōm u-vayn loylo,	וּמַבְדִּיל בֵּין יוֹם וּבֵין לָיְלָה,

and separates between day and night —

Adōnoy Tz'vo-ōs sh'mō.	יהוה צְבָאוֹת שְׁמוֹ.

HASHEM, Master of Legions, is His Name.

❖ Ayl chai v'ka-yom, tomid yimlōch olaynu	אֵל חַי וְקַיָּם, תָּמִיד יִמְלוֹךְ עָלֵינוּ,

May the living and enduring God continuously reign over us,

l'ōlom vo-ed.	לְעוֹלָם וָעֶד.

for all eternity.

Boruch ato Adōnoy, hama-ariv arovim.	בָּרוּךְ אַתָּה יהוה, הַמַּעֲרִיב עֲרָבִים.

Blessed are You, HASHEM, Who brings on evenings.

CONGREGATION RESPONDS AMEN: Omayn — אָמֵן

■ Second blessing preceding the *Shema:* God's love of Israel manifested itself by His giving the Jewish people the Torah and *mitzvos*. We reciprocate with our pledge to study and observe His Torah and *mitzvos*.

AHAVAS ŌLOM / אַהֲבַת עוֹלָם

[With] an eternal love

bays yisro-ayl am'cho ohovto,	בֵּית יִשְׂרָאֵל עַמְּךָ אָהָבְתָּ.

have You loved the House of Israel, Your people;

tōro u-mitzvōs, chukim u-mishpotim,	תּוֹרָה וּמִצְוֹת, חֻקִּים וּמִשְׁפָּטִים,

Torah and commandments, decrees and ordinances

ōsonu limadto	אוֹתָנוּ לִמַּדְתָּ.

have You taught us.

Al kayn Adōnoy Elōhaynu,	עַל כֵּן יהוה אֱלֹהֵינוּ,

Therefore HASHEM, our God,

מעריב לחול / 408

b'shoch-vaynu uvkumaynu — בְּשָׁכְבֵנוּ וּבְקוּמֵנוּ
upon our retiring and our arising,

nosi-ach b'chukecho, — נָשִׂיחַ בְּחֻקֶּיךָ,
we will discuss Your decrees

v'nismach b'divray sōrosecho — וְנִשְׂמַח בְּדִבְרֵי תוֹרָתֶךָ,
and we will rejoice with the words of Your Torah

uvmitzvōsecho l'ōlom vo-ed, — וּבְמִצְוֹתֶיךָ לְעוֹלָם וָעֶד,
and with Your commandments for all eternity,

ki haym cha-yaynu v'ōrech yomaynu, — ❖ כִּי הֵם חַיֵּינוּ, וְאֹרֶךְ יָמֵינוּ,
for they are our life and the length of our days

u-vohem neh-ge yōmom voloylo. — וּבָהֶם נֶהְגֶּה יוֹמָם וָלָיְלָה.
and about them we will meditate day and night.

V'ahavos'cho — וְאַהֲבָתְךָ,
al tosir mimenu l'ōlomim. — אַל תָּסִיר מִמֶּנּוּ לְעוֹלָמִים.
May You not remove Your love from us forever.

Boruch ato Adōnoy, — בָּרוּךְ אַתָּה יהוה,
ōhayv amō yisro-ayl. — אוֹהֵב עַמּוֹ יִשְׂרָאֵל.
Blessed are You, HASHEM, Who loves His people Israel.

CONGREGATION RESPONDS: Omayn — אָמֵן

THE SHEMA

■ The *Shema* is our acceptance of and submission to the absolute Sovereignty of God.

IMMEDIATELY BEFORE THE RECITATION OF THE *SHEMA*, CONCENTRATE ON FULFILLING THE POSITIVE COMMANDMENT OF RECITING THE *SHEMA* DAILY, ONCE IN THE EVENING AND ONCE IN THE MORNING. IT IS IMPORTANT TO ENUNCIATE EACH WORD CLEARLY AND NOT TO RUN WORDS TOGETHER. ONE PRAYING WITHOUT A *MINYAN* BEGINS WITH THE FOLLOWING THREE-WORD FORMULA:

Ayl melech ne-emon. — אֵל מֶלֶךְ נֶאֱמָן.
God, trustworthy King.

RECITE THE FIRST VERSE ALOUD, WITH YOUR RIGHT HAND COVERING YOUR EYES, AND CONCENTRATE INTENSELY UPON ACCEPTING GOD'S ABSOLUTE SOVEREIGNTY.

SH'MA yisro-ayl, — **שְׁמַע** יִשְׂרָאֵל,
Adōnoy Elōhaynu, Adōnoy e-chod. — יהוה אֱלֹהֵינוּ, יהוה אֶחָד.
Hear, O Israel: HASHEM is our God, HASHEM, the One [and Only].

IN AN UNDERTONE:

Boruch shaym k'vōd malchusō — בָּרוּךְ שֵׁם כְּבוֹד מַלְכוּתוֹ
l'ōlom vo-ed. — לְעוֹלָם וָעֶד.
Blessed is the Name of His glorious kingdom for all eternity.

■ We return God's love by studying the Torah and committing ourselves to observe His Torah with all our resources and being.

SHEMA AND ITS BLESSINGS

WHILE RECITING THE FOLLOWING PARAGRAPH, CONCENTRATE ON ACCEPTING THE COMMANDMENT TO LOVE GOD.

V'OHAVTO ays
Adōnoy Elōhecho,
וְאָהַבְתָּ אֵת יהוה ׀ אֱלֹהֶיךָ,
You shall love H<small>ASHEM</small>, *your God,*

b'chol l'vov'cho,
בְּכָל לְבָבְךָ,
with all your heart,

uvchol nafsh'cho, uvchol m'ōdecho.
וּבְכָל נַפְשְׁךָ, וּבְכָל מְאֹדֶךָ.
with all your soul and with all your resources.

V'ho-yu had'vorim ho-ayle,
asher onōchi m'tzav'cho ha-yōm,
וְהָיוּ הַדְּבָרִים הָאֵלֶּה, אֲשֶׁר אָנֹכִי מְצַוְּךָ הַיּוֹם,
Let these matters that I command you today

al l'vovecho.
עַל לְבָבֶךָ.
be upon your heart.

V'shinantom l'vonecho,
וְשִׁנַּנְתָּם לְבָנֶיךָ,
Teach them thoroughly to your children

v'dibarto bom
וְדִבַּרְתָּ בָּם,
and speak of them

b'shivt'cho b'vaysecho,
uvlecht'cho vaderech
בְּשִׁבְתְּךָ בְּבֵיתֶךָ, וּבְלֶכְתְּךָ בַדֶּרֶךְ,
while you sit in your home, while you walk on the way,

uv'shochb'cho uvkumecho.
וּבְשָׁכְבְּךָ וּבְקוּמֶךָ.
when you retire and when you arise.

Ukshartom l'ōs al yodecho,
וּקְשַׁרְתָּם לְאוֹת עַל יָדֶךָ,
And you shall bind them as a sign upon your arm

v'ho-yu l'tōtofōs bayn aynecho.
וְהָיוּ לְטֹטָפֹת בֵּין עֵינֶיךָ.
and they shall be tefillin between your eyes.

Uchsavtom al m'zuzōs bay-secho
u-vish-orecho.
וּכְתַבְתָּם עַל מְזֻזוֹת בֵּיתֶךָ, וּבִשְׁעָרֶיךָ.
And write them on the doorposts of your house and upon your gates.

■ *We declare our collective commitment to observe God's* mitzvos, *and the recognition that our national success or failure is dependent on this observance.*

V'HO-YO im shomō-a tishm'u
el mitzvōsai,
וְהָיָה, אִם־שָׁמֹעַ תִּשְׁמְעוּ אֶל מִצְוֹתַי,
And it will come to pass that if you continually hearken to My commandments

asher onōchi
m'tza-ve eschem ha-yōm,
אֲשֶׁר אָנֹכִי מְצַוֶּה אֶתְכֶם הַיּוֹם,
that I command you today,

l'ahavo es Adōnoy Elōhaychem,	לְאַהֲבָה אֶת יהוה אֱלֹהֵיכֶם

to love H‍ASHEM*, your God,*

ul-ovdō וּלְעָבְדוֹ,

and to serve Him,

b'chol l'vavchem uvchol nafsh'chem. בְּכָל לְבַבְכֶם, וּבְכָל נַפְשְׁכֶם.

with all your heart and with all your soul —

V'nosati m'tar artz'chem b'itō, וְנָתַתִּי מְטַר אַרְצְכֶם בְּעִתּוֹ,

then I will provide rain for your land in its proper time,

yōre u-malkōsh, יוֹרֶה וּמַלְקוֹשׁ,

the early rains and the late rains,

v'osafto d'gonecho v'sirōsh'cho וְאָסַפְתָּ דְגָנֶךָ וְתִירֹשְׁךָ
v'yitzhorecho. וְיִצְהָרֶךָ.

that you may gather in your grain, your wine, and your oil.

V'nosati aysev וְנָתַתִּי עֵשֶׂב
b'sod'cho livhemtecho, בְּשָׂדְךָ לִבְהֶמְתֶּךָ,

I will provide grass in your field for your cattle

v'ochalto v'sovo-to. וְאָכַלְתָּ וְשָׂבָעְתָּ.

and you will eat and you will be satisfied.

Hi-shom'ru lochem, הִשָּׁמְרוּ לָכֶם,

Beware for yourselves,

pen yifte l'vavchem, פֶּן יִפְתֶּה לְבַבְכֶם,

lest your heart be seduced

v'sartem va-avadtem וְסַרְתֶּם וַעֲבַדְתֶּם
elōhim a-chayrim אֱלֹהִים אֲחֵרִים,

and you turn astray and serve gods of others

v'hishtachavisem lohem. וְהִשְׁתַּחֲוִיתֶם לָהֶם.

and bow to them.

V'choro af Adōnoy bochem, וְחָרָה אַף יהוה בָּכֶם,

Then the wrath of H‍ASHEM *will blaze against you;*

v'otzar es ha-shoma-yim וְעָצַר אֶת הַשָּׁמַיִם,
v'lō yih-ye motor, וְלֹא יִהְיֶה מָטָר,

He will restrain the heaven so there will be no rain

v'ho-adomo lō sitayn es y'vuloh וְהָאֲדָמָה לֹא תִתֵּן אֶת יְבוּלָהּ,

and the ground will not yield its produce;

va-avadtem m'hayro וַאֲבַדְתֶּם מְהֵרָה

and you will swiftly be banished

may-al ho-oretz hatōvo מֵעַל הָאָרֶץ הַטֹּבָה

from the goodly land

asher Adōnoy nōsayn lochem.	אֲשֶׁר יהוה נֹתֵן לָכֶם.

which H<small>ASHEM</small> *gives you.*

V'samtem es d'vorai ayle	וְשַׂמְתֶּם אֶת דְּבָרַי אֵלֶּה,

You shall place these words of Mine

al l'vavchem v'al nafsh'chem	עַל לְבַבְכֶם וְעַל נַפְשְׁכֶם,

upon your heart and upon your soul;

ukshartem ōsom l'ōs al yedchem,	וּקְשַׁרְתֶּם אֹתָם לְאוֹת עַל יֶדְכֶם,

and you shall bind them for a sign upon your arm

v'ho-yu l'tōtofōs bayn aynaychem.	וְהָיוּ לְטוֹטָפֹת בֵּין עֵינֵיכֶם.

and they shall be tefillin between your eyes.

V'limadtem ōsom es b'naychem,	וְלִמַּדְתֶּם אֹתָם אֶת בְּנֵיכֶם,

You shall teach them to your children,

l'dabayr bom,	לְדַבֵּר בָּם,

to discuss them,

b'shivt'cho b'vay-secho,	בְּשִׁבְתְּךָ בְּבֵיתֶךָ,
uvlecht'cho vaderech,	וּבְלֶכְתְּךָ בַדֶּרֶךְ,

while you sit in your home, while you walk on the way,

uv'shochb'cho uvkumecho.	וּבְשָׁכְבְּךָ וּבְקוּמֶךָ.

when you retire and when you arise.

Uchsavtom al m'zuzōs bay-secho	וּכְתַבְתָּם עַל מְזוּזוֹת בֵּיתֶךָ,
u-vish-orecho.	וּבִשְׁעָרֶיךָ.

And write them on the doorposts of your house and upon your gates.

L'ma-an yirbu y'maychem	לְמַעַן יִרְבּוּ יְמֵיכֶם
vimay v'naychem	וִימֵי בְנֵיכֶם,

In order to prolong your days and the days of your children

al ho-adomo asher nishba	עַל הָאֲדָמָה אֲשֶׁר נִשְׁבַּע
Adōnoy la-avōsaychem	יהוה לַאֲבֹתֵיכֶם

upon the ground that H<small>ASHEM</small> *has sworn to your ancestors*

losays lohem,	לָתֵת לָהֶם,

to give them,

kimay ha-shoma-yim al ho-oretz.	כִּימֵי הַשָּׁמַיִם עַל הָאָרֶץ.

like the days of the heavens on the earth.

■ We acknowledge the Divine providence over Israel as demonstrated by the Exodus from Egypt, thus obligating us to observe His *mitzvos*.

VA-YŌMER Adōnoy	וַיֹּאמֶר יהוה
el mōshe laymōr.	אֶל מֹשֶׁה לֵּאמֹר.

And H<small>ASHEM</small> *said to Moses saying:*

Dabayr el b'nay yisro-ayl	דַּבֵּר אֶל בְּנֵי יִשְׂרָאֵל,
v'omarto alayhem,	וְאָמַרְתָּ אֲלֵהֶם,

Speak to the Children of Israel and say to them

v'osu lohem tzitzis	וְעָשׂוּ לָהֶם צִיצִת,

that they are to make themselves tzitzis

al kanfay vigdayhem	עַל כַּנְפֵי בִגְדֵיהֶם

on the corners of their garments,

l'dōrōsom,	לְדֹרֹתָם,

throughout their generations.

v'nos'nu al tzitzis hakonof	וְנָתְנוּ עַל צִיצִת הַכָּנָף,
p'sil t'chayles.	פְּתִיל תְּכֵלֶת.

And they are to place upon the tzitzis of each corner a thread of turquoise wool.

V'ho-yo lochem l'tzitzis,	וְהָיָה לָכֶם לְצִיצִת,

And it shall constitute tzitzis for you,

ur-isem ōsō	וּרְאִיתֶם אֹתוֹ,

that you may see it

uz-chartem	וּזְכַרְתֶּם
es kol mitzvōs Adōnoy,	אֶת כָּל מִצְוֹת יהוה,

and remember all the commandments of HASHEM

va-asisem ōsom,	וַעֲשִׂיתֶם אֹתָם,

and perform them;

v'lō sosuru acharay l'vavchem	וְלֹא תָתוּרוּ אַחֲרֵי לְבַבְכֶם
v'acharay aynaychem,	וְאַחֲרֵי עֵינֵיכֶם,

and you shall not explore after your heart and after your eyes

asher atem zōnim acharayhem.	אֲשֶׁר אַתֶּם זֹנִים אַחֲרֵיהֶם.

after which you stray.

L'ma-an tizk'ru	לְמַעַן תִּזְכְּרוּ
va-asisem es kol mitzvōsoy,	וַעֲשִׂיתֶם אֶת כָּל מִצְוֹתָי,

So that you may remember and perform all My commandments;

vih-yisem k'dōshim Laylōhaychem.	וִהְיִיתֶם קְדֹשִׁים לֵאלֹהֵיכֶם.

and be holy to your God.

CONCENTRATE ON FULFILLING THE COMMANDMENT TO REMEMBER THE EXODUS FROM EGYPT.

Ani Adōnoy Elohaychem,	אֲנִי יהוה אֱלֹהֵיכֶם,

I am HASHEM, your God,

asher hōtzaysi eschem	אֲשֶׁר הוֹצֵאתִי אֶתְכֶם
may-eretz mitzra-yim,	מֵאֶרֶץ מִצְרַיִם,

Who has removed you from the land of Egypt

lih-yōs lochem Laylōhim,	לִהְיוֹת לָכֶם לֵאלֹהִים,

to be a God to you;

ani Adōnoy Elōhaychem. Emes . . .   . . . אֱמֶת. אֱלֹהֵיכֶם. יהוה אֲנִי

I am HASHEM your God. It is true . . .

Chazzan repeats — יהוה אֱלֹהֵיכֶם אֱמֶת.

■ **First blessing following *Shema*:** Our national deliverance in the past, exemplified by the Egyptian Exodus, serves as a source of trust in God in difficult times, strengthening our faith and commitment in the future Redemption.

VE-EMUNO kol zōs,   וֶאֱמוּנָה כָּל זֹאת,
    v'ka-yom olaynu,   וְקַיָּם עָלֵינוּ,
. . . and faithful is all this, and it is firmly established for us

ki hu Adōnoy Elōhaynu   כִּי הוּא יהוה אֱלֹהֵינוּ
that He is HASHEM our God,

v'ayn zulosō,   וְאֵין זוּלָתוֹ,
and there is none but Him,

va-anachnu yisro-ayl amō.   וַאֲנַחְנוּ יִשְׂרָאֵל עַמּוֹ.
and we are Israel, His people.

Hapōdaynu miyad m'lochim,   הַפּוֹדֵנוּ מִיַּד מְלָכִים,
He redeems us from the power of kings,

malkaynu hagō-alaynu   מַלְכֵּנוּ הַגּוֹאֲלֵנוּ
    mikaf kol he-oritzim,   מִכַּף כָּל הֶעָרִיצִים,
our King Who delivers us from the hand of all the cruel tyrants;

ho-Ayl hanifro lonu mitzoraynu,   הָאֵל הַנִּפְרָע לָנוּ מִצָּרֵינוּ,
the God Who exacts vengeance for us from our foes

v'ham'shalaym g'mul   וְהַמְשַׁלֵּם גְּמוּל
    l'chol ō-y'vay nafshaynu,   לְכָל אֹיְבֵי נַפְשֵׁנוּ,
and Who brings just retribution upon all enemies of our soul;

ho-ōse g'dōlōs ad ayn chayker,   הָעֹשֶׂה גְדֹלוֹת עַד אֵין חֵקֶר,
He performs great deeds that are beyond comprehension,

v'niflo-ōs ad ayn mispor,   וְנִפְלָאוֹת עַד אֵין מִסְפָּר,
and wonders beyond number;

hasom nafshaynu ba-cha-yim,   הַשָּׂם נַפְשֵׁנוּ בַּחַיִּים,
He set our soul in life

v'lō nosan lamōt raglaynu,   וְלֹא נָתַן לַמּוֹט רַגְלֵנוּ,
and did not allow our foot to falter;

hamad-richaynu al bomōs ōy'vaynu,   הַמַּדְרִיכֵנוּ עַל בָּמוֹת אוֹיְבֵינוּ,
He led us upon the heights of our enemies

va-yorem karnaynu al kol sōn'aynu,   וַיָּרֶם קַרְנֵנוּ עַל כָּל שׂוֹנְאֵינוּ,
and raised our pride above all who hate us;

ho-ōse lonu nisim un-komō b'faro,	הָעֹשֶׂה לָּנוּ נִסִּים וּנְקָמָה בְּפַרְעֹה,

He wrought for us miracles and vengeance upon Pharaoh,

ōsōs u-mōf'sim
   b'admas b'nay chom,   אוֹתוֹת וּמוֹפְתִים בְּאַדְמַת בְּנֵי חָם,

signs and wonders on the land of the offspring of Ham;

hama-ke v'evrosō
   kol b'chōray mitzro-yim,   הַמַּכֶּה בְעֶבְרָתוֹ כָּל בְּכוֹרֵי מִצְרָיִם,

He struck with His anger all the firstborn of Egypt

va-yōtzay es amō yisro-ayl
   mitōchom,   וַיּוֹצֵא אֶת עַמּוֹ יִשְׂרָאֵל מִתּוֹכָם,

and removed His people Israel from their midst

l'chayrus ōlom,   לְחֵרוּת עוֹלָם,

to everlasting freedom;

hama-avir bonov
   bayn gizray yam suf,   הַמַּעֲבִיר בָּנָיו בֵּין גִּזְרֵי יַם סוּף,

He brought His children through the split parts of the Sea of Reeds

es rōd'fayhem v'es sōn'ayhem,
   bis-hōmōs tiba.   אֶת רוֹדְפֵיהֶם וְאֶת שׂוֹנְאֵיהֶם בִּתְהוֹמוֹת טִבַּע.

while their pursuers and their enemies He caused to sink into the depths.

V'rō-u vonov g'vurosō,   וְרָאוּ בָנָיו גְּבוּרָתוֹ,

When His children perceived His power,

shib'chu v'hōdu lishmō,   שִׁבְּחוּ וְהוֹדוּ לִשְׁמוֹ,

they lauded and gave grateful praise to His Name;

u-malchusō v'rotzōn
   kib'lu alayhem.   ❖ וּמַלְכוּתוֹ בְּרָצוֹן קִבְּלוּ עֲלֵיהֶם.

and His Kingship they willingly accepted upon themselves.

Mōshe uvnay yisro-ayl
   l'cho onu shiro,   מֹשֶׁה וּבְנֵי יִשְׂרָאֵל לְךָ עָנוּ שִׁירָה,

Moses and the Children of Israel exclaimed to You in song,

b'simcho rabo,   בְּשִׂמְחָה רַבָּה,

with abundant gladness —

v'om'ru chulom: וְאָמְרוּ כֻלָּם:

and they said unanimously:

MI chomōcho bo-aylim Adōnoy,   **מִי** כָמֹכָה בָּאֵלִם יהוה,

*Who is like You among the heavenly powers, H*ASHEM*!*

mi komōcho nedor bakōdesh,   מִי כָּמֹכָה נֶאְדָּר בַּקֹּדֶשׁ,

Who is like You, mighty in holiness,

nōro s'hilōs, ōsay fele.	נוֹרָא תְהִלֹּת עֹשֵׂה פֶלֶא.

too awesome for praise, doing wonders!

❖ Malchus'cho ro-u vonecho   מַלְכוּתְךָ רָאוּ בָנֶיךָ

Your children beheld Your majesty,

bōkay-a yom lifnay mōshe,   בּוֹקֵעַ יָם לִפְנֵי מֹשֶׁה,

as You split the Sea before Moses,

zeh Ayli onu v'om'ru: זֶה אֵלִי עָנוּ וְאָמְרוּ:

"This is my God!" they exclaimed, then they said:

ADŌNOY yimlōch l'ōlom vo-ed.   יהוה יִמְלֹךְ לְעֹלָם וָעֶד.

"HASHEM shall reign for all eternity!"

❖ V'ne-emar: וְנֶאֱמַר:

    Ki fodo Adōnoy es ya-akōv,   כִּי פָדָה יהוה אֶת יַעֲקֹב,

And it is further said: "For HASHEM has redeemed Jacob

ug-olō mi-yad chozok mimenu.   וּגְאָלוֹ מִיַּד חָזָק מִמֶּנּוּ.

and delivered him from a power mightier than he."

Boruch ato Adōnoy,   בָּרוּךְ אַתָּה יהוה,

    go-al yisro-ayl.   גָּאַל יִשְׂרָאֵל.

Blessed are You, HASHEM, Who redeemed Israel.

CONGREGATION RESPONDS: Omayn — אָמֵן

■ *Second blessing following Shema:* We have complete trust in the protection that God grants us always. We request His assistance to utilize the tranquility of the night for personal resolutions and to plan for a better tomorrow.

HASHKIVAYNU Adōnoy Elōhaynu   הַשְׁכִּיבֵנוּ יהוה אֱלֹהֵינוּ

    l'sholōm,   לְשָׁלוֹם,

Lay us down to sleep, HASHEM, our God, in peace,

v'ha-amidaynu malkaynu l'cha-yim,   וְהַעֲמִידֵנוּ מַלְכֵּנוּ לְחַיִּים,

raise us erect, our King, to life;

ufrōs olaynu sukas sh'lōmecho,   וּפְרוֹשׂ עָלֵינוּ סֻכַּת שְׁלוֹמֶךָ,

spread over us the shelter of Your peace;

v'sak'naynu b'aytzo tōvo   וְתַקְּנֵנוּ בְּעֵצָה טוֹבָה

    mil'fonecho,   מִלְּפָנֶיךָ,

set us aright with good counsel from before Your Presence;

v'hōshi-aynu l'ma-an sh'mecho.   וְהוֹשִׁיעֵנוּ לְמַעַן שְׁמֶךָ.

and save us for Your Name's sake.

V'hogayn ba-adaynu,   וְהָגֵן בַּעֲדֵנוּ,

    Shield us,

מעריב לחול / 416

v'hosayr may-olaynu ō-yayv,	וְהָסֵר מֵעָלֵינוּ אוֹיֵב,
dever v'cherev v'ro-ov v'yogōn,	דֶּבֶר, וְחֶרֶב, וְרָעָב, וְיָגוֹן,

remove from us foe, plague, sword, famine, and woe;

v'hosayr soton mil'fonaynu
u-may-acharaynu,
וְהָסֵר שָׂטָן מִלְּפָנֵינוּ וּמֵאַחֲרֵינוּ,

and remove spiritual impediment from before us and from behind us,

uvtzayl k'nofecho tastiraynu,
וּבְצֵל כְּנָפֶיךָ תַּסְתִּירֵנוּ,

and in the shadow of Your wings shelter us —

ki Ayl shōm'raynu u-matzilaynu oto,
כִּי אֵל שׁוֹמְרֵנוּ וּמַצִּילֵנוּ אָתָּה,

for God Who protects and rescues us are You;

ki Ayl melech chanun v'rachum oto.
כִּי אֵל מֶלֶךְ חַנּוּן וְרַחוּם אָתָּה.

for God, the Gracious and Compassionate King, are You.

❖ Ushmōr tzaysaynu u-vō-aynu,
וּשְׁמוֹר צֵאתֵנוּ וּבוֹאֵנוּ,

Safeguard our going and coming,

l'cha-yim ulsholōm
לְחַיִּים וּלְשָׁלוֹם

for life and for peace,

may-ato v'ad ōlom.
מֵעַתָּה וְעַד עוֹלָם.

from now to eternity.

Boruch ato Adōnoy,
shōmayr amō yisro-ayl lo-ad.
בָּרוּךְ אַתָּה יהוה, שׁוֹמֵר עַמּוֹ יִשְׂרָאֵל לָעַד.

Blessed are You, HASHEM, Who protects His people Israel forever.

CONGREGATION RESPONDS: Omayn — אָמֵן

■ This prayer contains the Name of God eighteen times, corresponding to the original number of blessings in the *Amidah*. At a time and place when synagogues were in remote and unsafe areas, this prayer was substituted for the *Amidah* when it was not safe to be outside the towns after dark.

BORUCH Adōnoy l'ōlom,
omayn v'omayn.
בָּרוּךְ יהוה לְעוֹלָם, אָמֵן וְאָמֵן.

Blessed is HASHEM forever, Amen and Amen.

Boruch Adōnoy mitziyōn,
בָּרוּךְ יהוה מִצִּיּוֹן,

Blessed is HASHEM from Zion,

shōchayn y'rusholoyim hal'luyoh.
שֹׁכֵן יְרוּשָׁלָיִם, הַלְלוּיָהּ.

Who dwells in Jerusalem, Praise God!

Boruch Adōnoy Elōhim
בָּרוּךְ יהוה אֱלֹהִים

Blessed is HASHEM, God,

Elōhay yisro-ayl,
אֱלֹהֵי יִשְׂרָאֵל,

the God of Israel,

ōsay niflo-ōs l'vadō.	עֹשֵׂה נִפְלָאוֹת לְבַדּוֹ.

Who alone does wondrous things.

U-voruch shaym k'vōdō l'ōlom,	וּבָרוּךְ שֵׁם כְּבוֹדוֹ לְעוֹלָם,

Blessed is His glorious Name forever,

v'yimolay ch'vōdō	וְיִמָּלֵא כְבוֹדוֹ
es kol ho-oretz, omayn v'omayn.	אֶת כָּל הָאָרֶץ, אָמֵן וְאָמֵן.

and may all the earth be filled with His glory, Amen and Amen.

Y'hi ch'vōd Adōnoy l'ōlom,	יְהִי כְבוֹד יהוה לְעוֹלָם,

May the glory of HASHEM endure forever,

yismach Adōnoy b'ma-asov.	יִשְׂמַח יהוה בְּמַעֲשָׂיו.

let HASHEM rejoice in His works.

Y'hi shaym Adōnoy m'vōroch,	יְהִי שֵׁם יהוה מְבֹרָךְ,

Blessed be the Name of HASHEM

may-ato v'ad ōlom.	מֵעַתָּה וְעַד עוֹלָם.

from this time and forever.

Ki lō yitōsh Adōnoy es amō	כִּי לֹא יִטֹּשׁ יהוה אֶת עַמּוֹ

For HASHEM will not cast off His people

ba-avur sh'mō hagodōl,	בַּעֲבוּר שְׁמוֹ הַגָּדוֹל,

for the sake of His Great Name,

ki hō-il Adōnoy	כִּי הוֹאִיל יהוה
la-asōs eschem lō l'om.	לַעֲשׂוֹת אֶתְכֶם לוֹ לְעָם.

for HASHEM has vowed to make you His own people.

Va-yar kol ho-om va-yip'lu	וַיַּרְא כָּל הָעָם וַיִּפְּלוּ
al p'nayhem,	עַל פְּנֵיהֶם,

Then the entire people saw and fell on their faces

va-yōmru, Adōnoy hu ho-Elōhim,	וַיֹּאמְרוּ, יהוה הוּא הָאֱלֹהִים,
Adōnoy hu ho-Elōhim.	יהוה הוּא הָאֱלֹהִים.

and said, "HASHEM — only He is God! HASHEM — only He is God!"

V'hoyo Adōnoy l'melech	וְהָיָה יהוה לְמֶלֶךְ
al kol ho-oretz,	עַל כָּל הָאָרֶץ,

Then HASHEM will be King over all the world,

ba-yōm hahu yih-ye	בַּיּוֹם הַהוּא יִהְיֶה
Adōnoy e-chod ush'mō e-chod.	יהוה אֶחָד וּשְׁמוֹ אֶחָד.

on that day HASHEM will be One and His Name will be One.

Y'hi chasd'cho Adōnoy olaynu,	יְהִי חַסְדְּךָ יהוה עָלֵינוּ,
ka-asher yichalnu loch.	כַּאֲשֶׁר יִחַלְנוּ לָךְ.

May Your kindness, HASHEM, be upon us, just as we awaited You.

מעריב לחול

קריאת שמע וברכותיה

Hōshi-aynu Adōnoy Elōhaynu,	הוֹשִׁיעֵנוּ יהוה אֱלֹהֵינוּ,
Save us, Hashem, our God,	
v'kab'tzaynu min hagō-yim,	וְקַבְּצֵנוּ מִן הַגּוֹיִם,
gather us from the nations,	
l'hōdōs l'shaym kod'shecho,	לְהוֹדוֹת לְשֵׁם קָדְשֶׁךָ,
to thank Your Holy Name	
l'hishtabay-ach bis-hilosecho.	לְהִשְׁתַּבֵּחַ בִּתְהִלָּתֶךָ.
and to glory in Your praise!	
Kol gō-yim asher osiso yovō-u	כָּל גּוֹיִם אֲשֶׁר עָשִׂיתָ יָבוֹאוּ
All the nations that You made will come	
v'yishtachavu l'fonecho Adōnoy,	וְיִשְׁתַּחֲווּ לְפָנֶיךָ אֲדֹנָי,
and bow before You, My Lord,	
vichab'du lishmecho.	וִיכַבְּדוּ לִשְׁמֶךָ.
and shall glorify Your Name.	
Ki godōl ato v'ōse niflo-ōs,	כִּי גָדוֹל אַתָּה וְעֹשֵׂה נִפְלָאוֹת,
For You are great and work wonders;	
ato Elōhim l'vadecho.	אַתָּה אֱלֹהִים לְבַדֶּךָ.
You alone, O God.	
Va-anachnu am'cho v'tzōn mar-isecho,	וַאֲנַחְנוּ עַמְּךָ וְצֹאן מַרְעִיתֶךָ,
Then we, Your people and the sheep of Your pasture,	
nōde l'cho l'ōlom,	נוֹדֶה לְּךָ לְעוֹלָם,
shall thank You forever;	
l'dōr vodōr n'sapayr t'hilosecho.	לְדוֹר וָדֹר נְסַפֵּר תְּהִלָּתֶךָ.
for generation after generation we will relate Your praise.	
Boruch Adōnoy ba-yōm,	בָּרוּךְ יהוה בַּיּוֹם,
Blessed is Hashem by day;	
boruch Adōnoy baloylo,	בָּרוּךְ יהוה בַּלָּיְלָה,
blessed is Hashem by night;	
boruch Adōnoy b'shoch'vaynu,	בָּרוּךְ יהוה בְּשָׁכְבֵנוּ,
blessed is Hashem when we retire;	
boruch Adōnoy b'kumaynu.	בָּרוּךְ יהוה בְּקוּמֵנוּ.
blessed is Hashem when we arise.	
Ki v'yod'cho nafshōs hacha-yim v'hamaysim.	כִּי בְיָדְךָ נַפְשׁוֹת הַחַיִּים וְהַמֵּתִים.
For in Your hand are the souls of the living and the dead.	
Asher b'yodō nefesh kol choy,	אֲשֶׁר בְּיָדוֹ נֶפֶשׁ כָּל חָי,
He in Whose hand is the soul of all the living	

v'ru-ach kol b'sar ish.	וְרוּחַ כָּל בְּשַׂר אִישׁ.

and the spirit of every human being.

B'yod'cho afkid ruchi,	בְּיָדְךָ אַפְקִיד רוּחִי,

In Your hand I shall entrust my spirit,

podiso ōsi, Adōnoy Ayl emes.	פָּדִיתָה אוֹתִי, יהוה אֵל אֱמֶת.

You redeemed me, Hashem, God of truth.

Elōhaynu, sheba-shoma-yim,	אֱלֹהֵינוּ שֶׁבַּשָּׁמַיִם,

Our God, Who is in heaven,

yachayd shimcho,	יַחֵד שִׁמְךָ,
v'ka-yaym malchus'cho tomid,	וְקַיֵּם מַלְכוּתְךָ תָּמִיד,

bring unity to Your Name; establish Your kingdom forever

umlōch olaynu l'ōlom vo-ed.	וּמְלוֹךְ עָלֵינוּ לְעוֹלָם וָעֶד.

and reign over us for all eternity.

YIR-U aynaynu v'yismach libaynu	**יִרְאוּ** עֵינֵינוּ וְיִשְׂמַח לִבֵּנוּ

May our eyes see, our heart rejoice

v'sogayl nafshaynu	וְתָגֵל נַפְשֵׁנוּ
bishu-os'cho be-emes,	בִּישׁוּעָתְךָ בֶּאֱמֶת,

and our soul exult in Your salvation in truth,

be-emōr l'tziyōn molach Elōhoyich.	בֶּאֱמֹר לְצִיּוֹן מָלַךְ אֱלֹהָיִךְ.

when Zion is told, "Your God has reigned!"

Adōnoy melech, Adōnoy moloch,	יהוה מֶלֶךְ, יהוה מָלָךְ,
Adōnoy yimlōch l'ōlom vo-ed.	יהוה יִמְלֹךְ לְעוֹלָם וָעֶד.

Hashem reigns, Hashem has reigned, Hashem will reign for all eternity.

Ki hamalchus shel'cho hi,	❖ כִּי הַמַּלְכוּת שֶׁלְּךָ הִיא,
ul-ōl'may ad timlōch b'chovōd,	וּלְעוֹלְמֵי עַד תִּמְלוֹךְ בְּכָבוֹד,

For the kingdom is Yours and for all eternity You will reign in glory,

ki ayn lonu melech elo oto.	כִּי אֵין לָנוּ מֶלֶךְ אֶלָּא אָתָּה.

for we have no King but You.

Boruch ato Adōnoy,	בָּרוּךְ אַתָּה יהוה,

Blessed are You, Hashem,

hamelech bichvōdō tomid	הַמֶּלֶךְ בִּכְבוֹדוֹ תָּמִיד
yimlōch olaynu l'ōlom vo-ed,	יִמְלוֹךְ עָלֵינוּ לְעוֹלָם וָעֶד,

the King in His glory — He shall constantly reign over us forever and ever,

v'al kol ma-asov.	וְעַל כָּל מַעֲשָׂיו.

and over all His creatures.

CONGREGATION RESPONDS: **Omayn** — אָמֵן

THE *CHAZZAN* RECITES *HALF-KADDISH*.
(Congregational responses are indicated by parentheses.)

יִתְגַּדַּל וְיִתְקַדַּשׁ שְׁמֵהּ רַבָּא. (Omayn – אָמֵן.) בְּעָלְמָא דִּי בְרָא כִרְעוּתֵהּ. וְיַמְלִיךְ מַלְכוּתֵהּ, בְּחַיֵּיכוֹן וּבְיוֹמֵיכוֹן וּבְחַיֵּי דְכָל בֵּית יִשְׂרָאֵל, בַּעֲגָלָא וּבִזְמַן קָרִיב. וְאִמְרוּ: אָמֵן.

(אָמֵן. יְהֵא שְׁמֵהּ רַבָּא מְבָרַךְ לְעָלַם וּלְעָלְמֵי עָלְמַיָּא.)

(Omayn. Y'hay sh'mayh rabo m'vorach l'olam ul-ol'may ol'ma-yo)

יְהֵא שְׁמֵהּ רַבָּא מְבָרַךְ לְעָלַם וּלְעָלְמֵי עָלְמַיָּא. יִתְבָּרַךְ וְיִשְׁתַּבַּח וְיִתְפָּאַר וְיִתְרוֹמַם וְיִתְנַשֵּׂא וְיִתְהַדָּר וְיִתְעַלֶּה וְיִתְהַלָּל שְׁמֵהּ דְּקֻדְשָׁא בְּרִיךְ הוּא (בְּרִיךְ הוּא – B'rich hu) °לְעֵלָּא מִן כָּל [substitute Rosh Hashanah to Yom Kippur from — °לְעֵלָּא לְעֵלָּא מִכָּל] בִּרְכָתָא וְשִׁירָתָא תֻּשְׁבְּחָתָא וְנֶחֱמָתָא, דַּאֲמִירָן בְּעָלְמָא. וְאִמְרוּ: אָמֵן. (אָמֵן – Omayn).

⌁{ SHEMONEH ESREI — AMIDAH }⌁

IN THE SYNAGOGUE THE *SHEMONEH ESREI* IS RECITED WHILE FACING THE ARK; ELSEWHERE IT IS RECITED WHILE FACING THE DIRECTION OF THE LAND OF ISRAEL. TAKE THREE STEPS BACKWARD, LEFT, RIGHT, LEFT, THEN THREE STEPS FORWARD, RIGHT, LEFT, RIGHT. REMAIN STANDING WITH FEET TOGETHER DURING *SHEMONEH ESREI*. RECITE IT WITH QUIET DEVOTION AND WITHOUT ANY INTERRUPTION. ALTHOUGH IT SHOULD NOT BE AUDIBLE TO OTHERS, ONE MUST PRAY LOUDLY ENOUGH TO HEAR ONESELF.

Adōnoy s'fosai tiftoch, אֲדֹנָי שְׂפָתַי תִּפְתָּח,
My Lord, open my lips,
u-fi yagid t'hilosecho. וּפִי יַגִּיד תְּהִלָּתֶךָ.
that my mouth may declare Your praise.

■ First Blessing: In the merit of our Patriarchs whose actions reflected Godliness, Hashem pledged to always be with Israel and protect them.

BEND THE KNEES AT Boruch; BOW AT ato; STRAIGHTEN UP AT Adōnoy.

BORUCH ato Adōnoy **בָּרוּךְ** אַתָּה יהוה
Blessed are You, HASHEM,
Elōhaynu Vaylōhay avōsaynu, אֱלֹהֵינוּ וֵאלֹהֵי אֲבוֹתֵינוּ,
our God and the God of our forefathers,
Elōhay avrohom, Elōhay yitzchok, אֱלֹהֵי אַבְרָהָם, אֱלֹהֵי יִצְחָק,
Vaylōhay ya-akōv, וֵאלֹהֵי יַעֲקֹב,
God of Abraham, God of Isaac, and God of Jacob;
ho-Ayl hagodōl hagibōr v'hanōro, הָאֵל הַגָּדוֹל הַגִּבּוֹר וְהַנּוֹרָא,
Ayl elyōn, אֵל עֶלְיוֹן,
the great, mighty, and awesome God, the supreme God,

gōmayl chasodim tōvim
  v'kōnay hakōl,
גּוֹמֵל חֲסָדִים טוֹבִים
וְקוֹנֵה הַכֹּל,

Who bestows beneficial kindnesses and creates everything,

v'zōchayr chasday ovōs,
וְזוֹכֵר חַסְדֵי אָבוֹת,

Who recalls the kindnesses of the Patriarchs

u-mayvi gō-ayl livnay v'nayhem,
וּמֵבִיא גוֹאֵל לִבְנֵי בְנֵיהֶם,

and brings a Redeemer to their children's children,

l'ma-an sh'mō b'ahavo.
לְמַעַן שְׁמוֹ בְּאַהֲבָה.

for His Name's sake, with love.

FROM ROSH HASHANAH TO YOM KIPPUR ADD:

Zochraynu l'cha-yim,
  melech chofaytz bacha-yim,
זָכְרֵנוּ לְחַיִּים,
מֶלֶךְ חָפֵץ בַּחַיִּים,

Remember us for life, O King Who desires life,

v'chosvaynu b'sayfer hacha-yim,
l'ma-ancho Elōhim cha-yim.
וְכָתְבֵנוּ בְּסֵפֶר הַחַיִּים,
לְמַעַנְךָ אֱלֹהִים חַיִּים.

and inscribe us in the Book of Life — for Your sake, O Living God.

Melech ōzayr u-mōshi-a u-mogayn.
מֶלֶךְ עוֹזֵר וּמוֹשִׁיעַ וּמָגֵן.

O King, Helper, Savior, and Shield.

BEND THE KNEES AT Boruch; BOW AT ato; STRAIGHTEN UP AT Adōnoy.

Boruch ato Adōnoy, mogayn avrohom.
בָּרוּךְ אַתָּה יהוה, מָגֵן אַבְרָהָם.

*Blessed are You, H*ASHEM*, Shield of Abraham.*

■ Second Blessing: God's might as it is manifest in nature and man

---

ATO gibōr l'ōlom Adōnoy,
אַתָּה גִּבּוֹר לְעוֹלָם אֲדֹנָי,

You are eternally mighty, my Lord,

m'cha-yay maysim ato,
מְחַיֵּה מֵתִים אַתָּה,

the Resuscitator of the dead are You,

rav l'hōshi-a.
רַב לְהוֹשִׁיעַ.

abundantly able to save,

BETWEEN SHEMINI ATZERES AND PESACH, ADD:

Mashiv horu-ach u-mōrid hageshem.
מַשִּׁיב הָרוּחַ וּמוֹרִיד הַגֶּשֶׁם.

Who makes the wind blow and makes the rain descend;

M'chalkayl cha-yim b'chesed,
מְכַלְכֵּל חַיִּים בְּחֶסֶד,

Who sustains the living with kindness,

m'cha-yay maysim b'rachamim rabim,
מְחַיֵּה מֵתִים בְּרַחֲמִים רַבִּים,

resuscitates the dead with abundant mercy,

סוֹמֵךְ נוֹפְלִים, וְרוֹפֵא חוֹלִים,
sōmaych nōf'lim, v'rōfay chōlim,
supports the fallen, heals the sick,

וּמַתִּיר אֲסוּרִים,
u-matir asurim,
releases the confined,

וּמְקַיֵּם אֱמוּנָתוֹ לִישֵׁנֵי עָפָר.
umka-yaym emunosō li-shaynay ofor.
and maintains His faith to those asleep in the dust.

מִי כָמוֹךָ בַּעַל גְּבוּרוֹת,
Mi cho-mōcho ba-al g'vurōs,
Who is like You, O Master of mighty deeds,

וּמִי דּוֹמֶה לָּךְ,
u-mi dōme loch,
and who is comparable to You,

מֶלֶךְ מֵמִית וּמְחַיֶּה
melech maymis umcha-ye
   וּמַצְמִיחַ יְשׁוּעָה.
   u-matzmi-ach y'shu-o.
O King Who causes death and restores life and makes salvation sprout!

■ FROM ROSH HASHANAH TO YOM KIPPUR ADD:

מִי כָמוֹךָ אַב הָרַחֲמִים,
Mi cho-mōcho av horachamim,
Who is like You, O Merciful Father,

זוֹכֵר יְצוּרָיו לְחַיִּים
zōchayr y'tzurov l'cha-yim
   בְּרַחֲמִים.
   b'rachamim.
Who recalls His creatures mercifully for life!

וְנֶאֱמָן אַתָּה לְהַחֲיוֹת מֵתִים.
V'ne-emon ato l'hacha-yōs maysim.
And You are faithful to resuscitate the dead.

בָּרוּךְ אַתָּה יהוה,
Boruch ato Adōnoy,
   מְחַיֵּה הַמֵּתִים.
   m'cha-yay hamaysim.
*Blessed are You, H*ASHEM*, Who resuscitates the dead.*

■ Third Blessing: Regarding the holiness of God's Name

אַתָּה קָדוֹשׁ וְשִׁמְךָ קָדוֹשׁ,
ATO kodōsh v'shimcho kodōsh,
You are holy and Your Name is holy,

וּקְדוֹשִׁים בְּכָל יוֹם
ukdōshim b'chol yōm
   יְהַלְלוּךָ סֶּלָה.
   y'hal'lucho, selo.
and holy ones praise You, every day, forever.

בָּרוּךְ אַתָּה יהוה,
Boruch ato Adōnoy,
   °הָאֵל הַקָּדוֹשׁ.
   °ho-Ayl hakodōsh.
*Blessed are You, H*ASHEM*, the holy God.*

FROM ROSH HASHANAH TO YOM KIPPUR SUBSTITUTE:

   °הַמֶּלֶךְ הַקָּדוֹשׁ.
   °hamelech hakodōsh.
the holy King.

■ **Fourth Blessing: Supplication for the gift of intellect**

ATO chōnayn l'odom da-as,   אַתָּה חוֹנֵן לְאָדָם דַּעַת,
You graciously endow man with wisdom
umlamayd le-enōsh bino.   וּמְלַמֵּד לֶאֱנוֹשׁ בִּינָה.
and teach insight to a frail mortal.

AFTER THE SABBATH OR A FESTIVAL, ADD THE FOLLOWING:

ATO chōnantonu   אַתָּה חוֹנַנְתָּנוּ
l'mada tōrosecho,   לְמַדַּע תּוֹרָתֶךָ,
You have graced us* with intelligence to study Your Torah
vat'lam'daynu la-asōs   וַתְּלַמְּדֵנוּ לַעֲשׂוֹת
chukay r'tzōnecho.   חֻקֵּי רְצוֹנֶךָ.
and You have taught us to perform the decrees You have willed.
Vatavdayl Adōnoy Elōhaynu   וַתַּבְדֵּל יהוה אֱלֹהֵינוּ
HASHEM, *our God, You have distinguished*
bayn kōdesh l'chōl,   בֵּין קֹדֶשׁ לְחוֹל,
between the sacred and the secular,*
bayn ōr l'chōshech,   בֵּין אוֹר לְחֹשֶׁךְ,
between light and darkness,
bayn yisro-ayl lo-amim,   בֵּין יִשְׂרָאֵל לָעַמִּים,
between Israel and the peoples,
bayn yōm hash'vi-i   בֵּין יוֹם הַשְּׁבִיעִי
l'shayshes y'may hama-ase.   לְשֵׁשֶׁת יְמֵי הַמַּעֲשֶׂה.
between the Seventh Day and the six days of labor.
Ovinu malkaynu hochayl olaynu   אָבִינוּ מַלְכֵּנוּ הָחֵל עָלֵינוּ
Our Father, our King, begin for us
ha-yomim habo-im likrosaynu   הַיָּמִים הַבָּאִים לִקְרָאתֵנוּ
l'sholōm,   לְשָׁלוֹם,
the days approaching us for peace,
chasuchim mikol chayt   חֲשׂוּכִים מִכָּל חֵטְא
free from all sin,
umnukim mikol ovōn   וּמְנֻקִּים מִכָּל עָוֹן
cleansed from all iniquity
umdubokim b'yiro-secho. V' ...   וּמְדֻבָּקִים בְּיִרְאָתֶךָ. וְ ...
and attached to fear of You. And ...

אַתָּה חוֹנַנְתָּנוּ — *You have graced us.* The *Havdalah* blessing that differentiates between the Sabbath and the weekdays is quite properly inserted in the blessing of wisdom because of the well-known dictum of the Sages: "If there is no wisdom, how can there be differentiation?" (*Yerushalmi, Berachos* 5:20).

בֵּין קֹדֶשׁ לְחוֹל — *Between the sacred and the secular.* Four distinctions are enumerated here: (1) Between the holy and the secular —

chonaynu may-it'cho
day-o bino v'haskayl.
חָנֵּנוּ מֵאִתְּךָ
דֵּעָה בִּינָה וְהַשְׂכֵּל.
endow us graciously from Yourself with wisdom, insight, and discernment.

Boruch ato Adōnoy, chōnayn hado-as. בָּרוּךְ אַתָּה יהוה, חוֹנֵן הַדָּעַת.
Blessed are You, Hashem, gracious Giver of wisdom.

■ Fifth Blessing: Supplication for Divine assistance in repentance

---

HASHIVAYNU ovinu l'sōrosecho, הֲשִׁיבֵנוּ אָבִינוּ לְתוֹרָתֶךָ,
Bring us back, our Father, to Your Torah,

v'kor'vaynu malkaynu la-avōdosecho, וְקָרְבֵנוּ מַלְכֵּנוּ לַעֲבוֹדָתֶךָ,
and bring us near, our King, to Your service,

v'hachaziraynu bis-shuvo sh'laymo l'fonecho.
וְהַחֲזִירֵנוּ בִּתְשׁוּבָה שְׁלֵמָה לְפָנֶיךָ.
and return us in perfect repentance before You.

Boruch ato Adōnoy,
horōtze bis-shuvo.
בָּרוּךְ אַתָּה יהוה,
הָרוֹצֶה בִּתְשׁוּבָה.
Blessed are You, Hashem, Who desires repentance.

■ Sixth Blessing: Supplication for forgiveness

STRIKE THE LEFT SIDE OF THE CHEST WITH THE RIGHT FIST
WHILE RECITING THE WORDS ki chotonu AND ki foshonu.

S'LACH lonu ovinu ki chotonu, סְלַח לָנוּ אָבִינוּ כִּי חָטָאנוּ,
Forgive us, our Father, for we have erred;

m'chal lonu malkaynu ki foshonu, מְחַל לָנוּ מַלְכֵּנוּ כִּי פָשָׁעְנוּ,
pardon us, our King, for we have willfully sinned;

ki mōchayl v'sōlayach oto. כִּי מוֹחֵל וְסוֹלֵחַ אָתָּה.
for You pardon and forgive.

Boruch ato Adōnoy,
chanun hamarbe lislō-ach.
בָּרוּךְ אַתָּה יהוה,
חַנּוּן הַמַּרְבֶּה לִסְלֹחַ.
Blessed are You, Hashem, the gracious One Who pardons abundantly.

■ Seventh Blessing: Supplication for personal redemption
from the perils and problems of daily life

R'AY v'on-yaynu, v'rivo rivaynu, רְאֵה בְעָנְיֵנוּ, וְרִיבָה רִיבֵנוּ,
Behold our affliction, take up our grievance,

---

not the profane, but the mundane factors in life that prevent us from recognizing and achieving holiness; (2) between light and darkness, which also symbolizes the distinctions between good and evil; (3) the fact that God took Israel to be His chosen people from among all the nations; and (4) between the day that testifies to God as the Creator and the days when His Presence is less apparent.

WEEKDAY MAARIV — SHEMONEH ESREI

ug-olaynu m'hayro l'ma-an sh'mecho,   וּגְאָלֵנוּ מְהֵרָה לְמַעַן שְׁמֶךָ,
and redeem us speedily for Your Name's sake,

ki gō-ayl chozok oto.   כִּי גּוֹאֵל חָזָק אָתָּה.
for You are a powerful Redeemer.

Boruch ato Adōnoy, gō-ayl yisro-ayl.   בָּרוּךְ אַתָּה יהוה, גּוֹאֵל יִשְׂרָאֵל.
Blessed are You, HASHEM, Redeemer of Israel.

■ **Eighth Blessing: Supplication for health and healing of body and soul**

R'FO-AYNU Adōnoy, v'nayrofay,   רְפָאֵנוּ יהוה וְנֵרָפֵא,
Heal us, HASHEM — then we will be healed;

hōshi-aynu v'nivoshay-o,   הוֹשִׁיעֵנוּ וְנִוָּשֵׁעָה,
save us — then we will be saved,

ki s'hilosaynu oto,   כִּי תְהִלָּתֵנוּ אָתָּה,
for You are our praise;

v'ha-alay r'fu-o sh'laymo   וְהַעֲלֵה רְפוּאָה שְׁלֵמָה
    l'chol makōsaynu,   לְכָל מַכּוֹתֵינוּ,
and bring complete recovery for all our ailments,

ki Ayl melech   כִּי אֵל מֶלֶךְ
    rōfay ne-emon v'rachamon oto.   רוֹפֵא נֶאֱמָן וְרַחֲמָן אָתָּה.
for You are God, King, the faithful and compassionate Healer.

Boruch ato Adōnoy,   בָּרוּךְ אַתָּה יהוה,
    rōfay chōlay amō yisro-ayl.   רוֹפֵא חוֹלֵי עַמּוֹ יִשְׂרָאֵל.
Blessed are You, HASHEM, Who heals the sick of His people Israel.

■ **Ninth Blessing: Supplication for a year of prosperity**

FOR THE FOLLOWING BLESSING, SUMMER IS DEFINED AS THE PERIOD FROM PESACH THROUGH *MINCHAH* OF DECEMBER 4TH (OR 5TH, IN THE YEAR BEFORE A CIVIL LEAP YEAR); WINTER IS DEFINED AS THE REST OF THE YEAR.

BORAYCH olaynu, Adōnoy Elōhaynu,   בָּרֵךְ עָלֵינוּ יהוה אֱלֹהֵינוּ
    es ha-shono ha-zōs   אֶת הַשָּׁנָה הַזֹּאת
Bless on our behalf, O HASHEM, our God, this year

v'es kol minay s'vu-oso l'tōvo,   וְאֶת כָּל מִינֵי תְבוּאָתָהּ לְטוֹבָה,
and all its kinds of crops for the best,

IN SUMMER SAY:

v'sayn b'rocho   וְתֵן בְּרָכָה
and give a blessing

IN WINTER SAY:

v'sayn tal u-motor livrocho   וְתֵן טַל וּמָטָר לִבְרָכָה
and give dew and rain for a blessing

al p'nay ho-adomo,	עַל פְּנֵי הָאֲדָמָה,
on the face of the earth,	
v'sab'aynu mituvecho,	וְשַׂבְּעֵנוּ מִטּוּבֶךָ,
and satisfy us from Your bounty,	
u-voraych sh'nosaynu ka-shonim hatōvōs.	וּבָרֵךְ שְׁנָתֵנוּ כַּשָּׁנִים הַטּוֹבוֹת.
and bless our year like the best years.	
Boruch ato Adōnoy, m'voraych ha-shonim.	בָּרוּךְ אַתָּה יהוה, מְבָרֵךְ הַשָּׁנִים.
Blessed are You, HASHEM, Who blesses the years.	

■ **Tenth Blessing:** Supplication for the ingathering of the exiles

T'KA b'shōfor godōl l'chayrusaynu, תְּקַע בְּשׁוֹפָר גָּדוֹל לְחֵרוּתֵנוּ,
Sound the great shofar for our freedom,
v'so nays l'kabaytz golu-yōsaynu, וְשָׂא נֵס לְקַבֵּץ גָּלֻיּוֹתֵינוּ,
raise a banner to gather our exiles
v'kab'tzaynu yachad may-arba kanfōs ho-oretz. וְקַבְּצֵנוּ יַחַד מֵאַרְבַּע כַּנְפוֹת הָאָרֶץ.
and gather us together from the four corners of the earth.
Boruch ato Adōnoy, m'kabaytz nidchay amō yisro-ayl. בָּרוּךְ אַתָּה יהוה, מְקַבֵּץ נִדְחֵי עַמּוֹ יִשְׂרָאֵל.
Blessed are You, HASHEM, Who gathers in the dispersed of His people Israel.

■ **Eleventh Blessing:** Supplication for the restoration of justice to the Jewish judiciary

HOSHIVO shōf'taynu k'vorishōno הָשִׁיבָה שׁוֹפְטֵינוּ כְּבָרִאשׁוֹנָה,
Restore our judges as in earliest times
v'yō-atzaynu k'vat'chilo, וְיוֹעֲצֵינוּ כְּבַתְּחִלָּה,
and our counselors as at first;
v'hosayr mimenu yogōn va-anocho, וְהָסֵר מִמֶּנּוּ יָגוֹן וַאֲנָחָה,
remove from us sorrow and groan;
umlōch olaynu ato, Adōnoy, l'vad'cho וּמְלוֹךְ עָלֵינוּ אַתָּה יהוה לְבַדְּךָ
and reign over us, You, HASHEM, alone,
b'chesed uvrachamim, בְּחֶסֶד וּבְרַחֲמִים,
with kindness and with compassion,
v'tzad'kaynu bamishpot. וְצַדְּקֵנוּ בַּמִּשְׁפָּט.
and justify us through judgment.

Boruch ato Adōnoy,	בָּרוּךְ אַתָּה יהוה,
°melech ōhayv tz'doko u-mishpot.	°מֶלֶךְ אוֹהֵב צְדָקָה וּמִשְׁפָּט.

Blessed are You, HASHEM, the King Who loves righteousness and judgment.

FROM ROSH HASHANAH TO YOM KIPPUR SUBSTITUTE:

°hamelech hamishpot.	°הַמֶּלֶךְ הַמִּשְׁפָּט.

the King of Judgment.

■ **Twelfth Blessing:** Supplication for the eradication of heretic influences that threaten Jewish life

---

V'LAMALSHINIM al t'hi sikvo,   **וְלַמַּלְשִׁינִים** אַל תְּהִי תִקְוָה,

And for the slanderers let there be no hope;

v'chol horish-o k'rega tōvayd.   וְכָל הָרִשְׁעָה כְּרֶגַע תֹּאבֵד.

and may all wickedness perish in an instant;

v'chol ō-y'vecho m'hayro yikoraysu.   וְכָל אֹיְבֶיךָ מְהֵרָה יִכָּרֵתוּ.

and may all Your enemies be cut down speedily.

V'hazaydim m'hayro s'akayr   וְהַזֵּדִים מְהֵרָה תְעַקֵּר

The wanton sinners — may You speedily uproot,

us-shabayr usmagayr v'sachni-a   וּתְשַׁבֵּר וּתְמַגֵּר וְתַכְנִיעַ

smash, cast down, and humble —

bimhayro v'yomaynu.   בִּמְהֵרָה בְיָמֵינוּ.

speedily in our days.

Boruch ato Adōnoy,   בָּרוּךְ אַתָּה יהוה,

shōvayr ōy'vim u-machni-a zaydim.   שׁוֹבֵר אֹיְבִים וּמַכְנִיעַ זֵדִים.

Blessed are You, HASHEM, Who breaks enemies and humbles wanton sinners.

■ **Thirteenth Blessing:** Supplication on behalf of the righteous and recognition of their significance

---

AL hatzadikim v'al hachasidim   **עַל** הַצַּדִּיקִים וְעַל הַחֲסִידִים,

On the righteous, on the devout,

v'al ziknay am'cho bays yisro-ayl,   וְעַל זִקְנֵי עַמְּךָ בֵּית יִשְׂרָאֵל,

on the elders of Your people the Family of Israel,

v'al p'laytas sōf'rayhem,   וְעַל פְּלֵיטַת סוֹפְרֵיהֶם,

on the remnant of their scholars,

v'al gayray hatzedek v'olaynu.   וְעַל גֵּרֵי הַצֶּדֶק וְעָלֵינוּ.

on the righteous converts and on ourselves —

yehemu rachamecho,   יֶהֱמוּ רַחֲמֶיךָ

Adōnoy Elōhaynu,   יהוה אֱלֹהֵינוּ,

may Your compassion be aroused, HASHEM, our God;

v'sayn sochor tōv l'chol habōt'chim b'shimcho be-emes,	וְתֵן שָׂכָר טוֹב לְכָל הַבּוֹטְחִים בְּשִׁמְךָ בֶּאֱמֶת,

and give goodly reward to all who sincerely believe in Your Name;

v'sim chelkaynu i-mohem l'ōlom,   וְשִׂים חֶלְקֵנוּ עִמָּהֶם לְעוֹלָם,
and place our lot with them forever,

v'lō nayvōsh ki v'cho botoch'nu.   וְלֹא נֵבוֹשׁ כִּי בְךָ בָּטָחְנוּ.
and we will not feel ashamed, for we trust in You.

Boruch ato Adōnoy,   בָּרוּךְ אַתָּה יהוה,
mish-on u-mivtoch latzadikim.   מִשְׁעָן וּמִבְטָח לַצַּדִּיקִים.
*Blessed are You, H*ASHEM*, Mainstay and Assurance of the righteous.*

■ Fourteenth Blessing: Supplication for the physical and spiritual rebuilding of Jerusalem

V'LIRUSHOLA-YIM ir'cho   **וְלִירוּשָׁלַיִם** עִירְךָ
b'rachamim toshuv,   בְּרַחֲמִים תָּשׁוּב,
And to Jerusalem, Your city, may You return in compassion,

v'sishkōn b'sōchoh ka-asher dibarto,   וְתִשְׁכּוֹן בְּתוֹכָהּ כַּאֲשֶׁר דִּבַּרְתָּ,
and may You rest within it, as You have spoken;

uvnay ōsoh b'korōv b'yomaynu   וּבְנֵה אוֹתָהּ בְּקָרוֹב בְּיָמֵינוּ
binyan ōlom,   בִּנְיַן עוֹלָם,
may You rebuild it soon in our days as an eternal structure,

v'chisay dovid   וְכִסֵּא דָוִד
m'hayro l'sōchoh tochin   מְהֵרָה לְתוֹכָהּ תָּכִין.
and the throne of David may You speedily establish within it.

Boruch ato Adōnoy,   בָּרוּךְ אַתָּה יהוה,
bōnay y'rusholo-yim.   בּוֹנֵה יְרוּשָׁלָיִם.
*Blessed are You, H*ASHEM*, the Builder of Jerusalem.*

■ Fifteenth Blessing: Supplication that the Messiah restore the Davidic reign

ES TZEMACH dovid avd'cho   **אֶת צֶמַח** דָּוִד עַבְדְּךָ
m'hayro satzmi-ach,   מְהֵרָה תַצְמִיחַ,
The offspring of Your servant David may You speedily cause to flourish,

v'karnō torum bi-shu-osecho,   וְקַרְנוֹ תָּרוּם בִּישׁוּעָתֶךָ,
and enhance his pride through Your salvation,

ki lishu-os'cho kivinu kol ha-yom   כִּי לִישׁוּעָתְךָ קִוִּינוּ כָּל הַיּוֹם.
for we hope for Your salvation all day long.

Boruch ato Adōnoy,   בָּרוּךְ אַתָּה יהוה,
matzmi-ach keren y'shu-o.   מַצְמִיחַ קֶרֶן יְשׁוּעָה.
*Blessed are You, H*ASHEM*, Who causes the pride of salvation to flourish.*

■ Sixteenth Blessing: Supplication for God's acceptance of our prayer

SH'MA KOLAYNU Adōnoy Elōhaynu, שְׁמַע קוֹלֵנוּ יהוה אֱלֹהֵינוּ,
Hear our voice, HASHEM, our God,
chus v'rachaym olaynu, חוּס וְרַחֵם עָלֵינוּ,
pity and be compassionate to us,
v'kabayl b'rachamim uvrotzōn וְקַבֵּל בְּרַחֲמִים וּבְרָצוֹן
    es t'filosaynu, אֶת תְּפִלָּתֵנוּ,
and accept — with compassion and favor — our prayer,
ki Ayl shōmay-a כִּי אֵל שׁוֹמֵעַ
    t'filōs v'sachanunim oto, תְּפִלּוֹת וְתַחֲנוּנִים אָתָּה.
for God Who hears prayers and supplications are You;
u-mil'fonecho, malkaynu, וּמִלְּפָנֶיךָ מַלְכֵּנוּ,
from before Yourself, our King,
raykom al t'shivaynu, רֵיקָם אַל תְּשִׁיבֵנוּ,
turn us not away empty-handed,
ki ato shōmay-a t'filas כִּי אַתָּה שׁוֹמֵעַ תְּפִלַּת
    am'cho yisro-ayl b'rachamim. עַמְּךָ יִשְׂרָאֵל בְּרַחֲמִים.
for You hear the prayer of Your people Israel with compassion.
Boruch ato Adōnoy, בָּרוּךְ אַתָּה יהוה,
    shōmay-a t'filo. שׁוֹמֵעַ תְּפִלָּה.
Blessed are You, HASHEM, Who hears prayer.

■ Seventeenth Blessing: Prayer for restoration of the Temple service

R'TZAY, Adōnoy Elōhaynu רְצֵה יהוה אֱלֹהֵינוּ
Be favorable, HASHEM, our God,
b'am'cho yisro-ayl u-visfilosom, בְּעַמְּךָ יִשְׂרָאֵל וּבִתְפִלָּתָם,
toward Your people Israel and their prayer
v'hoshayv es ho-avōdo וְהָשֵׁב אֶת הָעֲבוֹדָה
    lidvir bay-secho. לִדְבִיר בֵּיתֶךָ.
and restore the service to the Holy of Holies of Your Temple.
V'i-shay yisro-ayl, usfilosom וְאִשֵּׁי יִשְׂרָאֵל וּתְפִלָּתָם
    b'ahavo s'kabayl b'rotzōn, בְּאַהֲבָה תְקַבֵּל בְּרָצוֹן,
The fire-offerings of Israel and their prayer accept with love and favor,
us-hi l'rotzōn tomid וּתְהִי לְרָצוֹן תָּמִיד
    avōdas yisro-ayl amecho. עֲבוֹדַת יִשְׂרָאֵל עַמֶּךָ.
and may the service of Your people Israel always be favorable to You.

- **Yaaleh Veyavo:** We petition God to have compassion on Israel and Jerusalem, and to reinstate the Temple service, to enable us to bring the appropriate offerings for the particular occasion.

ON *ROSH CHODESH* AND *CHOL HAMOED* RECITE THE FOLLOWING:

ELŌHAYNU Vaylōhay avōsaynu, אֱלֹהֵינוּ וֵאלֹהֵי אֲבוֹתֵינוּ,
Our God and the God of our forefathers,

ya-a-le v'yovō v'yagi-a v'yayro-e יַעֲלֶה, וְיָבֹא, וְיַגִּיעַ, וְיֵרָאֶה,
may there rise, come, reach, be noted,

v'yayro-tze v'yi-shoma v'yipokayd וְיֵרָצֶה, וְיִשָּׁמַע, וְיִפָּקֵד,
be favored, be heard, be considered,

v'yizochayr zichrōnaynu u-fikdōnaynu, וְיִזָּכֵר זִכְרוֹנֵנוּ וּפִקְדוֹנֵנוּ,
and be remembered — the remembrance and consideration of ourselves;

v'zichrōn avōsaynu, וְזִכְרוֹן אֲבוֹתֵינוּ,
the remembrance of our forefathers;

v'zichrōn moshi-ach וְזִכְרוֹן מָשִׁיחַ
ben dovid avdecho, בֶּן דָּוִד עַבְדֶּךָ,
the remembrance of Messiah, son of David, Your servant;

v'zichrōn y'rushola-yim וְזִכְרוֹן יְרוּשָׁלַיִם
ir kod-shecho, עִיר קָדְשֶׁךָ,
the remembrance of Jerusalem, Your Holy City;

v'zichrōn kol am'cho bays yisro-ayl וְזִכְרוֹן כָּל עַמְּךָ בֵּית יִשְׂרָאֵל
and the remembrance of Your entire people the Family of Israel —

l'fonecho, lif-layto l'tōvo לְפָנֶיךָ, לִפְלֵיטָה לְטוֹבָה
before You for deliverance, for goodness,

l'chayn ulchesed ulrachamim, לְחֵן וּלְחֶסֶד וּלְרַחֲמִים,
for grace, for kindness, and for compassion,

l'cha-yim ulsholōm לְחַיִּים וּלְשָׁלוֹם
for life, and for peace

--- ON ROSH CHODESH ---

b'yōm rōsh hachōdesh ha-ze. בְּיוֹם רֹאשׁ הַחֹדֶשׁ הַזֶּה.
on this day of Rosh Chodesh.

--- ON PESACH ---

b'yōm chag hamatzōs ha-ze. בְּיוֹם חַג הַמַּצּוֹת הַזֶּה.
on this day of the Festival of Matzos.

--- ON SUCCOS ---

b'yōm chag hasukōs ha-ze. בְּיוֹם חַג הַסֻּכּוֹת הַזֶּה.
on this day of the Succos Festival.

WEEKDAY MAARIV — SHEMONEH ESREI

Zoch'raynu Adōnoy Elōhaynu　　　זָכְרֵנוּ יהוה אֱלֹהֵינוּ
　bō l'tōvo,　　　בּוֹ לְטוֹבָה,
　　Remember us on it, Hashem, our God, for goodness,
u-fokdaynu vō livrocho,　　　וּפָקְדֵנוּ בּוֹ לִבְרָכָה,
　　consider us on it for blessing
v'hōshi-aynu vō l'cha-yim.　　　וְהוֹשִׁיעֵנוּ בוֹ לְחַיִּים.
　　and help us on it for life.
U-vidvar y'shu-o v'rachamim,　　　וּבִדְבַר יְשׁוּעָה וְרַחֲמִים,
　　In the matter of salvation and compassion,
chus v'chonaynu　　　חוּס וְחָנֵּנוּ
v'rachaym olaynu v'hōshi-aynu,　　　וְרַחֵם עָלֵינוּ וְהוֹשִׁיעֵנוּ,
　　pity, be gracious and compassionate with us and help us,
ki aylecho aynaynu,　　　כִּי אֵלֶיךָ עֵינֵינוּ,
　　for our eyes are turned to You,
ki Ayl melech　　　כִּי אֵל מֶלֶךְ
chanun v'rachum oto.　　　חַנּוּן וְרַחוּם אָתָּה.
　　because You are God, the gracious and compassionate King.

V'SECHEZENO aynaynu　　　וְתֶחֱזֶינָה עֵינֵינוּ
　　May our eyes behold
b'shuv'cho l'tziyōn b'rachamim.　　　בְּשׁוּבְךָ לְצִיּוֹן בְּרַחֲמִים.
　　Your return to Zion in compassion.
Boruch ato Adōnoy,　　　בָּרוּךְ אַתָּה יהוה,
hamachazir sh'chinosō l'tziyōn.　　　הַמַּחֲזִיר שְׁכִינָתוֹ לְצִיּוֹן.
　　Blessed are You, Hashem, Who restores His Presence unto Zion.

■ Eighteenth Blessing: Acknowledgment of our debt of gratitude

---

BOW AT Mōdim anachnu loch; STRAIGHTEN UP AT Adōnoy.

MŌDIM anachnu loch,　　　מוֹדִים אֲנַחְנוּ לָךְ,
　　We gratefully thank You,
sho-ato hu Adōnoy Elōhaynu　　　שָׁאַתָּה הוּא יהוה אֱלֹהֵינוּ
　　for it is You Who are Hashem, our God,
Vaylōhay avōsaynu　　　וֵאלֹהֵי אֲבוֹתֵינוּ
　　and the God of our forefathers
l'ōlom vo-ed,　　　לְעוֹלָם וָעֶד,
　　forever and ever;
tzur cha-yaynu, mogayn yish-aynu　　　צוּר חַיֵּינוּ, מָגֵן יִשְׁעֵנוּ
　　Rock of our lives, Shield of our salvation

אַתָּה הוּא לְדוֹר וָדוֹר.
ato hu l'dōr vodōr.
are You from generation to generation.

נוֹדֶה לְךָ וּנְסַפֵּר תְּהִלָּתֶךָ
Nōde l'cho unsapayr t'hilosecho
We shall thank You and relate Your praise —

עַל חַיֵּינוּ הַמְּסוּרִים בְּיָדֶךָ,
al cha-yaynu ham'surim b'yodecho,
for our lives which are committed to Your power,

וְעַל נִשְׁמוֹתֵינוּ הַפְּקוּדוֹת לָךְ,
v'al nishmōsaynu hap'kudōs loch,
and for our souls that are entrusted to You,

וְעַל נִסֶּיךָ שֶׁבְּכָל יוֹם עִמָּנוּ,
v'al nisecho sheb'chol yōm i-monu,
and for Your miracles that are with us every day,

וְעַל נִפְלְאוֹתֶיךָ וְטוֹבוֹתֶיךָ שֶׁבְּכָל עֵת,
v'al nifl'ōsecho v'tōvōsecho sheb'chol ays,
and for Your wonders and favors in every season —

עֶרֶב וָבֹקֶר וְצָהֳרָיִם.
erev vovōker v'tzohorō-yim.
evening, morning, and afternoon.

הַטּוֹב כִּי לֹא כָלוּ רַחֲמֶיךָ,
Hatōv ki lō cholu rachamecho,
The Beneficent One, for Your compassions were never exhausted,

וְהַמְרַחֵם כִּי לֹא תַמּוּ חֲסָדֶיךָ,
v'ham'rachaym ki lō samu chasodecho,
and the Compassionate One, for Your kindnesses never ended —

מֵעוֹלָם קִוִּינוּ לָךְ.
may-ōlom kivinu loch.
always have we put our hope in You.

ON ALL DAYS OTHER THAN CHANUKAH AND PURIM CONTINUE V'al kulom (P. 435).

ON CHANUKAH AND PURIM CONTINUE BELOW:

עַל הַנִּסִּים, וְעַל הַפֻּרְקָן,
AL hanisim, v'al hapurkon,
For the miracles, and for the salvation,

וְעַל הַגְּבוּרוֹת, וְעַל הַתְּשׁוּעוֹת,
v'al hag'vurōs, v'al hat'shu-ōs,
and for the mighty deeds, and for the victories,

וְעַל הַמִּלְחָמוֹת,
v'al hamilchomōs,
and for the battles

שֶׁעָשִׂיתָ לַאֲבוֹתֵינוּ
she-osiso la-avōsaynu
which You performed for our forefathers

בַּיָּמִים הָהֵם בַּזְּמַן הַזֶּה.
ba-yomim hohaym baz'man ha-ze.
in those days, at this time.

ON CHANUKAH CONTINUE HERE; ON PURIM TURN TO P. 434.

בִּימֵי מַתִּתְיָהוּ בֶּן יוֹחָנָן
BIMAY matisyohu ben yōchonon
In the days of Mattisyahu, the son of Yochanan,

כֹּהֵן גָּדוֹל חַשְׁמוֹנָאִי וּבָנָיו,
kōhayn godōl chashmōno-i u-vonov,
the High Priest, the Hasmonean, and his sons —

ON CHANUKAH CONTINUE HERE:

k'she-om'do malchus yovon / כְּשֶׁעָמְדָה מַלְכוּת יָוָן
hor'sho-o al am'cho yisro-ayl, / הָרְשָׁעָה עַל עַמְּךָ יִשְׂרָאֵל,
when the wicked Greek kingdom rose up against Your people Israel

l'hashkichom tōrosecho, / לְהַשְׁכִּיחָם תּוֹרָתֶךָ,
to make them forget Your Torah

ulha-avirom maychukay r'tzōnecho. / וּלְהַעֲבִירָם מֵחֻקֵּי רְצוֹנֶךָ.
and compel them to stray from the statutes of Your will.

V'ato b'rachamecho horabim, / וְאַתָּה בְּרַחֲמֶיךָ הָרַבִּים,
But You, in Your abundant mercy,

omadto lohem b'ays tzorosom, / עָמַדְתָּ לָהֶם בְּעֵת צָרָתָם,
stood up for them in the time of their distress.

Ravto es rivom, danto es dinom, / רַבְתָּ אֶת רִיבָם, דַּנְתָּ אֶת דִּינָם,
You took up their grievance, You judged their claim,

nokamto es nikmosom. / נָקַמְתָּ אֶת נִקְמָתָם.
and You avenged their wrong.

Mosarto gibōrim b'yad chaloshim, / מָסַרְתָּ גִבּוֹרִים בְּיַד חַלָּשִׁים,
You delivered the strong into the hand of the weak,

v'rabim b'yad m'atim, / וְרַבִּים בְּיַד מְעַטִּים,
the many into the hand of the few,

utmay-im b'yad t'hōrim, / וּטְמֵאִים בְּיַד טְהוֹרִים,
the impure into the hand of the pure,

ursho-im b'yad tzadikim / וּרְשָׁעִים בְּיַד צַדִּיקִים
the wicked into the hand of the righteous,

v'zaydim b'yad ōs'kay sōrosecho. / וְזֵדִים בְּיַד עוֹסְקֵי תוֹרָתֶךָ.
and the wanton into the hand of the diligent students of Your Torah.

Ulcho osiso / וּלְךָ עָשִׂיתָ
For Yourself You made

shaym godōl v'kodōsh b'ōlomecho, / שֵׁם גָּדוֹל וְקָדוֹשׁ בְּעוֹלָמֶךָ,
a great and holy Name in Your world,

ul-am'cho yisro-ayl / וּלְעַמְּךָ יִשְׂרָאֵל
and for Your people Israel

osiso t'shu-o g'dōlo u-furkon / עָשִׂיתָ תְּשׁוּעָה גְדוֹלָה וּפֻרְקָן
k'ha-yōm ha-ze. / כְּהַיּוֹם הַזֶּה.
You performed a great victory and salvation as this very day.

V'achar kayn bo-u vonecho / וְאַחַר כֵּן בָּאוּ בָנֶיךָ
lidvir bay-secho, / לִדְבִיר בֵּיתֶךָ,
Thereafter, Your children came to the Holy of Holies of Your House,

ON CHANUKAH CONTINUE HERE:

u-finu es haycholecho,   וּפִנּוּ אֶת הֵיכָלֶךָ,
they cleansed Your Temple,

v'tiharu es mikdoshecho,   וְטִהֲרוּ אֶת מִקְדָּשֶׁךָ,
they purified the site of Your Holiness;

v'hidliku nayrōs   וְהִדְלִיקוּ נֵרוֹת
    b'chatzrōs kod-shecho,   בְּחַצְרוֹת קָדְשֶׁךָ,
and they kindled lights in the Courtyards of Your Sanctuary;

v'kov'u   וְקָבְעוּ
    sh'mōnas y'may chanuko aylu,   שְׁמוֹנַת יְמֵי חֲנֻכָּה אֵלּוּ,
and they established these eight days of Chanukah

l'hōdōs ulhalayl   לְהוֹדוֹת וּלְהַלֵּל
l'shimcho hagodōl.   לְשִׁמְךָ הַגָּדוֹל.
to express thanks and praise to Your great Name.

CONTINUE V'al kulom (P. 435).

ON PURIM CONTINUE HERE:

BIMAY mord'chai v'estayr   **בִּימֵי** מָרְדְּכַי וְאֶסְתֵּר
In the days of Mordechai and Esther,

b'shushan habiro,   בְּשׁוּשַׁן הַבִּירָה,
in Shushan, the capital,

k'she-omad alayhem homon horosho,   כְּשֶׁעָמַד עֲלֵיהֶם הָמָן הָרָשָׁע,
when Haman, the wicked, rose up against them

bikaysh l'hashmid laharōg ul-abayd   בִּקֵּשׁ לְהַשְׁמִיד לַהֲרֹג וּלְאַבֵּד
and sought to destroy, to slay, and to exterminate

es kol ha-y'hudim,   אֶת כָּל הַיְּהוּדִים,
    mina-ar v'ad zokayn, taf v'noshim   מִנַּעַר וְעַד זָקֵן, טַף וְנָשִׁים
all the Jews, young and old, infants and women,

b'yōm e-chod,   בְּיוֹם אֶחָד,
on the same day,

bishlōsho osor l'chōdesh   בִּשְׁלוֹשָׁה עָשָׂר לְחֹדֶשׁ
    sh'naym osor, hu chōdesh ador,   שְׁנֵים עָשָׂר, הוּא חֹדֶשׁ אֲדָר,
on the thirteenth of the twelfth month which is the month of Adar,

ushlolom lovōz.   וּשְׁלָלָם לָבוֹז.
and to plunder their possessions.

V'ato b'rachamecho horabim   וְאַתָּה בְּרַחֲמֶיךָ הָרַבִּים
But You, in Your abundant mercy,

hayfarto es atzosō,   הֵפַרְתָּ אֶת עֲצָתוֹ,
nullified his counsel

ON PURIM CONTINUE HERE:

v'kilkalto es machashavtō, וְקִלְקַלְתָּ אֶת מַחֲשַׁבְתּוֹ,
and frustrated his intention
vaha-shayvōso lō g'mulō b'rōshō, וַהֲשֵׁבוֹתָ לּוֹ גְּמוּלוֹ בְרֹאשׁוֹ,
and caused his design to return upon his own head,
v'solu ōsō v'es bonov al ho-aytz. וְתָלוּ אוֹתוֹ וְאֶת בָּנָיו עַל הָעֵץ.
and they hanged him and his sons on the gallows.

V'AL kulom yisborach v'yisrōmam וְעַל כֻּלָּם יִתְבָּרַךְ וְיִתְרוֹמַם
shimcho, malkaynu שִׁמְךָ מַלְכֵּנוּ
For all these, may Your Name be blessed and exalted, our King,
tomid l'ōlom vo-ed. תָּמִיד לְעוֹלָם וָעֶד.
continually, forever and ever.

FROM ROSH HASHANAH TO YOM KIPPUR ADD:

Uchsōv l'cha-yim tōvim וּכְתוֹב לְחַיִּים טוֹבִים
kol b'nay v'risecho. כָּל בְּנֵי בְרִיתֶךָ.
And inscribe all the children of Your covenant for a good life.

V'chōl hacha-yim yōducho selo, וְכֹל הַחַיִּים יוֹדוּךָ סֶּלָה,
Everything alive will gratefully acknowledge You, Selah!
vihal'lu es shimcho be-emes, וִיהַלְלוּ אֶת שִׁמְךָ בֶּאֱמֶת,
and praise Your Name sincerely,
ho-Ayl y'shu-osaynu הָאֵל יְשׁוּעָתֵנוּ
v'ezrosaynu selo. וְעֶזְרָתֵנוּ סֶלָה.
O God of our salvation and help, Selah!

BEND THE KNEES AT Boruch; BOW AT ato; STRAIGHTEN UP AT Adōnoy.

Boruch ato Adōnoy, בָּרוּךְ אַתָּה יְהֹוָה,
hatōv shimcho הַטּוֹב שִׁמְךָ
ulcho no-e l'hōdōs. וּלְךָ נָאֶה לְהוֹדוֹת.
Blessed are You, HASHEM, Your Name is "The Beneficent One"
and to You it is fitting to give thanks.

■ Nineteenth Blessing: Prayer for peace and harmony
amongst the Jewish people

SHOLŌM ROV al yisro-ayl שָׁלוֹם רָב עַל יִשְׂרָאֵל
am'cho tosim l'ōlom, עַמְּךָ תָּשִׂים לְעוֹלָם,
Establish abundant peace upon Your people Israel forever,

ki ato hu melech,	כִּי אַתָּה הוּא מֶלֶךְ
odōn l'chol ha-sholōm.	אָדוֹן לְכָל הַשָּׁלוֹם.

for You are King, Master of all peace.

V'tōv b'aynecho l'voraych	וְטוֹב בְּעֵינֶיךָ לְבָרֵךְ
es am'cho yisro-ayl,	אֶת עַמְּךָ יִשְׂרָאֵל,

And may it be good in Your eyes to bless Your people Israel

b'chol ays uvchol sho-o bish-lōmecho. בְּכָל עֵת וּבְכָל שָׁעָה בִּשְׁלוֹמֶךָ.

at every time and at every hour, with Your peace.

°Boruch ato Adōnoy,	בָּרוּךְ אַתָּה יהוה,
ham'voraych es amō yisro-ayl	הַמְבָרֵךְ אֶת עַמּוֹ יִשְׂרָאֵל
ba-sholōm.	בַּשָּׁלוֹם.

°Blessed are You, HASHEM, Who blesses His people Israel with peace.

° FROM ROSH HASHANAH TO YOM KIPPUR SUBSTITUTE THE FOLLOWING:

B'sayfer cha-yim b'rocho v'sholōm,	בְּסֵפֶר חַיִּים בְּרָכָה וְשָׁלוֹם,
u-farnoso tōvo,	וּפַרְנָסָה טוֹבָה,

In the book of life, blessing, and peace, and good livelihood,

nizochayr v'nikosayv l'fonecho, נִזָּכֵר וְנִכָּתֵב לְפָנֶיךָ,

may we be remembered and inscribed before You —

anachnu v'chol am'cho	אֲנַחְנוּ וְכָל עַמְּךָ
bays yisro-ayl,	בֵּית יִשְׂרָאֵל,

we and Your entire people the Family of Israel —

l'cha-yim tōvim ulsholōm. לְחַיִּים טוֹבִים וּלְשָׁלוֹם.

for a good life and for peace.

Boruch ato Adōnoy,	בָּרוּךְ אַתָּה יהוה,
ō-se ha-sholōm.	עוֹשֶׂה הַשָּׁלוֹם.

Blessed are You, HASHEM, Who makes the peace.

Yih-yu l'rotzōn imray fi	יִהְיוּ לְרָצוֹן אִמְרֵי פִי
v'hegyōn libi l'fonecho,	וְהֶגְיוֹן לִבִּי לְפָנֶיךָ,

May the expressions of my mouth and the thoughts of my heart find favor before You,

Adōnoy tzuri v'gō-ali. יהוה צוּרִי וְגֹאֲלִי.

HASHEM, my Rock and my Redeemer.

■ I pray that, having completed my *Amidah*, I have been changed in a positive way, especially with regard to my interpersonal relationships.

ELŌHAI, n'tzōr l'shōni mayro, אֱלֹהַי, נְצוֹר לְשׁוֹנִי מֵרָע,

My God, guard my tongue from evil

usfosai midabayr mirmo,	וּשְׂפָתַי מִדַּבֵּר מִרְמָה,

and my lips from speaking deceitfully.

V'limkal'lai nafshi sidōm,	וְלִמְקַלְלַי נַפְשִׁי תִדּוֹם,

To those who curse me, let my soul be silent;

v'nafshi ke-ofor lakōl tih-ye.	וְנַפְשִׁי כֶּעָפָר לַכֹּל תִּהְיֶה.

and let my soul be like dust to everyone.

P'sach libi b'sōrosecho,	פְּתַח לִבִּי בְּתוֹרָתֶךָ,
uvmitzvōsecho tirdōf nafshi.	וּבְמִצְוֹתֶיךָ תִּרְדּוֹף נַפְשִׁי.

Open my heart to Your Torah, then my soul will pursue Your commandments.

V'chol hachōsh'vim olai ro-o,	וְכָל הַחוֹשְׁבִים עָלַי רָעָה,

As for all those who design evil against me,

m'hayro hofayr atzosom	מְהֵרָה הָפֵר עֲצָתָם
v'kalkayl machashavtom.	וְקַלְקֵל מַחֲשַׁבְתָּם.

speedily nullify their counsel and disrupt their design.

asay l'ma-an sh'mecho,	עֲשֵׂה לְמַעַן שְׁמֶךָ,
asay l'ma-an y'minecho,	עֲשֵׂה לְמַעַן יְמִינֶךָ,

Act for Your Name's sake; act for Your right hand's sake;

asay l'ma-an k'dushosecho,	עֲשֵׂה לְמַעַן קְדֻשָּׁתֶךָ,
asay l'ma-an tōrosecho.	עֲשֵׂה לְמַעַן תּוֹרָתֶךָ.

act for Your sanctity's sake; act for Your Torah's sake.

L'ma-an yaychol'tzun y'didecho,	לְמַעַן יֵחָלְצוּן יְדִידֶיךָ,

That Your beloved ones may be given rest;

hōshi-o y'min'cho va-anayni.	הוֹשִׁיעָה יְמִינְךָ וַעֲנֵנִי.

let Your right hand save, and respond to me.

Yih-yu l'rotzōn imray fi	יִהְיוּ לְרָצוֹן אִמְרֵי פִי
v'hegyōn libi l'fonecho,	וְהֶגְיוֹן לִבִּי לְפָנֶיךָ,

May the expressions of my mouth and the thoughts of my heart find favor before You,

Adōnoy tzuri v'gō-ali.	יהוה צוּרִי וְגֹאֲלִי.

Hashem, my Rock and my Redeemer.

BOW. TAKE THREE STEPS BACK. BOW LEFT AND SAY:

Ō-se sholōm bimrōmov,	עֹשֶׂה שָׁלוֹם בִּמְרוֹמָיו,

He Who makes peace in His heights,

BOW RIGHT AND SAY:

hu ya-a-se sholōm olaynu,	הוּא יַעֲשֶׂה שָׁלוֹם עָלֵינוּ,

may He make peace upon us,

BOW FORWARD AND SAY:

v'al kol yisro-ayl. V'imru: Omayn.	וְעַל כָּל יִשְׂרָאֵל. וְאִמְרוּ: אָמֵן.

and upon all Israel. Now respond: Amen.

Y'HI ROTZŌN mil'fonecho, יְהִי רָצוֹן מִלְּפָנֶיךָ
May it be Your will,
Adōnoy Elōhaynu יהוה אֱלֹהֵינוּ
Vaylōhay avōsaynu, וֵאלֹהֵי אֲבוֹתֵינוּ,
Hashem, our God and the God of our forefathers,
she-yibo-ne bays hamikdosh שֶׁיִּבָּנֶה בֵּית הַמִּקְדָּשׁ
bimhayro v'yomaynu, בִּמְהֵרָה בְיָמֵינוּ,
that the Holy Temple be rebuilt, speedily in our days;
v'sayn chelkaynu b'sōrosecho, וְתֵן חֶלְקֵנוּ בְּתוֹרָתֶךָ,
and grant us our share in Your Torah;
v'shom na-avod-cho b'yiro, וְשָׁם נַעֲבָדְךָ בְּיִרְאָה,
and may we serve You there with reverence,
kimay ōlom uchshonim kadmōniyōs. כִּימֵי עוֹלָם וּכְשָׁנִים קַדְמוֹנִיּוֹת.
as in days of old and in former years.
V'or'vo Ladōnoy וְעָרְבָה לַיהוה
minchas y'hudo virusholo-yim מִנְחַת יְהוּדָה וִירוּשָׁלָיִם,
Then the offering of Judah and Jerusalem will be pleasing to Hashem,
kimay ōlom uchshonim kadmōniyōs. כִּימֵי עוֹלָם וּכְשָׁנִים קַדְמוֹנִיּוֹת.
as in days of old and in former years.

SHEMONEH ESREI ENDS HERE. REMAIN STANDING IN PLACE AT LEAST FOR A FEW MOMENTS
THEN TAKE THREE STEPS FORWARD.

THE CHAZZAN RECITES FULL KADDISH

(congregational responses are indicated by parentheses):

יִתְגַּדַּל וְיִתְקַדַּשׁ שְׁמֵהּ רַבָּא. (אָמֵן–Omayn). בְּעָלְמָא דִּי בְרָא כִרְעוּתֵהּ. וְיַמְלִיךְ מַלְכוּתֵהּ, בְּחַיֵּיכוֹן וּבְיוֹמֵיכוֹן וּבְחַיֵּי דְכָל בֵּית יִשְׂרָאֵל, בַּעֲגָלָא וּבִזְמַן קָרִיב. וְאִמְרוּ: אָמֵן.

(אָמֵן. יְהֵא שְׁמֵהּ רַבָּא מְבָרַךְ לְעָלַם וּלְעָלְמֵי עָלְמַיָּא.)
(Omayn. Y'hay sh'mayh rabo m'vorach l'olam ulol'may ol'ma-yo.)

יְהֵא שְׁמֵהּ רַבָּא מְבָרַךְ לְעָלַם וּלְעָלְמֵי עָלְמַיָּא. יִתְבָּרַךְ וְיִשְׁתַּבַּח וְיִתְפָּאַר וְיִתְרוֹמַם וְיִתְנַשֵּׂא וְיִתְהַדָּר וְיִתְעַלֶּה וְיִתְהַלָּל שְׁמֵהּ דְקֻדְשָׁא בְּרִיךְ הוּא (בְּרִיךְ הוּא – B'rich hu). °לְעֵלָּא מִן כָּל [substitute לְעֵלָּא לְעֵלָּא מִכָּל° – from Rosh Hashanah to Yom Kippur] בִּרְכָתָא וְשִׁירָתָא תֻּשְׁבְּחָתָא וְנֶחֱמָתָא, דַּאֲמִירָן בְּעָלְמָא. וְאִמְרוּ: אָמֵן.
(אָמֵן–Omayn).

תִּתְקַבֵּל צְלוֹתְהוֹן וּבָעוּתְהוֹן דְּכָל (בֵּית) יִשְׂרָאֵל קֳדָם אֲבוּהוֹן דִּי בִשְׁמַיָּא. וְאִמְרוּ: אָמֵן. (אָמֵן–Omayn).

יְהֵא שְׁלָמָא רַבָּא מִן שְׁמַיָּא, וְחַיִּים עָלֵינוּ וְעַל כָּל יִשְׂרָאֵל. וְאִמְרוּ:
אָמֵן. (Omayn – אָמֵן).

Bow. Take three steps back. Bow left and say, . . . עֹשֶׂה; bow right and say, . . . הוּא יַעֲשֶׂה; bow forward and say, . . . וְעַל כָּל. Remain in place for a few moments, then take three steps forward.

עֹשֶׂה שָׁלוֹם בִּמְרוֹמָיו, הוּא יַעֲשֶׂה שָׁלוֹם עָלֵינוּ, וְעַל כָּל יִשְׂרָאֵל.
וְאִמְרוּ: אָמֵן. (Omayn – אָמֵן).

BETWEEN PESACH AND SHAVUOS, THE *OMER* IS COUNTED (P. 448).
ON PURIM THE *MEGILLAH* IS READ; ON TISHAH B'AV *EICHAH* IS READ.

■ As we take leave of the synagogue and God's presence, we fortify ourselves with the resolve and commitment that the lofty ideals of prayer can be implemented and actualized in our mundane pursuits.

STAND WHILE RECITING *ALEINU*.

OLAYNU l'shabay-ach la-adōn hakōl, עָלֵינוּ לְשַׁבֵּחַ לַאֲדוֹן הַכֹּל,
It is our duty to praise the Master of all,

losays g'dulo l'yōtzayr b'rayshis, לָתֵת גְּדֻלָּה לְיוֹצֵר בְּרֵאשִׁית,
to ascribe greatness to the Molder of primeval Creation,

shelō osonu k'gōyay ho-arotzōs, שֶׁלֹּא עָשָׂנוּ כְּגוֹיֵי הָאֲרָצוֹת,
for He has not made us like the nations of the lands

v'lō somonu k'mishp'chōs ho-adomo, וְלֹא שָׂמָנוּ כְּמִשְׁפְּחוֹת הָאֲדָמָה.
and has not emplaced us like the families of the earth;

shelō som chelkaynu kohem, שֶׁלֹּא שָׂם חֶלְקֵנוּ כָּהֶם,
for He has not assigned our portion like theirs

v'gōrolaynu k'chol hamōnom וְגוֹרָלֵנוּ כְּכָל הֲמוֹנָם.
nor our lot like all their multitudes.

SOME CONGREGATIONS OMIT THE PARENTHESIZED VERSE:

(Shehaym mishta-chavim (שֶׁהֵם מִשְׁתַּחֲוִים
l'hevel vorik לְהֶבֶל וָרִיק,
(For they bow to vanity and emptiness

u-mispal'lim el ayl lō yōshi-a.) וּמִתְפַּלְלִים אֶל אֵל לֹא יוֹשִׁיעַ.)
and pray to a god which helps not.)

BOW WHILE RECITING THE NEXT PHRASE.

Va-anachnu kōr'im u-mishta-chavim וַאֲנַחְנוּ כּוֹרְעִים וּמִשְׁתַּחֲוִים
u-mōdim, וּמוֹדִים,
But we bend our knees, bow, and acknowledge our thanks

lifnay melech malchay ham'lochim, לִפְנֵי מֶלֶךְ מַלְכֵי הַמְּלָכִים
before the King Who reigns over kings,

hakodōsh boruch hu. הַקָּדוֹשׁ בָּרוּךְ הוּא.
the Holy One, Blessed is He.

Shehu nōte shoma-yim v'yōsayd oretz,	שֶׁהוּא נוֹטֶה שָׁמַיִם וְיֹסֵד אָרֶץ,
He stretches out heaven and establishes earth's foundation,	
u-mōshav y'korō ba-shoma-yim mima-al,	וּמוֹשַׁב יְקָרוֹ בַּשָּׁמַיִם מִמַּעַל,
the seat of His homage is in the heavens above	
ushchinas u-zō b'gov-hay m'rōmim.	וּשְׁכִינַת עֻזּוֹ בְּגָבְהֵי מְרוֹמִים.
and His powerful Presence is in the loftiest heights.	
Hu Elōhaynu ayn ōd.	הוּא אֱלֹהֵינוּ, אֵין עוֹד.
He is our God and there is none other.	
Emes malkaynu, efes zulosō,	אֱמֶת מַלְכֵּנוּ, אֶפֶס זוּלָתוֹ,
True is our King, there is nothing beside Him,	
kakosuv b'sōrosō:	כַּכָּתוּב בְּתוֹרָתוֹ:
as it is written in His Torah:	
V'yodato ha-yōm vaha-shayvōso el l'vovecho,	וְיָדַעְתָּ הַיּוֹם וַהֲשֵׁבֹתָ אֶל לְבָבֶךָ,
"You are to know this day and take to your heart	
ki Adōnoy hu ho-Elōhim	כִּי יהוה הוּא הָאֱלֹהִים
that HASHEM *is the only God —*	
ba-shoma-yim mima-al	בַּשָּׁמַיִם מִמַּעַל
in heaven above	
v'al ho-oretz mitochas, ayn ōd.	וְעַל הָאָרֶץ מִתָּחַת, אֵין עוֹד.
and on the earth below — there is none other."	
AL KAYN n'kave l'cho Adōnoy Elōhaynu	**עַל כֵּן** נְקַוֶּה לְךָ יהוה אֱלֹהֵינוּ
Therefore we put our hope in You, HASHEM, *our God,*	
lir-ōs m'hayro b'sif-eres u-zecho,	לִרְאוֹת מְהֵרָה בְּתִפְאֶרֶת עֻזֶּךָ,
that we may soon see Your mighty splendor,	
l'ha-avir gilulim min ho-oretz,	לְהַעֲבִיר גִּלּוּלִים מִן הָאָרֶץ,
to remove detestable idolatry from the earth,	
v'ho-elilim korōs yikoraysun,	וְהָאֱלִילִים כָּרוֹת יִכָּרֵתוּן,
and false gods will be utterly cut off,	
l'sakayn ōlom b'malchus Shadai.	לְתַקֵּן עוֹלָם בְּמַלְכוּת שַׁדַּי.
to perfect the universe through the Almighty's sovereignty.	
V'chol b'nay vosor yikr'u vishmecho,	וְכָל בְּנֵי בָשָׂר יִקְרְאוּ בִשְׁמֶךָ,
Then all humanity will call upon Your Name,	
l'hafnōs aylecho kol rish-ay oretz.	לְהַפְנוֹת אֵלֶיךָ כָּל רִשְׁעֵי אָרֶץ.
to turn all the earth's wicked toward You.	
Yakiru v'yayd'u kol yōsh'vay sayvayl,	יַכִּירוּ וְיֵדְעוּ כָּל יוֹשְׁבֵי תֵבֵל,
All the world's inhabitants will recognize and know	

WEEKDAY MAARIV — ALEINU

ki l'cho tichra kol berech,   כִּי לְךָ תִּכְרַע כָּל בֶּרֶךְ,
tishova kol loshōn.   תִּשָּׁבַע כָּל לָשׁוֹן.
that to You every knee should bend, every tongue should swear.

L'fonecho Adōnoy Elōhaynu   לְפָנֶיךָ יהוה אֱלֹהֵינוּ
yichr'u v'yipōlu,   יִכְרְעוּ וְיִפֹּלוּ,
Before You, HASHEM, our God, they will bend every knee and cast themselves down,

v'lichvōd shimcho y'kor yitaynu,   וְלִכְבוֹד שִׁמְךָ יְקָר יִתֵּנוּ,
and to the glory of Your Name they will render homage,

vikab'lu chulom es ōl malchusecho,   וִיקַבְּלוּ כֻלָּם אֶת עוֹל מַלְכוּתֶךָ,
and they will all accept upon themselves the yoke of Your kingship

v'simlōch alayhem m'hayro   וְתִמְלֹךְ עֲלֵיהֶם מְהֵרָה
l'ōlom vo-ed.   לְעוֹלָם וָעֶד.
that You may reign over them soon and for all eternity.

Ki hamalchus shelcho hi   כִּי הַמַּלְכוּת שֶׁלְּךָ הִיא
ul-ōl'may ad timlōch b'chovōd,   וּלְעוֹלְמֵי עַד תִּמְלוֹךְ בְּכָבוֹד,
For the kingdom is Yours and You will reign for all eternity in glory,

kakosuv b'sōrosecho: כַּכָּתוּב בְּתוֹרָתֶךָ:
as it is written in Your Torah:

Adōnoy yimlōch l'ōlom vo-ed.   יהוה יִמְלֹךְ לְעֹלָם וָעֶד.
"HASHEM shall reign for all eternity."

V'ne-emar: ❖ וְנֶאֱמַר:
And it is said:

V'ho-yo Adōnoy l'melech   וְהָיָה יהוה לְמֶלֶךְ
al kol ho-oretz,   עַל כָּל הָאָרֶץ,
"HASHEM will be King over all the world —

ba-yōm hahu yih-ye   בַּיּוֹם הַהוּא יִהְיֶה
Adōnoy e-chod, ushmō e-chod.   יהוה אֶחָד וּשְׁמוֹ אֶחָד.
on that day HASHEM will be One and His Name will be One."

SOME CONGREGATIONS RECITE THE FOLLOWING AT THIS POINT.

AL TIRO mipachad pis-ōm,   **אַל תִּירָא** מִפַּחַד פִּתְאֹם,
Do not fear sudden terror,

u-mishō-as r'sho-im ki sovō.   וּמִשֹּׁאַת רְשָׁעִים כִּי תָבֹא.
or the holocaust of the wicked when it comes.

Utzu aytzo v'sufor,   עֻצוּ עֵצָה וְתֻפָר,
Plan a conspiracy and it will be annulled;

dab'ru dovor v'lō yokum,   דַּבְּרוּ דָבָר וְלֹא יָקוּם,
speak your piece and it shall not stand,

| | מעריב לחול / 442 | קדיש יתום |

| ki i-monu Ayl. | כִּי עִמָּנוּ אֵל. |
for God is with us.

| V'ad zikno ani hu, | וְעַד זִקְנָה אֲנִי הוּא, |
Even till your seniority, I remain unchanged;

| v'ad sayvo ani esbōl, | וְעַד שֵׂיבָה אֲנִי אֶסְבֹּל, |
and even till your ripe old age, I shall endure;

ani osisi va-ani eso, אֲנִי עָשִׂיתִי וַאֲנִי אֶשָּׂא,
   va-ani esbōl va-amalayt. וַאֲנִי אֶסְבֹּל וַאֲמַלֵּט.
I created [you] and I shall bear [you]; I shall endure and rescue.

MOURNER'S KADDISH
KADDISH IS RECITED ONLY IN THE PRESENCE OF A MINYAN.

MOURNER:

YISGADAL v'yiskadash **יִתְגַּדַּל** וְיִתְקַדַּשׁ
  sh'mayh rabo. שְׁמֵהּ רַבָּא.
May His great Name grow exalted and sanctified

CONGREGATION RESPONDS: Omayn – אָמֵן

B'ol'mo di v'ro chir-usayh. בְּעָלְמָא דִּי בְרָא כִרְעוּתֵהּ.
in the world that He created as He willed.

V'yamlich malchusayh, וְיַמְלִיךְ מַלְכוּתֵהּ,
May He give reign to His kingship

b'cha-yaychōn uvyōmaychōn בְּחַיֵּיכוֹן וּבְיוֹמֵיכוֹן
  uvcha-yay d'chol bays yisro-ayl, וּבְחַיֵּי דְכָל בֵּית יִשְׂרָאֵל,
in your lifetimes and in your days and in the lifetimes of the entire Family of Israel,

ba-agolo u-vizman koriv. בַּעֲגָלָא וּבִזְמַן קָרִיב.
swiftly and soon.

V'imru: Omayn. וְאִמְרוּ: אָמֵן.
Now respond: Amen.

CONGREGATION RESPONDS:

Omayn. Y'hay sh'mayh rabo m'vorach אָמֵן. יְהֵא שְׁמֵהּ רַבָּא מְבָרַךְ
  l'olam ul-ol'may ol'ma-yo. לְעָלַם וּלְעָלְמֵי עָלְמַיָּא.
Amen. May His great Name be blessed forever and ever.

MOURNER CONTINUES:

Y'hay sh'mayh rabo m'vorach יְהֵא שְׁמֵהּ רַבָּא מְבָרַךְ
  l'olam ul-ol'may ol'ma-yo, לְעָלַם וּלְעָלְמֵי עָלְמַיָּא,
May His great Name be blessed forever and ever;

yisborach v'yishtabach v'yispo-ar יִתְבָּרַךְ וְיִשְׁתַּבַּח וְיִתְפָּאַר
  v'yisrōmam v'yisnasay וְיִתְרוֹמַם וְיִתְנַשֵּׂא
blessed, praised, glorified, exalted, extolled,

WEEKDAY MAARIV — MOURNER'S KADDISH

v'yis-hador v'yis-ale v'yis-halol — וְיִתְהַדָּר וְיִתְעַלֶּה וְיִתְהַלָּל
mighty, upraised, and lauded

sh'mayh d'kudsho b'rich hu — שְׁמֵהּ דְּקֻדְשָׁא בְּרִיךְ הוּא
be the Name of the Holy One, Blessed is He,

CONGREGATION RESPONDS:

B'rich hu. *Blessed is He.* — בְּרִיךְ הוּא.

MOURNER CONTINUES:

°l'aylo min kol — °לְעֵלָּא מִן כָּל
beyond any

FROM ROSH HASHANAH TO YOM KIPPUR SUBSTITUTE:

°l'aylo l'aylo mikol — °לְעֵלָּא לְעֵלָּא מִכָּל
exceedingly beyond any

birchoso v'shiroso — בִּרְכָתָא וְשִׁירָתָא
tushb'choso v'nechemoso, — תֻּשְׁבְּחָתָא וְנֶחֱמָתָא,
blessing and song, praise and consolation

da-amiron b'ol'mo. — דַּאֲמִירָן בְּעָלְמָא.
that are uttered in the world.

V'imru: Omayn. — וְאִמְרוּ: אָמֵן.
Now respond: Amen.

CONGREGATION RESPONDS: Omayn — אָמֵן

Y'hay sh'lomo rabo min sh'mayo — יְהֵא שְׁלָמָא רַבָּא מִן שְׁמַיָּא,
May there be abundant peace from Heaven,

v'cha-yim olaynu v'al kol yisro-ayl. — וְחַיִּים עָלֵינוּ וְעַל כָּל יִשְׂרָאֵל.
and life, upon us and upon all Israel.

V'imru: Omayn: — וְאִמְרוּ: אָמֵן.
Now respond: Amen.

CONGREGATION RESPONDS: Omayn — אָמֵן

MOURNER BOWS, THEN TAKES THREE STEPS BACK, BOWS LEFT AND SAYS:

Ō-se sholōm bimrōmov — עֹשֶׂה שָׁלוֹם בִּמְרוֹמָיו,
He Who makes peace in His heights,

MOURNER BOWS RIGHT AND SAYS:

hu ya-a-se sholōm olaynu — הוּא יַעֲשֶׂה שָׁלוֹם עָלֵינוּ,
may He make peace upon us,

MOURNER BOWS FORWARD AND SAYS:

v'al kol yisro-ayl. V'imru: Omayn. — וְעַל כָּל יִשְׂרָאֵל. וְאִמְרוּ: אָמֵן.
and upon all Israel. Now respond: Amen.

CONGREGATION RESPONDS: Omayn — אָמֵן

MOURNER REMAINS IN PLACE FOR A FEW MOMENTS, THEN TAKES THREE STEPS FORWARD.

FROM *ROSH CHODESH* ELUL THROUGH SHEMINI ATZERES, THE FOLLOWING PSALM IS RECITED.

L'DOVID, Adōnoy ōri v'yish-i mimi iro, — לְדָוִד, יהוה אוֹרִי וְיִשְׁעִי, מִמִּי אִירָא,

Of David: HASHEM *is my light and my salvation, whom shall I fear?*

Adōnoy mo-ōz cha-yai, mimi efchod. — יהוה מָעוֹז חַיַּי, מִמִּי אֶפְחָד.

HASHEM *is my life's strength, whom shall I dread?*

Bikrōv olai m'ray-im le-echōl es b'sori, — בִּקְרֹב עָלַי מְרֵעִים לֶאֱכֹל אֶת בְּשָׂרִי,

When evildoers approach me to devour my flesh,

tzorai v'ō-y'vai li, haymo kosh'lu v'nofolu. — צָרַי וְאֹיְבַי לִי, הֵמָּה כָּשְׁלוּ וְנָפָלוּ.

my tormentors and my foes against me — it is they who stumble and fall.

Im tachane olai machane, lō yiro libi, — אִם תַּחֲנֶה עָלַי מַחֲנֶה, לֹא יִירָא לִבִּי,

Though an army would besiege me, my heart would not fear;

im tokum olai milchomo, b'zōs ani vōtay-ach. — אִם תָּקוּם עָלַי מִלְחָמָה, בְּזֹאת אֲנִי בוֹטֵחַ.

though war would arise against me, in this I trust.

Achas sho-alti may-ays Adōnoy, ōsoh avakaysh, — אַחַת שָׁאַלְתִּי מֵאֵת יהוה, אוֹתָהּ אֲבַקֵּשׁ,

One thing I asked of HASHEM, *that shall I seek:*

shivti b'vays Adōnoy kol y'may cha-yai, — שִׁבְתִּי בְּבֵית יהוה כָּל יְמֵי חַיַּי,

that I dwell in the House of HASHEM *all the days of my life;*

la-chazōs b'nō-am Adōnoy, ulvakayr b'haycholō. — לַחֲזוֹת בְּנֹעַם יהוה, וּלְבַקֵּר בְּהֵיכָלוֹ.

to behold the sweetness of HASHEM *and to contemplate in His Sanctuary.*

Ki yitzp'nayni b'sukō b'yōm ro-o, — כִּי יִצְפְּנֵנִי בְּסֻכֹּה בְּיוֹם רָעָה,

Indeed, He will hide me in His shelter on the day of evil;

yastirayni b'sayser oholō, — יַסְתִּרֵנִי בְּסֵתֶר אָהֳלוֹ,

He will conceal me in the concealment of His Tent,

b'tzur y'rōm'mayni. — בְּצוּר יְרוֹמְמֵנִי.

He will lift me upon a rock.

V'ato yorum rōshi al ō-y'vai s'vivōsai, — וְעַתָּה יָרוּם רֹאשִׁי עַל אֹיְבַי סְבִיבוֹתַי,

Now my head is raised above my enemies around me,

v'ezb'cho v'oholō zivchay s'ru-o, — וְאֶזְבְּחָה בְאָהֳלוֹ זִבְחֵי תְרוּעָה,

and in His Tent I will slaughter offerings accompanied by joyous song;

oshiro va-azam'ro Ladōnoy. — אָשִׁירָה וַאֲזַמְּרָה לַיהוה.

I will sing and make music to HASHEM.

PSALM 27

Sh'ma Adōnoy kōli ekro,   שְׁמַע יהוה קוֹלִי אֶקְרָא,
v'chonayni va-anayni.   וְחָנֵּנִי וַעֲנֵנִי.
HASHEM, hear my voice when I call, and be gracious toward me and answer me.

L'cho omar libi bak'shu fonoy,   לְךָ אָמַר לִבִּי בַּקְּשׁוּ פָנָי,
In Your behalf, my heart has said, "Seek My Presence";

es ponecho Adōnoy avakaysh.   אֶת פָּנֶיךָ יהוה אֲבַקֵּשׁ.
Your Presence, HASHEM, do I seek.

Al tastayr ponecho mimeni,   אַל תַּסְתֵּר פָּנֶיךָ מִמֶּנִּי,
al tat b'af avdecho,   אַל תַּט בְּאַף עַבְדֶּךָ,
Conceal not Your Presence from me, repel not Your servant in anger.

ezrosi ho-yiso,   עֶזְרָתִי הָיִיתָ,
You have been my Helper,

al tit'shayni v'al ta-azvayni,   אַל תִּטְּשֵׁנִי וְאַל תַּעַזְבֵנִי,
Elōhay yish-i.   אֱלֹהֵי יִשְׁעִי.
abandon me not, forsake me not, O God of my salvation.

Ki ovi v'imi azovuni,   כִּי אָבִי וְאִמִּי עֲזָבוּנִי,
Vadōnoy ya-asfayni.   וַיהוה יַאַסְפֵנִי.
Though my father and mother have forsaken me, HASHEM will gather me in.

Hōrayni Adōnoy dar-kecho,   הוֹרֵנִי יהוה דַּרְכֶּךָ,
un-chayni b'ōrach mi-shōr,   וּנְחֵנִי בְּאֹרַח מִישׁוֹר,
Teach me Your way, HASHEM, and lead me on the path of integrity,

l'ma-an shōr'roy.   לְמַעַן שׁוֹרְרָי.
because of my watchful foes.

Al tit'nayni b'nefesh tzoroy,   אַל תִּתְּנֵנִי בְּנֶפֶשׁ צָרָי,
Deliver me not to the wishes of my tormentors,

ki komu vi   כִּי קָמוּ בִי
ayday sheker vifay-ach chomos.   עֵדֵי שֶׁקֶר, וִיפֵחַ חָמָס.
for there have arisen against me false witnesses who breathe violence.

❖ Lulay he-emanti   ❖ לוּלֵא הֶאֱמַנְתִּי
Had I not trusted

lir-ōs b'tuv Adōnoy b'eretz cha-yim.   לִרְאוֹת בְּטוּב יהוה בְּאֶרֶץ חַיִּים.
that I would see the goodness of HASHEM in the land of life!

Kavay el Adōnoy,   קַוֵּה אֶל יהוה,
Hope to HASHEM,

chazak v'ya-amaytz libecho,   חֲזַק וְיַאֲמֵץ לִבֶּךָ,
strengthen yourself and He will give your heart courage;

v'kavay el Adōnoy.   וְקַוֵּה אֶל יהוה.
and hope to HASHEM.

MOURNERS RECITE THE MOURNER'S *KADDISH* (P. 442).

IN A HOUSE OF MOURNING, PSALM 49 IS RECITED:

▪ Psalm 49 teaches that man should use his sojourn on earth to enhance his spiritual development so that he will be better prepared for the World to Come. This concept is a source of comfort for those who have lost a close relative; therefore it is customary to recite this psalm after *Shacharis* and *Maariv* in the home of someone observing *shivah*, the seven-day period of mourning.

LAM'NATZAY-ACH livnay kōrach mizmōr.   לַמְנַצֵּחַ לִבְנֵי קֹרַח מִזְמוֹר.
For the Conductor, by the sons of Korach, a psalm.

Shim-u zōs kol ho-amim,   שִׁמְעוּ זֹאת כָּל הָעַמִּים,
ha-azinu kol yōsh'vay choled.   הַאֲזִינוּ כָּל יֹשְׁבֵי חָלֶד.
Hear this all you peoples, give ear all you dwellers of decaying earth.

Gam b'nay odom, gam b'nay ish,   גַּם בְּנֵי אָדָם, גַּם בְּנֵי אִישׁ,
yachad oshir v'evyōn.   יַחַד עָשִׁיר וְאֶבְיוֹן.
Sons of Adam and sons of man alike; together — rich man, poor man.

Pi y'dabayr chochmōs,   פִּי יְדַבֵּר חָכְמוֹת,
v'hogus libi s'vunōs.   וְהָגוּת לִבִּי תְבוּנוֹת.
My mouth shall speak wisdom, and the meditations of my heart are insightful.

A-te l'moshol ozni,   אַטֶּה לְמָשָׁל אָזְנִי,
eftach b'chinōr chidosi.   אֶפְתַּח בְּכִנּוֹר חִידָתִי.
I will incline my ear to the parable, with a harp I will solve my riddle.

Lomo iro bimay ro,   לָמָּה אִירָא בִּימֵי רָע,
Why should I have to fear in days of evil,

avon akayvai y'subayni.   עֲוֹן עֲקֵבַי יְסֻבֵּנִי.
when the injunctions that I trod upon will surround me?

Habōt'chim al chaylom,   הַבֹּטְחִים עַל חֵילָם,
Those who rely on their possessions,

uvrōv osh'rom yis-halolu.   וּבְרֹב עָשְׁרָם יִתְהַלָּלוּ.
and of their great wealth they are boastful —

Och lō fodō yifde ish,   אָח לֹא פָדֹה יִפְדֶּה אִישׁ,
lō yitayn Laylōhim kofrō.   לֹא יִתֵּן לֵאלֹהִים כָּפְרוֹ.
yet a man cannot redeem a brother, nor give to God his ransom.

V'yaykar pidyōn nafshom,   וְיֵקַר פִּדְיוֹן נַפְשָׁם,
v'chodal l'ōlom.   וְחָדַל לְעוֹלָם.
Too costly is their soul's redemption and unattainable forever.

Vichi ōd lonetzach,   וִיחִי עוֹד לָנֶצַח,
lō yir-e ha-shochas.   לֹא יִרְאֶה הַשָּׁחַת.
Can one live eternally, never to see the pit?

Ki yir-e chachomim yomusu,	כִּי יִרְאֶה חֲכָמִים יָמוּתוּ,
yachad k'sil vova-ar yōvaydu,	יַחַד כְּסִיל וָבַעַר יֹאבֵדוּ,

Though he sees that wise men die, that the foolish and boorish perish together

v'oz'vu la-achayrim chaylom.	וְעָזְבוּ לַאֲחֵרִים חֵילָם.

and leave their possessions to others — [nevertheless,]

Kirbom botaymō l'ōlom,	קִרְבָּם בָּתֵּימוֹ לְעוֹלָם,

in their imagination their houses are forever,

mish-k'nōsom l'dōr vodōr,	מִשְׁכְּנֹתָם לְדוֹר וָדֹר,

their dwellings for generation after generation;

kor'u vishmōsom alay adomōs.	קָרְאוּ בִשְׁמוֹתָם עֲלֵי אֲדָמוֹת.

they have proclaimed their names throughout the lands.

V'odom bikor bal yolin,	וְאָדָם בִּיקָר בַּל יָלִין,
nimshal kab'haymōs nidmu.	נִמְשַׁל כַּבְּהֵמוֹת נִדְמוּ.

But as for man — in glory he shall not repose, he is likened to the silenced animals.

Ze darkom, kesel lomō,	זֶה דַרְכָּם, כֵּסֶל לָמוֹ,

This is their way — folly is theirs,

v'a-charayhem b'fihem yirtzu, selo.	וְאַחֲרֵיהֶם בְּפִיהֶם יִרְצוּ, סֶלָה.

yet of their destiny their mouths speak soothingly, Selah!

Katzōn lish-ōl shatu,	כַּצֹאן לִשְׁאוֹל שַׁתּוּ,
mo-ves yir-aym,	מָוֶת יִרְעֵם,

Like sheep, they are destined for the Lower World, death shall consume them;

va-yirdu vom y'shorim labōker,	וַיִּרְדּוּ בָם יְשָׁרִים לַבֹּקֶר,

and the upright shall dominate them at daybreak,

v'tzurom l'valōs sh'ōl miz'vul lō.	וְצוּרָם לְבַלּוֹת שְׁאוֹל מִזְּבֻל לוֹ.

their essence is doomed to rot in the grave, each from his dwelling.

Ach Elōhim yifde nafshi	אַךְ אֱלֹהִים יִפְדֶּה נַפְשִׁי
miyad sh'ōl,	מִיַּד שְׁאוֹל,

But God will redeem my soul from the grip of the Lower World,

ki yikochayni selo.	כִּי יִקָּחֵנִי סֶלָה.

for He will take me, Selah!

Al tiro ki ya-ashir ish,	אַל תִּירָא כִּי יַעֲשִׁר אִישׁ,
ki yirbe k'vōd bay-sō.	כִּי יִרְבֶּה כְּבוֹד בֵּיתוֹ.

Fear not when a man grows rich, when he increases the splendor of his house.

Ki lō v'mōsō yikach hakōl,	כִּי לֹא בְמוֹתוֹ יִקַּח הַכֹּל,

For upon his death he will not take anything,

lō yayrayd acharov k'vōdō.	לֹא יֵרֵד אַחֲרָיו כְּבוֹדוֹ.

his splendor will not descend after him.

Ki nafshō b'chayov y'voraych,	כִּי נַפְשׁוֹ בְּחַיָּיו יְבָרֵךְ,

Though he may bless himself in his lifetime,

v'yōducho ki saytiv loch.	וְיוֹדֻךָ כִּי תֵיטִיב לָךְ.

others will praise you if you improve yourself.

Tovō ad dōr avōsov,	תָּבוֹא עַד דּוֹר אֲבוֹתָיו,
ad naytzach lō yir-u ōr.	עַד נֵצַח לֹא יִרְאוּ אוֹר.

It shall come to the generation of its fathers — unto eternity they shall see no light.

❖ Odom bikor v'lō yovin,	❖ אָדָם בִּיקָר וְלֹא יָבִין,
nimshal kab'haymōs nidmu.	נִמְשַׁל כַּבְּהֵמוֹת נִדְמוּ.

Man is glorious but understands not, he is likened to the silenced animals.

IF A MOURNER IS PRESENT, HE RECITES THE MOURNER'S *KADDISH* (PAGE 442).

⊰{ COUNTING THE OMER }⊱

THE *CHAZZAN*, FOLLOWED BY THE CONGREGATION, RECITES THE BLESSING AND COUNT.
ONE PRAYING WITHOUT A *MINYAN* SHOULD ALSO RECITE THE *OMER* SERVICE.

BORUCH ato Adōnoy	**בָּרוּךְ** אַתָּה יהוה
Elōhaynu melech ho-ōlom,	אֱלֹהֵינוּ מֶלֶךְ הָעוֹלָם,

Blessed are You, HASHEM, our God, King of the universe,

asher kid'shonu b'mitzvōsov	אֲשֶׁר קִדְּשָׁנוּ בְּמִצְוֹתָיו

Who has sanctified us with His commandments

v'tzivonu al s'firas ho-ōmer.	וְצִוָּנוּ עַל סְפִירַת הָעוֹמֶר.

and has commanded us regarding the counting of the Omer.

INSERT THE APPROPRIATE DAY'S COUNT. SEE CHART PP. 449-453.

HORACHAMON hu yachazir lonu	**הָרַחֲמָן** הוּא יַחֲזִיר לָנוּ

The Compassionate One! May He return for us

avōdas bays hamikdosh	עֲבוֹדַת בֵּית הַמִּקְדָּשׁ
limkōmo,	לִמְקוֹמָהּ,

the service of the Temple to its place,

bimhayro v'yomaynu . Omayn selo.	בִּמְהֵרָה בְיָמֵינוּ. אָמֵן סֶלָה.

speedily in our days. Amen, Selah.

⇜§ Counting the Omer

The Torah commands that from the second day of Pesach — the day the *Omer*-offering of new barley is brought in the Temple — forty-nine days are to be counted, and the festival of Shavuos celebrated on the fiftieth day. This period is called *Sefiras HaOmer*, the Counting of the *Omer*. The *Sefirah* count also recalls an earlier event. During the seven weeks following the Exodus, our ancestors prepared themselves for receiving the Torah at Mount Sinai. This responsibility to prepare oneself to receive the Torah is present every year, as we relive the Exodus from bondage and materialism, and strive to be worthy of the gift of Torah. In ancient times, the *Sefirah* period was a time of rejoicing, but it is now observed as a time of semi-mourning because of several reasons: the absence of the Temple; the death of Rabbi Akiva's 24,000 students during thirty-three days of the *Sefirah;* and a series of bloody massacres befalling Jewish communities during the Crusades.

MAARIV FOR WEEKDAYS — COUNTING OF THE OMER

1	Ha-yōm yōm e-chod bo-ōmer. *Today is one day of the Omer.*	הַיּוֹם יוֹם אֶחָד בָּעוֹמֶר.
2	Ha-yōm sh'nay yomim bo-ōmer. *Today is two days of the Omer.*	הַיּוֹם שְׁנֵי יָמִים בָּעוֹמֶר.
3	Ha-yōm sh'lōsho yomim bo-ōmer. *Today is three days of the Omer.*	הַיּוֹם שְׁלֹשָׁה יָמִים בָּעוֹמֶר.
4	Ha-yōm arbo-o yomim bo-ōmer. *Today is four days of the Omer.*	הַיּוֹם אַרְבָּעָה יָמִים בָּעוֹמֶר.
5	Ha-yōm chami-sho yomim bo-ōmer. *Today is five days of the Omer.*	הַיּוֹם חֲמִשָּׁה יָמִים בָּעוֹמֶר.
6	Ha-yōm shi-sho yomim bo-ōmer. *Today is six days of the Omer.*	הַיּוֹם שִׁשָּׁה יָמִים בָּעוֹמֶר.
7	Ha-yōm shiv-o yomim shehaym shovu-a e-chod bo-ōmer. *Today is seven days, which are one week of the Omer.*	הַיּוֹם שִׁבְעָה יָמִים, שֶׁהֵם שָׁבוּעַ אֶחָד, בָּעוֹמֶר.
8	Ha-yōm sh'mōno yomim shehaym shovu-a e-chod v'yōm e-chod bo-ōmer. *Today is eight days, which are one week and one day of the Omer.*	הַיּוֹם שְׁמוֹנָה יָמִים, שֶׁהֵם שָׁבוּעַ אֶחָד וְיוֹם אֶחָד, בָּעוֹמֶר.
9	Ha-yōm tish-o yomim shehaym shovu-a e-chod ushnay yomim bo-ōmer. *Today is nine days, which are one week and two days of the Omer.*	הַיּוֹם תִּשְׁעָה יָמִים, שֶׁהֵם שָׁבוּעַ אֶחָד וּשְׁנֵי יָמִים, בָּעוֹמֶר.
10	Ha-yōm asoro yomim shehaym shovu-a e-chod ushlōsho yomim bo-ōmer. *Today is ten days, which are one week and three days of the Omer.*	הַיּוֹם עֲשָׂרָה יָמִים, שֶׁהֵם שָׁבוּעַ אֶחָד וּשְׁלֹשָׁה יָמִים, בָּעוֹמֶר.
11	Ha-yōm achad osor yōm shehaym shovu-a e-chod v'arbo-o yomim bo-ōmer. *Today is eleven days, which are one week and four days of the Omer.*	הַיּוֹם אַחַד עָשָׂר יוֹם, שֶׁהֵם שָׁבוּעַ אֶחָד וְאַרְבָּעָה יָמִים, בָּעוֹמֶר.
12	Ha-yōm sh'naym osor yōm shehaym shovu-a e-chod vachami-sho yomim bo-ōmer. *Today is twelve days, which are one week and five days of the Omer.*	הַיּוֹם שְׁנֵים עָשָׂר יוֹם, שֶׁהֵם שָׁבוּעַ אֶחָד וַחֲמִשָּׁה יָמִים, בָּעוֹמֶר.

13	Ha-yōm sh'lōsho osor yōm, shehaym shovu-a e-chod v'shisho yomim bo-ōmer. *Today is thirteen days, which are one week and six days of the Omer.*	הַיּוֹם שְׁלֹשָׁה עָשָׂר יוֹם, שֶׁהֵם שָׁבוּעַ אֶחָד וְשִׁשָּׁה יָמִים, בָּעוֹמֶר.
14	Ha-yōm arbo-o osor yōm shehaym sh'nay shovu-ōs bo-ōmer. *Today is fourteen days, which are two weeks of the Omer.*	הַיּוֹם אַרְבָּעָה עָשָׂר יוֹם, שֶׁהֵם שְׁנֵי שָׁבוּעוֹת, בָּעוֹמֶר.
15	Ha-yōm chami-sho osor yōm shehaym sh'nay shovu-ōs v'yōm e-chod bo-ōmer. *Today is fifteen days, which are two weeks and one day of the Omer.*	הַיּוֹם חֲמִשָּׁה עָשָׂר יוֹם, שֶׁהֵם שְׁנֵי שָׁבוּעוֹת וְיוֹם אֶחָד, בָּעוֹמֶר.
16	Ha-yōm shi-sho osor yōm shehaym sh'nay shovu-ōs ushnay yomim bo-ōmer. *Today is sixteen days, which are two weeks and two days of the Omer.*	הַיּוֹם שִׁשָּׁה עָשָׂר יוֹם, שֶׁהֵם שְׁנֵי שָׁבוּעוֹת וּשְׁנֵי יָמִים, בָּעוֹמֶר.
17	Ha-yōm shiv-o osor yōm shehaym sh'nay shovu-ōs ushlōsho yomim bo-ōmer. *Today is seventeen days, which are two weeks and three days of the Omer.*	הַיּוֹם שִׁבְעָה עָשָׂר יוֹם, שֶׁהֵם שְׁנֵי שָׁבוּעוֹת וּשְׁלֹשָׁה יָמִים, בָּעוֹמֶר.
18	Ha-yōm sh'mōno osor yōm shehaym sh'nay shovu-ōs v'arbo-o yomim bo-ōmer. *Today is eighteen days, which are two weeks and four days of the Omer.*	הַיּוֹם שְׁמוֹנָה עָשָׂר יוֹם, שֶׁהֵם שְׁנֵי שָׁבוּעוֹת וְאַרְבָּעָה יָמִים, בָּעוֹמֶר.
19	Ha-yōm tish-o osor yōm shehaym sh'nay shovu-ōs vachami-sho yomim bo-ōmer. *Today is nineteen days, which are two weeks and five days of the Omer.*	הַיּוֹם תִּשְׁעָה עָשָׂר יוֹם, שֶׁהֵם שְׁנֵי שָׁבוּעוֹת וַחֲמִשָּׁה יָמִים, בָּעוֹמֶר.
20	Ha-yōm esrim yōm shehaym sh'nay shovu-ōs v'shisho yomim bo-ōmer. *Today is twenty days, which are two weeks and six days of the Omer.*	הַיּוֹם עֶשְׂרִים יוֹם, שֶׁהֵם שְׁנֵי שָׁבוּעוֹת וְשִׁשָּׁה יָמִים, בָּעוֹמֶר.
21	Ha-yōm e-chod v'esrim yōm shehaym sh'lōsho shovu-ōs bo-ōmer. *Today is twenty-one days, which are three weeks of the Omer.*	הַיּוֹם אֶחָד וְעֶשְׂרִים יוֹם, שֶׁהֵם שְׁלֹשָׁה שָׁבוּעוֹת, בָּעוֹמֶר.
22	Ha-yōm sh'na-yim v'esrim yōm shehaym sh'lōsho shovu-ōs v'yōm e-chod bo-ōmer. *Today is twenty-two days, which are three weeks and one day of the Omer.*	הַיּוֹם שְׁנַיִם וְעֶשְׂרִים יוֹם, שֶׁהֵם שְׁלֹשָׁה שָׁבוּעוֹת וְיוֹם אֶחָד, בָּעוֹמֶר.

23	Ha-yōm sh'lōsho v'esrim yōm shehaym sh'lōsho shovu-ōs ushnay yomim bo-ōmer. *Today is twenty-three days, which are three weeks and two days of the Omer.*	הַיּוֹם שְׁלֹשָׁה וְעֶשְׂרִים יוֹם, שֶׁהֵם שְׁלֹשָׁה שָׁבוּעוֹת וּשְׁנֵי יָמִים, בָּעוֹמֶר.
24	Ha-yōm arbo-o v'esrim yōm shehaym sh'lōsho shovu-ōs ushlōsho yomim bo-ōmer. *Today is twenty-four days, which are three weeks and three days of the Omer.*	הַיּוֹם אַרְבָּעָה וְעֶשְׂרִים יוֹם, שֶׁהֵם שְׁלֹשָׁה שָׁבוּעוֹת וּשְׁלֹשָׁה יָמִים, בָּעוֹמֶר.
25	Ha-yōm chami-sho v'esrim yōm shehaym sh'lōsho shovu-ōs v'arbo-o yomim bo-ōmer. *Today is twenty-five days, which are three weeks and four days of the Omer.*	הַיּוֹם חֲמִשָּׁה וְעֶשְׂרִים יוֹם, שֶׁהֵם שְׁלֹשָׁה שָׁבוּעוֹת וְאַרְבָּעָה יָמִים, בָּעוֹמֶר.
26	Ha-yōm shi-sho v'esrim yōm shehaym sh'lōsho shovu-ōs vachami-sho yomim bo-ōmer. *Today is twenty-six days, which are three weeks and five days of the Omer.*	הַיּוֹם שִׁשָּׁה וְעֶשְׂרִים יוֹם, שֶׁהֵם שְׁלֹשָׁה שָׁבוּעוֹת וַחֲמִשָּׁה יָמִים, בָּעוֹמֶר.
27	Ha-yōm shiv-o v'esrim yōm shehaym sh'lōsho shovu-ōs v'shisho yomim bo-ōmer. *Today is twenty-seven days, which are three weeks and six days of the Omer.*	הַיּוֹם שִׁבְעָה וְעֶשְׂרִים יוֹם, שֶׁהֵם שְׁלֹשָׁה שָׁבוּעוֹת וְשִׁשָּׁה יָמִים, בָּעוֹמֶר.
28	Ha-yōm sh'mōno v'esrim yōm shehaym arbo-o shovu-ōs bo-ōmer. *Today is twenty-eight days, which are four weeks of the Omer.*	הַיּוֹם שְׁמוֹנָה וְעֶשְׂרִים יוֹם, שֶׁהֵם אַרְבָּעָה שָׁבוּעוֹת בָּעוֹמֶר.
29	Ha-yōm tish-o v'esrim yōm shehaym arbo-o shovu-ōs v'yōm e-chod bo-ōmer. *Today is twenty-nine days, which are four weeks and one day of the Omer.*	הַיּוֹם תִּשְׁעָה וְעֶשְׂרִים יוֹם, שֶׁהֵם אַרְבָּעָה שָׁבוּעוֹת וְיוֹם אֶחָד, בָּעוֹמֶר.
30	Ha-yōm sh'lōshim yōm shehaym arbo-o shovu-ōs ushnay yomim bo-ōmer. *Today is thirty days, which are four weeks and two days of the Omer.*	הַיּוֹם שְׁלֹשִׁים יוֹם, שֶׁהֵם אַרְבָּעָה שָׁבוּעוֹת וּשְׁנֵי יָמִים, בָּעוֹמֶר.
31	Ha-yōm e-chod ushlōshim yōm shehaym arbo-o shovu-ōs ushlōsho yomim bo-ōmer. *Today is thirty-one days, which are four weeks and three days of the Omer.*	הַיּוֹם אֶחָד וּשְׁלֹשִׁים יוֹם, שֶׁהֵם אַרְבָּעָה שָׁבוּעוֹת וּשְׁלֹשָׁה יָמִים, בָּעוֹמֶר.

#		
32	Ha-yōm sh'na-yim ushlōshim yōm shehaym arbo-o shovu-ōs v'arbo-o yomim bo-ōmer.	הַיּוֹם שְׁנַיִם וּשְׁלֹשִׁים יוֹם, שֶׁהֵם אַרְבָּעָה שָׁבוּעוֹת וְאַרְבָּעָה יָמִים, בָּעוֹמֶר.
	Today is thirty-two days, which are four weeks and four days of the Omer.	
33	Ha-yōm sh'lōsho ushlōshim yōm shehaym arbo-o shovu-ōs vachami-sho yomim bo-ōmer	הַיּוֹם שְׁלֹשָׁה וּשְׁלֹשִׁים יוֹם, שֶׁהֵם אַרְבָּעָה שָׁבוּעוֹת וַחֲמִשָּׁה יָמִים, בָּעוֹמֶר.
	Today is thirty-three days, which are four weeks and five days of the Omer.	
34	Ha-yōm arbo-o ushlōshim yōm shehaym arbo-o shovu-ōs v'shisho yomim bo-ōmer.	הַיּוֹם אַרְבָּעָה וּשְׁלֹשִׁים יוֹם, שֶׁהֵם אַרְבָּעָה שָׁבוּעוֹת וְשִׁשָּׁה יָמִים, בָּעוֹמֶר.
	Today is thirty-four days, which are four weeks and six days of the Omer.	
35	Ha-yōm chami-sho ushlōshim yōm shehaym chami-sho shovu-ōs bo-ōmer.	הַיּוֹם חֲמִשָּׁה וּשְׁלֹשִׁים יוֹם, שֶׁהֵם חֲמִשָּׁה שָׁבוּעוֹת, בָּעוֹמֶר.
	Today is thirty-five days, which are five weeks of the Omer.	
36	Ha-yōm shi-sho ushlōshim yōm shehaym chami-sho shovu-ōs v'yōm e-chod bo-ōmer.	הַיּוֹם שִׁשָּׁה וּשְׁלֹשִׁים יוֹם, שֶׁהֵם חֲמִשָּׁה שָׁבוּעוֹת וְיוֹם אֶחָד, בָּעוֹמֶר.
	Today is thirty-six days, which are five weeks and one day of the Omer.	
37	Ha-yōm shiv-o ushlōshim yōm shehaym chami-sho shovu-ōs ushnay yomim bo-ōmer.	הַיּוֹם שִׁבְעָה וּשְׁלֹשִׁים יוֹם, שֶׁהֵם חֲמִשָּׁה שָׁבוּעוֹת וּשְׁנֵי יָמִים, בָּעוֹמֶר.
	Today is thirty-seven days, which are five weeks and two days of the Omer.	
38	Ha-yōm sh'mōno ushlōshim yōm shehaym chami-sho shovu-ōs ushlōsho yomim bo-ōmer.	הַיּוֹם שְׁמוֹנָה וּשְׁלֹשִׁים יוֹם, שֶׁהֵם חֲמִשָּׁה שָׁבוּעוֹת וּשְׁלֹשָׁה יָמִים, בָּעוֹמֶר.
	Today is thirty-eight days, which are five weeks and three days of the Omer.	
39	Ha-yōm tish-o ushlōshim yōm shehaym chami-sho shovu-ōs v'arbo-o yomim bo-ōmer.	הַיּוֹם תִּשְׁעָה וּשְׁלֹשִׁים יוֹם, שֶׁהֵם חֲמִשָּׁה שָׁבוּעוֹת וְאַרְבָּעָה יָמִים, בָּעוֹמֶר.
	Today is thirty-nine days, which are five weeks and four days of the Omer.	
40	Ha-yōm arbo-im yōm shehaym chami-sho shovu-ōs v'chami-sho yomim bo-ōmer.	הַיּוֹם אַרְבָּעִים יוֹם, שֶׁהֵם חֲמִשָּׁה שָׁבוּעוֹת וַחֲמִשָּׁה יָמִים, בָּעוֹמֶר.
	Today is forty days, which are five weeks and five days of the Omer.	

41	Ha-yōm e-chod v'arbo-im yōm shehaym chami-sho shovu-ōs v'shisho yomim bo-ōmer.	הַיּוֹם אֶחָד וְאַרְבָּעִים יוֹם, שֶׁהֵם חֲמִשָּׁה שָׁבוּעוֹת וְשִׁשָּׁה יָמִים, בָּעוֹמֶר.
	Today is forty-one days, which are five weeks and six days of the Omer.	
42	Ha-yōm sh'na-yim v'arbo-im yōm shehaym shisho shovu-ōs bo-ōmer.	הַיּוֹם שְׁנַיִם וְאַרְבָּעִים יוֹם, שֶׁהֵם שִׁשָּׁה שָׁבוּעוֹת, בָּעוֹמֶר.
	Today is forty-two days, which are six weeks of the Omer.	
43	Ha-yōm sh'lōsho v'arbo-im yōm shehaym shisho shovu-ōs v'yōm e-chod bo-ōmer.	הַיּוֹם שְׁלֹשָׁה וְאַרְבָּעִים יוֹם, שֶׁהֵם שִׁשָּׁה שָׁבוּעוֹת וְיוֹם אֶחָד, בָּעוֹמֶר.
	Today is forty-three days, which are six weeks and one day of the Omer.	
44	Ha-yōm arbo-o v'ar'bo-im yōm shehaym shisho shovu-ōs ushnay yomim bo-ōmer.	הַיּוֹם אַרְבָּעָה וְאַרְבָּעִים יוֹם, שֶׁהֵם שִׁשָּׁה שָׁבוּעוֹת, וּשְׁנֵי יָמִים, בָּעוֹמֶר.
	Today is forty-four days, which are six weeks and two days of the Omer.	
45	Ha-yōm chami-ho v'arbo-im yōm shehaym shisho shovu-ōs ushlōsho yomim bo-ōmer.	הַיּוֹם חֲמִשָּׁה וְאַרְבָּעִים יוֹם, שֶׁהֵם שִׁשָּׁה שָׁבוּעוֹת וּשְׁלֹשָׁה יָמִים, בָּעוֹמֶר.
	Today is forty-five days, which are six weeks and three days of the Omer.	
46	Ha-yōm shi-sho v'arbo-im yōm shehaym shisho shovu-ōs v'arbo-o yomim bo-ōmer.	הַיּוֹם שִׁשָּׁה וְאַרְבָּעִים יוֹם, שֶׁהֵם שִׁשָּׁה שָׁבוּעוֹת וְאַרְבָּעָה יָמִים, בָּעוֹמֶר.
	Today is forty-six days, which are six weeks and four days of the Omer.	
47	Ha-yōm shiv-o v'arbo-im yōm shehaym shisho shovu-ōs vachami-sho yomim bo-ōmer.	הַיּוֹם שִׁבְעָה וְאַרְבָּעִים יוֹם, שֶׁהֵם שִׁשָּׁה שָׁבוּעוֹת וַחֲמִשָּׁה יָמִים, בָּעוֹמֶר.
	Today is forty-seven days, which are six weeks and five days of the Omer.	
48	Ha-yōm sh'mōno v'arbo-im yōm shehaym shisho shovu-ōs v'shisho yomim bo-ōmer.	הַיּוֹם שְׁמוֹנָה וְאַרְבָּעִים יוֹם, שֶׁהֵם שִׁשָּׁה שָׁבוּעוֹת וְשִׁשָּׁה יָמִים, בָּעוֹמֶר.
	Today is forty-eight days, which are six weeks and six days of the Omer.	
49	Ha-yōm tish-o v'arbo-im yōm shehaym shiv-o shovu-ōs bo-ōmer.	הַיּוֹם תִּשְׁעָה וְאַרְבָּעִים יוֹם, שֶׁהֵם שִׁבְעָה שָׁבוּעוֹת, בָּעוֹמֶר.
	Today is forty-nine days, which are seven weeks of the Omer.	

⸪ SANCTIFICATION OF THE MOON/KIDDUSH LEVANAH ⸫

■ I joyously greet the "Divine Presence" by acknowledging the renewal of Creation as evidenced by the renewal of the moon. My joy is compounded when I realize the potential for renewal and striving for perfection that both I and the Jewish People — who are compared to the moon — are afforded monthly.

HAL'LUYOH,   **הַלְלוּיָהּ,**
Praise God!

hal'lu es Adōnoy min ha-shoma-yim,   הַלְלוּ אֶת יהוה מִן הַשָּׁמַיִם,
Praise HASHEM *from the heavens;*

hal'luhu bam'rōmim.   הַלְלוּהוּ בַּמְּרוֹמִים.
praise Him in the heights.

Hal'luhu chol mal-ochov,   הַלְלוּהוּ כָל מַלְאָכָיו,
   hal'luhu kol tz'vo-ov.   הַלְלוּהוּ כָּל צְבָאָיו.
Praise Him, all His angels; praise Him, all His legions.

Hal'luhu shemesh v'yoray-ach,   הַלְלוּהוּ שֶׁמֶשׁ וְיָרֵחַ,
   hal'luhu kol kōch'vay ōr.   הַלְלוּהוּ כָּל כּוֹכְבֵי אוֹר.
Praise Him, sun and moon; praise Him, all bright stars.

Hal'luhu sh'may ha-shomo-yim,   הַלְלוּהוּ שְׁמֵי הַשָּׁמָיִם,
Praise Him, the most exalted of the heavens

v'hama-yim asher may-al   וְהַמַּיִם אֲשֶׁר מֵעַל
ha-shomo-yim.   הַשָּׁמָיִם.
and the waters that are above the heavens.

Y'hal'lu es shaym Adōnoy,   יְהַלְלוּ אֶת שֵׁם יהוה,
Let them praise the Name of HASHEM,

ki hu tzivo v'nivro-u.   כִּי הוּא צִוָּה וְנִבְרָאוּ.
for He commanded and they were created.

Va-ya-amidaym lo-ad l'ōlom,   וַיַּעֲמִידֵם לָעַד לְעוֹלָם,
And He established them forever and ever,

chok nosan v'lō ya-avōr.   חָק נָתַן וְלֹא יַעֲבוֹר.
He issued a decree that will not change.

⸪ Sanctification of the Moon

The Sanctification of the Moon [*Kiddush Levanah*] has no calendrical significance. Rather, there are two bases for this ritual: The Talmud (*Sanhedrin* 42a) states that one who blesses the new moon in its proper time is regarded like one who greets God's Presence. This is because one of the ways we can recognize the existence of God is through the orderly functioning of the enormously complex heavenly bodies. We may note that as science unfolds more and more of the vastness of the universe, the presence of a Creator becomes more and more obvious to one who wishes to see; indeed, to deny Him is ludicrous. This phenomenon is most apparent in the cycles of the moon, because its changes are more visible than those of any other body. Thus, when we greet the moon, we greet its Creator and Guide.

SANCTIFICATION OF THE MOON

SOME ADD THIS KABBALISTIC DECLARATION OF INTENT BEFORE THE BLESSING:

Harayni muchon umzumon   הֲרֵינִי מוּכָן וּמְזֻמָּן
   Behold I am prepared and ready
l'ka-yaym hamitzvo   לְקַיֵּם הַמִּצְוָה
   l'kadaysh hal'vono.   לְקַדֵּשׁ הַלְּבָנָה.
   to perform the commandment to sanctify the moon.
L'shaym yichud kudsho   לְשֵׁם יִחוּד קֻדְשָׁא
   b'rich hu ushchintayh,   בְּרִיךְ הוּא וּשְׁכִינְתֵּיהּ,
For the sake of the unification of the Holy One, Blessed is He, and His Presence,
al y'day hahu tomir v'nelom,   עַל יְדֵי הַהוּא טָמִיר וְנֶעְלָם,
   through Him Who is hidden and inscrutable —
b'shaym kol yisro-ayl.   בְּשֵׁם כָּל יִשְׂרָאֵל.
   [I pray] in the name of all Israel.

ONE SHOULD LOOK AT THE MOON BEFORE RECITING THIS BLESSING:

BORUCH ato Adōnoy,   בָּרוּךְ אַתָּה יהוה,
   Blessed are You, HASHEM,
Elōhaynu melech ho-ōlom,   אֱלֹהֵינוּ מֶלֶךְ הָעוֹלָם,
   our God, King of the Universe,
asher b'ma-amorō boro sh'chokim,   אֲשֶׁר בְּמַאֲמָרוֹ בָּרָא שְׁחָקִים,
   Who with His utterance created* the heavens,
uvru-ach piv kol tz'vo-om.   וּבְרוּחַ פִּיו כָּל צְבָאָם.
   and with the breath of His mouth all their legion.
Chōk uzman nosan lohem   חֹק וּזְמַן נָתַן לָהֶם
   A decree and a schedule did He give them*
shelō y'shanu es tafkidom.   שֶׁלֹּא יְשַׁנּוּ אֶת תַּפְקִידָם.
   that they not alter their assigned task.
Sosim usmaychim   שָׂשִׂים וּשְׂמֵחִים
   la-asōs r'tzōn kōnom,   לַעֲשׂוֹת רְצוֹן קוֹנָם,
   They are joyous and glad* to perform the will of their Maker —

The second aspect of the prayer is its significance for the history of Israel. Just as the moon is reborn after a period of decline and total disappearance, so too, Israel's decline will end and its light will once again blaze to fullness.

בָּרוּךְ... אֲשֶׁר בְּמַאֲמָרוֹ בָּרָא — *Blessed ... Who with His utterance created.* God created heaven and its infinite bodies with nothing more than His word. The very existence of so many galaxies and solar systems testifies undeniably to Creation because so huge and complex a universe could not have come about by chance.

חֹק וּזְמַן נָתַן לָהֶם — *A decree and a schedule did He give them.* After creating the heavenly bodies, God set them in their specified orbits, giving each an unchangeable role in the cosmos.

שָׂשִׂים וּשְׂמֵחִים — *They are joyous and glad.* Despite the apparent tedium of their permanently assigned tasks, the heavenly bodies joyously serve their Maker because they know that by doing His will they have a role in Creation. This is a lesson to man to revel in his opportunity to serve God.

456 / קדוש לבנה

פּוֹעֵל אֱמֶת שֶׁפְּעֻלָּתוֹ אֱמֶת.	pō-ayl emes shep'ulosō emes.

the Worker of truth Whose work is truth.

וְלַלְּבָנָה אָמַר   V'lal'vono omar
שֶׁתִּתְחַדֵּשׁ עֲטֶרֶת תִּפְאֶרֶת   shetischadaysh ateres tiferes

To the moon He said that it should renew itself as a crown of splendor

לַעֲמוּסֵי בָטֶן,   la-amusay voten,

for those borne [by Him] from the womb,

שֶׁהֵם עֲתִידִים   shehaym asidim
לְהִתְחַדֵּשׁ כְּמוֹתָהּ,   l'hischadaysh k'mōsoh,

those who are destined to renew themselves like it,

וּלְפָאֵר לְיוֹצְרָם   ulfo-ayr l'yōtz'rom
עַל שֵׁם כְּבוֹד מַלְכוּתוֹ.   al shaym k'vōd malchusō.

and to glorify their Molder for the name of His glorious kingdom.

בָּרוּךְ אַתָּה יהוה,   Boruch ato Adōnoy,
מְחַדֵּשׁ חֳדָשִׁים.   m'chadaysh chodoshim.

Blessed are You, HASHEM, Who renews the months.

RECITE THREE TIMES:

בָּרוּךְ יוֹצְרֵךְ, בָּרוּךְ עוֹשֵׂךְ,   **BORUCH** yōtz'raych, boruch ōsaych,

Blessed is your Molder; blessed is your Maker;

בָּרוּךְ קוֹנֵךְ, בָּרוּךְ בּוֹרְאֵךְ.   boruch kōnaych, boruch bōr'aych.

blessed is your Owner; blessed is your Creator.

RECITE THREE TIMES:

כְּשֵׁם שֶׁאֲנִי רוֹקֵד כְּנֶגְדֵּךְ   K'shaym she-ani rōkayd k'negdaych

Just as I dance* toward you

וְאֵינִי יָכוֹל לִנְגּוֹעַ בָּךְ,   v'ayni yochōl lin-gō-a boch,

but cannot touch you,

כָּךְ לֹא יוּכְלוּ כָּל אוֹיְבַי   kach lō yuchlu kol ō-y'vai
לִנְגּוֹעַ בִּי לְרָעָה.   lin-gō-a bi l'ro-o.

so may none of my enemies be able to touch me for evil.

RECITE THREE TIMES:

תִּפֹּל עֲלֵיהֶם אֵימָתָה וָפַחַד,   Tipōl alayhem aymoso vofachad,

Let fall upon them fear and terror;

בִּגְדֹל זְרוֹעֲךָ יִדְּמוּ כָּאָבֶן.   bigdōl z'rō-acho yid'mu ko-oven.

at the greatness of Your arm, let them be still as stone.

כְּשֵׁם שֶׁאֲנִי רוֹקֵד — *Just as I dance.* Often in Scripture, a prophecy is accompanied by a physical act. This has the effect of making the prophecy irreversible. Here, too, we, in a sym- bolic way, exert ourselves to touch the moon while remaining on earth, and we pray that, in like fashion, the exertions of our enemies against us will be of no avail. Thus, we rein-

SANCTIFICATION OF THE MOON

RECITE THREE TIMES:

Ko-oven yid'mu z'rō-acho bigdōl   כָּאֶבֶן יִדְּמוּ זְרוֹעֲךָ בִּגְדֹל

As stone let them be still,* at Your arm's greatness;

vofachad aymoso alayhem tipōl.   וָפַחַד אֵימָתָה עֲלֵיהֶם תִּפֹּל.

terror and fear, upon them let fall.

RECITE THREE TIMES:

Dovid melech yisro-ayl chai v'ka-yom.   דָּוִד מֶלֶךְ יִשְׂרָאֵל חַי וְקַיָּם.

David, King of Israel, is alive and enduring.

EXTEND GREETINGS THREE TIMES:

Sholōm alay-chem.   שָׁלוֹם עֲלֵיכֶם.

Peace upon you.*

THE PERSON WHO WAS GREETED RESPONDS:

Alay-chem sholōm.   עֲלֵיכֶם שָׁלוֹם.

Upon you, peace.

RECITE THREE TIMES:

Simon tōv u-mazol tōv y'hay lonu   סִמָּן טוֹב וּמַזָּל טוֹב יְהֵא לָנוּ

May there be a good sign and a good fortune for us

ulchol yisro-ayl, omayn.   וּלְכָל יִשְׂרָאֵל. אָמֵן.

and for all Israel. Amen.

KŌL dōdi hinay ze bo,   קוֹל דּוֹדִי הִנֵּה זֶה בָּא

The voice of my beloved — Behold! It came suddenly,

m'dalayg al hehorim,   מְדַלֵּג עַל הֶהָרִים,

m'kapaytz al hag'vo-ōs.   מְקַפֵּץ עַל הַגְּבָעוֹת.

leaping over mountains, skipping over hills.

Dō-me dōdi litzvi   דּוֹמֶה דוֹדִי לִצְבִי

ō l'ōfer ho-ayolim,   אוֹ לְעֹפֶר הָאַיָּלִים,

My beloved is like a gazelle or a young hart.

hinay ze ōmayd achar kos'laynu,   הִנֵּה זֶה עוֹמֵד אַחַר כָּתְלֵנוּ,

Behold! He was standing behind our wall,

mashgi-ach min hachalōnōs   מַשְׁגִּיחַ מִן הַחֲלֹנוֹת,

observing through the windows,

maytzitz min hacharakim.   מֵצִיץ מִן הַחֲרַכִּים.

peering through the lattices.

---

force the point by a physical act.

כָּאֶבֶן יִדְּמוּ — *As stone let them be still.* We now repeat the previous verse, but we reverse the order of the words. This reversal implies that the natural order of nature, too, may sometimes be reversed. In other words, God will sometimes protect us through the natural order of events; at other times He will perform open miracles to thwart those who seek our harm.

שָׁלוֹם עֲלֵיכֶם — *Peace upon you.* Various reasons are given for the inclusion of this greeting.

▪ As the monthly development of the moon testifies to Hashem's direction and orchestration of nature, so do I derive optimism and faith recognizing that my deliverance comes directly from Hashem.

SHIR LAMA-ALŌS,   שִׁיר לַמַּעֲלוֹת,
   A song to the ascents.

eso aynai el hehorim,   אֶשָּׂא עֵינַי אֶל הֶהָרִים,
   may-a-yin yovō ezri.   מֵאַיִן יָבֹא עֶזְרִי.
   I raise my eyes to the mountains; whence will come my help?

Ezri may-im Adōnoy,   עֶזְרִי מֵעִם יהוה,
   ōsay shoma-yim vo-oretz.   עֹשֵׂה שָׁמַיִם וָאָרֶץ.
   My help is from HASHEM, *Maker of heaven and earth.*

Al yitayn lamōt raglecho,   אַל יִתֵּן לַמּוֹט רַגְלֶךָ,
   al yonum shōm'recho.   אַל יָנוּם שֹׁמְרֶךָ.
   He will not allow your foot to falter; your Guardian will not slumber.

Hinay lō yonum v'lō yishon   הִנֵּה לֹא יָנוּם וְלֹא יִישָׁן,
   shōmayr yisro-ayl.   שׁוֹמֵר יִשְׂרָאֵל.
   Behold, He neither slumbers nor sleeps — the Guardian of Israel.

Adōnoy shōm'recho,   יהוה שֹׁמְרֶךָ,
   HASHEM *is your Guardian;*

Adōnoy tzil'cho al yad y'minecho.   יהוה צִלְּךָ עַל יַד יְמִינֶךָ.
   HASHEM *is your Shade at your right hand.*

Yōmom ha-shemesh lō yakeko,   יוֹמָם הַשֶּׁמֶשׁ לֹא יַכֶּכָּה
   v'yorayach baloy'lo.   וְיָרֵחַ בַּלָּיְלָה.
   By day the sun will not harm you, nor the moon by night.

Adōnoy yishmor'cho mikol ro   יהוה יִשְׁמָרְךָ מִכָּל רָע,
   yishmōr es nafshecho.   יִשְׁמֹר אֶת נַפְשֶׁךָ.
   HASHEM *will protect you from every evil; He will guard your soul.*

Adōnoy yishmor tzays'cho u-vō-echo   יהוה יִשְׁמָר צֵאתְךָ וּבוֹאֶךָ,
   HASHEM *will guard your departure and your arrival,*

may-ato v'ad ōlom.   מֵעַתָּה וְעַד עוֹלָם.
   from this time and forever.

Having greeted the *Shechinah*, we joyously wish the blessing of peace upon one another; after cursing our enemies, we make clear that we wish no ill to our brethren. At the beginning of Creation, as recorded in the Talmud (*Chullin* 60b), the sun and moon were of equal size. When the moon complained that two kings cannot wear the same crown — i.e., it wished to be larger than the sun — the moon was made smaller. Nevertheless, the sun continues to shine its brilliant light upon the moon, thus providing a lesson to man not to harbor a grudge against others who have wronged him. We express this resolve by wishing peace upon our fellow Jews.

SANCTIFICATION OF THE MOON

HAL'LUYOH,   הַלְלוּיָהּ,
hal'lu Ayl b'kod'shō,   הַלְלוּ אֵל בְּקָדְשׁוֹ,
Praise God! Praise God in His Sanctuary;
hal'luhu birki-a u-zō.   הַלְלוּהוּ בִּרְקִיעַ עֻזּוֹ.
praise Him in the firmament of His power.
Hal'luhu bigvurōsov,   הַלְלוּהוּ בִגְבוּרֹתָיו,
Praise Him for His mighty acts;
hal'luhu k'rōv gudlō.   הַלְלוּהוּ כְּרֹב גֻּדְלוֹ.
praise Him as befits His abundant greatness.
Hal'luhu b'sayka shōfor,   הַלְלוּהוּ בְּתֵקַע שׁוֹפָר,
Praise Him with the blast of the shofar;
hal'luhu b'nayvel v'chinōr.   הַלְלוּהוּ בְּנֵבֶל וְכִנּוֹר.
praise Him with lyre and harp.
Hal'luhu b'sōf u-mochōl,   הַלְלוּהוּ בְּתֹף וּמָחוֹל,
Praise Him with drum and dance;
hal'luhu b'minim v'ugov.   הַלְלוּהוּ בְּמִנִּים וְעֻגָב.
praise Him with organ and flute.
Hal'luhu b'tziltz'lay shoma,   הַלְלוּהוּ בְצִלְצְלֵי שָׁמַע,
Praise Him with clanging cymbals;
hal'luhu b'tziltz'lay s'ru-o.   הַלְלוּהוּ בְּצִלְצְלֵי תְרוּעָה.
praise him with resonant trumpets.
Kōl han'shomo t'halayl Yoh,   כֹּל הַנְּשָׁמָה תְּהַלֵּל יָהּ,
Let all souls praise God,
hal'luyoh.   הַלְלוּיָהּ.
Praise God!

TONO d'vay rabi yishmo-ayl.   תָּנָא דְּבֵי רַבִּי יִשְׁמָעֵאל.
The Academy of Rabbi Yishmael taught:
Ilmolay lō zochu yisro-ayl   אִלְמָלֵי לֹא זָכוּ יִשְׂרָאֵל
Had Israel not been privileged
elo l'hakbil p'nay avihem   אֶלָּא לְהַקְבִּיל פְּנֵי אֲבִיהֶם
   sheba-shoma-yim   שֶׁבַּשָּׁמַיִם
to greet the countenance of their Father in Heaven
pa-am achas bachōdesh, da-yom.   פַּעַם אַחַת בַּחֹדֶשׁ, דַּיָּם.
except for once a month — it would have sufficed them.
Omar aba-yay,   אָמַר אַבַּיֵי.
Abaye said:

hilkoch tzorich l'maym'ro m'umod.	הִלְכָךְ צָרִיךְ לְמֵימְרָא מְעֻמָּד.

Therefore one must recite it while standing.

Mi zōs ōlo min hamidbor	מִי זֹאת עֹלָה מִן הַמִּדְבָּר

Who is this who rises from the desert

misrapekes al dōdoh.	מִתְרַפֶּקֶת עַל דּוֹדָהּ.

clinging to her Beloved!

VI-HI ROTZŌN mil'fonecho — וִיהִי רָצוֹן מִלְּפָנֶיךָ

May it be Your will,

Adōnoy Elōhai Vaylōhay avōsai, — יהוה אֱלֹהַי וֵאלֹהֵי אֲבוֹתַי,

Hashem, my God and the God of my forefathers,

l'malōs p'gimas hal'vono — לְמַלֹּאת פְּגִימַת הַלְּבָנָה,

to fill the flaw of the moon*

v'lō yih-ye voh shum mi-ut, — וְלֹא יִהְיֶה בָהּ שׁוּם מִעוּט,

that there be no diminution in it.

vi-hi ōr hal'vono k'ōr ha-chamo, — וִיהִי אוֹר הַלְּבָנָה כְּאוֹר הַחַמָּה,

May the light of the moon be like the light of the sun

uch-ōr shiv-as y'may v'rayshis, — וּכְאוֹר שִׁבְעַת יְמֵי בְרֵאשִׁית,

and like the light of the seven days of Creation,

k'mō sheho-y'so kōdem mi-utoh, — כְּמוֹ שֶׁהָיְתָה קוֹדֶם מִעוּטָהּ,

as it was before it was diminished,

shene-emar: — שֶׁנֶּאֱמַר:

as it is said:

Es sh'nay ham'ōrōs hag'dōlim. — אֶת שְׁנֵי הַמְּאֹרֹת הַגְּדֹלִים.

"The two great luminaries."

V'yiska-yaym bonu mikro shekosuv: — וְיִתְקַיֵּם בָּנוּ מִקְרָא שֶׁכָּתוּב:

And may there be fulfilled upon us the verse that is written:

U-vikshu es Adōnoy Elōhayhem — וּבִקְשׁוּ אֶת יהוה אֱלֹהֵיהֶם,

They shall seek Hashem, their God,

v'ays dovid malkom. Omayn. — וְאֵת דָּוִיד מַלְכָּם. אָמֵן.

and David, their king. Amen.

לְמַלֹּאת פְּגִימַת הַלְּבָנָה — *To fill the flaw of the moon.* The references to diminution of the moon and its restoration to its primeval status refer to spiritual concepts. The Sages teach that the spiritual illumination of those earliest days was concealed because God knew that man would prove unworthy of it. That was only a temporary phenomenon, however. When the Final Redemption comes, that splendor will be returned to the earth, thus removing the stigma from the moon. Since the moon symbolizes Israel and the House of David, it is natural that man's lack of spiritual fulfillment — the concealment of the light — should be expressed in the smallness of the moon.

SANCTIFICATION OF THE MOON

LAM'NATZAY-ACH bin-ginōs   לַמְנַצֵּחַ בִּנְגִינֹת
mizmōr shir.   מִזְמוֹר שִׁיר.
For the Conductor, upon Neginos, a psalm, a song.

Elōhim y'chonaynu vi-vor'chaynu,   אֱלֹהִים יְחָנֵּנוּ וִיבָרְכֵנוּ,
May God favor us and bless us,

yo-ayr ponov itonu selo.   יָאֵר פָּנָיו אִתָּנוּ סֶלָה.
may He illuminate His countenance with us, Selah.

Loda-as bo-oretz dar-kecho,   לָדַעַת בָּאָרֶץ דַּרְכֶּךָ,
To make known Your way on earth,

b'chol gō-yim y'shu-osecho.   בְּכָל גּוֹיִם יְשׁוּעָתֶךָ.
among all the nations Your salvation.

Yōducho amim Elōhim,   יוֹדוּךָ עַמִּים אֱלֹהִים,
The peoples will acknowledge You, O God,

yōducho amim kulom.   יוֹדוּךָ עַמִּים כֻּלָּם.
all of the peoples will acknowledge You.

Yism'chu viran'nu l'umim,   יִשְׂמְחוּ וִירַנְּנוּ לְאֻמִּים,
Nations will be glad and sing for joy,

ki sishpōt amim mishōr,   כִּי תִשְׁפֹּט עַמִּים מִישֹׁר,
because You will judge the peoples fairly

ul-umim bo-oretz tanchaym selo.   וּלְאֻמִּים בָּאָרֶץ תַּנְחֵם סֶלָה.
and guide the nations on earth, Selah.

Yōducho amim Elōhim,   יוֹדוּךָ עַמִּים אֱלֹהִים,
Then peoples will acknowledge You, O God,

yōducho amim kulom.   יוֹדוּךָ עַמִּים כֻּלָּם.
the peoples will acknowledge You, all of them.

Eretz nos'no y'vuloh,   אֶרֶץ נָתְנָה יְבוּלָהּ,
The earth has yielded its produce,

y'vor'chaynu Elōhim Elōhaynu.   יְבָרְכֵנוּ אֱלֹהִים אֱלֹהֵינוּ.
may God, our own God, bless us.

Y'vor'chaynu Elōhim,   יְבָרְכֵנוּ אֱלֹהִים,
May God bless us

v'yir'u ōsō kol afsay oretz.   וְיִירְאוּ אוֹתוֹ כָּל אַפְסֵי אָרֶץ.
and may all the ends of the earth fear Him.

IN MOST CONGREGATIONS, ALEINU,* (PAGE 439), FOLLOWED BY THE MOURNER'S *KADDISH*, IS REPEATED AT THIS POINT.

עלינו – *Aleinu*. Lest our ecstatic greeting of the moon be interpreted as worship of a heavenly body, God forbid, we recite *Aleinu*, which is our declaration that we serve only God and none other.

The Bedtime Shema

❧ The Bedtime Shema

Rabbi Yehoshua ben Levi, in the Talmud (*Berachos* 4b) taught: "Even though a person recited the *Shema* in the synagogue during the evening prayer, there is a *mitzvah* to recite it again at one's bedside before going to sleep." It is important to note that if one already recited the *Shema* as part of the *Maariv* prayer after nightfall, he has thereby fulfilled the Biblical *mitzvah* to recite the *Shema* at night. Then it is sufficient to recite but the first paragraph of the *Shema* (*V'ahavta* until *u'visharecha*) before retiring. However, if one recited the *Shema* at *Maariv* while it was still day (as many do especially when they make an early Shabbos in the summer months), then they must repeat the entire three paragraphs of the *Shema* before going to bed. The *Mishnah Berurah* (Chapter 239:1) recommends always repeating the three paragraphs of the *Shema*, as they contain 248 words and thus provide protection for the 248 limbs of one's body.

The Scriptural source for the recitation of the bedtime *Shema* is *Psalms* 4:5: "Tremble and sin not, reflect in your hearts on your beds and be utterly silent. Selah." As this verse calls for a "reflection of the heart" and a recitation "on your beds" and the *Shema* contains both of these elements, we see that this verse teaches one to recite the *Shema* prior to retiring. It is interesting to note that the verse concludes "and be utterly silent," which teaches that one should preferably not speak after the recitation of the *Shema*, but rather, as *Rashi* explains, "fall silent in sleep after reciting these words."

The Talmud (*Berachos* 5a) continues and teaches that if one is a Torah scholar he does not need to repeat the *Shema* before going to sleep. The commentaries explain that since a scholar is constantly reviewing what he studies during the day, the Torah thoughts which preoccupy his mind are sufficient to protect him during his sleep. Abaye taught that even a Torah scholar must recite one verse that makes mention of God's mercy before going to sleep, for example "In Your hand I entrust my spirit; You redeemed me Hashem, God of truth" (*Psalms* 31:6).

The Talmud continues and teaches in the name of Rabbi Yitzchak: "Whoever recites the *Shema* at his bedside before going to sleep is considered as though he holds a double-edged sword in his hand to ward off the forces of evil." Moreover, continued Rabbi Yitzchak, "The recitation of *Shema* at the bedside protects the individual from demons, i.e., harmful forces."

Thus, the recitation of the *Shema* at bedtime provides the individual protection and sanctity. The Talmud (*Berachos* 57b) teaches that sleep is 1/60 of death, and thus we require both physical and psychological protection during the night.

We pray that the ideas and fantasies that we entertain during our wakeful hours not cause disturbing nightmares or immoral dreams. Just as we dream at night about the thoughts and notions that pre-occupied us by day, similarly, suggests Rabbi Munk in his *World of Prayer*, "bad dreams adversely effect the purity of our thoughts and feelings even during our waking hours." Proof that the recitation of the *Shema* is for protection comes from the *Shulchan Orach* (*Orach Chaim*, Chapter 481) where the *Rama* relates the practice to recite only the first paragraph of the *Shema* on the night of the Pesach Seder, and not the other accompanying prayers. Since the Torah calls this night "a night of watching" (*Exodus* 12:42), signifying that greater Divine protection is extended that night, the usual recitation of prayers for protection is unnecessary.

Rashi in his commentary on *Numbers* (23:24) cites the *Midrash Tanchuma* in praise of the Jewish nation, "He shall not lie down until he eats of the prey." He does not lie down on his bed at night until he consumes and destroys those forces which come to harm him by reciting the *Shema* and entrusting his spirit into Hashem's hands. Moreover, teaches the *Tanchuma*, he does not retire until he affirms the Kingship of Hashem. Thus, the Jew begins his day by acknowledging the Kingship of Hashem and ends his day the same way.

The Talmud (*Berachos* 60b) legislates the blessing of *HaMapil* — "Who casts the bonds of sleep upon my eyes and slumber upon my eyelids." There is a difference of opinion as to the sequence of the *Shema* and this blessing. Most codifiers held that the blessing of *HaMapil* is to precede the recitation of the *Shema* (*Rambam, Rif, Rosh*). Others felt that since this blessing refers to the gift of sleep, that rejuvenates man, it should be recited as close as possible to the actual onset of sleep, after the recitation of the *Shema* (*Shulchan Orach, Orach Chaim* 231:1). The *Mishnah Berurah* (239:2) rules that it depends on the individual. If one usually falls asleep in the middle of the recitation of the bedtime *Shema*, then *HaMapil* should be recited first, prior to the *Shema*. If, however, this is not usually the case, then it would be preferable to recite *HaMapil* at the end. The *Magen Avraham* (*Orach Chaim* 239) felt that since this recitation of *Shema* is said only at night, women are exempt therefrom as it is considered to be a positive *mitzvah* that is governed by a specific time. *Mishnah Kiddushin* (29a), *Eliyahu Rabbah* and *Pri Megadim,* however, opine that women are obligated to recite the bedtime *Shema* as they too require the protection afforded by its recitation. Most authorities follow the latter opinion and certainly women too should recite the blessing of *HaMapil* thanking Hashem for the phenomenon of sleep.

The ensuing paragraphs of the bedtime *Shema*, beginning with *Yoshaiv b'seser elyon*, are not considered an interruption between the blessing and sleep, as they are said to reinforce the theme of Divine protection at night. Many begin with the recitation of *Ribono Shel Olam,* Master of the Universe, I hereby forgive anyone who angered or antagonized me during the day. This prayer declares that we forgive one and all and do not hold a grudge in our heart. We are not going to bed angry. This is based on the practice of Mar Zutra as cited in *Megillah* (28a), who announced that he forgave all who had wronged him that

day. Our Rabbis teach us that the way we act with others is the way Hashem will reciprocate with us. If we wish to be forgiven daily for our transgressions, we should forgive others.

We conclude the bedtime *Shema* with *Adon Olam,* a beautiful hymn which ends with "Into His hand I entrust my spirit," paraphrasing *Psalms* 31:6 as cited above from Tractate *Berachos.* A *"pikadon"* is a collateral that the borrower provides the lender until the loan is repaid. Every night we extend our most precious possession — our soul — as a *pikadon,* collateral, to Hashem in lieu of all we owe Him. Hashem, in His kindness, goes beyond the letter of the law in dealing with us and graciously returns our soul to us in the morning. May we be privileged to learn from Him and deal with others generously and beyond the exact letter of the law, generating love, brotherhood and peace in our midst.

⊰{ THE BEDTIME SHEMA }⊱

■ Commensurate with our belief and trust in Hashem is the protection He affords each of us. The Talmud (*Berachos* 57b) teaches that sleep constitutes one sixtieth of death. In response to the need for greater protection, we recite the *Shema* and Scriptural verses portraying Hashem's protection.

RIBÔNO shel ôlom — רִבּוֹנוֹ שֶׁל עוֹלָם
Master of the universe,

harayni môchayl l'chol mi — הֲרֵינִי מוֹחֵל לְכָל מִי
she-hich-is v'hik-nit o-si — שֶׁהִכְעִיס וְהִקְנִיט אוֹתִי,
I hereby forgive anyone who angered or antagonized me

ō shechoto k'negdi — אוֹ שֶׁחָטָא כְּנֶגְדִּי —
or who sinned against me —

bayn b'gufi bayn b'momôni, — בֵּין בְּגוּפִי, בֵּין בְּמָמוֹנִי,
whether against my body, my property,

bayn bichvôdi bayn b'chol asher li; — בֵּין בִּכְבוֹדִי, בֵּין בְּכָל אֲשֶׁר לִי;
my honor or against anything of mine;

bayn b'ōnes bayn b'rotzōn — בֵּין בְּאוֹנֶס, בֵּין בְּרָצוֹן,
whether he did so accidentally, willfully,

bayn b'shōgayg bayn b'mayzid; — בֵּין בְּשׁוֹגֵג, בֵּין בְּמֵזִיד;
carelessly, or purposely;

bayn b'dibur bayn b'ma-a-se — בֵּין בְּדִבּוּר, בֵּין בְּמַעֲשֶׂה,
whether through speech, deed,

bayn b'machshovo bayn b'hirhur; — בֵּין בְּמַחֲשָׁבָה, בֵּין בְּהִרְהוּר;
thought, or notion;

bayn b'gilgul ze — בֵּין בְּגִלְגּוּל זֶה,
bayn b'gilgul achayr — בֵּין בְּגִלְגּוּל אַחֵר —
whether in this transmigration or another transmigration —

l'chol bar yisro-ayl — לְכָל בַּר יִשְׂרָאֵל,
I forgive every Jew.

v'lo yay-onaysh shum odom b'sibosi. — וְלֹא יֵעָנֵשׁ שׁוּם אָדָם בִּסְבָתִי.
May no man be punished because of me.

Y'hi rotzon mil'fonecho — יְהִי רָצוֹן מִלְּפָנֶיךָ
Adōnoy Elōhai Vaylōhay avosai — יהוה אֱלֹהַי וֵאלֹהֵי אֲבוֹתַי,
May it be Your will, HASHEM, my God and the God of my forefathers,

shelō e-cheto ōd — שֶׁלֹּא אֶחֱטָא עוֹד,
that I may sin no more,

u-ma shechotosi l'fonecho	וּמַה שֶּׁחָטָאתִי לְפָנֶיךָ

and whatever sins I have done before You,

m'chōk b'rachamecho horabim	מְחוֹק בְּרַחֲמֶיךָ הָרַבִּים,

may You blot out in Your abundant mercies,

avol lō al y'day yisurim	אֲבָל לֹא עַל יְדֵי יִסּוּרִים
vocholo-yim ro-im.	וָחֳלָיִים רָעִים.

but not through suffering or bad illnesses.

Yih-yu l'rotzōn imray fi	יִהְיוּ לְרָצוֹן אִמְרֵי פִי
v'hegyōn libi lifonecho	וְהֶגְיוֹן לִבִּי לְפָנֶיךָ,

May the expressions of my mouth and the thoughts of my heart find favor before You,

Adōnoy tzuri v'gō-ali	יהוה צוּרִי וְגֹאֲלִי.

Hashem, my Rock and my Redeemer.

BORUCH ato Adōnoy	**בָּרוּךְ** אַתָּה יהוה
Elōhaynu melech ho-ōlom	אֱלֹהֵינוּ מֶלֶךְ הָעוֹלָם,

Blessed are You, Hashem, our God, King of the universe,

hamapil chevlay shayno al aynoi	הַמַּפִּיל חֶבְלֵי שֵׁנָה עַל עֵינָי,

Who casts the bonds of sleep upon my eyes

us-numo al af-apoi.	וּתְנוּמָה עַל עַפְעַפָּי.

and slumber upon my eyelids.

Vi-hi rotzōn mil'fonecho	וִיהִי רָצוֹן מִלְּפָנֶיךָ
Adōnoy Elohai Vaylōhay avosai,	יהוה אֱלֹהַי וֵאלֹהֵי אֲבוֹתַי,

May it be Your will, Hashem, my God, and the God of my forefathers,

shetashkivayni l'sholōm	שֶׁתַּשְׁכִּיבֵנִי לְשָׁלוֹם
v'sa-amidayni l'sholōm.	וְתַעֲמִידֵנִי לְשָׁלוֹם.

that You lay me down to sleep in peace and raise me erect in peace.

V'al y'va-haluni ra-yōnai,	וְאַל יְבַהֲלוּנִי רַעְיוֹנַי,
vachalōmōs ro-im	וַחֲלוֹמוֹת רָעִים,
v'harhōrim ro-im.	וְהִרְהוּרִים רָעִים.

May my ideas, bad dreams, and bad notions not confound me.

Us-hay mitosi sh'laymo l'fonecho.	וּתְהֵא מִטָּתִי שְׁלֵמָה לְפָנֶיךָ.

May my offspring be perfect before You,

V'ho-ayr aynai pen i-shan hamo-ves,	וְהָאֵר עֵינַי פֶּן אִישַׁן הַמָּוֶת,

and may You illuminate my eyes lest I die in sleep,

ki ato hamayir l'i-shōn bas o-yin.	כִּי אַתָּה הַמֵּאִיר לְאִישׁוֹן בַּת עָיִן.

for it is You Who illuminates the pupil of the eye.

קריאת שמע על המטה / 470

Boruch ato Adōnoy
בָּרוּךְ אַתָּה יהוה,
Blessed are You, HASHEM,

hamay-ir lo-ōlom kulō bichvodō.
הַמֵּאִיר לָעוֹלָם כֻּלּוֹ בִּכְבוֹדוֹ.
Who illuminates the entire world with His glory.

AYL melech ne-emon.
אֵל מֶלֶךְ נֶאֱמָן.
God, trustworthy King.

RECITE THE FIRST VERSE ALOUD, WITH YOUR RIGHT HAND COVERING YOUR EYES, AND CONCENTRATE INTENSELY UPON ACCEPTING GOD'S ABSOLUTE SOVEREIGNTY.

SH'MA yisro-ayl,
שְׁמַע יִשְׂרָאֵל,
Adōnoy Elōhaynu, Adōnoy e-chod.
יהוה אֱלֹהֵינוּ, יהוה אֶחָד.
Hear, O Israel: HASHEM is our God, HASHEM, the One [and Only].

IN AN UNDERTONE:

Boruch shaym k'vōd malchusō
בָּרוּךְ שֵׁם כְּבוֹד מַלְכוּתוֹ
l'ōlom vo-ed.
לְעוֹלָם וָעֶד.
Blessed is the Name of His glorious kingdom for all eternity.

V'OHAVTO ays
וְאָהַבְתָּ אֵת
Adōnoy Elōhecho,
יהוה ׀ אֱלֹהֶיךָ,
You shall love HASHEM, your God,

b'chol l'vov'cho,
בְּכָל לְבָבְךָ,
with all your heart,

uvchol nafsh'cho, uvchol m'ōdecho.
וּבְכָל נַפְשְׁךָ, וּבְכָל מְאֹדֶךָ.
with all your soul and with all your resources.

V'ho-yu had'vorim ho-ayle,
וְהָיוּ הַדְּבָרִים הָאֵלֶּה,
asher onōchi m'tzav'cho ha-yōm,
אֲשֶׁר אָנֹכִי מְצַוְּךָ הַיּוֹם,
Let these matters that I command you today

al l'vovecho.
עַל לְבָבֶךָ.
be upon your heart.

V'shinantom l'vonecho,
וְשִׁנַּנְתָּם לְבָנֶיךָ,
Teach them thoroughly to your children

v'dibarto bom
וְדִבַּרְתָּ בָּם,
and speak of them

b'shivt'cho b'vay'secho,
בְּשִׁבְתְּךָ בְּבֵיתֶךָ,
uvlecht'cho vaderech
וּבְלֶכְתְּךָ בַדֶּרֶךְ,
while you sit in your home, while you walk on the way,

uv'shochb'cho, uvkumecho.
וּבְשָׁכְבְּךָ וּבְקוּמֶךָ.
when you retire and when you arise.

Ukshartom l'ōs al yodecho,
וּקְשַׁרְתָּם לְאוֹת עַל יָדֶךָ,
And you shall bind them as a sign upon your arm

v'ho-yu l'tōtofōs bayn aynecho.	וְהָיוּ לְטֹטָפֹת בֵּין עֵינֶיךָ.

and they shall be tefillin between your eyes.

Uchsavtom al m'zuzōs bay-secho u-vish-orecho.	וּכְתַבְתָּם עַל מְזֻזוֹת בֵּיתֶךָ, וּבִשְׁעָרֶיךָ.

And write them on the doorposts of your house and upon your gates.

VI-HI nō-am Adōnoy Elōhaynu olaynu,	**וִיהִי** נֹעַם אֲדֹנָי אֱלֹהֵינוּ עָלֵינוּ,

May the pleasantness of my Lord, our God, be upon us –

u-ma-asay yodaynu kōn'no olaynu,	וּמַעֲשֵׂה יָדֵינוּ כּוֹנְנָה עָלֵינוּ,

and our handiwork, may You establish for us;

u-ma-asay yodaynu kōn'nayhu.	וּמַעֲשֵׂה יָדֵינוּ כּוֹנְנֵהוּ.

and our handiwork, may You establish.

YŌSHAYV b'sayser elyōn,	**יֹשֵׁב** בְּסֵתֶר עֶלְיוֹן,

Whoever sits in the refuge of the Most High,

b'tzayl Shadai yislōnon.	בְּצֵל שַׁדַּי יִתְלוֹנָן.

he shall dwell in the shadow of the Almighty.

Ōmar Ladōnoy machsi umtzudosi,	אֹמַר לַיהוה מַחְסִי וּמְצוּדָתִי,

I will say of HASHEM, "He is my refuge and my fortress,

Elōhai evtach bō.	אֱלֹהַי אֶבְטַח בּוֹ.

my God, I will trust in Him."

Ki hu yatzil'cho mipach yokush,	כִּי הוּא יַצִּילְךָ מִפַּח יָקוּשׁ,

For He will deliver you from the ensnaring trap,

mi-dever havōs.	מִדֶּבֶר הַוּוֹת.

from devastating pestilence.

B'evrosō yosech loch,	בְּאֶבְרָתוֹ יָסֶךְ לָךְ,

With His pinion He will cover you,

v'sachas k'nofov techse,	וְתַחַת כְּנָפָיו תֶּחְסֶה,

and beneath His wings you will be protected;

tzino v'sōchayro amitō.	צִנָּה וְסֹחֵרָה אֲמִתּוֹ.

shield and armor is His truth.

Lō siro mipachad loylo,	לֹא תִירָא מִפַּחַד לָיְלָה,

You shall not fear the terror of night;

maychaytz yo-uf yōmom.	מֵחֵץ יָעוּף יוֹמָם.

nor the arrow that flies by day;

Mi-dever bo-ōfel yahalōch,	מִדֶּבֶר בָּאֹפֶל יַהֲלֹךְ,

nor the pestilence that walks in gloom;

miketev yoshud tzohoro-yim.	מִקֶּטֶב יָשׁוּד צָהֳרָיִם.

nor the destroyer who lays waste at noon.

Yipōl mitzid'cho elef,	יִפֹּל מִצִּדְּךָ אֶלֶף,
ur'vovo miminecho,	וּרְבָבָה מִימִינֶךָ,

Let a thousand encamp at your side and a myriad at your right hand,

aylecho lō yigosh.	אֵלֶיךָ לֹא יִגָּשׁ.

but to you they shall not approach.

Rak b'aynecho sabit,	רַק בְּעֵינֶיךָ תַבִּיט,
v'shilumas r'sho-im tir-e.	וְשִׁלֻּמַת רְשָׁעִים תִּרְאֶה.

You will merely peer with your eyes and you will see the retribution of the wicked.

Ki ato Adōnoy machsi,	כִּי אַתָּה יהוה מַחְסִי,

Because [you said,] "You, HASHEM, are my refuge,"

elyōn samto m'ōnecho.	עֶלְיוֹן שַׂמְתָּ מְעוֹנֶךָ.

you have made the Most High your dwelling place.

Lō s'une aylecho ro-o,	לֹא תְאֻנֶּה אֵלֶיךָ רָעָה,
v'nega lō yikrav b'oholecho.	וְנֶגַע לֹא יִקְרַב בְּאָהֳלֶךָ.

No evil will befall you, nor will any plague come near your tent.

Ki mal-ochov y'tza-ve loch,	כִּי מַלְאָכָיו יְצַוֶּה לָּךְ,
lishmorcho b'chol d'rochecho.	לִשְׁמָרְךָ בְּכָל דְּרָכֶיךָ.

He will charge His angels for you, to protect you in all your ways.

Al kapa-yim yiso-uncho,	עַל כַּפַּיִם יִשָּׂאוּנְךָ,
pen tigōf bo-even raglecho.	פֶּן תִּגֹּף בָּאֶבֶן רַגְלֶךָ.

On [their] palms they will carry you, lest you strike your foot against a stone.

Al shachal vofesen tidrōch,	עַל שַׁחַל וָפֶתֶן תִּדְרֹךְ,

Upon the lion and the viper you will tread;

tirmōs k'fir v'sanin.	תִּרְמֹס כְּפִיר וְתַנִּין.

you will trample the young lion and the serpent.

Ki vi choshak va-afal'tayhu,	כִּי בִי חָשַׁק וַאֲפַלְּטֵהוּ,

For he has yearned for Me and I will deliver him;

asag'vayhu ki yoda sh'mi.	אֲשַׂגְּבֵהוּ כִּי יָדַע שְׁמִי.

I will elevate him because he knows My Name.

Yikro-ayni v'e-enayhu,	יִקְרָאֵנִי וְאֶעֱנֵהוּ,

He will call upon Me and I will answer him,

imō onōchi v'tzoro,	עִמּוֹ אָנֹכִי בְצָרָה,
achal'tzayhu va-achab'dayhu.	אֲחַלְּצֵהוּ וַאֲכַבְּדֵהוּ.

I am with him in distress, I will release him and I will honor him.

THE BEDTIME SHEMA

Ōrech yomim asbi-ayhu,
v'ar-ayhu bishu-osi.

אֹרֶךְ יָמִים אַשְׂבִּיעֵהוּ,
וְאַרְאֵהוּ בִּישׁוּעָתִי.

With long life will I satisfy him, and I will show him My salvation.

Ōrech yomim asbi-ayhu,
v'ar-ayhu bishu-osi.

אֹרֶךְ יָמִים אַשְׂבִּיעֵהוּ,
וְאַרְאֵהוּ בִּישׁוּעָתִי.

With long life will I satisfy him, and I will show him My salvation.

ADONOY mo rabu tzoroy
rabim komim oloy.

יהוה מָה רַבּוּ צָרָי,
רַבִּים קָמִים עָלָי.

Hᴀꜱʜᴇᴍ, *how many are my tormentors! The great rise up against me!*

Rabim ōm'rim l'nafshi

רַבִּים אֹמְרִים לְנַפְשִׁי,

The great say of my soul,

ayn yishu-oso lō Baylōhim selo.

אֵין יְשׁוּעָתָה לּוֹ בֵאלֹהִים סֶלָה.

"There is no salvation for him from God — Selah!"

V'ato Adōnoy mogayn ba-adi
k'vōdi u-mayrim rōshi.

וְאַתָּה יהוה מָגֵן בַּעֲדִי,
כְּבוֹדִי וּמֵרִים רֹאשִׁי.

But You Hᴀꜱʜᴇᴍ *are a shield for me, for my soul, and the One Who raises my head.*

kōli el Adōnoy ekro

קוֹלִי אֶל יהוה אֶקְרָא,

With my voice I call out to Hᴀꜱʜᴇᴍ,

va-ya-anayni may-har kodshō selo.

וַיַּעֲנֵנִי מֵהַר קָדְשׁוֹ סֶלָה.

and He answers me from His holy mountain — Selah.

Ani shochavti vo-ishono,

אֲנִי שָׁכַבְתִּי וָאִישָׁנָה,

I lay down and slept,

hekitzōsi ki Adōnoy yism'chayni

הֱקִיצוֹתִי, כִּי יהוה יִסְמְכֵנִי.

yet I awoke, for Hᴀꜱʜᴇᴍ *supports me.*

Lō iro mayriv'vōs om
asher soviv shosu oloy.

לֹא אִירָא מֵרִבְבוֹת עָם,
אֲשֶׁר סָבִיב שָׁתוּ עָלָי.

I fear not the myriad people deployed against me from every side.

Kumo Adōnoy hōshi-ayni Elōhai

קוּמָה יהוה, הוֹשִׁיעֵנִי אֱלֹהַי,

Rise up, Hᴀꜱʜᴇᴍ; *save me, my God;*

ki hikiso es kōl ō-y'vai lechi

כִּי הִכִּיתָ אֶת כָּל אֹיְבַי לֶחִי,

for You struck all of my enemies on the cheek,

shinay r'sho-im shibarto.

שִׁנֵּי רְשָׁעִים שִׁבַּרְתָּ.

You broke the teeth of the wicked.

Ladōnoy hai-shu-o
al amcho virchosecho selo.

לַיהוה הַיְשׁוּעָה,
עַל עַמְּךָ בִרְכָתֶךָ סֶּלָה.

Salvation is Hᴀꜱʜᴇᴍ'ꜱ, *upon Your people is Your blessing — Selah.*

HASHKIVAYNU Adōnoy Elōhaynu l'sholōm,	הַשְׁכִּיבֵנוּ יהוה אֱלֹהֵינוּ לְשָׁלוֹם,

Lay us down to sleep, HASHEM, our God, in peace,

v'ha-amidaynu malkaynu l'cha-yim, וְהַעֲמִידֵנוּ מַלְכֵּנוּ לְחַיִּים,

raise us erect, our King, to life;

ufrōs olaynu sukas sh'lōmecho, וּפְרוֹשׂ עָלֵינוּ סֻכַּת שְׁלוֹמֶךָ,

spread over us the shelter of Your peace;

v'sak'naynu b'aytzo tōvo mil'fonecho, וְתַקְּנֵנוּ בְּעֵצָה טוֹבָה מִלְּפָנֶיךָ,

set us aright with good counsel from before Your Presence;

v'hōshi-aynu l'ma-an sh'mecho. וְהוֹשִׁיעֵנוּ לְמַעַן שְׁמֶךָ.

and save us for Your Name's sake.

V'hogayn ba-adaynu, וְהָגֵן בַּעֲדֵנוּ,

Shield us,

v'hosayr may-olaynu ō-yayv, וְהָסֵר מֵעָלֵינוּ אוֹיֵב,
dever v'cherev v'ro-ov v'yogōn, דֶּבֶר, וְחֶרֶב, וְרָעָב, וְיָגוֹן,

remove from us foe, plague, sword, famine, and woe;

v'hosayr soton mil'fonaynu u-may-acharaynu, וְהָסֵר שָׂטָן מִלְּפָנֵינוּ וּמֵאַחֲרֵינוּ,

and remove spiritual impediment from before us and from behind us,

uvtzayl k'nofecho tastiraynu, וּבְצֵל כְּנָפֶיךָ תַּסְתִּירֵנוּ,

and in the shadow of Your wings shelter us —

ki Ayl shōm'raynu u-matzilaynu oto, כִּי אֵל שׁוֹמְרֵנוּ וּמַצִּילֵנוּ אָתָּה,

for God Who protects and rescues us are You;

ki Ayl melech chanun v'rachum oto. כִּי אֵל מֶלֶךְ חַנּוּן וְרַחוּם אָתָּה.

for God, the Gracious and Compassionate King, are You.

Ushmōr tzaysaynu u-vō-aynu, l'cha-yim ulsholōm וּשְׁמוֹר צֵאתֵנוּ וּבוֹאֵנוּ, לְחַיִּים וּלְשָׁלוֹם

Safeguard our going and coming, for life and for peace,

may-ato v'ad ōlom. מֵעַתָּה וְעַד עוֹלָם.

from now to eternity.

BORUCH Adōnoy ba-yōm, בָּרוּךְ יהוה בַּיּוֹם,
boruch Adōnoy baloylo, בָּרוּךְ יהוה בַּלָּיְלָה,

Blessed is HASHEM by day; blessed is HASHEM by night;

THE BEDTIME SHEMA

boruch Adōnoy b'shoch'vaynu,   בָּרוּךְ יהוה בְּשָׁכְבֵנוּ,
boruch Adōnoy b'kumaynu.   בָּרוּךְ יהוה בְּקוּמֵנוּ.
Blessed is HASHEM *when we retire; blessed is* HASHEM *when we arise.*

Ki v'yod'cho nafshōs   כִּי בְיָדְךָ נַפְשׁוֹת
hacha-yim v'hamaysim.   הַחַיִּים וְהַמֵּתִים.
For in Your hand are the souls of the living and the dead.

Asher b'yodō nefesh kol choy,   אֲשֶׁר בְּיָדוֹ נֶפֶשׁ כָּל חָי,
He in Whose hand is the soul of all the living

v'ru-ach kol b'sar ish.   וְרוּחַ כָּל בְּשַׂר אִישׁ.
and the spirit of every human being.

B'yod'cho afkid ruchi,   בְּיָדְךָ אַפְקִיד רוּחִי,
In Your hand I shall entrust my spirit,

podiso ōsi, Adōnoy Ayl emes.   פָּדִיתָה אוֹתִי, יהוה אֵל אֱמֶת.
You redeemed me, HASHEM, *God of truth.*

Elōhaynu, sheba-shoma-yim,   אֱלֹהֵינוּ שֶׁבַּשָּׁמַיִם,
Our God, Who is in heaven,

yachayd shimcho,   יַחֵד שִׁמְךָ,
v'ka-yaym malchus'cho tomid,   וְקַיֵּם מַלְכוּתְךָ תָּמִיד,
bring unity to Your Name; establish Your kingdom forever

umlōch olaynu l'ōlom vo-ed.   וּמְלוֹךְ עָלֵינוּ לְעוֹלָם וָעֶד.
and reign over us for all eternity.

YIR-U aynaynu v'yismach libaynu   **יִרְאוּ** עֵינֵינוּ וְיִשְׂמַח לִבֵּנוּ
May our eyes see, our heart rejoice

v'sogayl nafshaynu   וְתָגֵל נַפְשֵׁנוּ
bishu-os'cho be-emes,   בִּישׁוּעָתְךָ בֶּאֱמֶת,
and our soul exult in Your salvation in truth,

be-emōr l'tziyōn molach Elōhoyich.   בֶּאֱמֹר לְצִיּוֹן מָלַךְ אֱלֹהָיִךְ.
when Zion is told, "Your God has reigned!"

Adōnoy melech, Adōnoy moloch,   יהוה מֶלֶךְ, יהוה מָלָךְ,
Adōnoy yimlōch l'ōlom vo-ed.   יהוה יִמְלֹךְ לְעֹלָם וָעֶד.
HASHEM *reigns,* HASHEM *has reigned,* HASHEM *will reign for all eternity.*

Ki hamalchus shel'cho hi,   כִּי הַמַּלְכוּת שֶׁלְּךָ הִיא,
ul-ōl'may ad timlōch b'chovōd,   וּלְעוֹלְמֵי עַד תִּמְלוֹךְ בְּכָבוֹד,
For the kingdom is Yours and for all eternity You will reign in glory,

ki ayn lonu melech elo oto.   כִּי אֵין לָנוּ מֶלֶךְ אֶלָּא אָתָּה.
for we have no King but You.

476 / קריאת שמע על המטה

הַמַּלְאָךְ הַגֹּאֵל אֹתִי מִכָּל רָע **HAMAL-OCH** hagō-ayl ōsi mikol ro
The angel who redeems me from all evil

יְבָרֵךְ אֶת הַנְּעָרִים, y'voraych es han'orim
   וְיִקָּרֵא בָהֶם שְׁמִי, v'yikoray vohem sh'mi
may he bless the lads, and may my name be declared upon them —

וְשֵׁם אֲבֹתַי אַבְרָהָם וְיִצְחָק, v'shaym avosai avrohom v'yitzchok
and the names of my forefathers Abraham and Isaac —

וְיִדְגּוּ לָרֹב בְּקֶרֶב הָאָֽרֶץ. v'yidgu lorōv b'kerev ho-oretz.
and may they proliferate abundantly like fish within the land.

וַיֹּֽאמֶר, אִם שָׁמֽוֹעַ תִּשְׁמַע **VAYŌMER** im shomō-a tishma
   לְקוֹל יהוה אֱלֹהֶֽיךָ, l'kōl Adōnoy Elōhecha
He said: "If you diligently heed the voice of HASHEM, your God,

וְהַיָּשָׁר בְּעֵינָיו תַּעֲשֶׂה, v'hayoshor b'aynov ta-a-se
and do what is proper in His eyes,

וְהַאֲזַנְתָּ לְמִצְוֺתָיו, v'ha-azanto l'mitzvōsov
   וְשָׁמַרְתָּ כָּל חֻקָּיו, v'shomarto kol chukov
and you listen closely to His commandments and observe His decrees —

כָּל הַמַּחֲלָה kol hamachalo
   אֲשֶׁר שַֽׂמְתִּי בְמִצְרַֽיִם asher sam-ti v'mitzra-yim
   לֹא אָשִׂים עָלֶֽיךָ, lō osim olecho
the entire malady that I inflicted upon Egypt I will not inflict upon you,

כִּי אֲנִי יהוה רֹפְאֶֽךָ. ki ani Adōnoy ro-f'echo.
for I am HASHEM your Healer."

וַיֹּֽאמֶר יהוה אֶל הַשָּׂטָן, **VA-YŌMER** Adōnoy el hasoton
HASHEM said to the Satan,

יִגְעַר יהוה בְּךָ הַשָּׂטָן, yig-ar Adōnoy b'cho hasoton
"HASHEM shall denounce you, O Satan,

וְיִגְעַר יהוה בְּךָ v'yig-ar Adōnoy b'cho
   הַבֹּחֵר בִּירוּשָׁלָֽיִם, habochayr birushalo-yim
and HASHEM, Who selects Jerusalem, shall denounce you again.

הֲלוֹא זֶה אוּד מֻצָּל מֵאֵשׁ. halō ze ud mutzol may-aysh.
This is indeed a firebrand rescued from flames."

הִנֵּה מִטָּתוֹ שֶׁלִּשְׁלֹמֹה, Hinay mitosō she-lishlōmo
Behold! The couch of Shlomo!

שִׁשִּׁים גִּבֹּרִים סָבִיב לָהּ, shishim gibōrim soviv lo
Sixty mighty ones round about it,

THE BEDTIME SHEMA

migiboray yisro-ayl.	מִגִּבֹּרֵי יִשְׂרָאֵל.

of the mighty ones of Israel.

Kulom achuzay cherev	כֻּלָּם אֲחֻזֵי חֶרֶב,
m'lumday milchomo	מְלֻמְּדֵי מִלְחָמָה,

All gripping the sword, learned in warfare,

ish charbo al y'raycho	אִישׁ חַרְבּוֹ עַל יְרֵכוֹ
mipachad balaylos.	מִפַּחַד בַּלֵּילוֹת.

each with his sword on his thigh, from fear in the nights.

——————— RECITE THREE TIMES: ———————

Y'vorech'cho Adonoy v'yishm'recho	יְבָרֶכְךָ יהוה וְיִשְׁמְרֶךָ.

May HASHEM bless you and safeguard you.

Yo-air Adonoy	יָאֵר יהוה
ponov aylecho vichuneko.	פָּנָיו אֵלֶיךָ, וִיחֻנֶּךָּ.

May HASHEM illuminate His countenance for you and be gracious to you.

Yiso Adonoy ponov ay-lecho	יִשָּׂא יהוה פָּנָיו אֵלֶיךָ,
v'yosaym l'cho sholom.	וְיָשֵׂם לְךָ שָׁלוֹם.

May HASHEM turn His countenance to you and establish peace for you.

——————— RECITE THREE TIMES: ———————

Hinay lo yonum v'lo yishon	הִנֵּה לֹא יָנוּם וְלֹא יִישָׁן,
shomayr yisro-ayl.	שׁוֹמֵר יִשְׂרָאֵל.

Behold, the Guardian of Israel neither slumbers nor sleeps.

——————— RECITE THREE TIMES: ———————

Lishu-oscho kivisi Adonoy.	לִישׁוּעָתְךָ קִוִּיתִי יהוה.

For Your salvation do I long HASHEM.

Kivisi Adonoy lishu-oscho.	קִוִּיתִי יהוה לִישׁוּעָתְךָ.

I do long, HASHEM, for your salvation.

Adonoy lishu-oscho kivisi.	יהוה לִישׁוּעָתְךָ קִוִּיתִי.

HASHEM, for Your salvation do I long.

——————— RECITE THREE TIMES: ———————

B'shaym Adonoy Elohay yisro-ayl,	בְּשֵׁם יהוה אֱלֹהֵי יִשְׂרָאֵל,

In the Name of HASHEM, God of Israel:

mi-mini micho-ayl,	מִימִינִי מִיכָאֵל,
u-mismoli gavri-ayl,	וּמִשְּׂמֹאלִי גַּבְרִיאֵל,

May Michael be at my right, Gabriel at my left,

u-milfonai u-ri-el,	וּמִלְּפָנַי אוּרִיאֵל,
u-may-achorai r'fo-ayl,	וּמֵאֲחוֹרַי רְפָאֵל,

Uriel before me, and Rephael behind me;

v'al rōshi sh'chinas Ayl.	וְעַל רֹאשִׁי שְׁכִינַת אֵל.

and above my head the Presence of God.

SHIR HAMA-ALŌS

שִׁיר הַמַּעֲלוֹת,

A song of ascents:

ashray kol y'ray Adōnoy,	אַשְׁרֵי כָּל יְרֵא יהוה,
hahōlaych bidrochov.	הַהֹלֵךְ בִּדְרָכָיו.

Praiseworthy is each person who fears HASHEM, who walks in His paths.

Y'gi-a kapecho ki sōchayl,	יְגִיעַ כַּפֶּיךָ כִּי תֹאכֵל,

When you eat the labor of your hands,

ashrecho v'tōv loch.	אַשְׁרֶיךָ וְטוֹב לָךְ.

you are praiseworthy, and it is well with you.

Esht'cho k'gefen pōriyo	אֶשְׁתְּךָ כְּגֶפֶן פֹּרִיָּה
b'yark'say vay-secho	בְּיַרְכְּתֵי בֵיתֶךָ,

Your wife shall be like a fruitful vine in the inner chambers of your home;

bonecho kish-silay zaysim,	בָּנֶיךָ כִּשְׁתִלֵי זֵיתִים,
soviv l'shulchonecho.	סָבִיב לְשֻׁלְחָנֶךָ.

your children shall be like olive shoots surrounding your table.

Hinay chi chayn y'vōrach gover	הִנֵּה כִי כֵן יְבֹרַךְ גָּבֶר
y'ray Adōnoy.	יְרֵא יהוה.

Behold! For so is blessed the man who fears HASHEM.

Y'vorech'cho Adōnoy mitziyōn,	יְבָרֶכְךָ יהוה מִצִּיּוֹן,

May HASHEM bless you from Zion,

ur-ay b'tuv y'rusholo-yim,	וּרְאֵה בְּטוּב יְרוּשָׁלָיִם,

and may you gaze upon the goodness of Jerusalem,

kōl y'may cha-yecho.	כֹּל יְמֵי חַיֶּיךָ.

all the days of your life.

Ur-ay vonim l'vonecho,	וּרְאֵה בָנִים לְבָנֶיךָ,
sholōm al yisro-ayl.	שָׁלוֹם עַל יִשְׂרָאֵל.

And may you see children born to your children, peace upon Israel.

--- RECITE THREE TIMES: ---

Rigzu v'al techeto-u	רִגְזוּ וְאַל תֶּחֱטָאוּ,

Tremble and sin not.

imru vilvavchem al mishkavchem	אִמְרוּ בִלְבַבְכֶם עַל מִשְׁכַּבְכֶם,

Reflect in your hearts while on your beds,

v'dōmu selo.	וְדֹמּוּ סֶלָה.

and be utterly silent. Selah.

THE BEDTIME SHEMA

ADŌN ŌLOM asher molach, אֲדוֹן עוֹלָם אֲשֶׁר מָלַךְ,
Master of the universe, Who reigned
b'terem kol y'tzir nivro. בְּטֶרֶם כָּל־יְצִיר נִבְרָא.
before any form was created.
L'ays na-aso v'cheftzō kōl, לְעֵת נַעֲשָׂה בְחֶפְצוֹ כֹּל,
At the time when His will brought all into being –
azai melech sh'mō nikro. אֲזַי מֶלֶךְ שְׁמוֹ נִקְרָא.
then as "King" was His Name proclaimed.
V'a-charay kichlōs hakōl, וְאַחֲרֵי כִּכְלוֹת הַכֹּל,
l'vadō yimlōch nōro. לְבַדּוֹ יִמְלוֹךְ נוֹרָא.
After all has ceased to be, He, the Awesome One, will reign alone.
V'hu ho-yo, v'hu hōve, וְהוּא הָיָה וְהוּא הֹוֶה,
v'hu yih-ye, b'siforo. וְהוּא יִהְיֶה בְּתִפְאָרָה.
It is He Who was, He Who is, and He Who shall remain, in splendor.
V'hu e-chod v'ayn shayni, וְהוּא אֶחָד וְאֵין שֵׁנִי,
He is One – there is no second
l'hamshil lō l'hachbiro. לְהַמְשִׁיל לוֹ לְהַחְבִּירָה.
to compare to Him, to declare as His equal.
B'li rayshis b'li sachlis, בְּלִי רֵאשִׁית בְּלִי תַכְלִית,
Without beginning, without conclusion –
v'lō ho-ōz v'hamisro. וְלוֹ הָעֹז וְהַמִּשְׂרָה.
His is the power and dominion.
V'hu Ayli v'chai gō-ali, וְהוּא אֵלִי וְחַי גֹּאֲלִי,
He is my God, my living Redeemer,
v'tzur chevli b'ays tzoro. וְצוּר חֶבְלִי בְּעֵת צָרָה.
Rock of my pain in time of distress.
V'hu nisi u-monōs li וְהוּא נִסִּי וּמָנוֹס לִי
m'nos kōsi b'yōm ekro. מְנָת כּוֹסִי בְּיוֹם אֶקְרָא.
He is my banner, a refuge for me, the portion in my cup on the day I call.
B'yodō afkid ruchi, בְּיָדוֹ אַפְקִיד רוּחִי,
b'ays i-shan v'o-iro. בְּעֵת אִישַׁן וְאָעִירָה.
Into His hand I shall entrust my spirit when I go to sleep – and I shall awaken!
V'im ruchi g'viyosi, וְעִם רוּחִי גְוִיָּתִי,
With my spirit shall my body remain.
Adōnoy li v'lō iro. יהוה לִי וְלֹא אִירָא.
HASHEM is with me, I shall not fear.

Hallel

🛯 Hallel

🛯 Day of Praise

That *Hallel* is recited on the festivals may be understood by the fact that the Torah commands וְשָׂמַחְתָּ בְּחַגֶּךָ, *You shall rejoice on your festivals* (*Deuteronomy* 16:14). In the physical sense, this happiness manifests itself in the form of special food and drink, clothing, and treats for the children (see *Orach Chaim* 529). It is interesting to note, Rabbi Soloveitchik taught, that the Torah often connects happiness with being before and in the presence of Hashem as found, for example, in *Leviticus* (23:40). On Pesach, Shavuos, and Succos, the festivals when the Torah ordains a pilgrimage to Jerusalem and visiting the Temple (*Deuteronomy* 16:16), the privilege of participating in this spiritually uplifting experience elicits songs of praise and thanksgiving. While we do not yet have the Third Temple, the festivals remain the Biblically designated holy days when the Jew is privileged to have a rendezvous with Hashem, and this warrants the recitation of *Hallel*.

🛯 Whole and Half-Hallel

The Talmud (*Arachin* 10b) differentiates between Pesach and Succos. Whereas on Succos the Full *Hallel* is recited each day, on Pesach it is recited only on the first two days (in Israel only on the first day). On the rest of Pesach, we recite the so-called Half-*Hallel*, or more exactly the abridged *Hallel*, which omits the first eleven verses of Psalm 115, and the first eleven verses of Psalm 116. The Talmud explains that on Succos the composition of the *mussaf* offering changed each day, thus each day has its own unique character and warrants its own recitation of *Hallel*. On Pesach, however, the sacrifices for all the days are identical. Since there is no new character, there is no independent obligation for *Hallel* after the first day(s). However, it is customary to recite *Hallel* on the rest of Pesach, since the Intermediate Days possess a flavor of the holiday — which is why many do not don *tefillin* — and the last days are Yom Tov. To mark the difference between an obligatory and customary *Hallel*, the latter is abridged. A second reason for the abridged *Hallel* during the remainder of Pesach will be explained below.

Rambam (*Hil. Chanukah* 3:6) explains that *Hallel* is not recited on Rosh Hashanah and Yom Kippur, because "they are days of repentance, awe, and dread, not days of excessive joy." Rabbi Chaim Soloveitchik of Brisk wonders: Why not recite *Hallel* on these days as an expression of our optimism? After all, we bathe and take haircuts in honor of Rosh Hashanah and we do not fast on that day, as we are optimistic that the Jewish nation will emerge victorious and meritorious in their judgment (*Orach Chaim* 581:4). Reb Chaim answers, based on *Psalms* 13:6: "As for me, I trust in Your kindness, my heart will rejoice in

Your salvation yet I will sing to Hashem, for He dealt kindly with me." King David declares that although he trusts and rejoices, he will actually *sing* out in joy only after God has *dealt kindly with* him. From this we derive that one does not recite *Hallel* in *anticipation;* one recites *Hallel* only after the actual salvation has occurred.

◆§ Reasons for Recitation

There is a difference of opinion regarding the commandment of reciting *Hallel* on the holidays. The *Bahag* — *Baal Halachos Gedolos* — maintains that it is a Biblical commandment. *Ramban* maintains that it is part of the Biblical command to rejoice on the holidays, not necessarily a separate independent command. *Rambam* maintains that *Hallel* is always a Rabbinic commandment.

The second obligation for the recitation of *Hallel* is deliverance from an impending danger to the Jewish nation. *Midrash Tanchuma (Parashas Beshalach)* teaches that the Torah says: "Then Moses and the children of Israel chose to sing this song to Hashem, and they said the following." Why must the Torah include the word לֵאמֹר, *the following?* Let it simply proceed with the text of the song and we would know what they sang. Therefore the Midrash teaches that the word לֵאמֹר, literally *to say,* is meant to teach that whenever God delivers Jews from a potential disaster, they should respond with songs of praise, i.e., *Hallel.* This requirement to recite *Hallel* applies not only when the actual deliverance occurs, but annually on the anniversary of the event. We literally relive Jewish history. We not only eat matzah, receive the Torah, and reside in *succos* as the Jews of Moses' time did, but fast when they did and feast when they did.

For the same reason, *Hallel* is recited all eight days of Chanukah. While it is not a Biblically ordained festival, having occurred long after the giving of the Torah, we recite *Hallel* because of the miracle of the oil and the military victory over the Syrian-Greek oppressors.

◆§ Purim

The Talmud (*Megillah* 14a) asks why do we not recite *Hallel* on Purim. If on Pesach, upon emerging from slavery to freedom, we recite *Hallel,* then surely on Purim, when we were threatened with annihilation, we should sing *Hallel.* The Talmud gives three answers. The last one is that in a sense we *do* recite *Hallel,* for the reading of *Megillas Esther* on Purim is a fulfillment of *Hallel.* While the Name of Hashem does not appear explicitly in the *Megillah,* our Rabbis teach that often the word מֶלֶךְ, *king,* refers not only to Ahasuerus, but to Hashem. For example, the beginning of Chapter 6, "That night the king could not sleep," refers to the King of kings, as well as Ahasuerus. Thus, the reading of the *Megillah* is not just the retelling of an exciting slice of history and an example of God's guiding hand, but the fulfillment of our obligation to recite *Hallel.* So much so, that *Meiri* holds that if one cannot hear the *Megillah* on Purim, one should recite *Hallel.* Although the *halachah* does not follow *Meiri's* view, his teaching helps us focus on the role of the *Megillah.* The other two reasons given

by the Talmud are that from the time the Jewish people entered their land, *Hallel* is recited only for miracles that occurred in *Eretz Yisrael*. Lastly, even after the miracle of Purim, the Jews were still subjects of King Ahasuerus, and *Hallel* is recited only if the national freedom is more complete.

◆§ My Creatures Are Drowning

Yalkut Shimoni §654 gives a reason why the Full *Hallel* is not recited on the last day of Pesach, in celebration of the miraculous salvation at the Sea of Reeds, which took place on that day. When the sea was split and the Egyptian army was drowned, the angels wished to sing praise to Hashem for saving the Jewish nation, whereupon Hashem stopped them, saying, "My creatures are drowning in the sea and you wish to sing?" Thus, because of the loss of human life, albeit our enemy, we do not recite Full *Hallel* on the seventh day of Pesach. This accords with the verse, "When your enemy falls, be not glad, and when he stumbles, let your heart not be joyous" (*Proverbs* 24:17). What a powerful lesson regarding the worth, value, and potential of life!

◆§ Rosh Chodesh and Hallel

Although *Rosh Chodesh* is included in the Torah's chapter of festivals, it is not considered a full-fledged festival because it is permissible to work on *Rosh Chodesh*. Nevertheless, it has been customary since Talmudic times to recite Half-*Hallel*. *Meiri* (*Taanis* 28b) comments that the basis of the custom was to provide a remembrance of the ceremony of sanctifying the month that was done in *Eretz Yisrael*, or simply to serve as a reminder that the day was *Rosh Chodesh*.

The halachic codifiers differ regarding whether or not a blessing should be recited prior to the *Hallel* of *Rosh Chodesh*, since it began as a custom, rather that a requirement (see *Orach Chaim* 422). Ashkenazic Jewry follows the opinion of the *Rama*, that a blessing should be recited.

◆§ On the Seder Night

Finally, it is interesting to note that the Mishnah (*Megillah* 20b) identifies *Hallel* as one of the *mitzvos* that is done only during the day and not at night. The exception to the rule is that of *Hallel* on the night of the Pesach *Seder*. Rav Hai Gaon (cited by *Ran*, on the *Rif*, *Pesachim* 26b) explains that *Hallel* on the night of the Pesach *Seder* is not in response to the occasion of the Yom Tov — that *Hallel* is said only during the day. Rather as the Mishnah teaches (*Pesachim* 116b), "Every year the Jew is to look upon himself as if he personally left Egypt." Therefore the motivation for the recitation of *Hallel* on the night of the Pesach *Seder* is in response to the miracle that is happening to us "now" on that night. Therefore we recite *Hallel* at night in praise for the miracle that is presently occurring.

❧ HALLEL ❧

HALLEL IS RECITED AFTER THE SHEMONEH ESREI OF SHACHARIS ON CHANUKAH AND ROSH CHODESH. ON ROSH CHODESH (EXCEPT ON ROSH CHODESH TEVES) TWO PARAGRAPHS (AS INDICATED IN THE TEXT) ARE OMITTED.

THE CHAZZAN RECITES THE BLESSING. THE CONGREGATION, AFTER RESPONDING AMEN, REPEATS IT, AND CONTINUES WITH THE FIRST PSALM.

BORUCH ato Adonoy בָּרוּךְ אַתָּה יהוה
Elōhaynu melech ho-ōlom, אֱלֹהֵינוּ מֶלֶךְ הָעוֹלָם,
Blessed are You, HASHEM, our God, King of the universe,
asher kid'shonu b'mitzvōsov אֲשֶׁר קִדְּשָׁנוּ בְּמִצְוֹתָיו,
Who has sanctified us with His commandments
v'tzivonu likrō es ha-halayl. וְצִוָּנוּ לִקְרוֹא אֶת הַהַלֵּל.
and has commanded us to read the Hallel.

■ I proudly join the People of Israel in extolling Hashem as the Creator and Master of the world — particularly His ability to transform man's condition.

HAL'LUYOH, הַלְלוּיָהּ
hal'lu avday Adōnoy, הַלְלוּ עַבְדֵי יהוה,
Praise God! Give praise, you servants of HASHEM;
hal'lu es shaym Adōnoy. הַלְלוּ אֶת שֵׁם יהוה.
praise the Name of HASHEM!
Y'hi shaym Adōnoy m'vōroch, יְהִי שֵׁם יהוה מְבֹרָךְ,
may-ato v'ad ōlom. מֵעַתָּה וְעַד עוֹלָם.
Blessed be the Name of HASHEM, from this time and forever.
Mimizrach shemesh ad m'vō-ō, מִמִּזְרַח שֶׁמֶשׁ עַד מְבוֹאוֹ,
m'hulol shaym Adōnoy. מְהֻלָּל שֵׁם יהוה.
From the rising of the sun to its setting, HASHEM's Name is praised.
Rom al kol gō-yim Adōnoy, רָם עַל כָּל גּוֹיִם יהוה,
High above all nations is HASHEM,

◆§ **Hallel**

The prophets ordained that the six psalms (113-118) of *Hallel* [literally, *praise*] be recited on each Festival, and to commemorate times of national deliverance from peril. Moreover, the Talmud (*Pesachim* 117a) states that before David redacted and incorporated these psalms into the Book of *Psalms*, *Hallel* was already known to the nation: Moses and Israel had recited it after being saved from the Egyptians at the Sea; Joshua, after defeating the kings of Canaan; Deborah and Barak, after defeating Sisera; Hezekiah, after defeating Sennacherib; Chananyah, Mishael and Azariah, after being saved from the wicked Nebuchadnezzar; and Mordechai and Esther, after the defeat of the wicked Haman.

These psalms were singled out as the unit of praise because they contain five fundamental themes of Jewish faith: the Exodus, the Splitting of the Sea, the Giving of the Torah at Sinai, the future Resurrection of the Dead, and the coming of the Messiah.

הַלְלוּ עַבְדֵי ה׳ — *Give praise, you servants of HASHEM.* Only after their liberation from Pharaoh's bondage could the Jews be considered the *servants of HASHEM*, because they no longer vowed allegiance to any other ruler.

al ha-shoma-yim k'vōdō.	עַל הַשָּׁמַיִם כְּבוֹדוֹ.

above the heavens is His glory.

Mi Kadōnoy Elōhaynu,	מִי כַּיהוה אֱלֹהֵינוּ,
hamagbihi lo-shoves.	הַמַּגְבִּיהִי לָשָׁבֶת.

Who is like HASHEM, our God, Who is enthroned on high —

Hamashpili lir-ōs,	הַמַּשְׁפִּילִי לִרְאוֹת,
ba-shoma-yim u-vo-oretz.	בַּשָּׁמַיִם וּבָאָרֶץ.

yet deigns to look upon the heaven and the earth?*

M'kimi may-ofor dol,	מְקִימִי מֵעָפָר דָּל,
may-ashpōs yorim evyōn.	מֵאַשְׁפֹּת יָרִים אֶבְיוֹן.

He raises the needy from the dust, from the trash heaps He lifts the destitute.

L'hōshivi im n'divim,	לְהוֹשִׁיבִי עִם נְדִיבִים,
im n'divay amō.	עִם נְדִיבֵי עַמּוֹ.

To seat them with nobles, with the nobles of His people.

Mōshivi akeres haba-yis,	מוֹשִׁיבִי עֲקֶרֶת הַבַּיִת,
aym habonim s'maycho,	אֵם הַבָּנִים שְׂמֵחָה,

He transforms the barren wife into a glad mother of children.

hal'luyoh.	הַלְלוּיָהּ.

Praise God!

■ I sing in grateful appreciation and reverence, recalling the miraculous transformation of the natural order that accompanied the Exodus from Egypt and the Revelation at Sinai.

B'TZAYS yisro-ayl mimitzro-yim,	**בְּצֵאת** יִשְׂרָאֵל מִמִּצְרָיִם,

When Israel went out of Egypt,*

bays ya-akōv may-am lō-ayz.	בֵּית יַעֲקֹב מֵעַם לֹעֵז.

Jacob's household from a people of alien tongue* —

Hoy'so y'hudo l'kod-shō,	הָיְתָה יְהוּדָה לְקָדְשׁוֹ,
yisro-ayl mamsh'lōsov.	יִשְׂרָאֵל מַמְשְׁלוֹתָיו.

Judah became His sanctuary,* Israel His dominions.

הַמַּשְׁפִּילִי לִרְאוֹת בַּשָּׁמַיִם וּבָאָרֶץ — *Yet deigns to look* [lit. *bends down low to see*] *upon the heaven and the earth*. This is the challenging and exciting aspect of God's relationship to man: As we act towards God, so does He react to us. If we ignore His presence, He withdraws high above the heavens; but if we welcome His proximity, He lovingly involves Himself in every phase of our lives.

בְּצֵאת יִשְׂרָאֵל מִמִּצְרָיִם — *When Israel went out of Egypt*. The second chapter of *Hallel* continues the theme of the first chapter, which praises God for raising up the needy and destitute. Israel was thus elevated when they left Egypt and risked their lives by entering the Sea at God's command.

בֵּית יַעֲקֹב מֵעַם לֹעֵז — *Jacob's household from a people of alien tongue*. Even the Jews who were forced to communicate with the Egyptians in the language of the land did so only under duress. Among themselves, however, they spoke only the Holy Tongue and regarded Egyptian as a foreign language.

הָיְתָה יְהוּדָה לְקָדְשׁוֹ — *Judah became His sanctu-*

| | הַלֵּל / 488 |

| Ha-yom ro-o va-yonōs, | הַיָּם רָאָה וַיָּנֹס, |
| ha-yardayn yisōv l'ochōr. | הַיַּרְדֵּן יִסֹּב לְאָחוֹר. |

The sea saw and fled; the Jordan turned backward.

| Hehorim rok'du ch'aylim, | הֶהָרִים רָקְדוּ כְאֵילִים, |
| g'vo-ōs kivnay tzōn. | גְּבָעוֹת כִּבְנֵי צֹאן. |

The mountains skipped like rams,* the hills like young lambs.

| Ma l'cho ha-yom ki sonus, | מַה לְּךָ הַיָּם כִּי תָנוּס, |
| ha-yardayn tisōv l'ochōr. | הַיַּרְדֵּן תִּסֹּב לְאָחוֹר. |

What ails you, O sea, that you flee? O Jordan, that you turn backward?

| Hehorim tirk'du ch'aylim, | הֶהָרִים תִּרְקְדוּ כְאֵילִים, |
| g'vo-ōs kivnay tzōn. | גְּבָעוֹת כִּבְנֵי צֹאן. |

O mountains, that you skip like rams? O hills, like young lambs?

| Milifnay odōn chuli oretz, | מִלִּפְנֵי אָדוֹן חוּלִי אָרֶץ, |

Before the Lord's Presence — did I, the earth, tremble —

| milifnay Elō-a ya-akōv. | מִלִּפְנֵי אֱלוֹהַּ יַעֲקֹב. |

before the presence of the God of Jacob,

| Hahōf'chi hatzur agam mo-yim, | הַהֹפְכִי הַצּוּר אֲגַם מָיִם, |

Who turns the rock into a pond of water,*

| chalomish l'ma-y'nō mo-yim. | חַלָּמִישׁ לְמַעְיְנוֹ מָיִם. |

the flint into a flowing fountain.

■ I beseech Hashem to reveal Himself, again enabling all of mankind to recognize and appreciate His true essence.

ON *ROSH CHODESH* (EXCEPT TEVES) THE FOLLOWING PARAGRAPH IS OMITTED.

LŌ LONU, Adōnoy, lō lonu,   **לֹא לָנוּ**, יהוה, לֹא לָנוּ,

Not for our sake,* HASHEM, not for our sake,

ki l'shimcho tayn kovōd,   כִּי לְשִׁמְךָ תֵּן כָּבוֹד,

but for Your Name's sake give glory,*

---

ary. God singled out the tribe of Judah to be the family of royalty, because they sanctified God's Name at the Sea of Reeds. Led by their prince, Nachshon ben Aminadav, this tribe was the first to jump into the threatening waters (*Rosh*).

הֶהָרִים רָקְדוּ כְאֵילִים — *The mountains skipped like rams.* When Israel received the Torah, Sinai and the neighboring mountains and hills shook and trembled at the manifestation of God's Presence and the thunder and lightning that accompanied it.

הַהֹפְכִי הַצּוּר אֲגַם מָיִם — *Who turns the rock into a pond of water.* When the Jews thirsted for water in the wilderness, God instructed Moses (*Exodus* 17:6), "You shall smite the rock and water shall come out of it, so that the people may drink."

לֹא לָנוּ — *Not for our sake.* The preceding psalm depicts the awe inspired by God's miracles. Here the Psalmist describes the aftermath of that inspiration. Although Israel remained imbued with faith, our oppressors soon began to scoff, "Where is your God?" We pray that God will intervene again in the affairs of man, not for our sake, but for His.

כִּי לְשִׁמְךָ תֵּן כָּבוֹד ... לֹא לָנוּ ה׳ — *Not for our sake, HASHEM ... but for Your Name's sake give glory.* We beg You to redeem us, not because we are personally worthy, nor because of the merit of our forefathers. Rather we urgently strive to

al chasd'cho al amitecho.	עַל חַסְדְּךָ עַל אֲמִתֶּךָ.

for Your kindness and for Your truth!

Lomo yōm'ru hagōyim,	לָמָּה יֹאמְרוּ הַגּוֹיִם,
a-yay no Elōhayhem.	אַיֵּה נָא אֱלֹהֵיהֶם.

Why should the nations say, "Where is their God now?"

Vaylōhaynu va-shomo-yim,	וֵאלֹהֵינוּ בַשָּׁמָיִם,
kōl asher chofaytz oso.	כֹּל אֲשֶׁר חָפֵץ עָשָׂה.

Our God is in the heavens; whatever He pleases, He does!

Atzabayhem kesef v'zohov,	עֲצַבֵּיהֶם כֶּסֶף וְזָהָב,
ma-asay y'day odom.	מַעֲשֵׂה יְדֵי אָדָם.

Their idols are silver and gold, the handiwork of man.

Pe lohem v'lō y'dabayru,	פֶּה לָהֶם וְלֹא יְדַבֵּרוּ,
ayna-yim lohem v'lō yir-u.	עֵינַיִם לָהֶם וְלֹא יִרְאוּ.

They have a mouth, but cannot speak; they have eyes, but cannot see.

Ozna-yim lohem v'lō yishmo-u,	אָזְנַיִם לָהֶם וְלֹא יִשְׁמָעוּ,

They have ears, but cannot hear;

af lohem v'lō y'ri-chun.	אַף לָהֶם וְלֹא יְרִיחוּן.

they have a nose, but cannot smell.

Y'dayhem v'lō y'mi-shun,	יְדֵיהֶם וְלֹא יְמִישׁוּן,
raglayhem v'lō y'halaychu,	רַגְלֵיהֶם וְלֹא יְהַלֵּכוּ,

Their hands — they cannot feel; their feet — they cannot walk;

lō yegu bigrōnom.	לֹא יֶהְגּוּ בִּגְרוֹנָם.

they cannot utter a sound from their throat.

K'mōhem yih-yu ōsayhem,	כְּמוֹהֶם יִהְיוּ עֹשֵׂיהֶם,
kōl asher bōtay-ach bohem.	כֹּל אֲשֶׁר בֹּטֵחַ בָּהֶם.

Those who make them should become like them, whoever trusts in them!

Yisro-ayl b'tach Badōnoy,	❖ יִשְׂרָאֵל בְּטַח בַּיהוה,
ezrom u-moginom hu.	עֶזְרָם וּמָגִנָּם הוּא.

O Israel, trust in H{\sc ashem}; their help and their shield is He!

Bays aharōn bitchu Vadōnoy,	בֵּית אַהֲרֹן בִּטְחוּ בַיהוה,
ezrom u-moginom hu.	עֶזְרָם וּמָגִנָּם הוּא.

House of Aaron, trust in H{\sc ashem}; their help and their shield is He!

Yir-ay Adōnoy bitchu Vadōnoy,	יִרְאֵי יהוה בִּטְחוּ בַיהוה,
ezrom u-moginom hu.	עֶזְרָם וּמָגִנָּם הוּא.

You who fear H{\sc ashem}, trust in H{\sc ashem}; their help and their shield is He!

---

protect Your glorious Name, so that no one can deny Your mastery and dominion.

■ **Reciprocal Appreciation:** Hashem blesses Israel, and I pledge that as long as I have the gift of life, I will enthusiastically praise Hashem.

ADŌNOY z'choronu y'voraych,   יהוה זְכָרָנוּ יְבָרֵךְ,
Hashem Who has remembered us will bless* —
y'voraych es bays yisro-ayl,   יְבָרֵךְ אֶת בֵּית יִשְׂרָאֵל,
He will bless the House of Israel;
y'voraych es bays aharōn.   יְבָרֵךְ אֶת בֵּית אַהֲרֹן.
He will bless the House of Aaron;
Y'voraych yir-ay Adōnoy,   יְבָרֵךְ יִרְאֵי יהוה,
hak'tanim im hag'dōlim.   הַקְּטַנִּים עִם הַגְּדֹלִים.
He will bless those who fear Hashem, the small as well as the great.
Yōsayf Adōnoy alaychem,   יֹסֵף יהוה עֲלֵיכֶם,
alaychem v'al b'naychem.   עֲלֵיכֶם וְעַל בְּנֵיכֶם.
May Hashem increase upon you, upon you and upon your children!*
B'ruchim atem Ladōnoy,   בְּרוּכִים אַתֶּם לַיהוה,
ōsay shoma-yim vo-oretz.   עֹשֵׂה שָׁמַיִם וָאָרֶץ.
You are blessed of Hashem, maker of heaven and earth.
❖ Ha-shoma-yim shoma-yim Ladōnoy,   הַשָּׁמַיִם שָׁמַיִם לַיהוה,
As for the heavens — the heavens are Hashem's,
v'ho-oretz nosan livnay odom.   וְהָאָרֶץ נָתַן לִבְנֵי אָדָם.
but the earth He has given to mankind.*
Lō ha-maysim y'hal'lu Yoh,   לֹא הַמֵּתִים יְהַלְלוּ יָהּ,
v'lō kol yōr'day dumo.   וְלֹא כָּל יֹרְדֵי דוּמָה.
Neither the dead can praise God,* nor any who descend into silence;

ה׳ זְכָרָנוּ יְבָרֵךְ — *Hashem Who has remembered us will bless.* The Psalmist expresses confidence that just as God has blessed His people in the past, so He will bless them in the future.

יֹסֵף ה׳ עֲלֵיכֶם, עֲלֵיכֶם וְעַל בְּנֵיכֶם — *May Hashem increase upon you, upon you and upon your children!* The true nature of בְּרָכָה, "blessing," means increase and abundance. The Psalmist foresaw that Israel would suffer from attrition in exile and they would fear eventual extinction. Therefore, he offers the assurance that, at the advent of Messiah, their number will increase dramatically.

הַשָּׁמַיִם שָׁמַיִם לַה׳ וְהָאָרֶץ נָתַן לִבְנֵי אָדָם — *As for the heavens — the heavens are Hashem's, but the earth He has given to mankind.* Since the heavens remain under God's firm control, all celestial bodies are forced to act in accordance with His will without freedom of choice. On earth, however, man was granted the freedom to determine his own actions and beliefs.

This verse can be explained homiletically. Man need not perfect heaven because it is already dedicated to the holiness of God. But the earth is man's province. Man is bidden to perfect it and transform its material nature into something spiritual. Indeed, man was created to make the earth heavenly.

לֹא הַמֵּתִים יְהַלְלוּ יָהּ — *Neither the dead can praise God.* The people who fail to recognize God's omnipresence and influence over the world resemble the dead, who are insensitive to all external stimuli and who are oblivious to reality. However, the souls of the righteous continue to praise God even after they depart from their bodies.

Va-anachnu n'voraych Yoh, may-ato v'ad ōlom, hal'luyoh.	וַאֲנַחְנוּ נְבָרֵךְ יָהּ, מֵעַתָּה וְעַד עוֹלָם, הַלְלוּיָהּ.

but we will bless God from this time and forever. Bless God!

■ *I invoke the Name of Hashem in times of trouble and sorrow.*

ON *ROSH CHODESH* (EXCEPT TEVES) THE FOLLOWING PARAGRAPH IS OMITTED.

OHAVTI ki yishma Adōnoy
es kōli tachanunoy.
אָהַבְתִּי כִּי יִשְׁמַע יהוה
אֶת קוֹלִי תַּחֲנוּנָי.

I love [Him],* for HASHEM *hears my voice, my supplications.*

Ki hito oznō li, uvyomai ekro.
כִּי הִטָּה אָזְנוֹ לִי, וּבְיָמַי אֶקְרָא.

As He has inclined His ear to me, so in my days shall I call.

Afofuni chevlay mo-ves,
umtzoray sh'ōl m'tzo-uni,
אֲפָפוּנִי חֶבְלֵי מָוֶת,
וּמְצָרֵי שְׁאוֹל מְצָאוּנִי,

The pains of death* encircled me; the confines of the grave have found me;

tzoro v'yogōn emtzo.
צָרָה וְיָגוֹן אֶמְצָא.

trouble and sorrow I would find.

Uvshaym Adōnoy ekro,
ono Adōnoy mal'to nafshi.
וּבְשֵׁם יהוה אֶקְרָא,
אָנָּה יהוה מַלְּטָה נַפְשִׁי.

Then I would invoke the Name of HASHEM*: "Please,* HASHEM*, save my soul."*

Chanun Adōnoy v'tzadik,
Vaylōhaynu m'rachaym.
חַנּוּן יהוה וְצַדִּיק,
וֵאלֹהֵינוּ מְרַחֵם.

Gracious is HASHEM *and righteous, our God is merciful.*

Shōmayr p'so-yim Adōnoy,
dalōsi v'li y'hōshi-a.
שֹׁמֵר פְּתָאיִם יהוה,
דַּלּוֹתִי וְלִי יְהוֹשִׁיעַ.

HASHEM *protects the simple; I was brought low, but He saved me.*

Shuvi nafshi limnuchoychi,
ki Adōnoy gomal oloychi.
שׁוּבִי נַפְשִׁי לִמְנוּחָיְכִי,
כִּי יהוה גָּמַל עָלָיְכִי.

Return, my soul, to your rest;* for HASHEM *has been kind to you.*

Ki chilatzto nafshi mimo-ves,
כִּי חִלַּצְתָּ נַפְשִׁי מִמָּוֶת,

For You have delivered my soul from death,

אָהַבְתִּי — *I love [Him]*. The Psalmist foresaw that Israel would feel completely alone in exile. The nations would taunt them, "Your prayers and pleas are worthless, because God has turned a deaf ear to you." Therefore, he composed this psalm to encourage the downcast exiles with the assurance that indeed: "HASHEM hears my voice, my supplications."

חֶבְלֵי מָוֶת — *The pains of death*. This is an apt description of the exile, when Israel is encircled by violent enemies who seek to kill them.

שׁוּבִי נַפְשִׁי לִמְנוּחָיְכִי — *Return, my soul, to your rest*. When misery and persecution upset me, I told my soul that it would find peace and comfort only if it would *return* to God.

	הלל / 492
es ayni min dim-o,	אֶת עֵינִי מִן דִּמְעָה,
es ragli midechi.	אֶת רַגְלִי מִדֶּחִי.

my eyes from tears, my feet from stumbling.

❖ Es-halaych lifnay Adōnoy,   ❖ אֶתְהַלֵּךְ לִפְנֵי יהוה,
   b'artzōs hacha-yim.   בְּאַרְצוֹת הַחַיִּים.

I shall walk before HASHEM in the lands of the living.

He-emanti ki adabayr,   הֶאֱמַנְתִּי כִּי אֲדַבֵּר,
   ani onisi m'ōd.   אֲנִי עָנִיתִי מְאֹד.

I have kept faith although I say: "I suffer exceedingly."

Ani omarti v'chofzi,   אֲנִי אָמַרְתִּי בְחָפְזִי,
   kol ho-odom kōzayv.   כָּל הָאָדָם כֹּזֵב.

I said in my haste: "All mankind is deceitful."

■ *I invoke the Name of Hashem in times of rejoicing and success.*

MO OSHIV Ladōnoy,   **מָה אָשִׁיב** לַיהוה,
   kol tagmulōhi oloy.   כָּל תַּגְמוּלוֹהִי עָלָי.

How can I repay HASHEM* for all His kindness to me?

Kōs y'shu-ōs eso,   כּוֹס יְשׁוּעוֹת אֶשָּׂא,
   uvshaym Adōnoy ekro.   וּבְשֵׁם יהוה אֶקְרָא.

I will raise the cup of salvations and the Name of HASHEM I will invoke.

N'dorai Ladōnoy ashalaym,   נְדָרַי לַיהוה אֲשַׁלֵּם,
   negdo no l'chol amō.   נֶגְדָה נָּא לְכָל עַמּוֹ.

My vows to HASHEM I will pay, in the presence, now, of His entire people.

Yokor b'aynay Adōnoy   יָקָר בְּעֵינֵי יהוה
   hamovso lachasidov.   הַמָּוְתָה לַחֲסִידָיו.

Difficult in the eyes of HASHEM is the death of His devout ones.

Ono Adōnoy ki ani avdecho,   אָנָּה יהוה כִּי אֲנִי עַבְדֶּךָ,

Please, HASHEM — for I am Your servant,

ani avd'cho, ben amosecho,   אֲנִי עַבְדְּךָ, בֶּן אֲמָתֶךָ,
   pitachto l'mōsayroy.   פִּתַּחְתָּ לְמוֹסֵרָי.

I am Your servant, son of Your handmaid — You have released my bonds.

❖ L'cho ezbach zevach tōdo,   ❖ לְךָ אֶזְבַּח זֶבַח תּוֹדָה,

To You I will sacrifice thanksgiving offerings,

מָה אָשִׁיב לַה' — *How can I repay HASHEM?* What gift can I give to the King who owns everything? How can I possibly repay His acts of kindness, for they are too numerous to recount? How can I even approach Him? He is eternal and I am finite; He is the highest, and I am the lowest!

uvshaym Adōnoy ekro.
וּבְשֵׁם יהוה אֶקְרָא.
and the Name of HASHEM I will invoke.

N'dorai Ladōnoy ashalaym,
נְדָרַי לַיהוה אֲשַׁלֵּם,
   negdo no l'chol amō.
נֶגְדָה נָּא לְכָל עַמּוֹ.
My vows to HASHEM I will pay, in the presence, now, of His entire people.

B'chatzrōs bays Adōnoy,
בְּחַצְרוֹת בֵּית יהוה,
   b'sōchaychi y'rusholo-yim,
בְּתוֹכֵכִי יְרוּשָׁלָיִם,
In the Courtyards of the House of HASHEM, in your midst, O Jerusalem,

hal'luyoh.
הַלְלוּיָהּ.
Praise God!

■ The shortest chapter in Scripture depicts the universal recognition and praise of Hashem's Divine protection of the Jewish people which will prevail in Messianic times.

HAL'LU es Adōnoy, kol gōyim,
הַלְלוּ אֶת יהוה, כָּל גּוֹיִם,
   shab'chuhu kol ho-umim.
שַׁבְּחוּהוּ כָּל הָאֻמִּים.
Praise HASHEM, all nations; praise Him, all the states!*

Ki govar olaynu chasdō,
כִּי גָבַר עָלֵינוּ חַסְדּוֹ,
For His kindness has overwhelmed us,

ve-emes Adōnoy l'ōlom
וֶאֱמֶת יהוה לְעוֹלָם,
   hal'luyoh.
הַלְלוּיָהּ.
and the truth of HASHEM is eternal, Praise God!

■ I affirm that Hashem's kindness endures forever,
even at times when it is not apparent.

EACH OF THE FOLLOWING FOUR VERSES IS RECITED ALOUD BY THE *CHAZZAN*. AFTER EACH VERSE, THE CONGREGATION RESPONDS WITH THE VERSE: Hōdu Ladōnoy ki tōv, ki l'ōlom chasdō, AND THEN RECITES THE SUCCEEDING VERSE.

HŌDU Ladōnoy ki tōv,
הוֹדוּ לַיהוה כִּי טוֹב,
   ki l'ōlom chasdō.
כִּי לְעוֹלָם חַסְדּוֹ.
Give thanks to HASHEM for He is good; His kindness endures forever!*

Yōmar no yisro-ayl,
יֹאמַר נָא יִשְׂרָאֵל,
   ki l'ōlom chasdō.
כִּי לְעוֹלָם חַסְדּוֹ.
Let Israel say now: His kindness endures forever!

Yōm'ru no vays aharōn,
יֹאמְרוּ נָא בֵית אַהֲרֹן,
   ki l'ōlom chasdō.
כִּי לְעוֹלָם חַסְדּוֹ.
Let the House of Aaron say now: His kindness endures forever!

הַלְלוּ אֶת ה' — *Praise HASHEM.* The brevity of this psalm symbolizes the simplicity of the world order which will prevail after the advent of the Messiah.

הוֹדוּ לַה' כִּי טוֹב — *Give thanks to HASHEM for He is good.* This is a general expression of thanks to God. No matter what occurs, God is always good and everything He does is for the best,

Yōm'ru no yir-ay Adōnoy,
ki l'ōlom chasdō.

יֹאמְרוּ נָא יִרְאֵי יהוה,
כִּי לְעוֹלָם חַסְדּוֹ.

Let those who fear HASHEM say now: His kindness endures forever!

■ I express my confidence that despite the difficult circumstances of my people, our destiny is to be triumphant, and when we experience redemption, I will recognize that all that Hashem has done has been for the good.

MIN HAMAYTZAR korosi Yoh, מִן הַמֵּצַר קָרָאתִי יָּהּ,

From the straits* did I call upon God;

ononi vamerchov Yoh.   עָנָנִי בַמֶּרְחָב יָהּ.

God answered me with expansiveness.

Adōnoy li lō iro,
ma ya-ase li odom.

יהוה לִי לֹא אִירָא,
מַה יַּעֲשֶׂה לִּי אָדָם.

HASHEM is with me, I have no fear; how can man affect me?

Adōnoy li b'ōz'roy,
va-ani er-e v'sōn'oy.

יהוה לִי בְּעֹזְרָי,
וַאֲנִי אֶרְאֶה בְשֹׂנְאָי.

HASHEM is with me through my helpers;* therefore I can face my foes.

Tōv la-chasōs Badōnoy,
mib'tō-ach bo-odom.

טוֹב לַחֲסוֹת בַּיהוה,
מִבְּטֹחַ בָּאָדָם.

It is better to take refuge in HASHEM than to rely on man.*

Tōv la-chasōs Badōnoy,
mib'tō-ach bindivim.

טוֹב לַחֲסוֹת בַּיהוה,
מִבְּטֹחַ בִּנְדִיבִים.

It is better to take refuge in HASHEM than to rely on nobles.

Kol gōyim s'vovuni,
b'shaym Adōnoy ki amilam.

כָּל גּוֹיִם סְבָבוּנִי,
בְּשֵׁם יהוה כִּי אֲמִילַם.

All the nations surround me; in the Name of HASHEM I cut them down!

Sabuni gam s'vovuni,

סַבּוּנִי גַם סְבָבוּנִי,

They encircle me, they also surround me;

b'shaym Adōnoy ki amilam.

בְּשֵׁם יהוה כִּי אֲמִילַם.

in the Name of HASHEM, I cut them down!

מן הַמֵּצַר — *From the straits*. This psalm expresses gratitude and confidence. Just as David himself was catapulted from his personal straits to a reign marked by accomplishment and glory, so too Israel can look forward to Divine redemption from the straits of exile and oppression.

ה' לִי בְעֹזְרִי — *HASHEM is with me through my helpers*. I have many helpers, but I place confidence in them only because HASHEM is with them. If my helpers were not granted strength by God, their assistance would be futile.

טוֹב לַחֲסוֹת בַּה' מִבְּטֹחַ בָּאָדָם — *It is better to take refuge in HASHEM than to rely on man*. It is far better to put one's trust in God's protection, even without a pledge from Him, than to rely on the most profuse assurances of human beings.

even though this may not be immediately apparent to man.

Sabuni chidvōrim	סַבּוּנִי כִדְבֹרִים

They encircle me like bees,

dō-achu k'aysh kōtzim,	דֹּעֲכוּ כְּאֵשׁ קוֹצִים,

but they are extinguished as a fire does thorns;

b'shaym Adōnoy ki amilam.	בְּשֵׁם יהוה כִּי אֲמִילַם.

in the Name of HASHEM I cut them down!

Dochō d'chisani linpōl,	דָּחֹה דְחִיתַנִי לִנְפֹּל,
Vadōnoy azoroni.	וַיהוה עֲזָרָנִי.

You pushed me hard that I might fall, but HASHEM assisted me.

Ozi v'zimros Yoh, vai-hi li li-shu-o.	עָזִּי וְזִמְרָת יָהּ, וַיְהִי לִי לִישׁוּעָה.

God is my might and my praise, and He was a salvation for me.

Kōl rino vi-shu-o,	קוֹל רִנָּה וִישׁוּעָה,
b'oholay tzadikim,	בְּאָהֳלֵי צַדִּיקִים,

The sound of rejoicing and salvation is in the tents of the righteous:

Y'min Adōnoy ōso cho-yil.	יְמִין יהוה עֹשָׂה חָיִל.

"HASHEM's right hand does valiantly.

Y'min Adōnoy rōmaymo,	יְמִין יהוה רוֹמֵמָה,

HASHEM's right hand is raised triumphantly;

y'min Adōnoy ōso cho-yil.	יְמִין יהוה עֹשָׂה חָיִל.

HASHEM's right hand does valiantly!"

Lō omus ki echye,	לֹא אָמוּת כִּי אֶחְיֶה,
va-asapayr ma-asay Yoh.	וַאֲסַפֵּר מַעֲשֵׂי יָהּ.

I shall not die! But I shall live and relate the deeds of God.

Yasōr yis'rani Yoh,	יַסֹּר יִסְּרַנִּי יָּהּ,
v'lamo-ves lō n'sononi.	וְלַמָּוֶת לֹא נְתָנָנִי.

God has chastened me exceedingly, but He did not let me die.*

Pischu li sha-aray tzedek,	פִּתְחוּ לִי שַׁעֲרֵי צֶדֶק,

Open for me the gates of righteousness,

ovō vom ōde Yoh.	אָבֹא בָם אוֹדֶה יָהּ.

I will enter them and thank God.

Ze ha-sha-ar Ladōnoy,	זֶה הַשַּׁעַר לַיהוה,
tzadikim yovō-u vō.	צַדִּיקִים יָבֹאוּ בוֹ.

This is the gate of HASHEM; the righteous shall enter through it.*

יַסֹּר יִסְּרַנִּי יָּהּ וְלַמָּוֶת לֹא נְתָנָנִי — *God has chastened me exceedingly, but He did not let me die.* Throughout the duration of the exile, I survived because whatever suffering God decreed was only to atone for my sins.

זֶה הַשַּׁעַר לַה׳ צַדִּיקִים יָבֹאוּ בוֹ — *This is the gate of HASHEM; the righteous shall enter through it.* This refers to the Temple gate, through which the righteous will enter after the exile, thanking God for answering their plea for redemption.

Ōd'cho ki anisoni,	אוֹדְךָ כִּי עֲנִיתָנִי,
vat'hi li li-shu-o.	וַתְּהִי לִי לִישׁוּעָה.

I thank You for You have answered me and become my salvation.

Ōd'cho ki anisoni,	אוֹדְךָ כִּי עֲנִיתָנִי,
vat'hi li li-shu-o.	וַתְּהִי לִי לִישׁוּעָה.

I thank You for You have answered me and become my salvation.

Even mo-asu habōnim,	אֶבֶן מָאֲסוּ הַבּוֹנִים,
ho-y'so l'rōsh pino.	הָיְתָה לְרֹאשׁ פִּנָּה.

The stone the builders despised has become the cornerstone.*

Even mo-asu habōnim,	אֶבֶן מָאֲסוּ הַבּוֹנִים,
ho-y'so l'rōsh pino.	הָיְתָה לְרֹאשׁ פִּנָּה.

The stone the builders despised has become the cornerstone.

May-ays Adōnoy ho-y'so zōs,	מֵאֵת יהוה הָיְתָה זֹּאת,
hi niflos b'aynaynu.	הִיא נִפְלָאת בְּעֵינֵינוּ.

This emanated from HASHEM; it is wondrous in our eyes.

May-ays Adōnoy ho-y'so zōs,	מֵאֵת יהוה הָיְתָה זֹּאת,
hi niflos b'aynaynu.	הִיא נִפְלָאת בְּעֵינֵינוּ.

This emanated from HASHEM; it is wondrous in our eyes.

Ze ha-yōm oso Adōnoy,	זֶה הַיּוֹם עָשָׂה יהוה,
nogilo v'nism'cho vō.	נָגִילָה וְנִשְׂמְחָה בוֹ.

This is the day HASHEM has made; let us rejoice and be glad on it.

Ze ha-yōm oso Adōnoy	זֶה הַיּוֹם עָשָׂה יהוה,
nogilo v'nism'cho vō.	נָגִילָה וְנִשְׂמְחָה בוֹ.

This is the day HASHEM has made; let us rejoice and be glad on it.

THE NEXT FOUR LINES ARE RECITED RESPONSIVELY, CHAZZAN THEN CONGREGATION.

ONO Adōnoy hōshi-o no.	**אָנָּא** יהוה הוֹשִׁיעָה נָּא.

Please, HASHEM, save now!

Ono Adōnoy hōshi-o no.	אָנָּא יהוה הוֹשִׁיעָה נָּא.

Please, HASHEM, save now!

Ono Adōnoy hatzlicho no.	אָנָּא יהוה הַצְלִיחָה נָּא.

Please, HASHEM, bring success now!

Ono Adōnoy hatzlicho no.	אָנָּא יהוה הַצְלִיחָה נָּא.

Please, HASHEM, bring success now.

אֶבֶן מָאֲסוּ הַבּוֹנִים הָיְתָה לְרֹאשׁ פִּנָּה — *The stone the builders despised has become the cornerstone.* This verse refers to David, who was rejected by his own father and brothers. When the prophet Samuel announced that one of Jesse's sons was to be anointed king, no one even thought of summoning David, who was out tending the sheep (see *I Samuel* 16:4-13).

HALLEL

BORUCH HABO b'shaym Adōnoy, בָּרוּךְ הַבָּא בְּשֵׁם יהוה,
Blessed is he who comes in the Name of HASHEM;
bayrachnuchem mibays Adōnoy. בֵּרַכְנוּכֶם מִבֵּית יהוה.
we bless you from the House of HASHEM.

Boruch habo b'shaym Adōnoy, בָּרוּךְ הַבָּא בְּשֵׁם יהוה,
Blessed is he who comes in the Name of HASHEM;
bayrachnuchem mibays Adōnoy. בֵּרַכְנוּכֶם מִבֵּית יהוה.
we bless you from the House of HASHEM.

Ayl Adōnoy va-yo-er lonu, אֵל יהוה וַיָּאֶר לָנוּ,
HASHEM is God, He illuminated for us;
isru chag ba-avōsim, אִסְרוּ חַג בַּעֲבֹתִים,
bind the festival-offering with cords
ad karnōs hamizbay-ach. עַד קַרְנוֹת הַמִּזְבֵּחַ.
until the corners of the Altar.

Ayl Adōnoy va-yo-er lonu, אֵל יהוה וַיָּאֶר לָנוּ,
HASHEM is God, He illuminated for us;
isru chag ba-avōsim, אִסְרוּ חַג בַּעֲבֹתִים,
bind the festival-offering with cords
ad karnōs hamizbay-ach. עַד קַרְנוֹת הַמִּזְבֵּחַ.
until the corners of the Altar.

Ayli ato v'ōdeko, אֵלִי אַתָּה וְאוֹדֶךָּ,
You are my God, and I will thank You;
Elōhai arōm'meko. אֱלֹהַי אֲרוֹמְמֶךָּ.
my God, I will exalt You.

Ayli ato v'ōdeko, אֵלִי אַתָּה וְאוֹדֶךָּ,
You are my God, and I will thank You;
Elōhai arōm'meko. אֱלֹהַי אֲרוֹמְמֶךָּ.
my God, I will exalt You.

Hōdu Ladōnoy ki tōv, הוֹדוּ לַיהוה כִּי טוֹב,
Give thanks to HASHEM, *for He is good;*
ki l'ōlom chasdō. כִּי לְעוֹלָם חַסְדּוֹ.
His kindness endures forever.

Hōdu Ladōnoy ki tōv, הוֹדוּ לַיהוה כִּי טוֹב,
Give thanks to HASHEM, *for He is good;*
ki l'ōlom chasdō. כִּי לְעוֹלָם חַסְדּוֹ.
His kindness endures forever.

■ The concluding blessing of *Hallel* reaffirms my belief and confidence that all mankind will join in the praise of Hashem.

Y'HAL'LUCHO Adōnoy Elōhaynu יְהַלְלוּךָ יהוה אֱלֹהֵינוּ
kol ma-asecho, כָּל מַעֲשֶׂיךָ,
All Your works shall praise You,* HASHEM, our God;

vachasidecho tzadikim וַחֲסִידֶיךָ צַדִּיקִים
ōsay r'tzōnecho, עוֹשֵׂי רְצוֹנֶךָ,
and Your devout ones, the righteous who do Your will,

v'chol am'cho bays yisro-ayl וְכָל עַמְּךָ בֵּית יִשְׂרָאֵל
and Your entire people, the House of Israel,

b'rino yōdu vi-vor'chu בְּרִנָּה יוֹדוּ וִיבָרְכוּ
with glad song will thank, bless,

vi-shab'chu vifo-aru virōm'mu וִישַׁבְּחוּ וִיפָאֲרוּ וִירוֹמְמוּ
praise, glorify, exalt,

v'ya-aritzu v'yakdishu v'yamlichu וְיַעֲרִיצוּ וְיַקְדִּישׁוּ וְיַמְלִיכוּ
extol, sanctify, and proclaim the sovereignty

es shimcho malkaynu אֶת שִׁמְךָ מַלְכֵּנוּ.
of Your Name, our King.

Ki l'cho tōv l'hōdōs כִּי לְךָ טוֹב לְהוֹדוֹת
For to You it is fitting to give thanks,

ulshimcho no-e l'zamayr, וּלְשִׁמְךָ נָאֶה לְזַמֵּר,
and unto Your Name it is proper to sing praises,

ki may-ōlom v'ad ōlom ato Ayl. כִּי מֵעוֹלָם וְעַד עוֹלָם אַתָּה אֵל.
for from this world to the World to Come You are God.

Boruch ato Adōnoy, בָּרוּךְ אַתָּה יהוה,
melech m'hulol ba-tishbochōs. מֶלֶךְ מְהֻלָּל בַּתִּשְׁבָּחוֹת.
Blessed are You, HASHEM, the King Who is lauded with praises.

CONGREGATION RESPONDS: Omayn — אָמֵן

ON *ROSH CHODESH* MANY RECITE THE FOLLOWING VERSE AFTER *HALLEL*:

V'avrohom zokayn bo ba-yomim וְאַבְרָהָם זָקֵן בָּא בַּיָּמִים
Now Abraham was old, well on in years,

Vadonoy bay-rach es avrohom bakol. וַיהוה בֵּרַךְ אֶת אַבְרָהָם בַּכֹּל.
and HASHEM had blessed Abraham with everything.

יְהַלְלוּךָ ... כָּל מַעֲשֶׂיךָ — *All Your works shall praise You.* This paragraph is a concluding blessing that sums up the broad theme of *Hallel,* that Israel and the entire universe will join in praising God. In the perfect world of the future, the entire universe, including the vast variety of human beings, will function harmoniously according to God's will. This is the highest form of praise, for without it all the beautiful spoken and sung words and songs of praise are insincere and meaningless.

Rosh Chodesh

৵ঌ Rosh Chodesh

৵ঌ The Biblical Status

The institution of *Rosh Chodesh*, the New Moon, is Biblical. It was the first commandment given to the Jewish nation as a people: "This month shall be for you the beginning of the months" (*Exodus* 12:2). Even before the Jewish slaves were liberated and brought to their own land, they were given the gift of time, their own calendar. This verse contains the commandment to establish a Jewish calendar based on the moon, yet regulated by the sun. The time span between one new moon and the next is a bit over $29^{1}/_{2}$ days, and since a month must be composed of complete days, the months of the Jewish calendar alternate between 29 and 30 days, so that a typical 12-month year contains 354 days. Because the lunar year is eleven days shorter than the solar year, and the Torah has prescribed that Passover is to be observed annually in the springtime (*Deuteronomy* 16:1), it was necessary to regulate the calendar by adding seven additional months — making for years of thirteen lunar months — in a nineteen-year cycle. These additional months are called Adar II.

The Torah prescribes that, "On a day of your gladness and on your festivals, and on your new moons, you shall sound the trumpets over your elevation-offerings, and your feast peace offerings; and they shall be a remembrance for you, before your God" (*Numbers* 10:10). We are further taught that in addition to the daily morning offering, there were additional offerings on the New Moon (ibid. 28:11-15).

The Torah does not set forth the character of *Rosh Chodesh*, nor does it prohibit work on the day. The *Tur* (*Orach Chaim* 531) explains that the twelve New Moons were in honor of the twelve tribes, but when the men participated in the sin of the Golden Calf, the holiday of *Rosh Chodesh* was taken from the men and given primary to the women of Israel, who demonstrated by their enthusiastic contribution to the Sanctuary that their unwillingness to give their jewelry for the Calf was not because they did not want to part with their jewelry, but because of their abhorrence of idolatry.

৵ঌ Day of Atonement

The *Mussaf Shemoneh Esrei* of *Rosh Chodesh* provides us with the insight to understand how our Sages viewed *Rosh Chodesh* and the impact the day should have upon us. The middle blessing, which defines the essence of the day, begins "New Moons have You given Your people, a time of atonement for all their offspring." As Rosh Hashanah once a year is a day of spiritual reckoning and self-examination, so, too, is *Rosh Chodesh* a monthly call to the Jew to emulate the moon. As the moon is renewed, so the Jew is given a new opportunity to

improve his life, right the wrongs around him, both internally within his character and personality and externally in his community and environment. It is for this reason that the day before *Rosh Chodesh* is called *Yom Kippur Katan,* a minor Yom Kippur, and some fast on this day. Rabbi Samson Refael Hirsch (*Horeb* (paragraph 150) notes that Shabbos is a day of sanctity to prepare the individual for the forthcoming week, while *Rosh Chodesh* is a time of atonement and repentance for the past.

What is the specific nature of this atonement? And what is the reason for the unique *Rosh Chodesh* offering? Several insightful explanations are offered. The Talmud *(Shavuos* 2a, 9a) understands that this offering atones for a sin that only Hashem knows about, namely that of entering the Temple in a state of impurity.

The Talmud (*Chullin* 60b) notes that of all the festival additional offerings, only that of *Rosh Chodesh* is described as "a sin offering *to Hashem*" (*Numbers* 28:15). Thus the Talmud quotes Reish Lakish that Hashem asks the Jewish nation to bring an atonement on *His* behalf for having diminished the size of the moon. This refers to the apparent contradiction found in the account of creation on the fourth day. First the Torah says "And Hashem made the two great luminaries," i.e., the sun and the moon, implying that the two were equal. Then the verse continues, "The greater luminary to dominate the day, and the lesser luminary to dominate the night" (*Genesis* 1:16), stating clearly that the sun was larger. The Talmud explains that the two were created equal, whereupon the moon complained to Hashem that "two kings cannot share one crown," meaning that one should be superior to the other. Hashem immediately commanded the moon to diminish itself. The moon then protested, "Because I have rightfully complained, is it fair that I be diminished?" The Talmud informs us that Hashem did not successfully appease the moon, and therefore He instructs the Jews, "Bring an atonement on My behalf for having diminished the moon."

The above Talmudic passage is most difficult to comprehend. The commentary *Baruch She'amar,* of Rabbi Baruch HaLevi Epstein, suggests that Hashem had two alternatives in response to the moon's protest. He could have intensified the light of the sun, or diminished the light of the moon. He refrained from adding to the sun because *Bnei Yisrael*, the Jewish nation, was unworthy of such brilliant light. (See *Rashi* to *Genesis* 1:4, citing *Chagigah* 12a, who states that the original light created on the first day one was "too good" for this world, due to man's unworthiness, and therefore it is reserved for the righteous in the World to Come.) Therefore when the Torah refers to the New Moon *mussaf* as a "sin offering to Hashem," it is a euphemistic reference to the unworthiness of the Jewish nation, and it is for this that we are seeking atonement. It is noteworthy that this is one of the many examples of how man's performance impacts upon the natural environment about him. Not only is this a major theme in the second paragraph of the *Shema*, but the Talmud (*Berachos* 35b) teaches that if the Jewish people refrain from reciting blessings, the quality of the taste of fruit is diminished.

The commentary *Iyun Tefillah* understands the atonement of *Rosh Chodesh* to refer to our failure to have been worthy as yet of the Messiah and the reinstatement of the Kingship of the House of David in this past month. As we are taught in the *Yerushalmi* (*Yoma* 1:1): Every generation that does not bring about the rebuilding of the Temple in its day, is as if it had caused the destruction of the Temple. Similarly, our improper behavior this past month, both individually and communally, has delayed the ultimate redemption of our people, and for this we seek atonement on *Rosh Chodesh*. Appropriately and understandably, the *Mussaf Shemoneh Esrei* continues with the prayer and yearning for the restoration of the Jewish nation to Jerusalem and the building of the Third Temple, where speedily in our day we shall once again perform all the offerings prescribed by the Torah, daily offerings and those for the festivals.

◆§ Mussaf

The term *mussaf* means extra or additional, and it refers to the additional prayer that is added on Shabbos, festivals, and *Rosh Chodesh,* and also to the additional offering in the Temple service on those days. As mentioned earlier, there are two reasons for our prayers (*Berachos* 26b). We pray as did our forefathers, and our prayers correspond to the daily offerings in the Temple. *Mussaf*, however, has one motivation exclusively; it is, as the prophet Hosea (14:3) taught, "Let our lips substitute for bulls." That is to say, let God view the *Mussaf Amidah* as if we actually brought the offering in the Temple.

Rabbi Yitzchak Hutner noted that we do not mention the daily *tamid*, continual offering, in the *Shacharis* or *minchah* prayer, but we do recount the exact composition of the various *mussaf* offerings that were brought in the Temple. He explains that the daily prayers focus on various motifs, not only the offerings; these prayers *correspond* to the offerings, but are not devoted exclusively to them. Regarding the *Mussaf* prayer, however, the offerings are their exclusive focus (*Pachad Yitzchak*, *Pesach* §67).

⸨ MUSSAF FOR ROSH CHODESH ⸩

IN THE SYNAGOGUE THE *SHEMONEH ESREI* IS RECITED WHILE FACING THE ARK; ELSEWHERE IT IS RECITED WHILE FACING THE DIRECTION OF THE LAND OF ISRAEL. TAKE THREE STEPS BACKWARD, LEFT, RIGHT, LEFT, THEN THREE STEPS FORWARD, RIGHT, LEFT, RIGHT. REMAIN STANDING WITH FEET TOGETHER DURING *SHEMONEH ESREI*. RECITE IT WITH QUIET DEVOTION AND WITHOUT ANY INTERRUPTION. ALTHOUGH IT SHOULD NOT BE AUDIBLE TO OTHERS, ONE MUST PRAY LOUDLY ENOUGH TO HEAR ONESELF.

Ki shaym Adōnoy ekro,   כִּי שֵׁם יהוה אֶקְרָא,
When I call out the Name of HASHEM,

hovu gōdel Laylōhaynu.   הָבוּ גֹדֶל לֵאלֹהֵינוּ.
ascribe greatness to our God.

Adōnoy s'fosai tiftoch,   אֲדֹנָי שְׂפָתַי תִּפְתָּח,
My Lord, open my lips,

u-fi yagid t'hilosecho.   וּפִי יַגִּיד תְּהִלָּתֶךָ.
that my mouth may declare Your praise.

■ **First Blessing:** In the merit of our Patriarchs whose actions reflected Godliness, Hashem pledged to always be with Israel and protect them.

BEND THE KNEES AT Boruch; BOW AT ato; STRAIGHTEN UP AT Adōnoy.

BORUCH ato Adōnoy   בָּרוּךְ אַתָּה יהוה
    Elōhaynu Vaylōhay avōsaynu,   אֱלֹהֵינוּ וֵאלֹהֵי אֲבוֹתֵינוּ,
Blessed are You, HASHEM, *our God and the God of our forefathers,*

Elōhay avrohom, Elōhay yitzchok,   אֱלֹהֵי אַבְרָהָם, אֱלֹהֵי יִצְחָק,
    Vaylōhay ya-akōv,   וֵאלֹהֵי יַעֲקֹב,
God of Abraham, God of Isaac, and God of Jacob;

ho-Ayl hagodōl hagibōr v'hanōro,   הָאֵל הַגָּדוֹל הַגִּבּוֹר וְהַנּוֹרָא,
    Ayl elyōn,   אֵל עֶלְיוֹן,
the great, mighty, and awesome God, the supreme God,

gōmayl chasodim tōvim   גּוֹמֵל חֲסָדִים טוֹבִים
    v'kōnay hakōl,   וְקוֹנֵה הַכֹּל,
Who bestows beneficial kindnesses and creates everything,

v'zōchayr chasday ovōs,   וְזוֹכֵר חַסְדֵי אָבוֹת,
Who recalls the kindnesses of the Patriarchs

u-mayvi gō-ayl livnay v'nayhem,   וּמֵבִיא גוֹאֵל לִבְנֵי בְנֵיהֶם,
and brings a Redeemer to their children's children,

l'ma-an sh'mō b'ahavo.   לְמַעַן שְׁמוֹ בְּאַהֲבָה.
for His Name's sake, with love.

Melech ōzayr u-mōshi-a u-mogayn.   מֶלֶךְ עוֹזֵר וּמוֹשִׁיעַ וּמָגֵן.
O King, Helper, Savior, and Shield.

BEND THE KNEES AT Boruch; BOW AT ato; STRAIGHTEN UP AT Adōnoy.

Boruch ato Adōnoy, בָּרוּךְ אַתָּה יהוה,
mogayn avrohom. מָגֵן אַבְרָהָם.

Blessed are You, HASHEM, Shield of Abraham.

■ Second Blessing: God's might as it is manifest in nature and man

---

ATO gibōr l'ōlom Adōnoy, אַתָּה גִּבּוֹר לְעוֹלָם אֲדֹנָי,

You are eternally mighty, my Lord,

m'cha-yay maysim ato, מְחַיֵּה מֵתִים אַתָּה,

the Resuscitator of the dead are You,

rav l'hōshi-a. רַב לְהוֹשִׁיעַ.

abundantly able to save,

BETWEEN SHEMINI ATZERES AND PESACH, ADD:

Mashiv horu-ach u-mōrid hageshem. מַשִּׁיב הָרוּחַ וּמוֹרִיד הַגֶּשֶׁם.

Who makes the wind blow and makes the rain descend;

M'chalkayl cha-yim b'chesed, מְכַלְכֵּל חַיִּים בְּחֶסֶד,

Who sustains the living with kindness;

m'cha-yay maysim b'rachamim rabim, מְחַיֵּה מֵתִים בְּרַחֲמִים רַבִּים,

resuscitates the dead with abundant mercy,

sōmaych nōf'lim, v'rōfay chōlim, סוֹמֵךְ נוֹפְלִים, וְרוֹפֵא חוֹלִים,

supports the fallen, heals the sick,

u-matir asurim, וּמַתִּיר אֲסוּרִים,

releases the confined,

umka-yaym emunosō li-shaynay ofor. וּמְקַיֵּם אֱמוּנָתוֹ לִישֵׁנֵי עָפָר.

and maintains His faith to those asleep in the dust.

Mi cho-mōcho ba-al g'vurōs, מִי כָמוֹךָ בַּעַל גְּבוּרוֹת,

Who is like You, O Master of mighty deeds,

u-mi dōme loch, וּמִי דּוֹמֶה לָּךְ,

and who is comparable to You,

melech maymis umcha-ye מֶלֶךְ מֵמִית וּמְחַיֶּה
u-matzmi-ach y'shu-o. וּמַצְמִיחַ יְשׁוּעָה.

O King Who causes death and restores life and makes salvation sprout!

V'ne-emon ato l'hacha-yōs maysim. וְנֶאֱמָן אַתָּה לְהַחֲיוֹת מֵתִים.

And You are faithful to resuscitate the dead.

Boruch ato Adōnoy, בָּרוּךְ אַתָּה יהוה,
m'cha-yay hamaysim. מְחַיֵּה הַמֵּתִים.

Blessed are You, HASHEM, Who resuscitates the dead.

MUSSAF FOR ROSH CHODESH

DURING THE *CHAZZAN'S* REPETITION, *KEDUSHAH* (BELOW) IS RECITED;
INDIVIDUALS CONTINUE ON P. 506.

■ **Third Blessing: Regarding the holiness of God's Name**

DURING *KEDUSHAH* STAND WITH FEET TOGETHER AND AVOID ANY INTERRUPTIONS.
RISE ON TOES WHEN SAYING Kodōsh, kodōsh, kodōsh; Boruch; AND Yimlōch.

CONGREGATION, THEN *CHAZZAN*:

N'KADAYSH es shimcho bo-ōlom,   נְקַדֵּשׁ אֶת שִׁמְךָ בָּעוֹלָם,
We shall sanctify Your Name in this world,

k'shaym shemakdishim ōsō   כְּשֵׁם שֶׁמַּקְדִּישִׁים אוֹתוֹ
bishmay morōm,   בִּשְׁמֵי מָרוֹם,
just as they sanctify it in heaven above,

kakosuv al yad n'vi-echo,   כַּכָּתוּב עַל יַד נְבִיאֶךָ,
as it is written by the hand of Your prophet,

v'koro ze el ze v'omar: וְקָרָא זֶה אֶל זֶה וְאָמַר:
"And one [angel] will call another and say:

ALL IN UNISON:

Kodōsh, kodōsh, kodōsh   קָדוֹשׁ קָדוֹשׁ קָדוֹשׁ
Adōnoy Tz'vo-ōs,   יהוה צְבָאוֹת,
'Holy, holy, holy is HASHEM, *Master of Legions,*

m'lō chol ho-oretz k'vōdō.   מְלֹא כָל הָאָרֶץ כְּבוֹדוֹ.
the whole world is filled with His glory.'"

CHAZZAN:

L'u-mosom boruch yōmayru: לְעֻמָּתָם בָּרוּךְ יֹאמֵרוּ:
Those facing them say, "Blessed":

ALL IN UNISON:

Boruch k'vōd Adōnoy, mim'kōmō.   בָּרוּךְ כְּבוֹד יהוה, מִמְּקוֹמוֹ.
"Blessed is the glory of HASHEM *from His place."*

CHAZZAN:

Uvdivray kodsh'cho kosuv laymōr: וּבְדִבְרֵי קָדְשְׁךָ כָּתוּב לֵאמֹר:
And in Your holy Writings the following is written:

ALL IN UNISON:

Yimlōch Adōnoy l'ōlom,   יִמְלֹךְ יהוה לְעוֹלָם,
*"*HASHEM *shall reign forever —*

Elōha-yich tziyōn l'dōr vodōr,   אֱלֹהַיִךְ צִיּוֹן לְדֹר וָדֹר,
hal'luyoh.   הַלְלוּיָהּ.
your God, O Zion — from generation to generation: Praise God!"

CHAZZAN CONCLUDES:

לְדוֹר וָדוֹר נַגִּיד גָּדְלֶךָ וּלְנֵצַח נְצָחִים קְדֻשָּׁתְךָ נַקְדִּישׁ, וְשִׁבְחֲךָ אֱלֹהֵינוּ מִפִּינוּ לֹא יָמוּשׁ לְעוֹלָם וָעֶד, כִּי אֵל מֶלֶךְ גָּדוֹל וְקָדוֹשׁ אָתָּה. בָּרוּךְ אַתָּה יהוה, הָאֵל הַקָּדוֹשׁ.

THE *CHAZZAN* CONTINUES Roshay chodoshim (P. 506).

ATO kodōsh v'shimcho kodōsh,   אַתָּה קָדוֹשׁ וְשִׁמְךָ קָדוֹשׁ,
You are holy and Your Name is holy,

ukdōshim b'chol yōm   וּקְדוֹשִׁים בְּכָל יוֹם
   y'hal'lucho, selo.   יְהַלְלוּךָ סֶּלָה.
and holy ones praise You, every day, forever.

Boruch ato Adōnoy, ho-Ayl hakodōsh.   בָּרוּךְ אַתָּה יהוה, הָאֵל הַקָּדוֹשׁ.
*Blessed are You, H*ASHEM*, the holy God.*

■ Fourth Blessing: the holiness of the Day. Saddened by the absence of the Temple in Jerusalem, we recount the special atonement offerings of the New Month, and beseech God to restore to the Jewish People the glory of His Temple and its Service.

ROSHAY CHODOSHIM   רָאשֵׁי חֳדָשִׁים
   l'am'cho nosoto,   לְעַמְּךָ נָתָתָּ,
New Moons have You given Your people,

z'man kaporo l'chol tōl'dōsom,   זְמַן כַּפָּרָה לְכָל תּוֹלְדוֹתָם,
a time of atonement for all their offspring,

bi-yōsom makrivim l'fonecho   בִּהְיוֹתָם מַקְרִיבִים לְפָנֶיךָ
   zivchay rotzōn,   זִבְחֵי רָצוֹן,
when they would bring before You offerings for favor

usiray chatos l'chapayr ba-adom.   וּשְׂעִירֵי חַטָּאת לְכַפֵּר בַּעֲדָם.
and goats of sin-offering to atone on their behalf.

Zikorōn l'chulom yih-yu,   זִכָּרוֹן לְכֻלָּם יִהְיוּ,
They would serve as a remembrance for them all

us-shu-as nafshom miyad sōnay.   וּתְשׁוּעַת נַפְשָׁם מִיַּד שׂוֹנֵא.
and a salvation for their soul from the hand of the enemy.

Mizbayach chodosh b'tziyōn tochin,   מִזְבֵּחַ חָדָשׁ בְּצִיּוֹן תָּכִין,
May You establish a new Altar in Zion,

v'ōlas rōsh chōdesh na-ale olov,   וְעוֹלַת רֹאשׁ חוֹדֶשׁ נַעֲלֶה עָלָיו,
and may we bring up upon it the elevation-offering of the New Moon,

us-iray izim na-ase v'rotzōn.   וּשְׂעִירֵי עִזִּים נַעֲשֶׂה בְרָצוֹן.
and prepare he-goats with favor.

U-va-avōdas bays hamikdosh   וּבַעֲבוֹדַת בֵּית הַמִּקְדָּשׁ
   nismach kulonu,   נִשְׂמַח כֻּלָּנוּ,
In the service of the Holy Temple may we all rejoice

uvshiray dovid avdecho   וּבְשִׁירֵי דָוִד עַבְדֶּךָ
   hanishmo-im b'irecho,   הַנִּשְׁמָעִים בְּעִירֶךָ,
and in the songs of Your servant David that are heard in Your City,

ho-amurim lifnay mizb'checho,   הָאֲמוּרִים לִפְנֵי מִזְבְּחֶךָ,
when they are recited before Your Altar.

MUSSAF FOR ROSH CHODESH

אַהֲבַת עוֹלָם תָּבִיא לָהֶם, — ahavas ōlom tovi lohem,
May You bring them an eternal love

וּבְרִית אָבוֹת לַבָּנִים תִּזְכּוֹר. — uvris ovōs labonim tizkōr.
and the covenant of the forefathers may You recall upon the children.

וַהֲבִיאֵנוּ לְצִיּוֹן עִירְךָ בְּרִנָּה, — Vahavi-aynu l'tziyōn ir'cho b'rino,
May You bring us to Zion, Your city, in glad song,

וְלִירוּשָׁלַיִם בֵּית מִקְדָּשְׁךָ — v'lirushola-yim bays mikdosh'cho
בְּשִׂמְחַת עוֹלָם. — b'simchas ōlom.
and to Jerusalem, Your Holy Temple, in eternal gladness.

וְשָׁם נַעֲשֶׂה לְפָנֶיךָ — V'shom na-ase l'fonecho
אֶת קָרְבְּנוֹת חוֹבוֹתֵינוּ, — es korb'nōs chōvōsaynu,
There we shall perform before You our obligated offerings,

תְּמִידִים כְּסִדְרָם, — t'midim k'sidrom,
the continual-offerings according to their order

וּמוּסָפִים כְּהִלְכָתָם. — u-musofim k'hilchosom.
and the additional offerings according to their law.

וְאֶת מוּסַף יוֹם — V'es musaf yōm
רֹאשׁ הַחֹדֶשׁ הַזֶּה — rōsh ha-chōdesh ha-ze,
And the additional offering of this New Moon day

נַעֲשֶׂה וְנַקְרִיב לְפָנֶיךָ בְּאַהֲבָה, — na-ase v'nakriv l'fonecho b'ahavo,
we shall perform and bring before You with love

כְּמִצְוַת רְצוֹנֶךָ, — k'mitzvas r'tzōnecho,
according to the commandment of Your favor,

כְּמוֹ שֶׁכָּתַבְתָּ עָלֵינוּ בְּתוֹרָתֶךָ, — k'mō shekosavto olaynu b'sōrosecho,
as You have written for us in Your Torah,

עַל יְדֵי מֹשֶׁה עַבְדֶּךָ, — al y'day mōshe avdecho,
מִפִּי כְבוֹדֶךָ, כָּאָמוּר: — mipi ch'vōdecho ko-omur:
through Moses Your servant, from Your glorious expression, as it is said:

■ We pray that Hashem consider our reciting the verses of Torah enumerating the offerings of *Rosh Chodesh* as if we actually brought them in His Holy Temple.

וּבְרָאשֵׁי חָדְשֵׁיכֶם — **UVROSHAY** chod'shaychem
תַּקְרִיבוּ עֹלָה לַיהוה, — takrivu ōlo Ladōnoy,
And on your New Moons you are to bring an elevation-offering to HASHEM;

פָּרִים בְּנֵי בָקָר שְׁנַיִם, — porim b'nay vokor sh'na-yim,
וְאַיִל אֶחָד, — v'a-yil e-chod,
two young bulls; one ram;

כְּבָשִׂים בְּנֵי שָׁנָה שִׁבְעָה תְּמִימִם. — k'vosim b'nay shono shivo t'mimim.
seven (male) first-year lambs — unblemished.

U-minchosom v'niskayhem kimdubor, וּמִנְחָתָם וְנִסְכֵּיהֶם כִּמְדֻבָּר,
And their meal-offerings and their drink-offerings as specified:

sh'lōsho esrōnim lapor, שְׁלֹשָׁה עֶשְׂרֹנִים לַפָּר,
ush'nay esrōnim lo-oyil, וּשְׁנֵי עֶשְׂרֹנִים לָאַיִל,
three tenth-ephah for each bull; two tenth-ephah for the ram;

v'isorōn lakeves, v'ya-yin k'niskō, וְעִשָּׂרוֹן לַכֶּבֶשׂ וְיַיִן כְּנִסְכּוֹ,
one tenth-ephah for each lamb; and wine for its drink offering.

v'so-ir l'chapayr, וְשָׂעִיר לְכַפֵּר,
A he-goat for atonement

ush'nay s'midim k'hilchosom. וּשְׁנֵי תְמִידִים כְּהִלְכָתָם.
and two continual-offerings according to their law.

■ I pray that Hashem fill the new month with every form of happiness and blessing.

DURING *CHAZZAN'S* REPETITION, THE CONGREGATION RESPONDS *AMEN*, AS INDICATED.

ELŌHAYNU Vaylōhay avōsaynu. אֱלֹהֵינוּ וֵאלֹהֵי אֲבוֹתֵינוּ,
Our God and the God of our forefathers,

chadaysh olaynu es ha-chōdesh ha-ze, חַדֵּשׁ עָלֵינוּ אֶת הַחֹדֶשׁ הַזֶּה
inaugurate for us this month

l'tōvo v'livrocho (Omayn), לְטוֹבָה וְלִבְרָכָה (אָמֵן),
for good and for blessing (Amen),

l'sosōn ulsimcho (Omayn), לְשָׂשׂוֹן וּלְשִׂמְחָה (אָמֵן),
for joy and for gladness (Amen),

li-shu-o ulnechomo (Omayn), לִישׁוּעָה וּלְנֶחָמָה (אָמֵן),
for salvation and for consolation (Amen),

l'farnoso ulchalkolo (Omayn), לְפַרְנָסָה וּלְכַלְכָּלָה (אָמֵן),
for sustenance and for support (Amen),

l'cha-yim ulsholōm (Omayn), לְחַיִּים וּלְשָׁלוֹם (אָמֵן),
for life and for peace (Amen),

limchilas chayt v'lislichas ovōn (Omayn). לִמְחִילַת חֵטְא וְלִסְלִיחַת עָוֹן (אָמֵן).
for pardon of sin and forgiveness of iniquity (Amen).

——— DURING A JEWISH LEAP YEAR ADD: ———

ulchaporas posha (Omayn). וּלְכַפָּרַת פָּשַׁע (אָמֵן).
and for atonement of willful sin (Amen).

Ki v'am'cho yisro-ayl bocharto כִּי בְעַמְּךָ יִשְׂרָאֵל בָּחַרְתָּ
mikol ho-umōs, מִכָּל הָאֻמּוֹת,
For You have chosen Your people Israel from all the nations,

v'chukay roshay chodoshim lohem kovo'to.	וְחֻקֵּי רָאשֵׁי חֳדָשִׁים לָהֶם קָבָעְתָּ.

and You have set forth the decrees of the New Moons for them.

Boruch ato Adōnoy,	בָּרוּךְ אַתָּה יהוה,

Blessed are You HASHEM,

m'kadaysh yisro-ayl v'roshay chodoshim.	מְקַדֵּשׁ יִשְׂרָאֵל וְרָאשֵׁי חֳדָשִׁים.

Who sanctifies Israel and the New Moons.

■ Fifth Blessing: Prayer for restoration of the Temple service

---

R'TZAY, Adōnoy Elōhaynu b'am'cho yisro-ayl u-visfilosom,	**רְצֵה** יהוה אֱלֹהֵינוּ בְּעַמְּךָ יִשְׂרָאֵל וּבִתְפִלָּתָם,

Be favorable, HASHEM, our God, toward Your people Israel and their prayer

v'hoshayv es ho-avōdo lidvir bay-secho.	וְהָשֵׁב אֶת הָעֲבוֹדָה לִדְבִיר בֵּיתֶךָ.

and restore the service to the Holy of Holies of Your Temple.

V'i-shay yisro-ayl, usfilosom b'ahavo s'kabayl b'rotzōn,	וְאִשֵּׁי יִשְׂרָאֵל וּתְפִלָּתָם בְּאַהֲבָה תְקַבֵּל בְּרָצוֹן,

The fire-offerings of Israel and their prayer accept with love and favor,

us-hi l'rotzōn tomid avōdas yisro-ayl amecho.	וּתְהִי לְרָצוֹן תָּמִיד עֲבוֹדַת יִשְׂרָאֵל עַמֶּךָ.

and may the service of Your people Israel always be favorable to You.

V'SECHEZENO aynaynu b'shuv'cho l'tziyōn b'rachamim.	**וְתֶחֱזֶינָה** עֵינֵינוּ בְּשׁוּבְךָ לְצִיּוֹן בְּרַחֲמִים.

May our eyes behold Your return to Zion in compassion.

Boruch ato Adōnoy, hamachazir sh'chinosō l'tziyōn.	בָּרוּךְ אַתָּה יהוה, הַמַּחֲזִיר שְׁכִינָתוֹ לְצִיּוֹן.

Blessed are You, HASHEM, Who restores His Presence unto Zion.

■ Sixth Blessing: Acknowledgment of our debt of gratitude

BOW AT Mōdim anachnu loch; STRAIGHTEN UP AT Adōnoy.
IN HIS REPETITION THE CHAZZAN SHOULD RECITE THE ENTIRE MODIM ALOUD,
WHILE THE CONGREGATION RECITES MODIM OF THE RABBIS (P. 510) SOFTLY.

MŌDIM anachnu loch,	**מוֹדִים** אֲנַחְנוּ לָךְ,

We gratefully thank You,

sho-ato hu Adōnoy Elōhaynu Vaylōhay avōsaynu	שָׁאַתָּה הוּא יהוה אֱלֹהֵינוּ וֵאלֹהֵי אֲבוֹתֵינוּ

for it is You Who are HASHEM, our God, and the God of our forefathers

l'ōlom vo-ed,	לְעוֹלָם וָעֶד,

forever and ever;

tzur cha-yaynu, mogayn yish-aynu ato hu l'dōr vodōr.	צוּר חַיֵּינוּ, מָגֵן יִשְׁעֵנוּ אַתָּה הוּא לְדוֹר וָדוֹר.

Rock of our lives, Shield of our salvation are You from generation to generation.

Nōde l'cho unsapayr t'hilosecho	נוֹדֶה לְּךָ וּנְסַפֵּר תְּהִלָּתֶךָ

We shall thank You and relate Your praise —

al cha-yaynu ham'surim b'yodecho,	עַל חַיֵּינוּ הַמְּסוּרִים בְּיָדֶךָ,

for our lives, which are committed to Your power,

v'al nishmōsaynu hap'kudōs loch,	וְעַל נִשְׁמוֹתֵינוּ הַפְּקוּדוֹת לָךְ,

and for our souls that are entrusted to You,

v'al nisecho sheb'chol yōm i-monu,	וְעַל נִסֶּיךָ שֶׁבְּכָל יוֹם עִמָּנוּ,

and for Your miracles that are with us every day,

v'al nifl'ōsecho v'tōvōsecho sheb'chol ays,	וְעַל נִפְלְאוֹתֶיךָ וְטוֹבוֹתֶיךָ שֶׁבְּכָל עֵת,

and for Your wonders and favors in every season —

erev vovōker v'tzohoro-yim.	עֶרֶב וָבֹקֶר וְצָהֳרָיִם.

evening, morning, and afternoon.

Hatōv ki lō cholu rachamecho,	הַטּוֹב כִּי לֹא כָלוּ רַחֲמֶיךָ,

The Beneficent One, for Your compassions were never exhausted,

v'ham'rachaym ki lō samu chasodecho,	וְהַמְרַחֵם כִּי לֹא תַמּוּ חֲסָדֶיךָ,

and the Compassionate One, for Your kindnesses never ended —

may-ōlom kivinu loch.	מֵעוֹלָם קִוִּינוּ לָךְ.

always have we put our hope in You.

MODIM OF THE RABBIS

RECITED SOFTLY BY CONGREGATION WHILE *CHAZZAN* RECITES THE REGULAR MODIM ALOUD

MŌDIM anachnu loch,	**מוֹדִים** אֲנַחְנוּ לָךְ,

We gratefully thank You,

sho-ato hu Adōnoy Elōhaynu Vaylōhay avōsaynu,	שָׁאַתָּה הוּא יהוה אֱלֹהֵינוּ וֵאלֹהֵי אֲבוֹתֵינוּ,

for it is You Who are HASHEM, *our God and the God of our forefathers,*

Elōhay chol bosor,	אֱלֹהֵי כָל בָּשָׂר,

the God of all flesh,

yōtz'raynu, yōtzayr b'rayshis.	יוֹצְרֵנוּ, יוֹצֵר בְּרֵאשִׁית.

our Molder, the Molder of the universe.

B'rochōs v'hōdo-ōs l'shimcho hagodōl v'hakodōsh,	בְּרָכוֹת וְהוֹדָאוֹת לְשִׁמְךָ הַגָּדוֹל וְהַקָּדוֹשׁ,

Blessings and thanks are due Your great and holy Name

MUSSAF FOR ROSH CHODESH

al sheheche-yisonu v'ki-yamtonu.   עַל שֶׁהֶחֱיִיתָנוּ וְקִיַּמְתָּנוּ.
for You have given us life and sustained us.

Kayn t'cha-yaynu uska-y'maynu,   כֵּן תְּחַיֵּנוּ וּתְקַיְּמֵנוּ,
So may You continue to give us life and sustain us

v'se-esōf golu-yōsaynu   וְתֶאֱסוֹף גָּלֻיּוֹתֵינוּ
l'chatzrōs kod-shecho,   לְחַצְרוֹת קָדְשֶׁךָ,
and gather our exiles to the Courtyards of Your Sanctuary,

lishmōr chukecho v'la-asōs r'tzōnecho,   לִשְׁמוֹר חֻקֶּיךָ וְלַעֲשׂוֹת רְצוֹנֶךָ,
ul-ovd'cho b'layvov sholaym,   וּלְעָבְדְּךָ בְּלֵבָב שָׁלֵם,
to observe Your decrees, to do Your will and to serve You wholeheartedly.

al she-anachnu mōdim loch.   עַל שֶׁאֲנַחְנוּ מוֹדִים לָךְ.
[We thank You] for inspiring us to thank You.

Boruch Ayl hahōdo-ōs.   בָּרוּךְ אֵל הַהוֹדָאוֹת.
Blessed is the God of thanksgivings.

ON CHANUKAH CONTINUE BELOW. ON ALL OTHER DAYS TURN TO P. 513.

ON CHANUKAH ADD THE FOLLOWING:

AL hanisim, v'al hapurkon,   **עַל** הַנִּסִּים, וְעַל הַפֻּרְקָן,
For the miracles, and for the salvation,

v'al hag'vurōs, v'al hat'shu-ōs,   וְעַל הַגְּבוּרוֹת, וְעַל הַתְּשׁוּעוֹת,
v'al hamilchomōs,   וְעַל הַמִּלְחָמוֹת,
and for the mighty deeds, and for the victories, and for the battles

she-osiso la-avōsaynu   שֶׁעָשִׂיתָ לַאֲבוֹתֵינוּ
ba-yomim hohaym baz'man ha-ze.   בַּיָּמִים הָהֵם בַּזְּמַן הַזֶּה.
which You performed for our forefathers in those days, at this time.

BIMAY matisyohu ben yōchonon   **בִּימֵי** מַתִּתְיָהוּ בֶּן יוֹחָנָן
In the days of Mattisyahu, the son of Yochanan,

kōhayn godōl chashmōno-i u-vonov,   כֹּהֵן גָּדוֹל חַשְׁמוֹנָאִי וּבָנָיו,
the High Priest, the Hasmonean, and his sons —

k'she-om'do malchus yovon   כְּשֶׁעָמְדָה מַלְכוּת יָוָן
hor'sho-o al am'cho yisro-ayl,   הָרְשָׁעָה עַל עַמְּךָ יִשְׂרָאֵל,
when the wicked Greek kingdom rose up against Your people Israel

l'hashkichom tōrosecho.   לְהַשְׁכִּיחָם תּוֹרָתֶךָ,
to make them forget Your Torah

ulha-avirom maychukay r'tzōnecho.   וּלְהַעֲבִירָם מֵחֻקֵּי רְצוֹנֶךָ.
and compel them to stray from the statutes of Your will.

V'ato b'rachamecho horabim,   וְאַתָּה בְּרַחֲמֶיךָ הָרַבִּים,
But You, in Your abundant mercy,

omadto lohem b'ays tzorosom,	עָמַדְתָּ לָהֶם בְּעֵת צָרָתָם,

stood up for them in the time of their distress;

ravto es rivom, danto es dinom,	רַבְתָּ אֶת רִיבָם, דַּנְתָּ אֶת דִּינָם,

You took up their grievance, You judged their claim,

nokamto es nikmosom.	נָקַמְתָּ אֶת נִקְמָתָם.

and You avenged their wrong.

Mosarto gibōrim b'yad chaloshim,	מָסַרְתָּ גִבּוֹרִים בְּיַד חַלָּשִׁים,
v'rabim b'yad m'atim,	וְרַבִּים בְּיַד מְעַטִּים,

You delivered the strong into the hand of the weak, the many into the hand of the few,

utmay-im b'yad t'hōrim,	וּטְמֵאִים בְּיַד טְהוֹרִים,
ursho-im b'yad tzadikim	וּרְשָׁעִים בְּיַד צַדִּיקִים,

the impure into the hand of the pure, the wicked into the hand of the righteous,

v'zaydim b'yad ōs'kay sōrosecho.	וְזֵדִים בְּיַד עוֹסְקֵי תוֹרָתֶךָ.

and the wanton into the hand of the diligent students of Your Torah.

Ulcho osiso	וּלְךָ עָשִׂיתָ
shaym godōl v'kodōsh b'ōlomecho,	שֵׁם גָּדוֹל וְקָדוֹשׁ בְּעוֹלָמֶךָ,

For Yourself You made a great and holy Name in Your world,

ul-am'cho yisro-ayl	וּלְעַמְּךָ יִשְׂרָאֵל

and for Your people Israel

osiso t'shu-o g'dōlo u-furkon	עָשִׂיתָ תְּשׁוּעָה גְדוֹלָה וּפֻרְקָן
k'ha-yōm ha-ze.	כְּהַיּוֹם הַזֶּה.

You performed a great victory and salvation as this very day.

V'achar kayn bo-u vonecho	וְאַחַר כֵּן בָּאוּ בָנֶיךָ
lidvir bay-secho,	לִדְבִיר בֵּיתֶךָ,

Thereafter, Your children came to the Holy of Holies of Your House,

u-finu es haycholecho,	וּפִנּוּ אֶת הֵיכָלֶךָ,
v'tiharu es mikdoshecho,	וְטִהֲרוּ אֶת מִקְדָּשֶׁךָ,

they cleansed Your Temple, they purified the site of Your Holiness;

v'hidliku nayrōs	וְהִדְלִיקוּ נֵרוֹת
b'chatzrōs kod-shecho,	בְּחַצְרוֹת קָדְשֶׁךָ,

and they kindled lights in the Courtyards of Your Sanctuary;

v'kov'u sh'mōnas y'may chanuko aylu,	וְקָבְעוּ שְׁמוֹנַת יְמֵי חֲנֻכָּה אֵלּוּ,

and they established these eight days of Chanukah

l'hōdōs ulhalayl	לְהוֹדוֹת וּלְהַלֵּל
l'shimcho hagodōl.	לְשִׁמְךָ הַגָּדוֹל.

to express thanks and praise to Your great Name.

513 / MUSSAF FOR ROSH CHODESH

ON ALL DAYS CONTINUE HERE:

V'AL kulom yisborach v'yisromam shimcho, malkaynu

וְעַל כֻּלָּם יִתְבָּרַךְ וְיִתְרוֹמַם שִׁמְךָ מַלְכֵּנוּ

For all these, may Your Name be blessed and exalted, our King,

tomid l'ōlom vo-ed.

תָּמִיד לְעוֹלָם וָעֶד.

continually forever and ever.

V'chōl hacha-yim yōducho selo,

וְכֹל הַחַיִּים יוֹדוּךָ סֶּלָה,

Everything alive will gratefully acknowledge You, Selah!

vihal'lu es shimcho be-emes,

וִיהַלְלוּ אֶת שִׁמְךָ בֶּאֱמֶת,

and praise Your Name sincerely,

ho-Ayl y'shu-osaynu v'ezrosaynu selo.

הָאֵל יְשׁוּעָתֵנוּ וְעֶזְרָתֵנוּ סֶּלָה.

O God of our salvation and help, Selah!

BEND THE KNEES AT Boruch; BOW AT ato; STRAIGHTEN UP AT Adōnoy.

Boruch ato Adōnoy,

בָּרוּךְ אַתָּה יהוה,

*Blessed are You, H*ASHEM*,*

hatōv shimcho ulcho no-e l'hōdōs.

הַטּוֹב שִׁמְךָ וּלְךָ נָאֶה לְהוֹדוֹת.

Your Name is "The Beneficent One" and to You it is fitting to give thanks.

■ Seventh Blessing: Prayer for peace and harmony amongst the Jewish people

---

THE *CHAZZAN* RECITES THE PRIESTLY BLESSING
DURING HIS REPETITION, EXCEPT IN A HOUSE OF MOURNING.

אֱלֹהֵינוּ, וֵאלֹהֵי אֲבוֹתֵינוּ, בָּרְכֵנוּ בַבְּרָכָה הַמְשֻׁלֶּשֶׁת בַּתּוֹרָה הַכְּתוּבָה עַל יְדֵי מֹשֶׁה עַבְדֶּךָ, הָאֲמוּרָה מִפִּי אַהֲרֹן וּבָנָיו, כֹּהֲנִים עַם קְדוֹשֶׁךָ, כָּאָמוּר:

יְבָרֶכְךָ יהוה, וְיִשְׁמְרֶךָ. — Cong.) — כֵּן יְהִי רָצוֹן – (kayn y'hi rotzōn)
יָאֵר יהוה פָּנָיו אֵלֶיךָ וִיחֻנֶּךָ. — Cong.) — כֵּן יְהִי רָצוֹן – (kayn y'hi rotzōn)
יִשָּׂא יהוה פָּנָיו אֵלֶיךָ וְיָשֵׂם לְךָ שָׁלוֹם. — Cong.) — כֵּן יְהִי רָצוֹן – (kayn y'hi rotzōn)

SIM SHOLŌM tōvo uvrocho,

שִׂים שָׁלוֹם, טוֹבָה, וּבְרָכָה,

Establish peace, goodness, blessing,

chayn vochesed v'rachamim

חֵן וָחֶסֶד וְרַחֲמִים

graciousness, kindness, and compassion

olaynu v'al kol yisro-ayl amecho.

עָלֵינוּ וְעַל כָּל יִשְׂרָאֵל עַמֶּךָ.

upon us and upon all of Your people Israel.

מוסף לראש חודש / 514

Bor'chaynu, ovinu,	בָּרְכֵנוּ, אָבִינוּ,
Bless us, our Father,	
kulonu k'e-chod	כֻּלָּנוּ כְּאֶחָד
all of us as one,	
b'ōr ponecho,	בְּאוֹר פָּנֶיךָ,
with the light of Your countenance,	
ki v'ōr ponecho nosato lonu,	כִּי בְאוֹר פָּנֶיךָ נָתַתָּ לָּנוּ,
Adōnoy Elōhaynu,	יהוה אֱלֹהֵינוּ,
*for with the light of Your countenance, You, H*ASHEM*, our God, gave us*	
tōras cha-yim v'ahavas chesed,	תּוֹרַת חַיִּים וְאַהֲבַת חֶסֶד,
the Torah of life and a love of kindness,	
utz-doko uvrocho v'rachamim	וּצְדָקָה וּבְרָכָה וְרַחֲמִים
righteousness, blessing, compassion,	
v'cha-yim v'sholōm.	וְחַיִּים וְשָׁלוֹם.
life, and peace.	
V'tōv b'aynecho	וְטוֹב בְּעֵינֶיךָ
And may it be good in Your eyes	
l'voraych es am'cho yisro-ayl,	לְבָרֵךְ אֶת עַמְּךָ יִשְׂרָאֵל,
to bless Your people Israel	
b'chol ays uvchol sho-o	בְּכָל עֵת וּבְכָל שָׁעָה
at every time and at every hour,	
bish-lōmecho.	בִּשְׁלוֹמֶךָ.
with Your peace.	
Boruch ato Adōnoy,	בָּרוּךְ אַתָּה יהוה,
*Blessed are You, H*ASHEM*,*	
ham'voraych es amō yisro-ayl	הַמְבָרֵךְ אֶת עַמּוֹ יִשְׂרָאֵל
ba-sholōm.	בַּשָּׁלוֹם.
Who blesses His people Israel with peace.	

THE CHAZZAN'S REPETITION ENDS HERE; THE SERVICE CONTINUES WITH FULL KADDISH (P. 255). INDIVIDUALS CONTINUE.

Yih-yu l'rotzōn imray fi	יִהְיוּ לְרָצוֹן אִמְרֵי פִי
v'hegyōn libi l'fonecho,	וְהֶגְיוֹן לִבִּי לְפָנֶיךָ,
May the expressions of my mouth and the thoughts of my heart find favor before You,	
Adōnoy tzuri v'gō-ali.	יהוה צוּרִי וְגֹאֲלִי.
*H*ASHEM*, my Rock and my Redeemer.*	

MUSSAF FOR ROSH CHODESH

■ *I pray that, having completed my Amidah, I have been changed in a positive way, especially with regard to my interpersonal relationships.*

ELŌHAI, n'tzōr l'shōni mayro, אֱלֹהַי, נְצוֹר לְשׁוֹנִי מֵרָע,
My God, guard my tongue from evil

usfosai midabayr mirmo, וּשְׂפָתַי מִדַּבֵּר מִרְמָה,
and my lips from speaking deceitfully.

V'limkal'lai nafshi sidōm, וְלִמְקַלְלַי נַפְשִׁי תִדּוֹם,
To those who curse me, let my soul be silent;

v'nafshi ke-ofor lakōl tih-ye. וְנַפְשִׁי כֶּעָפָר לַכֹּל תִּהְיֶה.
and let my soul be like dust to everyone.

P'sach libi b'sōrosecho, פְּתַח לִבִּי בְּתוֹרָתֶךָ,
Open my heart to Your Torah,

uvmitzvōsecho tirdōf nafshi. וּבְמִצְוֹתֶיךָ תִּרְדּוֹף נַפְשִׁי.
then my soul will pursue Your commandments.

V'chol hachōsh'vim olai ro-o, וְכָל הַחוֹשְׁבִים עָלַי רָעָה,
As for all those who design evil against me,

m'hayro hofayr atzosom מְהֵרָה הָפֵר עֲצָתָם
   v'kalkayl machashavtom. וְקַלְקֵל מַחֲשַׁבְתָּם.
speedily nullify their counsel and disrupt their design.

Asay l'ma-an sh'mecho, עֲשֵׂה לְמַעַן שְׁמֶךָ,
Act for Your Name's sake;

asay l'ma-an y'minecho, עֲשֵׂה לְמַעַן יְמִינֶךָ,
act for Your right hand's sake;

asay l'ma-an k'dushosecho, עֲשֵׂה לְמַעַן קְדֻשָּׁתֶךָ,
act for Your sanctity's sake;

asay l'ma-an tōrosecho. עֲשֵׂה לְמַעַן תּוֹרָתֶךָ.
act for Your Torah's sake.

L'ma-an yaychol'tzun y'didecho, לְמַעַן יֵחָלְצוּן יְדִידֶיךָ,
That Your beloved ones may be given rest;

hōshi-o y'min'cho va-anayni. הוֹשִׁיעָה יְמִינְךָ וַעֲנֵנִי.
let Your right hand save, and respond to me.

Yih-yu l'rotzōn imray fi יִהְיוּ לְרָצוֹן אִמְרֵי פִי
   v'hegyōn libi l'fonecho, וְהֶגְיוֹן לִבִּי לְפָנֶיךָ,
May the expressions of my mouth and the thoughts of my heart find favor before You,

Adōnoy tzuri v'gō-ali. יהוה צוּרִי וְגֹאֲלִי.
HASHEM, my Rock and my Redeemer.

516 / מוסף לראש חודש

BOW. TAKE THREE STEPS BACK. BOW LEFT AND SAY:
Ō-se sholōm bimrōmov, עֹשֶׂה שָׁלוֹם בִּמְרוֹמָיו,
He Who makes peace in His heights,

BOW RIGHT AND SAY:
hu ya-a-se sholōm olaynu, הוּא יַעֲשֶׂה שָׁלוֹם עָלֵינוּ,
may He make peace upon us,

BOW FORWARD AND SAY:
v'al kol yisro-ayl. V'imru: Omayn. וְעַל כָּל יִשְׂרָאֵל. וְאִמְרוּ: אָמֵן.
and upon all Israel. Now respond: Amen.

Y'HI ROTZŌN mil'fonecho, **יְהִי רָצוֹן** מִלְּפָנֶיךָ
May it be Your will,

Adōnoy Elōhaynu יהוה אֱלֹהֵינוּ
HASHEM, *our God*

Vaylōhay avōsaynu, וֵאלֹהֵי אֲבוֹתֵינוּ,
and the God of our forefathers,

she-yibo-ne bays hamikdosh שֶׁיִּבָּנֶה בֵּית הַמִּקְדָּשׁ
that the Holy Temple be rebuilt,

bimhayro v'yomaynu, בִּמְהֵרָה בְיָמֵינוּ,
speedily in our days;

v'sayn chelkaynu b'sōrosecho, וְתֵן חֶלְקֵנוּ בְּתוֹרָתֶךָ,
and grant us our share in Your Torah;

v'shom na-avod-cho b'yiro, וְשָׁם נַעֲבָדְךָ בְּיִרְאָה,
and may we serve You there with reverence,

kimay ōlom כִּימֵי עוֹלָם
    uchshonim kadmōniyōs. וּכְשָׁנִים קַדְמוֹנִיּוֹת.
as in days of old and in former years.

V'or'vo Ladōnoy וְעָרְבָה לַיהוה
    minchas y'hudo virusholo-yim מִנְחַת יְהוּדָה וִירוּשָׁלָיִם,
Then the offering of Judah and Jerusalem will be pleasing to HASHEM,

kimay ōlom כִּימֵי עוֹלָם
    uchshonim kadmōniyōs. וּכְשָׁנִים קַדְמוֹנִיּוֹת.
as in days of old and in former years.

THE INDIVIDUAL'S RECITATION OF *SHEMONEH ESREI* ENDS HERE.
REMAIN STANDING IN PLACE UNTIL THE *CHAZZAN* REACHES *KEDUSHAH* —
OR AT LEAST FOR A FEW MOMENTS — THEN TAKE THREE STEPS FORWARD.
THE *CHAZZAN* RECITES THE FULL *KADDISH* (P. 255);
INDIVIDUALS CONTINUE Aleinu (P. 256).

Erev Yom Kippur

⊰{ KAPAROS/ATONEMENT }⊱

B'NAY odom **בְּנֵי** אָדָם
  yōsh'vay chōshech v'tzalmo-ves, יֹשְׁבֵי חֹשֶׁךְ וְצַלְמָוֶת,
Children of Man, who sit in darkness and the shadow of death,
asiray oni u-varzel. אֲסִירֵי עֳנִי וּבַרְזֶל.
shackled in affliction and iron.
Yōtzi-aym may-chōshech v'tzalmo-ves יוֹצִיאֵם מֵחֹשֶׁךְ וְצַלְמָוֶת,
He removed them from darkness and the shadow of death,
umōs'rōsay-hem y'natayk. וּמוֹסְרוֹתֵיהֶם יְנַתֵּק.
and broke open their shackles.
Evilim mi-derech pishom, אֱוִלִים מִדֶּרֶךְ פִּשְׁעָם,
The fools — because of their sinful path
umay-avōnōsay-hem yisanu וּמֵעֲוֺנֹתֵיהֶם יִתְעַנּוּ.
and their iniquities they were afflicted.
Kol ōchel t'sa-ayv nafshom, כָּל אֹכֶל תְּתַעֵב נַפְשָׁם,
Their soul abhorred all food,
va-yagi-u ad sha-aray mo-ves. וַיַּגִּיעוּ עַד שַׁעֲרֵי מָוֶת.
and they reached the portals of death.
Va-yizaku el Adōnoy batzar lo-hem, וַיִּזְעֲקוּ אֶל יהוה בַּצַּר לָהֶם,
Then they cried out to Hashem in their distress;
mim'tzukōsay-hem yōshi-aym. מִמְּצֻקוֹתֵיהֶם יוֹשִׁיעֵם.
from their woes He spared them.
Yishlach d'vorō v'yirpo-aym, יִשְׁלַח דְּבָרוֹ וְיִרְפָּאֵם,
He dispatched His word and cured them,
vi-malayt mish'chisōsom. וִימַלֵּט מִשְּׁחִיתוֹתָם.
and let them escape their destruction.
Yōdu Ladōnoy chasdō, יוֹדוּ לַיהוה חַסְדּוֹ,
Let them thank Hashem for His kindness
v'nifl'ōsov livnay odom. וְנִפְלְאוֹתָיו לִבְנֵי אָדָם.
and for His wonders to mankind.
Im yaysh olov maloch maylitz echod אִם יֵשׁ עָלָיו מַלְאָךְ מֵלִיץ אֶחָד
If there will be for someone but a single defending angel
mini olef מִנִּי אָלֶף,
out of a thousand

⊰• **Kaparos/Atonement**
  There is an ancient custom to take a white rooster for males and a white hen for females on the day before Yom Kippur and perform the *Kaparos* [Atonement] ritual. Money may be substituted for the fowl, and the ritual may be

l'hagid l'odom yoshrō,	לְהַגִּיד לְאָדָם יָשְׁרוֹ,
to declare a man's uprightness on his behalf,	
vai-chunenu va-yōmer:	וַיְחֻנֶּנּוּ וַיֹּאמֶר:
then He will be gracious to him and say,	
P'do-ayhu may-redes shachas,	פְּדָעֵהוּ מֵרֶדֶת שָׁחַת,
"Redeem him from descending to the Pit;	
mo-tzosi chofer.	מָצָאתִי כֹפֶר.
I have found atonement."	

——————— A MAN PERFORMING THE RITUAL FOR HIMSELF ———————

WITH A ROOSTER:

Ze chalifosi, ze t'murosi,	זֶה חֲלִיפָתִי, זֶה תְּמוּרָתִי,
This is my exchange, this is my substitute,	
ze kaporosi.	זֶה כַּפָּרָתִי.
this is my atonement.	
Ze hatarn'gōl yaylaych l'miso,	זֶה הַתַּרְנְגוֹל יֵלֵךְ לְמִיתָה,
This rooster will go to its death	
va-ani ekonays v'aylaych	וַאֲנִי אֶכָּנֵס וְאֵלֵךְ
while I will enter and proceed	
l'chayim tōvim aruchim ulsholōm.	לְחַיִּים טוֹבִים אֲרוּכִים וּלְשָׁלוֹם.
to a good long life, and to peace.	

WITH MONEY:

Ze chalifosi, ze t'murosi,	זֶה חֲלִיפָתִי, זֶה תְּמוּרָתִי,
This is my exchange, this is my substitute,	
ze kaporosi.	זֶה כַּפָּרָתִי.
this is my atonement.	
Ze hakesef yaylaych litz-doko,	זֶה הַכֶּסֶף יֵלֵךְ לִצְדָקָה,
This money will go to charity	
va-ani ekonays v'aylaych	וַאֲנִי אֶכָּנֵס וְאֵלֵךְ
while I will enter and proceed	
l'chayim tōvim aruchim ulsholōm.	לְחַיִּים טוֹבִים אֲרוּכִים וּלְשָׁלוֹם.
to a good long life, and to peace.	

performed before Erev Yom Kippur if necessary. It is most important to realize, however, that the atonement results from giving the bird (or its value) to the poor. Only that, as part of repentance, gives meaning to the ceremony. Some use a different chicken for each person, while others use a single rooster for many men or a single hen for many women.

A pregnant woman customarily takes a hen and a rooster, a hen for herself and a rooster in case she is carrying a male. Those who use a separate bird for each person take three birds for a pregnant women, two hens, one for herself and one in case she is carrying a female, and a rooster in case she is carrying a male.

כפרות / 520

TWO OR MORE MEN PERFORMING THE RITUAL FOR THEMSELVES

WITH A ROOSTER:

Ze chalifosaynu, ze t'murosaynu,   זֶה חֲלִיפָתֵנוּ, זֶה תְּמוּרָתֵנוּ,
This is our exchange, this is our substitute,

ze kaporosaynu.   זֶה כַּפָּרָתֵנוּ.
this is our atonement.

Ze hatarn'gōl yaylaych l'miso,   זֶה הַתַּרְנְגוֹל יֵלֵךְ לְמִיתָה,
This rooster will go to its death

va-anchnu nikonays v'naylaych   וַאֲנַחְנוּ נִכָּנֵס וְנֵלֵךְ
while we will enter and proceed

l'chayim tōvim aruchim ulsholōm.   לְחַיִּים טוֹבִים אֲרוּכִים וּלְשָׁלוֹם.
to a good long life, and to peace.

WITH MONEY:

Ze chalifosaynu, ze t'murosaynu,   זֶה חֲלִיפָתֵנוּ, זֶה תְּמוּרָתֵנוּ,
This is our exchange, this is our substitute,

ze kaporosaynu.   זֶה כַּפָּרָתֵנוּ.
this is our atonement.

Ze hakesef yaylaych litz-doko,   זֶה הַכֶּסֶף יֵלֵךְ לִצְדָקָה,
This money will go to charity

va-anchnu nikonays v'naylaych   וַאֲנַחְנוּ נִכָּנֵס וְנֵלֵךְ
while we will enter and proceed

l'chayim tōvim aruchim ulsholōm.   לְחַיִּים טוֹבִים אֲרוּכִים וּלְשָׁלוֹם.
to a good long life, and to peace.

ONE PERFORMING THE RITUAL FOR A MAN

WITH A ROOSTER:

Ze chalifos'cho, ze t'muros'cho,   זֶה חֲלִיפָתְךָ, זֶה תְּמוּרָתְךָ,
This is your exchange, this is your substitute,

ze kaporos'cho.   זֶה כַּפָּרָתְךָ.
this is your atonement.

Ze hatarn'gōl yaylaych l'miso,   זֶה הַתַּרְנְגוֹל יֵלֵךְ לְמִיתָה,
This rooster will go to its death

v'ato tikonays v'saylaych   וְאַתָּה תִּכָּנֵס וְתֵלֵךְ
while you will enter and proceed

l'chayim tōvim aruchim ulsholōm.   לְחַיִּים טוֹבִים אֲרוּכִים וּלְשָׁלוֹם.
to a good long life, and to peace.

WITH MONEY:

Ze chalifos'cho, ze t'muros'cho,   זֶה חֲלִיפָתְךָ, זֶה תְּמוּרָתְךָ,
This is your exchange, this is your substitute,

521 / KAPAROS/ATONEMENT

ze kaporos'cho.	זֶה כַּפָּרָתֶךָ.
this is your atonement.	
Ze hakesef yaylaych litz-doko,	זֶה הַכֶּסֶף יֵלֵךְ לִצְדָקָה,
This money will go to charity	
v'ato tikonays v'saylaych	וְאַתָּה תִּכָּנֵס וְתֵלֵךְ
while you will enter and proceed	
l'chayim tōvim aruchim ulsholōm.	לְחַיִּים טוֹבִים אֲרוּכִים וּלְשָׁלוֹם.
to a good long life, and to peace.	

———— ONE PERFORMING THE RITUAL FOR TWO OR MORE MEN ————

WITH A ROOSTER:

Ze chalifaschem, ze t'muraschem,	זֶה חֲלִיפַתְכֶם, זֶה תְּמוּרַתְכֶם,
This is your exchange, this is your substitute,	
ze kaporaschem.	זֶה כַּפָּרַתְכֶם.
this is your atonement.	
Ze hatarn'gōl yaylaych l'miso,	זֶה הַתַּרְנְגוֹל יֵלֵךְ לְמִיתָה,
This rooster will go to its death	
v'atem tikon'su v'sayl'chu	וְאַתֶּם תִּכָּנְסוּ וְתֵלְכוּ
while you will enter and proceed	
l'chayim tōvim aruchim ulsholōm.	לְחַיִּים טוֹבִים אֲרוּכִים וּלְשָׁלוֹם.
to a good long life, and to peace.	

WITH MONEY:

Ze chalifaschem, ze t'muraschem,	זֶה חֲלִיפַתְכֶם, זֶה תְּמוּרַתְכֶם,
This is your exchange, this is your substitute,	
ze kaporaschem.	זֶה כַּפָּרַתְכֶם.
this is your atonement.	
Ze hakesef yaylaych litz-doko,	זֶה הַכֶּסֶף יֵלֵךְ לִצְדָקָה,
This money will go to charity	
v'atem tikon'su v'sayl'chu	וְאַתֶּם תִּכָּנְסוּ וְתֵלְכוּ
while you will enter and proceed	
l'chayim tōvim aruchim ulsholōm.	לְחַיִּים טוֹבִים אֲרוּכִים וּלְשָׁלוֹם.
to a good long life, and to peace.	

———— A WOMAN PERFORMING THE RITUAL FOR HERSELF ————

WITH A HEN:

Zōs chalifosi, zōs t'murosi,	זֹאת חֲלִיפָתִי, זֹאת תְּמוּרָתִי,
This is my exchange, this is my substitute,	
zōs kaporosi.	זֹאת כַּפָּרָתִי.
this is my atonement.	

כפרות / 522

Zōs hatarn'gōles taylaych l'miso,   זֹאת הַתַּרְנְגֹלֶת תֵּלֵךְ לְמִיתָה,
This hen will go to its death

va-ani ekonays v'aylaych   וַאֲנִי אֶכָּנֵס וְאֵלֵךְ
while I will enter and proceed

l'chayim tōvim aruchim ulsholōm.   לְחַיִּים טוֹבִים אֲרוּכִים וּלְשָׁלוֹם.
to a good long life, and to peace.

WITH MONEY:

Ze chalifosi, ze t'murosi,   זֶה חֲלִיפָתִי, זֶה תְּמוּרָתִי,
This is my exchange, this is my substitute,

ze kaporosi.   זֶה כַּפָּרָתִי.
this is my atonement.

Ze hakesef yaylaych litz-doko,   זֶה הַכֶּסֶף יֵלֵךְ לִצְדָקָה,
This money will go to charity

va-ani ekonays v'aylaych   וַאֲנִי אֶכָּנֵס וְאֵלֵךְ
while I will enter and proceed

l'chayim tōvim aruchim ulsholōm.   לְחַיִּים טוֹבִים אֲרוּכִים וּלְשָׁלוֹם.
to a good long life, and to peace.

TWO OR MORE WOMEN PERFORMING THE RITUAL FOR THEMSELVES

WITH A HEN:

Zōs chalifosaynu, zōs t'murosaynu,   זֹאת חֲלִיפָתֵנוּ, זֹאת תְּמוּרָתֵנוּ,
This is our exchange, this is our substitute,

zōs kaporosaynu.   זֹאת כַּפָּרָתֵנוּ.
this is our atonement.

Zōs hatarn'gōles taylaych l'miso,   זֹאת הַתַּרְנְגֹלֶת תֵּלֵךְ לְמִיתָה,
This hen will go to its death

va-anchnu nikonays v'naylaych   וַאֲנַחְנוּ נִכָּנֵס וְנֵלֵךְ
while we will enter and proceed

l'chayim tōvim aruchim ulsholōm.   לְחַיִּים טוֹבִים אֲרוּכִים וּלְשָׁלוֹם.
to a good long life, and to peace.

WITH MONEY:

Ze chalifosaynu, ze t'murosaynu,   זֶה חֲלִיפָתֵנוּ, זֶה תְּמוּרָתֵנוּ,
This is our exchange, this is our substitute,

ze kaporosaynu.   זֶה כַּפָּרָתֵנוּ.
this is our atonement.

Ze hakesef yaylaych litz-doko,   זֶה הַכֶּסֶף יֵלֵךְ לִצְדָקָה,
This money will go to charity

KAPAROS/ATONEMENT

---- ONE PERFORMING THE THE RITUAL FOR A PREGNANT WOMAN ----
WITH A HEN AND A ROOSTER:

Aylu chalifōsaychem, אֵלּוּ חֲלִיפוֹתֵיכֶם,
These are your exchanges,

aylu t'murōsaychem, אֵלּוּ תְּמוּרוֹתֵיכֶם,
these are your substitutes,

aylu kaporōsaychem. אֵלּוּ כַּפָּרוֹתֵיכֶם.
these are your atonements.

Aylu hatarn'gōlim yayl'chu l'miso, אֵלּוּ הַתַּרְנְגוֹלִים יֵלְכוּ לְמִיתָה,
These chickens will go to their deaths

v'atem tikon'su v'sayl'chu וְאַתֶּם תִּכָּנְסוּ וְתֵלְכוּ
while you will enter and proceed

l'chayim tōvim aruchim ulsholōm. לְחַיִּים טוֹבִים אֲרוּכִים וּלְשָׁלוֹם.
to a good long life, and to peace.

WITH MONEY:

Ze chalifaschem, ze t'muraschem, זֶה חֲלִיפַתְכֶם, זֶה תְּמוּרַתְכֶם,
This is your exchange, this is your substitute,

ze kaporaschem. זֶה כַּפָּרַתְכֶם.
this is your atonement.

Ze hakesef yaylaych litz-doko, זֶה הַכֶּסֶף יֵלֵךְ לִצְדָקָה,
This money will go to charity

v'atem tikon'su v'sayl'chu וְאַתֶּם תִּכָּנְסוּ וְתֵלְכוּ
while you will enter and proceed

l'chayim tōvim aruchim ulsholōm. לְחַיִּים טוֹבִים אֲרוּכִים וּלְשָׁלוֹם.
to a good long life, and to peace.

Chanukah

◈§ Chanukah

◈§ Lesson of the Miracle

The Talmud (*Shabbos* 21b) teaches the significance of Chanukah. The Syrian-Greeks had overrun and defiled the Second Temple. After the outnumbered Jews miraculously defeated the enemy, the task of restoring the Temple was at hand. The *Kohanim* sought to fulfill the Biblical commandment to light the Menorah in the Temple daily (*Leviticus* 24:3), but there was only one flask of oil that had not been defiled by the enemy. It had the capacity to light the Menorah in the Temple for one day, and it would have taken another week for uncontaminated oil to be produced. But a miracle occurred and the oil burned for eight days. To commemorate the miracle, the Rabbis ordained that we celebrate Chanukah and light our menorahs for eight days.

The Temple service was replete with miracles, as the *Mishnah* (*Avos* 5:7) teaches, "Ten miracles were performed for our ancestors in the holy Temple." Since we were already conditioned to an environment of miracles in the Temple, why then did our Rabbis focus on the miracle of the oil to institute an annual *mitzvah*?

The *Bach*, in his commentary to the laws of Chanukah (*Orach Chaim*, Chapter 670) cites the following insightful explanation, from the *Maharam* of Rothenburg: There is a cause and effect to historical events; the problem is that most often we do not understand the true underlying reason why events occur and how to respond. The real reason the Syrian-Greek enemy was successful in gaining control of the Temple was because the Jews became lax in their observance of the laws related to it. They took the Divine residence for granted, and failed to show sufficient honor and reverence for the Sanctuary in their midst. When they subsequently repented and demonstrated a willingness to sacrifice themselves to restore the Temple to its former glory, Hashem responded in kind, showing His approval by causing two miracles to occur: the military victory and the miracle of the oil. Our Sages understand that God performed the miracle of the Menorah to demonstrate that the military victory was indeed a miracle, that not by chance did the few defeat the many and the weak defeat the strong. The miracle of the Menorah, which happened at the same time, shed light on the military campaign.

It is thus understandable why we commemorate this happening by lighting the menorah. The major threat to the Jewish nation at that moment in their history was the attempt to destroy their religious, Torah-observant life; the Syrian-Greeks had no designs against their physical being and welfare. Thus we celebrate Chanukah by focusing on a rededication to our religious commitment, and not by partying and feasting and gladdening the body. The primary *mitzvos* of Chanukah — the lighting of the menorah each night and the recitation of *Hallel* each day — are spiritual in nature. There is no obligation to have a

Chanukah meal, as by contrast there is such a *mitzvah* on Purim. The recitation of the blessing each night, "Who has wrought miracles for our forefathers, in those days at this season," reminds us that just as Hashem played a direct, obvious role in their life, in accordance with their commitment and dedication to Torah, so does He continue to conduct Himself with His nation. Indeed, this spiritual aspect of the miracle is emphasized by the fact that the military campaign was headed by the *Kohanim*, the priests who officiated in the Temple.

Thus the main lesson to be learned from Chanukah is this: Hashem relates to us as we do to Him. If we live a life of devotion to His Torah, which includes the rituals between man and Hashem and the laws that govern the interaction between man to man, we can then be assured His special attention and protection.

৩ Desire for Perfection

This concept is highlighted by the *P'nei Yehoshua* in his commentary to the Talmud (*Shabbos* ibid.). The law of *tumah*, ritual contamination, is that if the majority of the Jewish community is impure, the laws of impurity in the Temple service are suspended. Consequently the Jews of that era could have used impure oil for the week they needed to secure pure oil; why then, *the P'nei Yehoshua* asks, was it necessary to have the miracle of the Menorah in the first place? Moreover, they could have divided the oil into eight parts and used especially thin wicks to enable them to make do with this one cruse for eight days. *P'nei Yehoshua* responds that it was the strong desire on the part of the Jewish nation to perform the lighting of the Menorah in the best way possible that caused the miracle to happen. Their not resorting to the alternatives, rather showing the resolve that the *mitzvah* be done perfectly, is what caused Hashem to miraculously let them fulfill that desire. As we conducted ourselves beyond the letter of the law, so did He.

৩ Publicizing Commitment

Another important aspect of Chanukah is evidenced by the requirement that the lights should be displayed publicly. There is no law suggesting that one's *succah* be constructed in a place that will attract the most public notice. Nor must one's curtains be opened to the public when the Shabbos candles are lit. Chanukah is different. This is called *"pirsumai nissa"* — publicizing the miracle. Why, specifically, on Chanukah? Perhaps we are reliving the essence of the holiday. The Syrian-Greeks prohibited the observance of circumcision, Shabbos and the proclamation of the New Moon, without which the Jewish calendar, and hence the festivals, could not exist. If a Jew went along with these laws and assimilated to the Syrian-Greco way of life, his life was spared. The challenge to Jews was to identify themselves, join ranks with the Maccabees and fight both the enemy from within, the assimilationists, and the enemy from without, the Syrian-Greeks. Our lighting of the Chanukah lights in public is our formal declaration, "I am proud to be a Jew committed to the observance of Torah and *mitzvos.*"

Chanukah enjoys much popularity in all Jewish circles, both among the observant and the not-yet observant. I pray that the lighting of the Menorah will

kindle not only specific lights in the window, but the spark of sanctity that each Jew possesses.

The very name Chanukah, our Rabbis teach, is a combination of two words: חָנוּ [*Chanu*], *they rested* from their battles on כה [*kuf-hay*], which has the numerical value of 25, referring to the twenty-fifth of the month of Kislev, the day when the Maccabees kindled the Menorah. In addition, the word Chanukah is related to the word חֲנוּךְ, *dedication,* or *inauguration,* which refers to the rededication of the Temple and the celebration that accompanied this event. The word *chinuch* also means education, symbolizing that the lighting of the menorah must remind us that ultimately the survival of our people is dependent upon its religious and Torah education.

On the first night we kindle one light and on each subsequent night we add a light (*Orach Chaim* Ch. 671). This is the preferable manner of fulfilling the *mitzvah*, but, if necessary, one can fulfill the *mitzvah* by lighting one candle per night. Sephardic practice is that one menorah is lit for each household, while Ashkenazim follow the *Rama* who rules that it is preferable for each male to kindle his own lights.

It is preferable to use an oil menorah, rather than candles. While the Chanukah menorah may be lit at any time during the night, it is best to light it in the early evening, prior to one's meal, approximately forty minutes after sunset. The Chanukah lights must burn for at least half-an-hour into the night. If one lights the candles prior to the ideal time, one must use candles large enough to burn at least half-an-hour into the night. It is for this reason that on Friday during Chanukah, when we light the Chanukah menorah about twenty minutes before sunset, we cannot use the small, colorful Chanukah candles, as they will not last the required time of half-an-hour into the night. It is therefore recommended that one use either the regular Shabbos candles or the long, tapered, specially made Chanukah candles for the Friday of Chanukah.

Many have the practice of beautifying the *mitzvah* by using a silver or ornate menorah of some other material, but if one does not have a menorah, one may still perform the *mitzvah* by lighting the appropriate number of candles.

On the first night three blessings are recited prior to the lighting of the menorah, and each subsequent night the two blessings of *"Lehadlik"* — to light the Chanukah lights — and *"She'asah nissim"* — Who has wrought miracles — are recited prior to the lighting. If one neglected to recite the *"Shehecheyanu"* blessing on the first night, it should be said before lighting the menorah on a succeeding night. The first candle is placed on the extreme right of the person facing the menorah. On each succeeding day, the newest candle, to the left, is kindled first. After lighting one candle on each night, while lighting the other candles, the paragraph *"Haneiros Halalu"* — these lights we kindle — is recited. In it we are reminded that the Chanukah lights are not to be utilized for any purpose whatsoever, even for the purpose of a *mitzvah*, such as to learn or pray by their light; the Chanukah lights are exclusively for the glory of the *mitzvah*, not for any manner of personal use. In addition, the lights of the menorah in the Temple were not to be used for any other purpose other than the *mitzvah*.

CHANUKAH

⊰{ KINDLING THE CHANUKAH MENORAH }⊱

■ The *menorah* is lit in public to proclaim the miracle of Chanukah, which demonstrated the omnipotence of Hashem.

ALL THREE BLESSINGS ARE PRONOUNCED BEFORE KINDLING THE CHANUKAH *MENORAH* FOR THE FIRST TIME. ON ALL SUBSEQUENT NIGHTS, THE THIRD BLESSING, *SHEHECHEYANU*, IS OMITTED.

BORUCH ato Adōnoy בָּרוּךְ אַתָּה יהוה
Elōhaynu melech ho-ōlom, אֱלֹהֵינוּ מֶלֶךְ הָעוֹלָם,
Blessed are You, HASHEM, our God, King of the universe,
asher kid'shonu b'mitzvōsov, אֲשֶׁר קִדְּשָׁנוּ בְּמִצְוֹתָיו,
Who has sanctified us with His commandments,
v'tzivonu l'hadlik nayr shel chanuko. וְצִוָּנוּ לְהַדְלִיק נֵר שֶׁל חֲנֻכָּה.
and has commanded us to kindle the Chanukah light.

ALL PRESENT RESPOND: Omayn — אָמֵן

BORUCH ato Adōnoy בָּרוּךְ אַתָּה יהוה
Elōhaynu melech ho-ōlom, אֱלֹהֵינוּ מֶלֶךְ הָעוֹלָם,
Blessed are You, HASHEM, our God, King of the universe,
she-oso nisim la-avōsaynu, שֶׁעָשָׂה נִסִּים לַאֲבוֹתֵינוּ,
ba-yomim hohaym baz'man ha-ze. בַּיָּמִים הָהֵם בַּזְּמַן הַזֶּה.
Who has wrought miracles for our forefathers, in those days at this season.

ALL PRESENT RESPOND: Omayn — אָמֵן

BORUCH ato Adōnoy בָּרוּךְ אַתָּה יהוה
Elōhaynu melech ho-ōlom, אֱלֹהֵינוּ מֶלֶךְ הָעוֹלָם,
Blessed are You, HASHEM, our God, King of the universe,
sheheche-yonu v'ki-y'monu v'higi-onu שֶׁהֶחֱיָנוּ וְקִיְּמָנוּ וְהִגִּיעָנוּ
laz'man ha-ze. לַזְּמַן הַזֶּה.
Who has kept us alive, sustained us, and brought us to this season.

ALL PRESENT RESPOND: Omayn — אָמֵן

ON THE FIRST NIGHT, THE LIGHT TO THE EXTREME RIGHT IS KINDLED. ON EACH SUBSEQUENT NIGHT, A NEW LIGHT IS ADDED TO THE LEFT OF THE PREVIOUS NIGHT'S LIGHTS. THE NEW LIGHT IS ALWAYS KINDLED FIRST, THE ONE TO ITS RIGHT SECOND, AND SO ON. AFTER ONE LIGHT HAS BEEN KINDLED, *HANAIROS HALALU* IS RECITED. THE ADDITIONAL LIGHTS ARE KINDLED DURING ITS RECITATION.

HANAYRŌS halolu הַנֵּרוֹת הַלָּלוּ
anachnu madlikin אֲנַחְנוּ מַדְלִיקִין
These lights we kindle
al hanisim v'al haniflo-ōs, עַל הַנִּסִּים וְעַל הַנִּפְלָאוֹת,
upon the miracles, the wonders,
v'al hat'shu-ōs v'al hamilchomōs, וְעַל הַתְּשׁוּעוֹת וְעַל הַמִּלְחָמוֹת,
the salvations, and the battles

she-osiso la-avōsaynu שֶׁעָשִׂיתָ לַאֲבוֹתֵינוּ
which You performed for our forefathers

ba-yomim hohaym baz'man ha-ze, בַּיָּמִים הָהֵם בַּזְּמַן הַזֶּה,
in those days at this season,

al y'day kōhanecho hak'dōshim. עַל יְדֵי כֹּהֲנֶיךָ הַקְּדוֹשִׁים.
through Your holy priests.

V'chol sh'mōnas y'may chanuko, וְכָל שְׁמוֹנַת יְמֵי חֲנֻכָּה,
During all eight days of Chanukah

hanayrōs halolu kōdesh haym. הַנֵּרוֹת הַלָּלוּ קֹדֶשׁ הֵם.
these lights are sacred,

V'ayn lonu r'shus וְאֵין לָנוּ רְשׁוּת
l'hishtamaysh bohem, לְהִשְׁתַּמֵּשׁ בָּהֶם,
and we are not permitted to make ordinary use of them, *

elo lir-ōsom bilvod, אֶלָּא לִרְאוֹתָם בִּלְבָד,
but to look at them,

k'day l'hōdōs ulhalayl כְּדֵי לְהוֹדוֹת וּלְהַלֵּל
l'shimcho hagodōl לְשִׁמְךָ הַגָּדוֹל
in order to express thanks and praise to Your great Name *

al nisecho v'al nifl'ōsecho עַל נִסֶּיךָ וְעַל נִפְלְאוֹתֶיךָ
v'al y'shu-osecho. וְעַל יְשׁוּעָתֶךָ.
for Your miracles, Your wonders and Your salvation.

AFTER THE LIGHTS HAVE BEEN KINDLED, *MAOZ TZUR* IS CHANTED:

MO-ŌZ TZUR y'shu-osi, **מָעוֹז צוּר** יְשׁוּעָתִי
l'cho no-e l'shabay-ach, לְךָ נָאֶה לְשַׁבֵּחַ,
O mighty Rock of my salvation, to praise You is a delight.

tikōn bays t'filosi, תִּכּוֹן בֵּית תְּפִלָּתִי
v'shom tōdo n'zabay-ach. וְשָׁם תּוֹדָה נְזַבֵּחַ.
Restore my House of Prayer and there we will bring a thanksgiving offering.

וְאֵין לָנוּ רְשׁוּת לְהִשְׁתַּמֵּשׁ בָּהֶם — *And we are not permitted to make ordinary use of them.* The prohibition against enjoying the lights for any personal purpose — such as reading or doing work by their illumination — makes it manifestly clear to all that they were kindled for the sole purpose of commemorating the miracle.

In compliance with the prohibition against enjoying the lights, we light a *shamash*, (a servant) flame, which is not holy, so that any incidental pleasure that comes from the lights can be considered as coming from the *shamash*.

כְּדֵי לְהוֹדוֹת וּלְהַלֵּל לְשִׁמְךָ הַגָּדוֹל — *In order to express thanks and praise to Your great Name*. By utilizing the Chanukah lights only for the *mitzvah* and contemplating them while they burn, we make it apparent to all that our intent is to publicize the miracle and to praise God's great Name in acknowledgment of His great miracles.

ଓ§ מָעוֹז צוּר / **Maoz Tzur**

This *piyut* (liturgical poem) opens with a plea for the reestablishment of the Temple; the rededication of the Altar; and the renewal of the services there. It then recalls various exiles that the Jewish people endured, praises God for redeeming us from each of them, and prays for the restoration of the Temple and for the dawn of the Messianic Redemption.

L'ays tochin matbay-ach,   לְעֵת תָּכִין מַטְבֵּחַ,
  mitzor ham'nabay-ach,   מִצָּר הַמְנַבֵּחַ,

When You will have prepared the slaughter for the blaspheming foe,

oz egmōr, b'shir mizmōr,   אָז אֶגְמוֹר, בְּשִׁיר מִזְמוֹר,
  chanukas hamizbay-ach.   חֲנֻכַּת הַמִּזְבֵּחַ.

then I shall complete with a song of hymn the dedication of the Altar.

RO-ŌS sov'o nafshi,   **רְעוֹת** שָׂבְעָה נַפְשִׁי,
  b'yogōn kōchi chilo,   בְּיָגוֹן כֹּחִי כִּלָּה,

Troubles sated my soul, when with grief my strength was consumed.

cha-yai mayr'ru b'kōshi,   חַיַּי מֵרְרוּ בְּקֹשִׁי,
  b'shibud malchus eglo,   בְּשִׁעְבּוּד מַלְכוּת עֶגְלָה,

They had embittered my life with hardship, with the calf-like kingdom's bondage.

uvyodō hag'dōlo,   וּבְיָדוֹ הַגְּדוֹלָה,
  hōtzi es has'gulo,   הוֹצִיא אֶת הַסְּגֻלָּה,

But with His great power He brought forth the treasured ones.

chayl par-ō, v'chol zar-ō,   חֵיל פַּרְעֹה, וְכָל זַרְעוֹ,
  yor'du k'even bimtzulo.   יָרְדוּ כְּאֶבֶן בִּמְצוּלָה.

Pharaoh's army and all his offspring went down like a stone into the deep.

D'VIR kodshō hevi-ani,   **דְּבִיר** קָדְשׁוֹ הֱבִיאַנִי,
  v'gam shom lō shokat-ti,   וְגַם שָׁם לֹא שָׁקַטְתִּי,

To the abode of His holiness He brought me, but there, too, I had no rest;

u-vo nōgays v'higlani,   וּבָא נוֹגֵשׂ וְהִגְלַנִי,
  ki zorim ovadti,   כִּי זָרִים עָבַדְתִּי,

and an oppressor came and exiled me. For I had served aliens,

v'yayn ra-al mosachti,   וְיֵין רַעַל מָסַכְתִּי,
  kim-at she-ovarti,   כִּמְעַט שֶׁעָבַרְתִּי,

and had drunk benumbing wine. Scarcely had I departed [my land]

kaytz bovel, z'rubovel,   קֵץ בָּבֶל, זְרֻבָּבֶל,
  l'kaytz shiv-im nōshoti.   לְקֵץ שִׁבְעִים נוֹשָׁעְתִּי.

when at Babylonia's demise Zerubabel came.
At the end of seventy years I was saved.

K'RŌS kōmas b'rōsh,   **כְּרוֹת** קוֹמַת בְּרוֹשׁ,
  bikaysh agogi ben ham'doso,   בִּקֵּשׁ אֲגָגִי בֶּן הַמְּדָתָא,

To sever the towering cypress* sought the Aggagite, son of Hammedatha,

---

כְּרוֹת קוֹמַת בְּרוֹשׁ — *To sever the towering cypress*. The Talmud (*Megillah* 10b) expounds on an obscure prophecy of *Isaiah* (55:13): "In place of the thorn shall come up the cypress," the prickly

v'nih-y'so lō l'fach ulmōkaysh,	וַנְהִיתָה לּוֹ לְפַח וּלְמוֹקֵשׁ,
v'ga-avosō nishboso,	וְגַאֲוָתוֹ נִשְׁבָּתָה,

but it became a snare and a stumbling block to him and his arrogance was stilled.

rōsh y'mini nisay-so,	רֹאשׁ יְמִינִי נִשֵּׂאתָ,
v'ōyayv sh'mō mochiso,	וְאוֹיֵב שְׁמוֹ מָחִיתָ,

The head of the Benjaminite You lifted, and the enemy, his name You blotted out.

rōv bonov, v'kinyonov,	רֹב בָּנָיו, וְקִנְיָנָיו,
al ho-aytz toliso.	עַל הָעֵץ תָּלִיתָ.

His numerous progeny — his possessions — on the gallows You hanged.

Y'VONIM nikb'tzu olai,	**יְוָנִים** נִקְבְּצוּ עָלַי,
azai bimay chashmanim,	אֲזַי בִּימֵי חַשְׁמַנִּים,

Greeks* gathered against me then in Hasmonean days.

u-for'tzu chōmōs migdolai,	וּפָרְצוּ חוֹמוֹת מִגְדָּלַי,
v'tim'u kol hash'monim,	וְטִמְּאוּ כָּל הַשְּׁמָנִים,

They breached the walls of my towers and they defiled all the oils;

u-minōsar kankanim,	וּמִנּוֹתַר קַנְקַנִּים,
na-aso nays la-shōshanim,	נַעֲשָׂה נֵס לַשּׁוֹשַׁנִּים,

and from the one remnant of the flasks a miracle was wrought for the roses.

b'nay vino, y'may sh'mōno,	בְּנֵי בִינָה, יְמֵי שְׁמוֹנָה,
kov'u shir urnonim.	קָבְעוּ שִׁיר וּרְנָנִים.

Men of insight — eight days established for song and jubilation.

CHASŌF z'rō-a kodshecho.	**חֲשׂוֹף** זְרוֹעַ קָדְשֶׁךָ,
v'korayv kaytz hai-shu-o,	וְקָרֵב קֵץ הַיְשׁוּעָה,

Bare Your holy arm and hasten the End for salvation.

n'kōm nikmas dam avodecho,	נְקֹם נִקְמַת דַּם עֲבָדֶיךָ,
may-umo hor'sho-o,	מֵאֻמָּה הָרְשָׁעָה,

Avenge the vengeance of Your servant's blood from the wicked nation.

ki or'cho lonu hai-shu-o,	כִּי אָרְכָה לָּנוּ הַיְשׁוּעָה,
v'ayn kaytz limay horo-o,	וְאֵין קֵץ לִימֵי הָרָעָה,

For the triumph is too long delayed for us, and there is no end to days of evil.

d'chay admōn, b'tzayl tzalmōn,	דְּחֵה אַדְמוֹן, בְּצֵל צַלְמוֹן,
hokaym lonu rō-im shiv-o.	הָקֵם לָנוּ רוֹעִים שִׁבְעָה.

Repel the Red One in the nethermost shadow and establish for us the seven shepherds.

"thorn" Haman who attempted to destroy Mordechai, the stately "cypress." But Haman's own sinister plans ensnared him and he was hung on the gallows he had prepared for Mordechai.

יְוָנִים — *Greeks*. This refers to the Syrian-Greeks, especially Antiochus IV Epiphanes, the monarch who attempted through force to impose Greek culture on the Land of Israel.

Purim

✺ Purim

✺ Two Themes

Two primary themes underlay the observance of Purim: the physical salvation of the Jewish people, and the nation's joyous renewed acceptance of the Torah.

Purim, which occurred toward the end of the seventy years between the First and Second Temple eras, is the celebration of our having survived the threat of extinction from Haman and the many tens of thousands of his followers. This component is built into the day by the requirement that each person should partake in a special festive meal. Since the physical body of the Jew was threatened, we celebrate in a way that pleases and satisfies the body. Moreover, our Rabbis teach that the threat against the Jewish people emanated from their participation in the feast of Ahasuerus (*Esther* 1:5-8), where both non-kosher food and wine was served, and where the utensils looted from the Temple were used. At the eleventh hour, Queen Esther called for a public fast (ibid. 4:16), providing the nation with an opportunity for repentance, and our annual *mitzvah* of partaking in a kosher feast is an additional form of righting that historic wrong.

The commentary *Maasei Hashem* contrasts Purim and Chanukah, and observes that Purim has the *mitzvah* of *simchah*, joy, as not a single Jewish casualty was lost in the wars against their enemy. Chanukah, on the other hand, does not have *simchah* as part of its character, because many casualties fell in the battles against the Syrian-Greek armies, including even some of the Maccabee brothers who led the revolt.

✺ No Hallel

The Talmud (*Megillah* 14a) infers the obligation to celebrate and acknowledge the Purim salvation from Israel's song of deliverance after the threat of the Egyptians had been removed by their drowning in Sea of Reeds. If we sing His praises upon being freed from slavery, then certainly we should recite *Hallel* on Purim, when we were saved from death and annihilation. Why, then, do we not recite *Hallel* on Purim? The Talmud gives several answers. One of them is that the reading of the Book of *Esther* is equivalent to *Hallel*. At first glance this seems difficult, as the Name of Hashem is not explicitly mentioned in *Megillas Esther,* although it is clear that His hand directed the salvation.

✺ Two Kinds of Miracles

To appreciate how the *Megillah* constitutes not only the Purim story but praise of Hashem, we need to recognize that two types of miracles are performed on our behalf: open, obvious miracles, and those that are hidden and concealed, yet,

nonetheless, are the workings of Hashem. The Talmud (*Chullin* 131b) asks where the Torah alludes to Queen Esther. At first glance the question seems strange, as the heroine of the Purim story lived over 1,000 years after the completion of the Five Books of Moses! The answer given by the Talmud is a verse in *Deuteronomy* (31:18), וְאָנֹכִי הַסְתֵּר אַסְתִּיר, "But I will surely have concealed My face on that day because of all the evil that it did." The Hebrew *hasteir astir*, which means to conceal, and has the same root as Esther, is the reference to her in the Torah. Our Rabbis explained that not only do the name of Esther and the Hebrew word *to hide* sound alike, but the story of Esther occurred after the destruction of the First Temple and the end of the period of prophecy. At that time it was no longer clear to Israel why such things were happening and what the correct response should be. A case in point: As soon as Mordechai learned of Haman's evil plot of destruction, he urged Esther to appeal immediately to the king on behalf of her people (4:8). Esther, however, did things her own way. She first invited King Ahasuerus to a wine party and then a second one. Only then did she plead for her people. There was no prophetic message to tell Israel what God wanted of them — His Name is not found in the *Megillah* — but we celebrate every year to affirm that the story is not a series of unconnected coincidences, but rather the hand of God directing history.

❧ Second Theme

The second theme of Purim is the re-acquisition of Torah on the part of the Jewish people. The Talmud (*Shabbos* 88a) understands that Israel's acceptance of the Torah at Sinai was under a degree of duress. "And they stood at the bottom of the mountain" (*Exodus* 19:17) is understood by Rabbi Avdimi to indicate that Hashem suspended Mount Sinai above the Jewish nation declaring, "If you accept the Torah all will be well, but if not there shall be your grave." The *Meshech Chochmah* explains that given the fact that at Sinai the entire nation actually saw Hashem and experienced communication from Him, it was as if their free will had been removed. They had no choice but to accept the Torah. If Sinai represents the open, revealed miracle, then Purim represents the concealed miracle. It is thus understandable that at the time of the Purim miracle, realizing that Hashem had orchestrated both the threat and the salvation, they now accepted His Torah of their own volition.

❧ Miracle in Exile

The *Vilna Gaon*, in his commentary to the Book of *Esther* (1:2), focuses on the fact that specifically because the miracle of Purim occurred outside the land of Israel was its impact so great on the Jewish people. When they realize that even in exile, outside *Eretz Yisrael*, Hashem protects them, they are filled with greater love and appreciation of Him. It is for this reason that the *Gaon* considers the miracle of Purim to be even greater than that of Chanukah, which happened in Israel during the era of the Second Temple. He uses an allegory to explain the Purim salvation: There was a prince who angered his father and was exiled to a forest. The son thought this meant his father didn't care about him

anymore and forgot about him. Unbeknownst to him, however, the king stationed servants in the forest to protect his son. A few days later he was attacked by a bear, and the servant of his father "happened to be in the vicinity" to save him. When an enemy of the king tried to harm the prince, once again he was saved at the last minute. Slowly realizing that the "coincidences" were orchestrated by his father, the prince was filled with new love for his father.

Similarly, when Hashem casts his nation into exile, He stations His emissaries in the form of miracles to protect the Jewish people. As in the allegory of the prince, the circumstance of being saved filled the nation with tremendous love and appreciation for their Heavenly Father. It was in this grateful environment and with these emotions that on Purim they willingly accepted His Torah anew.

∽§ The Festive Seudah

This second theme of Purim marking the re-acceptance of Torah is an additional explanation for the *mitzvah* of having a special festival meal — a Purim *seudah*. Commenting on the verse at Sinai, "They gazed at God, yet they ate and drank" (*Exodus* 24:11), *Ramban* writes that this is the source for the custom that a festive meal should accompany the celebration of Torah. Thus a *siyum* — the completion of a tractate or other unit of the Torah — is marked by a festive meal. In discussing the ideal nature of Yom Tov observance, the Talmud *(Pesachim* 68b) records a dispute between Rabbi Eliezer and Rabbi Yehoshua. Rabbi Eliezer teaches that either the Yom Tov is to be spent immersed in Torah study and prayer, or by celebrating in a feasting environment. Rabbi Yehoshua rules that the day should be split, "half for Hashem and half for you" — part of the day in prayer and study and the other half eating and enjoying with family and friends. We follow the opinion of Rabbi Yehoshua. What is noteworthy, however, is that the Talmud says that there are certain days when even Rabbi Eliezer agrees we should enjoy good food, namely Shavuos, marking the day we received the Torah, this time willingly.

∽§ The Other Two Mitzvos

The other *mitzvos* of Purim are the reading of the *Megillah,* evening and morning, gifts to the poor, and gifts of food to friends. Both men and women are obligated in all the *mitzvos* of Purim including the reading of the *Megillah.* While often it is more convenient to hear the *Megillah* reading on Purim night, the reading of the *Megillah* by day is even more important. Therefore everyone should make a special effort to hear the *Megillah* both times. If one cannot hear the *Megillah* in the synagogue — which is preferable, based on the verse "A multitude of people is a king's glory" (*Proverbs* 14:28) — one should hear it at home. In addition, the public reading of the *Megillah* fulfills the obligation of *pirsumei nissa,* or publicizing the miracle (*Megillah* 4a).

The last two *mitzvos* are mentioned in the *Megillah* itself: "They were to observe them as days of feasting and gladness, and for sending delicacies to one another and gifts to the poor" (9:22).

The Jew attains true happiness when he provides not only for himself and his

family, but also for those who are less fortunate. The *Rambam* (*Laws of Yom Tov* 6:18) codifies that if people tend only to their own needs on Yom Tov, it is not true joy of a *mitzvah*, but only selfish satisfaction. *Simchah* for the Jew is helping others. The preparations for Pesach and the beginning of the *Seder* involve concern that others have sufficient provisions for the holiday. On Purim, too, *halachah* requires that we assist at least two poor persons. While we are not told how much to give, a suggested barometer would be to assist them by giving at least two individuals the cost of a Purim *seudah*.

The fourth *mitzvah* of the day is *mishloach manos*, sending delicacies to one another. Haman's description of the Jews as "a certain people scattered and dispersed" (*Esther* 3:8) is understood by our Rabbis to mean not only geographic, but social dispersion, by not caring for one another, which would make the task of their destruction much easier. We counter this charge of Haman annually by demonstrating our true concern one for the other. By sending at least two different, ready-to-eat foods to at least one person, we are saying, "I wish you could join me for the Purim *seudah*, and here is a part of it." Whereas giving gifts to the needy is a form of kindness by responding to the needs of the next one, *mishloach manos* to friends is a kindness of initiation, going out of one's way to extend joy to another. I strongly recommend that you not only send *mishloach manos* to your best friends – they will remain your good friends regardless – but rather to those individuals you don't usually greet on Shabbos, those persons who are not especially close to you. This is an opportunity to strengthen the bonds of friendship in the community. Moreover, don't forget the aged, shut-ins, and other lonely individuals; send *mishloach manos* to them, as well.

◆§ Like Purim

It is interesting to note that, phonetically, Purim and Yom Kippurim sound alike. The *Arizal*, however, not only saw a connection, but interpreted the name יוֹם כִּפּוּרִים to mean that Yom Kippur is *a day **like** Purim* (since the letter *kuf* is used as an indication of comparison). At first glance this is most difficult, as Yom Kippur is our holiest day of the year, when we *desist* from food and drink, while Purim is the one day that we not only partake of food and drink but are taught, "One is obligated to imbibe on Purim until he cannot differentiate between cursed is Haman and blessed is Mordechai" (*Megillah* 7b). One answer might be that it is easier to *fast* for Hashem than to *feast* for Him. When we are in the synagogue enwrapped in our prayer shawls and wearing a *kittel*, the white robe worn on Yom Kippur, it is relatively easy to focus on spirituality. However, to eat and drink and revel for the sake of a *mitzvah* – that is more difficult; hence the revelry of Purim is even on a more exalted level.

Regarding the drinking, the important thing to remember is that though one has consumed more wine or drink than usual, one dare not act destructively or in such a way that he will bring disrepute upon the Torah, himself, or his community. If one is unsure of how he will act or whether he will say words of Torah or, God forbid, matters that will bring embarrassment to himself or the

audience, then he should not drink. Moreover, everything must be put in the proper prospective. We dare not allow this aspect of the Purim *seudah* to negatively influence the day either, God forbid, by endangering those who are driving or by sending a wrong message.

܀ৡ Fast of Esther

The day before Purim is *Taanis Esther,* the Fast of Esther. The *Rosh* in his commentary on Talmud (*Megillah*), explains that the Jewish people fasted on the day they fought their enemy. Rather than think that military success is due to their fighting ability and strategy, they fast to demonstrate that only due to God's assistance could they be victorious. Just as they fasted on the thirteenth of Adar when they fought, and celebrated their victory on the fourteenth, which was Purim, we do likewise to relive their accomplishments.

Thus *Taanis Esther,* the Fast of Esther, is different from all other communal fasts. The other fast days (with the exception of Yom Kippur) commemorate tragedies that were related to the destruction to the Temples; here, as the *Raavad* notes, it is a fast of joy. The *Beis Yosef* (*Orach Chaim* Chapter 686) notes that the Fast of Esther reminds us that Hashem sees and responds to each individual who returns to Him sincerely, just as He answered the Jews in the time of Purim.

܀ৡ Noisemaking

In his commentary to the laws of Purim (*Orach Chaim* 690:17), *Rama* refers to the custom that children respond with various forms of noisemakers each time the name of Haman is recited, and writes that all customs are to be treated with respect and reverence. This is a symbolic fulfillment of the Biblical directive, "You shall wipe out the memory of Amalek" (*Deuteronomy* 25:19), as Haman, the villain of Purim, was a descendant of Amalek.

On a deeper level, one can suggest that we are educating our children at an early age to protest evil in their midst. The *Chofetz Chaim,* however, writes that while it is important for the children to participate in the response to the name Haman, that should not be their sole purpose in coming to the synagogue, and certainly their noisemaking should not interfere with the adults' fulfillment of the *mitzvah* of hearing each word of the *Megillah* (*Mishnah Berurah* 689:18).

⊰{ READING OF THE MEGILLAH }⊱

■ The *Megillah* reflects our realization that Hashem protects His nation Israel even in the Diaspora.

BEFORE READING *MEGILLAS ESTHER* ON PURIM [BOTH AT NIGHT AND AGAIN IN THE MORNING], THE READER RECITES THE FOLLOWING THREE BLESSINGS. [THE BLESSINGS ARE RECITED WHETHER OR NOT A *MINYAN* IS PRESENT.] THE CONGREGATION SHOULD ANSWER AMEN AFTER EACH BLESSING, AND HAVE IN MIND THAT THEY THEREBY FULFILL THE OBLIGATION OF RECITING THE BLESSINGS THEMSELVES. DURING THE MORNING READING, THEY SHOULD ALSO HAVE IN MIND THAT THE THIRD BLESSING APPLIES TO THE OTHER *MITZVOS* OF PURIM — *MISHLOACH MANOS*, GIFTS TO THE POOR, AND THE FESTIVE PURIM MEAL — AS WELL AS TO THE *MEGILLAH* READING.

BORUCH ato Adōnoy   בָּרוּךְ אַתָּה יהוה
*Blessed are You, H*ASHEM,
Elōhaynu melech ho-ōlom,   אֱלֹהֵינוּ מֶלֶךְ הָעוֹלָם,
our God, King of the universe,
asher kid'shonu b'mitzvōsov,   אֲשֶׁר קִדְּשָׁנוּ בְּמִצְוֹתָיו,
Who has sanctified us with His commandments
v'tzivonu al mikro m'gilo.   וְצִוָּנוּ עַל מִקְרָא מְגִלָּה.
and has commanded us regarding the reading of the Megillah.

CONGREGATION RESPONDS: Omayn — אָמֵן

BORUCH ato Adōnoy   בָּרוּךְ אַתָּה יהוה
*Blessed are You, H*ASHEM,
Elōhaynu melech ho-ōlom,   אֱלֹהֵינוּ מֶלֶךְ הָעוֹלָם,
our God, King of the universe,
she-oso nisim la-avōsaynu,   שֶׁעָשָׂה נִסִּים לַאֲבוֹתֵינוּ,
Who has wrought miracles for our forefathers,
ba-yomim hohaym baz'man ha-ze.   בַּיָּמִים הָהֵם בַּזְּמַן הַזֶּה.
in those days at this season.

CONGREGATION RESPONDS: Omayn — אָמֵן

BORUCH ato Adōnoy   בָּרוּךְ אַתָּה יהוה
*Blessed are You, H*ASHEM,
Elōhaynu melech ho-ōlom,   אֱלֹהֵינוּ מֶלֶךְ הָעוֹלָם,
our God, King of the universe,
sheheche-yonu v'ki-y'monu   שֶׁהֶחֱיָנוּ וְקִיְּמָנוּ
Who has kept us alive, sustained us
v'higi-onu laz'man ha-ze.   וְהִגִּיעָנוּ לַזְּמַן הַזֶּה.
and brought us to this season.

CONGREGATION RESPONDS: Omayn — אָמֵן

THE *MEGILLAH* IS READ.

PURIM

AFTER THE *MEGILLAH* READING, EACH MEMBER OF THE CONGREGATION RECITES THE FOLLOWING BLESSING. [THIS BLESSING IS NOT RECITED UNLESS A *MINYAN* IS PRESENT FOR THE READING.]

BORUCH ato Adōnoy   בָּרוּךְ אַתָּה יהוה
*Blessed are You, H*ASHEM,

Elōhaynu melech ho-ōlom,   אֱלֹהֵינוּ מֶלֶךְ הָעוֹלָם,
our God, King of the universe,

horov es rivaynu,   הָרָב אֶת רִיבֵנוּ,
Who takes up our grievance,

v'hadon es dinaynu,   וְהַדָּן אֶת דִּינֵנוּ,

v'hanōkaym es nikmosaynu,   וְהַנּוֹקֵם אֶת נִקְמָתֵנוּ,
judges our claim, avenges our wrong;

v'ham'shalaym g'mul   וְהַמְשַׁלֵּם גְּמוּל
l'chol ō-y'vay nafshaynu,   לְכָל אֹיְבֵי נַפְשֵׁנוּ,
Who brings just retribution upon all enemies of our soul

v'hanifro lonu mitzoraynu.   וְהַנִּפְרָע לָנוּ מִצָּרֵינוּ.
and exacts vengeance for us from our foes.

Boruch ato Adōnoy,   בָּרוּךְ אַתָּה יהוה,
*Blessed are You, H*ASHEM,

hanifro l'amō yisro-ayl   הַנִּפְרָע לְעַמּוֹ יִשְׂרָאֵל
mikol tzorayhem,   מִכָּל צָרֵיהֶם,
Who exacts vengeance for His people Israel from all their foes,

ho-Ayl hamōshi-a.   הָאֵל הַמּוֹשִׁיעַ.
the God Who brings salvation.

CONGREGATION RESPONDS: Omayn — אָמֵן

AFTER THE NIGHTTIME *MEGILLAH* READING, THE FOLLOWING TWO PARAGRAPHS ARE RECITED. AFTER THE DAYTIME READING, CONTINUE WITH SHOSHANAS YAAKOV, P. 546.

ASHER HAYNI atzas gō-yim,   אֲשֶׁר הֵנִיא עֲצַת גּוֹיִם,
Who balked the counsel of the nations

va-yofer machsh'vōs arumim,   וַיָּפֶר מַחְשְׁבוֹת עֲרוּמִים,
and annulled the designs of the cunning,

b'kum olaynu odom rosho,   בְּקוּם עָלֵינוּ אָדָם רָשָׁע,
when a wicked man stood up against us,

naytzer zodōn mizera amolayk.   נֵצֶר זָדוֹן מִזֶּרַע עֲמָלֵק.
a wantonly evil branch of Amalek's offspring.

Go-o v'oshrō v'choro lō bōr,   גָּאָה בְעָשְׁרוֹ וְכָרָה לוֹ בוֹר,
Haughty with his wealth he dug himself a grave,

ugdulosō yok'sho lō loched.   וּגְדֻלָּתוֹ יָקְשָׁה לּוֹ לָכֶד.
and his very greatness snared him in a trap.

דָּמָה בְנַפְשׁוֹ לִלְכֹּד וְנִלְכָּד,	Dimo v'nafshō lilkōd v'nilkad,

Fancying to trap, he became entrapped;

בִּקֵּשׁ לְהַשְׁמִיד וְנִשְׁמַד מְהֵרָה.	bikaysh l'hashmid v'nishmad m'hayrō.

attempting to destroy, he was swiftly destroyed.

הָמָן הוֹדִיעַ אֵיבַת אֲבוֹתָיו,	Homon hōdi-a ayvas avōsov,

Haman showed his forebears' enmity,

וְעוֹרֵר שִׂנְאַת אַחִים לַבָּנִים.	v'ōrayr sin-as achim labonim.

and aroused the brotherly hate of Esau on the children.

וְלֹא זָכַר רַחֲמֵי שָׁאוּל,	V'lō zochar rachamay sho-ul,

He would not remember Saul's compassion,

כִּי בְחֶמְלָתוֹ עַל אֲגָג נוֹלַד אוֹיֵב.	ki v'chemlosō al agog nōlad ō-yayv.

that through his pity on Agag the foe was born.

זָמַם רָשָׁע לְהַכְרִית צַדִּיק,	Zomam rosho l'hachris tzadik,

The wicked one conspired to cut away the righteous,

וְנִלְכַּד טָמֵא בִּידֵי טָהוֹר.	v'nilkad tomay biday tohōr.

but the impure was trapped in the pure one's hands.

חֶסֶד גָּבַר עַל שִׁגְגַת אָב,	Chesed govar al shig'gas ov,

Kindness overcame the father's error,

וְרָשָׁע הוֹסִיף חֵטְא עַל חֲטָאָיו.	v'rosho hōsif chayt al chato-ov.

and the wicked one piled sin on sins.

טָמַן בְּלִבּוֹ מַחְשְׁבוֹת עֲרוּמָיו,	Toman b'libō machsh'vōs arumov,

In his heart he hid his cunning thoughts,

וַיִּתְמַכֵּר לַעֲשׂוֹת רָעָה.	va-yismakayr la-asōs ro-o.

and devoted himself to evildoing.

יָדוֹ שָׁלַח בִּקְדוֹשֵׁי אֵל,	Yodō sholach bikdōshay Ayl,

He stretched his hand against God's holy ones,

כַּסְפּוֹ נָתַן לְהַכְרִית זִכְרָם.	kaspō nosan l'hachris zichrom.

he spent his silver to destroy their memory.

כִּרְאוֹת מָרְדְּכַי כִּי יָצָא קֶצֶף,	Kir-ōs mord'chai ki yotzo ketzef,

When Mordechai saw the wrath commence,

וְדָתֵי הָמָן נִתְּנוּ בְשׁוּשָׁן,	v'dosay homon nit'nu v'shushon,

and Haman's decrees issued in Shushan,

לָבַשׁ שַׂק וְקָשַׁר מִסְפֵּד,	lovash sak v'koshar mispayd,

he put on sackcloth and bound himself in mourning,

v'gozar tzōm va-yayshev al ho-ayfer.	וְגָזַר צוֹם וַיֵּשֶׁב עַל הָאֵפֶר.
decreed a fast and sat on ashes;	
Mi ze ya-amōd l'chapayr sh'gogo,	**מִי** זֶה יַעֲמֹד לְכַפֵּר שְׁגָגָה,
"Who would arise to atone for error,	
v'limchōl chatas avōn avōsaynu.	וְלִמְחֹל חַטַּאת עֲוֹן אֲבוֹתֵינוּ.
to gain forgiveness for our ancestors' sins?"	
Naytz porach milulov,	**נֵץ** פָּרַח מִלּוּלָב,
A blossom bloomed from a lulav branch —	
hayn hadaso om'do l'ōrayr y'shaynim.	הֵן הֲדַסָּה עָמְדָה לְעוֹרֵר יְשֵׁנִים.
behold! Hadassah stood up to arouse the sleeping.	
Soriseho hivhilu l'homon,	**סָרִיסֶיהָ** הִבְהִילוּ לְהָמָן,
His servants hastened Haman,	
l'hashkōsō yayn chamas taninim.	לְהַשְׁקוֹתוֹ יֵין חֲמַת תַּנִּינִים.
to serve him wine of serpent's poison.	
Omad b'oshrō v'nofal b'rish-ō,	**עָמַד** בְּעָשְׁרוֹ וְנָפַל בְּרִשְׁעוֹ,
He stood tall through his wealth and toppled through his evil —	
oso lō aytz v'nislo olov.	עָשָׂה לוֹ עֵץ וְנִתְלָה עָלָיו.
he built the gallows on which he was hung.	
Pihem pos'chu kol yōsh'vay sayvayl,	**פִּיהֶם** פָּתְחוּ כָּל יוֹשְׁבֵי תֵבֵל,
The earth's inhabitants opened their mouths,	
ki fur homon nepach l'furaynu.	כִּי פוּר הָמָן נֶהְפַּךְ לְפוּרֵנוּ.
for Haman's lot became our Purim.	
Tzadik nechelatz miyad rosho,	**צַדִּיק** נֶחֱלַץ מִיַּד רָשָׁע,
The righteous man was saved from the wicked's hand;	
ō-yayv nitan tachas nafshō.	אוֹיֵב נִתַּן תַּחַת נַפְשׁוֹ.
the foe was substituted for him.	
Ki-y'mu alayhem la-asōs purim,	**קִיְּמוּ** עֲלֵיהֶם לַעֲשׂוֹת פּוּרִים,
They undertook to establish Purim,	
v'lismō-ach b'chol shono v'shono.	וְלִשְׂמֹחַ בְּכָל שָׁנָה וְשָׁנָה.
to rejoice in every single year.	
Ro-iso es t'filas	**רָאִיתָ** אֶת תְּפִלַּת
mord'chai v'estayr,	מָרְדֳּכַי וְאֶסְתֵּר,
You noted the prayer of Mordechai and Esther;	
homon u-vonov al ho-aytz toliso.	הָמָן וּבָנָיו עַל הָעֵץ תָּלִיתָ.
Haman and his sons You hung on the gallows.	

THE FOLLOWING IS RECITED AFTER BOTH *MEGILLAH* READINGS.

SHŌSHANAS ya-akōv	**שׁוֹשַׁנַּת** יַעֲקֹב
The rose of Jacob	
tzohalo v'somaycho,	צָהֲלָה וְשָׂמֵחָה,
was cheerful and glad,	
bir-ōsom yachad	בִּרְאוֹתָם יַחַד
when they jointly saw	
t'chayles mord'choy.	תְּכֵלֶת מָרְדְּכָי.
Mordechai robed in royal blue.	
T'shu-osom ho-yiso lo-netzach,	תְּשׁוּעָתָם הָיִיתָ לָנֶצַח,
You have been their eternal salvation,	
v'sikvosom b'chol dōr vodōr.	וְתִקְוָתָם בְּכָל דּוֹר וָדוֹר.
and their hope throughout generations.	
L'hōdi-a shekol kōvecho lō yayvōshu,	לְהוֹדִיעַ שֶׁכָּל קֹוֶיךָ לֹא יֵבֹשׁוּ,
To make known that all who hope in You will not be shamed;	
v'lō yikol'mu lo-netzach	וְלֹא יִכָּלְמוּ לָנֶצַח
nor ever be humiliated,	
kol ha-chōsim boch.	כָּל הַחוֹסִים בָּךְ.
those taking refuge in You.	
Orur homon asher bikaysh l'ab'di,	אָרוּר הָמָן אֲשֶׁר בִּקֵּשׁ לְאַבְּדִי,
Accursed be Haman who sought to destroy me,	
boruch mord'chai ha-y'hudi.	בָּרוּךְ מָרְדְּכַי הַיְּהוּדִי.
blessed be Mordechai the Yehudi.	
Aruro zeresh ayshes mafchidi,	אֲרוּרָה זֶרֶשׁ אֵשֶׁת מַפְחִידִי,
Accursed be Zeresh the wife of my terrorizer,	
b'rucho estayr ba-adi,	בְּרוּכָה אֶסְתֵּר בַּעֲדִי,
blessed be Esther [who sacrificed] for me —	
v'gam charvōno zochur latōv.	וְגַם חַרְבוֹנָה זָכוּר לַטּוֹב.
and Charvonah, too, be remembered for good.	

Death and Bereavement

~§ Inyanei Semachos — Bereavement

One of the most difficult phenomena for man to respond to is death. This is one of the very few areas where all agree that ultimately man has no control. The Jew looks at death as part of life. It is a transition from one state of being to another. From this world to the next. From a world that demands the difficult balancing act between the body and soul, to a world that is all soul. The following citations from our traditional sources, I hope, will pave the way for not only more study but a healthier response at the time of the ultimate transition, death.

~§ Knowing That There Is a Reason

We conclude the *Aleinu* prayer thrice daily with the statement: "And it is said, Hashem will be King over all the world — on that day Hashem will be One, and His Name will be One" (*Zechariah* 14:9). The Talmud (*Pesachim* 50b) asks, "On *that* day He will be One — is He not one today?" Rather the next world is not like this world. In this world there are two blessings, one in response to good tidings, good news, the blessing of *HaTov VeHaMeitiv*, that Hashem is good and bestows His good upon others. But when one hears tragic, sad news of someone dying, the response is *Dayan HaEmes*, that Hashem is the true Judge. In the future, however, there will be but one blessing: that of *Hatov VeHaMeitiv* for all circumstances and situations, because people will understand that everything Hashem does is for the good.

The Talmud (*Berachos* 60b) further teaches that nowadays we are to recite the blessing over tragedy in the same way that one recites the blessing for good, meaning that both blessings should be recited with joy. Once again this seems most difficult and unrealistic. Rabbi Soloveitchik responded that *simchah* — happiness — does not simply mean singing and dancing; it also involves a state of mind. The verb שמח, *to be glad*, is often found in conjunction with לִפְנֵי ה, *before Hashem*, as the Torah commands, "And you shall rejoice before Hashem your God for a seven-day period" (*Leviticus* 23:40). Being before Hashem, in His presence, is what creates joy. The realization that everything that occurs happens only with the direct involvement of Hashem makes it easier to respond to difficult situations. Events do not happen in a vacuum. No body and soul enter this world without the invitation of Hashem and nobody leaves this world without being beckoned by Him.

~§ Two Worlds

In describing the creation of man in *Genesis* 2:7, the Torah informs us, "And Hashem formed the man of dust from the ground, and He blew into his nostrils

the soul of life; and man became a living being." The word וַיִּיצֶר, *and He formed*, is found twice in this chapter, once in the above verse describing the creation of man and once in verse 19 describing the creation of the animals. With regard to the animals, the word is spelled with one *yud*, which is the common and correct spelling, but the same word used earlier describing the creation of man has two *yuds*. What a difference a *yud* makes. The *Midrash Tanchuma* explains that the two letters denote that man was created for two worlds, for this world and for the next. On this same verse, which states, "and He blew into his nostrils the soul of life," *Chizkuni* understands this to refer to the eternal and immortal soul, which does not die with the body of man. As Hashem is eternal, that which He blew into man to energize him is likewise eternal. A simple metaphor is to look upon the soul as a battery from Hashem. As long as the battery is functioning, so is the appliance or toy. Similarly, as long as the soul is within the body, there is life.

When the soul leaves the body, rather than be discarded like a spent battery, the soul is judged and evaluated as to how it fared in this world. If it influenced the bearer of that soul to a meaningful life of Torah, *mitzvos*, and kindness, it is rewarded. If it succumbed to a life of selfishness and pursuit only of pleasure, without yielding to a Higher Authority, it will pay for its foolishness by being denied access to Heaven, and be consigned to a state of being that can be called Gehinnom, or Hell.

◆§ There Is Life

That there is a world beyond this world is portrayed brilliantly by Rabbi Yechiel Michel Tukachinsky, in his classic work *Gesher HaChaim* (literally: The Bridge of Life), where he speaks of the transition from one world to another. He compares it to twin brothers who are being nurtured and developed in the womb. One believes that there is a life beyond the womb, and the other is a non-believer who is convinced that everything comes to an abrupt end when the newborn exits the womb. This debate continues throughout the pregnancy with the believing brother asserting that someday they will feed themselves, walk, talk, and develop and enhance a great big world out there. The atheist denies it all, forever claiming that what you see is all there is. The time of birth comes and the believing brother is born first. His brother, left temporarily behind and alone, is convinced that the crying of his brother only affirms his worst fears, and moreover the shouts of all the adults substantiate his conviction that his brother has fallen into an endless abyss. In reality the newborn's crying demonstrates his healthy, functioning lungs and body, and the shouts were those of *mazel tov*! Similarly, not having seen yet a video of the World to Come, many may deny its existence. Others would rather enjoy the here and now and not focus on the serious consequences that await them.

Fortunate are those, however, who remember the teaching of Rabbi Yaakov (*Avos* 4:21), "This world is like a lobby before the World to Come; prepare yourself in the lobby so that you may enter the banquet hall." A traveler once visited the late saintly Rabbi Yisrael Meir HaCohen of Radin, known as the

Chofetz Chaim, after his classic work on the laws of *lashon hara*, or evil speech. The visitor was amazed at the simple furnishings in the great man's home. When he asked the *Chofetz Chaim* where his furniture was, the *Chofetz Chaim* returned the question and asked where *his* furniture was. The traveler thought the question was very strange, "Oh, I'm only passing through, my furniture is at home." The *Chofetz Chaim* said, "I, too, am only passing through this world, my furniture is in the next world." While this is a level of realization to which only the saintly can relate, it behooves all of us to allow the significance of his remark to impact on us. There is a World to Come!

Our sacred tradition teaches us that there is not an extra word in the Torah. "You shall observe the commandment and the decrees and the ordinances that I command you today, to perform them" (*Deuteronomy* 7:11). What does the superfluous word "today" contribute to the verse? Rabbi Yehoshua ben Levi, in the Talmud (*Eruvin* 22a), responds, "The word 'today' means to say that the commandments can be performed in this world, but not tomorrow in the World to Come. Moreover, today, i.e., this world, was made to perform them, while tomorrow, the World to Come, was made for receiving their reward."

◆§ Honor Your Mother

Rabbi Chanania ben Akashia says: "The Holy One, Blessed is He, wished to confer merit upon Israel; therefore He gave them Torah and *mitzvos* in abundance, as it is said, Hashem desired, for the sake of [Israel's] righteousness that the Torah be made great and glorious" (*Makkos* 23b). The *Rambam,* in his commentary on this Mishnah, teaches that while a Jew must perform all the commandments, if he performs but one *mitzvah* perfectly, he will merit his share in the World to Come *Rambam* is addressing the question of why there are so many *mitzvos*, why 613. He answers that the character and personality of each individual differs from that of the next one. Some are introverted, others more sociable; some are studious, others find prayers, charity or communal work more fulfilling and expressive of their being. By providing so many *mitzvos* encompassing all aspects of life, Hashem gives man the opportunity to develop himself and acquire his share in the World to Come. While the Jew must perform all *mitzvos*, he is given the opportunity to specialize in one *mitzvah* to fulfill his mission and purpose, and thereby acquire his place in the World to Come.

What our mission is in life most often eludes us. The following insightful teaching will illustrate this concept. The *Yerushalmi (Kiddushin)* speaks of the remarkable character of the Talmudic sage Rabbi Tarfon. Once, when he was ill, his colleagues came to visit him. His mother said to his colleagues, "Pray for my son Tarfon, he is such a good son." Questioning the proud mother as to what made her son so special in his fulfillment of the fifth commandment, she responded, "Once we were out on a walk and the strap of my sandal broke; rather than allow me to walk barefoot on the dirty, rocky road, he got down on his knees and held out his hands, and I walked on his hands." When the Rabbis heard this, they responded, "He didn't even fulfill half his devotion as a son."

◈§ To Complete the Mission

Rabbi Soloveitchik presented an intriguing understanding of the above incident. He suggested that if one were to ask any of the participants in this story, either Rav Tarfon, his mother, or the Rabbis, what is Rav Tarfon's mission on earth, they would respond, "To be one of the rabbis who clarify and explain Torah law." When they heard the response of Rav Tarfon's mother and the incredible extent of honor he rendered her, they reasoned that perhaps he was put in this world to teach how far the *mitzvah* of honoring a parent goes. If that was indeed his mission, maybe they are now calling him back in heaven, as he has already fulfilled his purpose for living. They therefore responded, he didn't even do half his potential as a son, meaning they were praying on his behalf that he should be permitted to do much more. This incident teaches that we do not know what our mission is, but whatever it is, we believe that once an individual has fulfilled his mission he is ready to return to his Maker.

This is substantiated by the teaching of King Solomon, "Sweet is the sleep of the laborer, whether he eats little or much" (*Ecclesiastes* 5:11). The *Midrash* understands this verse to mean that how long a person lives is not important; what matters is how well. Substantiation for this principle comes from the verse cited in the *Midrash,* "Moses and Aaron were among His priests, and Samuel among those who invoked His Name" (*Psalms* 96:6). Moses lived for 120 years and Aaron for 123 years and Samuel for 52 years, yet they are linked and equated one to another.

◈§ Two Choices

The Torah teaches, "You are children to Hashem, your God, you shall not cut yourselves and you shall not make a bald spot between your eyes for a dead person" (*Deuteronomy* 14:1). The *Ramban* and *Ibn Ezra* understand the flow of this verse to mean that because you are children of Hashem, you are not to respond to death in the manner of non-believing pagans. As young children cannot always understand their father, but trust him, similarly we must realize that it is our loving Father in Heaven Who is causing this to happen. In addition, the *Ramban* says, the next verse, "For you are a holy people to Hashem, your God," refers to the sanctity and eternity of the soul. Thus one dare not mar the body in response to death, even for an individual who died at a young age. By right there should not be any allowance or permission for mourning and crying other than the fact that this is the natural way one takes leave of a loved one, often even if it is for a very long trip. Based on this verse, however, the Talmud (*Moed Katan* 27b) teaches that it is prohibited for one to mourn excessively. For example, it is contrary to Jewish law and philosophy for one to say, "I love this individual, so I will extend the period of *shivah* from seven days to nine or ten days."

The Talmud (*Menachos* 37b) utilizes this verse as the source for a very important aspect of Jewish law. The Torah mandates regarding the head *tefillin*

that they are to be an ornament "between your eyes" (*Exodus* 13:16). How do we know, asks the Talmud, that "between the eyes" is not to be taken literally, but rather on the top of one's head where the skull of a baby is still tender and pulsates? The above-cited verse proves this point. Just as in this verse, the prohibition of pulling out one's hair in grief does not mean literally from between one's eyes but rather from the top of one's head, so, too, regarding the *mitzvah* of *tefillin* are they to be worn on the top of the head.

In reality this "equation of terms," known as *gezeirah shavah*, whereby similar words in different contexts are meant to clarify one another, teaches not only where the *tefillin* are worn but what role the *tefillin* are to play. On the very spot from which the pagan rips out his hair in mourning the total devastation of death, the Jew dons *tefillin* acknowledging his belief and trust, and, indeed, his love of Hashem. There are but two choices: to rip one's hair or to don the *tefillin*. To the believer, therefore, there are no questions, and to the non-believer there are no answers.

CONFESSIONAL ON THE DEATHBED

■ King Solomon teaches (*Proverbs* 28:13): "He who confesses and forsakes his sins will obtain mercy." Realizing that death is a transition from one world to the next, my soul prays for life in order to continue to serve Hashem; or, it can be cleansed by returning to Hashem even at the final moments of life.

THE FOLLOWING CONFESSION IS RECITED BY OR WITH
A PERSON NEAR DEATH, HEAVEN FORBID.

MŌ-DE ANI l'fonecho מוֹדֶה אֲנִי לְפָנֶיךָ
I acknowledge before You,

Adōnoy Elōhai Vaylōhay avōsai, יהוה אֱלֹהַי וֵאלֹהֵי אֲבוֹתַי,
Hashem, my God, and the God of my forefathers,

sher'fu-osi u-misosi v'yodecho. שֶׁרְפוּאָתִי וּמִיתָתִי בְּיָדֶךָ.
that my recovery and death are in Your hand.

Y'hi rotzon mil'fonecho יְהִי רָצוֹן מִלְּפָנֶיךָ
May it be Your will

shet'rap'ayni r'fu-o sh'laymo, שֶׁתְּרַפְּאֵנִי רְפוּאָה שְׁלֵמָה,
that You heal me with total recovery,

v'im omus, וְאִם אָמוּת,
but, if I die,

t'hay misosi chaporo תְּהֵא מִיתָתִי כַּפָּרָה
may my death be an atonement

al kol chato'im עַל כָּל חֲטָאִים
for all the errors,

avōnōs ufsho'im עֲוֹנוֹת וּפְשָׁעִים
iniquities, and willful sins

shechotosi v'she-ovisi שֶׁחָטָאתִי וְשֶׁעָוִיתִי
that I have erred, sinned

v'sheposha-ti lifonecho. וְשֶׁפָּשַׁעְתִּי לְפָנֶיךָ.
and transgressed before You.

V'sayn chelki v'gan ayden וְתֵן חֶלְקִי בְּגַן עֵדֶן
May You grant my share in the Garden of Eden,

v'zakayni l'ōlom habo וְזַכֵּנִי לְעוֹלָם הַבָּא
and privilege me for the World to Come

hatzofun latzadikim. הַצָּפוּן לַצַּדִּיקִים.
that is concealed for the righteous.

⊰ FUNERAL SERVICES ⊱

■ As difficult as it might be, I accept Divine Justice.

THE MOURNERS RECITE THE FOLLOWING BLESSING
WHEN THEY RIP THEIR OUTER GARMENTS.

BORUCH ato Adōnoy,   בָּרוּךְ אַתָּה יהוה,
*Blessed are You, H*ASHEM*,*

Elōhaynu melech ho-ōlom,   אֱלֹהֵינוּ מֶלֶךְ הָעוֹלָם,
our God, King of the universe,

dayan ho-emes.   דַּיַּן הָאֱמֶת.
the true Judge.

THOSE WHO HAVE NOT SEEN A CEMETERY FOR THIRTY DAYS
RECITE THE FOLLOWING BLESSING WHEN COMING THERE:

BORUCH ato Adōnoy,   בָּרוּךְ אַתָּה יהוה,
*Blessed are You, H*ASHEM*,*

Elōhaynu melech ho-ōlom,   אֱלֹהֵינוּ מֶלֶךְ הָעוֹלָם,
our God, King of the universe,

asher yotzar eschem ba-din,   אֲשֶׁר יָצַר אֶתְכֶם בַּדִּין,
Who fashioned you with justice,

v'zon v'chilkayl eschem ba-din,   וְזָן וְכִלְכֵּל אֶתְכֶם בַּדִּין,
nourished and sustained you with justice,

v'haymis eschem ba-din,   וְהֵמִית אֶתְכֶם בַּדִּין,
took your lives with justice,

v'yōday-a mispar kul-chem ba-din,   וְיוֹדֵעַ מִסְפַּר כֻּלְכֶם בַּדִּין,
knows the sum total of all of you with justice,

v'hu osid l'hacha-yōs-chem   וְהוּא עָתִיד לְהַחֲיוֹתְכֶם
and Who in the future will resuscitate

ul-ka-yaym eschem ba-din.   וּלְקַיֵּם אֶתְכֶם בַּדִּין.
and restore you with justice.

Boruch ato Adōnoy,   בָּרוּךְ אַתָּה יהוה,
*Blessed are You, H*ASHEM*,*

m'cha-yay hamaysim.   מְחַיֵּה הַמֵּתִים.
Who resuscitates the dead.

ATO gibōr l'ōlom Adōnoy,   אַתָּה גִבּוֹר לְעוֹלָם אֲדֹנָי,
You are eternally mighty, my Lord,

m'cha-yay maysim ato,   מְחַיֵּה מֵתִים אַתָּה,
the Resuscitator of the dead are You;

rav l'hōshi-a.	רַב לְהוֹשִׁיעַ.
abundantly able to save.	
M'chalkayl cha-yim b'chesed,	מְכַלְכֵּל חַיִּים בְּחֶסֶד,
Who sustains the living with kindness,	
m'cha-yay maysim b'rachamim rabim,	מְחַיֶּה מֵתִים בְּרַחֲמִים רַבִּים,
resuscitates the dead with abundant mercy,	
sōmaych nōf'lim v'rōfay chōlim,	סוֹמֵךְ נוֹפְלִים, וְרוֹפֵא חוֹלִים,
supports the fallen, heals the sick,	
u-matir asurim,	וּמַתִּיר אֲסוּרִים,
releases the confined,	
umka-yaym emunosō li-shaynay ofor.	וּמְקַיֵּם אֱמוּנָתוֹ לִישֵׁנֵי עָפָר.
and maintains His faith to those asleep in the dust.	
Mi chomōcho ba-al g'vurōs,	מִי כָמוֹךָ בַּעַל גְּבוּרוֹת,
Who is like You, O Master of mighty deeds,	
u-mi dō-me loch,	וּמִי דּוֹמֶה לָּךְ,
and who is comparable to You,	
melech maymis um-cha-ye,	מֶלֶךְ מֵמִית וּמְחַיֶּה,
O King Who causes death and restores life	
u-matzmi-ach y'shu-o.	וּמַצְמִיחַ יְשׁוּעָה.
and makes salvation sprout.	
V'ne-e-mon ato l'hacha-yos maysim.	וְנֶאֱמָן אַתָּה לְהַחֲיוֹת מֵתִים.
And You are faithful to resuscitate the dead.	

ACCEPTANCE OF JUDGMENT

■ Death is more acceptable when one acknowledges that Hashem personally directs life and death.

WHEN THE DECEASED IS BROUGHT TO THE CEMETERY, THE FOLLOWING IS RECITED. HOWEVER, IT IS OMITTED ON DAYS WHEN *TACHANUN* IS NOT RECITED.

HATZUR tomim po-olō,	הַצוּר תָּמִים פָּעֳלוֹ,
The Rock! — perfect is His work,	
ki chol d'rochov mishpot,	כִּי כָל דְּרָכָיו מִשְׁפָּט,
for all His paths are justice;	
Ayl emuna v'ayn ovel,	אֵל אֱמוּנָה וְאֵין עָוֶל,
a God of faith without iniquity,	
tzadik v'yoshor hu.	צַדִּיק וְיָשָׁר הוּא.
righteous and fair is He.	

ענייני שמחות / הלוית המת

HATZUR tomim b'chol po-al,	הַצוּר תָּמִים בְּכָל פֹּעַל,
The Rock! — perfect in every work.	
mi yōmar lo ma tifol,	מִי יֹאמַר לוֹ מַה תִּפְעָל,
Who can say to Him, "What have You done?"	
ha-shalit b'mato uv-ma'al,	הַשַׁלִיט בְּמַטָּה וּבְמַעַל,
He rules below and above,	
maymis um-cha-ye,	מֵמִית וּמְחַיֶּה,
brings death and resuscitates,	
mōrid sh'ōl va-yo-al.	מוֹרִיד שְׁאוֹל וַיָּעַל.
brings down to the grave and raises up.	
HATZUR tomim b'chol ma-a-se,	הַצוּר תָּמִים בְּכָל מַעֲשֶׂה,
The Rock — perfect in every deed.	
mi yōmar aylov ma ta-a-se,	מִי יֹאמַר אֵלָיו מַה תַּעֲשֶׂה,
Who can say to Him, "What do You do?"	
ho-ōmayr v'ō-se,	הָאוֹמֵר וְעֹשֶׂה,
O He Who says and does,	
chesed chinom lonu sa-a-se,	חֶסֶד חִנָּם לָנוּ תַּעֲשֶׂה,
do undeserved kindness with us.	
u-viz-chus hane-ekod k'se,	וּבִזְכוּת הַנֶּעֱקַד כְּשֶׂה,
In the merit of him [Isaac] who was bound like a lamb,	
hakshivo va-asay.	הַקְשִׁיבָה וַעֲשֵׂה.
hearken and act.	
TZADIK b'chol d'rochov	צַדִּיק בְּכָל דְּרָכָיו
O righteous One in all His ways,	
hatzur tomim,	הַצוּר תָּמִים,
O Rock Who is perfect —	
erech apa-yim u-molay rachamim,	אֶרֶךְ אַפַּיִם וּמָלֵא רַחֲמִים,
slow to anger and full of mercy —	
chamol no v'chus no	חֲמָל נָא וְחוּס נָא
al ovōs u-vonim,	עַל אָבוֹת וּבָנִים,
take pity and please spare parents and children,	
ki l'cho odōn	כִּי לְךָ אָדוֹן
for Yours, O master,	
has'lichōs v'horachamim.	הַסְּלִיחוֹת וְהָרַחֲמִים.
are forgiveness and mercy.	

TZADIK ato Adōnoy   צַדִּיק אַתָּה יהוה
Righteous are You, Hashem,
l'homis ulhacha-yōs,   לְהָמִית וּלְהַחֲיוֹת,
to bring death and to resuscitate,
asher b'yod'cho pikdōn kol ruchōs,   אֲשֶׁר בְּיָדְךָ פִּקְדוֹן כָּל רוּחוֹת,
for in Your hand is the safekeeping of all spirits.
cholilo l'cho zichrōnaynu limchōs,   חָלִילָה לְךָ זִכְרוֹנֵנוּ לִמְחוֹת,
It would be sacrilegious for You to erase our memory.
v'yih-yu no aynecho b'rachamim   וְיִהְיוּ נָא עֵינֶיךָ בְּרַחֲמִים
May Your eyes mercifully
olaynu p'ku-chōs,   עָלֵינוּ פְקוּחוֹת,
take cognizance of us,
ki l'cho odōn   כִּי לְךָ אָדוֹן
for Yours, O Master,
horachamim v'has'lichōs.   הָרַחֲמִים וְהַסְּלִיחוֹת.
are mercy and forgiveness.

ODOM im ben shono yih-ye,   אָדָם אִם בֶּן שָׁנָה יִהְיֶה,
A man, whether he be a year old,
ō elef shonim yich-ye,   אוֹ אֶלֶף שָׁנִים יִחְיֶה,
or whether he lives a thousand years,
ma yisrōn lō,   מַה יִּתְרוֹן לוֹ,
what does it profit him?
k'lo ho-yo yih-ye,   כְּלֹא הָיָה יִהְיֶה,
— As if he has never been shall he be.
boruch da-yan ho-emes,   בָּרוּךְ דַּיַּן הָאֱמֶת,
Blessed is the true Judge,
maymis um-cha-ye.   מֵמִית וּמְחַיֶּה.
Who brings death and resuscitates.

BORUCH hu ki emes dino,   בָּרוּךְ הוּא, כִּי אֱמֶת דִּינוֹ,
Blessed is He, for His judgment is true,
umshōtayt hakol b'ayno   וּמְשׁוֹטֵט הַכֹּל בְּעֵינוֹ
He scans everything with His eye,
umshalaym l'odom   וּמְשַׁלֵּם לְאָדָם
cheshbōnō v'dino,   חֶשְׁבּוֹנוֹ וְדִינוֹ,
and He recompenses man according to his account and his just sentence.

v'hakol lishmo hōdo-yo yitaynu.	וְהַכֹּל לִשְׁמוֹ הוֹדָיָה יִתֵּנוּ.

All must give His Name acknowledgment.

YODA-NU Adōnoy   **יָדַעְנוּ** יהוה

We know, HASHEM,

ki tzedek mishpotecho,   כִּי צֶדֶק מִשְׁפָּטֶךָ,

that Your judgment is righteous,

titzdak b'dovrecho   תִּצְדַּק בְּדָבְרֶךָ

You are righteous when You speak

v'siz-ke b'shoftecho,   וְתִזְכֶּה בְשָׁפְטֶךָ,

and pure when You judge;

v'ayn l'har-hayr   וְאֵין לְהַרְהֵר

and there is no complaining

achar midas shoftecho,   אַחַר מִדַּת שָׁפְטֶךָ,

about the attribute of Your judgment.

tzadik ato Adōnoy,   צַדִּיק אַתָּה יהוה,

Righteous are You, O HASHEM,

v'yoshor mishpotecho.   וְיָשָׁר מִשְׁפָּטֶיךָ.

and Your judgments are fair.

DAYAN emes,   **דַּיָּן** אֱמֶת,

shōfayt tzedek ve-emes,   שׁוֹפֵט צֶדֶק וֶאֱמֶת,

O true Judge, Judge of righteousness and truth.

boruch dayan ho-emes,   בָּרוּךְ דַּיַּן הָאֱמֶת,

Blessed is the true Judge,

shekol mish-potov tzedek v'emes.   שֶׁכָּל מִשְׁפָּטָיו צֶדֶק וֶאֱמֶת.

for all of His judgments are righteous and true.

NEFESH kol chai b'yo-de-cho,   **נֶפֶשׁ** כָּל חַי בְּיָדֶךָ,

The soul of all the living is in Your hand,

tzedek mol-o y'min'cho v'yo-de-cho,   צֶדֶק מָלְאָה יְמִינְךָ וְיָדֶךָ,

righteousness fills Your right hand and Your power.

rachaym al p'laytas tzōn yo-de-cho,   רַחֵם עַל פְּלֵיטַת צֹאן יָדֶךָ,

Have mercy on the remnant of the sheep of Your hand,

v'sōmar lamal-och heref yo-de-cho.   וְתֹאמַר לַמַּלְאָךְ הֶרֶף יָדֶךָ.

and say to the Angel [of Death], "Hold back your hand!"

FUNERAL SERVICES

גְּדֹל הָעֵצָה וְרַב הָעֲלִילִיָּה,
G'DŌL ho-aytzo v'rav ho-alili-yo,
Great in counsel and abundant in deed,

אֲשֶׁר עֵינֶיךָ פְקֻחוֹת
asher ay-ne-cho f'kuchos
Your eyes are open

עַל כָּל דַּרְכֵי בְּנֵי אָדָם,
al kol darchay b'nay odom,
upon all the ways of the children of man,

לָתֵת לְאִישׁ כִּדְרָכָיו
lo-says l'ish kid-rochov
וְכִפְרִי מַעֲלָלָיו.
v'chifri ma-alolov.
to give man according to his ways and according to the fruit of his deeds.

לְהַגִּיד כִּי יָשָׁר יהוה,
L'hagid ki yoshor Adōnoy,
צוּרִי וְלֹא עַוְלָתָה בּוֹ.
tzuri v'lō avloso bō.
To declare that Hashem *is just, my Rock, in Whom there is no wrong.*

יהוה נָתַן, וַיהוה לָקָח,
Adōnoy nosan, Vadōnoy lokoch,
Hashem *gave and* Hashem *took.*

יְהִי שֵׁם יהוה מְבֹרָךְ.
y'hi shaym Adōnoy m'vōroch.
Blessed be the Name of Hashem.

וְהוּא רַחוּם,
V'hu rachum,
יְכַפֵּר עָוֹן וְלֹא יַשְׁחִית,
y'chapayr ovōn v'lō yash-chis,
He, the Merciful One, is forgiving of iniquity and does not destroy,

וְהִרְבָּה לְהָשִׁיב אַפּוֹ,
v'hirbo l'hoshiv apō,
וְלֹא יָעִיר כָּל חֲמָתוֹ.
v'lō yo-ir kol chamosō.
frequently withdrawing His anger, not arousing His entire rage.

KADDISH AFTER BURIAL

■ *Immediately upon burying a loved one, the mourner proclaims his trust and belief that Hashem will bring the dead to life.*

יִתְגַּדַּל וְיִתְקַדַּשׁ שְׁמֵהּ רַבָּא
YISGADAL v'yiskadash sh'mayh rabo
May His great Name grow exalted and sanctified
CONGREGATION RESPONDS: Omayn — אָמֵן

בְּעָלְמָא דִּי הוּא עָתִיד לְאִתְחַדָּתָא,
b'olmo di hu osid l'is-chadoso,
in the world which will be renewed,

וּלְאַחֲיָאָה מֵתַיָּא,
ul-acha-yo-o maysa-yo,
and where He will resuscitate the dead

ul-asoko yos-hōn l'cha-yay olmo,	וּלְאַסָּקָא יָתְהוֹן לְחַיֵּי עָלְמָא,

and raise them up to eternal life,

ulmivnay karto dirushlaym,	וּלְמִבְנֵא קַרְתָּא דִירוּשְׁלֵם,

and rebuild the city of Jerusalem

ulshachlayl haychlayh b'gavoh,	וּלְשַׁכְלֵל הֵיכְלֵהּ בְּגַוַּהּ,

and complete His Temple within it,

ulme-kar pulchono nuchro-o may-ar-o,	וּלְמֶעְקַר פֻּלְחָנָא נֻכְרָאָה מֵאַרְעָא,

and uproot alien worship from the earth,

v'la-asovo pulchono dishmaya l'asrayh.	וְלַאֲתָבָא פֻּלְחָנָא דִשְׁמַיָּא לְאַתְרֵהּ,

and return the service of Heaven to its place,

v'yamlich kudsho b'rich hu	וְיַמְלִיךְ קֻדְשָׁא בְּרִיךְ הוּא

and where the Holy One, Blessed is He,

b'malchusayh vi-korayh,	בְּמַלְכוּתֵהּ וִיקָרֵהּ,

will reign in His sovereignty and splendor,

b'cha-yaychōn uvyōmaychōn	בְּחַיֵּיכוֹן וּבְיוֹמֵיכוֹן

in your lifetimes and in your days

uvcha-yay d'chol bays yisro-ayl,	וּבְחַיֵּי דְכָל בֵּית יִשְׂרָאֵל,

and in the lifetimes of the entire Family of Israel,

ba-agolo u-vizman koriv.	בַּעֲגָלָא וּבִזְמַן קָרִיב.

swiftly and soon.

V'imru: Omayn.	וְאִמְרוּ: אָמֵן.

Now respond: Amen.

CONGREGATION RESPONDS:

Omayn. Y'hay sh'mayh rabo m'vorach l'olam ul-ol'may ol'ma-yo.	אָמֵן. יְהֵא שְׁמֵהּ רַבָּא מְבָרַךְ לְעָלַם וּלְעָלְמֵי עָלְמַיָּא.

Amen. May His great Name be blessed forever and ever.

MOURNER CONTINUES:

Y'hay sh'mayh rabo m'vorach l'olam ul-ol'may ol'ma-yo,	יְהֵא שְׁמֵהּ רַבָּא מְבָרַךְ לְעָלַם וּלְעָלְמֵי עָלְמַיָּא,

May His great Name be blessed forever and ever;

yisborach v'yishtabach v'yispo-ar	יִתְבָּרַךְ וְיִשְׁתַּבַּח וְיִתְפָּאַר

blessed, praised, glorified,

v'yisrōmam v'yisnasay	וְיִתְרוֹמַם וְיִתְנַשֵּׂא

exalted, extolled,

FUNERAL SERVICES

v'yis-hador v'yis-ale v'yis-halol   וְיִתְהַדָּר וְיִתְעַלֶּה וְיִתְהַלָּל
mighty, upraised, and lauded

sh'mayh d'kudsho b'rich hu   שְׁמֵהּ דְּקֻדְשָׁא בְּרִיךְ הוּא
be the Name of the Holy One, Blessed is He,

CONGREGATION RESPONDS:

B'rich hu.   Blessed is He.   בְּרִיךְ הוּא.

MOURNER CONTINUES:

°l'aylo min kol   °לְעֵלָּא מִן כָּל
beyond any

FROM ROSH HASHANAH TO YOM KIPPUR SUBSTITUTE:

°l'aylo l'aylo mikol   °לְעֵלָּא לְעֵלָּא מִכָּל
exceedingly beyond any

birchoso v'shiroso   בִּרְכָתָא וְשִׁירָתָא
blessing and song,

tushb'choso v'nechemoso,   תֻּשְׁבְּחָתָא וְנֶחֱמָתָא,
praise and consolation

da-amiron b'ol'mo.   דַּאֲמִירָן בְּעָלְמָא.
that are uttered in the world.

V'imru: Omayn.   וְאִמְרוּ: אָמֵן.
Now respond: Amen.

CONGREGATION RESPONDS: Omayn — אָמֵן

Y'hay sh'lomo rabo min sh'mayo,   יְהֵא שְׁלָמָא רַבָּא מִן שְׁמַיָּא,
May there be abundant peace from Heaven,

v'cha-yim olaynu v'al kol yisro-ayl.   וְחַיִּים עָלֵינוּ וְעַל כָּל יִשְׂרָאֵל.
and life, upon us and upon all Israel.

V'imru: Omayn.   וְאִמְרוּ: אָמֵן.
Now respond: Amen.

CONGREGATION RESPONDS: Omayn — אָמֵן

MOURNER BOWS, THEN TAKES THREE STEPS BACK, BOWS LEFT AND SAYS:

O-se sholom bimromov,   עֹשֶׂה שָׁלוֹם בִּמְרוֹמָיו,
He Who makes peace in His heights,

MOURNER BOWS RIGHT AND SAYS:

hu ya-a-se sholom olaynu,   הוּא יַעֲשֶׂה שָׁלוֹם עָלֵינוּ,
may He make peace upon us,

MOURNER BOWS FORWARD AND SAYS:

v'al kol yisro-ayl. V'imru: Omayn.   וְעַל כָּל יִשְׂרָאֵל. וְאִמְרוּ: אָמֵן.
and upon all Israel. Now respond: Amen.

CONGREGATION RESPONDS: Omayn — אָמֵן

MOURNER REMAINS IN PLACE FOR A FEW MOMENTS, THEN TAKES THREE STEPS FORWARD.

CONSOLING THE MOURNERS

HAMOKÔM y'nachaym   הַמָּקוֹם יְנַחֵם

───────── TO A MALE MOURNER: ─────────
ōs-cho   אוֹתְךָ

───────── TO A FEMALE MOURNER: ─────────
ō-soch   אוֹתָךְ

───────── TO A GROUP OF MOURNERS: ─────────
eschem   אֶתְכֶם

May the Omnipresent console you

b'soch sh'or   בְּתוֹךְ שְׁאָר
    among the other
avaylay tzi-yon virusholo-yim.   אֲבֵלֵי צִיּוֹן וִירוּשָׁלָיִם.
    mourners of Zion and Jerusalem.

V'YOTZITZU may-ir   וְיָצִיצוּ מֵעִיר
    k'aysev ho-oretz.   כְּעֵשֶׂב הָאָרֶץ.
May they blossom forth from the city like the grass of the earth.

Zochur ki ofor anoch-nu   זָכוּר כִּי עָפָר אֲנָחְנוּ.
    Remember that we are but dust.

BILA ha-moves lo-netzach,   בִּלַּע הַמָּוֶת לָנֶצַח,
    May He swallow up death forever,
u-mocho Adōnoy Elō-him   וּמָחָה אֲדֹנָי יֱהוִה
    and may HASHEM *the God*
dim-o may-al kol ponim,   דִּמְעָה מֵעַל כָּל פָּנִים,
    wipe away tears from every face
v'cherpas amō yosir   וְחֶרְפַּת עַמּוֹ יָסִיר
    and remove the scorn of His people
may-al kol ho-oretz,   מֵעַל כָּל הָאָרֶץ,
    from throughout the world,
ki Adōnoy dibayr.   כִּי יהוה דִּבֵּר.
    for HASHEM *has spoken.*

Weekday Torah Readings

קריאת התורה לימות החול
Torah Reading for Weekdays

פ׳ בראשית / BEREISHIS
(Genesis 1:1-13)

כהן: בְּרֵאשִׁית בָּרָא אֱלֹהִים אֵת הַשָּׁמַיִם וְאֵת הָאָרֶץ: וְהָאָרֶץ הָיְתָה תֹהוּ וָבֹהוּ וְחֹשֶׁךְ עַל־פְּנֵי תְהוֹם וְרוּחַ אֱלֹהִים מְרַחֶפֶת עַל־פְּנֵי הַמָּיִם: וַיֹּאמֶר אֱלֹהִים יְהִי אוֹר וַיְהִי־אוֹר: וַיַּרְא אֱלֹהִים אֶת־הָאוֹר כִּי־טוֹב וַיַּבְדֵּל אֱלֹהִים בֵּין הָאוֹר וּבֵין הַחֹשֶׁךְ: וַיִּקְרָא אֱלֹהִים ׀ לָאוֹר יוֹם וְלַחֹשֶׁךְ קָרָא לָיְלָה וַיְהִי־עֶרֶב וַיְהִי־בֹקֶר יוֹם אֶחָד:

לוי: וַיֹּאמֶר אֱלֹהִים יְהִי רָקִיעַ בְּתוֹךְ הַמָּיִם וִיהִי מַבְדִּיל בֵּין מַיִם לָמָיִם: וַיַּעַשׂ אֱלֹהִים אֶת־הָרָקִיעַ וַיַּבְדֵּל בֵּין הַמַּיִם אֲשֶׁר מִתַּחַת לָרָקִיעַ וּבֵין הַמַּיִם אֲשֶׁר מֵעַל לָרָקִיעַ וַיְהִי־כֵן: וַיִּקְרָא אֱלֹהִים לָרָקִיעַ שָׁמָיִם וַיְהִי־עֶרֶב וַיְהִי־בֹקֶר יוֹם שֵׁנִי:

ישראל: וַיֹּאמֶר אֱלֹהִים יִקָּווּ הַמַּיִם מִתַּחַת הַשָּׁמַיִם אֶל־מָקוֹם אֶחָד וְתֵרָאֶה הַיַּבָּשָׁה וַיְהִי־כֵן: וַיִּקְרָא אֱלֹהִים ׀ לַיַּבָּשָׁה אֶרֶץ וּלְמִקְוֵה הַמַּיִם קָרָא יַמִּים וַיַּרְא אֱלֹהִים כִּי־טוֹב: וַיֹּאמֶר אֱלֹהִים תַּדְשֵׁא הָאָרֶץ דֶּשֶׁא עֵשֶׂב מַזְרִיעַ זֶרַע עֵץ פְּרִי עֹשֶׂה פְּרִי לְמִינוֹ אֲשֶׁר זַרְעוֹ־בוֹ עַל־הָאָרֶץ וַיְהִי־כֵן: וַתּוֹצֵא הָאָרֶץ דֶּשֶׁא עֵשֶׂב מַזְרִיעַ זֶרַע לְמִינֵהוּ וְעֵץ עֹשֶׂה־פְּרִי אֲשֶׁר זַרְעוֹ־בוֹ לְמִינֵהוּ וַיַּרְא אֱלֹהִים כִּי־טוֹב: וַיְהִי־עֶרֶב וַיְהִי־בֹקֶר יוֹם שְׁלִישִׁי:

פ׳ נח / NOACH
(Genesis 6:9-22)

כהן: אֵלֶּה תּוֹלְדֹת נֹחַ נֹחַ אִישׁ צַדִּיק תָּמִים הָיָה בְּדֹרֹתָיו אֶת־הָאֱלֹהִים הִתְהַלֶּךְ־נֹחַ: וַיּוֹלֶד נֹחַ שְׁלֹשָׁה בָנִים אֶת־שֵׁם אֶת־חָם וְאֶת־יָפֶת: וַתִּשָּׁחֵת הָאָרֶץ לִפְנֵי הָאֱלֹהִים וַתִּמָּלֵא הָאָרֶץ חָמָס: וַיַּרְא אֱלֹהִים אֶת־הָאָרֶץ וְהִנֵּה נִשְׁחָתָה כִּי־הִשְׁחִית כָּל־בָּשָׂר אֶת־דַּרְכּוֹ עַל־הָאָרֶץ: וַיֹּאמֶר אֱלֹהִים לְנֹחַ קֵץ כָּל־בָּשָׂר בָּא לְפָנַי כִּי־מָלְאָה הָאָרֶץ חָמָס מִפְּנֵיהֶם וְהִנְנִי מַשְׁחִיתָם אֶת־הָאָרֶץ: עֲשֵׂה לְךָ תֵּבַת עֲצֵי־גֹפֶר קִנִּים תַּעֲשֶׂה אֶת־הַתֵּבָה וְכָפַרְתָּ אֹתָהּ מִבַּיִת וּמִחוּץ בַּכֹּפֶר: וְזֶה אֲשֶׁר תַּעֲשֶׂה אֹתָהּ שְׁלֹשׁ מֵאוֹת אַמָּה אֹרֶךְ הַתֵּבָה חֲמִשִּׁים אַמָּה רָחְבָּהּ וּשְׁלֹשִׁים אַמָּה קוֹמָתָהּ: צֹהַר ׀ תַּעֲשֶׂה לַתֵּבָה וְאֶל־אַמָּה תְּכַלֶּנָּה מִלְמַעְלָה וּפֶתַח הַתֵּבָה בְּצִדָּהּ תָּשִׂים תַּחְתִּיִּם שְׁנִיִּם וּשְׁלִשִׁים תַּעֲשֶׂהָ:

לוי: וַאֲנִי הִנְנִי מֵבִיא אֶת־הַמַּבּוּל מַיִם עַל־הָאָרֶץ לְשַׁחֵת כָּל־בָּשָׂר אֲשֶׁר־בּוֹ רוּחַ חַיִּים מִתַּחַת הַשָּׁמָיִם כֹּל אֲשֶׁר־בָּאָרֶץ יִגְוָע: וַהֲקִמֹתִי אֶת־בְּרִיתִי אִתָּךְ וּבָאתָ אֶל־הַתֵּבָה אַתָּה וּבָנֶיךָ וְאִשְׁתְּךָ וּנְשֵׁי־בָנֶיךָ אִתָּךְ: וּמִכָּל־הָחַי מִכָּל־בָּשָׂר שְׁנַיִם מִכֹּל תָּבִיא אֶל־הַתֵּבָה לְהַחֲיֹת אִתָּךְ זָכָר וּנְקֵבָה יִהְיוּ:

ישראל: מֵהָעוֹף לְמִינֵהוּ וּמִן־הַבְּהֵמָה לְמִינָהּ מִכֹּל רֶמֶשׂ הָאֲדָמָה לְמִינֵהוּ שְׁנַיִם מִכֹּל יָבֹאוּ אֵלֶיךָ לְהַחֲיוֹת: וְאַתָּה קַח־לְךָ מִכָּל־מַאֲכָל אֲשֶׁר יֵאָכֵל וְאָסַפְתָּ אֵלֶיךָ וְהָיָה לְךָ וְלָהֶם לְאָכְלָה: וַיַּעַשׂ נֹחַ כְּכֹל אֲשֶׁר צִוָּה אֹתוֹ אֱלֹהִים כֵּן עָשָׂה:

פ׳ לך לך / LECH LECHA
(Genesis 12:1-13)

כהן: וַיֹּאמֶר יהוה אֶל־אַבְרָם לֶךְ־לְךָ מֵאַרְצְךָ וּמִמּוֹלַדְתְּךָ וּמִבֵּית אָבִיךָ אֶל־הָאָרֶץ אֲשֶׁר אַרְאֶךָּ: וְאֶעֶשְׂךָ לְגוֹי גָּדוֹל וַאֲבָרֶכְךָ וַאֲגַדְּלָה שְׁמֶךָ וֶהְיֵה בְּרָכָה: וַאֲבָרְכָה מְבָרְכֶיךָ וּמְקַלֶּלְךָ אָאֹר וְנִבְרְכוּ בְךָ כֹּל מִשְׁפְּחֹת הָאֲדָמָה:

לוי: וַיֵּלֶךְ אַבְרָם כַּאֲשֶׁר דִּבֶּר אֵלָיו יהוה וַיֵּלֶךְ אִתּוֹ לוֹט וְאַבְרָם בֶּן־חָמֵשׁ שָׁנִים וְשִׁבְעִים שָׁנָה בְּצֵאתוֹ מֵחָרָן: וַיִּקַּח אַבְרָם אֶת־שָׂרַי אִשְׁתּוֹ וְאֶת־לוֹט בֶּן־אָחִיו וְאֶת־כָּל־רְכוּשָׁם אֲשֶׁר רָכָשׁוּ וְאֶת־הַנֶּפֶשׁ אֲשֶׁר־עָשׂוּ בְחָרָן וַיֵּצְאוּ לָלֶכֶת אַרְצָה כְּנַעַן וַיָּבֹאוּ אַרְצָה

כְּנָעַן: וַיַּעֲבֹר אַבְרָם בָּאָרֶץ עַד מְקוֹם שְׁכֶם עַד אֵלוֹן מוֹרֶה וְהַכְּנַעֲנִי אָז בָּאָרֶץ: וַיֵּרָא יהוה אֶל־אַבְרָם וַיֹּאמֶר לְזַרְעֲךָ אֶתֵּן אֶת־הָאָרֶץ הַזֹּאת וַיִּבֶן שָׁם מִזְבֵּחַ לַיהוה הַנִּרְאֶה אֵלָיו: וַיַּעְתֵּק מִשָּׁם הָהָרָה מִקֶּדֶם לְבֵית־אֵל וַיֵּט אָהֳלֹה בֵּית־אֵל מִיָּם וְהָעַי מִקֶּדֶם וַיִּבֶן־שָׁם מִזְבֵּחַ לַיהוה וַיִּקְרָא בְּשֵׁם יהוה: וַיִּסַּע אַבְרָם הָלוֹךְ וְנָסוֹעַ הַנֶּגְבָּה:

ישראל: וַיְהִי רָעָב בָּאָרֶץ וַיֵּרֶד אַבְרָם מִצְרַיְמָה לָגוּר שָׁם כִּי־כָבֵד הָרָעָב בָּאָרֶץ: וַיְהִי כַּאֲשֶׁר הִקְרִיב לָבוֹא מִצְרָיְמָה וַיֹּאמֶר אֶל־שָׂרַי אִשְׁתּוֹ הִנֵּה־נָא יָדַעְתִּי כִּי אִשָּׁה יְפַת־מַרְאֶה אָתְּ: וְהָיָה כִּי־יִרְאוּ אֹתָךְ הַמִּצְרִים וְאָמְרוּ אִשְׁתּוֹ זֹאת וְהָרְגוּ אֹתִי וְאֹתָךְ יְחַיּוּ: אִמְרִי־נָא אֲחֹתִי אָתְּ לְמַעַן יִיטַב־לִי בַעֲבוּרֵךְ וְחָיְתָה נַפְשִׁי בִּגְלָלֵךְ:

פ׳ וירא / VAYEIRA
(Genesis 18:1-14)

כהן: וַיֵּרָא אֵלָיו יהוה בְּאֵלֹנֵי מַמְרֵא וְהוּא יֹשֵׁב פֶּתַח־הָאֹהֶל כְּחֹם הַיּוֹם: וַיִּשָּׂא עֵינָיו וַיַּרְא וְהִנֵּה שְׁלֹשָׁה אֲנָשִׁים נִצָּבִים עָלָיו וַיַּרְא וַיָּרָץ לִקְרָאתָם מִפֶּתַח הָאֹהֶל וַיִּשְׁתַּחוּ אָרְצָה: וַיֹּאמַר אֲדֹנָי אִם־נָא מָצָאתִי חֵן בְּעֵינֶיךָ אַל־נָא תַעֲבֹר מֵעַל עַבְדֶּךָ: יֻקַּח־נָא מְעַט־מַיִם וְרַחֲצוּ רַגְלֵיכֶם וְהִשָּׁעֲנוּ תַּחַת הָעֵץ: וְאֶקְחָה פַת־לֶחֶם וְסַעֲדוּ לִבְּכֶם אַחַר תַּעֲבֹרוּ כִּי־עַל־כֵּן עֲבַרְתֶּם עַל־עַבְדְּכֶם וַיֹּאמְרוּ כֵּן תַּעֲשֶׂה כַּאֲשֶׁר דִּבַּרְתָּ:

לוי: וַיְמַהֵר אַבְרָהָם הָאֹהֱלָה אֶל־שָׂרָה וַיֹּאמֶר מַהֲרִי שְׁלֹשׁ סְאִים קֶמַח סֹלֶת לוּשִׁי וַעֲשִׂי עֻגוֹת: וְאֶל־הַבָּקָר רָץ אַבְרָהָם וַיִּקַּח בֶּן־בָּקָר רַךְ וָטוֹב וַיִּתֵּן אֶל־הַנַּעַר וַיְמַהֵר לַעֲשׂוֹת אֹתוֹ: וַיִּקַּח חֶמְאָה וְחָלָב וּבֶן־הַבָּקָר אֲשֶׁר עָשָׂה וַיִּתֵּן לִפְנֵיהֶם וְהוּא־עֹמֵד עֲלֵיהֶם תַּחַת הָעֵץ וַיֹּאכֵלוּ:

ישראל: וַיֹּאמְרוּ אֵלָיו אַיֵּה שָׂרָה אִשְׁתֶּךָ וַיֹּאמֶר הִנֵּה בָאֹהֶל: וַיֹּאמֶר שׁוֹב אָשׁוּב אֵלֶיךָ כָּעֵת חַיָּה וְהִנֵּה־בֵן לְשָׂרָה אִשְׁתֶּךָ וְשָׂרָה שֹׁמַעַת פֶּתַח הָאֹהֶל וְהוּא אַחֲרָיו: וְאַבְרָהָם וְשָׂרָה זְקֵנִים בָּאִים בַּיָּמִים חָדַל לִהְיוֹת לְשָׂרָה אֹרַח כַּנָּשִׁים: וַתִּצְחַק שָׂרָה בְּקִרְבָּהּ לֵאמֹר אַחֲרֵי בְלֹתִי הָיְתָה־לִּי עֶדְנָה וַאדֹנִי זָקֵן: וַיֹּאמֶר יהוה אֶל־אַבְרָהָם לָמָּה זֶּה צָחֲקָה שָׂרָה לֵאמֹר הַאַף אֻמְנָם אֵלֵד וַאֲנִי זָקַנְתִּי: הֲיִפָּלֵא מֵיהוה דָּבָר לַמּוֹעֵד אָשׁוּב אֵלֶיךָ כָּעֵת חַיָּה וּלְשָׂרָה בֵן:

פ׳ חיי שרה / CHAYEI SARAH
(Genesis 23:1-16)

כהן: וַיִּהְיוּ חַיֵּי שָׂרָה מֵאָה שָׁנָה וְעֶשְׂרִים שָׁנָה וְשֶׁבַע שָׁנִים שְׁנֵי חַיֵּי שָׂרָה: וַתָּמָת שָׂרָה בְּקִרְיַת אַרְבַּע הִוא חֶבְרוֹן בְּאֶרֶץ כְּנָעַן וַיָּבֹא אַבְרָהָם לִסְפֹּד לְשָׂרָה וְלִבְכֹּתָהּ: וַיָּקָם אַבְרָהָם מֵעַל פְּנֵי מֵתוֹ וַיְדַבֵּר אֶל־בְּנֵי־חֵת לֵאמֹר: גֵּר־וְתוֹשָׁב אָנֹכִי עִמָּכֶם תְּנוּ לִי אֲחֻזַּת־קֶבֶר עִמָּכֶם וְאֶקְבְּרָה מֵתִי מִלְּפָנָי: וַיַּעֲנוּ בְנֵי־חֵת אֶת־אַבְרָהָם לֵאמֹר לוֹ: שְׁמָעֵנוּ ׀ אֲדֹנִי נְשִׂיא אֱלֹהִים אַתָּה בְּתוֹכֵנוּ בְּמִבְחַר קְבָרֵינוּ קְבֹר אֶת־מֵתֶךָ אִישׁ מִמֶּנּוּ אֶת־קִבְרוֹ לֹא־יִכְלֶה מִמְּךָ מִקְּבֹר מֵתֶךָ: וַיָּקָם אַבְרָהָם וַיִּשְׁתַּחוּ לְעַם־הָאָרֶץ לִבְנֵי־חֵת:

לוי: וַיְדַבֵּר אִתָּם לֵאמֹר אִם־יֵשׁ אֶת־נַפְשְׁכֶם לִקְבֹּר אֶת־מֵתִי מִלְּפָנַי שְׁמָעוּנִי וּפִגְעוּ־לִי בְּעֶפְרוֹן בֶּן־צֹחַר: וְיִתֶּן־לִי אֶת־מְעָרַת הַמַּכְפֵּלָה אֲשֶׁר־לוֹ אֲשֶׁר בִּקְצֵה שָׂדֵהוּ בְּכֶסֶף מָלֵא יִתְּנֶנָּה לִי בְּתוֹכְכֶם לַאֲחֻזַּת־קָבֶר: וְעֶפְרוֹן יֹשֵׁב בְּתוֹךְ בְּנֵי־חֵת וַיַּעַן עֶפְרוֹן הַחִתִּי אֶת־אַבְרָהָם בְּאָזְנֵי בְנֵי־חֵת לְכֹל בָּאֵי שַׁעַר־עִירוֹ לֵאמֹר: לֹא־אֲדֹנִי שְׁמָעֵנִי הַשָּׂדֶה נָתַתִּי לָךְ וְהַמְּעָרָה אֲשֶׁר־בּוֹ לְךָ נְתַתִּיהָ לְעֵינֵי בְנֵי־עַמִּי נְתַתִּיהָ לָּךְ קְבֹר מֵתֶךָ: וַיִּשְׁתַּחוּ אַבְרָהָם לִפְנֵי עַם הָאָרֶץ:

ישראל: וַיְדַבֵּר אֶל־עֶפְרוֹן בְּאָזְנֵי עַם־הָאָרֶץ לֵאמֹר אַךְ אִם־אַתָּה לוּ שְׁמָעֵנִי נָתַתִּי כֶּסֶף הַשָּׂדֶה קַח מִמֶּנִּי וְאֶקְבְּרָה אֶת־מֵתִי שָׁמָּה: וַיַּעַן עֶפְרוֹן אֶת־אַבְרָהָם לֵאמֹר לוֹ: אֲדֹנִי שְׁמָעֵנִי אֶרֶץ אַרְבַּע מֵאֹת שֶׁקֶל־כֶּסֶף בֵּינִי וּבֵינְךָ מַה־הִוא וְאֶת־מֵתְךָ קְבֹר: וַיִּשְׁמַע

TOLDOS-VAYEITZEI

אַבְרָהָם אֶל־עֶפְרוֹן וַיִּשְׁקֹל אַבְרָהָם לְעֶפְרֹן אֶת־הַכֶּסֶף אֲשֶׁר דִּבֶּר בְּאָזְנֵי בְנֵי־חֵת אַרְבַּע מֵאוֹת שֶׁקֶל כֶּסֶף עֹבֵר לַסֹּחֵר:

פ׳ תּוֹלְדֹת / TOLDOS
(Genesis 25:19 — 26:5)

כה/יט וְאֵלֶּה תּוֹלְדֹת יִצְחָק בֶּן־אַבְרָהָם אַבְרָהָם הוֹלִיד אֶת־יִצְחָק: וַיְהִי יִצְחָק בֶּן־אַרְבָּעִים שָׁנָה בְּקַחְתּוֹ אֶת־רִבְקָה בַּת־בְּתוּאֵל הָאֲרַמִּי מִפַּדַּן אֲרָם אֲחוֹת לָבָן הָאֲרַמִּי לוֹ לְאִשָּׁה: וַיֶּעְתַּר יִצְחָק לַיהוָה לְנֹכַח אִשְׁתּוֹ כִּי עֲקָרָה הִוא וַיֵּעָתֶר לוֹ יְהוָה וַתַּהַר רִבְקָה אִשְׁתּוֹ: וַיִּתְרֹצֲצוּ הַבָּנִים בְּקִרְבָּהּ וַתֹּאמֶר אִם־כֵּן לָמָּה זֶּה אָנֹכִי וַתֵּלֶךְ לִדְרֹשׁ אֶת־יְהוָה:

לוי וַיֹּאמֶר יְהוָה לָהּ שְׁנֵי גוֹיִם בְּבִטְנֵךְ וּשְׁנֵי לְאֻמִּים מִמֵּעַיִךְ יִפָּרֵדוּ וּלְאֹם מִלְאֹם יֶאֱמָץ וְרַב יַעֲבֹד צָעִיר: וַיִּמְלְאוּ יָמֶיהָ לָלֶדֶת וְהִנֵּה תוֹמִם בְּבִטְנָהּ: וַיֵּצֵא הָרִאשׁוֹן אַדְמוֹנִי כֻּלּוֹ כְּאַדֶּרֶת שֵׂעָר וַיִּקְרְאוּ שְׁמוֹ עֵשָׂו: וְאַחֲרֵי־כֵן יָצָא אָחִיו וְיָדוֹ אֹחֶזֶת בַּעֲקֵב עֵשָׂו וַיִּקְרָא שְׁמוֹ יַעֲקֹב וְיִצְחָק בֶּן־שִׁשִּׁים שָׁנָה בְּלֶדֶת אֹתָם:

ישראל וַיִּגְדְּלוּ הַנְּעָרִים וַיְהִי עֵשָׂו אִישׁ יֹדֵעַ צַיִד אִישׁ שָׂדֶה וְיַעֲקֹב אִישׁ תָּם יֹשֵׁב אֹהָלִים: וַיֶּאֱהַב יִצְחָק אֶת־עֵשָׂו כִּי־צַיִד בְּפִיו וְרִבְקָה אֹהֶבֶת אֶת־יַעֲקֹב: וַיָּזֶד יַעֲקֹב נָזִיד וַיָּבֹא עֵשָׂו מִן־הַשָּׂדֶה וְהוּא עָיֵף: וַיֹּאמֶר עֵשָׂו אֶל־יַעֲקֹב הַלְעִיטֵנִי נָא מִן־הָאָדֹם הָאָדֹם הַזֶּה כִּי עָיֵף אָנֹכִי עַל־כֵּן קָרָא־שְׁמוֹ אֱדוֹם: וַיֹּאמֶר יַעֲקֹב מִכְרָה כַיּוֹם אֶת־בְּכֹרָתְךָ לִי: וַיֹּאמֶר עֵשָׂו הִנֵּה אָנֹכִי הוֹלֵךְ לָמוּת וְלָמָּה־זֶּה לִי בְּכֹרָה: וַיֹּאמֶר יַעֲקֹב הִשָּׁבְעָה לִּי כַּיּוֹם וַיִּשָּׁבַע לוֹ וַיִּמְכֹּר אֶת־בְּכֹרָתוֹ לְיַעֲקֹב: וְיַעֲקֹב נָתַן לְעֵשָׂו לֶחֶם וּנְזִיד עֲדָשִׁים וַיֹּאכַל וַיֵּשְׁתְּ וַיָּקָם וַיֵּלַךְ וַיִּבֶז עֵשָׂו אֶת־הַבְּכֹרָה: וַיְהִי רָעָב בָּאָרֶץ מִלְּבַד הָרָעָב הָרִאשׁוֹן אֲשֶׁר הָיָה בִּימֵי אַבְרָהָם וַיֵּלֶךְ יִצְחָק אֶל־אֲבִימֶלֶךְ מֶלֶךְ־פְּלִשְׁתִּים גְּרָרָה: וַיֵּרָא אֵלָיו יְהוָה וַיֹּאמֶר אַל־תֵּרֵד מִצְרַיְמָה שְׁכֹן בָּאָרֶץ אֲשֶׁר אֹמַר אֵלֶיךָ: גּוּר בָּאָרֶץ הַזֹּאת וְאֶהְיֶה עִמְּךָ וַאֲבָרְכֶךָּ כִּי־לְךָ וּלְזַרְעֲךָ אֶתֵּן אֶת־כָּל־הָאֲרָצֹת הָאֵל וַהֲקִמֹתִי אֶת־הַשְּׁבֻעָה אֲשֶׁר נִשְׁבַּעְתִּי לְאַבְרָהָם אָבִיךָ: וְהִרְבֵּיתִי אֶת־זַרְעֲךָ כְּכוֹכְבֵי הַשָּׁמַיִם וְנָתַתִּי לְזַרְעֲךָ אֵת כָּל־הָאֲרָצֹת הָאֵל וְהִתְבָּרֲכוּ בְזַרְעֲךָ כֹּל גּוֹיֵי הָאָרֶץ: עֵקֶב אֲשֶׁר־שָׁמַע אַבְרָהָם בְּקֹלִי וַיִּשְׁמֹר מִשְׁמַרְתִּי מִצְוֹתַי חֻקּוֹתַי וְתוֹרֹתָי:

פ׳ וַיֵּצֵא / VAYEITZEI
(Genesis 28:10-22)

כהן וַיֵּצֵא יַעֲקֹב מִבְּאֵר שָׁבַע וַיֵּלֶךְ חָרָנָה: וַיִּפְגַּע בַּמָּקוֹם וַיָּלֶן שָׁם כִּי־בָא הַשֶּׁמֶשׁ וַיִּקַּח מֵאַבְנֵי הַמָּקוֹם וַיָּשֶׂם מְרַאֲשֹׁתָיו וַיִּשְׁכַּב בַּמָּקוֹם הַהוּא: וַיַּחֲלֹם וְהִנֵּה סֻלָּם מֻצָּב אַרְצָה וְרֹאשׁוֹ מַגִּיעַ הַשָּׁמָיְמָה וְהִנֵּה מַלְאֲכֵי אֱלֹהִים עֹלִים וְיֹרְדִים בּוֹ:

לוי וְהִנֵּה יְהוָה נִצָּב עָלָיו וַיֹּאמַר אֲנִי יְהוָה אֱלֹהֵי אַבְרָהָם אָבִיךָ וֵאלֹהֵי יִצְחָק הָאָרֶץ אֲשֶׁר אַתָּה שֹׁכֵב עָלֶיהָ לְךָ אֶתְּנֶנָּה וּלְזַרְעֶךָ: וְהָיָה זַרְעֲךָ כַּעֲפַר הָאָרֶץ וּפָרַצְתָּ יָמָּה וָקֵדְמָה וְצָפֹנָה וָנֶגְבָּה וְנִבְרְכוּ בְךָ כָּל־מִשְׁפְּחֹת הָאֲדָמָה וּבְזַרְעֶךָ: וְהִנֵּה אָנֹכִי עִמָּךְ וּשְׁמַרְתִּיךָ בְּכֹל אֲשֶׁר־תֵּלֵךְ וַהֲשִׁבֹתִיךָ אֶל־הָאֲדָמָה הַזֹּאת כִּי לֹא אֶעֱזָבְךָ עַד אֲשֶׁר אִם־עָשִׂיתִי אֵת אֲשֶׁר־דִּבַּרְתִּי לָךְ: וַיִּיקַץ יַעֲקֹב מִשְּׁנָתוֹ וַיֹּאמֶר אָכֵן יֵשׁ יְהוָה בַּמָּקוֹם הַזֶּה וְאָנֹכִי לֹא יָדָעְתִּי: וַיִּירָא וַיֹּאמַר מַה־נּוֹרָא הַמָּקוֹם הַזֶּה אֵין זֶה כִּי אִם־בֵּית אֱלֹהִים וְזֶה שַׁעַר הַשָּׁמָיִם:

ישראל וַיַּשְׁכֵּם יַעֲקֹב בַּבֹּקֶר וַיִּקַּח אֶת־הָאֶבֶן אֲשֶׁר־שָׂם מְרַאֲשֹׁתָיו וַיָּשֶׂם אֹתָהּ מַצֵּבָה וַיִּצֹק שֶׁמֶן עַל־רֹאשָׁהּ: וַיִּקְרָא אֶת־שֵׁם־הַמָּקוֹם הַהוּא בֵּית־אֵל וְאוּלָם לוּז שֵׁם־הָעִיר לָרִאשֹׁנָה: וַיִּדַּר יַעֲקֹב נֶדֶר לֵאמֹר אִם־יִהְיֶה אֱלֹהִים עִמָּדִי וּשְׁמָרַנִי בַּדֶּרֶךְ הַזֶּה אֲשֶׁר אָנֹכִי הוֹלֵךְ וְנָתַן־לִי לֶחֶם לֶאֱכֹל וּבֶגֶד לִלְבֹּשׁ: וְשַׁבְתִּי בְשָׁלוֹם אֶל־בֵּית אָבִי וְהָיָה יְהוָה לִי לֵאלֹהִים: וְהָאֶבֶן הַזֹּאת אֲשֶׁר־

פ׳ וישלח / VAYISHLACH
(Genesis 32:4-13)

כהן: וַיִּשְׁלַח יַעֲקֹב מַלְאָכִים לְפָנָיו אֶל־עֵשָׂו אָחִיו אַרְצָה שֵׂעִיר שְׂדֵה אֱדוֹם: וַיְצַו אֹתָם לֵאמֹר כֹּה תֹאמְרוּן לַאדֹנִי לְעֵשָׂו כֹּה אָמַר עַבְדְּךָ יַעֲקֹב עִם־לָבָן גַּרְתִּי וָאֵחַר עַד־עָתָּה: וַיְהִי־לִי שׁוֹר וַחֲמוֹר צֹאן וְעֶבֶד וְשִׁפְחָה וָאֶשְׁלְחָה לְהַגִּיד לַאדֹנִי לִמְצֹא־חֵן בְּעֵינֶיךָ: לוי: וַיָּשֻׁבוּ הַמַּלְאָכִים אֶל־יַעֲקֹב לֵאמֹר בָּאנוּ אֶל־אָחִיךָ אֶל־עֵשָׂו וְגַם הֹלֵךְ לִקְרָאתְךָ וְאַרְבַּע־מֵאוֹת אִישׁ עִמּוֹ: וַיִּירָא יַעֲקֹב מְאֹד וַיֵּצֶר לוֹ וַיַּחַץ אֶת־הָעָם אֲשֶׁר־אִתּוֹ וְאֶת־הַצֹּאן וְאֶת־הַבָּקָר וְהַגְּמַלִּים לִשְׁנֵי מַחֲנוֹת: וַיֹּאמֶר אִם־יָבוֹא עֵשָׂו אֶל־הַמַּחֲנֶה הָאַחַת וְהִכָּהוּ וְהָיָה הַמַּחֲנֶה הַנִּשְׁאָר לִפְלֵיטָה:

ישראל: וַיֹּאמֶר יַעֲקֹב אֱלֹהֵי אָבִי אַבְרָהָם וֵאלֹהֵי אָבִי יִצְחָק יְהוָה הָאֹמֵר אֵלַי שׁוּב לְאַרְצְךָ וּלְמוֹלַדְתְּךָ וְאֵיטִיבָה עִמָּךְ: קָטֹנְתִּי מִכֹּל הַחֲסָדִים וּמִכָּל־הָאֱמֶת אֲשֶׁר עָשִׂיתָ אֶת־עַבְדֶּךָ כִּי בְמַקְלִי עָבַרְתִּי אֶת־הַיַּרְדֵּן הַזֶּה וְעַתָּה הָיִיתִי לִשְׁנֵי מַחֲנוֹת: הַצִּילֵנִי נָא מִיַּד אָחִי מִיַּד עֵשָׂו כִּי־יָרֵא אָנֹכִי אֹתוֹ פֶּן־יָבוֹא וְהִכַּנִי אֵם עַל־בָּנִים: וְאַתָּה אָמַרְתָּ הֵיטֵב אֵיטִיב עִמָּךְ וְשַׂמְתִּי אֶת־זַרְעֲךָ כְּחוֹל הַיָּם אֲשֶׁר לֹא־יִסָּפֵר מֵרֹב:

פ׳ וישב / VAYEISHEV
(Genesis 37:1-11)

כהן: וַיֵּשֶׁב יַעֲקֹב בְּאֶרֶץ מְגוּרֵי אָבִיו בְּאֶרֶץ כְּנָעַן: אֵלֶּה | תֹּלְדוֹת יַעֲקֹב יוֹסֵף בֶּן־שְׁבַע־עֶשְׂרֵה שָׁנָה הָיָה רֹעֶה אֶת־אֶחָיו בַּצֹּאן וְהוּא נַעַר אֶת־בְּנֵי בִלְהָה וְאֶת־בְּנֵי זִלְפָּה נְשֵׁי אָבִיו וַיָּבֵא יוֹסֵף אֶת־דִּבָּתָם רָעָה אֶל־אֲבִיהֶם: וְיִשְׂרָאֵל אָהַב אֶת־יוֹסֵף מִכָּל־בָּנָיו כִּי־בֶן־זְקֻנִים הוּא לוֹ וְעָשָׂה לוֹ כְּתֹנֶת פַּסִּים: לוי: וַיִּרְאוּ אֶחָיו כִּי־אֹתוֹ אָהַב אֲבִיהֶם מִכָּל־אֶחָיו וַיִּשְׂנְאוּ אֹתוֹ וְלֹא יָכְלוּ דַּבְּרוֹ לְשָׁלֹם: וַיַּחֲלֹם יוֹסֵף חֲלוֹם וַיַּגֵּד לְאֶחָיו וַיּוֹסִפוּ עוֹד שְׂנֹא אֹתוֹ: וַיֹּאמֶר אֲלֵיהֶם שִׁמְעוּ־נָא הַחֲלוֹם הַזֶּה אֲשֶׁר חָלָמְתִּי: וְהִנֵּה אֲנַחְנוּ מְאַלְּמִים אֲלֻמִּים בְּתוֹךְ הַשָּׂדֶה וְהִנֵּה קָמָה אֲלֻמָּתִי וְגַם־נִצָּבָה וְהִנֵּה תְסֻבֶּינָה אֲלֻמֹּתֵיכֶם וַתִּשְׁתַּחֲוֶיןָ לַאֲלֻמָּתִי: ישראל: וַיֹּאמְרוּ לוֹ אֶחָיו הֲמָלֹךְ תִּמְלֹךְ עָלֵינוּ אִם־מָשׁוֹל תִּמְשֹׁל בָּנוּ וַיּוֹסִפוּ עוֹד שְׂנֹא אֹתוֹ עַל־חֲלֹמֹתָיו וְעַל־דְּבָרָיו: וַיַּחֲלֹם עוֹד חֲלוֹם אַחֵר וַיְסַפֵּר אֹתוֹ לְאֶחָיו וַיֹּאמֶר הִנֵּה חָלַמְתִּי חֲלוֹם עוֹד וְהִנֵּה הַשֶּׁמֶשׁ וְהַיָּרֵחַ וְאַחַד עָשָׂר כּוֹכָבִים מִשְׁתַּחֲוִים לִי: וַיְסַפֵּר אֶל־אָבִיו וְאֶל־אֶחָיו וַיִּגְעַר־בּוֹ אָבִיו וַיֹּאמֶר לוֹ מָה הַחֲלוֹם הַזֶּה אֲשֶׁר חָלָמְתָּ הֲבוֹא נָבוֹא אֲנִי וְאִמְּךָ וְאַחֶיךָ לְהִשְׁתַּחֲוֹת לְךָ אָרְצָה: וַיְקַנְאוּ־בוֹ אֶחָיו וְאָבִיו שָׁמַר אֶת־הַדָּבָר:

פ׳ מקץ / MIKEITZ
(Genesis 41:1-14)

כהן: וַיְהִי מִקֵּץ שְׁנָתַיִם יָמִים וּפַרְעֹה חֹלֵם וְהִנֵּה עֹמֵד עַל־הַיְאֹר: וְהִנֵּה מִן־הַיְאֹר עֹלֹת שֶׁבַע פָּרוֹת יְפוֹת מַרְאֶה וּבְרִיאֹת בָּשָׂר וַתִּרְעֶינָה בָּאָחוּ: וְהִנֵּה שֶׁבַע פָּרוֹת אֲחֵרוֹת עֹלוֹת אַחֲרֵיהֶן מִן־הַיְאֹר רָעוֹת מַרְאֶה וְדַקּוֹת בָּשָׂר וַתַּעֲמֹדְנָה אֵצֶל הַפָּרוֹת עַל־שְׂפַת הַיְאֹר: וַתֹּאכַלְנָה הַפָּרוֹת רָעוֹת הַמַּרְאֶה וְדַקֹּת הַבָּשָׂר אֵת שֶׁבַע הַפָּרוֹת יְפֹת הַמַּרְאֶה וְהַבְּרִיאֹת וַיִּיקַץ פַּרְעֹה: לוי: וַיִּישָׁן וַיַּחֲלֹם שֵׁנִית וְהִנֵּה | שֶׁבַע שִׁבֳּלִים עֹלוֹת בְּקָנֶה אֶחָד בְּרִיאוֹת וְטֹבוֹת: וְהִנֵּה שֶׁבַע שִׁבֳּלִים דַּקּוֹת וּשְׁדוּפֹת קָדִים צֹמְחוֹת אַחֲרֵיהֶן: וַתִּבְלַעְנָה הַשִּׁבֳּלִים הַדַּקּוֹת אֵת שֶׁבַע הַשִּׁבֳּלִים הַבְּרִיאוֹת וְהַמְּלֵאוֹת וַיִּיקַץ פַּרְעֹה וְהִנֵּה חֲלוֹם: ישראל: וַיְהִי בַבֹּקֶר וַתִּפָּעֶם רוּחוֹ וַיִּשְׁלַח וַיִּקְרָא אֶת־כָּל־חַרְטֻמֵּי מִצְרַיִם וְאֶת־כָּל־חֲכָמֶיהָ וַיְסַפֵּר פַּרְעֹה לָהֶם אֶת־חֲלֹמוֹ וְאֵין־פּוֹתֵר אוֹתָם לְפַרְעֹה: וַיְדַבֵּר שַׂר

◈ פ׳ ויחי / VAYECHI ◈
(Genesis 47:28 – 48:9)

כהן: וַיְחִ֤י יַעֲקֹב֙ בְּאֶ֣רֶץ מִצְרַ֔יִם שְׁבַ֥ע עֶשְׂרֵ֖ה שָׁנָ֑ה וַיְהִ֤י יְמֵי־יַעֲקֹב֙ שְׁנֵ֣י חַיָּ֔יו שֶׁ֣בַע שָׁנִ֔ים וְאַרְבָּעִ֥ים וּמְאַ֖ת שָׁנָֽה: וַיִּקְרְב֣וּ יְמֵֽי־יִשְׂרָאֵל֮ לָמוּת֒ וַיִּקְרָ֣א ׀ לִבְנ֣וֹ לְיוֹסֵ֗ף וַיֹּ֤אמֶר לוֹ֙ אִם־נָ֨א מָצָ֤אתִי חֵן֙ בְּעֵינֶ֔יךָ שִֽׂים־נָ֥א יָדְךָ֖ תַּ֣חַת יְרֵכִ֑י וְעָשִׂ֤יתָ עִמָּדִי֙ חֶ֣סֶד וֶאֱמֶ֔ת אַל־נָ֥א תִקְבְּרֵ֖נִי בְּמִצְרָֽיִם: וְשָֽׁכַבְתִּי֙ עִם־אֲבֹתַ֔י וּנְשָׂאתַ֨נִי֙ מִמִּצְרַ֔יִם וּקְבַרְתַּ֖נִי בִּקְבֻֽרָתָ֑ם וַיֹּאמַ֕ר אָנֹכִ֖י אֶעֱשֶׂ֥ה כִדְבָרֶֽךָ: וַיֹּ֗אמֶר הִשָּֽׁבְעָה֙ לִ֔י וַיִּשָּׁבַ֖ע ל֑וֹ וַיִּשְׁתַּ֥חוּ יִשְׂרָאֵ֖ל עַל־רֹ֥אשׁ הַמִּטָּֽה:

לוי: וַיְהִ֗י אַחֲרֵי֙ הַדְּבָרִ֣ים הָאֵ֔לֶּה וַיֹּ֣אמֶר לְיוֹסֵ֔ף הִנֵּ֥ה אָבִ֖יךָ חֹלֶ֑ה וַיִּקַּ֞ח אֶת־שְׁנֵ֤י בָנָיו֙ עִמּ֔וֹ אֶת־מְנַשֶּׁ֖ה וְאֶת־אֶפְרָֽיִם: וַיַּגֵּ֣ד לְיַעֲקֹ֔ב וַיֹּ֕אמֶר הִנֵּ֛ה בִּנְךָ֥ יוֹסֵ֖ף בָּ֣א אֵלֶ֑יךָ וַיִּתְחַזֵּק֙ יִשְׂרָאֵ֔ל וַיֵּ֖שֶׁב עַל־הַמִּטָּֽה: וַיֹּ֤אמֶר יַעֲקֹב֙ אֶל־יוֹסֵ֔ף אֵ֥ל שַׁדַּ֛י נִרְאָֽה־אֵלַ֥י בְּל֖וּז בְּאֶ֣רֶץ כְּנָ֑עַן וַיְבָ֖רֶךְ אֹתִֽי:

ישראל: וַיֹּ֣אמֶר אֵלַ֗י הִנְנִ֤י מַפְרְךָ֙ וְהִרְבִּיתִ֔ךָ וּנְתַתִּ֖יךָ לִקְהַ֣ל עַמִּ֑ים וְנָ֨תַתִּ֜י אֶת־הָאָ֧רֶץ הַזֹּ֛את לְזַרְעֲךָ֥ אַחֲרֶ֖יךָ אֲחֻזַּ֥ת עוֹלָֽם: וְעַתָּ֡ה שְׁנֵֽי־בָנֶיךָ֩ הַנּוֹלָדִ֨ים לְךָ֜ בְּאֶ֣רֶץ מִצְרַ֗יִם עַד־בֹּאִ֥י אֵלֶ֛יךָ מִצְרַ֖יְמָה לִי־הֵ֑ם אֶפְרַ֨יִם֙ וּמְנַשֶּׁ֔ה כִּרְאוּבֵ֥ן וְשִׁמְע֖וֹן יִֽהְיוּ־לִֽי: וּמוֹלַדְתְּךָ֛ אֲשֶׁר־הוֹלַ֥דְתָּ אַחֲרֵיהֶ֖ם לְךָ֣ יִהְי֑וּ עַ֣ל שֵׁ֧ם אֲחֵיהֶ֛ם יִקָּרְא֖וּ בְּנַחֲלָתָֽם: וַאֲנִ֣י ׀ בְּבֹאִ֣י מִפַּדָּ֗ן מֵ֩תָה֩ עָלַ֨י רָחֵ֜ל בְּאֶ֤רֶץ כְּנַ֨עַן֙ בַּדֶּ֔רֶךְ בְּע֥וֹד כִּבְרַת־אֶ֖רֶץ לָבֹ֣א אֶפְרָ֑תָה וָאֶקְבְּרֶ֤הָ שָּׁם֙ בְּדֶ֣רֶךְ אֶפְרָ֔ת הִ֖וא בֵּ֥ית לָֽחֶם: וַיַּ֥רְא יִשְׂרָאֵ֖ל אֶת־בְּנֵ֣י יוֹסֵ֑ף וַיֹּ֖אמֶר מִי־אֵֽלֶּה: וַיֹּ֤אמֶר יוֹסֵף֙ אֶל־אָבִ֔יו בָּנַ֣י הֵ֔ם אֲשֶׁר־נָֽתַן־לִ֥י אֱלֹהִ֖ים בָּזֶ֑ה וַיֹּאמַ֕ר קָֽחֶם־נָ֥א אֵלַ֖י וַאֲבָרֲכֵֽם:

◈ פ׳ שמות / SHEMOS ◈
(Exodus 1:1-17)

כהן: וְאֵ֗לֶּה שְׁמוֹת֙ בְּנֵ֣י יִשְׂרָאֵ֔ל הַבָּאִ֖ים מִצְרָ֑יְמָה אֵ֣ת יַעֲקֹ֔ב אִ֥ישׁ וּבֵית֖וֹ בָּֽאוּ: רְאוּבֵ֣ן שִׁמְע֔וֹן לֵוִ֖י וִיהוּדָֽה: יִשָּׂשכָ֥ר זְבוּלֻ֖ן וּבִנְיָמִֽן: דָּ֥ן וְנַפְתָּלִ֖י גָּ֥ד וְאָשֵֽׁר: וַֽיְהִ֗י כָּל־נֶ֛פֶשׁ יֹצְאֵ֥י

הַמַּשְׁקִ֣ים אֶת־פַּרְעֹ֑ה לֵאמֹ֕ר אֶת־חֲטָאַ֕י אֲנִ֖י מַזְכִּ֥יר הַיּֽוֹם: פַּרְעֹ֖ה קָצַ֣ף עַל־עֲבָדָ֑יו וַיִּתֵּ֨ן אֹתִ֜י בְּמִשְׁמַ֗ר בֵּ֚ית שַׂ֣ר הַטַּבָּחִ֔ים אֹתִ֕י וְאֵ֖ת שַׂ֥ר הָאֹפִֽים: וַנַּֽחַלְמָ֥ה חֲל֛וֹם בְּלַ֥יְלָה אֶחָ֖ד אֲנִ֣י וָה֑וּא אִ֛ישׁ כְּפִתְר֥וֹן חֲלֹמ֖וֹ חָלָֽמְנוּ: וְשָׁ֨ם אִתָּ֜נוּ נַ֣עַר עִבְרִ֗י עֶ֚בֶד לְשַׂ֣ר הַטַּבָּחִ֔ים וַנְּ֨סַפֶּר־ל֔וֹ וַיִּפְתָּר־לָ֖נוּ אֶת־חֲלֹמֹתֵ֑ינוּ אִ֥ישׁ כַּחֲלֹמ֖וֹ פָּתָֽר: וַיְהִ֛י כַּאֲשֶׁ֥ר פָּֽתַר־לָ֖נוּ כֵּ֣ן הָיָ֑ה אֹתִ֛י הֵשִׁ֥יב עַל־כַּנִּ֖י וְאֹת֥וֹ תָלָֽה: וַיִּשְׁלַ֤ח פַּרְעֹה֙ וַיִּקְרָ֣א אֶת־יוֹסֵ֔ף וַיְרִיצֻ֖הוּ מִן־הַבּ֑וֹר וַיְגַלַּח֙ וַיְחַלֵּ֣ף שִׂמְלֹתָ֔יו וַיָּבֹ֖א אֶל־פַּרְעֹֽה:

◈ פ׳ ויגש / VAYIGASH ◈
(Genesis 44:18-30)

כהן: וַיִּגַּ֨שׁ אֵלָ֜יו יְהוּדָ֗ה וַיֹּאמֶר֮ בִּ֣י אֲדֹנִי֒ יְדַבֶּר־נָ֨א עַבְדְּךָ֤ דָבָר֙ בְּאָזְנֵ֣י אֲדֹנִ֔י וְאַל־יִ֥חַר אַפְּךָ֖ בְּעַבְדֶּ֑ךָ כִּ֥י כָמ֖וֹךָ כְּפַרְעֹֽה: אֲדֹנִ֣י שָׁאַ֔ל אֶת־עֲבָדָ֖יו לֵאמֹ֑ר הֲיֵשׁ־לָכֶ֥ם אָ֖ב אוֹ־אָֽח: וַנֹּ֨אמֶר֙ אֶל־אֲדֹנִ֔י יֶשׁ־לָ֨נוּ֙ אָ֣ב זָקֵ֔ן וְיֶ֥לֶד זְקֻנִ֖ים קָטָ֑ן וְאָחִ֣יו מֵ֔ת וַיִּוָּתֵ֨ר ה֧וּא לְבַדּ֛וֹ לְאִמּ֖וֹ וְאָבִ֥יו אֲהֵבֽוֹ:

לוי: וַתֹּ֨אמֶר֙ אֶל־עֲבָדֶ֔יךָ הֽוֹרִדֻ֖הוּ אֵלָ֑י וְאָשִׂ֥ימָה עֵינִ֖י עָלָֽיו: וַנֹּ֨אמֶר֙ אֶל־אֲדֹנִ֔י לֹא־יוּכַ֥ל הַנַּ֖עַר לַעֲזֹ֣ב אֶת־אָבִ֑יו וְעָזַ֥ב אֶת־אָבִ֖יו וָמֵֽת: וַתֹּ֨אמֶר֙ אֶל־עֲבָדֶ֔יךָ אִם־לֹ֥א יֵרֵ֛ד אֲחִיכֶ֥ם הַקָּטֹ֖ן אִתְּכֶ֑ם לֹ֥א תֹסִפ֖וּן לִרְא֥וֹת פָּנָֽי: וַיְהִי֙ כִּ֣י עָלִ֔ינוּ אֶֽל־עַבְדְּךָ֖ אָבִ֑י וַנַּ֨גֶּד־ל֔וֹ אֵ֖ת דִּבְרֵ֥י אֲדֹנִֽי:

ישראל: וַיֹּ֖אמֶר אָבִ֑ינוּ שֻׁ֖בוּ שִׁבְרוּ־לָ֥נוּ מְעַט־אֹֽכֶל: וַנֹּ֕אמֶר לֹ֥א נוּכַ֖ל לָרֶ֑דֶת אִם־יֵשׁ֩ אָחִ֨ינוּ הַקָּטֹ֤ן אִתָּ֨נוּ֙ וְיָרַ֔דְנוּ כִּי־לֹ֣א נוּכַ֗ל לִרְאוֹת֙ פְּנֵ֣י הָאִ֔ישׁ וְאָחִ֥ינוּ הַקָּטֹ֖ן אֵינֶ֥נּוּ אִתָּֽנוּ: וַיֹּ֛אמֶר עַבְדְּךָ֥ אָבִ֖י אֵלֵ֑ינוּ אַתֶּ֣ם יְדַעְתֶּ֔ם כִּ֥י שְׁנַ֖יִם יָֽלְדָה־לִּ֥י אִשְׁתִּֽי: וַיֵּצֵ֤א הָֽאֶחָד֙ מֵֽאִתִּ֔י וָאֹמַ֕ר אַ֖ךְ טָרֹ֣ף טֹרָ֑ף וְלֹ֥א רְאִיתִ֖יו עַד־הֵֽנָּה: וּלְקַחְתֶּ֧ם גַּם־אֶת־זֶ֛ה מֵעִ֥ם פָּנַ֖י וְקָרָ֑הוּ אָס֕וֹן וְהוֹרַדְתֶּ֧ם אֶת־שֵׂיבָתִ֛י בְּרָעָ֖ה שְׁאֹֽלָה: וְעַתָּ֗ה כְּבֹאִי֙ אֶל־עַבְדְּךָ֣ אָבִ֔י וְהַנַּ֖עַר אֵינֶ֣נּוּ אִתָּ֑נוּ וְנַפְשׁ֖וֹ קְשׁוּרָ֥ה בְנַפְשֽׁוֹ:

פ׳ וארא / VAEIRA
(Exodus 6:2-13)

כהן וַיְדַבֵּ֥ר אֱלֹהִ֖ים אֶל־מֹשֶׁ֑ה וַיֹּ֥אמֶר אֵלָ֖יו אֲנִ֥י יהוֹה: וָאֵרָ֗א אֶל־אַבְרָהָ֛ם אֶל־יִצְחָ֥ק וְאֶֽל־יַעֲקֹ֖ב בְּאֵ֣ל שַׁדָּ֑י וּשְׁמִ֣י יהוֹ֔ה לֹ֥א נוֹדַ֖עְתִּי לָהֶֽם: וְגַ֨ם הֲקִמֹ֤תִי אֶת־בְּרִיתִי֙ אִתָּ֔ם לָתֵ֥ת לָהֶ֖ם אֶת־אֶ֣רֶץ כְּנָ֑עַן אֵ֛ת אֶ֥רֶץ מְגֻרֵיהֶ֖ם אֲשֶׁר־גָּ֥רוּ בָֽהּ: וְגַ֣ם ׀ אֲנִ֣י שָׁמַ֗עְתִּי אֶֽת־נַאֲקַת֙ בְּנֵ֣י יִשְׂרָאֵ֔ל אֲשֶׁ֥ר מִצְרַ֖יִם מַעֲבִדִ֣ים אֹתָ֑ם וָאֶזְכֹּ֖ר אֶת־בְּרִיתִֽי:

לוי לָכֵ֞ן אֱמֹ֥ר לִבְנֵֽי־יִשְׂרָאֵל֮ אֲנִ֣י יהוֹה֒ וְהוֹצֵאתִ֣י אֶתְכֶ֗ם מִתַּ֙חַת֙ סִבְלֹ֣ת מִצְרַ֔יִם וְהִצַּלְתִּ֥י אֶתְכֶ֖ם מֵעֲבֹדָתָ֑ם וְגָאַלְתִּ֤י אֶתְכֶם֙ בִּזְר֣וֹעַ נְטוּיָ֔ה וּבִשְׁפָטִ֖ים גְּדֹלִֽים: וְלָקַחְתִּ֨י אֶתְכֶ֥ם לִי֙ לְעָ֔ם וְהָיִ֥יתִי לָכֶ֖ם לֵֽאלֹהִ֑ים וִֽידַעְתֶּ֗ם כִּ֣י אֲנִ֤י יהוֹה֙ אֱלֹ֣הֵיכֶ֔ם הַמּוֹצִ֣יא אֶתְכֶ֔ם מִתַּ֖חַת סִבְל֥וֹת מִצְרָֽיִם: וְהֵבֵאתִ֣י אֶתְכֶ֗ם אֶל־הָאָ֙רֶץ֙ אֲשֶׁ֤ר נָשָׂ֙אתִי֙ אֶת־יָדִ֔י לָתֵ֣ת אֹתָ֔הּ לְאַבְרָהָ֥ם לְיִצְחָ֖ק וּֽלְיַעֲקֹ֑ב וְנָתַתִּ֨י אֹתָ֥הּ לָכֶ֛ם מוֹרָשָׁ֖ה אֲנִ֥י יהוֹֽה: וַיְדַבֵּ֥ר מֹשֶׁ֛ה כֵּ֖ן אֶל־בְּנֵ֣י יִשְׂרָאֵ֑ל וְלֹ֤א שָֽׁמְעוּ֙ אֶל־מֹשֶׁ֔ה מִקֹּ֣צֶר ר֔וּחַ וּמֵעֲבֹדָ֖ה קָשָֽׁה:

ישראל וַיְדַבֵּ֥ר יהוֹ֖ה אֶל־מֹשֶׁ֥ה לֵּאמֹֽר: בֹּ֣א דַבֵּ֔ר אֶל־פַּרְעֹ֖ה מֶ֣לֶךְ מִצְרָ֑יִם וִֽישַׁלַּ֥ח אֶת־בְּנֵֽי־יִשְׂרָאֵ֖ל מֵאַרְצֽוֹ: וַיְדַבֵּ֣ר מֹשֶׁ֔ה לִפְנֵ֥י יהוֹ֖ה לֵאמֹ֑ר הֵ֤ן בְּנֵֽי־יִשְׂרָאֵל֙ לֹֽא־שָׁמְע֣וּ אֵלַ֔י וְאֵיךְ֙ יִשְׁמָעֵ֣נִי פַרְעֹ֔ה וַאֲנִ֖י עֲרַ֥ל שְׂפָתָֽיִם: וַיְדַבֵּ֤ר יהוֹה֙ אֶל־מֹשֶׁ֣ה וְאֶֽל־אַהֲרֹ֔ן וַיְצַוֵּם֙ אֶל־בְּנֵ֣י יִשְׂרָאֵ֔ל וְאֶל־פַּרְעֹ֖ה מֶ֣לֶךְ מִצְרָ֑יִם לְהוֹצִ֥יא אֶת־בְּנֵֽי־יִשְׂרָאֵ֖ל מֵאֶ֥רֶץ מִצְרָֽיִם:

פ׳ בא / BO
(Exodus 10:1-11)

כהן וַיֹּ֤אמֶר יהוֹה֙ אֶל־מֹשֶׁ֔ה בֹּ֖א אֶל־פַּרְעֹ֑ה כִּֽי־אֲנִ֞י הִכְבַּ֤דְתִּי אֶת־לִבּוֹ֙ וְאֶת־לֵ֣ב עֲבָדָ֔יו לְמַ֗עַן שִׁתִ֛י אֹתֹתַ֥י אֵ֖לֶּה בְּקִרְבּֽוֹ: וּלְמַ֡עַן תְּסַפֵּר֩ בְּאָזְנֵ֨י בִנְךָ֜ וּבֶן־בִּנְךָ֗ אֵ֣ת אֲשֶׁ֤ר הִתְעַלַּ֙לְתִּי֙ בְּמִצְרַ֔יִם וְאֶת־אֹתֹתַ֖י אֲשֶׁר־שַׂ֣מְתִּי בָ֑ם וִֽידַעְתֶּ֖ם כִּי־אֲנִ֥י יהוֹֽה: וַיָּבֹ֨א מֹשֶׁ֤ה וְאַהֲרֹן֙ אֶל־פַּרְעֹ֔ה וַיֹּאמְר֣וּ אֵלָ֗יו כֹּֽה־אָמַ֤ר יהוֹה֙ אֱלֹהֵ֣י הָֽעִבְרִ֔ים עַד־מָתַ֣י מֵאַ֔נְתָּ לֵעָנֹ֖ת מִפָּנָ֑י שַׁלַּ֥ח עַמִּ֖י וְיַֽעַבְדֻֽנִי:

לוי כִּ֛י אִם־מָאֵ֥ן אַתָּ֖ה לְשַׁלֵּ֣חַ אֶת־עַמִּ֑י הִנְנִ֨י מֵבִ֥יא מָחָ֛ר אַרְבֶּ֖ה בִּגְבֻלֶֽךָ: וְכִסָּה֙ אֶת־עֵ֣ין הָאָ֔רֶץ וְלֹ֥א יוּכַ֖ל לִרְאֹ֣ת אֶת־הָאָ֑רֶץ וְאָכַ֣ל ׀ אֶת־יֶ֣תֶר הַפְּלֵטָ֗ה הַנִּשְׁאֶ֤רֶת לָכֶם֙ מִן־הַבָּרָ֔ד וְאָכַל֙ אֶת־כָּל־הָעֵ֔ץ הַצֹּמֵ֥חַ לָכֶ֖ם מִן־הַשָּׂדֶֽה: וּמָלְא֨וּ בָתֶּ֜יךָ וּבָתֵּ֣י כָל־עֲבָדֶיךָ֮ וּבָתֵּ֣י כָל־מִצְרַיִם֒ אֲשֶׁ֨ר לֹֽא־רָא֤וּ אֲבֹתֶ֙יךָ֙ וַאֲב֣וֹת אֲבֹתֶ֔יךָ מִיּ֗וֹם הֱיוֹתָם֙ עַל־הָ֣אֲדָמָ֔ה עַ֖ד הַיּ֣וֹם הַזֶּ֑ה וַיִּ֥פֶן וַיֵּצֵ֖א מֵעִ֥ם פַּרְעֹֽה:

ישראל וַיֹּאמְרוּ֩ עַבְדֵ֨י פַרְעֹ֜ה אֵלָ֗יו עַד־מָתַי֙ יִהְיֶ֨ה זֶ֥ה לָ֙נוּ֙ לְמוֹקֵ֔שׁ שַׁלַּח֙ אֶת־הָ֣אֲנָשִׁ֔ים

וַיַּֽעַבְד֥וּ אֶת־יְהֹוָ֖ה אֱלֹֽהֵיהֶ֑ם הֲטֶ֣רֶם תֵּדַ֔ע כִּ֥י אָבְדָ֖ה מִצְרָֽיִם: וַיּוּשַׁ֞ב אֶת־מֹשֶׁ֤ה וְאֶֽת־אַהֲרֹן֙ אֶל־פַּרְעֹ֔ה וַיֹּ֥אמֶר אֲלֵהֶ֖ם לְכ֣וּ עִבְד֣וּ אֶת־יְהֹוָ֣ה אֱלֹֽהֵיכֶ֑ם מִ֥י וָמִ֖י הַהֹֽלְכִֽים: וַיֹּ֣אמֶר מֹשֶׁ֗ה בִּנְעָרֵ֤ינוּ וּבִזְקֵנֵ֙ינוּ֙ נֵלֵ֔ךְ בְּבָנֵ֥ינוּ וּבִבְנוֹתֵ֛נוּ בְּצֹאנֵ֥נוּ וּבִבְקָרֵ֖נוּ נֵלֵ֑ךְ כִּ֥י חַג־יְהֹוָ֖ה לָֽנוּ: וַיֹּ֣אמֶר אֲלֵהֶ֗ם יְהִ֨י כֵ֤ן יְהֹוָה֙ עִמָּכֶ֔ם כַּאֲשֶׁ֛ר אֲשַׁלַּ֥ח אֶתְכֶ֖ם וְאֶֽת־טַפְּכֶ֑ם רְא֕וּ כִּ֥י רָעָ֖ה נֶ֥גֶד פְּנֵיכֶֽם: לֹ֣א כֵ֗ן לְכֽוּ־נָ֤א הַגְּבָרִים֙ וְעִבְד֣וּ אֶת־יְהֹוָ֔ה כִּ֥י אֹתָ֖הּ אַתֶּ֣ם מְבַקְשִׁ֑ים וַיְגָ֣רֶשׁ אֹתָ֔ם מֵאֵ֖ת פְּנֵ֥י פַרְעֹֽה:

◈ פ׳ בשלח / BESHALACH

(Exodus 13:17 — 14:8)

כהן: וַיְהִ֗י בְּשַׁלַּ֣ח פַּרְעֹה֮ אֶת־הָעָם֒ וְלֹא־נָחָ֣ם אֱלֹהִ֗ים דֶּ֚רֶךְ אֶ֣רֶץ פְּלִשְׁתִּ֔ים כִּ֥י קָר֖וֹב ה֑וּא כִּ֣י ׀ אָמַ֣ר אֱלֹהִ֗ים פֶּן־יִנָּחֵ֥ם הָעָ֛ם בִּרְאֹתָ֥ם מִלְחָמָ֖ה וְשָׁ֥בוּ מִצְרָֽיְמָה: וַיַּסֵּ֨ב אֱלֹהִ֧ים ׀ אֶת־הָעָ֛ם דֶּ֥רֶךְ הַמִּדְבָּ֖ר יַם־ס֑וּף וַחֲמֻשִׁ֛ים עָל֥וּ בְנֵֽי־יִשְׂרָאֵ֖ל מֵאֶ֥רֶץ מִצְרָֽיִם: וַיִּקַּ֥ח מֹשֶׁ֛ה אֶת־עַצְמ֥וֹת יוֹסֵ֖ף עִמּ֑וֹ כִּי֩ הַשְׁבֵּ֨עַ הִשְׁבִּ֜יעַ אֶת־בְּנֵ֤י יִשְׂרָאֵל֙ לֵאמֹ֔ר פָּקֹ֨ד יִפְקֹ֤ד אֱלֹהִים֙ אֶתְכֶ֔ם וְהַעֲלִיתֶ֧ם אֶת־עַצְמֹתַ֛י מִזֶּ֖ה אִתְּכֶֽם: וַיִּסְע֖וּ מִסֻּכֹּ֑ת וַיַּחֲנ֣וּ בְאֵתָ֔ם בִּקְצֵ֖ה הַמִּדְבָּֽר: וַֽיהֹוָ֡ה הֹלֵךְ֩ לִפְנֵיהֶ֨ם יוֹמָ֜ם בְּעַמּ֤וּד עָנָן֙ לַנְחֹתָ֣ם הַדֶּ֔רֶךְ וְלַ֛יְלָה בְּעַמּ֥וּד אֵ֖שׁ לְהָאִ֣יר לָהֶ֑ם לָלֶ֖כֶת יוֹמָ֥ם וָלָֽיְלָה: לֹֽא־יָמִ֞ישׁ עַמּ֤וּד הֶֽעָנָן֙ יוֹמָ֔ם וְעַמּ֥וּד הָאֵ֖שׁ לָ֑יְלָה לִפְנֵ֖י הָעָֽם: לוי: וַיְדַבֵּ֥ר יְהֹוָ֖ה אֶל־מֹשֶׁ֥ה לֵּאמֹֽר: דַּבֵּר֘ אֶל־בְּנֵ֣י יִשְׂרָאֵל֒ וְיָשֻׁ֗בוּ וְיַחֲנוּ֙ לִפְנֵי֙ פִּ֣י הַֽחִירֹ֔ת בֵּ֥ין מִגְדֹּ֖ל וּבֵ֣ין הַיָּ֑ם לִפְנֵי֙ בַּ֣עַל צְפֹ֔ן נִכְח֥וֹ תַחֲנ֖וּ עַל־הַיָּֽם: וְאָמַ֤ר פַּרְעֹה֙ לִבְנֵ֣י יִשְׂרָאֵ֔ל נְבֻכִ֥ים הֵ֖ם בָּאָ֑רֶץ סָגַ֥ר עֲלֵיהֶ֖ם הַמִּדְבָּֽר: וְחִזַּקְתִּ֣י אֶת־לֵב־פַּרְעֹה֮ וְרָדַ֣ף אַחֲרֵיהֶם֒ וְאִכָּבְדָ֤ה בְּפַרְעֹה֙ וּבְכָל־חֵיל֔וֹ וְיָדְע֥וּ מִצְרַ֖יִם כִּֽי־אֲנִ֣י יְהֹוָ֑ה וַיַּֽעֲשׂוּ־כֵֽן: ישראל: וַיֻּגַּד֙ לְמֶ֣לֶךְ מִצְרַ֔יִם כִּ֥י בָרַ֖ח הָעָ֑ם וַ֠יֵּהָפֵ֠ךְ לְבַ֨ב פַּרְעֹ֤ה וַעֲבָדָיו֙ אֶל־הָעָ֔ם וַיֹּֽאמְרוּ֙ מַה־זֹּ֣את עָשִׂ֔ינוּ כִּֽי־שִׁלַּ֥חְנוּ אֶת־יִשְׂרָאֵ֖ל מֵעָבְדֵֽנוּ: וַיֶּאְסֹ֖ר אֶת־רִכְבּ֑וֹ וְאֶת־

עַמּ֖וֹ לָקַ֥ח עִמּֽוֹ: וַיִּקַּ֗ח שֵׁשׁ־מֵא֥וֹת רֶ֙כֶב֙ בָּח֔וּר וְכֹ֖ל רֶ֣כֶב מִצְרָ֑יִם וְשָׁלִשִׁ֖ם עַל־כֻּלּֽוֹ: וַיְחַזֵּ֣ק יְהֹוָ֗ה אֶת־לֵ֤ב פַּרְעֹה֙ מֶ֣לֶךְ מִצְרַ֔יִם וַיִּרְדֹּ֕ף אַחֲרֵ֖י בְּנֵ֣י יִשְׂרָאֵ֑ל וּבְנֵ֣י יִשְׂרָאֵ֔ל יֹצְאִ֖ים בְּיָ֥ד רָמָֽה:

◈ פ׳ יתרו / YISRO

(Exodus 18:1-12)

כהן: וַיִּשְׁמַ֞ע יִתְר֨וֹ כֹהֵ֤ן מִדְיָן֙ חֹתֵ֣ן מֹשֶׁ֔ה אֵת֩ כָּל־אֲשֶׁ֨ר עָשָׂ֤ה אֱלֹהִים֙ לְמֹשֶׁ֔ה וּלְיִשְׂרָאֵ֖ל עַמּ֑וֹ כִּֽי־הוֹצִ֧יא יְהֹוָ֛ה אֶת־יִשְׂרָאֵ֖ל מִמִּצְרָֽיִם: וַיִּקַּ֗ח יִתְרוֹ֙ חֹתֵ֣ן מֹשֶׁ֔ה אֶת־צִפֹּרָ֖ה אֵ֣שֶׁת מֹשֶׁ֑ה אַחַ֖ר שִׁלּוּחֶֽיהָ: וְאֵ֖ת שְׁנֵ֣י בָנֶ֑יהָ אֲשֶׁ֨ר שֵׁ֤ם הָֽאֶחָד֙ גֵּֽרְשֹׁ֔ם כִּ֣י אָמַ֔ר גֵּ֣ר הָיִ֔יתִי בְּאֶ֖רֶץ נָכְרִיָּֽה: וְשֵׁ֥ם הָאֶחָ֖ד אֱלִיעֶ֑זֶר כִּֽי־אֱלֹהֵ֤י אָבִי֙ בְּעֶזְרִ֔י וַיַּצִּלֵ֖נִי מֵחֶ֥רֶב פַּרְעֹֽה: לוי: וַיָּבֹ֞א יִתְר֨וֹ חֹתֵ֥ן מֹשֶׁ֛ה וּבָנָ֥יו וְאִשְׁתּ֖וֹ אֶל־מֹשֶׁ֑ה אֶל־הַמִּדְבָּ֗ר אֲשֶׁר־ה֛וּא חֹנֶ֥ה שָׁ֖ם הַ֥ר הָאֱלֹהִֽים: וַיֹּ֙אמֶר֙ אֶל־מֹשֶׁ֔ה אֲנִ֛י חֹתֶנְךָ֥ יִתְר֖וֹ בָּ֣א אֵלֶ֑יךָ וְאִ֨שְׁתְּךָ֔ וּשְׁנֵ֥י בָנֶ֖יהָ עִמָּֽהּ: וַיֵּצֵ֨א מֹשֶׁ֜ה לִקְרַ֣את חֹֽתְנ֗וֹ וַיִּשְׁתַּ֙חוּ֙ וַיִּשַּׁק־ל֔וֹ וַיִּשְׁאֲל֥וּ אִישׁ־לְרֵעֵ֖הוּ לְשָׁל֑וֹם וַיָּבֹ֖אוּ הָאֹֽהֱלָה: וַיְסַפֵּ֤ר מֹשֶׁה֙ לְחֹ֣תְנ֔וֹ אֵת֩ כָּל־אֲשֶׁ֨ר עָשָׂ֤ה יְהֹוָה֙ לְפַרְעֹ֣ה וּלְמִצְרַ֔יִם עַ֖ל אוֹדֹ֣ת יִשְׂרָאֵ֑ל אֵ֤ת כָּל־הַתְּלָאָה֙ אֲשֶׁ֣ר מְצָאָ֣תַם בַּדֶּ֔רֶךְ וַיַּצִּלֵ֖ם יְהֹוָֽה: ישראל: וַיִּ֣חַדְּ יִתְר֔וֹ עַ֚ל כָּל־הַטּוֹבָ֔ה אֲשֶׁר־עָשָׂ֥ה יְהֹוָ֖ה לְיִשְׂרָאֵ֑ל אֲשֶׁ֥ר הִצִּיל֖וֹ מִיַּ֥ד מִצְרָֽיִם: וַיֹּ֘אמֶר֘ יִתְרוֹ֒ בָּר֣וּךְ יְהֹוָ֔ה אֲשֶׁ֨ר הִצִּ֤יל אֶתְכֶם֙ מִיַּ֣ד מִצְרַ֔יִם וּמִיַּ֖ד פַּרְעֹ֑ה אֲשֶׁ֤ר הִצִּיל֙ אֶת־הָעָ֔ם מִתַּ֖חַת יַד־מִצְרָֽיִם: עַתָּ֣ה יָדַ֔עְתִּי כִּֽי־גָד֥וֹל יְהֹוָ֖ה מִכָּל־הָאֱלֹהִ֑ים כִּ֣י בַדָּבָ֔ר אֲשֶׁ֥ר זָד֖וּ עֲלֵיהֶֽם: וַיִּקַּ֞ח יִתְר֨וֹ חֹתֵ֥ן מֹשֶׁ֛ה עֹלָ֥ה וּזְבָחִ֖ים לֵֽאלֹהִ֑ים וַיָּבֹ֨א אַהֲרֹ֜ן וְכֹ֣ל ׀ זִקְנֵ֣י יִשְׂרָאֵ֗ל לֶאֱכָל־לֶ֛חֶם עִם־חֹתֵ֥ן מֹשֶׁ֖ה לִפְנֵ֥י הָאֱלֹהִֽים:

◈ פ׳ משפטים / MISHPATIM

(Exodus 21:1-19)

כהן: וְאֵ֙לֶּה֙ הַמִּשְׁפָּטִ֔ים אֲשֶׁ֥ר תָּשִׂ֖ים לִפְנֵיהֶֽם: כִּ֤י תִקְנֶה֙ עֶ֣בֶד עִבְרִ֔י שֵׁ֥שׁ שָׁנִ֖ים יַעֲבֹ֑ד וְאֶת־

וּבַשְּׁבִעִת יֵצֵא לַחָפְשִׁי חִנָּם: אִם־בְּגַפּוֹ יָבֹא בְּגַפּוֹ יֵצֵא אִם־בַּעַל אִשָּׁה הוּא וְיָצְאָה אִשְׁתּוֹ עִמּוֹ: אִם־אֲדֹנָיו יִתֶּן־לוֹ אִשָּׁה וְיָלְדָה־לּוֹ בָנִים אוֹ בָנוֹת הָאִשָּׁה וִילָדֶיהָ תִּהְיֶה לַאדֹנֶיהָ וְהוּא יֵצֵא בְגַפּוֹ: וְאִם־אָמֹר יֹאמַר הָעֶבֶד אָהַבְתִּי אֶת־אֲדֹנִי אֶת־אִשְׁתִּי וְאֶת־בָּנָי לֹא אֵצֵא חָפְשִׁי: וְהִגִּישׁוֹ אֲדֹנָיו אֶל־הָאֱלֹהִים וְהִגִּישׁוֹ אֶל־הַדֶּלֶת אוֹ אֶל־הַמְּזוּזָה וְרָצַע אֲדֹנָיו אֶת־אָזְנוֹ בַּמַּרְצֵעַ וַעֲבָדוֹ לְעֹלָם:

לוי: וְכִי־יִמְכֹּר אִישׁ אֶת־בִּתּוֹ לְאָמָה לֹא תֵצֵא כְּצֵאת הָעֲבָדִים: אִם־רָעָה בְּעֵינֵי אֲדֹנֶיהָ אֲשֶׁר־לא יְעָדָהּ וְהֶפְדָּהּ לְעַם נָכְרִי לֹא־יִמְשֹׁל לְמָכְרָהּ בְּבִגְדוֹ־בָהּ: וְאִם־לִבְנוֹ יִיעָדֶנָּה כְּמִשְׁפַּט הַבָּנוֹת יַעֲשֶׂה־לָּהּ: אִם־אַחֶרֶת יִקַּח־לוֹ שְׁאֵרָהּ כְּסוּתָהּ וְעֹנָתָהּ לֹא יִגְרָע: וְאִם־שְׁלָשׁ־אֵלֶּה לֹא יַעֲשֶׂה לָהּ וְיָצְאָה חִנָּם אֵין כָּסֶף:

ישראל: מַכֵּה אִישׁ וָמֵת מוֹת יוּמָת: וַאֲשֶׁר לֹא צָדָה וְהָאֱלֹהִים אִנָּה לְיָדוֹ וְשַׂמְתִּי לְךָ מָקוֹם אֲשֶׁר יָנוּס שָׁמָּה: וְכִי־יָזִד אִישׁ עַל־רֵעֵהוּ לְהָרְגוֹ בְעָרְמָה מֵעִם מִזְבְּחִי תִּקָּחֶנּוּ לָמוּת: וּמַכֵּה אָבִיו וְאִמּוֹ מוֹת יוּמָת: וְגֹנֵב אִישׁ וּמְכָרוֹ וְנִמְצָא בְיָדוֹ מוֹת יוּמָת: וּמְקַלֵּל אָבִיו וְאִמּוֹ מוֹת יוּמָת: וְכִי־יְרִיבֻן אֲנָשִׁים וְהִכָּה־אִישׁ אֶת־רֵעֵהוּ בְּאֶבֶן אוֹ בְאֶגְרֹף וְלֹא יָמוּת וְנָפַל לְמִשְׁכָּב: אִם־יָקוּם וְהִתְהַלֵּךְ בַּחוּץ עַל־מִשְׁעַנְתּוֹ וְנִקָּה הַמַּכֶּה רַק שִׁבְתּוֹ יִתֵּן וְרַפֹּא יְרַפֵּא:

פ׳ תרומה / TERUMAH

(Exodus 25:1-16)

כהן: וַיְדַבֵּר יְהוָה אֶל־מֹשֶׁה לֵּאמֹר: דַּבֵּר אֶל־בְּנֵי יִשְׂרָאֵל וְיִקְחוּ־לִי תְּרוּמָה מֵאֵת כָּל־אִישׁ אֲשֶׁר יִדְּבֶנּוּ לִבּוֹ תִּקְחוּ אֶת־תְּרוּמָתִי: וְזֹאת הַתְּרוּמָה אֲשֶׁר תִּקְחוּ מֵאִתָּם זָהָב וָכֶסֶף וּנְחֹשֶׁת: וּתְכֵלֶת וְאַרְגָּמָן וְתוֹלַעַת שָׁנִי וְשֵׁשׁ וְעִזִּים: וְעֹרֹת אֵילִם מְאָדָּמִים וְעֹרֹת תְּחָשִׁים וַעֲצֵי שִׁטִּים:

לוי: שֶׁמֶן לַמָּאֹר בְּשָׂמִים לְשֶׁמֶן הַמִּשְׁחָה וְלִקְטֹרֶת הַסַּמִּים: אַבְנֵי־שֹׁהַם וְאַבְנֵי מִלֻּאִים לָאֵפֹד וְלַחֹשֶׁן: וְעָשׂוּ לִי מִקְדָּשׁ וְשָׁכַנְתִּי בְּתוֹכָם: כְּכֹל אֲשֶׁר אֲנִי מַרְאֶה אוֹתְךָ אֵת תַּבְנִית הַמִּשְׁכָּן וְאֵת תַּבְנִית כָּל־כֵּלָיו וְכֵן תַּעֲשׂוּ:

ישראל: וְעָשׂוּ אֲרוֹן עֲצֵי שִׁטִּים אַמָּתַיִם וָחֵצִי אָרְכּוֹ וְאַמָּה וָחֵצִי רָחְבּוֹ וְאַמָּה וָחֵצִי קֹמָתוֹ: וְצִפִּיתָ אֹתוֹ זָהָב טָהוֹר מִבַּיִת וּמִחוּץ תְּצַפֶּנּוּ וְעָשִׂיתָ עָלָיו זֵר זָהָב סָבִיב: וְיָצַקְתָּ לּוֹ אַרְבַּע טַבְּעֹת זָהָב וְנָתַתָּה עַל אַרְבַּע פַּעֲמֹתָיו וּשְׁתֵּי טַבָּעֹת עַל־צַלְעוֹ הָאֶחָת וּשְׁתֵּי טַבָּעֹת עַל־צַלְעוֹ הַשֵּׁנִית: וְעָשִׂיתָ בַדֵּי עֲצֵי שִׁטִּים וְצִפִּיתָ אֹתָם זָהָב: וְהֵבֵאתָ אֶת־הַבַּדִּים בַּטַּבָּעֹת עַל צַלְעֹת הָאָרֹן לָשֵׂאת אֶת־הָאָרֹן בָּהֶם: בְּטַבְּעֹת הָאָרֹן יִהְיוּ הַבַּדִּים לֹא יָסֻרוּ מִמֶּנּוּ: וְנָתַתָּ אֶל־הָאָרֹן אֵת הָעֵדֻת אֲשֶׁר אֶתֵּן אֵלֶיךָ:

פ׳ תצוה / TETZAVEH

(Exodus 27:20—28:12)

כהן: וְאַתָּה תְּצַוֶּה | אֶת־בְּנֵי יִשְׂרָאֵל וְיִקְחוּ אֵלֶיךָ שֶׁמֶן זַיִת זָךְ כָּתִית לַמָּאוֹר לְהַעֲלֹת נֵר תָּמִיד: בְּאֹהֶל מוֹעֵד מִחוּץ לַפָּרֹכֶת אֲשֶׁר עַל־הָעֵדֻת יַעֲרֹךְ אֹתוֹ אַהֲרֹן וּבָנָיו מֵעֶרֶב עַד־בֹּקֶר לִפְנֵי יְהוָה חֻקַּת עוֹלָם לְדֹרֹתָם מֵאֵת בְּנֵי יִשְׂרָאֵל: וְאַתָּה הַקְרֵב אֵלֶיךָ אֶת־אַהֲרֹן אָחִיךָ וְאֶת־בָּנָיו אִתּוֹ מִתּוֹךְ בְּנֵי יִשְׂרָאֵל לְכַהֲנוֹ־לִי אַהֲרֹן נָדָב וַאֲבִיהוּא אֶלְעָזָר וְאִיתָמָר בְּנֵי אַהֲרֹן: וְעָשִׂיתָ בִגְדֵי־קֹדֶשׁ לְאַהֲרֹן אָחִיךָ לְכָבוֹד וּלְתִפְאָרֶת: וְאַתָּה תְּדַבֵּר אֶל־כָּל־חַכְמֵי־לֵב אֲשֶׁר מִלֵּאתִיו רוּחַ חָכְמָה וְעָשׂוּ אֶת־בִּגְדֵי אַהֲרֹן לְקַדְּשׁוֹ לְכַהֲנוֹ־לִי: וְאֵלֶּה הַבְּגָדִים אֲשֶׁר יַעֲשׂוּ חֹשֶׁן וְאֵפוֹד וּמְעִיל וּכְתֹנֶת תַּשְׁבֵּץ מִצְנֶפֶת וְאַבְנֵט וְעָשׂוּ בִגְדֵי־קֹדֶשׁ לְאַהֲרֹן אָחִיךָ וּלְבָנָיו לְכַהֲנוֹ־לִי: וְהֵם יִקְחוּ אֶת־הַזָּהָב וְאֶת־הַתְּכֵלֶת וְאֶת־הָאַרְגָּמָן וְאֶת־תּוֹלַעַת הַשָּׁנִי וְאֶת־הַשֵּׁשׁ:

לוי: וְעָשׂוּ אֶת־הָאֵפֹד זָהָב תְּכֵלֶת וְאַרְגָּמָן תּוֹלַעַת שָׁנִי וְשֵׁשׁ מָשְׁזָר מַעֲשֵׂה חֹשֵׁב: שְׁתֵּי

TORAH READING — KI SISA-VAYAKHEL

פ׳ כי תשא / KI SISA
(Exodus 30:11-21)

כה וַיְדַבֵּר יְהוָה אֶל־מֹשֶׁה לֵּאמֹר: כִּי תִשָּׂא אֶת־רֹאשׁ בְּנֵי־יִשְׂרָאֵל לִפְקֻדֵיהֶם וְנָתְנוּ אִישׁ כֹּפֶר נַפְשׁוֹ לַיהוָה בִּפְקֹד אֹתָם וְלֹא־יִהְיֶה בָהֶם נֶגֶף בִּפְקֹד אֹתָם: זֶה ׀ יִתְּנוּ כָּל־הָעֹבֵר עַל־הַפְּקֻדִים מַחֲצִית הַשֶּׁקֶל בְּשֶׁקֶל הַקֹּדֶשׁ עֶשְׂרִים גֵּרָה הַשֶּׁקֶל מַחֲצִית הַשֶּׁקֶל תְּרוּמָה לַיהוָה:

לוי כֹּל הָעֹבֵר עַל־הַפְּקֻדִים מִבֶּן עֶשְׂרִים שָׁנָה וָמָעְלָה יִתֵּן תְּרוּמַת יְהוָה: הֶעָשִׁיר לֹא־יַרְבֶּה וְהַדַּל לֹא יַמְעִיט מִמַּחֲצִית הַשָּׁקֶל לָתֵת אֶת־תְּרוּמַת יְהוָה לְכַפֵּר עַל־נַפְשֹׁתֵיכֶם: וְלָקַחְתָּ אֶת־כֶּסֶף הַכִּפֻּרִים מֵאֵת בְּנֵי יִשְׂרָאֵל וְנָתַתָּ אֹתוֹ עַל־עֲבֹדַת אֹהֶל מוֹעֵד וְהָיָה לִבְנֵי יִשְׂרָאֵל לְזִכָּרוֹן לִפְנֵי יְהוָה לְכַפֵּר עַל־נַפְשֹׁתֵיכֶם:

ישראל וַיְדַבֵּר יְהוָה אֶל־מֹשֶׁה לֵּאמֹר: וְעָשִׂיתָ כִּיּוֹר נְחֹשֶׁת וְכַנּוֹ נְחֹשֶׁת לְרָחְצָה וְנָתַתָּ אֹתוֹ בֵּין־אֹהֶל מוֹעֵד וּבֵין הַמִּזְבֵּחַ וְנָתַתָּ שָׁמָּה מָיִם: וְרָחֲצוּ אַהֲרֹן וּבָנָיו מִמֶּנּוּ אֶת־יְדֵיהֶם וְאֶת־רַגְלֵיהֶם: בְּבֹאָם אֶל־אֹהֶל מוֹעֵד יִרְחֲצוּ־מַיִם וְלֹא יָמֻתוּ אוֹ בְגִשְׁתָּם אֶל־הַמִּזְבֵּחַ לְשָׁרֵת לְהַקְטִיר אִשֶּׁה לַיהוָה: וְרָחֲצוּ יְדֵיהֶם וְרַגְלֵיהֶם וְלֹא יָמֻתוּ וְהָיְתָה לָהֶם חָק־עוֹלָם לוֹ וּלְזַרְעוֹ לְדֹרֹתָם:

פ׳ ויקהל / VAYAKHEL
(Exodus 35:1-20)

כה וַיַּקְהֵל מֹשֶׁה אֶת־כָּל־עֲדַת בְּנֵי יִשְׂרָאֵל וַיֹּאמֶר אֲלֵהֶם אֵלֶּה הַדְּבָרִים אֲשֶׁר־צִוָּה יְהוָה לַעֲשֹׂת אֹתָם: שֵׁשֶׁת יָמִים תֵּעָשֶׂה מְלָאכָה וּבַיּוֹם הַשְּׁבִיעִי יִהְיֶה לָכֶם קֹדֶשׁ שַׁבַּת שַׁבָּתוֹן לַיהוָה כָּל־הָעֹשֶׂה בוֹ מְלָאכָה יוּמָת: לֹא־תְבַעֲרוּ אֵשׁ בְּכֹל מֹשְׁבֹתֵיכֶם בְּיוֹם הַשַּׁבָּת:

לוי וַיֹּאמֶר מֹשֶׁה אֶל־כָּל־עֲדַת בְּנֵי־יִשְׂרָאֵל לֵאמֹר זֶה הַדָּבָר אֲשֶׁר־צִוָּה יְהוָה לֵאמֹר: קְחוּ מֵאִתְּכֶם תְּרוּמָה לַיהוָה כֹּל נְדִיב לִבּוֹ יְבִיאֶהָ אֵת תְּרוּמַת יְהוָה זָהָב וָכֶסֶף וּנְחֹשֶׁת: וּתְכֵלֶת וְאַרְגָּמָן וְתוֹלַעַת שָׁנִי וְשֵׁשׁ וְעִזִּים: וְעֹרֹת אֵילִם מְאָדָּמִים וְעֹרֹת תְּחָשִׁים וַעֲצֵי שִׁטִּים: וְשֶׁמֶן לַמָּאוֹר וּבְשָׂמִים לְשֶׁמֶן הַמִּשְׁחָה וְלִקְטֹרֶת הַסַּמִּים: וְאַבְנֵי־שֹׁהַם וְאַבְנֵי מִלֻּאִים לָאֵפוֹד וְלַחֹשֶׁן: וְכָל־חֲכַם־לֵב בָּכֶם יָבֹאוּ וְיַעֲשׂוּ אֵת כָּל־אֲשֶׁר צִוָּה יְהוָה:

ישראל אֶת־הַמִּשְׁכָּן אֶת־אָהֳלוֹ וְאֶת־מִכְסֵהוּ אֶת־קְרָסָיו וְאֶת־קְרָשָׁיו אֶת־בְּרִיחָו אֶת־עַמֻּדָיו וְאֶת־אֲדָנָיו: אֶת־הָאָרֹן וְאֶת־בַּדָּיו אֶת־הַכַּפֹּרֶת וְאֵת פָּרֹכֶת הַמָּסָךְ: אֶת־הַשֻּׁלְחָן וְאֶת־בַּדָּיו וְאֶת־כָּל־כֵּלָיו וְאֵת לֶחֶם הַפָּנִים: וְאֶת־מְנֹרַת הַמָּאוֹר וְאֶת־כֵּלֶיהָ וְאֶת־נֵרֹתֶיהָ וְאֵת שֶׁמֶן הַמָּאוֹר: וְאֶת־מִזְבַּח הַקְּטֹרֶת וְאֶת־בַּדָּיו וְאֵת שֶׁמֶן הַמִּשְׁחָה וְאֵת קְטֹרֶת הַסַּמִּים וְאֶת־מָסַךְ הַפֶּתַח לְפֶתַח הַמִּשְׁכָּן: אֵת ׀ מִזְבַּח הָעֹלָה וְאֶת־מִכְבַּר הַנְּחֹשֶׁת אֲשֶׁר־לוֹ אֶת־בַּדָּיו וְאֶת־כָּל־כֵּלָיו אֶת־הַכִּיֹּר וְאֶת־כַּנּוֹ: אֵת קַלְעֵי הֶחָצֵר אֶת־עַמֻּדָיו וְאֶת־אֲדָנֶיהָ וְאֵת מָסַךְ שַׁעַר הֶחָצֵר: אֶת־יִתְדֹת הַמִּשְׁכָּן וְאֶת־יִתְדֹת הֶחָצֵר וְאֶת־מֵיתְרֵיהֶם: אֶת־בִּגְדֵי הַשְּׂרָד לְשָׁרֵת בַּקֹּדֶשׁ אֶת־בִּגְדֵי הַקֹּדֶשׁ לְאַהֲרֹן הַכֹּהֵן וְאֶת־בִּגְדֵי בָנָיו לְכַהֵן: וַיֵּצְאוּ כָּל־עֲדַת בְּנֵי־יִשְׂרָאֵל מִלִּפְנֵי מֹשֶׁה:

כְּתֵפֹת חֹבְרֹת יִהְיֶה־לּוֹ אֶל־שְׁנֵי קְצוֹתָיו וְחֻבָּר: וְחֵשֶׁב אֲפֻדָּתוֹ אֲשֶׁר עָלָיו כְּמַעֲשֵׂהוּ מִמֶּנּוּ יִהְיֶה זָהָב תְּכֵלֶת וְאַרְגָּמָן וְתוֹלַעַת שָׁנִי וְשֵׁשׁ מָשְׁזָר: וְלָקַחְתָּ אֶת־שְׁתֵּי אַבְנֵי־שֹׁהַם וּפִתַּחְתָּ עֲלֵיהֶם שְׁמוֹת בְּנֵי יִשְׂרָאֵל:

ישראל שִׁשָּׁה מִשְּׁמֹתָם עַל הָאֶבֶן הָאֶחָת וְאֶת־שְׁמוֹת הַשִּׁשָּׁה הַנּוֹתָרִים עַל־הָאֶבֶן הַשֵּׁנִית כְּתוֹלְדֹתָם: מַעֲשֵׂה חָרַשׁ אֶבֶן פִּתּוּחֵי חֹתָם תְּפַתַּח אֶת־שְׁתֵּי הָאֲבָנִים עַל־שְׁמֹת בְּנֵי יִשְׂרָאֵל מֻסַבֹּת מִשְׁבְּצוֹת זָהָב תַּעֲשֶׂה אֹתָם: וְשַׂמְתָּ אֶת־שְׁתֵּי הָאֲבָנִים עַל כִּתְפֹת הָאֵפֹד אַבְנֵי זִכָּרֹן לִבְנֵי יִשְׂרָאֵל וְנָשָׂא אַהֲרֹן אֶת־שְׁמוֹתָם לִפְנֵי יְהוָה עַל־שְׁתֵּי כְתֵפָיו לְזִכָּרֹן:

פ׳ פקודי / PEKUDEI
(Exodus 38:21 – 39:1)

כהן: אֵ֣לֶּה פְקוּדֵ֤י הַמִּשְׁכָּן֙ מִשְׁכַּ֣ן הָעֵדֻ֔ת אֲשֶׁ֥ר פֻּקַּ֖ד עַל־פִּ֣י מֹשֶׁ֑ה עֲבֹדַת֙ הַלְוִיִּ֔ם בְּיַד֙ אִֽיתָמָ֔ר בֶּֽן־אַהֲרֹ֖ן הַכֹּהֵֽן: וּבְצַלְאֵ֛ל בֶּן־אוּרִ֥י בֶן־ח֖וּר לְמַטֵּ֣ה יְהוּדָ֑ה עָשָׂ֕ה אֵ֛ת כָּל־אֲשֶׁר־צִוָּ֥ה יְהֹוָ֖ה אֶת־מֹשֶֽׁה: וְאִתּ֗וֹ אָהֳלִיאָ֞ב בֶּן־אֲחִֽיסָמָ֛ךְ לְמַטֵּה־דָ֖ן חָרָ֣שׁ וְחֹשֵׁ֑ב וְרֹקֵ֗ם בַּתְּכֵ֙לֶת֙ וּבָֽאַרְגָּמָ֔ן וּבְתוֹלַ֥עַת הַשָּׁנִ֖י וּבַשֵּֽׁשׁ:

לוי: כָּל־הַזָּהָ֗ב הֶֽעָשׂוּי֙ לַמְּלָאכָ֔ה בְּכֹ֖ל מְלֶ֣אכֶת הַקֹּ֑דֶשׁ וַיְהִ֣י ׀ זְהַ֣ב הַתְּנוּפָ֗ה תֵּ֤שַׁע וְעֶשְׂרִים֙ כִּכָּ֔ר וּשְׁבַ֨ע מֵא֧וֹת וּשְׁלֹשִׁ֛ים שֶׁ֖קֶל בְּשֶׁ֥קֶל הַקֹּֽדֶשׁ: וְכֶ֛סֶף פְּקוּדֵ֥י הָעֵדָ֖ה מְאַ֣ת כִּכָּ֑ר וְאֶ֩לֶף֩ וּשְׁבַ֨ע מֵא֜וֹת וַחֲמִשָּׁ֧ה וְשִׁבְעִ֛ים שֶׁ֖קֶל בְּשֶׁ֥קֶל הַקֹּֽדֶשׁ: בֶּ֚קַע לַגֻּלְגֹּ֔לֶת מַחֲצִ֥ית הַשֶּׁ֖קֶל בְּשֶׁ֣קֶל הַקֹּ֑דֶשׁ לְכֹ֨ל הָעֹבֵ֜ר עַל־הַפְּקֻדִ֗ים מִבֶּ֨ן עֶשְׂרִ֤ים שָׁנָה֙ וָמַ֔עְלָה לְשֵׁשׁ־מֵא֥וֹת אֶ֙לֶף֙ וּשְׁלֹ֣שֶׁת אֲלָפִ֔ים וַחֲמֵ֥שׁ מֵא֖וֹת וַחֲמִשִּֽׁים: וַיְהִ֗י מְאַת֙ כִּכַּ֣ר הַכֶּ֔סֶף לָצֶ֗קֶת אֵ֚ת אַדְנֵ֣י הַקֹּ֔דֶשׁ וְאֵ֖ת אַדְנֵ֣י הַפָּרֹ֑כֶת מְאַ֧ת אֲדָנִ֛ים לִמְאַ֥ת הַכִּכָּ֖ר כִּכָּ֥ר לָאָֽדֶן:

ישראל: וְאֶת־הָאֶ֜לֶף וּשְׁבַ֤ע הַמֵּאוֹת֙ וַחֲמִשָּׁ֣ה וְשִׁבְעִ֔ים עָשָׂ֥ה וָוִ֖ים לָֽעַמּוּדִ֑ים וְצִפָּ֥ה רָאשֵׁיהֶ֖ם וְחִשַּׁ֥ק אֹתָֽם: וּנְחֹ֥שֶׁת הַתְּנוּפָ֖ה שִׁבְעִ֣ים כִּכָּ֑ר וְאַלְפַּ֥יִם וְאַרְבַּע־מֵא֖וֹת שָֽׁקֶל: וַיַּ֣עַשׂ בָּ֗הּ אֶת־אַדְנֵי֙ פֶּ֚תַח אֹ֣הֶל מוֹעֵ֔ד וְאֵת֙ מִזְבַּ֣ח הַנְּחֹ֔שֶׁת וְאֶת־מִכְבַּ֥ר הַנְּחֹ֖שֶׁת אֲשֶׁר־ל֑וֹ וְאֵ֖ת כָּל־כְּלֵ֥י הַמִּזְבֵּֽחַ: וְאֶת־אַדְנֵ֤י הֶֽחָצֵר֙ סָבִ֔יב וְאֶת־אַדְנֵ֖י שַׁ֣עַר הֶֽחָצֵ֑ר וְאֵ֨ת כָּל־יִתְדֹ֧ת הַמִּשְׁכָּ֛ן וְאֶת־כָּל־יִתְדֹ֥ת הֶֽחָצֵ֖ר סָבִֽיב: וּמִן־הַתְּכֵ֤לֶת וְהָֽאַרְגָּמָן֙ וְתוֹלַ֣עַת הַשָּׁנִ֔י עָשׂ֥וּ בִגְדֵי־שְׂרָ֖ד לְשָׁרֵ֣ת בַּקֹּ֑דֶשׁ וַֽיַּעֲשׂ֞וּ אֶת־בִּגְדֵ֤י הַקֹּ֙דֶשׁ֙ אֲשֶׁ֣ר לְאַהֲרֹ֔ן כַּאֲשֶׁ֛ר צִוָּ֥ה יְהֹוָ֖ה אֶת־מֹשֶֽׁה:

פ׳ ויקרא / VAYIKRA
(Leviticus 1:1-13)

כהן: וַיִּקְרָ֖א אֶל־מֹשֶׁ֑ה וַיְדַבֵּ֤ר יְהֹוָה֙ אֵלָ֔יו מֵאֹ֥הֶל מוֹעֵ֖ד לֵאמֹֽר: דַּבֵּ֞ר אֶל־בְּנֵ֤י יִשְׂרָאֵל֙ וְאָמַרְתָּ֣ אֲלֵהֶ֔ם אָדָ֗ם כִּֽי־יַקְרִ֥יב מִכֶּ֛ם קָרְבָּ֖ן לַֽיהֹוָ֑ה מִן־הַבְּהֵמָ֗ה מִן־הַבָּקָר֙ וּמִן־הַצֹּ֔אן תַּקְרִ֖יבוּ אֶת־קָרְבַּנְכֶֽם: אִם־עֹלָ֤ה קָרְבָּנוֹ֙ מִן־הַבָּקָ֔ר זָכָ֥ר תָּמִ֖ים יַקְרִיבֶ֑נּוּ אֶל־פֶּ֜תַח אֹ֤הֶל מוֹעֵד֙ יַקְרִ֣יב אֹת֔וֹ לִרְצֹנ֖וֹ לִפְנֵ֥י יְהֹוָֽה: וְסָמַ֣ךְ יָד֔וֹ עַ֖ל רֹ֣אשׁ הָעֹלָ֑ה וְנִרְצָ֥ה ל֖וֹ לְכַפֵּ֥ר עָלָֽיו:

לוי: וְשָׁחַ֛ט אֶת־בֶּ֥ן הַבָּקָ֖ר לִפְנֵ֣י יְהֹוָ֑ה וְ֠הִקְרִ֠יבוּ בְּנֵ֨י אַהֲרֹ֤ן הַכֹּֽהֲנִים֙ אֶת־הַדָּ֔ם וְזָרְק֨וּ אֶת־הַדָּ֤ם עַל־הַמִּזְבֵּ֙חַ֙ סָבִ֔יב אֲשֶׁר־פֶּ֖תַח אֹ֥הֶל מוֹעֵֽד: וְהִפְשִׁ֖יט אֶת־הָעֹלָ֑ה וְנִתַּ֥ח אֹתָ֖הּ לִנְתָחֶֽיהָ: וְ֠נָתְנ֠וּ בְּנֵ֨י אַהֲרֹ֧ן הַכֹּהֵ֛ן אֵ֖שׁ עַל־הַמִּזְבֵּ֑חַ וְעָרְכ֥וּ עֵצִ֖ים עַל־הָאֵֽשׁ: וְעָרְכ֗וּ בְּנֵ֤י אַהֲרֹן֙ הַכֹּ֣הֲנִ֔ים אֵ֚ת הַנְּתָחִ֔ים אֶת־הָרֹ֖אשׁ וְאֶת־הַפָּ֑דֶר עַל־הָֽעֵצִים֙ אֲשֶׁ֣ר עַל־הָאֵ֔שׁ אֲשֶׁ֖ר עַל־הַמִּזְבֵּֽחַ: וְקִרְבּ֥וֹ וּכְרָעָ֖יו יִרְחַ֣ץ בַּמָּ֑יִם וְהִקְטִ֨יר הַכֹּהֵ֤ן אֶת־הַכֹּל֙ הַמִּזְבֵּ֔חָה עֹלָ֛ה אִשֵּׁ֥ה רֵֽיחַ־נִיח֖וֹחַ לַֽיהֹוָֽה:

ישראל: וְאִ֨ם־מִן־הַצֹּ֧אן קָרְבָּנ֛וֹ מִן־הַכְּשָׂבִ֥ים א֛וֹ מִן־הָעִזִּ֖ים לְעֹלָ֑ה זָכָ֥ר תָּמִ֖ים יַקְרִיבֶֽנּוּ: וְשָׁחַ֨ט אֹת֜וֹ עַ֣ל יֶ֧רֶךְ הַמִּזְבֵּ֛חַ צָפֹ֖נָה לִפְנֵ֣י יְהֹוָ֑ה וְזָרְק֡וּ בְּנֵי֩ אַהֲרֹ֨ן הַכֹּהֲנִ֧ים אֶת־דָּמ֛וֹ עַל־הַמִּזְבֵּ֖חַ סָבִֽיב: וְנִתַּ֤ח אֹתוֹ֙ לִנְתָחָ֔יו וְאֶת־רֹאשׁ֖וֹ וְאֶת־פִּדְר֑וֹ וְעָרַ֤ךְ הַכֹּהֵן֙ אֹתָ֔ם עַל־הָֽעֵצִים֙ אֲשֶׁ֣ר עַל־הָאֵ֔שׁ אֲשֶׁ֖ר עַל־הַמִּזְבֵּֽחַ: וְהַקֶּ֥רֶב וְהַכְּרָעַ֖יִם יִרְחַ֣ץ בַּמָּ֑יִם וְהִקְרִ֨יב הַכֹּהֵ֤ן אֶת־הַכֹּל֙ וְהִקְטִ֣יר הַמִּזְבֵּ֔חָה עֹלָ֣ה ה֗וּא אִשֵּׁ֛ה רֵ֥יחַ נִיחֹ֖חַ לַיהֹוָֽה:

פ׳ צו / TZAV
(Leviticus 6:1-11)

כהן: וַיְדַבֵּ֥ר יְהֹוָ֖ה אֶל־מֹשֶׁ֥ה לֵּאמֹֽר: צַ֤ו אֶֽת־אַהֲרֹן֙ וְאֶת־בָּנָ֣יו לֵאמֹ֔ר זֹ֥את תּוֹרַ֖ת הָֽעֹלָ֑ה הִ֣וא הָֽעֹלָ֡ה עַל֩ מוֹקְדָ֨ה עַל־הַמִּזְבֵּ֤חַ כָּל־הַלַּ֙יְלָה֙ עַד־הַבֹּ֔קֶר וְאֵ֥שׁ הַמִּזְבֵּ֖חַ תּ֥וּקַד בּֽוֹ: וְלָבַ֨שׁ הַכֹּהֵ֜ן מִדּ֣וֹ בַ֗ד וּמִכְנְסֵי־בַד֮ יִלְבַּ֣שׁ עַל־בְּשָׂרוֹ֒ וְהֵרִ֣ים אֶת־הַדֶּ֗שֶׁן אֲשֶׁ֨ר תֹּאכַ֥ל הָאֵ֛שׁ אֶת־הָֽעֹלָ֖ה עַל־הַמִּזְבֵּ֑חַ וְשָׂמ֕וֹ אֵ֖צֶל הַמִּזְבֵּֽחַ:

לוי: וּפָשַׁט֙ אֶת־בְּגָדָ֔יו וְלָבַ֖שׁ בְּגָדִ֣ים אֲחֵרִ֑ים

SHEMINI-TAZRIA

וְהוֹצִ֣יא אֶת־הַדֶּ֗שֶׁן אֶל־מִח֨וּץ לַֽמַּחֲנֶ֜ה אֶל־מָק֣וֹם טָה֑וֹר: וְהָאֵ֨שׁ עַל־הַמִּזְבֵּ֤חַ תּֽוּקַד־בּוֹ֙ לֹ֣א תִכְבֶּ֔ה וּבִעֵ֨ר עָלֶ֧יהָ הַכֹּהֵ֛ן עֵצִ֖ים בַּבֹּ֣קֶר בַּבֹּ֑קֶר וְעָרַ֤ךְ עָלֶ֨יהָ֙ הָֽעֹלָ֔ה וְהִקְטִ֥יר עָלֶ֖יהָ חֶלְבֵ֥י הַשְּׁלָמִֽים: אֵ֗שׁ תָּמִ֛יד תּוּקַ֥ד עַל־הַמִּזְבֵּ֖חַ לֹ֥א תִכְבֶּֽה:

ישראל וְזֹ֥את תּוֹרַ֖ת הַמִּנְחָ֑ה הַקְרֵ֨ב אֹתָ֤הּ בְּנֵֽי־אַהֲרֹן֙ לִפְנֵ֣י יְהֹוָ֔ה אֶל־פְּנֵ֖י הַמִּזְבֵּֽחַ: וְהֵרִ֨ים מִמֶּ֜נּוּ בְּקֻמְצ֗וֹ מִסֹּ֤לֶת הַמִּנְחָה֙ וּמִשַּׁמְנָ֔הּ וְאֵת֙ כׇּל־הַלְּבֹנָ֔ה אֲשֶׁ֖ר עַל־הַמִּנְחָ֑ה וְהִקְטִ֣יר הַמִּזְבֵּ֗חַ רֵ֧יחַ נִיחֹ֛חַ אַזְכָּרָתָ֖הּ לַֽיהֹוָֽה: וְהַנּוֹתֶ֣רֶת מִמֶּ֔נָּה יֹֽאכְל֖וּ אַהֲרֹ֣ן וּבָנָ֑יו מַצּ֤וֹת תֵּֽאָכֵל֙ בְּמָק֣וֹם קָדֹ֔שׁ בַּחֲצַ֥ר אֹֽהֶל־מוֹעֵ֖ד יֹאכְלֽוּהָ: לֹ֤א תֵֽאָפֶה֙ חָמֵ֔ץ חֶלְקָ֛ם נָתַ֥תִּי אֹתָ֖הּ מֵֽאִשָּׁ֑י קֹ֤דֶשׁ קָֽדָשִׁים֙ הִ֔וא כַּחַטָּ֖את וְכָאָשָֽׁם: כׇּל־זָכָ֞ר בִּבְנֵ֤י אַהֲרֹן֙ יֹֽאכְלֶ֔נָּה חׇק־עוֹלָם֙ לְדֹרֹ֣תֵיכֶ֔ם מֵֽאִשֵּׁ֖י יְהֹוָ֑ה כֹּ֛ל אֲשֶׁר־יִגַּ֥ע בָּהֶ֖ם יִקְדָּֽשׁ:

פ׳ שמיני / SHEMINI
(Leviticus 9:1-16)

כה׳ וַיְהִי֙ בַּיּ֣וֹם הַשְּׁמִינִ֔י קָרָ֣א מֹשֶׁ֔ה לְאַהֲרֹ֖ן וּלְבָנָ֑יו וּלְזִקְנֵ֖י יִשְׂרָאֵֽל: וַיֹּ֣אמֶר אֶֽל־אַהֲרֹ֗ן קַח־לְךָ֠ עֵ֣גֶל בֶּן־בָּקָ֧ר לְחַטָּ֛את וְאַ֥יִל לְעֹלָ֖ה תְּמִימִ֑ם וְהַקְרֵ֖ב לִפְנֵ֥י יְהֹוָֽה: וְאֶל־בְּנֵ֥י יִשְׂרָאֵ֖ל תְּדַבֵּ֣ר לֵאמֹ֑ר קְח֤וּ שְׂעִיר־עִזִּים֙ לְחַטָּ֔את וְעֵ֨גֶל וָכֶ֧בֶשׂ בְּנֵי־שָׁנָ֛ה תְּמִימִ֖ם לְעֹלָֽה: וְשׁ֨וֹר וָאַ֜יִל לִשְׁלָמִ֗ים לִזְבֹּ֨חַ֙ לִפְנֵ֣י יְהֹוָ֔ה וּמִנְחָ֖ה בְּלוּלָ֣ה בַשָּׁ֑מֶן כִּ֣י הַיּ֔וֹם יְהֹוָ֖ה נִרְאָ֥ה אֲלֵיכֶֽם: וַיִּקְח֗וּ אֵ֚ת אֲשֶׁ֣ר צִוָּ֣ה מֹשֶׁ֔ה אֶל־פְּנֵ֖י אֹ֣הֶל מוֹעֵ֑ד וַֽיִּקְרְבוּ֙ כׇּל־הָ֣עֵדָ֔ה וַיַּעַמְד֖וּ לִפְנֵ֥י יְהֹוָֽה: וַיֹּ֣אמֶר מֹשֶׁ֔ה זֶ֧ה הַדָּבָ֛ר אֲשֶׁר־צִוָּ֥ה יְהֹוָ֖ה תַּעֲשׂ֑וּ וְיֵרָ֥א אֲלֵיכֶ֖ם כְּב֥וֹד יְהֹוָֽה:

לוי וַיֹּ֤אמֶר מֹשֶׁה֙ אֶֽל־אַהֲרֹ֔ן קְרַ֣ב אֶל־הַמִּזְבֵּ֗חַ וַעֲשֵׂ֞ה אֶת־חַטָּֽאתְךָ֙ וְאֶת־עֹ֣לָתֶ֔ךָ וְכַפֵּ֥ר בַּֽעַדְךָ֖ וּבְעַ֣ד הָעָ֑ם וַעֲשֵׂ֞ה אֶת־קׇרְבַּ֤ן הָעָם֙ וְכַפֵּ֣ר בַּֽעֲדָ֔ם כַּאֲשֶׁ֖ר צִוָּ֥ה יְהֹוָֽה: וַיִּקְרַ֥ב אַהֲרֹ֖ן אֶל־הַמִּזְבֵּ֑חַ וַיִּשְׁחַ֛ט אֶת־עֵ֥גֶל הַחַטָּ֖את אֲשֶׁר־לֽוֹ: וַ֠יַּקְרִ֠בוּ בְּנֵ֨י אַהֲרֹ֣ן

אֶת־הַדָּם֮ אֵלָיו֒ וַיִּטְבֹּ֤ל אֶצְבָּעוֹ֙ בַּדָּ֔ם וַיִּתֵּ֖ן עַל־קַרְנ֣וֹת הַמִּזְבֵּ֑חַ וְאֶת־הַדָּ֣ם יָצַ֔ק אֶל־יְס֖וֹד הַמִּזְבֵּֽחַ: וְאֶת־הַחֵ֤לֶב וְאֶת־הַכְּלָיֹת֙ וְאֶת־הַיֹּתֶ֨רֶת֙ מִן־הַכָּבֵ֔ד מִן־הַֽחַטָּ֖את הִקְטִ֣יר הַמִּזְבֵּ֑חָה כַּאֲשֶׁ֛ר צִוָּ֥ה יְהֹוָ֖ה אֶת־מֹשֶֽׁה:

ישראל וְאֶת־הַבָּשָׂ֖ר וְאֶת־הָע֑וֹר שָׂרַ֣ף בָּאֵ֔שׁ מִח֖וּץ לַֽמַּחֲנֶֽה: וַיִּשְׁחַ֖ט אֶת־הָעֹלָ֑ה וַ֠יַּמְצִ֠אוּ בְּנֵ֨י אַהֲרֹ֤ן אֵלָיו֙ אֶת־הַדָּ֔ם וַיִּזְרְקֵ֥הוּ עַל־הַמִּזְבֵּ֖חַ סָבִֽיב: וְאֶת־הָ֣עֹלָ֔ה הִמְצִ֥יאוּ אֵלָ֛יו לִנְתָחֶ֖יהָ וְאֶת־הָרֹ֑אשׁ וַיַּקְטֵ֖ר עַל־הַמִּזְבֵּֽחַ: וַיִּרְחַ֥ץ אֶת־הַקֶּ֖רֶב וְאֶת־הַכְּרָעָ֑יִם וַיַּקְטֵ֤ר עַל־הָעֹלָ֖ה הַמִּזְבֵּֽחָה: וַיַּקְרֵ֕ב אֵ֖ת קׇרְבַּ֣ן הָעָ֑ם וַיִּקַּ֞ח אֶת־שְׂעִ֤יר הַֽחַטָּאת֙ אֲשֶׁ֣ר לָעָ֔ם וַיִּשְׁחָטֵ֥הוּ וַֽיְחַטְּאֵ֖הוּ כָּרִאשֽׁוֹן: וַיַּקְרֵ֖ב אֶת־הָעֹלָ֑ה וַֽיַּעֲשֶׂ֖הָ כַּמִּשְׁפָּֽט:

פ׳ תזריע / TAZRIA
(Leviticus 12:1–13:5)

כה׳ וַיְדַבֵּ֥ר יְהֹוָ֖ה אֶל־מֹשֶׁ֥ה לֵּאמֹֽר: דַּבֵּ֞ר אֶל־בְּנֵ֤י יִשְׂרָאֵל֙ לֵאמֹ֔ר אִשָּׁה֙ כִּ֣י תַזְרִ֔יעַ וְיָלְדָ֖ה זָכָ֑ר וְטָֽמְאָה֙ שִׁבְעַ֣ת יָמִ֔ים כִּימֵ֛י נִדַּ֥ת דְּוֺתָ֖הּ תִּטְמָֽא: וּבַיּ֖וֹם הַשְּׁמִינִ֑י יִמּ֖וֹל בְּשַׂ֥ר עׇרְלָתֽוֹ: וּשְׁלֹשִׁ֥ים יוֹם֙ וּשְׁלֹ֣שֶׁת יָמִ֔ים תֵּשֵׁ֖ב בִּדְמֵ֣י טׇהֳרָ֑ה בְּכׇל־קֹ֣דֶשׁ לֹֽא־תִגָּ֗ע וְאֶל־הַמִּקְדָּשׁ֙ לֹ֣א תָבֹ֔א עַד־מְלֹ֖את יְמֵ֥י טׇהֳרָֽהּ:

לוי וְאִם־נְקֵבָ֣ה תֵלֵ֔ד וְטָמְאָ֥ה שְׁבֻעַ֖יִם כְּנִדָּתָ֑הּ וְשִׁשִּׁ֥ים יוֹם֙ וְשֵׁ֣שֶׁת יָמִ֔ים תֵּשֵׁ֖ב עַל־דְּמֵ֥י טׇהֳרָֽה: וּבִמְלֹ֣את ׀ יְמֵ֣י טׇהֳרָ֗הּ לְבֵן֮ א֣וֹ לְבַת֒ תָּבִ֞יא כֶּ֤בֶשׂ בֶּן־שְׁנָתוֹ֙ לְעֹלָ֔ה וּבֶן־יוֹנָ֥ה אוֹ־תֹ֛ר לְחַטָּ֖את אֶל־פֶּ֣תַח אֹֽהֶל־מוֹעֵ֑ד אֶל־הַכֹּהֵֽן: וְהִקְרִיב֞וֹ לִפְנֵ֤י יְהֹוָה֙ וְכִפֶּ֣ר עָלֶ֔יהָ וְטָהֲרָ֖ה מִמְּקֹ֣ר דָּמֶ֑יהָ זֹ֤את תּוֹרַת֙ הַיֹּלֶ֔דֶת לַזָּכָ֖ר א֥וֹ לַנְּקֵבָֽה: וְאִם־לֹ֨א תִמְצָ֣א יָדָהּ֮ דֵּ֣י שֶׂה֒ וְלָקְחָ֣ה שְׁתֵּֽי־תֹרִ֗ים א֤וֹ שְׁנֵי֙ בְּנֵ֣י יוֹנָ֔ה אֶחָ֥ד לְעֹלָ֖ה וְאֶחָ֣ד לְחַטָּ֑את וְכִפֶּ֥ר עָלֶ֛יהָ הַכֹּהֵ֖ן וְטָהֵֽרָה:

ישראל וַיְדַבֵּ֣ר יְהֹוָ֔ה אֶל־מֹשֶׁ֥ה וְאֶֽל־אַהֲרֹ֖ן לֵאמֹֽר: אָדָ֗ם כִּֽי־יִהְיֶ֤ה בְעוֹר־בְּשָׂרוֹ֙ שְׂאֵ֤ת אֽוֹ־סַפַּ֨חַת֙ א֣וֹ בַהֶ֔רֶת וְהָיָ֥ה בְעוֹר־בְּשָׂר֖וֹ

לְנֶגַע צָרַעַת וְהוּבָא אֶל־אַהֲרֹן הַכֹּהֵן אוֹ אֶל־אַחַד מִבָּנָיו הַכֹּהֲנִים: וְרָאָה הַכֹּהֵן אֶת־הַנֶּגַע בְּעוֹר־הַבָּשָׂר וְשֵׂעָר בַּנֶּגַע הָפַךְ ׀ לָבָן וּמַרְאֵה הַנֶּגַע עָמֹק מֵעוֹר בְּשָׂרוֹ נֶגַע צָרַעַת הוּא וְרָאָהוּ הַכֹּהֵן וְטִמֵּא אֹתוֹ: וְאִם־בַּהֶרֶת לְבָנָה הִוא בְּעוֹר בְּשָׂרוֹ וְעָמֹק אֵין־מַרְאֶהָ מִן־הָעוֹר וּשְׂעָרָה לֹא־הָפַךְ לָבָן וְהִסְגִּיר הַכֹּהֵן אֶת־הַנֶּגַע שִׁבְעַת יָמִים: וְרָאָהוּ הַכֹּהֵן בַּיּוֹם הַשְּׁבִיעִי וְהִנֵּה הַנֶּגַע עָמַד בְּעֵינָיו לֹא־פָשָׂה הַנֶּגַע בָּעוֹר וְהִסְגִּירוֹ הַכֹּהֵן שִׁבְעַת יָמִים שֵׁנִית:

◃ פ׳ מצורע / METZORA ▹
(Leviticus 14:1-12)

כהן וַיְדַבֵּר יְהוָה אֶל־מֹשֶׁה לֵּאמֹר: זֹאת תִּהְיֶה תּוֹרַת הַמְּצֹרָע בְּיוֹם טָהֳרָתוֹ וְהוּבָא אֶל־הַכֹּהֵן: וְיָצָא הַכֹּהֵן אֶל־מִחוּץ לַמַּחֲנֶה וְרָאָה הַכֹּהֵן וְהִנֵּה נִרְפָּא נֶגַע־הַצָּרַעַת מִן־הַצָּרוּעַ: וְצִוָּה הַכֹּהֵן וְלָקַח לַמִּטַּהֵר שְׁתֵּי־צִפֳּרִים חַיּוֹת טְהֹרוֹת וְעֵץ אֶרֶז וּשְׁנִי תוֹלַעַת וְאֵזֹב: וְצִוָּה הַכֹּהֵן וְשָׁחַט אֶת־הַצִּפּוֹר הָאֶחָת אֶל־כְּלִי־חֶרֶשׂ עַל־מַיִם חַיִּים:

לוי אֶת־הַצִּפֹּר הַחַיָּה יִקַּח אֹתָהּ וְאֶת־עֵץ הָאֶרֶז וְאֶת־שְׁנִי הַתּוֹלַעַת וְאֶת־הָאֵזֹב וְטָבַל אוֹתָם וְאֵת ׀ הַצִּפֹּר הַחַיָּה בְּדַם הַצִּפֹּר הַשְּׁחֻטָה עַל הַמַּיִם הַחַיִּים: וְהִזָּה עַל הַמִּטַּהֵר מִן־הַצָּרַעַת שֶׁבַע פְּעָמִים וְטִהֲרוֹ וְשִׁלַּח אֶת־הַצִּפֹּר הַחַיָּה עַל־פְּנֵי הַשָּׂדֶה: וְכִבֶּס הַמִּטַּהֵר אֶת־בְּגָדָיו וְגִלַּח אֶת־כָּל־שְׂעָרוֹ וְרָחַץ בַּמַּיִם וְטָהֵר וְאַחַר יָבוֹא אֶל־הַמַּחֲנֶה וְיָשַׁב מִחוּץ לְאָהֳלוֹ שִׁבְעַת יָמִים: וְהָיָה בַיּוֹם הַשְּׁבִיעִי יְגַלַּח אֶת־כָּל־שְׂעָרוֹ אֶת־רֹאשׁוֹ וְאֶת־זְקָנוֹ וְאֵת גַּבֹּת עֵינָיו וְאֶת־כָּל־שְׂעָרוֹ יְגַלֵּחַ וְכִבֶּס אֶת־בְּגָדָיו וְרָחַץ אֶת־בְּשָׂרוֹ בַּמַּיִם וְטָהֵר:

ישראל וּבַיּוֹם הַשְּׁמִינִי יִקַּח שְׁנֵי־כְבָשִׂים תְּמִימִם וְכַבְשָׂה אַחַת בַּת־שְׁנָתָהּ תְּמִימָה וּשְׁלֹשָׁה עֶשְׂרֹנִים סֹלֶת מִנְחָה בְּלוּלָה בַשֶּׁמֶן וְלֹג אֶחָד שָׁמֶן: וְהֶעֱמִיד הַכֹּהֵן הַמְטַהֵר אֵת הָאִישׁ הַמִּטַּהֵר וְאֹתָם לִפְנֵי יְהוָה פֶּתַח אֹהֶל מוֹעֵד: וְלָקַח הַכֹּהֵן אֶת־הַכֶּבֶשׂ הָאֶחָד וְהִקְרִיב אֹתוֹ לְאָשָׁם וְאֶת־לֹג הַשָּׁמֶן וְהֵנִיף אֹתָם תְּנוּפָה לִפְנֵי יְהוָה:

◃ פ׳ אחרי מות / ACHAREI MOS ▹
(Leviticus 16:1-17)

כהן וַיְדַבֵּר יְהוָה אֶל־מֹשֶׁה אַחֲרֵי מוֹת שְׁנֵי בְּנֵי אַהֲרֹן בְּקָרְבָתָם לִפְנֵי־יְהוָה וַיָּמֻתוּ: וַיֹּאמֶר יְהוָה אֶל־מֹשֶׁה דַּבֵּר אֶל־אַהֲרֹן אָחִיךָ וְאַל־יָבֹא בְכָל־עֵת אֶל־הַקֹּדֶשׁ מִבֵּית לַפָּרֹכֶת אֶל־פְּנֵי הַכַּפֹּרֶת אֲשֶׁר עַל־הָאָרֹן וְלֹא יָמוּת כִּי בֶּעָנָן אֵרָאֶה עַל־הַכַּפֹּרֶת: בְּזֹאת יָבֹא אַהֲרֹן אֶל־הַקֹּדֶשׁ בְּפַר בֶּן־בָּקָר לְחַטָּאת וְאַיִל לְעֹלָה: כְּתֹנֶת־בַּד קֹדֶשׁ יִלְבָּשׁ וּמִכְנְסֵי־בַד יִהְיוּ עַל־בְּשָׂרוֹ וּבְאַבְנֵט בַּד יַחְגֹּר וּבְמִצְנֶפֶת בַּד יִצְנֹף בִּגְדֵי־קֹדֶשׁ הֵם וְרָחַץ בַּמַּיִם אֶת־בְּשָׂרוֹ וּלְבֵשָׁם: וּמֵאֵת עֲדַת בְּנֵי יִשְׂרָאֵל יִקַּח שְׁנֵי־שְׂעִירֵי עִזִּים לְחַטָּאת וְאַיִל אֶחָד לְעֹלָה: וְהִקְרִיב אַהֲרֹן אֶת־פַּר הַחַטָּאת אֲשֶׁר־לוֹ וְכִפֶּר בַּעֲדוֹ וּבְעַד בֵּיתוֹ:

לוי וְלָקַח אֶת־שְׁנֵי הַשְּׂעִירִם וְהֶעֱמִיד אֹתָם לִפְנֵי יְהוָה פֶּתַח אֹהֶל מוֹעֵד: וְנָתַן אַהֲרֹן עַל־שְׁנֵי הַשְּׂעִירִם גֹּרָלוֹת גּוֹרָל אֶחָד לַיהוָה וְגוֹרָל אֶחָד לַעֲזָאזֵל: וְהִקְרִיב אַהֲרֹן אֶת־הַשָּׂעִיר אֲשֶׁר עָלָה עָלָיו הַגּוֹרָל לַיהוָה וְעָשָׂהוּ חַטָּאת: וְהַשָּׂעִיר אֲשֶׁר עָלָה עָלָיו הַגּוֹרָל לַעֲזָאזֵל יָעֳמַד־חַי לִפְנֵי יְהוָה לְכַפֵּר עָלָיו לְשַׁלַּח אֹתוֹ לַעֲזָאזֵל הַמִּדְבָּרָה: וְהִקְרִיב אַהֲרֹן אֶת־פַּר הַחַטָּאת אֲשֶׁר־לוֹ וְכִפֶּר בַּעֲדוֹ וּבְעַד בֵּיתוֹ וְשָׁחַט אֶת־פַּר הַחַטָּאת אֲשֶׁר־לוֹ:

ישראל וְלָקַח מְלֹא־הַמַּחְתָּה גַּחֲלֵי־אֵשׁ מֵעַל הַמִּזְבֵּחַ מִלִּפְנֵי יְהוָה וּמְלֹא חָפְנָיו קְטֹרֶת סַמִּים דַּקָּה וְהֵבִיא מִבֵּית לַפָּרֹכֶת: וְנָתַן אֶת־הַקְּטֹרֶת עַל־הָאֵשׁ לִפְנֵי יְהוָה וְכִסָּה ׀ עֲנַן הַקְּטֹרֶת אֶת־הַכַּפֹּרֶת אֲשֶׁר עַל־הָעֵדוּת וְלֹא יָמוּת: וְלָקַח מִדַּם הַפָּר וְהִזָּה בְאֶצְבָּעוֹ

פ׳ אמור / EMOR

(Leviticus 21:1-15)

כהן וַיֹּאמֶר יהוה אֶל־מֹשֶׁה אֱמֹר אֶל־הַכֹּהֲנִים בְּנֵי אַהֲרֹן וְאָמַרְתָּ אֲלֵהֶם לְנֶפֶשׁ לֹא־יִטַּמָּא בְּעַמָּיו: כִּי אִם־לִשְׁאֵרוֹ הַקָּרֹב אֵלָיו לְאִמּוֹ וּלְאָבִיו וְלִבְנוֹ וּלְבִתּוֹ וּלְאָחִיו: וְלַאֲחֹתוֹ הַבְּתוּלָה הַקְּרוֹבָה אֵלָיו אֲשֶׁר לֹא־הָיְתָה לְאִישׁ לָהּ יִטַּמָּא: לֹא יִטַּמָּא בַּעַל בְּעַמָּיו לְהֵחַלּוֹ: לֹא־יקרחה קָרְחָה בְּרֹאשָׁם וּפְאַת זְקָנָם לֹא יְגַלֵּחוּ וּבִבְשָׂרָם לֹא יִשְׂרְטוּ שָׂרָטֶת: קְדֹשִׁים יִהְיוּ לֵאלֹהֵיהֶם וְלֹא יְחַלְּלוּ שֵׁם אֱלֹהֵיהֶם כִּי אֶת־אִשֵּׁי יהוה לֶחֶם אֱלֹהֵיהֶם הֵם מַקְרִיבִם וְהָיוּ קֹדֶשׁ: לוי אִשָּׁה זֹנָה וַחֲלָלָה לֹא יִקָּחוּ וְאִשָּׁה גְּרוּשָׁה מֵאִישָׁהּ לֹא יִקָּחוּ כִּי־קָדֹשׁ הוּא לֵאלֹהָיו: וְקִדַּשְׁתּוֹ כִּי־אֶת־לֶחֶם אֱלֹהֶיךָ הוּא מַקְרִיב קָדֹשׁ יִהְיֶה־לָּךְ כִּי קָדוֹשׁ אֲנִי יהוה מְקַדִּשְׁכֶם: וּבַת אִישׁ כֹּהֵן כִּי תֵחֵל לִזְנוֹת אֶת־אָבִיהָ הִיא מְחַלֶּלֶת בָּאֵשׁ תִּשָּׂרֵף: וְהַכֹּהֵן הַגָּדוֹל מֵאֶחָיו אֲשֶׁר־יוּצַק עַל־רֹאשׁוֹ ׀ שֶׁמֶן הַמִּשְׁחָה וּמִלֵּא אֶת־יָדוֹ לִלְבֹּשׁ אֶת־הַבְּגָדִים אֶת־רֹאשׁוֹ לֹא יִפְרָע וּבְגָדָיו לֹא יִפְרֹם: וְעַל כָּל־נַפְשֹׁת מֵת לֹא יָבֹא לְאָבִיו וּלְאִמּוֹ לֹא יִטַּמָּא: וּמִן־הַמִּקְדָּשׁ לֹא יֵצֵא וְלֹא יְחַלֵּל אֵת מִקְדַּשׁ אֱלֹהָיו כִּי נֵזֶר שֶׁמֶן מִשְׁחַת אֱלֹהָיו עָלָיו אֲנִי יהוה: ישראל וְהוּא אִשָּׁה בִבְתוּלֶיהָ יִקָּח: אַלְמָנָה וּגְרוּשָׁה וַחֲלָלָה זֹנָה אֶת־אֵלֶּה לֹא יִקָּח כִּי אִם־בְּתוּלָה מֵעַמָּיו יִקַּח אִשָּׁה: וְלֹא־יְחַלֵּל זַרְעוֹ בְּעַמָּיו כִּי אֲנִי יהוה מְקַדְּשׁוֹ:

פ׳ בהר / BEHAR

(Leviticus 25:1-13)

כהן וַיְדַבֵּר יהוה אֶל־מֹשֶׁה בְּהַר סִינַי לֵאמֹר: דַּבֵּר אֶל־בְּנֵי יִשְׂרָאֵל וְאָמַרְתָּ אֲלֵהֶם כִּי תָבֹאוּ אֶל־הָאָרֶץ אֲשֶׁר אֲנִי נֹתֵן לָכֶם וְשָׁבְתָה הָאָרֶץ שַׁבָּת לַיהוה: שֵׁשׁ שָׁנִים תִּזְרַע שָׂדֶךָ וְשֵׁשׁ שָׁנִים תִּזְמֹר כַּרְמֶךָ וְאָסַפְתָּ אֶת־תְּבוּאָתָהּ: לוי וּבַשָּׁנָה הַשְּׁבִיעִת שַׁבַּת שַׁבָּתוֹן יִהְיֶה

עַל־פְּנֵי הַכַּפֹּרֶת קֵדְמָה וְלִפְנֵי הַכַּפֹּרֶת יַזֶּה שֶׁבַע־פְּעָמִים מִן־הַדָּם בְּאֶצְבָּעוֹ: וְשָׁחַט אֶת־שְׂעִיר הַחַטָּאת אֲשֶׁר לָעָם וְהֵבִיא אֶת־דָּמוֹ אֶל־מִבֵּית לַפָּרֹכֶת וְעָשָׂה אֶת־דָּמוֹ כַּאֲשֶׁר עָשָׂה לְדַם הַפָּר וְהִזָּה אֹתוֹ עַל־הַכַּפֹּרֶת וְלִפְנֵי הַכַּפֹּרֶת: וְכִפֶּר עַל־הַקֹּדֶשׁ מִטֻּמְאֹת בְּנֵי יִשְׂרָאֵל וּמִפִּשְׁעֵיהֶם לְכָל־חַטֹּאתָם וְכֵן יַעֲשֶׂה לְאֹהֶל מוֹעֵד הַשֹּׁכֵן אִתָּם בְּתוֹךְ טֻמְאֹתָם: וְכָל־אָדָם לֹא־יִהְיֶה ׀ בְּאֹהֶל מוֹעֵד בְּבֹאוֹ לְכַפֵּר בַּקֹּדֶשׁ עַד־צֵאתוֹ וְכִפֶּר בַּעֲדוֹ וּבְעַד בֵּיתוֹ וּבְעַד כָּל־קְהַל יִשְׂרָאֵל:

פ׳ קדשים / KEDOSHIM

(Leviticus 19:1-14)

כהן וַיְדַבֵּר יהוה אֶל־מֹשֶׁה לֵּאמֹר: דַּבֵּר אֶל־כָּל־עֲדַת בְּנֵי־יִשְׂרָאֵל וְאָמַרְתָּ אֲלֵהֶם קְדֹשִׁים תִּהְיוּ כִּי קָדוֹשׁ אֲנִי יהוה אֱלֹהֵיכֶם: אִישׁ אִמּוֹ וְאָבִיו תִּירָאוּ וְאֶת־שַׁבְּתֹתַי תִּשְׁמֹרוּ אֲנִי יהוה אֱלֹהֵיכֶם: אַל־תִּפְנוּ אֶל־הָאֱלִילִים וֵאלֹהֵי מַסֵּכָה לֹא תַעֲשׂוּ לָכֶם אֲנִי יהוה אֱלֹהֵיכֶם: לוי וְכִי תִזְבְּחוּ זֶבַח שְׁלָמִים לַיהוה לִרְצֹנְכֶם תִּזְבָּחֻהוּ: בְּיוֹם זִבְחֲכֶם יֵאָכֵל וּמִמָּחֳרָת וְהַנּוֹתָר עַד־יוֹם הַשְּׁלִישִׁי בָּאֵשׁ יִשָּׂרֵף: וְאִם הֵאָכֹל יֵאָכֵל בַּיּוֹם הַשְּׁלִישִׁי פִּגּוּל הוּא לֹא יֵרָצֶה: וְאֹכְלָיו עֲוֹנוֹ יִשָּׂא כִּי־אֶת־קֹדֶשׁ יהוה חִלֵּל וְנִכְרְתָה הַנֶּפֶשׁ הַהִוא מֵעַמֶּיהָ: וּבְקֻצְרְכֶם אֶת־קְצִיר אַרְצְכֶם לֹא תְכַלֶּה פְּאַת שָׂדְךָ לִקְצֹר וְלֶקֶט קְצִירְךָ לֹא תְלַקֵּט: וְכַרְמְךָ לֹא תְעוֹלֵל וּפֶרֶט כַּרְמְךָ לֹא תְלַקֵּט לֶעָנִי וְלַגֵּר תַּעֲזֹב אֹתָם אֲנִי יהוה אֱלֹהֵיכֶם: ישראל לֹא תִּגְנֹבוּ וְלֹא־תְכַחֲשׁוּ וְלֹא־תְשַׁקְּרוּ אִישׁ בַּעֲמִיתוֹ: וְלֹא־תִשָּׁבְעוּ בִשְׁמִי לַשָּׁקֶר וְחִלַּלְתָּ אֶת־שֵׁם אֱלֹהֶיךָ אֲנִי יהוה: לֹא־תַעֲשֹׁק אֶת־רֵעֲךָ וְלֹא תִגְזֹל לֹא־תָלִין פְּעֻלַּת שָׂכִיר אִתְּךָ עַד־בֹּקֶר: לֹא־תְקַלֵּל חֵרֵשׁ וְלִפְנֵי עִוֵּר לֹא תִתֵּן מִכְשֹׁל וְיָרֵאתָ מֵּאֱלֹהֶיךָ אֲנִי יהוה:

לָאָרֶץ שַׁבָּת לַיהוה: שָׂדְךָ לֹא תִזְרָע וְכַרְמְךָ לֹא תִזְמֹר: אֵת סְפִיחַ קְצִירְךָ לֹא תִקְצוֹר וְאֶת־עִנְּבֵי נְזִירֶךָ לֹא תִבְצֹר שְׁנַת שַׁבָּתוֹן יִהְיֶה לָאָרֶץ: וְהָיְתָה שַׁבַּת הָאָרֶץ לָכֶם לְאָכְלָה לְךָ וּלְעַבְדְּךָ וְלַאֲמָתֶךָ וְלִשְׂכִירְךָ וּלְתוֹשָׁבְךָ הַגָּרִים עִמָּךְ: וְלִבְהֶמְתְּךָ וְלַחַיָּה אֲשֶׁר בְּאַרְצֶךָ תִּהְיֶה כָל־תְּבוּאָתָהּ לֶאֱכֹל:

ישראל: וְסָפַרְתָּ לְךָ שֶׁבַע שַׁבְּתֹת שָׁנִים שֶׁבַע שָׁנִים שֶׁבַע פְּעָמִים וְהָיוּ לְךָ יְמֵי שֶׁבַע שַׁבְּתֹת הַשָּׁנִים תֵּשַׁע וְאַרְבָּעִים שָׁנָה: וְהַעֲבַרְתָּ שׁוֹפַר תְּרוּעָה בַּחֹדֶשׁ הַשְּׁבִעִי בֶּעָשׂוֹר לַחֹדֶשׁ בְּיוֹם הַכִּפֻּרִים תַּעֲבִירוּ שׁוֹפָר בְּכָל־אַרְצְכֶם: וְקִדַּשְׁתֶּם אֵת שְׁנַת הַחֲמִשִּׁים שָׁנָה וּקְרָאתֶם דְּרוֹר בָּאָרֶץ לְכָל־יֹשְׁבֶיהָ יוֹבֵל הִוא תִּהְיֶה לָכֶם וְשַׁבְתֶּם אִישׁ אֶל־אֲחֻזָּתוֹ וְאִישׁ אֶל־מִשְׁפַּחְתּוֹ תָּשֻׁבוּ: יוֹבֵל הִוא שְׁנַת הַחֲמִשִּׁים שָׁנָה תִּהְיֶה לָכֶם לֹא תִזְרָעוּ וְלֹא תִקְצְרוּ אֶת־סְפִיחֶיהָ וְלֹא תִבְצְרוּ אֶת־נְזִרֶיהָ: כִּי יוֹבֵל הִוא קֹדֶשׁ תִּהְיֶה לָכֶם מִן־הַשָּׂדֶה תֹּאכְלוּ אֶת־תְּבוּאָתָהּ: בִּשְׁנַת הַיּוֹבֵל הַזֹּאת תָּשֻׁבוּ אִישׁ אֶל־אֲחֻזָּתוֹ:

❧ פ' בחוקתי / BECHUKOSAI ❧
(Leviticus 26:3-13)

כהן: אִם־בְּחֻקֹּתַי תֵּלֵכוּ וְאֶת־מִצְוֹתַי תִּשְׁמְרוּ וַעֲשִׂיתֶם אֹתָם: וְנָתַתִּי גִשְׁמֵיכֶם בְּעִתָּם וְנָתְנָה הָאָרֶץ יְבוּלָהּ וְעֵץ הַשָּׂדֶה יִתֵּן פִּרְיוֹ: וְהִשִּׂיג לָכֶם דַּיִשׁ אֶת־בָּצִיר וּבָצִיר יַשִּׂיג אֶת־זָרַע וַאֲכַלְתֶּם לַחְמְכֶם לָשֹׂבַע וִישַׁבְתֶּם לָבֶטַח בְּאַרְצְכֶם:

לוי: וְנָתַתִּי שָׁלוֹם בָּאָרֶץ וּשְׁכַבְתֶּם וְאֵין מַחֲרִיד וְהִשְׁבַּתִּי חַיָּה רָעָה מִן־הָאָרֶץ וְחֶרֶב לֹא־תַעֲבֹר בְּאַרְצְכֶם: וּרְדַפְתֶּם אֶת־אֹיְבֵיכֶם וְנָפְלוּ לִפְנֵיכֶם לֶחָרֶב: וְרָדְפוּ מִכֶּם חֲמִשָּׁה מֵאָה וּמֵאָה מִכֶּם רְבָבָה יִרְדֹּפוּ וְנָפְלוּ אֹיְבֵיכֶם לִפְנֵיכֶם לֶחָרֶב: וּפָנִיתִי אֲלֵיכֶם וְהִפְרֵיתִי אֶתְכֶם וְהִרְבֵּיתִי אֶתְכֶם וַהֲקִימֹתִי אֶת־בְּרִיתִי אִתְּכֶם:

ישראל: וַאֲכַלְתֶּם יָשָׁן נוֹשָׁן וְיָשָׁן מִפְּנֵי חָדָשׁ תּוֹצִיאוּ: וְנָתַתִּי מִשְׁכָּנִי בְּתוֹכְכֶם וְלֹא־תִגְעַל נַפְשִׁי אֶתְכֶם: וְהִתְהַלַּכְתִּי בְּתוֹכְכֶם וְהָיִיתִי לָכֶם לֵאלֹהִים וְאַתֶּם תִּהְיוּ־לִי לְעָם: אֲנִי יְהוה אֱלֹהֵיכֶם אֲשֶׁר הוֹצֵאתִי אֶתְכֶם מֵאֶרֶץ מִצְרַיִם מִהְיֹת לָהֶם עֲבָדִים וָאֶשְׁבֹּר מֹטֹת עֻלְּכֶם וָאוֹלֵךְ אֶתְכֶם קוֹמְמִיּוּת:

❧ פ' במדבר / BAMIDBAR ❧
(Numbers 1:1-19)

כהן: וַיְדַבֵּר יְהוה אֶל־מֹשֶׁה בְּמִדְבַּר סִינַי בְּאֹהֶל מוֹעֵד בְּאֶחָד לַחֹדֶשׁ הַשֵּׁנִי בַּשָּׁנָה הַשֵּׁנִית לְצֵאתָם מֵאֶרֶץ מִצְרַיִם לֵאמֹר: שְׂאוּ אֶת־רֹאשׁ כָּל־עֲדַת בְּנֵי־יִשְׂרָאֵל לְמִשְׁפְּחֹתָם לְבֵית אֲבֹתָם בְּמִסְפַּר שֵׁמוֹת כָּל־זָכָר לְגֻלְגְּלֹתָם: מִבֶּן עֶשְׂרִים שָׁנָה וָמַעְלָה כָּל־יֹצֵא צָבָא בְּיִשְׂרָאֵל תִּפְקְדוּ אֹתָם לְצִבְאֹתָם אַתָּה וְאַהֲרֹן: וְאִתְּכֶם יִהְיוּ אִישׁ אִישׁ לַמַּטֶּה אִישׁ רֹאשׁ לְבֵית־אֲבֹתָיו הוּא:

לוי: וְאֵלֶּה שְׁמוֹת הָאֲנָשִׁים אֲשֶׁר יַעַמְדוּ אִתְּכֶם לִרְאוּבֵן אֱלִיצוּר בֶּן־שְׁדֵיאוּר: לְשִׁמְעוֹן שְׁלֻמִיאֵל בֶּן־צוּרִישַׁדָּי: לִיהוּדָה נַחְשׁוֹן בֶּן־עַמִּינָדָב: לְיִשָּׂשכָר נְתַנְאֵל בֶּן־צוּעָר: לִזְבוּלֻן אֱלִיאָב בֶּן־חֵלֹן: לִבְנֵי יוֹסֵף לְאֶפְרַיִם אֱלִישָׁמָע בֶּן־עַמִּיהוּד לִמְנַשֶּׁה גַּמְלִיאֵל בֶּן־פְּדָהצוּר: לְבִנְיָמִן אֲבִידָן בֶּן־גִּדְעֹנִי: לְדָן אֲחִיעֶזֶר בֶּן־עַמִּישַׁדָּי: לְאָשֵׁר פַּגְעִיאֵל בֶּן־עָכְרָן: לְגָד אֶלְיָסָף בֶּן־דְּעוּאֵל: לְנַפְתָּלִי אֲחִירַע בֶּן־עֵינָן: אֵלֶּה קְרוּאֵי הָעֵדָה נְשִׂיאֵי מַטּוֹת אֲבוֹתָם רָאשֵׁי אַלְפֵי יִשְׂרָאֵל הֵם:

ישראל: וַיִּקַּח מֹשֶׁה וְאַהֲרֹן אֵת הָאֲנָשִׁים הָאֵלֶּה אֲשֶׁר נִקְּבוּ בְּשֵׁמוֹת: וְאֵת כָּל־הָעֵדָה הִקְהִילוּ בְּאֶחָד לַחֹדֶשׁ הַשֵּׁנִי וַיִּתְיַלְדוּ עַל־מִשְׁפְּחֹתָם לְבֵית אֲבֹתָם בְּמִסְפַּר שֵׁמוֹת מִבֶּן עֶשְׂרִים שָׁנָה וָמַעְלָה לְגֻלְגְּלֹתָם: כַּאֲשֶׁר צִוָּה יְהוה אֶת־מֹשֶׁה וַיִּפְקְדֵם בְּמִדְבַּר סִינָי:

TORAH READING — NASSO-SHELACH

פ׳ נשא / NASSO

(Numbers 4:21-37)

כא וַיְדַבֵּר יהוה אֶל־מֹשֶׁה לֵּאמֹר: נָשֹׂא אֶת־רֹאשׁ בְּנֵי גֵרְשׁוֹן גַּם־הֵם לְבֵית אֲבֹתָם לְמִשְׁפְּחֹתָם: מִבֶּן שְׁלֹשִׁים שָׁנָה וָמַעְלָה עַד בֶּן־חֲמִשִּׁים שָׁנָה תִּפְקֹד אוֹתָם כָּל־הַבָּא לִצְבֹא צָבָא לַעֲבֹד עֲבֹדָה בְּאֹהֶל מוֹעֵד: זֹאת עֲבֹדַת מִשְׁפְּחֹת הַגֵּרְשֻׁנִּי לַעֲבֹד וּלְמַשָּׂא:

לוי וְנָשְׂאוּ אֶת־יְרִיעֹת הַמִּשְׁכָּן וְאֶת־אֹהֶל מוֹעֵד מִכְסֵהוּ וּמִכְסֵה הַתַּחַשׁ אֲשֶׁר־עָלָיו מִלְמָעְלָה וְאֶת־מָסַךְ פֶּתַח אֹהֶל מוֹעֵד: וְאֵת קַלְעֵי הֶחָצֵר וְאֶת־מָסַךְ ׀ פֶּתַח ׀ שַׁעַר הֶחָצֵר אֲשֶׁר עַל־הַמִּשְׁכָּן וְעַל־הַמִּזְבֵּחַ סָבִיב וְאֵת מֵיתְרֵיהֶם וְאֶת־כָּל־כְּלֵי עֲבֹדָתָם וְאֵת כָּל־אֲשֶׁר יֵעָשֶׂה לָהֶם וְעָבָדוּ: עַל־פִּי אַהֲרֹן וּבָנָיו תִּהְיֶה כָּל־עֲבֹדַת בְּנֵי הַגֵּרְשֻׁנִּי לְכָל־מַשָּׂאָם וּלְכֹל עֲבֹדָתָם וּפְקַדְתֶּם עֲלֵהֶם בְּמִשְׁמֶרֶת אֵת כָּל־מַשָּׂאָם: זֹאת עֲבֹדַת מִשְׁפְּחֹת בְּנֵי הַגֵּרְשֻׁנִּי בְּאֹהֶל מוֹעֵד וּמִשְׁמַרְתָּם בְּיַד אִיתָמָר בֶּן־אַהֲרֹן הַכֹּהֵן:

ישראל: בְּנֵי מְרָרִי לְמִשְׁפְּחֹתָם לְבֵית־אֲבֹתָם תִּפְקֹד אֹתָם: מִבֶּן שְׁלֹשִׁים שָׁנָה וָמַעְלָה וְעַד בֶּן־חֲמִשִּׁים שָׁנָה תִּפְקְדֵם כָּל־הַבָּא לַצָּבָא לַעֲבֹד אֶת־עֲבֹדַת אֹהֶל מוֹעֵד: וְזֹאת מִשְׁמֶרֶת מַשָּׂאָם לְכָל־עֲבֹדָתָם בְּאֹהֶל מוֹעֵד קַרְשֵׁי הַמִּשְׁכָּן וּבְרִיחָיו וְעַמּוּדָיו וַאֲדָנָיו: וְעַמּוּדֵי הֶחָצֵר סָבִיב וְאַדְנֵיהֶם וִיתֵדֹתָם וּמֵיתְרֵיהֶם לְכָל־כְּלֵיהֶם וּלְכֹל עֲבֹדָתָם וּבְשֵׁמֹת תִּפְקְדוּ אֶת־כְּלֵי מִשְׁמֶרֶת מַשָּׂאָם: זֹאת עֲבֹדַת מִשְׁפְּחֹת בְּנֵי מְרָרִי לְכָל־עֲבֹדָתָם בְּאֹהֶל מוֹעֵד בְּיַד אִיתָמָר בֶּן־אַהֲרֹן הַכֹּהֵן:

Some end the reading at this point.

וַיִּפְקֹד מֹשֶׁה וְאַהֲרֹן וּנְשִׂיאֵי הָעֵדָה אֶת־בְּנֵי הַקְּהָתִי לְמִשְׁפְּחֹתָם וּלְבֵית אֲבֹתָם: מִבֶּן שְׁלֹשִׁים שָׁנָה וָמַעְלָה וְעַד בֶּן־חֲמִשִּׁים שָׁנָה כָּל־הַבָּא לַצָּבָא לַעֲבֹדָה בְּאֹהֶל מוֹעֵד: וַיִּהְיוּ פְקֻדֵיהֶם לְמִשְׁפְּחֹתָם אַלְפַּיִם שְׁבַע מֵאוֹת

וַחֲמִשִּׁים: אֵלֶּה פְקוּדֵי מִשְׁפְּחֹת הַקְּהָתִי כָּל־הָעֹבֵד בְּאֹהֶל מוֹעֵד אֲשֶׁר פָּקַד מֹשֶׁה וְאַהֲרֹן עַל־פִּי יהוה בְּיַד־מֹשֶׁה:

פ׳ בהעלתך / BEHA'ALOSCHA

(Numbers 8:1-14)

כהן וַיְדַבֵּר יהוה אֶל־מֹשֶׁה לֵּאמֹר: דַּבֵּר אֶל־אַהֲרֹן וְאָמַרְתָּ אֵלָיו בְּהַעֲלֹתְךָ אֶת־הַנֵּרֹת אֶל־מוּל פְּנֵי הַמְּנוֹרָה יָאִירוּ שִׁבְעַת הַנֵּרוֹת: וַיַּעַשׂ כֵּן אַהֲרֹן אֶל־מוּל פְּנֵי הַמְּנוֹרָה הֶעֱלָה נֵרֹתֶיהָ כַּאֲשֶׁר צִוָּה יהוה אֶת־מֹשֶׁה: וְזֶה מַעֲשֵׂה הַמְּנֹרָה מִקְשָׁה זָהָב עַד־יְרֵכָהּ עַד־פִּרְחָהּ מִקְשָׁה הִוא כַּמַּרְאֶה אֲשֶׁר הֶרְאָה יהוה אֶת־מֹשֶׁה כֵּן עָשָׂה אֶת־הַמְּנֹרָה:

לוי וַיְדַבֵּר יהוה אֶל־מֹשֶׁה לֵּאמֹר: קַח אֶת־הַלְוִיִּם מִתּוֹךְ בְּנֵי יִשְׂרָאֵל וְטִהַרְתָּ אֹתָם: וְכֹה־תַעֲשֶׂה לָהֶם לְטַהֲרָם הַזֵּה עֲלֵיהֶם מֵי חַטָּאת וְהֶעֱבִירוּ תַעַר עַל־כָּל־בְּשָׂרָם וְכִבְּסוּ בִגְדֵיהֶם וְהִטֶּהָרוּ: וְלָקְחוּ פַּר בֶּן־בָּקָר וּמִנְחָתוֹ סֹלֶת בְּלוּלָה בַשָּׁמֶן וּפַר־שֵׁנִי בֶן־בָּקָר תִּקַּח לְחַטָּאת: וְהִקְרַבְתָּ אֶת־הַלְוִיִּם לִפְנֵי אֹהֶל מוֹעֵד וְהִקְהַלְתָּ אֶת־כָּל־עֲדַת בְּנֵי יִשְׂרָאֵל:

ישראל: וְהִקְרַבְתָּ אֶת־הַלְוִיִּם לִפְנֵי יהוה וְסָמְכוּ בְנֵי־יִשְׂרָאֵל אֶת־יְדֵיהֶם עַל־הַלְוִיִּם: וְהֵנִיף אַהֲרֹן אֶת־הַלְוִיִּם תְּנוּפָה לִפְנֵי יהוה מֵאֵת בְּנֵי יִשְׂרָאֵל וְהָיוּ לַעֲבֹד אֶת־עֲבֹדַת יהוה: וְהַלְוִיִּם יִסְמְכוּ אֶת־יְדֵיהֶם עַל רֹאשׁ הַפָּרִים וַעֲשֵׂה אֶת־הָאֶחָד חַטָּאת וְאֶת־הָאֶחָד עֹלָה לַיהוה לְכַפֵּר עַל־הַלְוִיִּם: וְהַעֲמַדְתָּ אֶת־הַלְוִיִּם לִפְנֵי אַהֲרֹן וְלִפְנֵי בָנָיו וְהֵנַפְתָּ אֹתָם תְּנוּפָה לַיהוה: וְהִבְדַּלְתָּ אֶת־הַלְוִיִּם מִתּוֹךְ בְּנֵי יִשְׂרָאֵל וְהָיוּ לִי הַלְוִיִּם:

פ׳ שלח / SHELACH

(Numbers 13:1-20)

כהן וַיְדַבֵּר יהוה אֶל־מֹשֶׁה לֵּאמֹר: שְׁלַח־לְךָ אֲנָשִׁים וְיָתֻרוּ אֶת־אֶרֶץ כְּנַעַן אֲשֶׁר־אֲנִי נֹתֵן לִבְנֵי יִשְׂרָאֵל אִישׁ אֶחָד אִישׁ אֶחָד

לְמַטֵּה אֲבֹתָיו תִּשְׁלָחוּ כֹּל נָשִׂיא בָהֶם: וַיִּשְׁלַח אֹתָם מֹשֶׁה מִמִּדְבַּר פָּארָן עַל־פִּי יהוה כֻּלָּם אֲנָשִׁים רָאשֵׁי בְנֵי־יִשְׂרָאֵל הֵמָּה: לוי וְאֵלֶּה שְׁמוֹתָם לְמַטֵּה רְאוּבֵן שַׁמּוּעַ בֶּן־זַכּוּר: לְמַטֵּה שִׁמְעוֹן שָׁפָט בֶּן־חוֹרִי: לְמַטֵּה יְהוּדָה כָּלֵב בֶּן־יְפֻנֶּה: לְמַטֵּה יִשָּׂשכָר יִגְאָל בֶּן־יוֹסֵף: לְמַטֵּה אֶפְרָיִם הוֹשֵׁעַ בִּן־נוּן: לְמַטֵּה בִנְיָמִן פַּלְטִי בֶּן־רָפוּא: לְמַטֵּה זְבוּלֻן גַּדִּיאֵל בֶּן־סוֹדִי: לְמַטֵּה יוֹסֵף לְמַטֵּה מְנַשֶּׁה גַּדִּי בֶּן־סוּסִי: לְמַטֵּה דָן עַמִּיאֵל בֶּן־גְּמַלִּי: לְמַטֵּה אָשֵׁר סְתוּר בֶּן־מִיכָאֵל: לְמַטֵּה נַפְתָּלִי נַחְבִּי בֶּן־וָפְסִי: לְמַטֵּה גָד גְּאוּאֵל בֶּן־מָכִי: אֵלֶּה שְׁמוֹת הָאֲנָשִׁים אֲשֶׁר־שָׁלַח מֹשֶׁה לָתוּר אֶת־הָאָרֶץ וַיִּקְרָא מֹשֶׁה לְהוֹשֵׁעַ בִּן־נוּן יְהוֹשֻׁעַ:

ישראל: וַיִּשְׁלַח אֹתָם מֹשֶׁה לָתוּר אֶת־אֶרֶץ כְּנָעַן וַיֹּאמֶר אֲלֵהֶם עֲלוּ זֶה בַּנֶּגֶב וַעֲלִיתֶם אֶת־הָהָר: וּרְאִיתֶם אֶת־הָאָרֶץ מַה־הִוא וְאֶת־הָעָם הַיֹּשֵׁב עָלֶיהָ הֶחָזָק הוּא הֲרָפֶה הַמְעַט הוּא אִם־רָב: וּמָה הָאָרֶץ אֲשֶׁר־הוּא יֹשֵׁב בָּהּ הֲטוֹבָה הִוא אִם־רָעָה וּמָה הֶעָרִים אֲשֶׁר־הוּא יוֹשֵׁב בָּהֵנָּה הַבְּמַחֲנִים אִם בְּמִבְצָרִים: וּמָה הָאָרֶץ הַשְּׁמֵנָה הִוא אִם־רָזָה הֲיֵשׁ־בָּהּ עֵץ אִם־אַיִן וְהִתְחַזַּקְתֶּם וּלְקַחְתֶּם מִפְּרִי הָאָרֶץ וְהַיָּמִים יְמֵי בִּכּוּרֵי עֲנָבִים:

פ׳ קרח / KORACH
(Numbers 16:1-13)

כהן: וַיִּקַּח קֹרַח בֶּן־יִצְהָר בֶּן־קְהָת בֶּן־לֵוִי וְדָתָן וַאֲבִירָם בְּנֵי אֱלִיאָב וְאוֹן בֶּן־פֶּלֶת בְּנֵי רְאוּבֵן: וַיָּקֻמוּ לִפְנֵי מֹשֶׁה וַאֲנָשִׁים מִבְּנֵי־יִשְׂרָאֵל חֲמִשִּׁים וּמָאתָיִם נְשִׂיאֵי עֵדָה קְרִאֵי מוֹעֵד אַנְשֵׁי־שֵׁם: וַיִּקָּהֲלוּ עַל־מֹשֶׁה וְעַל־אַהֲרֹן וַיֹּאמְרוּ אֲלֵהֶם רַב־לָכֶם כִּי כָל־הָעֵדָה כֻּלָּם קְדֹשִׁים וּבְתוֹכָם יהוה וּמַדּוּעַ תִּתְנַשְּׂאוּ עַל־קְהַל יהוה:

לוי: וַיִּשְׁמַע מֹשֶׁה וַיִּפֹּל עַל־פָּנָיו: וַיְדַבֵּר אֶל־קֹרַח וְאֶל־כָּל־עֲדָתוֹ לֵאמֹר בֹּקֶר וְיֹדַע יהוה אֶת־אֲשֶׁר־לוֹ וְאֶת־הַקָּדוֹשׁ וְהִקְרִיב אֵלָיו וְאֵת אֲשֶׁר יִבְחַר־בּוֹ יַקְרִיב אֵלָיו: זֹאת עֲשׂוּ קְחוּ־לָכֶם מַחְתּוֹת קֹרַח וְכָל־עֲדָתוֹ: וּתְנוּ בָהֵן ׀ אֵשׁ וְשִׂימוּ עֲלֵיהֶן ׀ קְטֹרֶת לִפְנֵי יהוה מָחָר וְהָיָה הָאִישׁ אֲשֶׁר־יִבְחַר יהוה הוּא הַקָּדוֹשׁ רַב־לָכֶם בְּנֵי לֵוִי:

ישראל: וַיֹּאמֶר מֹשֶׁה אֶל־קֹרַח שִׁמְעוּ־נָא בְּנֵי לֵוִי: הַמְעַט מִכֶּם כִּי־הִבְדִּיל אֱלֹהֵי יִשְׂרָאֵל אֶתְכֶם מֵעֲדַת יִשְׂרָאֵל לְהַקְרִיב אֶתְכֶם אֵלָיו לַעֲבֹד אֶת־עֲבֹדַת מִשְׁכַּן יהוה וְלַעֲמֹד לִפְנֵי הָעֵדָה לְשָׁרְתָם: וַיַּקְרֵב אֹתְךָ וְאֶת־כָּל־אַחֶיךָ בְנֵי־לֵוִי אִתָּךְ וּבִקַּשְׁתֶּם גַּם־כְּהֻנָּה: לָכֵן אַתָּה וְכָל־עֲדָתְךָ הַנֹּעָדִים עַל־יהוה וְאַהֲרֹן מַה־הוּא כִּי תַלִּינוּ עָלָיו: וַיִּשְׁלַח מֹשֶׁה לִקְרֹא לְדָתָן וְלַאֲבִירָם בְּנֵי אֱלִיאָב וַיֹּאמְרוּ לֹא נַעֲלֶה: הַמְעַט כִּי הֶעֱלִיתָנוּ מֵאֶרֶץ זָבַת חָלָב וּדְבַשׁ לַהֲמִיתֵנוּ בַּמִּדְבָּר כִּי־תִשְׂתָּרֵר עָלֵינוּ גַּם־הִשְׂתָּרֵר:

פ׳ חקת / CHUKAS
(Numbers 19:1-17)

כהן: וַיְדַבֵּר יהוה אֶל־מֹשֶׁה וְאֶל־אַהֲרֹן לֵאמֹר: זֹאת חֻקַּת הַתּוֹרָה אֲשֶׁר־צִוָּה יהוה לֵאמֹר דַּבֵּר ׀ אֶל־בְּנֵי יִשְׂרָאֵל וְיִקְחוּ אֵלֶיךָ פָרָה אֲדֻמָּה תְּמִימָה אֲשֶׁר אֵין־בָּהּ מוּם אֲשֶׁר לֹא־עָלָה עָלֶיהָ עֹל: וּנְתַתֶּם אֹתָהּ אֶל־אֶלְעָזָר הַכֹּהֵן וְהוֹצִיא אֹתָהּ אֶל־מִחוּץ לַמַּחֲנֶה וְשָׁחַט אֹתָהּ לְפָנָיו: וְלָקַח אֶלְעָזָר הַכֹּהֵן מִדָּמָהּ בְּאֶצְבָּעוֹ וְהִזָּה אֶל־נֹכַח פְּנֵי אֹהֶל־מוֹעֵד מִדָּמָהּ שֶׁבַע פְּעָמִים: וְשָׂרַף אֶת־הַפָּרָה לְעֵינָיו אֶת־עֹרָהּ וְאֶת־בְּשָׂרָהּ וְאֶת־דָּמָהּ עַל־פִּרְשָׁהּ יִשְׂרֹף: וְלָקַח הַכֹּהֵן עֵץ אֶרֶז וְאֵזוֹב וּשְׁנִי תוֹלָעַת וְהִשְׁלִיךְ אֶל־תּוֹךְ שְׂרֵפַת הַפָּרָה:

לוי: וְכִבֶּס בְּגָדָיו הַכֹּהֵן וְרָחַץ בְּשָׂרוֹ בַּמַּיִם וְאַחַר יָבֹא אֶל־הַמַּחֲנֶה וְטָמֵא הַכֹּהֵן עַד־הָעָרֶב: וְהַשֹּׂרֵף אֹתָהּ יְכַבֵּס בְּגָדָיו בַּמַּיִם וְרָחַץ בְּשָׂרוֹ בַּמָּיִם וְטָמֵא עַד־הָעָרֶב: וְאָסַף ׀ אִישׁ טָהוֹר אֵת אֵפֶר הַפָּרָה וְהִנִּיחַ מִחוּץ לַמַּחֲנֶה בְּמָקוֹם טָהוֹר וְהָיְתָה לַעֲדַת בְּנֵי־יִשְׂרָאֵל לְמִשְׁמֶרֶת לְמֵי נִדָּה חַטָּאת הִוא:

ישראל: וְכִבֶּס הָאֹסֵף אֶת־אֵפֶר הַפָּרָה אֶת־בְּגָדָיו וְטָמֵא עַד־הָעָרֶב וְהָיְתָה לִבְנֵי יִשְׂרָאֵל וְלַגֵּר הַגָּר בְּתוֹכָם לְחֻקַּת עוֹלָם: הַנֹּגֵעַ בְּמֵת לְכָל־נֶפֶשׁ אָדָם וְטָמֵא שִׁבְעַת יָמִים: הוּא יִתְחַטָּא־בוֹ בַּיּוֹם הַשְּׁלִישִׁי וּבַיּוֹם הַשְּׁבִיעִי יִטְהָר וְאִם־לֹא יִתְחַטָּא בַּיּוֹם הַשְּׁלִישִׁי וּבַיּוֹם הַשְּׁבִיעִי לֹא יִטְהָר: כָּל־הַנֹּגֵעַ בְּמֵת בְּנֶפֶשׁ הָאָדָם אֲשֶׁר־יָמוּת וְלֹא יִתְחַטָּא אֶת־מִשְׁכַּן יְהוָה טִמֵּא וְנִכְרְתָה הַנֶּפֶשׁ הַהִוא מִיִּשְׂרָאֵל כִּי מֵי נִדָּה לֹא־זֹרַק עָלָיו טָמֵא יִהְיֶה עוֹד טֻמְאָתוֹ בוֹ: זֹאת הַתּוֹרָה אָדָם כִּי־יָמוּת בְּאֹהֶל כָּל־הַבָּא אֶל־הָאֹהֶל וְכָל־אֲשֶׁר בָּאֹהֶל יִטְמָא שִׁבְעַת יָמִים: וְכֹל כְּלִי פָתוּחַ אֲשֶׁר אֵין־צָמִיד פָּתִיל עָלָיו טָמֵא הוּא: וְכֹל אֲשֶׁר־יִגַּע עַל־פְּנֵי הַשָּׂדֶה בַּחֲלַל־חֶרֶב אוֹ בְמֵת אוֹ־בְעֶצֶם אָדָם אוֹ בְקָבֶר יִטְמָא שִׁבְעַת יָמִים: וְלָקְחוּ לַטָּמֵא מֵעֲפַר שְׂרֵפַת הַחַטָּאת וְנָתַן עָלָיו מַיִם חַיִּים אֶל־כֶּלִי:

פ׳ בלק / BALAK
(Numbers 22:2-12)

כה: וַיַּרְא בָּלָק בֶּן־צִפּוֹר אֵת כָּל־אֲשֶׁר־עָשָׂה יִשְׂרָאֵל לָאֱמֹרִי: וַיָּגָר מוֹאָב מִפְּנֵי הָעָם מְאֹד כִּי רַב־הוּא וַיָּקָץ מוֹאָב מִפְּנֵי בְּנֵי יִשְׂרָאֵל: וַיֹּאמֶר מוֹאָב אֶל־זִקְנֵי מִדְיָן עַתָּה יְלַחֲכוּ הַקָּהָל אֶת־כָּל־סְבִיבֹתֵינוּ כִּלְחֹךְ הַשּׁוֹר אֵת יֶרֶק הַשָּׂדֶה וּבָלָק בֶּן־צִפּוֹר מֶלֶךְ לְמוֹאָב בָּעֵת הַהִוא:
לוי: וַיִּשְׁלַח מַלְאָכִים אֶל־בִּלְעָם בֶּן־בְּעוֹר פְּתוֹרָה אֲשֶׁר עַל־הַנָּהָר אֶרֶץ בְּנֵי־עַמּוֹ לִקְרֹא־לוֹ לֵאמֹר הִנֵּה עַם יָצָא מִמִּצְרַיִם הִנֵּה כִסָּה אֶת־עֵין הָאָרֶץ וְהוּא יֹשֵׁב מִמֻּלִי: וְעַתָּה לְכָה־נָּא אָרָה־לִּי אֶת־הָעָם הַזֶּה כִּי־עָצוּם הוּא מִמֶּנִּי אוּלַי אוּכַל נַכֶּה־בּוֹ וַאֲגָרְשֶׁנּוּ מִן־הָאָרֶץ כִּי יָדַעְתִּי אֵת אֲשֶׁר־תְּבָרֵךְ מְבֹרָךְ וַאֲשֶׁר תָּאֹר יוּאָר: וַיֵּלְכוּ זִקְנֵי מוֹאָב וְזִקְנֵי מִדְיָן וּקְסָמִים בְּיָדָם וַיָּבֹאוּ אֶל־בִּלְעָם וַיְדַבְּרוּ אֵלָיו דִּבְרֵי בָלָק:
ישראל: וַיֹּאמֶר אֲלֵיהֶם לִינוּ פֹה הַלַּיְלָה

וַהֲשִׁבֹתִי אֶתְכֶם דָּבָר כַּאֲשֶׁר יְדַבֵּר יְהוָה אֵלַי וַיֵּשְׁבוּ שָׂרֵי־מוֹאָב עִם־בִּלְעָם: וַיָּבֹא אֱלֹהִים אֶל־בִּלְעָם וַיֹּאמֶר מִי הָאֲנָשִׁים הָאֵלֶּה עִמָּךְ: וַיֹּאמֶר בִּלְעָם אֶל־הָאֱלֹהִים בָּלָק בֶּן־צִפֹּר מֶלֶךְ מוֹאָב שָׁלַח אֵלָי: הִנֵּה הָעָם הַיֹּצֵא מִמִּצְרַיִם וַיְכַס אֶת־עֵין הָאָרֶץ עַתָּה לְכָה קָבָה־לִּי אֹתוֹ אוּלַי אוּכַל לְהִלָּחֶם בּוֹ וְגֵרַשְׁתִּיו: וַיֹּאמֶר אֱלֹהִים אֶל־בִּלְעָם לֹא תֵלֵךְ עִמָּהֶם לֹא תָאֹר אֶת־הָעָם כִּי בָרוּךְ הוּא:

פ׳ פנחס / PINCHAS
(Numbers 25:10—26:4)

כה: וַיְדַבֵּר יְהוָה אֶל־מֹשֶׁה לֵּאמֹר: פִּינְחָס בֶּן־אֶלְעָזָר בֶּן־אַהֲרֹן הַכֹּהֵן הֵשִׁיב אֶת־חֲמָתִי מֵעַל בְּנֵי־יִשְׂרָאֵל בְּקַנְאוֹ אֶת־קִנְאָתִי בְּתוֹכָם וְלֹא־כִלִּיתִי אֶת־בְּנֵי־יִשְׂרָאֵל בְּקִנְאָתִי: לָכֵן אֱמֹר הִנְנִי נֹתֵן לוֹ אֶת־בְּרִיתִי שָׁלוֹם:
לוי: וְהָיְתָה לּוֹ וּלְזַרְעוֹ אַחֲרָיו בְּרִית כְּהֻנַּת עוֹלָם תַּחַת אֲשֶׁר קִנֵּא לֵאלֹהָיו וַיְכַפֵּר עַל־בְּנֵי יִשְׂרָאֵל: וְשֵׁם אִישׁ יִשְׂרָאֵל הַמֻּכֶּה אֲשֶׁר הֻכָּה אֶת־הַמִּדְיָנִית זִמְרִי בֶּן־סָלוּא נְשִׂיא בֵית־אָב לַשִּׁמְעֹנִי: וְשֵׁם הָאִשָּׁה הַמֻּכָּה הַמִּדְיָנִית כָּזְבִּי בַת־צוּר רֹאשׁ אֻמּוֹת בֵּית־אָב בְּמִדְיָן הוּא:
ישראל: וַיְדַבֵּר יְהוָה אֶל־מֹשֶׁה לֵּאמֹר: צָרוֹר אֶת־הַמִּדְיָנִים וְהִכִּיתֶם אוֹתָם: כִּי צֹרְרִים הֵם לָכֶם בְּנִכְלֵיהֶם אֲשֶׁר־נִכְּלוּ לָכֶם עַל־דְּבַר־פְּעוֹר וְעַל־דְּבַר כָּזְבִּי בַת־נְשִׂיא מִדְיָן אֲחֹתָם הַמֻּכָּה בְיוֹם־הַמַּגֵּפָה עַל־דְּבַר־פְּעוֹר: וַיְהִי אַחֲרֵי הַמַּגֵּפָה וַיֹּאמֶר יְהוָה אֶל־מֹשֶׁה וְאֶל אֶלְעָזָר בֶּן־אַהֲרֹן הַכֹּהֵן לֵאמֹר: שְׂאוּ אֶת־רֹאשׁ | כָּל־עֲדַת בְּנֵי־יִשְׂרָאֵל מִבֶּן עֶשְׂרִים שָׁנָה וָמַעְלָה לְבֵית אֲבֹתָם כָּל־יֹצֵא צָבָא בְּיִשְׂרָאֵל: וַיְדַבֵּר מֹשֶׁה וְאֶלְעָזָר הַכֹּהֵן אֹתָם בְּעַרְבֹת מוֹאָב עַל־יַרְדֵּן יְרֵחוֹ לֵאמֹר: מִבֶּן עֶשְׂרִים שָׁנָה וָמַעְלָה כַּאֲשֶׁר צִוָּה יְהוָה אֶת־מֹשֶׁה וּבְנֵי יִשְׂרָאֵל הַיֹּצְאִים מֵאֶרֶץ מִצְרָיִם:

◃{ פ׳ מטות / MATOS }▹

(Numbers 30:2-17)

כהן: וַיְדַבֵּר מֹשֶׁה אֶל־רָאשֵׁי הַמַּטּוֹת לִבְנֵי יִשְׂרָאֵל לֵאמֹר זֶה הַדָּבָר אֲשֶׁר צִוָּה יְהֹוָה: אִישׁ כִּי־יִדֹּר נֶדֶר לַיהֹוָה אִוֹ־הִשָּׁבַע שְׁבֻעָה לֶאְסֹר אִסָּר עַל־נַפְשׁוֹ לֹא יַחֵל דְּבָרוֹ כְּכָל־הַיֹּצֵא מִפִּיו יַעֲשֶׂה: וְאִשָּׁה כִּי־תִדֹּר נֶדֶר לַיהֹוָה וְאָסְרָה אִסָּר בְּבֵית אָבִיהָ בִּנְעֻרֶיהָ: וְשָׁמַע אָבִיהָ אֶת־נִדְרָהּ וֶאֱסָרָהּ אֲשֶׁר אָסְרָה עַל־נַפְשָׁהּ וְהֶחֱרִישׁ לָהּ אָבִיהָ וְקָמוּ כָּל־נְדָרֶיהָ וְכָל־אִסָּר אֲשֶׁר־אָסְרָה עַל־נַפְשָׁהּ יָקוּם: וְאִם־הֵנִיא אָבִיהָ אֹתָהּ בְּיוֹם שָׁמְעוֹ כָּל־נְדָרֶיהָ וֶאֱסָרֶיהָ אֲשֶׁר־אָסְרָה עַל־נַפְשָׁהּ לֹא יָקוּם וַיהֹוָה יִסְלַח־לָהּ כִּי־הֵנִיא אָבִיהָ אֹתָהּ: וְאִם־הָיוֹ תִהְיֶה לְאִישׁ וּנְדָרֶיהָ עָלֶיהָ אוֹ מִבְטָא שְׂפָתֶיהָ אֲשֶׁר אָסְרָה עַל־נַפְשָׁהּ: וְשָׁמַע אִישָׁהּ בְּיוֹם שָׁמְעוֹ וְהֶחֱרִישׁ לָהּ וְקָמוּ נְדָרֶיהָ וֶאֱסָרֶהָ אֲשֶׁר־אָסְרָה עַל־נַפְשָׁהּ יָקֻמוּ: וְאִם בְּיוֹם שְׁמֹעַ אִישָׁהּ יָנִיא אוֹתָהּ וְהֵפֵר אֶת־נִדְרָהּ אֲשֶׁר עָלֶיהָ וְאֵת מִבְטָא שְׂפָתֶיהָ אֲשֶׁר אָסְרָה עַל־נַפְשָׁהּ וַיהֹוָה יִסְלַח־לָהּ:

לוי: וְנֵדֶר אַלְמָנָה וּגְרוּשָׁה כֹּל אֲשֶׁר־אָסְרָה עַל־נַפְשָׁהּ יָקוּם עָלֶיהָ: וְאִם־בֵּית אִישָׁהּ נָדָרָה אוֹ־אָסְרָה אִסָּר עַל־נַפְשָׁהּ בִּשְׁבֻעָה: וְשָׁמַע אִישָׁהּ וְהֶחֱרִשׁ לָהּ לֹא הֵנִיא אֹתָהּ וְקָמוּ כָּל־נְדָרֶיהָ וְכָל־אִסָּר אֲשֶׁר־אָסְרָה עַל־נַפְשָׁהּ יָקוּם: וְאִם־הָפֵר יָפֵר אֹתָם ׀ אִישָׁהּ בְּיוֹם שָׁמְעוֹ כָּל־מוֹצָא שְׂפָתֶיהָ לִנְדָרֶיהָ וּלְאִסַּר נַפְשָׁהּ לֹא יָקוּם אִישָׁהּ הֲפֵרָם וַיהֹוָה יִסְלַח־לָהּ:

ישראל: כָּל־נֵדֶר וְכָל־שְׁבֻעַת אִסָּר לְעַנֹּת נָפֶשׁ אִישָׁהּ יְקִימֶנּוּ וְאִישָׁהּ יְפֵרֶנּוּ: וְאִם־הַחֲרֵשׁ יַחֲרִישׁ לָהּ אִישָׁהּ מִיּוֹם אֶל־יוֹם וְהֵקִים אֶת־כָּל־נְדָרֶיהָ אוֹ אֶת־כָּל־אֱסָרֶיהָ אֲשֶׁר עָלֶיהָ הֵקִים אֹתָם כִּי־הֶחֱרִשׁ לָהּ בְּיוֹם שָׁמְעוֹ: וְאִם־הָפֵר יָפֵר אֹתָם אַחֲרֵי שָׁמְעוֹ וְנָשָׂא אֶת־עֲוֺנָהּ: אֵלֶּה הַחֻקִּים אֲשֶׁר צִוָּה יְהֹוָה אֶת־מֹשֶׁה בֵּין אִישׁ לְאִשְׁתּוֹ בֵּין־אָב לְבִתּוֹ בִּנְעֻרֶיהָ בֵּית אָבִיהָ:

◃{ פ׳ מסעי / MASEI }▹

(Numbers 33:1-10)

כהן: אֵלֶּה מַסְעֵי בְנֵי־יִשְׂרָאֵל אֲשֶׁר יָצְאוּ מֵאֶרֶץ מִצְרַיִם לְצִבְאֹתָם בְּיַד־מֹשֶׁה וְאַהֲרֹן: וַיִּכְתֹּב מֹשֶׁה אֶת־מוֹצָאֵיהֶם לְמַסְעֵיהֶם עַל־פִּי יְהֹוָה וְאֵלֶּה מַסְעֵיהֶם לְמוֹצָאֵיהֶם: וַיִּסְעוּ מֵרַעְמְסֵס בַּחֹדֶשׁ הָרִאשׁוֹן בַּחֲמִשָּׁה עָשָׂר יוֹם לַחֹדֶשׁ הָרִאשׁוֹן מִמָּחֳרַת הַפֶּסַח יָצְאוּ בְנֵי־יִשְׂרָאֵל בְּיָד רָמָה לְעֵינֵי כָּל־מִצְרָיִם:

לוי: וּמִצְרַיִם מְקַבְּרִים אֵת אֲשֶׁר הִכָּה יְהֹוָה בָּהֶם כָּל־בְּכוֹר וּבֵאלֹהֵיהֶם עָשָׂה יְהֹוָה שְׁפָטִים: וַיִּסְעוּ בְנֵי־יִשְׂרָאֵל מֵרַעְמְסֵס וַיַּחֲנוּ בְּסֻכֹּת: וַיִּסְעוּ מִסֻּכֹּת וַיַּחֲנוּ בְאֵתָם אֲשֶׁר בִּקְצֵה הַמִּדְבָּר:

ישראל: וַיִּסְעוּ מֵאֵתָם וַיָּשָׁב עַל־פִּי הַחִירֹת אֲשֶׁר עַל־פְּנֵי בַּעַל צְפוֹן וַיַּחֲנוּ לִפְנֵי מִגְדֹּל: וַיִּסְעוּ מִפְּנֵי הַחִירֹת וַיַּעַבְרוּ בְתוֹךְ־הַיָּם הַמִּדְבָּרָה וַיֵּלְכוּ דֶּרֶךְ שְׁלֹשֶׁת יָמִים בְּמִדְבַּר אֵתָם וַיַּחֲנוּ בְּמָרָה: וַיִּסְעוּ מִמָּרָה וַיָּבֹאוּ אֵילִמָה וּבְאֵילִם שְׁתֵּים עֶשְׂרֵה עֵינֹת מַיִם וְשִׁבְעִים תְּמָרִים וַיַּחֲנוּ־שָׁם: וַיִּסְעוּ מֵאֵילִם וַיַּחֲנוּ עַל־יַם־סוּף:

◃{ פ׳ דברים / DEVARIM }▹

(Deuteronomy 1:1-11)

כהן: אֵלֶּה הַדְּבָרִים אֲשֶׁר דִּבֶּר מֹשֶׁה אֶל־כָּל־יִשְׂרָאֵל בְּעֵבֶר הַיַּרְדֵּן בַּמִּדְבָּר בָּעֲרָבָה מוֹל סוּף בֵּין־פָּארָן וּבֵין־תֹּפֶל וְלָבָן וַחֲצֵרֹת וְדִי זָהָב: אַחַד עָשָׂר יוֹם מֵחֹרֵב דֶּרֶךְ הַר־שֵׂעִיר עַד קָדֵשׁ בַּרְנֵעַ: וַיְהִי בְּאַרְבָּעִים שָׁנָה בְּעַשְׁתֵּי־עָשָׂר חֹדֶשׁ בְּאֶחָד לַחֹדֶשׁ דִּבֶּר מֹשֶׁה אֶל־בְּנֵי יִשְׂרָאֵל כְּכֹל אֲשֶׁר צִוָּה יְהֹוָה אֹתוֹ אֲלֵהֶם:

לוי: אַחֲרֵי הַכֹּתוֹ אֵת סִיחֹן מֶלֶךְ הָאֱמֹרִי אֲשֶׁר יוֹשֵׁב בְּחֶשְׁבּוֹן וְאֵת עוֹג מֶלֶךְ הַבָּשָׁן אֲשֶׁר־יוֹשֵׁב בְּעַשְׁתָּרֹת בְּאֶדְרֶעִי: בְּעֵבֶר הַיַּרְדֵּן בְּאֶרֶץ מוֹאָב הוֹאִיל מֹשֶׁה בֵּאֵר אֶת־הַתּוֹרָה הַזֹּאת לֵאמֹר: יְהֹוָה אֱלֹהֵינוּ

דִּבֶּר אֵלֵינוּ בְּחֹרֵב לֵאמֹר רַב־לָכֶם שֶׁבֶת בָּהָר הַזֶּה: פְּנוּ ׀ וּסְעוּ לָכֶם וּבֹאוּ הַר הָאֱמֹרִי וְאֶל־כָּל־שְׁכֵנָיו בָּעֲרָבָה בָהָר וּבַשְּׁפֵלָה וּבַנֶּגֶב וּבְחוֹף הַיָּם אֶרֶץ הַכְּנַעֲנִי וְהַלְּבָנוֹן עַד־הַנָּהָר הַגָּדֹל נְהַר־פְּרָת:

ישראל׃ רְאֵה נָתַתִּי לִפְנֵיכֶם אֶת־הָאָרֶץ בֹּאוּ וּרְשׁוּ אֶת־הָאָרֶץ אֲשֶׁר נִשְׁבַּע יְהֹוָה לַאֲבֹתֵיכֶם לְאַבְרָהָם לְיִצְחָק וּלְיַעֲקֹב לָתֵת לָהֶם וּלְזַרְעָם אַחֲרֵיהֶם: וָאֹמַר אֲלֵכֶם בָּעֵת הַהִוא לֵאמֹר לֹא־אוּכַל לְבַדִּי שְׂאֵת אֶתְכֶם: יְהֹוָה אֱלֹהֵיכֶם הִרְבָּה אֶתְכֶם וְהִנְּכֶם הַיּוֹם כְּכוֹכְבֵי הַשָּׁמַיִם לָרֹב: יְהֹוָה אֱלֹהֵי אֲבוֹתֵכֶם יֹסֵף עֲלֵיכֶם כָּכֶם אֶלֶף פְּעָמִים וִיבָרֵךְ אֶתְכֶם כַּאֲשֶׁר דִּבֶּר לָכֶם:

◈ פ׳ ואתחנן / VA'ESCHANAN ◈
(Deuteronomy 3:23–4:8)

כה׃ וָאֶתְחַנַּן אֶל־יְהֹוָה בָּעֵת הַהִוא לֵאמֹר: אֲדֹנָי יֱהֹוִה אַתָּה הַחִלּוֹתָ לְהַרְאוֹת אֶת־עַבְדְּךָ אֶת־גָּדְלְךָ וְאֶת־יָדְךָ הַחֲזָקָה אֲשֶׁר מִי־אֵל בַּשָּׁמַיִם וּבָאָרֶץ אֲשֶׁר־יַעֲשֶׂה כְמַעֲשֶׂיךָ וְכִגְבוּרֹתֶךָ: אֶעְבְּרָה־נָּא וְאֶרְאֶה אֶת־הָאָרֶץ הַטּוֹבָה אֲשֶׁר בְּעֵבֶר הַיַּרְדֵּן הָהָר הַטּוֹב הַזֶּה וְהַלְּבָנֹן:

לוי׃ וַיִּתְעַבֵּר יְהֹוָה בִּי לְמַעַנְכֶם וְלֹא שָׁמַע אֵלָי וַיֹּאמֶר יְהֹוָה אֵלַי רַב־לָךְ אַל־תּוֹסֶף דַּבֵּר אֵלַי עוֹד בַּדָּבָר הַזֶּה: עֲלֵה ׀ רֹאשׁ הַפִּסְגָּה וְשָׂא עֵינֶיךָ יָמָּה וְצָפֹנָה וְתֵימָנָה וּמִזְרָחָה וּרְאֵה בְעֵינֶיךָ כִּי־לֹא תַעֲבֹר אֶת־הַיַּרְדֵּן הַזֶּה: וְצַו אֶת־יְהוֹשֻׁעַ וְחַזְּקֵהוּ וְאַמְּצֵהוּ כִּי־הוּא יַעֲבֹר לִפְנֵי הָעָם הַזֶּה וְהוּא יַנְחִיל אוֹתָם אֶת־הָאָרֶץ אֲשֶׁר תִּרְאֶה: וַנֵּשֶׁב בַּגָּיְא מוּל בֵּית פְּעוֹר: וְעַתָּה יִשְׂרָאֵל שְׁמַע אֶל־הַחֻקִּים וְאֶל־הַמִּשְׁפָּטִים אֲשֶׁר אָנֹכִי מְלַמֵּד אֶתְכֶם לַעֲשׂוֹת לְמַעַן תִּחְיוּ וּבָאתֶם וִירִשְׁתֶּם אֶת־הָאָרֶץ אֲשֶׁר יְהֹוָה אֱלֹהֵי אֲבֹתֵיכֶם נֹתֵן לָכֶם: לֹא תֹסִפוּ עַל־הַדָּבָר אֲשֶׁר אָנֹכִי מְצַוֶּה אֶתְכֶם וְלֹא תִגְרְעוּ מִמֶּנּוּ לִשְׁמֹר אֶת־מִצְוֺת יְהֹוָה אֱלֹהֵיכֶם אֲשֶׁר אָנֹכִי מְצַוֶּה אֶתְכֶם: עֵינֵיכֶם

הָרֹאוֹת אֵת אֲשֶׁר־עָשָׂה יְהֹוָה בְּבַעַל פְּעוֹר כִּי כָל־הָאִישׁ אֲשֶׁר הָלַךְ אַחֲרֵי בַעַל־פְּעוֹר הִשְׁמִידוֹ יְהֹוָה אֱלֹהֶיךָ מִקִּרְבֶּךָ: וְאַתֶּם הַדְּבֵקִים בַּיהֹוָה אֱלֹהֵיכֶם חַיִּים כֻּלְּכֶם הַיּוֹם:

ישראל׃ רְאֵה ׀ לִמַּדְתִּי אֶתְכֶם חֻקִּים וּמִשְׁפָּטִים כַּאֲשֶׁר צִוַּנִי יְהֹוָה אֱלֹהָי לַעֲשׂוֹת כֵּן בְּקֶרֶב הָאָרֶץ אֲשֶׁר אַתֶּם בָּאִים שָׁמָּה לְרִשְׁתָּהּ: וּשְׁמַרְתֶּם וַעֲשִׂיתֶם כִּי הִוא חָכְמַתְכֶם וּבִינַתְכֶם לְעֵינֵי הָעַמִּים אֲשֶׁר יִשְׁמְעוּן אֵת כָּל־הַחֻקִּים הָאֵלֶּה וְאָמְרוּ רַק עַם־חָכָם וְנָבוֹן הַגּוֹי הַגָּדוֹל הַזֶּה: כִּי מִי־גוֹי גָּדוֹל אֲשֶׁר־לוֹ אֱלֹהִים קְרֹבִים אֵלָיו כַּיהֹוָה אֱלֹהֵינוּ בְּכָל־קָרְאֵנוּ אֵלָיו: וּמִי גּוֹי גָּדוֹל אֲשֶׁר־לוֹ חֻקִּים וּמִשְׁפָּטִים צַדִּיקִם כְּכֹל הַתּוֹרָה הַזֹּאת אֲשֶׁר אָנֹכִי נֹתֵן לִפְנֵיכֶם הַיּוֹם:

◈ פ׳ עקב / EIKEV ◈
(Deuteronomy 7:12–8:10)

כה׃ וְהָיָה ׀ עֵקֶב תִּשְׁמְעוּן אֵת הַמִּשְׁפָּטִים הָאֵלֶּה וּשְׁמַרְתֶּם וַעֲשִׂיתֶם אֹתָם וְשָׁמַר יְהֹוָה אֱלֹהֶיךָ לְךָ אֶת־הַבְּרִית וְאֶת־הַחֶסֶד אֲשֶׁר נִשְׁבַּע לַאֲבֹתֶיךָ: וַאֲהֵבְךָ וּבֵרַכְךָ וְהִרְבֶּךָ וּבֵרַךְ פְּרִי־בִטְנְךָ וּפְרִי־אַדְמָתֶךָ דְּגָנְךָ וְתִירֹשְׁךָ וְיִצְהָרֶךָ שְׁגַר־אֲלָפֶיךָ וְעַשְׁתְּרֹת צֹאנֶךָ עַל הָאֲדָמָה אֲשֶׁר־נִשְׁבַּע לַאֲבֹתֶיךָ לָתֶת לָךְ: בָּרוּךְ תִּהְיֶה מִכָּל־הָעַמִּים לֹא־יִהְיֶה בְךָ עָקָר וַעֲקָרָה וּבִבְהֶמְתֶּךָ: וְהֵסִיר יְהֹוָה מִמְּךָ כָּל־חֹלִי וְכָל־מַדְוֵי מִצְרַיִם הָרָעִים אֲשֶׁר יָדַעְתָּ לֹא יְשִׂימָם בָּךְ וּנְתָנָם בְּכָל־שֹׂנְאֶיךָ: וְאָכַלְתָּ אֶת־כָּל־הָעַמִּים אֲשֶׁר יְהֹוָה אֱלֹהֶיךָ נֹתֵן לָךְ לֹא־תָחוֹס עֵינְךָ עֲלֵיהֶם וְלֹא תַעֲבֹד אֶת־אֱלֹהֵיהֶם כִּי־מוֹקֵשׁ הוּא לָךְ: כִּי תֹאמַר בִּלְבָבְךָ רַבִּים הַגּוֹיִם הָאֵלֶּה מִמֶּנִּי אֵיכָה אוּכַל לְהוֹרִישָׁם: לֹא תִירָא מֵהֶם זָכֹר תִּזְכֹּר אֵת אֲשֶׁר־עָשָׂה יְהֹוָה אֱלֹהֶיךָ לְפַרְעֹה וּלְכָל־מִצְרָיִם: הַמַּסֹּת הַגְּדֹלֹת אֲשֶׁר־רָאוּ עֵינֶיךָ וְהָאֹתֹת וְהַמֹּפְתִים וְהַיָּד הַחֲזָקָה וְהַזְּרֹעַ הַנְּטוּיָה אֲשֶׁר הוֹצִאֲךָ יְהֹוָה אֱלֹהֶיךָ

כֵּן יַעֲשֶׂה יהוה אֱלֹהֶיךָ לְכָל־הָעַמִּים אֲשֶׁר־אַתָּה יָרֵא מִפְּנֵיהֶם: וְגַם אֶת־הַצִּרְעָה יְשַׁלַּח יהוה אֱלֹהֶיךָ בָּם עַד־אֲבֹד הַנִּשְׁאָרִים וְהַנִּסְתָּרִים מִפָּנֶיךָ: לֹא תַעֲרֹץ מִפְּנֵיהֶם כִּי־יהוה אֱלֹהֶיךָ בְּקִרְבֶּךָ אֵל גָּדוֹל וְנוֹרָא: לוי וְנָשַׁל יהוה אֱלֹהֶיךָ אֶת־הַגּוֹיִם הָאֵל מִפָּנֶיךָ מְעַט מְעָט לֹא תוּכַל כַּלֹּתָם מַהֵר פֶּן־תִּרְבֶּה עָלֶיךָ חַיַּת הַשָּׂדֶה: וּנְתָנָם יהוה אֱלֹהֶיךָ לְפָנֶיךָ וְהָמָם מְהוּמָה גְדֹלָה עַד הִשָּׁמְדָם: וְנָתַן מַלְכֵיהֶם בְּיָדֶךָ וְהַאֲבַדְתָּ אֶת־שְׁמָם מִתַּחַת הַשָּׁמָיִם לֹא־יִתְיַצֵּב אִישׁ בְּפָנֶיךָ עַד הִשְׁמִדְךָ אֹתָם: פְּסִילֵי אֱלֹהֵיהֶם תִּשְׂרְפוּן בָּאֵשׁ לֹא־תַחְמֹד כֶּסֶף וְזָהָב עֲלֵיהֶם וְלָקַחְתָּ לָךְ פֶּן תִּוָּקֵשׁ בּוֹ כִּי תוֹעֲבַת יהוה אֱלֹהֶיךָ הוּא: וְלֹא־תָבִיא תוֹעֵבָה אֶל־בֵּיתֶךָ וְהָיִיתָ חֵרֶם כָּמֹהוּ שַׁקֵּץ | תְּשַׁקְּצֶנּוּ וְתַעֵב | תְּתַעֲבֶנּוּ כִּי־חֵרֶם הוּא: כָּל־הַמִּצְוָה אֲשֶׁר אָנֹכִי מְצַוְּךָ הַיּוֹם תִּשְׁמְרוּן לַעֲשׂוֹת לְמַעַן תִּחְיוּן וּרְבִיתֶם וּבָאתֶם וִירִשְׁתֶּם אֶת־הָאָרֶץ אֲשֶׁר־נִשְׁבַּע יהוה לַאֲבֹתֵיכֶם: וְזָכַרְתָּ אֶת־כָּל־הַדֶּרֶךְ אֲשֶׁר הוֹלִיכְךָ יהוה אֱלֹהֶיךָ זֶה אַרְבָּעִים שָׁנָה בַּמִּדְבָּר לְמַעַן עַנֹּתְךָ לְנַסֹּתְךָ לָדַעַת אֶת־אֲשֶׁר בִּלְבָבְךָ הֲתִשְׁמֹר מִצְוֹתָו אִם־לֹא: וַיְעַנְּךָ וַיַּרְעִבֶךָ וַיַּאֲכִלְךָ אֶת־הַמָּן אֲשֶׁר לֹא־יָדַעְתָּ וְלֹא יָדְעוּן אֲבֹתֶיךָ לְמַעַן הוֹדִיעֲךָ כִּי לֹא עַל־הַלֶּחֶם לְבַדּוֹ יִחְיֶה הָאָדָם כִּי עַל־כָּל־מוֹצָא פִי־יהוה יִחְיֶה הָאָדָם: ישראל שִׂמְלָתְךָ לֹא בָלְתָה מֵעָלֶיךָ וְרַגְלְךָ לֹא בָצֵקָה זֶה אַרְבָּעִים שָׁנָה: וְיָדַעְתָּ עִם־לְבָבֶךָ כִּי כַּאֲשֶׁר יְיַסֵּר אִישׁ אֶת־בְּנוֹ יהוה אֱלֹהֶיךָ מְיַסְּרֶךָּ: וְשָׁמַרְתָּ אֶת־מִצְוֹת יהוה אֱלֹהֶיךָ לָלֶכֶת בִּדְרָכָיו וּלְיִרְאָה אֹתוֹ: כִּי יהוה אֱלֹהֶיךָ מְבִיאֲךָ אֶל־אֶרֶץ טוֹבָה אֶרֶץ נַחֲלֵי מָיִם עֲיָנֹת וּתְהֹמֹת יֹצְאִים בַּבִּקְעָה וּבָהָר: אֶרֶץ חִטָּה וּשְׂעֹרָה וְגֶפֶן וּתְאֵנָה וְרִמּוֹן אֶרֶץ־זֵית שֶׁמֶן וּדְבָשׁ: אֶרֶץ אֲשֶׁר לֹא בְמִסְכֵּנֻת תֹּאכַל־בָּהּ לֶחֶם לֹא־תֶחְסַר כֹּל בָּהּ אֶרֶץ אֲשֶׁר אֲבָנֶיהָ בַרְזֶל וּמֵהֲרָרֶיהָ תַּחְצֹב נְחֹשֶׁת: וְאָכַלְתָּ וְשָׂבָעְתָּ וּבֵרַכְתָּ אֶת־יהוה אֱלֹהֶיךָ עַל־הָאָרֶץ הַטֹּבָה אֲשֶׁר נָתַן־לָךְ:

פ׳ ראה / RE'EH

(Deuteronomy 11:26 – 12:10)

כה רְאֵה אָנֹכִי נֹתֵן לִפְנֵיכֶם הַיּוֹם בְּרָכָה וּקְלָלָה: אֶת־הַבְּרָכָה אֲשֶׁר תִּשְׁמְעוּ אֶל־מִצְוֹת יהוה אֱלֹהֵיכֶם אֲשֶׁר אָנֹכִי מְצַוֶּה אֶתְכֶם הַיּוֹם: וְהַקְּלָלָה אִם־לֹא תִשְׁמְעוּ אֶל־מִצְוֹת יהוה אֱלֹהֵיכֶם וְסַרְתֶּם מִן־הַדֶּרֶךְ אֲשֶׁר אָנֹכִי מְצַוֶּה אֶתְכֶם הַיּוֹם לָלֶכֶת אַחֲרֵי אֱלֹהִים אֲחֵרִים אֲשֶׁר לֹא־יְדַעְתֶּם: וְהָיָה כִּי יְבִיאֲךָ יהוה אֱלֹהֶיךָ אֶל־הָאָרֶץ אֲשֶׁר־אַתָּה בָא־שָׁמָּה לְרִשְׁתָּהּ וְנָתַתָּה אֶת־הַבְּרָכָה עַל־הַר גְּרִזִּים וְאֶת־הַקְּלָלָה עַל־הַר עֵיבָל: הֲלֹא־הֵמָּה בְּעֵבֶר הַיַּרְדֵּן אַחֲרֵי דֶּרֶךְ מְבוֹא הַשֶּׁמֶשׁ בְּאֶרֶץ הַכְּנַעֲנִי הַיֹּשֵׁב בָּעֲרָבָה מוּל הַגִּלְגָּל אֵצֶל אֵלוֹנֵי מֹרֶה: כִּי אַתֶּם עֹבְרִים אֶת־הַיַּרְדֵּן לָבֹא לָרֶשֶׁת אֶת־הָאָרֶץ אֲשֶׁר־יהוה אֱלֹהֵיכֶם נֹתֵן לָכֶם וִירִשְׁתֶּם אֹתָהּ וִישַׁבְתֶּם־בָּהּ: לוי וּשְׁמַרְתֶּם לַעֲשׂוֹת אֵת כָּל־הַחֻקִּים וְאֶת־הַמִּשְׁפָּטִים אֲשֶׁר אָנֹכִי נֹתֵן לִפְנֵיכֶם הַיּוֹם: אֵלֶּה הַחֻקִּים וְהַמִּשְׁפָּטִים אֲשֶׁר תִּשְׁמְרוּן לַעֲשׂוֹת בָּאָרֶץ אֲשֶׁר נָתַן יהוה אֱלֹהֵי אֲבֹתֶיךָ לְךָ לְרִשְׁתָּהּ כָּל־הַיָּמִים אֲשֶׁר־אַתֶּם חַיִּים עַל־הָאֲדָמָה: אַבֵּד תְּאַבְּדוּן אֶת־כָּל־הַמְּקֹמוֹת אֲשֶׁר עָבְדוּ־שָׁם הַגּוֹיִם אֲשֶׁר אַתֶּם יֹרְשִׁים אֹתָם אֶת־אֱלֹהֵיהֶם עַל־הֶהָרִים הָרָמִים וְעַל־הַגְּבָעוֹת וְתַחַת כָּל־עֵץ רַעֲנָן: וְנִתַּצְתֶּם אֶת־מִזְבְּחֹתָם וְשִׁבַּרְתֶּם אֶת־מַצֵּבֹתָם וַאֲשֵׁרֵיהֶם תִּשְׂרְפוּן בָּאֵשׁ וּפְסִילֵי אֱלֹהֵיהֶם תְּגַדֵּעוּן וְאִבַּדְתֶּם אֶת־שְׁמָם מִן־הַמָּקוֹם הַהוּא: לֹא־תַעֲשׂוּן כֵּן לַיהוה אֱלֹהֵיכֶם: כִּי אִם־אֶל־הַמָּקוֹם אֲשֶׁר־יִבְחַר יהוה אֱלֹהֵיכֶם מִכָּל־שִׁבְטֵיכֶם לָשׂוּם אֶת־שְׁמוֹ שָׁם לְשִׁכְנוֹ תִדְרְשׁוּ וּבָאתָ שָּׁמָּה:

יִשְׂרָאֵל: וֶהֱבִיאתֶ֣ם שָׁ֔מָּה עֹלֹתֵיכֶ֖ם וְזִבְחֵיכֶ֑ם וְאֵת֙ מַעְשְׂרֹ֣תֵיכֶ֔ם וְאֵ֖ת תְּרוּמַ֣ת יֶדְכֶ֑ם וְנִדְרֵיכֶם֙ וְנִ֣דְבֹתֵיכֶ֔ם וּבְכֹרֹ֥ת בְּקַרְכֶ֖ם וְצֹאנְכֶֽם: וַאֲכַלְתֶּם־שָׁ֗ם לִפְנֵי֙ יהו֣ה אֱלֹֽהֵיכֶ֔ם וּשְׂמַחְתֶּ֗ם בְּכֹל֙ מִשְׁלַ֣ח יֶדְכֶ֔ם אַתֶּ֖ם וּבָֽתֵּיכֶ֑ם אֲשֶׁ֥ר בֵּֽרַכְךָ֖ יהו֥ה אֱלֹהֶֽיךָ: לֹ֣א תַֽעֲשׂ֔וּן כְּ֠כֹל אֲשֶׁ֨ר אֲנַ֧חְנוּ עֹשִׂ֛ים פֹּ֖ה הַיּ֑וֹם אִ֖ישׁ כָּל־הַיָּשָׁ֥ר בְּעֵינָֽיו: כִּ֥י לֹֽא־בָאתֶ֖ם עַד־עָ֑תָּה אֶל־הַמְּנוּחָה֙ וְאֶל־הַֽנַּחֲלָ֔ה אֲשֶׁר־יהו֥ה אֱלֹהֶ֖יךָ נֹתֵ֥ן לָֽךְ: וַעֲבַרְתֶּם֮ אֶת־הַיַּרְדֵּן֒ וִישַׁבְתֶּ֣ם בָּאָ֔רֶץ אֲשֶׁר־יהו֥ה אֱלֹֽהֵיכֶ֖ם מַנְחִ֣יל אֶתְכֶ֑ם וְהֵנִ֨יחַ לָכֶ֧ם מִכָּל־אֹֽיְבֵיכֶ֛ם מִסָּבִ֖יב וִֽישַׁבְתֶּם־בֶּֽטַח:

פ׳ שׁוֹפְטִים / SHOFTIM
(Deuteronomy 16:18–17:13)

כה: שֹֽׁפְטִ֣ים וְשֹֽׁטְרִ֗ים תִּֽתֶּן־לְךָ֙ בְּכָל־שְׁעָרֶ֔יךָ אֲשֶׁ֨ר יהו֧ה אֱלֹהֶ֛יךָ נֹתֵ֥ן לְךָ֖ לִשְׁבָטֶ֑יךָ וְשָֽׁפְט֥וּ אֶת־הָעָ֖ם מִשְׁפַּט־צֶֽדֶק: לֹֽא־תַטֶּ֣ה מִשְׁפָּ֔ט לֹ֥א תַכִּ֖יר פָּנִ֑ים וְלֹֽא־תִקַּ֣ח שֹׁ֔חַד כִּ֣י הַשֹּׁ֗חַד יְעַוֵּר֙ עֵינֵ֣י חֲכָמִ֔ים וִֽיסַלֵּ֖ף דִּבְרֵ֥י צַדִּיקִֽם: צֶ֥דֶק צֶ֖דֶק תִּרְדֹּ֑ף לְמַ֤עַן תִּֽחְיֶה֙ וְיָֽרַשְׁתָּ֣ אֶת־הָאָ֔רֶץ אֲשֶׁר־יהו֥ה אֱלֹהֶ֖יךָ נֹתֵ֥ן לָֽךְ:

לוי: לֹֽא־תִטַּ֥ע לְךָ֛ אֲשֵׁרָ֖ה כָּל־עֵ֑ץ אֵ֗צֶל מִזְבַּ֛ח יהו֥ה אֱלֹהֶ֖יךָ אֲשֶׁ֥ר תַּֽעֲשֶׂה־לָּֽךְ: וְלֹֽא־תָקִ֥ים לְךָ֖ מַצֵּבָ֑ה אֲשֶׁ֥ר שָׂנֵ֖א יהו֥ה אֱלֹהֶֽיךָ: לֹֽא־תִזְבַּח֩ לַֽיהו֨ה אֱלֹהֶ֜יךָ שׁ֣וֹר וָשֶׂ֗ה אֲשֶׁ֨ר יִֽהְיֶ֥ה בוֹ֙ מ֔וּם כֹּ֖ל דָּבָ֣ר רָ֑ע כִּ֧י תֽוֹעֲבַ֛ת יהו֥ה אֱלֹהֶ֖יךָ הֽוּא: כִּֽי־יִמָּצֵ֤א בְקִרְבְּךָ֙ בְּאַחַ֣ד שְׁעָרֶ֔יךָ אֲשֶׁר־יהו֥ה אֱלֹהֶ֖יךָ נֹתֵ֣ן לָ֑ךְ אִ֣ישׁ אֽוֹ־אִשָּׁ֗ה אֲשֶׁ֨ר יַֽעֲשֶׂ֧ה אֶת־הָרַ֛ע בְּעֵינֵ֥י יהוֽה־אֱלֹהֶ֖יךָ לַֽעֲבֹ֣ר בְּרִית֑וֹ: וַיֵּ֗לֶךְ וַֽיַּעֲבֹד֙ אֱלֹהִ֣ים אֲחֵרִ֔ים וַיִּשְׁתַּ֖חוּ לָהֶ֑ם וְלַשֶּׁ֣מֶשׁ ׀ א֣וֹ לַיָּרֵ֗חַ א֛וֹ לְכָל־צְבָ֥א הַשָּׁמַ֖יִם אֲשֶׁ֥ר לֹֽא־צִוִּֽיתִי: וְהֻגַּד־לְךָ֖ וְשָׁמָ֑עְתָּ וְדָֽרַשְׁתָּ֣ הֵיטֵ֔ב וְהִנֵּ֤ה אֱמֶת֙ נָכ֣וֹן הַדָּבָ֔ר נֶֽעֶשְׂתָ֛ה הַתֹּֽעֵבָ֥ה הַזֹּ֖את בְּיִשְׂרָאֵֽל: וְהֽוֹצֵאתָ֣ אֶת־הָאִ֣ישׁ הַה֡וּא א֣וֹ אֶת־הָֽאִשָּׁ֣ה הַהִוא֩ אֲשֶׁ֨ר עָשׂ֜וּ אֶת־הַדָּבָ֤ר הָרַע֙ הַזֶּ֔ה אֶל־שְׁעָרֶ֔יךָ אֶת־הָאִ֕ישׁ א֖וֹ אֶת־הָֽאִשָּׁ֑ה וּסְקַלְתָּ֥ם בָּֽאֲבָנִ֖ים וָמֵֽתוּ: עַל־פִּ֣י

ישראל: שְׁנַ֣יִם עֵדִ֗ים א֛וֹ שְׁלֹשָׁ֥ה עֵדִ֖ים יוּמַ֣ת הַמֵּ֑ת לֹ֣א יוּמַ֔ת עַל־פִּ֖י עֵ֥ד אֶחָֽד: יַ֣ד הָֽעֵדִ֞ים תִּֽהְיֶה־בּ֤וֹ בָרִֽאשֹׁנָה֙ לַֽהֲמִית֔וֹ וְיַ֥ד כָּל־הָעָ֖ם בָּאַֽחֲרֹנָ֑ה וּבִֽעַרְתָּ֥ הָרָ֖ע מִקִּרְבֶּֽךָ: כִּ֣י יִפָּלֵא֩ מִמְּךָ֨ דָבָ֜ר לַמִּשְׁפָּ֗ט בֵּֽין־דָּ֨ם ׀ לְדָ֜ם בֵּֽין־דִּ֣ין לְדִ֗ין וּבֵ֥ין נֶ֨גַע֙ לָנֶ֔גַע דִּבְרֵ֥י רִיבֹ֖ת בִּשְׁעָרֶ֑יךָ וְקַמְתָּ֣ וְעָלִ֔יתָ אֶל־הַ֨מָּק֔וֹם אֲשֶׁ֥ר יִבְחַ֛ר יהו֥ה אֱלֹהֶ֖יךָ בּֽוֹ: וּבָאתָ֗ אֶל־הַכֹּֽהֲנִים֙ הַלְוִיִּ֔ם וְאֶל־הַ֨שֹּׁפֵ֔ט אֲשֶׁ֥ר יִֽהְיֶ֖ה בַּיָּמִ֣ים הָהֵ֑ם וְדָֽרַשְׁתָּ֙ וְהִגִּ֣ידוּ לְךָ֔ אֵ֖ת דְּבַ֥ר הַמִּשְׁפָּֽט: וְעָשִׂ֗יתָ עַל־פִּ֤י הַדָּבָר֙ אֲשֶׁ֣ר יַגִּ֣ידוּ לְךָ֔ מִן־הַמָּק֣וֹם הַה֔וּא אֲשֶׁ֖ר יִבְחַ֣ר יהו֑ה וְשָֽׁמַרְתָּ֣ לַֽעֲשׂ֔וֹת כְּכֹ֖ל אֲשֶׁ֥ר יוֹרֽוּךָ:

ישראל: עַל־פִּ֨י הַתּוֹרָ֜ה אֲשֶׁ֣ר יוֹר֗וּךָ וְעַל־הַמִּשְׁפָּ֛ט אֲשֶׁר־יֹֽאמְר֥וּ לְךָ֖ תַּֽעֲשֶׂ֑ה לֹ֣א תָס֗וּר מִן־הַדָּבָ֛ר אֲשֶׁר־יַגִּ֥ידוּ לְךָ֖ יָמִ֥ין וּשְׂמֹֽאל: וְהָאִ֞ישׁ אֲשֶׁר־יַֽעֲשֶׂ֣ה בְזָד֗וֹן לְבִלְתִּ֨י שְׁמֹ֤עַ אֶל־הַכֹּהֵן֙ הָֽעֹמֵ֞ד לְשָׁ֤רֶת שָׁם֙ אֶת־יהו֣ה אֱלֹהֶ֔יךָ א֖וֹ אֶל־הַשֹּׁפֵ֑ט וּמֵת֙ הָאִ֣ישׁ הַה֔וּא וּבִֽעַרְתָּ֥ הָרָ֖ע מִיִּשְׂרָאֵֽל: וְכָל־הָעָ֖ם יִשְׁמְע֣וּ וְיִרָ֑אוּ וְלֹ֥א יְזִיד֖וּן עֽוֹד:

פ׳ כי תצא / KI SEITZEI
(Deuteronomy 21:10-21)

כה: כִּֽי־תֵצֵ֥א לַמִּלְחָמָ֖ה עַל־אֹֽיְבֶ֑יךָ וּנְתָנ֞וֹ יהו֧ה אֱלֹהֶ֛יךָ בְּיָדֶ֖ךָ וְשָׁבִ֥יתָ שִׁבְיֽוֹ: וְרָאִ֨יתָ֙ בַּשִּׁבְיָ֔ה אֵ֖שֶׁת יְפַת־תֹּ֑אַר וְחָֽשַׁקְתָּ֣ בָ֔הּ וְלָֽקַחְתָּ֥ לְךָ֖ לְאִשָּֽׁה: וַֽהֲבֵאתָ֖הּ אֶל־תּ֣וֹךְ בֵּיתֶ֑ךָ וְגִלְּחָה֙ אֶת־רֹאשָׁ֔הּ וְעָֽשְׂתָ֖ה אֶת־צִפָּרְנֶֽיהָ: וְהֵסִ֩ירָה֩ אֶת־שִׂמְלַ֨ת שִׁבְיָ֜הּ מֵֽעָלֶ֗יהָ וְיָֽשְׁבָה֙ בְּבֵיתֶ֔ךָ וּבָֽכְתָ֛ה אֶת־אָבִ֥יהָ וְאֶת־אִמָּ֖הּ יֶ֣רַח יָמִ֑ים וְאַ֨חַר כֵּ֜ן תָּב֤וֹא אֵלֶ֨יהָ֙ וּבְעַלְתָּ֔הּ וְהָֽיְתָ֥ה לְךָ֖ לְאִשָּֽׁה: וְהָיָ֞ה אִם־לֹ֧א חָפַ֣צְתָּ בָּ֗הּ וְשִׁלַּחְתָּהּ֙ לְנַפְשָׁ֔הּ וּמָכֹ֥ר לֹֽא־תִמְכְּרֶ֖נָּה בַּכָּ֑סֶף לֹֽא־תִתְעַמֵּ֣ר בָּ֔הּ תַּ֖חַת אֲשֶׁ֥ר עִנִּיתָֽהּ:

לוי: כִּי־תִֽהְיֶ֨יןָ לְאִ֜ישׁ שְׁתֵּ֣י נָשִׁ֗ים הָֽאַחַ֤ת אֲהוּבָה֙ וְהָֽאַחַ֣ת שְׂנוּאָ֔ה וְיָֽלְדוּ־ל֣וֹ בָנִ֔ים הָֽאֲהוּבָ֖ה וְהַשְּׂנוּאָ֑ה וְהָיָ֛ה הַבֵּ֥ן הַבְּכ֖וֹר לַשְּׂנִיאָֽה: וְהָיָ֗ה בְּיוֹם֙ הַנְחִיל֣וֹ אֶת־בָּנָ֔יו אֶת

אֲשֶׁר־יִֽהְיֶה־לּ֔וֹ לֹ֣א יוּכַ֗ל לְבַכֵּר֙ אֶת־בֶּן־הָ֣אֲהוּבָ֔ה עַל־פְּנֵ֥י בֶן־הַשְּׂנוּאָ֖ה הַבְּכֹֽר: כִּי֩ אֶת־הַבְּכֹ֨ר בֶּן־הַשְּׂנוּאָ֜ה יַכִּ֗יר לָ֤תֶת לוֹ֙ פִּ֣י שְׁנַ֔יִם בְּכֹ֥ל אֲשֶׁר־יִמָּצֵ֖א ל֑וֹ כִּי־הוּא֙ רֵאשִׁ֣ית אֹנ֔וֹ ל֖וֹ מִשְׁפַּ֥ט הַבְּכֹרָֽה:

ישראל: כִּֽי־יִהְיֶ֣ה לְאִ֗ישׁ בֵּ֚ן סוֹרֵ֣ר וּמוֹרֶ֔ה אֵינֶ֣נּוּ שֹׁמֵ֔עַ בְּק֥וֹל אָבִ֖יו וּבְק֣וֹל אִמּ֑וֹ וְיִסְּר֣וּ אֹת֔וֹ וְלֹ֥א יִשְׁמַ֖ע אֲלֵיהֶֽם: וְתָ֥פְשׂוּ ב֖וֹ אָבִ֣יו וְאִמּ֑וֹ וְהוֹצִ֧יאוּ אֹת֛וֹ אֶל־זִקְנֵ֥י עִיר֖וֹ וְאֶל־שַׁ֥עַר מְקֹמֽוֹ: וְאָ֣מְר֞וּ אֶל־זִקְנֵ֣י עִיר֗וֹ בְּנֵ֤נוּ זֶה֙ סוֹרֵ֣ר וּמֹרֶ֔ה אֵינֶ֥נּוּ שֹׁמֵ֖עַ בְּקֹלֵ֑נוּ זוֹלֵ֖ל וְסֹבֵֽא: וּרְגָמֻ֠הוּ כָּל־אַנְשֵׁ֨י עִיר֤וֹ בָֽאֲבָנִים֙ וָמֵ֔ת וּבִֽעַרְתָּ֥ הָרָ֖ע מִקִּרְבֶּ֑ךָ וְכָל־יִשְׂרָאֵ֖ל יִשְׁמְע֥וּ וְיִרָֽאוּ:

◆ פ׳ כי תבוא / KI SAVO ◆
(Deuteronomy 26:1-15)

כהן: וְהָיָה֙ כִּֽי־תָב֣וֹא אֶל־הָאָ֔רֶץ אֲשֶׁר֙ יְהוָ֣ה אֱלֹהֶ֔יךָ נֹתֵ֥ן לְךָ֖ נַחֲלָ֑ה וִֽירִשְׁתָּ֖הּ וְיָשַׁ֥בְתָּ בָּֽהּ: וְלָקַחְתָּ֞ מֵרֵאשִׁ֣ית ׀ כָּל־פְּרִ֣י הָאֲדָמָ֗ה אֲשֶׁ֨ר תָּבִ֧יא מֵֽאַרְצְךָ֛ אֲשֶׁ֨ר יְהוָ֧ה אֱלֹהֶ֛יךָ נֹתֵ֥ן לָ֖ךְ וְשַׂמְתָּ֣ בַטֶּ֑נֶא וְהָֽלַכְתָּ֙ אֶל־הַמָּק֔וֹם אֲשֶׁ֤ר יִבְחַר֙ יְהוָ֣ה אֱלֹהֶ֔יךָ לְשַׁכֵּ֥ן שְׁמ֖וֹ שָֽׁם: וּבָאתָ֙ אֶל־הַכֹּהֵ֔ן אֲשֶׁ֥ר יִהְיֶ֖ה בַּיָּמִ֣ים הָהֵ֑ם וְאָמַרְתָּ֣ אֵלָ֗יו הִגַּ֤דְתִּי הַיּוֹם֙ לַיהוָ֣ה אֱלֹהֶ֔יךָ כִּי־בָ֙אתִי֙ אֶל־הָאָ֔רֶץ אֲשֶׁ֨ר נִשְׁבַּ֧ע יְהוָ֛ה לַאֲבֹתֵ֖ינוּ לָ֥תֶת לָֽנוּ:

לוי: וְלָקַ֧ח הַכֹּהֵ֛ן הַטֶּ֖נֶא מִיָּדֶ֑ךָ וְהִ֨נִּיח֔וֹ לִפְנֵ֕י מִזְבַּ֖ח יְהוָ֥ה אֱלֹהֶֽיךָ: וְעָנִ֨יתָ וְאָמַרְתָּ֜ לִפְנֵ֣י ׀ יְהוָ֣ה אֱלֹהֶ֗יךָ אֲרַמִּי֙ אֹבֵ֣ד אָבִ֔י וַיֵּ֣רֶד מִצְרַ֔יְמָה וַיָּ֥גָר שָׁ֖ם בִּמְתֵ֣י מְעָ֑ט וַֽיְהִי־שָׁ֕ם לְג֥וֹי גָּד֖וֹל עָצ֥וּם וָרָֽב: וַיָּרֵ֧עוּ אֹתָ֛נוּ הַמִּצְרִ֖ים וַיְעַנּ֑וּנוּ וַיִּתְּנ֥וּ עָלֵ֖ינוּ עֲבֹדָ֥ה קָשָֽׁה: וַנִּצְעַ֕ק אֶל־יְהוָ֖ה אֱלֹהֵ֣י אֲבֹתֵ֑ינוּ וַיִּשְׁמַ֤ע יְהוָה֙ אֶת־קֹלֵ֔נוּ וַיַּ֧רְא אֶת־עָנְיֵ֛נוּ וְאֶת־עֲמָלֵ֖נוּ וְאֶת־לַחֲצֵֽנוּ: וַיּוֹצִאֵ֤נוּ יְהוָה֙ מִמִּצְרַ֔יִם בְּיָ֤ד חֲזָקָה֙ וּבִזְרֹ֣עַ נְטוּיָ֔ה וּבְמֹרָ֖א גָּדֹ֑ל וּבְאֹת֖וֹת וּבְמֹפְתִֽים: וַיְבִאֵ֖נוּ אֶל־הַמָּק֣וֹם הַזֶּ֑ה וַיִּתֶּן־לָ֙נוּ֙ אֶת־הָאָ֣רֶץ הַזֹּ֔את אֶ֛רֶץ זָבַ֥ת חָלָ֖ב וּדְבָֽשׁ: וְעַתָּ֗ה הִנֵּ֤ה הֵבֵ֙אתִי֙ אֶת־רֵאשִׁית֙ פְּרִ֣י הָֽאֲדָמָ֔ה אֲשֶׁר־נָתַ֥תָּה לִּ֖י

יְהוָ֑ה וְהִנַּחְתּ֗וֹ לִפְנֵי֙ יְהוָ֣ה אֱלֹהֶ֔יךָ וְהִֽשְׁתַּחֲוִ֔יתָ לִפְנֵ֖י יְהוָ֥ה אֱלֹהֶֽיךָ: וְשָׂמַחְתָּ֣ בְכָל־הַטּ֗וֹב אֲשֶׁ֧ר נָֽתַן־לְךָ֛ יְהוָ֥ה אֱלֹהֶ֖יךָ וּלְבֵיתֶ֑ךָ אַתָּה֙ וְהַלֵּוִ֔י וְהַגֵּ֖ר אֲשֶׁ֥ר בְּקִרְבֶּֽךָ:

ישראל: כִּ֣י תְכַלֶּ֞ה לַ֠עְשֵׂ֠ר אֶת־כָּל־מַעְשַׂ֧ר תְּבוּאָתְךָ֛ בַּשָּׁנָ֥ה הַשְּׁלִישִׁ֖ת שְׁנַ֣ת הַֽמַּעֲשֵׂ֑ר וְנָתַתָּ֣ה לַלֵּוִ֗י לַגֵּר֙ לַיָּת֣וֹם וְלָֽאַלְמָנָ֔ה וְאָכְל֥וּ בִשְׁעָרֶ֖יךָ וְשָׂבֵֽעוּ: וְאָמַרְתָּ֡ לִפְנֵי֩ יְהוָ֨ה אֱלֹהֶ֜יךָ בִּעַ֧רְתִּי הַקֹּ֣דֶשׁ מִן־הַבַּ֗יִת וְגַ֨ם נְתַתִּ֤יו לַלֵּוִי֙ וְלַגֵּר֙ לַיָּת֣וֹם וְלָֽאַלְמָנָ֔ה כְּכָל־מִצְוָתְךָ֖ אֲשֶׁ֣ר צִוִּיתָ֑נִי לֹֽא־עָבַ֥רְתִּי מִמִּצְוֹתֶ֖יךָ וְלֹ֥א שָׁכָֽחְתִּי: לֹא־אָכַ֨לְתִּי בְאֹנִ֜י מִמֶּ֗נּוּ וְלֹא־בִעַ֤רְתִּי מִמֶּ֙נּוּ֙ בְּטָמֵ֔א וְלֹא־נָתַ֥תִּי מִמֶּ֖נּוּ לְמֵ֑ת שָׁמַ֗עְתִּי בְּקוֹל֙ יְהוָ֣ה אֱלֹהָ֔י עָשִׂ֕יתִי כְּכֹ֖ל אֲשֶׁ֥ר צִוִּיתָֽנִי: הַשְׁקִ֩יפָה֩ מִמְּע֨וֹן קָדְשְׁךָ֜ מִן־הַשָּׁמַ֗יִם וּבָרֵ֤ךְ אֶֽת־עַמְּךָ֙ אֶת־יִשְׂרָאֵ֔ל וְאֵת֙ הָֽאֲדָמָ֔ה אֲשֶׁ֥ר נָתַ֖תָּה לָ֑נוּ כַּאֲשֶׁ֤ר נִשְׁבַּ֙עְתָּ֙ לַֽאֲבֹתֵ֔ינוּ אֶ֛רֶץ זָבַ֥ת חָלָ֖ב וּדְבָֽשׁ:

◆ פ׳ נצבים / NITZAVIM ◆
(Deuteronomy 29:9-28)

כהן: אַתֶּ֨ם נִצָּבִ֤ים הַיּוֹם֙ כֻּלְּכֶ֔ם לִפְנֵ֖י יְהוָ֣ה אֱלֹהֵיכֶ֑ם רָאשֵׁיכֶ֣ם שִׁבְטֵיכֶ֗ם זִקְנֵיכֶם֙ וְשֹׁ֣טְרֵיכֶ֔ם כֹּ֖ל אִ֥ישׁ יִשְׂרָאֵֽל: טַפְּכֶ֣ם נְשֵׁיכֶ֔ם וְגֵ֣רְךָ֔ אֲשֶׁ֖ר בְּקֶ֣רֶב מַחֲנֶ֑יךָ מֵחֹטֵ֣ב עֵצֶ֔יךָ עַ֖ד שֹׁאֵ֥ב מֵימֶֽיךָ: לְעָבְרְךָ֗ בִּבְרִ֛ית יְהוָ֥ה אֱלֹהֶ֖יךָ וּבְאָלָת֑וֹ אֲשֶׁר֙ יְהוָ֣ה אֱלֹהֶ֔יךָ כֹּרֵ֥ת עִמְּךָ֖ הַיּֽוֹם:

לוי: לְמַ֣עַן הָקִֽים־אֹתְךָ֩ הַיּ֨וֹם ׀ ל֜וֹ לְעָ֗ם וְה֤וּא יִֽהְיֶה־לְּךָ֙ לֵֽאלֹהִ֔ים כַּאֲשֶׁ֖ר דִּבֶּר־לָ֑ךְ וְכַאֲשֶׁ֤ר נִשְׁבַּע֙ לַאֲבֹתֶ֔יךָ לְאַבְרָהָ֥ם לְיִצְחָ֖ק וּֽלְיַעֲקֹֽב: וְלֹ֥א אִתְּכֶ֖ם לְבַדְּכֶ֑ם אָנֹכִ֗י כֹּרֵת֙ אֶת־הַבְּרִ֣ית הַזֹּ֔את וְאֶת־הָאָלָ֖ה הַזֹּֽאת: כִּי֩ אֶת־אֲשֶׁ֨ר יֶשְׁנ֜וֹ פֹּ֗ה עִמָּ֙נוּ֙ עֹמֵ֣ד הַיּ֔וֹם לִפְנֵ֖י יְהוָ֣ה אֱלֹהֵ֑ינוּ וְאֵ֨ת אֲשֶׁ֥ר אֵינֶ֛נּוּ פֹּ֖ה עִמָּ֥נוּ הַיּֽוֹם:

ישראל: כִּֽי־אַתֶּ֣ם יְדַעְתֶּ֔ם אֵ֥ת אֲשֶׁר־יָשַׁ֖בְנוּ בְּאֶ֣רֶץ מִצְרָ֑יִם וְאֵ֧ת אֲשֶׁר־עָבַ֛רְנוּ בְּקֶ֥רֶב הַגּוֹיִ֖ם אֲשֶׁ֥ר עֲבַרְתֶּֽם: וַתִּרְאוּ֙ אֶת־שִׁקּ֣וּצֵיהֶ֔ם וְאֵ֖ת גִּלֻּלֵיהֶ֑ם עֵ֣ץ וָאֶ֔בֶן כֶּ֥סֶף וְזָהָ֖ב אֲשֶׁ֥ר עִמָּהֶֽם: פֶּן־יֵ֣שׁ בָּ֠כֶ֠ם אִ֣ישׁ אוֹ־אִשָּׁ֞ה א֧וֹ מִשְׁפָּחָ֣ה אוֹ־שֵׁ֗בֶט אֲשֶׁר֩ לְבָב֨וֹ פֹנֶ֤ה הַיּוֹם֙

VAYEILECH-HA'AZINU

מֵעִם יְהוָה אֱלֹהֵינוּ לָלֶכֶת לַעֲבֹד אֶת־אֱלֹהֵי הַגּוֹיִם הָהֵם פֶּן־יֵשׁ בָּכֶם שֹׁרֶשׁ פֹּרֶה רֹאשׁ וְלַעֲנָה: וְהָיָה בְּשָׁמְעוֹ אֶת־דִּבְרֵי הָאָלָה הַזֹּאת וְהִתְבָּרֵךְ בִּלְבָבוֹ לֵאמֹר שָׁלוֹם יִהְיֶה־לִּי כִּי בִּשְׁרִרוּת לִבִּי אֵלֵךְ לְמַעַן סְפוֹת הָרָוָה אֶת־הַצְּמֵאָה: לֹא־יֹאבֶה יְהוָֹה סְלֹחַ לוֹ כִּי אָז יֶעְשַׁן אַף־יְהוָה וְקִנְאָתוֹ בָּאִישׁ הַהוּא וְרָבְצָה בּוֹ כָּל־הָאָלָה הַכְּתוּבָה בַּסֵּפֶר הַזֶּה וּמָחָה יְהוָה אֶת־שְׁמוֹ מִתַּחַת הַשָּׁמָיִם: וְהִבְדִּילוֹ יְהוָה לְרָעָה מִכֹּל שִׁבְטֵי יִשְׂרָאֵל כְּכֹל אָלוֹת הַבְּרִית הַכְּתוּבָה בְּסֵפֶר הַתּוֹרָה הַזֶּה: וְאָמַר הַדּוֹר הָאַחֲרוֹן בְּנֵיכֶם אֲשֶׁר יָקוּמוּ מֵאַחֲרֵיכֶם וְהַנָּכְרִי אֲשֶׁר יָבֹא מֵאֶרֶץ רְחוֹקָה וְרָאוּ אֶת־מַכּוֹת הָאָרֶץ הַהִוא וְאֶת־תַּחֲלֻאֶיהָ אֲשֶׁר־חִלָּה יְהוָה בָּהּ: גָּפְרִית וָמֶלַח שְׂרֵפָה כָל־אַרְצָהּ לֹא תִזָּרַע וְלֹא תַצְמִחַ וְלֹא־יַעֲלֶה בָהּ כָּל־עֵשֶׂב כְּמַהְפֵּכַת סְדֹם וַעֲמֹרָה אַדְמָה וּצְבֹיִים אֲשֶׁר הָפַךְ יְהוָה בְּאַפּוֹ וּבַחֲמָתוֹ: וְאָמְרוּ כָּל־הַגּוֹיִם עַל־מֶה עָשָׂה יְהוָה כָּכָה לָאָרֶץ הַזֹּאת מֶה חֳרִי הָאַף הַגָּדוֹל הַזֶּה: וְאָמְרוּ עַל אֲשֶׁר עָזְבוּ אֶת־בְּרִית יְהוָה אֱלֹהֵי אֲבֹתָם אֲשֶׁר כָּרַת עִמָּם בְּהוֹצִיאוֹ אֹתָם מֵאֶרֶץ מִצְרָיִם: וַיֵּלְכוּ וַיַּעַבְדוּ אֱלֹהִים אֲחֵרִים וַיִּשְׁתַּחֲווּ לָהֶם אֱלֹהִים אֲשֶׁר לֹא־יְדָעוּם וְלֹא חָלַק לָהֶם: וַיִּחַר־אַף יְהוָה בָּאָרֶץ הַהִוא לְהָבִיא עָלֶיהָ אֶת־כָּל־הַקְּלָלָה הַכְּתוּבָה בַּסֵּפֶר הַזֶּה: וַיִּתְּשֵׁם יְהוָה מֵעַל אַדְמָתָם בְּאַף וּבְחֵמָה וּבְקֶצֶף גָּדוֹל וַיַּשְׁלִכֵם אֶל־אֶרֶץ אַחֶרֶת כַּיּוֹם הַזֶּה: הַנִּסְתָּרֹת לַיהוָה אֱלֹהֵינוּ וְהַנִּגְלֹת לָנוּ וּלְבָנֵינוּ עַד־עוֹלָם לַעֲשׂוֹת אֶת־כָּל־דִּבְרֵי הַתּוֹרָה הַזֹּאת:

◆{ VAYEILECH / פ׳ וילך }◆
(Deuteronomy 31:1-13)

כה: וַיֵּלֶךְ מֹשֶׁה וַיְדַבֵּר אֶת־הַדְּבָרִים הָאֵלֶּה אֶל־כָּל־יִשְׂרָאֵל: וַיֹּאמֶר אֲלֵהֶם בֶּן־מֵאָה וְעֶשְׂרִים שָׁנָה אָנֹכִי הַיּוֹם לֹא־אוּכַל עוֹד לָצֵאת וְלָבוֹא וַיהוָה אָמַר אֵלַי לֹא תַעֲבֹר אֶת־הַיַּרְדֵּן הַזֶּה: יְהוָה אֱלֹהֶיךָ הוּא ׀ עֹבֵר לְפָנֶיךָ הוּא־יַשְׁמִיד אֶת־הַגּוֹיִם הָאֵלֶּה מִלְּפָנֶיךָ וִירִשְׁתָּם יְהוֹשֻׁעַ הוּא עֹבֵר לְפָנֶיךָ כַּאֲשֶׁר דִּבֶּר יְהוָה:

לוי: וְעָשָׂה יְהוָה לָהֶם כַּאֲשֶׁר עָשָׂה לְסִיחוֹן וּלְעוֹג מַלְכֵי הָאֱמֹרִי וּלְאַרְצָם אֲשֶׁר הִשְׁמִיד אֹתָם: וּנְתָנָם יְהוָה לִפְנֵיכֶם וַעֲשִׂיתֶם לָהֶם כְּכָל־הַמִּצְוָה אֲשֶׁר צִוִּיתִי אֶתְכֶם: חִזְקוּ וְאִמְצוּ אַל־תִּירְאוּ וְאַל־תַּעַרְצוּ מִפְּנֵיהֶם כִּי ׀ יְהוָה אֱלֹהֶיךָ הוּא הַהֹלֵךְ עִמָּךְ לֹא יַרְפְּךָ וְלֹא יַעַזְבֶךָּ:

ישראל: וַיִּקְרָא מֹשֶׁה לִיהוֹשֻׁעַ וַיֹּאמֶר אֵלָיו לְעֵינֵי כָל־יִשְׂרָאֵל חֲזַק וֶאֱמָץ כִּי אַתָּה תָּבוֹא אֶת־הָעָם הַזֶּה אֶל־הָאָרֶץ אֲשֶׁר נִשְׁבַּע יְהוָה לַאֲבֹתָם לָתֵת לָהֶם וְאַתָּה תַּנְחִילֶנָּה אוֹתָם: וַיהוָה הוּא ׀ הַהֹלֵךְ לְפָנֶיךָ הוּא יִהְיֶה עִמָּךְ לֹא יַרְפְּךָ וְלֹא יַעַזְבֶךָּ לֹא תִירָא וְלֹא תֵחָת: וַיִּכְתֹּב מֹשֶׁה אֶת־הַתּוֹרָה הַזֹּאת וַיִּתְּנָהּ אֶל־הַכֹּהֲנִים בְּנֵי לֵוִי הַנֹּשְׂאִים אֶת־אֲרוֹן בְּרִית יְהוָה וְאֶל־כָּל־זִקְנֵי יִשְׂרָאֵל: וַיְצַו מֹשֶׁה אוֹתָם לֵאמֹר מִקֵּץ ׀ שֶׁבַע שָׁנִים בְּמֹעֵד שְׁנַת הַשְּׁמִטָּה בְּחַג הַסֻּכּוֹת: בְּבוֹא כָל־יִשְׂרָאֵל לֵרָאוֹת אֶת־פְּנֵי יְהוָה אֱלֹהֶיךָ בַּמָּקוֹם אֲשֶׁר יִבְחָר תִּקְרָא אֶת־הַתּוֹרָה הַזֹּאת נֶגֶד כָּל־יִשְׂרָאֵל בְּאָזְנֵיהֶם: הַקְהֵל אֶת־הָעָם הָאֲנָשִׁים וְהַנָּשִׁים וְהַטַּף וְגֵרְךָ אֲשֶׁר בִּשְׁעָרֶיךָ לְמַעַן יִשְׁמְעוּ וּלְמַעַן יִלְמְדוּ וְיָרְאוּ אֶת־יְהוָה אֱלֹהֵיכֶם וְשָׁמְרוּ לַעֲשׂוֹת אֶת־כָּל־דִּבְרֵי הַתּוֹרָה הַזֹּאת: וּבְנֵיהֶם אֲשֶׁר לֹא־יָדְעוּ יִשְׁמְעוּ וְלָמְדוּ לְיִרְאָה אֶת־יְהוָה אֱלֹהֵיכֶם כָּל־הַיָּמִים אֲשֶׁר אַתֶּם חַיִּים עַל־הָאֲדָמָה אֲשֶׁר אַתֶּם עֹבְרִים אֶת־הַיַּרְדֵּן שָׁמָּה לְרִשְׁתָּהּ:

◆{ HA'AZINU / פ׳ האזינו }◆
(Deuteronomy 32:1-12)

כה: הַאֲזִינוּ הַשָּׁמַיִם וַאֲדַבֵּרָה וְתִשְׁמַע הָאָרֶץ אִמְרֵי־פִי: יַעֲרֹף כַּמָּטָר לִקְחִי תִּזַּל כַּטַּל אִמְרָתִי כִּשְׂעִירִם עֲלֵי־דֶשֶׁא וְכִרְבִיבִים עֲלֵי־עֵשֶׂב: כִּי שֵׁם יְהוָה אֶקְרָא הָבוּ גֹדֶל לֵאלֹהֵינוּ:

ברכה-ראש חודש

הַצּוּר תָּמִים פָּעֳלוֹ כִּי כָל־דְּרָכָיו מִשְׁפָּט אֵל אֱמוּנָה וְאֵין עָוֶל צַדִּיק וְיָשָׁר הוּא: שִׁחֵת לוֹ לֹא בָּנָיו מוּמָם דּוֹר עִקֵּשׁ וּפְתַלְתֹּל: הֲ־לַיהוה תִּגְמְלוּ־זֹאת עַם נָבָל וְלֹא חָכָם הֲלוֹא־הוּא אָבִיךָ קָּנֶךָ הוּא עָשְׂךָ וַיְכֹנְנֶךָ:

ישראל: זְכֹר יְמוֹת עוֹלָם בִּינוּ שְׁנוֹת דֹּר־וָדֹר שְׁאַל אָבִיךָ וְיַגֵּדְךָ זְקֵנֶיךָ וְיֹאמְרוּ לָךְ: בְּהַנְחֵל עֶלְיוֹן גּוֹיִם בְּהַפְרִידוֹ בְּנֵי אָדָם יַצֵּב גְּבֻלֹת עַמִּים לְמִסְפַּר בְּנֵי יִשְׂרָאֵל: כִּי חֵלֶק יהוה עַמּוֹ יַעֲקֹב חֶבֶל נַחֲלָתוֹ: יִמְצָאֵהוּ בְּאֶרֶץ מִדְבָּר וּבְתֹהוּ יְלֵל יְשִׁמֹן יְסֹבְבֶנְהוּ יְבוֹנְנֵהוּ יִצְּרֶנְהוּ כְּאִישׁוֹן עֵינוֹ: כְּנֶשֶׁר יָעִיר קִנּוֹ עַל־גּוֹזָלָיו יְרַחֵף יִפְרֹשׂ כְּנָפָיו יִקָּחֵהוּ יִשָּׂאֵהוּ עַל־אֶבְרָתוֹ: יהוה בָּדָד יַנְחֶנּוּ וְאֵין עִמּוֹ אֵל נֵכָר:

פ׳ ברכה / BERACHAH
(Deuteronomy 33:1-17)

כהן: וְזֹאת הַבְּרָכָה אֲשֶׁר בֵּרַךְ מֹשֶׁה אִישׁ הָאֱלֹהִים אֶת־בְּנֵי יִשְׂרָאֵל לִפְנֵי מוֹתוֹ: וַיֹּאמַר יהוה מִסִּינַי בָּא וְזָרַח מִשֵּׂעִיר לָמוֹ הוֹפִיעַ מֵהַר פָּארָן וְאָתָה מֵרִבְבֹת קֹדֶשׁ מִימִינוֹ אֵשׁ דָּת לָמוֹ: אַף חֹבֵב עַמִּים כָּל־קְדֹשָׁיו בְּיָדֶךָ וְהֵם תֻּכּוּ לְרַגְלֶךָ יִשָּׂא מִדַּבְּרֹתֶיךָ: תּוֹרָה צִוָּה־לָנוּ מֹשֶׁה מוֹרָשָׁה קְהִלַּת יַעֲקֹב: וַיְהִי בִישֻׁרוּן מֶלֶךְ בְּהִתְאַסֵּף רָאשֵׁי עָם יַחַד שִׁבְטֵי יִשְׂרָאֵל: יְחִי רְאוּבֵן וְאַל־יָמֹת וִיהִי מְתָיו מִסְפָּר: וְזֹאת לִיהוּדָה וַיֹּאמַר שְׁמַע יהוה קוֹל יְהוּדָה וְאֶל־עַמּוֹ תְּבִיאֶנּוּ יָדָיו רָב לוֹ וְעֵזֶר מִצָּרָיו תִּהְיֶה:

לוי: וּלְלֵוִי אָמַר תֻּמֶּיךָ וְאוּרֶיךָ לְאִישׁ חֲסִידֶךָ אֲשֶׁר נִסִּיתוֹ בְּמַסָּה תְּרִיבֵהוּ עַל־מֵי מְרִיבָה: הָאֹמֵר לְאָבִיו וּלְאִמּוֹ לֹא רְאִיתִיו וְאֶת־אֶחָיו לֹא הִכִּיר וְאֶת־בָּנָיו לֹא יָדָע כִּי שָׁמְרוּ אִמְרָתֶךָ וּבְרִיתְךָ יִנְצֹרוּ: יוֹרוּ מִשְׁפָּטֶיךָ לְיַעֲקֹב וְתוֹרָתְךָ לְיִשְׂרָאֵל יָשִׂימוּ קְטוֹרָה בְּאַפֶּךָ וְכָלִיל עַל־מִזְבְּחֶךָ: בָּרֵךְ יהוה חֵילוֹ וּפֹעַל יָדָיו תִּרְצֶה מְחַץ מָתְנַיִם קָמָיו וּמְשַׂנְאָיו מִן־יְקוּמוּן: לְבִנְיָמִן אָמַר יְדִיד יהוה יִשְׁכֹּן לָבֶטַח עָלָיו חֹפֵף עָלָיו כָּל־הַיּוֹם וּבֵין

כְּתֵפָיו שָׁכֵן:

ישראל: וּלְיוֹסֵף אָמַר מְבֹרֶכֶת יהוה אַרְצוֹ מִמֶּגֶד שָׁמַיִם מִטָּל וּמִתְּהוֹם רֹבֶצֶת תָּחַת: וּמִמֶּגֶד תְּבוּאֹת שָׁמֶשׁ וּמִמֶּגֶד גֶּרֶשׁ יְרָחִים: וּמֵרֹאשׁ הַרְרֵי־קֶדֶם וּמִמֶּגֶד גִּבְעוֹת עוֹלָם: וּמִמֶּגֶד אֶרֶץ וּמְלֹאָהּ וּרְצוֹן שֹׁכְנִי סְנֶה תָּבוֹאתָה לְרֹאשׁ יוֹסֵף וּלְקָדְקֹד נְזִיר אֶחָיו: בְּכוֹר שׁוֹרוֹ הָדָר לוֹ וְקַרְנֵי רְאֵם קַרְנָיו בָּהֶם עַמִּים יְנַגַּח יַחְדָּו אַפְסֵי־אָרֶץ וְהֵם רִבְבוֹת אֶפְרַיִם וְהֵם אַלְפֵי מְנַשֶּׁה:

ראש חודש / ROSH CHODESH

כהן: וַיְדַבֵּר יהוה אֶל־מֹשֶׁה לֵּאמֹר: צַו אֶת־בְּנֵי יִשְׂרָאֵל וְאָמַרְתָּ אֲלֵהֶם אֶת־קָרְבָּנִי לַחְמִי לְאִשַּׁי רֵיחַ נִיחֹחִי תִּשְׁמְרוּ לְהַקְרִיב לִי בְּמוֹעֲדוֹ: וְאָמַרְתָּ לָהֶם זֶה הָאִשֶּׁה אֲשֶׁר תַּקְרִיבוּ לַיהוה כְּבָשִׂים בְּנֵי־שָׁנָה תְמִימִם שְׁנַיִם לַיּוֹם עֹלָה תָמִיד:

לוי: וְאָמַרְתָּ לָהֶם זֶה הָאִשֶּׁה אֲשֶׁר תַּקְרִיבוּ לַיהוה כְּבָשִׂים בְּנֵי־שָׁנָה תְמִימִם שְׁנַיִם לַיּוֹם עֹלָה תָמִיד: אֶת־הַכֶּבֶשׂ אֶחָד תַּעֲשֶׂה בַבֹּקֶר וְאֵת הַכֶּבֶשׂ הַשֵּׁנִי תַּעֲשֶׂה בֵּין הָעַרְבָּיִם: וַעֲשִׂירִית הָאֵיפָה סֹלֶת לְמִנְחָה בְּלוּלָה בְּשֶׁמֶן כָּתִית רְבִיעִת הַהִין:

ישראל: עֹלַת תָּמִיד הָעֲשֻׂיָה בְּהַר סִינַי לְרֵיחַ נִיחֹחַ אִשֶּׁה לַיהוה: וְנִסְכּוֹ רְבִיעִת הַהִין לַכֶּבֶשׂ הָאֶחָד בַּקֹּדֶשׁ הַסֵּךְ נֶסֶךְ שֵׁכָר לַיהוה: וְאֵת הַכֶּבֶשׂ הַשֵּׁנִי תַּעֲשֶׂה בֵּין הָעַרְבָּיִם כְּמִנְחַת הַבֹּקֶר וּכְנִסְכּוֹ תַּעֲשֶׂה אִשֵּׁה רֵיחַ נִיחֹחַ לַיהוה: וּבְיוֹם הַשַּׁבָּת שְׁנֵי־כְבָשִׂים בְּנֵי־שָׁנָה תְּמִימִם וּשְׁנֵי עֶשְׂרֹנִים סֹלֶת מִנְחָה בְּלוּלָה בַשֶּׁמֶן וְנִסְכּוֹ: עֹלַת שַׁבַּת בְּשַׁבַּתּוֹ עַל־עֹלַת הַתָּמִיד וְנִסְכָּהּ:

רביעי: וּבְרָאשֵׁי חָדְשֵׁיכֶם תַּקְרִיבוּ עֹלָה לַיהוה פָּרִים בְּנֵי־בָקָר שְׁנַיִם וְאַיִל אֶחָד כְּבָשִׂים בְּנֵי־שָׁנָה שִׁבְעָה תְּמִימִם: וּשְׁלֹשָׁה עֶשְׂרֹנִים סֹלֶת מִנְחָה בְּלוּלָה בַשֶּׁמֶן לַפָּר הָאֶחָד וּשְׁנֵי עֶשְׂרֹנִים סֹלֶת מִנְחָה בְּלוּלָה בַשֶּׁמֶן לָאַיִל הָאֶחָד: וְעִשָּׂרֹן עִשָּׂרוֹן סֹלֶת מִנְחָה בְּלוּלָה בַשֶּׁמֶן לַכֶּבֶשׂ הָאֶחָד עֹלָה

רֵיחַ נִיחֹחַ אִשֶּׁה לַיהוָה: וְנִסְכֵּיהֶם חֲצִי הַהִין יִהְיֶה לַפָּר וּשְׁלִישִׁת הַהִין לָאַיִל וּרְבִיעִת הַהִין לַכֶּבֶשׂ יָיִן זֹאת עֹלַת חֹדֶשׁ בְּחָדְשׁוֹ לְחָדְשֵׁי הַשָּׁנָה: וּשְׂעִיר עִזִּים אֶחָד לְחַטָּאת לַיהוָה עַל־עֹלַת הַתָּמִיד יֵעָשֶׂה וְנִסְכּוֹ:

◄ CHANUKAH / חנוכה ►

FIRST DAY CHANUKAH

Some congregations begin at this point:

כהו: וַיְדַבֵּר יְהוָה אֶל־מֹשֶׁה לֵּאמֹר: דַּבֵּר אֶל־אַהֲרֹן וְאֶל־בָּנָיו לֵאמֹר כֹּה תְבָרְכוּ אֶת־בְּנֵי יִשְׂרָאֵל אָמוֹר לָהֶם: יְבָרֶכְךָ יְהוָה וְיִשְׁמְרֶךָ: יָאֵר יְהוָה ׀ פָּנָיו אֵלֶיךָ וִיחֻנֶּךָּ: יִשָּׂא יְהוָה ׀ פָּנָיו אֵלֶיךָ וְיָשֵׂם לְךָ שָׁלוֹם: וְשָׂמוּ אֶת־שְׁמִי עַל־בְּנֵי יִשְׂרָאֵל וַאֲנִי אֲבָרֲכֵם:

Some congregations begin at this point:

וַיְהִי בְּיוֹם כַּלּוֹת מֹשֶׁה לְהָקִים אֶת־הַמִּשְׁכָּן וַיִּמְשַׁח אֹתוֹ וַיְקַדֵּשׁ אֹתוֹ וְאֶת־כָּל־כֵּלָיו וְאֶת־הַמִּזְבֵּחַ וְאֶת־כָּל־כֵּלָיו וַיִּמְשָׁחֵם וַיְקַדֵּשׁ אֹתָם: וַיַּקְרִיבוּ נְשִׂיאֵי יִשְׂרָאֵל רָאשֵׁי בֵּית אֲבֹתָם הֵם נְשִׂיאֵי הַמַּטֹּת הֵם הָעֹמְדִים עַל־הַפְּקֻדִים: וַיָּבִיאוּ אֶת־קָרְבָּנָם לִפְנֵי יְהוָה שֵׁשׁ־עֶגְלֹת צָב וּשְׁנֵי־עָשָׂר בָּקָר עֲגָלָה עַל־שְׁנֵי הַנְּשִׂאִים וְשׁוֹר לְאֶחָד וַיַּקְרִיבוּ אוֹתָם לִפְנֵי הַמִּשְׁכָּן: וַיֹּאמֶר יְהוָה אֶל־מֹשֶׁה לֵּאמֹר: קַח מֵאִתָּם וְהָיוּ לַעֲבֹד אֶת־עֲבֹדַת אֹהֶל מוֹעֵד וְנָתַתָּה אוֹתָם אֶל־הַלְוִיִּם אִישׁ כְּפִי עֲבֹדָתוֹ: וַיִּקַּח מֹשֶׁה אֶת־הָעֲגָלֹת וְאֶת־הַבָּקָר וַיִּתֵּן אוֹתָם אֶל־הַלְוִיִּם: אֵת ׀ שְׁתֵּי הָעֲגָלוֹת וְאֵת אַרְבַּעַת הַבָּקָר נָתַן לִבְנֵי גֵרְשׁוֹן כְּפִי עֲבֹדָתָם: וְאֵת ׀ אַרְבַּע הָעֲגָלֹת וְאֵת שְׁמֹנַת הַבָּקָר נָתַן לִבְנֵי מְרָרִי כְּפִי עֲבֹדָתָם בְּיַד אִיתָמָר בֶּן־אַהֲרֹן הַכֹּהֵן: וְלִבְנֵי קְהָת לֹא נָתָן כִּי־עֲבֹדַת הַקֹּדֶשׁ עֲלֵהֶם בַּכָּתֵף יִשָּׂאוּ: וַיַּקְרִיבוּ הַנְּשִׂאִים אֵת חֲנֻכַּת הַמִּזְבֵּחַ בְּיוֹם הִמָּשַׁח אֹתוֹ וַיַּקְרִיבוּ הַנְּשִׂיאִם אֶת־קָרְבָּנָם לִפְנֵי הַמִּזְבֵּחַ: וַיֹּאמֶר יְהוָה אֶל־מֹשֶׁה נָשִׂיא אֶחָד לַיּוֹם נָשִׂיא אֶחָד לַיּוֹם יַקְרִיבוּ אֶת־קָרְבָּנָם לַחֲנֻכַּת הַמִּזְבֵּחַ:

לוי: וַיְהִי הַמַּקְרִיב בַּיּוֹם הָרִאשׁוֹן אֶת־קָרְבָּנוֹ נַחְשׁוֹן בֶּן־עַמִּינָדָב לְמַטֵּה יְהוּדָה: וְקָרְבָּנוֹ קַעֲרַת־כֶּסֶף אַחַת שְׁלֹשִׁים וּמֵאָה מִשְׁקָלָהּ מִזְרָק אֶחָד כֶּסֶף שִׁבְעִים שֶׁקֶל בְּשֶׁקֶל הַקֹּדֶשׁ שְׁנֵיהֶם ׀ מְלֵאִים סֹלֶת בְּלוּלָה בַשֶּׁמֶן לְמִנְחָה: כַּף אַחַת עֲשָׂרָה זָהָב מְלֵאָה קְטֹרֶת:

ישראל: פַּר אֶחָד בֶּן־בָּקָר אַיִל אֶחָד כֶּבֶשׂ־אֶחָד בֶּן־שְׁנָתוֹ לְעֹלָה: שְׂעִיר־עִזִּים אֶחָד לְחַטָּאת: וּלְזֶבַח הַשְּׁלָמִים בָּקָר שְׁנַיִם אֵילִם חֲמִשָּׁה עַתּוּדִים חֲמִשָּׁה כְּבָשִׂים בְּנֵי־שָׁנָה חֲמִשָּׁה זֶה קָרְבַּן נַחְשׁוֹן בֶּן־עַמִּינָדָב:

SECOND DAY CHANUKAH

כהו: בַּיּוֹם הַשֵּׁנִי הִקְרִיב נְתַנְאֵל בֶּן־צוּעָר נְשִׂיא יִשָּׂשכָר: הִקְרִב אֶת־קָרְבָּנוֹ קַעֲרַת־כֶּסֶף אַחַת שְׁלֹשִׁים וּמֵאָה מִשְׁקָלָהּ מִזְרָק אֶחָד כֶּסֶף שִׁבְעִים שֶׁקֶל בְּשֶׁקֶל הַקֹּדֶשׁ שְׁנֵיהֶם ׀ מְלֵאִים סֹלֶת בְּלוּלָה בַשֶּׁמֶן לְמִנְחָה: כַּף אַחַת עֲשָׂרָה זָהָב מְלֵאָה קְטֹרֶת:

לוי: פַּר אֶחָד בֶּן־בָּקָר אַיִל אֶחָד כֶּבֶשׂ־אֶחָד בֶּן־שְׁנָתוֹ לְעֹלָה: שְׂעִיר־עִזִּים אֶחָד לְחַטָּאת: וּלְזֶבַח הַשְּׁלָמִים בָּקָר שְׁנַיִם אֵילִם חֲמִשָּׁה עַתֻּדִים חֲמִשָּׁה כְּבָשִׂים בְּנֵי־שָׁנָה חֲמִשָּׁה זֶה קָרְבַּן נְתַנְאֵל בֶּן־צוּעָר:

ישראל: בַּיּוֹם הַשְּׁלִישִׁי נָשִׂיא לִבְנֵי זְבוּלֻן אֱלִיאָב בֶּן־חֵלֹן: קָרְבָּנוֹ קַעֲרַת־כֶּסֶף אַחַת שְׁלֹשִׁים וּמֵאָה מִשְׁקָלָהּ מִזְרָק אֶחָד כֶּסֶף שִׁבְעִים שֶׁקֶל בְּשֶׁקֶל הַקֹּדֶשׁ שְׁנֵיהֶם ׀ מְלֵאִים סֹלֶת בְּלוּלָה בַשֶּׁמֶן לְמִנְחָה: כַּף אַחַת עֲשָׂרָה זָהָב מְלֵאָה קְטֹרֶת: פַּר אֶחָד בֶּן־בָּקָר אַיִל אֶחָד כֶּבֶשׂ־אֶחָד בֶּן־שְׁנָתוֹ לְעֹלָה: שְׂעִיר־עִזִּים אֶחָד לְחַטָּאת: וּלְזֶבַח הַשְּׁלָמִים בָּקָר שְׁנַיִם אֵילִם חֲמִשָּׁה עַתֻּדִים חֲמִשָּׁה כְּבָשִׂים בְּנֵי־שָׁנָה חֲמִשָּׁה זֶה קָרְבַּן אֱלִיאָב בֶּן־חֵלֹן:

THIRD DAY CHANUKAH

כהו: בַּיּוֹם הַשְּׁלִישִׁי נָשִׂיא לִבְנֵי זְבוּלֻן אֱלִיאָב בֶּן־חֵלֹן: קָרְבָּנוֹ קַעֲרַת־כֶּסֶף אַחַת שְׁלֹשִׁים

וּמֵאָה מִשְׁקָלָהּ מִזְרָק אֶחָד כֶּסֶף שִׁבְעִים שֶׁקֶל בְּשֶׁקֶל הַקֹּדֶשׁ שְׁנֵיהֶם ׀ מְלֵאִים סֹלֶת בְּלוּלָה בַשֶּׁמֶן לְמִנְחָה: כַּף אַחַת עֲשָׂרָה זָהָב מְלֵאָה קְטֹרֶת: לוי: פַּר אֶחָד בֶּן־בָּקָר אַיִל אֶחָד כֶּבֶשׂ־אֶחָד בֶּן־שְׁנָתוֹ לְעֹלָה: שְׂעִיר־עִזִּים אֶחָד לְחַטָּאת: וּלְזֶבַח הַשְּׁלָמִים בָּקָר שְׁנַיִם אֵילִם חֲמִשָּׁה עַתּוּדִים חֲמִשָּׁה כְּבָשִׂים בְּנֵי־שָׁנָה חֲמִשָּׁה זֶה קָרְבַּן אֱלִיאָב בֶּן־חֵלֹן:

ישראל: בַּיּוֹם הָרְבִיעִי נָשִׂיא לִבְנֵי רְאוּבֵן אֱלִיצוּר בֶּן־שְׁדֵיאוּר: קָרְבָּנוֹ קַעֲרַת־כֶּסֶף אַחַת שְׁלֹשִׁים וּמֵאָה מִשְׁקָלָהּ מִזְרָק אֶחָד כֶּסֶף שִׁבְעִים שֶׁקֶל בְּשֶׁקֶל הַקֹּדֶשׁ שְׁנֵיהֶם ׀ מְלֵאִים סֹלֶת בְּלוּלָה בַשֶּׁמֶן לְמִנְחָה: כַּף אַחַת עֲשָׂרָה זָהָב מְלֵאָה קְטֹרֶת: פַּר אֶחָד בֶּן־בָּקָר אַיִל אֶחָד כֶּבֶשׂ־אֶחָד בֶּן־שְׁנָתוֹ לְעֹלָה: שְׂעִיר־עִזִּים אֶחָד לְחַטָּאת: וּלְזֶבַח הַשְּׁלָמִים בָּקָר שְׁנַיִם אֵילִם חֲמִשָּׁה עַתֻּדִים חֲמִשָּׁה כְּבָשִׂים בְּנֵי־שָׁנָה חֲמִשָּׁה זֶה קָרְבַּן אֱלִיצוּר בֶּן־שְׁדֵיאוּר:

FOURTH DAY CHANUKAH

כהן: בַּיּוֹם הָרְבִיעִי נָשִׂיא לִבְנֵי רְאוּבֵן אֱלִיצוּר בֶּן־שְׁדֵיאוּר: קָרְבָּנוֹ קַעֲרַת־כֶּסֶף אַחַת שְׁלֹשִׁים וּמֵאָה מִשְׁקָלָהּ מִזְרָק אֶחָד כֶּסֶף שִׁבְעִים שֶׁקֶל בְּשֶׁקֶל הַקֹּדֶשׁ שְׁנֵיהֶם ׀ מְלֵאִים סֹלֶת בְּלוּלָה בַשֶּׁמֶן לְמִנְחָה: כַּף אַחַת עֲשָׂרָה זָהָב מְלֵאָה קְטֹרֶת: לוי: פַּר אֶחָד בֶּן־בָּקָר אַיִל אֶחָד כֶּבֶשׂ־אֶחָד בֶּן־שְׁנָתוֹ לְעֹלָה: שְׂעִיר־עִזִּים אֶחָד לְחַטָּאת: וּלְזֶבַח הַשְּׁלָמִים בָּקָר שְׁנַיִם אֵילִם חֲמִשָּׁה עַתֻּדִים חֲמִשָּׁה כְּבָשִׂים בְּנֵי־שָׁנָה חֲמִשָּׁה זֶה קָרְבַּן אֱלִיצוּר בֶּן־שְׁדֵיאוּר:

ישראל: בַּיּוֹם הַחֲמִישִׁי נָשִׂיא לִבְנֵי שִׁמְעוֹן שְׁלֻמִיאֵל בֶּן־צוּרִישַׁדָּי: קָרְבָּנוֹ קַעֲרַת־כֶּסֶף אַחַת שְׁלֹשִׁים וּמֵאָה מִשְׁקָלָהּ מִזְרָק אֶחָד כֶּסֶף שִׁבְעִים שֶׁקֶל בְּשֶׁקֶל הַקֹּדֶשׁ שְׁנֵיהֶם ׀ מְלֵאִים סֹלֶת בְּלוּלָה בַשֶּׁמֶן לְמִנְחָה: כַּף אַחַת עֲשָׂרָה זָהָב מְלֵאָה קְטֹרֶת: פַּר אֶחָד בֶּן־בָּקָר אַיִל אֶחָד כֶּבֶשׂ־אֶחָד בֶּן־שְׁנָתוֹ לְעֹלָה: שְׂעִיר־עִזִּים אֶחָד לְחַטָּאת: וּלְזֶבַח הַשְּׁלָמִים בָּקָר שְׁנַיִם אֵילִם חֲמִשָּׁה עַתֻּדִים חֲמִשָּׁה כְּבָשִׂים בְּנֵי־שָׁנָה חֲמִשָּׁה זֶה קָרְבַּן שְׁלֻמִיאֵל בֶּן־צוּרִישַׁדָּי:

FIFTH DAY CHANUKAH

כהן: בַּיּוֹם הַחֲמִישִׁי נָשִׂיא לִבְנֵי שִׁמְעוֹן שְׁלֻמִיאֵל בֶּן־צוּרִישַׁדָּי: קָרְבָּנוֹ קַעֲרַת־כֶּסֶף אַחַת שְׁלֹשִׁים וּמֵאָה מִשְׁקָלָהּ מִזְרָק אֶחָד כֶּסֶף שִׁבְעִים שֶׁקֶל בְּשֶׁקֶל הַקֹּדֶשׁ שְׁנֵיהֶם ׀ מְלֵאִים סֹלֶת בְּלוּלָה בַשֶּׁמֶן לְמִנְחָה: כַּף אַחַת עֲשָׂרָה זָהָב מְלֵאָה קְטֹרֶת: לוי: פַּר אֶחָד בֶּן־בָּקָר אַיִל אֶחָד כֶּבֶשׂ־אֶחָד בֶּן־שְׁנָתוֹ לְעֹלָה: שְׂעִיר־עִזִּים אֶחָד לְחַטָּאת: וּלְזֶבַח הַשְּׁלָמִים בָּקָר שְׁנַיִם אֵילִם חֲמִשָּׁה עַתֻּדִים חֲמִשָּׁה כְּבָשִׂים בְּנֵי־שָׁנָה חֲמִשָּׁה זֶה קָרְבַּן שְׁלֻמִיאֵל בֶּן־צוּרִישַׁדָּי:

ישראל: בַּיּוֹם הַשִּׁשִּׁי נָשִׂיא לִבְנֵי גָד אֶלְיָסָף בֶּן־דְּעוּאֵל: קָרְבָּנוֹ קַעֲרַת־כֶּסֶף אַחַת שְׁלֹשִׁים וּמֵאָה מִשְׁקָלָהּ מִזְרָק אֶחָד כֶּסֶף שִׁבְעִים שֶׁקֶל בְּשֶׁקֶל הַקֹּדֶשׁ שְׁנֵיהֶם ׀ מְלֵאִים סֹלֶת בְּלוּלָה בַשֶּׁמֶן לְמִנְחָה: כַּף אַחַת עֲשָׂרָה זָהָב מְלֵאָה קְטֹרֶת: פַּר אֶחָד בֶּן־בָּקָר אַיִל אֶחָד כֶּבֶשׂ־אֶחָד בֶּן־שְׁנָתוֹ לְעֹלָה: שְׂעִיר־עִזִּים אֶחָד לְחַטָּאת: וּלְזֶבַח הַשְּׁלָמִים בָּקָר שְׁנַיִם אֵילִם חֲמִשָּׁה עַתֻּדִים חֲמִשָּׁה כְּבָשִׂים בְּנֵי־שָׁנָה חֲמִשָּׁה זֶה קָרְבַּן אֶלְיָסָף בֶּן־דְּעוּאֵל:

SIXTH DAY CHANUKAH

Two Torah Scrolls are removed from the Ark. Three *olim* are called to the first Torah for the Rosh Chodesh reading. A fourth *oleh* is called to the second Torah for the Chanukah reading.

כהן: וַיְדַבֵּר יהוה אֶל־מֹשֶׁה לֵּאמֹר: צַו אֶת־בְּנֵי יִשְׂרָאֵל וְאָמַרְתָּ אֲלֵהֶם אֶת־קָרְבָּנִי לַחְמִי לְאִשַּׁי רֵיחַ נִיחֹחִי תִּשְׁמְרוּ לְהַקְרִיב לִי בְּמוֹעֲדוֹ: וְאָמַרְתָּ לָהֶם זֶה הָאִשֶּׁה אֲשֶׁר

TORAH READING/CHOL HAMOED — CHANUKAH

SEVENTH DAY CHANUKAH

In most years the seventh day of Chanukah is also Rosh Chodesh. The Rosh Chodesh reading is the same as that of the sixth day. The following is the Chanukah reading for the fourth *oleh*:

רביעי: בַּיּוֹם֙ הַשְּׁבִיעִ֔י נָשִׂ֖יא לִבְנֵ֣י אֶפְרָ֑יִם אֱלִישָׁמָ֖ע בֶּן־עַמִּיהֽוּד: קׇרְבָּנ֞וֹ קַֽעֲרַת־כֶּ֣סֶף אַחַ֗ת שְׁלֹשִׁ֣ים וּמֵאָה֮ מִשְׁקָלָהּ֒ מִזְרָ֤ק אֶחָד֙ כֶּ֔סֶף שִׁבְעִ֥ים שֶׁ֖קֶל בְּשֶׁ֣קֶל הַקֹּ֑דֶשׁ שְׁנֵיהֶ֣ם ׀ מְלֵאִ֗ים סֹ֛לֶת בְּלוּלָ֥ה בַשֶּׁ֖מֶן לְמִנְחָֽה: כַּ֥ף אַחַ֛ת עֲשָׂרָ֥ה זָהָ֖ב מְלֵאָ֥ה קְטֹֽרֶת: פַּ֣ר אֶחָ֞ד בֶּן־בָּקָ֗ר אַ֧יִל אֶחָ֛ד כֶּֽבֶשׂ־אֶחָ֥ד בֶּן־שְׁנָת֖וֹ לְעֹלָֽה: שְׂעִיר־עִזִּ֥ים אֶחָ֖ד לְחַטָּֽאת: וּלְזֶ֣בַח הַשְּׁלָמִים֮ בָּקָ֣ר שְׁנַ֒יִם֒ אֵילִ֤ם חֲמִשָּׁה֙ עַתּוּדִ֣ים חֲמִשָּׁ֔ה כְּבָשִׂ֥ים בְּנֵֽי־שָׁנָ֖ה חֲמִשָּׁ֑ה זֶ֛ה קׇרְבַּ֥ן אֱלִישָׁמָ֖ע בֶּן־עַמִּיהֽוּד:

In years when only the sixth day of Chanukah is Rosh Chodesh, the following is the reading for the seventh day.

כהן: בַּיּוֹם֙ הַשְּׁבִיעִ֔י נָשִׂ֖יא לִבְנֵ֣י אֶפְרָ֑יִם אֱלִישָׁמָ֖ע בֶּן־עַמִּיהֽוּד: קׇרְבָּנ֞וֹ קַֽעֲרַת־כֶּ֣סֶף אַחַ֗ת שְׁלֹשִׁ֣ים וּמֵאָה֮ מִשְׁקָלָהּ֒ מִזְרָ֤ק אֶחָד֙ כֶּ֔סֶף שִׁבְעִ֥ים שֶׁ֖קֶל בְּשֶׁ֣קֶל הַקֹּ֑דֶשׁ שְׁנֵיהֶ֣ם ׀ מְלֵאִ֗ים סֹ֛לֶת בְּלוּלָ֥ה בַשֶּׁ֖מֶן לְמִנְחָֽה: כַּ֥ף אַחַ֛ת עֲשָׂרָ֥ה זָהָ֖ב מְלֵאָ֥ה קְטֹֽרֶת:

לוי: פַּ֣ר אֶחָ֞ד בֶּן־בָּקָ֗ר אַ֧יִל אֶחָ֛ד כֶּֽבֶשׂ־אֶחָ֥ד בֶּן־שְׁנָת֖וֹ לְעֹלָֽה: שְׂעִיר־עִזִּ֥ים אֶחָ֖ד לְחַטָּֽאת: וּלְזֶ֣בַח הַשְּׁלָמִים֮ בָּקָ֣ר שְׁנַ֒יִם֒ אֵילִ֤ם חֲמִשָּׁה֙ עַתּוּדִ֣ים חֲמִשָּׁ֔ה כְּבָשִׂ֥ים בְּנֵֽי־שָׁנָ֖ה חֲמִשָּׁ֑ה זֶ֛ה קׇרְבַּ֥ן אֱלִישָׁמָ֖ע בֶּן־עַמִּיהֽוּד:

ישראל: בַּיּוֹם֙ הַשְּׁמִינִ֔י נָשִׂ֖יא לִבְנֵ֣י מְנַשֶּׁ֑ה גַּמְלִיאֵ֖ל בֶּן־פְּדָהצֽוּר: קׇרְבָּנ֞וֹ קַֽעֲרַת־כֶּ֣סֶף אַחַ֗ת שְׁלֹשִׁ֣ים וּמֵאָה֮ מִשְׁקָלָהּ֒ מִזְרָ֤ק אֶחָד֙ כֶּ֔סֶף שִׁבְעִ֥ים שֶׁ֖קֶל בְּשֶׁ֣קֶל הַקֹּ֑דֶשׁ שְׁנֵיהֶ֣ם ׀ מְלֵאִ֗ים סֹ֛לֶת בְּלוּלָ֥ה בַשֶּׁ֖מֶן לְמִנְחָֽה: כַּ֥ף אַחַ֛ת עֲשָׂרָ֥ה זָהָ֖ב מְלֵאָ֥ה קְטֹֽרֶת: פַּ֣ר אֶחָ֞ד בֶּן־בָּקָ֗ר אַ֧יִל אֶחָ֛ד כֶּֽבֶשׂ־אֶחָ֥ד בֶּן־שְׁנָת֖וֹ לְעֹלָֽה: שְׂעִיר־עִזִּ֥ים אֶחָ֖ד לְחַטָּֽאת: וּלְזֶ֣בַח הַשְּׁלָמִים֮ בָּקָ֣ר שְׁנַ֒יִם֒ אֵילִ֤ם חֲמִשָּׁה֙ עַתּוּדִ֣ים

תַּקְרִ֖יבוּ לַֽיהוָ֑ה כְּבָשִׂ֧ים בְּנֵֽי־שָׁנָ֛ה תְּמִימִ֖ם שְׁנַ֣יִם לַיּ֥וֹם עֹלָ֖ה תָמִֽיד: אֶת־הַכֶּ֤בֶשׂ אֶחָד֙ תַּֽעֲשֶׂ֣ה בַבֹּ֔קֶר וְאֵת֙ הַכֶּ֣בֶשׂ הַשֵּׁנִ֔י תַּֽעֲשֶׂ֖ה בֵּ֣ין הָֽעַרְבָּ֑יִם: וַֽעֲשִׂירִ֧ית הָֽאֵיפָ֛ה סֹ֖לֶת לְמִנְחָ֑ה בְּלוּלָ֛ה בְּשֶׁ֥מֶן כָּתִ֖ית רְבִיעִ֥ת הַהִֽין:

לוי: עֹלַ֖ת תָּמִ֑יד הָֽעֲשֻׂיָה֙ בְּהַ֣ר סִינַ֔י לְרֵ֣יחַ נִיחֹ֔חַ אִשֶּׁ֖ה לַֽיהוָֽה: וְנִסְכּוֹ֙ רְבִיעִ֣ת הַהִ֔ין לַכֶּ֖בֶשׂ הָֽאֶחָ֑ד בַּקֹּ֗דֶשׁ הַסֵּ֛ךְ נֶ֥סֶךְ שֵׁכָ֖ר לַֽיהוָֽה: וְאֵת֙ הַכֶּ֣בֶשׂ הַשֵּׁנִ֔י תַּֽעֲשֶׂ֖ה בֵּ֣ין הָֽעַרְבָּ֑יִם כְּמִנְחַ֨ת הַבֹּ֤קֶר וּכְנִסְכּוֹ֙ תַּֽעֲשֶׂ֔ה אִשֵּׁ֛ה רֵ֥יחַ נִיחֹ֖חַ לַֽיהוָֽה: וּבְיוֹם֙ הַשַּׁבָּ֔ת שְׁנֵֽי־כְבָשִׂ֥ים בְּנֵֽי־שָׁנָ֖ה תְּמִימִ֑ם וּשְׁנֵ֣י עֶשְׂרֹנִ֗ים סֹ֧לֶת מִנְחָ֛ה בְּלוּלָ֥ה בַשֶּׁ֖מֶן וְנִסְכּֽוֹ: עֹלַ֥ת שַׁבַּ֖ת בְּשַׁבַּתּ֑וֹ עַל־עֹלַ֥ת הַתָּמִ֖יד וְנִסְכָּֽהּ:

ישראל: וּבְרָאשֵׁי֙ חׇדְשֵׁיכֶ֔ם תַּקְרִ֥יבוּ עֹלָ֖ה לַֽיהוָ֑ה פָּרִ֣ים בְּנֵֽי־בָקָ֤ר שְׁנַ֙יִם֙ וְאַ֣יִל אֶחָ֔ד כְּבָשִׂ֧ים בְּנֵֽי־שָׁנָ֛ה שִׁבְעָ֖ה תְּמִימִֽם: וּשְׁלֹשָׁ֣ה עֶשְׂרֹנִ֗ים סֹ֤לֶת מִנְחָה֙ בְּלוּלָ֣ה בַשֶּׁ֔מֶן לַפָּ֖ר הָֽאֶחָ֑ד וּשְׁנֵ֣י עֶשְׂרֹנִ֗ים סֹ֤לֶת מִנְחָה֙ בְּלוּלָ֣ה בַשֶּׁ֔מֶן לָאַ֖יִל הָֽאֶחָֽד: וְעִשָּׂרֹ֨ן עִשָּׂר֜וֹן סֹ֤לֶת מִנְחָה֙ בְּלוּלָ֣ה בַשֶּׁ֔מֶן לַכֶּ֖בֶשׂ הָֽאֶחָ֑ד עֹלָה֙ רֵ֣יחַ נִיחֹ֔חַ אִשֶּׁ֖ה לַֽיהוָֽה: וְנִסְכֵּיהֶ֗ם חֲצִ֣י הַהִ֞ין יִֽהְיֶ֣ה לַפָּ֗ר וּשְׁלִישִׁ֧ת הַהִ֛ין לָאַ֖יִל וּרְבִיעִ֥ת הַהִ֖ין לַכֶּ֣בֶשׂ יָ֑יִן זֹ֣את עֹלַ֥ת חֹ֙דֶשׁ֙ בְּחׇדְשׁ֔וֹ לְחׇדְשֵׁ֖י הַשָּׁנָֽה: וּשְׂעִ֨יר עִזִּ֥ים אֶחָ֛ד לְחַטָּ֖את לַֽיהוָ֑ה עַל־עֹלַ֧ת הַתָּמִ֛יד יֵֽעָשֶׂ֖ה וְנִסְכּֽוֹ:

רביעי: בַּיּוֹם֙ הַשִּׁשִּׁ֔י נָשִׂ֖יא לִבְנֵ֣י גָ֑ד אֶלְיָסָ֖ף בֶּן־דְּעוּאֵֽל: קׇרְבָּנ֞וֹ קַֽעֲרַת־כֶּ֣סֶף אַחַ֗ת שְׁלֹשִׁ֣ים וּמֵאָה֮ מִשְׁקָלָהּ֒ מִזְרָ֤ק אֶחָד֙ כֶּ֔סֶף שִׁבְעִ֥ים שֶׁ֖קֶל בְּשֶׁ֣קֶל הַקֹּ֑דֶשׁ שְׁנֵיהֶ֣ם ׀ מְלֵאִ֗ים סֹ֛לֶת בְּלוּלָ֥ה בַשֶּׁ֖מֶן לְמִנְחָֽה: כַּ֥ף אַחַ֛ת עֲשָׂרָ֥ה זָהָ֖ב מְלֵאָ֥ה קְטֹֽרֶת: פַּ֣ר אֶחָ֞ד בֶּן־בָּקָ֗ר אַ֧יִל אֶחָ֛ד כֶּֽבֶשׂ־אֶחָ֥ד בֶּן־שְׁנָת֖וֹ לְעֹלָֽה: שְׂעִיר־עִזִּ֥ים אֶחָ֖ד לְחַטָּֽאת: וּלְזֶ֣בַח הַשְּׁלָמִים֮ בָּקָ֣ר שְׁנַ֒יִם֒ אֵילִ֤ם חֲמִשָּׁה֙ עַתּוּדִ֣ים חֲמִשָּׁ֔ה כְּבָשִׂ֥ים בְּנֵֽי־שָׁנָ֖ה חֲמִשָּׁ֑ה זֶ֛ה קׇרְבַּ֥ן אֶלְיָסָ֖ף בֶּן־דְּעוּאֵֽל:

חֲמִשָּׁה כְבָשִׂים בְּנֵי־שָׁנָה חֲמִשָּׁה זֶה קָרְבַּן גַּמְלִיאֵל בֶּן־פְּדָהצוּר:

EIGHTH DAY CHANUKAH

כה) בַּיּוֹם הַשְּׁמִינִי נָשִׂיא לִבְנֵי מְנַשֶּׁה גַּמְלִיאֵל בֶּן־פְּדָהצוּר: קָרְבָּנוֹ קַעֲרַת־כֶּסֶף אַחַת שְׁלֹשִׁים וּמֵאָה מִשְׁקָלָהּ מִזְרָק אֶחָד כֶּסֶף שִׁבְעִים שֶׁקֶל בְּשֶׁקֶל הַקֹּדֶשׁ שְׁנֵיהֶם ׀ מְלֵאִים סֹלֶת בְּלוּלָה בַשֶּׁמֶן לְמִנְחָה: כַּף אַחַת עֲשָׂרָה זָהָב מְלֵאָה קְטֹרֶת:

לוי: פַּר אֶחָד בֶּן־בָּקָר אַיִל אֶחָד כֶּבֶשׂ־אֶחָד בֶּן־שְׁנָתוֹ לְעֹלָה: שְׂעִיר־עִזִּים אֶחָד לְחַטָּאת: וּלְזֶבַח הַשְּׁלָמִים בָּקָר שְׁנַיִם אֵילִם חֲמִשָּׁה עַתּוּדִים חֲמִשָּׁה כְּבָשִׂים בְּנֵי־שָׁנָה חֲמִשָּׁה זֶה קָרְבַּן גַּמְלִיאֵל בֶּן־פְּדָהצוּר:

ישראל: בַּיּוֹם הַתְּשִׁיעִי נָשִׂיא לִבְנֵי בִנְיָמִן אֲבִידָן בֶּן־גִּדְעֹנִי: קָרְבָּנוֹ קַעֲרַת־כֶּסֶף אַחַת שְׁלֹשִׁים וּמֵאָה מִשְׁקָלָהּ מִזְרָק אֶחָד כֶּסֶף שִׁבְעִים שֶׁקֶל בְּשֶׁקֶל הַקֹּדֶשׁ שְׁנֵיהֶם ׀ מְלֵאִים סֹלֶת בְּלוּלָה בַשֶּׁמֶן לְמִנְחָה: כַּף אַחַת עֲשָׂרָה זָהָב מְלֵאָה קְטֹרֶת: פַּר אֶחָד בֶּן־בָּקָר אַיִל אֶחָד כֶּבֶשׂ־אֶחָד בֶּן־שְׁנָתוֹ לְעֹלָה: שְׂעִיר־עִזִּים אֶחָד לְחַטָּאת: וּלְזֶבַח הַשְּׁלָמִים בָּקָר שְׁנַיִם אֵילִם חֲמִשָּׁה עַתּוּדִים חֲמִשָּׁה כְּבָשִׂים בְּנֵי־שָׁנָה חֲמִשָּׁה זֶה קָרְבַּן אֲבִידָן בֶּן־גִּדְעֹנִי: בַּיּוֹם הָעֲשִׂירִי נָשִׂיא לִבְנֵי דָן אֲחִיעֶזֶר בֶּן־עַמִּישַׁדָּי: קָרְבָּנוֹ קַעֲרַת־כֶּסֶף אַחַת שְׁלֹשִׁים וּמֵאָה מִשְׁקָלָהּ מִזְרָק אֶחָד כֶּסֶף שִׁבְעִים שֶׁקֶל בְּשֶׁקֶל הַקֹּדֶשׁ שְׁנֵיהֶם ׀ מְלֵאִים סֹלֶת בְּלוּלָה בַשֶּׁמֶן לְמִנְחָה: כַּף אַחַת עֲשָׂרָה זָהָב מְלֵאָה קְטֹרֶת: פַּר אֶחָד בֶּן־בָּקָר אַיִל אֶחָד כֶּבֶשׂ־אֶחָד בֶּן־שְׁנָתוֹ לְעֹלָה: שְׂעִיר־עִזִּים אֶחָד לְחַטָּאת: וּלְזֶבַח הַשְּׁלָמִים בָּקָר שְׁנַיִם אֵילִם חֲמִשָּׁה עַתּוּדִים חֲמִשָּׁה כְּבָשִׂים בְּנֵי־שָׁנָה חֲמִשָּׁה זֶה קָרְבַּן אֲחִיעֶזֶר בֶּן־עַמִּישַׁדָּי: בְּיוֹם עַשְׁתֵּי עָשָׂר יוֹם נָשִׂיא לִבְנֵי אָשֵׁר פַּגְעִיאֵל בֶּן־עָכְרָן: קָרְבָּנוֹ קַעֲרַת־כֶּסֶף אַחַת שְׁלֹשִׁים וּמֵאָה מִשְׁקָלָהּ מִזְרָק אֶחָד כֶּסֶף שִׁבְעִים שֶׁקֶל בְּשֶׁקֶל הַקֹּדֶשׁ שְׁנֵיהֶם ׀ מְלֵאִים סֹלֶת בְּלוּלָה בַשֶּׁמֶן לְמִנְחָה: כַּף אַחַת עֲשָׂרָה זָהָב מְלֵאָה קְטֹרֶת: פַּר אֶחָד בֶּן־בָּקָר אַיִל אֶחָד כֶּבֶשׂ־אֶחָד בֶּן־שְׁנָתוֹ לְעֹלָה: שְׂעִיר־עִזִּים אֶחָד לְחַטָּאת: וּלְזֶבַח הַשְּׁלָמִים בָּקָר שְׁנַיִם אֵילִם חֲמִשָּׁה עַתּוּדִים חֲמִשָּׁה כְּבָשִׂים בְּנֵי־שָׁנָה חֲמִשָּׁה זֶה קָרְבַּן פַּגְעִיאֵל בֶּן־עָכְרָן: בְּיוֹם שְׁנֵים עָשָׂר יוֹם נָשִׂיא לִבְנֵי נַפְתָּלִי אֲחִירַע בֶּן־עֵינָן: קָרְבָּנוֹ קַעֲרַת־כֶּסֶף אַחַת שְׁלֹשִׁים וּמֵאָה מִשְׁקָלָהּ מִזְרָק אֶחָד כֶּסֶף שִׁבְעִים שֶׁקֶל בְּשֶׁקֶל הַקֹּדֶשׁ שְׁנֵיהֶם ׀ מְלֵאִים סֹלֶת בְּלוּלָה בַשֶּׁמֶן לְמִנְחָה: כַּף אַחַת עֲשָׂרָה זָהָב מְלֵאָה קְטֹרֶת: פַּר אֶחָד בֶּן־בָּקָר אַיִל אֶחָד כֶּבֶשׂ־אֶחָד בֶּן־שְׁנָתוֹ לְעֹלָה: שְׂעִיר־עִזִּים אֶחָד לְחַטָּאת: וּלְזֶבַח הַשְּׁלָמִים בָּקָר שְׁנַיִם אֵילִם חֲמִשָּׁה עַתֻּדִים חֲמִשָּׁה כְּבָשִׂים בְּנֵי־שָׁנָה חֲמִשָּׁה זֶה קָרְבַּן אֲחִירַע בֶּן־עֵינָן: זֹאת ׀ חֲנֻכַּת הַמִּזְבֵּחַ בְּיוֹם הִמָּשַׁח אֹתוֹ מֵאֵת נְשִׂיאֵי יִשְׂרָאֵל קַעֲרֹת כֶּסֶף שְׁתֵּים עֶשְׂרֵה מִזְרְקֵי־כֶסֶף שְׁנֵים עָשָׂר כַּפּוֹת זָהָב שְׁתֵּים עֶשְׂרֵה: שְׁלֹשִׁים וּמֵאָה הַקְּעָרָה הָאַחַת כֶּסֶף וְשִׁבְעִים הַמִּזְרָק הָאֶחָד כָּל כֶּסֶף הַכֵּלִים אַלְפַּיִם וְאַרְבַּע־מֵאוֹת בְּשֶׁקֶל הַקֹּדֶשׁ: כַּפּוֹת זָהָב שְׁתֵּים־עֶשְׂרֵה מְלֵאֹת קְטֹרֶת עֲשָׂרָה עֲשָׂרָה הַכַּף בְּשֶׁקֶל הַקֹּדֶשׁ כָּל־זְהַב הַכַּפּוֹת עֶשְׂרִים וּמֵאָה: כָּל־הַבָּקָר לָעֹלָה שְׁנֵים עָשָׂר פָּרִים אֵילִם שְׁנֵים־עָשָׂר כְּבָשִׂים בְּנֵי־שָׁנָה שְׁנֵים עָשָׂר וּמִנְחָתָם וּשְׂעִירֵי עִזִּים שְׁנֵים עָשָׂר לְחַטָּאת: וְכֹל בְּקַר ׀ זֶבַח הַשְּׁלָמִים עֶשְׂרִים וְאַרְבָּעָה פָּרִים אֵילִם שִׁשִּׁים עַתֻּדִים שִׁשִּׁים כְּבָשִׂים בְּנֵי־שָׁנָה שִׁשִּׁים זֹאת חֲנֻכַּת הַמִּזְבֵּחַ אַחֲרֵי הִמָּשַׁח אֹתוֹ: וּבְבֹא מֹשֶׁה אֶל־אֹהֶל מוֹעֵד לְדַבֵּר אִתּוֹ וַיִּשְׁמַע אֶת־הַקּוֹל מִדַּבֵּר אֵלָיו מֵעַל הַכַּפֹּרֶת אֲשֶׁר עַל־אֲרֹן הָעֵדֻת מִבֵּין שְׁנֵי הַכְּרֻבִים וַיְדַבֵּר אֵלָיו: וַיְדַבֵּר יְהֹוָה אֶל־מֹשֶׁה לֵּאמֹר: דַּבֵּר אֶל־אַהֲרֹן וְאָמַרְתָּ אֵלָיו בְּהַעֲלֹתְךָ אֶת־הַנֵּרֹת אֶל־מוּל פְּנֵי הַמְּנוֹרָה יָאִירוּ שִׁבְעַת

593 / TORAH READING/CHOL HAMOED — PURIM — FAST DAY

הַנֵּרֹת: וַיַּעַשׂ כֵּן אַהֲרֹן אֶל־מוּל' פְּנֵי הַמְּנוֹרָה הֶעֱלָה נֵרֹתֶיהָ כַּאֲשֶׁר צִוָּה יהוה אֶת־מֹשֶׁה: וְזֶה מַעֲשֵׂה הַמְּנֹרָה מִקְשָׁה זָהָב עַד־יְרֵכָהּ עַד־פִּרְחָהּ מִקְשָׁה הִוא כַּמַּרְאֶה אֲשֶׁר הֶרְאָה יהוה אֶת־מֹשֶׁה כֵּן עָשָׂה אֶת־הַמְּנֹרָה:

◆{ פורים / PURIM }◆
(Exodus 17:8-16)

כהן: וַיָּבֹא עֲמָלֵק וַיִּלָּחֶם עִם־יִשְׂרָאֵל בִּרְפִידִם: וַיֹּאמֶר מֹשֶׁה אֶל־יְהוֹשֻׁעַ בְּחַר־לָנוּ אֲנָשִׁים וְצֵא הִלָּחֵם בַּעֲמָלֵק מָחָר אָנֹכִי נִצָּב עַל־רֹאשׁ הַגִּבְעָה וּמַטֵּה הָאֱלֹהִים בְּיָדִי: וַיַּעַשׂ יְהוֹשֻׁעַ כַּאֲשֶׁר אָמַר־לוֹ מֹשֶׁה לְהִלָּחֵם בַּעֲמָלֵק וּמֹשֶׁה אַהֲרֹן וְחוּר עָלוּ רֹאשׁ הַגִּבְעָה:

לוי: וְהָיָה כַּאֲשֶׁר יָרִים מֹשֶׁה יָדוֹ וְגָבַר יִשְׂרָאֵל וְכַאֲשֶׁר יָנִיחַ יָדוֹ וְגָבַר עֲמָלֵק: וִידֵי מֹשֶׁה כְּבֵדִים וַיִּקְחוּ־אֶבֶן וַיָּשִׂימוּ תַחְתָּיו וַיֵּשֶׁב עָלֶיהָ וְאַהֲרֹן וְחוּר תָּמְכוּ בְיָדָיו מִזֶּה אֶחָד וּמִזֶּה אֶחָד וַיְהִי יָדָיו אֱמוּנָה עַד־בֹּא הַשָּׁמֶשׁ: וַיַּחֲלֹשׁ יְהוֹשֻׁעַ אֶת־עֲמָלֵק וְאֶת־עַמּוֹ לְפִי־חָרֶב:

ישראל: וַיֹּאמֶר יהוה אֶל־מֹשֶׁה כְּתֹב זֹאת זִכָּרוֹן בַּסֵּפֶר וְשִׂים בְּאָזְנֵי יְהוֹשֻׁעַ כִּי־מָחֹה אֶמְחֶה אֶת־זֵכֶר עֲמָלֵק מִתַּחַת הַשָּׁמָיִם: וַיִּבֶן מֹשֶׁה מִזְבֵּחַ וַיִּקְרָא שְׁמוֹ יהוה ׀ נִסִּי: וַיֹּאמֶר כִּי־יָד עַל־כֵּס יָהּ מִלְחָמָה לַיהוה בַּעֲמָלֵק מִדֹּר דֹּר:

◆{ תענית ציבור / FAST DAY }◆

During *Shacharis* of public fast days (except for Tishah B'Av, see next page) three *olim* are called to the Torah. At *Minchah*, the same Torah reading is repeated, but the third *oleh* also reads the *Haftarah*. Upon reaching the words in bold type, the reader pauses. The congregation recites these verses, which are then repeated by the reader.

(Exodus 32:11-14; 34:1-10)

כהן: וַיְחַל מֹשֶׁה אֶת־פְּנֵי יהוה אֱלֹהָיו וַיֹּאמֶר לָמָה יהוה יֶחֱרֶה אַפְּךָ בְּעַמֶּךָ אֲשֶׁר הוֹצֵאתָ מֵאֶרֶץ מִצְרַיִם בְּכֹחַ גָּדוֹל וּבְיָד חֲזָקָה: לָמָּה יֹאמְרוּ מִצְרַיִם לֵאמֹר בְּרָעָה הוֹצִיאָם לַהֲרֹג

אֹתָם בֶּהָרִים וּלְכַלֹּתָם מֵעַל פְּנֵי הָאֲדָמָה **שׁוּב מֵחֲרוֹן אַפֶּךָ וְהִנָּחֵם עַל־הָרָעָה לְעַמֶּךָ:** זְכֹר לְאַבְרָהָם לְיִצְחָק וּלְיִשְׂרָאֵל עֲבָדֶיךָ אֲשֶׁר נִשְׁבַּעְתָּ לָהֶם בָּךְ וַתְּדַבֵּר אֲלֵהֶם אַרְבֶּה אֶת־זַרְעֲכֶם כְּכוֹכְבֵי הַשָּׁמָיִם וְכָל־הָאָרֶץ הַזֹּאת אֲשֶׁר אָמַרְתִּי אֶתֵּן לְזַרְעֲכֶם וְנָחֲלוּ לְעֹלָם: וַיִּנָּחֶם יהוה עַל־הָרָעָה אֲשֶׁר דִּבֶּר לַעֲשׂוֹת לְעַמּוֹ:

לוי: וַיֹּאמֶר יהוה אֶל־מֹשֶׁה פְּסָל־לְךָ שְׁנֵי־לֻחֹת אֲבָנִים כָּרִאשֹׁנִים וְכָתַבְתִּי עַל־הַלֻּחֹת אֶת־הַדְּבָרִים אֲשֶׁר הָיוּ עַל־הַלֻּחֹת הָרִאשֹׁנִים אֲשֶׁר שִׁבַּרְתָּ: וֶהְיֵה נָכוֹן לַבֹּקֶר וְעָלִיתָ בַבֹּקֶר אֶל־הַר סִינַי וְנִצַּבְתָּ לִי שָׁם עַל־רֹאשׁ הָהָר: וְאִישׁ לֹא־יַעֲלֶה עִמָּךְ וְגַם־אִישׁ אַל־יֵרָא בְּכָל־הָהָר גַּם־הַצֹּאן וְהַבָּקָר אַל־יִרְעוּ אֶל־מוּל הָהָר הַהוּא:

ישראל/מפטיר: וַיִּפְסֹל שְׁנֵי־לֻחֹת אֲבָנִים כָּרִאשֹׁנִים וַיַּשְׁכֵּם מֹשֶׁה בַבֹּקֶר וַיַּעַל אֶל־הַר סִינַי כַּאֲשֶׁר צִוָּה יהוה אֹתוֹ וַיִּקַּח בְּיָדוֹ שְׁנֵי לֻחֹת אֲבָנִים: וַיֵּרֶד יהוה בֶּעָנָן וַיִּתְיַצֵּב עִמּוֹ שָׁם וַיִּקְרָא בְשֵׁם יהוה: וַיַּעֲבֹר יהוה ׀ עַל־פָּנָיו וַיִּקְרָא יהוה ׀ **יהוה אֵל רַחוּם וְחַנּוּן אֶרֶךְ אַפַּיִם וְרַב־חֶסֶד וֶאֱמֶת: נֹצֵר חֶסֶד לָאֲלָפִים נֹשֵׂא עָוֺן וָפֶשַׁע וְחַטָּאָה וְנַקֵּה לֹא** יְנַקֶּה פֹּקֵד ׀ עֲוֺן אָבוֹת עַל־בָּנִים וְעַל־בְּנֵי בָנִים עַל־שִׁלֵּשִׁים וְעַל־רִבֵּעִים: וַיְמַהֵר מֹשֶׁה וַיִּקֹּד אַרְצָה וַיִּשְׁתָּחוּ: וַיֹּאמֶר אִם־נָא מָצָאתִי חֵן בְּעֵינֶיךָ אֲדֹנָי יֵלֶךְ־נָא אֲדֹנָי בְּקִרְבֵּנוּ כִּי עַם־קְשֵׁה־עֹרֶף הוּא **וְסָלַחְתָּ לַעֲוֺנֵנוּ וּלְחַטָּאתֵנוּ וּנְחַלְתָּנוּ:** וַיֹּאמֶר הִנֵּה אָנֹכִי כֹּרֵת בְּרִית נֶגֶד כָּל־עַמְּךָ אֶעֱשֶׂה נִפְלָאֹת אֲשֶׁר לֹא־נִבְרְאוּ בְכָל־הָאָרֶץ וּבְכָל־הַגּוֹיִם וְרָאָה כָל־הָעָם אֲשֶׁר־אַתָּה בְקִרְבּוֹ אֶת־מַעֲשֵׂה יהוה כִּי־נוֹרָא הוּא אֲשֶׁר אֲנִי עֹשֶׂה עִמָּךְ:

HAFTARAH — MINCHAH OF FAST DAY

בָּרוּךְ אַתָּה יהוה אֱלֹהֵינוּ מֶלֶךְ הָעוֹלָם, אֲשֶׁר בָּחַר בִּנְבִיאִים טוֹבִים, וְרָצָה

בְּדִבְרֵיהֶם הַנֶּאֱמָרִים בֶּאֱמֶת, בָּרוּךְ אַתָּה יהוה, הַבּוֹחֵר בַּתּוֹרָה וּבְמֹשֶׁה עַבְדּוֹ, וּבְיִשְׂרָאֵל עַמּוֹ, וּבִנְבִיאֵי הָאֱמֶת וָצֶדֶק.

CONGREGATION RESPONDS: Omayn – אָמֵן

Isaiah 55:6-56:8

דִּרְשׁוּ יהוה בְּהִמָּצְאוֹ קְרָאֻהוּ בִּהְיוֹתוֹ קָרוֹב: יַעֲזֹב רָשָׁע דַּרְכּוֹ וְאִישׁ אָוֶן מַחְשְׁבֹתָיו וְיָשֹׁב אֶל־יהוה וִירַחֲמֵהוּ וְאֶל־אֱלֹהֵינוּ כִּי־יַרְבֶּה לִסְלוֹחַ: כִּי לֹא מַחְשְׁבוֹתַי מַחְשְׁבוֹתֵיכֶם וְלֹא דַרְכֵיכֶם דְּרָכָי נְאֻם יהוה: כִּי־גָבְהוּ שָׁמַיִם מֵאָרֶץ כֵּן גָּבְהוּ דְרָכַי מִדַּרְכֵיכֶם וּמַחְשְׁבֹתַי מִמַּחְשְׁבֹתֵיכֶם: כִּי כַּאֲשֶׁר יֵרֵד הַגֶּשֶׁם וְהַשֶּׁלֶג מִן־הַשָּׁמַיִם וְשָׁמָּה לֹא יָשׁוּב כִּי אִם־הִרְוָה אֶת־הָאָרֶץ וְהוֹלִידָהּ וְהִצְמִיחָהּ וְנָתַן זֶרַע לַזֹּרֵעַ וְלֶחֶם לָאֹכֵל: כֵּן יִהְיֶה דְבָרִי אֲשֶׁר יֵצֵא מִפִּי לֹא־יָשׁוּב אֵלַי רֵיקָם כִּי אִם־עָשָׂה אֶת־אֲשֶׁר חָפַצְתִּי וְהִצְלִיחַ אֲשֶׁר שְׁלַחְתִּיו: כִּי־בְשִׂמְחָה תֵצֵאוּ וּבְשָׁלוֹם תּוּבָלוּן הֶהָרִים וְהַגְּבָעוֹת יִפְצְחוּ לִפְנֵיכֶם רִנָּה וְכָל־עֲצֵי הַשָּׂדֶה יִמְחֲאוּ־כָף: תַּחַת הַנַּעֲצוּץ יַעֲלֶה בְרוֹשׁ וְתַחַת הַסִּרְפַּד יַעֲלֶה הֲדַס וְהָיָה לַיהוה לְשֵׁם לְאוֹת עוֹלָם לֹא יִכָּרֵת: כֹּה אָמַר יהוה שִׁמְרוּ מִשְׁפָּט וַעֲשׂוּ צְדָקָה כִּי־קְרוֹבָה יְשׁוּעָתִי לָבוֹא וְצִדְקָתִי לְהִגָּלוֹת: אַשְׁרֵי אֱנוֹשׁ יַעֲשֶׂה־זֹּאת וּבֶן־אָדָם יַחֲזִיק בָּהּ שֹׁמֵר שַׁבָּת מֵחַלְּלוֹ וְשֹׁמֵר יָדוֹ מֵעֲשׂוֹת כָּל־רָע: וְאַל־יֹאמַר בֶּן־הַנֵּכָר הַנִּלְוָה אֶל־יהוה לֵאמֹר הַבְדֵּל יַבְדִּילַנִי יהוה מֵעַל עַמּוֹ וְאַל־יֹאמַר הַסָּרִיס הֵן אֲנִי עֵץ יָבֵשׁ: כִּי־כֹה ׀ אָמַר יהוה לַסָּרִיסִים אֲשֶׁר יִשְׁמְרוּ אֶת־שַׁבְּתוֹתַי וּבָחֲרוּ בַּאֲשֶׁר חָפָצְתִּי וּמַחֲזִיקִים בִּבְרִיתִי: וְנָתַתִּי לָהֶם בְּבֵיתִי וּבְחוֹמֹתַי יָד וָשֵׁם טוֹב מִבָּנִים וּמִבָּנוֹת שֵׁם עוֹלָם אֶתֶּן־לוֹ אֲשֶׁר לֹא יִכָּרֵת: וּבְנֵי הַנֵּכָר הַנִּלְוִים עַל־יהוה לְשָׁרְתוֹ וּלְאַהֲבָה אֶת־שֵׁם יהוה לִהְיוֹת לוֹ לַעֲבָדִים כָּל־שֹׁמֵר שַׁבָּת מֵחַלְּלוֹ וּמַחֲזִיקִים בִּבְרִיתִי: וַהֲבִיאוֹתִים אֶל־הַר קָדְשִׁי וְשִׂמַּחְתִּים בְּבֵית תְּפִלָּתִי עוֹלֹתֵיהֶם וְזִבְחֵיהֶם לְרָצוֹן עַל־

מִזְבְּחִי כִּי בֵיתִי בֵּית־תְּפִלָּה יִקָּרֵא לְכָל־הָעַמִּים: נְאֻם אֲדֹנָי יֱהֹוִה מְקַבֵּץ נִדְחֵי יִשְׂרָאֵל עוֹד אֲקַבֵּץ עָלָיו לְנִקְבָּצָיו:

בָּרוּךְ אַתָּה יהוה אֱלֹהֵינוּ מֶלֶךְ הָעוֹלָם, צוּר כָּל הָעוֹלָמִים, צַדִּיק בְּכָל הַדּוֹרוֹת, הָאֵל הַנֶּאֱמָן הָאוֹמֵר וְעֹשֶׂה, הַמְדַבֵּר וּמְקַיֵּם, שֶׁכָּל דְּבָרָיו אֱמֶת וָצֶדֶק. נֶאֱמָן אַתָּה הוּא יהוה אֱלֹהֵינוּ, וְנֶאֱמָנִים דְּבָרֶיךָ, וְדָבָר אֶחָד מִדְּבָרֶיךָ אָחוֹר לֹא יָשׁוּב רֵיקָם, כִּי אֵל מֶלֶךְ נֶאֱמָן (וְרַחֲמָן) אָתָּה. בָּרוּךְ אַתָּה יהוה, הָאֵל הַנֶּאֱמָן בְּכָל דְּבָרָיו.

CONGREGATION RESPONDS: Omayn – אָמֵן

רַחֵם עַל צִיּוֹן כִּי הִיא בֵּית חַיֵּינוּ, וְלַעֲלוּבַת נֶפֶשׁ תּוֹשִׁיעַ בִּמְהֵרָה בְיָמֵינוּ. בָּרוּךְ אַתָּה יהוה, מְשַׂמֵּחַ צִיּוֹן בְּבָנֶיהָ.

CONGREGATION RESPONDS: Omayn – אָמֵן

שַׂמְּחֵנוּ יהוה אֱלֹהֵינוּ בְּאֵלִיָּהוּ הַנָּבִיא עַבְדֶּךָ, וּבְמַלְכוּת בֵּית דָּוִד מְשִׁיחֶךָ, בִּמְהֵרָה יָבֹא וְיָגֵל לִבֵּנוּ, עַל כִּסְאוֹ לֹא יֵשֵׁב זָר וְלֹא יִנְחֲלוּ עוֹד אֲחֵרִים אֶת כְּבוֹדוֹ, כִּי בְשֵׁם קָדְשְׁךָ נִשְׁבַּעְתָּ לּוֹ, שֶׁלֹּא יִכְבֶּה נֵרוֹ לְעוֹלָם וָעֶד. בָּרוּךְ אַתָּה יהוה, מָגֵן דָּוִד.

CONGREGATION RESPONDS: Omayn – אָמֵן

☙ תשעה באב / TISHAH B'AV ❧

During *Shacharis* of Tishah B'Av, three *olim* are called to the Torah. The third *oleh* also reads the *Haftarah* of the day. During *Minchah* the Torah reading and the *Haftarah* are the same as for other public fast days (see page 591).

(Deuteronomy 4:25-40)

כה כִּי־תוֹלִיד בָּנִים וּבְנֵי בָנִים וְנוֹשַׁנְתֶּם בָּאָרֶץ וְהִשְׁחַתֶּם וַעֲשִׂיתֶם פֶּסֶל תְּמוּנַת כֹּל וַעֲשִׂיתֶם הָרַע בְּעֵינֵי־יהוה אֱלֹהֶיךָ לְהַכְעִיסוֹ: הַעִידֹתִי בָכֶם הַיּוֹם אֶת־הַשָּׁמַיִם וְאֶת־הָאָרֶץ כִּי־אָבֹד תֹּאבֵדוּן מַהֵר מֵעַל הָאָרֶץ אֲשֶׁר אַתֶּם עֹבְרִים אֶת־הַיַּרְדֵּן שָׁמָּה לְרִשְׁתָּהּ לֹא־תַאֲרִיכֻן יָמִים עָלֶיהָ כִּי הִשָּׁמֵד תִּשָּׁמֵדוּן: וְהֵפִיץ יהוה אֶתְכֶם בָּעַמִּים וְנִשְׁאַרְתֶּם מְתֵי מִסְפָּר בַּגּוֹיִם אֲשֶׁר יְנַהֵג

יְהוָה אֶתְכֶם שָׁמָּה: וַעֲבַדְתֶּם־שָׁם אֱלֹהִים מַעֲשֵׂה יְדֵי אָדָם עֵץ וָאֶבֶן אֲשֶׁר לֹא־יִרְאוּן וְלֹא יִשְׁמְעוּן וְלֹא יֹאכְלוּן וְלֹא יְרִיחֻן: וּבִקַּשְׁתֶּם מִשָּׁם אֶת־יְהוָה אֱלֹהֶיךָ וּמָצָאתָ כִּי תִדְרְשֶׁנּוּ בְּכָל־לְבָבְךָ וּבְכָל־נַפְשֶׁךָ: לוי׳ בַּצַּר לְךָ וּמְצָאוּךָ כֹּל הַדְּבָרִים הָאֵלֶּה בְּאַחֲרִית הַיָּמִים וְשַׁבְתָּ עַד־יְהוָה אֱלֹהֶיךָ וְשָׁמַעְתָּ בְּקֹלוֹ: כִּי אֵל רַחוּם יְהוָה אֱלֹהֶיךָ לֹא יַרְפְּךָ וְלֹא יַשְׁחִיתֶךָ וְלֹא יִשְׁכַּח אֶת־ בְּרִית אֲבֹתֶיךָ אֲשֶׁר נִשְׁבַּע לָהֶם: כִּי שְׁאַל־ נָא לְיָמִים רִאשֹׁנִים אֲשֶׁר־הָיוּ לְפָנֶיךָ לְמִן־ הַיּוֹם אֲשֶׁר בָּרָא אֱלֹהִים ׀ אָדָם עַל־הָאָרֶץ וּלְמִקְצֵה הַשָּׁמַיִם וְעַד־קְצֵה הַשָּׁמָיִם הֲנִהְיָה כַּדָּבָר הַגָּדוֹל הַזֶּה אוֹ הֲנִשְׁמַע כָּמֹהוּ: הֲשָׁמַע עָם קוֹל אֱלֹהִים מְדַבֵּר מִתּוֹךְ־הָאֵשׁ כַּאֲשֶׁר־שָׁמַעְתָּ אַתָּה וַיֶּחִי: אוֹ ׀ הֲנִסָּה אֱלֹהִים לָבוֹא לָקַחַת לוֹ גוֹי מִקֶּרֶב גּוֹי בְּמַסֹּת בְּאֹתֹת וּבְמוֹפְתִים וּבְמִלְחָמָה וּבְיָד חֲזָקָה וּבִזְרוֹעַ נְטוּיָה וּבְמוֹרָאִים גְּדֹלִים כְּכֹל אֲשֶׁר־עָשָׂה לָכֶם יְהוָה אֱלֹהֵיכֶם בְּמִצְרַיִם לְעֵינֶיךָ: אַתָּה הָרְאֵתָ לָדַעַת כִּי יְהוָה הוּא הָאֱלֹהִים אֵין עוֹד מִלְבַדּוֹ:

מפטיר׳ מִן־הַשָּׁמַיִם הִשְׁמִיעֲךָ אֶת־קֹלוֹ לְיַסְּרֶךָּ וְעַל־הָאָרֶץ הֶרְאֲךָ אֶת־אִשּׁוֹ הַגְּדוֹלָה וּדְבָרָיו שָׁמַעְתָּ מִתּוֹךְ הָאֵשׁ: וְתַחַת כִּי אָהַב אֶת־אֲבֹתֶיךָ וַיִּבְחַר בְּזַרְעוֹ אַחֲרָיו וַיּוֹצִאֲךָ בְּפָנָיו בְּכֹחוֹ הַגָּדֹל מִמִּצְרָיִם: לְהוֹרִישׁ גּוֹיִם גְּדֹלִים וַעֲצֻמִים מִמְּךָ מִפָּנֶיךָ לַהֲבִיאֲךָ לָתֶת־לְךָ אֶת־אַרְצָם נַחֲלָה כַּיּוֹם הַזֶּה: וְיָדַעְתָּ הַיּוֹם וַהֲשֵׁבֹתָ אֶל־לְבָבֶךָ כִּי יְהוָה הוּא הָאֱלֹהִים בַּשָּׁמַיִם מִמַּעַל וְעַל־ הָאָרֶץ מִתָּחַת אֵין עוֹד: וְשָׁמַרְתָּ אֶת־חֻקָּיו וְאֶת־מִצְוֹתָיו אֲשֶׁר אָנֹכִי מְצַוְּךָ הַיּוֹם אֲשֶׁר יִיטַב לְךָ וּלְבָנֶיךָ אַחֲרֶיךָ וּלְמַעַן תַּאֲרִיךְ יָמִים עַל־הָאֲדָמָה אֲשֶׁר יְהוָה אֱלֹהֶיךָ נֹתֵן לְךָ כָּל־הַיָּמִים:

HAFTARAH — SHACHARIS OF TISHAH B'AV

בָּרוּךְ אַתָּה יהוה אֱלֹהֵינוּ מֶלֶךְ הָעוֹלָם,

אֲשֶׁר בָּחַר בִּנְבִיאִים טוֹבִים, וְרָצָה בְדִבְרֵיהֶם הַנֶּאֱמָרִים בֶּאֱמֶת, בָּרוּךְ אַתָּה יהוה, הַבּוֹחֵר בַּתּוֹרָה וּבְמֹשֶׁה עַבְדּוֹ, וּבְיִשְׂרָאֵל עַמּוֹ, וּבִנְבִיאֵי הָאֱמֶת וָצֶדֶק.

CONGREGATION RESPONDS: Omayn – אָמֵן

Jeremiah 8:13-9:23

אָסֹף אֲסִיפֵם נְאֻם־יְהֹוָה אֵין עֲנָבִים בַּגֶּפֶן וְאֵין תְּאֵנִים בַּתְּאֵנָה וְהֶעָלֶה נָבֵל וָאֶתֵּן לָהֶם יַעַבְרוּם: עַל־מָה אֲנַחְנוּ יֹשְׁבִים הֵאָסְפוּ וְנָבוֹא אֶל־עָרֵי הַמִּבְצָר וְנִדְּמָה־שָּׁם כִּי יְהוָה אֱלֹהֵינוּ הֲדִמָּנוּ וַיַּשְׁקֵנוּ מֵי־רֹאשׁ כִּי חָטָאנוּ לַיהוָה: קַוֵּה לְשָׁלוֹם וְאֵין טוֹב לְעֵת מַרְפֵּה וְהִנֵּה בְעָתָה: מִדָּן נִשְׁמַע נַחְרַת סוּסָיו מִקּוֹל מִצְהֲלוֹת אַבִּירָיו רָעֲשָׁה כָּל־הָאָרֶץ וַיָּבוֹאוּ וַיֹּאכְלוּ אֶרֶץ וּמְלוֹאָהּ עִיר וְיֹשְׁבֵי בָהּ: כִּי הִנְנִי מְשַׁלֵּחַ בָּכֶם נְחָשִׁים צִפְעֹנִים אֲשֶׁר אֵין־לָהֶם לָחַשׁ וְנִשְּׁכוּ אֶתְכֶם נְאֻם־יְהוָה: מַבְלִיגִיתִי עֲלֵי יָגוֹן עָלַי לִבִּי דַוָּי: הִנֵּה־קוֹל שַׁוְעַת בַּת־עַמִּי מֵאֶרֶץ מַרְחַקִּים הַיהוָה אֵין בְּצִיּוֹן אִם־מַלְכָּהּ אֵין בָּהּ מַדּוּעַ הִכְעִסוּנִי בִּפְסִלֵיהֶם בְּהַבְלֵי נֵכָר: עָבַר קָצִיר כָּלָה קָיִץ וַאֲנַחְנוּ לוֹא נוֹשָׁעְנוּ: עַל־שֶׁבֶר בַּת־עַמִּי הָשְׁבָּרְתִּי קָדַרְתִּי שַׁמָּה הֶחֱזִקָתְנִי: הַצֳרִי אֵין בְּגִלְעָד אִם־רֹפֵא אֵין שָׁם כִּי מַדּוּעַ לֹא עָלְתָה אֲרֻכַת בַּת־עַמִּי: מִי־יִתֵּן רֹאשִׁי מַיִם וְעֵינִי מְקוֹר דִּמְעָה וְאֶבְכֶּה יוֹמָם וָלַיְלָה אֵת חַלְלֵי בַת־עַמִּי: מִי־יִתְּנֵנִי בַמִּדְבָּר מְלוֹן אֹרְחִים וְאֶעֶזְבָה אֶת־עַמִּי וְאֵלְכָה מֵאִתָּם כִּי כֻלָּם מְנָאֲפִים עֲצֶרֶת בֹּגְדִים: וַיַּדְרְכוּ אֶת־לְשׁוֹנָם קַשְׁתָּם שֶׁקֶר וְלֹא לֶאֱמוּנָה גָּבְרוּ בָאָרֶץ כִּי מֵרָעָה אֶל־רָעָה ׀ יָצָאוּ וְאֹתִי לֹא־יָדָעוּ נְאֻם־יְהוָה: אִישׁ מֵרֵעֵהוּ הִשָּׁמֵרוּ וְעַל־כָּל־אָח אַל־תִּבְטָחוּ כִּי כָל־אָח עָקוֹב יַעְקֹב וְכָל־רֵעַ רָכִיל יַהֲלֹךְ: וְאִישׁ בְּרֵעֵהוּ יְהָתֵלּוּ וֶאֱמֶת לֹא יְדַבֵּרוּ לִמְּדוּ לְשׁוֹנָם דַּבֶּר־שֶׁקֶר הַעֲוֵה נִלְאוּ: שִׁבְתְּךָ בְּתוֹךְ מִרְמָה בְּמִרְמָה מֵאֲנוּ דַעַת־אוֹתִי נְאֻם־יְהוָה: לָכֵן כֹּה אָמַר יְהוָה צְבָאוֹת הִנְנִי צוֹרְפָם וּבְחַנְתִּים כִּי־אֵיךְ אֶעֱשֶׂה מִפְּנֵי בַּת־עַמִּי:

חֵץ שָׁחוּט לְשׁוֹנָם מִרְמָה דִבֵּר בְּפִיו שָׁלוֹם אֶת־רֵעֵהוּ יְדַבֵּר וּבְקִרְבּוֹ יָשִׂים אָרְבּוֹ: הַעַל־אֵלֶּה לֹא־אֶפְקָד־בָּם נְאֻם־יְהֹוָה אִם בְּגוֹי אֲשֶׁר־כָּזֶה לֹא תִתְנַקֵּם נַפְשִׁי: עַל־הֶהָרִים אֶשָּׂא בְכִי וָנֶהִי וְעַל־נְאוֹת מִדְבָּר קִינָה כִּי נִצְּתוּ מִבְּלִי־אִישׁ עֹבֵר וְלֹא שָׁמְעוּ קוֹל מִקְנֶה מֵעוֹף הַשָּׁמַיִם וְעַד־בְּהֵמָה נָדְדוּ הָלָכוּ: וְנָתַתִּי אֶת־יְרוּשָׁלַםִ לְגַלִּים מְעוֹן תַּנִּים וְאֶת־עָרֵי יְהוּדָה אֶתֵּן שְׁמָמָה מִבְּלִי יוֹשֵׁב: מִי־הָאִישׁ הֶחָכָם וְיָבֵן אֶת־זֹאת וַאֲשֶׁר דִּבֶּר פִּי־יְהֹוָה אֵלָיו וְיַגִּדָהּ עַל־מָה אָבְדָה הָאָרֶץ נִצְּתָה כַמִּדְבָּר מִבְּלִי עֹבֵר: וַיֹּאמֶר יְהֹוָה עַל־עָזְבָם אֶת־תּוֹרָתִי אֲשֶׁר נָתַתִּי לִפְנֵיהֶם וְלֹא־שָׁמְעוּ בְקוֹלִי וְלֹא־הָלְכוּ בָהּ: וַיֵּלְכוּ אַחֲרֵי שְׁרִרוּת לִבָּם וְאַחֲרֵי הַבְּעָלִים אֲשֶׁר לִמְּדוּם אֲבוֹתָם: לָכֵן כֹּה־אָמַר יְהֹוָה צְבָאוֹת אֱלֹהֵי יִשְׂרָאֵל הִנְנִי מַאֲכִילָם אֶת־הָעָם הַזֶּה לַעֲנָה וְהִשְׁקִיתִים מֵי־רֹאשׁ: וַהֲפִצוֹתִים בַּגּוֹיִם אֲשֶׁר לֹא יָדְעוּ הֵמָּה וַאֲבוֹתָם וְשִׁלַּחְתִּי אַחֲרֵיהֶם אֶת־הַחֶרֶב עַד כַּלּוֹתִי אוֹתָם: כֹּה אָמַר יְהֹוָה צְבָאוֹת הִתְבּוֹנְנוּ וְקִרְאוּ לַמְקוֹנְנוֹת וּתְבוֹאֶינָה וְאֶל־הַחֲכָמוֹת שִׁלְחוּ וְתָבוֹאנָה: וּתְמַהֵרְנָה וְתִשֶּׂנָה עָלֵינוּ נֶהִי וְתֵרַדְנָה עֵינֵינוּ דִּמְעָה וְעַפְעַפֵּינוּ יִזְּלוּ־מָיִם: כִּי קוֹל נְהִי נִשְׁמַע מִצִּיּוֹן אֵיךְ שֻׁדָּדְנוּ בֹּשְׁנוּ מְאֹד כִּי־עָזַבְנוּ אָרֶץ כִּי הִשְׁלִיכוּ מִשְׁכְּנוֹתֵינוּ: כִּי־שְׁמַעְנָה נָשִׁים דְּבַר־יְהֹוָה וְתִקַּח אָזְנְכֶם דְּבַר־פִּיו וְלַמֵּדְנָה בְנוֹתֵיכֶם נֶהִי וְאִשָּׁה רְעוּתָהּ קִינָה: כִּי־עָלָה מָוֶת בְּחַלּוֹנֵינוּ בָּא בְּאַרְמְנוֹתֵינוּ לְהַכְרִית עוֹלָל מִחוּץ בַּחוּרִים מֵרְחֹבוֹת: דַּבֵּר כֹּה נְאֻם־יְהֹוָה וְנָפְלָה נִבְלַת הָאָדָם כְּדֹמֶן עַל־פְּנֵי הַשָּׂדֶה וּכְעָמִיר מֵאַחֲרֵי הַקֹּצֵר וְאֵין מְאַסֵּף: כֹּה ׀ אָמַר יְהֹוָה אַל־יִתְהַלֵּל חָכָם בְּחָכְמָתוֹ וְאַל־יִתְהַלֵּל הַגִּבּוֹר בִּגְבוּרָתוֹ אַל־יִתְהַלֵּל עָשִׁיר בְּעָשְׁרוֹ: כִּי אִם־בְּזֹאת יִתְהַלֵּל הַמִּתְהַלֵּל הַשְׂכֵּל וְיָדֹעַ אוֹתִי כִּי אֲנִי יְהֹוָה עֹשֶׂה חֶסֶד מִשְׁפָּט וּצְדָקָה בָּאָרֶץ כִּי־בְאֵלֶּה חָפַצְתִּי נְאֻם־יְהֹוָה:

בָּרוּךְ אַתָּה יהוה אֱלֹהֵינוּ מֶלֶךְ הָעוֹלָם, צוּר כָּל הָעוֹלָמִים, צַדִּיק בְּכָל הַדּוֹרוֹת, הָאֵל הַנֶּאֱמָן הָאוֹמֵר וְעֹשֶׂה, הַמְדַבֵּר וּמְקַיֵּם, שֶׁכָּל דְּבָרָיו אֱמֶת וָצֶדֶק. נֶאֱמָן אַתָּה הוּא יהוה אֱלֹהֵינוּ, וְנֶאֱמָנִים דְּבָרֶיךָ, וְדָבָר אֶחָד מִדְּבָרֶיךָ אָחוֹר לֹא יָשׁוּב רֵיקָם, כִּי אֵל מֶלֶךְ נֶאֱמָן (וְרַחֲמָן) אָתָּה. בָּרוּךְ אַתָּה יהוה, הָאֵל הַנֶּאֱמָן בְּכָל דְּבָרָיו.

CONGREGATION RESPONDS: Omayn — אָמֵן

רַחֵם עַל צִיּוֹן כִּי הִיא בֵּית חַיֵּינוּ, וְלַעֲלוּבַת נֶפֶשׁ תּוֹשִׁיעַ בִּמְהֵרָה בְיָמֵינוּ. בָּרוּךְ אַתָּה יהוה, מְשַׂמֵּחַ צִיּוֹן בְּבָנֶיהָ.

CONGREGATION RESPONDS: Omayn — אָמֵן

שַׂמְּחֵנוּ יהוה אֱלֹהֵינוּ בְּאֵלִיָּהוּ הַנָּבִיא עַבְדֶּךָ, וּבְמַלְכוּת בֵּית דָּוִד מְשִׁיחֶךָ, בִּמְהֵרָה יָבֹא וְיָגֵל לִבֵּנוּ, עַל כִּסְאוֹ לֹא יֵשֶׁב זָר וְלֹא יִנְחֲלוּ עוֹד אֲחֵרִים אֶת כְּבוֹדוֹ, כִּי בְשֵׁם קָדְשְׁךָ נִשְׁבַּעְתָּ לּוֹ, שֶׁלֹּא יִכְבֶּה נֵרוֹ לְעוֹלָם וָעֶד. בָּרוּךְ אַתָּה יהוה, מָגֵן דָּוִד.

CONGREGATION RESPONDS: Omayn — אָמֵן